Twentieth-Century Literary Criticism

Topics Volume

Guide to Gale Literary Criticism Series

For criticism on	Consult these Gale series
Authors now living or who died after December 31, 1999	*CONTEMPORARY LITERARY CRITICISM (CLC)*
Authors who died between 1900 and 1999	*TWENTIETH-CENTURY LITERARY CRITICISM (TCLC)*
Authors who died between 1800 and 1899	*NINETEENTH-CENTURY LITERATURE CRITICISM (NCLC)*
Authors who died between 1400 and 1799	*LITERATURE CRITICISM FROM 1400 TO 1800 (LC)* *SHAKESPEAREAN CRITICISM (SC)*
Authors who died before 1400	*CLASSICAL AND MEDIEVAL LITERATURE CRITICISM (CMLC)*
Authors of books for children and young adults	*CHILDREN'S LITERATURE REVIEW (CLR)*
Dramatists	*DRAMA CRITICISM (DC)*
Poets	*POETRY CRITICISM (PC)*
Short story writers	*SHORT STORY CRITICISM (SSC)*
Literary topics and movements	*HARLEM RENAISSANCE: A GALE CRITICAL COMPANION (HR)* *THE BEAT GENERATION: A GALE CRITICAL COMPANION (BG)*
Asian American writers of the last two hundred years	*ASIAN AMERICAN LITERATURE (AAL)*
Black writers of the past two hundred years	*BLACK LITERATURE CRITICISM (BLC)* *BLACK LITERATURE CRITICISM SUPPLEMENT (BLCS)*
Hispanic writers of the late nineteenth and twentieth centuries	*HISPANIC LITERATURE CRITICISM (HLC)* *HISPANIC LITERATURE CRITICISM SUPPLEMENT (HLCS)*
Native North American writers and orators of the eighteenth, nineteenth, and twentieth centuries	*NATIVE NORTH AMERICAN LITERATURE (NNAL)*
Major authors from the Renaissance to the present	*WORLD LITERATURE CRITICISM, 1500 TO THE PRESENT (WLC)* *WORLD LITERATURE CRITICISM SUPPLEMENT (WLCS)*

ISSN 0276-8178

Volume 194

Twentieth-Century Literary Criticism

**Commentary on Various Topics
in Twentieth-Century Literature, including Literary
and Critical Movements, Prominent Themes and
Genres, Anniversary Celebrations, and Surveys
of National Literatures**

**Thomas J. Schoenberg
Lawrence J. Trudeau**
Project Editors

THOMSON
GALE

Detroit • New York • San Francisco • New Haven, Conn. • Waterville, Maine • London

Twentieth-Century Literary Criticism, Vol. 194

Project Editors
Thomas J. Schoenberg and Lawrence J. Trudeau

Editorial
Dana Ramel Barnes, Tom Burns, Elizabeth A. Cranston, Kathy D. Darrow, Kristen A. Dorsch, Jeffrey W. Hunter, Jelena O. Krstović, Michelle Lee, Russel Whitaker

Data Capture
Frances Monroe, Gwen Tucker

Rights and Acquisitions
Scott Bragg, Lisa Kincade, Aja Perales

Composition and Electronic Capture
Tracey L. Matthews

Manufacturing
Cynde Bishop

Associate Product Manager
Marc Cormier

LIBRARY OF CONGRESS CATALOG CARD NUMBER 76-46132

ISBN-13: 978-0-7876-9969-7
ISBN-10: 0-7876-9969-1
ISSN 0276-8178

Printed in the United States of America
10 9 8 7 6 5 4 3 2 1

Contents

Preface

Since its inception *Twentieth-Century Literary Criticism* (*TCLC*) has been purchased and used by some 10,000 school, public, and college or university libraries. *TCLC* has covered more than 1000 authors, representing over 60 nationalities and nearly 50,000 titles. No other reference source has surveyed the critical response to twentieth-century authors and literature as thoroughly as *TCLC*. In the words of one reviewer, "there is nothing comparable available." *TCLC* "is a gold mine of information—dates, pseudonyms, biographical information, and criticism from books and periodicals—which many librarians would have difficulty assembling on their own."

Scope of the Series

TCLC is designed to serve as an introduction to authors who died between 1900 and 1999 and to the most significant interpretations of these author's works. Volumes published from 1978 through 1999 included authors who died between 1900 and 1960. The great poets, novelists, short story writers, playwrights, and philosophers of the period are frequently studied in high school and college literature courses. In organizing and reprinting the vast amount of critical material written on these authors, *TCLC* helps students develop valuable insight into literary history, promotes a better understanding of the texts, and sparks ideas for papers and assignments. Each entry in *TCLC* presents a comprehensive survey on an author's career or an individual work of literature and provides the user with a multiplicity of interpretations and assessments. Such variety allows students to pursue their own interests; furthermore, it fosters an awareness that literature is dynamic and responsive to many different opinions.

Every fourth volume of *TCLC* is devoted to literary topics. These topics widen the focus of the series from the individual authors to such broader subjects as literary movements, prominent themes in twentieth-century literature, literary reaction to political and historical events, significant eras in literary history, prominent literary anniversaries, and the literatures of cultures that are often overlooked by English-speaking readers.

TCLC is designed as a companion series to Thomson Gale's *Contemporary Literary Criticism*, (*CLC*) which reprints commentary on authors who died after 1999. Because of the different time periods under consideration, there is no duplication of material between *CLC* and *TCLC*.

Organization of the Book

A *TCLC* entry consists of the following elements:

■ The **Author Heading** cites the name under which the author most commonly wrote, followed by birth and death dates. Also located here are any name variations under which an author wrote, including transliterated forms for authors whose native languages use nonroman alphabets. If the author wrote consistently under a pseudonym, the pseudonym is listed in the author heading and the author's actual name is given in parenthesis on the first line of the biographical and critical information. Uncertain birth or death dates are indicated by question marks. Single-work entries are preceded by a heading that consists of the most common form of the title in English translation (if applicable) and the name of its author.

■ The **Introduction** contains background information that introduces the reader to the author, work, or topic that is the subject of the entry.

■ The list of **Principal Works** is ordered chronologically by date of first publication and lists the most important works by the author. The genre and publication date of each work is given. In the case of foreign authors whose works have been translated into English, the English-language version of the title follows in brackets. Unless otherwise indicated, dramas are dated by first performance, not first publication. Lists of **Representative Works** by different authors appear with topic entries.

- Reprinted **Criticism** is arranged chronologically in each entry to provide a useful perspective on changes in critical evaluation over time. The critic's name and the date of composition or publication of the critical work are given at the beginning of each piece of criticism. Unsigned criticism is preceded by the title of the source in which it originally appeared. All titles by the author featured in the text are printed in boldface type. Footnotes are reprinted at the end of each essay or excerpt. In the case of excerpted criticism, only those footnotes that pertain to the excerpted texts are included. Criticism in topic entries is arranged chronologically under a variety of subheadings to facilitate the study of different aspects of the topic.

- A complete **Bibliographical Citation** of the original essay or book precedes each piece of criticism. Source citations in the Literary Criticism Series follow University of Chicago Press style, as outlined in *The Chicago Manual of Style,* 15th ed. (Chicago: The University of Chicago Press, 2003).

- Critical essays are prefaced by brief **Annotations** explicating each piece.

- An annotated bibliography of **Further Reading** appears at the end of each entry and suggests resources for additional study. In some cases, significant essays for which the editors could not obtain reprint rights are included here. Boxed material following the further reading list provides references to other biographical and critical sources on the author in series published by Thomson Gale.

Indexes

A **Cumulative Author Index** lists all of the authors that appear in a wide variety of reference sources published by Thomson Gale, including *TCLC*. A complete list of these sources is found facing the first page of the Author Index. The index also includes birth and death dates and cross references between pseudonyms and actual names.

A **Cumulative Topic Index** lists the literary themes and topics treated in *TCLC* as well as other Literature Criticism series.

A **Cumulative Nationality Index** lists all authors featured in *TCLC* by nationality, followed by the numbers of the *TCLC* volumes in which their entries appear.

An alphabetical **Title Index** accompanies each volume of *TCLC*. Listings of titles by authors covered in the given volume are followed by the author's name and the corresponding page numbers where the titles are discussed. English translations of foreign titles and variations of titles are cross-referenced to the title under which a work was originally published. Titles of novels, dramas, nonfiction books, and poetry, short story, or essay collections are printed in italics, while individual poems, short stories, and essays are printed in roman type within quotation marks.

In response to numerous suggestions from librarians, Thomson Gale also produces a paperbound edition of the *TCLC* cumulative title index. This annual cumulation, which alphabetically lists all titles reviewed in the series, is available to all customers. Additional copies of this index are available upon request. Librarians and patrons will welcome this separate index; it saves shelf space, is easy to use, and is recyclable upon receipt of the next edition.

Citing *Twentieth-Century Literary Criticism*

When citing criticism reprinted in the Literary Criticism Series, students should provide complete bibliographic information so that the cited essay can be located in the original print or electronic source. Students who quote directly from reprinted criticism may use any accepted bibliographic format, such as University of Chicago Press style or Modern Language Association (MLA) style. Both the MLA and the University of Chicago formats are acceptable and recognized as being the current standards for citations. It is important, however, to choose one format for all citations; do not mix the two formats within a list of citations.

The examples below follow recommendations for preparing a bibliography set forth in *The Chicago Manual of Style,* 15th ed. (Chicago: The University of Chicago Press, (2003); the first example pertains to material drawn from periodicals, the second to material reprinted from books:

Morrison, Jago. "Narration and Unease in Ian McEwan's Later Fiction." *Critique* 42, no. 3 (spring 2001): 253-68. Reprinted in *Twentieth-Century Literary Criticism.* Vol. 127, edited by Janet Witalec, 212-20. Detroit: Thomson Gale, 2003.

Brossard, Nicole. "Poetic Politics." In *The Politics of Poetic Form: Poetry and Public Policy,* edited by Charles Bernstein, 73-82. New York: Roof Books, 1990. Reprinted in *Twentieth-Century Literary Criticism.* Vol. 127, edited by Janet Witalec, 3-8. Detroit: Thomson Gale, 2003.

The examples below follow recommendations for preparing a works cited list set forth in the *MLA Handbook for Writers of Research Papers,* 5th ed. (New York: The Modern Language Association of America, 1999); the first example pertains to material drawn from periodicals, the second to material reprinted from books:

Morrison, Jago. "Narration and Unease in Ian McEwan's Later Fiction." *Critique* 42.3 (spring 2001): 253-68. Reprinted in *Twentieth-Century Literary Criticism.* Ed. Janet Witalec. Vol. 127. Detroit: Thomson Gale, 2003. 212-20.

Brossard, Nicole. "Poetic Politics." *The Politics of Poetic Form: Poetry and Public Policy.* Ed. Charles Bernstein. New York: Roof Books, 1990. 73-82. Reprinted in *Twentieth-Century Literary Criticism.* Ed. Janet Witalec. Vol. 127. Detroit: Thomson Gale, 2003. 3-8.

Suggestions are Welcome

Readers who wish to suggest new features, topics, or authors to appear in future volumes, or who have other suggestions or comments are cordially invited to call, write, or fax the Associate Product Manager:

Associate Product Manager, Literary Criticism Series
Thomson Gale
27500 Drake Road
Farmington Hills, MI 48331-3535
1-800-347-4253 (GALE)
Fax: 248-699-8054

Acknowledgments

The editors wish to thank the copyright holders of the criticism included in this volume and the permissions managers of many book and magazine publishing companies for assisting us in securing reproduction rights. Following is a list of the copyright holders who have granted us permission to reproduce material in this volume of *TCLC*. Every effort has been made to trace copyright, but if omissions have been made, please let us know.

COPYRIGHTED MATERIAL IN *TCLC*, VOLUME 194, WAS REPRODUCED FROM THE FOLLOWING PERIODICALS:

American Drama, v. 13, winter, 2004. Copyright © 2004 American Drama Institute. Reproduced by permission.—*boundary 2*, v. 31, spring, 2004. Copyright, 2004, Duke University Press. All rights reserved. Used by permission of the publisher.—*Critique*, v. 43, summer, 2002. Copyright © 2002 by Helen Dwight Reid Educational Foundation. Reproduced with permission of the Helen Dwight Reid Educational Foundation, published by Heldref Publications, 1319 18th Street, NW, Washington, DC 20036-1802.—*Great Plains Quarterly*, v. 2, fall, 1982. Copyright 1982 by the Center for Great Plains Studies. Reproduced by permission.—*Journal of American Studies*, v. 27, August, 1993, for "Frederick Jackson Turner's Frontier Thesis and the Self-Consciousness of America" by Tiziano Bonazzi. Copyright © 1993 Cambridge University Press. Reprinted with the permission of the author and Cambridge University Press.—*Langston Hughes Review*, v. 16, fall-spring, 1999-2001. Copyright, 1999-2001, by The Langston Hughes Society. Reproduced by permission.—*McNeese Review*, v. XXVIII, 1981-82. Reproduced by permission.—*Missouri Review*, v. 7, fall, 1983. Copyright © 1983 by The Curators of the University of Michigan. Reproduced by permission.—*Philological Papers*, v. 51, 2004 for "Wartime Propaganda: Enemies Defined by Race" by Erin E. Sapre. Reproduced by permission of the publisher and the author.—*Soundings: An Interdisciplinary Journal*, v. LXIV, summer, 1981. Copyright © 1981 by the Society for Values in Higher Education and Vanderbilt University. Reproduced by permission.—*Western American Literature*, v. 21, November, 1986. Copyright © 1986 by The Western Literature Association. Reproduced by permission.

COPYRIGHTED MATERIAL IN *TCLC*, VOLUME 194, WAS REPRODUCED FROM THE FOLLOWING BOOKS:

Barsanti, Michael. From "Little Magazines," in *The Oxford Encyclopedia of American Literature*. Edited by Jay Parini. Oxford University Press, 2004. Copyright © 2004 by Oxford University Press, Inc. Reproduced by permission of Oxford University Press, Inc.—Brunnhuber, Nicole M. T. From "After the Prison Ships: Internment Narratives in Canada," in *"Totally Un-English"? Britain's Internment of "Enemy Aliens" in Two World Wars*. Edited by Richard Dove. Rodopi, 2005. Copyright © 2005 Editions Rodopi B. V. Reproduced by permission.—Busby, Mark. From "The Significance of the Frontier in Contemporary American Fiction," in *The Frontier Experience and the American Dream: Essays on American Literature*. Edited by David Mogen, Mark Busby, and Paul Bryant. Texas A&M University, 1989. Copyright © by David Mogen, Mark Busby, and Paul Bryant. All rights reserved. Reproduced by permission.—Calder, Robert. From *Beware the British Serpent: The Role of Writers in British Propaganda in the United States, 1939-1945*. McGill-Queen's University Press, 2004. Copyright © 2004 McGill-Queen's University Press. Reproduced by permission.—Cloonan, William. From *The Writing of War: French and German Fiction and World War II*. University Press of Florida, 1999. Copyright © 1999 by the Board of Commissioners of State Institutions of Florida. Reprinted with permission of the University Press of Florida.—Ellis, R. J. From "Mapping the UK Little Magazine Field," in *New British Poetries: The Scope of the Possible*. Edited by Robert Hampson and Peter Barry. Manchester University Press, 1993. Copyright © 1993 by R. J. Ellis. Reproduced by permission of the author.—Görtschacher, Wolfgang. From *Contemporary Views on the Little Magazine Scene*. Poetry Salzburg at the University of Salzburg, 2000. © Wolfgang Görtschacher. Reproduced by permission.—Hamblin, Robert W. From "Beyond the Edge of the Map: Faulkner, Turner, and the Frontier Line," in *Faulkner in the Twenty-First Century: Faulkner and Yoknapatawpha, 2000*. Edited by Robert W. Hamblin and Ann J. Abadie. University Press of Mississippi, 2003. Copyright © 2003 by University Press of Mississippi. All rights reserved. Reproduced by permission.—Hamilton, Ian. From *The Little Magazines: A Study of Six Editors*. Weidenfeld and Nicolson, 1976. Copyright © 1976 Ian Hamilton. All rights reserved. Reproduced by permission of Aitken Alexander Associates Ltd., on behalf of the author's estate. In the UK and British Commonwealth by permission of Weidenfeld and Nicolson, a division of The Orion Publishing Group.—Harris, Frederick J. From *Encounters with Darkness: French and German Writers on World War II*. Oxford

Thomson Gale Literature Product Advisory Board

The members of the Thomson Gale Literature Product Advisory Board—reference librarians from public and academic library systems—represent a cross-section of our customer base and offer a variety of informed perspectives on both the presentation and content of our literature products. Advisory board members assess and define such quality issues as the relevance, currency, and usefulness of the author coverage, critical content, and literary topics included in our series; evaluate the layout, presentation, and general quality of our printed volumes; provide feedback on the criteria used for selecting authors and topics covered in our series; provide suggestions for potential enhancements to our series; identify any gaps in our coverage of authors or literary topics, recommending authors or topics for inclusion; analyze the appropriateness of our content and presentation for various user audiences, such as high school students, undergraduates, graduate students, librarians, and educators; and offer feedback on any proposed changes/enhancements to our series. We wish to thank the following advisors for their advice throughout the year.

American Frontier Literature

Fiction, poetry, and essays based on the American migration experience to the western frontier beginning in the nineteenth century.

INTRODUCTION

During the nineteenth century, many Americans migrated across the Mississippi River and onto the plains, mountains, and deserts of the West, seeking new land and new opportunities. Writers chronicled this westward migration, composing stories about the individuals who struggled to survive and prosper under harsh and often dangerous conditions while freeing themselves from the constrictions of civilization. Stories about these characters and the land they set out to conquer resulted in the creation of many archetypal characters of frontier literature–including cowboys, mountain men, and settlers—and featured vivid descriptions of the natural beauty of the western landscape. In these works, writers of frontier literature were able to construct a mythology of the American West, and beginning in the nineteenth century and into the early years of the twentieth century, frontier literature remained an immensely popular genre in the United States. Readers were fascinated by images of majestic mountains, unending prairie landscapes, and inhospitable deserts, as well as the dangers posed by Native Americans, wild animals, and harsh environmental conditions. Although the term frontier literature is typically associated with the nineteenth-century American West, critics acknowledge that the description covers a broad range of settings and is used to refer to a vast collection of works deriving from the clash between the civilized and natural worlds. Represented by European thinking and the rules and customs of traditional society, civilization was thought to symbolize the past while the frontier—with its promises of adventure, opportunity, and individual freedom—was regarded as the future. However, the frontier also represented danger, alienation, and even violence.

In his seminal 1893 lecture, "The Significance of the Frontier in American History," better known as the Frontier Thesis, Frederick Jackson Turner maintained that it was America's frontier that best explained the distinctive history of the United States. He linked the settling of the American frontier with American exceptionalism: as Americans moved westward across the continent, communities became more democratic, less hierarchical, and allowed more individual freedoms.

The Frontier Thesis was widely disseminated amongst scholars and is considered one of the most influential theories in American history. With the onset of the twentieth century came the realization that the American frontier was closing. As civilization and its culture and traditions encroached upon the open frontier, writers began to reflect on the clash of cultures that formed the American experience, the death of the frontier and its values, and the impact of this demise on the concept of American exceptionalism. In the meantime, many writers have used the themes and concerns of traditional frontier literature to explore new avenues, such as the Far North or outer space; or have touched on a reversal of the frontier migration, as Americans confronted Old World values in Europe. Other authors have explored new frontiers in the form of social or political movements. However, traditional frontier novels and short stories remain popular in American literature and continue to be successfully translated into other mediums. These stories revisit themes central to American mythology and literature and reflect concerns integral to the American consciousness in the twenty-first century.

REPRESENTATIVE WORKS

Edward Abbey
The Brave Cowboy (novel) 1958
Desert Solitaire: A Season in the Wilderness (nonfiction) 1968
The Monkey Wrench Gang (novel) 1975

Rex Beach
The Winds of Chance (novel) 1918

Saul Bellow
Henderson the Rain King (novel) 1959
Herzog (novel) 1964

Willa Cather
O Pioneers! (novel) 1913
The Song of the Lark (novel) 1915
A Lost Lady (novel) 1923

James Oliver Curwood
The Alaskan: A Novel of the North (novel) 1923

William Faulkner
The Wild Palms (novel) 1939
Go Down, Moses (short stories) 1942

A. B. Guthrie
The Big Sky (novel) 1947
The Way West (novel) 1950
These Thousand Hills (novel) 1956

Ken Kesey
One Flew over the Cuckoo's Nest (novel) 1962

Jack London
The Call of the Wild (novel) 1903
The Valley of the Moon (novel) 1913

Frederick Manfred
Lord Grizzly (novel) 1954
Riders of Judgment (novel) 1957

Cormac McCarthy
All the Pretty Horses (novel) 1992
The Crossing (novel) 1994
Cities of the Plain (novel) 1998
No Country for Old Men (novel) 2005

Larry McMurtry
Horseman, Pass By (novel) 1961
Lonesome Dove (novel) 1985
Buffalo Girls (novel) 1990
Streets of Laredo (novel) 1993

Frank Norris
The Octopus (novel) 1901

Jack Shaefer
Shane (novel) 1949
Monte Walsh (novel) 1963

Nevil Shute
A Town Like Alice (novel) 1950
The Far Country (novel) 1952

John Steinbeck
Grapes of Wrath (novel) 1939; revised ed., 1972

Wallace Stegner
The Big Rock Candy Mountain (novel) 1942

Frederick Jackson Turner
The Significance of the Frontier in American History
  (nonfiction) 1894

Nathanael West
Miss Lonelyhearts (novel) 1933
The Day of the Locust (novel) 1939

OVERVIEWS AND GENERAL STUDIES

Ann-Janine Morey-Gaines (essay date summer 1981)

SOURCE: Morey-Gaines, Ann-Janine. "Of Menace and Men: The Sexual Tensions of the American Frontier Metaphor." *Soundings: An Interdisciplinary Journal* 64, no. 2 (summer 1981): 132-49.

[*In the following essay, Morey-Gaines examines the role of women in the male-dominated genre of frontier literature.*]

"His career was like a prairie—vast, uncluttered, straight away."[1] So read one epitaph in remembrance of John Wayne, a man who represents one of the most essential archetypes of American culture. The current of emotion called forth by his death suggests that when Marshall McLuhan asks: "How long can the urban male live imaginatively on the frontier of eighty years ago?" the question is largely rhetorical.[2] The frontier has become an enduring metaphor of a history remembered with keen nostalgia by those who never lived it.

The frontier metaphor is essentially dependent upon the land for its various expressions. Early observers equated geographic horizons with the horizons of the American soul. Lyman Beecher, for example, announced that "all of the West is on a great scale and the minds and the views of the people correspond with these relative proportions."[3] The quality of American morality was associated with the quantity of American territory and valued features of American character came to be integrally connected with the western landscape. This cultural conviction, renewed with the visible loss of each remaining emblem of the frontier, makes the task of understanding the metaphor very difficult. Metaphor works by balancing seemingly disparate descriptions against one another, holding a complexity of meanings "in solution." To describe the American frontier mythos as metaphor is to make an important statement about its complexity, ambiguity, and value tension.

The frontier metaphor involves two distinct but interrelated zones, the wild West and the agrarian West. The geographic qualities of each zone are applied to the human beings who live in the West and a metaphoric reasoning from place to person produces at least two kinds of American heroes, the farmer and the gunfighter. While both types of hero are for a time visible in the agrarian and wild West, only the gunfighter gains cultural ascendency. The popularity of the gunfighter and the obscurity of the farmer are heavily influenced by the literal and metaphoric location of woman in each zone. The agrarian West, more associated with woman, seems unable to sustain its male hero. The wild West, defined in part by its defiance of woman, produces our lasting cultural heroes.

Women inhabit the shadows of a metaphor that is understood, however unconsciously, to have as its special referent the white, male American. Accordingly, this paper uses American literature written by men as a principal formative artifact of the frontier metaphor. Yet in spite of the understood exclusivity of the literature examined here, woman—idealized, suppressed, and finally vilified—is also a principal subject of this body of literature. Sexual tension is rendered metaphorically in the struggle between the agrarian West and the wild West and from the dust of that struggle the archetypal American hero and his archetypal antagonist is formed. The images of each shift within the metaphor of the frontier as the culture moves from the nineteenth to twentieth centuries. In that shift is recorded a classic conversation about values, ideals, and dreams.

II

Although the symbol of the agrarian West as a garden of the world was common to American political rhetoric of the mid-nineteenth century, it never arrived as a permanent motive in male-authored fiction. The domination of the wild West mythos over the agrarian mythos illumines the value preference of cultural imagination. In *Virgin Land,* Henry Nash Smith offers several reasons for the recessive profile of the agrarian West. Briefly summarized, these include the fact that the self-declared center of civilization—the East—persisted in regarding the West as an area interesting only for its rusticity, an interest quickly worn thin. Furthermore, "rain follows the plow" oratory was so false to the facts that its idealized version of rural life was doomed to early obscurity.[4]

In addition to these weaknesses of the agrarian myth, there is also a serious problem with the image of the agrarian hero as he is environmentally situated. In both the agrarian novel and the wild West novel the hero—whether gunfighter or farmer—is defined in terms of his relationship to the land. Both types of frontier novels present nature as an impersonal force that is at once beautiful and terrible in the power of its elements. Yet in one kind of frontier novel the hero thrives in his association with nature and in the other he falters; the deification of the frontier hero through association with the natural world is as common in the novel of the wild West as it is uncommon in the agrarian novel.

The agrarian works of Hamlin Garland and Frank Norris both contain repeated patterns of imagery that make it difficult to sustain an agrarian hero. In each, the vast beauty of the landscape is recorded back to back with the squalor and unhappiness that is visible upon closer examination. Thus Garland may present us with the cool tranquility of a rural sunset whose chief detail is the weary, sweating farmer trying to milk a hot and fly-tormented cow. In Norris's *The Octopus,* the western epic envisioned by the ambitious young poet is always derailed by the intrusion of the people who populate the West. Against the magnificent backdrop of western landscape, they are "uncouth brutes . . . , grimed with the soil they worked on."[5] From a distance, the rural countryside is a model of bucolic splendor, but a closer inspection reveals a life of toil and grim resolution.

In contrast, the wild West hero is magnified in proportion to the landscape, as in the oft-remarked passage from *The Prairie* that introduces the reader to Leatherstocking,[6] or, as in a more recent example, Max Brand's description of the outlaw Annan Rhiannon:

> When they look up there, what do they see? Do they see Mt. Laurel? No, you damn well bet they don't. They see Annan Rhiannon standing in the middle of the sky with his black beard on his face; and the clouds that blow over the shoulder of Mt. Laurel, they're the hair blowing over the back of Rhiannon.[7]

The title character of Jack Schaefer's *Shane* embodies this land/man imagery carried to the limits of romantic mythologizing. More at home with his horse than human company, Shane is initially set apart from the human world by his effortless communion with the natural world. Man and horse are "like a single being," and like his horse, Shane moves with a "quiet sureness and power."[8] In moments of solitude or crisis, Shane instinctively turns toward the western mountains for sustenance. In the Gethsemane-like moment when Shane must choose whether or not to apply his power to change the situation between farmer and rancher, he turns to the sunset-lit mountains and stretches "his arms up, the fingers reaching to their utmost limits, grasping and grasping, it seemed, at the glory glowing in the sky" (p. 100).

Although Shane is physically small in stature, his presence commands and overwhelms all ideas of physical proportion so that he is, in fact, larger than life. The uncanny physical presence he gains through his association with the natural world is translated into an imposing metaphysical presence, giving him a legendary and Christ-like omniscience. Shane "was the man who rode into our little valley out of the heart of the great glowing West and when his work was done, rode back whence he had come" (p. 119). At once immanent in and transcendent of nature, the wild West hero is magnified to the limits of spiritual and physical boundaries, his immortality secured through his oneness with "the great glowing West." In the language of the makers of those heroes and myths, the "courageous" but often "broken" characters of the agrarian novel "are no match for" the olympian characters produced by the novel of the wild West.

In many instances the same landscape that enhances the reputation of the gunfighter may only serve to emphasize the farmer's precarious hold upon his world. The important variable in the picture may not be so much landscape, or even occupation, although one may be inherently more romantic than the other. The truly crucial explanation for the failure of the agrarian novel has yet to be examined in current commentary *and it has to do with the ascendency of women in the agrarian landscape in contrast to the helplessness of men*. The hidden problem of the agrarian myth is the gender associations that pervade the garden, and the metaphoric position of women as they relate to these images. The agrarian mythos suggests a feminine personification of the earth, lending metaphoric power to women rather than men. The archetypal association of women with land and nature further diminishes the farmer's heroic possibilities.[9]

Frank Norris's turn of the century plea for the small rancher in *The Octopus* provides an embarrassment of examples of the woman-as-land metaphor, parallel in image and purpose to the later Steinbeck novel, *The Grapes of Wrath*. Norris sees in the act of farming representations of "elemental Male and Female, locked in colossal embrace . . . , untamed, savage, natural, sublime." He struggles to give the wheat farmer epic proportions through imagery of cosmic sexual assault concretized by the plowing of the fields. Aided by the plow, a "multitude of iron hands," the farmer's "heroic embrace" of the earth is "so violent as to be veritably brutal," and the "warm, brown flesh of the mother earth is "responsive and passionate under this assault" (pp. 127-31). The earth is given a feminine personification, and the processes of seedtime, growth, and harvest are all expressed in sexual metaphors.

This aspect of the metaphor stresses domination of the earth mother; other aspects present her as a supreme, sensuous power. One of several examples in *The Octopus* is the milkmaid Hilma Tree. She is an earth mother figure, and like the male hero of the wild West novel, she is glorified and enlarged by her mystical connection with nature:

> He saw her standing there in the scintillating light of the morning, her smooth arms wet with milk, redolent and fragrant of milk, her whole desirable figure moving in the golden glory of the sun, steeped in a lambent flame, saturated with it, joyous as the dawn itself.
>
> (p. 210)

Motherhood is the finishing touch to the "delicacy of an elemental existence," and in one of Norris's more contrived moments he has her sitting upon a natural throne formed by tree roots, "the radiance of the unseen crown of motherhood glowing from her forehead, the beauty of the perfect woman surrounding her like a glory" (p. 504).

The poet, Presley, comes to see in her a "perfect maturity" and "infinite capacity for love," and with this realization, the long awaited inspiration for his epic comes to him, described by Norris in the following suggestive language:

> A longing . . . to be strong and noble because of her, to reshape his purposeless, half-wasted life with her nobility and purity and gentleness . . . his inspiration leaped all at once within him, leaped and stood firm, hardening to a resolve stronger than any he had ever known.
>
> (pp. 629-30)

In a very real sense she is the last hope of the farmer, for only she endures to nurture and inspire in the scattered farmers and the aimless poet the courage needed to continue their life-long struggles.

For Norris, nature is the "Force," the mystery of creation and life embodied by the growing wheat and the motherhood of Hilma Tree. Furthermore, truth and justice will prosper in the impersonal power of natural cycles, a Norris conviction illustrated by the grim death scene of the evil railroad agent. Trapped in the belly of a grain vessel, he is smothered by streams of wheat, the "nourisher of nations," the agent of the feminine-personified earth (p. 652). Given this pattern of intense sexual metaphor attached to the earth, it is no surprise that it is woman's uncompromised mutuality with earth that leaves her the transcendent figure closing each epic agrarian narrative. It is the women who endure and triumph.

Like the "Force" that runs the world in *The Octopus*, Ma Joad holds the migrant family together in *The Grapes of Wrath*, and she is an earth mother figure straight from the archetype. In Steinbeck's world women have an innate understanding of cyclic immortality, and with motherhood, woman comes into her own as a special elemental being. Thus, the whiney young girl, Rose of Sharon, joins the ranks of the Great Mother in the powerful closing image of *The Grapes of Wrath*. Left destitute by seasonal rains and perpetual unemployment, the Joad family seeks refuge in an old barn, finding there another worker near death from starvation. Rose of Sharon has recently lost a baby, and her breasts are swollen with milk. She and Ma communicate silently, on some intuitive level, and in the final sentences of *The Grapes of Wrath* the girl-grown-mother insists the dying man take the life nourishment she offers. Smiling mysteriously, she suckles him as she would a baby.

On the most universal level of the archetype, woman embodies life while man is the potential master of life who must transcend the claims of the Mother in order to achieve his heroic status.[10] Yet the overpowering natural strength suggested by the metaphoric reciprocity between woman and land in the agrarian mythos creates a female, rather than a male hero. As an emblem of the rural agrarian frontier, woman represents the life and land he cultivates, farming and marriage become equivalent (and ambivalently regarded) actions. The mixed blessing of woman and the agrarian frontier is that while farming and marriage bring forth new abundance (crops/children), the woman-as-land metaphor only highlights the transience and frailty of manhood in this frontier. The relatively few examples of a true earth mother figure in American frontier literature suggests that American culture will not give mythological approval to the strong, dignified woman-image that the archetype might yield.[11]

The remedy for the threatened male hero is a shift to the landscape of the wild West where woman's connection to the land is minimal. In the literature of the wild West the agrarian West represents civilization. Woman serves as an ambivalently regarded symbol of the progress of the domesticated West upon the wild West. However, the power of the idealized earth mother imagery disappears in wild West novels. Instead, woman's weakness is insured by her separation from the earth, and her civility is emphasized. She seems to be a very minor character in wild West novels. The male who profits from her diminution, however, is the wild West hero. A plow cannot seem to replace a horse or a gun as the true tool of the American hero, and the destruction of life rather than its cultivation becomes the primary interest of the frontier metaphor. In the last analysis, the real American hero is the individualistic gunslinger whose embattled identity is the subject of the wild West novel.

III

The hero of the wild West is sworn to protect civilization and its tender messenger even though his identity as male is threatened by the imposition of civilized structures upon the frontier. To lose touch with civilization is to relinquish a host of traditional virtues that are considered essential to a superior race. On the other hand, to plunge into the primitive state demanded by the wild West (or the wilderness) is to regain a sexual and spiritual potency that is sapped by the structures of civilization. The frontier serves as the arena wherein these ambivalences and cultural uncertainties can be played out.

Jack Schaefer's *Shane* is an excellent illustration of how tensions between the values of the agrarian and wild West frontier are juxtaposed and resolved. The drama in the simple-seeming story of *Shane* is double-leveled and cross-purposed in its message. The external action leads to a symbolic and literal showdown between the agrarian West (represented by the farmer Joe

Starrett) and the wild West (the cowboys and cattle ranchers). The internal action of the story belongs to Shane who struggles to honor his renunciation of a violent past. While his resolve is strengthened by the temporary assumption of a farmer's garb and way of life, it is also threatened by the clear imperative he feels to defend the Starrett family with the power he has renounced.

The real interest of the story is not the farmer-rancher struggle, but the carefully anticipated moment when Shane will fling off his self-imposed exile and reveal his true identity as a joyous and powerful frontier god. The irony of having such a savior for the peaceful agrarian way is the ancient one that peace and justice are attainable only through the acts that are presumably repugnant to a civilized way of life. Thus the triumph of the agrarian West over the wild West is undercut at every point by the tormented hero who makes it possible, and the contrast between the inevitable helplessness of the farmer and the equally inevitable strength of the gunslinger cannot fail to diminish the farmer, the agrarian West, and the civilized values they represent. The uprooting of an old tree stump on Joe Starrett's farm is one of several double-messaged episodes in which the symbolic action persistently weakens the literal, physical action of the characters.

The invincible old tree stump is, like Shane, a resiliant reminder of a wilder way of life and the order of things that preceded the domestication of the wilderness. Shane's decision to aid the farmer in his struggle against the rancher is symbolized in his willingness to help Joe cut the old root from the ground. Heretofore, Joe has been unable to remove the stump, but with the aid of the disguised gunfighter, the monstrous stump is finally dislodged (pp. 26-27). Only with Shane's cooperation is the triumph of the cultivated West over the wild secured. Another reading of this episode simultaneously suggests that the giant stump and root is also a phallic symbol and the inevitable cutting of the root symbolizes a severance of potency and loss of manhood in the winning of the agrarian West.

The sexual symbolism involved in this presentation of the winning of the West must not be underestimated. Sexual as well as national identity is linked to the conquest of the land. While Joe Starrett is unarguably a strong and admirable man, Shane is his acknowledged master in all things, including male sex dominance. For the classic precautionary reasons, Shane takes the dinner table seat facing the door of the kitchen. For symbolic reasons, however, the seat he so naturally assumes is Joe Starrett's chair, and Joe gives it up willingly (p. 35).

The prize that accompanies the seat of the father is the only woman in the novel, maid/mother Marian Starrett. Her status as a cherished but transferable possession is made quite clear. Starrett is willing to relinquish his claim upon his wife as just compensation for Shane's protection, yet Shane is too honorable to take her, and Marian too honorable to be disloyal to her husband, in spite of the obvious mutual attraction between herself and the gunman (pp. 80 and 104). The farmer is "all man," but he is no match for the potency of the wild West hero, and they all know it.

It is no accident that Shane's superior status is revealed, in part, through covertly presented sexual themes. He has not simply renounced a violent past, but the full sexuality that is expressed in the violence of the wild West. The underlying sexual tension of the novel surfaces most clearly once the ultimate source of his innate power is revealed—his guns. Shane's "intangible and terrifying presence," hinting at dominion over more than one world, is seen to derive partly from his glorified association with the natural world, but is completed preternaturally when he straps on the gunbelt, noticeably absent throughout most of the novel:

> Belt and holster and gun. . . . These were not things he was wearing or carrying. They were part of him, part of the man, of the full sum of the integrate force that was Shane. You could see now that for the first time this man who had been living with us, who was one of us, was complete, was himself in the final effect of his being. . . . Slim and dark in the doorway, he seemed somehow to fill the whole frame.

(pp. 101-102)

With the addition of the phallic guns, Shane is finally set apart as Exalted and Other in his revealed identity as the righteous arbiter of justice and administrator of death. This omniscient identity is integrally linked with his identity as a powerful sexual being. Thus, in addition to his special relationship to an unfeminized natural world, the guns are a further source of heroic power that is alien and unavailale to the farmer.

The sexual longing so discreetly displayed in *Shane* is often much bolder in other wild West novels[12] suggesting that at least one critical function of the wild West novel is the resolution of the sexual anxiety generated by woman's presence in the diminishing territory of American manhood. In every gun battle the hero secures a physical and moral territory that proclaims his manhood and the fitness of his judgmental prerogatives. Ostensibly, part of the territory he defends is that adoring woman, but in actuality every gun battle is as much a defense against her as for her. In *Shane,* as with other wild West novels, it is important that the woman give assent to the gunfight and that she witness or eagerly await the details of the battle. The witnessed act of violence publicly confirms a manhood unavailable to the agrarian hero, shows the gunslinger to be a righteous defender of civilization, and yet immediately removes him from the realm of woman's influence. It is perhaps

not surprising to find that the wild West hero is rarely seen in the embrace of the waiting woman, for the consummated sexual act is performed between men, with guns.

The motivating sexual tension of the wild West novel is played out in the language of violence, and the compliance of woman the civilizer to man the righteous destroyer is a critical part of the formula of American manhood. As this violent communion is separated from the geographic context that gave it credence, the execution of that act becomes increasingly vital as an affirmation of manhood and sexual domination. The modern-day winning of the West finally becomes more a matter of sexual than national aggrandizement, and the view of American womanhood shifts drastically once the special western landscape no longer exists to give the wild West hero strength and moral sanction.

IV

In the twentieth-century frontier novel the once-positive mother image is no longer supported by its natural setting. Woman becomes fearsome in her disregard of traditional mores of passivity and self-sacrifice. Will and sexual menace increase proportionally in twentieth-century images of the modern woman. The original tension between the wild and agrarian West, the struggle to control the frontier, is transformed into a desperate sexual contest between the gunfighter and the modern woman. She is the sexual dragon who prowls the highroads of American culture. She is the hunter who must be hunted and slain if the original hunter is to regain the sexual security once promised by the frontier metaphor. The metaphor has shifted, and the frontier is now located on new ground—an insane asylum in Ken Kesey's *One Flew Over the Cuckoo's Nest*; Africa, South America, or Europe in Ernest Hemingway's works. These new battlefields suggest strange and intimately linked domains of sexuality, madness, and death that have come to be the important frontiers of the twentieth century.

An early short story by Hemingway establishes the ethos under consideration here, suggesting that in the twentieth century death is a most fearsome territory (even though human sexuality may be the far more treacherous and uncertain ground). "The Short Happy Life of Frances Macomber" is set in the jungles of darkest Africa, but the territory in question is sexual. Margaret Macomber is Hemingway's idea of the twentieth-century woman, "the hardest, the cruelest, the most predatory and the most attractive" in the world.[13] Frances Macomber is the "great American boy-man" who seeks to come of age through that classic ritual of manhood, the hunt. The modernity of the story is demonstrated by the fact that it does not end with Macomber's undisputed dominion over a villain, the land, death, or a woman. When Macomber at last fearlessly encounters his prey, he is shot from behind by his wife before the primal hunting scene can be completed. Hemingway's portrayal of Margaret leaves no doubt that she shoots her husband, not accidentally or out of fear for his safety, but out of revenge for his belated claim to manhood that spells the end of her castrating domination over him. The once-adoring, waiting woman has become the biggest enemy the American male faces in the new frontier.

Margaret's sins against the American man are several. In an early incident, when Frances Macomber abdicates his place as master by showing himself to be afraid of his quarry, Margaret is quick to claim an analogous role as a sexual hunter. She dispenses her sexual favors to the safari guide as a sign of her disdain for her cowardly husband, in effect preying upon his masculinity. Her sexual defiance is, in itself, a violation of the sexual politics of American life. For a time, she is unnaturally autonomous. The extent of her transgression is not fully concretized, however, until she picks up her husband's weapon and uses this tool to become the hunter of her own husband. While her sexual betrayal is made clear only by suggestion, the shooting of Frances Macomber is vividly depicted for the reader. Violent intercourse takes the place of sexual intercourse.

In the same way, Ken Kesey's Irish cowboy, McMurphy, in *One Flew Over the Cuckoo's Nest* is also presented in a struggle that is primordially sexual. In this novel, mental health practices represent a mindless, mechanical conspiracy against freedom and individuality. Acting autonomously on the ward as the single identifiable source of repression, McMurphy's antagonist, Nurse Ratched, represents modern woman. Randle P. McMurphy seems to represent freedom of mind for all people. He champions, however, a romantic frontier ambience in which the male struggles for a balance of power that is to be sexually determined and reinforced. Thus, *One Flew Over the Cuckoo's Nest* is most accurately described as a wild West tale rendered in the savage polemic of sexual contest.

McMurphy is a modern-day Shane, the rugged individual who reluctantly but courageously takes up the cause of the weak and oppressed. He enters the ward like the gunfighter who is inseparable from his horse, and his several showdowns with Nurse Ratched evoke all the repressed hysteria of *High Noon*:

> He walked with long steps, too long, and he had his thumbs hooked in his pockets again, the iron in his boot heels cracked lightning out of the tile. He was the logger again, the swaggering gambler, the big redheaded brawling Irishman, the cowboy out of the TV set walking down the middle of the street to meet a dare.[14]

His weapon is his sexuality, madness the fierce expression of his manhood against the brutality of the "normal," "sane" Nurse Ratched.

"Madness" as a desirable state of mind and sexual freedom are specifically associated with the male organ. Nurse Ratched, McMurphy discovers and announces to the ward, is a ball breaker. And, he goes on to explain by analogy, there is an indivisible connection between freedom of mind and male potency:

> Seen 'em all over the country and in the homes—people who try to make you weak so they can get you to toe the line, . . . You ever been kneed in the nuts in a brawl, buddy? . . . If you're up against a guy who wants to win by making you weaker instead of making himself stronger, then watch for his knee, he's gonna go for your vitals. And that's what the old buzzard is doing, going for your vitals.
>
> (p. 57)

When McMurphy later realizes how serious his situation is, he articulates the terror of Nurse Ratched's power. Lobotomy is the extreme measure she can order for her patients, nothing less than "frontal-lobe castration. I guess if she can't cut below the belt she'll do it above the eyes" (p. 165). Intentionally or not, this kind of metaphor decisively denies woman a place among the free and the brave. At best, she can have no mind at all. At worst, she is the sworn enemy of that which she cannot possess.

As if these values are not already clearly visible in the stereotypes of the genre, Kesey, by calling upon the spirit of Melville, has attempted to give the frontier formula a deeper metaphysical significance. The lineaments of good and evil are quite simplistic here, but the intention is unmistakable. McMurphy wears black boxer shorts with large, white whales leaping about upon them because a literature major said he "was a symbol." The double entendre is unavoidable as the whale's name simultaneously suggests the physical size and metaphysical significance of the organ that is the center of attention. McMurphy has got himself a whale of a dick and a whale of a cause. Even the nurse acknowledges the source of his power. Just as she is "rolling along at her biggest and meanest," McMurphy steps in front of her with nothing but a wet, skintight towel around him. "She shrinks to about head-high to where that towel covers him" while he towers above her (p. 87). Like a vampire checked by a cross, she is temporarily thwarted by the unseen organ. Billy Bibbitt, whose euphonious name and childish stutter evoke Melville's Billy Budd, is the innocent who is martyred in the struggle between these forces of good and evil. Nurse Ratched, of course, is the evil one.

Nurse Ratched is a fearsome parody of the nineteenth-century image of the benevolent and self-sacrificing mother (pp. 58-59). She is a classic Great Bitch Mother who devours or cripples her wayward children. The gentle haze of natural earth imagery which once surrounded the image of mother has been replaced by the imagery of mechanical bestiality. As Chief Bromden sees it, Nurse Ratched is the representative of "the Combine, which is a huge organization that aims to adjust the Outside as well as she has the Inside" (p. 30). She is the incarnation of the organization (slyly named after a harvesting and threshing machine used in modern agriculture) which has taken over not only the garden, but now threatens the wild western frontier as well. When she unleashes her fury she is like beast and machine together, a mechanical hunter driven by rage and repressed sexuality:

> Her nostrils flare open, and every breath she draws she gets bigger, as big and tough-looking's I seen her get over a patient since Taber was here. She works the hinges in her elbows and fingers. I hear a small squeak. She starts moving, and I get back against the wall, and when she rumbles past she's already big as a truck, trailing that wicker bag behind in her exhaust like a semi behind a Jimmy Diesel. Her lips are parted, and her smile's going out before her like a radiator grill. I can smell the hot oil and magneto spark when she goes past, and as every step hits the floor she blows up a size bigger, blowing and puffing, roll down anything in her path.
>
> (p. 87)

This is the manifestation of her true self.[15]

Most of the time, however, she is a well-oiled robot, tending the machinery of the Combine. Her public face is "smooth, calculated and precision made, like an expensive baby-doll, skin like flesh-colored enamel, blend of white and cream and baby-blue eyes" (p. 11). She is the demonic underside of Marshall McLuhan's "Mechanical Bride."[16] The only chinks in Nurse Ratched's machinery are betrayed by the smoldering color of her lips and fingers (pp. 10 and 136) and the "size of her bosom. A mistake was made somehow in manufacturing, putting those big womanly breasts on what would otherwise have been a perfect work, and you can see how bitter she is about it" (p. 11). Her repressed femininity is her fatal flaw, and she must be conquered sexually, or not at all. McMurphy's crusade must be against the "juggernaut of modern matriarchy" (p. 66).

At first, McMurphy seems to think that a good screw is all she needs to straighten her out. But when one of the men challenges him to do the job, McMurphy concedes the impossibility of that assignment. Only an act of sexual violence will defeat her, and to that end McMurphy is finally driven. He attacks the implacable monster in a sequence in which sexuality and violence are one. He rips open her uniform and exposes her breasts, which are "warm and pink," and "bigger than anybody ever imagined." These "outsized badges of femininity,"

should have kept her power in check. But even the suggested rape and its symbolic imposition of her natural role upon her are not enough to recall her to her true self, and McMurphy knows that only violence and death rather than sexual congress will restore this world to its natural order. So, after ripping open her uniform, he attempts to strangle her (p. 267). He is partially successful, for when she returns to the ward she is wearing a new uniform that *"could no longer conceal the fact that she was a woman"* (p. 268, emphasis mine).

The lethal power that obviously stemmed from her denial of her feminine sexuality has been broken. Even the callow display of McMurphy's lobotomized body is not enough to recall the men to their old position of emasculated subservience. Gradually they leave the ward. Chief Bromden, McMurphy's alter spirit, smothers the "castrated" McMurphy. Taking the gift of new man-self called forth by McMurphy, he breaks out of the ward and heads back to open country and free spaces.

It is impossible not to be utterly in sympathy with this modern-day cowboy in the heroic and unequal struggle. Respect for the larger theme of freedom of mind and body need not obscure, however, the very disturbing images of antagonism which are used as the vehicle. The propagandistic utility of polemic is cheapened and degraded by this presentation of one of the most fearsome Mother figures in modern fiction contrasted with a heroism and reluctant high-mindedness which is exclusively male-identified. The novel extolls a brawling, sexually abusive man whom we must admire and support or find ourselves on the side of repression and social tyranny. The reduction of complex cultural choices to simple, easy-to-follow diagrams is a fatal legacy of the ascendancy of the wild West hero over the agrarian hero.

The frontier story has always been a simplistic formula for separating heroes and villains and assuring the victory of the self-righteous.[17] The noticeable alteration in the twentieth-century formula is the centrality of the female characters to ritual violence. While it is possible to discuss most nineteenth-century wild western literature without ever mentioning the female characters, twentieth-century female characters are crucial to the resolution. They are, in fact, the precipitators of the action. Their prominence has not necessarily enhanced their reputation. No longer complementary, protected accessories to the ritualized slaying of the evil one, woman is either the victim or the excuse for the modern recreation of the frontier showdown. Often, she is the evil one who has taken over the hunting skills of the hunter. She now presumes to determine who shall live and who shall perish. Unlike their nineteenth-century ancestors, then, the women in these novels are the reason for the narrative. It is safe to conclude that in terms of the American drama of the frontier, attitudes about, and images of, women have changed considerably since the nineteenth century, while the standard for the male hero has remained constant, with a shift in the scenery, perhaps, but not a shift in substance.

The analogy, which works from the wide open spaces of the land to the wide open spaces of the male mind, made size and gender the first requirements for moral decision making. Even when the land vanishes as the century turns and progresses, the habit of mind engendered by that precious freedom of space remains. This individualistic turn of mind would be far more of a treasure were it not so virulently associated with an exclusive male prerogative, and were it not so dependent upon violence for its ultimate fulfillment. Figuratively speaking, the male hero began as a frontiersman hunting game and Indians. As he stalked west and toward the end of the nineteenth century, Indians and wilderness became scarce, and the new villains became those who challenge the traditional order the hero himself so ambivalently championed. The territory for resolving those ambivalences, however, has long since disappeared by the middle of the twentieth century. The hero, accustomed to a certain moral ascendancy and in innocent, lawless autonomy, finds himself facing east with a western state of mind, finds himself the hunted rather than the hunter, finds himself defending a frontier ethos moved into the territory of sexual metaphor. Woman, always less secure in her ties to the land, always more a symbol of civilization in American fiction, becomes the villain responsible for the disappearance of the anarchic, adolescent freedom of the wild western frontier. In the twentieth century the American frontier metaphor is reduced to phallic proportions and to the poisonous warfare for sexual supremacy. In *The Return of the Vanishing American,* Leslie Fiedler makes a remark to the effect that the warfare between white and Indian has created some fine tragic themes in American fiction, while the escalated war between the sexes has created for the most part only a little low comedy.[18] Mr. Fiedler is quite wrong. The gender antagonism which currently infuses American fiction betokens one of the most profound failures of the questing American spirit.

Notes

1. *The Herald Examiner,* headline, Tuesday, June 12, 1979, p. A-1.

2. Marshall McLuhan, *The Mechanical Bride: Folklore of Industrial Man* (Boston: Beacon, 1967), pp. 154-57.

3. *A Plea for the West,* 2nd ed. (New York: Leavitt, Lord and Company, 1935), p. 40. For similar expressions see also: Josiah Strong, *Our Country: Its Possible Future and Its Present Crisis,* intro. Jurgen Herbst (New York: The Baker and Taylor Company, for the American Home Missionary Society, 1891; reprint ed., Cambridge, Mass.: Belknap, 1963); "The Passing of the Frontier," *Dial* 67 (October 1919): 286; "Exit Frontier Morality," *New Republic* 37 (January 1924): 137-38; "Frontier America," *Nation* 104 (January 1917): 66-67.

4. Henry Nash Smith, *Virgin Land: The American West as Myth and Symbol* (Cambridge, Mass.: Harvard University, 1950).

5. Hamlin Garland, *Main Travelled Roads,* afterword by Mark Schorer (New York: New American Library, Signet, 1962), pp. 78-79, and Frank Norris, *The Octopus: A Story of California* (New York: Doubleday, Page and Company, 1901), p. 5. All references to *The Octopus* are from this Doubleday edition. Subsequent page references are given after the quotation.

6. James Fenimore Cooper, *The Prairie: A Tale,* ed. Henry Nash Smith (New York: Rinehart and Company, 1956), p. 8.

7. Max Brand (Frederick Faust), *Singing Guns* (New York: Grosset and Dunlap, 1938), p. 23.

8. Jack Schaefer, *Shane* (New York: Houghton Mifflin, 1949; Bantam Pathfinder, 1972), pp. 4 and 63. All references to *Shane* are from the Bantam edition. Subsequent page references are given after the quotation.

9. This archetypal association of woman and land has been well documented. For example: Erich Neuman, *The Great Mother: An Analysis of the Archetype,* trans. Ralph Manheim (Princeton University, 1972); Joseph Campbell, *The Hero with a Thousand Faces* (New York: Bollinger, 1949), and Carl Gustav Jung, *The Archetypes and the Collective Unconscious,* in *The Collected Works of Carl Gustav Jung,* 17 vols., trans. R. F. C. Hull (Princeton: Princeton University, 1959), 9, i.

Feminist scholarship has pursued the archetype beyond these traditional sources in an effort to understand the negative and positive capacities of the woman-earth archetype. For example: Rosemary Ruether, *New Woman, New Earth: Sexist Ideologies and Human Liberation* (New York: Seabury, 1975), pp. 137-61 and pp. 186-214; Annette Kolodny, *The Lay of the Land: Metaphor as Experience and History in American Life and Letters* (Chapel Hill: University of North Carolina, 1975); Simone deBeauvoir, *The Second Sex* (New York: Alfred A. Knopf, 1952; Vintage, 1974), pp. 157-223, and Sherry B. Ortner, "Is Female to Male as Nature is to Culture," in *Woman, Culture, and Society,* ed. Michelle Zimbalist Rosaldo and Louise Lamphere (Stanford: Stanford University, 1974), pp. 67-87.

10. Joseph Campbell, *Hero with a Thousand Faces* (New York: Bollinger, 1949), pp. 113-47.

11. The number of agrarian novels by male authors is sparse in comparison to those of the wild West, and of the agrarian novels, by no means do all present woman as earth mother figures. Hamlin Garland's works present men and woman as battered and drained by nature, but then, Garland presumed to be in the business of telling the truth about the agrarian West. Agrarian works by *women,* especially some of our neglected regionalists, might provide an important counterpoint to the themes discussed in this essay.

12. One of the many such examples is found in Zane Grey's *Riders of The Purple Sage* (New York: Harper and Brothers, 1921), pp. 286-88:

> "Lassiter, *I do love you!* . . . You are a man! I never knew it till now. Some wonderful change came over me when you buckled on these guns and showed that gray, awful face . . ."
>
> She lifted her face closer and closer to his, until their lips nearly touched, and she hung upon his neck and with strength almost spent pressed and still pressed her palpitating body to his . . . As she whirled in endless chaos she seemed to be falling at the feet of a luminous figure—a man—Lassiter—who had saved her from herself, who could not be changed, who would slay rightfully.

13. Ernest Hemingway, "The Short Happy Life of Frances Macomber," in *The Short Stories of Ernest Hemingway,* preface by Ernest Hemingway (New York: Charles Scribner's Sons, 1966), p. 8.

14. Ken Kesey, *One Flew Over the Cuckoo's Nest* (New York: Viking, 1962; Signet, 1976), p. 172. All references to *One Flew* are from the Signet edition. Subsequent page references are given after the quotation.

15. A similar description makes her sound uncannily like a human incarnation of Norris's octopus railroad:

> She goes into a crouch and advances on where they're trapped in a huddle at the end of the corridor . . . She's swelling up, swells till her back's splitting out the white uniform and she's let her arms section out long enough to wrap around the three of them five, six times.
>
> (p. 10)

16. In *The Mechanical Bride: Folklore of Industrial Man* (Boston: Beacon, 1967), McLuhan observes: "The Hiroshima Bomb was named 'Gilda' in honor of Rita Hayworth" (p. 99).

17. See John Cawelti's discussion of the game formula of the Western in *The Six-Gun Mystique* (Bowling Green, Ohio: Bowling Green University, n.d.), pp. 71-74.

18. Leslie A. Fiedler, *The Return of the Vanishing American* (New York: Stein and Day, 1968), p. 53.

Mark Busby (essay date 1989)

SOURCE: Busby, Mark. "The Significance of the Frontier in Contemporary American Fiction." In *The Frontier Experience and the American Dream: Essays on American Literature,* edited by David Mogen, Mark Busby, and Paul Bryant, pp. 95-103. College Station: Texas A&M University, 1989.

[*In the following essay, Busby contends that frontier imagery and mythology is central to the work of not only writers of Westerns, but also of many contemporary mainstream writers.*]

Although Frederick Jackson Turner's frontier thesis has been widely attacked by historians over the years, it is clear that images of the frontier continue to be important to American writers. Certainly the frontier remains central to writers of formula Westerns, for they set their stories during the golden days of the American West. But the frontier is significant in works by "mainstream" American writers too. Saul Bellow, Ralph Ellison, Ken Kesey, Joseph Heller, Kurt Vonnegut, John Barth, Alice Walker, Joan Didion, Edward Abbey, Larry McMurtry, Ray Bradbury, Philip Caputo, even a "nonfiction" novelist such as Michael Herr—all continue to use frontier imagery as significant elements of their works. Most of these writers express a deep ambivalence toward the frontier. On one hand, they nod longingly toward some frontier American values and recognize positive traits associated with the pastoral frontier. On the other hand, they acknowledge the limitations that a nostalgic, rearward-looking frontier emphasis produces, and they recognize the problems spawned by playing what McMurtry calls "symbolic frontiersman." Many of these writers, therefore, feel a greater affinity for the gothic frontier of the Puritans and American Renaissance writers such as Poe, Hawthorne, and Melville.

Let me specify what I mean by "frontier" before turning to specific contemporary writers who use images associated with the frontier. Although we usually associate the frontier with the American West of the 1800s, I do not refer to a specific place but to a cluster of images and values that grew out of the confrontation between the uncivilized and the civilized world, what Turner called the "meeting point between savagery and civilization."[1] Civilization has generally been associated with the past and with Europe, which for early American thinkers was withering and moribund, the "dead hand" of the past. Civilization, then, is associated with society—its institutions, laws, and restrictions, its demands for compromise and restriction, its cultural refinement and emphasis on manners, its industrial development, and its class distinctions.

The wilderness that civilization confronts suggests many opposite ideas. Rather than the restrictive demands of society, the wilderness offers the possibility of individual freedom, where individuals can test their sense of self against nature without the demand for social responsibility and the compromise of being part of a community. Cultural refinement and emphasis on manners give way to pragmatic empiricism. Rather than industrialism, agrarianism is the major force. Class distinctions disappear. In the wilderness breathes the all-enfolding spirit, a deity worshiped alike by Indians, Transcendentalists, and Naturalists.

These positive images are associated with the pastoral frontier, made familiar through Cooper and Thoreau. But another image cluster has grown out of the gothic frontier, the product of the Puritans' confrontation with the dark forces represented to them by the Indians. Violence, captivity, and metamorphosis are the major aspects of this strain of frontier imagery.

The literary importance of these image clusters appears in many works of literature through archetypal patterns such as those identified by D. H. Lawrence in *Studies in Classic American Literature,* Henry Nash Smith in *Virgin Land,* R. W. B. Lewis in *The American Adam,* Leo Marx in *The Machine in the Garden,* Roderick Nash in *Wilderness and the American Mind,* and Richard Slotkin in *Regeneration through Violence* and *The Fatal Environment.* Let me try to simplify this archetypal pattern. Over and over, American literature concerns itself with innocent American individuals who find themselves in conflict with the oppositions suggested by the east/west, civilization/wilderness grid I described earlier. The archetypal American figure, attempting to free himself from the constrictions of civilization, has moved into the wilderness where, as R. W. B. Lewis has demonstrated, he has become a new Adam in the Garden. The process, though, according to Richard Slotkin, often involves a ritualistic hunt in which the American hunter regenerates himself through violence so that he can return to the familial bonds of civilization with a renewed awareness of his own individuality. The change, Leslie Fiedler and D. H. Lawrence have pointed out, often involves a coming to terms with the nonrational forces that the native American has come to represent.

With the end of the frontier, how can the contemporary American novelist present any of these same concerns, since the primary field of action—the Wilderness, and its principal representative, the native American—have almost vanished from the physical world?

In fact, many important critics specializing in post-World War II fiction deny or ignore the significance of frontier images for contemporary American writers. Raymond Olderman, for example, in *Beyond the Waste Land: The American Novel in the Nineteen-Sixties,* goes so far as to assert categorically that some of the important frontier images have disappeared. Olderman states:

> Eden, Utopia, and the New Adam have no major significance in the novel of the sixties. If the memory of Eden and a related sense of loss continue to appear, they appear only as the universal remembrance of the eden of childhood. . . . As images haunting our imagination, these memories no longer connect to a sense of a lost America. If the promise of Utopia should continue to appear in the novel of the sixties, it exists as the universal hope for self-discovery. The old theme of the American Adam aspiring to move ever forward in time and space unencumbered by guilt or reflection on human limitation is certainly unavailable to the guilt-ridden psyche of modern man.[2]

And Josephine Hendin, in *Vulnerable People: A View of American Fiction since 1945,* finds that American writers react to the changes in contemporary life by moving in one of two directions—through "holistic" or "anarchic" fiction: "Fiction divides over the methods that will reduce emotional vulnerability and alternates between two extremes. One is holistic, stressing the virtues of management, wholeness and reason. The other is anarchic, stressing the mystical values of self-effacement and disintegration."[3] These impulses grow from contemporary American life, particularly from the successes of American capitalism. Both appear "memoryless," with little concern for the ideas produced by the frontier past.

Jerry Bryant in *The Open Decision* finds European philosophy, particularly Existentialism, to be the nurturing agent for contemporary fiction.[4] Jack Hicks in *In the Singer's Temple* concludes that diversity prevails in contemporary American fiction, that contemporary writing reveals the diversity and fragmentation of American life, and that little coherence exists.[5] Warner Berthoff, in *A Literature without Qualities: American Writing since 1945,* seems to despair when he examines contemporary writing, for, as his title suggests, he sees little of quality, and he finds a retreat from distinguishing qualities as well.[6]

If one were to read the last few years' entries by Jerome Klinkowitz on "Fiction: 1950 to the Present" in *American Literary Scholarship,* the inevitable conclusion would be that the only significant concerns among contemporary novelists revolve around innovation or reaction. For Klinkowitz, the only legitimate choice is for them to throw their lots in with the postmodernists, who embrace experimentation and plow the fields of self-reflexive fiction. God forbid that writers—or critics—cast their buckets down with the reactionaries like John Gardner or Gerald Graff, who call for referential and moral fiction. Klinkowitz discusses literature of the American West as a "subgenre" that he includes with "Native American, Chicano Writers and Oriental-American Literature."

How then can one approach contemporary American fiction in any coherent way? The standard approach is exemplified by the organization of the *Harvard Guide to Contemporary American Writing,* edited by Daniel Hoffman, and that is to categorize writers by region, ethnic background, style, or sex. Thus, the chapters are titled "Southern Fiction," "Jewish Writers," "Experimental Fiction," "Women's Literature," and so forth.[7] But among the diverse groups of mainstream American writers are discernible ideas that grow out of these American writers' concerns with "frontier" images, and these concerns cut across these standard categories.

Contemporary novelists embed elements of the frontier mythos into their novels in various ways. In some cases they use some remaining natural wilderness: Saul Bellow removes the title character in *Herzog* to the Berkshires, where he contemplates his existence; James Dickey sets *Deliverance* in the southern backwoods; and Flannery O'Connor does the same in *The Violent Bear It Away*; John Barth uses the early Maryland frontier in *The Sot Weed Factor*; William Styron in *The Confessions of Nat Turner* explores the diminishing wilderness of Virginia in 1831; and Thomas Berger examines the historical west in *Little Big Man*; Edward Abbey used the post-war West in *The Brave Cowboy* and *The Monkey Wrench Gang*. Philip Caputo employs Hemingway country up in Michigan in *Indian Country*. Some introduce elements of the natural world to suggest the power of the mythical West. Ken Kesey, for example, used the flight of the geese in *One Flew Over the Cuckoo's Nest* to remind Chief Bromden of this connection to the healing power of nature.

In other cases these wilderness concerns take place on a new field of action rather than in the West itself. Bellow has Henderson travel to Africa in *Henderson the Rain King*. The war becomes the focus of action in *Catch-22, Slaughterhouse-Five,* Tim O'Brien's *Going After Cacciato,* and Michael Herr's *Dispatches*. For Ralph Ellison's *Invisible Man* it is the city. For John Irving it is the old world of Vienna, and for Garp it is a young girl's rape in Central Park. Larry McMurtry's new frontiersman in *Cadillac Jack* is a junk dealer who finds the world of possibility in the flea markets of the world. Ray Bradbury replicates these concerns on the Martian frontier. Kurt Vonnegut in *Galapagos* and Bernard Malamud in *God's Grace* create post-apocalyptic frontier islands.

At the center of many of these novels we find the frontier paradigm. An innocent figure (or more likely an ignorant one) undergoes an initiatory experience that grows out of the elements he confronts in the transformed wilderness he faces. Ironically, the difficulties he faces often result from elements of the pastoral frontier myth, which emphasizes the primary need for unfettered individual freedom of action. Bellow's Henderson must escape the submerged voice crying "I want" before he can dissolve the sense of having a separate self when he confronts Dahfu's lion. Kesey's gambler, rounder, cartoon-cowboy hero in *One Flew Over the Cuckoo's Nest* must give up his selfish concerns before he can regenerate himself and the inhabitants of the asylum. John Irving's Garp must learn how to sympathize with the oppressed and recognize the human potential for violence so that he can become a redemptive figure. Styron's Nat Turner must turn from the "Old Testament God of Hate" and embrace the "New Testament God of Love" before he can sense the morning star. Heller's Yossarian, inspired by the innocent Orr of the apple cheeks who hails from the undefined border territory outside New York City, must give up his singular desire for survival and strive to save the kid sister of Nately's whore. Michael Herr's persona in *Dispatches* must confront the dislocations he discovers in the Vietnam wilderness before he can use language to attempt to come to terms with that disquieting experience.

One major element in the character's metamorphosis—and another theme inherited from frontier mythology—concerns captivity. From Mary Rowlandson and other Puritan captivity narratives to Cooper's tales about Leatherstocking's quests to recapture white maidens, captivity has been an important element of the narrative. Likewise, captivity of various sorts enters the contemporary American novel. For many writers, the captivity comes from the military: Yossarian cannot escape flying in *Catch-22,* and Billy Pilgrim is first captured by the military and later by the Germans in *Slaughterhouse-Five*. Vietnam novels like *Going After Cacciato* or Herr's new-journalism *Dispatches* also concentrate on the military, but the military during Vietnam takes on a more sinister nature than in the other two books mentioned. In *Cuckoo's Nest* it is the asylum that encaptures; in *Nat Turner* it is slavery; in *Deliverance* the hillbilly capturers are dispatched ironically by the hero's bow and arrow; in John Cheever's *Falconer* and Vonnegut's *Jailbird* it is prison. Captivity is important to Flannery O'Connor too; in *Wise Blood* Haze Motes is uprooted from home by the army, and Old Tarwater captures both Rayber and young Tarwater. For some contemporary women writers, such as Alice Walker and Joan Didion, marriage is captivity.

Another element important to older American literature that reappears in contemporary fiction concerns the confrontation between the Old and the New World presented through the American's journey to the Old World. Twain and James traveled with the innocent abroad to point to these differences. Likewise, the motif appears in contemporary American fiction. Saul Bellow has Charlie Citrine travel to Europe in *Humboldt's Gift.* In *The Dean's December* Bellow narrows the focus: Chicago represents the anarchic American world where death and captivity permeate the texture of life: Bucharest is the old, entropic world of restriction. John Irving uses Vienna in several of his novels to represent the Old World, especially in *The Hotel New Hampshire,* where the escape-and-return pattern familiar to American literature appears when the characters move from a hotel in America to one in Vienna and then return to one in America.

Another aspect of the frontier emphasis in contemporary fiction concerns the continuing appearance of the innocent figure identified by R. W. B. Lewis as the American Adam. In the nineteenth century, when the pastoral vision of the wilderness took predominance over the Puritan one of evil, the figure that often personified the new American was the New Adam, innocent, full of possibility and potential. Contemporary American novelists do not use the Adam figure as a realistically possible heroic figure, but many of them do present the innocent Adam in the process of becoming Adam's counterpointing figure in religious typology: Christ. The tension between the innocent Adam and the aware Christ is a sustaining part of the narrative pattern in *Invisible Man, Henderson the Rain King, One Flew Over the Cuckoo's Nest, Catch-22, The Confessions of Nat Turner, Slaughterhouse-Five, Going After Cacciato,* and *The World According to Garp.* In these works the main character begins as an American Adam who believes some of the illusions spawned by the vision of the American wilderness as Eden and the American as innocent (characterized by self-centered individuality, desire for simplicity and harmony, recoil from death, materialism, anarchic freedom, and self-righteousness). The character is established as Adamic through his grappling with these problems; often, too, clusters of images are associated with the American as Adam (nakedness, blindness or sleep, garden, tree, snake, open air). Occasionally the main character is also associated with the various transformations of the American Adam as he moved west across the American frontier—frontiersman, riverboatman, tinker, trickster, logger, cowboy. Events challenge the reality of the character's illusions, and often some form of captivity or attempted escape from captivity causes the transformation. As a result the character's illusions are challenged, and he is forced toward experience or knowledge. Usually the main character must face the reality of death; either his own life is threatened or he witnesses the death of another character. The resulting awareness dawns slowly in most cases, suggesting a gap between seeing and understanding and the difficulty in overcoming illusions.

When the main character finally achieves knowledge, he attempts to become a conscious Messiah who sees clearly that his purpose is to transform the world into one of hope, community, and love, or at least one in which it is easier to live. The character usually comes to understand the illusory nature of his world, and he knows that for destructive illusions to be overthrown they must be clearly articulated. Contemporary writers emphasize the importance of language that creates illusions and that conversely can be used to strip away inhumane beliefs and create humane ones. Usually when the character becomes Christlike, he also becomes a writer (*logos*). Besides an awareness of language, the Christlike traits are an awareness of discord, complexity, human limitation, the problems of the past, and the need for community and love. Various images are associated with Christ—cross, tree, burdens, suffering, crown of thorns, rebirth, baptism, light, sight, and seed, among other aspects of Jesus' life.

The metamorphosis from Adam to Christ owes much to the Puritan emphasis on biblical typology, where, as Ursula Brumm has demonstrated, "characters and events of the Old Testament are prefigurations and prophecies of future events, mainly of Christ and His works."[8] What gives the transformation its particular connection with elements of the frontier myth is the corresponding movement in native-American culture. Joseph Campbell in *The Masks of God* points out the significance of two opposing figures—the "hunter" or "warrior," and the "shaman." Slotkin examines the similarity between the "warrior" and the Adam figure and the "shaman" and Christ:

> Both the hunter and the shaman had their counterparts in white mythology. Indians were generally quick to notice the similarity between the laws of shamans like Quetzalcoatl and Deganawidah and the tenets of Christianity (especially those of Quaker Christianity). The spirit of the hunter likewise corresponded to the entrepreneurial spirit of the colonist-adventurers; the traders in furs and hides and land.[9]

Another similarity to native-American culture concerns the pattern the characters follow toward spiritual redemption. Joseph Epes Brown in *The Spiritual Legacy of the American Indian* identifies a three-stage pattern common to native-American cultures:

> All true spiritual progress involves three stages, which are not successfully experienced and left behind, but rather each in turn is realized and then integrated within the next stage, so that ultimately they become one in the individual who attains the ultimate goal. Different terms may be used for these stages, but essentially they constitute purification, perfection or expansion, and union.[10]

So it is not unexpected to find variations of this pattern in native-American literature, where the main character must transform from warrior or hunter to shaman who, like the Christ-logos figure, values the power of language. N. Scott Momaday's *House Made of Dawn* is the prototype of the native-American novel, and Leslie Silko in *Ceremony* and James Welch in *Winter in the Blood* present similar patterns. In these novels the hunter/warrior must be initiated into a shamanistic view of the world and must strip away the demands of the warrior ideal. Some form of captivity (the military for Momaday's and Silko's main characters, the past for Welch's) must be overcome. In each case a shamanistic mentor aids in the process of returning to some fundamental ideas about native-American culture. These native-American writers have made a major impact on contemporary American fiction, so much so that they have moved into the mainstream of American literature, and it is important to note how the frontier elements provide the basis for the narrative structure of various works.

Hispanic writers have also moved into the mainstream, as is illustrated by Rudolfo Anaya's *Bless Me, Ultima,* which adapts the pattern for a Hispanic novel. His youthful character, Tony, witnesses death in various forms before he escapes from the potential captivity of a life as a Catholic priest. He will become a shaman for the Christlike teachings of the Golden Carp as he is reintegrated into a primitivistic approach to the world, and he becomes the writer who tells his own story.

Although the Adamic figure seems inherently masculine, some contemporary women writers present women main characters who undergo an initiatory experience similar to the one I have described. In Alice Walker's critically acclaimed *The Color Purple* Celie must break out of her captivity and establish a singular identity outside of her forced marriage to Albert. Her journey is a tenuous one, but aided by the model that Shug Avery provides and guided by the letters her sister Nettie writes about her confrontation with the African frontier, Celie uses her own writing first to become independent and then to establish her own community. Her letter-writing is compared to her sewing, first with Sofia in making a quilt and later by making pants and becoming independent through her own work. Along the way she learns from Shug (a shaman in her own right) the native-American emphasis on the spirit that exists in all things.

To summarize how these various elements of frontier mythos inform contemporary American fiction, let me concentrate on a single novel, *One Flew Over the Cuckoo's Nest*. McMurphy in Ken Kesey's novel initially represents the Western figure, a cowboy, gambler, logger—a composite of stereotyped Western heroes. McMurphy's captivity is in an insane asylum, where his principal antagonist is Big Nurse, a figure of control and restriction associated with the East and civilization in the frontier paradigm. McMurphy's Adamic inno-

cence involves first his ignorance of the system in which he finds himself and later his childlike self-interest, which he ultimately relinquishes to become a Christlike martyr. His metamorphosis—symbolized by a violent confrontation with Big Nurse—is effected partially by his association with the native-American shaman, Chief Bromden, who follows a path to redemption similar to McMurphy's. In fact, McMurphy's death has a profound effect on all the men in the insane asylum, but especially on Chief Bromden, who also moves from innocence to knowledge, from withdrawal to participation. Chief Bromden becomes the conscious writer who tells McMurphy's story.

This loop I toss is wide, encompassing much, but I think it is important to round up as much as possible to prove my point—that, contrary to what many critics have stated about contemporary American literature, significant elements of frontier mythology continue to appear in American fiction. And those elements cut across the categories popularly used to classify contemporary American fiction: Eastern—Bellow, Irving, Heller, Cheever; Southern—Styron, O'Connor; Western—McMurtry, Abbey, Kesey; Women—O'Connor, Silko, Walker; black—Ellison; native American—Momaday, Silko, Welch; Hispanic—Anaya; Experimental—Vonnegut, Barth, Irving. I do not mean to suggest that the frontier has arisen Phoenix-like in these novels. Rather, like Proteus or Coyote, it has simply taken new shapes to adapt to new circumstances.

Notes

1. Frederick Jackson Turner, "The Significance of the Frontier in American History," in *Selected Essays of Frederick Jackson Turner: Frontier and Section,* ed. Ray Allen Billington (Englewood Cliffs, N.J.: Prentice-Hall, 1961), p. 38.

2. Raymond Olderman, *Beyond the Waste Land: The American Novel in the Nineteen-Sixties* (New Haven, Conn.: Yale Univ. Press, 1972), p. 9.

3. Josephine Hendin, *Vulnerable People: A View of American Fiction since 1945* (New York: Oxford Univ. Press, 1978), p. 6.

4. Jerry Bryant, *The Open Decision: The Contemporary American Novel and Its Intellectual Background* (Detroit: The Free Press, 1970).

5. Jack Hicks, *In the Singer's Temple* (Chapel Hill: Univ. of North Carolina Press, 1981).

6. Warner Berthoff, *A Literature without Qualities: American Writing since 1945* (Berkeley: Univ. of California Press, 1979).

7. Daniel Hoffman, ed., *The Harvard Guide to Contemporary American Writing* (Cambridge, Mass.: Harvard Univ. Press, 1979).

8. Ursula Brumm, *American Thought and Religious Typology* (New Brunswick, N.J.: Rutgers Univ. Press, 1970), p. 23.

9. Richard Slotkin, *Regeneration through Violence* (Middletown, Conn.: Wesleyan Univ. Press, 1973), p. 49.

10. Joseph Epes Brown, *The Spiritual Legacy of the American Indian* (New York: Crossroad, 1982), p. 45.

Delbert E. Wylder (essay date 1989)

SOURCE: Wylder, Delbert E. "The Western Novel as Literature of the Last Frontier." In *The Frontier Experience and the American Dream: Essays on American Literature,* edited by David Mogen, Mark Busby, and Paul Bryant, pp. 120-31. College Station: Texas A&M University, 1989.

[*In the following essay, Wylder surveys several major novels that focus on the American frontier, noting that the literature of the American West is based in history, and that it celebrates the achievements of frontier pioneers somewhat nostalgically.*]

Since the conclusion of World War II, attempts have been made to re-create, or at least to revitalize, the "frontier" concept in American society. There have been many "new frontiers," some denoting social or political movements, some in the areas of science and technology. The most famous of all, of course, is the "new frontier" of space. Evidently, the concept of the frontier, originally thought of in terms of horizontal—rather than vertical—space, remains not only very much a part of the usable American vocabulary, what with all its connotations, but also a part of the American consciousness or, perhaps even more appropriately, the American unconscious. At least the frontier concept appeals to that large part of the population which considers itself descended, not necessarily biologically nor even ethnically, from the Anglo-Saxon invaders of this continent.

Despite the fact that all of America was a frontier for these Western Europeans at one time in our history, the trans-Mississippi West remains the "true" frontier in the American imagination. The towering mountains, the seemingly unending prairies, the hostile deserts—the very magnitude of space that beggared the eighteenth- and nineteenth-century imaginations and that still, despite our ability to fly over it in a matter of hours, has the power to amaze as we see it from thirty thousand feet—are reasons enough. The cast of characters in this drama of expansion and settlement adds further to the longevity of the appeal of the American West. From the Lewis and Clark expedition, through the mountain men

and fur traders, through the dogged and deliberate trains of covered wagons, the inexorable progress of the railroads, and later the cattle drives, the American West provided characters in conflict with space, with the elements and, perhaps even more important, with antagonists as romantic as any group of human beings in history, or the history of literature—the native American on horseback.

It is little wonder, then, that the literature of the American West has been such a large part historically oriented, and that it is both a celebration of the heroic activities of those who managed to push a modified Western civilization into the trans-Mississippi West and at the same time a literature filled with nostalgia for the past and what that past meant to the American spirit and a large but decreasing segment of the American people. What becomes more clear in every decade since Turner published his famous thesis is that the settlement of the Western frontier marked the end of that mass-movement of Anglo-Saxons toward the setting sun. When, in *The Great Gatsby,* F. Scott Fitzgerald has Nick Carraway describe World War I as "that delayed Teutonic migration known as the Great War,"[1] we know that he is talking about a reverse migration—a wave, broken against the shore, receding into the sea.

What is true of Western literature in general is particularly true of the first two of three subgenres we might call "Mountain Man," "Cowboy," and "Indian" novels. As with any sweeping generalization, of course, there are some exceptions—even some outstanding exceptions. For the most part, however, Mountain Man and Cowboy novels concentrate on the conquest of space, on battles with the elements, and on the defeat of an enemy within that space. In many of these novels, especially the "popular" novels, there is a celebration of the final conquest by the Anglo-Saxon. In almost all of them, especially the literary novels, there is the constant sadness of the *ubi sunt* theme, for the frontier itself is seen as a land unpeopled by anyone but savages, a virgin land that must be shaped into the Anglo-Saxon man's own image, and that in the shaping has been raped and ravaged—destroyed, in a very important sense, not only ironically for those who have unwittingly destroyed it, but tragically for posterity which will never be able to experience it. The passage of time and its relationship to the activities of people, then, becomes another of the important conflicts in Western novels.

These novels also frequently bewail the loss not only of the virgin land but of a primitive way of life that is extremely masculine in requiring physical strength, adaptability to nature, resourcefulness, courage, and an almost stoic self-control. Both the mountain man and the cowboy must be able to survive alone, although their chances of survival are increased through male-bonding with a relatively few of their own kind, as in primitive hunting societies.

Finally, the novels, for the most part, present protagonists who revel in their freedoms, whose loss creates nostalgia for the way things were. The typical Mountain Man protagonist, for example, has created a life in which he sees himself free from the responsibilities of domesticity, from laws created by communities of men and women, and even from the future. He is motivated by an unreflecting commitment to individualism, a distrust of other human beings in groups, a failure to understand cause and effect relationships, and an almost aboriginal passion for the hunting life. He has, in actuality, left the community of men behind him and not only distrusts that community but hates it.

He detests the lawyer, the merchant, and the farmer. He feels threatened by the lawyer because lawyers represent a legal authoritarian structure that deprives the free-spirited of their freedom through a complex maze of written proscriptions, and by the merchant because he amasses wealth not by work but by financial manipulations. He has contempt for the farmer because the farmer has abandoned the free, more dangerous, style of living of the hunting societies and has substituted, out of fear or weakness or apathy, a life-style typical of agricultural societies. The farmer has betrayed his masculinity by trading the hunter's commitment to male-bonding for family-bonding, and has lost his independence. The farmer tills the soil, making him dependent not only on the weather but on the community and the marketplace. For the mountain-man protagonists, the marketplace is so distant it seems not to exist in reality; its representatives may form the only community that exists with any regularity during the yearly rendezvous, but it does not pervade his life. For the most part, he does not see it as intruding into his life.

The mountain-man protagonists operate within a code that had evolved with very little change from warrior and hunting societies. One of the major tenets of that code was courage in the face of danger. Another was patience and persistence under stress. Another was silence—the acceptance of hardship without complaint, and self-protective silence in dangerous situations. The most important tenet, as demonstrated in Manfred's *Lord Grizzly,* was loyalty to the group, as well as to a way of life that was viewed as masculine and natural.

Whether part of a "code" or not, mountain men and cowboys see woman, at least the Anglo-saxon woman, as threatening to the male, for she embodies the concept of civilization. She carries with her not only the "trappings" of civilization, but is the "trap" that can destroy freedom and the masculine way of life. She must be sheltered from nature, she and her offspring must be provided for, and she brings with her the concept of the future. In this sense, she is more dangerous than the wild animals in the forest.

It is interesting to note that this same code and the attitude toward women exist, for the most part, in the "cowboy" novels as well, and perhaps provide for the tremendous appeal of popular Westerns to the male reading audience. Even in "literary" Westerns, much of the code remains but, as we shall see, the archetypal cowboy novels would serve as transitions into a "contemporary" novel if, indeed, the force of the "last frontier," that tremendous sense of loss, were not so strong.

Aristotle used *Oedipus Rex* as the typical basis for his discussion of tragedy, and any literary critic would have a difficult time selecting a novel other than Guthrie's *The Big Sky* for paradigmatic purposes, for *The Big Sky* is the most typical, the most archetypal of them all. This is not to say that it is necessarily the most successful, but that it is quintessential. It is a celebration of the mountain men and their wilderness, and it also strongly emphasizes the mutability theme. The three males who have bonded together to battle the elements, the Indians, and, on occasion, other mountain men, are an interesting trio. Dick Summers, the oldest, most experienced of them all, is obviously the tutor figure who is gradually replaced by the more dominant Boone Caudill. Caudill has run away from his Kentucky home because his independence and his developing manliness are being threatened, and he fears that he is being trapped and stultified within the confines of civilization. "It wasn't right to set the law on a man, making him feel small and alone, making him run away."[2] Boone escapes to the wilderness. He learns quickly, and is so ego-centered that nothing he does is wrong in his own eyes. Yet, he is bonded closely to both Summers and Jim Deakins, the third member of the group, who is more sensitive and less capable than Caudill. Boone's murder of Deakins, after he has saved his life, is typical of the unthinking Boone, as is his inability to come to grips with his own emotions about Teal Eye or Jim Deakins.

What is most important about the novel in this context, however, is that there is a constant celebration of the immensity and beauty of the country that almost everyone sees except Boone. Even Peabody, the Easterner who has come to map the country, is awed by the power and the beauty. Boone is also almost completely impervious to time and change, two forces which become thematic early in the novel, but most obviously when Zeb Callaway, Boone's uncle, exclaims, "The whole shitaree. Gone, by God, and naught to care savin' some of us who seen her new" (p. 435). The theme is emphasized further as Jim Deakins contemplates the changes he experiences, when Summers thinks about the companions of his younger days who have all now "gone under" and when everyone finally becomes aware of the gradual disappearance of the beaver. All of the ironies implicit in the novel are summed up beautifully in Summers' statement:

> "There was beaver for us and free country and a big way of livin', and everything we done it looks like we done against ourselves and couldn't do different if we knowed. We went to get away and to enj'y ourselves free and easy, but folks was bound to foller and beaver to get scarce and Injuns to be killed or tamed, and all the time the country gettin' safer and better known. We ain't seen the end of it yet, Boone, not to what the mountain man does against hisself. . . . It's like we heired money and had to spend it, and now it's nigh gone."

(Pp. 168-69)

John R. Milton, rightly, I believe, identifies *The Big Sky,* Harvey Fergusson's *Wolf Song,* and Frederick Manfred's *Lord Grizzly* as the "three novels being the best fictional treatment of the mountain men,"[3] although I might quarrel with the selection of Fergusson's novel. Fisher's *Mountain Man,* Guthrie's recent novel, *Fair Land, Fair Land,* which was published after Milton's analysis, and even the almost-forgotten *The Shining Mountains,* by Dale Van Every, seem equal in almost all ways, except stylistically, to the Fergusson novel. Another novel published since Milton's evaluation, Bill Hotchkiss' *The Medicine Calf,* a novel based on the life of Jim Beckwourth, must also be considered seriously.

All of these novels are celebratory in nature. The praise is, once again, not only for the land but for the men who, for a short moment in time, made an impression upon it, or at least put a mark on man's record of the passing of time and the changes that occurred. Manfred's *Lord Grizzly* celebrates the courage, hardihood, and the patience of Hugh Glass, the protagonist, in one of the more complex of the mountain-man novels. Glass, true to his calling, does not leave the mountains to return to "civilization" as does, say, the protagonist of *The Shining Mountains,* but his newly found self-understanding and his willingness, as a result, to forgive the companions who, he has thought, have deserted him mark a change from the self-centered lack of awareness of a Boone Caudill and a deviation from the absolutist Old Testament and tribal concept of revenge which, ironically, has kept him alive.

Dick Summers, the mountain-man mentor in *The Big Sky* is, of course, the transitional figure in Guthrie's works. Committed to the ways of mountain men, he instructs Boone Caudill and Jim Deakins in the wiles and ways of this hunting clan. When he realizes, for himself, that the old days are gone and that his own body can no longer cope with the rigors of life in the wilderness, he returns East, only to betray his former companions by leading a wagonload of settlers into the no-longer virgin land in *The Way West.* He had damned Tom Fitzpatrick at the end of *The Big Sky* for just such

an undertaking. His understanding of the elements and of the country and of the Indians, learned as a mountain man, is the required knowledge the settlers must have to be successful. And finally, in *Fair Land, Fair Land,* Summers returns to the mountains in an attempt to live out his life in peace and contentment. But it is useless. The beaver is gone, the game is scarce, and his few years of idyllic life with Teal Eye are doomed by the "relentless march" of the Anglo-Saxons. Sam Lash, the protagonist of *Wolf Song,* having established himself within a small hunting group, adjusted to the wilderness and even, in hand-to-hand combat, killed the archetypal enemy, becomes a true mountain man. But Lash trades his passion for the wilderness and the camaraderie of male companions for the love of a Spanish woman, and through the very act of winning her for his bride, he suffers a great loss, for he has been, in a sense, tamed.

Although their roles may not be significant in terms of the space allotted them, women play a significant role in novels about cowboys and the life of the range. It is only in the popular genre, and in cinematic adaptations, that the final scene shows the cowboy hero "riding off into the sunset," thus turning his back on women and the civilized community that she represents. Owen Wister's *The Virginian* is the archetype of the cowboy novel. The protagonist seems perfectly adapted to his life on the range. He is superior in riding, roping, and shooting, and at the beginning of the novel he is carefree, youthfully rebellious, and protective of his freedom. But he is also reflective and ambitious, especially after he falls in love with the schoolteacher who has come from the East. He takes his responsibilities seriously, not only to the owner of the ranch where he finally becomes foreman but to the unwritten laws of th range concerning rustling. He is willing to sacrifice his best friend to the concept of private ownership of cattle. A law higher than the law of the male hunting group becomes operational in the cowboy novels. Boone Caudill would never have betrayed one of his small group; only what he thought was a personal and sexual affront led him to kill Jim Deakins.

The Virginian is no Boone Caudill. He travels to the East and is accepted by the Easterners as almost a model of the reinvigorated man. He has an aesthetic appreciation of the landscape in which he lives. He reads, and he thinks of the future. At the end of the novel, he is finding ways to make the ranching more efficient. Much of his inspiration and motivation comes from his educated Eastern wife, although, one must admit, he is not willing to bow to her pacifism when his integrity is challenged by Trampas. In that sense, he is true to the code of the West.

Constance Ellsworth, in Emerson Hough's *Heart's Desire,* is another Eastern woman who has a dramatic effect upon male-oriented society in a tiny New Mexican town devoid of women except for "the girls from Kansas," who are essentially homemakers and thus not dangerous in Hough's scenario. Even these women cause difficulties, for Curly, a cowboy who has married one of them, is unable to go with a posse to capture Billy the Kid because he has become a "family man" with responsibilities. But the educated, cultured Constance Ellsworth is the real "Eve" in the Garden of Eden, and it is only the weakness of the hero, Dan Anderson, that allows him to invite her into the Garden of Heart's Desire. Dan Anderson is able, by the end of the novel, to arrange something of a compromise between the "corruption" of the railroad representatives from the East and the code that binds him to his friends in the Western hamlet. But *Heart's Desire* is not a typical Western novel. The men who live in the town can hardly be described as energetic, dynamic Westerners; Heart's Desire could be called a "sleepy" town at best.

It would be hard to compile a list of the "best" four or five literary range novels, for there are so many good ones. A. B. Guthrie's *These Thousand Hills* is one of them. Like Wister's *Virginian*, the protagonist of Guthrie's novel chooses responsibility over his earlier carefree life, but his seeming desertion of the prostitute who has helped him prosper, and his return to his colder but cultured wife is a scene far different from the idyllic honeymoon near the end of *The Virginian*, where the Virginian's bride quite obviously fits very well into the Edenic setting. Perhaps the novel is too realistic to have gained the popularity of Guthrie's other novels, but it illustrates very well the acceptance of a settled way of life and a turning from the masculine society to a family society dominated by a responsibility to women and children. For the most part, the best of the range novels show, if not the actual decay, at least the deterioration of the frontier spirit and the life of freedom. Walter Van Tilburg Clark's *The Ox-Bow Incident* is one, Larry McMurtry's *Horseman, Pass By* another, and Frederick Manfred's *Riders of Judgment* still another. These novels concentrate on human weaknesses or on the "darker side" of human nature as causes of the change, while Jack Shaefer's *Monte Walsh* shows the effect of economic and social changes on the life of the cowboy.

Two highly symbolic novels, Shaefer's *Shane* and Edward Abbey's *The Brave Cowboy*, illustrate quite well the "lastness" of the American frontier. Shane is the epitome of the popular cowboy hero. He rides into the farm and then into town, straightening out the problems that the homesteader and his family are having with the corrupted rancher, and then rides off into the sunset. He has saved the farmers and made a lasting and inspiring impression on the boy narrator and his parents, but he has also caused the beginning of the end of a way of life. The life of the cowboy will be superseded by the life of the farmer and the townsman, an occurrence illustrated in *Monte Walsh*.

In Edward Abbey's *The Brave Cowboy*, made into the cinematically successful *Lonely Are the Brave*, the protagonist Jack Burns is, in a sense, the "last cowboy." He no longer punches cattle but has been reduced to herding sheep and now has come to rescue his friend from a term in prison for aiding "wetbacks." A living champion of freedom, Burns is totally unable to understand his friend's refusal, on philosophical grounds, to escape the punishment of the law. Burns escapes alone, across the mesa and into the mountains on his skittish young horse, Whiskey, only to be killed along with his horse by a truck (although he miraculously reappears in two later Abbey novels), while trying to cross a highway that divides one range of mountains from the range that, he thinks, will provide him with a safe exit to Mexico.

Throughout the novel, Abbey makes it clear that Burns is a ghost from the past. Riding through the modern industrialized Duke City, Burns is seen as an anachronism. The sheriff of the search party trying to capture him speaks of him as a "ghost." Thus the final scene, when he and his horse are hit by the truck carrying flush toilets to Duke City and which throughout the novel has symbolized "over-organized society," depicts the sudden end of a way of life that has been gradually disappearing.

Appropriately to "Indian" novels, such as Frederick Manfred's *Conquering Horse*, in which the capture of a horse is symbolic of the continuation and fulfilling celebration of a way of life—the death of the horse becomes in contrast symbolic in cowboy novels. The cowboy was equally dependent on the horse for his way of life. Another novel in which the death of a horse signals the end of an era is Tom Lea's neglected *The Wonderful Country*, a novel which moves back and forth across the border between Texas and Mexico with descriptions of landscape on both sides, descriptions that are almost unrivaled in their ability to call up southwestern scenes to the mind's eye in order to celebrate the beauty and magnificence of the Southwest.

Lea's novel, of course, is not the only cowboy novel that is celebratory of Western landscapes. As in the mountain-man novels, there is such a concern with descriptions of landscape in cowboy and mountain-man novels that for many critics landscape has almost become a character in the development of individual Westerns. If true, that character is aging; seams and wrinkles show on his face in the cowboy novels. Gone is the purity, the freedom of movement, as towns begin to dot the landscape, and barbed-wire fence and dirt roads divide the land into parcels. Thus, even the descriptions of the land remind the reader of the *ubi sunt* theme that becomes predominant, finally, in the best of both the mountain-man and cowboy novels. There is a sad undertone, even in the otherwise hilarious Max Evans comic novel *The Rounders*.

Gone, too, is the strongly male-bonded hunting group, a victim of both the times and the demands of a hero-oriented, or at least a "protagonist-oriented" novel form. Only in some of the novels of Eugene Manlove Rhodes or in trail narratives like Andy Adams's *The Log of a Cowboy* do we find "men in groups" as the unified hero figure in literature of the range. The Virginian is a hero, as in Dan McMasters in Hough's trail-drive novel *North of 36*; even Jack Burns in *The Brave Cowboy* is a hero.

It would be logical to assume that the "Indian" novel would be the most concerned with the sense of loss—the *ubi sunt* theme—since, at least chronologically, the native-American civilization was the first to inhabit the Western mountains, plains, and deserts, only to be replaced by what Hough called "the relentless march" of the Anglo-Saxons. That would be a mistaken assumption, however; some of the best of the native-American novels concentrate on the human dilemmas of the central characters, and the authors usually depend on the reader's awareness of the loss of the whole native-American culture to the advancing whites. Frank Waters's *The Man Who Killed the Deer,* for example, places the focus on the problems of the protagonist, Martiniano, not only in his attempts to find a place between the white community and the Pueblo community but in his battle with his own ego, and the conclusion, in which Martiniano subordinates his ego to the more important spiritual domination of the tribe and its religion and tradition, is a triumphant affirmation of the human, though particularly native-American, spirit. Frederick Manfred's *Conquering Horse* and the more recent lyrical *Manly Hearted Woman* are both celebrations of the culture of the native American but, even more, novels of the development of the individual but distinctly native-American psyche within that culture.

There have been, of course, many novels, as well as narratives and biographies, which delineate the loss of native-American land and autonomy to the advancing white culture. The story is told in novels as disparate in time and tone as Will Levington Comfort's *Apache* and Thomas Berger's well-researched *Little Big Man,* but the story has been much more emotionally reported in such narratives and collections as Neihardt's *Black Elk Speaks* and Dee Brown's compilation of materials on Wounded Knee.

Novels in which the protagonist attempts to enter the white civilization but finally returns to his native-American heritage are many. The best of these is Waters's *The Man Who Killed the Deer,* although Oliver La Farge's romanticized *Laughing Boy* should certainly not be forgotten. Neither should La Farge's far more naturalistic novel, *The Enemy Gods.* Hal Borland's *When the Legends Die* follows somewhat the same pattern as the latter novel but adds a very symbolic bear for good measure. Leslie Silko's *Ceremony* also de-

serves mention here, although it belongs to a very distinct group of novels.

This group is written by native-American novelists, and their characters wander, often listlessly, through an almost Kafkaesque landscape and an incomprehensible world until they somehow find themselves and their own Indianness away from the meaningless white culture that surrounds and stifles them. N. Scott Momaday's *House Made of Dawn* is the most complex of these, perceptively showing the conflicts between the Spanish, Mexican, Anglo, and native-American cultures within a contemporary framework, but Jim Welch's *Winter in the Blood* is a beautifully and almost surrealistic depiction of the absurdities, to the native American, of American culture in the West. Silko's novel is far more naturalistic, but also effective, particularly in picturing the despair of native-American males in the twentieth century. These novels written by native Americans point up most dramatically, in one sense, the loss of freedoms symbolized by the closing of the frontier, for the protagonists find themselves almost totally isolated within an alien culture, with only themselves, their heritage, and their spirituality to save them.

But perhaps the most significant statements about mountain men, cowboys, and native Americans as characters who represent the finality of the frontier is in contemporary novels, which either reject the civilization that has followed the settling of the West or which suggest the incorporation of the mountain man's "clear vision" into the structure of that civilization. Edward Abbey's Hayduke, in *The Monkey Wrench Gang,* is an example, though certainly an atypical one. Hayduke is a "happy-go-lucky" throwback to the mountain man. Careless of the environment himself, he fights against all major attempts to restructure that environment in the name of civilization. Though his cause seems hopeless, his cleverness both in nature and in his understanding of the law allow him to survive both nature and the law. Despite the open-ended conclusion of the novel, however, Abbey's novel presents a pathetic picture of the end of the frontier itself, if not the end of the frontier spirit.

William Eastlake's *The Bronc People* presents another portrait of the mountain-man image which has survived the closing of the frontier. Blue-eyed Billy Peersall is an old Indian fighter who has survived the wars and, by the end of the novel, becomes the tutor for both Little Sant Bowman, the "really cowboy," and his friend Alistair Benjamin, the black boy raised by the Bowmans. The novel celebrates the beauty and the immutability of nature, but the plaintive note of the lost frontier and the last frontier can be found in the following passage when Little Sant and Alistair interview the old Indian fighter.

> "Well, we made the wrong arrangements. We fought the wrong people. We should have joined the Indians, fought the whites, the Easterners. That's why we come

here, mountain men, the plainsmen, to escape all that. And then we joined them to fight the people who were the same, who wanted to live like us—the Indians. I don't know why we did it except we were confused by the color of their skins, the Easterners' skins, their language. Because they were the same color, spoke the same language, we must have been confused into thinking, into forgetting we had come out here to escape them."[4]

Eastlake's lament, through his character Blue-eyed Billy Peersall, is a lament that permeates almost all contemporary Western literary novels—the sense of loss of male companionship and the loss of freedom to "do what I please," as Boone Caudill would say.

Blue-eyed Billy's commitment, at the end of *The Bronc People,* to be the inspirational mentor for the young black man, Alistair Benjamin, along with his championing of the Mexican children in the public school system, is highly significant for not only the future of the United States but for the future of Western American literature. The fact that astronauts and scientists have, in the latter decades of the twentieth century, walked on the moon and created a new frontier in space seems much less important to literature than another fact—the complexion of the American people is rapidly changing.

The influx of Eastern and Southern Europeans toward the end of the nineteenth century that so upset hardened Anglo-Saxon Americans like Emerson Hough seems to pale almost into insignificance when compared to immigration statistics since World War II. Refugees came from Korea after the "police action" there, and in even greater numbers from South Vietnam after that unfortunate war, tremendously increasing the numbers of Americans with Asian backgrounds. From the Spanish-speaking countries, there have been refugees from Castro's Cuba, political refugees from Central America, particularly El Salvador, and a stream of Mexicans attempting to find work and a higher standard of living north of the border. Furthermore, though there have been a relatively small number of black immigrants from Haiti, American black citizens have at least made a beginning to finding a measure of equality. To further complicate the situation, American women have insisted on equality of rights, and have, perhaps, made more gains than any of the other groups.

What all this will mean to society is difficult to say. What it means to literature, however, is that it will present a new era of human problems that, though not necessarily new, will be found in different contexts that will appeal not only to naturalistic but romantic writers.

For Western American literature, the shift away from Anglo-Saxon majorities in the reading public may result in a change of interest. The predominant subject matter of Western American literature has been male-

oriented, white Anglo-Saxon pantheistic, if not atheistic, hunting or warrior-like societies and individuals who have cherished freedom to live their own way of life despite the rest of society. How such a literature will appeal to the reading public of the future is difficult to guess. Although Western films and television programs seem to be on the decline, the popularity of Westerns where such themes seem to be even more blatantly expressed seems to have remained as strong as ever. And courses in Western American literature seem to be thriving.

But Western American literature has had its Homers, singing of the magnificent days of the past—A. B. Guthrie, Jr., Frank Waters, Frederick Manfred, Vardis Fisher, Harvey Fergusson, Conrad Richter, and many, many more. And it is beginning to see the dilemmas of the contemporary scene through the mixture of the past and the present, as in Wallace Stegner's masterful *Angle of Repose,* or William Eastlake's *Bronc People,* or through a study of the contemporary scene, as we find in some of Larry McMurtry's best novels.

Although the geographical frontier has closed, and there is a strong sense that it was, for Americans at least, the last meaningful frontier on this planet, the possibilities remain great for not only the continued exploration and reinterpretation of that frontier in literature but for an expansion of literature in the social and human problems that change will bring—changes that will cause even greater human problems and conflicts, but also, hopefully, expressions of understanding, tolerance, and love—precisely because the frontier has closed and America must turn in on itself, finally, and find answers to, rather than escape from, its problems.

Notes

1. F. Scott Fitzgerald, *The Great Gatsby* (New York: Charles Scribner's Sons, 1925), p. 3.

2. A. B. Guthrie, Jr., *The Big Sky* (New York: Cardinal Edition, Pocket Books, Inc., 1962) p. 7. Subsequent references in the text are to this edition.

3. John R. Milton, *The Novel of the American West* (Lincoln: Univ. of Nebraska Press, 1980), p. 234.

4. William Eastlake, *The Bronc People* (Albuquerque: Univ. of New Mexico Press, 1975), p. 156.

Aron Senkpiel (essay date 1992)

SOURCE: Senkpiel, Aron. "From the Wild West to the Far North: Literary Representations of North America's Last Frontier." In *Desert, Garden, Margin, Range: Literature on the American Frontier,* edited by Eric Heyne, pp. 133-42. New York: Twayne Publishers, 1992.

[*In the following essay, Senkpiel maintains that the exploration of the Northern frontier is an integral aspect of Canada's national identity and traces the relationship between Canadian and American frontier literature.*]

> When cold and dark followed the clouds, the rain became snow and the water ice. That is why the world is the way it is.
>
> —Ikpakhauq and Uloqsaq[1]

> The "North" is not merely a point on the compass. It has filled our minds for thousands of years. . . ."
>
> —Louis-Edmond Hamelin[2]

It is a truism that Canada is a northern nation. From the perspective of most Americans, all of Canada is "up there," a distant place far to the north that is often seen as a geographical as well as cultural wasteland: North America's own Siberia. Canadians and Americans alike even joke about it, often together. On "SCTV," for example, one of the more popular comedy routines had two "eh"-saying, beer-drinking brothers sitting in front of a map of Canada that was an expansive void marked "the Great White North." Viewers were never certain which was emptier: the area represented by the map or the area between the two fellows' ears. For many Americans, says Margaret Atwood, "Canada is just that vague, cold place where their uncle used to go fishing."[3]

From the perspective of most Canadians, who live within spitting distance of the forty-ninth parallel, the North is not viewed much differently. It's just closer; it begins a few hundred miles up the road. Most of the provinces have a community or two that boast to be the "gateway to the North." In Manitoba it's the Pas. In Saskatchewan it's Prince Albert. In Alberta it's Fort McMurray. In British Columbia it's Prince George. If these are the cities beyond which the North lies, they are also the places beyond which few Canadians travel. While the North may be a place many dream about, few choose to visit and fewer choose to stay.[4]

Despite the imprecision that characterizes many Americans' and Canadians' knowledge of the North, they seem to agree on a number of basic points. Asked to point northward, most will turn in a direction roughly approximate to the line of a compass needle and say it's "somewhere up there" or "somewhere out there," where houses and paved highways give way to trees and gravel roads.

Not everyone is so imprecise. The noted Canadian geographer Louis-Edmond Hamelin wrote that if he had to accept a "single human factor . . . to define and delimit the North" he would use "the northern fringe of the continuous ecumene."[5] However, when he developed his northern index, he decided on "a family of ten significant, converging factors" that allowed him to

quantify a particular place's "nordicity" (*Canadian Nordicity,* 17). Six are "physical": latitude, temperature, cold, presence of ice, precipitation, and ground cover. That is, the higher the latitude, the colder and icier and more barren the place, the more northern it is. But of more significance to us are the four that are, in geographical terms, "human": accessibility, air service, population, and level of economic activity. That is, the less accessible a place, the sparser the population, the smaller the economy, the more northern a place is. In short, using the measurement tools of the geographer, Hamelin quantified—empirically validated in space and time—the artist's notion of the North as a vast, remote area lying just at the edge of most people's experiences. Shelagh Grant, for example, notes that "the North is often referred to as 'wilderness,' a place beyond southern civilisation, agricultural settlement, or urban life."[6] From a Canadian perspective, quantifiable fact confirms the reality of the North. Quite simply, it exists; not only can you read about it, you can walk into it.

Admittedly, it's getting harder to step out the door and amble northward because the North, like all frontiers, is shrinking. Toward the end of the last century, for example, the "southern boundary of the North [was] at the 49th parallel" (*Canadian Nordicity,* 35). Now, a hundred years later, it has receded northward several hundred miles. However, about 70 percent of Canada remains "northern." As Northrop Frye mused in his influential conclusion to *A Literary History of Canada*: "One wonders if any other national consciousness has had so large an amount of the unknown, the unrealized, the humanly undigested, so built into it."[7] Importantly, then, the "frontier was the immediate datum of [the Canadian's] imagination, the thing that had to be dealt with first" ("Conclusion," 221). Most Canadians, therefore, "believe that the North has somehow imparted a unique quality to the character of the nation" (Grant, 13).

But the North has not just shaped the country's past. For Canadians, it has to be contended with in the present and—in a deterministic, even fatalistic way—in the future. Shelagh Grant notes that "since the time of Confederation, the people of Canada have looked upon their North as a symbol of identity and destiny" (13). "In the North," writes Thomas Berger, "lies the future of Canada."[8] It is a statement that has been made many, many times.

Given the contiguity of the northern wilderness to the experiences of Canadians, it is not surprising that it has had a special, formative impact on their identity, particularly as it has been developed through their literature. Indeed, the North and its exploration—in both geographical and psychological terms—are fundamental, even definitive features of Canada's national identity. In her classic thematic study of Canadian literature,

Survival, Atwood suggests that in Canada "the answer to the question 'Who am I?' is at least partly the same as the answer to another question: 'Where is here?' 'Who am I?' is a question appropriate in countries where the environment, the 'here,' is already well-defined. . . . 'Where is here?' is a different kind of question. It is what a man asks when he finds himself in unknown territory."[9] So we discover that the quest for the North is, in Canadian terms, also the search for a meaningful identity. That search, which began several centuries ago in a "north" that we now think of as eastern and southern Canada, is not only recorded by but continues today in Canada's literature.

This literature is, if not the lineal descendant of the frontier literature of the American West, its first cousin. What Frye has said about the "Laurentian" movement in Canada—which he mistakenly calls "western" rather than "northern" as Hamelin properly does—echoes what has so often been noted about the westward expansion of the United States: it "has attracted to itself nearly everything that is heroic and romantic in the Canadian tradition" ("Conclusion," 217). Romantic in its language and epic in its proportions, this literature describes an imaginative realm often searched for but rarely found.

It is history, more than geography, that separates the frontier West from the Far North. This is important. When the last corners of the West were surveyed and fenced, it could no longer support the wild fantasies and utopian dreams it had sustained for so long. Therefore, as several contributors to this volume suggest, enthusiastic dreams about the "Wild West" have given way to wistful regard for the "Old West." What "was"—rather than what "is" or "could be"—now fuels speculation about the West. Today, cowboy boots are a fashion statement one is apt to see on city sidewalks, not a practical response to the need to keep one's feet firmly planted in a saddle's stirrups. The West, as frontier, quite simply no longer exists except, of course, as one of America's most potent imaginative constructs.

Thus, there is a correlation—if not a causal connection—between the waning of the Wild West and the rise of the Far North. The North is to the twentieth century what the West was to the late eighteenth and nineteenth centuries: a place with more future than past, more unexplored reaches than carefully mapped topography. Even today the North, especially the Far North, is a region suited to the grand speculations of the romantic as well as the matter-of-fact observations of the chronicler. Whereas a century ago, young men may have been urged to "go west" to make their fortunes, today they are often urged to turn north. In doing so, they often not only follow routes first traveled by the early northern explorers but model habits borrowed from them.

As *A Literary History of Canada* attests, many of the early explorers' accounts offer compelling personal narratives. Some, such as Radisson's *Voyages,* are badly written blends of "truth and fancy."[10] Others, such as Samuel Hearne's *Journey from Prince of Wales's Fort in Hudson's Bay to the Northern Ocean*[11] and John Rae's *Narrative of an Expedition to the Shores of the Arctic Sea in 1846 and 1847*[12], offer at times profound observations about the landscape, its original inhabitants, and the physical and psychological challenges frequently faced by the travelers. Taken together, their work is of great importance; as Victor Hopwood suggests, the origins of a Canadian, as distinct from British or American, literature can be found in the writings of these often solitary Europeans who moved out into what the French called *"le pays d'en haut"* and what the English came to call, with the founding of the Hudson's Bay Company in 1670, "Rupert's Land": "The protoform of our still largely unwritten foundation literature is of necessity the record of our explorers, fur traders and pioneers. The transformation of such material has already begun" ("Explorers By Land," 19). There are now numerous examples—some successful, some not—of that transformation. Some events and characters have particularly attracted the attention of Canadian writers. For example, Albert Johnson's efforts to elude the Royal Canadian Mounted Police in the western Northwest Territories, which earned him the epithet "mad trapper," have been the subject of countless articles and several novels. Two of these—Wiebe's *Mad Trapper*[13] and York's *Trapper*[14]—are rightly considered "northern" classics. As well, countless stories have been written in an effort not just to retell but to reevaluate the contribution of the "giants" of the exploration of the Northwest. Brian Fawcett, for example, adopts a style and diction reminiscent of Mackenzie's own to create "The Secret Journal of Alexander Mackenzie." In it the narrator describes his discovery of a previously "lost" manuscript that shows the explorer "close to the very core and home of the continent's savagery."[15]

But as Fawcett's rather Conradian tale suggests, this preoccupation with things northern goes beyond the simple recasting of familiar northern historical events and personages in modern literary terms. The North has, in the last century, become the favored imaginative terrain across which an individual can travel, usually alone and facing great odds, in search of wealth and knowledge.

This oft-told story of the individual's quest northward is, I believe, reduced to its bare essentials in J. Michael Yates's "The Hunter Who Loses His Human Scent."[16] The story begins with a quotation from the writings of Sono Nis, Yates's alter ego, who suggests that some men are instinctually driven north:

> . . . we come then to the polar particle adrift somewhere in the chromosomes of the equatorial man—that atavism (auxin in the plant, Man, which causes its

leaves to bear around toward a small high window through which—it knows or dreams—sunlight streams) which brings few, nearly no men north. Figuratively, it is possible to say that all of us are born at the equator. Order there is other than north. Most live out their lives at the equator. Those who vanish one day—frequently with promises of return—become regarded, finally, as lost souls. As if in defiance of all human gravities, they go up and do not come down.

("Hunter," 52)

The hunter in the story has been "moving north through the south of the northern hemisphere . . . always" ("Hunter," 52). His travel is made difficult—"his way north labyrinthine" ("Hunter," 53)—by the distractions and obstacles of a "civilized" south: "There are the other impediments—museums of natural history, municipal administration offices, baseball diamonds, and cemeteries which appear suddenly to turn the streets or truncate them altogether" ("Hunter," 53). The pattern is one not of investiture but of divestiture. He travels north first by "public conveyances," then by hitchhiking and finally by foot; he finds walking "a relief." He travels north from a comfortable home to a series of one-room cabins and finally abandons even them for the wide open. He travels north from the humidity and heat of summer to the dessicated air and the cold of winter. Finally, he divests himself of everything, pack, rifle, snowshoes, even his human scent. And it is then that he symbolically "arrives" in a state of pure, simple existence.

Yates, an expatriate American, clearly views the North as the last place in North America where one can psychologically as well as geographically free oneself from the civilized, "equatorial" world of the South and, no longer encumbered by its materialism, find oneself. Thus, the journey north becomes for the individual in search of self-knowledge—Yates's symbolic hunter—a "hunt in an unmapped interior."[17]

Yates's work is characteristic of the Thoreauvian turn that "mainstream" northern Canadian writing has taken in the last several decades. For writers like Margaret Atwood, Aritha van Herk, Robert Kroetsch, and M. T. Kelly, the North represents a last chance to escape the errors and terrors of the "civilized"—that is, industrialized, polluted, and overpopulated—south. It offers a last chance to find a simpler life in a purer world. In van Herk's *No Fixed Address,* the northern Yukon is called "the ultimate frontier, a place where the civilized melt away."[18] In *Surfacing,* Atwood's heroine returns north—to her "home ground, foreign territory"[19]—in an effort to heal the psychological wounds acquired from too much city living. M. T. Kelly's autobiographical main character in *A Dream Like Mine* travels north to Kenora where he is kidnapped by a couple of Indians who carry him into the wilderness where he experiences something akin to a revelation.[20] According to Al-

lison Mitcham, "the pattern of northward flight in pursuit of a utopian dream is clearly a dominant pattern in contemporary Canadian fiction."[21]

While the "frontiersman," that man with Hercules' strength and Odysseus's wit, was traditionally a trapper or factor or missionary or outlaw or even a policeman, today he or she is just as often a writer. As we look more closely at modern exempla of northern quest literature, we discover that they do not merely recount a character's northward search for self-knowledge, but proceed from a prevalent view among contemporary Canadian writers that in the North can be found what has so often eluded them in the South: inspiration. Indeed, over the last three decades the quest for a "voice" has, in contemporary Canadian terms, almost always been northward. The "trip north" has almost become an obligatory rite of passage. Almost every major contemporary Canadian writer has made the pilgrimage. A surprising number of modern Canadian classics are, consequently, "northern." Three—Al Purdy's *North of Summer*[22], Atwood's *Surfacing,* and M. T. Kelly's *A Dream Like Mine*—come immediately to mind. So pronounced is this northward-looking imagination that Allison Mitcham speaks of a distinctive, modern "northern imagination" (9). She notes that "many contemporary Canadian novelists—French and English—[focus] on the northern wilderness in the [continuing] belief that it is what makes Canada distinctive and original" (17).

Just as the literature of the western frontier is largely an eastern creation, the literature of the northern frontier is largely a southern one.[23] It has been written largely outside the area of study, first in Europe and more recently in the United States and southern Canada. At best, writers working within this tradition have made occasional forays into the North, usually returning south to turn their field notes into finished productions destined for a largely southern readership. This pattern was also set by the early explorers and factors. While they wintered in the North, they went "outside" to sell their furs and to Europe for their vacations and retirement. Robert Service, who perhaps more than any other writer popularized the Yukon, did much the same, moving out as soon as his income allowed him to.[24] And the pattern continues; today, however, many writers journey north with the assistance of Canada Council's "Exploration Grants" and the logistical support of the Continental Polar Shelf Project.

Despite the number of literary texts that comprise this literature, only a limited and very imperfect criticism has grown up around it,[25] which has more often than not enthusiastically adopted a "frontier" perspective and perpetuated the frontier myths rather than challenged them. Nevertheless, what many critics have said about the North is validated by many southern Canadians' imaginative perceptions of the North, if not by most northerners' firsthand experiences of it. And, as should now be clear, the south-north axis along which so many of Canada's writers are moving has all the historical and imaginative impetus that the east-west axis did a century ago.

So far, we have looked northward, adopting a national, pan-Canadian or North American perspective, looking up from the South. But there is a small handful of people for whom the North is not "up there" but "right here." When asked to point at a boundary, a line of demarcation, they will do so by turning south and pointing "down there" or "outside." Clearly, the first group is separated from the second by more than a geopolitical boundary, the timberline, or the line of discontinuous permafrost. They are separated by their experiences of the North and, consequently, by how they think and write about it.[26]

Despite the difficulty of drawing a precise boundary between the sparsely populated north and the settled south, we must make a fundamental distinction between "here" and "there"—that is, if we are to differentiate critically among the vast number of texts about the North. While there has been at least one recent attempt to classify the types of northern literature,[27] we in fact need to distinguish between two literary traditions, both of which are about the North but each of which reflects a fundamentally different relationship with or stance toward the North. So far we have, as I have suggested, looked at a tradition that, while imaginatively focused on the North, is written and read largely outside it and that is preoccupied, ultimately, with the North as a frontier. But there is another tradition we need to examine, one which focuses on a fundamentally different north: the one that Justice Thomas Berger first brought to the public's attention when he said he wanted Canadians to learn about a north that was not the south's frontier but an ancient homeland.[28]

For several decades these two views of the North have been colliding violently. They have collided in virtually every arena: politics, history, economics, and even religion. Out of this collision a new literature of the North is beginning to emerge. Protean as it is, this new regional literature has many identifiable and unique features. The most important, perhaps, is that it is, to use Reed Way Dasenbrock's phrase, "the discourse of the insider about his or her own region,"[29] and much of its impetus comes from a desire to confront, even repudiate, what Dasenbrock appropriately calls the "received notions" of traditional "northern" writers. For example, a recent publication of the Dene Cultural Institute reexamines Alexander Mackenzie's accomplishments; its title alone announces the challenge it intends to conventional thinking about the exploration of the North: *Dehcho: Mom, We've Been Discovered!*[30] Such works, on the one hand, challenge the romantic notions of the South's northern imaginings and, on the other, take inspiration from the North's oral traditions. Even when they are not especially good, they are provocative. As Frye suggests, "It is much easier to see what literature is trying to do when we are studying a literature that has not quite done it" ("Conclusion," 214).

If the accounts of the early explorers and traders represent the protoform of the frontier tradition, then the protoform of this emergent tradition is provided by the oral tales of the North's indigenous peoples. Once passed by mouth from generation to generation, they have been written down by anthropologists and, more recently, by a new generation of native writers. These tales document a world much different than that found in the frontier literature of the North. In them one crosses no frontier (unless it is that which lies between the physical and spiritual worlds) and gets lost in no northern "wilderness"—a word with no counterpart in any Athapaskan dialect.[31] Rather, one walks across a familiar, even comforting landscape called quite simply "the land" or "home." In this literature, which is so intimately tied to the northern landscape, the northern frontier, as Anglo-and Franco-Canadians think and write about it, has no existence, except occasionally as a target for satire.[32] Indeed, from an Inuit perspective the great unknown lies south of the tree line.

Elsewhere, I have discussed the gradual evolution of oral material from unattributed quotation scattered in anthropologists' writings into mature, "authored" texts.[33] This foundation-building process continues. Two Alaskans—Nora Marks Dauenhauer and Richard Dauenhauer—are, for example, editing *Classics of Tlingit Oral Literature,* the first volume of which, *Haa Shuka, Our Ancestors,* appeared in 1987.[34] In Canada, *Northern Voices: Inuit Writing in English*[35] has recently been published by the University of Toronto, thus making easily available a wide range of Inuit writing for the first time. Despite the great distance that separates the Tlingit and Inuit cultures, these recent works express remarkably similar attitudes about the land, ones diametric to a traditional European, frontier attitude.

At the same time that native people in the north are authoring their own texts, a number of northern anthropologists are producing texts that are consciously "literary" in that they mix traditional scholarship and personal narrative. In Hugh Brody's *Maps and Dreams,* chapters of personal narrative alternate with chapters of conventional scholarship.[36] Similarly, Robin Ridington has said that his *Trail to Heaven* describes "moments in the life of a northern Indian community . . . from the point of view of my own involvement with the community and its people." Moreover, he says that it is "to the best of [his] ability, a true story and a very personal one."[37] Clearly, such texts are mapping a new literary territory, not just thematically but structurally as well.

While these efforts first occurred outside the literary world as narrowly defined, they are now clearly having an impact on mainstream Canadian writing. Richard Davis writes: "Many Canadian writers are today recognizing that the oral legends and myths of Chipweyan, Cree, Montagnais, Inuit, Algonkian, and other indigenous cultures—which were here long before Europeans "discovered" North America—have immense relevance to Canada, and modern authors are drawing from this rich well of Canadian "stories" that pre-date even the records of the first European explorers" ("The North in Canadian Literature," 14). One of the most impressive recent examples of this recognition is to be found in Rudy Wiebe's *Playing Dead: A Contemplation Concerning the Arctic*. In it, we see, for the first time perhaps, a Canadian writer of considerable stature turning his attention away from the grand names and events of northern exploration and focusing on a more immediate and, somehow, more truly northern world.

Quite simply, the North confronts him. "When one personally goes to the Mackenzie Delta," says Wiebe, "Franklin and Richardson seem amazingly irrelevant."[38] Even when Wiebe ponders over the "historical record"—presumably someplace outside the North—it is not Franklin that captures his attention, but an ordinary seaman—the "excellent old Mr. Hepburn" (Wiebe, 35)—and a young Yellowknife woman called Greenstockings.

In *Playing Dead*, Wiebe thinks about a north that is "here" and "now." The result is not just a complete "restructuring" of his artistic sense of the northern landscape—shifting him from a European's lineal conceptualization of space to an Inuit's areal one (Wiebe, 49-78)—but an effort to explore its aesthetic and artistic ramifications. It is significant, not just for Wiebe but for all of us who "desire true NORTH, not PASSAGE to anywhere" (Wiebe, 114), that Wiebe contemplates a world that begins with the words of two of the North's most eloquent Inuit—Ikpakhuaq and Uloqsaq—but ends with a contemporary writer saying, "So, I am trying to . . . prepare myself. To walk into the true north of my own head between the stones and the ocean. If I do, I will get a new song. If I do, I will sing it for you" (Wiebe, 119).

If Wiebe and other writers like him are successful—if they find new songs that integrate their own firsthand experiences with the Inuit's and Dene's understanding of the landscape—our literature will be the richer for it. Certainly, the northern frontier will, like some tired glacier warmed by a summer sun, retract even more. But, perhaps for the first time ever, the reading public will travel north and see a world that, as any number of Inuit and Dene will confirm, has existed here for millennia.

Notes

1. Quoted in Rudy Wiebe, *Playing Dead: A Contemplation Concerning the Arctic* (Edmonton: Newest, 1989), 5.

2. Louis-Edmond Hamelin, *The Canadian North and Its Conceptual Referents* (Ottawa: Supply and Services Canada, 1988), 12.

3. Margaret Atwood, "Canadians: What Do They Want?" in *75 Readings: An Anthology,* 2d ed. (New York: McGraw-Hill, 1989), 290-91.

4. Aron Senkpiel, "Of Kiwi Fruit and Moosemeat: Contradictory Perceptions of Canada's North," *History and Social Science Teacher* 23 (1988): 77-81.

5. Louis-Edmond Hamelin, *Canadian Nordicity: It's Your North Too* (Montreal: Harvest House, 1978), 17; hereafter cited in text as *Canadian Nordicity*.

6. S. D. Grant, "Myths of the North in the Canadian Ethos," *The Northern Review,* 3-4 (Summer-Winter 1989), 14; hereafter cited in text.

7. Northrop Frye, "Conclusion to *A Literary History of Canada,*" in *The Bush Garden* (Toronto: Anansi, 1971), 220; hereafter cited in text as "Conclusion."

8. Thomas Berger, *Northern Frontier, Northern Homeland: Report of the Mackenzie Valley Pipeline Inquiry,* rev. ed. (Vancouver: Douglas & MacIntyre, 1988), 12.

9. Margaret Atwood, *Survival: A Thematic Guide to Canadian Literature* (Toronto: Anansi, 1972), 17.

10. Victor Hopwood, "Explorers by Land (to 1867)," in vol. 1 of *A Literary History of Canada,* ed. Carl F. Klinck, 2d ed., 3 vols. (Toronto: University of Toronto Press, 1976), 23; hereafter cited in text as "Explorers by Land."

11. Samuel Hearne, *Journey from Prince of Wales's Fort in Hudson's Bay to the Northern Ocean,* ed. Richard Glover (Toronto: Macmillan, 1958).

12. John Rae, *Narrative of an Expedition to the Shores of the Arctic Sea in 1846 and 1847,* referred to by Victor Hopwood, "Explorers by Land (to 1867)," 47.

13. Rudy Wiebe, *The Mad Trapper* (Toronto: McClelland & Stewart, 1980).

14. Thomas York, *Trapper* (Toronto: Doubleday, 1981).

15. Brian Fawcett, "The Secret Journal of Alexander Mackenzie," in *The Secret Journal of Alexander Mackenzie* (Vancouver: Talonbooks, 1985), 24.

16. J. Michael Yates, "The Hunter Who Loses His Scent," in *Man in the Glass Octopus* (Vancouver: Sono Nis Press, 1968), 52-61.

17. J. Michael Yates, *Hunt in an Unmapped Interior* (Francestown, N. H.: Golden Quill, 1967), 47.

18. Aritha van Herk, *No Fixed Address* (Toronto: McClelland & Stewart, 1986), 316.

19. Margaret Atwood, *Surfacing* (Toronto: General, 1972), 11.

20. M. T. Kelly, *A Dream Like Mine* (Toronto: Stoddart, 1987).

21. Allison Mitcham, *The Northern Imagination: A Study of Northern Canadian Literature* (Moonbeam, Ontario: Penumbra Press, 1983), 20; hereafter cited in text.

22. Al Purdy, *North of Summer* (Toronto: McClelland & Stewart, 1967).

23. This point is discussed by Eric Heyne in his article in this volume, "The Lasting Frontier: Reinventing America."

24. Carl F. Klinck, *Robert Service: A Biography* (Toronto: McGraw-Hill, 1976), 72.

25. This point is made by Richard Davis in his essay, "The North in Canadian Literature," which is to be published in *New Bearings on Northern Scholarship,* ed. Aron Senkpiel and Kenneth Coates, which is to be released by University of British Columbia Press in Vancouver in 1991; hereafter cited in text as "The North in Canadian Literature."

26. Aron Senkpiel, "Of Kiwi Fruit and Moosemeat," 78.

27. Richard Davis, "The North in Canadian Literature," 1-4.

28. Thomas Berger, *Northern Frontier, Northern Homeland,* 31-33.

29. This point is made by Reed Way Dasenbrock in his article, "Southwest of What?", in this volume.

30. *Dehco: Mom, We've Been Discovered!* (Yellowknife: Dene Cultural Institute, 1989).

31. S. D. Grant, "Myths of the North in the Canadian Ethos," 16.

32. Alootook Ipellie, "Damn Those Invaders," in *Northern Voices,* ed. Penny Petrone (Toronto: University of Toronto, 1988), 248-52.

33. Aron Senkpiel and N. Alexander Easton, "New Bearings on Northern Scholarship," *The Northern Review* 1 (Summer 1988): 15-17.

34. Nora Marks Dauenhauer and Richard Dauenhauer, *Haa Shuka, Our Ancestors,* vol. 1 of *Classics of Tlingit Oral Narrative* (Seattle: University of Washington, 1987).

35. Penny Petrone, ed., *Northern Voices: Inuit Writing in English* (Toronto: University of Toronto Press, 1988).

36. Hugh Brody, *Maps and Dreams: Indians and the British Columbia Frontier* (Vancouver: Douglas & McIntyre, 1981).

37. Robin Ridington, *Trail to Heaven: Knowledge and Narrative in a Northern Native Community* (Vancouver: Douglas & McIntyre, 1988), ix, xi.

38. Rudy Wiebe, *Playing Dead: A Contemplation Concerning the Arctic* (Edmonton: Newest, 1989), 40; hereafter cited in text.

THE FRONTIER THESIS AND FRONTIER LITERATURE

Tiziano Bonazzi (essay date August 1993)

SOURCE: Bonazzi, Tiziano. "Frederick Jackson Turner's Frontier Thesis and the Self-Consciousness of America." *Journal of American Studies* 27, no. 2 (August 1993): 149-71.

[*In the following essay, Bonazzi perceives Frederick Jackson Turner's "Frontier Thesis" as a culmination of a new approach to history that Turner had been developing for many years.*]

In their work on Turner's formative period, Ray A. Billington and Fulmer Mood[1] have shown that the Frontier Thesis, formulated in 1893 in "The Significance of the Frontier in American History,"[2] is not so much a brilliant early effort by a young scholar as a mature study in which Turner gave his ideas an organization that proved to be final. During the rest of his life he developed but never disclaimed or modified them. Billington and Mood also add that the Frontier Thesis is meant to test a new approach to history that Turner had been developing since the beginning of his academic career. We can fully understand it, then, only by setting it within the framework of the assumptions and goals of his 1891 essay, "The Significance of History,"[3] Turner's only attempt to sketch a philosophy of history.

In "The Significance of History" Turner defines from an evolutionary perspective the relationship between history as science and its role among the social sciences.

Historiography to him is a science insofar as it is the consciousness and demonstration of the evolution inherent in social life. A genetic approach will show history to be a continuous process of societies—understood as *social organisms*[4]—developing by adapting themselves to ever new environments, marked by ever different sets of dominant conditions: "History . . . is ever becoming, never completed."[5] Historians are conditioned by the age in which they live; they must be conscious of the fact that they will not find final answers in their study of the past, because their approach and interests are rooted in and dependent on the problems and dominant conditions of their age. As Turner states: "Each generation writes the history of the past anew with reference to the conditions uppermost in its own time."[6] This statement, far from being relativistic, gives expression to the author's evolutionary anthropology and, as a consequence, allows his triumphant assertion of history's relevance to the present: "The historian strives to show the present to itself by revealing its origin from the past. The goal of the antiquarian is the dead past; the goal of the historian is the living present."[7] Evolutionary history, then, is a discipline of the present for the present. Through a genetic study of their social environment people will become better equipped to deal with the problems of their age and to ensure a rapid and smooth passage to a more advanced social stage.

Turner is no ivory tower intellectual; the past is meaningful to him only as far as it shows the dominant conditions of the present and helps to change them. His Darwinian evolution amounts to making historical research a necessary prerequisite to politics, although he is not making a plea for the historian to take an active stance in politics or to write politically "relevant" history. A true positivist, Turner is a devotee of pure science. The new age of industrialism, however, needs science not only to organize its economy rationally, but also to foster good citizenship and "an intellectual regeneration of the state."[8] By being a scientist and an educator the historian is a true politician.

History, then, is a practical discipline that, if rightly approached, can lead to an understanding of the unity and continuity of the evolutionary process. This means that it can help mankind comprehend itself, or, in the words of Droysen quoted by Turner, "history is the 'know thyself' of humanity—the selfconsciousness of mankind."[9] Here we can see the scope of Turner's ambitious project, his attempt to make history the leading discipline of the modern age: a necessary step toward the solution of the problems of the present. Entirely practical and fully ethical, Turnerian history aims to be a shining example of the positivistic ideal of a science which becomes man's self-consciousness.

II

The Frontier Thesis was Turner's answer to the challenge of putting his ideas about history into practice. Its meaning, then, does not simply lie in a new interpretation of the past, but in a new use of the past for the present. This implied building a theory whose very structure would change man's understanding of himself. The key to the transformation of evolutionary historical science into man's self-consciousness, then, is hidden in the organization of the historical discourse.

Turner's reversal of the traditional approach to American history, which focused on the Eastern states, a reversal on which the Frontier Thesis rests, is a splendid example of just how evolutionism helped him shape his historical discourse. His emphasis on western expansion as the key to American history[10] was born out of his early perceptions and research, but its rationale and the frame in which it is cast are based on his scientific credo. Following the ideas of evolutionary human geography and anthropology—the cutting edge of science during his formative period in the 1880s[11]—Turner equated societies to organisms and, as a consequence, their history to the development of new species. His task as a scientist was to trace the process of adaptation through which the social organism he was dealing with, the United States, had become a distinct organism with an identity of its own. The champions of neo-Lamarckian evolutionism taught him that the process of identification is one of differentiation and of growing inner cohesion depending on the organism's response to its environment. Therefore, the distinctiveness of a nation like the United States, whose history is marked by expansion into ever new and different geographic regions, cannot but be based on the consequences of this process and must be looked for in those very areas where the process occurred. Turner's scientific assurance is reflected in his matter of fact style: "The existence of an area of free land, its continuous recession, and the advance of the American settlement westward, explain American development. Behind institutions, behind constitutional forms and modifications, lie the vital forces that call these organs into life and shape them to meet changing conditions."[12]

Evolutionary theory, moreover, offered a normative diachronic model that could be analogically used in the historical field. Biological evolution proceeds, according to Darwin, by following a temporal pattern of differentiation through adaptation that creates ever more complex organisms. In the 1860s and 1870s this model merged with earlier evolutionary theories applied to society—those of Comte, Spencer and Maine—to give life to a model of human development by social stages with which Turner got acquainted at Johns Hopkins in the early 1880s. In the case of the United States this model seemed at first sight to substantiate the point of view of the supercilious Easterners, who thought of themselves as "civilized" while the West was still "savage". Turner's own understanding of the theory of social stages, however, exposed their formalistic approach to evolutionism, unable to understand the nature of the *process* of change. In America, in fact, Turner says, the temporal process of evolutionary anthropology has a spatial dimension that excludes the possibility of a mere repetition of social development. Each new frontier environment starts a process of adaptation with new consequences: "American development has exhibited not merely advance along a single line, but a return to primitive conditions on a continually advancing frontier line, and a new development for that area. American social development has been continually beginning over again on the frontier."[13]

Turner's coherence in making use of evolutionism not as a model to be superimposed on reality, but as an ongoing process to be understood qualitatively step-by-step had important consequences for the structure of his work. This can be seen in the meaning given to movement, the main feature of frontier life. In the Frontier Thesis movement, both as territorial expansion and as individual nomadism, is equated with change.[14] We know that change is a prerequisite for survival in evolutionary theory and that in evolutionary anthropology social change is a prerequisite for progress; in both cases immutability amounts to decay and death. Thus, by being considered synonymous with change, movement acquires a normative meaning for American history. The *fact* of moving becomes normative, a *vital* need for society, the positive value *par excellence* and a yardstick against which to judge all historical facts. In order to be a positive factor of development, moreover, movement cannot be disordered like an explosion of brute energy. Evolutionary anthropology privileges sequential processes, where modifications are continuous but gradual—the unity and continuity of history. Moreover, it reads them teleologically, as having an inner rationality that brings about an ever increasing mastery over the environment—that is complexity. Rational complexity is the goal of change as shown in the history of civilization. Turner, accordingly, interprets western expansion as a sequential, ordered process leading to economic and technical complexity—that is progress: "The United States lies like a huge page in the history of society. Line by line as we read this continental page from West to East we find the record of social evolution."[15] This is also the reason why he tones down all references to conflict or chaos on the frontier. He does not deny their existence but is led by the logic of evolutionism to turn them into factors of social integration. Conflict, if structural, is a symptom of failure in adapting to the environment. As a moment of the process of adaptation, on the other hand, it is proof that society

moves forward and is ready to change.[16] The constant use by Turner of terms like "transformation," "development," and "growth" must be seen as normative, not as descriptive. They refer to the integration of conflict into gradual change that adaptation to nature on the frontier brings about. They all climax in that term "opportunity" depicting the teleology of progress contained in frontier history: "America has been another name for opportunity, and the people of the United States have taken their tone from the incessant expansion which has not only been open but has even been forced upon them."[17]

Positivist science, therefore, sets the stage for an interpretation in which change creates unity and continuity. Making use of it Turner could maintain that the frontier is the key to American history. It was the frontier—as movement and expansion—that gave an identity to America, because it was in the process of adaptation to ever new environments that the social organism "United States" developed its peculiar characteristics. These characteristics, moreover, grow ever more distinctive, because the "recurrence of the process of evolution" that we have on the frontier is not a mere repetition. Neo-Lamarckism offered Turner the instruments with which to explain the survival of useful frontier traits—those peculiar features born out of adaptation to every new environment—in the developed Western societies, and geology gave him the right images: "As successive terminal moraines result from successive glaciations, so each frontier leaves its traces behind it, and when it becomes a settled area the region still partakes of the frontier characteristics."[18] A devotion to movement and change is what gave the American social organism a unity and a biography. American culture is a process, we cannot depict it in static terms. We ought always to speak of "Americanization" as the true description of what America is. In a sense, "America as process" is the paradigm of every social organism conscious of its evolutionary nature, and "America the paradigm" can be true to itself only by further, incessant Americanization.

III

All that has been so far said points to a sort of "manifest structure" of the Frontier Thesis stressing the creative side of history, seen as a purely human evolutionary process, and supplying an antiformalistic interpretation of both evolutionism and American history.

For the purposes of this essay it is not necessary to analyse the strictures that Turner's radical application of his method put on his substantive interpretation. It is, for instance, true that his idea that the American social organism developed by differentiation from Europe compelled him to underestimate the role of the Atlantic economy, as can be seen from the following passage:

The West as a phase of social organization, began with the Atlantic coast, and passed through the continent. But the colonial tidewater area was in close touch with the Old World, and soon lost its western aspects . . . On the coast were the fishermen and the skippers, the merchants and planters, with eyes turned toward Europe.[19]

They did not go West, they were not Americanized enough and Turner soon forgets them. All this is entirely coherent with the "order of discourse"[20] of the manifest structure. This coherence is what interests us here. Subsequent interpretations of the frontier up to contemporary "New frontier history" and the demise of Turner's substantive views of the West are outside the scope of this essay.[21]

What is of paramount importance to us, instead, is that when we reach the core of the Frontier Thesis the coherence of the manifest structure suddenly disappears. The frontier to Turner is "the line of most rapid and effective americanization,"[22] the social phase where the American human and social characteristics are born. The frontier Americanizes the frontiersman by destroying his inherited culture. It strips him naked and teaches him everything anew: in Turner's vocabulary it "breaks the cake of custom"[23] and it offers the pioneer new opportunities, new ideals once he has overcome the ordeal of being mastered by the wilderness. The frontier brings man back to an original state of freedom, marked by a rude, but energetic and practical turn of mind—a "forest philosophy."[24] So wide is the gap between the frontiersman and the original European immigrant, that Turner speaks of the process as a "rebirth."[25]

The final, and climactic part of the Frontier Thesis interrupts the coherent application of the manifest structure to history, because it is flawed from the point of view of both evolutionary biology and evolutionary anthropology. Biological evolutionism does not imply a reversal to primitive or original life forms as a consequence of adaptation to new environments. There is, in fact, no "original" life form to which to go back. Evolutionary retrogression, moreover, easily means the beginning of the end for the species that undertakes it. It is evolutionary anthropology that speaks of a first or original stage of civilization, and Turner no doubt makes reference to it.[26] But he goes against the logic of the theory when he maintains that the reversal to primitive conditions on the frontier is a *prerequisite* for the creation of a new civilization *because* it destroys inherited culture. He does not seem to be aware of the fact that the idea of a "perennial rebirth" on the frontier, on which he founds American identity, endangers his evolutionary approach to history. It is true that ambiguities of this kind can be detected in evolutionist authors like Richard T. Ely and Achille Loria, two of the scholars that influenced him most,[27] but this does not free us from trying to understand the meaning of this central feature of the Frontier Thesis.

Turner's approach to the opportunities offered by the frontier is at first strictly economic: "obviously the immigrant was attracted by the cheap lands of the frontier, and even the native farmer felt their influence strongly"; however, he goes immediately beyond this and frontier opportunities take a more exalted meaning: "each frontier did indeed furnish a new field of opportunity, a gate of escape from the bondage of the past; and freshness, and confidence, and scorn of old society. . . ."[28] In this statement as in most descriptions of the frontier, economic elements are submerged by new features that overturn the evolutionist time model and scale of values, showing the strong appearance of an *"elsewhere"* that annihilates the positivist approach.

The framework of the manifest structure is, in fact, a diachronic system of stages of social growth organized in a necessary series. The effects of the frontier on the pioneer, on the other hand, are organized in dichotomic pairs, the most basic of which is the present-past one. The present, born out of purifying frontier experience, is always better than the past. However primitive, the frontier is superior to the already settled areas. The contradiction between this dichotomic arrangement and the one shown by the "process of civilization, marching single file," social stage after social stage that Turner imagines witnessing from Cumberland Gap,[29] is glaring, and it suggests that he unconsciously makes use of two different models in building the Frontier Thesis. The one we find in the manifest structure interprets the birth of American identity as orderly change in the direction of progress, unfolding itself through the development of material civilization. The second, shown in the dichotomic organization of frontier life, is founded on the contrast between a series of irreconcilable spiritual values. According to the latter model, the meaning of frontier experience does not consist in progressive development, but in a dramatic clash between values:

> The wilderness masters the colonists. It finds him a European in dress, industries, tools, modes of travel, and thought. It takes him from the railroad car and puts him in the birch canoe. It strips off the garments of civilization and arrays him in the hunting shirt and mocassins . . . He must accept the conditions which it furnishes or perish . . . Little by little he transforms the wilderness, but the outcome is not the old Europe . . . The fact is, that here is a new product that is American.[30]

From this ordeal a "new" and "liberated" man is born.

Turner describes the effects of the frontier as if they were an initiation rite, something that helps us understand the present-past dichotomy. The post-initiation phase, emerging from the "return to origins" that takes place on the frontier, cannot but be qualitatively different from and superior to the pre-initiation phase. If we accept the hypothesis that Turner unconsciously deals with frontier life as if it were a religious experience, the Frontier Thesis can be said to be built on two opposed, but interlaced structures: the manifest one, founded on Turner's avowed evolutionism, and a "latent" one, based on the model of an initiatory rite which appears at crucial moments to redirect the meaning of the former.

The present-past dichotomy is merely the first of a series of dichotomies that takes us deeper and deeper into the latent structure. Along with it we find that of nature-civilization, involving the pair simplicity-complexity. As is well known, they all lead to the ultimate dichotomy, America-Europe. Whenever these pairs emerge the manifest structure is overturned and its main value, civilization, becomes the "cake of custom"[31] that frontier life is called upon to destroy. Yet it would be dangerous to believe that because Turner sees a return to nature as a positive value he indulges in a sort of inverse evolutionism, a return, that is, to primitivism. Such a reading misunderstands both Turner's intention and the relationship between the manifest and the latent structure.

The two structures answer different needs and are entirely separate. The pairs of terms making up the dichotomies of the latent structure are spiritual values, they are not social stages and therefore do not invalidate social evolution. They express the change of state undergone by the pioneers, their purification and cleansing that entails the opportunity to rebuild civilization along natural lines. Here is the core of Turner's argument. Civilization as a product of evolution is not rejected. Turner seems to regard civilization as being made up of two related, but different elements, man the moral agent and human science or technology. The second element, born out of adaptation to the environment, is deemed to have an objective history of its own. Turner sees no need to refute or even to discuss it and simply accepts the tenets of evolutionary anthropology. It is man who must be purified, because in Europe man has built social institutions that enslave him; his adaptive achievements are not to be abandoned. The frontier purifies man by freeing him "from the bondage of the past," that is by "breaking the cake of custom", by compelling him to do without time-honored institutions and therefore by making him an individual again.

An *individual,* why? Evolutionary anthropology put the horde at the beginning of human evolution and thought the individual to be the final expression of civilization as shown in 19th century European liberal societies.[32] Evolutionary social science offered Turner no opportunity to turn this model upside down and find individualism in a primitive context. He could find historical evidence to the fact that "Complex society is precipitated by the wilderness into a kind of primitive organization based on the family. The tendency is anti-social." However, it does not follow from this "antipathy to con-

trol"[33] that frontier individualism corresponds to the "hunter type" of the anthropologists. The two human models cannot be reconciled in scientific terms. We have to return to the latent structure and its rite of initiation to find an answer. By reenacting through frontier experience the "time of origins", the pioneer reaches back to his archetypal nature and becomes an individual not so much in a utilitarian-psychological or sociological sense as in a religious one. He is the *New Adam.* He has returned to his original true nature. As such he does not need the forest any more; Arcadic simplicity is not his lot. He is ready to build civilization anew, and the process of social stages can be restored. This is why America reads like a palimpsest of social evolution, and why the whole of America, not the frontier alone makes up the social organism called America. In spite of all contradictions the two structures of the Frontier Thesis reinforce each other and live in symbiosis.

American civilization then, is not technologically different from Europe. Nonetheless it is far superior to it, because Americans can build a natural civilization, that is, a civilization expressive of true human nature. The consequence of continuous adaptation-initiation on the frontier is not Arcadic simplicity, but the reconquest of an immediately operative posture as against the intellectualist impotence of Europe: "that practical, inventive turn of mind, quick to find expedients; that masterful grasp of material things, lacking in the artistic but powerful to affect great ends," "the fundamental traits of the man of the interior were due to the free lands of the West. These turned his attention to the great task of subduing them to the purpose of civilization."[34] The "forest philosophy" of the pioneer cannot simply be termed "practical", because it is true *praxis*: reason smoothly turning into constructive action, action based on reconstituted reason. The contrast between America and Europe, then, does not depend on a choice of primitivism as against progress. It is, on the contrary, a contrast between a civilization whose goals are in tune with *being,* and one that has forgotten human nature and follows artificial values. The first one is always simple because it is whole; the second is artificially complex whatever its degree of technical development.

Two further elements prove the role of the latent structure in redirecting the meaning of the Frontier Thesis. We have seen that movement is a central feature of the manifest structure, where it is equated to change and where it is a sequential, ordered process having strong anticonflictual overtones. In the latent structure, on the other hand, westward expansion corresponds to a repetition of the nature-civilization fracture. It is a prerequisite for the ordeal of initiation. It is not a material element concerning adaptation; it is a spiritual quality, the true mark of the original human condition. As such it is an explosion of pure energy coming from the renewed union with the fountainhead of life: "Energy, incessant activity became the lot of this new American" Turner writes; freshness, confidence, impatience are his main characteristics.[35] Movement in the latent structure gives expression to the creative freedom of the spirit, to its operative potential. Therefore, it can be sudden like an explosion without bringing about chaos; on the contrary, it restores the chaotic historical man to his original perfection and allows him to start the civilization process anew.

In the latent structure, then, movement and change are no longer sociohistorical elements, nor are they a requisite for adaptation. They allow a "rebirth" or "regeneration" that validates adaptation. An important passage of "The Significance of the Frontier" consists of a long quotation from a speech of a Western politician, who, after praising "the energy which the mountain breezes and western habits import on those emigrants," concludes: "They are regenerated, politically, I mean."[36] In "The Problem of the West" we read: "The self-made man was the Western man's ideal . . . Out of the wilderness experience, out of the freedom of his opportunities, he fashioned a formula of social regeneration."[37] Undoubtedly Turner's intention was not to use these expressions of the Reformed tradition literally, as he was personally indifferent to religious problems,[38] but they turn up in his vocabulary as symptoms of a religious intellectual framework on which he unconsciously relies.

The present analysis has brought to light the presence of two contradictory structures in the Frontier Thesis. This contradiction, however, does not invalidate the thesis and the intellectual appeal of Turner's construction seems to derive precisely from their coexistence. This is partly due to Turner's rhetorical and artistic ability; but rhetoric and art alone do not explain the symbiotic union of the two structures. Nor do they explain whether the contradiction explodes at a deeper level of the Frontier Thesis.

IV

To American Studies scholars the latent structure of the Frontier Thesis has a familiar ring. It embodies a myth that has been widely explored by intellectual historians, and that we might call the "American Promise."[39] The core of the myth is a rite of passage, whose primal situation is a rite of initiation, a baptism: the crossing of the Atlantic Ocean.[40] Beyond the ocean is the New Canaan, where the European emigrant freed from Babylon will dwell in peace enjoying a special relationship with God. The pioneer ideal, particularly strong in the Mid West, was a further development of this theme, and the Frontier Thesis shows its persistence in the age of the second industrial revolution and outside its Christian cradle.

The presence of the myth of the Promise in the Frontier Thesis has already been studied at length from Henry Nash Smith's *Virgin Land* onward.[41] It is, however, to David W. Noble that we owe an in-depth analysis of the myth in American historiography. In his writings[42] Noble maintains that American historians have been the keepers of the myth of American a-historical uniqueness, and he sees Turner as a dramatic example of a scholar caught in the contradictions of the myth. According to Noble, Turner struggled to reconcile the fulfilling of the Promise on the frontier with the complexity of the post-frontier industrial world, and failed. He tried to maintain that industrialism is a natural process, like the frontier, but was unable to demonstrate that industrialization is in the hands of the common people as the frontier had been, and had to admit that in a frontierless nation democracy can be saved only by *artificial* control of the social environment. This proposition spells the doom for democracy in industrial America, because it runs against his main tenet, that democracy can only stem *naturally* from the environment. David Noble's interpretation of American historiography is important, but his analysis of Turner's Frontier Thesis does not reach deep enough, because Noble does not make the all important distinctions between the two structures. A full analysis of the symbiosis between them can help us carry Noble's argument a step further.

In order to understand why the two structures, however contradictory, are in symbiosis, we must go back to Turner's self-assigned role as a historian. More than once he pointedly remarked that he conceived his work "as that of dealing with the processes of American history rather than with a geographic section,"[43] a statement that stems from his goal to turn history into the self-consciousness of mankind, and that made him plan work in American history as that of giving "a connected and unified account of the progress of civilization across this continent, with the attendant results. Until this work is finished we shall have no real national self-consciousness."[44] The evolutionary consciousness of the American social organism, then, must be historical and political at the same time. Turner opened the way for multicausal and multidisciplinary history, but history to him culminates in political history, because political institutions are expressive of the ethical element of civilization. Although democracy, not the state, is to him the depository of ethical values, Turner writes in the grand tradition of 19th century German historiography.

The political aura permeating the Frontier Thesis penetrates both the manifest and the latent structures. In the manifest one, Turner imaginatively explains social evolution as a process moving from the "physiographic basis of history," "the arteries made by geology," through "the economic and social consolidation of the country" to political institutions, thus explaining "why we are today a nation rather than a collection of isolated states."[45] The latent structure, in turn, is thoroughly political in nature, in that it contains both a political myth dealing with the restoring of the earthly social experience of man in America, and a foundation myth of the American nation:

> But free lands and the consciousness of working out their social destiny did more than turn the Westerner to material interests and devote him to a restless existence. They promoted equality among the Western settlers . . . The West was another name for opportunity . . . The self-made man was the Western man's ideal, was the kind of man that all men might become. Out of his wilderness experience, out of the freedom of his opportunities, he fashioned a formula for social regeneration—the freedom of the individual to seek his own.[46]

The latent structure does not answer the mystical longings of isolated men, it answers needs of social and political identification that can also be found in the manifest structure.

Politics, then, is the ground where the two structures meet and can be analysed in their interrelatedness. This can best be done at that very logical and historical point where Smith and Noble locate the main contradiction of the Frontier Thesis, 1890, at the end of the "free lands": the moment when the frontiersman was bound to consider "that his conditions were exceptional and temporary".[47]

A correct reading of the often quoted, or misquoted, last sentence of "The Significance of the Frontier" substantiates my point. "The frontier has gone, and its going has closed the first period of American history."[48] Here Turner quietly points out that a stage of development of the American social organism—the first—has ended; a stage in which America was able to adapt and, as a consequence, to produce social harmony among the moral monads, the individuals. Turner does not go any further, he does not foretell the future, because the task of the social scientist, as he understands it, is to have the past itself lead men to self-consciousness. From the vantage point of his method, then, his last sentence is not meant to point to a tragic *caesura* between past and present. On the contrary, it is the gateway to a consciousness of historical continuity through change. The peculiar characteristics that the American social organism has acquired are there to help it adapt to the new environment. The West still exists:

> It has its characteristically Western ideals and social traits, at the time when it especially is in the position to arrest tendencies in the industrial life and society of the East, which if continued might result in the European type . . . The end of the free lands doesn't mean the end of creative activity in the West.[49]

The Frontier Thesis is meant to be a gateway to a consciousness of historical continuity through change. Turner constructed it in order to show his countrymen

that their basic political ideals, individualism and democracy, are not secured once and for ever, but exist only as a result of successful adaptations to ever-changing environments. He wants his readers to understand that the present is a new environment—a "socialistic" one; that old means are inadequate to keep democracy alive, and that a novel adaptation is needed. Evolutionism shows that there is nothing inherently tragic in the passing of the frontier: the real tragedy would be to keep fast to old customs and ideas. This is how history works as the self-consciousness of America.

If nothing in Turner's method and in the manifest structure necessarily links the political message of the Frontier Thesis to frontier conditions, the same is true of the latent structure. This second structure, in fact, prevents us from reading the thesis as an agrarian utopia, because the American Promise, as a promise of spiritual rebirth and liberation of the true energies of *homo faber*, cannot be confined to any one environment or historical period, but transcends them all. No confusion is possible between human transcendent nature and the natural environment. Although it is true that the two have very often come together in western intellectual history, and that in the neo-platonic tradition, for instance, nature leads to God, Christian theology, on which the myth of the Promise rests, never maintained that a return to nature is a substitute or a necessary precondition for spiritual experience. The latter alone can lead man to his original nature as a creature of God. Therefore, pivotal as the contact with nature has been in the American experience, it would not be in keeping with the Christian roots of American culture and of its foundation myth to claim for nature a position as the sole repository of salvation or the only possible environment in which the Promise can be fulfilled.

Moreover, the Promise, as a myth, cannot contain a detailed project. Myths create intellectual horizons; they circumscribe the field of acceptable meaning and give direction to it, but they cannot have a precise content. This is why they have to be made actual in a rite. In the case of a foundation myth like that of the American Promise there is a need for a positive historical project that will fulfill it: the latent structure, embodying the myth, must live in symbiosis with the manifest structure serving the purpose of a rite. The theory of social stages and of their continuous repetition on the frontier can be such a ritual, because it provides a dynamic model based on the possibility of repeating over and over again the spiritual experience of rebirth.

"The Significance of the Frontier" does not relate a tragedy, and its last sentence is no more than an introduction to Turner's later meditation on the present.

V

It should not come as a surprise that in Turner's view the frontier *naturally,* if too rapidly, gives way to industrial society. The frontier, as it has been shown, was not the place of an Arcadian utopia, and life in it was simple and pure because the pioneer was purified, not because he lived in a simple, primitive way. Pioneers created a human, that is a progressively more and more complex, environment out of the free lands of the West, and an industrial society got under way as a consequence. Turner the positivist and evolutionist scholar could not but see things this way. The complexity of the industrial environment, being a product of evolution, is not a problem, it is a challenge. European complexity, in fact, is "artificial" not *per se,* but because European man is impure.

Adaptation, however, is difficult and Turner readily admits that Americans might fail. In this context it is illuminating to comment on his attitude towards the tycoons of his age. They are the product of frontier virtues, he writes. They are individualistic, self-reliant and practical, but the sheer efficiency of industrial economy allows them to accumulate so much personal power that they endanger democracy. They might prove to be an "incipient aristocracy" that would introduce power and hierarchy in American society, thus destroying the American Promise and the American social organism with it.[50] We face an interesting paradox here. The captains of industry might prove to be a hindrance to adaptation just because their rough individualism is a survival from the past. In the new "socialistic" age "the freedom of the individual to seek his own" is an enemy to evolution. Turner's perplexities about the survival of democracy in the present, then, do not derive from the difficulty of keeping frontier individualism alive in the industrial society. He does not believe such a thing to be desirable. If the individual must survive, we may add, it is the moral monad of the latent structure, not a historically bound social type, a point brought home by Turner's analysis of the fading away of the individualistic pioneer on the frontier itself.

Turner devoted a great deal of attention to the frontier in the Mississippi Basin and in the trans-Mississippi region, an area that he saw as a turning point in American history and that became the core of his meditation on the present:

> When the arid lands and the mineral resources of the Far West were reached, no conquest was possible by the old individual pioneer methods. Here expensive irrigation works must be constructed, cooperative activity was demanded in the utilization of the water supply, capital beyond the reach of the small farmer was required. In a word, the physiographic province itself decreed that the destiny of this new frontier should be social rather than individual . . . There has been a steady development of the industrial ideal, and a steady increase of the social tendency, in this later movement of Western democracy.[51]

That very nature—the "physiographic province"—that on the old frontier creates the individual, in the Far

West gives life to social tendencies and requires a strong government. Should we say that nature itself undercuts democracy? Or should not we explore whether Turner's emphasis on the novel features of the trans-Mississippi frontier is an evolutionary transition to present conditions?

Turner forcefully maintains that beginning with the trans-Allegheny frontier a western man was born that had considerable homogeneity "and began to stand as a new social type."[52] This type took a stand against the strict construction of the Constitution and substituted nationalism for sectionalism, being aware of the magnitude of the problems involved in subjugating an area "as large as an empire." Magnitude was the main characteristic of the far western frontier, as the forest had been of the old one, and magnitude required combination to tame an environment too strong for the individual:

> The Western radical became convinced that he must sacrifice his ideal of individualism and free competition in order to maintain his ideal of democracy . . . capital, labor, and the Western pioneer, all deserted the ideal of competitive individualism in order to organize their interests in more effective combinations.[53]

They all did this, because it was the rational thing to do: combination, control, complexity were strategies necessary to adaptation in the Mississippi Basin, and as such they must be considered natural. Almost a social stage in itself, this region constituted a bridge showing the evolutionary continuity between the old frontier with its individualistic forest philosophy and the frontierless, social, industrial society.

Turner, however, could not simply demonstrate to his and his readers' satisfaction that evolution required an end to competitive individualism. He had to find in the stage of industrialism a rite of initiation reenacting the process of Americanization. This he did finding inspiration, he might say, in himself. As a historian, he wrote that he had "to take some lessons from the scientist"[54] and make history an evolutionary science in order to help his generation reach consciousness and adjust to the present. Like him, Americans of the industrial age ought to make recourse to science:

> General experience and rules of the thumb information are inadequate for the solution of the problems of a democracy which no longer owns the safety fund of an unlimited quantity of untouched resources . . . The test tube and the microscope are needed rather than ax and rifle in this new ideal of conquest.[55]

In an unpublished fragment on "The State University" he also wrote:

> The work of the pioneer in finding the best lands, opening to settlement the most eligible sites, finding and exploiting the best timber forties, the best coal, iron,

gold, silver mines—has its companion in the work of the curious, questful, adventurous scholar, the pioneer in the field of knowledge . . . The simplicity of the early squatter exploration is replaced by the complexity of knowledge of scientific process.[56]

This is a powerful statement in the hands of the author of the Frontier Thesis. A statement whose climax can be found in the following words: "In the place of the old frontiers of wilderness there are new frontiers of unwon fields of science, fruitful for the needs of the race; there are frontiers of better social domains yet unexplored."[57]

The themes found in these quotations and in many others consistently stating the same ideas, can be properly understood only in the light of the dual structure of the Frontier Thesis. The scholar dressed in pioneer's garb as a "curious, adventurous" social type; the "fields" of knowledge, a new frontier to be explored; the parallel between the squatter's simplicity and the complexity of knowledge, a parallel replacing the contrast between American simplicity and European complexity—all these elements point to a central role of science in the latent structure. In the manifest structure science is the true mark of the industrial age; in the latent one it plays the same role that nature plays on the frontier.

Turner's analysis of the Mississippi Basin reinforces this interpretation, in that it demonstrates that the need for a scientific control of the environment naturally springs from frontier *praxis* and turns into a continuation and preservation of *praxis* under new conditions. As a product of free human rationality science can, in fact, take man back to his original status as a creature made in God's image, exactly as nature does. Objective, disinterested, passionless, anti-authoritarian, science has a regenerative power. The man of science—or the scientifically trained technician—can tame complexity as the pioneer tamed the forest; he can act as a countervailing force to the tycoons' attempts to use modern industry for their selfish interests. As the history of the end of the 19th century shows, tycoons would turn necessary change into a social and political conflict endangering adaptation. Their individualism, then, must give way to the superior solutions to the problems of the industrial age provided by science. People trained in the sciences have the same capacity to harmonize change and cooperation that the pioneer showed on the frontier. They can fulfill the Promise. Science is today's nature; it provides the framework for a society based on cooperation and efficient procedures. It is the rite opening up new free spaces to a society without free lands; it will regenerate *individuals* ready to cooperate for the common good.

The rite, however, must be open to plain people as the frontier was. Turner understands that science cannot regenerate society without mass scientific education. This explains his devotion to the State University, that peculiar fruit of the Mississippi Basin frontier, as he writes, which for Turner must be seen both as an intellectual necessity and as a positive political act.[58] The State University, in fact, is in the hands of the plain people as the frontier was; it is the safety valve of industrial society, opening to everybody what we might call the *vertical* frontier of science. There is a clear parallel in Turner's thought between the frontier, nature and free lands on one hand and industrialism, science and public education on the other. Both allow the birth of a non-authoritarian, rational society: a democracy.

Far from being tied to primitivism and to an idyllic view of the agrarian past, Turner was able to produce a forward looking set of ideas that moved coherently from historical analysis to the study of the present and to a project for the solution of its problems. There is an inner consistency in his work—due to the symbiotic relationship between the manifest and the latent structure—that should not be underestimated. Turner is not the historian of a back-to-the-woods utopia, or the messenger of the end of the American dream; he is the historian of American continuity, and he can be said to have achieved—within bounds—the objective he set himself, that of bringing self-consciousness to the present. He demonstrated, however unsystematically, that science is an evolutionary sequel to nature, or that science and nature share the same regenerative virtues. "In history there is unity and continuity,"[59] Turner wrote in 1893, an apt summary to his lifetime's work.

VI

However certain that the reconstruction of the structure of Frederick Jackson Turner's Frontier Thesis made in this paper is not a breakthrough in the "self-consciousness of humanity," I do not either believe it to be an instance of that "antiquarianism" that Turner decries in his 1891 essay "The Significance of History."[60]

Turner's writings provide a late example of those meta-narratives that have been used to legitimize modernity in the western world.[61] As such they belong to a tradition that is common both to Europe and America. His attempt to appropriate the true heritage of Europe for America corresponds to similar attempts that have been made everywhere in the West, and must, therefore, be seen as unexceptional and *European*. The culture of Western modernity has been historically embodied in individual states, nationalities, churches and ideologies, each one of them pretending to be the heir to Western universal values. American exceptionalism and the Frontier Thesis are a part of the Western world-system.[62] They might even be said to be the expression of a culture pushing the "order of discourse" of the Western system to an extreme—to its final frontier.

All this may make sense only if we do not lose touch with history. Meta-narratives, in fact, are a product of history. In the case of the Frontier Thesis we face a meta-narrative with a peculiar importance in early 20th-century American history, because it became a factor in the renewal of the national covenant in a period of crisis. The Frontier Thesis provides us with an extraordinary *melange* of myth and of perceptions about contemporary reality mediated by historical research. Its success can be understood only if we suppose that American historians, the media that popularized the thesis, and the general public did not see it as a tragic narrative, but were driven by its rhetoric and content to read it as a jeremiad, to use Sacvan Bercovitch's expression;[63] that is, if they identified themselves with the virtues of the vanishing pioneer and realized that they could still live by them, however challenging this would be. Turner's parallel between nature and science in an age enthralled not only by scientific marvels, but by the promise of order contained in scientific reasoning, answered this need and allowed the jeremiad to run its course. What made the sacred song—the *mythos*—of the "vertical" frontier of science heal the wounds and fears of an industrial society torn by social strife, was the agreement between the promises of science and the hopes and projects of the nationalistic "new middle class" to which Turner belonged.[64]

Cast in scientific language, the Frontier Thesis was a part of the attempt made by the progressive "new middle class" to turn science and its two handmaidens—efficiency and organization—into the moral soul of economics. As such the Frontier Thesis contributed to the birth of 20th-century American social consensus; a consensus built on the political promise that everyone would share, however unequally, the coming "abundance"[65] that efficient, organized economics would create.

The cultural legitimation of this social consensus, however, rested on the founding myth of America, the political myth of the Promise present in the Frontier Thesis. In the context of this essay political myths can be adequately described as cultural entities building a public "square", an ideal place where people meet and solve conflicts of roles and interests through shared mechanisms of adjudication. The "public square" metaphor also indicates that political entities—states in the modern western world system—live through a process of inclusion-exclusion. Groups, or individuals, are admitted into the square on the basis of a given set of cultural or social markers identifying them as *sodales,* as members of the community, and giving them a legitimate "place". Everyone else is outside the square, is not allowed to speak and therefore is classified as "other", potentially a *hostis.*[66]

The American Promise functions in precisely this way, as the latent structure of the Frontier Thesis shows. We may add that the thesis could work as a jeremiad only

because it reenacted the political myth of America. What it did, in fact, was to inject new life into the Promise by demonstrating that in the contemporary and higher stage of industrial civilization the initiation rite allowing regeneration was still in place and that the American public square still existed. The fearless individuals, the reform-minded "pioneers" who were ready to devote their life to science and to scientific institutions, as Turner did as a historian and as a prominent figure at the State University of Wisconsin, would be stripped of the garments of the past—the frontier individualism linked to the free lands—and would create a brand-new individualism suited to the new age of cooperation and team work. Regenerated as moral monads—true *homines fabri*—they would meet in a public square founded on mutual recognition and equality. Americans were thus assured that America would continue to Americanize itself.

Ronald Barthes[67] has taught us to detect ideology in modern myths and the Frontier Thesis, linked as it is to progressive reform, is no exception. The same, of course, is true of the American Promise, one of the founding myths of modernity. In our age of political and cultural redefinition, however, it is not so much the presence as the quality of ideology that must be scrutinized. In the case of Turner, what he was able to do was to cast in new forms, using the values of the rising progressive ideology, the myth of America as a community founded on an act of separation of its members from the past, on a voluntary denial of one's own origins and roots in a different community. America, in this way, would be based solely on the mutual recognition of these rootless individuals: a recognition that would set them *free* to decide on their own identity. Turner even radicalized the myth, to the point of linking American identity to an evolutionary process of Americanization that implied an act of separation from one's own American past.

It would not be of any value to recollect early 20th century policies aimed at the Americanization of the European immigrants and Turner's own "melting pot" mentality[68] in order to disprove the myth. The ideology of Americanization is as much a part of American history as Turner's meta-narrative is. The two are necessarily linked in history, although they are different. The Promise that the Frontier Thesis reenacts is meant to define the normative identity of America. It indicates the kind of culture that can legitimately be called American. The result is a radically *political* community, that is, a community founded only on the agreement of its members and continuously redefined by the free, rational will of individuals unhampered by the strictures of a cultural past. Each American generation, as Thomas Jefferson understood quite well, should—because it can—change the Constitution. The social contract in America is an ongoing process open to all those who have the stamina to deny their past. As such it is normatively democratic, because its members, having lost their past identity, are equals as moral monads.

The Frontier Thesis is dead as a substantive interpretation of American history. As a meta-narrative, on the other hand, it allows us to probe a cultural "order of discourse" that reaches deep into American and western history. Jacques Derrida speaks of the true identity of Europe as being the urge to differ from itself and to be like a promontory facing the open sea.[69] Turner's narrative of the myth of America as frontier—as "the outer edge"[70]—identifies the United States as *the* modern European nation, a nation so radically modern and European as to contain the "germs" of the end of the modern European system. In good Turnerian fashion I go no further and stop here, on the threshold of a new stage of civilization.

Notes

1. Ray A. Billington, *The Genesis of the Frontier Thesis: A Study in Historical Creativity* (San Marino, Ca.: The Huntington Library, 1971); Fulmer Mood, "The Development of Frederick J. Turner as a Historical Thinker," *Transactions of the Colonial Society of Massachusetts, 1937-42,* 34, (1943), 283-352.

2. Frederick J. Turner, "The Significance of the Frontier in American History," *Proceedings of the State Historical Society of Wisconsin,* 14 December 1893.

3. Frederick J. Turner, "The Significance of History," *Wisconsin Journal of Education,* 21 (October 1891), 230-4, (November 1891), 253-6.

4. Turner, "The Significance of History," in *Frontier and Section: Selected Essays of F. J. Turner,* Ray A. Billington ed. (Englewood Cliffs, N.J.: Prentice-Hall, 1961), 20.

5. Turner, "The Significance of History," 17.

6. Ibid.

7. Ibid., 18.

8. Ibid., 27.

9. Ibid., 18.

10. Frederick J. Turner, "Problems in American History," in *Frontier and Section,* Billington, ed., 29.

11. Ray A. Billington, *Frederick J. Turner: Historian, Scholar, Teacher* (New York: Oxford University Press, 1973), chapter 5; William Coleman, "Science and Symbol in Turner Frontier Hypothesis," *American Historical Review,* 72, 3 (1966), 22-49.

12. Turner, "The Significance of the Frontier," 1-2; see also "Problems in American History," 29.

13. Turner, "The Significance of the Frontier," 2.

14. The link between the "instinct for moving" and the development of human history and culture was forcefully made by Turner in an 1891 address to the Madison Literary Club: "The colonizing spirit is one form of the nomadic instinct. The immigrant train on its way to the far west or the steamer laden with passengers for Australia is but the last embodiment of the impulse that took Abraham out of Ur of the Chaldees and sent our Aryan forefathers from their primitive pasture lands to Greece and Italy and India and Scandinavia": Frederick J. Turner, "American Colonization," published in Ronald H. Carpenter, *The Eloquence of Frederick J. Turner* (San Marino, Ca.: The Huntington Library, 1893), 176.

15. Turner, "The Significance of the Frontier," 11.

16. See, for instance, his treatment of populism, "The Significance of the Frontier," 32.

17. Ibid., 37.

18. Ibid., 4.

19. Turner, "The Problem of the West," in *Frontier and Section,* Billington ed., 206; also: "At first the frontier was the Atlantic coast. It was the frontier of Europe in a very real sense. Moving westward, the frontier became more and more American," Turner, "The Significance of the Frontier," 4.

20. Michel Foucault, *L'ordre du discours* (Paris: 1970).

21. See, *Trails: Toward a New Western History,* Patricia Nelson Limerick, Clyde A. Milner II, Charles E. Rankin eds. (University Press of Kansas).

22. Turner, "The Significance of the Frontier," 3-4.

23. Turner, "The Problem of the West," 205.

24. Ibid., 207.

25. Turner, "The Significance of the Frontier," 2.

26. See Lewis Henry Morgan, *Ancient Society* (1877).

27. Billington, *Frederick Jackson Turner,* 76-9, 122-3.

28. Turner, "The Significance of the Frontier," 21, 38.

29. Ibid., 12.

30. Ibid., 4.

31. Turner, "The Problem of the West," 205.

32. See Lewis H. Morgan, *Ancient Society* (1877), and Walter Bagehot, *Physics and Politics: An Application of the Principles of Natural Selection and Heredity to Political Society* (1872), on the first and second points respectively. The pervasive

influence in late 19th century culture of Sumner Maine's theory of the transition from status to contract should also be kept in mind.

33. Turner, "The Significance of the Frontier," 30.

34. Ibid., 37; "The problem of the West," 211.

35. Ibid., quoted.

36. Turner, "The Significance of the Frontier," 31.

37. Turner, "The Problem of the West," 213.

38. Billington, *Frederick Jackson Turner,* 425.

39. Tiziano Bonazzi, "Un'analisi della American Promise: ordine e senso nel discorso storico-politico," in Tiziano Bonazzi, *Struttura e meta-morfosi della civilta' progressista* (Venezia: Marsilio, 1974), 41-140.

40. Loren Baritz, "The Idea of the West," *American Historical Review,* 66, 3 (1961), 618-40. An important parallel can also be made with Michael Walzer, *Exodus and Revolution* (New York: Basic Books, 1985).

41. Henry Nash Smith, *Virgin Land: The American West As Symbol and Myth* (Cambridge, Mass.: Harvard University Press, 1950). On the importance of foundation myths, see Eric Voegelin, *The New Science of Politics* (Chicago: University of Chicago Press, 1952).

42. David W. Noble, *Historians against History. The Frontier Thesis and the National Covenant in American Historical Writing since 1830* (Minneapolis: University of Minnesota Press, 1965), and *The End of American History* (Minneapolis: University of Minnesota Press, 1985).

43. Turner to Carl Becker, 21 January 1911, in Wilbur R. Jacobs, *The Historical World of Frederick J. Turner* (New Haven-London: Yale University Press, 1968), 135; also, Turner to Constance Lindsay Skinner, 15 March 1922, in Jacobs, *The Historical World,* 56.

44. Turner, "Problems in American History," 29.

45. Ibid., 32.

46. Turner, "The Problem of the West," 68-9.

47. Ibid., 69. This expression follows immediately upon the sentence previously quoted.

48. Turner, "The Significance of the Frontier," 38.

49. Turner to Carl Becker, in Jacobs, *The Historical World,* 135.

50. Turner, "Contributions of the West to American Democracy," in Turner, *The Frontier in American History,* 264-6.

51. Ibid., 258.

52. Turner, "The Problem of the West," 216.

53. Turner, "The West and American Ideals," in Turner, *The Frontier in American History,* 305.

54. Turner, "Social Forces in American History," in Turner, *The Frontier in American History,* 331.

55. Turner, "Pioneer Ideals and the State University," in Turner, *The Frontier in American History,* 284.

56. Turner, "The State University," in *America's Great Frontier and Sections: Frederick Jackson Turner's Unpublished Essays,* Wilbur R. Jacobs ed. (Lincoln: University of Nebraska Press, 1969), 196.

57. Turner, "The West and American Ideals," 300.

58. See his "Pioneer Ideals and the State University," 269-89.

59. Turner, "The Significance of History," in *Frontier and Section,* Billington ed., 21.

60. Ibid., 18.

61. Jean-Francois Lyotard, *La condition postmoderne* (Paris: Les Editions de Minuit, 1979).

62. Reference is made here to Immanuel Wallerstein, *The Modern World-System* (New York: Academic Press, 1976).

63. Sacvan Bercovitch, *The American Jeremiad* (Madison: Wisconsin University Press, 1978); also Sacvan Bercovitch, "The Rites of Assent: Rhetoric, Ritual, and the Ideology of American Consensus," in *The American Self: Myth, Ideology and Popular Culture,* Sam B. Girgus ed. (Albuquerque: New Mexico University Press, 1980), 5-45. On the "rhetorical impact" of the Frontier Thesis upon the American public mind see Ronald H. Carpenter, *The Eloquence of F. J. Turner,* 47-95.

64. Robert H. Wiebe, *The Search for Order, 1877-1920* (New York: Hill and Wang, 1967), ch. 5.

65. The idea of a transition from an age of scarcity to an age of abundance was articulated by Simon N. Patten, professor of economics at the Wharton School of the University of Pennsylvania, in *The New Basis of Civilization* (New York: Macmillan, 1907).

66. Henry Tudor, *Political Myth* (London: 1972); also, Tiziano Bonazzi, "Mito politico," in *Dizionario di politica,* Norberto Bobbio and Nicola Matteucci eds. (Torino: UTET, 1976), 587-94. The most important interpretation of politics based on the dialectics *amicus-hostis* is that of Carl Schmitt, see, among his many publications, *Der Bergriff des Politischen. Text von 1932 mit einem Vorwort und drei Corollarien* (Berlin: Duncker und Humblot, 1963).

67. Ronald Barthes, *Mythologies* (Paris: Editions du Seuil, 1957).

68. See Turner's articles on immigration in *Chicago Record-Herald,* 28 Aug., 4, 11, 18, 25 Sept., 16 Oct. 1901. Let us not forget, however, that Marcus Hansen was one of Turner's students.

69. Jacques Derrida, *L'autre cap* (Paris: Les Editions de Minuit, 1991).

70. Turner, "The Significance of the Frontier," 3.

Brook Thomas (essay date 1996)

SOURCE: Thomas, Brook. "Turner's 'Frontier Thesis' as a Narrative of Reconstruction." In *Centuries' Ends, Narrative Means,* edited by Robert Newman, pp. 117-37. Stanford, Calif.: Stanford University Press, 1996.

[*In the following essay, Thomas argues that Frederick Jackson Turner's "Frontier Thesis" provided a powerful impetus to twentieth century critical discussions about the frontier and its significance in American history and culture.*]

In 1893 Frederick Jackson Turner delivered a paper to the American Historical Association that arguably remains the most influential piece ever presented to that organization. In it he describes simultaneously the significance of the frontier in the history of the United States and the closing—forever—of the western frontier. Seventy-two years later, in what deservedly remains an insignificant moment in the country's history, my senior year high school yearbook appeared with "New Frontiers" as its theme. I risk moving from the sublime to the ridiculous with this juxtaposition in order to illustrate one of the most often-noted paradoxes about Turner's "frontier thesis": whereas it seems to announce the end to the exceptional conditions of the United States, it in fact launched a new tradition of interpretations of American exceptionalism.

Turner so powerfully generated a new beginning in understanding American history that considerable energy during the twentieth century has been spent debating whether we have finally reached the end of his influential narrative about an end. That debate itself suggests, as William Cronon puts it, that "we have not yet figured out a way to escape him."[1] In this essay I argue that the durability of the frontier thesis is linked to its structure as a narrative of reconstruction. In the first part I contend that its reconstructive capacity distinguishes it from alternative narratives at the time. In the second I examine reasons for recent attacks on Turner's narrative and how they are linked to his definition of the word "frontier." I conclude by offering two conflicted, yet re-lated, ways of reading Turner that suggest an alternative narrative structure for us at the end of the twentieth century, one that, nonetheless, cannot do without the reconstructive capacity of Turner's narrative.

I

A good place to begin an analysis of that reconstructive capacity is with Turner's famous ending. "The frontier," he concludes, "has gone, and its going has closed the first period of American history."[2] This ending does not, as Tiziano Bonazzi has recently argued, mean that the "formula for social regeneration" that the frontier allowed is also at an end.[3] It does not because, as Michael P. Malone puts it, the frontier was "defined both as a place—a zone of free land beyond the western edge of settlement—and as process—where social atomization shattered mores. Turner's frontier was a sociocultural furnace that forged a new Americanism embodying democracy, individualism, pragmatism, and a healthy nationalism."[4] The process described by Turner may be threatened by the closing of the frontier, but it is not necessarily at an end because the social organism that it formed has acquired characteristics that can help it adapt to ever-changing conditions. As Turner wrote Carl Becker, "The end of the free lands doesn't mean the end of creative activity in the West."[5] For Turner that creative activity meant, according to Bonazzi, "a gateway to a consciousness of historical continuity through change" (163). If in announcing the end of the frontier Turner warns his countrymen that their basic political ideals of individualism and democracy are not secured once and forever but must be continually renewed while being tested by new conditions, his narrative of progressive emergence implies that such an end is not a moment of tragic closure but the opportunity for a new beginning. As Bonazzi puts it, "There is nothing inherently tragic in the passing of the frontier: the real tragedy would be to keep fast to the old customs and ideas" (163).

One reason that the passing of the frontier is not tragic is that the frontier functions in Turner's narrative as a metaphor; that is, as a space of displacement in which something or someone is reconstructed as something or someone else. The actual space that Turner designates the "frontier" may be at an end, but the end that that space serves can be maintained by various metaphoric substitutions. In subsequent accounts of American history we have seen numerous designations for what became the new frontier. For instance, analyzing transformations at the turn of the century, Martin Sklar claims, "For many Americans, the corporation became the new frontier of opportunity that the western lands had once symbolized."[6] Indeed, Turner suggests that his own narrative can serve as an imaginative substitute for the frontier whose end it proclaims. Noting that the aim or end of his paper "is simply to call attention to the frontier as a *fertile field* for investigation" (3, my emphasis), Turner offers his narrative as a metaphoric space to initiate the regeneration necessary to face changing conditions. The frontier's role as a metaphor of displacement highlights the need to study documents of American cultural history in terms of metaphorology as opposed to symbology. If symbols suggest organic unity and seamless continuity, metaphors call attention to the displacements necessary to maintain continuities and the appearance of unity.

To understand Turner's narrative in terms of its specific metaphoric displacements is to distinguish it from competing narratives at the end of the nineteenth century that were faced with a bizarre phenomenon. The new political entity called the United States now had an existing constitution older than any in the "old" world. In 1890 James Harvey Robinson, later to become famous as a founder of the New History, begins his first major publication with the following:

> Not many months ago the hundredth anniversary of the inauguration of our present constitutional form of government was celebrated in the city of New York. To realize fully the significance of this event, one should consider not only how many years must still elapse before it will be permitted to any one of the states of Europe to solemnize the corresponding event in its national history, but also that this government, established in 1789, has outlived a century of change in social life and political institutions without precedent in the history of the world.[7]

Like the young Robinson, most contemplating the state of the United States in the 1890s were less self-conscious about the end of a century than the coincidence that that end corresponded with a series of anniversaries that granted a history to a land that supposedly lacked one.

Centennial celebrations of the Declaration of Independence, the Constitution, and the Bill of Rights were followed by the 400th anniversary of Columbus's arrival in the Americas, an anniversary that provided the occasion for the meeting that Turner addressed in conjunction with the Chicago World Exposition. In "The Figure of Columbus" in 1892 a writer for the *Atlantic Monthly* notes:

> Nearly a score of years ago the study of American history received a singular impetus through the series of centennial celebrations which began. There can be no question that not only were popular conceptions of the men and events connected with the War for Independence readjusted and greatly enriched, but the scientific pursuit of American history, especially the history of institutions, received an emphatic impulse.[8]

"Especially the history of institutions." For many trying to explain how the United States had survived a century of unprecedented change the answer lay in the stability of its political institutions. Of course fascination with American political institutions did not suddenly spring up at the end of the century. The most famous European chronicler of the American way of life, Alexis de Tocqueville, emphasized the influence that the country's political institutions had in shaping its national character. But de Tocqueville stressed the novelty of those institutions. Less than fifty years after *Democracy in America* the same institutions were the subject of numerous histories. Institutional histories require that institutions have histories, and by the end of the nineteenth century institutions in the United States clearly did—often longer ones than comparable institutions in Europe.

To be sure, an end-of-the-century series of centennial celebrations was not the only cause for the rise of institutional histories. Another reason was the popularity of institutional histories with German historians, who were the model for the "scientific pursuit" of history. Germans influenced American historians through training those who studied at German universities and through the establishment of a German-style seminar system at Johns Hopkins University. The history seminars of Herbert Baxter Adams institutionalized institutional histories in the United States.

Designed in part to account for stability in a time of change, most institutional histories were politically conservative. Indeed, the focus of Adams's seminars was neither to stress the novelty of American institutions nor to seek their potential for stability in the special circumstances of the New World. Instead, relying on a biological metaphor, they sought the "seed" of those institutions in the distant past. Disputing the "theory of spontaneous generation," Adams insisted, "Whenever organic life occurs there must have been some seed for that life. . . . It is just as improbable that free local institutions should spring up without a germ along American shores as that English wheat should have grown here without planting."[9] For Adams's students those seeds were to be found in the forests of Germany during the fifth and sixth centuries. Tracing the transportation of that seed from Germanic forests to Britain and then to the New World, the so-called Teutonic germ theory has narrative similarities with that of *translatio imperi* or the transfer of empire westward. In a time of heavy immigration from Southern and Eastern Europe, it also served the convenient function of denying a Mediterranean and Roman origin to the democratic institutions of the United States. As a result, it stressed not only the Anglo-Saxon nature of the country, but also the difference between the Protestant institutions of North America and the Catholic ones of Latin America.

Linking national character to institutions whose germ could be found over 1,000 years in the past, institutional histories were an early attempt at what Robert

Wiebe has called the "search for order" in a period of rapid social and economic change.[10] They were, however, a failed attempt, a victim of the very forces of change that they tried to combat. Some of the most important challenges to them were mounted by students from Adams's seminars. A particularly significant one came from Woodrow Wilson.

In 1889 Wilson received James Bryce's *The American Commonwealth*. Published the year before, Bryce's book was the most important European account of the United States since de Tocqueville's. On the one hand, Wilson's review reveals his indebtedness to Adams's training. Denying de Tocqueville's argument about the novelty of political institutions in the United States, Wilson praised Bryce for realizing that "there is really, when American institutions are compared with English, nothing essentially novel in our political arrangements: they are simply the normal institutions of the Englishman in America."[11] But if Wilson agreed with institutional historians that American institutions are not novel, he questioned the importance that they granted to institutions. More attention, he argued, should be paid to "material, economic, and social conditions" (181). Furthermore, he disputed the assumption that institutions shape national character. Bryce, according to Wilson, deserves credit for "perceiving that democracy is not a cause but an effect." More important, he sees "that our politics are no explanation of our character, but that our character, rather, is the explanation of our politics" (182-83). The "only stable foundation" of democracy, Wilson argues, is "character." "America has democracy because she is free; she is not free because she has democracy" (187).

The liberation of national character from political institutions was a crucial part of one of Wilson's major contributions to the nature of American political institutions: the development of a bureaucratic, administrative state. Many Americans resisted the institutionalization of what they felt was a continental European bureaucracy, fearing that it would destroy the special quality of American republicanism. For instance, a traditional Republican like Albion W. Tourgée, the lawyer-novelist who pleaded the case of Homer Plessy, opposed civil service reform because it would create a permanent class of governmental bureaucrats and thus take government out of the hands of the people.[12] In contrast, Wilson, believing that American democracy was founded on its people's character rather than vice versa, felt that borrowing efficient administrative structures from continental Europe would pose no threat to the country.[13]

Like his friend Wilson, whom he met while studying at Johns Hopkins, Turner challenged institutional histories by stressing the importance of material, economic, and social forces. But despite similarities, his challenge has a significant difference from Wilson's. Wilson may have separated the question of national character from national institutions, but he did not challenge the notion that those institutions were basically the same as English ones. In contrast, Turner continues to link the question of character and institutions, but insists on the differences between American and English, as well as all European, institutions. "Our early history," he writes, "is the study of European germs developing in an American environment. Too exclusive attention has been paid by institutional students to the Germanic origins, too little to the American factors" (3). "Behind institutions, behind constitutional forms and modifications, lie the vital forces that call these organs into life and shape them to meet changing conditions" (2). The most important forces for Turner are, of course, those connected with the frontier. Those forces shape, not only institutions, but also character. "The outcome is not the old Europe, not simply the development of Germanic germs" (4).

This difference between Wilson and Turner has important implications for the question of race. As we have seen, advocates of the Teutonic germ theory posited a narrative that stressed the Anglo-Saxon character of American democracy. Relying on a particular interpretation of the period's predominant neo-Lamarckianism, they connected institutions and race. Anglo-Saxon institutions were shaped by the Anglo-Saxon character, which was in turn reinforced by its institutions.

As racist as this interpretation of the interrelation between institutions and race seems, it was not inevitable. For instance, Tourgée also linked the democratic character of the Anglo-Saxon race with its institutions. For him, however, that link required a redefinition of what it means to be Anglo-Saxon. "The seventy-odd millions of people who constitute the population of the American Republic, whether white or black, Celt or Slav, or from whatever European stock they may be descended, in political ideals are purely American and derivatively Anglican."[14] At a time when a crucial question was whether African-Americans would achieve responsible political maturity if allowed to vote, Wilson's separation of character and institutions implicitly undercut an argument like Tourgée's that made American blacks as well as whites Anglo-Saxon.

For Wilson, as for advocates of the Teutonic germ theory *and* Tourgée, the United States is an Anglo-Saxon country. But, like the former and unlike the latter, Anglo-Saxon for Wilson meant English. American "character is the result of the operation of forces permanent in the history of the English race, modified in our case by peculiar influences, subtle or obvious" (183), influences that do not include political institutions. By separating racial character from the influence of political institutions Wilson, like another friend of his days at

Johns Hopkins, Thomas Dixon Jr., the author of *The Clansman,* mystified the determination of race. That mystification warned against "experiments," such as those granting newly freed blacks the right to vote. Indeed, Wilson chided Bryce for describing the American system as "'an experiment' in government. . . . We are in fact but living an old life under new conditions. Where there is conservative continuity there can hardly be said to be experiment" (184).

Wilson's stress on "conservative continuity" raises the question of how he, like his friend Turner, became associated with progressive thought. A partial answer to that question is that progressivism had many strains and that Wilson's is different from Turner's. Nonetheless, Turner and Wilson do have much in common. In a passage that almost anticipates Turner's "frontier thesis," Wilson warned, "America is now sauntering through her resources and through the mazes of her politics with easy nonchalance; but presently there will come a time when she will be surprised to find herself grown old,—a country crowded, strained, perplexed" (182). "That," he argues, "will be the time of change" (182). If Wilson's emphasis on a moment of closure as a time of important change signaled his similarity with Turner, his difference came in his narrative of how that change would occur. According to Wilson change will come because the country "will be obliged to fall back upon her conservatism, obliged to pull herself together, adopt a new regime of life, husband her resources, concentrate her strength, steady her methods, sober her views, restrict her vagaries, trust her best, not her average, members" (182). An example of what David Noble has called the "paradox of progressive thought,"[15] Wilson's narrative imagines change, but change based on the "conservative continuity" of a basically unchanging national character. In contrast, Turner's narrative responds to a moment of crisis by imagining change that is founded, not on an essential character, but on the nation's ability perpetually to reconstruct itself.

For Turner up until 1890 the frontier had served as the space in which such reconstruction occurred. The challenge for the future was to find a way for it to continue. If that challenge was difficult because of the closing of the frontier, it was in part possible to meet because there is a connection between institutions and character. Having shaped flexible and democratic institutions, the character forged from the experience of the frontier might in turn be further influenced by those institutions as it faced the material, social, and economic conditions of the country's next stage of development, provided that those institutions were reformed in the proper manner. Such reform depended, not on the inherent conservatism of Englishness, but the innovative spirit of an American people shaped by the frontier spirit. "In the crucible of the frontier," Turner writes in one of his most memorable passages, "the immigrants were Ameri-

canized, liberated, and fused into a mixed race. English in neither nationality nor characteristics" (23). The incomplete grammar in the second phase of the passage helps to dramatize that in the space created by Turner's narrative the process of Americanization is not necessarily over, that in responding to new conditions the American people can—and must, if they are to retain the special characteristics of being American—reconstruct themselves.

It's not hard to see why the implications of Turner's narrative, rather than those of the Teutonic germ theorists, Wilson, or even Tourgée, caught the imagination of the generation to which my high school classmates belonged. In the midst of the civil rights movement, with the nation attempting to reconstruct itself as "the great society," we found the idea of a new frontier compelling. Nonetheless, one hundred years after it was delivered, Turner's thesis finds itself under fundamental attack. We need to look both at the justifiable reasons for those attacks and how Turner continues, nonetheless, to pose a challenge to his critics.

II

Criticism of Turner is nothing new. But, to indulge in a dangerous generalization, I would argue that for the most part earlier attacks focused on Turner's definition of the frontier as the *place* of American renewal. For instance, Arthur M. Schlesinger Sr. argued that it was in cities, not the frontier, that Americanization took place.[16] David M. Potter claimed that the frontier was only one factor, even if an important one, in the primary shaping force of American character: material abundance.[17] Turner's critics, like Schlesinger and Potter, might have challenged his emphasis on the frontier, but they continued to share his belief in a unique process of Americanization.

Recently, however, there has been a full-fledged attack on narratives of American exceptionalism. For instance, in his important book *The End of American History* David Noble announced the end of a historical project that located the United States as the *telos* of history.[18] Today Turner's narrative is challenged not only because of its emphasis on the *place* of the frontier but also because of the way in which it links that *place* to a particular *process*. To understand the terms of this challenge, we need briefly to return to and expand upon how Turner constructs a narrative of continuity through change.

As Bonazzi points out, Turner's narrative is punctuated by a series of conflicts that would seem to threaten the continuity of national progress. How these conflicts transform into progressive change rather than revolution, repetition, or decline is at the heart of Turner's progressive vision for America and helps to account for the most important conflict that his narrative constructs, that between America and Europe. For instance, just a few years earlier Henry Adams had described the early United States as a place with "no arts, a provincial literature, a cancerous disease of negro slavery, and differences of political theory fortified within geographic lines." "What," Adams asked, "could be hoped for such a country except to repeat the story of violence and brutality which the world already knew by heart, until repetition for thousands of years had wearied and sickened mankind?" (722-23).[19]

Turner's answer to why that story was not repeated is the frontier. As such, the story he tells gives narrative form to a comment made by Hegel that the existence of free western land in the United States served as a safety valve to potential conflicts.[20] Providing a space of what we might call supplementation, the frontier made possible a narrative of American history in which conflicts could be endlessly deferred rather than dialectically resolved. Even if American history did not produce a classless society, it did, according to Turner, produce one in which class interests were complementary rather than oppositional. For instance, he quotes a description of how three classes—pioneers, settlers, and men of capital and enterprise—lived off and profited from one another by arriving in succession. "Like the waves of the ocean," these three "have rolled one after the other" (19), one after the other in diachronic sequence, not synchronic conflict. By providing a space in which synchronic conflicts could be avoided by transferring them into diachronic sequence, the frontier allowed for an organic synthesis of a diverse population without the need of a dialectical resolution. But it could do so only if Turner's notion of an ever-expanding frontier could displace Adams's description of political differences "fortified within geographic lines." That displacement required a redefinition of "frontier."

"The American frontier," Turner asserts, "is sharply distinguished from the European frontier" (3). The European frontier is "a fortified boundary line running through dense populations. The most significant thing about the American frontier is, that it lies at the hither edge of free land" (3). This distinction between American and European definitions of "frontier" is one of the most significant aspects of Turner's essay.

As John T. Juricek has pointed out, Turner is right to note that "frontier" took on a new meaning in the United States. That meaning did not develop, however, until the late nineteenth century; that is, about the time that Turner announced its closure. This philological detail is highly significant, for it means that, although Turner claimed to be using a peculiarly American notion of the frontier to account for the peculiar nature of American history, he was in fact, as Juricek argues, "reading a late nineteenth-century world view back into the past."[21]

Turner's use of the new definition of frontier suggests, in other words, that his compelling narrative of the nation's ability perpetually to reconstruct itself is itself an act of historical reconstruction. What, we might ask, is at stake in that act of reconstruction? As we shall see, quite a lot.

First of all, defining the frontier "to mean the edge of settlement, rather than, as in Europe, the political boundary"[22] allows Turner to shift the focus of previous interpretations of the frontier. Much has been written, Turner acknowledges, "about the frontier from the point of view of border warfare and the chase" (3). Turner, however, as we have seen, is interested in how the United States avoids conflict, not how it perpetuates it. Nonetheless, so long as the frontier is defined as a political boundary, any expansion of it immediately raises the possibility of "border warfare." Indeed, "frontier" derives from the later medieval Latin term "fronteria," which means "line of battle," and an earlier meaning of the term in English is "a barrier against attack."[23] But if a frontier is no longer seen as between two political entities, its function can dramatically change. Rather than a site of conflict, it becomes, for Turner, a site in which conflicts and differences are overcome. It becomes, in other words, what a later Turner, Victor, would call a space of "liminality."

Liminality involves release from normal constraints. "In liminality what is mundanely bound in sociostructural form may be unbound and rebound." Thus it is in the frontier that the immigrants cast off their old cultures. But they cast them off in order to participate in the construction of a new, composite one. Allowing for a "rite of passage" in which the culture renews itself, the frontier shapes what Victor Turner calls *communitas,* which "breaks in through the interstices of structure, in liminality; at the edges of structure, in marginality."[24]

To see the frontier as a liminal space is to understand its function as a space of cultural regeneration. It regenerates by transforming cultural difference into commonality and community. Whereas many of Frederick Jackson Turner's contemporaries linked race and culture as a way of stressing irreconcilable differences, Turner imagines a space in which people of different cultural backgrounds become one. Strangely enough, then, what is probably the most famous narrative of American exceptionalism is simultaneously a narrative about the universality of human nature. We can get a better feel for the progressive nature of that narrative by comparing it to a powerful European narrative constructed in the late 1890s: Joseph Conrad's *Heart of Darkness.*

Conrad's story is in part a response to conditions that produced a study like Charles Pearson's *National Life and Character,* which appeared in 1893.[25] Noting that there were no new lands to explore and conquer, the

Englishman Pearson predicted the inevitable and gradual decline of the influence of European and especially Anglo-Saxon people, whose exemplary individualistic character also happened to be incompatible with life in tropical lands where future economic growth would occur. Conrad too recognizes that there are no new lands for Europeans to explore and conquer when he has Marlow recall his youthful fascination with the remaining "blank spaces on the earth" as designated by Western maps and then remark that the Congo, "the biggest, the most blank," by the time of his trip "was not a blank space anymore."[26] Indeed, Marlow's journey in part confirms Pearson's view that Europeans have experienced their twilight, for the heart of Africa turns out to conquer the would-be conquerors. But Conrad's reason for the European's defeat is quite different from Pearson's. If Pearson argues that Europeans are constitutionally incapable of living in a tropical climate, Conrad constructs a narrative exposing what Pearson values as an inherent European character to be nothing more than the cloak of civilization. It is in Africa that Marlow discovers his "remote kinship" (51) with "savages" that other Europeans dismiss as "inhuman" (51).

But if Conrad's narrative, like Turner's, posits the commonality of all human beings, it does so through a temporal movement backward, not forward. In Conrad's imagination the former blank space of Africa enables a narrative that journeys against the course of history, so that as a wanderer "on a prehistoric earth" (50) Marlow can encounter a terrible "truth stripped of its cloak of time" (51). In contrast, in Turner's imagination the liminal space of the frontier enables a narrative in which a common human community overcoming cultural differences can be constructed through the progressive march of history. Ironically, however, this common history can progress only through a ritual process in which human beings forget their pasts. If it was the German Nietzsche who at the end of the century most loudly called for regeneration through an active forgetting, for Turner it was in America, not Europe with its burden of the past, that such a ritual could occur.

Thus, as much as Turner's narrative celebrates the potential commonality of all human beings, it, nonetheless, locates the United States as the place where universal history can unfold. Indeed, Turner favorably quotes the Italian economist Achille Loria: "America . . . has the key to the historical enigma which Europe has sought for centuries in vain, and the land which has no history reveals luminously the course of universal history" (11). Although Conrad's universal narrative moves backward in time and Turner's forward, both, it turns out, reveal a European perspective by denying non-European lands a history. That denial helps to explain why in Turner's narrative universal history culminates in the United States. If the liminal qualities of Turner's new definition of the frontier open up univer-

sal possibilities, its location in the American West limits those possibilities to the United States.

As I have already argued, Turner's notion of the frontier creates a space in which the United States can avoid the conflicts that have plagued European history. This opposition *between* the United States and Europe is possible, however, only because the United States is *between* Europe and the frontier. If Turner's image of the frontier lay in the east of Europe rather than in the west of the United States the narrative would move in the other direction. For instance, later historians, recognizing the universal potential to Turner's thesis, tried to apply it to German and Russian history.[27] But to do so they had to posit an Eastern frontier. Turner's narrative remains a document of American exceptionalism because it maintains a westward movement in which the United States, not Europe, becomes the site where history unfolds.

Paradoxically, however, if the United States's location between Europe and the frontier makes possible an opposition between Europe and America, it also establishes a link between them. This link occurs because the American frontier also serves as Europe's. Even though the frontier does not affect Europe directly, it does affect it. Its effect generates a countermovement to the predominantly westward movement of Turner's narrative. "Steadily the frontier of settlement advanced and carried with it individualism, democracy, and nationalism, and powerfully affected the East and the Old World" (35).

Less noticeable than the opposition between the United States and Europe, this link between the two is important. If the presence of a frontier in the European sense of a political boundary inevitably raises the possibility of conflict, Americans had traditionally felt protected from a conflict with Europe because they were separated by the vast expanse of the Atlantic Ocean. By locating a new sort of frontier in the American West, Turner provides a somewhat different explanation of why the United States faced no threat from Europe. If, on the one hand, the frontier created an opposition between Europe and the United States by exempting the latter from the former's problems, on the other, it transformed what seemed a clearcut opposition into an interconnection. Although the presence of the ocean is important, even without it the boundary between Europe and the United States would be special because of the westward movement of Turner's narrative of progressive history. The major threat to the internal security of the United States in Turner's narrative had not been Europe but barriers to westward movement. As a result, the "common danger" to the country, according to Turner, was the "Indian frontier" (15). By 1893, of course, Indians no longer posed a threat. Appropriately, Turner's new definition of the frontier transforms the

"Indian frontier" into simply "the frontier," a transformation that allows a former site of conflict to become a site of *communitas*.

Turner's transformation of a place of historical conflict into a narrative of progress opens him to criticism by those intent on escaping a tradition of American exceptionalism that his narrative so powerfully renewed and reconstructed. If, as Warren I. Susman argues, "The escape from history leads us to the world of myth,"[28] Turner seems to offer us more a myth about the frontier than an accurate historical account. Indeed, by emphasizing the frontier as a site of national renewal rather than a site of "border warfare," Turner would seem to dramatize Richard Slotkin's well-known thesis about the mythical quality of the United States's "regeneration through violence."[29] For critics concerned about historical accuracy the mythical quality of Turner's narrative demands that they reverse the process by which he constructs his narrative and reveal the historical actuality disguised by the mythologization.

Such readings of Turner are, of course, part of a larger project of demystification that has captivated the energy of a generation of U.S. critics at the end of the twentieth century. As important as this project of demystification is, however, it meets with resistance when confronted with the reconstructive powers of Turner's narrative. A sign of that resistance is Slotkin's treatment of Turner. Although he is critical of Turner for indulging in the myth of the frontier, Slotkin indirectly acknowledges his debt to him by titling the introduction of his latest book "The Significance of the Frontier Myth in American History." Despite that debt, Slotkin in fact downplays Turner's significance. Comparing Turner's account of the frontier with Teddy Roosevelt's, Slotkin argues, "Although Turner's work has had the greater influence on academic historiography and has received the greater acknowledgment from historically minded policy-makers, Roosevelt's version of the Myth is closer in style, emphasis, and content to the productions of industrial popular culture and (as the body of the study will show) has had a greater (though unacknowledged) impact on the ideological underpinnings and policy-practice of twentieth-century administrations."[30]

Slotkin's choice of Roosevelt as the more ideologically corrupt of the two fits into his myth of the Myth for a number of reasons. First, as he points out, Roosevelt is much more embedded in turn-of-the-century racialism than Turner. Second, whereas in Roosevelt "the history of the Indian wars *is* the history of the West," Turner's work "is remarkable for the degree to which it marginalizes the role of violence."[31] Roosevelt's overt racism and celebration of violence make him much easier to demystify.

The relative ease by which we can draw on present assumptions to demystify Roosevelt rather than Turner points to the continuing influence that Turner has upon us. That influence is signaled once again by a title in Slotkin's latest book. Slotkin calls the first section in a chapter on the early 1960s "Modernizing Turner: The Ideology of the New Frontier." One reason that Turner rather than Roosevelt could be modernized in the 1960s was because his narrative helps to construct the utopian image of a racial melting pot. Another is that as much as it might seem to dramatize Slotkin's thesis about violence in the country's imagination, it in fact, as Slotkin himself recognizes, has a subtle, but crucial, difference from that myth. Rather than identify the frontier as a space in which the nation regenerates itself *through* violence, Turner imagines it as a space in which the nation regenerates itself by *displacing* violence. As important a part of the national imagination as the attitude toward violence that Slotkin has spent his career identifying, Turner's utopian vision does not invite immediate demystification.

Turner's resistance to complete demystification suggests two conflicted—yet complementary—readings of his thesis for us today. On the one hand, because it minimizes the role of conflict in the nation's history, it invites its own demystification. On the other, by trying to imagine a space in which regeneration can occur without a repetition of the violent conflicts that have plagued human history, it evokes a utopian possibility that would seem to lend itself to those trying to break with a past of violent exploitation. Seemingly opposed, these two ways of reading are structurally related to the reconstructive capacity of Turner's narrative. That reconstructive capacity is, in turn, related to the position that the frontier occupies in Turner's narrative as a space of displacement.

Turner's narrative invites demystification because it constructs a history of national renewal out of a history of internal conflict. In order to do so, however, it represses the involuntary displacement that westward expansion caused to Native Americans and others already occupying land in the West. At the same time, cultural renewal, according to Turner, is possible on the frontier because it allows settlers to undergo a voluntary displacement that allows them to take on a new identity. Similarly, Turner's narrative is potentially renewable because it allows for a perpetual displacement of the actual frontier by metaphoric "new frontiers," new frontiers that take on the function of national renewal.[32] By bringing a demystified and utopian reading together it should be possible to reconstruct the narrative of reconstruction that Turner constructed a hundred years ago.

III

Because it is almost always easier to do, I'll start with demystification. The most obvious way to proceed is to follow the path laid down by Slotkin and insist on the history of "border warfare" that Turner's narrative displaces. To do so is to recognize, as I have already suggested, that such a displacement can occur in the 1890s precisely because the Indians had virtually been eliminated as a threat. But there is a less obvious way to demystify Turner's celebration of the West, one that sees him producing a narrative of reconstruction in a sense quite different from how I have used that phrase so far.

If, on the one hand, Turner's frontier thesis is an important precursor to progressive narratives of the twentieth century, on the other, it is part of a general project at the end of the nineteenth century by which American historians dramatically revised accounts of the era of Reconstruction.[33] As we have seen, Turner constructs an opposition *between* Europe and America based on the latter's ability to avoid the former's history of dialectical confrontation. But that opposition helps to minimize a conflict *within* the United States that a generation earlier had threatened to tear the country apart: the Civil War and its Reconstruction aftermath. Rather than construct a narrative of American history that focuses on the Mason-Dixon line separating North and South, Turner focuses on a frontier common to both. Not a fixed boundary like the one that created an absolute division between free and slave states, the frontier, as defined by Turner, allowed for expansion rather than internal conflict. Indeed, "the economic and social characteristics of the frontier worked against sectionalism." A space of consensus, it produced people who "had closer resemblances to the Middle region than to either of the other sections" (27).

To be sure, by 1893 the frontier was closed. But by evoking a history in which a "common danger" along it demanded "united action," Turner hopes once again to use it "as a consolidating agent in our history" (15). Thus twice he feels compelled to challenge Hermann Edward von Holst, the German institutional historian of the United States Constitution, who insisted that the dispute over slavery was the formative event in shaping national character.[34] "When American history comes to be rightly viewed," Turner asserts, "it will be seen that the slavery question is an incident" (24). As if to signal his consolatory message, Turner in his second paragraph uses the southerner John C. Calhoun to define the "distinguishing feature of American life": "We are great, and rapidly—I was about to say fearfully—growing" (2).

Turner, of course, is a westerner, not a southerner, and later in the essay he makes clear that he does not condone Calhoun's states' rights philosophy. Evoking the dedication of the Calhoun monument, he quotes a Mr. Lamar who declared that "in 1789 the States were the creators of the Federal Government: in 1861 the Federal Government was the creator of a large majority of

the States" (25). More important, Turner cites "the greatest of frontiersmen," Lincoln, "who declared: 'I believe this Government can not endure permanently half slave and half free. It will become all of one thing or all of the other'" (29-30).

Turner's appeal to Lincoln might seem to indicate a clear Northern sympathy. But by 1893 advocates of the New South were also willing to condemn slavery and stress the need for national reconciliation, so long as the North admitted the folly of Reconstruction and gave the South control over the "Negro problem." Thus, in his address entitled "The New South," delivered to the New England Club of New York in 1886, Henry W. Grady drew on Lincoln's western birth to anoint him the "first typical American," one who united "Puritans and Cavaliers" by "straightening" their purposes and "crossing" their blood.[35] Eleven years after Turner's own address, Dixon appealed to Lincoln in *The Clansman* as someone whose love of his country would have kept him from imposing Reconstruction on the South. "I love the South!" declares Dixon's Lincoln. "It is part of the Union. I love every foot of its soil, every hill and valley, mountain, lake, and sea, and every man, woman, and child that breathes beneath its skies. I am an American." That love does not, however, extend to African-Americans, as Dixon plays on Lincoln's house-divided rhetoric to have him proclaim, "The Nation cannot exist half white and half black, anymore than it could exist half slave and half free."[36] Dixon's Lincoln advocates the return of blacks to Africa to help with the birth of a nation in the aftermath of the Civil War.

As I have already made clear, Turner's image of the frontier as the crucible in which "immigrants were Americanized, liberated, and fused into a mixed race" (23) is not only different from but potentially at odds with the racism of people like Grady and Dixon. Nonetheless, by deflecting attention from the nation's failed reconstruction in the South, Turner's account of national reconstruction in the West leaves an important part of the country's history and people unaccounted for. Paradoxically, that lack of accountability grows out of Turner's efforts to provide a reconstructed account of American history that pays attention to aspects ignored by existing histories.

While at Johns Hopkins, Turner and Wilson agreed that American history had too often been written from a Northeastern perspective. Their combined effort to remedy that situation saw fruition in 1893. The same year that Turner's "frontier thesis" emphasized the role of the West in overcoming sectional conflict, Wilson's *Division and Reunion, 1829-1889* provided an "unbiased" Southern perspective on the long conflict between North and South.[37] Turner and Wilson share a number of assumptions. But if in his essay Turner acknowledges Wilson for recognizing "the West as a factor in American history" (1n.), the way in which Turner's narrative complements Wilson's perspective has not been properly acknowledged, perhaps because its relationship is so complex.

Looking at American history from the perspective of the West, not that of either North or South, Turner stresses reconciliation, not conflict. One result, as we have seen, is that his narrative is not generated by dialectical confrontation. Instead, for Turner, in the West the American people achieved an organic synthesis through perpetually deferring conflict rather than through dialectical confrontation. But precisely because Turner's image of national synthesis depends on deferring conflict, it opens itself to charges that it represses it. Indeed, an image of immigrants in the West fusing into a mixed race is possible only because Turner fails to take into account the country's inability to achieve the racial inclusion promised by radical Reconstruction. As a result, Turner's effort to reconstruct American history by providing a neglected perspective from the West needs itself to be reconstructed by supplementing it with another end-of-the-century account of the formative conditions of American character, that of W. E. B. Du Bois.

In an 1897 essay written in the wake of the *Plessy* decision and later to appear in revised form in *The Souls of Black Folk* (1903), Du Bois, sounding almost like Turner, looks back on the period since emancipation as "thirty years of renewal and development." Nonetheless, for Du Bois the failure of Reconstruction means that despite such renewal:

> The swarthy ghost of Banquo sits in its old place at the national feast. In vain does the nation cry to its vastest problem,—
>
> "Take any shape but that, and my firm nerves shall never tremble!"[38] The freedman has not yet found in his freedom his promised land.

Pondering what it means for the Negro to be considered by the nation a "problem," Du Bois offers his justly famous description of "double-consciousness, this sense of always looking at one's self through the eyes of others, of measuring one's soul by the tape of a world that looks on in amused contempt and pity. One ever feels his twoness,—an American, a Negro; two souls, two thoughts, two unreconciled strivings; two warring ideals in one dark body, whose dogged strength alone keeps it from being torn asunder" (194). Rather than achieve an identity of organic synthesis, the African-American, left out of Turner's narrative of progressive emergence, has an unresolved, double identity.

Indeed, in his narrative that celebrates the regenerative powers of open space, Turner allows no space for not only African-Americans, but other hyphenated Ameri-cans, such as Mexican-Americans and Asian-Americans. If Native Americans are present as a common enemy, other non-European groups remain invisible in his account, even though the march westward that he describes brought American settlers in contact with what today is described as the "Spanish Frontier" and even though Chinese played such an important role in building the transcontinental railroad that helped spell an end to the frontier.[39]

Of course, at this moment in the late twentieth century to point out the invisibility of non-Europeans in our national narratives is a commonplace, if not an obligation. Their invisibility in Turner's narrative is certainly not surprising. A more interesting question is whether the structure of his progressive narrative inevitably excludes them. As I have already suggested, the renewal power of Turner's narrative complicates any exclusions that it seems to perpetuate. Although at the moment of its production it does not account for non-Europeans, its definition of Americanization as fusion into a "mixed race" implies that those previously excluded are welcome to join in a newly reconstructed mixture. Nonetheless, the dependence of Turner's narrative on the existence of some liminal space for that fusion to occur demands closer scrutiny.

Neither Frederick Jackson Turner's notion of the frontier nor Victor Turner's notion of the liminal can accommodate what the later Turner calls "marginals." Marginals are "simultaneously (by ascription, optation, self-definition, or achievement) of two or more groups whose social definitions and cultural norms are distinct from, and often even opposed to, one another. . . . Marginals like liminars are also betwixt and between, but unlike ritual liminars they have no cultural assurance of a final stable resolution of their ambiguity."[40] Rather than achieve the synthetic, unified identity implied by Frederick Turner's metaphor of immigrants fusing into a "mixed race," the marginal, like Du Bois's description of the African-American, is in a state of internal "border warfare."

As inclusive and regenerative as it promises to be, the liminal seems to have no place for the marginal. Its inability to accommodate or find a home for the marginal has opened it to attack by "border" anthropologists like Renato Rosaldo.[41] In this regard it is important to remember that in redefining "frontier" Frederick Jackson Turner effaced the existence of borderlands in American history. A liminal space on the "edge of settlement" rather than a political boundary around which a border can develop, Turner's frontier creates a community of inclusiveness only through a subtle process of repression.

Nonetheless, if the liminal marginalizes the marginal, it also holds out the promise that even marginals can be included. For instance, according to Du Bois, the Negro strives to overcome his twoness. He longs "to attain self-conscious manhood, to merge his double self into a better and truer self" (195). Liminality, it seems, can provide the "cultural assurance" and "final stable resolution of . . . ambiguity" that so troubles the marginal. But it does so at a price. For, if Du Bois's Negro longs to overcome twoness, he also hopes that in his "better and truer self . . . neither of the older selves" will be lost. Americanization, according to Turner, requires precisely this loss of a past self.

For years the positive aspects of the process of Americanization described by Turner have been emphasized. But today more and more critics question the process of forgetting necessary for it to occur. One reason for their resistance is the growing awareness that the only way to understand the marginalized position of many in today's society is to remember an oppressive past that created the conditions of double-consciousness as described by Du Bois. Because part of the power of Turner's narrative grows out of its tendency to displace such oppressions caused by literal and metaphoric "border warfare," it is justly viewed with suspicion.

Nonetheless, as we have seen, the nature of that displacement creates a moment of resistance of its own for those operating solely within a hermeneutics of suspicion. As important as it is to reconstruct a past of oppression, we need to ask if such a reconstructive project is possible without some space of displacement, like that provided in Turner's narrative. We also need to ask whether we want to privilege as normative the double consciousness that such a past created. Indeed, is it possible that various celebrations of border identities growing out of the physical displacement of people result from various cultural critics imposing their self-image as free-floating (dare I say, Enlightenment?) intellectuals whose permanent mental displacement grants them a space of independence?[42] Are we guilty of conflating that metaphoric space of displacement with actual spaces of displacement and thus perpetuating the sense of homelessness felt by so many of today's marginalized? In other words, do we want to perpetuate a permanent feeling of displacement for marginalized people, or should we strive to create conditions in which those on the border can feel at home?

Of course, our choice need not be one of either/or, nor need we embrace a logic of both/and.[43] If the reconstructive powers of Turner's narrative depend on the space of displacement that he designates "the frontier," we need to ask ourselves if there is a way of reimagining that space. One way to do so is to return to the notion of "frontier" as a boundary around which a border space emerges. To understand the significance of the frontier in terms of borders is to construct narratives that dramatically alter Turner's structure.

Such narratives, I need to point out, are becoming commonplace in the growing field of cultural studies. I will note just a few of their differences from Turner's. First of all, they do not posit Europe as the origin of civilization. Instead, they assume the simultaneous existence of various civilizations with none at the center. Furthermore, they replace the linear movement of Turner's narrative with a reciprocal one. Rather than a narrative about the westward march of civilization, they are about exchanges and conflicts—often uneven—among cultures. As we have seen, even Turner's narrative implies some such reciprocity. But he confines it to an exchange between Europe and America. The new narratives try to describe exchanges occurring in various directions across various borders around the globe.[44]

As such, these narratives imply a different interpretation of the final image that Turner evokes to describe the role of the frontier. "What the Mediterranean Sea was to the Greeks breaking the bond of custom, offering new experiences, calling out new institutions and activities, that, and more, the ever retreating frontier has been to the United States directly, and to the nations of Europe more remotely" (38). Instead of seeing the Mediterranean as the edge of civilization, we need to see it, as present historians tell us it was, in the middle of various civilizations, a space allowing for trade and the exchange of ideas among cultures of three different continents. Spaces of cultural regeneration, it seems, are border spaces, not "frontier" spaces as defined by Turner.

Nonetheless, as we imagine new narratives in which the frontier is reconstructed as a place of borders—spaces between, not spaces on the edge—we should not forget the military roots of the word "frontier." Borderlands are the sites of war as well as exchange. Indeed, as much as we feel the need to reconstruct Turner's use of the frontier to displace a past history of violence, his narrative remains extremely attractive if we view it, not as a narrative about the past, but as a vision for the future. For instance, given the horrendous problem of violence in American society today and its clear link to issues of race and battles over turf, the vision of a nation regenerating itself by displacing violence is as relevant to the end of the twentieth century as it was to the end of the nineteenth.

Of course, one reason that it retains its relevance is that narratives like Turner's helped to divert attention away from Du Bois's prophetic insight that "the problem of the Twentieth Century is the problem of the color-line."[45] Our challenge today seems to be to come up with narratives that will construct regenerative spaces where, historically, not only lines of color, but also lines of nationality, ethnicity, gender, and class have created boundaries.

Such narratives require an important reconstruction of Turner's notion of the frontier, but they haven't, it seems to me, completely escaped his narrative structure. After all, to announce the end of the usefulness of Turner's notion of the frontier is in one sense merely to repeat—with a difference—what he announced one hundred years ago when he proclaimed the end of one stage of American history and the need to move on to a new one. As much as our new narratives show—as to an extent mine does—that the frontier, as defined by Turner, was always at an end in American history, and as much as we call for the need to confront the conditions of a new age, whether we call it "postmodernity," "postindustrial capitalism," or "postcolonialism," it is hard to imagine coming up with new narratives and new meanings of culture without relying on some space of displacement that Turner in his narrative calls a no-longer-existing frontier.

Notes

1. William Cronon, "Revisiting the Vanishing Frontier: The Legacy of Frederick Jackson Turner," *Western Historical Quarterly* 18 (1987): 160. Some of the debate is collected in George Rogers Taylor, ed., *The Turner Thesis* (Boston: D. C. Heath, 1949). For fascinating appraisals by two revisionist historians of the West see *The Frontier in American Culture: Essays by Richard White and Patricia Limerick,* ed. James R. Grossman (Berkeley: University of California Press, 1994).

2. Frederick Jackson Turner, "The Significance of the Frontier in American History," in *The Frontier in American History* (New York: Henry Holt, 1920), 38.

3. Tiziano Bonazzi, "Frederick Jackson Turner's Frontier Thesis and the Self-Consciousness of America," *Journal of American Studies* 27 (1993): 162.

4. Michael P. Malone, "Beyond the Last Frontier: Toward a New Approach to Western History," *Western Historical Quarterly* 22 (1989): 410. Malone's claim that the frontier for Turner is a space of "social atomization" is commonplace. I argue that it is also for Turner a space for the creation of reconstructed *communitas*. See also Gerald Thompson, "Frontier West: Process of Place," *Journal of the Southwest* 29 (1987): 364-75.

5. Quoted in Wilbur R. Jacobs, *The Historical World of Frederick J. Turner* (New Haven, Conn.: Yale University Press, 1968), 135.

6. Martin Sklar, *The Corporate Reconstruction of American Capitalism, 1890-1916* (New York: Cambridge University Press, 1988), 26.

7. James Harvey Robinson, "The Original and Derived Features of the Constitution," *Annals of the American Academy of Political and Social Science* 1 (1890): 203.

8. "The Figure of Columbus," *Atlantic Monthly* 69 (March 1892): 409. This anonymous reviewer urges that Americans need to supplement their understanding of the Teutonic origins of their civilization by reestablishing "our connection with Latin Christianity in all its forms" (409). The Spanish-American War derailed that project.

9. Herbert Baxter Adams, "The Germanic Origins of New England Towns with Notes on Cooperation in University Work," *Johns Hopkins University Studies,* 1st ser., 2 (1882): 1.

10. Robert H. Wiebe, *The Search for Order, 1877-1920* (New York: Hill & Wang, 1967).

11. Woodrow Wilson, "Bryce's *American Commonwealth*: A Review," in *Bryce's "American Commonwealth": Fiftieth Anniversary,* ed. Robert C. Brooks (New York: Macmillan, 1939), 181.

12. Albion W. Tourgée, "Reform versus Reformation," *The North American Review* 293 (1881): 305-19.

13. Woodrow Wilson, "The Study of Administration," *Political Science Quarterly* 2 (1887): 197-222.

14. Albion W. Tourgée, "The Twentieth Century Peacemakers," *The Contemporary Review* 75 (1899): 888.

15. David W. Noble, *The Paradox of Progressive Thought* (Minneapolis: University of Minnesota Press, 1958).

16. Arthur M. Schlesinger, "The City in American History," *Mississippi Valley Historical Review* 27 (1940): 43-66. Turner was not unaware of the importance of cities. In 1922 he proposed writing an essay on "the significance of the city in American history."

17. David M. Potter, *People of Plenty* (Chicago: University of Chicago Press, 1954).

18. David W. Noble, *The End of American History* (Minneapolis: University of Minnesota Press, 1985). For an excellent supplement to Noble's book that focuses on the history of the American West, see David M. Wrobel, *The End of American Exceptionalism* (Lawrence: University Press of Kansas, 1993). Turner's claim that the United States avoided European class conflict was challenged during the Depression. See Charles A. Beard, "The Myth of Rugged American Individualism," *Harpers,* December 1931, 13-22, and "The Frontier in American History," *New Republic,* February 1, 1939, 359-62, and Louis M. Hacker, "Sections—of Classes?" *Nation,* July 26, 1933, 108-10. Nonetheless, as Noble points out, even Beard maintained a vision of American exceptionalism.

19. Henry Adams, *History of the United States of America* vol. 1, *During the First Administration of Thomas Jefferson* (New York: Charles Scribner's Sons, 1891-96), 156.

20. G. W. F. Hegel, *Lectures on the Philosophy of History,* trans. J. Sibree (New York: Colonial Press, 1900), 85-87.

21. John T. Juricek, "American Usage of the Word 'Frontier' from Colonial Times to Frederick Jackson Turner," *Proceedings of the American Philosophical Society* 110 (1966): 33. The new use of "frontier" by no means completely drove out the old. In the same year that Turner presented the frontier thesis, Senator Thomas J. Geary of California defended his 1892 bill extending the exclusion of Chinese and severely punishing Chinese illegally caught in the United States by detaining the expense needed to maintain "guards and inspectors upon our frontiers and at our different seaports, in order to prevent the infraction of our laws by a race of people who never have shown any respect for them." "Should the Chinese Be Excluded?" *North American Review* 158 (1893): 61.

22. Frederick Jackson Turner, "The First Official Frontier of the Massachusetts Bay," in *The Frontier in American History,* 41.

23. Juricek, "The Word 'Frontier,'" 10-11.

24. Victor Turner, *From Ritual to Theatre* (New York: Performing Arts Journal Publications, 1982), 84, and *The Ritual Process* (Chicago: Aldine Publishing, 1969), 128. Sacvan Bercovitch draws heavily on Turner's notion of liminality to describe how an American *communitas* is forged out of a "Ritual of Consensus" in *The American Jeremiad* (Madison: University of Wisconsin Press, 1978), 132-75 and 204-5n.

25. Charles H. Pearson, *National Life and Character: A Forecast* (London: Macmillan, 1893).

26. Joseph Conrad, *Heart of Darkness* (New York: St. Martin's Press, 1989), 22.

27. James Westfall, "Profitable Fields of Investigation in Medieval History," *American Historical Review* 8 (1913): 490-504, and Joseph L. Wieczynski, *The Russian Frontier* (Charlottesville: University of Virginia Press, 1976).

28. Warren I. Susman, *Culture as History* (New York: Pantheon, 1984), 25.

29. Richard Slotkin, *Regeneration through Violence: The Mythology of The American Frontier, 1600-1860* (Wesleyan, Conn.: Wesleyan University Press, 1973). Although critical of the "myth" of the frontier, Slotkin to a large extent remains captive to Turner's construction of it. For instance, he accepts Turner's definition of the frontier, as a permanent fixture of American culture, not a late-nineteenth-century construction, going so far as to claim to identify "one of the *cultural archetypes* which emerged from the historical experience of the American *colonial* frontier to function as myth in our culture" (9, my emphasis).

30. Richard Slotkin, *Gunfighter Nation: The Myth of the Frontier in Twentieth-Century America* (New York: Atheneum, 1992), 26.

31. Ibid., 55.

32. My emphasis on metaphoric displacement as a space for reconstructing history has some similarities with Paul de Man's argument about "modernity" in "Literary History and Literary Modernity," *Blindness and Insight* (New York: Oxford University Press, 1971), 142-65. I am certainly indebted to de Man's criticism of the privileged status given to the symbol in studies of romanticism. But I am more strongly influenced by Hans Blumenberg's work on metaphor. See especially "An Anthropological Approach to the Contemporary Significance of Rhetoric," in *After Philosophy: End or Transformation?* ed. Kenneth Baynes, James Bohman, and Thomas McCarthy (Cambridge, Mass.: MIT Press, 1988), 421-58. One important aspect of Blumenberg's work is his awareness that the concrete metaphors that we use matter. This commonsensical point complicates attempts, like Hayden White's, to explain the enduring status of powerful historical texts like Turner's by formalizing their content. See White's *Content of the Form* (Baltimore, Md.: Johns Hopkins University Press, 1987). If, indeed, the form of Turner's narrative allows for perpetual reconstruction, it also designates a specific place for the frontier. That designation opens his narrative to demystification.

33. See Peter Novick, *That Noble Dream* (New York: Cambridge University Press, 1988), 72-85, and John David Smith, *An Old Creed for the New South* (Westport, Conn.: Greenwood Press, 1985).

34. On Von Holst, see Eric F. Goldman, "Hermann Eduard Von Holst: Plumed Knight of American Historiography," *Mississippi Valley Historical Review* 23 (1937): 511-32.

35. Henry W. Grady, "The New South," in *Life of Henry W. Grady Including His Writings and Speeches,* ed. Joel Chandler Harris; reprint, 1886 (New York: Haskell House Publishers, 1972), 85.

36. Thomas Dixon Jr., *The Clansman* (Lexington: University Press of Kentucky, 1970), 54, 47.

37. Woodrow Wilson, *Division and Reunion, 1829-1889* (New York: Longmans, Green, 1893). Also in 1893 Wilson published a review attacking the bias of James Ford Rhodes's treatment of white Southerners. "Anti-Slavery History and Biography," *Atlantic Monthly,* August 1893, 272-74. Turner also faults Rhodes (24). On Turner and Wilson, see documents collected by Wendell H. Stephenson, ed., "The Influence of Woodrow Wilson on Frederick Jackson Turner," *Agricultural History* 19 (1945): 249-53. In addition, Turner was a powerful influence on Ulrich B. Phillips, whose *American Negro Slavery* (1918) is credited with authoritatively making the Southern perspective on race a national perspective until after World War II. In 1902 Turner hired Phillips to teach Southern history at Wisconsin, and when Turner died Phillips wrote his memorial for the American Historical Association's annual report. These connections should not, however, lead us uncritically to condemn Turner on the issue of race. What they suggest is that the reconstructive potential of Turner's narrative opens it to different political appropriations. Indeed, Phillips's youthful descriptions of Turner's influence highlight, not a specific content, but a spirit of endless renewal. "The best of this is that [Turner's] disciples are not content (the good ones) to walk in his steps, but are eager to blaze paths of their own." Turner's "great function" was "to stimulate and exhilarate young scholars in a way to make them stimulate others, and so on in a ripple which though it must lessen in the lapse of time and the spread of space, never quite reaches an end." Quoted in Merton L. Dillon, *Ulrich Bonnell Phillips* (Baton Rouge: Louisiana State University Press, 1985), 17.

38. W. E. Burghardt Du Bois, "Strivings of the Negro People," *Atlantic Monthly* 80 (August 1897): 195. In *The Souls of Black Folk,* Du Bois drops the specific reference to Banquo's ghost, while retaining the lines from *Macbeth.* In *Souls* the first two sentences of the quotation read: "The swarthy spectre sits in its accustomed seat at the Nation's feast. In vain do we cry to this our vastest social problem." Du Bois also revises "thirty years" to "forty years." *The Souls of Black Folk* (New York: Penguin, 1989), 7. On Du Bois and Turner, see William Toll, "W. E. B. Du Bois and Frederick Jackson Turner: The Unveiling and Preemption of America's Inner History," *Pacific Northwest Quarterly* 65 (1974): 66-78. See also Kathleen Diffley, "Home on the Range: Turner, Slavery, and the Landscape Illustrations in *Harper's New Monthly Magazine,* 1861-1876," *Prospects* 14 (1989): 175-202.

39. David J. Weber, *The Spanish Frontier in North America* (New Haven, Conn.: Yale University Press, 1992). Weber is indebted to Herbert Eugene Bolton, who established the study of "Spanish Borderlands." Insofar as individualism was a sign of progressive democracy Chinese were seen as a blocking force because they were associated with feudal forms of collectivity. On the frontier with China, see note 21.

40. Victor Turner, *Dramas, Fields, and Metaphors* (Ithaca, N.Y.: Cornell University Press, 1974), 232-33.

41. Renato Rosaldo, *Culture and Truth* (Boston: Beacon Press, 1989). My understanding of Victor Turner and the recent challenge to him is heavily indebted to Donald Weber's "From Limen to Border: The Legacy of Victor Turner for American Studies" (paper delivered at the annual meeting of the ASA, Boston, November 7, 1993).

42. In the twelfth century Hugh of St. Victor wrote: "The man who finds his country sweet is only a raw beginner; the man for whom each country is as his own is only strong; but only the man for whom the whole world is as a foreign country is perfect." He is cited by Tzvetan Todorov, citing Edward Said, citing Erich Auerbach, to express the position of the displaced intellectual. Tzvetan Todorov, *The Conquest of America,* trans. Richard Howard (New York: Harper & Row, 1984), 250.

43. On the liberal logic of "both/and," see Sacvan Bercovitch, *The Office of "The Scarlet Letter"* (Baltimore: Johns Hopkins University Press, 1991). According to Victor Turner, *Blazing the Trail* (Tucson: University of Arizona Press, 1992), 49, "The most characteristic midliminal symbolism is that of paradox, of being *both* this *and* that."

44. The need for a global narrative to replace the exceptionalist one spawned by Turner's legacy has been especially felt in studies of the American West. For instance, Malone, "Beyond the Last Frontier," 424, urges that the word "frontier" be replaced by the term "globalization." See also Spencer C. Olin Jr., "Towards a Synthesis of the Political and Social History of the American West," *Pacific Historical Review* 55 (1986): 599-611. For an attempt to analyze the notion of "frontier" at times in relation to the notion of "border," see the special issue "Frontiers," *Oxford Literary Review* 14 (1992). Contributions are mostly from a series of seminars on the topic at the University of Sussex under the auspices of the College Internationale de Philosophie. The volume was also affected by the "Borderlines" conference at Sussex in March 1991. According to editor Geoffrey Bennington, "frontiers" were defined in a seminar on

Kant as "the place where violent lawlessness of the 'state of nature' returns inevitably to haunt the supposed lawfulness of political organization, this 'return' in fact originally constituting the concept of a 'state of nature.'" As a result, Bennington wonders, "if a radical political thinking would not have to attempt to start from the relations *between* States as a condition for anything like 'the' state in the first place." Bennington, "Frontiers: Two Seminar Sessions," 198, 199. It is unclear, however, what German term Bennington refers to in Kant to develop his definition of "frontier." Indeed, although the volume is full of etymological investigations, I discovered none devoted to "frontier" itself.

45. W. E. B. Du Bois, *The Souls of Black Folk* 1, 13, 35. An example of understanding the frontier as a metaphoric space on the color line occurs in a Frenchman's autobiographical account of an exchange year in Virginia in the 1950s. A diner called Steve's is described as "sort of a frontier post between the white and black sections of town." Phillipe Labro, *The Frontier Student*, trans. Williams R. Byron (New York: Ballantine, 1988), 81.

MAJOR AUTHORS OF FRONTIER LITERATURE

Christopher Baker (essay date 1981-82)

SOURCE: Baker, Christopher. "The Death of the Frontier in the Novels of Larry McMurtry." *McNeese Review* 28 (1981-82): 44-54.

[*In the following essay, Baker identifies the demise of the American frontier and its related values as one of the central themes of Larry McMurtry's novels.*]

I would like to begin with four items of historical interest. Item: Between 1870 and 1885 in five of the most important cattle towns in Kansas there was an average of only 1.5 homicide "per cattle trading season." Contemporary newspapers record "no evidence that there was ever a shoot-out on main street at high noon" in either Abilene, Dodge City, Ellsworth, Wichita, or Caldwell.[1] Item: In 1858 an Austin newspaper stated that it was a "common thing here to see boys from 10 to 14 years of age carrying about their persons Bowie knives and pistols. By the time he was eighteen, John Wesley Hardin had killed twenty-five men and was said to "handle a pistol faster than a frog can lick flies."[2] Item:

interviews with persons who helped settle the Oklahoma Territory in the 1880's and 1890's recall that a dominant feature of their lives then was "the wretched loneliness and almost total lack of excitement in their lives."[3] Item: "Leadville, Colorado, one of the last 'Wild West' towns, in 1879, in addition to its 110 saloons, boasted four daily newspapers, five churches, three schools and a branch of the YMCA."[4] What these items all have in common is that each describes an aspect of the American frontier: peaceful yet violent, lonely but bustling. Together, they illustrate the paradoxical character of this much-debated element of American social growth. And the paradox continues: the Census Bureau declared in 1890 that the frontier had closed, yet the direct impact of that era has only recently begun to die out, amalgamated into lesser importance by admixture with other social and historical factors.

The novels of Larry McMurtry, who has been called the finest regional novelist Texas has produced,[5] have as a major theme the death of the frontier and its values and the impact of this death on the lives of contemporary Texans. His novels, in their dispassionate and acerbic picture of a modern urban Texas, in their lament of a lost age of strong values rooted in a life on the land, and in their contrast between the proud but outmoded ranchers and the prosperous but anxiety-ridden urbanites, all document the loss of certain frontier attitudes first outlined by historian Frederick Jackson Turner seventy years before McMurtry was born in 1936 in Wichita Falls, Texas. His first three novels, *Horseman, Pass By* (adapted for the movie *Hud* in 1963), *Leaving Cheyenne*, and *The Last Picture Show*, are all set in the prairie towns of West Texas. His last three novels leave the plains behind as he studies life in contemporary Houston and other Texas cities: *Moving On, All My Friends are Going to be Strangers*, and *Terms of Endearment*. McMurtry is probably the best contemporary chronicler of what has been called the "major social problem" of the Southwest, the "imperfect transition from a rural to an urban society."[6] His novels reveal not so much the death of frontier behavior, as the death of what might be called the frontier attitude—a set of expectations which defined that behavior. The underlying mood of optimism which contributed to the settling of the "free land" to the West of the Eastern seaboard during the nineteenth century counterbalanced, if it did not lessen, the frequent loneliness, isolation and nomadic existence of many of the early settlers, who also benefited from generally close-knit families and mining and cattle cooperatives. The closing of the frontier, however, brought with it the end of this mood of popular expectation. This social disorientation in the wake of the frontier's death is a strong contributing factor to the random violence, personal alienation, and wandering life-style which marks so many of McMurtry's characters. This theme could be profitably traced through both trilogies, but I shall here focus only on *The Last Picture Show* and *All My Friends are Going to be Strangers.*

Like McMurtry, Frederick Jackson Turner was raised in a region having immediate ties to the frontier. As he grew up in the 1860's in Portage, Wisconsin, a firsthand knowledge of the wilderness helped impress upon him the importance of the land, and a migration into it, as a significant social factor in American life. John Stuart Mill, Karl Marx, Josiah Strong, and James Bryce had already begun to comment on the effect of a diminishing supply of land upon "man's social evolution,"[7] and they were only a few of many influences which ultimately led to Turner's paper on "The Significance of the Frontier in American History," first read in 1893. His basic thesis is by now familiar. The westward migration of settlers, beginning in the mid-eighteenth century, introduced the "disintegrating forces of civilization" into the wilderness as trappers, traders, and adventurers subdued both land and Indians. This process placed a premium on individual effort. "The frontier is productive of individualism," wrote Turner. "Complex society is precipitated by the wilderness into a kind of primitive organization based on the family. The tendency is anti-social. It produces antipathy to control and particularly to any direct control."[8] Following the Italian economist Achille Loria, Turner also seized upon the concept of available free land as a spawning ground for other related features of American political and social behavior. While acknowledging that the frontier experience had its negative points, Turner sees it as one source for a host of features basic to the American "intellect": "That coarseness and strength combined with acuteness and inquisitiveness; that practical, inventive turn of mind, quick to find expedients; that masterful grasp of material things, lacking in the artistic but powerful to effect great ends; that restless, nervous energy; that dominant individualism, working for good and evil, and withal that buoyancy and exuberance which comes with freedom."[9]

Billington suggests that Turner's concept of the frontier can be usefully understood as both *place* (a geographical location having a low man-land ratio) and as *process* (the act and opportunity for self-advancement made possible by the low ratio). Men and women moved westward driven by both a "deficiency motivation" (the desire to escape negative social factors) and an "abundancy motivation" (the seeking of positive factors).[10] Though the actual presence of a "safety-valve" of available jobs and wages for Easterners once they reached the frontier is debatable, a "socio-psychological" safety-valve seems to have been at work: the settlers headed west prompted by what they hoped they would find or could create.

One reason for the paradoxical nature of the items noted earlier was the presence of at least three categories of westward travellers. The trappers, explorers, and backwoodsmen were the first to reach a frontier place and valued its freedom at the price of extreme physical isolation. The small-propertied farmers cultivated the land first infiltrated by the backwoodsmen and created a market for the services of the townspeople, whose social organizations were often as conformist as the backwoodsmen were iconoclastic. The mood within the towns was defined more by a desire for upward mobility and the accumulation of wealth, both of which helped engender conformity. Kit Carson would not have felt at home in a little house on the prairie, but both were part of the frontier ethos.

Indeed, the mountain men and trappers, even if not outlaws, scorned the more civilized towns and ranches in favor of a wandering life and were, as a contemporary traveller noted, "never satisfied if there [were] any white man between them and sundown."[11] Billington feels they were victims of *anomie,* "a state of mind in which the individual's sense of social cohesion is weakened or broken, and [which] arises when he leaves a familiar environment with a corresponding disruption of connection, social status and economic security." From the deep sense of hostility thus fostered sprang arrogance, aggression, and indolence.[12] The small ranchers were able to curb these traits somewhat by their greater acceptance of responsibility, their sense of belonging to a social group, and their need to take part in a money economy, among other reasons. Each, however, displays qualities of the character type which Georg Simmel has called "the stranger." Each is a potential wanderer, each is a newcomer to an environment of which he was not an original member, and each is not radically committed to the "unique ingredients and peculiar tendencies" of the dominant group (the townspeople).[13] It is not surprising to recall that one of the most clichéd lines in Western films has been "Howdy, stranger," or that McMurtry would entitle one of his books *All My Friends are Going to be Strangers.*

Such negative characteristics were outweighed by the more affirmative qualities of the frontier attitude, the values which made for "abundancy motivation." Travellers from Europe and the East noted that the frontiersmen (and they were primarily men, in both numbers and significance) exhibited great self-confidence, a desire for self-improvement, a dislike of artificiality or lying ("a man's word is his bond"), strong support of democracy and nationalism, "manliness in respect to women," practicality, materialism, restlessness, and "aggressive optimism."[14] These features found expression in all three categories of settlers; and even in the towns, which were built upon hard work, cooperation (and a sense of community) was often so strong that it was "almost stultifying in its parochialism."[15]

McMurtry's novels record the dilemmas of those who must live in the moral and emotional vacuum left after the death of this age of exuberance. What had been a transition into the "free land" has now become a transition into a "controlled land" society. In the first trilogy, the older men who see Texas, as does McMurtry, as a "lost frontier,"[16] are the only ones who remember the ideals of the open plains, but are powerless to live by them. As Turner wrote, "inherited ideals persist long after environment has changed,"[17] and McMurtry agrees when he says "the cowboy's temperament has not changed much since the nineteenth century; it is his world that has changed, and the change has been a steady shrinkage. There are no more trail herds, no more wide open cattle towns, no longer that vast stretch of unfenced land between Laredo and Calgary. . . . The effect of this has been to diminish the cowboy's sense of isolation, his sense of himself as a man alone . . . he is being drawn toward the confusions of the urban or suburban neighborhood" (*ING* [*In a Narrow Grave*], 26).

In *The Last Picture Show,* Sam the Lion (no one knew how he got his nickname) is the owner of the poolhall and picture show in the town of Thalia, and is its last remnant of the frontier cowboy culture of the plains. A rancher and later rodeo rider whose three sons died before they reached eighteen, he now looks after the idiot Billy and is a father-figure to Duane and Sonny, two adolescents who frequent the pool hall. Sentimental, he reminisces with Sonny as the two of them sit near a watering tank, remarking "I used to own this land, you know. It's been right at fifty years since I watered a horse at this tank."[18] It was also the place where he courted women: isolated, uninhibited, romantic. Sam embodies the silent aloofness of the frontier rancher whose isolation conveys a sense of gravity and deeply held values, unlike the drifting solitude of the backwoodsmen. He "personifies the quiet masculine dignity, honesty and strength of the cowboy archetype—a vestigial remnant of the old West of the ranges amid the drab town of the new West whose boys define their masculinity through high school athletics, zoophilia and group sex."[19] To Sonny he "was the man who took care of things . . . and Sonny did not like to think that he might die" (*LPS* [*Last Picture Show*], 4). For these reasons Sam is far less lonely—though alone—than the rest of Thalia's citizens. He contrasts sharply with Herman Popper, a crude, abusive, latent homosexual who is also the high school coach. Unlike Sam, who laments the loss of what he was, Popper longs for what he never will be: namely, the kind of man he sees on *Gunsmoke* each week.

The rest of the town exhibits other features of frontier behavior, but without the corresponding frontier attitudes of optimism and self-reliance. The loneliness of the women n this novel stems from their emotional isolation, not a physical solitude. Popper's wife Ruth is desperately driven into Sonny's arms in an attempt to cope with her emptiness. Herman has ignored the tumor in her breast and complains about the cost of her prescriptions with the false bravado of a masculinity he lacks. "I could have bought a new deer rifle with what she's spent on pills just this last year, and I wish I had by God. A good gun beats a woman any day" (*LPS*, 60). "The pioneer women had to cope with deprivation and hardship," but the post-frontier woman of the twenties and thirties, in McMurtry's opinion, found it even harder to cope with more modern concepts of womanhood which stressed sexual equality.[20] The men, intimidated by this unique assertiveness, retreated from the responsibilities it brought, producing a loneliness far different from that dictated by a division of labor for the sake of survival on the open plains. As Ruth Popper tells Sonny, "the reason I'm so crazy is that nobody cares anything about me" (*LPS*, 58).

The town itself shares the dulling sameness which marked many frontier towns, but again it is a product not of the move into new territory, but of the death of that sense of newness. "There ain't no sure-nuff rich people in this town now," says Sam. "I doubt there'll ever be any more. The oil fields are about to dry up and the cattle business looks like it's going to peter out" (*LPS*, 62-63). Lois Farrow, the rich wife of a boorish oilman, feels bored: "Everything's flat and empty and there's nothing to do but spend money." In some of the most unselfish words she ever speaks, she warns her spoiled daughter Jacy of what life in Thalia means. "The only really important thing I came in to tell you was that life is very monotonous. Things happen the same way over and over again. I think it's more monotonous in this part of the country than it is in other places, but I don't really know that—it may be monotonous everywhere. I'm sick of it myself" (*LPS*, 49).

Duane and Sonny must cope with this stultifying dullness as they emerge into manhood. Each is essentially an orphan; their only remaining parents have neglected them and they lack any adult model except for Sam. Their desire to escape Thalia is not only an expression of adolescent restlessness, but reveals the desire to seek new and better frontiers of their own; only one of them manages to break away. They drive to the valley for a few days of liquor and sex south of the border, and to Ft. Worth for a taste of the big city. "'We got to go *somewhere*,' Sonny said." Ft. Worth "was part of the big world, and he always came back from a trip there with the satisfying sense that he had traveled" (*LPS*, 67). Duane decides there's no future in Thalia. "'There's not a goddamn thing to stay for,' he says. 'I'm going to Midland'" (*LPS*, 200). But he soon returns, disgusted with the Odessa desert, and finally enlists in the Army, bound for Korea. For Sonny, the pull of the familiar, even though depressing, is too strong to escape. His marriage to Jacy is annulled by her mother before they reach their honeymoon destination, Sam has died, and the innocent Billy is run down by a cattle truck; but Sonny cannot leave the town. Driving to work one afternoon, he stops his pickup outside the city limits, and seems threatened by what lies beyond. "The gray pastures and the distant brown ridges looked too empty. He himself felt too empty. . . . From the road the town looked raw, scraped by the wind, as empty as the country. It didn't look like the town it had been in high school, in the days of Sam the Lion" (*LPS*, 277). He returns to Ruth Popper and their reunion only deepens their private loneliness. The *anomie* Sonny feels at the end of the novel, his longing, his sense of dislocation, is not the result of his distance from a culture with whose values he strongly disagreed, as was the case with the backwoodsmen. He feels unable to leave a place which now has no values at all, and there is nothing beckoning him away from Thalia. "As empty as he felt and as empty as the country looked it was too risky going out into it—he might be blown around for days like a broom weed in the wind" (*LPS*, 277). The land still holds him, but neither he nor it is in any sense "free."

Though the inhabitants of Thalia live within the *place* of the frontier, its prosperity has long since gone and they have ceased to benefit from the invigorating frontier *process*. The characters in *All My Friends are Going to be Strangers* are even further removed from the frontier ethos, living their lives in Houston, Los Angeles, and New York, a fact which mirrors McMurtry's contention that "the Metropolis swallowed the Frontier like a small snake swallows a large frog: slowly, not without strain, but inexorably. And if something of the Frontier remains alive in the innards of the Metropolis, it is because the process of digestion has only just begun" (*ING*, 44). Danny Deck, the novel's hero and in places an alter-ego of McMurtry himself, has just had his first novel published, has married Sally after knowing her a week, and leaves Rice University for San Francisco. The novel revolves around Danny's aimless travels, his various sexual adventures and disintegrating marriage, and leads finally to an ambiguous ending as he wades into the Rio Grande River near Roma, drowning the manuscript of his new novel as he heads for the lights of Mexico.

Danny lacks practically all of the positive attitudes which Turner felt the frontier had bequeathed to the American individual. He is bewildered rather than optimistic, diffident rather than self-confident, expedient rather than principled, and artistic without being practical. His decision to leave Houston is clearly "deficiency-motivated." "Suddenly I didn't fit it any more," he says. "All the furniture of my life had been changed around. Sally was there, the apartment was too small, I couldn't see much of the Hortons, I had sold my novel, I didn't want to study anymore, Jenny wanted me, Godwin was around—it was all too much. Without wanting it to

happen, I had let myself be dislodged. Dislodged was exactly how I felt."[21] There is no hint of a distant goal in his leaving, even though he is living out the frontier *wanderlust*; and as he leaves, he senses a loss of the one thing which really defines him—Texas itself and his ancestry there. As he drove into New Mexico, he could feel the authority of the land. "It was all behind me, north to south, not lying there exactly, but more like looming there over the car, not a state or a stretch of land, but some giant, some genie, some god, towering over the road. . . . Texas let me go, ominously quiet. It hadn't gone away" (*AMF* [*All My Friends are Going to be Strangers*], 67).

Though an urbanite himself, Danny is viewed as a son of the pioneers by the city-dwellers. His wife is scandalized to discover he has shot a squirrel with his .22 and is cooking it for supper, but he is proud of his "perfect" shot, hitting a moving animal eighty-five feet off the ground with the sun in his eyes. At a cocktail party an English biologist tells him "if you propose to walk among us as an equal you must begin to cultivate one or two more of the more basic of the civilized graces." Godwin, the lecherous literature professor, mockingly defends him, saying "The boy's a frontier genius, don't you know? The fact that he farts in public is part of his appeal" (*AMF*, 41).

Danny is no hayseed, but his deep affinity for the lost life of the frontier is most clearly revealed in his respect for his Uncle Laredo, a ninety-two year-old black sheep of the family who lives on a decrepit ranch called Hacienda of the Bitter Waters near Van Horn with three Mexican hands, all of whom he calls "Pierre." It was from his uncle that Danny thinks he inherited his good shooting eye. Uncle Laredo and his friend Lorenzo had fought with Zapata and Villa in Mexico, with the Texas Rangers, and with the Seventh Cavalry in Wyoming in 1890, and time had not mellowed him a bit. Laredo's wife Martha lived on her own ranch some miles away, their individualism so strong that not even marriage could keep them under one roof. Danny knows he doesn't live by their values and he doesn't even really like them as people, but his admiration for their tenacity and sense of identity is profound and tragic:

> I always thought of Uncle L as near death, because he was ninety-two, but it was obvious to me that that was a wrong way to think. I was probably nearer death. It was as if Uncle L and Martha and Lorenzo had already contested Time and won. The contest was over. They had made life theirs. So far as life was concerned they could go on living until they got bored with living, with butchering goats and digging postholes and cooking buffalo steaks.

> I felt really insubstantial. I didn't know if I would ever make life mine. Martha was right about Uncle L, though. He was an old sonofabitch. The Hacienda of the Bitter Waters wasn't the Old West I liked to believe

in—it was the bitter end of something. I knew I would never want to visit it again.

(*AMF,* 170)

Uncle L is a magnificent, comical anachronism, but he possesses a greater sense of identity and vitality than Danny thinks he will ever achieve himself in his "dislodged" life.

Danny's sense of dislocation, of displacement, is a "central concern" of McMurtry's as R. L. Neinstein has noted.[22] McMurtry writes that "the place where all my stories start is the heart faced suddenly with the loss of its country, its customary and legendary range" (*ING,* 140) and his reference to the land links his characters' sense of loss to the historical change they are forced to confront. Unlike Sam the Lion or Uncle L, Danny and Sonny are, in Matthew Arnold's words, "caught between two worlds, one dead, the other powerless to be born." Danny is what Robert E. Park has called "the marginal man." "When the traditional organization of society breaks down, as a result of contact and collision with a new invading culture, the effect is, so to speak, to emancipate the individual man. . . . The individual is free for new adventures, but he is more or less without direction and control." Just such a clash, of course, is occurring as the frontier meets the metropolis. Danny is "a man on the margin of two cultures and two societies," and has links with the character type of the "stranger" mentioned earlier. Unlike the stranger, however, he lacks a private sense of values which distinguishes him from the crowd; unlike him, the stranger does not exist in a crisis of transition. "But in the case of the marginal man the period of crisis is relatively permanent;" he exhibits "spiritual instability, intensified self-consciousness, restlessness, and *malaise.*"[23] Park sees the marginal man's instability as a necessary step in the synthesis of a new stage in the progress of civilization, but McMurtry does not leave us with the sense that Danny is forging a new life for either himself or his society.

To conclude, we must return to paradoxes. McMurtry's people all possess a love-hate relationship with their native locale: a love for what it was and a hatred of what it has become. The values of the frontier still seem desirable, but no longer attainable. His characters are crossing a new frontier which has less freedom, fewer clearly defined principles, and greater personal anonymity than the old. There is isolation, but it is internal, not geographical; there is restlessness, but it is spiritual more than economic; there is resistance to control and defiance of authority, but without a corresponding social bonding in either family or friendship to balance that rebellion. McMurtry views the frontier cowboy as an essentially tragic figure, and it is hard not to conclude that the same urbanization which spelled his demise has lost in him the embodiment of certain values which it itself desperately needs.

Notes

1. W. Eugene Hollon, *Frontier Violence: Another Look* (New York: Oxford University Press, 1974), p. 200.

2. Hollon, p. 54.

3. Hollon, p. 196.

4. Ray Allen Billington, *America's Frontier Heritage* (Holt, Rinehart and Winston: New York, 1966), p. 78.

5. Charles D. Peavy, *Larry McMurtry* (Twayne: Boston, 1977), p. 118.

6. Peavy, p. 140.

7. Billington, p. 6.

8. *The Turner Thesis Concerning The Role of the Frontier in American History,* ed. G. R. Taylor (D. C. Heath: Lexington, Mass., 1956), p. 6.

9. *Turner Thesis,* p. 20.

10. Billington, pp. 25-26.

11. Billington, p. 42.

12. Billington, pp. 42-43.

13. Georg Simmel, "The Stranger" in *The Sociology of Georg Simmel,* trans. Kurt H. Wolf (Free Press: 1950, 1978), repr. in *The Pleasures of Sociology,* ed. Lewis Coser (New American Library, 1980), p. 237.

14. Billington, p. 59.

15. Billington, p. 144.

16. *In a Narrow Grave: Essays on Texas* (Austin: Encino Press, 1968), chapter 5. References to this book are cited as *ING.*

17. Billington, p. 26.

18. *The Last Picture Show* (New York: Dial Press, 1966), p. 153. References to this book are cited as *LPS.*

19. Peavy, p. 124, n. 17.

20. *ING,* pp. 68-69.

21. *All My Friends are Going to be Strangers* (New York: Pocket Books, 1973), p. 47. References to this book are cited as *AMF.*

22. *The Ghost Country: A Study of the Novels of Larry McMurtry* (Berkely: Creative Arts Book Co., 1976).

23. Robert E. Park, "Migration and the Marginal Man," *American Journal of Sociology,* 33 (May, 1928), 200-206. Repr. in Coser, pp. 241-247.

Susan J. Rosowski (essay date fall 1982)

SOURCE: Rosowski, Susan J. "Willa Cather's *A Lost Lady*: Art Versus the Closing Frontier." *Great Plains Quarterly* 2, no. 4 (fall 1982): 240-48.

[*In the following essay, Rosowski assesses Willa Cather's achievement with her novel* A Lost Lady, *maintaining that the story concerns the decline of the West and the exploitation of the frontier.*]

When *A Lost Lady* appeared in 1923, readers immediately recognized Willa Cather's achievement. T. K. Whipple wrote, "with *A Lost Lady,* Miss Cather arrived at what can only be called perfection in her art";[1] Joseph Wood Krutch termed it "nearly perfect."[2] Later readers continued the praise, calling it "perfectly modulated"[3] and "a flawless classic"[4] and generally judging it the finest of Cather's novels. While acknowledging its art, however, critics have stressed its themes in their interpretations, reading it as telling of the frontier's downfall, of the noble pioneer's passing, of materialism's onslaught, of woman's plight in a patriarchal society. These themes run through the novel, certainly; Cather begins her story with the historical decline of the West and she traces the passing of the noble pioneer and the exploitation of the land. But she posits against this decline a human need for primitive or sacred understanding, for spiritual attitudes and intuitive, symbolic art forms.[5] Cather's art lies in perfectly incorporating the two kinds of experience and, in the end, celebrating symbolic possibility in the face of historical loss.

A Lost Lady presents the age-old tension between possibility and loss against a background of an American frontier that promised a pioneer experience of boundless opportunity at the same time it restricted that experience to a strikingly brief period.[6] It does so through the story of Marian Forrester, brought as a bride to the small town of Sweet Water by her road-making husband, one of the last of the pioneer aristocrats. A generation younger than Captain Forrester, Mrs. Forrester is caught in the increasingly narrow circumstances of a closing frontier: her husband suffers a loss of fortune and health, and then dies, leaving her apparently at the mercy of grasping, materialistic elements in Sweet Water. Her story is told primarily from the point of view of Niel Herbert. A generation younger than Mrs. Forrester and two generations younger than the pioneers who settled the West, Niel realizes he lives at "the very end of the road-making West. . . . It was already gone, that age; nothing could ever bring it back,"[7] and he seeks ennobling symbolic value in the face of this loss.

Tension between possibility and loss is further evident in the two quite different effects the book produces. *A Lost Lady* contains a bustle of activity that forms an overall pattern of rising and falling motion, of expectation and disappointment. The pioneers live and die, people come and go, the economy grows and declines, light dawns and fades, flowers open and close—even Mrs. Forrester's laugh rises and descends. The plot reflects this pattern: Marian Forrester comes to Sweet Water as the young bride of Captain Forrester and she leaves after his death; at the beginning of the action, the boy Niel Herbert first enters the Forrester place, and at its ending an older Niel departs "for the last time." Scenes suggest this pattern in miniature, characteristically beginning with Niel's coming up the hill approaching the Forrester house and ending with his going down the hill after leaving it.

Although movement surrounds episodes of *A Lost Lady,* there is a profound stillness at its center. Episodes contain moments of recognition that seem frozen in time, and these moments make up the essential substance of the novel. Like Ántonia, who could "leave images in the mind that did not fade—that grew stronger with time,"[8] so does *A Lost Lady* leave such images; Mrs. Forrester bringing cookies to the boys in the marsh; listening to Captain Forrester tell their dinner guests of first coming to Sweet Water and, later, presiding over her own dinner party, telling quite different guests of her meeting Captain Forrester; Niel, stooping to place a bouquet of flowers outside her bedroom window, then hearing from within the sound of her laughter mingled with that of her lover.

These effects of movement and stillness derive from two impulses that run through the novel—one historical, the other symbolic, and both focusing on Marian Forrester, the lost lady of the title. In the historical narrative, Mrs. Forrester is a woman who lives in time: she comes to Sweet Water and presides over her husband's home as a brilliant hostess, takes a lover, cares for her husband during his prolonged illness, abandons principles of his generation after his death, has an affair with a shyster lawyer, and moves from Sweet Water to seek her fortune elsewhere. Throughout this progression, she participates in cause-and-effect relationships in time: she flourishes as a result of her husband's prosperity and suffers by his loss of fortune; she enjoys youthful beauty, then gradually grows old.

But as the historical account progresses, Cather presents a second level of significance in her characterization of Marian Forrester—a symbolic one. While the events of her life exist within time and in terms of cause-and-effect relationships, her symbolic meaning exists out of time and comes from the integration of apparently disparate elements: her suspicious past and her respectability as Captain Forrester's wife; her aesthetic otherworldliness and her sensuality; her fragility and her strength; her exquisiteness and her coarseness; her artlessness and her artifice; her mocking, guarded veneer and the living reality beneath it.

The novel's intensity builds on both levels. First, there are the increasingly desperate circumstances of Mrs. Forrester's life—of her struggle to avoid entrapment by the restricting effects of her husband's loss of fortune and death, of living in Sweet Water, of growing old. Second, and far more important, intensity builds as Mrs. Forrester expands as a symbol by incorporating ever greater discrepancies. Initially, the contrasts she presents are relatively easy to resolve: she seems a lady far above and detached from other people, yet she enters the ordinary world of childhood play when she brings cookies to young boys playing in the marsh. Gradually, she reveals wider contrasts—between the spiritual and the physical, the common and the uncommon, fidelity and betrayal—and resolution becomes correspondingly more difficult.

Niel Herbert, the sensitive observer of Marian Forrester, is the major vehicle for this expanding symbolic meaning. It is Niel who feels most intensely her "magic of contradictions" (p. 79), and it is he who attempts most arduously to deny those contradictions. The overall symbolic movement of the novel follows Niel's responses and consists of two major imaginative expansions and contractions, followed by a resolution.[9] In the first part, scenes expand the symbolic significance of Mrs. Forrester through a dialectic between her otherworldly grace and her physical reality. Early expansive movement occurs when the young Niel thinks of her as a spiritual goddess, then perceives her playful, teasing, human qualities. Expansion continues as the adolescent Niel becomes aware of other incongruities in her: a scandalous past and a present respectability, a mocking manner and a deep interest in people, fragility and vitality: "from that disparity, he believed, came the subtlest thrill of her fascination. She . . . inherited the magic of contradictions" (p. 79). As other readers have observed, Niel's imaginative, emotional response is far deeper than he is conscious of: in terms of the aesthetic experience of the novel, Mrs. Forrester's symbolic meaning greatly exceeds the adolescent Niel's capacity to comprehend her. Cather prepares for this disparity by a sequence of episodes: the dinner party, culminating Niel's initial response to Mrs. Forrester, is followed by the cedarbough-cutting episode, which occurs outside Niel's knowledge and in which the non-judgmental Adolph Blum provides the lens for presenting profoundly sexual qualities in Mrs. Forrester. Thus in the following chapter, when Niel attempts to explain his interest in Mrs. Forrester, there is an enormous ironic difference between his explanation that "it was as Captain Forrester's wife that she most interested Niel, and it was in her relation to her husband that he most admired her" (p. 78) and the reader's knowledge of qualities in her that lie far outside this explanation.

Through this expansion, tension builds with intrusions by Frank Ellinger, Mrs. Forrester's lover, and culmi-nates when Niel overhears Mrs. Forrester with Ellinger in her bedroom. Unable to accommodate sexuality in his imaginative conception of her, Niel draws back in bitter disillusionment, breaking the imaginative expansion with logic: "he burned to ask her one question, to get the truth out of her and to set his mind at rest: What did she do with all her exquisiteness when she was with a man like Ellinger? Where did she put it away? And having put it away, how could she recover herself, and give one—give even him—the sense of tempered steel, a blade that could fence with anyone and never break" (p. 100). Niel's question reveals an analytic impulse and an underlying denial of paradoxes. He assumes that Mrs. Forrester puts away her exquisiteness when she is with her lover and that, after having given herself up to sexuality, she "recovers herself," putting aside sexuality and resuming her former nature. Intensifying the question is Niel's almost violent impulse to force a response from her, a yielding to him, as he "burned . . . *to get the truth out of her*" (my emphasis).

In the novel's second part, Niel's response is again expansive as scenes further present Mrs. Forrester's complexity, this time primarily through disparities between her self-renunciation and her independence. Seldom leaving Sweet Water during her husband's last years, Mrs. Forrester reveals gentleness in her ministrations to her dying husband and fierceness in her own desire to live, exhaustion and strength, generosity and greed. This expansion culminates when Mrs. Forrester presides at her own dinner party after her husband's death and, despite her great fatigue and her guests' insensitivity, transforms those present with the story of her first meeting Captain Forrester.

Throughout this expansion, tension builds as Ivy Peters assumes the role previously held by Frank Ellinger—on a narrative level of lover, on a symbolic level of eliciting contradictory features in Mrs. Forrester. Contraction occurs when Niel, seeing Ivy Peters "unconcernedly put both arms around her, his hands meeting over her breast" (p. 169), turns from her in bitter disillusionment, resolving never to return to the Forrester place. Again Niel attempts to deny contradictions in her: she is either common or uncommon, worthy or unworthy. Recalling her, Niel wishes to "challenge [her], demand the secret of that ardour," just as he had earlier wished "to get the truth out of her." Yet the futility of this last wish is apparent. Mrs. Forrester "had drifted out of his ken"—she had moved to South America, remarried, and died—and the image of her drifting away combines with Niel's wish "to call up the shade of the young Mrs. Forrester, as the witch of Endor called up Samuel's" (p. 171), to convey a dreamlike, imaginative quality in his response.

Resolution comes when Niel, ceasing his attempts to explain Mrs. Forrester or to force her to explain herself, acknowledges her value on another level. Removed in time and place from the cause-and-effect relationships of the narrative, Niel hears once again of his "long-lost lady," an account relayed by a childhood friend, Ed Elliott. In this final description, Mrs. Forrester remains enigmatic: she had aged, yet hadn't changed in essentials; she had married a man reputed to be "quarrelsome and rather stingy," yet "she seemed to have everything"; most remarkably, she had "come up again" after having "pretty well gone to pieces before she left Sweet Water." But Niel responds, "'So we may feel sure that she was well cared for to the end . . . Thank God for that!'" The resolution here is in Niel's attitude to Mrs. Forrester, an acknowledgment of the truth of his subjective experience of her. His "'Thank God!'" reveals the strength of his feeling; his friend interprets the reaction as feeling ("'I knew you'd feel that way'"); then the narrator affirms this interpretation in the novel's final clause, "a warm wave of feeling passed over his face" (pp. 172-74).

At the end, we too try to "get at" Mrs. Forrester's secret—to explain and judge her as strong or weak, noble or fallen. But just as there is a problem with the "real" meaning in "Ode on a Grecian Urn," so there is a problem with the "real" meaning of Marian Forrester and, through her, of *A Lost Lady.* We finally return to the images of the woman that live in the book and, as we do so, recognize as Niel does the expanding significance that radiates from her, infusing every part of the novel: "she had always the power of suggesting things much lovelier than herself, as the perfume of a single flower may call up the whole sweetness of spring" (p. 172).

This infusing power of the symbol is its essential quality. As Coleridge wrote, a symbol "partakes of the reality which it renders intelligible [and] . . . abides itself as a living part in that unity, of which it is a representative."[10] It follows then that we would expect the parts of a symbolic prose narrative—as Karl Kroeber does those of a symbolic poem—"to be dynamically interrelated."[11] And so they are. To develop the expanding symbolic significance that radiates from Mrs. Forrester, Cather uses a form of incremental repetition, repeating descriptive phrases so that the significance of the reference changes in the progress of the novel. By repetition, the things to which phrases refer become familiar: they appear, then reappear, with each reappearance bringing forward the accumulated associations of their past. When the boy Niel is taken into Mrs. Forrester's bedroom after breaking his arm, for example, he sees light coming through closed green shutters; later, an older Niel, having gathered a bouquet for Mrs. Forrester in the early morning, goes "softly round the still house to the north side of Mrs. Forrester's own room, where the door-like green shutters were closed" (p. 86). The familiar shutters subtly evoke the earlier scene in which

Niel was inside the room and secure in his youthful idealization of Mrs. Forrester, and thus they contribute to the dramatic impact of the disillusionment scene.

As the effect of incremental repetition expands, objects take on qualities of their perceivers, further suggesting a world informed with symbolic significance. The poplars bordering the road to the Forrester place are initially simply objects in a rather flat nature: "the Captain's private land [was] bordered by Lombardy poplars" (p. 11). Gradually, however, the trees become sentinels of the coming and going of visitors to the Forrester place, familiar landmarks in a world we come to recognize. Eventually, they participate in the symbolic meaning that radiates from Mrs. Forrester, transformed by Niel following his experiences with her. Leaving the Forrester place, "Niel paused for a moment at the end of the lane to look up at the last skeleton poplar in the long row; just above its pointed tip hung the hollow, silver winter moon" (p. 42). When Niel leaves the Forrester place "'for the last time,'" the narrator affirms, "it was even so; he never went up the poplar-bordered road again" (p. 170)—and the reference to the poplars, with their many associations from the past, suggests the symbolic resonances Niel is turning from.

Finally, by building to symbolic climaxes, the accumulative meaning of images enables moments of recognition. Rose imagery, for example, underlies the novel's first major expansive movement. When Mrs. Forrester sees Niel and the other boys on their way to the marsh, she is arranging roses; when she comes to the door to talk with them, she is holding a single rose. The rose, apparently tamed and domesticated inside Mrs. Forrester's parlor, reappears in the marsh in profusion as "wild roses [that] were wide open and brilliant" (p. 17), the image subtly foreshadowing the sensual, even wild potential in Mrs. Forrester's own nature and suggesting Niel's response to that potential. On the one hand, the intimation of sensuality is a major element in his fascination with her; on the other hand, it is this quality in her that he is unable to face. Rose imagery climaxes in the early morning scene in which Niel gathers a bouquet for Mrs. Forrester. The extended image begins with a relatively objective description of "thickets of wild roses, with flaming buds, just beginning to open." Then, as if the objects by their own beauty and by their past association with Mrs. Forrester draw forth fuller perception, the description moves from the roses themselves to Niel's mind as he perceives them: "Where they had opened, their petals were stained with that burning rose-colour which is always gone by noon,—a dye made of sunlight and morning and moisture, so intense that it cannot possibly last . . . must fade, like ecstasy." The image unifies aesthetic and sensual responses into a single intense moment. Finally, Niel begins to cut stems of the flowers, resolving, in highly metaphorical terms, that "he would make a bouquet for a lovely lady; a bouquet gathered off the cheeks of morning . . . these roses, only half awake, in the defenselessness of utter beauty" (p. 85). Far more than the action, the imagery here conveys the transitoriness of such a moment and the vulnerability of one who experiences it, anticipating Niel's disillusionment at the end of that scene. As preceding rose imagery foreshadows this scene, succeeding imagery echoes it. Roses, again reduced to objects but now containing symbolic resonances, reappear after Captain Forrester's death when the Blum brothers bring a box of yellow roses to Mrs. Forrester and, later, when she resolves to plant some of her husband's rose bushes over his grave (pp. 145-46).

Incremental repetition illustrates, then, the way in which symbolic meaning works by accumulation, expansion, and infusion, its movement quite different from the sequential movement characteristic of the cause-and-effect patterns in the historical account. Through this contrast, the symbolic and historic elements work off one another. Scenes customarily begin in time, move to a core episode that contains a moment of recognition and an escape from time, then return abruptly to the historical, real world. The Forrester place resides at the center of this movement, offering apparent security and constancy and containing Mrs. Forrester, with her magical power of transformation. But experiences there are surrounded by ominous images of incompletion, change, and death that suggest inevitable intrusions from the real world. When Niel is taken to Mrs. Forrester's room after breaking his arm, he becomes aware of a "different world from any he had ever known" (p. 42). His involvement intensifies until, when "Mrs. Forrester ran her fingers through his black hair and lightly kissed him on the forehead," he loses himself in the fullness of the experience: "Oh, how sweet, how sweet she smelled!" With the next line, however, the world of change intrudes—"'Wheels on the bridge; it's Doctor Dennison. Go and show him in, Mary.'" Niel's return is dramatized as Doctor Dennison "took him home," a home "set off on the edge of the prairie" and "usually full of washing in various stages of incompletion" (p. 29). The wholeness Niel felt with Mrs. Forrester intensifies his later sense of incompletion; his happiness sharpens his dissatisfaction; his fleeting sense of belonging heightens the loneliness of his daily life.

Subsequent episodes follow a similar pattern. Niel feels exultation over an evening talk with Mrs. Forrester; then, leaving the Forrester place, he stops "at the end of the lane" to look at the last skeletal poplar pointing to a hollow winter moon (p. 42). At Captain Forrester's dinner party, Niel again feels a deep sense of security, this time through loss of self in Captain Forrester's story of coming to Sweet Water; then "just before midnight" he returns to a world of separation and incompletion as the guests sing "Auld Lang Syne" and "hadn't got to the end of it" when they hear "a hollow rumbling down on

the bridge" and then "see the judge's funeral coach come lurching up the hill, with only one of the side lanterns lit" (p. 57). Other scenes come to mind: Niel's gathering flowers for Mrs. Forrester and reveling in the "almost religious purity about the morning air," then abruptly returning to the real world at the sound of laughter from within (pp. 84-87); Niel's losing himself in Mrs. Forrester's story of first meeting Captain Forrester, and then, in the next scene, planning to leave Sweet Water and feeling he was "making the final break with everything that had been dear to him in his boyhood" (p. 168).

What emerges is a buildup of tension between the encroaching real world of change and experiences of unity—of symbolic meaning—that become increasingly difficult to reach in that world. The contrasting dinner parties illustrate the heightening of tension. In the first, a young Mrs. Forrester appears effortless as she assists her husband in transforming the evening; in the second, an older, widowed, impoverished Mrs. Forrester appears haggard, and it is only by a supreme act of will that she again electrifies her guests. The strong sense of incompletion throughout the narrative contributes to this tension: Sweet Water does not fulfill its early promise; Captain Forrester's career as a builder is cut short by an accident; the heirs apparent to the pioneer generation—Marian Forrester and Niel Herbert—leave without bringing renewal.

Finally, changes in point of view reinforce this tension. The overall progression of point of view is from the public meaning of a storyteller to the private meaning of subjective experience. The novel begins with a narrator who recalls, "thirty or forty years ago, in one of those grey towns along the Burlington railroad, which are so much greyer today than they were then, there was a house well known from Omaha to Denver for its hospitality and for a certain charm of atmosphere," then modifies this observation—"well known, that is to say, to the railroad aristocracy of that time." The effect is of ongoing reminiscence, of the actual presence of a storyteller who offers an observation as it occurs to her. Because she is casual about time (referring to "thirty or forty years ago" and to "long ago") as well as about place (referring to "one of those grey towns along the Burlington railroad"), the storyteller herself emerges strongly in the opening passage, seeming more immediate, real, and accessible than her subject.

Recounting comings and goings, sequences and changes, the storyteller provides a logical, rational organization of these movements. She establishes a chronology of events ("for the next few years Niel saw very little of Mrs. Forrester"; "during that winter . . . Niel came to know her very well"; "Captain Forrester's death . . . occurred early in December"), and she explains events through their sequence of cause and effect within that chronology ("For the Forresters that winter was a sort of isthmus between two estates; soon afterward came a change in their fortunes. And for Niel, it was a natural turning point" (pp. 31, 69, 103, 144). The narrative conveys a sense of movement; its meaning is objective, factual, settled.

But the stillness at *A Lost Lady*'s center derives from a quite different experience—one that is subjective, imaginative, and expanding. For it Cather moves from the storyteller's omniscience to the limited points of view of individual characters, such as Niel. This movement involves a gradual narrowing from the storyteller's long view to a specific episode, to one character within the episode, and, finally, to the episode as it is being processed in that character's mind. Beginning with the long view, for example, the storyteller explains, "It was two years before Niel Herbert came home again," then presents Niel having come to the Forrester place, summarizes his meeting with Captain Forrester, and follows Niel "round the house to the gate that gave into the grove," where he saw first a hammock between two cottonwoods, then a still, slender, white figure in it. The account gains in immediacy as Niel, approaching, discerns more details: "as he hurried across the grass he saw that a white garden hat lay over her face" and was "just wondering if she were asleep, when he heard a soft delighted laugh," stepped forward, and caught her suspended figure. Suddenly, the point of view presents Niel's mind encountering the object: "How light and alive she was! like a bird caught in a net. If only he could rescue her and carry her off like this" (pp. 103-10).

Within specific scenes, Cather interweaves omniscience with individual perceptions, keeping the point of view in motion and maintaining dialectical tension through which symbolic meaning emerges. The storyteller contrasts descriptions from the "long ago" past (of the young Mrs. Forrester, "bareheaded, a basket on her arm, her blue-black hair shining in the sun") to later time ("it was not until years afterward that she began to wear veils and sun hats," pp. 17-18). Similar movement occurs as a result of changes in Niel. Niel's youthful idealization of Mrs. Forrester contrasts with his later disillusionment and his still later gratitude to her. And the storyteller contrasts individual points of view: Adolph Blum, seeing Mrs. Forrester come from an assignation with her lover, contrasts with Niel's seeing her only as Captain Forrester's wife; Captain Forrester, watching her with Niel and thinking of her "as very, very young" (p. 75) contrasts with Niel's general view of her as an older woman.

Within the novel as a whole, changes in point of view suggest the effects of a disintegration of traditional, communal values and a corresponding stress on personal symbolic meaning. Initially, the storyteller identi-

fies individuals in terms of her community: Marian Forrester, seeing a group of boys approach, "knew most of them" as members of the community. Niel is "Judge Pommeroy's nephew"; the others include the "son of a gentleman rancher," "the leading grocer's . . . twins," and "the two sons of the German tailor." Recognition is personal and intimate, based on gossip about as well as the professional standing of their fathers. Ed Elliot, for example, is the boy "whose flirtatious old father kept a shoe store and was the Don Juan of the lower world of Sweet Water" (p. 14). Similarly, the boy Niel approaches the Forrester place in terms of alignment and congruity: it represents the values he upholds and the life to which he aspires.

By the end of Part II, however, Niel returns to a community from which he is alienated. Cather has replaced Marian Forrester with Ivy Peters to describe Niel's return, and Peters identifies Niel not by community relationships but by his clothes. A shift in power and in communal values is suggested by the shift from Mrs. Forrester, who greets guests as a representative of her husband and the best of Sweet Water, to Ivy Peters, who greets guests as the leader of materialistic, unscrupulous elements that have gained power in the same community. Tension heightens as Niel believes Mrs. Forrester is aligning herself with the new "generation of shrewd young men, trained to petty economies" (p. 107), represented by Ivy Peters.

As Niel's alienation deepens, his subjective, imaginative response is increasingly at odds with his rational appraisal of the "lost lady." Logically and objectively, Niel comes to believe that Mrs. Forrester's generosity and her greed, her exquisiteness and her coarseness, her fidelity and her betrayal, are irreconcilable contradictions. He judges her harshly and keeps his distance from her. When Mrs. Forrester invites him to her dinner party, for example, he resists, arguing, "'What do you want me for?'" and later feeling "angry with himself for having been persuaded" to accept; on the night of the dinner, he is "the last guest to arrive" (p. 158). Yet against all rational preconceptions, at this dinner party Niel is still moved by Mrs. Forrester's "indomitable self," and his apprehension of her telling of first meeting Captain Forrester is one of the timeless moments of recognition at the heart of the novel (pp. 164-67).

Niel's conflict may be illustrated by the motif "always" that runs through the novel. Initially, "always" refers to apparent permanence within time—to rituals, for example, that by repetition seem constant. Captain Forrester's toast, "Happy Days," is such a ritual, "the toast he always drank at dinner." As a hostess, Mrs. Forrester carries out other such rituals: "she was always there" (p. 12) to greet visitors; to the young Niel, she seemed "always the same" (p. 39). Such rituals serve their function: they provide a sense of security and stability. But eventually the world of change exerts itself and, in retrospect, the apparent stability offered by rituals seems illusory. Captain Forrester falls from power; Mrs. Forrester is neither always there nor always the same. But even as Niel must accept the loss of Mrs. Forrester within the historical narrative (indeed, he must accept that he never possessed her, and never could have), he comes to realize her permanence on a symbolic level. *Always* runs through the symbolic elements of the novel also, referring to a permanence that exists outside of time. In the end, Niel is certain that Mrs. Forrester "had always the power of suggesting things much lovelier than herself, as the perfume of a single flower may call up the whole sweetness of spring" (p. 172).

Significantly, Niel casts his reflection in the past tense—for him, Mrs. Forrester "*had* always the power of suggesting things"—and with this past tense, the reader departs from Niel. Niel's resolution comes with his subjective sense that Mrs. Forrester had the power to evoke a symbolic mode of perception; he has reached the point that he is no longer analyzing and judging—no longer holding it against her that "she was not willing to immolate herself, like the widow of all these great men, and die with the pioneer period to which she belonged, that she preferred life on any terms." Ironically, however, his resolution comes only after she, whom Niel believed "preferred life on any terms," has died, and we suspect that Niel's longing for permanence, forever frustrated in a world of change, ends with the secure distance and detachment of an experience "recollected in tranquillity."[12]

For the reader, however, Marian Forrester continues to live in the novel, for in reading we, like Niel with his uncle's books, meet "living creatures, caught in the very behaviour of living" (p. 81). As a result, it is impossible to settle Marian Forrester into a fixed meaning, to put her into the past tense and set one's mind to rest about her. Although she recedes in the reader's memory, she comes forward again with each rereading and, by continuing to exert her intense individuality, evokes fresh responses and forces the reader to expand his or her perception of her. In so doing, the reader takes up where Niel left off. Each reading contains moments of recognition and resolution in which Mrs. Forrester is seen as a whole, combining contrary qualities that are logically irreconcilable. Once read, the novel evokes questions which, in turn, lead back into the work. And each time we return to the novel, expansion continues. By offering "an expanding potentiality for formulating values, an expanding area of sympathy and insight out of which values of lasting refinement can emerge and to which they can return," *A Lost Lady* is a novel of experience in Robert Langbaum's sense. The reader is "always in the process of formulating values, although he never arrives at a final formulation."[13] As Karl Kroeber observes, experiences of symbolic meaning "are subjective and creative; they cannot be told about; we must . . . participate."[14] Unlimited opportunity for the individual to engage in personal experience, to formulate values, and to create anew—the description could be of the American frontier—or of *A Lost Lady*. For in *A Lost Lady*, Cather celebrates the constantly expanding possibilities of symbolic art even as she laments the closed frontier of history.

Notes

1. *New York Evening Post*, December 8, 1923; 1928 revised version reprinted in *Spokesmen* (Berkeley: University of California Press, 1963), p. 143; reprinted in *Willa Cather and Her Critics,* ed. by James Schroeter (Ithaca: Cornell University Press, 1967), p. 38.

2. *Nation*, November 28, 1923; reprinted in Schroeter, *Willa Cather and Her Critics,* p. 52.

3. David Daiches, *Willa Cather: A Critical Introduction* (1951; reprint ed., Westport, Conn.: Greenwood Press, 1971), p. 86.

4. John Davenport, *Observer,* May 7, 1966.

5. See John Milton's description of the fourth phase "in the relationship between plainsman (or his artistic representatives) and the landscape." Milton describes the four phases as an initial "romantic, idealized, Edenic vision," which gives way to a realistic shattering of vision, then "an industrialized and technological revision of the land," and, finally, "a reaction to the exploitation of the land; a partial return to a primitive or sacred understanding of the land, spiritual in attitude and intuitive and symbolic in art forms"; "Plains Landscapes and Changing Visions," *Great Plains Quarterly* 2 (Winter 1982): 61. In my view, Cather affirms symbolic art in response to her perception of the exploitation of the land and the decline of American life and letters.

6. David Lowenthal, in "The Pioneer Landscape: An American Dream," writes, "the sense of a pioneer environment rarely endured in toto more than a few years before giving way to a settled order"; *Great Plains Quarterly* 2 (Winter 1982): 10.

7. *A Lost Lady* (1923; reprint ed., New York: Knopf, 1963), pp. 168-69. All references are to this text.

8. *My Ántonia* (1918; reprint ed., Boston: Houghton Mifflin, 1961), p. 352.

9. Niel's response, coming from his deep longing for permanence in a world of change, is remarkably similar in motive and form to Keats's response to the objects of his odes. The odes characteristically begin with the observer feeling the impact of the object's fullness—for example, the Grecian urn's paradoxical combination of activity and immobility, of silence and expression:

> Thou still unravished bride of quietness
>   Thou foster child of silence and slow time,
> Sylvan historian, who canst thus express
>   A flowery tale more sweetly than our rhyme.

This initial sense of value is followed by the pain of separation from the object and an attempt to bridge that separation—to make the object give itself up to the observer. Tension builds between reason and imagination: the reason, an analyzing faculty, seeks to separate, divide, and categorize, while the imagination, a synthesizing faculty, seeks to perceive similarities, to unite, and to enter into. Increasingly intense questions addressed to the urn are frustrated by the object's self-sufficiency, and resolution comes only when the observer, ceasing his attempt to force the object to reveal its secrets, allows himself to experience it in all its paradoxical fullness. It is at this point that the observer moves beyond the object as object and experiences it as a symbol; the experience forms the lyric climax of the ode. This experience is transitory, however, and so the observer drops back into separation—but a separation different from that at the poem's beginning, for he retains a sense of the symbolic richness he participated in.

10. Samuel T. Coleridge, *The Statesman's Manual* (London: Gale and Fenner, 1816), p. 37. Coleridge includes here his famous description of a symbol as "characterized by a translucence of the Special in the Individual or of the General in the Especial or of the Universal in the General. Above all the translucence of the Eternal through and in the Temporal." In *Willa Cather's Gift of Sympathy,* Edward A. Bloom and Lillian D. Bloom write, "the fundamental understanding of Cather's work is, indeed, dependent upon an understanding of her meaningful employment of a set of symbols, all of which are segments of the total theme"; they use Coleridge's definition to clarify Cather's symbolism (Carbondale: Southern Illinois Press, 1962), p. 26.

11. Karl Kroeber, *Romantic Narrative Art* (Madison: University of Wisconsin Press, 1966), p. 53.

12. In response to a draft of this essay, Patricia Yongue (University of Houston) commented on the paradox implicit in Niel's aestheticism: "there is aesthetic value . . . in Marian Forrester's expanding symbolic significance for Niel and for the reader. . . . Yet the same aesthetic process which gives Mrs. Forrester a dignity and makes her interesting as a symbol also limits her humanity and freedom. Insofar as Niel and the Captain . . . ask Marian to remain unchanged, they are asking her to be an object, an urn which depicts motion but does not move in terms of human growth and expansion. It is a request, of course, which she denies, and so she moves on to California and finally to South America" (personal correspondence, October 16, 1981). For Yongue's general treatment of this "allegiance to an aristocratic ideal which often serves as a fundamental component in the dynamics of [Cather's] fiction," see her essay, "Willa Cather's Aristocrats," in two parts, *Southern Humanities Review* 14 and 15 (1980). For my own general treatment of the relationship between Cather's narrators and the objects they describe, see "Willa Cather's Women," *Studies in American Fiction* 9 (Autumn 1981): 261-75.

13. Robert Langbaum, *The Poetry of Experience* (London: Chatto and Windus, 1957), p. 26.

14. Kroeber, *Romantic Narrative Art,* p. 58.

Fred Erisman (essay date November 1986)

SOURCE: Erisman, Fred. "Nevil Shute and the Closed Frontier." *Western American Literature* 21, no. 3 (November 1986): 207-17.

[*In the following essay, Erisman considers Nevil Shute's treatment of the Australian frontier theme in his novels, contending that the author offers perceptive commentary about the mythical power of the frontier and the impact of its closing.*]

When the British novelist Nevil Shute (1899-1960) immigrated to Australia in 1950, he did so for reasons more economic and emotional than artistic. As a best-selling author with growing international sales, he was frustrated by the heavy tax burden that Labourite England imposed upon him; out of expected royalties of fifteen thousand pounds on his most recent book, he would net approximately three thousand, whereas the Australian tax scale would let him keep almost six thousand. Moreover, as a trained aeronautical engineer, an experienced corporate entrepreneur, and a dedicated believer in a meritocracy based upon individualism and competence, he was equally frustrated by what he perceived as the Socialist government's deliberate stifling of individual initiative and effort. He knew and liked Australia, having been there for a six-month visit in 1948-1949, so, when circumstances permitted, he moved.

The move was a fortuitous one, economically, emotionally, and artistically. It freed him from the financial constraints that had chafed him in England and enabled him to accumulate a substantial fortune. It confirmed his deep-seated belief that the self-sufficient individual was the foundation of a nation's cultural and economic growth. And, most significantly, it led him to write a three-novel sequence that constitutes a little-known but provocative exploration of the frontier hypothesis and its implications. He was, to be sure, an engineer and a novelist, not a profound student of either history or literature; even so, he knew (and admired) the "rough vitality [and] optimism" of Americans and he was professionally sensitive to the presence and power of myth.[1] These traits stood him in good stead as he looked at Australia and the United States, so that, in *A Town Like Alice* (1950), *The Far Country* (1952), and *Beyond the Black Stump* (1956), Nevil Shute, an Englishman turned Australian, emerges as a perceptive commentator upon the mythic power of the frontier and upon the consequences of its closing.

As Shute develops his ideas over the six-year span of the three books, he proceeds in straightforward, systematic fashion. Thus, the first of the three, *A Town Like Alice,* published in the United States as *The Legacy* and given a new audience by its television dramatization on *Masterpiece Theatre* in the early 1980s, is a simple statement of the possibilities that a frontier environment holds for those willing to adapt themselves to its circumstances. Jean Paget, a London typist who has been a prisoner of the Japanese on Malaya during the Second World War, inherits a windfall fortune from a long-forgotten uncle. When she travels to Malaya to build a well for the natives who had befriended her, she crosses the path of another wartime acquaintance, Joe Harmon, an Australian ringer (i.e., cowboy) whom she had thought executed by the Japanese. She traces him to his cattle station, they fall in love and marry, and she devotes the residue of her legacy to modernizing the dreary outback village of Willstown.

Thus summarized, the novel seems little more than a conventional love story suitable for light reading on a summer afternoon. Within its sentimental plot, however, Shute hides considerable substance, for he shapes the action in a way that pointedly echoes Frederick Jackson Turner's vision of the American frontier. In this instance, the events parallel Turner's observation that "the peculiarity of American institutions is, the fact that they have been compelled to adapt themselves to the changes of an expanding people . . . and in developing at each area of this progress out of the primitive economic and political conditions of the frontier into the complexity of city life."[2] Turner speaks of the United States and Shute of Australia, yet both see the same processes at work.

The processes, for Shute as much as for Turner, are a combination of the environmental and the personal. Shute presents Australia as a land of vast spaces, of challenges and of enormous difficulties. A cattle station embracing twenty-seven hundred square miles and supporting eighteen thousand cattle is commonplace, and hardships are as much a part of outback life as the challenge; as Harmon says, "It's a grand country for a man to live and work in, and good money, too. But it's a crook place for a woman." Yet the potential of the country is equally real, and if a person shows initiative and adaptability, rapid progress is sure to result. When Jean outlines her plans for Willstown to a bank manager, he replies: "Joe Harmon may be on to a good thing up there. . . . The Gulf Country's not much just at present, but he's a young man, and things can happen very quickly in Australia."[3] And, stimulated by Jean's capital and Australia's opportunities, things do happen.

By story's end, Jean is a flourishing capitalist (also a contented wife and mother); Joe is a substantial landholder; and Willstown, like a case history for Turner, is a thriving community complete with ice cream shop, laundromat, swimming pool, and beauty parlor. Jean herself, as her aging London attorney notes, has "ceased to write as an Englishwoman living in a strange, hard, foreign land [and] gradually began to write about the people as if she was one of them, about the place as if it was her place." She and Joe, Shute remarks in a telling aside, are planning a holiday in the United States, where "their problems must be just the same as ours, and they've been at it longer." (*TLA* [*A Town Like Alice*], pp. 290, 305) And the old attorney, in the closing paragraphs of the story, puts an appropriately Turnerian finish to it all: "It is," he says, "no small matter to assist in the birth of a new city." (*TLA,* p. 306) For Jean and Joe, and, behind them, for Nevil Shute, the open frontier of Australia has proven as stimulating and as productive as did the American frontier for its people.

Having established Australia as a Turnerian frontier, Shute develops his ideas in his second novel set in the country, *The Far Country.* Here his concern is with the differences between conditions there and those prevailing in England in the mid-1950s, so that his story becomes a deliberate contrasting of the two countries, one new and flourishing, the other old and stagnant. Jennifer Morton, daughter of a Leicester physician, travels to Australia to visit her aunt and uncle, Jane and Jack Dorman, the now-prosperous owners of a sheep station. She meets Carl Zlinter, a refugee physician from Czechoslovakia who is working as a lumberman, and falls in love. Compelled by the death of her mother to return to England, she is increasingly oppressed by the colorlessness of life there, and, when Zlinter appears to complete his recertification as a doctor in London, they agree to return to Australia and start their new life.

The Far Country, like *A Town Like Alice,* is primarily a conventional love-story aimed at the women in Shute's middle-brow audience. Yet, like the earlier novel, it contains significant parallels with certain of Turner's ideas. As he closed his essay, the historian listed a number of attributes that had accrued to American life because of the frontier experience (among them practicality, individualism, energy, and materialism), and concluded by hinting at the frontier's role as safety valve, its presence supplying a chance for all to start anew. "Each frontier," he wrote, "did indeed furnish a new field of opportunity, a gate of escape from the bondage of the past." (*FJT* [*The Frontier in American History*], pp. 37-38) For Shute, the new country of Australia surpasses the old country of England—or, for that matter, Europe—in what it offers its citizens, and in what they can make of themselves.

Shute builds his argument carefully, presenting Labourite England as a place of unrelieved dreariness and burgeoning mediocrity. Jennifer's father, thinking of the future, can conjure up little hope: "It was easy to say that good times would come again in England, but was it true? In each year of the peace food had got shorter and shorter, more and more expensive, and taxation had risen higher and higher. He was now living on a lower scale than in the war-time years; the decline had gone on steadily, if anything increasing in momentum, and there seemed no end to it." A young woman echoes her lawyer fiancé's pessimism: "What's the good of being successful in England? They only take it all away from you, with tax and supertax." And Jennifer herself, talking with her aunt, has to concede that in England the quality most in demand is conformity: "I don't think it a very good thing to be different in England. . . . It's better if you go along like everybody else."[4] Clearly, England offers little to its people beyond mere survival.

In contrast, Australia offers all the incentives of a frontier society. It offers, for example, tangible, material rewards that are directly in proportion to the amount of work that a person chooses to expend. Jennifer, after watching her aunt and uncle spend close to fourteen hundred pounds in a morning's shopping, has to readjust her thinking: "[She] felt that surely there must be something wrong in spending so much money; her upbringing in the austerities of England insisted that this must be so. The queer thing was that here it all seemed natural and right. The Dormans had worked for thirty years without much recompense and now had won through to their reward; in spite of the violation of all her traditions Jennifer was pleased for them, and pleased with a country that allowed rewards like that." (*FC* [*The Far Country*], p. 126) It is, moreover, a country that fosters forthright individualism, producing persons who act on their convictions and stand by the consequences. When Jim Forrest, manager of the lumber company, authorizes Zlinter to proceed with a necessary but dangerous and highly illegal piece of surgery, he does so because "he was Australian to the core, bred in the country with only a few years of school in town, an individualist to the bone, a foe of all regimentation and control." (*FC*, p. 160) The contrast with England's economic and emotional poverty is obvious.

Even more obvious is Shute's belief that Australia provides the same safety valve of opportunity that Turner

saw in the American frontier. Thus, as early as 1919, Jane Dorman, ostracized by her aristocratic kin in England because of Jack's colonial roughness, looks with relief to life in Australia, where she can escape "all the complications and unpleasantness and [be] able to start fresh in a new place with Jack." (*FC*, p. 75) The most overt and eloquent testimonial to the Australian safety valve, however, comes from Carl Zlinter. A Czech surgeon, a displaced person, and a former prisoner of war, he can equally consider giving up the profession of medicine and starting life anew in Australia, for, as he tells Jennifer, "Here is a beautiful, empty country . . . with freedom, and opportunity. . . . Here is a country where a man can live a sane and proper life, even if it is only one little log hut in the middle of the woods for a home." (*FC*, pp. 209-11) The images that Shute puts into Zlinter's mouth are resonant ones, for they attribute to Australia all the mystique of the American frontier: its freedom, its opportunity, and even its log cabins. The images, like the colors of the Australian vegetation and the spaciousness of its land, constitute a dramatic contrast to the cramped, stifling colorlessness of England, and they enable Shute, like Brigham Young, to say: "This is the place."[5]

Four years later, with two other novels, his autobiography, and a trip to the United States (during which he paid a lengthy visit to friends in Oregon and made a horseback trip into the mountains) under his belt, Shute returns to his consideration of the two frontiers in *Beyond the Black Stump*. Now, however, he confronts the issue squarely, contrasting Australia, where the frontier and its effects are still real, with the United States, where the frontier has closed but the myth endures. Stanton Laird, an Oregon-born geologist employed by the Topeka Exploration Co., goes to prospect for oil on the million-acre Laragh Station in the Lunatic Range of West Australia. He falls in love with Molly Regan, daughter of the unschooled but prosperous homesteader at Laragh, proposes to her, and brings her back to Oregon to meet his family before they marry. Molly, at first amused and later appalled by the Oregonians' glorification of themselves as frontiersmen, realizes that her ways and values are not those of the New—or is it for her the Old?—World, rejects Stanton's proposal, and returns to Laragh to marry the young stockman living on the adjoining station.

Within the novel, Shute echoes two of Turner's particular concerns. The first is the persistence of frontier elements in a society after the line of settlement has moved on, for, as Turner points out, there is a degree of cultural lag inherent in the process of settlement: "As successive terminal moraines result from successive glaciations, so each frontier leaves its traces behind it, and when it becomes a settled area the region still partakes of the frontier characteristics." The second is the realization that the American frontier has closed, ending all that the frontier experience provided for the country and its people: "Now," says Turner in 1893, "four centuries from the discovery of America, at the end of a hundred years of life under the Constitution, the frontier has gone, and with its going has closed the first period of American history." (*FJT,* pp. 4, 38) The crucial point here is Turner's reference to the *first* period of American history; other periods, he implies, will follow, and they may well be less vital than the first. And, indeed, the degree to which Australia retains the vitality that the United States has lost becomes the heart of Shute's story.

Shute has not changed his attitude toward Australia in the intervening four years: it remains for him the place where human institutions confront nature and produce a vital synthesis. His consciousness of the frontier, though, has intensified, and, for the first time, he makes explicit reference to it in his text. He dwells upon the vast expanses of the country, and repeatedly has his characters speak of the effects of its roughness upon their lives—as, for example, when Molly describes her home to an Oregon matron: "We live three hundred miles from the nearest town, and that's only got two stores, two hotels, and an airstrip. We're nine hundred miles from a paved road, and three hundred miles from a gas station. Our property is just under a million acres—that's about fifteen hundred square miles. The priest comes to see us once a year. Things are different in that kind of place to what they would be here. . . . Our country is The Frontier now."[6]

And indeed it is, in Shute's vision. In it origins have no bearing on outcomes: the conditions of Laragh Station, primitive though they are, have produced among the Regan children a Harley Street physician, a civil servant in the Australian Department of External Affairs, and a chartered accountant in Perth, all of whom had their first schooling in a makeshift classroom conducted by a disbarred and alcoholic judge. (*BBS [Beyond the Black Stump],* pp. 64-66) In it the safety valve still operates. Molly's father and uncle, renegade gunmen in the Irish Republican Army with a price on their heads, flee the Troubles, start over in Australia in 1921, and establish themselves as solid citizens, while, thirty years later, Stanton Laird can think of his hell-raising friend, Chuck Sheraton, killed playing the fool in an airplane, and reflect: "In this country, harsh and arid as it was, Chuck might have found fulfillment . . . ; his daily living might have given him the adventure that he needed." (*BBS,* pp. 79, 180) And in it lies the prospect of infinite possibility, of infinite challenge, where "everything is still to do." (*BBS,* p. 308) Idealized and sentimental Shute's version of the Australian frontier may be, but it is one wholly in keeping with that of Frederick Jackson Turner.

Not so, however, the circumstances of the United States. When Shute turns his attention to the Pacific North-

west, he paints an understanding yet critical picture of a society dominated by its past, a society in which the legacy of the frontier has become feeble, debased, and even pernicious. Stanton's home town of Hazel, Oregon, has, to be sure, a legitimate frontier past: it was once an outpost on the Oregon Trail and Stanton's grandfather has many times told him "the history of Hazel as it had grown in one man's lifetime from the first shack in the virgin prairie on the edge of the forests and the mountains to the place that it was now." Now, however, it is just another 1950s-vintage small town, located in a still largely unspoiled part of the country, but indistinguishable from hundreds of other American communities, all comfortably equipped with supermarkets, television, and service stations. (*BBS,* pp. 23, 265)

In Hazel, nevertheless, traces of frontier consciousness remain, just as Turner predicted. Stanton's father, for example, a person of "restless energy," has the frontiersman's drive, though he must express it in civilized ways: intially owner of a cold-storage company and later a rancher, he now runs the local Ford agency and aspires to develop a contracting business, for "the urge to move earth lies deep in the heart of a number of Americans." Moreover, certain of the town's institutional attitudes retain a degree of frontier pragmatism; when Stanton and Chuck run afoul of the law as teenagers, their punishment is summary but token: "In such a place [as Hazel] the legislature acts more directly and with fewer inhibitions than in districts with a longer record as communities . . . [and] it seemed profitless to Judge Hadley to start anyone upon a road that might end at the penitentiary." (*BBS,* pp. 13-14, 17, 50) The frontier has, indeed, affected Hazel and its people, and some of the effects are positive.

Yet, as Shute makes clear, the frontier for America generally has become little more than a simplistic myth that does the society no good at all. Stanton can naively say to his father, in all sincerity, "It's still The Frontier here. Hazel's not the same as a small town back East, say in Connecticut. It's still pioneering here, opening things up and getting new things started. Why, lots of the roads around here aren't paved yet, an' you can go thirty miles and never pass a gas station. It's pioneering here, Dad, still—and will be for a long time," but the once-vital materialism of earlier days has degenerated into an innocent but all-pervasive consumerism. "To look at the magazines," the Laragh schoolmaster tells Mrs. Regan, "one would suppose that everything would be completely different in America, a hedonistic paradise where human jealousies, depravities, and infamies would be unknown. A land where every woman is young and smiling on a sunny background, a land where every man is young and bronzed and wears an Arrow collar and a Stetson hat." (*BBS,* pp. 52, 203) Indeed, as Shute intuitively perceives, the frontier has closed, and there is trouble in Eden.

Molly Regan becomes the agent through which he details life in the closed frontier. The owner of the Hazel hardware store tells her how rugged life is, as she buys a new can opener and looks at the air-conditioned cinema across the street. Although enriched white bread can be bought at the local supermarket, orange bread cannot, and the Laird women ingenuously suggest to her that their home-baking of the delicacy is an expression of frontier hardiness. Her memory of the fifteen-hundred-square-mile expanse of Laragh Station tempers her admiration when natives sing the praises of the three-hundred-square-mile wilderness area outside Hazel. It comes, therefore, as no surprise when Shute remarks that, "little by little, as the weeks went by, The Frontier began to get her down." (*BBS,* pp. 269-70)

Far more disturbing to Molly, however, is her discovery that the frontier vigor and openmindedness that she takes for granted in Australia have been replaced in America by narrowmindedness and social rigidity equal to that of Gopher Prairie. Hazel, for all its claims to frontier roughness, is set a-twitter by her casual remark that her father once sired half-breed children among the aboriginal women, while the Laird family is totally incapable of seeing the parallels between Pat Regan's gunman past in Ireland and the powder-stained exploits of their favorite television horse opera hero. (*BBS,* pp. 290-92, 302-03) Reflecting on these and other incidents, Molly at last speaks out, articulating her grasp of change, progress, and the closing of the frontier: "Everybody here talks about The Frontier, and says this is a frontier town. You're pretty proud of that. But you've forgotten what The Frontier's like. . . . When your first tough guys broke through the Rockies from the East and found this lovely place, they married Indian girls. You know it, and you're rather proud of it. It's part of the frontier legend. Well, The Frontier's moved on." (*BBS,* pp. 298-99) Distressing though the discovery is to Molly, it is nonetheless eye-opening, and she comes to see the United States in a new light.

That new vision enables Shute to drive home his point even as he resolves the tensions of his novel. Molly gently but firmly breaks off her engagement, telling Stanton that she prefers the genuine frontier of Laragh Station to the mythic and mythical one of Hazel: "Where I come from, everything is still to do. I know you'll say that there are still roads to be paved, that you can only get two channels on the television when you ought to be able to get six, and that you can go thirty miles in one direction without seeing a gas station. *There's more to do than that back in the Lunatic.* I'd like to go back and have a hand in doing it." (*BBS,* p. 308; italics added) Molly here clearly speaks for Shute.

The frontier in the United States has closed irrevocably, but that in Australia remains, offering its vitality, its opportunity, and its salvation to those with the vision and fortitude to confront it. His statement is complete.

Nevil Shute is a novelist, not a historian, and to suggest that he began writing of Australia with the Turner thesis in mind is to do injustice to his craftsmanship; there is ample evidence to establish that his initial use of Australian materials grew out of his customary practice of building novels upon his travels and other experiences, and that he thought of *A Town Like Alice* as little more than a story written to pay its own way.[7] Yet there is equally persuasive evidence to establish that, as he warmed to his subject and himself became more at home in Australia, he came to see the country as a frontier society in the American mold, with all that that vision entails. What he saw there appealed to him and led him further into his exploration of frontier elements, culminating in the overt pairing of the two frontiers appearing in *Beyond the Black Stump.*

Shute's fascination with the frontier seems almost inevitable. Trained as a young man as an engineer, he brought to his work an engineer's sense of the appropriateness of mankind's confronting nature, so that in a commentary upon his autobiography he notes: "When I was a student I was taught that engineering was 'the art of directing the great sources of Power in Nature to the use and convenience of man.'" This attitude, moreover, colors many of his early novels, where he explores "the theme of organization: the organizing of enterprises and the coördinating of people." He was, therefore, by virtue of his professional training and early literary inclinations, receptive to the opportunity for community growth and the exploitation of nature that Australia provided, and able to see in that opportunity an expression of the mythic belief that through the frontier experience a person "could battle nature's inscrutable ways and, through strength and resourcefulness, triumph over them."[8] When he set out to apply this belief to Australia, he found in the frontier a vivid and compelling metaphor for his ideas.

His acceptance of that metaphor is enhanced by the events of his later literary career. Prior to the Second World War, he looked to technology for the themes of his fiction; after the war, wearied by his work in weapons development and somewhat disenchanted with technology, he began to explore a more satisfying cluster of themes, "the role of the 'little man' in history and society [and] the joys of finding a new life in a new land." This exploration, in turn, led him to the growing conviction that "history is made by plain and simple people . . . doing the best we can with each job as it comes along." He found ready confirmation of his belief in Australia, with its open land, easy-going democracy, and seemingly endless opportunity; from there to the

Turnerian belief that "on the open frontier a person could be reborn; he could have a second chance" was but a small step, and he took it readily.[9]

Nevil Shute is not, of course, the first author to see Australia as a frontier state, and he quietly ignores many of the ways in which the Australian frontier experience differs from that of the United States.[10] These matters are, however, of little consequence: as a writer he is more concerned with human than with historical truths, and his achievement is of another order of magnitude entirely. Like other writers he speaks eloquently of the freedom offered by unspoiled nature, like them he argues for the importance of individualism in contemporary society, and like them he suggests how the frontier stimulates that individualism. But he then goes on, as others do not, to consider what happens when the frontier no longer exists. His picture of mid-twentieth-century America, still a country of immense potential but one dragging about the corpse of its memory, is a haunting one, for it speaks volumes to his readers, whether British, Australian, or American. England and the United States, he reminds us, were once the lands of opportunity; now, in the 1950s, Australia has become that land. Yet, if only the two older countries can shake off the myths that oppress them, realistically assess their circumstances, and set their goals accordingly, they can regain their lost ideal.

For Shute, the individualist, the literal frontier of Australia is appealing, but as his last three novels seem to affirm, the ultimate frontier is that of the individual person's potential. *The Rainbow and the Rose* (1958) and *Trustee from the Toolroom* (1960) make clear just how far a sincere, resourceful person can go in overcoming the obstacles of ordinary life, while *On the Beach* (1957) speaks memorably of individual fortitude in the face of extraordinary and inescapable—but not necessarily inevitable—disaster.[11] Thus, though he does not explicitly concern himself in these books with comparative frontiers, Shute nevertheless stands by his point. If a society and its citizens can shake off the artificial constraints that an outdated myth—be it Labourite economics, national chauvinism, or Turnerian history—imposes and build instead to the enduring abilities of the people themselves, the glories of national promise may yet become realities.

Notes

1. Julian Smith, *Nevil Shute,* TEAS 190 (Boston: Twayne Publishers, 1976), pp. 9, 104-05, 126. This Twayne volume is surprisingly the only extended study of Shute and his work to date. For a consideration of some of his characteristic themes and narrative devices, see Fred Erisman, "The Ageless Adventure Hero," *Illinois Quarterly,* 43 (Fall, 1980), 40-48.

2. Frederick Jackson Turner, "The Significance of the Frontier in American History," *The Frontier in American History* (New York: Henry Holt & Co., 1920), p. 2. Further references to this work will appear in the text, designated *FJT*.

3. Nevil Shute, *The Legacy* (New York: William Morrow & Co., 1950), pp. 74, 142, 161. Further references to this work, which I will discuss using its British title, will appear in the text, designated *TLA*.

4. Nevil Shute, *The Far Country* [1952] (London: Heinemann, 1965), pp. 76-77, 88, 137. Further references to this work will appear in the text, designated *FC*.

5. Smith unconsciously responds to Shute's use of frontier materials, commenting that the novelist found in Australia "subject matter as potent as that of James Fenimore Cooper—the civilization of a new land" (p. 105).

6. Nevil Shute, *Beyond the Black Stump* (New York: William Morrow & Co., 1956), pp. 298-299. Further references to this work will appear in the text, designated *BBS*. The capitalization of "The Frontier" here, as in later quotations from this book, is Shute's.

7. Smith, pp. 100-101.

8. Nevil Shute, quoted in Smith, p. 127; David Martin, "The Mind That Conceived *On The Beach,*" *Meanjin* 19 (June, 1960), 197; Harold P. Simonson, *The Closed Frontier: Studies in American Literary Tragedy* (New York: Holt, Rinehart, & Winston, 1970), pp. 4-5.

9. Smith, p. 69; Nevil Shute, *Vinland The Good* (New York: William Morrow & Co., 1946), p. 125; Simonson, pp. 4-5.

10. For comparative discussions of the Australian frontier in fiction and in history, see Roy W. Meyer, "The Outback and the West: Australian and American Frontier Fiction," *Western American Literature,* 6 (Spring, 1971), 3-19, or Robin W. Winks, *The Myth of the American Frontier: Its Relevance to America, Canada and Australia* (Leicester, England: Leicester University Press, 1971).

11. *On the Beach,* readers will recall, tells of the waning days of the human race as fallout from the final thermonuclear war inexorably permeates the Southern Hemisphere. It is tempting to read this book as the ultimate closed-frontier story, since, for humanity, there is truly nowhere else to go. Nevertheless, Shute's characters, Australian and American, remain true to his vision of the forthright individual and go on about their business, with matter-of-fact gallantry, to the end.

Harold P. Simonson (essay date 1989)

SOURCE: Simonson, Harold P. "California, Nathanael West and the Journey's End." In *Beyond the Frontier: Writers, Western Regionalism, and a Sense of Place*, pp. 101-22. Fort Worth: Texas Christian University Press, 1989.

[*In the following essay, Simonson argues that the work of Nathanael West can be read as an interpretation of how the great American frontier myth ends, concluding that* The Day of the Locust *is one of the most powerful American novels that deals with this theme.*]

As if by destiny, Walt Whitman's song calling for all Americans to enlarge their souls harmonized perfectly with President James K. Polk's intention to enlarge America's soil. By the time the poet's song was heard, America indeed had swelled to the Pacific. The achievement following Polk's inauguration was remarkable: Texas in 1845, the Oregon Territory and California in 1848. As counterpoint were the pulse-tingling words "manifest destiny," handily introduced in 1845 by the editor of the *New York Morning News,* John L. O'Sullivan, who wrote of "our manifest destiny to overspread and to possess the whole continent which Providence has given us." By the end of the century this moral mandate sent Americans seeking still other continents which, perhaps, Providence had also given them. But within this continent alone, the mandate was sufficient reason to allow the United States to fulfill its role as mother of freedom, a role that in the West meant liberating those people suffering under the bondage of England and Mexico. As one western crusader wrote of the Mexican Californians: "They are only a grade above the aborigines, and like them will be compelled by the very nature of things, to yield to the swelling tide of Anglo-Saxon adventure." The story is, of course, rich in drama. In looking back over the days of the Oregon and California trails, the Gold Rush, the railroads, and all those dreamers of the frontier dream, one must agree with critic Edmund Wilson, who said that California, especially since we took it away from the Mexicans, "had always presented itself to Americans as one of the strangest and most exotic of our adventures."[1]

It would be in California, if at all, where the American frontier dream would be authenticated. Here was the literal end of the trail, and here the Great Promise had to be revealed. Suggestive of this fulfillment is Bayard Taylor's account of the Santa Clara Valley. Commissioned by Horace Greeley to report on the California Gold Rush to the *New-York Tribune,* Taylor wrote that "the unvarying yellow hue of mountain and plain, except where they were transversed by broad belts of dark-green timber, gave a remarkable effect to the view." The mountains "seemed to have arrayed themselves in cloth of gold, as if giving testimony to the

royal metal [in] which their veins abound." The more prosaic reasons pioneers headed west, and on to California, are well known. Ray Allen Billington uses the term, "abundance motivation," meaning "a desire to find new pleasures, gratifications, experiences, and achievements." Most of these reasons had to do in some way with economic or social advantage, explained by Frederick Jackson Turner's "safety valve" theory and the mobility enjoyed by those who went west. But there was that other motivation as well, the one that spelled the call of the wild, the unknown, the mystical. California's gold served as the perfect symbol. For his millions of readers Zane Grey's explanation was as good as any: that men in his western land could come "to a supreme proof of the evolution of man, to a realization of God."[2]

To find in California what is strange and exotic is also to discover its tragic groundwork. With desperate effort the frontiersman had crossed the continent; and, decades later, with similar effort, the man from Iowa had saved his money or had planned his career so that, at last, he could go to California to live the good life. As if the continent tilted toward Southern California, the people journeyed to Los Angeles, which, like some vast organism, spread out for miles while its population increased from some fifty thousand in 1890 to over half a million thirty years later. The prospering oil, film and aircraft industries were in Los Angeles, but people came also to wrest nothing less than human fulfillment and God's special providence for America. By the 1920s, as one historian says, California had come to be

> a sort of middle-class Methodist paradise, with enough sunshine and oranges to give color, enough innovations in the way of airplanes and automobiles and cafeterias to lend excitement, and enough ruggedness—with its jack rabbits and stingarees [stingrays] and hiking trails and surf bathing—to provide adventure.

For the non-Methodists, life in Los Angeles promised to be "one long cocktail of orange blossoms, ocean beaches, and Spring Street." Intent upon creating an exotic Mediterranean culture, enthusiasts named their towns Arcadia, Hesperia, Morocco, Verona; Abbot Kinney spent a fortune developing "Venice," a cultural center near Pasadena complete with canals, weeping willow trees, gondolas, singing gondoliers and imported Venetian pigeons; and with the help of Henry Huntington and others, Frank Miller of Riverside built Mission Inn, called "the Alhambra" of the Pacific Coast by its many renowned visitors who sat quietly in the shade of lemon trees and bougainvillea to listen to mission bells.[3]

All these efforts to create a paradise where dreams come true, where physical and spiritual health is restored after one's long years on the severe Nebraska or Dakota prairie, and where fullness of life has something to do with exotic surroundings kept pace with the flow of newcomers. Los Angeles became the mecca for cultists of all description—"sick survivors of New England transcendentalism," said Paul Jordan-Smith, a long-time Los Angeles spokesman who, in his essay, "Los Angeles: Ballyhooers in Heaven," noted that the milder climate enabled them "to keep the illusion that they have conquered disease through spiritual power." During the 1920s the "religious awakening" in Los Angeles reached such proportions that legislation finally forced soothsayers, fortune-tellers and swamis to operate under license. As the oasis for divine healing, occult science, reincarnation and astrological revelations, the city in 1926 had seven separate churches of the American Theosophical Society and twenty-one churches of the National Spiritualist Association. Living in palaces of opulent optimism or surging along Spring Street, the people seized at whatever offered uplift, be it the faith of some newly arrived prophet, or only a pamphlet announcing still another real estate subdivision, this one perhaps named Eve's Garden. As Paul Jordan-Smith observed, Los Angeles was "less a city of angels than a paradise of realtors and a refuge for the rheumatics." The point, as he notes, is that the newcomers hoped to find their Promised Land in Los Angeles, their "American Port Said," and instead discovered a population of "Iowa farmers and sunburned old maids in an endless chain of cafeterias, movie palaces and state picnics." The city of angels was "just as dull as the traditional kingdom of heaven."[4]

Wherein lies the tragedy? Simply and profoundly in the disparity between illusion and reality, between the promise and its denial. In the American Westward Movement, California came to symbolize the logical conclusion of America itself. Not only had a continent been crossed but in the West lived a new breed (some even called them a new species, endowed, said occultists P. D. Ouspensky, Annie Besant and others, with "higher consciousness") that had sloughed off the past with its stale traditions and built a civilization more uniquely American than anything in the Ohio Valley or the Virginia Piedmont. But if at the trail's end there was only fool's gold, if fulfillment failed to square with expectation, if with unabated frenzy Californians were *still* seeking their Promised Land, then what follows must be despair, first mute, then violent, according to the extent of hope originally proffered. It is this scene of the American Westerner with nowhere left to go, with the frontier closed, with only California at his feet, with shore and waves but no "passage to India," that the pioneer never dared to imagine. The one dream he dared not dream was exactly the one he did not need to dream, for he now confronted the reality that his transcendental self, which had previously been supported by the metaphor of the open frontier, no longer found a safety valve through which to escape. Space had closed in upon him.

It was not merely the need to readjust to a closed-space existence in the literal sense. Living in cities rather than on prairies, accepting more governmental restriction, getting along within complex communication and transportation systems, coping with automation, or adjusting to a thousand other situations unique to twentieth-century urban America have little to do with what it means to face the closed frontier as a metaphor of tragedy. Nor was it that Westerners had not asked the fateful questions about existence. It was instead that they had not asked such questions in terms of their own existence. It became obvious, after finding California something less than what the rainbow had promised, that Westerners still would not force questions upon existence but would rather manufacture the dreamworld they so desperately sought, or else destroy the dream factories, and themselves in a single apocalyptic holocaust.

II

If it is legitimate to trace the Westward Movement to its logical end in California, and if the whole incremental symbolism of this movement can be given a California setting, then the work of Nathanael West must be read as a profound interpretation of how the great myth of the West comes to an end. Many writers of stature have written about California. One immediately thinks of F. Scott Fitzgerald and John Steinbeck, or such satirists as Aldous Huxley and Evelyn Waugh. One also thinks of all those writers who spent their last years in Southern California: Julian Hawthorne in Pasadena; Hamlin Garland and Theodore Dreiser who found Hollywood culture perfect for their spiritualistic pursuits; a potpourri of other writers including Upton Sinclair, Edgar Rice Burroughs, Gene Stratton Porter, Rupert Hughes and Zane Grey; and a handful of foreign authors including Huxley, Franz Werfel and, for a time, Thomas Mann. Yet, strangely enough, Nathanael West was like none of these, just as his *The Day of the Locust* (1939) brings the frontier to a close as does no other American novel.

The critical attention West has received since his death in California in 1940 makes clear that his works—especially *Miss Lonelyhearts* (1933) and *The Day of the Locust*—have found an important place in American literature, primarily because they capture the inevitable tragedy in American frontierism. West's writing is not restricted to this American theme, nor does it place him among only American writers of his own day. Several scholars suggest strong resemblances between West and Dostoevsky; or they see West as living in the haunted castles of Salvador Dali and Giorgio de Chirico; they find echoes of T. S. Eliot's *The Waste Land* nearly everywhere in West. Even West himself in his writing of *Miss Lonelyhearts* acknowledges indebtedness to William James, John Bunyan and Leo Tolstoy. In fact, Nathanael West has contributed greatly to an American view of tragedy. And, as this view relates to the dominant metaphor of the closed frontier, his position in American literature grows ever stronger.

Even in his independence, his work reflects interesting similarities to that of Sherwood Anderson and F. Scott Fitzgerald. Randall Reid, for example, gives considerable attention to the way *The Day of the Locust* and *Winesburg, Ohio* are similar. Like Homer Simpson in West's novel, Anderson's characters long to return to Eden, which "beckons somewhere in the distance." But at the moment of release—defined as "expressive communion with someone else"—they are irrevocably thwarted, and the tragic fact is that in both Anderson and West, "the grotesque is normal." As for West and Fitzgerald, one discovers many similarities as well as the uncanny coincidence that the two writers died only a few miles apart on successive days. Both men came from American minorities, one Jewish and the other Irish Catholic; both went to Paris after college; both created unforgettable images of the waste land, one of old movie lots and the other of the Valley of Ashes; both wrote "last" novels about Hollywood; both, observes David D. Galloway, had "an agonized sense of the ironies of life, and their heroes all embarked on the fatal race for a green light or a silver screen image that continually receded before them," and, according to Edmund Wilson, who epitomized eastern critical opinion, both failed "to get the best out of their best years" because, in part at least, they succumbed to Hollywood "with its already appalling record of talent depraved and wasted."[5]

Instead of succumbing to Hollywood, however, West found there the instant symbol for the theme he had been developing ever since his first novel, *The Dream Life of Balso Snell* (1931). The same relationship with Hollywood prevails in his style, which takes on the kind of radical distortion he later found pervading life in Southern California. More than either Anderson or Fitzgerald, West artistically wove something monstrous and misshapen into his novels, the same qualities the French surrealist painters brought to their work. Like them West recreated a twisted, demented world. It is true he did this before he saw Hollywood, for even in his first two books, *Balso Snell* and *Miss Lonelyhearts,* this kind of bizarre world exists. But his trip to Hollywood in 1933 and his return for good in 1935 confirmed the American correlative. His third novel, *A Cool Million* (1934), demolishes the American Horatio Alger myth, and *The Day of the Locust* does the same to the frontier myth. West's last novel incorporates many of the concepts, themes and styles of his earlier work, but the author uses Hollywood as the locus for this, his darkest and most tragic scene. In Hollywood, West transmogrifies his apocalyptic theme into something uniquely American. One might speculate how far he would have carried his dark ideas, but West was killed in an automobile accident on December 22, 1940, when he was only thirty-seven years old.

III

Balso Snell was published the same year (1931) Nathanael West legally changed his name from Nathan Weinstein, although he had written the novel six years earlier when he was living in Paris. Considering that he was only twenty-two at the time, it is remarkable that this first novel should have contained the key to all his later works. It is equally striking that he chose the name he did for himself. When questioned about this, West answered, "Horace Greeley said, 'Go West young man.' So I did."[6] Since West was always careful in choosing names for his fictional characters, he could not have missed what his new name implied. As an explicit metaphor in his last novel, it also announces the theme found in all four novels and introduced by Balso Snell with the opening epigram: "After all, my dear fellow, life, Anaxagoras has said, is a journey." What preoccupied West in this key novel was the nature of the journey.[7]

The one Balso takes seems little more than an outrageous parody. After entering the "mystic portal," ("O Anus Mirabilis!") of the Greeks' famous wooden horse, Balso sees "a beautiful Doric prostate gland"; he enters "the large intestine" and, while talking with his guide about art as "sublime excrement," makes headway "up the tube." Down "the great tunnel" he comes upon Maloney the Areopagite who, "naked except for a derby in which thorns were sticking," was trying "to crucify himself with thumbtacks." After listening to Maloney's biography of Saint Puce, a flea who lived in the armpit of Christ, Balso turns "a bend in the intestine" and encounters a boy with a diary supposedly written for his teacher, Miss McGeeney. The entries are mostly his "Crime Journal," one signed "John Raskolnikov Gilson" and another containing the boy's long Dostoevskian dreamlike account of how he murdered an idiot neighbor. Putting the diary aside, Balso takes up a pamphlet, again supposedly written by Miss McGeeney's young student, who reflects upon the death of Saniette, a smart and sophisticated woman representing the type of audience for whom he, the youthful student, writer and actor, sees himself as "a tragic clown," one who must "burlesque the mystery of feeling at its source" and then "laugh at the laugh." Balso next spies Miss McGeeney herself—"a middle aged woman dressed in a mannish suit and wearing hornrimmed glasses"—who succeeds in grabbing Balso and forcing him to listen to her new biography, *Samuel Perkins: Smeller.* He finally frees himself, hits her "a terrific blow in the gut," throws her into a fountain, and then wonders if the only people inhabiting the wooden horse are "writers in search of an audience."

He next encounters Janey Davenport, called "the Lepi," a hunchback with a "beautiful, hydrocephalic forehead," who agrees to "yield" to Balso after he kills her lover,

Beagle Darwin. Nothing comes from this arrangement except that Balso reads two letters Beagle had written to Janey explaining that he, Beagle, refused to take her to Paris because he was convinced the trip would result in her suicide. Actually the letters recapitulate her hypothetical suicide and Beagle's feigned madness following it. At this point in his journey Balso "awoke" to see Miss McGeeney, who explains that she has written the two letters as part of a novel. She identifies herself as Mary, Balso's old friend. They make love, his ejaculation being nothing more than a wet dream as the novel ends.

Fantastic parody that this novel is, West is deadly serious about the subjects he treats. There is no mistaking his indictment against art and the patronizing art-lovers over whose heads, he says at one point, the ceiling of the theater ought to be made to open and "cover the occupants with tons of loose excrement." His position against church and culture, especially the commercialization of both, is equally petulant. West subjects "Home and Duty, Love and Art" to scathing parody, sustained throughout by what Balso Snell's initials clearly stand for.

On a deeper level West condemns whatever gets in the way of honest feeling. Here is his castigation of literature, if what one knows about "Death, Love, Beauty" or "Love, Life, Death" consists merely of words that protect one from experience. Equally intolerable as protection against reality is philosophic idealism, which reconciles the Plural into the Singular, does away with beginnings and ends, and appropriates the circle as its illusory symbol of human existence. Such monism, Balso reads in the pamphlet, is like Saniette's "hiding under the blankets of her hospital bed and invoking the aid of Mother [Mary Baker] Eddy . . . 'I won't die! I'm getting better and better. I won't die.'" In the same way Beagle Darwin speculates about ways to avoid the fact of death as he imagines Janey Davenport's suicide. His alternatives are to remain "cold, calm, collected, almost stolid"; to stay in his ivory tower of thought and refuse to disturb "that brooding white bird, my spirit"; to call himself the "Buffoon of the New Eternities" and, like Mary Baker Eddy, preach that life is merely "the absence of Death" and Death merely "the absence of Life"; or to feign either sadness or madness. In short, like a tragic clown, to "convert everything into fantastic entertainment," finally laughing at the laugh itself.

At the heart of the novel is Dante's dark wood, described in the pamphlet and the two letters Balso reads. Here is where Balso's journey takes him. "It seems to me," he reads in the pamphlet,

> as though all the materials of life—wood, glass, wool, skin—are rubbing against my sty, my cold sore and my pimples; rubbing in such a way as not to satisfy the

itch or convert irritation into active pain, but so as to increase the size of the irritation, magnify it and make it seem to cover everything—hysteria, despair.

For this condition, for this irritation of the spirit, there is neither relief nor escape: no Keats, music, mathematics or architecture. This tragic condition is not to be surmounted or transcended. No mystic revelation, no pantheistic apotheosis will come either to justify or to annul it. Only by playing the clown can one cope with it. And, asks Beagle Darwin, "What is more tragic than the role of clown?" The clown pretends the illusions are real, but he knows that

> Life is but the span from womb to tomb; a sigh, a smile; a chill, a fever; a throe of pain, a spasm of volupty [sic]: then a gasping for breath and the comedy is over, the song is ended, ring down the curtain, the clown is dead.

The novel depicts human birth, signaled not by the Three Kings, the Dove, or the Star of Bethlehem, but only by "old Doctor Haasenschweitz who wore rubber gloves and carried a towel over his arm like a waiter." "The tragedy of all of us" is that we are only human, that our father came not as the mythical swan, bull or shower of gold; he came only from the bathroom and "with his pants unsupported by braces." We were conceived, not like Christ, Dionysus or Gargantua, but like the deformed Janey Davenport—"in an offhand manner on a rainy afternoon."

The crucial ambiguity of the novel is whether or not Balso understands what he has read in the pamphlet and in Beagle Darwin's two letters. Does he know where his journey has taken him, and does he discover what it means to play the role of tragic clown? It seems clear that Balso's mystical experience at the end of the novel when the "Two became One," paralleling the moment when he and Mary McGeeney copulate, can only be West's parodical *coup de grâce* suggesting something more closely akin to Sartre's horrible ecstasy. If, then, Balso Snell's dreamworld is one of total delusion, if what he takes as a miracle is only hysteria and despair, then the ambiguity perfectly serves the novel's irony: Balso Snell journeys to what for him is meaningless. His journey to the tragic depths brings him nothing more than the grandest of all illusions—his "shout of triumph . . . victorious, relieved."

More than Balso, Miss Lonelyhearts, in West's next novel, understands that life is a "stinking business." To those who endure it because they are either too witless or, like Melville's Bartleby, too honest to run from it, Miss Lonelyhearts compassionately murmurs, "Ah, humanity." But in his public statements, printed as advice in his newspaper lovelorn column, Miss Lonelyhearts offers much more. To Sick-of-it-all and Desperate and Brokenhearted and Disillusioned-with-tubercular-husband he writes that "Life *is* worth while, for it is full of dreams and peace, gentleness and ecstasy, and faith that burns like a clear white flame on a grim dark altar." At the same time he knows his words fail to meet the needs of those persons who seek his help. The words also fail to assuage his own life of quiet desperation. Miss Lonelyhearts' journey is a *via dolorosa*, a forbidding effort to support promises with facts. "Christ is love" is the promise; the letters heaped on his desk each day are the facts. An abyss lies between.

If only Miss Lonelyhearts himself could believe the promise, then everything would be simple and the letters extremely easy to answer. But he is caught in the condition of one to whom knowledge and belief are vastly disparate. Various escapes beguile him from this trap: nature, the South Seas, hedonism, art, sex, humanism, marriage and home, even drugs and suicide. Each offers some reconciliation; each answers some of his questions. Instead of peace, however, they leave him with only a strange exhaustion, yet with a desperate compulsion to continue seeking, even though no signs of spring, no "target" in the sky, offer hope.

What makes Miss Lonelyhearts a tragic figure is that in a belittered world he seeks order, Christian order founded on Christ's love. "If you love everything," Miss Lonelyhearts reads in *The Brothers Karamazov*, "you will perceive the divine mystery in things. . . . And you will come at last to love the whole world with an all-embracing love." These words spoken by Father Zossima to Alyosha were now taken by Miss Lonelyhearts into the Dismal Swamp, where he has a vision of the world as a great pawnshop and of himself as one who was appointed to set its litter aright. All the fur coats, diamond rings, watches, shotguns, fishing tackle, mandolins—all this "paraphernalia of suffering"—Miss Lonelyhearts confronts, first arranging everything into a giant phallus, then a diamond, and after these a circle, triangle, square, swastika. Not until he has fashioned a gigantic cross is his vision complete. Each shape symbolizes a *Weltanschauung*. The cross symbolizes his own. His decision to act upon this Christ-dream, to reconcile his actions with the Christ-promise, is the desperate wager. "He had played with this thing ['this Christ business'], but had never allowed it to come alive." His gamble is to battle the world's chaos with love.

This gamble is like the turning point of Melville's novel *Pierre*, when Pierre throws himself upon the Chronometrical instead of the Horological. To Pierre chronometrical standards come to represent "ideas celestial" whereas the horological ones represent "things terrestrial." The analogy is to a Greenwich chronometer; when it indicates twelve o'clock high noon locally, watches elsewhere will indicate a different time, say, twelve o'clock midnight. Melville says the former "will

always" contradict the latter. Thus heavenly wisdom, analogous with chronometrical or absolute time, is earthly folly. Melville explains that, for the human masses, heavenly or chronometrical righteousness "is not only impossible, but would be entirely out of place, and positively wrong" in our horological, everyday and relative world. Christ's injunction, for example, that when struck on one cheek we turn the other is chronometrical; so also his injunction that we give all we have to the poor. The chronometrical and horological conceit teaches that "in things terrestrial [horological] a man must not be governed by things celestial [chronometrical]."[8] If he is, Christ's crucifixion makes clear the consequence.

In *Miss Lonelyhearts* the character Shrike embodies the horological. With terrifying insight he knows the folly of Miss Lonelyhearts' living in this world by the standards of the other. But like Pierre, Miss Lonelyhearts crosses the Rubicon and gambles on the chronometrical. He admits to a "Christ complex," and even though his friends mockingly call him a "leper licker," he declares himself a "humanity lover." In the novel's final chapter, "Miss Lonelyhearts Has a Religious Experience," a mystic vision comes to him as he stares at a figure of Christ hung on his bedroom wall. He sees that the real Christ is "life and light." For a moment his room is "full of grace," his identification with God "complete." He has seen Christian order; his pawnshop world fits together into a beautiful Oneness and he with it.

But like the fateful knocking on the gate in *Macbeth*, a doorbell shatters the vision of Miss Lonelyhearts, who goes to the top of the stairs to watch Peter Doyle, a cripple, trudging up toward him. Fresh from his religious experience, Miss Lonelyhearts takes Doyle for another Desperate, Broken-hearted, Sick-of-it-all, and rushes to embrace him with love. A bullet from the gun of Doyle, who has had his own grievances against Miss Lonelyhearts, sends the deluded savior tumbling down the stairs, down into the very horological world he had thought he could transform. Christian love has been shattered by murderous life.

At the end of their respective journeys both Balso Snell and Miss Lonelyhearts supposedly experience a mystical Oneness with all things. As if absorbed in God and made God, Balso merges with "the One that is all things and yet no one of them" and Miss Lonelyhearts experiences "two rhythms that were slowly becoming one. . . . His heart was the one heart, the heart of God." But nothing in West could be more ironic. Balso's expanded consciousness was only sexual fantasy and Miss Lonelyhearts' Truth is only the stage setting for the real truth, namely, that life is violent, not loving.

One might strenuously argue that Miss Lonelyhearts is a religious saint: he first withdraws from the world in order to correct it, he subdues selfhood, he undergoes a dark night of the soul, and then he finally knows the joy of mystical union with God. To support this interpretation, critic Thomas M. Lorch cites West's statement, found in a short piece West called "Some Notes on Miss L.," that "Miss Lonelyhearts became the portrait of a priest of our time who has a religious experience."[9] It must be noted, however, that in the novel Shrike makes an almost identical observation: "Did I myself not say that the Miss Lonelyhearts are the priests of twentieth-century America?" That Shrike jokes at the hollowness of such priesthood is not too different from the way Nathanael West mockingly brings each of his protagonists' journeys to a dead end. To Miss Lonelyhearts and Lemuel Pitkin in *A Cool Million,* West ironically bestows martyrdom. ("He [Miss Lonelyhearts] smiled at Shrike as the saints are supposed to have smiled at those about to martyr them.") Rather than showing Miss Lonelyhearts as a religious saint, West shows the grotesqueness of this identity. Thinking himself another Christ, Miss Lonelyhearts rushes to make the cripple, Peter Doyle, "whole again," but instead, the savior, felled by the bullet, drags the cripple down with him in a crazy reversal of the resurrection. His mystical union with God and his vision of himself as a savior parallel those of Lemuel Pitkin, another crippled martyr, whose last words before an assassin's bullet found *its* mark were: "I am a clown . . . but there are times when even clowns must grow serious. This is such a time. I. . . ."

IV

In his third novel, *A Cool Million,* written after his 1933 visit to Hollywood, West sends his deluded protagonist, Lemuel Pitkin, on a journey that literally costs him his teeth, an eye, a thumb, his scalp, a leg and finally his life. Comic as this business is, the underlying seriousness concerns West's devastating treatment of American capitalism and his complete renunciation of the myth of the open frontier. Out to seek his fortune like a western Horatio Alger, Lemuel encounters frauds and con men of every description, each carrying out the great American prerogative of free enterprise. Deluded by the notion that others are as innocently engaged as himself, Lemuel goes his way, incredulously finding himself in one dead-end after another. The biggest fraud of all is Nathan "Shagpoke" Whipple, former president of the United States as well as of the Rat River National Bank. It is with "Shagpoke" that the guileless Lemuel goes to California to dig gold, an outrageous adventure that leaves Lemuel without his scalp and a leg; and it is also with him that Lemuel travels "many weary months" as the chief attraction of their tent show, in which Lemuel, showing off his scalped skull, is hailed as the only survivor of the Yuba River massacre. For a while the two adventurers—one as naive as the other is cunning—work for S. Snodgrasse's road show, which

features the "Chamber of American Horrors / Animate and Inanimate / Hideosities." With a gigantic, electrically lighted hemorrhoid in the center, the "inanimate" exhibit displays objects "whose distinction lay in the great skill with which their materials had been disguised": paper made to look like wood, "wood like rubber, rubber like steel, steel like cheese, cheese like glass, and, finally, glass like paper . . . pencil sharpeners that could also be used as earpicks, can openers as hair brushes . . . flower pots that were really victrolas, revolvers that held candy, candy that held collar buttons and so forth." The "animate" part of the show is a pageant showing Quakers "being branded, Indians brutalized and cheated, Negroes sold, children sweated to death." Culminating the pageant is a playlet set first in "a typical American home" where a white-haired grandmother is hoodwinked out of her money by a "sleek salesman," and then on a busy street where the grandmother and her three starved grandchildren lie dead while two laughing millionaires, almost tripping over the corpses, curse "the street cleaning department for its negligence."

Duped, defrauded and literally decimated, Lemuel is still not shaken by what has clearly become an American nightmare, complete with West's surrealism. Lemuel, whose grotesque disfigurement contrasts with his innocence, continues to believe in the American Dream, which West shows as defrauding all Americans who, holding desperately to it, go to California to have it come true. Calling on the "Golden Gates Employment Bureau," Lemuel gratefully takes a job as stooge in still another road show, this one featuring a team of men who in the last act bring out an enormous wooden mallet called "The Works" and proceed to "demolish" him. First his toupee flies off, then his glass eye and false teeth pop out, and finally his wooden leg is knocked into the audience which, at this point, is "convulsed with joy."

In this novel West is working toward the kind of mob violence marking certain scenes in *Huckleberry Finn.* But with West this violence more sharply reflects people ready for catastrophe. These are the people self-justified by their own innocent righteousness. The more fanatically they defend the illusion, the more violently and joyfully they make victims of those who, by their existence alone, vex it. This fanaticism coupled with a suspicion that they themselves are victims of some gigantic fraud brings on the riot marking the end of what Nathanael West saw for the American frontier journey. The sweeping, engulfing violence in West's last novel is only incipient in *A Cool Million.* But its terror is nonetheless real, as seen not only in Lemuel's disfigurement but in the riot "Shagpoke" incited in the name of his fascist National Revolutionary Party, a riot in which southern white Protestant citizens of Beulah raise the Confederate flag on their courthouse staff and then proceed to parade the heads of Blacks on poles, nail a Jew to the door of his hotel room and rape the local Catholic priest's housekeeper.

Unlike Huck Finn, Lemuel has nowhere "to light out" to. Illusory as Huck's escape was, Lemuel's open frontier is an even greater illusion. For Lemuel the frontier was closed even before he started his journey, and his innocence could never survive, let alone be reborn. In Huck's world there was still nature, and there was love between him and Jim. In Lemuel's world neither exists. There is only the chaos of violence, brutality, fanaticism and dissemblance—a closed world in which nature is synthetic and people are hell. The great difference between Huck and Lemuel is that whereas Huck recognized evil for what it was, Lemuel perceives nothing beyond his dreamworld. Huck's innocence felt the crush of reality. Lemuel's innocence, on the other hand, feels nothing, even though he is literally torn apart by the real world. Actually Lemuel's is not innocence at all but a parody of it. Nothing tragic marks Lemuel as a character because he realizes nothing about either himself or his world. Thoroughly duped and deceived he dies a martyr for a cause he neither understands nor upholds. He dies a spokesman for the same forces of destruction that hail him as a martyr, the same forces that are intent upon making America "again American," the kind of fascism that will *have* its American Dream, come fire or brimstone.

That Lemuel Pitkin is not a tragic figure does not mean that West suspended this view in *A Cool Million*. Even though West never created a character of fully tragic dimensions, he did portray what can be called a tragic society. It is also true that he depicted certain characters whose dreams led to tragic consequences. Especially with Miss Lonelyhearts, these consequences are psychologically and spiritually credible. But West's creative insights focus more sharply upon masses than upon individuals. His concern is what happens to a society whose collective dream contradicts reality, and whose only way of confronting a closed frontier is by dreaming it is still open. This is why his insights are peculiarly American. As early as his first novel and his reference in it to Mary Baker Eddy, West identified the society as American, and in his next novel he refers to Miss Lonelyhearts as representative of "the priests of twentieth-century America." The society is unmistakably American in *A Cool Million,* and by the time he wrote *The Day of the Locust,* West concentrates all his vitriol upon a single place, Hollywood, and upon a single dream, the frontier. West's cynicism, anger, mockery and disgust cover the general malaise of the modern era; but it is to the twentieth-century American that he brings his full creative attention. Even though his first three books have their own artistic integrity, they serve as a long prelude to his final masterpiece. All that is in the earlier novels is to be found in *The Day of*

the Locust (1939) and the powerful concentration is almost overwhelming. No angrier book in American literature has been written since *The Confidence-Man* and *The Mysterious Stranger.*

V

An inevitability distinguishes West's last novel, as if by fate it was indeed to be his final work. In it the assumptions of the earlier works are not only elaborated but they carry eschatological importance. The masses in *The Day of the Locust* are waiting for the end. They dream with latent "messianic rage" of the last big miracle. No longer are they individually tragic clowns like the characters Abe Kusich and Harry Greener or even little Adore. They are now the "locust" with "wild, disordered minds" and the "awful, anarchic power" to destroy civilization. They are the cultists and mad dreamers, standing before their New Thought shrines and awaiting the apotheosis that the Golden West promised. The sex dream, the Christ dream, the million-dollar dream—all tried and untrue—must now make way for the paradise dream: "Why," says Maybelle Loomis (an old-time Westerner of six years), California is "a paradise on earth."

Like Harry Greener who once restricted his clowning to the stage but who now clowns continuously as "his sole method of defense," the hordes dare not see Hollywood for the dream dump it is. To do so would be, as Lemuel Pitkin discovered, to "grow serious," and at such a moment reality crashes in. In West's novel, society has become clownlike—the fat lady in the yachting cap who goes shopping, not boating, for example; or the man in the Tyrolean hat who returns home from an insurance office, not a mountain. Hollywood, once a stage, is now a way of life, a paradise for masqueraders.

West seems to have had no choice in making Hollywood the setting for this novel. Daniel Aaron points out that West does not merely give a "superficial arraignment of the film colony," nor does he intend "a romantic evocation of Hollywood as epic," after the manner of Evelyn Waugh or F. Scott Fitzgerald. Instead, says Aaron, Hollywood is a "symbol of despair and unfulfillment."[10] It symbolizes the fateful destiny of a society living on illusions.

There is also a terrible inevitability in what Tod Hackett will paint. Hired to learn set and costume designing, Tod had left the Yale School of Fine Arts to come west. It is through his eyes we see the people whom he felt he had to paint. At first he knew little about them except that "they had come to California to die." But as this "very complicated young man" wanders amid the sets and costumes of the real Hollywood, the painting takes shape in his mind. Each fragment, a little more terrifying than the last, falls into place. As prophet-artist he plans "The Burning of Los Angeles" to show the flames like "bright flags." Los Angeles will have a "gala air" as it burns. The people who set it on fire will be a "holiday crowd." As prophet he sees more than a single city gone mad. Angelenos may be the "cream" of America's madmen, and their city may be the first to be consumed in flame, but "their comrades all over the country would follow. There would be civil war." Amid a screaming tidal wave of humanity—a crowd turned "demoniac"—Tod imagines what his painting will show when finished. His vision becomes the fact; his dream of doom, doom itself. Tod, who from the first has made every effort to remain detached and objective, is at the end broken in both body and mind. With his leg fractured by the mob, he is lifted into a police car, its siren only a little louder than his own hysterical scream.

West said that this novel showed "the peculiar half-world" of Hollywood.[11] Randall Reid speculates that the force in this half-world resembles a Freudian "revolt of a mass id against those 'higher' powers which have denied it and tricked it"; or a Marxian "outrage of victims who have been cynically exploited by a system"; or a Nietzschean "revenge of Dionysian frenzy against a fraudulent Apollonian dream."[12] More striking than these suggestions is what D. H. Lawrence called the "inner diabolism" below the surface of American life, or what Melville called the "power of blackness." It is a power only the greatest American writers have probed. It is a power of tragedy, that fateful nemesis which, to prove its agency, destroys the dreamer.

West shows a power of violence beneath Hollywood's facade, a surging force not to be placated by swimming pools, fast cars and movie premieres, and emphatically not by Hollywood's bizarre cults. Throughout all of West's novels this ominous force lies under the surface, breaking out in Balso's dream of murder; in *Miss Lonelyhearts* it is the violence accompanying the sacrament, or stories of gang rape, or Miss Lonelyhearts' own violence against an old man sitting on the toilet cover who refused to tell his life story like another Broken-hearted or Sick-of-it-all. American success-at-any-price accounts for much of the violence in *A Cool Million*. In *The Day of the Locust* violence and prophecies of violence shatter nearly every scene. In a short piece entitled "Some Notes on Violence," written in 1932 when West joined William Carlos Williams in editing the little magazine *Contact*, he observed that "almost every manuscript we receive has violence for its core." The manuscripts came "from every state in the Union, from every type of environment, yet their highest common denominator is violence." "In America," West wrote, "violence is idiomatic."[13] In his own novels there is that peculiarly American penchant for what in *Miss Lonelyhearts* West calls an "orgy of stone breaking." Beneath the physical acts of violence West probes for reasons (which become evident in *The Day of the Locust*) why

Americans have smashed their cultural heritage. Rather than merely sloughing off their Old-World traditions, they have rebelled against them; they have smashed them, much in the manner of Rölvaag's *Peder Victorious*. With desperation they seek a new order.

The new order is the frontier and, inevitably, Southern California. As with Miss Lonelyhearts, who developed "an almost insane sensitiveness to order," Americans who saved their dollars and rejected their heritage journeyed west to the land of sunshine and oranges, accepting the desperate wager to unite with this order celebrated by cultists like Maybelle Loomis, the "raw-foodist" and follower of character Dr. Pierce, whose motto was "Know-All Pierce-All."

One such American in West's last novel is Homer Simpson, whom Tod recognized as "an exact model" for the westward bound. Homer had worked for years as a hotel bookkeeper in Wayneville, Iowa. He had saved his money and had migrated to California for his health. Homer's life in Iowa had been "without variety or excitement," a life of "totaling figures and making entries." Vulnerable as he is to the Hollywood dream befitting his name, Homer instead is stunned by the crazy, violent half-world represented especially by Harry Greener and his daughter Faye. Moreover, Homer confronts his own emptiness, his constantly trembling hands signaling the existential panic he feels within himself. Knowing his "anguish is basic," he thinks of yet other frontiers—of Mexico "only a few hundred miles away" or of the boats leaving daily for Hawaii. Unlike Faye, who has the wild energy for violence, and unlike Harry Greener, who can laugh a horrible, "machinelike-screech," Homer can only cry and, in the end, coil fetus-like on his bed, an escape far better, thinks Tod, than Religion, Art or South Sea Islands.

Homer's "Uterine Flight" as an alternative to the acceptance of life contrasts with that other alternative—violence. Both lead to self-destruction, but it is the destruction of society that preoccupies West, the kind of anarchic energy that impels the mob to have its own blood. Having dreamed the great dream and found it fraudulent, having gone to California and found even the sun a joke, the people feed on violence. With nothing else to titillate their ennui, they devour the newspapers and movies, the endless suppliers of sex crimes, explosions, murder and war. Yet this fare is not sufficient, for theirs is a deeper sickness than boredom. Not only do they feel cheated but, more importantly, they feel lost. They no longer know who or where they are, so successful has been their masquerading and so monstrous are their phony Swiss chalets, Mediterranean villas, Egyptian temples and Mexican ranch houses. Their anonymity breeds fear and their fear breeds hate. These are the dark powers too voracious to be satisfied by cock fights or a staged Waterloo.

The final scene of the novel is like nothing else in American literature, unless it be Hawthorne's "Earth's Holocaust," a story set on the western prairie, where an Emersonian philosopher tends a giant fire intended to consume "the weight of dead men's thoughts." Whatever is associated with the weight of tradition—books, trappings of religion, monarchies, inventions—and impedes human progress towards a utopia of spirituality fuels the reformer's holocaust. What stays untouched is "that foul cavern" the human heart. "Purify that inward sphere," Hawthorne writes, "and the many shapes of evil that haunt the outward, and which now seem almost our only realities, will turn to shadowy phantoms, and vanish of their own accord." Hawthorne, however, expected no such millennium, for what he saw lying in that dark cavern was human pride. Nathanael West likewise envisioned no millennium, and he too perceived that lying more deeply than fear and hate is pride—the pride that leads to war abroad and, when the locusts turn on each other, to Waterloo at home. The Waterloo this time is not on some collapsing Hollywood set.

What West sees is the collapsing American myth of the open frontier, the tragedy of a society too proud to accept the disparity between promises and realities. It is in no way ironic that one of Miss Lonelyhearts' detractors should utter what may be the final truth in West's fiction, and the final significance of its journey theme: "we have no outer life, only an inner one, and that by necessity."

Notes

1. Quoted in Ray Allen Billington, *The Far Western Frontier* (New York, 1962), p. 149; Edmund Wilson, *The Boys in the Back Room: Notes on California Novelists* (San Francisco, 1941), p. 63.

2. Bayard Taylor, *Eldorado: or Adventures in the Path of Empire* (New York, 1949), p. 97; Billington, *America's Frontier Heritage* (New York, 1966), p. 26; Zane Grey, "Breaking Through: The Story of My Life," *The American Magazine*, XCVIII (July 1924), p. 80.

3. Franklin Walker, *A Literary History of Southern California* (Berkeley, 1950), p. 231; Zona Gale, *Frank Miller of Mission Inn* (New York, 1938).

4. Paul Jordan-Smith, "Los Angeles: Ballyhooers in Heaven," from Duncan Aikman (ed)., *The Taming of the Frontiers* (New York, 1925), pp. 285, 271, 279; *Religious Bodies: 1926* (Government Printing Office, 1930), pp. 457-459; *Los Angeles, a Guide to the City and Its Environs*, American Guide Series (New York, 1941), pp. 68-73.

5. James F. Light, *Nathanael West: An Interpretive Study* (Evanston, Illinois, 1961); Angel Flores, "Miss Lonelyhearts in the Haunted Castle," *Con-*

tempo, III (July 25, 1933), p. 11; Victor Comerchero, *Nathanael West: The Ironic Prophet* (Seattle, 1967); Nathanael West, "Some Notes on Miss L.," *Contempo*, III (May 15, 1933), p. 2; Randall Reid, *The Fiction of Nathanael West: No Redeemer, No Promised Land* (Chicago, 1968), pp. 141-144; David D. Galloway, "Nathanael West's Dream Dump," *Critique: Studies in Modern Fiction*, VI (Winter 1963), pp. 60-61.

6. Quoted in Light, p. 69.

7. All subsequent references to West's novels are taken from *A Cool Million* and *The Dream Life of Balso Snell*, both novels in one volume (New York, 1965); and *Miss Lonelyhearts* and *The Day of the Locust* both novels also in one volume (New York, 1962). The four novels are available in one volume, *The Complete Works of Nathanael West* (New York, 1957).

8. Herman Melville, *Pierre, or The Ambiguities* (New York, 1949), pp. 247-253.

9. Thomas M. Lorch, "West's Miss Lonelyhearts: Skepticism Mitigated?" *Renascence*, XVIII (Winter 1966), pp. 99-109; "Religion and Art in Miss Lonelyhearts," *Renascence*, XX (Autumn 1967), pp. 11-17; West, "Some Notes on Miss L.," p. 2.

10. Daniel Aaron, "Waiting for the Apocalypse," *The Hudson Review*, III (Winter 1951), p. 634.

11. West to Jack Conway, quoted in Richard Gehman's introduction to *The Day of the Locust* (New York, 1950), pp. ix-x.

12. Reid, p. 154.

13. West, "Some Notes on Violence," *Contact*, I (October 1932), p. 132.

Conrad Ostwalt (essay date 1997)

SOURCE: Ostwalt, Conrad. "Boundaries and Marginality in Willa Cather's Frontier Fiction." In *Dissent and Marginality: Essays on the Borders of Literature and Religion*, edited by Kiyoshi Tsuchiya, pp. 102-14. London: Macmillan, 1997.

[*In the following essay, Ostwalt asserts that Willa Cather's fiction depicts an American frontier that isolates and marginalizes her characters and ultimately helps to redefine predominant popular notions about the American frontier and its inhabitants.*]

The announcement for the 1994 'Dissent and Marginality' conference described frontiers as having 'disconcerting properties—neither inside nor outside neither known nor unknown. They are where change takes place, and certainties are questioned'. In the case of the American frontier, we might add that 'frontiers are neither old nor new', and in the case of popular American mythology, we might describe frontiers as places 'where self-definition and self-understanding emerge from change'. Certainly, few images have contributed as much to the sense of self-understanding for North Americans as that of the American frontier, at one time boundless and inviting, a testament to courage, it represents the impulse for exploration and the relentless drive to conquer and master the environment. Indeed, in much American literature and popular thought, the American frontier, the Western boundary, exists as that which provides opportunity, unbounded freedom, and prosperity. In American iconography, the Western frontier has and in many ways still symbolizes the New World experiment of the Americas and the democratic experiment of the United States.

Willa Cather's prairie fiction is dominated by this symbolic setting—the American frontier.[1] Yet, quite different from much of nineteenth and twentieth-century American fiction, which tends to romanticize the American West, Cather's narratives represent dissent from the romanticized portrait of the West to paint the frontier in harsh terms. Unlike much popular fiction, Cather's work does not portray the frontier primarily as the place to realize human potential, rather her fictions present an American frontier that alienates and marginalizes her characters—a frontier that restricts and imprisons her pioneers—a frontier that threatens to crush and destroy those who seek to conquer its boundaries. Cather's characters are on the margins and borders of society, they are peripheral, and more often than not they are immigrants, women, or other marginalized groups of the nineteenth century. Thus, in Cather's frontier fiction, the American frontier, that which is 'neither known nor unknown', 'where change takes place', and 'where self-understanding emerges', helps to produce or attract characters who are marginal, who are caught up in this ever-changing and disconcerting place, and who often lose themselves to the harsh frontier.

Yet, Cather's fiction goes beyond stereotyping these characters as powerless in their hostile environment. Thus, she eclipses the naturalists who were her contemporaries and who portrayed characters as mechanical products of their universe. Rather, Cather enlivens her characters through the exploration of different responses to marginalization, and in the process, she redefines some predominant popular notions about the American frontier and pioneers. Cather's characters respond to their marginalization in one of two ways—either they try to dominate the frontier to overcome its oppressive power, or they seek harmony with the land rather than trying to subdue it. Cather's sympathies lie with the latter approach to the land, and this portrayal of pioneers

and their frontier constitutes a portrait of dissent—dissent from the predominant symbols embodying the American frontier—dissent from celebrating the drive to conquer and tame. In the end, Cather's peripheral characters overcome their marginality by learning to live harmoniously with the natural world that makes up their frontier and by participating in an alternative means of existing on frontiers and through boundaries.

In Cather's fiction, the American frontier, the setting and environment for her stories, creates boundaries that bring about the unknown and exist as 'otherness' to protagonists who are marginalized by these frontiers. Characters who embody the popular notions of the American pioneer by conquering frontiers, those who try to dominate the environment, are further marginalized. Yet, those characters who represent an alternative mode of approaching the frontier based upon cooperation and harmony change frontiers from boundaries to opportunities. Given these themes, Cather critiques dominant notions, assumptions, and mythologies of American life to give readers a fresh look at relationships, gender roles, and power structures. This critique becomes clear by examining Willa Cather's frontier as an ambiguous setting that marginalizes characters and by looking at the ways characters respond to this marginalization.

CATHER'S FRONTIER: THE SETTINGS THAT MARGINALIZE

The mid-Western frontier, the Nebraska plains, and the desert Southwest dominate the fiction of Willa Cather. These settings should not be surprising, because Cather's own life was affected greatly by the Western move across the American continent. While Willa Cather was a young girl (1883), her family set out from their Virginia home to seek a new life and promised opportunities 'out West' near Red Cloud, Nebraska. With Nebraska in the background, her own pioneering experience provides the backdrop for the frontier settings of her novels and short stories[2] to such an extent that many critics suggest that 'Willa Cather was under the spell of the Nebraska countryside'.[3]

The prairie became a metaphor for Willa Cather—it was literally without boundary, with no fences and few geographical disturbances to the flat landscape. Such a landscape was disturbing to a young Willa Cather and became for the artist the 'predominant, though silent protagonist propelling the plot forward'.[4] And this particular protagonist had a disquieting effect on the young girl's impressionable imagination. Willa Cather describes an early encounter with the prairie and communicates some of that disturbing sense the prairie was to represent in her fiction in the following:

> We drove out from Red Cloud to my grandfather's homestead one day in April. I was sitting on the hay in the bottom of a Studebaker wagon, holding on to the

side of the wagon box to steady myself—the roads were mostly faint trails over the bunch grass in those days. The land was open range and there was almost no fencing. As we drove further and further out into the country, I felt a good deal as if we had come to the end of everything—it was a kind of erasure of personality.[5]

Drawing from her own experiences on the prairie, Cather wrote not only about the pioneers, the immigrants, and the colorful characters who filled her life and pages; rather, she wrote first and foremost about 'the clash of character and environment'—the struggle between the pioneer and the frontier setting.[6] Furthermore, Cather's fiction is at its best when it deals primarily with this frontier environment that is, for Cather, 'the essence of life in America',[7] if not at least the essence of life in her frontier fiction. It is Cather's fictional environment that sets the agenda for what is possible in her stories. In other words, setting places constraints upon and grants possibilities to the characters and to the action within her fictional world,[8] and this particular setting, the boundary-less prairie, had the power to create the 'erasure of personality'.

Cather's frontier both places constraints upon and grants possibilities to her characters: 'the land is at once frustrating and liberating; harsh and salvific; stifling and enabling'.[9] Therefore, Cather's frontier is ambiguous and unpredictable, neither known nor unknown, neither good nor bad. However, in Cather's fictional world, the natural environment of the prairie is almost always hostile to the pioneers, and as a result, Cather's characters are peripheral and marginal, they are of little significance to the workings of the world; and the hostile magnitude of nature illustrates this.

Cather's prairie novels exemplify best the antagonistic role of the physical environment in her fiction. For example, *O Pioneers!* is the story of Alexandra Bergson's life on the American frontier and opens during Alexandra's childhood when the frontier is still 'The Wild Land'. This land can be endured only by the hardiest of settlers and only a few of them can survive on the untamed frontier. At the beginning of the book the land 'was an enigma. It was like a horse that no one knows how to break to harness, that runs wild and kicks things to pieces'.[10] *My Ántonia* also portrays the land as an antagonistic force that impedes the freedom of human beings. As in *O Pioneers!*, only a few survive the harsh conditions of the frontier. Cather symbolizes this power of the environment in a celebrated image from the novel. At sundown,

> as the lower edge of the red disk rested on the high fields against the horizon, a great black figure suddenly appeared on the face of the sun . . . In a moment we realized what it was. On some upland farm, a plough had been left standing in the field. The sun was sinking

just behind it. Magnified across the distance by the horizontal light, it stood out against the sun, was exactly contained within the circle of the disk; the handles, the tongue, the share-black against the molten red. There it was, heroic in size, a picture writing on the sun.[11]

The abandoned 'plough' is highly symbolic. On the one hand, it calls to mind the pioneer's heroic struggle to till and to tame the wild land; on the other hand, the 'plough' reminds the reader that many farmers abandoned their fields and fled the harsh prairie.

The antagonistic environment of the frontier—the 'bitter cold, scorching heat, and wind without rain—. . . unconsciously shaped and twisted the lives of the people'.[12] This life for Cather's fictional pioneers is physically intolerable; however, nature also governs the emotional as well as the physical characteristics of life and affects the characters' sense of 'self-identity'.[13] Thus, even the emotional states of Cather's characters seem to be intimately related to the physical environment they call home. Not only does the frontier isolate the pioneers physically from the rest of the world, but it also imprisons them emotionally[14] and leads to intense loneliness, insanity ('Lou the Prophet'), and desperate acts, such as suicide (*My Ántonia*), kidnapping (Canute, 'On the Divide'), and murder (Frank, *O Pioneers!*).

Cather's pioneers live on frontiers and boundaries that are counter to their needs and purposes and that create or intensify their marginality. This marginality exists because Cather's frontier is neither known nor unknown, neither new nor old, and her characters are caught between worlds to such an extent that their existence and self-understanding are threatened. The most obvious example of this marginality comes with Cather's extensive characterization of immigrant families who dominate her novels (especially her prairie and frontier novels) and who are trapped between two worlds. They try to continue the ways of the Old World while attempting to exist in the New, and as a result, they lose all sense of identity and purpose.[15]

Nevertheless, one does not have to be an immigrant in a strange land to be marginal in Cather's fictional world. In *One of Ours,* Claude Wheeler is a marginal figure who is caught between the battlefields of France and the cornfields of Nebraska. Marian Forrester, in *A Lost Lady,* lives isolated in the small town of Sweet Water while she dreams of a more exciting life in more intriguing places. She exists on a boundary—trapped between two worlds—the world of Sweet Water and the more exciting world that she desires, and she is as much out of place with her environment as are the immigrant families in *O Pioneers!* and in *My Ántonia.*

Perhaps Cather's most disinherited and dislocated character is the priest, Father Latour, in *Death Comes for the Archbishop.* As Latour nears his death, he contemplates returning to his native France to die after a life of missionary service in New Mexico. However, he had made a recent trip to his native land, and he was 'homesick for the New' World while in the Old.[16] At the end of his life, Father Latour is at home neither in the Old World nor in the New; he is a stranger to New Mexico even after long years of traveling across the desert, yet he is even more a stranger to his native land, France. Latour epitomizes the marginality of Cather's characters on the New World frontier—they are caught between places and times and are at home no where—neither inside nor outside.

Nevertheless, many of Cather's characters stage a dissent from this marginality by changing their frontiers from boundaries to opportunities. The very condition that produces the marginality in the first place also provides the means of escape; the setting, the environment, the character's world is that which makes it possible for the marginal person to overcome marginality. The setting, the Western frontier, is the great equalizer that not only handicaps its inhabitants to the same degree but that also provides them with the same starting point and possibilities. Thus, Cather's settings are neither deterministic nor naturalistic environments that only place constraints upon characters but are places that also provide them with opportunities.[17] These opportunities come through a character's response to the marginal situation created by the frontier. In Cather's fiction, how characters approach their frontiers makes all the difference.

DISSENT FROM MARGINALITY

Cather's characters respond to the harsh and antagonistic environment usually in one of two ways—either they try to dominate nature and bend the prairie to human and materialistic purposes, or they seek another way of relating to nature based on respect and awe for the natural realm. More often than not, the attempt to dominate the powerful forces of nature, to obey the biblical command to subdue the earth, is what marginalizes Cather's characters in the first place—they are simply not strong enough to conquer nature. On the other hand, those characters who receive a heightened insight about the true relation between human beings and the natural realm mold human life to fit natural rhythms rather than trying to shape nature to fit civilization. These characters escape their marginality and learn about themselves in the context of nature rather than in opposition to it. These characters represent dissent because their example runs counter to traditional views of humanity's place within popular American mythology. Cather's picture of proper relationships in the frontier setting not only denies the biblical image that human beings are commissioned to master the environment and bend it to their will, but she also denies the popular American assumption that strength and domination can lead to self-

fulfillment. Rather, self-fulfillment can come only through yielding to nature and, indeed, to others. This constitutes Cather's voice of dissent for those on the margins.

Once again, we see this dissent through Cather's portrait of the metaphorical frontier. The majority of Cather's settings occur on the frontier that is in the process of decline at the hands of eager pioneers who want to use the land for material gain. However, from time to time, Cather's reader encounters an environment that has not been humanized—an environment that still maintains empowering and, thus, sacred qualities. The primordial land, untouched by Euro-Americans, is a favorite image for Cather and a key to her fiction.[18] The ancient land, the land of the Native American cliff dwellers, maintains mystical and mysterious forces in the natural world and, thus, sacred significance. The experience of this land is beyond the grasp of the majority of Cather's characters, but its distant presence haunts these characters just the same.

Cather's enlightened characters who can live harmoniously in the natural and social environment are represented most often by the ancient Native Americans who populated the frontier before the arrival of Euro-Americans. The distinguishing mark of these ancient societies is that they manage to live in concert with the world around them in such a way that the physical environment retains its pristine and sacred character. This is in stark contrast to the advancing pioneers who tend to dominate and master the land in such a way that reduces the natural world to material value. The narratives describing the native relationship to the land are couched within larger narratives and lead to self-discovery for Cather's characters. As a result, Cather's picture of the ancient societies is not simply a romantic view of 'primitive' cultures (like one might find in James Fenimore Cooper's frontier fiction); rather, it is paradigmatic, and it extends beyond time and place to highlight the reason for the pioneer's failure.

Death Comes for the Archbishop represents Cather's use of ancient societies to describe heightened approaches to living in the world. In this book, nature takes on a most obvious sacred quality as ancient religion plays an important role to reinforce the nature of the land as sacred space. The Native Americans in New Mexico care only to preserve their land that is indispensable to the practice of their religion and to their existence. 'Their country . . . was a part of their religion; the two were inseparable . . . their gods dwelt there.'[19] Thus, the native presence, in *Death Comes for the Archbishop,* commands respect for the sacredness of the land and demands living harmoniously with it instead of trying to exert dominion over the land as do the pioneers.

This harmony involves an innate sense of awe toward nature—a sense of respect that leads humans to accommodate themselves to nature rather than attempting to accommodate nature to human desire. The ancient people do not try to master or violate a natural world that is sacred but learn to live in concert with nature, using nature to satisfy only the most basic survival needs.[20] Cather's fiction contrasts this native approach to the natural world to the Euro-American approach. The native inhabitants accommodate themselves to the natural world because they are awed by its sacred quality while the pioneering settler seeks to master and control the natural world in the search for prosperity. The native lands for those early inhabitants are, in Cather's words, 'places more sacred to them than churches, more sacred than any place is to the white man'.[21]

European settlers sometimes but rarely approximate this ideal of recognizing and respecting the sacred character of nature. Father Latour begins to recognize the sacred quality of the natural world. In his travels throughout the wild country of New Mexico, he often associates the land and nature with his religious beliefs and with religious symbols. A juniper tree reminds Latour of a crucifix and provides an appropriate place for prayer; a cave serves as a Gothic chapel; an outcropping rock signifies the relationship of Christ and Peter. Throughout the novel, events and forms in the natural surroundings remind Latour of his own religious heritage, symbolize 'religious realities . . . [and] "holy mysteries",' and allow Latour access to 'the one supreme spiritual experience'.[22] This spiritual experience of the sacred natural world is symbolized by the cathedral he builds from the native stone of the region. This is his statement on the harmonious existence one should seek with one's surroundings.

Besides Latour, a few other enlightened characters in Cather's fiction recognize the proper way to exist in one's environment should come through respect and harmony rather than through domination. This is Alexandra's insight in *O Pioneers!* when she recognizes that the wild land is superior to the settled land.[23] However, she does not make this recognition until after she spends her life in the effort to dominate and tame the land. Perhaps the character who best describes the harmonious relationship one should preserve with nature is Jim Burden, the narrator of *My Ántonia*. Jim's description of the prairie hints at the sacredness of the natural world. 'The whole prairie was like the bush that burned with fire and was not consumed.'[24] This clear reference to the burning bush of Moses implies that the prairie is holy ground that should not be tread upon and made unclean. Jim's description of the prairie is a description of the land that had not yet been plowed under and farmed—it was the land untarnished by the pioneers' humanizing tools. This is the land that is sacred in Cather's fiction, and this is the frontier that provides

opportunity rather than boundaries. This is the sacred land she so often represents in her depiction of Native American Cliff Dwelling societies.[25]

CONCLUSION

Willa Cather wrote about marginal characters—characters defined by the otherness of race, gender, and ethnicity. It probably made sense for her to do so since she herself was marginal in her time because of her ambiguous sexuality and her struggle to become a writer in a male dominated literary and social world.[26] Perhaps Cather expressed her own 'outsiderness' through those characters in her fiction who were outsiders: immigrants, women pioneers, Native Americans, priests separated from their homeland, and the like.[27] Many of these already marginal characters were made even more peripheral by their place on a harsh and unrelenting frontier. All of these characters were marginalized by predominant myths about the New World experiment centred on strength and domination. Yet, Cather, like her characters, was able to overcome those forces of society that pushed her to the margins by dissent from established norms. She rejected gender roles in her own personal life and in the lives of her characters (e.g. Alexandra); her dissent was against traditional ways of viewing male and female, and she demonstrated this through her experimental use of a male narrator (e.g. Jim Burden); she refused to allow immigrant characters to give up their heritage and history simply to fit into the predominant culture (e.g. Ántonia);[28] her dissent was against racism in her exploration of and admiration of Native American and Mexican American life. Cather's marginal characters on the frontier, when faced with the harsh realities of frontier life, either buckle under the pressure of the myth of domination-subjugation, or they rebel against that myth, and their dissent allows them to overcome that which marginalizes them. It is through this latter action that Cather's characters mimic the artist herself, and it is this model that provides Cather's readers hope in the face of their own frontiers and in the reality of their own marginality.

Notes

1. Portions of this chapter are based upon chapter two of Conrad Ostwalt's, *After Eden: The Secularization of American Space in the Fiction of Willa Cather and Theodore Dreiser* (Lewisburg: Bucknell University Press, 1990).

2. Cather scholarship is characterized by the critical biography. There are numerous studies that draw inferences between Cather's life and the effect her experiences played upon the creation of her fiction. Since my primary objective is not critical biography, I shall mention the best of these studies here for further reference. The best full length biographies of Willa Cather are Mildred R. Bennett,

The World of Willa Cather (New York: Dodd, Mead, and Company, 1951), E. K. Brown, *Willa Cather: A Critical Biography* (New York: Alfred A. Knopf, 1953), James Woodress, *Willa Cather: Her Life and Art* (New York: Pegasus, 1970, reprint, Lincoln: University of Nebraska Press, 1982), Sharon O'Brien, *Willa Cather: the Emerging Voice* (New York: Oxford University Press, 1987), and James Woodress, *Willa Cather: A Literary Life* (Lincoln: University of Nebraska Press, 1987). Although not an outright biography, Susan J. Rosowski's insightful book, *The Voyage Perilous: Willa Cather's Romanticism* (Lincoln: University of Nebraska Press, 1986) places Cather's work in the tradition of Romanticism. An older but excellent summary of Cather's life and works appears in Henry James Forman, 'Willa Cather: A Voice from the Prairie', *Southwest Review,* XLVII (Summer 1962) 248-58. See also David Stouck, *Willa Cather's Imagination* (Lincoln: University of Nebraska Press, 1975).

3. Brown, *Willa Cather,* pp. 48, *v-vi.*

4. Shelley Saposnik-Noire, 'The Silent Protagonist: The Unifying Presence of Landscape in Willa Cather's *My Ántonia*', *The Midwest Quarterly,* XXXI (1990) 171-9.

5. Willa Cather, *The Kingdom of Art: Willa Cather's First Principles and Critical Statements, 1893-1896,* ed. Bernice Slote (Lincoln: University of Nebraska Press, 1967) p. 448. This quotation was cited by James Woodress in *Willa Cather: A Literary Life* (Lincoln: University of Nebraska Press, 1987) p. 36. In his notation, Woodress indicates that the quotation first appeared in the 'Philadelphia Record', 9 August 1913 (Woodress, p. 517). See also Demaree Peck, '"Possession Granted by a Different Lease": Alexandra Bergson's Imaginative Conquest of Cather's Nebraska', *Modern Fiction Studies,* XXXVI (1990) 5-22.

6. Russell Blankenship, *American Literature As An Expression of the National Mind* (New York: Henry Holt and Company, 1931) p. 677. See also David Daiches, *Willa Cather: A Critical Introduction* (New York: Cornell University Press, 1951) p. 18.

7. John H. Randall, III, 'Willa Cather and the Pastoral Tradition', in John J. Murphy (ed.), *Five Essays on Willa Cather: The Merrimack Symposium* (North Andover, Massachusetts: Merrimack College, 1974).

8. For this understanding of setting or 'atmosphere', see Wesley A. Kort, *Narrative Elements and Religious Meaning* (Philadelphia: Fortress Press, 1975) p. 20ff. I have chosen to deal with setting, because setting seems to dominate Cather's prairie novels. Nevertheless, other critics tend to isolate one of the other four literary elements as the dominant characteristic of Cather's fiction. For example, John H. Randall and a myriad of critics isolate plot and narrative time as the predominant element in Cather's fiction. See John H. Randall, *The Landscape and the Looking Glass: Willa Cather's Search for Value* (Boston: Houghton Mifflin Company, 1960). Edward A. and Lillian D. Bloom reduce the importance of both setting and plot and tend to emphasize tone in Cather's work. See Edward A. and Lillian D. Bloom, 'Willa Cather's Novel's of the Frontier: A Study in Thematic Symbolism', *American Literature,* XXI (March 1949) 71-93. Finally, Lionel Trilling focuses upon the character of the pioneer in the face of failure as the dominant element in Cather's novels. See Lionel Trilling, 'Willa Cather' in James Schroeter (ed.), *Willa Cather and Her Critics* (New York: Cornell University Press, 1967) pp. 148-55.

9. Conrad Ostwalt, *After Eden: The Secularization of American Space in the Fiction of Willa Cather and Theodore Dreiser* (Lewisburg: Bucknell University Press, 1990) p. 38.

10. Willa Cather, *O Pioneers!* (Boston: Houghton Mifflin Company, 1913) pp. 21-2.

11. Willa Cather, *My Ántonia* (Boston: Houghton Mifflin Company, 1918) p. 159. The abandoned 'plough' image is one of the most famous and the most quoted of the passages from *My Ántonia*. Critics interpret its symbolic significance in a variety of ways ranging from a symbol of defeat and abandonment to a symbol of the heroic struggle that the pioneer exhibited. The predominant force of the symbol seems to be one of abandonment that highlights the futility of the pioneers' heroism in the face of an indifferent environment.

12. Robert Edson Lee, *From West to East: Studies in the Literature of the American West* (Urbana: University of Illinois Press, 1966) pp. 114-15.

13. Eudora Welty, 'The House of Cather', in the Alderman Library, *Miracles of Perception: The Art of Willa Cather* (Charlottesville: University of Virginia, 1980) pp. 22, 21. See also Randall, *The Landscape and the Looking Glass,* p. 84. Randall asserts that nature governs emotions. For example, in *O Pioneers!,* the passion of Marie and Emil, and Frank's rage, are emotions springing from the internal nature of the characters.

14. Arnold, *Willa Cather's Short Fiction,* p. 88. Imprisonment takes on a quite literal meaning in *Sapphira and the Slave Girl.* See Dorothy Canfield Fisher, 'Review of *Sapphira and the Slave*

Girl', in John J. Murphy (ed.), *Critical Essays on Willa Cather* (Boston: G. K. Hall and Company, 1984) p. 285.

15. Marginality in Cather's work is best identified in the prevalent theme of cultural complexity. Although Cather usually appears to be a regional writer, this conception is much too narrow for her. As Elizabeth Monroe writes, Cather writes of 'a new settlement of the frontier by Swedes, Norwegians, Poles, Slavs, Bohemians, and the French, the contrast between the civilizations involved in this settlement, the sweep of American religious history, and the triumph of great personalities over the hardships of American life'. See Elizabeth Monroe, *The Novel and Society* (UNC Press, 1941), quoted in Edward Wagenknecht, *Cavalcade of the American Novel: From the Birth of the Nation to the Middle of the Twentieth Century* (New York: Holt, Rinehart and Winston, 1952) p. 319. For a further discussion on the treatment of immigrants in Cather's work, see Howard Mumford Jones, *The Frontier in American Fiction: Four Lectures on the Relation of Landscape to Literature* (Jerusalem: The Magness Press, 1956) p. 78ff. The problem of cultural complexity usually occurs as a problem of new and old institutions clashing. 'Grounded deeply in the American soil, the novels of Willa Cather nevertheless are attached also by visible threads to roots in the Old World'. See Brown, *Willa Cather: A Critical Biography*, p. 99, and Cooper, 'Review' of *O Pioneers!*, pp. 16-17. Cultural complexity in Cather's work also occurs within the American boundaries. For example, in 'A Wagner Matinee', the cultural 'lack' of the West contrasts to the cultural forms of Boston. Furthermore, in 'Old Mrs. Harris', the cultural forms of European civilization clash on the frontier with traditional Southern feudalism and the new Western democracy. See Cather, 'A Wagner Matinee', and Cather, 'Old Mrs. Harris', in Cather, *Obscure Destinies* (New York: Vintage Books, Random House, 1974).

16. Willa Cather, *Death Comes for the Archbishop* (New York: Vintage Books, Random House, 1971) p. 274.

17. See Wesley Kort, *Narrative Elements*, pp. 20-39 for a development of this understanding of 'atmosphere'.

18. Van Ghent, *Willa Cather*, p. 6.

19. Cather, *Death Comes For the Archbishop*, p. 295.

20. See Judith Fryer, 'Cather's Felicitous Space', *Prairie Schooner*, LV (Spring/Summer 1981) 196; Fox, 'Proponents of Order: Tom Outland and Bishop

Latour', 111-12; and Schneider, 'Cather's "Land-Philosophy" in *Death Comes For the Archbishop*', p. 81 for descriptions of the Indian's sacred understanding of and approach to the land.

21. Cather, *Death Comes For the Archbishop*, p. 295.

22. Sullivan, 'Willa Cather's Southwest', p. 34.

23. See Brown, *Willa Cather: A Critical Biography*, pp. 176-7. The wild land appears superior in Cather's *Shadows on the Rock* as well. See Brown, *Willa Cather: A Critical Biography*, p. 285.

24. Cather, *My Ántonia*, p. 28.

25. Phyllis C. Robinson, *Willa: The Life of Willa Cather* (Garden City, New York: Doubleday and Company, 1983) p. 175. See also Fryer, 'Cather's Felicitous Space', pp. 185-6.

26. Katrina Irving, 'Displacing Homosexuality: The Use of Ethnicity in Willa Cather's *My Ántonia*', *Modern Fiction Studies*, XXXVI, (Spring 1990) 93.

27. Ibid., 92.

28. See Emmy Stark Zitter, 'The Unfinished Picture: Willa Cather's "The Marriage of Phaedra"', *Studies in Short Fiction*, XXX (1993) 153-8; Jeane Harris, 'Aspects of Athene in Willa Cather's Short Fiction', *Studies in Short Fiction*, XXVIII (1991) 177-82; and Reginald Dyck, 'Revisiting and Revising the West: Willa Cather's *My Ántonia* and Wright Morris' *Plains Song*', *Modern Fiction Studies*, XXXVI, (Spring 1990) 25-38.

Susan Kollin (essay date 2001)

SOURCE: Kollin, Susan. "Border Fictions: Frontier Adventure and the Literature of U. S. Expansion in Canada." In *Nature's State: Imagining Alaska as the Last Frontier*, pp. 59-89. Chapel Hill: University of North Carolina Press, 2001.

[*In the following essay, Kollin examines the shift of the frontier territory from the American West to the Far North through a study of the novels of Jack London, Rex Beach, and James Oliver Curwood, maintaining that these adventure narratives establish Alaska and the Canadian Yukon as significant wilderness regions in need of protection.*]

[A]dventure is the energizing myth of empire. . . . The American adventure stories represented . . . the policies and compromises, the punishments and rewards, and the stresses and problems involved in advancing a frontier at the expense of native populations and against natural obstacles. To read the adventures was to prepare oneself to go west and take part in the national work.

—Martin Green, *The Great American Adventure*

[T]he specifically American construction of the modern wilderness idea . . . serves increasingly to justify what are effectively imperialist interventions anywhere across the globe.

—Denis Cosgrove, "Habitable Earth: Wilderness, Empire, and Race in America"

In 1902, the frontier chronicler Frank Norris wrote that having gone as far west as possible, "suddenly we have found that there is no longer any Frontier." According to him, U.S. nation builders "went at the wilderness as only the Anglo-Saxon can," until they found they had arrived at the shores of the Pacific. The frontier reopened, he argued, when a "gun was fired in the Bay of Manila, still further Westward."[1] Facing a national landscape that seemed devoid of opportunities for adventure, many U.S. writers followed this expansionist move and sought new terrain in which to play out their western dramas of expansion and conquest. While some turn-of-the-century writers reconstructed U.S. frontiers overseas, still others such as Jack London, Rex Beach, and James Oliver Curwood relocated their western settings in the Far North.[2] At a time when environmental awareness was gaining popularity in the United States, these writers often discovered it was not enough to merely restage their narratives in a new setting. Thus, many of them struggled to preserve frontier experiences by framing their expansionist adventures in a conservationist rhetoric. In these narratives, the desire for an untrammeled land—an Other to the settled spaces of the western United States—reconstructed heroic acts as the struggle to save the environment. As a result, in many of these texts wilderness advocacy emerged as a form of imperial adventure in its own right.[3]

In his oft-cited "frontier thesis," Frederick Jackson Turner argued that the western frontier figured centrally in the production of European American identity. Using a language of nature, he contended that the frontier experience was crucial to the United States; the "forest clearings" were the "seed plots" of a national self that provided an "expansive character to American life."[4] By the late nineteenth century, however, national advancement across the continental frontier no longer seemed an infinite possibility; the "forest clearings" once considered important for the production of national identity were now transformed into signs of its exhaustion. Turner thus expressed new concerns, explaining that the "national problem is no longer how to cut and burn away the vast screen of the dense and daunting forest; it is how to save and wisely use the remaining timber."[5] Facing a scarcity of U.S. resources, Turner found he could no longer discuss expansion without addressing

environmental concerns. The decline of the western American landscape led him to advocate a conservationist ethic that complemented rather than replaced expansionism; by connecting the two projects, Turner presented both enterprises as central elements in the national mission.

As critics have pointed out, Turner's observations about the closing of the frontier should not be understood as a truth claim but as an elaborate narrative strategy that helped rationalize U.S. expansion. Because the frontier in American cultural discourse is never *not* receding but is thought to be continually threatened with extinction, the national narrative is shaped by a never-ending quest for new lands, the conditions enabling a renewal and extension of an American self across time and space.[6] Turner used this rhetoric to advocate U.S. expansion in Canada, a land seemingly empty, unclaimed, and full of promise. "If we turn to the Northern border," he wrote, "we see in progress, like a belated procession of our own history the spread of pioneers." The "American advance" is now "carried across the national border to the once lone plains" and the "desolate snows of the wild North Land."[7]

Frontier writers also adopted a similar rhetoric about lands located outside the nation's borders. In his numerous adventure stories about the Far North, for instance, Jack London describes the region as a vast "White Silence," one of the world's last untrammeled spaces. His writings typically portray the North as a shifting signifier that includes Alaska and the Canadian Yukon, places whose national identities are always fluid and contested. Depicting these areas as interchangeable terrain, London presents them as a single, unified territory whose undetermined borders and geopolitical location allow U.S. adventurers unrestricted expansion across "the top of the world." In doing so, he contributed to a growing American interest in the Far North. At the beginning of the twentieth century, U.S. desires for empire became increasingly directed toward the region; although still a vague geography for most Americans, the Far North in general and the Canadian Arctic in particular held great romantic appeal as some of the last "blank places" on the map.[8] Adventure narratives about U.S. polar expeditions as well as other excursions across the North functioned centrally in bringing this geography into national consciousness. London's stories of American heroes in the "vast, silent" region likewise advanced these larger sentiments, depicting the Far North as an important new terrain for U.S. frontier adventures.

Often situated in and around Dawson, a place one historian has called an "American city on Canadian soil," London's narratives helped establish a subgenre of the Western that featured U.S. adventurers moving north to Alaska and Canada in search of wilderness experiences, the continuation of their national mission.[9] The transnational frontier London described thus served an important role in expansion, and operated as a crucial staging ground for territorial struggles between natives, Russians, Canadians, and (U.S.) Americans.[10] As a way of justifying U.S. encroachment in the region, London framed his frontier adventures in an environmental rhetoric, depicting his heroes as "ecological subjects" whose care for the northern environment supposedly sets them off from other adventurers.[11] By placing this movement across the border, London's adventure narratives helped situate Alaska and the Canadian Yukon as an important wilderness region in need of protection as well as a new domain for U.S. nation-building enterprises.

Although he was perhaps the most famous U.S. writer of the Far North, London was not alone in drawing the area into the national orbit. Other American authors including Rex Beach and James Oliver Curwood also helped situate the region as an extension of the nation, creating an imagined community for the United States in a new northern setting. This chapter examines frontier adventure narratives written by London, Beach, and Curwood, and traces how a concern for nature in their novels helped shape understandings of Alaska while also aiding U.S. nation-building projects in the Far North. Although investigations of U.S./Mexico borderlands are increasingly challenging the ways we conceptualize American literary studies, U.S./Canadian relations still remain largely undertheorized, at least among scholars south of the border. An examination of frontier novels, however, allows us to trace the ways Alaska—a seemingly remote space on the nation's map—functions to resolve larger concerns about region, race, and nature. As a gateway for adventurers seeking new thrills in new lands, the Last Frontier aided U.S. projects of territorial expansion across the North in general and the Canadian border in particular.

THE GREENING OF AMERICAN EXPANSION

Although liberal ecological rhetoric typically presents nature advocacy as an inherently benevolent project, it is important to acknowledge the ways environmental awareness has also served larger national functions. Perhaps nowhere is this national project more notable than in the struggle over wilderness areas. As Denis Cosgrove points out, the history in which wilderness advocacy emerged in the United States suggests a "closer link with imperialist, xenophobic, and racist features of American nationalism than many Americans would feel comfortable espousing today."[12] This context has much to do with the connections drawn between the demise of the frontier and the racial discourses that shaped U.S. responses to immigration in the early twentieth century. Historians have argued, for instance, that both the perceived closing of the continental frontier and the rise of new immigration were seen as contribut-

ing factors in the decline of Anglo Saxon hegemony. In an era when white Americans felt overwhelmed by the growing numbers of new immigrants from other parts of the world, a beleaguered masculinity sought to reestablish itself through wilderness experiences, the continuation of the United States' frontier saga into the twentieth century. Outdoors adventures emerged as one means of reinvigorating U.S. men by allowing them to test their strength and endurance against the challenges of the wilderness.[13] In this context, the Far North functioned as a site of white flight, a new frontier where Anglo Saxon males could reenact conquest and reclaim their manliness.

A back-to-nature movement also arose during this period which advocated outdoors experiences as a crucial element of modern life. The movement had a wide urban constituency and included diverse interests such as hiking, gardening, scouting, nature study, mountaineering, and even voyages of discovery and Arctic exploration.[14] Although they lamented the unchecked development of the nation's natural resources, wilderness enthusiasts and back-to-nature advocates were typically not outside the very logic of development they criticized; by securing areas of the world as "wild," they themselves took part in transforming "natural" areas into social landscapes.[15] Moreover, in many instances, nature advocates also reenacted projects of conquest as the land they sought to preserve from development was often the home of native peoples.[16] Theodore Roosevelt as much as any other U.S. figure helps foreground the ties between nature advocacy and projects of expansion. As one of the nation's most famous wilderness enthusiasts and one of its most aggressive expansionists, Roosevelt argued that outdoors adventures created "masterful people" who contributed to the country's own virility. For him, the struggle in and for the environment operated as a new heroic adventure; the back-to-nature movement thus became both a means of promoting personal regeneration in the outdoors and a means of ensuring larger nation-building efforts.[17] By expanding into seemingly open spaces, U.S. adventurers could fulfill their nationalist destinies and help resolve the crisis of Anglo Saxonism. Rather than being opposed to acts of conquest, turn-of-the-century environmental discourses often functioned as the intellectual labor needed to ensure that expansionist projects remained an important element in national life.

In the late nineteenth century, western writers along with other adventure seekers traveled to the North—to Alaska and Canada—in search of wilderness opportunities that seemed largely curtailed in the continental United States. Jack London himself visited the Klondike in 1896 but returned to California in less than a year after contracting scurvy in the mining camps.[18] He stayed long enough in the region, however, to collect tales from miners about their gold rush experiences, information he later used as the basis for his short stories and novels. Known as the "Kipling of the Klondike," London did much to popularize the Far North as an important new frontier for U.S. readers, drawing this remote region into the nation's spatial imagination. What is interesting to notice about his tales of the Klondike, however, are the ways they typically erase Canada as a separate and distinct nation. In his discursive remappings of the North, London frequently depicts the Yukon and Alaska as one continuous territory, a primeval wilderness where adventuring U.S. miners struggle against the harsh conditions in order to prove their strength and survival as the fittest of all heroes.[19]

In "The God of His Fathers," for instance, London sets the story along the banks of the Yukon, a place where territorial conquest continues in all its "ancient brutality." British, Russian, and Indian presence in this multinational landscape eventually makes way for the arrival of the conquering Anglo Saxons from the South. The story opens with a description of this event:

> On every hand stretched the forest primeval. . . . Briton and Russian were still to overlap in the Land of the Rainbow's End. . . . The sparse aborigines still acknowledged the rule of their chiefs and medicine men, drove out bad spirits, burned their witches, fought their neighbors, and ate their enemies with a relish which spoke well of their bellies . . . it was at the moment when the stone age was drawing to a close. Already, over unknown trails and chartless wildernesses, were the harbingers of the steel arriving—fair-faced, blue-eyed, indomitable men, incarnations of the unrest of their race. . . . Like water seeping from some mighty reservoir, they trickled through the dark forests and mountain passes. . . . They came of a great breed. . . . So many an unsung wanderer fought his last and died under the cold fire of the aurora, as did his brothers in burning sand and reeking jungles, and as they shall continue to do till the fullness of time the destiny of their race be achieved.[20]

Through a strategy of unmapping, London presents the Far North as the destiny of Anglo Saxons from the United States whose white rule over the land is as assured as it is apparently elsewhere throughout the world. Portraying the struggle for conquest as a timeless U.S. activity, London uses organic tropes to describe American presence in the North, referring to the arrival of these men as a natural event, "like water" trickling through the wilderness. In this narrative, Euro-American expansion in the North emerges as a unique aspect of the national mission. The inevitable drive for U.S. rule throughout the continent brings new heights of civilization to this seemingly primitive land.

While western tales of this period typically featured the migration of an easterner whose own exhausted lands led them to move west, London's tales of expansion often chronicled the nation's expansionist drive to the North, and featured westerners who travel to Alaska and Canada in order to rejuvenate the United States' dying frontier ethic. Situating the North as an exotic new terrain in which to stage his local color literature, London once described the region as a "vast wilderness" encompassing "hundreds of thousands of square miles" that are "as dark and chartless as Darkest Africa."[21] Employing colonial motifs reminiscent of writers such as Rudyard Kipling and H. Rider Haggard, London conflated U.S. wilderness fantasies with British imperial desires in India and Africa, using a similar setting and plot in a manner that did not go unnoticed by audiences.[22] In a review of a collection of London's Northland tales, for instance, one writer suggested that "what Kipling has done for India . . . Jack London has done for the Arctic."[23] Another reviewer went on to praise London for outdoing the famous British adventure writer, claiming that he "goes farther than Kipling could go. His life in the North is more primitive, more elemental, than Kipling's Indian jungle life could possibly be."[24] Other reviewers elaborated on the importance of London's new choice of setting, especially appreciating the exotic possibilities offered by the Northland stories. "Life within the Arctic circle is so far beyond the stretch of our imagination that we scarcely reckon it in as a part of our world," one reviewer explained.[25] Another reviewer commented with enthusiasm that the Far North of London's narratives "has succeeded the Far West as the haunt of the adventurer, and opened up a new field to the writer of short stories."[26]

Born and raised in Oakland, California, London once expressed nostalgia for the western landscapes of the nation's past, lamenting what he considered to be the decline of the "old frontier." He confessed, "I realize that much of California's romance is passing away, and I intend to see to it that I, at least, shall preserve as much of that romance as is possible for me."[27] As historian Kevin Starr points out, frontier narratives written before the 1848 gold rush often portray California as an idealized agrarian landscape, the "cutting edge of the American Dream" where frontier experiences continue to be forged and where pastoral opportunities associated with Jeffersonian agrarian democracy might still be enacted. By the time London was writing, however, the Golden State no longer seemed to offer such promise. As Starr argues, London's descriptions of the California landscape often foreground the region's demise through signs of its ecological decline; his stories frequently portray the state as an exhausted space littered with "broken fences, overgrown roads, untended grapevines, crumbling adobe barns, and deserted mine shafts."[28]

In his Northland adventure narratives, London contrasts the decline of California with the possibilities offered by the Far North, a theme that figures centrally in his novel *Smoke Bellew*. The text opens as the main character, Christopher Bellew, is commissioned by a California newspaper editor to write stories about San Francisco that contain "the real romance and glamour and color of the place."[29] The job turns out to be a thinly veiled challenge, for, as the editor confesses, the project of writing "real" adventure stories set in San Francisco has become an almost impossible task. While California "has always had a literature of her own," he explains, "she hasn't any now." The literary exhaustion facing California leads Bellew on a quest for narrative. After hearing news of the gold strike in the Klondike, he proclaims that "the days of '49 are over." Later, Bellew follows the scores of Euro-American adventures on their way to the days of '98, thus reshaping the nation's east-west expansionist trajectory into a movement from south to north. As the character explains, the opportunities offered by the Yukon gold rush are too good to pass up; the stories that will soon emerge from the region, he argues, are sure "to be big" (1, 12-13).

London's most famous text, *The Call of the Wild,* also presents the Canadian North as an important wilderness area for U.S. adventurers. Buck, the canine hero of *The Call of the Wild,* travels between Alaska and the Yukon, enacting his own back-to-nature movement when he "goes native," leaving his human companion, John Thornton, for life with a pack of northern wolves. The text reverses the project of expansion; at one point, for instance, Buck is sold to two French Canadians, a "swarthy" figure named Perrault and a "black-faced giant" and "half-breed" named François, who enter the Southland and exploit U.S. resources in the form of animal labor.[30] As miners crisscross back and forth between the Yukon and Alaska in the story, London erases geographical distinctions, celebrating the primitive, uncultivated qualities of the Far North while imaginatively claiming Canadian terrain for the United States. The constantly shifting settings in the text have often confused U.S. critics who associate the narrative with Alaska; following in London's footsteps, they help contribute to a national habit of erasing distinctions between the United States and Canada.[31] Such instances of border confusion are more than mere geographical oversights on the part of U.S. critics and writers. Instead, they foreground the ways wilderness ideology itself operates in the service of domination: by presenting the Yukon as wild, uncultivated terrain, the discourse of wilderness in U.S. culture becomes an expansionist gesture that suspends territorial boundaries and national jurisdictions across a given space.

As the gold rush drives London's U.S. adventurers north to Canada, the characters also adopt a colonial attitude toward the region, moving through the land in hopes of amassing great wealth yet rarely staying in the region once they've made their fortunes. In his story "To the Man on Trail," for instance, London tells of U.S. miners situated north of the border who experience "vague yearnings for the sunnier pastures of the Southland,

where life promised something more than a barren struggle with cold and death."[32] London's novel *Burning Daylight* also opens with a depiction of the Far North as a silent, dead world, sealed off from the rest of "civilization" until the main character Elam Harnish arrives and brings it to life.[33] At one point while staying in the Yukon, London's hero tells other pioneers that he won't leave the region for the "outside" until he gets his "pile." He later announces his plans to "farm gold," an act that positions him as the quintessential U.S. figure, the agrarian hero situated, this time, in the Canadian North (32, 100).

Harnish's experiences in the "wild" also provide him with an expansive American self; he is described, for instance, as "too much" a man, "magnificently strong," and "almost bursting with a splendid virility," a figure unable to stay confined within the boundaries of the self or, as it turns out, the boundaries of his nation.[34] Because of these adventures, few men know him by any other name than "Burning Daylight," a title given to him "because of his habit of routing his comrades out of their blankets with the complaint that daylight was burning." A trailblazer, nation builder, and U.S. prospector on Canadian soil, Harnish is presented as the first white man to cross the "bleak, uncharted vastness" of the Chilkoot Pass to the Klondike, and a pioneer who "had made history and geography." This "King of the Klondike" secures U.S. rule throughout the "vast and frozen" terrain, earning a reputation for saving civilization from peril in the North. "Passing along the streets of Dawson, all heads turned to follow him . . . scarcely taking their eyes from him as long as he remained in their range of vision. . . . He was the Burning Daylight of scores of wild adventures, the man who carried word to the ice-bound whaling fleet across the tundra wilderness to the Arctic Sea, who raced mail from Circle to Salt Water and back again in sixty days, who saved the whole Tanana tribe from perishing in the winter of '91." As a frontier hero, Harnish helps stave off the threats to U.S. nation building in the Far North. He aids commercial whaling activities, keeps communication facilities intact, and helps to rescue rather than destroy the native population. His enormous reputation penetrates the farthest reaches of the "white wilderness," where he becomes an archetypal masculine figure for other Euro-American adventurers to emulate (5, 30, 68, 108, 124, 125).

In order to secure authority in the region, Harnish erases Anglo-Canadian and First Nations claims to the land and, through racial cross dressing, literally takes the place of the land's original inhabitants. At one point, for instance, we are told that Harnish's appearance has an "Indian effect": his hair is straight and black, his face lean and slightly long, and his garb made of "soft-tanned moccasins of moosehide, beaded in Indian designs." Yet in spite of these "native" qualities, the character's inherent domination as an Anglo-Saxon adventurer soon emerges; endowed with a unique destiny to rule the continent, Harnish and his conquering activities are accepted and even anticipated by the other characters in the novel. The Tagish guide Kama, for instance, describes Harnish as a nation-building figure whose presence overshadows all others in the region. Kama's "attitude toward Daylight was worshipful. Stoical, taciturn, proud of his physical prowess, he found all these qualities incarnated in his white companion. Here was one that excelled in the things worth excelling in, a man-god . . . Kama could not but worship. . . . No wonder the race of white men conquered, was his thought, when it bred men like this man. What chance had the Indian against such a dogged, enduring breed?" In staging this moment of racial envy, London establishes his own supremacy while presenting the Indian as doomed to vanish from the land. Kama thus greets the rise of U.S. rule in the Canadian North as an inevitable and unregrettable event. A spectator who contemplates the superiority of the Western "man-god," Kama watches as the Anglo-Saxon nation builders from the south descend upon the region in a conquering mode that necessarily contributes to his own demise (7-8, 44).

While London presents the downfall of indigenous rule as an unfortunate but inevitable result of U.S. encroachment in the region, he responds differently to the demise of wilderness. As Harnish soon learns, the frontier adventures that U.S. miners enact in the Canadian Yukon threaten to destroy the landscape so central to his personal and national rejuvenation. At one point in the novel, he gazes out over the mining grounds of Eldorado Creek and Bonanza, and comes face to face with the devastating ecological impact of the "stampeders":

> It was a scene of vast devastation. The hills, to their tops, had been shorn of trees, and their naked sides showed signs of goring and perforating that even the mantle of snow could not hide. . . . A blanket of smoke filled the valleys and turned the gray day to melancholy twilight. Smoke arose from a thousand holes in the snow, where, deep down on bed-rock, in the frozen muck and gravel, men crept and scratched and dug, and even built more fires to break the grip of the frost. . . . The wreckage of the spring washing appeared everywhere—piles of sluice-boxes, sections of elevated flumes, huge water-wheels,—all of the debris of an army of gold-mad men. . . . He looked at the naked hills and realized the enormous wastage of wood that had taken place.
>
> (117)

Like an invading army, the "gold-mad men" plunder and pillage the Yukon in search of their fortunes, leaving a ravaged landscape in their wake. This sight shocks Harnish, who realizes that frontier adventures cannot be sustained in the region unless careful planning is implemented. Becoming perhaps one of the earliest charac-

ters in U.S. literary history to grapple with the possibilities of "corporate green," Harnish decides something must be done to curb this waste. According to him, the ecological devastation emerged from the inefficient mining practices of individuals who extract natural resources with little interest in the cumulative impact on the environment. As he explains, this method "was a gigantic inadequacy. Each worked for himself, and the result was chaos . . . it cost one dollar to mine two dollars, and for every dollar taken out by their feverish, unthinking methods another dollar was left hopelessly in the earth" (118). Historians have recently documented similar scenes of environmental destruction in the region, pointing out that during their rush to the mine fields, careless stampeders set endless forest fires in the Yukon, depleted the region's wildlife, damaged nearby streams, and left huge tailings in their wake.[35]

In other writings, London also details the damage caused by miners who show little concern for treading lightly on the land. In his novel *Daughter of the Snows,* for instance, the main character Frona Welse feels "vaguely disturbed by the throbbing rush of gold-mad men" who cross Dyea on their way to the Canadian border.[36] On the grassy flat where she played as a child, "ten thousand men tramped ceaselessly up and down, grinding the tender herbage into the soil and mocking the stony silence. And just up the trail were ten thousand men who had passed by, and over the Chilcoot were ten thousand more." Frona Welse notes, too, that the miners cared little about their impact on the natural landscape: they "laughed at the old Dyea River and gored its banks deeper for the men who were to follow." On the other side of the pass in Canada, the men continued to trash the trails, leaving behind their "overthrown tents and caches." As they made their trek in an "endless string," the men formed a "black line across a dazzling stretch of ice," becoming fainter and smaller until they "squirmed and twisted like a column of ants" (17, 39).

In *Burning Daylight,* however, the main character tries to distinguish himself from other U.S. miners by halting the environmental damage. Using the discourses of efficiency and expertise so central to the Progressive-era conservation movement, Harnish advocates resource management as a means of solving the region's environmental problems.[37] This conservationist project authenticates his presence in the region, enbling him to become an exceptional figure in the Far North, no longer an enemy of nature but its advocate, someone who reconfigures the invasion of Canada as a green activity. By endowing his character with environmental expertise, London effectively reshapes nation-building events. Rewriting a history of conquest, he transforms U.S. expansionist activities in Canada into an ecofriendly enterprise. In her recent study of environmental history and the West, Patricia Limerick addresses the problems that arose in the wake of western mining rushes in a very different manner. As she explains, mining rushes often had profoundly negative consequences for the people living in the region. In particular, these events

> created the maximum degree of friction with Indians and set in motion the process that would leave them displaced, removed, and relocated. It is hard to imagine a system that could create more in the way of troubles for Indians: the discovery of precious metals and the movement to exploit them . . . flung white Americans around the Western landscape, into Indian terrain, in a way that left few areas untouched, and also left few reasons in the minds of the prospectors and miners as to why they should restrain themselves and their ambitions until a better arrangement could be made with the natives. . . . White Americans in mining rushes were clearly, unmistakably newcomers. . . . The recentness of their own arrival[, however,] did not cause them a moment's hesitation when it came to claiming the status of the legitimate occupants, the people who had the right to claim and use the local resources and to exclude and brand as illegitimate and undeserving people of other nationalities.[38]

London's narrative largely sidesteps this problem of legitimacy. Combining environmental awareness with an appeal to the regulated capitalist development of the region, the frontier hero in *Burning Daylight* gains a reputation by presenting U.S. rule in the Far North as an ecologically benevolent project. What sets this figure apart from other miners, London suggests, is his environmental vision, his foresight in noting that frontier adventures inevitably face exhaustion unless something is done to stop ecological devastation. According to this logic, the only way for the nation to curb economic catastrophe, the closing of the northern frontier, and the decline of Anglo-Saxon masculinity is to adopt a "green" lifestyle and a rhetoric of wilderness.

An American Leatherstocking in Canada

After the days of adventure begin to wane in the Far North, Harnish follows the lead of other U.S. miners who, "having made their strike . . . headed south for the States, taking a furlough from the grim Arctic battle." He leaves the frozen Northland and resettles in California to try his hand at a new "game," this time the world of high finance. As it turns out, Harnish's experiences in the Klondike enable him to "grubstake" his economic adventures in the Southland. Upon arriving in San Francisco, however, Harnish learns that his earlier fame had died out and that in "no blaze of glory" did he descend upon San Francisco. "Not only had he been forgotten, but the Klondike along with him. The world was interested in other things, and the Alaskan adventure, like the Spanish War, was an old story." The Klondike adventure—depicted here as an Alaskan event—appears in a league with other U.S. imperialist

adventures; both the gold rush and the Spanish American War are forgotten as the nation moves on to a new chapter of its history. Rather than feeling dejected, Harnish becomes excited by his invisibility, for it indicates to him how much "bigger this new game" is, when a man such as himself with his fortune and history passes unnoticed in a crowd. Entering what he calls "another kind of wilderness," the character confronts the world of capitalist adventures where he undergoes various losses and gains but finally multiplies his wealth several times.[39] The urban wilderness adventures Harnish experiences in San Francisco, however, prove less satisfying than the endeavors he carried out in the Far North. After spending several years battling other capitalists, he begins to feel the toll the urban wilderness has taken on his health, his "city-rotted body" no longer serving as the glorious receptacle of Anglo-Saxon virility (111, 123, 188).

The back-to-nature theme with its dual rhetoric of expansionism and environmentalism helps reverse the character's decline, a resolution London introduces through the figure of Dede Mason, a stenographer in Harnish's office. A lover of the outdoors and avid reader of Kipling's poetry, Mason disapproves of Harnish's capitalist enterprises and soon educates him about the regenerative qualities offered by the Californian landscape. Leading him through the mountains and the valleys, she teaches him to enjoy the "virgin wild," a natural landscape where "[n]o axe had invaded, and the trees died only of old age and stress of winter storm" (187). The novel ends as the main character gives up his financial struggles for a more peaceful agrarian existence in Sonoma Valley. The conversion to the pastoral dream appears at the close of the novel, when Harnish accidentally discovers gold on his plot of land; quickly covering it up with dirt, the character renounces his former way of life one last time.

Elizabeth Cook-Lynn has criticized white writers for their obsession with telling tales of a fondly remembered colonial past. The conquest of Indian lands by European peoples, she observes, is still largely portrayed in U.S. history and literature "as a benign movement directed by God, a movement of moral courage and physical endurance, a victory for all humanity."[40] Cook-Lynn's comments about the framing of conquest are meaningful in discussions of London's Northland adventure narratives. The environmental rhetoric featured in his stories invariably situates U.S. expansion as a "kinder, gentler" activity. This language appears in his adventure narratives as the Anglo-Saxon hero emerges not as a destroyer of the natural terrain or invader of indigenous lands, but a friend of the environment, a helpful ecological adviser. Throughout his texts, a concern for nature becomes incorporated into a national sense of self, where it prolongs U.S. frontier activities into the twentieth century. London's environmental writings thus foreground the territorial uses of wilderness rhetoric as nature advocacy becomes an important weapon in sustaining U.S. nation-building projects throughout the North. Denis Cosgrove makes a similar argument about contemporary nature rhetoric, pointing to connections between today's wilderness advocacy and U.S. colonial interventions across the globe. As Cosgrove observes, the wilderness rhetoric expressed today, though seemingly benign, often uses "the same language of pioneering adventure" and is frequently located "in the same theaters of snow, desert, and jungle" as "their colonial forebears" in the nineteenth century.[41]

APPROPRIATING THE NORTH

Throughout American literary history, London has been classified as a western writer, and his stories set in the wilds of Alaska and Canada have been largely understood as western narratives. This classification of London and his work as *western* appears mainly because the United States does not have a strong tradition of writing the North like Canada does. London's frontier narratives are thus interesting for the ways they borrow and further develop the idea of the North, an emerging icon of Canadian nationalism that appeared during the late nineteenth century as a means of establishing Canada's cultural differences from the United States.[42] While other non-Canadian writers also adopted the iconography of the North, London proved to be the most successful, his name so closely associated with the Klondike that the region is still commonly misrecognized as U.S. terrain.[43] His production of a "Northland Leatherstocking" points to the ways that frontier adventure involved northern as well as western lands.[44] Although U.S. expansion is still widely understood as a drive from east to west and north to south, London's stories remind us that the push also occurred in other geographical directions, toward the north through Alaska and from there east into Canada.

Throughout history, a long line of U.S. politicians have advanced a similar vision of expansion, endorsing an ideology of continentalism, the drive for U.S. rule from the "Arctic to the Tropics." Continentalism largely influenced the foreign policy of William Henry Seward, the secretary of state who negotiated the 1867 purchase of Alaska from Russia. In a speech he delivered in 1846, for instance, Seward contended that the United States was "destined to roll its resistless waves to the icy barrier of the North,"[45] and claimed that the "enterprising and ambitious people" in Canada were building "excellent states to be admitted into the American union."[46] As secretary of state, Seward later secured the purchase of Alaska in the hope that the rest of Canada would follow suit and join the United States. An emerging Canadian nationalism, however, ended the northward march of the United States. During the same year that the United States purchased Alaska, Canadian leaders bought out the Hudson's Bay Company and annexed British Columbia in order to stop U.S. encroachment in the region. Although they faced new obstacles, many U.S. leaders continued to express desires for continental expansion, and even after the 1860s fears emerged north of the border that the United States might claim areas in western and northern Canada.[47] These anxieties have not abated in the present era, as the United States continues to extend itself onto Canadian soil in new ways; a postwar transnational highway, environmental pollution, polar expeditions, military installations, free trade agreements, and various other forms of cultural imperialism represent only a few instances of more recent U.S. border violations in Canada.[48]

WRITING THE TRANSNATIONAL WEST

Jack London was not the only U.S. writer to popularize the Far North as a site for frontier adventures or to depict expansion into the region as a rightful and benevolent activity. Rex Beach has also been identified as a northern writer; his novel *The Spoilers* (1905), filmed five times beginning in the silent era, was loosely based on his experiences in the northern gold rushes at the turn of the last century.[49] The environmental narrative that London used to frame his adventure narratives also appears in Beach's novel *The World in His Arms*. Set in the 1860s in San Francisco and Sitka, the capital city of Russian America, the novel reminds readers that the region comprising present-day Alaska functioned at one time as a multinational frontier with Russian, Spanish, British, and U.S. commercial interests competing in the area. Even as the novel makes use of this history, however, Beach portrays the space as rightfully American. His protagonist, Jonathan Clark, is a Boston fur hunter who raids Russian waters in search of endangered sea otters. The character falls in love with Marina Selanova, the niece of the Russian governor, and then spends the rest of the novel convincing her to marry him. Clark also devises a clever scheme to enable U.S. expansion in the North, employing conservationist arguments that eventually convince the Russian government to turn the land over to the Americans.

Beach sets up this turn of events by describing the slaughter of seals in the U.S. fur industry. "It was bloody, heartless work which none of the white men enjoyed in the least. As a matter of fact, they hated it," he writes. "Jonathan Clark, for one, considered this wholesale destruction of harmless and bewildered creatures a thoroughly dirty and degrading business. He was ready to wash his hands of it in more ways than one."[50] As a poacher on foreign soil, Clark is an unlikely figure to espouse ideas of ecology in this context, yet he somehow makes a convincing argument to the governor after he is caught raiding Russian waters. "Your country took Alaska for the sea otters. They're gone, and the seals, which constitute the principal remaining source of revenue, are going the same way," Clark tells him. "You probably won't believe that a man of my sort can have a respect—a reverence, I may say—for the wonders of nature. But a rogue can revere beauty or grandeur and resent their destruction. Those fur seals are miraculous; it's a sacrilege to destroy them" (121). Persuading the governor to rethink Russia's territoriality, Clark sets in motion a series of events that enables the United States to purchase Alaska, a move imagined in the story as motivated as much by ecological concerns as by economic ones.

Throughout his career, Beach was a prolific writer of Westerns, with many of his stories published in the mass-circulation magazines that were a common venue for the genre in the early twentieth century. Like other short-story Westerns of the period, his narratives typically feature a male society in which women occupy minor roles. Set in a picturesque landscape always distinct from the urbanized East, the stories tended toward melodrama, employing over-the-top humor and emphasizing explosive physical action between the male characters who are presented as ideal frontier types, eager for adventure and intrigue.[51] After Glenister, the protaganist of *The Spoilers,* arrives in Nome, for instance, he announces, "This is my country. It's in my veins, this hunger for the North. I grow. I expand."[52] The description announces the arrival of a U.S. hero literally bursting with the urge for adventure. Like London's characters, Beach's expansionist heroes do not remain in Alaska; instead, their constant border crossings erase distinctions between Alaska and the Canadian Yukon as the characters struggle to take part in new outdoor adventures.

In a similar way, when Pierce Phillips, the protaganist in Beach's 1918 novel, *The Winds of Chance,* arrives at the international boundary on his way to the Klondike goldfields, he confronts the Canadian government's strict new mining regulations. "A ton of provisions and a thousand dollars!" the character exclaims. "Why that was absurd, out of all possible reason! It would bar the way to fully half this rushing army; it would turn men back at the very threshold of the golden North."[53] The "rushing army" or crowd of U.S. stampeders who follow in his wake share this frustration. Upon hearing the decree, they, too, voice their "indignation and bitter resentment." For Phillips, the Mounties' decision represents nothing less than the exercise of a "tyrannical power aimed at [his] ruin." Rather than becoming discouraged, however, he contends, "Most fellows would quit and go home but I shan't. I'm going to win out, somehow, for this is the real thing. This is Life, Adventure" (8-9).

The character's passionate insistence on his right to claim adventure in the Canadian Klondike captures the same sentiments London expressed in his narratives about the North. As Beach's hero explains, "Life and Adventure . . . that was what the gold-fields signified. . . . He had set out to see them, to taste the flavor of the world, and there it lay—his world, at least—just out of reach. A fierce impatience, a hot resentment at that senseless restriction which chained him in his tracks, ran through the boy. What right had any one to stop him here at the very door, when just inside great things were happening? . . . a new land lay, a radiant land of promise, of mystery, and of fascination; Pierce vowed that he would not, could not, wait" (11-12). Staging its conflict as the struggle of an imperiled male body at risk—a U.S. subject denied its right to expand—the text illustrates the colonial attitude many U.S. writers adopted toward Canada. These territorial designs reemerged in the patriotic names U.S. miners later placed on the map. After the gold rush abated, for instance, many U.S. miners crossed back into Alaska, settling in places they named Eagle, Star City, Nation, American Creek, Washington Creek, and Fourth of July Creek.[54]

In *The Winds of Chance,* the U.S. adventure seeker is likewise presented as a forthright, patriotic character, an innocent figure wronged by a Canadian government intent on violating the pact of friendship and neighborliness supposedly negotiated by the two nations. Like London's writings, Beach's narrative foregrounds the emergence of a national subject who is blameless, virtuous, and upright, a figure who justifies the actions of U.S. adventurers on the other side of the border. National expansion seems inevitable precisely because of the persistence of this extraordinary frontier figure. Beach foregrounds this drama and adventure in a description of the rush to the Klondike.

> The . . . scenes of the great autumn stampede to Dawson were picturesque, for the rushing river was crowded with boats all racing with one another . . . they went by ones and by twos, in groups and in flotillas, hourly the swifting current bore them along . . . Loud laughter, songs, yells of greeting and encouragement, ran back and forth; a triumphant joyfulness, a Jovian mirth, animated these men of brawn, for they had met the North and bested her . . . they reveled in a new-found freedom. There was license in the air, for Adventure was afoot and the Unknown beckoned.
>
> (288)

While the international conflict of Beach's text highlights the struggle to assert a U.S. presence on Canadian soil, his novel also functions as a divided narrative. Like other Westerns that are shaped by what Forrest G. Robinson calls "bad faith"—the deliberate attempt to evade an unsatisfying evidence of truth—Beach's novel reveals certain elements of historical fact only to later counter that impulse with an act of concealment.[55] For instance, in foregrounding the "hateful redjacketed police" who prevent Pierce Phillips and other U.S. miners from claiming their rightful adventure in Canada, Beach's narrative reveals a larger pattern of denial surrounding their advancement across the border, and in doing so, enacts a double erasure of both Anglo-Canadian and First Nations presence in the region (41). Throughout the text, Anglo-Canadians emerge as the encroaching figures, while the Indian characters are reduced to their role as packers for the U.S. stampeders. Depicted as eager profit-seeking businessmen, the native packers are presented in the novel as unfairly reaping rewards from the suffering U.S. miners forced to secure a ton of provisions before they are allowed across the border into Canada.

The central plot of *The Winds of Chance* concerns the experiences of U.S. miners and their struggles with unscrupulous, greedy claim jumpers who cheat them out of their fortunes in the Canadian Yukon, a problem that becomes elevated to the level of national threat. At one point, for instance, Phillips faces a possible lynch mob after he is wrongly accused of stealing another miner's gold. He responds with amazement, explaining, "Something must be done. . . . It's tough to be—disgraced, to have a thing like this hanging over you. I wouldn't mind it half so much if I were up for murder or arson or any man's sized crime. Anything except *stealing!*" (403). Foregrounding the character's code of honor—his belief that theft is a worse crime than murder—Beach evades the central conflict of his novel, the problem that threatens to undermine the logic of his narrative. One could, in fact, locate the unspoken crime of Beach's text in the long history of U.S. territorial encroachment across the North, the uses of Alaska in American attempts to expand into Canada. Beach buries this nagging truth, however, and instead presents innocent, upstanding U.S. miners as the real victims of a theft.

The American resentment expressed toward Canadian officials during the gold rush that Beach features in his novel has been well documented by a variety of other writers in the period. In his 1897 guide to the Klondike gold fields, for instance, U.S. author Byron Andrews addressed similar border conflicts between American miners and Canadian officials, warning his readers that a "good deal of intemperate discussion" was beginning to emerge between the two parties. He claimed that "among other things a revolution has been proposed" with U.S. miners threatening to "proclaim themselves independent of the Canadian government; to erect a Territory of their own" to be called "Klondike," and eventually "raise the American flag" on Canadian soil.[56] Another U.S. writer, A. C. Harris, also described the nation's expansionist interests in the region, suggesting that during the gold rush, the Klondike had emerged as a "magic word that is thrilling the whole country. It stands for millions of gold and great fortunes for hundreds of miners, who have risen from poverty to affluence in the brief period of a few months." Captivated

by the promise of an event so close to U.S. territory, he proclaimed that "[t]he old Spanish dreams of a wonderful realm somewhere in the Western Continent, made of gold and precious stones, seem almost on the point of being realized."[57] Describing the future of an American terrain in the Canadian North, Harris contended that an "interesting chapter" of history "is now in the making" and predicted that "in the near future the name of Lincoln will be given to a territory or state in the great northwest as that of Washington was some years ago" (277).

Such responses to the gold rush and desires toward territorial acquisition reveal how conceptions of U.S.-Canadian relations have been shaped in the American literary imagination and how the rhetoric of U.S. benevolence in Canada has produced its own fictions and fantasies. At the end of *The Winds of Chance*, Beach presents a fascinating resolution to the border conflict by staging Phillips's marriage to Josephine, the daughter of a Canadian mining official. The novel's conclusion functions as a thinly veiled wish fulfillment for a united relationship between Canada and the United States. The device allows the author to assert relations of power between the two nations as the feminized Canada becomes the subordinated party in the conventional tale of heterosexual union. First Nations claims, however, are erased in this marriage plot, which fails to script a role to third parties. In staging this political allegory, Beach's novel functions as part of an ongoing tradition aimed at absorbing Canadian claims of difference, independence, and sovereignty, and of overlooking an equally important indigenous history of displacement, dispossession, and erasure. In doing so, his narrative contributes to the fractious history that emerged as U.S. adventurers moved north into Canada in search of frontier experiences.

The arrival of American miners in the Klondike, in fact, had a profound impact on U.S.-Canadian relations and altered indigenous lifeways in the region in important ways. The boundary dispute that had been a source of international tension between the United States and Canada was eventually brought to a head as American opposition mounted against the 1825 treaty that had defined the boundaries of Russian and British possessions south of latitude 60. By 1898, however, both sides were increasingly interested in settling the controversy, especially as Canada's claims included Skagway and Dyea, towns that provided Canada with direct access to the sea without having to pass through U.S. territory. Recognizing they had much to lose, the Americans condemned Canada's claims, with Theodore Roosevelt refusing to allow the matter to rest. Fearing that the controversy would be settled to his nation's disadvantage, Roosevelt proposed that a tribunal of six members, three from each side, be constituted to assess the controversy. His U.S. delegates, not surprisingly, were less than neutral figures. In October 1903, Henry Cabot Lodge, Secretary of War Elihu Root, and Senator George Turner from Washington, a state that would be very much affected by the outcome of the decision about Alaska, helped sway the tribunal's vote in favor of the United States.[58]

Shortly after the decision was announced, a report in *The Dawson Daily News* indicated that, while Canadians opposed the outcome of the tribunal, they were not entirely surprised by the turn of events. The newspaper quoted one Canadian official who disapproved of the tribunal's decision to cede all territory to the states. "We wanted to live in peace and harmony with our neighbors, but it was time to call a halt. The states had established themselves to the west and the north. Was Canada to wait until she was entirely hemmed in by them?" Dismayed by this turn of events, he went on to predict that "[i]f the states discovered the north pole, then they would use it as a claim on Canadian territory."[59]

The U.S. and international response to the Canadian gold rush continues to have lasting effects in the history of the region, contributing to the imaginative production of the Yukon in ways that are often less than positive. The historian Ken Coates has pointed out, for instance, that in many ways the Yukon today is still unable to escape from what he calls "the limitations of an episodic history." The popularity of these adventure tales may be a determining factor for why the Klondike gold rush is still one of the few events in Canadian history that is widely known across the globe. Furthermore, while the U.S. onslaught in the Klondike displaced Canada's claims in the region, Canadian *Native* lifeways were also disrupted. Coates points out that the gold rush was almost overwhelmingly a nonnative event, as Indians in the region were continually placed at the margins of the action. Occasionally, Indians did participate directly in mining activity, staking claims on newly opened creeks but usually selling them at a huge profit to nonnative miners. Those Indians living near the vicinity of the mines were also involved in the rush but usually worked as packers, mine laborers, and traders, while Indians living farther away were involved primarily in trade with the whites.[60]

The marginalization of First Nations peoples is perhaps most telling in popular accounts of the Klondike's first gold strike. Conflicting national narratives continue to circulate across the continent as both countries argue whether the U.S. miner George Washington Carmack or the Canadian miner Robert Henderson made the first strike. The dominant version of this history credits the U.S. miner Carmack as the first miner to strike gold on Bonanza Creek, thus setting into motion the events that led to the Klondike stampede. It should come as no surprise to note that in London's novel, *Burning Daylight*,

the author stages this national rivalry between Henderson and Carmack, with the American Carmack emerging as the Klondike's true hero.[61] This story is, of course, the U.S. version. In other accounts, the Canadian Robert Henderson is credited with making the discovery. In either case, these competing national narratives serve to secure both U.S. and Anglo-Canadian claims in the North while removing Indian presence from the region, for what is overlooked in these more popular accounts are the native actors.[62] While the U.S. version fits well with larger narrative conventions established by American adventure writers in the wake of the gold rush and the Anglo-Canadian version operates well as a national counternarrative, over the years yet another version of the story has emerged, this time from native oral traditions rather than from written ones. According to oral accounts, George Carmack's Indian companion, Skookum Jim, and Carmack's native wife, Shaaw Tlàa (Kate Carmack), played a more central role in the discovery than George Carmack ever admitted. In the many versions he wrote about his experiences in the Yukon, however, Carmack always downplayed the role of his Indian companions, thus mirroring U.S. writers in the Far North who claimed the Klondike for their nation's history.

AN AMERICAN PROMOTER OF THE FAR NORTH

Like other frontier writers such as London and Beach, James Oliver Curwood also extended the United States' western experiences into the Far North by reimagining the Klondike gold rush as an American event, a project that likewise relied on an environmental rhetoric which allowed him to secure authority for his frontier heroes. Curwood was an active member of the U.S. conservation movement and eventually played an instrumental role in establishing legislation that preserved Superior National Forest in Michigan. Throughout his novels, he cultivated an awareness of nature, often expressing concerns that unchecked development would destroy the nation's "wild" landscapes. In his adventure narratives about the North, conservation operates not as a way of curtailing outdoor adventures but as a means of enabling and continuing the nation's frontier saga into the present era.

Curwood first gained fame for his stories set in the forests of the Midwest. His writings eventually caught the interests of the Canadian government, which offered him $1,800 a year plus expenses in 1901 to "explore the picturesque prairie provinces of the West." Curwood's task involved traveling throughout the Canadian prairies gathering materials for articles and stories that encouraged U.S. settlement in Canada, his career as an American promoter of the Canadian landscape resulting in over two dozen novels about an area he popularized as "God's Country." Curwood's adventure narratives were well read in the period; published in twelve languages, they sold more than four million hardcover copies in the United States alone. Over the years, Curwood came to regard his mission in Canada as an exciting experience, once confessing that "the opportunity to become a part of the great and glorious land whose far frontiers had been a part of my dreams for years thrilled me as no other event in my life."[63]

Curwood's interest in the Canadian landscape also led him to pursue Alaska as a setting for one of his frontier narratives. His 1923 novel, *The Alaskan: A Novel of the North,* for instance, is dedicated to "the strong-hearted men and women of Alaska, the new empire rising in the North." Like his other narratives, the novel functions as a thinly veiled promotional text advocating U.S. settlement in the Far North, an area of "immeasurable spaces into which civilization had not yet come with its clang and clamor."[64] As the author explains, while the North is a uniquely promising region, it is also not exempt from many of the problems other U.S. landscapes have faced. His novel thus begins with a depiction of the hero, aptly named Captain Rifle, who attempts to recapture the spirit of romance in an era when the boom of the Klondike had peaked and the mystique of the gold rush adventures in Skagway had died off. Set during a time when the region seemed threatened with the sense of exhaustion other U.S. regions previously faced, Curwood's text involves the struggle to preserve this endangered frontier.

The novel opens with a description of a die-hard U.S. adventurer whose name functions as a reminder of the nation's frontier past. "Captain Rifle . . . had not lost the spirit of his youth along with his years. Romance was not dead in him, and the fire which is built up of clean adventure and the association of strong men and a mighty country had not died out in his veins. He could still see the picturesque, feel the thrill of the unusual, and—at times—warm memories crowded upon him so closely that yesterday seemed today, and Alaska was young again, thrilling the world with her wild call." While the character associates the region with the promise and possibility of frontier adventure, he also notes a sense of sadness circulating among the residents who now seem nostalgic for the gold rush days. As he explains, "You can see it in their faces—always the memory of those days that are gone." Although the adventures that Alaska, and by extension the Canadian Klondike, once offered U.S. miners during the gold rush years appears a distant memory for the captain, he nevertheless tries to reclaim these glorious moments while seeking other means of rejuvenating the region (1, 6).

In order to promote Alaska as a site for present-day adventures, Curwood finds he has to counter dominant myths about the Far North. Although John Muir set in motion a different way of seeing the region that coun-

tered public perceptions of Alaska as a barren wasteland, a place devoid of any possible uses, this negative public sentiment was a force to be reckoned with even at the time Curwood was writing. In order to dismantle notions of Alaska as a god-forsaken terrain, he depicts his main character, Alan Holt, as an owner and manager of a reindeer herd, the northern equivalent of the American farmer. Curwood wasn't the first or the last U.S. figure to envision agrarian uses of Alaska. In an article published in the *Saturday Evening Post,* the chief of the Forest Service, Gifford Pinchot, also elaborated on Alaska's potential, telling of "the great stretches of agricultural land ready to produce in abundance the fruits, vegetables, and grains of Northern Europe," and the "cattle and the reindeer pastures, vast in extent," "the great resources of timber available for use in developing the mines," the general "fitness of this great land . . . to produce and support a population."[65] Such images promised to link Alaska to the rest of the United States, securing Euro-American dominion in the region. In his novel, Curwood helped stage these connections as well, in part by presenting Alaska Natives as employees on Holt's reindeer farm, an act that established them as part of an agrarian dream while dismantling their own claims to the land.

Addressing the region's status as a marginal U.S. territory in *The Alaskan,* Curwood highlighted the ways the land inflects larger themes about American national identity. His main character, Alan Holt, initially announces that his regional identity as an Alaskan holds more weight than his American identity. As an oldtimer in the region, Holt was "born in Alaska before Nome or Fairbanks or Dawson City were thought of." His love interest, who is aptly named Mary Standish, however, helps forge a more stable balance between Holt's regional and national identity. At one point after he foregrounds his regional interests over national ties, Standish interrupts him, crying out, "I am an American. I love America. I think I love it more than anything else in the world—more than my religion, even. . . . I love to think that I first came ashore in the *Mayflower.* That is why my name is Standish. And I just wanted to remind you that Alaska *is* America." Like his literary predecessor Owen Wister, who, in *The Virginian,* gave his New England heroine Molly Wood a revolutionary heritage that undergoes rebirth in the West, Curwood invokes a heroic American tradition in his heroine, Mary Standish, that is likewise rejuvenated by contact with the frontier.[66] Using images of the glorious founding of the nation to describe U.S. settlement in the North, he begins American history anew in Alaska by presenting the northern adventures as pilgrims in a New World, an act that further establishes an American tradition in the North (5, 14).

Once Alaska becomes incorporated into the United States, however, the region risks the same threat of exhaustion that other frontiers already experienced. Holt realizes this problem and ponders the future of Alaska, wondering whether it, too, will follow the tradition of other U.S. landscapes.

> He looked out at the stars and smiled up at them, and his soul was filled with an unspoken thankfulness that he was not born too late. Another generation and there would be no last frontier. Twenty-five years more and the world would lie utterly in the shackles of science and invention and what the human race called progress. So God had been good to him. He was helping to write the last page in that history . . . After him, there would be no frontiers. No more mysteries of unknown lands to solve. No more pioneering hazards to make. The earth would be tamed.
>
> (74)

While Holt feels fortunate to experience the last of the Last Frontier before it finally vanishes, he also realizes that the process of environmental decline is already unfolding before his eyes. The problem, as he explains, is that the once-promising gold fields have now become transformed into a popular tourist attraction. The steamships that earlier cruised through the Inside Passage to Skagway, taking U.S. miners to the start of their difficult trek to the Klondike, are now used as a "pleasure trip for flabby people" (16). According to Holt, this development signals an end to Alaska's status as a wild terrain. Tourism for him operates as a domesticated and feminized activity that transforms the region into an object of nostalgia rather than a manly terrain promising adventure and intrigue.

Holt's ambivalence toward the growing tourism industry stems from the ways it centers on older forms of adventure that the gold rush once offered. "Gold had its lure, its romance, its thrill. . . . It seemed to him the people he had met in the south had thought only of gold when they learned he was from Alaska. . . . It was gold that had been Alaska's doom. When people thought of it they visioned nothing beyond the old stampede days, the Chilkoot, White Horse, Dawson, and Circle City. Romance and glamor and the tragedies of dead men clung to their ribs" (42-43). According to him, the transformation of the gold-rush past into a modern tourist spectacle prevents Americans from realizing other opportunities offered by the region. His Alaska is thus endangered by a travel industry that has grown up unchecked in the short time since the end of the gold rush, by industrial development that remains unregulated, and by the ignorance with which most Americans still regard the region.

As a focal point for U.S. involvement in Alaska, however, the days of '98 also establish an important national tradition in the Far North. Thus, after criticizing the impact of tourism on the region, Holt himself becomes a travel guide for Standish, leading her around

the town of Skagway and describing the extraordinary events that made the region famous. Pointing to the mountain range before them, he paints an imagined past for her, describing "the wind-racked cañon where Skagway grew from one tent to hundreds in a day, from hundreds to thousands in a week." Holt envisions "the old days of romance, adventure, and death" and describes for her the changes that were "creeping slowly over Alaska, the replacement of mountain trails by stage and automobile highways, the building of railroads, the growth of cities where tents had stood a few years before" (67-68). He guides his companion through the city, ensuring that she receives a proper account of Alaska's past, and in doing so, presents the region as a site once bursting with adventure, describing the passing of a great city that was now being replaced by the encroachment of "civilization."

The problem for Holt is that many Americans do not appreciate "the immeasurable space of the big country," and refuse to acknowledge the region's worth. At one point, he cries out, "What fool had given to it the name of *Barren Lands*? What idiots people were to lie about it that way on the maps!" (143). According to him, most Americans are still largely ignorant about the vast opportunities offered by the nation's Last Frontier.

> [P]eople don't know what they ought to know about Alaska. In school they teach us that it's an eternal icebox full of gold, and is head-quarters for Santa Claus. . . . Why . . . it's nine times as large as the state of Washington, twelve times as big as the state of New York, and we bought it from Russia for less than two cents an acre. If you put it down on the face of the United States, the city of Juneau would be in St. Augustine, Florida, and Unalaska would be in Los Angeles. That's how big it is, and the geographical center of our country isn't Omaha or Sioux City, but exactly San Francisco, California.
>
> (19)

The United States' acquisitionist history in Alaska becomes significant to Holt precisely because it enables the nation to expand its contours, allowing the country to once again redraw its borders. Presenting Alaska as an entity that is as important in the nation's development as the Louisiana Purchase was more than a hundred years before, he argues that the incorporation of Alaska reconstructs U.S. regional identities, making California part of the Midwest rather than the Far West. By situating California at the center of the country, the purchase of Alaska shifts the point of reference for the West, moving the frontier away from its present location. Alaska therefore helps the country enact a project of remapping by repositioning the geographical center of the nation from Omaha to San Francisco.

Yet if Alaska enables a national redefinition, its location also makes it a dangerous place for national security. At various points throughout the novel, for instance, the region emerges as a vulnerable frontier, an exposed land situated in close proximity to the Soviet Union. One character notes this danger, arguing that Alaska is "only thirty-seven miles from Bolshevik Siberia . . . wireless messages are sent into Alaska by the Bolsheviks urging our people to rise against the Washington government." Holt also expresses concern about the new crisis now facing Alaska, lamenting the danger of Bolshevism hanging over the region "like a smoldering cloud." As he explains, Bolshevism is "the menace of blackest Russia. A disease which, if it crosses the little neck of water and gets hold of Alaska, will shake the American continent to bed-rock." The character thus makes conservation a key issue in the United States' national security, offering a solution that will allow Alaska to be developed carefully and profitably in order to guard against outside political influence. According to him, the real threat facing the region resides in the specter of its environmental and economical decline. Only through conservationism, the careful and efficient development of natural resources, can Alaskans be saved from the Bolshevik danger (19, 128).

Frontier adventures are therefore recast in the novel; rather than indiscriminately advancing northward, his heroes work instead to protect the land from selfish individuals whose careless acts threaten to destroy future adventures. Yet the frontier endeavors these characters advocate also require a certain kind of environmental vision. As Curwood's hero explains,

> We have ten times the wealth of California. We can care for a million people easily. But bad politics and bad judgment both here in Alaska and at Washington won't let them come. With coal enough under our feet to last a thousand years, we are buying fuel from the States. We've got billions in copper and oil, but can't touch them. We should have some of the world's greatest manufacturing plants, but we can not, because everything up here is locked away from us. I repeat that isn't conservation. . . . And the salmon are going, like the buffalo of the plains. The destruction of the salmon shows what will happen to us if the bars are let down all at once to the financial banditti.
>
> (129)

Describing the collapse of the buffalo on the plains as a symbol of the closing of the continental frontier, Holt seeks to prevent a similar disaster from occurring in Alaska, the Last Frontier. The region is best served, he argues, by conservationist management, the careful development of natural resources rather than preservationism, an activity that "locks up" the land.[67]

Ecological management of this sort promises to secure Alaska from both Bolshevik encroachment and environmental doom. Expressing trust in Roosevelt's conservationist agenda, Holt claims that while some citizens criticize the president for "putting what they called the

'conservation shackles' on their country . . . he, for one, did not." (43). As he explains, "Roosevelt's farsightedness had kept the body-snatchers at bay, and because he had foreseen what money-power and greed would do, Alaska was not entirely stripped today, but lay ready to serve with all her mighty resources the mother who had neglected her for a generation. But it was going to be a struggle, this opening up of a great land. It must be done resourcefully and with intelligence" (43-44). During the Roosevelt administration, the monopoly of land was a constant theme in national life, as large corporations threatened to exhaust the nation's natural resources. In an effort to prevent corporate control, conservation policy placed restrictions on private ownership, an act some westerners regarded as a "lock up" of the land.[68] In Curwood's novel, however, the main character suggests that Roosevelt's environmental policy is needed precisely in order to extend frontier adventures and ensure the future of Alaska as a viable American terrain. This vision is defined against preservationism, which, as Holt believes, closes off the land, in favor of conservation, which provides an "efficient and wise" use of the region's natural resources.[69]

Connecting ideologies of conservationism with expansionism, national security, and U.S. identity, Curwood's frontier hero argues that Alaska needs to be shaped by a foreign policy that situates nature as a crucial element in national security. Because uncontrolled industrial development threatens to turn U.S. citizens against the American way of life, he presents environmental politics as a constituting element of American identity and national security. Alaska's role in national security is also important for other reasons. According to the main character, the region is a crucial new territory, offering a jumping-off point for future expansion—not in the West or the North, but this time in the East. Holt elaborates on this idea, explaining that just across the Bering Sea lies Siberia, "the last and the greatest" frontier, where "not only men but nations would play their part in the breaking of it" (127). The novel's territorial vision thus links Curwood to London and Beach. Looking to the North for new frontiers, these three writers envision Alaska as a promising stepping stone that enables opportunities for U.S. expansion into other lands.

North to the West

In the stories and novels by early-twentieth-century frontier writers, the project of claiming new territory through Alaska helps recast expansion as an environmental act. The geographical oversights and the language of ecology that enable these authors to claim foreign land as U.S. terrain operate as part of a larger tendency among writers south of the border to blur, erase, or otherwise dismantle national boundaries. As James Doyle has argued, in the imaginative literature of the United States, Canada perennially figures "as a vague, peripheral, and ambiguous concept." Pointing to the U.S. habit of considering the northern country as merely an extension of itself, he suggests that Canada has always been an important element in developing an American national identity.[70] This use of an environmental rhetoric in nation-building projects becomes a means of greenwashing expansion, for in these narratives, U.S. encroachment in Canada is cast not for what it is, an act of territorial conquest, but as an ecofriendly gesture, a compassionate and charitable act. Discourses of nature thus emerge here much as they did in chapter one, as part of a larger expansionist gesture that operates centrally in the United States' national ecologies.

In an interesting turn of events in 1993 that might have unsettled popular frontier writers and their audiences, the right-wing Russian political leader Vladimir Zhirinovsky proposed that his country should likewise try to restore its previous "imperial greatness" by reclaiming Alaska, one of Russia's former American colonies. Noting the wealth of resources that Alaska has provided the United States since its purchase in 1867, Zhirinovsky argued that his nation should reextend its own frontier to include a significant portion of the Far North. Not surprisingly perhaps, the response among many Americans was disbelief that Zhirinovsky could suggest that Alaska still belonged to Russia, or that in some way ownership was contestable. In this instance, Americans were dismayed that another nation would attempt to make territorial designs on a region that was clearly a part of the United States.[71]

Notes

1. Norris, "The Frontier Gone at Last," 1728-29.

2. Several critics have discussed the use of U.S. frontier rhetoric in depicting overseas expansion. See, for instance, Drinnon, *Facing West*; and Kaplan, "Romancing the Empire." Other U.S. writers who used the Far North for their frontier settings include Emerson Hough, Robert Service, Hamlin Garland, and Frank Norris. Interestingly, the first figure hailed as a "real Alaskan novelist" was not a male but a female writer, Barrett Willoughby. For a study of her literary accomplishments during the 1920s and 1930s, see Ferrell, *Barrett Willoughby*.

3. This struggle shares much in common with the project that McClure addresses in *Late Imperial Romance*.

4. Turner, *The Frontier in American History*, 37, 206.

5. Ibid., 293.

6. Many critics have argued this point; for representative discussions, see Maltby, "John Ford and the Indians"; and Wrobel, *The End of American Exceptionalism*.

7. Turner, *The Frontier in American History*, 296.

8. Bloom, *Gender on Ice*, 1-3.

9. Canadian historian Pierre Berton refers to Dawson as an "American city on Canadian soil" in the documentary film *City of Gold* (1957). For a history of the Klondike gold rush, see Berton, *The Klondike Fever*; and Porschild, *Gamblers and Dreamers*.

10. In constructing a conceptual framework for the study of northern regions, Ken Coates suggests that a transnational approach might enable scholars to better understand such areas. Unlike London, however, Coates is sensitive to the ways political boundaries of the nation-state must also be recognized in studies of the North. For more on this point, see "The Rediscovery of the North," 15-43.

11. For further discussion of the modern "ecological subject," see Luke, "Green Consumerism," 156.

12. Cosgrove, "Habitable Earth," 36.

13. The literature on the turn-of-the-century crisis in Anglo-Saxon masculinity is vast. For a representative sample, see Cosgrove, "Habitable Earth," 34-36; Broun, "Foreword," in Truettner, *The West as America*, vii-ix; Peterson, "Jack London and the American Frontier"; Schmitt, *Back to Nature*; and Bederman, *Manliness and Civilization*.

14. Schmitt, *Back to Nature*, 23.

15. For more on the problems of "wilderness design," see Chaloupka and Cawley, "The Great Wild Hope," 5-6.

16. Many historians have noted the imperial politics of U.S. preservationism. For a representative discussion, see Darnovsky, "Stories Less Told," 15-16; and Gottlieb, *Forcing the Spring*, 27.

17. For a useful discussion of Roosevelt and the back-to-nature movement, see Gottlieb, *Forcing the Spring*, 213; and Peterson, "Jack London and the American Frontier," 138.

18. For more information about London as a writer of the Klondike, see Walker, *Jack London and the Klondike*.

19. The dime novels of the period also misrecognize the Klondike as U.S. terrain. The confusion is evident in the titles and plot summaries provided in Leithead, "Tales of Klondike Gold in Dime Novels." For a discussion of the divided and contested memory of Jack London among some Canadian residents, see Campbell, "Facing North."

20. London, "The God of His Fathers," *Complete Short Stories*, 1:382.

21. London, *Revolution and Other Essays,* 180.

22. For further discussion of the Western's origins in the British colonial adventure narrative, see Cawelti, *The Six-Gun Mystique Sequel,* 25; and Slotkin, *Gunfighter Nation,* 194.

23. Review of *The Son of the Wolf, The Beacon,* n.d., n.p. Collected in "The Scrapbooks," Jack London Papers, Huntington Library, San Marino, California.

24. Review of *The Son of the Wolf, The Wave,* May 12, 1900, n.a., n.p. Collected in ibid.

25. Review in *The Evening Transcript,* n.d, n.p. Collected in ibid.

26. "Alaskan Stories," *The Atlantic,* April 1900, n.a., n.p. Collected in ibid.

27. Quoted in Labor, "Jack London," 381.

28. Starr, *Americans and the California Dream,* 212.

29. London, *Smoke Bellew,* 1. Further references will appear parenthetically in the text.

30. London, *The Call of the Wild,* 21.

31. For a discussion of the ways this confusion informs Hollywood's production of Canada, see Berton, *Hollywood's Canada.* In a similar vein, Sherrill Grace refers to what she calls "literary Manifest Destiny," the process whereby U.S. critics claim Canadian writers as part of their own national tradition. For more on this idea, see Grace, "Comparing Mythologies: Ideas of West and North," 249.

32. London, "To the Man on Trail," *Complete Stories,* 1:157.

33. London, *Burning Daylight,* 38. Further references will appear parenthetically in the text.

34. According to Alfred Hornung, tropes of expansion play a central role in other London texts. In *John Barleycorn,* for instance, alcohol operates as a means of stimulating expansion; while under its influence, London feels that "all the world was mine." For more on this idea, see Hornung, "Evolution and Expansion in London's *The Road* and *John Barleycorn.*"

35. For further discussion of the environmental impact of the stampede, see Mayer, *Klondike Women*; and Porschild, "The Environmental Impact of the Klondike Stampede."

36. London, *Daughter of the Snows,* 16. Further references will appear parenthetically in the text.

37. For a historical discussion of this environmental approach, see Hays, *Conservation and the Gospel of Efficiency.*

38. Limerick, *Something in the Soil,* 215.

39. Here London replaces frontier rhetoric with the discourse of urban wilderness. For more on how U.S. writers imagined the city as a new wilderness needing to be tamed, see Light, "Urban Wilderness."

40. Cook-Lynn, *Why I Can't Read Wallace Stegner and Other Essays,* 29.

41. Cosgrove, "Habitable Earth," 39.

42. My discussion of the emergence of Canadian northern iconography comes from Osborne, "The Iconography of Nationhood in Canadian Art." For an analysis of the distinctions between the "Canadian Northern" and the "American Western" and the ways they fit into different national narratives, see Grace, "Comparing Mythologies." For a useful overview of Canadian literary constructions of the "mystic North," see Atwood, *Strange Things.*

43. For a discussion of non-Canadian literary uses of the Far North, see Gross, "From American Western to Canadian Northern."

44. For a discussion of Burning Daylight as a Leatherstocking figure, see Watson, *The Novels of Jack London,* 170-71.

45. Quoted in Graebner, *Manifest Destiny,* 330.

46. Quoted in LaFeber, *The New Empire,* 28.

47. Many historians have addressed these events; see, for instance, Sherwood, *Exploration in Alaska*; Van Alstyne, *The Rising American Empire*; and Kiernan, *America, The New Imperialism.*

48. For more on U.S. expansion in the Canadian North, see Honderich, *Arctic Imperative: Is Canada Losing the North?*; Coates and Morrison, *The Alaska Highway during World War II*; and Nielsen, *Armed Forces on a Northern Frontier.*

49. See entry for "Rex Beach" in Buscombe, *The BFI Companion to the Western,* 65.

50. Beach, *The World in His Arms,* 84. Further references will be incorporated parenthetically in the text.

51. See Hutchinson, "The Cowboy in Short Fiction," 516.

52. Beach, *The Spoilers,* 1.

53. Beach, *The Winds of Chance,* 8. Further references will appear parenthetically in the text.

54. McPhee addresses this history in *Coming into the Country,* 227-28.

55. Robinson, *Having It Both Ways.*

56. Andrews, "Alaska and Its Gold Fields," 4.

57. Harris, *Alaska and the Klondike Gold Fields,* iii.

58. See Naske and Slotnick, *Alaska,* 87.

59. "Decision Criticised," 1.

60. See Coates, *Best Left as Indians,* xv, 35-41.

61. George Carmack wrote an interesting series of accounts concerning the strike. In the years following the Klondike stampede, he produced at least three versions of his story, each one more elaborate and embellished than the first. The first two accounts are collected in the Snow Papers, MS 38, Alaska State Library, Historical Collections, Juneau, Alaska. Another version, *My Experiences in the Klondike,* privately printed by Marguerite Carmack, 1993, may be found in the Beinecke Library at Yale University. For Native accounts of the Klondike strike, see Cruikshank, *Life Lived Like a Story,* 128-39. Cruikshank's account foregrounds Shaaw Tlàa's role in particular. For more on Skookum Jim's role, see Rab Wilkie and the Skookum Jim Friendship Centre, *Skookum Jim,* copy in Alaska State Library, Historical Collections.

62. For an analysis of how myths of Canadian national identity also operate to erase the history of First Nations people, see Clarke, "White Like Canada."

63. Hepler, "Michigan's Forgotten Son"; and Curwood, *Son of the Forests,* 200-201.

64. Curwood, *The Alaskan,* 12. Further references will appear parenthetically in the text.

65. Quoted in Worster, *Under Western Skies,* 182.

66. For a discussion of how Molly Wood's revolutionary background figures into the logic of the novel, see Cawelti, *The Six-Gun Mystique Sequel,* 72-73. Incidentally, Wister's frontier romance also features a reference to a character who makes a journey to Alaska before returning to Wyoming. See Wister, *The Virginian,* 122.

67. White, *The Eastern Establishment and the Western Experience,* 181.

68. Ibid., 176-77.

69. For a discussion of ecology and the rhetoric of efficiency, see Hays, *Conservation and the Gospel of Efficiency.*

70. Doyle, *North of America,* 1, 150.

71. See McCarthy, "Zhirinovsky Upsets D.C.," 5; and Egan, "Alaskans Don't Want to Be Anyone's Siberia," 3.

Bibliography

Andrews, Byron. "Alaska and Its Gold Fields, and How to Get There." *National Tribune Library* 1, no. 22 (September 18, 1897): 4.

Atwood, Margaret. *Strange Things: The Malevolent North in Canadian Literature.* Oxford: Clarendon Press, 1995.

Beach, Rex. *The Spoilers.* New York: Harper and Brothers, 1905.

———. *The Winds of Chance.* New York: Harper and Brothers, 1918.

———. *The World in His Arms.* New York: Putnam, 1945.

Bederman, Gail. *Manliness and Civilization: A Cultural History of Gender and Race in the United States, 1880-1917.* Chicago: University of Chicago Press, 1995.

Berton, Pierre. *Hollywood's Canada: The Americanization of Our National Image.* Toronto: McClelland and Stewart, 1975.

———. *The Klondike Fever: The Life and Death of the Last Great Gold Rush.* New York: Alfred A. Knopf, 1967.

Bloom, Lisa. *Gender on Ice: American Ideologies of Polar Expeditions.* Minneapolis: University of Minnesota Press, 1993.

Broun, Elizabeth. "Foreword," in *The West as America: Reinterpreting Images of the Frontier, 1820-1920,* edited by William Truettner, vii-ix. Washington, D.C., and London: Smithsonian Institution Press, 1991.

Buscombe, Edward, ed. *The BFI Companion to the Western.* New York: Atheneum, 1988.

Campbell, Robert. "Facing North: Jack London's Imagined Indians on the Klondike Frontier." *Northern Review* 19 (Winter 1998): 122-40.

Carmack, George. *My Experiences in the Klondike.* Published privately by Marguerite Carmack, 1933.

Cawelti, John G. *The Six-Gun Mystique Sequel.* Bowling Green, Ohio: Bowling Green University Popular Press, 1999.

Chaloupka, William, and R. McGreggor Cawley. "The Great Wild Hope: Nature, Environmentalism, and the Open Secret." In *In the Nature of Things: Language, Politics, and the Environment,* edited by Jane Bennett and William Chaloupka, 3-23. Minneapolis: University of Minnesota Press, 1993.

Clarke, George Elliot. "White Like Canada." *Transition: An International Review* 7, no. 1 (1997): 98-109.

Coates, Kenneth S. *Best Left as Indians: Native-White Relations in the Yukon Territory, 1840-1973.* Montreal and Kingston: McGill-Queens University Press, 1991.

————. "The Rediscovery of the North: Towards a Conceptual Framework for the Study of Northern/ Remote Regions." *Northern Review* 12/13 (Summer/ Winter 1993-94): 15-43.

Coates, Kenneth S., and William R. Morrison. *The Alaska Highway during World War II: The U.S. Army Occupation of Canada's Northwest.* Norman: University of Oklahoma Press, 1992.

Cook-Lynn, Elizabeth. *Why I Can't Read Wallace Stegner and Other Essays: A Tribal Voice.* Madison: University of Wisconsin Press, 1996.

Cosgrove, Denis. "Habitable Earth: Wilderness, Empire, and Race in America." In *Wild Ideas,* edited by David Rothenberg, 27-41. Minneapolis: University of Minnesota Press, 1995.

Cruikshank, Julie, with Angela Sidney, Kitty Smith, and Annie Ned. *Life Lived Like a Story: Life Stories of Three Yukon Native Elders by Julie Cruikshank.* Lincoln: University of Nebraska Press, 1990.

Curwood, James Oliver. *The Alaskan: A Novel of the North.* New York: Grosset and Dunlap, 1922.

————. *Son of the Forests: An Autobiography.* Garden City, N.Y.: Doubleday, Doran and Company, 1930.

Darnovsky, Marcy. "Stories Less Told: Histories of the U.S. Environmentalism." *Socialist Review* 22, no. 4 (October/November 1992): 11-54.

Doyle, James. *North of America: Images of Canada in the Literature of the United States, 1775-1900.* Toronto: ECW Press, 1983.

Drinnon, Richard. *Facing West: The Metaphysics of Indian-Hating and Empire-Building.* Minneapolis, 1980. Reprint. New York: Schocken, 1990.

Egan, Timothy. "Alaskans Don't Want to Be Anyone's Siberia." *New York Times,* 19 December 1993, 3.

Ferrell, Nancy Warren. *Barrett Willoughby: Alaska's Forgotten Lady.* Fairbanks: University of Alaska Press, 1994.

Gottlieb, Robert. *Forcing the Spring: The Transformation of the American Environmental Movement.* Covelo, Calif., and Washington, D.C.: Island Press, 1993.

Grace, Sherrill. "Comparing Mythologies: Ideas of West and North." In *Borderlands: Essays in Canadian-American Relations,* edited by Robert Lecker, 243-62. Toronto: ECW Press, 1991.

Graebner, Norman, ed. *Manifest Destiny.* Indianapolis: Bobbs-Merrill, 1968.

Gross, Konrad. "From American Western to Canadian Northern: Images of the Canadian North in Early Twentieth-Century Popular Fiction in Canada." In *Das*

Natur/Kultur- Paradigma in der englischsprachigen Erzäahlliteratur des 19. Und 20. Jahrhunderts, edited by Konrad Gross, Kurt Müller, and Meinhard Winkgens, 354-66. Tübingen: Gunter Nerr Verlag, 1994.

Harris, A. C. *Alaska and the Klondike Gold Fields.* Washington, D.C.: Library of Congress, 1897.

Hays, Samuel P. *Conservation and the Gospel of Efficiency.* Cambridge, Mass.: Harvard University Press, 1959.

Hepler, John. "Michigan's Forgotten Son: James Oliver Curwood." *Midwestern Miscellany* 7 (1979): 25-33.

Honderich, John. *Arctic Imperative: Is Canada Losing the North?* Toronto: University of Toronto Press, 1987.

Hornung, Alfred. "Evolution and Expansion in Jack London's Personal Accounts: *The Road* and *John Barleycorn.*" In *An American Empire: Expansionist Cultures and Policies, 1881-1917,* edited by Serge Ricard, 197-213. Aix-en-Provence: Universite de Provence, 1990.

Hutchinson, W. H. "The Cowboy in Short Fiction." In *A Literary History of the American West,* edited by Thomas J. Lyon et al., 515-22. Fort Worth, Tex.: Texas Christian University Press, 1987.

Kaplan, Amy. "Romancing the Empire: The Embodiment of American Masculinity in the Popular Historical Novel of the 1890s." *American Literary History* 2, no. 4 (Winter 1990): 659-89.

Kiernan, V. G. *America: The New Imperialism, from White Settlement to World Hegemony.* London: Zed Press, 1978.

Labor, Earle. "Jack London." In *A Literary History of the American West,* edited by Thomas J. Lyon et. al., 381-97. Forth Worth, Tex.: Texas Christian University Press, 1987.

LaFeber, Walter. *The New Empire: An Interpretation of American Expansion, 1860-1898.* Ithaca, N.Y.: Cornell University Press, 1963.

Leithead, J. Edward. "Tales of Klondike Gold in Dime Novels." *Dime Novel Round-Up* 25, no. 10 (15 October 1957): 88-92.

Limerick, Patricia Nelson. *Something in the Soil: Legacies and Reckonings in the New West.* New York: W. W. Norton, 2000.

London, Jack. *Burning Daylight.* New York, 1910. Reprint. New York: Macmillan, 1913.

————. *The Call of the Wild.* New York, 1903. Reprint. New York: Penguin, 1960.

————. *The Complete Short Stories of Jack London.* 3 vols. Edited by Earle Labor, Robert C. Leitz III, and I. Milo Shepherd. Stanford, Calif.: Stanford University Press, 1993.

———. *Daughter of the Snows.* New York: Grosset and Dunlap, 1902.

———. *Revolution and Other Essays.* New York: Macmillan Company, 1912.

———. *Smoke Bellew.* New York, 1912. Reprint. New York: Dover Press, 1992.

Luke, Timothy W. "Green Consumerism: Ecology and the Ruse of Recycling." In *In the Nature of Things: Language, Politics, and the Environment,* edited by Jane Bennett and William Chaloupka, 154-72. Minneapolis: University of Minnesota Press, 1993.

McCarthy, Max. "Zhirinovsky Upsets D.C." *Buffalo News,* 26 December 1993, 5.

McClure, John. *Late Imperial Romance.* London: Verso, 1994.

McPhee, John. *Coming into the Country.* New York: Noonday Press, 1977.

Maltby, Richard. "John Ford and the Indians: Or, Tom Doniphon's History Lesson." In *Representing Others: White Views of Indigenous Peoples,* edited by Mick Gidley, 120-44. Exeter: Exeter University Press, 1992.

Mayer, Melanie. *Klondike Women: True Tales of the 1897-98 Gold Rush.* Athens, Ohio: Swallow Press/Ohio University Press, 1989.

Naske, Claus-M., and Herman E. Slotnick. *Alaska: A History of the 49th State.* 2d ed. Norman: University of Oklahoma Press, 1987.

Nielson, Jonathan M. *Armed Forces on a Northern Frontier: The Military in Alaska's History, 1867-1987.* Westport, Conn.: Greenwood Press, 1988.

Norris, Frank. "The Frontier Gone at Last." *The World's Work* 3, no. 4 (February 1902): 1728-31.

Osborne, Brian S. "The Iconography of Nationhood in Canadian Art." In *The Iconography of Landscape: Essays on the Symbolic Representation, Design, and Use of Past Environments,* edited by Denis Cosgrove and Stephen Daniels. 162-78. Cambridge: Cambridge University Press, 1988.

Peterson, Clell T. "Jack London and the American Frontier." Master's thesis, University of Minnesota, 1951.

Porschild, Charlene. "The Environmental Impact of the Klondike Stampede." Paper presented at the Association for Canadian Studies in the United States Biennial Meeting. Seattle, Wash., 15 November 1995.

———. *Gamblers and Dreamers: Women, Men, and Community in the Klondike.* Vancouver: University of British Columbia Press, 1998.

Robinson, Forrest G. *Having It Both Ways: Self-Subversion in Western Popular Classics.* Albuquerque: University of New Mexico Press, 1993.

Schmitt, Peter J. *Back to Nature: The Arcadian Myth in Urban America.* Foreword by John Stilgoe. New York, 1969. Reprint. Baltimore, Md.: Johns Hopkins University Press, 1990.

Sherwood, Morgan. *Exploration of Alaska, 1865-1900.* New Haven, Conn., 1965. Reprint. Fairbanks: University of Alaska Press, 1992.

Slotkin, Richard. *Gunfighter Nation: The Myth of the Frontier in Twentieth-Century America.* New York: HarperPerennial, 1993.

Starr, Kevin. *Americans and the California Dream, 1850-1915.* New York: 1973. Reprint. New York: Oxford University Press, 1986.

Turner, Frederick Jackson. *The Frontier in American History.* New York, 1920. Reprint. Tucson: University of Arizona Press, 1982.

Van Alstyne, Richard W. *The Rising American Empire.* Oxford, 1960. Reprint. New York: W. W. Norton, 1974.

Walker, Franklin. *Jack London and the Klondike: The Genesis of an American Writer.* 1966. Reprint. San Marino, Calif.: Huntington Library Press, 1994.

Watson, Charles N., Jr. *The Novels of Jack London: A Reappraisal.* Madison: University of Wisconsin Press, 1983.

White, G. Edward. *The Eastern Establishment and the Western Experience: The West of Frederic Remington, Theodore Roosevelt, and Owen Wister.* New Haven, Conn., 1968. Reprint. Austin: University of Texas Press, 1989.

Wilkie, Rab, and the Skookum Jim Friendship Centre. *Skookum Jim: Native and Non-Native Stories and Views about His Life and Times and the Klondike Gold Rush.* Whitehorse, Yukon: Heritage Branch/Department of Tourism, 1992.

Wister, Owen. *The Virginian: A Horseman of the Plains.* 1902. Reprint. New York: Signet, 1979.

Worster, Donald. *Under Western Skies: Nature and History in the American West.* New York and Oxford: Oxford University Press, 1992.

Wrobel, David M. *The End of American Exceptionalism: Frontier Anxiety from the Old West to the New Deal.* Lawrence: University of Kansas Press, 1993.

Robert C. Sickels and Marc Oxoby (essay date summer 2002)

SOURCE: Sickels, Robert C., and Marc Oxoby. "In Search of a Further Frontier: Cormac McCarthy's Border Trilogy." *Critique* 43, no. 4 (summer 2002): 347-60.

[*In the following essay, Sickels and Oxoby trace the development of the pastoral vision in Cormac McCarthy's Border Trilogy.*]

In 1998, McCarthy published the third volume of his Border Trilogy, *Cities of the Plain,* in which the protagonists of the previous two volumes, John Grady Cole and Billy Parham, are brought together; their previously disparate narratives intersect, effecting the trilogy's thematic unification. In the first two works, Cole and Parham, feeling the encroachment of increasing urbanization, leave the American Southwest to seek a simpler, more pastoral existence in Mexico. However, in the third novel the pastoral dream of an idyllic life on the edge of the Mexican frontier is superseded by the grim reality of the corrupt border city of Juárez and its American counterpart, El Paso. Accordingly, by the end of *Cities of the Plain* it becomes clear that McCarthy's trilogy chronicles the death of the traditional American pastoral dream.

Traditionally, American pastoralism has been closely identified with the American West, in which those seeking refuge and an agrarian existence escaped to live a kind of border life on their own terms. However, as the United States has grown in population and as technology such as television, movies, and the Internet has concurrently contributed to the cultural homogenization of the country, the West no longer seems much different from the East or any other region of the country. Every strip mall has the same stores, and every theater multiplex has the same movies. As Richard White argues,

> As sections of the West became powerful and populous, they became powerful and populous in ways that made them seem quite similar to older centers of power and population. The freeways and suburbs of Los Angeles, Dallas and Phoenix, after all, seemed generic freeways and suburbs, differing only in their shrubbery from the turnpikes and suburbs of the East, South, or Midwest [. . .].
>
> (538)

Contemporary pastoral theorist Lawrence Buell writes that the term "'pastoral' has become almost synonymous with the idea of (re)turn to a less urbanized, more 'natural' state of existence" (31). By this definition, if a movie star builds a mansion in Montana, he or she could be said to be living a pastoral existence. The West is no longer a pastoral land in which one can escape the pressures of urbanization and industrialization; instead it is a theme park, a place where middle-class Americans take their families to Disneyland. The increasingly urbanized American West is no longer an adequate setting for pastorals.

For Cole and Parham, merely living on the land does not make them feel as if they are living a "more natural state of existence." Like the earliest Greek pastoralists, they believe that a true connection with the land is predicated on working it as a way of life. Cole and Parham still believe in the possibility of what Richard Slotkin calls "a further frontier, a mythic space beyond

the frontier, a mythic space beyond the Western landscape and American history—whose possibilities have been thoroughly used up" (279). Over the course of the trilogy, the bulk of which occurs in Mexico, ostensibly a further frontier, the serenity of the pastoral landscape is repeatedly undermined by the naturalistic intrusion of violence and mechanization. The traditional American pastoral vision celebrated at the start of McCarthy's trilogy is forsaken by its end, replaced by what can be called a contemporary American pastoralism, which recognizes that regardless of one's desires a pastoral existence is not merely beyond the frontier, but permanently impossible.

ALL THE PRETTY HORSES

The trilogy begins with *All the Pretty Horses* and its sixteen-year-old protagonist, John Grady Cole. Early in the novel, which begins in 1949 and is initially set just outside of San Angelo, Texas, we find Cole's father dying from a condition he acquired while fighting in World War II. Cole's parents are divorced, so the ranch that he and his father once worked together now belongs to Cole's mother, whose father, the ranch's previous owner, has recently died. The ranch is no longer self-sufficient. Cole's mother, who "settled" for ranch life when she married his father, a gambler and a cowboy, sees her chance to follow her dreams of becoming a stage actress. She rejects Cole's pleas that she keep the ranch, thus denying him his pastoral birthright. Adding insult to injury, Cole's girlfriend has left him for an older boy with a car. With little ranch work available in the surrounding area and no compelling reason to stay, Cole and his friend Lacey Rawlins head to Mexico to pursue their dream of the cowboy life. Thus begins their quest for a further frontier.

However, even before the action begins, we know that we are reading what is ostensibly a traditional pastoral work. On the first page McCarthy uses the literary trope of what Leo Marx calls an "interrupted idyll"—a rupture in the otherwise harmonious relationship of humans and the natural world (27). As Marx writes, the sudden appearance of a machine on the landscape "is a metaphoric design which recurs everywhere" in American literature (16). McCarthy appears to be working squarely within this tradition, as evidenced when Cole walks out onto the prairie and hears the coming of a train: "He could feel it under his feet. It came boring out of the east like some ribald satellite of the coming sun howling and bellowing in the distance [. . .]" (3). The train has a greater significance than simply breaking the idyllic scene: It is juxtaposed with the death of Cole's way of life. That ownership of the ranch will soon leave the family and that Cole's opportunity to work the land is slipping away amplifies the "ground shudder" caused by the locomotive. With no viable options for continued ranch life on the Texas plains, Cole and Rawlins saddle up their horses and head for Mexico, where they hope to realize their dreams of cowboy life. After a series of misadventures with Jimmy Blevins, whom they meet shortly after they begin their journey, Cole and Rawlins end up at the utopian "Hacienda de Nuestra Señora de la Purísima Concepción [La Purísima . . .] a ranch of eleven thousand hectares situated along the edge of the Bolsón de Cuatro Ciénagas in the state of Coahuila" (97). As Alan Chuese notes, "The land is the promise, the promise is the land; alive, a symbol, a voice, a character" (142). Here at the ranch of Don Héctor Rocha y Villereal (Rocha) the boys think they have found their dream.

As its name suggests, the ranch is a mountain oasis above the harsh Mexican plains. Whereas McCarthy's earlier descriptions of the Mexican landscape concentrate on its aridity and barrenness, the ranch is characterized by its abundant fecundity:

> The western sections ran into the Sierra de Anteojo to elevations of nine thousand feet but south and east the ranch occupied part of the broad barrial or basin floor of the bolsón and was well watered with natural springs and clear streams and dotted with marshes and shallow lakes or lagunas. In the lakes and in the streams were species of fish not known elsewhere on earth and birds and lizards and other forms of life as well all long relict here for the desert stretched away on every side.
>
> (97)

On the night of their arrival Rawlins, dazzled by the ranch's promise, asks Cole "How long do you think you'd like to stay here?" "About a hundred years," Cole responds (96). It appears as though the ranch will provide refuge and solace for the travel-weary cowboys. Despite the ranch's pastoral landscape, the boys eventually learn that all is not as it initially appears at La Purísima.

While at the Ranch Cole's almost preternatural understanding of the ways of horses, to which McCarthy had earlier alluded—Cole sits a horse "not only as if he'd been born to it which he was but as if were he begot by malice or mischance into some queer land where horses never were he would have found them anyway" (23)—earns him the right to meet Rocha personally. Rocha appears to be the kind of person who Cole would like to emulate—a rancher living his life on the land. As such, Cole respects and trusts Rocha, but Rocha is not what he seems. Despite being "one of the few hacendados who actually lived on the land he claimed," it is not the ranch that gives Rocha his financial independence (97). Without his business interests in Mexico City Rocha would surely not have the luxury of his family's ranch. In addition, although Rocha clearly loves his ranch, he is not connected to it through working on it; he pays others to work it in his frequent and lengthy absences. Even as McCarthy writes of Rocha's love of

horses, he tells us that Rocha flies his own airplane, which at intervals throughout the novel's La Purísima section, ruptures tranquillity and reinforces the inevitable decline of the pastoral dream's feasibility. Although a refuge from industrialism, La Purísima is more a vacation home than a working ranch.

Cole believes he has found a kindred spirit in Alejandra, Rocha's horse-loving daughter; against his better judgment, he begins a clandestine affair with her. However, Alejandra, like her father, has made the jump into the modern world, even though she initially refuses to recognize the fact. She attends an elite prep school, a "fancy sort of school" as Rawlins calls it, in Mexico City. Indeed, Rawlins makes much of Alejandra's being "a fancy sort of girl," musing that "she probably dates guys got their own airplanes let alone cars" (118). While in Mexico City, Alejandra regularly attends the theatre and ballet with her mother, who does not understand the Hacienda's appeal. Alejandra does not share her mother's dislike of life on the Hacienda, but her mother knows Alejandra better than she knows herself, presciently telling her that she will change her mind about coming to the ranch, and, more ominously, "about everything" (124). Cole does not see it. He mistakenly thinks her love of horses and desire to ride them also indicates a desire to live the frontier life with a cowboy. Sadly, for him, one does not equal the other.

The illicit affair comes to the attention of "the Dueña Alfonsa," Alejandra's grandaunt and godmother, whose "life at the hacienda invested it with oldworld ties and with antiquity and tradition" (132). Alfonsa's intimate familiarity with "antiquity and tradition" informs her desire for a more "suitable" (i.e., affluent) match for Alejandra. Despite having similarly loved an inappropriate suitor during the years of the Revolution, the Dueña has, as Alejandra's mother believes Alejandra will, changed her mind "about everything." As the Dueña says "Whatever my appearance may suggest, I am not a particularly oldfashioned woman," which leads her to condemn Cole as an oldfashioned boy whose dreams are inappropriate to the developing face of the country (135). Significantly, Alfonsa remembers not a past Mexico of pastoral paradise, but explains "When I was a girl the poverty in this country was very terrible. What you see today cannot even suggest it [. . .]. The average family owned nothing machine-made except for a kitchen knife. Nothing. Not a pin or a plate or pot or a button" (231). Consequently, whereas Alejandra and Rocha still half-heartedly resist the passing of the rural era, Alfonsa attempts to cultivate the new world, which she sees as infinitely better than her past. Her rejection of Cole as a suitor is directly informed by her view of him as antiquated and obsolete in Mexico's new and increasingly modern urban context. As John C. Grammer notes, Cole's retreat into Mexico is driven by his "pastoral will to create a timeless order" (21). Instead he finds in Mexico what Tom Pilkington calls "an actual and metaphysical horror" (315). The way of life he seeks, the realization of his pastoral dream, is just as unattainable in Mexico as it was on the Texas plains.

Despite the Dueña's warnings, Cole's relationship with Alejandra intensifies, resulting in Cole and Rawlins being turned in to the authorities for crimes they ostensibly committed prior to their arrival at La Purísima. Despite their best intentions, they are, as Vereen Bell writes, "discredited and exiled from the ancient place of the good life, the Hacienda de Nuestra Señora de la Purísima Concepción, that they believe they have found" (921). The Dueña, at Alejandra's behest, secures their release from prison but only after Alejandra agrees to never see Cole again. On Cole's release, Alejandra breaks her word, but only for a brief time. She ultimately decides to adhere to her promise, which shocks Cole, who, as an American committed to the Code of the West, "believes in individualism, free will, volition" (Pilkington 320). After a violent interlude in which Cole retrieves the horses taken from him and Rawlins prior to their incarceration, he returns to Texas a broken and uncertain man, shattered by his realization that "even in Mexico, the modern world of politics and revolution, technology and cities is eroding and destroying the traditions of the countryside" (Cawelti 173).

The novel's elegiac ending portends the works to come. Cole wanders the plains of West Texas, returning to his hometown just long enough to seek out Rawlins, who encourages him to stay and work the oil rigs, which pay "awful good" (299). Much to Cole's chagrin, his country, "West Texas, once one of the last bastions of traditional pastoralism in America, has become a wasteland of oil derricks" (Cawelti 172). Cole opts to move on. Shortly thereafter he rides past an oil field, around the borders of which is an Indian encampment. Early in the novel, after the ranch has been sold, Cole tells his father that he is like "the Comanches was two hundred years ago" (25-26). The image of the Indian's wickiups "propped upon that scoured and trembling waste" reinforces Cole's earlier identification with displaced Native Americans (301). He has been beyond the frontier and back again, finding not a further frontier but more of the same.

THE CROSSING

The second volume of the trilogy, *The Crossing,* tells the story of a young boy's experiences in Mexico. *The Crossing* is, as its title suggests, a thematic segue between *All the Pretty Horses,* which takes its name "from a child's lullaby" and the biblically allusive *Cities of the Plain* (Luce 156). The novel's action centers around Billy Parham and his three "crossings" from New Mexico into Mexico. Each succeeding trip further emphasizes the fact that, despite its promising pastoral ap-

pearance, Mexico is as corrupt and fallen as its northern neighbor, if not more so.

The novel opens roughly ten years before *All the Pretty Horses,* with the simultaneous introduction of the Parham family—Billy, his parents, and younger brother Boyd—and the landscape of the extreme southwest corner of New Mexico: "When they came south out of Grant County Boyd was not much more than a baby and the newly formed county they'd named Hidalgo was itself little older than the child" (3). The freshness of the newborn baby parallels the freshness of this new county, a place of rebirth for the Parhams. But even as they live and work the land, dark clouds form, and by the "winter that Boyd turned fourteen the trees inhabiting the dry river bed were bare from early on and the sky was gray day after day and the trees were pale against it" (5). The changes are not merely meteorological. A man who lodges Billy Parham for a night explains, "Country crowdin up the way it is. You caint hardly keep up with your own neighbors even" (67). Indeed, the land first encountered by the family, the land in which they chose to establish their ranch, is no longer the same land.

The recent invasion of a wolf, which tears into ranchers' livestock, exacerbates the struggle of the Parham family. The visitation is unusual and foreboding. A neighbor explains: "There ain't no more wolves but what they come up out of Mexico, I reckon" (24). It is suggested that the wolves have left this land, fleeing perhaps the "crowdin up" of the country. The question of exactly what might have forced this particular wolf up out of Mexico is never raised. The wolf's behavior demonstrates an aversion to the technological and urban development of the country: "She would not cross a road or rail line in daylight. She would not cross under a wire fence twice in the same place. These were the new protocols. Strictures that had not existed before. Now they did" (25). In addition, McCarthy writes that "[t]he ranchers said [the wolves] brutalized the cattle in a way they did not the wild game. As if the cows evoked in them some anger. As if they were offended by some violation of an old order. Old ceremonies. Old protocols" (25). The wolf responds to her shrinking environment in the only way she knows: She attacks the new competition, not realizing that in the end she cannot possibly win.

Although Billy Parham eventually identifies with the wolf's plight, he initially sees her as a nuisance that must be stopped. He captures the wolf; but rather than execute his prisoner of war, he decides to take the animal back across the border into Mexico. But Billy and the wolf have not returned to the wild; the markings of civilization become more and more apparent. Their encounters with the people of northern Mexico end with the wolf being taken out of Billy's hands. Rather than being the wild infringing on civilization, the wolf becomes an entertainment for the people. She is used as just another fighting dog; her opponents are "mostly redbone and bluetick dogs bred in the country to the north but also nondescript animals from new-world bloodlines and dogs that were little more than pitbulls bred to fight" (115). The conflict between the old and new orders could not be more explicit: the natural world suffocated under the influx of unnaturally bred livestock. Before long, Billy realizes that there is only one way to get the wolf out of the situation; he shoots the wolf dead, ending her torment.

After the death of the wolf, Billy aimlessly wanders the Mexican countryside. At the outset of these wanderings McCarthy repeats the trope of an interrupted idyll. Billy guides his horse to a shelf of rock, a vantage point from which he can view the surrounding Mexican countryside. As Billy looks at the sky, a dark omen, "a single vulture hanging motionless in some high vector that the wind had chosen for it" interrupts his reverie. He turns his eyes back toward the landscape and sees "the smoke of a locomotive passing slowly downcountry over the plain forty mile away" (135). The vulture's presence over the wide open Mexican landscape serves notice of its future. Vultures feed on the dead and dying, and the remainder of the novel chronicles Billy's increasing familiarity with the inevitability of death, for his family and for the land where they sought refuge.

When Billy finally crosses back to the ranch he finds that it has been looted, his parents murdered, and their horses stolen. He reunites with his brother Boyd, but the Parham home, as it once was, is forever gone. Thus begins the wandering of Billy Parham, in search of a new life, which is actually his old way of life; he becomes like the wolf in his hopeless search for the old order, old ceremonies, old protocols, a pastoral existence free from modern interference. Shortly after their reunion, Billy and Boyd depart for Mexico with the ill-conceived idea of recapturing their horses, returning to their family ranch, and resuming the only life they have known. However, from the outset of this second crossing into Mexico it is clear that Billy's desired way of life is quickly becoming extinct. As McCarthy writes, "Doomed enterprises divide lives forever into the then and the now" (129).

McCarthy plays the two brothers against each other in this second crossing. Although Billy Parham and John Grady Cole are sometimes equated with one another, it is Boyd who parallels Cole in his association with the pastoral world. Boyd, for instance, engages Billy in a conversation about what horses know, and whereas Billy says "Hell, they don't know nothin. They're just in some mountains somewheres," Boyd objects, echoing Cole's sentiments in *All the Pretty Horses*. He argues that they could find their way back to the ranch if need

be, that "they just know where things are" (189). Other characters note a difference between Boyd and Billy. One remarks to Billy that "Your brother is young enough to believe that the past still exists" (202). On the other hand, although Billy laments the change from a pastoral existence, he does not seem so fully given over to it as Boyd. In truth, he is less like Cole and more like Lacey Rawlins in his ability to persevere, to survive the loss of the beloved lifestyle to which he has grown accustomed.

Conversely, when Billy determines that their ill-defined quest is futile, Boyd stays in Mexico rather than accompany Billy back north, even after a particularly harrowing series of events in which he is seriously wounded by gunfire. Boyd stays for love—for his love of the cowboy lifestyle and his love for a beautiful, naive young Mexican girl whom he and Billy earlier save from being gang raped. Like the wolf, Boyd suffers at the hands of men, and his end is ultimately like that of the wolf. But for Boyd that is perhaps not the worst of all possible fates; he becomes a kind of rebel legend in the country: mythic, grander in death than he could have been in life, given the shrinking accommodation of his relationship with the land. Learning of Boyd's death, Billy hears, "He is where he is supposed to be. And yet the place he has found is also of his own choosing. That is a piece of luck not to be despised" (387-88).

On his second return to the States from Mexico, Billy again faces a different world from the one he left. When he returned from his first crossing, he found his parents dead and his personal world irrevocably changed; however, the change he finds when he crosses into the States at Columbus, New Mexico, has more universal consequences. The border guard asks Billy if he has "come back to sign up," to which Billy, thinking the guard is referring to a ranch crew, answers "I reckon. If I can find an outfit that'll have me." "You neednt to worry about that" responds the guard. "You aint got flat feet have you?"

> "Flat feet?"
>
> "Yeah. You got flat feet they wont take you."
>
> "What the hell are you talking about?"
>
> "Talkin about the army."
>
> "Army?"
>
> "Yeah. The army. How long you been gone anyways?"
>
> "I dont have no idea. I dont even know what month this is."
>
> "You dont know what's happened?"
>
> "No. What's happened?"
>
> "Hell fire, boy. This country's at war."

(333)

With no family, no job, and no money, Billy decides to join the army, which would signal his transition from the old pastoral protocol to the new technological one. However, despite his willingness to make this transition, he is unsuccessful in his several attempts to join the military. Billy's irregular heartbeat and erratic pulse physically disqualify him from military service and metaphorically deny him the chance to fit into the new world order. Despondent and confused, Billy works as a hand at a series of southwestern ranches before making his last sojourn into Mexico.

Because McCarthy rarely makes his readers privy to the thoughts of his characters, it is initially unclear why Billy again descends into Mexico. The opportunity to reunite with his brother is significant, but the reunion is not what he might have hoped for. He soon confirms what his investigations have suggested, that his brother has been killed. His mission then changes from reunion to the retrieval of Boyd's remains, which, in a macabre episode, he unearths. He returns to New Mexico with his brother's bones and buries them in a cemetery outside Lordsburg. Of his third crossing into Mexico, Billy says "It's the only time I was ever down [there] that I got what I come after. But it sure as hell wasnt what I wanted" (416). Billy's belief in the superiority of a rural existence over that of city life dies with Boyd. Although he again works ranches, he never again sees in them the promise he once did.

CITIES OF THE PLAIN

The first two volumes of the Border Trilogy are coming of age tales set largely in Mexico, although the histories of John Grady Cole and Billy Parham do not seem especially congruent. However, their paths finally cross in *Cities of the Plain,* when the two are working on the ranch of Mac McGovern just outside El Paso, Texas. In this volume, which takes place in 1952, we finally learn their destinies. Cole's sentimental dream of a pastoral existence is permanently interrupted by the presence of cities on the plain, specifically the border towns of Juárez and El Paso. Metaphorically, the phrase "cities of the plain" aptly suggests a parallel between Juárez and El Paso and Sodom and Gomorra. Literally, "cities of the plain" implies that the open plains of Cole's and Parham's youth are now punctuated with cities, transforming Cole's pastoral dream into a nightmare and leaving Parham to live out his remaining days haunted by remembrances of all he has loved and lost.

The opening scene of the novel is familiar territory: "They stood in the doorway and stomped the rain from their boots and swung their hats and wiped the water from their faces": Cowboys in from the rain, perhaps after a hard day's work. What immediately follows places is new ground in the context of the trilogy:

> Out in the street the rain slashed through the standing
> water driving the gaudy red and green colors of the

neon signs to wander and seethe and rain danced on the steel tops of the cars parked along the curb.

> Damned if I aint half drowned, Billy said. He swung his dripping hat. Where's the all-american cowboy at?
>
> He's gone inside.
>
> Let's go. He'll have all them good fat ones picked out for hisself.

(3)

When Billy asks as to the whereabouts of "the all-american cowboy," it is clear he can mean only John Grady Cole. We realize McCarthy's cowboys are no longer out on the rangeland, nor have they returned to their ranch quarters. Instead, they are in a Juárez brothel. And so the new milieu is established. In the trilogy's earlier volumes, towns were intrusions on the western landscape; the reverse is the case in *Cities of the Plain.*

Part and parcel with the idea of a pastoral landscape is the existence of free ranging wild animals. In the wolf episode of *The Crossing,* the plausibility of wild animals coexisting with humans in an increasingly urbanized world is seriously challenged. In *Cities of the Plain,* McCarthy, through a series of bloody vignettes, makes the conflict even more explicit. Early in the novel, Billy and Troy, a co-worker, are on their way to visit Troy's brother. While en route Troy tells the tale of driving across Texas with a buddy, at high speeds in a brand new Oldsmobile 88. Along the way the Oldsmobile keeps hitting jackrabbits. They decide to ignore the near constant "thuds" and press on at high speeds. When they finally pull into a filling station, they nearly get into a fight with a man whose wife has an adverse reaction to what she sees in the Oldsmobile's grill. As Troy recounts,

> [. . .] when I got around to the front of the car it was just packed completely full of jackrabbit heads. I mean there was a hundred of em jammed in there and the front of the car and the bumper and all just covered with blood and rabbit guts and them rabbits I reckon they'd sort of turned their heads away just at impact cause they was all lookin out, eyes all crazy lookin. Teeth sideways. Grinnin.

(22)

If there is such a place as jackrabbit heaven, Texas is surely it. Or at least it was prior to the arrival en masse of the automobile. Troy's grisly story graphically illustrates the innate disadvantage of the natural world when forced to compete with technology.

Later, Cole talks with Mr. Johnson, Mac McGovern's father-in-law, who had "been born in east Texas in eighteen sixty-seven and come out to this country as a young man. In his time the country had gone from the oil lamp and the horse and buggy to jet planes and the atomic bomb" (106). Johnson, a figure revered by Cole, tells him of a time when wolves freely roamed the plains but that he "aint heard a wolf howl in thirty odd years. I dont know where you'd go to hear one. There may not be any such place" (126). Sadly, Mr. Johnson is correct in his suspicion. In *The Crossing* wolves still existed, albeit primarily in Mexico and in rapidly shrinking numbers; by the time of the events depicted in *Cities of the Plain* their existence has become hearsay and legend. The fate of wolves will ultimately be that of all plains animals, which are increasingly forced to compete with humans for resources in green spaces that shrink exponentially.

Just as the plains animals suffer from industrial encroachment, John Grady Cole, for whom the world he "has been born into is not the world for which he was made," also finds that he no longer functions as he once did (Arnold 261). The boy who demonstrated such a phenomenal relationship with horses has been reduced to a mere man; whereas John Grady Cole is described in *All the Pretty Horses* as one born to sit a horse, Cole now finds himself cast off the animals' backs. Early in *Cities of the Plain* Troy reports that Cole has been injured when a "horse fell backwards on him" (15). His astonishing fall serves as a graphic signal of the futility of Cole's attempts to stay atop the cowboy lifestyle. Cole cannot help but realize that in terms of equine empathy he is not as he once was. The cowboy lifestyle is vanishing not only on the landscape but within Cole, who says, "When I was a kid I thought I knew all there was to know about a horse. Where horses are concerned I've just got dumber and dumber" (53). Although still twice the horseman that anyone else is, he no longer measures up to the boy he once was.

Billy never held the dream quite as dear as Cole, but he nevertheless once believed in the superiority of cowboy life. After the events in *The Crossing,* he is no longer sure about the cowboy life, even though he continues to work as a ranch hand. However, Cole still has a pastoral vision of his future and thinks that perhaps he has found a kindred spirit in Billy. But he has not. Cole asks Billy, "You think you'd of liked to of lived back in the old days?" Without hesitation Billy replies, "No. I did when I was a kid. I used to think rawhidin a bunch of bony cattle in some outland country would be just as close to heaven as a man was likely to get. I wouldnt give you much for it now." Instead, he likes "When you throw a switch and the lights come on [. . .]. If I think about what I wanted as a kid and what I want now they aint the same thing. I guess what I wanted wasnt what I wanted" (77-78). Billy, older, wiser, and more realistic than Cole, has grown tired of fighting their changing world.

But John Grady Cole has not yet given the dream up as dead. Unbeknownst to his peers, while at the brothel in the novel's opening scene, Cole spotted a beautiful young epileptic prostitute named Magdalena. Although he did not pay for her services, he later tracks her down and begins a passionate love affair. He intends to free her from her life of prostitution and bring her back to a tiny house in the hills above the ranch. Cole envisions their life there as a refuge, free from the intrusion of the world's increasing urbanism. When Billy asks Cole if he could be anything other than a cowboy, Cole says "I wouldnt be nothin else" (95). But Cole's dream is deeply flawed. The U.S. Army is about to take McGovern's ranch and the surrounding area through eminent domain to expand the borders of neighboring Fort Bliss. Cole does not realize the inescapability of the Army's plan nor that World War II marked the beginning of a technological age from which there would be no turning back. Billy astutely observes that "this country aint the same. Nor anything in it. The war changed everything. I dont think people even know it yet." When Cole asks "how," Billy responds "It just did. It aint the same no more. It never will be" (78). In addition to his unwillingness to accept that his dream of a pastoral homestead can never be realized, Cole also refuses to acknowledge the risk associated with trying to remove a prostitute from the clutches of her pimp, who in Magdalena's case is a particularly dangerous man named Eduardo.

The pimp, revealingly, is depicted as standing with "His hands clasped behind him at the small of his back in a stance he had perhaps admired or read of but a stance native to some other country, not his" (79). Eduardo consciously situates himself in the new world, practicing the new protocols. In conversation with Billy, who Cole sent to gauge the possibility of buying Magdalena's freedom, Eduardo not only embraces these "new protocols," but disparages John Grady for his inability to see the world realistically. Their conversation cuts Billy deeply, evoking not only thoughts of John Grady Cole, but of Bill's brother Boyd. Billy later tells Cole "most people get smacked around enough after a while they start to pay attention. More and more you remind me of Boyd. Only way I could ever get him to do anything was to tell him not to" (146). Even as he warns Cole about the likely consequences of his continued pursuit of Magdalena, he seems to know that he cannot divert Cole from the path chosen by Boyd. Eduardo refuses to part with Magdalena; instead he has her killed, which causes Cole to seek revenge. He kills Eduardo in a knife fight, but not before sustaining fatal wounds himself. Shortly after the fight, he dies in the presence of Billy Parham, who arrives too late to save him.

For Billy Parham, Cole's death has a similar effect as had Boyd's. Once again he begins a period of wandering. In the epilogue we again meet Billy Parham, in "the spring of the second year of the new millennium" (264). Although it appears throughout *Cities of the Plain* as if Parham wanted to make the transition from a rural to an urban dweller, he never quite makes it. Instead, he bounces for years from ranch to ranch; we learn that his most recent job was as an extra in a movie, which is perhaps the only place where cowboys still live. When he has money he stays in fleabag hotels; otherwise, he survives the elements by staying under freeway overpasses and sleeping in concrete tiles by the highway. The future Cole wanted to forestall has arrived. And with its arrival, Parham has a new perspective. Despite his desire to live a life in which he could "throw a switch and the lights come on," he now is nostalgic for the pastoral life that Boyd and Cole pursued so fervently. He may never give in fully to their same urges, but with each loss he is closer to seeing what is vanishing. After the loss of Boyd, he is able to think, despite his earlier claims that horses are ignorant animals, that perhaps a horse really does know what is in a person's heart (84). Likewise, at the conclusion of *Cities of the Plain* he stops "to talk to children or to horses" in De Baca County, New Mexico; he drinks from a spring and McCarthy writes how "He'd not seen a cup at a spring in years and he held it in both hands as had thousands before him unknown to him yet joined in sacrament" (289-90). And more important, he dreams. He dreams of the rural life and Boyd and tells about how "He was awful good with horses. I always liked to watch him ride. Liked to watch him around horses. I'd give about anything to see him one more time" (291). Billy Parham, like Boyd and Cole, has become a dreamer. But unlike his brother and his friend, Billy cannot dream of an unattainable future, only of a long gone past.

And so concludes the trilogy that opened with such high hopes. Over its course, John Grady Cole slowly comes to think that maybe, just maybe, he will not be able to live his pastoral dream life on American soil. His stay in the utopian environs of La Purísima, leads him to think that even if he cannot find a pastoral life in America, he surely can in Mexico. Toward the end of *Cities of the Plain,* Cole asks Billy "Dont you think if there's anything left of this life it's down there?" to which Billy responds "I dont even know what this life is [. . .] I think it's in your head [. . .]. It's another world. Everybody I ever knew that ever went back [to Mexico] was goin after somethin. Or thought they was" (218). Sad to say, Billy is right. The Mexico represented in *Cities of the Plain* is not the idyllic pastoral fantasy land of La Purísima but the brutal and sordid urban reality of Juárez. Cumulatively, McCarthy's Border Trilogy chronicles the death of traditional American pastoralism. The result is a work that in earnestly recording that death concurrently became what is to date the defining work of contemporary American pastoralism, in which a nostalgia for what can never again be attained replaces dreams of a pastoral future.

Works Cited

Arnold, Edwin T. "*Cities of the Plain*." *World and I* 13.10 (Oct. 1998): 258-68.

Bell, Vereen. "'Between the Wish and the Thing the World Lies Waiting.'" *Southern Review* 28.4 (Autumn 1992): 920-27.

Buell, Lawrence. *The Environmental Imagination: Thoreau, Nature Writing, and the Formation of American Culture.* Cambridge: Belknap, 1995.

Cawelti, John G. "Cormac McCarthy: Restless Seekers." *Southern Writers at Century's End.* Ed. Jeffrey J. Folks and James A. Perkins. Lexington: U of Kentucky P, 1997. 164-76.

Cheuse, Alan. "A Note on Landscape in *All the Pretty Horses*." *Southern Quarterly* 30.4 (Summer 1992): 140-42.

Grammer, John M. "'A Thing Against Which Time Will Not Prevail': Pastoral and History in Cormac McCarthy's South." *Southern Quarterly* 30.4 (Summer 1992): 19-30.

Luce, Dianne C. "'When You Wake': John Grady Cole's Heroism in *All the Pretty Horses*." *Sacred Violence: A Reader's Companion to Cormac McCarthy.* Ed. Wade Hall and Rick Wallach. El Paso: Texas Western P, 1995. 155-67.

Marx, Leo. *The Machine in the Garden.* New York: Oxford UP, 1964.

McCarthy, Cormac. *All the Pretty Horses.* New York: Knopf, 1992.

———. *Cities of the Plain.* New York: Knopf, 1998.

———. *The Crossing.* New York: Knopf, 1994.

Pilkington, Tom. "Fate and Free Will on the American Frontier." *Western American Literature* 27.4 (Winter 1993): 311-22.

Slotkin, Richard. "John Ford's *Stagecoach* and the Mythic Space of the Western Movie." *The Big Empty: Essays on the Land as Narrative.* Ed. Leonard Engel. Albuquerque: U of New Mexico P, 1994. 261ff-82.

White, Richard. *"It's Your Misfortune and None of My Own": A New History of the American West.* Norman: U of Oklahoma P, 1991.

Robert W. Hamblin (essay date 2003)

SOURCE: Hamblin, Robert W. "Beyond the Edge of the Map: Faulkner, Turner, and the Frontier Line." In *Faulkner in the Twenty-First Century: Faulkner and*

Yoknapatawpha, 2000, edited by Robert W. Hamblin and Ann J. Abadie, pp. 154-71. Jackson: University Press of Mississippi, 2003.

[*In the following essay, Hamblin explores William Faulkner's preoccupation with the American frontier in his fiction, arguing that he was very interested in mapping out life at the frontier line, a place that Faulkner regarded as a significant meeting point for culture and wilderness.*]

1

James Cowan's fascinating novel, *A Mapmaker's Dream,* subtitled *The Meditations of Fra Mauro, Cartographer to the Court of Venice,*[1] records the lifelong efforts of a sixteenth-century monk to create an accurate and comprehensive map of the entire world. In his cloister of an island monastery Fra Mauro interviews explorers, merchants, and visitors from distant lands; reads letters and books by world travelers; and pores over maps created by other cartographers. In the process of conducting his research and mapping his findings, Fra Mauro comes to understand, and accept, the paradoxical and mysterious relationship between the known and the unknown, civilization and barbarity, culture and nature, science and myth, reality and ideality, experience and art. Ultimately, his life's work, the map, becomes the text in which he records his impressions of life, nature, and self.

Unlike Cowan, William Faulkner never wrote a philosophical novel about a mapmaker's quest for understanding and order; yet he too was a mapmaker of sorts (both literally and figuratively) who seriously explored the intersection of geography and culture. As demonstrated by the maps he drew of his imaginary Yoknapatawpha County,[2] his survey of the history of that county in *Requiem for a Nun* and "Mississippi," and the political and historical essays and addresses he produced during the 1950s, Faulkner was keenly interested in charting life and experience at the edge of the map, the frontier line—that point in the evolution of culture where wilderness and settlement meet, where nature and landscape are engaged and domesticated. Indeed, the story of Yoknapatawpha is one long chronicle of the advance of civilization, the repetitive cycle, as Faulkner expresses it in "Mississippi," of "the obsolescent, dispossessed tomorrow by the already obsolete"[3]: first the mound builders, then the Indians, then the white hunters and settlers who found Jefferson and establish a seat of government, then those like Thomas Sutpen who bring slaves and develop the plantations, then, during the Civil War and Reconstruction, the Northern soldiers and abolitionists and carpetbaggers, and eventually the lumbermen and bankers and industrialists who, in Faulkner's own time, "[push] what remain[s] of the wilderness further and further southward into the V of

the Big River and hills" (*ESPL* [*Essays, Speeches and Public Letters of William Faulkner*] 24). By 1945, when Faulkner drew the second of his maps of Yoknapatawpha, only a tiny part of the original wilderness yet remained, and that some two hundred miles to the southwest deep in the Mississippi Delta.

The Delta, beginning just to the west of Oxford and Lafayette County, played a significant role in William Faulkner's life and work. His lifelong friend and one-time literary agent and editor, Ben Wasson, came from Greenville, and Faulkner often visited him there. Another Greenvillian, Hodding Carter, the founding editor of the *Delta-Democrat Times,* strongly influenced Faulkner's views on race and sectionalism.[4] As a young man, in the company of another friend, Phil Stone, the Oxford lawyer, Faulkner frequently traveled to Clarksdale to visit Reno's Place, a popular nightclub and gambling spot of the 1920s. In 1952 Faulkner delivered the annual Delta Council address on the Delta State College campus in Cleveland. Sections of two of Faulkner's finest and most significant narratives are set in the Delta: *Go Down, Moses* and *If I Forget Thee, Jerusalem* [*The Wild Palms*].

In both Faulkner's personal life and his art the Mississippi Delta functions as a frontier society geographically and psychologically removed from the restraining social order of Oxford and Jefferson. The Delta is a place to explore personal freedom, to escape the censorious judgments of family and neighbors back home; it is a place to return to the primitive conditions of the wilderness, where bears and deer and squirrels outnumber humans, before the advent of plantations and lumber companies and railroads that would deplete the big woods and the animals; it is a place where individuals can test their mettle, where the worth of the individual and his place in the social order is based on integrity and personal skill and courage and effort and not on authoritative decree or aristocratic privilege. Significantly, Faulkner's Delta begins at the westernmost edge and continues beyond the border of the maps he drew of Yoknapatawpha County, thus representing unincorporated space, virgin land as yet unsettled, uncivilized and unspoiled. In this regard, as I shall subsequently demonstrate, Faulkner's Delta stands as a microcosm of that larger and continually expanding American frontier that Frederick Jackson Turner, in his highly influential *The Frontier in American History* and other works, argued was the single most important factor in the development of American character, values, and institutions.

2

The heart of Faulkner's vision of the Delta as frontier, of course, is "The Bear." Here Ike McCaslin serves his apprenticeship as hunter under the tutelage of Sam Fathers in "the wilderness, the big woods, bigger and older than any recorded document," "the same solitude, the same loneliness through which frail and timorous man had merely passed without altering it, leaving no mark nor scar, which looked exactly as it must have looked when the first ancestor of Sam Fathers' Chickasaw predecessors crept into it and looked about him, club or stone axe or bone arrow drawn and ready."[5] If Sam Fathers is the priest who guides Ike's novitiate in the ways of the wilderness, the god that Fathers serves is Old Ben, the bear that both rules and incarnates these woods. Modeled in part, it would appear, on the Sacred Bear of Frazer's *The Golden Bough,*[6] Old Ben (and to a lesser degree the other animals of the forest) is the totem god that offers himself in sacrifice for man's survival and renewal. Like Frazer's primitives, but with corn whiskey substituted for the animal blood employed in the religious rituals of precivilized men, Faulkner's hunters ingest "those fine fierce instants of heart and brain and courage and wiliness and speed [that] were concentrated and distilled into that brown liquor which not women, not boys and children, but only hunters drank, drinking not of the blood they spilled but some condensation of the wild immortal spirit, drinking it moderately, humbly even, not with the pagan's base and baseless hope of acquiring thereby the virtues of cunning and strength and speed but in salute to them" (*GDM* [*Go Down, Moses*] 192).

Ike's entry into this spiritual order occurs in his eleventh year when he is afforded his first view of the giant bear. The scene that records this event draws upon both primitive initiatory rites and ritual acts of Christian mystics in their quest for a vision of God. First Ike must purge himself of all the trappings of material culture—the gun, the compass, and the watch. Then, purified, lost to self, having given himself completely to the spirit of the wilderness, he is granted his vision. That Old Ben is more than mere bear, is mythic and divine, is suggested by the ghostly, almost supernatural, nature of his sudden appearance and disappearance: "Then he saw the bear. *It did not emerge,* appear: *it was just there,* immobile, fixed in the green and windless noon's hot dappling, . . . *dimensionless* against the dappled *obscurity,* looking at him. Then it moved. It crossed the glade without haste, walking for an instant into the sun's full glare and out of it. . . . Then it was gone. *It didn't walk* into the woods. It *faded,* sank back into the wilderness *without motion* [emphases added]" (209). Ike's novitiate is over; he has been accepted into the order of a spiritual, transcendent ideal.

To emphasize the ideal, even divine, quality of the wilderness, Faulkner compares the world of the big woods to the biblical Eden. Thus Ike links the existence of the Delta wilderness to the original creation story: "He told in the Book how He created the earth, made it and looked at it and said it was all right, and then He made man. He made the earth first and peopled it with dumb

creatures, and then He created man to be His overseer on the earth and to hold suzerainty over the earth and the animals on it in His name, not to hold for himself and his descendants inviolable title forever, generation after generation, to the oblongs and squares of the earth, but to hold the earth mutual and intact in the communal anonymity of brotherhood" (257). In the idyllic wilderness, then, there is no concern for ownership. Neither is social caste nor race a factor. In the big woods Southern aristocrats, poor whites, blacks, and Indians conjoin in mutual fellowship and brotherhood, and the worth of a man is determined by his own merits, not by artificial definitions society might impose. In the woods all men—white, black, and red—are literally and symbolically brothers.

In the dialogue with his cousin Cass in section 4 of "The Bear," Ike parallels this ideal wilderness ruled by Old Ben and Sam Fathers with the genesis of American civilization. The American continent, Ike points out, was settled in idealism and hope, a place where man could escape "the old world's worthless twilight" and create "a new world where a nation of people could be founded in humility and pity and sufferance and pride of one to another" (258). In this brave new world man would throw off the shackles of the past and begin anew to carve out an ideal commonwealth which would shun the sins and errors of previous civilizations. The bountiful and open frontier of the wilderness that settlers found in this new world contributed to the vision of perfection: "this land . . . for which [God] had done so much with woods for game and streams for fish and deep rich soil for seed and lush springs to sprout it and long summers to mature it and serene falls to harvest it and short mild winters for men and animals." Thus was born the American Dream, the belief that the "whole hopeful continent [was] dedicated as a refuge and sanctuary of liberty and freedom from . . . the old world's worthless evening" (283).

This dream, however, had not materialized, and Ike McCaslin's survey of the history of both the South and the nation explores some of the reasons why. For one thing there was the matter of how the white man had taken the land from the Indians. For another there was the curse of chattel slavery. America, which had been founded in freedom, had been built only in part on the noble virtues of courage, industry, and sacrifice: it was also based upon man's inhumanity to his fellow man, and this inhumanity was the practice of the New England slaver and manufacturer as well as the Southern planter. This violation of the original spirit of the dream had led to disappointment and suffering, to exile from Eden. America had ultimately proven to be not an escape from Europe but a repetition of Old World mistakes and atrocities: "not only that old world from which [God] had rescued them but this new one too which He had revealed and led them to as a sanctuary and refuge

[had] become the same worthless tideless rock cooling in the last crimson evening" (284). For Ike the symbol of this failure—and indeed of the judgment that comes to any society which substitutes greed and inhumanity and injustice for human brotherhood—is war and its horrible aftermath. The tragedies of the Civil War and Reconstruction, both of which pitted brother against brother and race against race, are interpreted as a working out of the curse which not only white Southerners but indeed all Americans have inherited because of their misdeeds.

In its broadest allegorical application, of course, "The Bear" becomes a commentary on the universal history of humankind. Ike McCaslin sees all history as a continual rise and fall of empires, each founded on romantic dreams of permanence and perfection and each in its turn falling prey to human folly and weakness. What has been said of the American Dream is here extended to embrace all mankind. This application accounts for the many historical and biblical allusions in "The Bear"—not only to the discovery of America and the fall of the antebellum South but also to the destruction of Noah's world by flood, to the rise and fall of the Roman empire, to the quest of the Jews for Canaan, and, as already noted and most importantly, to the fall of man in Eden. "Dispossessed of Eden" (257, 258)—this refrain serves as the unifying theme that links together all of the various allusions. The history of humanity, "The Bear" implies, is a cyclical reenactment of the loss of Eden and the quest to repossess the Garden experience in some "Promised Land" of the future. Thus caught between a forfeited Eden and a dreamed-of yet never-to-be-possessed Canaan, between community and frontier, man exists in a paradoxical state of stasis and motion, achievement and failure, gain and loss, memory and desire.

3

Readers must be cautious, however, of accepting Faulkner's (or is it merely Ike McCaslin's?) characterization of the wilderness in "The Bear" at face value. As Peter Froehlich has convincingly argued,[7] "The Bear" presents a highly romanticized and humanized view of nature, one that still lies very near to the civilized world, a user-friendly universe ruled by a benevolent God sympathetic to the needs and concerns of man. The characterization is decidedly Wordsworthian, a nature that with "One impulse from a vernal wood / May teach you more of man, / Of moral evil and of good, / Than all the sages can."[8] Yet Faulkner well knew there was another type of nature. Post-Darwinian and schooled in the literary naturalism of Theodore Dreiser and others, he knew of a nature that is indifferent, even hostile, to man: "nature red in tooth and claw,"[9] ruled by natural selection and chance and the survival of the fittest. This nature resides off the edge of the map; it is

the ultimate frontier, unexplored and terror-filled, beyond the known world, the place where land and water's end falls away into chaos and darkness. Before he wrote "The Bear," Faulkner had already presented this frightful view of nature, in the story of the tall convict in the "Old Man" section of *The Wild Palms* [*If I Forget Thee, Jerusalem*].

"Old Man" is set during the raging Mississippi River flood of 1927. At the height of the crisis a group of prisoners in Parchman penitentiary are commanded to assist in shoring up levees along the river and in locating and rescuing refugees who have had to abandon their homes. Two of the prisoners, the protagonist of the story identified only as "the tall convict" and a second called "the plump convict," are given a skiff and an oar and assigned the task of rescuing a woman clinging to a cypress snag and a man sitting on the ridgepole of a cotton house. Almost immediately the quest turns into a horror-filled struggle for survival pitting frail, solitary man against the malevolent and destructive power of the river, Old Man. On the rushing sweep of the flooding current the tall convict is swept uncontrollably on an atavistic journey backward through time, back to precivilization when, seemingly, the whole universe was one untraveled frontier. As in "The Bear," here Faulkner employs a biblical myth from Genesis, though in this case it is not the archetype of an idyllic Eden in which man communes with God but rather the image of Noah's flood which threatens to destroy man and all his endeavors, hurling nature back into chaos.

"Old Man" contains some of the most visually descriptive language in all of Faulkner's works, and even a small sampling of this magnificent prose will demonstrate what the tall convict is up against. Quickly separated from his companion, the tall convict is left to fend for himself, solitary and defenseless. As the plump convict later recounts the incident: "Just all of a sudden the boat whirled clean around and begun to run fast backward like it was hitched to a train and it whirled around again and I happened to look up and there was a limb right over my head and I grabbed it just in time and that boat was snatched out from under me like you'd snatch off a sock and I saw it one time more upside down and that fellow . . . holding to it with one hand and still holding the paddle in the other."[10]

Finally managing to upright and reboard the skiff and then, quite accidentally, discovering the woman, who is eight months' pregnant, the convict attempts to resume the search for the man on the cottonhouse, but the current is too strong and continues to sweep the skiff downstream: "During the next three or four hours after the thunder and lightning had spent itself the skiff ran in pitch streaming darkness upon a roiling expanse which, even if he could have seen, apparently had *no boundaries* [emphasis added]. Wild and invisible, it tossed and heaved about and beneath the boat, ridged with dirty phosphorescent foam and filled with a debris of destruction—objects nameless and enormous and invisible which struck and slashed at the skiff and whirled on" (*WP* [*Wild Palms*] 134). Now Faulkner presents the convict not only as Noah but also as Ulysses, lost on the vast water and seeking his way back home. When the woman inquires if he knows where they are, he says, "I dont even know where I used to be. Even if I knowed which way was north, I wouldn't know if that was where I wanted to go." "Which way you fixing to go?" she then asks. "Ask the boat [he replies]. I been in it since breakfast and I aint never knowed, where I aimed to go or where I was going either" (128-29).

Unable to deliver the woman to shore, unable even to surrender to the authorities, who mistake his circumstance as an attempted escape and fire upon him, the convict is eventually forced to serve as unwilling attendant for the birth of the child. Then, resuming the journey with a child as well as the woman, the convict is swept still farther beyond civilization and security, seemingly now beyond the boundaries marked by maps. Much later, when he tries to explain his experiences with the Louisiana Cajuns who speak no English, identifying them as "Not Americans," the plump convict responds in amazement: "Not Americans? You was clean out of *America* even?" (201). Symbolically, the region the convict has now entered is that populated by early cartographers with monsters and demons that waited to devour men who ventured too far and fell off the edge of the world.

The monsters here are snakes and alligators, the first of which he fights armed only with the broken boat paddle and the second with a small knife. It is in the hand-to-hand combats of the alligator hunts that Faulkner depicts the struggle of man versus nature in its most extreme and elemental form, a vivid description of what life is like at the farthest side of frontier: the convict "stooped straddling, the knife driving even as he grasped the near foreleg, this all in the same instant when the lashing tail struck him a terrific blow upon the back. But the knife was home, he knew that even on his back in the mud, the weight of the thrashing beast longwise upon him, its ridged back clutched to his stomach, his arm about its throat, the hissing head clamped against his jaw, the furious tail lashing and flailing, the knife in his other hand probing for the life and finding it, the hot fierce gush" (216-17).[11]

As terrible and painfully exhausting as the convict's struggle with elemental forces throughout "Old Man" proves to be, paradoxically it is also the means by which he discovers and acts upon his own strengths of character: courage, integrity, honor, honesty, fidelity ("I aint going without my boat" [227]), willfulness of purpose, ultimately the capacity to suffer, endure, and prevail. As

Faulkner writes, "[H]e who had never ceased to flail at the bland treacherous water with what he had believed to be the limit of his strength now from somewhere, some ultimate absolute reserve, produced a final measure of endurance, will to endure" (124). The crisis has also produced in him a curious though satisfying sense of freedom: "the being allowed to work and earn money, that right and privilege which he believed he had earned to himself unaided, asking no favor of anyone or anything save the right to be let alone to pit his will and strength against the sauric Protagonist of a land, a region" (226). Originally an obscure, anonymous prisoner without even a name, next a Noah looking for a place to land his ark, then Ulysses wandering in search of home, the convict is finally another legendary Greek hero, triumphing over insurmountable odds: "Do not concern yourself about food, O Hercules," the Cajun cries. "Catch alligators" (219). As I shall shortly seek to demonstrate, he has also become something of the type, if a reluctant one, of Frederick Jackson Turner's American pioneer and frontiersman, pushing the frontier line farther and farther and in the process discovering his tremendous capacity for courage, self-reliance, and responsibility. And the reader now understands that the word "tall" in the convict's description is a reference not merely to his height but also to his heroic character.

Readers should not be surprised that the tall convict, despite the gains of self-discovery and victory over external nature, readily forfeits his life beyond the edge of the map to return to the safety and security of the known world. Faulkner well understood (as he would later dramatize so poignantly in *A Fable*) that the masses of men are followers, not pioneers and trailblazers, and that the anxiety and sheer weight of total freedom and responsibility are so great as to cause most individuals to seek the security of the familiar and the comfortable, even in extreme cases choosing to become a ward of the bureaucratic state or live under the tyranny of despotic rule. In the final analysis, therefore, the convict is not a frontiersman, despite his initial appearance of being so. Ultimately he will travel not farther West (as, incidentally, Charlotte Rittenmeyer and Harry Wilbourne do in the companion story to "Old Man") but back East, recrossing the ocean (in this case a river), and gladly surrendering his newfound freedom to regain the secure footing of land, home, conventionality, community. But, even conceding this, we must also acknowledge that Faulkner understood the value of pioneering heroes, the need to keep alive the frontier spirit, the willingness to retain something of the wilderness mentality, to expand the map of experience by pushing the frontier line farther and farther into the unknown. (This is exactly what he did in his artistic life, of course, as he explored new forms of narrative and characterization and made his way into that unexplored territory with only his own genius and willpower as companions and without the aid of guide, mentor, institution, or government.) As I shall now seek to demonstrate, his views in this regard are remarkably similar to those of Frederick Jackson Turner.

4

Turner (1861-1932), a native of Wisconsin who became the foremost historian and theorist of the American frontier, taught history at the University of Wisconsin from 1889 to 1910 and at Harvard from 1910 to 1924. In July 1893 he delivered a paper at the annual meeting of the American Historical Association in Chicago entitled "The Significance of the Frontier in American History," published the following year. In succeeding years Turner expanded the application of his "frontier thesis" to various regions and stages of American history, finally publishing his most significant and influential book, *The Frontier in American History,* in 1920. Thus the rise to preeminence of Turner's ideas occurred during William Faulkner's formative years, and Faulkner is almost certain to have read or heard about Turner's thesis.

What Turner sought to do in the field of history was what Mark Twain had only recently accomplished in literature: to demonstrate that the American frontier was not a barren wasteland, greatly inferior to the more sophisticated and educated East, but a vital and viable part of American, even world, culture and thought. Turner opposed both the eighteenth-century historians, who focused almost entirely on the original colonies as an extension of European (primarily English) history and culture, and the nineteenth-century historians who interpreted American history primarily as the result of the North-South split over slavery. To really understand the uniqueness of the American experiment, Turner argued, one must examine the ongoing dialectic between the Eastern establishment and the continually expanding Western and Southwestern frontiers. "The West," Turner argued, "was a migrating region, a stage of society rather than a place," providing both individuals and the nation the opportunity of "beginning over on its outer edge as it advanced into the wilderness."[12]

Turner's basic ideas can be easily summarized. He contended that "the existence of an area of free land, its continuous recession, and the advance of American settlement westward, explain American development."[13] This development, which Turner saw as a near-Darwinian evolutionary process, results from the periodic return to primitive conditions on the advancing frontier that create an ongoing opposition between savagery and civilization, sectionalism and federalism, growth and stasis, freedom and restraint, opportunity and closure, West and East. "The West," he wrote, "opened a refuge from the rule of established classes, from the subordination of youth to age, from the sway of established and revered institutions" (*Sections* [*The*

Significance of Sections in American History] 25). What Turner viewed as the essential traits of the American character—a fervent individualism that is antagonistic toward centralized government, an egalitarian spirit that accepted immigrants from various ethnic backgrounds (not merely Anglo-Saxon), a preference for an agrarian over an industrial economy, a materialism that resulted from the opportunity for every individual to start over again and seek his fortune on the frontier, a pragmatism that resulted from the physical necessity of having to contend daily with the challenges of enemies and nature, a general optimism that resulted from success in overcoming obstacles and expanding onward—all of these evolve from the presence of a geographical frontier throughout the developing history of the American nation.

Turner, of course, was advancing these ideas at the time when the physical presence of an American frontier was coming to an end. He cited the report of the superintendent of the 1890 census, which stated: "Up to and including 1880 the country had a frontier of settlement, but at present the unsettled area has been so broken into by isolated bodies of settlement that there can hardly be said to be a frontier line. In the discussion of its extent, its westward movement, etc., it can not, therefore, any longer have a place in the census reports" (*Frontier* 1). Turner predicted that, just as the presence of the frontier had had profound effects on the American character, so now would its absence. While he never developed in great detail his theory of future development, his implications are quite clear, and quite logical. The loss of the frontier would reverse the effects of its presence: there would be, in twentieth-century America, an erosion of personal freedom and individuality; a rise in conformity and collectivism; an increase in federalism, urbanization, and socialism; a displacement of the agrarian life style by industrialization; and a general tendency toward national conformity rather than regional distinctiveness. As Turner wrote as early as 1907:

> The nationalizing tendencies are at the present time clearly in evidence. The control of great industries has passed to a striking extent into the hands of corporations or trusts, operating on a national basis and centered in a few hands. Banking and transportation systems show the same tendency to consolidation. Cities are growing at a rate disproportioned to the increase of general population, and their numerical growth is only a partial index of their influence upon the thought as well as the economic life of the country. On the whole, in spite of rivalry, the business world of these cities tends to act nationally and to promote national homogeneity. The labor organizations are national in their scope and purposes. Newspapers, telegraph, post-office—all the agencies of intercourse and the formation of thought—tend toward national uniformity and national consciousness. The cooperative publication of news furnished by national agencies, the existence of common ownership and editorial conduct of chains of

newspapers, all tend to produce simultaneous formation of a national public opinion. In general the forces of civilization are working toward uniformity.

(Sections 311-12)

The final, convincing evidence of both the geographical and psychological closing of the frontier, Turner pointed out, could be seen in the region of the frontier itself, where the policy of free land that had once promoted "old individualistic principles and the *laissez faire* conception of government" has now been replaced, through the actions of the federal Reclamation Service, by government ownership and management of land and resources (310).

It is these consequences of the disappearing frontier that seem most relevant to a reading of Faulkner, since Faulkner was writing at the time when the changes Turner predicted had already occurred and become entrenched in the national agenda.

5

Turner's ideas find echo throughout Faulkner's works, but most explicitly in the political essays and speeches like the one Faulkner presented at Delta State College in 1952. When Faulkner visited Delta State to speak to the Delta Council, an organization of planters, farmers, and businessmen, he was an internationally renowned figure who was being asked to express his views on any number of subjects, not only writing but also race relations, politics, religion, psychology, and international relations. Significantly, though, Faulkner chose to travel to Cleveland not under the persona of the world figure but under that of the common, ordinary citizen. Joseph Blotner records an interesting anecdote about Faulkner's dress for the occasion. When Bob and Alice Farley arrived at Rowan Oak to drive Faulkner to Cleveland, they found him dressed in wrinkled cotton seersucker trousers, a shirt with a badly frayed collar, an old, belted jacket that was now much too small for him, and a felt hat that Farley dated from about 1915. (Faulkner's attire, by the way, would prove especially fortuitous for Bern Keating, the photographer from Greenville, who was destined to shoot on this day some of the most impressive photographs of Faulkner ever made.) Blotner continues the story: "You ready to go to Cleveland," [Farley] asked. "Oh, is this the day?" Faulkner replied, his eyes glinting. "It sure is." "Can I go like this?" "You can if you want to." "Let's go."[14] This makes for an amusing story, but it is extremely hard to believe that anyone, even an absent-minded author, would forget the date scheduled for him to make a significant speech on an issue of grave concern at the invitation of an important organization and before a large audience that would include the governor of the state and other important dignitaries. More likely, Faulkner deliberately chose his attire to identify with the hard-working, self-reliant Americans who were the subject of his remarks.

The speech Faulkner delivered that day, May 15, 1952, in Whitfield Gymnasium contains the essence of his views on the proper relationship between the individual and government. Drawing upon ideas expressed in his fiction all the way back to the 1930s and early '40s,[15] as well as in the book that he was completing at the time of his visit to Cleveland, *A Fable,* Faulkner delivered, to a standing ovation, a scathing attack upon a federal welfare system that, he argued, devalued challenge and initiative and thus encouraged personal laziness and irresponsibility. Claiming that the contemporary American had forgotten that "the premise of the rights of man" (*ESPL* 127) carried with it a willingness "to be responsible for the consequences of his own acts, to pay his own score, owing nothing to any man" (129), Faulkner reviewed the historical accomplishments of "the old tough, durable, uncompromising men" (130) who "left [their] homes, the land and graves of [their] fathers and all familiar things" (128) to secure their independence from the Old World and then successively conquer wildernesses from the Atlantic seaboard to the Pacific Ocean, in the process creating "a land of opportunity, in which all a man needed were two legs to move to a new place on, and two hands to grasp and hold with, in order to amass to himself enough material substance to last him the rest of his days and, who knew? even something over for his and his wife's children" (130). In words that could have been written by Frederick Jackson Turner, Faulkner celebrated these heroic actions: "Even while we were still battling the wilderness with one hand, with the other we fended and beat off the power which would have followed us even into the wilderness we had conquered, to compel and hold us to the old way. But we did it. We founded a land, and founded in it not just our right to be free and independent and responsible, but the inalienable duty of man to be free and independent and responsible" (128-29).

Then "something happened to us" (129), Faulkner continued, offering his version of the nation that Turner had predicted at the turn of the century. Americans had discarded and forgotten the understanding that the word "rights" also implies duties and responsibilities and, as a result, had relinquished their freedom in order to "hold [their] individual place on a public relief roll or at a bureaucratic or political or any other organization's gravy-trough" (130). What made this development even more tragic and grievous, Faulkner claimed, was that the principal enemy of American freedom was no longer a foreign power across an ocean but rather one that "faces us now from beneath the eagle-perched domes of our capitols and from behind the alphabetical splatters on the doors of welfare and other bureaus of economic or industrial regimentation, dressed not in martial brass but in the habiliments of what the enemy himself has taught us to call peace and progress, a civilization and plenty where we never before had it as good, let alone better; his artillery is a debased and respectless currency which has emasculated the initiative for independence by robbing initiative of the only mutual scale it knew to measure independence by" (132). So seductive has been the beguiling power of this enemy to convert its subjects to "the right not to earn, but to be given" that "at last, by simple compound usage, we have made respectable and even elevated to a national system, that which the old tough fathers would have scorned and condemned: charity" (131).

Not all of Faulkner's remarks to the Delta Council, however, constituted a jeremiad of woe. In fact, he ended his speech with a glimmer of hope. Three times echoing a celebrated phrase from his Nobel Prize Acceptance Address, he emphasized that he "decline[d] to believe" that Americans were incapable of relearning and restoring the principle of self-reliant, responsible freedom. Americans could once again, with sufficient courage and fidelity and resolve, rediscover a social order based on the old frontier values, "where those who would stand on their own feet, could, and those who won't, might have to" (133). Only then, Faulkner concluded, could an appropriate type of welfare find its place in the republic. "Then the welfare, the relief, the compensation, instead of being nationally sponsored cash prizes for idleness and ineptitude, could go where the old independent uncompromising fathers themselves would have intended it and blessed it: to those who still cannot, until the day when even the last of them except the sick and the old, would also be among them who not only can, but will" (133-34).

Faulkner's appearance at Delta State, his dress for the occasion, and the speech he delivered there together form a symbolic representation of Faulkner's views of geography and culture. He had traveled beyond the edge of his map of Yoknapatawpha, to the area that still contained a remnant of the old lost wilderness, to express his continuing belief in frontier values in a nation that was becoming increasingly standardized and collectivist. He had traveled, as readers of his fiction would know, to the region he describes in "Delta Autumn."

6

"Delta Autumn" is the next to last story in *Go Down, Moses* and the one immediately following "The Bear." The present-tense action of "The Bear" occurs in the 1880s, exactly contemporaneous with the period in which the superintendent of the census noted that the American frontier had closed. Thus the simultaneous deaths of Old Ben, Lion, and Sam Fathers, which in Faulkner's chronology occur in 1883, may be taken as a symbolic representation of the larger event. And section 5 of the story, in which Major de Spain closes down the hunting camp but gives Ike permission to visit the site for one last time, stands as an elegy to the end of the wilderness not only in Yoknapatawpha County but in all of America.[16]

As the allusions to Hitler and war make clear, "Delta Autumn" is set in the early 1940s. It opens with a contrast of then and now, of how the annual hunts were conducted years ago and how they are conducted now. Ike McCaslin, now "Uncle Ike" to all of Yoknapatawpha County, is approaching eighty years old. Then they had entered the woods in wagons; now they go in cars. Then there had been bears and deer and wild turkey in the country; now there is left only a rapidly diminishing number of deer. Then one could hear the scream of panther in the wild; now one hears the long hoot of the locomotive. Then they had to travel only thirty miles from Jefferson to find big game; now they have to drive two hundred miles (roughly, as I calculate the actual distance, to what is today the Sharkey Delta National Forest located just north of Vicksburg) to find enough remaining woods to give habitat to deer. As Faulkner notes, "Now the land lay open from the cradling hills on the East to the rampart of levee on the West, standing horseman-tall with cotton for the world's looms— the rich black land, imponderable and vast, fecund up to the very doorsteps of the negroes who worked it and of the white men who owned it; which exhausted the hunting life of a dog in one year, the working life of a mule in five, and of a man in twenty—the land in which neon flashed past them from the little countless towns and countless shining this-year's automobiles sped past them on the broad plumb-ruled highways" (*GDM* 340-41). Nothing is left of the old time, Faulkner continues, but "the Indian names on the little towns and usually pertaining to water—Aluschaskuna, Tillatoba, Homochitto, Yazoo" (341).

A corresponding change has taken place in the character and behavior of the hunters. Paralleling the changes that Turner predicted would occur with the closing of the frontier, Faulkner presents the descendants of the old hunters as moral and physical lilliputians intruding into the former land of giants.[17] One of the hunters, in fact, Ike's cousin Roth Edmonds, the reader learns, has been coming to the woods not primarily to hunt but to engage in a love affair (thus all the inside jokes in the story about hunting does); and he has returned to the woods this time determined to end what has become a bothersome relationship. In Faulkner's characterization of Roth it quickly becomes clear that none of the lessons of the woods that Sam Fathers taught the young Ike McCaslin—courage, honor, responsibility—has been learned and assimilated by Roth. A hunter who indiscriminately shoots does as readily as bucks, and with a shotgun instead of a rifle, Roth refuses to meet his mistress face to face but instead leaves money and a one-word message, "No" (356), for Ike to give to her when she comes to the camp seeking Roth. "What did you promise her that you haven't the courage to face her and retract?" Ike asks (356).

When the woman shows up at the camp, Uncle Ike discovers not only that she has her and Roth's child with her but also that she is part black and a cousin of him and Roth, being the granddaughter of Tennie's Jim, one of the mulatto descendants of old L. Q. C. McCaslin. Now it is Uncle Ike who says no. "He cried, not loud, in a voice of amazement, pity, and outrage: 'You're a nigger!'" (361). Sadly, it would appear, even Uncle Ike in his old age has forgotten the lesson of universal brotherhood he learned under the tutelage of Sam Fathers, in whose veins ran the blood of three races. "Go back North," Uncle Ike advises the woman. "Marry: a man in your own race. That's the only salvation for you—for a while yet, maybe a long while yet. We will have to wait. Marry a black man" (363). Earlier he had thought: *"Maybe in a thousand or two thousand years in America. . . . But not now! Not now!"* (361, Faulkner's italics). The hunting horn that Uncle Ike subsequently gives to the woman for the boy, in lineage the last known surviving descendant of old Lucius Quintus Carothers McCaslin in Faulkner's work, seems nothing more than a hollow gesture. The meek may have inherited in this case, if not the earth at least some symbol of familial rights, but the legacy seems merely a sop to salve an old man's guilty conscience.

In terms of the map and frontier images I have employed throughout this essay, "Delta Autumn" suggests how far modern America has fallen from the rugged individualism of the old West/Southwest. In the post-frontier America, apparently, even old pioneers who had stood strong in the wilderness in support of their convictions now grow soft and conform to the will of the timid majority. The setting of "Delta Autumn" is far west of Faulkner's Yoknapatawpha, almost as far west as the tall convict's harrowing experiences in "Old Man." But there is something of the character of the old frontier still operative in "Old Man," whereas the frontier of "Delta Autumn" is a diminished, tamed one, both in terms of the woods and the men who frequent them. As Turner had predicted, with the closure of an authentic frontier, the West has been assimilated into the pattern of the East, both now standing in uniformed and unified defense of the status quo.

7

I have sought to demonstrate that there are considerable parallels between Faulkner's depiction of the western frontier of Yoknapatawpha County and Frederick Jackson Turner's characterization of the broader American frontier. In conclusion, however, I would like to emphasize a couple of key distinctions in the respective treatments.

Turner's theory of the influence of the presence and now absence of the frontier in America, as indeed his overall emphasis on the importance of geography upon a national consciousness, is highly deterministic in nature. Living and writing under the growing influence of Darwinian evolution, particularly as Darwin's ideas had been filtered and recycled by the British philosopher and sociologist Herbert Spencer, Turner allowed little room for human free will and choice in the development of a civilization and its values. His metaphors and ideas are drawn primarily from the sciences, particularly geography and geology, not from the traditional humanities and certainly not from the Bible. Humankind, along with its governments and institutions and values, is principally the result of environmental conditions. Logically and predictably, when those conditions change, the individuals and governments and institutions and values will likewise inevitably change. While Turner occasionally acknowledged that there are forces in human affairs other than climate and landscape, by and large he continued to advocate geographical determinism as the major factor in the development and decline of civilizations. In the final analysis, while brilliant in its conception, design, and application, it is nevertheless, as many later historians and cultural theorists have argued, a greatly oversimplified and reductionist approach to human history.[18]

Faulkner's views of history, civilization, and government, it seems to me, are both more moral and more complex than Turner's. Faulkner, too, was influenced by deterministic thought, Sherwood Anderson and Theodore Dreiser being two of his early influences, but Faulkner never became a convert to a wholly deterministic view of life. The Snopeses, Compsons, Sartorises, and McCaslins in his fiction are all products of a particular time and place, and of identifiable and influential economic and social conditions, but they are also possessed of a high degree of free will and alternative choice. For Faulkner the question of human history and destiny always remained a problem of "the heart's driving complexity" (*GDM* 260), of "the human heart in conflict with itself" (*ESPL* 119). Human beings are not primarily products of biological or environmental forces, but free moral agents who make choices either for good or for evil. Thus the Bible, with its insistence on a moral agency that produces salvation or damnation, would be, from beginning to end, a dominant influence upon Faulkner's work.

Still, despite their differences, it is helpful to place Faulkner's work alongside Turner's. They share a mutual love and respect for the land, for the men and women who live close to it, and for freedom and individuality; and they are both skeptical about the growing conformity and standardization that they see in the modern world. If nothing else, examining these two writers together serves at least partially to position Faulkner in the mainstream of American literature and history, as opposed to the tributaries of Southern regionalism or European modernism. And such positioning, I submit, provides the relevance of this presentation to the conference theme, "Faulkner in the Twenty-First Century." Over the years Faulkner's works have been extensively analyzed in relation to the peculiar history and culture of the American South and to the literary values and methods of modernism as exemplified by Joyce and Eliot. Just as Turner quarreled with those who interpreted American history altogether in terms of European or North-South elements, perhaps it is now time for Faulknerians to look beyond similar international and regional affinities and place Faulkner more centrally in the American literary tradition—as a writer far more concerned than is generally acknowledged with significant issues of national policy and import.[19]

Notes

1. (Boston: Shambhala, 1996).

2. Faulkner's first published map of Yoknapatawpha County was printed at the end of *Absalom, Absalom!* in 1936. He revised the map in 1945 for inclusion in Malcolm Cowley's *The Portable Faulkner.*

3. James B. Meriwether, ed., *Essays, Speeches & Public Letters of William Faulkner* (New York: Random House, 1965), 13. Cited hereafter in the text as *ESPL.*

4. See Robert W. Hamblin, "Teaching *Intruder in the Dust* through Its Political and Historical Context," *Teaching Faulkner: Approaches and Methods,* ed. Stephen Hahn and Robert W. Hamblin (Westport, Conn.: Greenwood Press, 2001), 151-62.

5. William Faulkner, *Go Down, Moses* (New York: Vintage, 1973), 191, 202. Cited hereafter in the text as *GDM.*

6. See Sir James George Frazer, *The Golden Bough: A Study in Magic and Religion,* abr. ed. (New York: Macmillan, 1963), 585-600.

7. See Froehlich, "Teaching 'The Bear' as an Artifact of Frontier Mythology," in *Teaching Faulkner: Approaches and Methods,* 137-49. Froehlich astutely argues that "the actual frontier experience, the settlement of Jefferson, occurs in Ike's grandfather's generation" and thus "[t]he main action of ["The Bear"] does not concern this primary frontier experience, but rather the situation of a young man of a later generation negotiating his relationship to the myth, struggling to come to terms with the legacy of the frontier and to revise the myth into something that will be practically and ethically useful in his life" (146).

8. William Wordsworth, "The Tables Turned," *Selected Poems* (New York: Gramercy Books, 1993), 77-78.

9. Now commonly used as a description of Darwin's view of nature, the phrase is from Tennyson's *In Memoriam.* See Alfred Lord Tennyson, *In Memoriam,* ed. Susan Shatto and Marion Shaw (Oxford: Clarendon Press, 1982), section 56.

10. William Faulkner, *If I Forget Thee, Jerusalem* [*The Wild Palms*] (New York: Vintage International, 1995), 66. Cited hereafter in the text as *WP.*

11. Compare the elemental savagery of this incident with Boon Hogganbeck's killing of the bear in *Go Down, Moses* and Thomas Sutpen's hand-to-hand combats with his slaves in *Absalom, Absalom!*

12. Frederick Jackson Turner, *The Significance of Sections in American History* (New York: Henry Holt and Company, 1932), 23. Cited hereafter in the text as *Sections.*

13. Frederick Jackson Turner, *The Frontier in American History* (New York: Henry Holt and Company, 1920), 1. Cited hereafter in the text as *Frontier.*

14. Joseph Blotner, *Faulkner: A Biography* (New York: Random House, 1974), 1415.

15. Consider, for example, the antifederalist views expressed in "Lo!" and "The Tall Men," both of which appear in *Collected Stories.*

16. Froehlich calls Faulkner's hunters "the McCaslin-DeSpain-Compson hunt club" (*Teaching Faulkner: Approaches and Methods,* 141) and argues, "In the end, the big woods of 'The Bear' functions in Faulkner's imagination the way Teddy Roosevelt envisioned the national parks would: as a space that would allow the residents of a modern, industrialized, fully settled culture access to the ethical and cultural lessons that can only be learned in contact with wild nature" (146-47).

17. John Steinbeck employs the same theme in his short story "The Leader of the People." See *The Portable Steinbeck,* rev. ed., ed. Pascal Covici, Jr. (New York: Viking, 1971), 397-415.

18. For a good critique of both the positive and negative aspects of Turner's views, see Richard Hofstadter, *The Progressive Historians: Turner, Beard, Parrington* (New York: Alfred A. Knopf, 1968), 118-64.

19. As indicated by the title of his biography, *William Faulkner, American Writer* (New York: Eidenfield and Nicolson, 1989), Frederick Karl has attempted to do precisely what I call for here. Earlier, R. W. B. Lewis linked Faulkner, most notably "The Bear," to his studies of Adamic innocence in American literature and history (see *The American*

Adam: Innocence, Tragedy, and Tradition in the Nineteenth Century [Chicago: University of Chicago Press, 1955] and "The Hero in the New World: William Faulkner's *The Bear,*" in *Bear, Man, and God: Seven Approaches to William Faulkner's "The Bear,"* ed. Francis Lee Utley and others [New York: Random House, 1964], 306-23). By contrast, more than a dozen books treat Faulkner as a modernist, while some two dozen examine his relationship to the American South. A major step toward placing Faulkner within a broader American context was taken with the 1998 Faulkner and Yoknapatawpha Conference, "Faulkner in America." See Joseph R. Urgo and Ann J. Abadie, eds., *Faulkner in America* (Jackson: University Press of Mississippi, 2001).

Joseph R. Urgo (essay date 2005)

SOURCE: Urgo, Joseph R. "The Cather Thesis: The American Empire of Migration." In *The Cambridge Companion to Willa Cather,* edited by Marilee Lindeman, pp. 35-50. Cambridge: Cambridge University Press, 2005.

[*In the following essay, Urgo formulates a thesis to encapsulate Willa Cather's attitude toward the frontier in her life and work, and contrasts it with Frederick Jackson Turner's Frontier Thesis.*]

> "She had heard the new call: 'Go East, young woman, and grow up with the steel and concrete and electric waves."
>
> —Sinclair Lewis, *Gideon Planish* (1943)

One thing to keep in mind when reading and thinking about Willa Cather is that she was, in both literal and figurative terms, an American pioneer. Her family migrated to Nebraska in the 1880s, a time when people lived in dug-outs and sod-houses (although when young Willa arrived, she had family contacts there to make her settlement relatively easier) and old-timers shared memories of Indian encounters. As an adult, with memories of one uprooting embedded in her consciousness, Cather moved to the Northeast with enthusiasm, finding opportunities for ambitious and intelligent women not in the small towns of Nebraska and the Midwest but in urban centers, amid "the steel and concrete and electric waves" of large cities such as Pittsburgh and New York. There, the figurative pioneer, Cather rose to the top of her field in journalism (in the first decade of the new century she was the editor of *McClure's Magazine,* one of the most famous and widely read magazines in American history) and then abandoned that career to become a novelist. In her fiction she did what is understood to be impossible: she wrote novels embraced as art by critics and read with passion and devotion by the popular reading public.

Willa Cather followed the path of the western pioneer in her lifetime, the path followed by at least half the nation's westward adventurers, though not the one immortalized in American movies and popular culture. In the popular national imagination, pioneers moved west and stayed there, established towns and cities, and expanded American civilization into western territories. Casualties, and there were many in this imaginary scenario, were those who succumbed to illness, madness, or death—death or madness in Indian warfare, death as a result of criminal activities, or illnesses aggravated by living so far from the medical benefits of civilization. What is left out of such popular portrayals for the most part are the stories of those pioneers who decided to turn around and go back east. (A lot more is left out, of course, including mundane matters of work accidents, loneliness, fatigue—not the stuff of legendary tale-telling.) The movement back east, when portrayed at all in popular culture, is often cast as one of failure, cowardice, or comedy. Historically, however, we know that a lot of people tried their fortunes out west and decided that east was preferable; just as millions of immigrants to the United States in the period of the Great Migration (1880-1920) decided that the home country was preferable to America and went back. Statistics show that about half of those who emigrated to America or tried their fortunes out west on the American continent either returned home or went to another location (sometimes trying a series of locations), and for various reasons. The historical record is rarely as simple as the myths it inspires.

Willa Cather was born in Virginia in 1873. In 1883, after the family's barn mysteriously burned down, the Cather family moved to Nebraska, where other family members had emigrated a few years before. Cather's biographers speculate that the barn may have been destroyed by neighbors who held a grudge against the Cathers for their Union sympathies during the Civil War. At the age of ten, Willa Cather undertook a traumatic relocation, one that would affect her profoundly for the rest of her life. Cather's childhood was spent among various dislocated peoples, including Virginians, like herself, but also including German, Swedish, Irish, English, Danish, and Bohemian immigrant settlers in the area. Her family settled in Red Cloud, in Webster Country, Nebraska, an agricultural area characterized by miles and miles of wheat and corn—and little else. Land companies advertised aggressively to recruit labor from Europe, enticing emigrants with American dreams of land ownership. However, while the overriding goal of most immigrants was to make a go of their lives in new territories, the trajectory of Cather's career seems, at least in hindsight, to have been characterized by an ambition to return east. She left Red Cloud to attend the University of Nebraska and graduated in 1895. In 1896, she took an editorial job in Pittsburgh and relocated to that city. She would never live in Nebraska again. Ten years later she moved to New York City, where she maintained a permanent address until her death in 1947. While her family stayed in Red Cloud, Nebraska, and went to rest, finally, in the family cemetery plot there, Willa Cather is buried in Jaffrey, New Hampshire, a favorite destination, one used especially for writing, and particularly for writing about western pioneers and their descendants.

As Cather moved east, she brought the West with her, as an idea. Cather traveled often—one might say she traveled incessantly—and took regular trips out west as well as to Maine, New Hampshire, Canada, and other locations. And so while she remained, throughout her adult life, an easterner, and, more specifically, a New Yorker, in terms of permanent residence, in her imagination Willa Cather was a Virginia, a Nebraska pioneer, a southwestern adventurer, a lover of the wilderness seeking refuge from the city. Those who wish to see where Willa Cather lived, or to answer the question "Where was Willa Cather's home?" must do some traveling. Her birthplace is in Back Creek Valley (near Winchester), Virginia and her childhood home is in Red Cloud, Nebraska; her Pittsburgh apartment was 1180 Murray Hill Avenue; she lived off Washington Square, in New York City, and on Park Avenue; she had regular summer destinations in Jaffrey, New Hampshire, Grand Manan Island in New Brunswick (where she built a small house), and Northeast Harbor on Mount Desert Island in Maine. And then there are the places Cather liked to visit: Walnut Canyon, Arizona; Santa Fe, New Mexico; Boston Garden; Manchester, Massachusetts; Cos Cob, Connecticut; Quebec City; and of course, she went to Nebraska, often. She told a friend once, referring to her travel schedule, that she kept her suitcases under her bed. Like a bee, Cather may be understood to have cross-pollinated ideas from one region to another, carrying the idea of Nebraskan immigrants to New York and transporting cosmopolitan vantage point to the West, Southwest, and Northeast, never forgetting her origins in the South. But to answer the question "Where was Willa Cather's home?" is no easy one. Perhaps the safest nominative for her is that she was quintessentially American.

The sentence below, taken from the opening paragraphs of Frederick Jackson Turner's "frontier thesis" (published as *The Significance of the Frontier in American History*), delivered first as a lecture at the Chicago World's Fair in 1893, is among the more famous summations in American historiography:

> The peculiarity of American institutions is the fact that they have been compelled to adapt themselves to the changes of an expanding people—to the changes involved in crossing a continent, in winning a wilderness, and in developing at each area of this progress out of the primitive economic and political conditions of the frontier into the complexity of city life.[1]

Turner argued that westward expansion in United States history was not simply a progressive movement, but constituted "a return to primitive conditions on a continually advancing frontier line," which meant that in American historical experience, progress meant "continually beginning over again on the frontier." As a result, the American character has been constructed by an experience marked by "perennial rebirth," by a "fluidity of American life," and by an "expansion westward with its new opportunities, [and] its continuous touch with the simplicity of primitive society" (p. 4).

"Americanization" is what happens in frontier conditions, according to Turner. The European immigrant arrives on the American frontier, sheds his European traits ("dress, industries, tools, modes of travel, and thought") and adapts to wilderness necessity ("planting Indian corn and plowing with a sharp stick"). The pioneer does not forget his origins in civilization; but at first, the frontier environment is "too strong for the man" and he must adapt or die (p. 5). Nevertheless, over time, he transforms the wilderness in ways that would never occur to the native Indian, and out of the clash of European and Indian, the return of civilization to frontier conditions, emerges the American. "And to study this advance," Turner claimed in 1893, "the men who grew up under these conditions, and the political, economic, and social results of it, is to study the really American part of our history" (p. 5).

Much of frontier history written in the twentieth century amounts to a series of footnotes to Turner, some elaborative, some challenging or revisionist. Women's history has revised the focus on "the men who grew up under these conditions" to include female frontier experience and the domestic adaptations made by mothers, daughters, wives, and independent female pioneers. Ethnic historians have challenged Turner's too-simplistic description of the process by which "immigrants were Americanized, liberated, and fused into a mixed race" (p. 17) in frontier conditions. Social historians have qualified Turner's claim that "to the frontier the American intellect owes its striking characteristics" (p. 27). Turner has subsequently been criticized or amended for the gaps or omissions in his historical method—his use of evidence, for example, and his employment of proof for his claims left much to be desired. Nevertheless, and despite the many faults and omissions of his essay, the Turner thesis remains the single most inspiring and provocative theory in American historiography. In many ways, the entire field of American studies finds its origins in Turner. If Turner was correct, the discipline may be seen as continuing a long tradition of establishing theories of American exceptionalism—how and why it is that the United States is unique among nations because of its historical experience. If Turner was not correct, if he was mistaken, the discipline may be seen as establishing a long tradition of examining how and why it is that Americans think they are exceptional (because of the frontier experience) when in fact they are not. Either way, Turner is at the root of it all.

Willa Cather never responded specifically to the Turner thesis, but as we extrapolate from her life and work, we can adapt Turner's language to formulate what might be called the Cather thesis:

> The peculiarity of American institutions is the fact that they have been compelled to adapt themselves to the restlessness of a migratory people—to the changes involved in crossing and then re-crossing the continent, in spending part of one's life in the wilderness only to return for a while to the city before moving on to another part of the country or to another city, and in influencing at each stopping point of this crisscrossing memories of someplace else, with ideas brought from another situation, making a frontier out of an established city and establishing a city out of a frontier. Incessant transit makes an American, the seeming inability to stay in one place for very long, or, if rendered stable by circumstances, the desire, nonetheless, to move, or the knowledge that one could have or should have moved.

Frederick Jackson Turner began his thesis about the American frontier by noting a statement from the 1890 Census that declared the absence of any significant large tracts of unsettled lands to report. For the first time in its history, the United States was not in the process of colonizing western territories. The closing of the frontier was a monumental event for Turner, as it was to the existence of the frontier that "the American intellect owes its striking characteristics." Turner enumerated such typical American traits, which he called "traits of the frontier," and listed them as "coarseness and strength combined with acuteness and inquisitiveness; that practical, inventive turn of mind, quick to find expedients; that masterful grasp of material things, lacking in the artistic but powerful to effect great ends; that restless, nervous energy; that dominant individualism, working for good and evil, and withal that buoyancy and exuberance which comes with freedom" (p. 27). Taking its starting point with the passing away of the unsettled lands, Turner's thesis is marked by a kind of nervousness itself, lamenting the disappearance of "a gate of escape from the bondage of the past" (p. 28) and marked by the pervasive sense of ending.

One may wonder what the pioneer and literary artist Willa Cather thought of Turner's assertion that frontier conditions resulted in minds "lacking in the artistic" sensibilities. There is no doubt that Turner was wrong about Willa Cather: it was the experience of frontier conditions in Nebraska, and "that restless, nervous energy; that dominant individualism," characteristic of Cather's intellect, that created the artist herself. Cather's frontier thesis, while not contradicting Turner's, and while not something to which Turner was oblivious by

any means, nevertheless refined Turner's focus. It was not the permanent settlers who formed American consciousness—though they certainly contributed to its material basis. Those who left cities to settle in frontier lands, never to return, did important work spreading American institutions by colonization, applying United States law to refine and eliminate primitive conditions, as Turner argued so eloquently. But these settlers did not affect those in the East, those in settled areas, except as the *idea* of progress and empire they represented, as an option, a safety-valve, a possibility of escape for settled Americans. Those who exerted more direct and more immediate influence were those who *did not remain* in the West, but who moved back and forth from one area to another. It is these, the great masses of unsettled people, writers, railroad lawyers, schoolteachers, land speculators, missionaries, fame-seekers, tourists—among many others—who embody Cather's version of the frontier thesis.

Exemplars of the Cather thesis include Jim Burden, the railroad man, born in Virginia, migrant to the Nebraska frontier, best friend to an immigrant woman (through whom he learns to write "The Pioneer Woman's Story," the title of Book IV of *My Ántonia* {1918]), and who, as an adult, "loves with a personal passion the great country through which his railway runs and branches."[2] While Ántonia has remained on the frontier, doing the work required to turn a wild landscape into the domestic basis of civilization, Jim returned east, to study law and then to become a railroad company lawyer. However, Cather makes explicit the debt Jim's intellect owes to the frontier experience, a debt symbolized in the novel by his memory of Ántonia. "More than any other person we remembered," the narrator explains, "this girl seemed to mean to us the country, the conditions, the whole adventure of our childhood" (pp. xi-xii). The country, in the novel, is the Nebraska frontier, what Jim refers to as "not a country at all, but the material out of which countries are made" (p. 7). The conditions were bleak: immigrant families living in dug-outs and sod-houses, men who committed suicide out of despair and loneliness, and a landscape so empty of human signs that Jim reports feeling so "erased, blotted out" (p. 8) that he was not even sure, as a child, whether God would hear his prayers from such exile. Nevertheless, it was "the whole adventure" of his childhood in Nebraska, which formed his eastern, urban, railroad attorney consciousness, that has made him renowned as an entrepreneur, one who "is always able to raise capital for new enterprises" and who has helped others "to do remarkable things in mines and timber and oil" (p. xi). He is, in short, a successful capitalist, with the kind of mind that has driven American expansion for two centuries.

Jim's mind may well be said to be the main focus of the novel. That is to say, while the novel is obviously about Ántonia, it is also quite clearly about Jim's view of her and the influence she has had on his mind—the ways in which she is important to him. At the end of Book IV, "The Pioneer Woman's Story," Jim makes his debt explicit. "The idea of you is a part of my mind," he tells Ántonia; "you influence my likes and dislikes, all my tastes, hundreds of times when I don't realize it. You really are a part of me" (p. 312). The Cather thesis is encapsulated in this moment, when Jim explains that while he did not remain on the frontier, while he returned east to work in New York, he carried with him the idea of Ántonia and all that she had come to mean to him. Jim's possession of the frontier as memory, as a dimension of his consciousness, is the psychic ingredient that makes him the quintessential New Yorker.

As we have seen, in her lifetime Cather moved west and she moved east, carrying with her the ideology of migration. In the Cather thesis, movement east, not west, is what strengthens the nation's idea of itself, and, not incidentally, what strengthens the nation's power and establishes the legitimacy of the American empire. Cather's western novels were all written in the East, and mark the infusion of the eastern establishment with western ideals—especially the ideals of expansion and national (as opposed to regional) identity. In her novels, energy flows east, back to such power centers as New York and Washington. And in Cather's prototypically American situations, pre-American loyalties (religion and ethnicity, for example) are supplanted by loyalties enacted by the experience of displacement, a displacement recognized as enabled by national expansion.

Very early in *The Song of the Lark* (1915) Cather makes connections between her main character's ambitions and the nation's movement towards empire. When Thea Kronborg and her friends take a Sunday expedition to the sand hills, a place of "constant tantalization" to Thea,[3] the narrative makes clear what will move east as Thea's career unfolds. She recalls an earlier trip with her father, to a "reunion of old frontiersmen" in Wyoming, when she came upon a site marked by the pathways of migratory pioneer wagon trains. Thea recalls being moved to tears when she saw the dozens of crisscrossing ruts,

> deep furrows, cut in the earth by heavy wagon-wheels, and not grown over with dry, whitish grass. The furrows ran side by side; when one trail had been worn too deep, the next party had abandoned it and made a new trail to the right or left. They were, indeed, only old wagon-ruts, running east and west, and grown over with grass. But as Thea ran about among the white stones, her skirts blowing this way and that, the wind brought to her eyes tears that might have come, anyway.

(pp. 47-8)

The furrows are evidence of continuous movement "running east and west" carrying settlers to the frontier and carrying restless people, their ideas as well as material goods and wealth, back east. *The Song of the Lark* will go on to suggest a parallel between Thea Kronborg's individual ascent (and her movement from a small western town to the cultural centers of the East and of Europe) with the progress of the American empire. Cather grounds Thea's consciousness thoroughly in "the spirit of human courage" that "seemed up there with the eagles," making the artist's story an epic of imperial significance as well as an individual story of great success. In *The Song of the Lark,* as in *My Ántonia,* Cather demonstrates essential links between what seem to be highly individualized traits of character and large, abstract historical movements. When Jim Burden takes the idea of the pioneer woman, Ántonia, back east to his railroad development office, he contributes one tiny element to what we call a historical force. When Thea Kronborg carries her great talent from Moonstone to New York and then to Paris, she also contributes to (and in her case, symbolizes) the movement of power from West to East.

American expansion moved west throughout the nineteenth century, transporting energies, resources, and labor to develop and settle new towns, cities, and states. At the same time, or as a result, the idea of an American empire moved east. As the West became settled, as the economic effects of Great Plains agriculture and livestock production became apparent, as gold and oil reserves were developed, as mines began to produce, and as populations soared, the ideas, the wealth, and the power generated by expansion flowed back to urban centers in the East. We know the story of the West. American pioneer tales, from James Fenimore Cooper's nineteenth-century Leatherstocking Tales through the western novels and movies of the twentieth century, Americans have provided themselves and the rest of the world with a steady supply of stories about "how the West was won," how pioneers overcame adversity, lawlessness, and countless challenges in order to bring American civilization to the frontier. Willa Cather was certainly interested in this idea, and she either told or referred to it in many of her novels. Nevertheless, another story captured her imagination, relayed intimately to it, but not as commonly told in her time.

It may be that the one obligation possessed exclusively by a country's literary artists is to render the story of the nation into poetic form. Willa Cather wrote her novels between 1913 and 1947, precisely the years in which the position of the United States as a world power solidified. Her life spans the close of the western continental frontier and the opening of the global imperial frontier, from the settling of the American continent to the height of what has been called the American Century. Of all her great contemporaries, however—including Faulkner and Hemingway—Cather alone confronted the poetic potential of a transnational, American empire in the process of formation. Although William Faulkner projected a global, indeed cosmic, scope in *A Fable,* the emphasis of his work overall is on relations within a fixed and established American national state. And while Ernest Hemingway sought to link continents in his fiction, portraying the fate of Americans in Europe socially and at war, a conception of the nation itself as a developing force was not foremost in his narrative purposes. Willa Cather, however, set about a serious project of writing that depicts a burgeoning American presence on the face of the earth as a historical force of spiritual dimensions.

One of Ours (1922) and *Death Comes for the Archbishop* (1927) are two novels most directly concerned with transforming the American empire into epic material. In both, the movement of ideas, power, and resources is to the East from the West. In *One of Ours,* a conquering army is raised among the millions of sons of western pioneers and settlers, and transported east for battle. The young male soldiers (and female missionaries) in this novel symbolize and embody the empowering of eastern urban centers with energies and lives originating in the West. In *Death Comes for the Archbishop,* the strength of the Catholic Church is enhanced by the claiming of western souls into its faith—as Archbishop Latour moves west, the souls he nourishes look east to the Roman church for salvation. In its plot development, the novel parallels the expansion of the nineteenth-century American empire with the spread of Christianity in pre-medieval Europe. The implied narrative correspondence in both novels suggests that the strength of empire depends on its people's possessing an idea that they can carry with them. The essential benevolence of this empire, or the potential evil within it, was beside the great fact of its presence; it was, simply, a force to reckon with in art. In Cather's vision empire requires motion, expansion, and restlessness; the American empire depends on a population convinced that it holds something transportable and, when as individuals they travel, they will take the idea with them as they move around the nation and the world, immune to local or native forces that may challenge their idea of themselves and their value. *One of Ours* focuses on an individual American man and demonstrates how the logic of empire—or its ideology—informs private decisions and makes sense of private dilemmas. What distinguishes Cather in these novels is that she takes empire as a political fact and depicts life within the context created by that historical contingency. The scope of her literary vision, while often grounded in very specific places, is consistently global in its projection of a spatialized and dynamic conception of history.

The cultural logic of imperialism suggested by Willa Cather implicates every American gesture towards individual distinction as contributing to American empire. Every act of immigration, every continental migration

(east and west, north and south), each man and woman's attempt to succeed by endorsement, critique, or attack on the social order or its ideology, is in and of itself an advance of the national culture as a whole towards an imperial position. Thea Kronborg, for example, is thinking not only of the purity of art as she advances her career. She is not committing herself solely to beauty or to voice or even to song. Her ambitions are clearly animated by such aesthetic devotions, but Cather explains that it is much more than this that motivates Thea Kronborg. Thea is rising from nowhere, from the comically named, lowbrow midwestern town of Moonstone, a few generations away from the frontier, from a preacher's family that, in Cather's treatment, is a prototype for Sinclair Lewis's more baldly satirical depictions of the Midwest. But Thea draws strength from the old faces of withered and wasted immigrant men and women at her father's church, faces that are "mysteriously marked by destiny" (p. 115), and which she will carry with her as ideas in her rise to prominence. In the same way that Alexandra Bergson, in *O Pioneers!,* was the first to look on the Great Divide and see agricultural wealth, Thea's is the first face to look on those "who have worked hard and who have always been poor" (p. 113) and see cultural wealth, her own potential for greatness, and the seeds of empire.

The final section of *The Song of the Lark* is titled "Kronborg," suggesting that Thea has become an icon, a great fact. She speaks, in her final textual appearance, with unchallenged authority. She has dwarfed her mentor, Howard Archie, she has withstood with unparalleled dignity the affair with Fred Ottenberg, and she has survived a near marriage to Nordquist. As an artist and as the textual personification of empire she is untouchable. She has become her own reason for being, and by each word uttered and with every gesture committed she articulates and defines what greatness is. Thea decides as well what she will remember and what she will discard, recalling only what contributes to her ascendancy, forgetting the things that may drag her down. At one point, earlier in the novel, she induces fear in Fred Ottenberg by the "elevation" in her eyes, a look described by Cather as one that "had no memories" but was purely "unconscious" (p. 314). As a woman of tremendous power and effect, Thea, as depicted in the novel's epilogue, has returned to Moonstone as an abstraction—she has become an icon in Moonstone, bringing comforting, compensatory memories to the old, and to the young dreams. The product of imperial forces, Thea brought the idea of the West through her tremendous voice east, emerged as a great force, and returned west as an idea to inspire others. In Thea's story is invested considerable value, and on her example is built a social system that implicitly rewards mobility, provisionality, and mutability. Traditional homage to home, fidelity, and stability are voiced as compensation for losses, but these notions hold little value to the ambitious. The successful ones at all levels, from simply "staying afloat" to world domination, move away from these values as easily as they migrate away from their sources—origins, families, and "permanent" residences.

Thea's angst at the end of the novel is real enough, but it is not the stuff of melancholy or regret. The fulfillment that her performances bring to others is "the only commensurate answer" to the question of her purpose or value. Outside of that function, she may indeed wonder about "the good of it all" (p. 399). At the novel's close she serves on the stage the same idea that had motivated her and those who produced her in the past, the idea that "closed roads" are to be opened and "all the gates dropped" (p. 398) that stand between stasis and movement. *The Song of the Lark* may be read as the story of female empowerment and voice, but only narrowly. In the context of the Cather thesis, the success story of individual eastern-moving female ambition becomes an imperial gesture, a definition of how and why out of this country and at this time greatness emerged, and the attention of the world is focused on an American voice.

In a novel at once very similar (in terms of its style and aspects of its form) and, in content, wholly distinct from *The Song of the Lark, One of Ours* traces the historical logic that follows when the destination country of the immigrant becomes an economic and military world power. The novel's context is the tremendous productivity of the United States: wheat-fields that feed the world, industries that power machines for domestic consumption and international export, and the main focus, a culture that produces eager, devoted soldiers willing to die for all that it produces, maintains, and symbolizes. The novel is a very political book for its concentration on the American turn, in 1917, towards active, global militarism. The wheat-fields over which Jim Burden rhapsodizes in *My Ántonia* are depicted now as having produced a world power; the "feeling of empire" at the core of Thea Kronborg's ambition in *The Song of the Lark* transfixes the nation; thousands of Thea-like women and men restlessly conceive the world as their personal theater of operations—the globe, in short, has become an American possession in *One of Ours*.

Claude Wheeler moves east to fulfill his destiny in an average sort of way. He is a Thea Kronborg mass-produced in wholesale quantities. He possesses none of her individual talent or genius but all of her dissatisfaction with the midwestern, provincial status quo. He feels that he deserves something more than his middle-brow, farmer-class origins can deliver. He is a small man with big plans, a limited, conventional mind with delusions of greatness. He is also, however, in command of tremendous resources. He has a very wealthy national benefactor known affectionately as his Uncle

Sam, who finds him "worth the watchfulness and devotion of so many men and machines, this extravagant consumption of fuel and energy."[4] Multiply Claude Wheeler by hundreds of thousands and extend his mind to the national culture as a whole, and what emerges is a clearly articulated sense of Cather's frontier thesis: moving east from the frontier, the birth of empire, the spread of US ideals on an international scale, packaged and delivered like canned goods across oceans and continents.

One of Ours situates itself on a liminal moment in American history and on a central dilemma in its culture. The moment is when the nation made its turn away from hemispheric isolation towards involvement in a major European war, thus introducing the term "world war" into the international vocabulary. Historically the process extended from the era before the Great War until the eve of World War II, continually refining and expanding the application of American interests abroad. Nevertheless, the terms of the transition are laid out clearly in the novel. These terms involve the unsolved "question of property" (p. 68) and the closing of the American frontier (p. 100), as Claude realizes. Also involved in the transition is the adaptation in the United States to the conditions of "the great argument" of German expansion: "preparation, organization, inexhaustible resources, inexhaustible men." What Cather centers on is not simply a historical moment but also a recurring dilemma in American culture. What is the global role of the nation of immigrants? Is the United States a safe refuge from the world or the next stage in world development? From the former come the American isolationists; from the latter emerges the American mission. In isolation one may cultivate the arts of music and agriculture as ends in themselves, but a nation with a mission knows music as something to march to and knows its farms as the wheatfields and cornfields that feed the world. The Cather thesis, extended to the global stage, is not so much concerned with the question whether the United States is exempt from historical forces or representative of the course of future development. In either case, having produced a migratory consciousness out of its own frontier development, the nation is not constrained by past examples of imperial excesses or failures. As depicted in the scenes of Claude in France, American soldiers march confidently over the ruins of a succession of historical empires.

To anyone raised on American wars, with no conception of a United States without a mobilized army, navy, air force, marine corps, CIA, or NASA, *One of Ours* can hardly be read without some sense of bewilderment. The novel's conclusions are not surprising. From our present vantage point, the entire history of the nation, from Indian-hating Puritans to the war on terror of the twenty-first century, has been a relentless expression of firepower. The historians who have written the story of America in this way were born in the middle of the last century, after global conflict had become a thoroughly naturalized structuring metaphor of American existence—the world's peacekeeper, mediator, and police force. However, Cather's novel reminds us that what appears to be a fact of existence in the present era came about as a result of historical choices, and the particular construction of the American national state. In other words, the national history as we know it today has been written by the heirs of Claude Wheeler, by historians who have written under the sound of the guns. Millions of Americans have since shared the sentiment of Claude's orphan friend, Albert Usher, that "the U.S. Marines are my family. Wherever they are, I'm at home" (p. 229). In the context of *One of Ours,* the American military is among the culture's most profound ideas. It is often at the forefront of social change, as seen later in the twentieth century, in the Civil Rights era. Its weapons research has poured into the marketplaces a steady flow of consumer goods and services, including internet technologies, microwave ovens, and mobile phones. Historically, it is difficult to find a great change in the United States that did not either result from or coincide with war-making of some sort: national independence, frontier settlement, the emancipation of slaves, women's suffrage, racial justice, civil rights.

Cather's novel projects a culture that is moving towards a conception of war as the ultimate articulation of national purpose, a conception as strong as any spiritual orthodoxy. This conclusion (which will be extended further in *Death Comes for the Archbishop*) is reached on numerous levels—economic, religious, social—that converge in the fate and figure of Claude Wheeler. To Claude, enlistment appears like a vision: it is a natural, salvational gesture on his part. After the war the efforts of soldiers were granted mythic significance by postwar initiatives that continued throughout the twentieth century with no signs of weakening. Yellow ribbons, heroes' welcomes,—such are the common aftermath of military service. The sacredness of war participation has become an indispensable component of American culture, embodied in public monuments, holidays, and civic rituals of remembrance and re-creation. In many ways, Cather's novel is concerned with the origins of this phenomenon as a national movement, and as the logical result of the frontier experience.

One of Ours turns directly to the production of American soldiers in the service of empire. Metaphors of harvest abound in the novel, suggesting that raising an army is an organic product of the culture as a whole. The section of the novel entitled "The Voyage of the Anchises" is a meditation on the movement of American minds from one way of thinking to another, from a variety of former occupations to soldiers. The ones who cannot make the transfer do not survive the passage.

Cather employs the metaphor of illness, or fever, a common usage of her time for what happens to the world when it goes to war. The metaphor serves another purpose, which is to cast the transformation of the idea of the United States from refuge to empire in naturalistic terms. Throughout the novel the dominant sense is that this metamorphosis is a kind of fulfillment, a harvesting, a logical culmination of the social order and an answer to the dilemma it had produced for itself. Claude articulates the national mission: "I've left everything behind me. I am going over" (p. 251). The descendant of pioneer settlers who left everything behind to go west, Claude, exemplar of the Cather thesis, heads east now, in full possession of a mission to conquer the world, or, in his case, to die in its accomplishment.

Cather's novel is thus a classic study of war culture from the citizen's perspective. College students who accept army reserve commitments in return for college tuition; criminal adolescents given the choice of prison or army enlistment; women and minorities expecting equal (and therefore relatively preferable) treatment under the auspices of the military code; the use of American soldiers in providing natural disaster relief, quelling urban rioting, or feeding starving people around the world—in each of these examples, the American military expands to encompass the culture. None of these examples represents an evil; on the contrary, each of them illustrates a version of the good. It was also good that Claude found service in the army, for otherwise he might have spent his life alone in his honeymoon house waiting for Enid to return, living a long life as a local oddity rather than a short one as a national hero. Nevertheless, what attracts Cather's attention is not the military per se but the conditions that have evolved to authenticate the military alternative as redemptive, and as the deepest and most profound expression of American ideals.

More than soldiers crossed the ocean in 1917; the very idea of America undertook a reverse migration. The immigrant nation returned east from its incubation in the West, where the same ethnic groups at war in Europe were working towards a relatively peaceful and benign domestic American "melting pot." The concept of ideas in transit, the mechanics involved in the projection and migration of an idea across an ocean and a continent, and the relationship between consciousness and materiality are central concerns of Cather's greatest novel of empire, *Death Comes for the Archbishop*. With her missionaries, Cather writes of intellectual colonists: Latour and Vaillant wish to plant ideas and colonize the minds of the Mexicans, the Americans, and (to a lesser extent) the indigenous peoples. The troopships in *One of Ours* embodied the idea of the United States evolving from nation to empire, returning to Europe as the force that would shape the destiny of the world throughout the twentieth century. In the same way, the thousands of immigrants who have come to the United States have embodied the idea that no particular place is necessarily or inevitably home to any human being and that as a species, human beings are movable and take well to being transplanted. The idea of movement is the idea of America as represented by the eagle, the bird of prey that will make its home on any rock high enough to provide a clear view. The eagle settles on the rock only to await its next move. An empire of migratory values, of transactions of power and focus, and of the adaptation of old ideas to contemporary necessity is of major concern to Cather's novel about an itinerant French bishop sent to the Spanish American Southwest by French and Italian cardinals to spread the faith of Rome in the New World.

Death Comes for the Archbishop opens in 1848, a pivotal year in the territorial expansion of the United States, and concludes near the end of the century, at the close of the frontier. But Cather is not concerned with the usual take of homesteads, forts, Indian wars, and gold rushes—although these material phenomena all figure in the background to the novel's events. Rather, *Death Comes for the Archbishop* centers on the business of transmission, the ways in which intellectual capital—ideas, spirituality, modes of thought—is carried from one place to another. Latour teaches his people, used to living in an isolated region, or as settlers in new territories, to face their minds and their souls east, back to the center of Catholicism and to the authority of Rome. It is out of the movement of ideas, from the structures that allow and foster intellectual and spiritual migration, that empire emerges. Throughout his career in the Southwest, Latour has moved from one place to another representing his faith. He is far from his origins in Auvergne, France, and far from his first position as parish priest on Lake Ontario. His career, as much as his preaching, is testimony to the idea that it does not matter where he lives; he is a missionary, he makes his home where he happens to be. His mobility, his missionary journeys and the simple fact that his faith is transplantable, contributes to the destruction of the indigenous cultures of America as much if not more than the Word he carries of Roman Catholicism.

In terms of the Cather thesis, one recognizes that America is settled by minds in which stability is an abstraction, in which national origins, religious faith, and ethnic identities are traded over time. A tremendous migration of human beings occurred in the nineteenth century, from east to west, from the Old World to the New. These human beings, emigrating from particular places in the eastern hemisphere, came to a new place that did not know their history and were inhabited by sparse populations without the means to hold this great migration at bay. The one common denominator to all emigrant groups was the fact of migration itself. Mobility has passed into the culture of the United States as a great fact of its national existence, a cornerstone to its

ideology. As movement becomes a quality of mind, all ideas and belief systems are leveled by the common experience of crossing, of having let go of some prior idea and moved to embrace another. As a French Catholic missionary in the Spanish American frontier, Latour embodies the principle of transitory ideas and mutable belief.

The faith that emerged from the experience of the American frontier, according to the Cather thesis, held that within the very quality of movement there exists an inherent progression of the human condition. "We're over," as the soldiers say in *One of Ours,* we have come here, and because we have crossed over, we achieve authenticity. The idea of America is accomplished through migration from one place to another, intellectually, physically, spiritually; Archbishop Latour is its patron saint. When Thea Kronborg thinks of herself in her relation to others, she imagines that "each of them concealed another person in himself, just as she did," and that everyone had "to guard them fiercely." The sense of spatialized multiplicity, allowing transactions among various potential selves, characterizes a culture of movement and migration. Thea considers her life progress "as if she had an appointment to meet the rest of herself sometime, somewhere. It was moving to meet her and she was moving to meet it" (p. 189). At the end of his life Archbishop Latour, "soon to have done with the calendared time," is described as being situated, spatially, "in the middle of his own consciousness; none of his former states of mind were lost or outgrown."[5] Even Claude Wheeler, before dying, articulates a sense of "beginning over again," possessing another life as a soldier in the Grand Army of the Republic (p. 322). The Cather thesis encapsulates one of the great paradoxes of American history, that out of the nation's great effort to settle the West emerged the idea that settlement itself was antithetical to human experience. While millions of human beings moved west to settle, it was the incessantly migratory American who brought the news that the West had been won. Moving east, back along the furrows of the wagon-ruts, is this new concept of rootedness, not in place, but in the experience, memory, or legacy of having traveled far and having grown up with the country.

Notes

1. George Rogers Taylor, ed. *The Turner Thesis: Concerning the Role of the Frontier in American History,* third edition (Lexington, MA: D. C. Heath and Co., 1972), p. 3. Future references will be made parenthetically.

2. Willa Cather, *My Ántonia* (1918; Boston: Houghton Mifflin, 1988), p. xi. Future references will be made parenthetically.

3. Willa Cather, *The Song of the Lark* (1915; New York: Penguin, 1991), p. 40. Future references will be made parenthetically.

4. Willa Cather, *One of Ours* (1922; New York: Vintage Classics, 1991), p. 230. Future references will be made parenthetically.

5. Willa Cather, *Death Comes for the Archbishop* (1927; New York: Vintage Classics, 1991), p. 288.

FURTHER READING

Criticism

Bloom, Edward A., and Lillian D. Bloom. "Willa Cather's Novels of the Frontier: A Study in Thematic Symbolism." *American Literature* 21, no. 1 (March 1949): 71-93.

Elucidates the major thematic concerns in Willa Cather's frontier novels.

Cleman, John. "The Belated Frontier: H. L. Davis and the Problem of Pacific Northwest Regionalism." *Western American Literature* 37 (winter 2003): 431-52.

Attributes the obscurity of H. L. Davis to his reputation as a regional writer and provides an assessment of his literary career.

Lawlor, Mary. *Recalling the Wild: Naturalism and the Closing of the American West.* New Brunswick, N.J.: Rutgers University Press, 224 p.

Full-length examination of American frontier literature and its major authors.

Thomas, Brook. "Frederick Jackson Turner, José Marti, and Finding a Home on the Range." In *José Marti's "Our America": From National to Hemispheric Cultural Studies,* edited by Jeffrey Belnap and Raúl Fernández, pp. 275-92. Durham, N.C.: Duke University Press, 1998.

Compares the visions of America offered by Frederick Jackson Turner and José Marti.

Little Magazines

INTRODUCTION

Often experimental and innovative in spirit, little magazines were generally not profitable, had a very small readership, and were sometimes quite short-lived. Nevertheless, they were enormously influential in introducing new writers and literary trends to the reading public and were particularly significant in promoting Modernism and black literature in the United States and abroad. Because of their pivotal role in literary history, little magazines, as Michael Barsanti has argued, are "best understood not as collections or samplers of artwork, but as works of art themselves."

Critics generally agree that the heyday of little magazines was approximately from the 1890s through the 1940s; some pinpoint the golden period, when hundreds of little magazines flourished, as 1912 through 1936. Little magazines began publishing in large numbers aided by a series of events, including advances in printing technology that made production easier and faster, and the opening of such new avenues of revenue as advertising and subscriptions, which made them less dependent upon the sponsorship of wealthy patrons. They were typically spearheaded by an energetic, discerning, and well-connected editor (for example, Harriet Monroe and Ezra Pound of *Poetry,* T. S. Eliot of *Criterion,* or W. E. B. Du Bois and Jessie R. Fauset of *Crisis*) who hoped to promote literature that was not found in mainstream commercial journals. Little magazines, therefore, could, and frequently did, promote emerging or alternative authors without the burden of having to show a profit. In some cases, established writers also used little magazines as a testing ground for new styles or themes. In a sense, little magazines existed to publish authors and works that could not get published anywhere else. They also materially promoted the notion of writers and publishers as an artistic community, and were instrumental in establishing strong ties between literary circles in the United States, Canada, Australia, and England.

There were several kinds of little magazines with distinct viewpoints and readerships. Some, like *Poetry, The Fugitive,* and *Palms* were devoted almost exclusively to advancing poetry; others, like *Hound and Horn, Symposium,* and *Criterion* specialized in reviews and literary criticism; still others, for example *Masses, The Liberator,* or *The Partisan Review,* had leftist leanings and were interested in providing a forum for social issues. Some little magazines were connected to universities, movements, or organizations. For instance, *Crisis* (edited by Du Bois and Fauset), *Opportunity* (edited by Zora Neale Hurston and Langston Hughes), and *Fire!!* (its single issue edited by Wallace Thurston) gave black writers the opportunity to publish their work and had a central role in the increasing popularity of black artists during the Harlem Renaissance.

There is consensus among commentators that little magazines were at their best starting around the year 1912, with such periodicals as *Poetry, Poetry Journal, Glebe, Masses,* and *The Little Review* playing a leading role in introducing some of the greatest modern writers. Pound published his basic principles of Imagism in the March 1913 issue of *Poetry,* while the June 1915 issue published Eliot's "The Love Song of J. Alfred Prufrock." *The Dial* and *Criterion* both published Eliot's "The Waste Land" in 1922. The works of William Carlos Williams, Wallace Stevens, and Djuna Barnes made their first appearance in *Glebe. The Double-Dealer* published Ernest Hemingway's first short story in 1922, as well as early works by Allen Tate and Jean Toomer. *The Little Review* serialized *Ulysses* in 1913, while *The Egoist* published James Joyce's *Portrait of the Artist as a Young Man* in 1914-15, and *transition* published *Finnegans Wake* as a work in progress in 1938. During the socially and politically turbulent 1930s, *The Masses* published the work of leading intellectuals like Lincoln Steffens, John Reed, and Upton Sinclair, while *The Partisan Review* featured the work of such avant garde writers as W. H. Auden, Vladimir Nabokov, and Jorge Luis Borges. Sometimes accused of elitism, little magazines took their mission of providing alternative publishing venues seriously. Modern scholars point out that this tradition continues in the twenty-first century with contemporary little magazines, as well as various online journals and Internet publications.

REPRESENTATIVE WORKS

Broom 1921-24
Challenge 1934-37
Chap Book 1894-98
The Chicago Review 1957-
Contemporary Verse 1916-29
Crisis 1910-76
Criterion 1922-39
The Double Dealer 1921-26

Egoist 1914-19
English Review 1908-
Fire!! 1926
The Fugitive 1922-25
Glebe 1913-14
The Hound and Horn 1927-34
Kenyon Review 1939-
The Liberator 1918-24
The Little Review 1914-29
The London Aphrodite 1928-29
The Masses 1911-17
The Measure 1921-26
Messenger 1917-28
The Midland 1915-33
Opportunity 1923-49
Others 1915-19
Pagany 1929-32
Palms 1932-40
The Partisan Review 1934-
Poetry: A Magazine of Verse 1912-
The Poetry Journal 1912-18
The Prairie Schooner 1927-
The Reviewer 1921-25
Secession 1922-24
Seven Arts 1916-17
Smoke 1931-37
Smart Set 1912-24
The Southern Review 1935-42
Stylus 1916-41
The Symposium 1930-33
transition 1927-38
Vision 1923-24

OVERVIEWS

Frederick J. Hoffman, Charles Allen, and Carolyn F. Ulrich (essay date 1947)

SOURCE: Hoffman, Frederick J., Charles Allen, and Carolyn F. Ulrich. Introduction to *The Little Magazine: A History and Bibliography*, pp. 1-17. Princeton, N.J.: Princeton University Press, 1947.

[*In the following essay, Hoffman, Allen, and Ulrich trace the history of little magazines beginning in approximately 1910, emphasizing their purpose, general character, and social and literary roles.*]

A character in William Saroyan's play, *The Time of Your Life*, suggests that all human problems might be solved if only there were enough magazines to go around.[1] Everyone, he implies, should have the opportu-

nity of seeing himself in print. The results might be most gratifying to politician and policeman alike. Man would no longer quarrel with his fellowman, for his greatest wish would be granted; he would be satisfied, happy, and amiably tolerant of the weaknesses in society. Of course, such a tremendous clearing house for man's literary pretensions has never been provided. Manuscripts still reside in trunks and in desk drawers. But one feature of twentieth century literary history must be noted: hundreds of writers have achieved publication—almost irrespective of their claims to merit or the significance of what they had to say. Since 1912 many of these persons have been published in the scores of literary magazines which have appeared and disappeared to the accompaniment of various forms of pretension, clamor, and editorial oratory.

What is important about this fact is that the best of our little magazines have stood, from 1912 to the present, defiantly in the front ranks of the battle for a mature literature. They have helped fight this battle by being the first to present such writers as Sherwood Anderson, Ernest Hemingway, William Faulkner, Erskine Caldwell, T. S. Eliot—by first publishing, in fact, about 80 per cent[2] of our most important post-1912 critics, novelists, poets, and storytellers. Further, they have introduced and sponsored every noteworthy literary movement or school that has made its appearance in America during the past thirty years.

There have been, conservatively estimated, over six hundred little magazines published in English since 1912. Many have been pale, harmless creatures. Fewer than one hundred of them have taken a decisive part in the battle for modern literature, or have sought persistently to discover good artists, or to promote the early work of talented innovators, or to sponsor literary movements. Many of the six hundred have been abortive—some lacking a definable purpose, others editorial discrimination, and still others plain common sense. Some, such as John Malcolm Brinnin's short-lived *Prelude*, irresponsibly followed the will-o'-the-wisp of novelty for novelty's sake.

A little magazine is a magazine designed to print artistic work which for reasons of commercial expediency is not acceptable to the money-minded periodicals or presses. Acceptance or refusal by commercial publishers at times has little to do with the quality of the work. If the little magazine can obtain artistic work from unknown or relatively unknown writers, the little magazine purpose is further accomplished. Little magazines are willing to lose money, to court ridicule, to ignore public taste, willing to do almost anything—steal, beg, or undress in public—rather than sacrifice their right to print good material, especially if it comes from the pen of an unknown Faulkner or Hemingway. Such periodicals are, therefore, noncommercial by intent, for their altruistic ideal usually rules out the hope of financial profit. No doubt little magazine editors would welcome a circulation of a million or two, but they know that their magazines will appeal only to a limited group, generally not more than a thousand persons. And so, financially limited, editors generally caution contributors to banish all thought of remuneration, to be satisfied with payment "in fame, not specie." When there is money for contributors, promises of payment are made triumphantly, always as though such payment is to be made in spite of, rather than because of, the bourgeois system of values.

To the extent that they are not money-minded, such reviews as *The Sewanee Review, The Southern Review, The Kenyon Review, The Yale Review,* and *The Virginia Quarterly Review* may be considered "little." Yet these excellent quarterlies are not little magazines. Intelligent, dignified, critical representatives of an intelligent, dignified, critical minority, they are conscious of a serious responsibility which does not often permit them the freedom to experiment or to seek out unknown writers.[3]

Many editors now contend that "advance guard" is a better name for their magazines than "little." Coming into use during the First World War, "little" did not refer to the size of the magazines, nor to their literary contents, nor to the fact that they usually did not pay for contributions. What the word designated above everything else was a limited group of intelligent readers: to be such a reader one had to understand the aims of the particular schools of literature that the magazines represented, had to be interested in learning about dadaism, vorticism, expressionism, and surrealism. In a sense, therefore, the word "little" is vague and even unfairly derogatory.

The commercial publishers—the large publishing houses and the big "quality" magazines—are the rear guard. In a few instances they are the rear guard because their editors are conservative in taste, slow to recognize good new writing; but more frequently the commercial publishers are the rear guard because their editors will accept a writer only after the advance guard has proved that he is, or can be made, commercially profitable. Whatever the reason for their backwardness, few commercial houses or magazines of the past thirty years can claim the honor of having served the advance guard banner: they have discovered and sponsored only about 20 per cent[4] of our post-1912 writers; they have done nothing to initiate the new literary groups. To their credit, it may be said that they have ultimately accepted any author, no matter how experimental, after he has been talked about for a period of years—sometimes a good many years.

Little magazine history provides us with a bewildering variety of personalities, but they do have certain characteristics in common. Drawing from the widely differ-

ing portraits of Ezra Pound, William Carlos Williams, Norman Macleod, Eugene Jolas, Ernest J. Walsh, and other *avant-garde* personalities, we may suggest a composite portrait of the little magazine editor or contributor. Such a man is stimulated by some form of discontent—whether with the constraints of his world or the negligence of publishers, at any rate with something he considers unjust, boring, or ridiculous. He views the world of publishers and popularizers with disdain, sometimes with despair. If he is a contributor and wishes to be published, he may have to abandon certain unorthodox aesthetic or moral beliefs. Often he is rebellious against the doctrines of popular taste and sincerely believes that our attitudes toward literature need to be reformed or at least made more liberal. More than that, he generally insists that publication should not depend upon the whimsy of conventional tastes and choices.

Certainly one of the great values of the little magazine for us, who are anxious to know more about the cultural history of our time, lies in its spirit of conscientious revolt against the guardians of public taste. Freedom from such control frequently leads to confusion. We can have little hope, therefore, for a simple clarification of our age from the little magazine, especially since editors were many and quarrels frequent. There is a tangled and delightful sense of contradiction in the total picture. One gets the impression that many writers, neither having had nor desiring the schooling which a calmer age grants somewhat pompously, were at the business of making up their minds, and liking it very much. The great seriousness with which some of the little magazines pronounced the dawn of a new cultural synthesis is forever being disturbed by the spirit of dada which animated certain others.

In view of the urgent conviction that he has something to say, a would-be editor finds that the resources for beginning a magazine are accessible, though he does not usually see beyond the publication of the first issue of the magazine. Generally he is deeply absorbed in the importance of what he has to say; but his interest in establishing and illustrating his own aesthetic beliefs leads him to neglect such matters as might insure either a wide distribution or a reasonable longevity for his periodical. He is of the advance guard simply because the form and content of his contributions are unusual or violate one or several of the principles upon which material is made acceptable to the commercial magazine.

Thus little magazines usually come into being for the purpose of attacking conventional modes of expression and of bringing into the open new and unorthodox literary theories and practices. One of the most significant contributions of these magazines to twentieth century literature is to give it an abundance of suggestions and styles which popular or academic taste scarcely could tolerate or accept. In summary we may say that little magazines have been founded for two reasons: rebellion against traditional modes of expression and the wish to experiment with novel (and sometimes unintelligible) forms; and a desire to overcome the commercial or material difficulties which are caused by the introduction of any writing whose commercial merits have not been proved.

There are some exceptions, of course; this pattern will not fit every one of the magazines whose individual histories the reader will find in the second half of this book. But it is appropriate to a surprisingly large number.

It has been suggested that the little magazines often pursue a perilous career, steering their courses uncertainly and erratically. Apparently the only certainty about them is the probability of early collapse. Morton Dauwen Zabel, reviewing the current literary magazines in the March 1933 issue of *Poetry*, remarks that "It becomes apparent that the multiplication of these periodicals atones for their individual impermanence; that despite their varying shades of policy and opinion, their functions are ultimately identical and their activities continuous." This is to say that though many die, many more are being born, and that this will continue to be true as long as there are young writers with courage, disregard for the requirements of the "dignified press," a few dollars in their pockets (or an interested friend or two who can pay the bills), and finally an abundance of sheer nerve. What makes the magazines "little" also insures their appearing everywhere and at any time—and disappearing without apparent cause.

It is not surprising that most little magazines are short-lived. The editors and contributors are often disrespectful of the ordinary and legitimate demands of the publishing world—the bare minimum of conformity which typesetters and copyreaders demand of their customers. Frequently editors lose interest in their magazines after the first few issues have appeared. Some editors set more or less definite dates at which the magazine will cease publication. Such, for example, was the reasoning of Director Gorham B. Munson, of *Secession*: "The Director pledges his energies for at least two years to the continuance of *Secession*. Beyond a two year span, observation shows, the vitality of most reviews is lowered and their contribution, accomplished, becomes repetitious and unnecessary. Secession will take care to avoid moribundity."[5] Jack Lindsay and P. R. Stephensen prescribed a life of six numbers for their magazine, *The London Aphrodite,* on the ground that "There has never yet been a literary periodical which has not gone dull after the first half-dozen numbers."[6]

Generally, however, the reason for suspending publication is less deliberate. The editor is at present in the hospital and will recover we know not when (*Dyn*); the editor has died, and the magazine cannot be the same without him (*Reedy's Mirror*); the editor has been inducted into the armed services, but the magazine will surely revive after his return (*Vice-Versa, The Little Man*). Most frequent of all reasons are these five: lack or loss of funds; lack or loss of interest; withdrawal of sustaining funds, because of some shift of policy, unpleasant to the backer; government prosecution for some reason or other, usually a matter of censorship; internecine quarrels or misunderstandings.

For the most part, each magazine serves its separate purpose before it dies: that purpose generally is to give finished form and some degree of distribution to the personality and the convictions of its editor or editors. Often these convictions are given editorial form. The editorial statement may be simply an expression of generosity to those who are akin in spirit; it may be (or become) a program or platform; and it may very well be (or become) the expression of some school of political or aesthetic thought which uses the magazine as its voice. A characteristic editorial statement from the little magazines is the following, from the ninth issue of *The New Talent*: "[Writers of *avant-garde* literature are motivated by] the spirit of revolt . . . against artificial boundaries of so-called good taste, against hypocritical 'sweetness and light,' against formalistic strictures of language. . . . [We demonstrate] an awakening . . . of a will to creative truth, a desire for frankness and freedom and honesty in the portraying of the people around us."[7] Such editorial remarks are indicative of the freedom and independence with which *avant-gardists* regarded their positions; they also suggest something of the urgency with which they felt a reform in modern letters was needed. And, in a sense, they underline an aesthetic preoccupation with the need to circumvent any and all restrictions upon experiment in literature. We find these simple ideals developed, practiced, and demonstrated in dozens of little magazines. Their justification is single and simple; their practice varied; their interpretation of literary experiment complex.

II

One should remember that there were advance guard magazines before 1912. The parent of the American little magazine was *The Dial* (1840-44), edited by Margaret Fuller and Ralph Waldo Emerson. Partly because it always held its standards high, *The Dial* never obtained over 300 subscribers, despite such contributors as Thoreau, Emerson, William Ellery Channing, and Theodore Parker. Most of our nineteenth century periodicals, however, were not very inspiring. Besides *The Dial* only four deserve serious recognition as predecessors of modern little magazines: Henry Clapp's *Saturday Press* (1858-66), and the Chicago *Chap Book, Lark, M'lle New York,* all of the nineties. The first decade of the twentieth century seemed as barren as any decade of the nineteenth.

The "renaissance" in the little magazines showed its first beginnings around 1910. In 1912 Harriet Monroe succeeded in starting her famous *Poetry: A Magazine of Verse*. Floyd Dell and Max Eastman decided to make *The Masses* a rebel literary magazine, and *The Poetry Journal* was founded in Boston. These and others that followed them in 1913 and 1914 were consciously established to promote a regenerative literature. Little magazine editors knew that there were already writers such as Robinson, Masters, and Sara Teasdale, poets with much to say provided they could find a place to publish consistently. And the editors suspected that there were many unknowns who could be encouraged to write if they were offered a fair chance of publication. How right the editors were we now know from the record of *Poetry, Glebe, Others, The Masses, The Little Review,* and the many other little magazines of those opening "renaissance" years. Besides firmly establishing the reputations of Edgar Lee Masters, Amy Lowell, Edwin Arlington Robinson, Sara Teasdale, and others who had received only the slightest attention before 1912, the little magazines, during their first three years, presented such previously almost unknown names as Carl Sandburg, Vachel Lindsay, T. S. Eliot, Wallace Stevens, Marianne Moore, John Reed, John Gould Fletcher, Maxwell Bodenheim, and Robert Frost.

It is impossible in this [essay] to do more than mention the influence of individual periodicals in shaping the literary milieu between the two great wars; impossible even to outline the fascinating and often incredible human stories that explain the accomplishments of the advance guard—stories sometimes of tragedy, more often of high comedy, nearly always of courageous sacrifice. In mentioning some of the more important of our post-1912 little magazines, it is convenient to list them as belonging to six major classes—poetry, leftist, regional, experimental, critical, and eclectic. Such a classification is made primarily in the interest of convenience; in many cases the divisions obviously overlap.

Among the more important little magazines devoted exclusively or largely to poetry we might name: *Poetry: A Magazine of Verse* (1912-), *The Poetry Journal* (1912-18), *Contemporary Verse* (1916-29), *The Fugitive* (1922-25), *The Measure* (1921-26), *Glebe* (1913-14), *Others* (1915-19), *Palms* (1932-40), *Voices* (1921-), and *Smoke* (1931-37). One can safely estimate not only that at least 95 per cent[8] of our post-1912 poets were introduced by such magazines, but that they remained the primary periodical outlets for most of our poets.

January 1911 to April 1917 are the dates of the socialist *Masses,* a magazine which, historically, must be considered a landmark. The first important literary voice of the left-wingers, *The Masses,* especially under the editorship of Max Eastman and Floyd Dell (1912-17), was the American inspiration for the so-called "proletarian"

movement of the sociologically minded thirties. The other famous leftwing little magazines are *The Liberator* (1918-24) and *The Partisan Review* (1934-). During the thirties there were many ephemeral voices such as *The Anvil, Left, Blast, The Monthly Review, Left-Front, The Little Magazine, The Windsor Quarterly, International Literature,* and *The New Quarterly.*

In 1915 the Midwest finally attempted to free itself from the domination of Eastern publishing influences. This domination usually took one of two forms, demanding either that the midland artist warp his material to conform to a preconceived notion of what represented the Midwest, or that he burlesque his native soil for the amusement of the East. John T. Frederick's *Midland,* printed in Iowa City from 1915 to 1933, was the first coherent voice to insist on the artist's right to present as he honestly saw it the spirit of the vast region between the Alleghenies and the Rockies. The right to interpret truthfully the cultural entity which the writer best knows became the ideal of several other little magazines in the Midwest, Southwest, and Far West. Such quarterlies as *The Frontier* (1920-39), *The Texas Review* (1915-24), *The Southwest Review* (1924-), *The Prairie Schooner* (1927-), and *The New Mexico Quarterly Review* (1931-) derive their inspiration from *The Midland.*

The advance guard magazines devoted to experimentalism in one form or another have been more numerous than any other type. They are the magazines that have introduced the literary movements or schools (imagism, dadaism, surrealism, etc.); they are the magazines that have cast a sympathetic eye on the more radical departures from conventional realism; they are the magazines, in short, that are concerned with widening the boundaries of an age dedicated to photographic realism and naturalism. Among scores of these periodicals the most important were the following: *The Little Review* (1914-29), *Broom* (1921-24), *Secession* (1922-24), *The Reviewer* (1921-25), *The Double Dealer* (1921-26), *The Dial* (1920-29), *This Quarter* (1925-32), and *transition* (1927-38). The poetry magazines that have been primarily experimental are: *Poetry, Glebe, Others,* and *The Fugitive.* One might also catalogue as experimental little magazine activities James Laughlin's New Directions Press (1936-) and Dorothy Norman's fat semiannual volume, *Twice a Year* (1938-).

A fifth group of little magazines specialized in criticism and reviewing, a group represented by *The Dial, The Hound and Horn* (1927-34), and *The Symposium* (1930-33). These reviews were designed as outlets for the intense, brilliant, and mannered critics, of whom T. S. Eliot, John Crowe Ransom, and R. P. Blackmur are fair representatives. Like *The Southern Review* (1935-42) and the present-day *Kenyon Review* (1939-), neither of which can be considered a little magazine, *The Hound and Horn* and *The Symposium* inherited much of their temperament from *The Dial* and from T. S. Eliot's British *Criterion* (1922-39), magazines that admired acuteness, urbanity, and sometimes preciousness.

The "eclectics" include some of our most interesting magazines, magazines open to most of the literary currents but generally favoring straight, realistic writing and more or less conventional structural patterns; they are the spiritual heirs of the commercial *Smart Set,* whose years of splendor were between 1912 and 1924. *The Seven Arts* (1916-17) and *Story* (1931-) can be included in this group. Many of the eclectic magazines have been and still are associated in some way with university campuses. They are not generally university magazines in the sense of existing simply to glorify the traditions or to inflate the literary accomplishments of the university environment, but they often reflect the tastes and preoccupations of the university community in which they originate. Such, for example, are the Midwestern magazines: *American Prefaces* (University of Iowa, 1935-43), *Accent* (University of Illinois, 1940-), *Diogenes* (University of Wisconsin, 1940-41), and *The University Review* (University of Kansas City, 1935-). Other magazines, like *The Chimera* (1942-) and *Furioso* (1939-), were born on a university campus but later moved away from their place of origin.

III

The individual histories of the magazines that have been mentioned above deserve close attention, and the later chapters will tell many of their stories. At present, for the purpose of illuminating what we have already said, it may be interesting to present an example, a thumbnail sketch, which will contribute to a concrete understanding of the aims and functions, merits and defects, of a typical little magazine. Let us look at the experimental *Double Dealer* for a moment.

The literary revival that began to grow in the East and Midwest in 1911 and 1912 did not take firm root in the South until around 1920. January 1921 saw the first issue of the sprightly New Orleans *Double Dealer,* and a month later *The Reviewer* made its first appearance in Richmond, Virginia.

The Double Dealer began by announcing itself "A National Magazine of the South." The editor, Julius Weis Friend, and his associates, Basil Thompson, Albert Goldstein, and John McClure, were out to deceive both the nation and the South "by speaking the truth."[9] It took some time, however, for the editors to determine exactly where to find the truth. At first they told the world (and they did have a worldwide, if scattered, circulation) that they had "no policy whatever but that of printing the very best material [they could] procure, regardless of popular appeal, moral or immoral stigmata, conventional or unconventional technique, new theme or old."[10] They were also worried about the bog into which Southern culture and literature had sunk since the days of the Civil War. In June 1921 *The Double Dealer* remarked: "It is high time, we believe, for some doughty, clear visioned penman to emerge from the sodden marshes of Southern literature. We are sick to death of the treacly sentimentalities with which our well-intentioned lady fictioneers regale us. The old traditions are no more. New peoples, customs prevail. The Confederacy has long since been dissolved. A storied realm of dreams, lassitude, pleasure, chivalry, and the Nigger no longer exists. We have our 'Main Streets' here, as elsewhere."[11]

This call for a regional Southern literature continued spasmodically until early in 1922. But gradually the editors found their true vision, a vision which they had half glimpsed from the beginning; for in that first issue they took the responsibility of appraising the existent magazines, finding that they approved only of *The Dial, The Pagan, The Little Review,* and *The Yale Review.* Since all of these periodicals except *The Yale Review* were interested in experimental writing, the editors of *The Double Dealer* gave some indication of their own purpose and direction by bestowing their blessings upon them.

But even during the first year a considerable quantity of experimental writing was published—and most of it did not come from the South. The work of Sherwood Anderson, Alfred Kreymborg, Babette Deutsch, Maxwell Bodenheim, and Lola Ridge gave the magazine its fire.

After the first year the periodical definitely found its true interest. It became a review that took its place alongside *The Dial* in establishing the early work of the 1920 experimentalists. We find many pages by Hart Crane, Edmund Wilson, Malcolm Cowley, Jean Toomer, John Crowe Ransom, Robert Penn Warren, Donald Davidson, Allen Tate, Ernest Hemingway, and others.

The few articles which have been written about little magazines have failed to give much attention to *The Double Dealer.* Certainly it was a magazine of great merit, one of the foremost leaders of the twenties. Jay B. Hubbell,[12] when discussing Southern magazines in 1934, failed wholly to appreciate the place of *The Double Dealer,* and the Southern commentators have had nothing to say of the three men who discovered some of the best work of their time.

The chief editor and founder, Julius Weis Friend, was born in 1896 in New Orleans, where he has lived most of his life. After serving in France for sixteen months during the First World War, he returned to New Orleans to establish his magazine and to try his hand at writing. When his association with *The Double Dealer* came to an end, he contributed essays and reviews to various magazines and newspapers. Later, during the thirties, he was co-author of three philosophical volumes: *Science and the Spirit of Man, The Unlimited Community,* and *What Science Really Means.* His philosophical interpretation of Western history, *The Odyssey of the Idea,* appeared in 1942. This is the man who wished to drive a "pile into the mud of this artistic stagnation which has been our portion since the Civil War."[13]

Friend had the assistance of the poet Basil Thompson, who served in the capacity of associate editor until his death early in 1924. Albert Goldstein was an associate editor for a time. And there was also John McClure, the man who wrote most of the excellent *Double Dealer* book reviews, the same John McClure who later gained some fame as a poet and as book critic on the *New Orleans Times-Picayune.*[14]

The year 1922 was the magazine's great year: it had broken with its regional aspirations and began seriously to sponsor experimental writing. It was the year when the general content of the review reached its highest level of excellence. It was the year when all but one of its important discoveries were printed.

The Double Dealer's first introduction of a new writer came in May 1922, with the publication of Ernest Hemingway's "A Divine Gesture." This short, two-page sketch has never been republished and there is no reason why it should be. It is a mildly amusing but slight account of an experience that the Lord God and Gabriel once had in the Garden of Eden. The next issue included the second Hemingway publication, a tough little quatrain, printed at the bottom of a page that also carried a poem written by another man who was soon to become famous.

This new writer was William Faulkner. The poetic "Portrait" of June 1922 tells in six stanzas of two brave young lovers who walk "clear with frank surprise," and "profound in youth," talk of "careful trivialities." The rapid accumulation of such mediocre and sentimental verse as "Portrait" resulted in Faulkner's first volume, *The Marble Faun.*

Jean Toomer and Thornton Wilder appeared for the first time in September 1922. Toomer, in a one-page sketch, writes about a soul called "Nora." Wilder's "Sentences," later to appear in *Cabala,* is a brief piece, probably published because the editor recognized an unusual style.

The October issue contained two poems, "Corymba" and "Dryad," by Donald Davidson, his first appearance outside of *The Fugitive.* The November issue offered verse by John Crowe Ransom, and within the next few months Allen Tate, Robert Penn Warren, and most of

the other *Fugitive* poets were appearing regularly. Hart Crane, Paul Eldridge, Matthew Josephson, Elizabeth Coatsworth, Malcolm Cowley, Edmund Wilson, and Kenneth Fearing also published some of their early work in *The Double Dealer,* though only Fearing appeared here for the first time (1923). The magazine issued its last number in May 1926. The editors felt that they could "no longer give the requisite time to it."[15]

Thus *The Double Dealer,* though it printed good criticism and book reviews, devoted most of its time to the unearthing of new poetry and fiction. Often it was purposely interested in encouraging a new writer rather than in the quality of his work. Consequently the magazine piled high its record of "discoveries" (whom we need not mention, for they have been long forgotten), and filled many of its pages with secondrate poetry and stories. We can submit in the editors' defense that they clearly recognized a most important function of the little magazine—that of encouraging unknown writers.

The Double Dealer, along with *The Fugitive* and *The Reviewer,* stands head and shoulders above the other Southern little magazines. The first discovered two of our best novelists, Hemingway and Faulkner; the second and third brought to fame a round half-dozen of our best present-day poets and critics. All three magazines can stand in the front rank with their more widely chronicled Northern brothers.

Each of the six groups of periodicals that we have mentioned contributed valuably to a regenerative literature. Perhaps those magazines devoted to the experimental philosophies and techniques, magazines such as *The Double Dealer* and *The Little Review,* have most clearly performed the advance guard function. The regionalists or proletarians might, and sometimes did, attain recognition without little magazine help, but the experimentalists rarely could rely on such fortune.

Though the periodicals we have discussed did publish much of the early work of our better writers, they did not actually discover many of them. Most of the reviews printed for the first time a modest two or three. *The Dial,* with its Albert Halper and Louis Zukofsky, is typical. *Poetry, Story, The Fugitive,* and *The Double Dealer* are the exceptions. *Poetry* has an impressive list that includes the names of many of our best poets. *The Double Dealer* first printed five important persons, and *The Fugitive* first published Donald Davidson, Robert Penn Warren, Laura Riding, and Merrill Moore. None of *Story's* many finds have yet had time to establish a solid reputation.

In what publications, then, did the writers, 80 per cent of whom first appeared in the advance guard reviews, receive their starts? They began their careers in the little, little magazines, in the very short-lived, often wild-eyed, periodicals, the ones such as *Blues* (first published James Farrell and Erskine Caldwell) or *Bruno's Bohemia* (Hart Crane). As we have suggested, there have been hundreds of these ephemera, some of which have been provocative, most of which have been unutterably dreary. Almost every one turns up a considerable number of discoveries. Once in a long while one of the discoveries manages to catch the attention of the more respectable little magazines; and, after a time, he may even attain a reputation that need no longer rely on the moneyless blessings of the advance guard.

IV

One may speak casually of an Ernest Hemingway's receiving his first half-dozen publications in little magazines and thereby gaining a reputation which the commercial publishers were eager to exploit. But let us be more specific. Hemingway publishes his first story in *The Double Dealer* in 1922. Assume that the editor and a few other people read this story and like it. These people talk enthusiastically of the story and perhaps twice as many read the next Hemingway offering. Soon many admirers are talking—a new name appears in the advance guard. A half-dozen little magazines are printing Hemingway stories and he has several thousand readers. A noncommercial press in Paris publishes his first thin volume, *Three Stories and Ten Poems*. The new writer attracts the attention of the Scribner's office. Finally in 1926 comes *The Sun Also Rises*. A writer has been started on the road to success—by the little magazines and their readers.

Though the best of our writers receive a wide enough acceptance through the little magazines to make them sought after by the conservative periodicals and publishing houses, one cannot help wondering what might have happened if these writers had not been offered a little magazine's encouragement. Many a Hart Crane or Sherwood Anderson might never have been heard from had there been no advance guard; for seeing one's work in print arouses a man's hope, stimulates further effort. This is what Stephen Vincent Benét has in mind when he writes: "The little magazines, of course, are absolutely indispensable. They give the beginning writer his first important step—a chance to see how the thing looks in print. And there's nothing as salutary."[16] This, indeed, is a primary justification.

Despite their promotion of the best of the new writers and literary movements, the advance guard magazines are easy targets for caustic ridicule. The most frequent accusation is that they do not print good writing. Of course there is a good deal of truth in this, and implied in the truth lies much of the strength and weakness of the little magazine. Few persons can take seriously the obvious nonsense that has filled many of the pages of *The Little Review, transition,* or *Broom.* Even the best

magazines, *Poetry* and *The Dial,* for instance, have frequently lost their critical balance, been deluded into bestowing praise on an upstart whose only virtue was a facile talent for novelty in phrasing. The readiness with which editors seek for materials of whatever quality is the weakness that plagues the little magazine. Our knowledge of *The Double Dealer* proves, however, that the editor may deliberately accept material which he knows to be second rate, for he sees the marks of a genuine talent behind the stumbling words or unsteady structure of a poem or story. In accepting a manuscript to give encouragement, the editor hopes that the discovery will soon outgrow his awkwardness. More often than not, awkwardness is not outgrown; thus the files of the little reviews lie heavy with frozen material that probably never interested anyone except the author and the hopeful, though probably skeptical, editor. And so, though one must willingly agree that the little magazines contain much that is not of first importance, one must just as willingly grant that there is justification in printing fledgling literary efforts. Nor must one forget that many of the more significant pieces of our time have found their way into the little magazines. The people who suggest that the little magazines do not publish literature might notice the "thanks for permission to reprint" acknowledgments in almost any first volume of reputable stories, poetry, or criticism.

Some persons also believe that the advance guard editors have a tendency to favor the "established" little magazine writers over the meritorious unknown. True enough. Little magazine editors are not free from vanity or oblivious of the desire for prestige. They do favor the "name" writers of their own circle. Yet they do not grant them the same favors that the commercial editor is likely to give his writers. The little magazine does not usually pay for its contributions, is not dependent on advertising, and can ignore names to a far greater extent than the commercial publisher. Several Hemingway stories were refused, perhaps unwisely, by little magazine editors in those first days of Hemingway glory.

Hostile observers also berate the "exhibitionism," "pretension," "snobbishness," and "adolescence" toward which some reviews incline. Exhibitionism there is, nor need one look far to discover pretension and snobbishness. But all of these words cannote, in varying degrees, conscious or semiconscious attitudinizing; yet such conscious posturing is rare, not only in literature but in any artistic or mental activity.

But when one comes to the charge that the little magazines are often adolescent, he is forced to grant that the critics have much firm ground under their feet. For if fear and uncertainty are signs of immaturity, as the psychologists contend, then many little magazine contributors and not a few editors are immature. The pioneer, whether he be the wielder of the broad axe, the explorer in the deep jungle of the unconscious mind, the rebel economic theorist, or the innovator of literary surrealism, is often a slightly maladjusted person. Not infrequently it is a feeling of insecurity that has driven him to pioneering, and it is insecurity, combined with an envy for the respectable, that leads the pioneer and rebel unknowingly, and sometimes knowingly, to apologize for his feeling of insecurity with considerable bizarre behavior and intellectual display—display which is designed to emphasize his uniqueness, his superiority. Thus a *Little Review* can convince itself of its ineffable critical discernment by insisting, in all high seriousness, that the dadaists and the machine reveal many of the highest aspirations of man. And *transition* can convince itself of its penetrating insight into the nature of man and the supernatural by talking of divine currents to which man must attune himself. One does not sense pretension nor exhibitionism here, but rather a lack of urbanity, an insecure mind.

Fortunately, one can afford to ignore a good deal of adolescence if courage and daring and genuine accomplishment are also present. All such comment is overshadowed, moreover, by very real contributions. In 1912, in 1920, in 1930, the little magazines were the innovators, and today they are still the innovators. A society needs ever-fresh interpretations and new writers to make these interpretations. Little magazine editors believe that a Hemingway or a Sandburg or a Faulkner may finally lose his power or die and that younger artists must be constantly encouraged. This is why advance guard editors sought out Erskine Caldwell, Albert Halper, and James Farrell in 1929, why they discovered most of the so-called proletarian writers of the thirties, and why in the forties they are still introducing new artists.

Notes

1. McCarthy, in Act Two. William Saroyan, *Three Plays,* New York, 1940, pp. 88-89.

2. Charles Allen, "The Advance Guard," *Sewanee Review,* ii, 425-29 (July/September 1943).

3. We have provided a place for such magazines in the supplementary list in the bibliography; they are important "fellow-travelers" of the little magazines and deserve comment.

4. See Allen, "The Advance Guard."

5. Editorial, *Secession,* i, n.p. (Spring 1922).

6. Editorial, *The London Aphrodite,* v, 400 (April 1929).

7. E. G. Arnold, Editorial, *The New Talent,* ix, 1-2 (July-August-September, 1935).

8. See Allen, "The Advance Guard."

9. Julius Weis Friend, Editorial, *The Double Dealer,* i, 1 (January 1921).

10. Friend, "The Magazine in America," *The Double Dealer,* i, 83 (March 1921).

11. Friend, "Southern Letters," *The Double Dealer,* i, 214 (June 1921).

12. Jay B. Hubbell, "Southern Magazines," *Culture in the South,* edited by W. T. Couch, Chapel Hill, N.C., 1934.

13. Friend, Editorial, *The Double Dealer,* i, 126 (April 1921).

14. Letter, Julius Weis Friend to Charles Allen, July 28, 1941 (unpublished).

15. See *Ibid.,* March 25, 1940. *The Double Dealer* cost on the average of $300 per issue, and "always ran a deficit over and above subscriptions and advertising, which was made up by donations from about forty individuals. Payment for material published started out at the rate of one cent per word for prose and fifty cents a line for verse. This was discontinued after about six issues due to a lack of funds, and for the remainder of the five years no payment was made for material." The average circulation was 1,500.

16. Letter, Stephen Vincent Benét to Charles Allen, September 1939 (unpublished).

List of References

Allen, Charles, "The Advance Guard," *Sewanee Review,* v. 51, no. 3, July/Sept. 1943, p. 410-29.

Hubbell, Jay B., "Southern Magazines," *Culture in the South,* edited by W. T. Couch, Chapel Hill, 1934, p. 159-82.

Wolfgang Görtschacher (essay date 2000)

SOURCE: Görtschacher, Wolfgang. "Putting the Record Straight: The Little Magazines and Literary History." In *Contemporary Views on the Little Magazine Scene,* pp. i-xiv. Salzburg, Austria: Poetry Salzburg at the University of Salzburg, 2000.

[*In the following essay, Görtschacher explores the significance of little magazines within the publishing industry.*]

> Hang a painting by Carlo Dolci beside a Cosimo Tura. You cannot prevent Mr Buggins from preferring the former, but you can very seriously impede his setting up a false tradition of teaching on the assumption that Tura has never existed, or that the qualities of the Tura are nonexistent or outside the scope of the possible.
>
> (Ezra Pound, *ABC of Reading*)

The importance of the little magazines vis-à-vis literary history was recently stressed by critics of eminent stature, such as Malcolm Bradbury and Marjorie Perloff. In a guest-lecture entitled "Barbed Wire Entanglements: Objectivist Poetics in the 1930s" at the University of Salzburg, Perloff argued, after an examination of *Pagany*'s Objectivist special issue, that the work published in the magazine prefigures what is done by postmodernists today. Perloff concludes that an examination and careful analysis of little magazines and small presses would be an overdue attempt at putting the record of literary history straight.

Both literary historians and university critics/lecturers have a tendency to accept the pre-selection by editors of mainstream publishers and degenerate to PR-agents or distribution managers of these publishing conglomerates. Thus many writers whose names are not on the poetry list of a big mainstream publisher are excluded from literary histories and university curricula because their writing is regarded as 'inferior'. In the "Introduction" to his anthology *Completing the Picture: Exiles, Outsiders and Independents* William Oxley perceptively maintains that the

> criticism that does exist today has become increasingly affected by media practices. In effect, the history of criticism—at least in the last fifty years—has become confused with the history of publicity. This is the only way to really account for the bright but brief 'stardom' of, for example, Brian Patten and Jeni Couzyn in the 1960s, Andrew Motion and Craig Raine in the 1970s/80s; and, very likely, the recently hyped Wendy Cope and Simon Armitage.[1]

For many neglected poets little magazines are the only possibility of getting their work published. Since the sixties, more and more writers, in particular those whose conception of poetry is based on radical, avant-garde and language-centred poetics, have decided to be published exclusively in little magazines and by small presses, because it suits them artistically and gives them more control over their work; examples include Ian Hamilton Finlay, Bob Cobbing, Allen Fisher, and Chris Torrance. One of the great contributions of small magazines and presses is the documentation of the still incomplete literary past. Often small magazines offer the only flexible forum for rounding out the black against the white, giving the present a more sober view of the past after the partisans have begun to grow old.

In order to understand the relative importance of this medium for publishing literary texts, one has to analyse the role of little magazines as part of the institutional network of publishers, reviewers, universities, arts organisations, newspapers, television, poetry prizes, public libraries, literary critics, bookstores, the Internet, etc., that sustain the dissemination of contemporary poetry. The medium also plays an important part in the perception of these texts as belonging to specific categories and representing a certain degree of literary quality. The institutional analysis of literature draws attention to the complex relations of production, distribution, exchange and reception in the literary field. In England the networks and cliques associated with the bigger publishing houses (Faber, Chatto & Windus, OUP, Bloodaxe Press, and the heavily subsidised Anvil Press), the Arts-Council-subsidised little magazines and literary reviews (*Poetry Review, London Magazine, The Times Literary Supplement, The London Review of Books*), the Literature Department of the Arts Council, and to a very important degree the universities of Oxford, Cambridge, and East Anglia, are cultural bases for the establishment of a canon of 'serious literature' or texts of 'literary merit', a criterion that has, over the years, proved to be indefinable, yet thought to be recognisable by Arts Council decision-makers. Texts owe their 'literary' or 'aesthetic' quality to the fact that specific social groups, usually those holding influential positions in the literary field, and institutions subject them to a valorisation process, based on their own conceptions of literature. "A conception of literature", to quote the Dutch critic Van Rees, "is a set of normative statements on the properties which texts ought to possess in order to be reckoned as literary and on the function to be assigned to literature".[2] Most important for this 'institutional' approach to the literary field are Pierre Bourdieu's studies, in which he conceives of the arts as being the object of incessant value-assessments by several cultural institutions, which constitute the literary field. Within and among these institutions a continuous struggle takes place for the monopoly of conferring cultural legitimacy to works of art. This line of research helps to demystify the notion of 'literary' or 'aesthetic' quality by undermining the wide-spread conviction that the assessment of literary quality can rest on 'purely literary' grounds. Arguments derived from institutional analyses necessitate the rejection of widespread conceptions: the view of the poet as autonomous executor of an individual creative project; that of the critic as an objective expert proficient in designating the qualities in a work of literature to which it owes its specific rank in the hierarchy; and that of the genuine poetry consumer who concerns himself intensively with high-quality poetry.[3]

A recent example might help to illustrate this argument. The quadriga of Craig Raine, Andrew Motion, Blake Morrison, and Christopher Reid have, since the early eighties, held important posts in the publishing trade and critical establishments. Thus they have succeeded in editing widely publicised anthologies with large print runs and, as editors and reviewers, accorded poems which deal with personal events, but fail to universalise convincingly whatever public connotations may underlie the personal experience (which started off as 'Martianism'), a favoured status. A comparison with the

Movement's poetry politics provides ample proof that Raine et al. seem to have perfectly copied their master poets, e.g. Amis, Larkin, Wain, Davie, etc. In his "Introduction" to *A Various Art,* Andrew Crozier suggests that the Movement's takeover, the establishment of a new orthodoxy by "a shift in taste", had been achieved "by means of a wholesale rewriting of and reorientation towards the history of modern poetry, and this included the virtual suppression of parts of it". The prevailing poetic orthodoxy was "an art in relation to its own conventions—and a pusillanimous set of conventions at that. It was not to be ambitious, or to seek to articulate ambition through the complex deployment of its technical means".[4] Morrison's influential study *The Movement* supplies the necessary data in support of Crozier's hypothesis. In it he describes how "the Movement inevitably produced a distorted picture of the decade [. . .] that allowed their own work to appear to be a radical departure, the 'new poetry'".[5] Through a network of Oxbridge contacts and a brilliantly organised publicity campaign that concentrated on the weeklies, e.g. the *Spectator,* the *New Statesman,* and the *Listener,* in order to gain access to the largest audience possible, they succeeded in shifting the taste of the fifties. As Donald Davie summed it up in "The Varsity March": "Precisely because the positions that matter are so few, it is entirely feasible for a group to secure one or two sub-editorial chairs and a few reviewing 'spots', so as to impose their shared proclivities and opinions as the reigning orthodoxy of a decade."[6] In *A Sinking Island* Hugh Kenner comes up with a similar portrait of British poetry in the eighties. He sees the few major publishing houses that still maintain poetry lists (Chatto, Faber, Secker, OUP) as under the control of a "Martian Mafia":

> The machinery, for those both knowledgeable and lucky, runs more reliably than at any time in the past [. . .] few publishers maintain poetry lists at all, and what gets selected for review, or for publication in the weekly journals, is consequently of much significance. Tie together publishing and reviewing and you have a lot of the action sewn up.[7]

I will try to chart some of the outlines of the map of poetry publishing and reviewing since the late seventies. Besides co-editing the very influential anthology *The Penguin Book of Contemporary Poetry* (1982), Morrison was fiction and poetry editor on the *TLS* from 1978 to 1981 and (deputy) literary editor on *The Observer* from 1981 to 1989. From 1990 until 1994/95 he was literary editor on *The Independent on Sunday.* His co-editor Motion held the posts of poetry editor and editorial director with Chatto & Windus between 1982 and 1989 and published his own *Natural Causes* (1987) and his pal's first two collections, *Dark Glasses* (1984; rev. and enl. ed. 1989) and *The Ballad of the Yorkshire Ripper* (1987) under his employer's imprint. In March 1993 Morrison commissioned Motion to write an article

on Philip Larkin, which was published in three instalments in *The Independent on Sunday*'s Review Supplement, as part of a PR campaign for his biography *Philip Larkin: A Writer's Life,* published by Faber. Even the affiliation with *The Observer*—quite supportive under Morrison's editorship—still seems to be operative: in the first six months of 1995 Motion managed to get six reviews published in the influential weekly. From April 1982 to July 1983 he was also *Poetry Review*'s editor. Between 1989 and 1990 he was project editor at Faber & Faber. Together with Malcolm Bradbury he co-edited the prestigious *New Writing 2,* a series of annual anthologies initiated by the Literature Department of the British Council in 1992 and sponsored from the outset by Booker, in 1993 and—obviously a sheer coincidence—became Bradbury's successor in February 1995 when the University of East Anglia appointed him to the chair of its creative writing programme. Together with Candice Rodd, Motion also co-edited *New Writing 3* in 1993. In early 1996 he became the chairman of the Arts Council of England's Literature Advisory Panel.

From 1981 until mid-1991 Craig Raine had a firm hold on Faber's poetry list which, some critics believe, led to an overrated prominence for poets like Andrew Motion, for example, by the sheer fact that they had—and, in Motion's case, still have—the majority of their books published by what may still be considered the major establishment poetry publisher. In 1985 Raine, who was Christopher Reid's teacher at Exeter College, Oxford for a term, did his former student a 'favour' and published his collection *Katerina Brac.* It came as no surprise that Reid, between March 1990 and March 1991 "Bookmark" and broadcasting reviewer for the *TLS,* replaced Raine in July 1991 and since then has been Faber's only poetry editor. Bearing in mind that there is always a sort of backlog when posts change hands, critics have to wait for another two or three years to be able to evaluate whether Reid has changed Faber's closed-shop policy or just followed in his predecessor's footsteps. An exchange of letters between Reid and Michael Hulse, who co-edited with David Kennedy and Brian Morley the immensely hyped Bloodaxe-anthology *The New Poetry* (1993), in the wake of Hulse's review of some Faber publications in *PN Review* 98 (1994) provides interested readers with a glimpse beneath the surface of the power struggle for market shares and a prominent place in literary history between two of the most influential British poetry presses. In his (pretended) attempt at summing up the Faber list, Hulse, after accusing Reid of taking on only those poets who are "closely approximate" to his "own style of poetry", concludes his review with the supposition that "the Faber list, under Reid's management [. . .] will probably never be open to the larger cultural, intellectual address of whatever latter-day Eliots or Pounds may be waiting in the wings". In the critical shadow-boxing Hulse's targets are the poets in the domestic strain, e.g.,

Simon Armitage, Hugo Williams and Don Paterson, carrying on in the main stream of British poetry the poetical ideals promoted by the Movement poets and their heirs, the Martians. On the other hand, Bloodaxe's intention is nothing more than to shake Britain's foremost poetry publisher to its foundations by making a claim for the top position: "Faber have too much their own way and like to believe they invented poetry and have a birthright to a monopoly of kudos." The time, however, is not yet ripe for a take-over. Hulse's blow was perhaps premature, diversionary tactics or even a PR-trick. In the end he even admits being "well aware of the qualities of Faber's list" and welcomes Reid's "decisions to publish Charles Simic and August Kleinzahler" because they "point in an extremely encouraging direction".[8]

Lack of time and space does not permit a close analysis of the supposed incestuousness of who-reviewed-whose-book-in-which-magazine, which would, I am certain, be quite enlightening as to who else belongs to the 'Martian' clique. But there is also another analogy with the Movement's poetry politics worth mentioning, i.e., the concentration of their publicity campaign on the weeklies and glossy monthlies, which, one has to add, usually pay the highest fees for poets, to the almost complete exclusion of little magazines. In his collections *Love in a Life* (1991) and *The Price of Everything* (1994) Motion acknowledges the first publication of some poems in *The Independent, The Independent on Sunday, The London Review of Books, The Times Literary Supplement, The Guardian, The Times, The Sunday Times, The Observer, Sunday Correspondent, Harpers & Queen,* among others. Alan Ross's *London Magazine,* highly subsidised by the ACGB, is the only literary magazine that is mentioned.

The initiation of Faber & Faber into the application of professional marketing strategies took place more than a decade ago under their sales and marketing director Desmond Clarke, who managed to increase poetry sales by 37 percent in 1985 and by more than 25 percent in 1986. After the firm's decision to change the format and design of Faber poetry volumes in order to market them as a coherent group, John McConnell at Pentagram, the firm of designers still responsible for the outward appearance of the books, designed the covers. The new austere jacket design, in which dark and light repetitions of the "ff" logo surround a white rectangle on which the title and the author's name are printed, reminded John Matthias of the old post-war Penguins, which included the transfer of associations of "quality, economy, democracy, and a canon in the making which is asking for one's trust" from the latter to the former.[9] The chief difference between Faber books and the old Penguins is the drawing or photograph or etching underneath the title, which Matthias interprets as "the manifestation of personality in the design's impersonal

context" and "the individual talent working through tradition."[10] Six months after Ted Hughes had been appointed Poet Laureate Clarke used his most prominent poet as the spearhead of a £22,000 national promotion campaign of 12 contemporary poets titled "The Best of Poetry Today,"[11] including adverts and features not only in literary publications, but in the daily press, the Sunday supplements, on radio and T.V., nationwide displays in the front of W. H. Smith's shops, a mailing bombardment of schools and universities, six public readings by Hughes, and the presentation to the winner of the Arvon Competition, which was judged by two Faber poets and the award presented to the winner by a third. In this context a study of the British poetry prizes, which are related to organisations and institutions in the literary field, the allocation of jury memberships to particular literary experts and practising poets and their technique of harmonizing opinion on certain authors would be valuable.

How do literary critics, university lecturers and literary historians as institutions in the literary field respond to literary market forces? How do they select their material for their critical studies? The majority of scholars seems to be quite willing to adhere to, and let themselves be governed by, extraneous considerations, such as value assessments by important critics, the status of the publishers, media-hype, subsidies, competitions, prizes, etc. Almost three decades ago Jeff Nuttall maintained that the "rebel styles in literature were blocked out of publishing, out of libraries, out of serious discussion, by the extensive influence of the universities who are too idle to reform their critical axioms and therefore try to preserve the critical status quo"[12]. I believe this hypothesis can still be applied to many Departments of English Studies.

On very rare occasions only have literary historians and editors of widely-publicised anthologies, which provide together with the publications of big presses the raw data for the former, paid attention to the little magazine and small press scene. The raison d'être of many little magazines and small presses, why they were founded in the first place, is a reaction to the establishment's literary orthodoxy that is felt to be too narrow-minded and to operate a system of cultural closure. A useful starting point to demonstrate the narrowness of poetic taste is *The Penguin Book of Contemporary British Poetry,* which belies the representative claim implicit in the title. In their introduction Morrison and Motion wanted to wipe off the literary historical map all the poetic achievements of the sixties and seventies, when little magazines and small presses provided, in the majority of cases, the main outlets for most British poets. They claimed that

> [A shift of sensibility] follows a stretch, occupying
> much of the 1960s and 70s, when very little—in Eng-
> land at any rate—seemed to be happening, when

achievements in British poetry were overshadowed by those in drama and fiction, and when, despite the presence of strong individual writers, there was a lack of overall shape and direction.[13]

Two anthologies, *A Various Art* (1990, first published by Carcanet in 1987) and *The New British Poetry* (1988), both published by Paladin, drawing on the wide variety of poetic production from the early sixties until the late eighties, indicate some of the segments of the poetic spectrum that had been ignored by Morrison and Motion: black British poetry, feminist poetry, the poetry of the British Poetry Revival[14] of the sixties and seventies, and the younger poets who developed in the context of the Poetry Revival. This samizdat publishing in little magazines and small presses that was a conscious reaction to the poetry orthodoxy of the fifties, was made possible by cheap mimeo and offset litho productions. Although for many poets little magazines have functioned as stepping stones to the poetry list of big publishers (e.g. Roy Fisher's *Collected Poems* were published by OUP), the publication of experimental poetry by big presses is only a recent development, after more than a quarter century, when Penguin had published its Modern Poets series and Michael Horovitz's *Children of Albion* anthology. From 1988 until 1993 the big press Paladin/Grafton Books, which was first a division of the Collins Publishing Group and in 1991 became an imprint of Harper Collins Publishers, tried to redress the imbalance. In its Re/Active poetry series Paladin, under its series editor Iain Sinclair, published important anthologies of experimental poetry and volumes of Selected Poems of poets whose work had hitherto appeared almost exclusively in little magazines and booklets of small presses, in inexpensive paperback editions.[15] Due to the large print run, the publicity campaign and the fact that these anthologies were on sale in almost every bookshop in the UK, experimental, anti-establishment poets, like Allen Fisher, Lee Harwood and Tom Raworth, were provided with the opportunity of reaching a wider reading public.

Seldom have histories of literature, in particular of British poetry, analysed—to quote Siegfried Schmidt—"the medium-system of a society, the socio-political positions of those who dispose of, and control, the system and its components, the hierarchy of the different media within the system, etc., in order to figure out the acting conditions of individuals and groups in co-present literary system."[16] Let us consider some examples! Vol. 8 entitled *The Present* of *The New Pelican Guide to English Literature* (1983), edited by Boris Ford, contains a short essay on the book market, but almost completely fades out on the question of little magazines: in his essay titled "The Literary Scene" John Holloway devotes ten lines to them mentioning *Critical Quarterly, Stand, Listen, Wave,* and *Lines Review* and the appendix, compiled by Joan Holloway, includes a one-page list of little magazines. In his *A Critical Guide to British Poetry 1964-84* Anthony Thwaite divides the poetry scene into seventeen segments, rather arbitrarily grouped I may add, including one page on Ian Hamilton's *The Review*. His simplistic résumé of the little magazines: they "have suffered in the bleak economic climate. Nevertheless, many come and go, and some persist."[17] It is as simple as that. *The Encyclopedia of Literature and Criticism* (Routledge 1990), edited by Martin Coyle, Peter Garside, Malcolm Kelsall and John Peck, contains a 13-page section, out of 1,300 pages, on "British Periodicals and Reading Publics". Although its author Jon Klancher maintains that "new understandings of English periodicals and audiences have helped generate fresh empirical researches that are redrawing the maps of English cultural transmission since 1688,"[18] the representation is totally inadequate. *The Oxford Companion to Twentieth-Century Poetry* (1994), edited by Ian Hamilton, one of the most influential figures in the poetry business and in the sixties and seventies editor of the highly subsidised magazines *The Review* and *The New Review,* pretends to be, in its editor's definition, "a history, a map of modern poetry in English"[19] that covers movements, genres, individual poets and magazines. Regarding the last, the book contains nineteen short entries discussing British little magazines but only four of them are still in existence: *Agenda, London Magazine, PN Review,* and *Stand.* Although restricted in their approach, Blake Morrison's *The Movement,* Jonathan Raban's *The Society of the Poem,* Alan Young's *Dada and After,* and Michael Schmidt and Grevel Lindop's *British Poetry since 1960,* draw attention to the importance of the little magazine and small press scene. On a completely different scale is *New British Poetry: The Scope of the Possible* (Manchester 1993), edited by Robert Hampson and Peter Barry. Although it does not live up to the expectations of all-inclusiveness raised by its title, it is a very important collection of essays about the wide range of innovative but neglected poetry which was published in little magazines and by small presses outside the mainstream during the period 1970-90. The most important publication to date is Alvin Sullivan's *British Literary Magazines: The Modern Age, 1914-1984.*

Why should little magazines and small press publications be studied in the first place? Why can't we just forget these manic obsessives with their numbered serial publications, mostly in paperback or A4 or a similar format, which regularly devote a major part of their total space to creative work, mainly poetry or poetry matters? In addition to some of the aspects I have already touched upon, I would like to mention that the majority of poets, and, indeed, some novelists and artists rely, at least at some point in their careers, for the publication of their work on these media. Secondly, the overwhelming majority of British literary experiments and developments first originated from publications in little magazines. In an interview for *The Times,* occasioned by the exhibition "Little Magazines" at the London Festival Hall in October 1990, its organiser, Geoffrey Soar, said, answering the journalists' question as to whether the proprietors of little magazines should not be a bit mad: "Oh yes, mad helps. But remember, without such madmen, and women, we might never have heard of Eliot, Hemingway, Joyce and many, many others."[20] In his statement about *Pagany* (1929-32), a little magazine that took its name from his novel *A Voyage to Pagany,* William Carlos Williams struck the same note: "The little magazine is something I have always fostered; for without it, I myself would have been early silenced."[21] Williams expressed the sentiments of many poets and writers of fiction.

On very rare occasions only have little magazines been stocked in bookshops. The medium's voluntary marginality on the literary market seems to be inscribed in the basic premises of its existence: its disregard of economic profit, its editor's desire to be completely independent, its relatively small circulation, its tight budget, and—in the case of several magazines—its irregularity of appearance and its functioning as a circular of communication for a restricted group of writers. As the information and distribution agents largely ignore the productivity of little magazines and small presses, which produce, due to inexpensive modern techniques, decent issues and pamphlets and books in both hardback and paperback editions, librarians, bookstore managers, and most of the potential reading public do not know of their existence and thus do not buy them. By publishing experimental poetry, little magazines are not "market consumption articles cater[ing] to the middle-class rapid reader, untrained in contemporary poetics and looking for instant significance and alibis with established, authenticated products".[22]

The use of little magazines in university courses could provide an instantaneous remedy, however incomplete, for this lack of educational training. Literary taste is so often governed by extraneous considerations, such as value assessments by important critics, the status of the publishers, media-hype, subsidies, competitions, etc., that little magazines with their welcome freedom from parochiality and modishness provide a real challenge, because they render impossible the usual abdication of responsibility on the part of many academics in favour of allowing critics of considerable stature and literary editors of big presses to determine and define the 'best' poetry. In the quest for excellence academics and students alike have to educate their own literary tastes by opening up the tradition-bound university curricula, libraries and classrooms. Little magazines enable the reader to study a wide range of both mainstream and non-Establishment poetry, in particular experimental and avant-garde poetry excluded by the dominant poetic culture: open-field poetry, concrete and soundtext

poetry, surrealism and dada, conceptual forms, the long poem in the tradition of Allen Fisher's 'content-specific' approach, language poetry, and performance poetry. The plethora of little magazines, which more than any lists of big mainstream presses and their anthologies represents the UK poetry spectrum in its entirety, enables readers to study these formal experiments alongside traditional and mainstream poetry.

Established poets gravitate towards little magazines at many stages of their careers, appreciating them as a testing ground for their latest projects, a source of inspiration and information. Many magazines are edited with the altruistic ideal of providing a crèche for young artists, publishing their work alongside that of their maturer colleagues. In their review sections, little magazines cover the poetry publications of establishment and small presses with a comprehensiveness that cannot be achieved by *The Times Literary Supplement* and *The London Review of Books.* That is why little magazines are the best source of information for anyone interested in recent developments on the literary market. Magazines also print recently conducted interviews with poets, and provide critical evaluation of the work of living authors, both famous and unknown, and make major contributions to a re-valuation of certain poets' work (e.g. *Agenda, Angel Exhaust, Pages, Chapman*). It is only with considerable delay, if at all, that these essays are anthologised or reprinted in a critic's collection of essays.

Little magazines are not the only remedy for the students' lack of interest in literature, poetry in particular. It is not *either* little magazines and small press publications *or* books from eminent commercial presses, but 'both—and'. Although attempts at poetry list extension occurred among major publishers in the early nineties, the pendulum of poetry publications—with the exception of Carcanet Press and Bloodaxe—seems to swing back to the other extreme, thus emphasising my thesis that little magazines and small presses are still the main outlets for poetry, matching the majors in attractive production and prestige. In the issues of these magazines we will not always come across the work of a future James Joyce or Ted Hughes or Seamus Heaney (these magazines also publish about ninety per cent of today's bad poetry), but they are the most promising searching ground for unknown serious poets.

Notes

1. "Introduction" in *Completing the Picture: Exiles, Outsiders and Independents,* ed. William Oxley (Exeter: Stride, 1995), p. 10.

2. C. J. Van Rees, "Introduction: Advances in the Empirical Sociology of Literature and the Arts: the Institutional Approach", *Poetics* 12 (1983), p. 286.

3. Pierre Bourdieu, "The Field of Cultural Production, or: The Economic World Reversed", *Poetics* 12 (1983), pp. 311-56; p. 322.

4. Andrew Crozier, "Introduction" in *A Various Art,* ed. A. Crozier and Tim Longville (London: Paladin, 1990), pp. 11-12.

5. Blake Morrison, *The Movement: English Poetry and Fiction of the 1950s* (Oxford UP, 1980), p. 25.

6. Donald Davie, "The Varsity March", *Poetry Nation* 2 (1974), p. 74.

7. Hugh Kenner, *A Sinking Island: The Modern English Writers* (London: Barrie and Jenkins, 1988), p. 256; pp. 254-5.

8. Christopher Reid, "Letter to the Editor"; Michael Hulse, "Letter to the Editor", *PN Review* 101 (Jan.-Feb. 1995), p. 2.

9. Cf. two facsimile messages by Christopher Reid, 3 May and 7 May 1996:

   The poetry list was redesigned at the same time as other Faber publications. In other words, it was no single person's decision [NOT Desmond Clarke's, who was Sales Director at the time], but the firm's. [. . .] Glad to have the opportunity to correct this bit of folklore.

10. John Matthias, "Of Publishers, Readings, and Festivals, Circa 1986" in *Reading Old Friends: Essays, Reviews, and Poems on Poetics 1975-1990* (State University of New York, 1992), p. 240.

11. The campaign featured the following poets: Ted Hughes, Seamus Heaney, Thom Gunn, Douglas Dunn, Philip Gross, Philip Larkin, Paul Muldoon, Norman Nicholson, Tom Paulin, Craig Raine, Derek Walcott, and Amy Clampitt.

12. Jeff Nuttall, *Bomb Culture* (London: MacGibbon & Kee, 1968), p. 45.

13. Blake Morrison and Andrew Motion, eds, "Introduction" in *The Penguin Book of Contemporary Poetry* (London: Penguin, 1982), p. 11.

14. Eric Mottram coined and defined this term when writing his two Catalogues for Poetry Conferences at the Polytechnic of Central London, 1974 and 1977:

   Since the 1930s, officially-sanctioned British poetry had favoured minimal invention and information, and maximum ironic finesse, with personal anecdote, covered with a social veneer or location of elements in the country. It favoured the urbanely witty or baroquely emotional rather than the thoroughly informed intelligence willing and eager to risk imaginative forms. Official preference could not tolerate an art that went beyond a leisure-hours consumer inclination to rapid reading; work which might necessitate concentration, trained ability to read, and a willingness to entertain the prospect of new forms and materials.

   Mottram: "The British Poetry Revival, 1960-75" in *New British Poetries,* ed. Robert Hampson and Peter Barry (Manchester UP, 1993), p. 26. Cf. Mottram, "The British Poetry Revival 1960-1974" in *Modern British Poetry Conference 1974* (London: The Polytechnic of Central London, 1974), p. 87.

15. Cf. the "Re/Active Anthologies" Allen Fisher, Bill Griffiths & Brian Catling, *Future Exiles: Three London Poets,* London: Paladin 1992; Andrew Crozier, Donald Davie & C. H. Sisson, *Ghosts in the Corridor,* London: Paladin, 1992; Thomas A. Clark, Barry MacSweeney & Chris Torrance, *The Tempers of Hazard,* London: Paladin, 1993. Paladin also published paperback editions of the Selected Poems of experimental poets, among them Lee Harwood, *Crossing the Frozen River: Selected Poems,* London: Paladin, 1988; Christopher Middleton, *Selected Writings,* London: Paladin, 1989; Tom Raworth, *Tottering State: New and Selected Poems 1963-1987,* London: Paladin, 1988.

16. Siegfried Schmidt, "On Writing Histories of Literature. Some Remarks from a Constructivist Point of View", *Poetics* 15 (1985), pp. 279-301; p. 299.

17. Anthony Thwaite, *A Critical Guide to British Poetry 1964-84* (London, New York: Longman, 1985), p. 130.

18. Jon Klancher, "British Periodicals and Reading Publics" in *The Encyclopedia of Literature and Criticism,* ed. Martin Coyle, Peter Garside, Malcolm Kelsall, and John Peck (London: Routledge, 1990), p. 876.

19. Ian Hamilton, ed., "Introduction" in *The Oxford Companion to Twentieth-Century Poetry* (Oxford, New York: OUP, 1994), p. v.

20. Joseph Connolly, "Licensed to Print Anything Except Money", *The Times,* 8 Oct. 1990, p. 19.

21. *A Return to 'Pagany': The History, Correspondence, and Selections from a Little Magazine,* ed Stephen A. Halpert and Richard Johns (Beacon Press, 1969), p. 3.

22. E. Mottram, "The British Poetry Revival" in *New British Poetries: The Scope of the Possible,* ed Robert Hampson and Peter Barry (Manchester New York: Manchester UP, 1993), p. 18.

Michael Barsanti (essay date 2004)

SOURCE: Barsanti, Michael. "Little Magazines." In *The Oxford Encyclopedia of American Literature,* edited by Jay Parini, pp. 462-68. Oxford: Oxford University Press, 2004.

[In the essay below, Barsanti surveys the major eras of little magazines, focusing on their historical and literary contexts.]

"Little magazines" is a term referring to a set of literary periodicals published between roughly 1912 and 1939 that are characterized by their small readership, financial fragility, and artistic innovation. Little magazines were the nursery of several literary movements but are most closely connected to the birth of American modernism. They provided a place where writers of new, unusual, and often iconoclastic work could get into print. Those who published little magazines were amateurs and often artists themselves. Their goals were more likely to be artistic than commercial, a distinction borne out by their overwhelming tendency to be short-lived. They were especially important in creating and developing new American poetry and in consolidating and establishing ties between literary communities all over the world, but especially those in the urban centers of Chicago, New York City, London, and Paris.

The little magazines were the product of several converging social, technological, and artistic forces. Technological improvements and efficiencies in the manufacture of printed materials in the late nineteenth century (such as Linotype machines, which dramatically increased the speed with which type could be set, and web-fed presses that made it possible to print large print runs quickly) made magazines significantly cheaper to produce. The expansion of literary and commercial markets across national and international borders and the creation of new ways for periodicals to earn money from advertising and subscriptions that were developed in the 1890s made smaller publications possible, though not always feasible. The growth of an educated middle class meant that there was a larger audience of consumers to which to sell. These factors alone produced a formidable popular press at the beginning of the twentieth century—a popular press that was responsible for the novel idea of popular culture. While the little magazines benefited from the technologies and strategies that the popular press had brought into being, popular culture gave them something to kick against.

Throughout the early twentieth century the rejection of conventional culture, the defiance of standard artistic and commercial practices, and the energetic search for new artists and new audiences characterized the attitude, if not always the practice, of the little magazine. While these elements remained constant, the kinds of things the magazines published and the range of magazines available changed over time, a change that can be roughly divided into four different periods. In the time immediately before 1912—the year of the watershed appearance of the Chicago publication, *Poetry: A Journal of Modern Verse*—several similar but unrelated periodicals made the idea of little magazines viable. From 1912 to 1920 they enjoyed a period of frenetic activity and diversification as magazines competed to lead the avant-garde of a new movement—a competition that at times appeared to be arranged if not entirely, than at least in part, by the poet, critic, and promoter of artists, Ezra Pound. By the 1920s the field began to become more organized and its members more specialized, while the threat of censorship loomed. Finally, in the decade that followed the stock market crash of 1929 and preceded World War II, many little magazines responded to economic and political uncertainty by becoming more closely affiliated with political movements and educational institutions. Little magazines—or publications like them—still exist; the rise of the Internet has produced a flood of online publications that exceeds that of the early twentieth century in diversity and volume. The phenomenon of the first little magazines, however, rises out of a distinct moment in American literary history where new ideas and artistic modes of expression found a new medium and a new audience, changing everything that came after them.

BEFORE 1912: ANTECEDENTS

The little magazines originated from several sources. They derived independence and stylistic innovation from the emergence in late Victorian Britain of avant-garde literary magazines, such as *The Yellow Book* (1894-1897) and *The Savoy* (1896), that combined elaborate visual presentation with audacious content. Closer to home, they are linked to a tradition of more sober, intellectual American reviews that go as far back as the original incarnation of *The Dial* (1840-1844), published by Ralph Waldo Emerson and Margaret Fuller. The idea of a literary review made up exclusively of work by new artists can be connected most immediately to the *Chap Book,* published in Chicago from 1894 to 1898, but also to the *English Review* of Ford Madox Hueffer (later Ford Madox Ford), which began publication in 1908.

Traditional accounts of the little magazines concentrate, for understandable reasons, on the literary journals. One of the distinguishing features of modernism as a movement, however, was the way in which it thrived on cross-pollination from different artistic spheres. Alfred Stieglitz's *Camera Work* (1903-1917) became best known for its pioneering advancement of photography as an art form, yet it also served (especially late in its career) as a forum for writers, such as Gertrude Stein and Mina Loy, who were interested in the textual representation of images. This broader interest survived into the successor journal to *Camera Work,* called *291,* which was named after Stieglitz's New York City gallery. The change from photographer's magazine to art journal alienated many of *Camera Work*'s original subscribers but attracted others who wanted to follow the dramatic change that Stieglitz was effecting in the art world. The pattern of a relatively small and specialized magazine becoming the harbinger of a new kind of artistic expression would be repeated many times in the following years.

1912-1920: THE OUTBURST

Prior to Harriet Monroe's first issue of *Poetry: A Magazine of Verse* in 1912, there were no national periodicals dedicated to publishing serious poetry. Monroe, an accomplished poet herself, saw this gap and sought to fill it with a small magazine that she would edit with her colleague, Alice Corbin Henderson. The plan for the magazine was simple: to find and publish the best new poetry available. Poetry was not very popular in America at the beginning of the twentieth century; its marginal position among the arts was not even widely seen as a problem.

Despite this, *Poetry*'s system of economic support was unusually solid. Unlike other founders of little magazines, Monroe was careful to get her financing in place first. With the help of H. C. Chatfield-Taylor, a businessman and patron of the arts, she spent months in 1911 and early 1912 seeking guarantors in Chicago's arts and business communities who would give the magazine fifty dollars a year for five years. Once she had over one hundred names, she proceeded to spend the summer of 1912 in the Chicago Public Library reading all the poetry that had been published in the previous five years and writing down all the names of writers who interested her.

While it is possible that *Poetry*'s roots in the practical world of businessmen and traditional patrons made it steer a safer course when it came to choosing work, it was never more radical than it was in its first five yeras of existence. Monroe invited the poets she found in her reading to submit work to her new magazine. Ezra Pound responded quickly and persuaded Monroe to accept not only his own work, but that of writers he had been cultivating for years. Monroe made Pound the "foreign editor" of *Poetry,* a title he held from 1912 to 1917, scouting talent from an exile's perch in London. Pound's tastes were very different from Monroe's. He preferred writers who looked to Europe (and to the French in particular) for inspiration and wrote compact, elliptical poems that emphasized visual experience, poets like H. D., Richard Aldington, Marianne Moore, and William Carlos Williams. In the March 1913 issue of *Poetry,* Pound defined the basic tenets of "imagism," a term he created (but would soon abandon).

Monroe, in contrast, seemed to prefer poets who spoke in a more distinctly American, even midwestern, voice, such as Carl Sandburg, Sherwood Anderson, and Vachel Lindsay. Overall, the two collaborated successfully for several years, but they came into conflict on several occasions involving prize contests. In 1913, for example, Pound argued that *Poetry*'s two-hundred-fifty-dollar Guarantor's Prize should go to Yeats for *The Grey Rock.* Though Monroe preferred Lindsay's *General William Booth Enters into Heaven,* she eventually deferred to Pound's wishes. She did not do so, however, in 1914, when she gave the newly named Levinson Prize to Carl Sandburg for *Chicago.* At around the same time, Pound submitted T. S. Eliot's "Love Song of J. Alfred Prufrock" to Monroe, who fretted over publishing it for nine months until, after urgent complaints from Pound, she finally put it at the back of the June 1915 issue. Pound began to shift his allegiance to other periodicals after this and left *Poetry* in 1917. *Poetry*'s roster of published work is as eclectic as it is impressive—most of the eminent poets of the twentieth century were first brought before an American public in its pages. Publication there meant, and still means, arrival on the national stage.

Poetry arrived first, but many others followed. William Stanley Braithwaite, an African-American poet and editor living in Boston, brought his *Poetry Journal* out within weeks of Monroe's first issue. He published more conservative work, however, and was not as successful in attracting attention or funding in the long run. In Ridgefield, New Jersey, Alfred Kreymborg, a writer and editor, combined with Man Ray, a painter who would soon become famous for his radical artistic photographs, to create *The Glebe* in 1913. *The Glebe* was as eccentric as it was short-lived (its last issue came out in 1915), but it is remembered mostly for the February 1914 issue, a special number called *Des Imagistes.* This issue, which was compiled by Pound and shortly thereafter published as a separate anthology, contained works by Aldington, H. D., Amy Lowell, Williams, James Joyce, and Pound himself, among others. *The Glebe* was succeeded by *Others,* a more viable journal edited by Kreymborg, with Walter Arensberg, that was dedicated to poetry and, as the title suggests, defined against a mainstream of poetic taste that *Poetry* magazine had begun to represent. Its contributors occasionally met at Kreymborg's house in Ridgefield and collectively decided what would go in to the next issue, conducting a sort of rural salon. It was published from 1915 to 1919 and featured the work of Mina Loy, William Carlos Williams, Moore, Kreymborg, Stevens, and Djuna Barnes, to name a few.

The use of the term "little magazine" to refer to a historically specific category has no certain origin, but it can be partly traced to another Chicago-born publication called *The Little Review* (1914-1929). In its fearless publication of difficult and controversial work, its always-desperate financial condition, and its importance to the literary circles of New York City and London, it serves as the paradigm of the little magazine. Its motto was "Making No Compromise with the Public Taste," and the confiscation of several issues by the U.S. Post Office proved they meant it.

Margaret Anderson founded *The Little Review* in 1914 not to compete with *Poetry* so much as to have an outlet for her own creative and spiritual energies, which were considerable. It is tempting to compare the two Chicago-born journals, launched within two years of each other by women who were part of the same intellectual moment. As has often been noted, their different temperaments are reflected in their journals. With relatively secure funding and a clear sense of its mission and market, *Poetry* published regularly into the twenty-first century. It took measured risks, especially in its early years, but balanced those risks with a diverse assortment of work. *The Little Review* had irregular funding at best and published erratically. (In the summer of 1915, Anderson was forced to move out of her apartment and live in a tent on Lake Michigan to save money.) Its mission was defined more by the intensity or vividness of the work it espoused (in Anderson's eyes) than by any more tangible or objective criteria. *The Little Review* took big risks and was both celebrated and prosecuted for them.

After Pound left *Poetry,* his allegiance (and his stable of writers) shifted to several other periodicals, including *The Glebe,* and then to *The Little Review.* Before Pound, Anderson went through several phases, first publishing work from the fringes of Chicago's avant-garde, then adopting Emma Goldman's anarchism, then Amy Lowell's brand of imagism. In February 1916, Anderson met Jane Heap; the two women became lovers and Heap joined the magazine, beginning a new, energetic phase. They spent the summer in California and, despairing of the meager material they had for the September 1916 issue, chose to publish it with many blank pages and to call the entire issue a "want ad" for new talent. The gesture caught Pound's attention, and he arranged to have his patron and friend, the New York lawyer John Quinn, contribute to *The Little Review* in exchange for Pound's service as "foreign editor" (as he had been for *Poetry*).

Pound's legacy as a talent scout and promoter is at least as significant as that left by his own work. The story of his involvement with *Poetry,* however, has often been told in such a way as to overshadow the importance of Monroe and Henderson, who made the final decisions of what to publish and when. Similar problems confront the reader who looks at Pound's relationship with Harriet Shaw Weaver at the *New Freewoman* (renamed the *Egoist* in 1914) or his experience with *The Little Review,* where Anderson and Heap were the principal editors. Recent scholars have noted the conspicuous number of women who wrote for, edited, and supported the little magazines. It was possible for women to have more influence and make a greater difference in these places than elsewhere because they were on the margins of the literary establishment and there was no pre-existing institutional bias to keep them out. Over time, their presence exerted a defining influence on the nature of modernism itself.

The high point of Pound's attachment to *The Little Review* was the publication of James Joyce's novel *Ulysses* (1922) in installments beginning in March 1918. Pound had first heard of Joyce through Yeats in 1913 and had placed Joyce's poetry and fiction in various magazines on both sides of the Atlantic—most prominently, he arranged for the publication of *Portrait of the Artist as a Young Man* (1916) in the *Egoist* in 1914 and 1915. Pound hoped to publish *Ulysses* simultaneously in the *Egoist* and *The Little Review,* but because of legal difficulties, only a few episodes came out in the British journal. Anderson and Heap moved to New York City in 1917, and their magazine immediately began to take on the city scene with pugnacity and a determined disregard for convention. They thought that the opportunity to publish *Ulysses* was the chance of a lifetime; after the first few chapters they did little or no censoring of it, and several issues were seized and destroyed by the post office. This outrage only emboldened them.

1920-1929: CONSOLIDATION

The Little Review continued publishing *Ulysses* in installments until the summer of 1920, when Anderson and Heap were arrested for publishing obscenity in the form of the Nausicaa episode of the novel, which depicts masturbation. John Quinn, who had warned them about sending unsolicited complimentary copies of *Ulysses* through the mails (the practice that got the attention of the New York Society for the Suppression of Vice), begrudgingly defended them by arguing that *Ulysses* was too difficult to understand to be obscene. The women were found guilty on Valentine's Day 1921, fined fifty dollars, and told to publish no more James Joyce. This derailed the book publication of the novel in the United States for over twelve years and nearly shut down *The Little Review,* but the magazine went on without Pound and eventually without Anderson, who left it to Heap in 1924. It continued into 1929 under Heap, changing direction by publishing more artwork and opening the Little Review Gallery. The trial, however, marked a small turning point for the little magazines. The exuberance that characterized the earlier decade was diminished, and those energies were redirected into the establishment and reinforcement of more secure, more focused publications.

One of the holdovers from the earlier period, however, was *Broom,* an international review first published by expatriate Americans in Italy that then moved on to Germany and New York City. It published many of the authors who had been affiliated with Kreymborg's *Others* during its three years of existence from 1921 to 1924, but was also known for its art reproductions, its avant-garde fiction, and its arresting design. *Secession* had a similar beginning in Europe and migration to America and is often linked with *Broom* through its shared history and several shared authors, though in its pages it vigorously defied any comparison. During *Secession's* two-year life from 1922 to 1924, it relentlessly advertised itself as the production of a discrete group of young artists who sought the furthest leading edge of the new, while it criticized its near-twin *Broom* for being like a serialized anthology that followed the leading trends. In practice, the magazines had far more in common than their quarreling would have suggested.

As mentioned earlier, one of the characteristics of modernism was the mutual influences that occurred between different art forms. Modernist writers were especially interested in the visual arts, and magazines like *Secession* and *Broom* emphasized their interrelationship. *The Dial,* probably the biggest and most influential little magazine of the 1920s, reported on different art forms and had reporters assigned to cover music, dance, and art. Emerson and Fuller's original *Dial* had ceased publishing in 1844, but the title was revived in 1880 for a political journal, again published out of Chicago, that also covered some literary subjects. By 1918 it had become stuck in financial and ideological quagmires and was purchased by the wealthy, well-connected, and intellectually expansive James Sibley Watson and Scofield Thayer. *The Dial* of the 1920s would be largely financed by Thayer, who also used his resources to build an important collection of modern art.

These works of art were regularly featured in *The Dial,* as were reviews of music, dance, and theater. *The Dial* was primarily a critical review; most of its contents in any given issue were prose pieces that set and described the tastes of the period. Because it was privately supported, it took no advertising and thus maintained greater independence. It was an expensive magazine to produce, however, both because of its high production values, its large staff, and the relatively generous amounts it paid to its contributors. One of *The Dial*'s greatest coups was the first American publication of Eliot's *The Waste Land* in November 1922, for which it paid Eliot over two thousand dollars. The lion's share of this payment came in the form of *The Dial*'s annual prize.

At the same time that *The Dial* was publishing *The Waste Land,* Eliot printed the poem in his own journal, *Criterion,* which was based in London. *Criterion* re-sembled *The Dial* in some respects—it, too, emphasized criticism over original work and occupied a position more elevated and authoritative than cutting edge in the literary marketplace. Eliot had been the assistant editor of the *Egoist* from 1915 to 1917 and was an editor for British publishers Faber and Faber, but *Criterion* allowed him his own arena. As the journal developed through the 1930s, it became increasingly interested in (and disturbed about) the rise of the competing ideologies of communism and fascism, often leaning away from the leftist sympathies that characterized the politics of so many other little magazines.

It was the nature of the little magazines, however, to speak for constituencies that had not had a voice in the larger cultural arena. As we have seen, this was first true for artists who were interested in jumping ahead of conventional tastes and producing modern work. It was also true, however, for underrepresented people of particular racial, class, gender, or even regional backgrounds. The *Double Dealer* was an early regional magazine started by Julius Weis Friend in New Orleans in 1921 and lasting until 1926. During those five years it initiated a southern literary renaissance, bringing out writing by Allen Tate, John Crowe Ransom, Thornton Wilder, and Jean Toomer. Its most famous discovery, however, was Ernest Hemingway, whose first short story was published there in 1922.

The Fugitive, a journal begun at Vanderbilt University, was part of the legacy of the *Double Dealer.* From 1922 to 1925 it was another platform for the growing southern school of literature and criticism as represented by the work of Tate and Ransom, but also later Robert Penn Warren. It spawned some of the most influential and enduring American literary magazines of the century, including the *Southern Review,* the *Kenyon Review,* and the *Sewanee Review.*

Within the African-American community, magazines also gave writers an important stage on which to present their work. While *The Crisis* (1910-), the official magazine of the National Association for the Advancement of Colored People (NAACP), might have been too large to qualify as a little magazine in the strictest sense, its role as an engine of the Harlem Renaissance, identifying and promoting African-American artists and writers under the editorship of W. E. B. Du Bois between 1910 and 1934 (with the novelist Jessie R. Fauset as literary editor from 1919 to 1926), makes it too important to omit from any account of the time. Its principal rival was *Opportunity* (1923-1949), a publication of the National Urban League that emphasized the representation of a New Negro in art. Together, these two magazines helped launch the careers of Fauset as well as Zora Neale Hurston, Countee Cullen, Langston Hughes, and Gwendolyn Bennett. More in the spirit of *Poetry* or *The Little Review* was *Fire!!,* created by Wallace Thurman in 1926 together with other Harlem Renaissance writers who wanted to establish an independent African-American review dedicated to the arts. While the group was unable to publish a second issue, *Fire!!* still broke important ground as the record of an African-American avant-garde.

1929-1939: Causes and Colleges

With the onset of the Great Depression, it became much harder to publish magazines. Many of those that were produced took activist stands to energize readers who sought social justice and economic reform. Little magazines had political agendas from the very beginning— *The Little Review* described itself as a magazine of "art and revolution" and published the writings of anarchist Emma Goldman next to its poetry and fiction. *The Masses* defined itself almost entirely through the application of literature and art to the causes of the left, including but not limited to socialism. Published from 1911 to 1917, *The Masses* was at its peak during the editorship of Floyd Dell and Max Eastman, which began in 1913. It published writers like Lincoln Steffens, Upton Sinclair, John Reed, and Louis Untermeyer, but it was also known for its striking graphic design and illustration. By the end of its short life (an end that was accelerated by its frequent run-ins with the post office and the law), *The Masses* was making decisions about the contents of each issue through consensus of its entire staff, which gave it even more of a polyglot, eccentric feel.

The Masses was succeeded in 1918 by *The Liberator,* which, though it did not survive the 1920s, became the model for many other politically engaged literary reviews. One of the foremost of these was the *Partisan Review,* which began publication in 1934 and continued past the twentieth century, combining liberal politics with writers from across a broad spectrum, such as W. H. Auden, Randall Jarrell, Vladimir Nabokov, Jorge Luis Borges, and Wallace Stevens. While the *Partisan Review* was explicit about its political orientation, it was criticized (as was *The Liberator* and *The Masses* itself) throughout the 1930s by those farther on the left who felt that a more urgent call to action to a more radical form of communism was needed—a position embodied by *The New Masses,* edited by the activist writers Mike Gold and John Sloan.

Other magazines found security and a critical mass of intellectual activity on college and university campuses. *Hound and Horn* began in 1927 as a student magazine at Harvard University edited by Lincoln Kirstein. Mostly a critical review, it became an early outlet for the work of the New Critics such as R. P. Blackmur. Similarly, *Contempo* began at the University of North Carolina at Chapel Hill, founded by Anthony Buttitta and Milton Abernethy in 1931. *Contempo* had a stron-

ger political orientation than *Hound and Horn,* devoting an issue to the support of the Scottsboro defendants (nine African-American youths who were accused of rape at an infamous 1931 trial in Alabama) but also to the work of William Faulkner and James Joyce.

The magazine *transition* carried forward the international type of little magazine, whose most immediate forerunners were *Broom* and *Secession.* Edited by Eugene Jolas in Paris, *transition* was published between 1927 and 1938. It called for a "revolution of the word" and selected critical and imaginative work from all over the world that called into question the most basic assumptions about the operations of language. For this reason, *transition* is often associated with the dada movement, but it is best known for its publication of James Joyce's "Work in Progress," which when published in book form in 1939 took on the more familiar name of *Finnegans Wake.*

As a phenomenon, the little magazines were produced by the confluence of several distinct forces and opportunities. Technological advancements made the production of magazines less expensive while the growth of consumer markets made subscriptions and the advertising of consumer products one viable, or nearly viable, way of generating revenue. For many magazines, however, support came from wealthy patrons whose interest in periodicals (as recipients of support analogous to artists themselves) constituted its own important trend. Meanwhile, the artistic forces behind trends that would come to be called literary modernism, as well as regionalism and the Harlem Renaissance, were generating material that needed ways to reach an audience. Because so much of this material was opposed, or even actively hostile, to the tastes and standards of the mainstream press, alternative outlets were required. Once set in motion, the system of little magazine publication acquired a momentum of its own that quickly radiated outwards, giving voice to otherwise-marginalized people and groups.

Literary movements are created in real and imaginary spaces, where kindred writers can associate with, be inspired by, or criticize one another. For writers of the pre-World War I period, these were often real spaces— salons, galleries, or cafés in major cities—but just as often those spaces were "virtual," existing between the covers of magazines. Writers became associated with the journals that published them, often forming clannish groups or schools that would seldom last very long but would help to define that group against a broader field. The editors of these magazines established the terms under which these communities operated and participated in them as artists themselves. One of the enduring legacies of the little magazine is this figure of the editor who answers to the artistic and political goals set by his or her community of writers, as well as to his or her own individual taste. It is this style of editorial leadership, whether by an individual or a group, that helps distinguish the little magazine from what came before or after it, as well as the energy with which it asserted its singular identity and its independence from the conventions and tastes not just of the broader society or of the marketplace, but of the other little magazines. They are therefore best understood not as collections or samplers of artwork, but as works of art themselves. . . .

Further Reading

Anderson, Elliott, and Mary Kinzie, eds. *The Little Magazine in America: A Modern Documentary History.* Yonkers, N.Y., 1978. While mostly concerned with little magazines published after World War II, this eclectic collection illuminates the legacy of the earlier generation.

Benstock, Shari, and Bernard Benstock. "The Role of Little Magazines in the Emergence of Modernism." *Library Chronicle of the University of Texas* 20, no. 4 (1991): 68-87. Discusses the importance of primary documents in tracing the relationships and communities at the heart of the little magazines.

Hoffman, Frederick J., Charles Allen, and Carolyn F. Ulrich. *The Little Magazine: A History and a Bibliography.* 2d ed. Princeton, N.J., 1947. This is the standard work on the subject, an excellent reference source, though it should not be considered comprehensive.

Johnson, Abby Arthur, and Ronald Mayberry Johnson. *Propaganda and Aesthetics: The Literary Politics of Afro-American Magazines in the Twentieth Century.* Amherst, Mass., 1979. One of the few books on the role of little magazines in the African-American arts community.

Marek, Jayne E. *Women Editing Modernism: "Little" Magazines and Literary History.* Lexington, Ky., 1995. Emphasizes the neglected importance of women to the little magazines.

Morrisson, Mark S. *The Public Face of Modernism: Little Magazines, Audiences, and Reception, 1905-1920.* Madison, Wis., 2001. On the little magazines and what they learned from mass-market publications.

Rainey, Lawrence. *Institutions of Modernism: Literary Elites and Public Culture.* The Henry McBride Series in Modernism and Modernity. New Haven, Conn., 1998. Rainey's book concentrates on the economic relationships at the center of many of the events of literary modernism.

Watson, Steven. *Strange Bedfellows: The First American Avant-Garde.* New York, 1991. An entertaining and readable history of the early years of modernism, ending in 1920.

Williams, Ellen. *Harriet Monroe and the Poetry Renaissance.* Urbana, Ill., 1977. A history of the first ten years of *Poetry* magazine.

LITTLE MAGAZINES AND AFRICAN AMERICAN LITERATURE

Eugene Redmond (essay date 1978)

SOURCE: Redmond, Eugene. "Stridency and the Sword: Literary and Cultural Emphasis in Afro-American Magazines." In *The Little Magazine in America: A Modern Documentary History,* edited by Elliott Anderson and Mary Kinzie, pp. 538-73. Yonkers, N.Y.: The Pushcart Press, 1978.

[*In the following essay, Redmond examines the history of black little magazines in the United States, noting their relationship to more prominent black publications and charting their "long trek from instability to an uneasy stability."*]

Origins and Evolution

For the purpose of developing a contemporary peak from which to survey beginnings of the Afro-American literary magazine, we could select any year, but let us settle for the year 1968. That was when *Black Fire: An Anthology of Afro-American Writing,* edited by LeRoi Jones and Larry Neal, made its provocative appearance. In April of the same year, the world mourned the assassination of Martin Luther King, Jr., apostle of peace and one of the most influential Afro-American leaders in history. Less than two months later, Henry Dumas and Conrad Kent Rivers, premier poetic voices of the "second renaissance," were silenced—Dumas by the bullets of a New York transit cop and Rivers by an "impulsive" act. Earlier in the decade, that missile-of-a-man named Malcolm X (*a.k.a.* Malcolm Little, Detroit Red, El-Hajj Malik El-Shabazz, "Black Shining Prince"), had been rammed by assassins' bullets at the Audubon Ballroom in Harlem. Black prophets and poets, activists and writers cried out, "If you talk too long and too loud about the hurt that's being put on you, you'll be long-gone." Hence Afro-American magazines such as *Liberator, Freedomways, Negro Digest, Dasein, Umbra, Soulbook, Black Dialogue, The Journal of Black Poetry, The Black Scholar,* and *Black Ascensions* became the cultural-literary offspring of the terrors and contradictions inherent in a society unable to practice what it preaches. *Black Fire,* in turn, was born of a disparate and far-flung, yet communalized, cultural spirit that completely remade the world of Afro-American arts and letters. Similarly, during the "renaissance" of the 1920s, Alain Locke's provocative *The New Negro* (1925), backdropped by Jim Crow laws, World War I, and lynchings, shored up the strength and perseverance of a kaleidoscopic battle line of black periodicals: *The Crisis, The Journal of Negro History, Southern Workman, The Messenger, Opportunity,* and others. This pattern was also seen in 1941, with the publication of *The Negro Caravan: Writings by American Negroes,* edited by Sterling A. Brown, Arthur P. Davis, and Ulysses Lee. *Caravan* performed what had become by then an important function of Afro-American editors and anthologists: to collect, at intervals, the best and most representative works from smaller black publications (journals, newsletters, pamphlets, broadsides, and newspapers) and put them into a substantial volume for posterity. Available to *Caravan's* editors was a rich new range of magazines and various periodicals, including *Challenge, New Challenge, Brown American, Journal of Negro Education, Negro History Bulletin,* and *Race.*

One sees in these and other new magazines of the thirties and forties—reflective as they were of the historical demands of the black struggle—an often part-time literary posture, since their primary function in each issue was to do battle with the forces of racism, oppression, and violence and to present basic usable data to Afro-American communities. The *Journal of Negro Education, Quarterly Review of Higher Education Among Negroes, Negro History Bulletin, Negro Digest,* and *Phylon: Atlanta University Review of Race and Culture* dealt with all areas of black development. On the other hand, a steady tradition of literary journal publishing had been established, as witnessed by magazines like the *Negro Quarterly, Challenge* and *New Challenge* (dedicated to the revitalization of black literature and art), *Negro Story,* and *Harlem Quarterly.* Often the editors and creative writers were one and the same. One found, for example, the following names on the editorial boards and in the tables of contents of these periodicals: W. E. B. DuBois, James Weldon Johnson, Wallace Thurman, Zora Neale Hurston, Langston Hughes, Countee Cullen, Claude McKay, Arna Bontemps, Ann Spencer, Angelina Grimké, Owen Dodson, Carter G. Woodson, Marcus Garvey, Margaret Walker, Horace Cayton, Richard Wright, Ralph Ellison, Gwendolyn Brooks, Robert Hayden, Melvin B. Tolson, E. Franklin Frazier, Chester Himes, and others.

BEARINGS AND FOCUSES: 1950-1960

Despite decades of vigorous effort to develop independent black literary and cultural magazines, these did not appear until the 1950s. Among the black literary journals to emerge at midcentury, *Free Lance* and *CLA Journal* have been the most influential, albeit for different reasons. Literarily speaking, the decade began auspiciously with several notable events: the reception of the works of Richard Wright (whose *Native Son* had been the first black-authored Book-of-the-Month Club selection); the establishment of several cultural and literary groups, such as the Harlem Writers' Club and the Committee for the Negro in the Arts; the awarding of the Pulitzer Prize for poetry (*Annie Allen,* 1950) to Gwendolyn Brooks; and the publication of the anthol-

ogy *The Poetry of the Negro* (1949), edited by Langston Hughes and Bontemps—further indication of large publishers' growing interest in black literature. But it was an already-established journal, *Phylon,* that carried the literary and cultural weight of the black experience during most of the 1950s.

Phylon's 1940s format, designed by W. E. B. DuBois (and colleagues), continued into the next decade: a good balance between sociological-historical analyses and cultural-artistic curatorship. The most advanced indigenous Afro-American social theories and concepts were reflected in its literary content. For example, the fourth quarter 1950 issue of *Phylon* was devoted to Afro-American literature and writers: "The Negro Writer Looks at His World" (William Gardner Smith, Ezra Bell Thompson, Langston Hughes, and *Phylon* editors); "Fiction and Folklore" (Thomas D. Jarrett and Sterling Brown); "Criticism and Literary Scholarship" (Ulysses Lee and Blyden Jackson); and "Poetry" (Margaret Walker and Arna Bontemps). In subsequent issues *Phylon* published "Contemporary French Negro Poets," "The Cuban Poetry of Nicholas Guillen" (Angel Augier, translated by Joseph Bernstein), an article by novelist René Maran (translated by Mercer Cook), and several pieces by the Dutch literary historian-anthologist Rosey E. Pool, including one on the "African Renaissance" (African writing in English). The poetry of Robert Hayden, Nanina Champney Alba, Hughes, Walker, Calvin C. Hernton, Ray Durem, Alvin Aubert, Raymond Patterson, Lance Jeffers, and James Emanuel also appeared in the journal along with short fiction by Hughes and Katherine Dunham ("Audrey"). In reviews and articles, writers waged critical wars, each adding to the wider portrait of the Afro-American literary legacy. Among books given extensive reviews in *Phylon* were all of Hughes's works, the autobiographies of Lena Horne and Ethel Waters, J. Saunders Redding's *On Being Black in America,* Wright's *The Outsider,* and Claude McKay's *Selected Poems,* Carl Rowan's *South of Freedom,* James Baldwin's *Go Tell It on the Mountain* and *Notes of a Native Son,* Gwendolyn Brooks's *Maud Martha,* Ann Petry's *The Narrows,* and George Lamming's *In the Castle of My Skin* (1953) and *The Emigrants* (1955). *Phylon's* book review pattern was reflected in almost all the black magazines of the fifties, including *Sepia* and *Ebony,* which irregularly published literary history and criticism. *Sepia* sustained a fine record for reviewing black literature, and both magazines carried in-depth stories on music and culture.

In 1953, *Free Lance* arrived as the first Afro-American literary journal destined to survive the handicaps and adversities usually visited on such efforts. Subtitled "A Publication of Free-Lance Poets and Prose Workshops, Inc.," this Cleveland-based little magazine played an as-yet-unsung role in the development of a multi-ethnic American literary underground, specifically the "Beat" movement in poetry, which prevailed between 1955 and 1965. *Free Lance* was directed by Casper Leroy Jordan, book reviewer and librarian at Wilberforce University, Ohio, and Russell Atkins, eccentric poet-composer and psycho-visualist. Early assistance also came from Helen J. Collins, Beatrice Augustus, and Helen Dobbins Dobbs. The first issues of *Free Lance* were hand done, so to speak, but it later took on a more professional look. Since it was devoted solely to the printing of short creative writings and occasional book reviews, the journal did not need the size or space of a *Phylon*. It became, by all definitions, a "little" magazine.

The first issue of *Free Lance* included work by Atkins, Augustus, Collins, Rose Green, Jordan, Budd Martin, Vera Steckles, Mott Wilson, and Jerry Davis. But the introduction—and the theme—were supplied by the literary father of all modern black writers, Langston Hughes:

> *Words are the paper and string to package experience, to wrap up from the inside out the poet's concentric waves of contact with the living world. Each poet makes of words his own highly individualized wrapping for life segments he wishes to present. Sometimes the paper and strings are more arresting than the contents of the package. Sometimes the poet creates a transparent wrapping revealing with great clarity and from all angles what is inside. Sometimes the word wrapping is clumsy and inept, and neither the inside nor the outside of the package is interesting. Sometimes the word wrapping contains nothing. But, regardless of quality or content, a poem reveals always the poet as a person. Skilled or unskilled, wise or foolish, nobody can write a poem without revealing something of himself. Here are people. Here are poems. Here is revolution.*

Hughes was talking, it seemed, almost directly to Atkins. The introduction was stripped of racial intensity, since the older writer knew that Atkins, like William Stanley Braithwaite, Countee Cullen, and Hayden, had protested against being judged purely on the basis of race. Precocious and brilliant, he had studied music and begun to develop provocative ideas and concepts connecting sound, dance, mathematics, drama, psychology, and language. In a January 1973 *Black World* article on "Black Art and Artists in Cleveland," Leatrice W. Emeruwa referred to *Free Lance* as the "oldest Black literary magazine extant" and said that Atkins was "to poetic, dramatic and musical innovation and leadership what Coltrane has been to jazz and avant-gardism."

In addition to printing the works of black poets (such as Hughes, Dudley Randall, and LeRoi Jones), *Free Lance* also opened its pages to white bards: Robert Sward, the Canadian Irving Layton, Don Silberger, and Robert Creeley (also critic and editor of *Black Mountain Review*). Stylistically, the poetry was traditional, experimental modern-formal, and offbeat; and much of it was iconoclastic, irreverent, pedantic, and didactic. Other writings ranged from a review of *Charles Waddell Chesnutt: Pioneer of the Color Line* to Philip Butcher's essay on Paul Laurence Dunbar and George Washington Cable, to Creeley's reflections on Hart Crane (including some letters of Crane). *Free Lance* also featured the fiction of Cleota Augustus, Adelaide Simon, Silberger, and Robert J. Shea. During the 1960s *Free Lance* would increase its review space, introduce some exciting new black poets to the public, and play an important role in the midwestern black arts scene.

CLA Journal appeared in 1957 as the brainchild of the College Language Association, formed in 1939 to protest the Modern Language Association's policy of excluding blacks. Its editor was Therman B. O'Daniel (Morgan State College); its associate editor, Blyden Jackson (Southern University); and its managing editor, Charles A. Ray (North Carolina College, Durham). Among its regional advisory editors were Hugh Gloster, Nathaniel P. Tillman, and Melvin B. Tolson. Contributing editors included Margaret Walker Alexander, Richard Barksdale, M. Carl Holman (of Clark College and editor of the *Atlanta Inquirer*), Redding, and Bertram L. Woodruff. Scholarly, erudite, and giving deference to linguistics and composition, the magazine's aims and objectives were stated by O'Daniel in the first issue: it would accept articles on "most languages." These languages, however, turned out to be "Greek and Latin, Old and Middle English, Modern English, and the Modern Foreign Languages." *CLA Journal*, as a black-based professional publication, was thus begun in something of a cultural limbo: it had no philosophical direction, no theoretical or conceptual framework with which to chart its direction, and hence no thrust that reflected, even from the magazine's high plane, the turbulence or beauty of the black sensibility that produced most of its staffers and contributors.

The cultural ambivalence of *CLA Journal*, born out of ideological tensions and conflicts that have historically mesmerized the black intelligentsia, was clearly seen in its allowance of twice as much space to writings on European and Euro-American culture as to African or Afro-American culture. Such a contradiction, hard to imagine when one recalls the social and racial factors that prompted the founding of the journal, would become even more glaring in the sixties and seventies when many new black-consciousness journals were being born. Whereas *Phylon* unashamedly grounded itself in black and Third World cultures (relegating its European concerns to notes and excerpts), *CLA Journal* repeatedly printed articles on Congreve, Shakespeare, Alain Robbe-Grillet, Poe, Baudelaire, Swift, Hawthorne, Tennessee Williams, and hundreds of other European and Euro-American subjects and writers. In all fairness, however, the foregoing comments must be balanced by a consideration of *CLA*'s contribution to black literature. Its first issue, for example, did contain a review of

Hughes's *Simple Stakes a Claim.* Later numbers of the quarterly carried articles on black authors and their work. During the sixties and seventies *CLA* would not be able to continue its immunity to the broad and intense cultural self-examination occurring in black communities. Like all other Afro-American publications, it would be substantially influenced by the social holocausts of the post-civil rights era.

Bob Kaufman, Ted Joans, LeRoi Jones, and Atkins come prominently to mind when one considers the "underground" movement. Kaufman, after an itinerant life, settled in San Francisco, where the West Coast pole of the Beat activity (Ferlinghetti's City Lights Bookstore) was centered. He published in *Beatitude* and numerous other little magazines, his work finally reaching France, where he became a literary sensation—occasionally being compared to Rimbaud and Baudelaire. Jazz poet Joans, trained as a painter, was among the first black artists to arrive in Greenwich Village, the East Coast center of the Beat school. Very early influenced by Hughes, he also published in many little magazines. The capricious LeRoi Jones was a central figure in the Greenwich Village movement (the New York literary underground), founding *Yugen* (1958-1961) with his Jewish wife, Hettie Cohen. Though Jones has always been irreverent and experimental in his posture and writing, the fact that he was black in 1958 was more or less incidental, since *Yugen* published mostly white authors. Occasionally, however, black writers were featured, as in the case of poets Allan Polite and Clarence Major. In addition to contributing to the avant-garde American poetry scene, these pioneers provided new experimental models for younger black poets tuned into the little magazine circuit.

ASCENDANCY'S SHARP MIRROR LIGHT: REAR VIEW TO A FUTURE (1960-1978)

By 1960 Afro-American periodicals, and their faithful editorial staffs, were well seasoned from several decades of training and experience. During this exciting history, countless publications had been founded by sororities, fraternities, college literary workshops, community organizations, unions, social clubs, reading guilds, and private individuals. Many of these older organs also wound their way into the 1960s and 1970s: *Crisis, Negro History Bulletin, Journal of Negro History, Phylon, Negro Educational Review, Free Lance,* and *CLA Journal. Phylon* maintained its previous leadership, though some fatigue was beginning to show in the later sixties—the journal having witnessed the death or dispersion of many of its original founders and contributors. Fresh talent, which would have naturally gravitated toward it, was attracted to the new black publications and the white periodicals opening their pages to black writers. Nevertheless, *Phylon* continued to present a solid offering of essays, reviews, poetry, and some fiction.

Among writers contributing articles to the journal during the sixties were Charles Hamilton (*Black Power,* with Stokely Carmichael), Eugene D. Genovese (*Roll, Jordan, Roll*), Eugenia Collier, John Henrik Clarke, Theodore L. Gross, Nathan Hare, Donald Henderson, B. I. Chukwukere (on African novelists), O. R. Dathorne (on Africa in West Indian literature), Charles Larsen, Addison Gayle, Jr., and Keneth Kinnamon. Older and newly discovered poets peppered the magazine's pages: Mary Graham Lund, Pinkie Gordon Lane, Dan Georgakas, Mari Evans, James Worley, Nanina Alba, George Douglass Johnson, James Emanuel, James Kilgore, and Julius Thompson. Of all the journals, *Phylon* in particular established an excellent record of good in-depth reviews.

On a smaller scale, but in steady pursuit of literary experimentation and freedom, *Free Lance* was realizing its goal of becoming a viable, if modest, alternative to the deaf ears and closed doors met by so many new young writers. *Free Lance* also upgraded its book review program and added a news column, "Occurrences." Among the black and white poets it published in the sixties were Major (editor, *The New Black Poetry*), Judson Crews, Charles Bukowski, Glen Grobos, Conrad Kent Rivers ("discovered" by *Free Lance*), Irene Dayton, Peter Jones (editor of *New Helios,* London), Hughes ("perhaps the only active link from the fabled period of the New York renaissance of the '20s"), David Rafael Wang (teacher at the University of Hawaii), Lewis Turco, L. S. Torgoff, Douglas Blazek, and Etheridge Knight (writing at this time from prison).

CLA Journal remained culturally adrift as the sixties unfolded. More than half of its space was still being devoted to the examination of European-American aesthetics. Granted the professional nature of the journal, with its emphases on composition and modern languages, one wonders why not even an experimental unit on Afro-American literary methodology was developed. The white-dominated MLA had established a Commission of Minority Literatures before the mid-seventies, but not until 1976 did *CLA Journal* begin its "Annual Bibliography of Afro-American Literature." Though hanging in a frustrating cultural limbo, it nevertheless published important articles on black culture, such as Jackson's "The Negro's Image of the Universe as Reflected in His Fiction," Barksdale's views on the teaching of poetry, Naomi Garrett's "French Poets of African Descent," Darwin Turner's "The Negro Dramatist's Image of the Universe, 1920-1960," Robert A. Smith on the folktales of Chesnutt, A. Russell Brooks's "The Comic Spirit in the Negro's New Look," and Arthur P. Davis' "The Black-and-Tan Motif in the Poetry of Gwendolyn Brooks" and "Gwendolyn Brooks: Poet of the Unheroic."

That a plethora of little magazines emerged during these years is obviously of more than mere incidental importance—even though so many were destined to a state of transiency or premature death. It is not always easy to record, or even locate, these publications. The most extensive listing of them, however, appears in various news and notes sections of *Negro Digest/Black World* (1961-1976), itself a product of the black cultural revival that swept the globe in the 1950s and 1960s. Other important magazines of the sixties were *Community, Dasein, Freedomways, Axiom, Approach, Adept, Negro Heritage, Floating Bear, Umbra, Harvard Journal of Afro-American Affairs,Soulbook, Vibration, Black Dialogue, Insurgent, Black America, Journal of Black Poetry, The Black Student, Echo, Negro American Literature Forum, Cricket, Shrewd, Issue: A Quarterly Journal of Africanist Opinion, Nommo, Pan-African Journal, Ex-Umbra, Newark Afro-American Magazine, The Feet* ("The Monthly Black Dance Magazine"), *Black Theater, Echoes from the Gumbo, The Black Scholar, Pound, Confrontation: A Journal of Third World Literature,* and *Nkombo.*

Literally before our very eyes, these journals did cultural somersaults and demographic cartwheels: being born, often experiencing immediate death, then being reborn in another place with a refurbished staff and a new name. Most of them, however, responded to, and some grew in the shadow of, the glitter of *Negro Digest*—resurrected in 1961 after a publishing hiatus of ten years. Its helm was manned by Hoyt W. Fuller, an Atlanta-born journalist who had worked for several newspapers and had formerly been associate editor of *Ebony.* Since *Digest* was a Johnson publication, it offered little opportunity for free and open experimentation and exploration. Moreover, like *CLA Journal,* it initially could not take an official editorial stand based on cultural theories or ideological concepts. But Fuller sought to compensate for these built-in restraints by cautiously indicating his evolving aesthetic in book reviews, various notes, articles, and news items. He charted a course that took that journal from civil rights through black arts/black power and into its new pan-Africanist posture as *Black World* (1970-1976).

During the first five years of its new life, *Digest* followed somewhat in the path of its forties predecessor, publishing general articles about black life, with an emphasis on stars. It also ran reprints from various other (mostly white) magazines as well as poems and articles by whites. From its very beginning, however, it had more of a literary thrust than the earlier *Digest.* Articles on black history and culture were contributed by C. Eric Lincoln, Bontemps, John Hope Franklin, Benjamin Quarles, Frank London Brown ("Chicago's Great Lady of Poetry," about Brooks), Babs Fafunwa ("An African Student Looks at America"), participants in a symposium on "The Negro's Role in American Culture" (Baldwin, Nat Hentoff, Lorraine Hansberry, Hughes, Emile Capouya, Alfred Kazin), Nathan Hare ("The

Black Anglo-Saxons"), Agnes Behling ("Father of Negro History," on Woodson), Casper Leroy Jordan (on Elizabeth Keckley, the black woman confidante to the wife of President Lincoln), Redding (interviewed by AMSAC on "An American Writer in Africa"), Kwame Nkrumah ("The Recovery of African History"), Louise Meriwether (on Baldwin), Horace Mann Bond, Arthur Schomburg, Lomax, Hernton ("White Liberals and Black Muslims"), Elijah Muhammad, Rivers (on Hughes), J. Noel Heermance ("The Modern Negro Novel"), Thomas Echewa ("Africa vs. Afro-Americans," part of a series of debates involving John A. Williams and John Oliver Killens), and Hamilton Bims ("The Plight of the Negro Writer in a Segregated Society").

Bontemps opened the decade appropriately enough with his November 1961 article, "The New Black Renaissance." Since he had participated in the "first" renaissance, he was aptly qualified to make comparisons between the two. He noted that "the new crop of Negro writers in the United States show more traits in common with the writers of the Harlem Renaissance than with the famous WPA group who were their literary parents so to speak." Wright, Yerby, Motley, Walker, and Brooks, Bontemps felt, did not have progeny in the newest group of authors (Paule Marshall, F. L. Brown, Jones, Gloria Oden, Killens, Herbert Simons, and William Melvin Kelley). A possible exception was Hansberry (*A Raisin in the Sun,* inspired by Hughes's "A Dream Deferred"), who may have been related "in some fundamental literary ways" to Wright. Her work reflected the "increase of technical skills" expected of "a second or third generation of writers." Bontemps warned that there was, after Wright's heroic efforts to master form and language, no excuse for poor writing by black authors. Such an admonishment was to become a source of great irritation to the still newer writers waiting in the wings—some of whom assumed that it represented a broadside against the new *Black Esthetic.*

In June 1964 Fuller's article on "The Role of the Negro Writer in an Era of Struggle" explored Baldwin's frustration at being acclaimed as an essayist while the same attention had not been given his fiction. Fuller noted that in a time of social crisis, readers and critics perhaps find more meaning in social essays than in novels. Ralph Ellison, he observed, emphasized craft, while Hughes remained very committed to civil rights. Many other articles dealt with the problems of black authors. Bims examined "The Plight of the Negro Writer in a Segregated Society" in a January 1965 issue, and lamented, "The current Negro Writer who does not have an unshakable faith in himself is frustrated in looking about him for justification of himself, of his chosen profession." In April of the same year, a symposium undertook a look at "The Task of the Negro Writer as Artist" with contributions from Lerone Bennett, Jr.

(author of *Before the Mayflower* and *Ebony* senior editor), Brooks, actor Ossie Davis, novelist William Demby, jazz critic Nat Hentoff, Hughes, Jones, Kelley, Killens, Redding, Harvey Swados, John A. Williams, Yerby, Hare, John Henrik Clarke, Rivers, Randall, Kristin Hunter, Bill Gunn, Lincoln, Ernest Gaines, Alex Haley (originator of *Playboy* magazine's famous "Interview" series, author of *Roots* and *The Autobiography of Malcolm X*), Lennox Raphael, Lomax, Hernton, playwright William B. Branch, Margaret Danner, Ronald Fair, and Emanuel. The committed Hughes remained basically true to his lifelong self, drawing away from the temporary *artiste*'s stance of his *Free Lance* introduction: "Contemporary white writers can perhaps afford to be utterly irresponsible in their moral and social viewpoints. The Negro writer cannot. Ours is a social as well as a literary responsibility."

Discussions and debates concerning the black writer's role had, in the mid-sixties, become an important arm of the black cultural enterprise, evidenced by the numerous conferences: AMSAC Student Editors Conference of Africans and Afro-Americans at Hampton Institute; a white literary luncheon in Chicago at which editors of *Digest* engaged in a touchy exchange with Roy Newquist over why his new book *Counterpoint* (featuring interviews with sixty-three writers) included no black authors; the Harlem Writers Guild-New School for Social Research symposium (Baldwin, Richard Gilman, Jones, Alice Childress, Sarah Wright, Marshall, Brown, Myrna Baines, Douglas Turner Ward, Killens, Gloria Oden, Allen, Walter Lowenfels, Loften Mitchell [*Black Drama*], Albert Murray, and others); and the Alabama A. and M. College Writers' Conference, where Rosey E. Pool, Hayden, Dodson, Evans, and Killens made presentations. Hayden, destined to figure prominently in the aesthetics controversy, talked about drama at the Alabama conference and labeled Baldwin's *Blues for Mr. Charlie* and Jones's *Dutchman* as "just bad plays." Notices of conferences and symposia were announced regularly in the columns of *Digest*—which developed into the best source of cultural news in black magazine history.

Jones and Major had been publishing in *Free Lance* and in myriad white-dominated little magazines (*Beatitude, Blue River, Beat Coast East, Statements*). With Spellman, Jones also wrote exciting jazz criticism in more widely circulated magazines such as *Nation, Jazz,* and *Downbeat*. In the meantime, Ted Joans (the itinerant jazz poet), Kaufman (the irreverent and brilliant Beat poet), and Atkins (the genius-experimentalist) had begun separate but—hindsight shows us—related assaults on the language traditionally employed in the service of poetry. Their efforts and those of others, however, were not confined exclusively to the often black-influenced but white-controlled cultural and literary undergrounds. Writing and theater arts workshops began

springing up all over black America. Following or preceding them were important social corollaries: political ideologies, religious sectarian theories, race pride philosophies, hero- and myth-makers, and an unprecedented consolidation of black activism (symbolized by freedom rides, sit-ins, and, most important, the 1963 March on Washington for Jobs and Freedom). It was not surprising, then, to find clusters of poets, writers, and activists developing their own journals: the Howard Poets and *Dasein*; "Liberation Committee for Africa" and *Liberator*; the New York activist-theoreticians and their *Freedomways*; the "Society of Umbra" and *Umbra*; the activist-writers workshops and their mirror-journal, *Soulbook* ("the Quarterly of Revolutionary Afro-America"); the Negro Student Association at San Francisco State College and *Black Dialogue*; the young poet-mystics who proudly announced their *Journal of Black Poetry* ("published for black people everywhere"); the Organization of Black American Culture's frank embrace of its Africanity in the name *Nommo* (Chicago); and the numerous others (most of them bearing names associated with the new mood and group spirit). It also goes without saying that because they took many and divergent ideological and cultural stances, they deserve more treatment than this essay can give them.

Dasein, one of the most consciously literary of the new journals, immediately established a link between the Harlem Renaissance and its progenitor of the sixties and seventies by organizing the following advisory board: Sterling Brown, Arthur P. Davis, Owen Dodson, and Eugene C. Holmes. Brought out by the Dasein Literary Society, the periodical was subtitled *A Quarterly of the Arts,* with Percy Johnston serving as publisher and Walter DeLegall as editor. Al Fraser, Oswald Govan, Lance Jeffers, Leroy O. Stone, and Joseph White were contributing editors. Original and experimental in content, design, and layout, *Dasein* remains one of the truly beautiful cultural art survivals of the much-discussed sixties. Bebop, Zen Buddhism, black language and folklore, the Beat poetry of coffee shops, nuclear armaments. racism, and the threat of World War III all influenced the writings of *Dasein*'s contributors. Like *Free Lance,* the journal did not restrict itself to printing works by blacks. Among the poets were Clyde Taylor, Delores ,Kendrick, Jeffers ("My Blackness Is the Beauty of This Land"), William Jackson, Vernon A. Butler, Laura Watkins, Govan, Dodson, Fraser, Karl Darmstadter, R. Orlando Jackson, DeLegall, Johnston ("On Her Senility," "To Paul Robeson, Opus no. 3"), Stone ("Calypso"), Richard Eberhart, and Carl Smith ("The Little Red-Bellied Woman"). The usually strong essays of the early sixties included Kermit Keith's "Approaching Architecture as an Art"; and among the writers of fiction were Theophis Shine, Jeffers, White, Barbarossa ("The Avengers"), Helmar Cooper ("Elizabeth"), E. L. Robertson, and Mel Cebulash ("The Price of Fame").

The early sixties continued to witness an outpouring of cultural and literary magazines, but they also saw their share of new political journals, most of them avowedly nationalistic and devoted primarily to the struggle. Such was *Freedomways,* established in 1961 by Shirley Graham (editor), W. Alphaeus Hunton (associate editor), Margaret Burroughs (art editor), and Esther Jackson (managing editor). Initiated as a "Quarterly Review of the Negro Freedom Movement," the magazine later dropped the word "Negro" and broadened its scope to deal with Africa and the Third World. However, its service to poets and writers was more than incidental, since it regularly featured creative literature and commentaries on the arts. Moreover, it received a boost from two veteran activists and magazine developers, John Henrik Clarke and Ernest Kaiser, who wrote on "The New Afro-American Nationalism" in a 1961 issue. The title of the article set the political and cultural tone for *Freedomways.* Other articles looked at freedom, jazz, W. E. B. DuBois, challenges to black artists, blacks in films, black poetry, Paul Robeson, social justice, new civil rights heroes, the significance of Lorraine Hansberry, "The Negro Woman in American Literature," and "The Free Southern Theatre." Handsome but rarely deviating from its basic design and layout, *Freedomways* soberly analyzed social and cultural developments, its pages reinforced by the fine art of Tom Feelings, Charles White, Elton Fax, and Lee Jack Morton. In 1963 the written and visual arts were combined in a special issue on "Harlem: A Community in Transition."

Taken together, the healthy group of black journals launched in the early sixties represented the Afro-American consciousness in all its many colors. It is to them that one must go to trace the weaving of black art and thought. They fashioned the new literary tapestry and published the new writers: Nathan Hare, Malcolm X, LeRoi Jones, James Emanuel, John A. Williams, Clarence Major, John Oliver Killens, Paule Marshall, Ernest Gaines, Jay Wright, Henry Dumas, June Jordan, Audre Lorde, Larry Neal, Frank London Brown, Herbert Simmons, Conrad Kent Rivers, and others.

Clarke, a regular *Freedomways* contributor, was also a founder of *Liberator,* along with L. P. Beveridge, Jr., and Evelyn Battle. *Liberator* brought the whole of black life into focus through its creative literature, social essays, reviews (books, plays, movies), cultural articles, photo-essays, and interviews. The first issue was dedicated to Patrice Lumumba: "a symbol of unity and freedom; the people know why he died and what he stood for. Lumumba has taken his place among millions of martyrs to 600 years of struggle against slavery and colonial exploitation in Africa." Because *Liberator,* like *Freedomways,* was born of struggle, it was hampered by none of the initial constraints imposed on *Negro Digest.* Very few subjects or styles were off limits—a fact

that was much more obvious after 1963, when the magazine became financially stable enough to use color and to experiment with different designs and formats.

Each month *Liberator* expressed its message in cover photographs of the new and old black heroes: Baldwin, Dick Gregory, Marcus Garvey, Cassius Clay, Martin Luther King, Jr., Jones, Hughes, Malcolm X, Paul Robeson, Ornette Coleman, and Julian Bond. Following the example of *Crisis, Opportunity,* and *CLA Journal,* in 1965 the magazine sought to encourage writers by instituting a $100 short story contest. However, it had already begun publishing the fiction of Bims, Clayton Riley, Carlos Russell, Joseph White ("O'Grady Says"), Len Holt ("The Bug Feeder"), and Alfred Gray ("Any Other Reason"). Riley, the main critic of drama and film, wrote reviews of *Nothing but a Man, The Pawnbroker, China,* and numerous other works. Chief essayists were Larry Neal and Chester Fuller. The perceptive Neal reviewed Jones's *The Slave* and *The Toilet* in February 1965 and made this synthesizing comment: "Jones' plays are the verbal companions to the expressions that have reached their greatest intensity in the music of Coltrane, Ornette Coleman, and more lately Archie Shepp." One function of a journal like *Liberator,* Neal said in September of the same year, "is a passionate and sincere examination of the role of Afro-American culture, e.g. the arts, in shaping the spiritual foundation for revolutionary change." Indeed *Liberator* seemed to wear Neal's suggested role, attempting to bring all black art forms into an arena of reenergized fluidity.

The first literary magazines of the 1960s published exclusively for black writers and readers were *Soulbook, Black Dialogue,* and *Journal of Black Poetry. Umbra* ("shadow region"), which chronologically preceded them, presaged and shared the excitement they caused. Founded by the Society of Umbra, a workshop of musicians, poets, fiction writers, and visual artists, the journal was not, like the other three mentioned, a black nationalist literary organ. Aesthetically, however, it was born of the black struggle, as evidenced by this statement in its first issue: "UMBRA is not another haphazard 'little literary' publication. UMBRA has a definite orientation: (1) the experience of being Negro, especially in America; and (2) that quality of human awareness often termed 'social consciousness.'" Though concerned primarily with issues facing Afro-Americans as these were reflected in creative literature ("poetry, short stories, articles, essays"), *Umbra* warned, "We will not print trash, no matter how relevantly it deals with race, social issues, or anything else." Neither was the publication a "self-deemed radical," but "as radical as society demands the truth to be." Its "unequivocal commitment," the editor-founders noted, was to "material of literary integrity and artistic excellence." This stand, with its implied preference for art over politics, may have been an overreaction to the attitudes of *Liberator* and *Freedomways,* both published "uptown." Once one read *Umbra,* however, there was no question of the journal's involvement in the struggle—or of the need for a purely literary black magazine to serve as a forum and laboratory for new aesthetic experiments and analyses. Finally, like *Free Lance* and *Dasein, Umbra* had a particular interest in linking the post-Beat movement with the (often ill-termed) avant-garde. Considering the magazine's financial and spatial limitations, its achievements were quite substantial.

One important by-product of the founding of *Umbra* and its cousins (*Liberator, Negro Digest, Soulbook, Black Dialogue, Journal of Black Poetry*) was an effort to reformulate a vision of black artistic reality. The family of black artists and theoreticians who participated in this effort served as a nucleus out of which evolved the scope and design of most of the later magazines. In the persistent search for a synthesis of the artistic and the political consciousness, *Umbra* assembled a wide range of opinions, personalities, and attitudes: editor Tom Dent (freedom fighter and son of the president of Dillard University in New Orleans), assistant editors Hernton (sociologist-novelist-poet, a product of black colleges) and David Henderson (a poet and former student of writing at the New School for Social Research), and editorial assistants William E. Day, Rolland Snellings, Pritchard, and Nora Hicks. The first issue was divided into four parts: "Figurine of the Dream Sometimes Nightmare," "Blues and Bitterness," "Time and Atavism," and "Umbra Through Ethos." These titles, with their *Dasein*-like evocation of sensuality, mystery, psychology, and social consciousness, pretty much established the breadth of interest of *Umbra's* first contributors. Interestingly, one of the poets was Julian Bond.

None of the new magazines was developed in isolated, self-contained cultural centers, but each bore some evidence of regionalism. That the editors and contributors were aware of national literary activities is chronicled in the notes, titles of poems (and dedicatory inscriptions), reviews, and news. More important to this sense of black nationality, however, was the appearance of the same names in most of the publications. These writer-editors—Neal, Jones, Cruse, Clarke, Snellings, William Keorepetse Kgositsile, Henderson, Hernton, Dent, Major, Joans, Hughes, Ishmael Reed, Joe Goncalves, Atkins, Bob Hamilton, Lorenzo Thomas, Ed Bullins, Jeffers, Donald Stone, Randall, and others—helped form the backbone of the new black periodicals. One finds this to be the case with *Soulbook, Black Dialogue,* and *Journal of Black Poetry,* all of which ironically, in view of their nationalistic orientation, sprang up in California, not in the compressed neo-African worlds of Chicago, Detroit, St. Louis, New York, or Washington, D.C. The on-again-off-again publication

schedule of the journals attested to the problems they faced as the first black literary magazines in history to try sustaining themselves purely on black resources. The forerunner of these, *Soulbook,* "the revolutionary journal of Afro-America," came from the Afro-American Research Institution in Berkeley. Its focus was on black music, economics, black poetry, and anti-imperialism. With Hamilton as editor, the journal received editorial support from Wananchi Donald Freeman, Isaac Moore, Ernie Allen, Alvin Morrell, Ken M. Freeman, Carroll Holmes, and Leo R. Huey. Its major associates and contributors, however, reflected an East Coast influence: Kgositsile, Jones, Major, Doug Allen, Cornwell, Bullins, and Alfredo Peña. Among subjects treated in articles were Frantz Fanon and the Third World, racism and the socialist society, Egypt in history, "Blackness, That's Where It's At!" "Racism in France," and the whole of the African past. Africa began to figure prominently in *Soulbook* and other journals. *Soulbook,* for example, employed numerous African phrases ("Kitabu Cha Weusi"), ideas, concepts, drawings, maps, and names.

Black Dialogue and *Journal of Black Poetry* were low-keyed in that they, like *Soulbook* but unlike *Digest,* avoided taking on the whole of the black cultural experience. *Dialogue,* born in 1965 at San Francisco State College, featured some articles and essays, reviews, poetry, and fiction. Its founding editor was Arthur A. Sheridan, a San Francisco State student who had published his writings in *Canadian Sun, San Francisco Sun Reporter,* and *Liberal Democrat.* The East Coast editor was Edward Spriggs, brilliant poet and artist, while the editorial board consisted of Abdul Kaliem, Joe Howard, Aubrey Labrie, and Sidney Schiffer. Brought out by Ari Publications, *Dialogue* was expected to appear every two months as "a meeting place for voices of the Black community wherever that community may exist." It symbolized the youthful vigor of black America, publishing articles on "Revolutionary Theatre," "Negritude Américaine," "The Future of 'Soul' in America," Santo Domingo, jazz, more on African negritude, revolutionary nationalism and the black artist, and Vietnam (by an eyewitness from Hanoi). Here the works of new young poets and occasionally those of older ones were printed: Al Young, Jon Lovett, Spriggs, Welton Smith, Neal, Conyus Calhoun, Alphonse Ngoma, Patricia Bullins, Goncalves, Senegalese David Diop, and Bisharo Al-Ausig. Here too were the fiction and drama of Marvin Jackmon ("Flowers for the Trashman"), Bullins ("How Do You Do"), Jane Clay (prize-winning author who had appeared in *New South* and *Negro Digest*), C. H. Fuller, and Melba Kgositsile. The talented, unpredictable LeRoi Jones led the roster of essay-article writers that included Saadat Ahmad, Romare Bearden, Neal, James T. Stewart, Bullins, and Eldridge Cleaver. The book review section, though sparse, was spiced with social undertones and ideological conflicts, as in reviews of *Glo-*

rious Age in Africa, Worth Fighting For, The Wretched of the Earth, and *Manchild in the Promised Land.* There were also reviews of movies (for example, of *Uptight* by Nikki Giovanni) and the Afro-American Folkloric Troupe. The middle years of the sixties were given a particular twist and impetus by Jones, who wrote in a 1965 issue of *Dialogue*: "Revolutionary Theatre must Accuse and Attack anything that can be accused and attacked. It must Accuse and Attack because it is a theatre of Victims. It looks at the sky with the victims' eyes, and moves the victims to look at the strength in their minds and their bodies." In that year of Watts, a major jolt would be given the American social consciousness, and certainly not the least affected would be black cultural institutions, especially the literary magazines.

"Published for all black people everywhere," the quarterly *Journal of Black Poetry* was founded by Goncalves and had a great impact on black arts groups during the late sixties and early seventies. No other periodical before or since has rivaled its leadership in publishing the best of the newest poetry from the black world. Yet while it focused on poems and poets, the journal included incisive book reviews and excellent art and illustrations. Unlike some of its contemporaries (such as *Negro Digest, Freedomways,* and *CLA Journal*), it energetically sought to establish an unbroken relationship between typography, content, and ideology. Following in the paths of *Soulbook* and *Dialogue,* it strove to achieve this synthesis by dismissing the Euro-American aesthetic and embracing neo-African criteria. An important component of this developing sensibility was the "new" music, which became increasingly important in the thinking of cultural philosophers, many of whom saw parallels between the ideas of Malcolm X and the "revolutionary" sounds. Goncalves' contribution to this vital breakthrough in black aesthetics was to provide a forum for the new poets and theoreticians. For over a decade this journal has remained the showplace for the best black poetry.

Part of the *Journal of Black Poetry's* appeal was in its cultural miscellany—a gumbo of criticism, reviews, news, and visual art. Articles, for example, covered such diverse subjects as Coltrane's music, black poetry from the Americas, "The Death of Yakub," "Toward a Purer Black Poetry Esthetic" (Crouch), "Letter to a Young Poet," "Black Magic" (on the new black poetry), "The Fire Must Be Permitted to Burn Full Up" (literary criticism), and "Black Arts Mexico" (Marvin X).

Battles over the new aesthetics continued to dominate the pages of *Journal* and other black cultural organs. One of the books contributing the most to this controversy was Cruse's *The Crisis of the Negro Intellectual*—a biting, searing indictment of black intellectuals and artists. It was simultaneously praised and attacked

in all quarters. Two examples of staunch positions, pro and con, taken by contemporaries were poet-artist Edward Spriggs's endorsement of the work as the "most significant book of the decade" (*Journal of Black Poetry,* 1967-1968) and *Black Scholar* editor Robert Chrisman's condemnation of it as "The Crisis of Harold Cruse" in a later issue of his own journal.

A kind of "blackening" process—which, in *Digest,* for example, took the form of ceasing to publish or endorse white writers and changing its name to *Black World*—occurred in most of these new journals. The pattern was quite apparent in their names or subtitles, as witness this very incomplete list: *Afro-America, Black America, Negro American Literature Forum, Black Expression, Black Theatre, Nommo, The Black Scholar, Confrontation* (Troupe: Ohio University, Athens), *Echoes from the Gumbo, Proud* (St. Louis), *Revolt!* (Nat Turner Theatre, New Orleans), *Cosmic Colors, Nkombo, Cricket* ("New Ark"), *Deep Down in My Soul* (Miami, Florida), *Spark* (Chicago), *Amistad* (John A. Williams and Charles Harris), *Black Academy Review* (A. Okechukwu, State University of New York, Buffalo), *Black Creation* (New York), *Black Review, Harvard Journal of Afro-American Affairs, The Mask* (Los Angeles), *Ex-Umbra, Chicory* (Baltimore), *Phat Mama* (New York, subtitled "Her Black Mind"), *Uptight* (El Paso), *Spirit* (London), *The Conch* ("Journal of Literary and Cultural Analysis"), *Rhythm* (Atlanta, African Expression, Inc.), *Black Lines* (Larry Coleman and Clarence Turner: Black Studies, University of Pittsburgh), *The Non-Aligned Third World Journal* (St. Louis), *Kushusu Vitabu* (Washington, D.C.), *Phase II* (Sarah Webster Fabio: Berkeley, "Journal of Black Art Renaissance"), *Onyx, Talking Drums* (London, monthly music magazine), *Yalode: Journal of Black Sister Poets* (Miami, Theatre of Afro-Arts), *Imani* (New York University, "Concepts of Education for Black People"), *Black History Museum Newsletter* (Philadelphia), *Roots* (Houston, Texas Southern University), *Hoo-Doo: A Journal of Black Arts* (later *Hoo-Doo Black Literature Series*; Up South-D.C. and Down South-DeRidder, Louisiana), *Transition* (later *Synergy*; D.C., Howard University Department of Afro-American Studies), *Pamoja Tutashinda* (Williamstown, Massachusetts), *Maongezi* (Detroit), *Renaissance 2: A Journal of Afro-American Studies* (Yale, Afro-American Cultural Center), *Watu* (Cornell University; "Journal of Black Literature and Art"), *Mwendo* (Coe College, Iowa), *The African Voice* (Camden, New Jersey, Black Cooperative Association), *Proud Black Images* (Ohio State University, Columbus; New World Arts Workshop), *Together Forever* (Chicago, Hirsch High School), *Poems by Blacks* (Lane; Baton Rouge and Fort Smith, Arkansas), *Shades* ("cultural, historical and literary magazine"), *Black Books Bulletin* (Chicago, Institute for Positive Education), *The Pan Africanist* ("quarterly of the international Black movement"; Claremont, California), *Black Music in Perspective* (Eileen

Southern), *Black-stage* (Adesanya Alokoya, "a monthly magazine reflecting the development of Black art and culture"), *Living Blues: A Journal of the Black American Blues Tradition* (Chicago), *Identity* (Detroit, Rapa House Writers Association), *Drum: Journal of the Black Experience* (University of Massachusetts, Amherst), *Hambone* (Stanford, Committee for Black Performing Arts), *Obsidian: Black Literature in Review* (Alvin Aubert; SUNY, Fredonia), *Studies in Black Literature, Movin' On in Space and Time* (Nora Bailey, Chicago: "Journal for the Fine Arts and Foreign Languages"), *Dues: An Annual of New Earth Writing* (Ron Welburn, New York), *Maji: A Journal of the Black Arts* (Philadelphia, The MAJI Collective), *Dark Waters* (Collen McElroy; Seattle, Washington), *Black Writers' News, Black Works* (New York), *Impressions, Spirit* (Jamaica, New York; Center for New Images, "A Black Arts and Communications Organization"), *Continuities: Words from the Communities of Pan-Africa* (Wilfred Cartey: New York), *BGI-18* (Black Graphics International, "Journal of Revolutionary Literature and Art"; Detroit), *Strive* (Montclair, New Jersey), *Gumbo: A Literary Magazine* (Yusef Komunyakaa), *Umoja: A Scholarly Journal of Black Studies* (Edward C. Okwu; University of Colorado, Boulder), *Blackprint* (Austin, Texas), and *Yardbird* (later *Y'bird*) (Reed and Young: Berkeley).

Many of these publications were patterned after their early and mid-sixties forebears. Some had radically new formats, reflecting the most advanced developments in print media technology; still others, like *CLA Journal* and *Phylon,* were more formal and academic in appearance. However, most were influenced by regional brands of black consciousness. This was particularly true of the Chicago-based *Negro Digest,* which, as the only national black literary magazine with a paid staff and a reliable publishing history, naturally assumed a position of leadership in the black arts movement. Until well into the seventies, Gayle, one of the most influential black aestheticians, dramatically aided Fuller in charting the journal's vision. He, along with Don Lee (Madhubuti) and Baraka (who later renounced *Black World*'s position), developed into a kind of axis force that monitored the evolution of the movement.

Of the other journals begun in the sixties, some, like *Dasein* and *Umbra,* changed paces and places. Others, such as *Liberator* and *Afro-America,* folded in the late sixties. Still others, among them *Freedomways* and *The Black Scholar,* remained strong and significant. Often the same editors simultaneously manned the staffs of several short-lived magazines. *Dasein,* which, like *Free Lance* and *Umbra,* had not been an exclusively black journal, reappeared in 1965 as a publication of the Dasein-Jupiter Hammom Press of New York. With this shift had come a change in mood and format. It remained beautifully laid out with attractive color covers

and fine-textured paper, but the obvious black context was gone, though all the black writers were not. The racially mixed contributors of poetry included Barbara Brown, Bruce Andrews, William Packard, Sue Abbot Boyd (white publisher of *Poems by Blacks*), Jeffers (who with J. William Meyers and Michael Winston had been added to the advisory board), Jack Crawford, and the talented young Jodi Braxton (*Sometimes I Think of Maryland*). Essays tended to be inspired by European-American academic ideas rerouted through an avant-garde consciousness. Very little fiction was published after the first two issues of *Dasein,* and there were few reviews. A current feature of the magazine is "The Young Writers' Salon," in which the work of new poets is introduced.

As nonliterary journals, *Freedomways* and *Liberator* nevertheless incorporated the essential black cultural spirit into their primary function. *Freedomways* opened its pages to dozens of poets. South African Bessie Head contributed short fiction ("Tao"), along with R. J. Meadough, Alice Walker, Loyle Hairston, Ann Shockley, and Mignon Holland Anderson. *Liberator,* with its larger size, made strategic use of visual arts and artists, featuring photo-essays on various black communities. Short fiction and plays were still its strong features in the late sixties, and its star-poet lineup was interspersed with occasional new names. However, publisher Daniel Watts and company were not able to keep *Liberator* in existence after 1970.

As for *Umbra,* the dispersion of its staff actually had a positive effect on the black literary world. Reed and Henderson went to Berkeley. Dent returned to New Orleans and, with the aid of Val Ferdinand (Kalamu Ya Salaam), organized two short-lived magazines: *Echoes from the Gumbo* and *Nkombo.* (Salaam, in turn, became a founding editor of *Black Collegian.*) In 1975 Dent joined Charles H. Rowell and Jerry Ward in establishing *Callaloo,* "born out of a specific desire to give expression to the new writers in the Deep South area." In the meantime, Henderson had revived *Umbra,* first in New York in the form of an anthology and later in California as a tabloid that has exerted considerable influence on Third World cultural programming. One of its most significant contributions was to bring together those writers and artists rarely published by the establishment with those from the black world. Only Troupe's three-issue *Confrontation* and Reed's five-issue *Yardbird* seemed similarly interested in tapping this broader base of creative expression. Most new journals, while not completely ignoring other colored artists, rarely attempted to show relationships between cultural expression and political events occurring in Latin America, the Middle East, and Southeast Asia. A prototype format for dealing with wider issues of color had been developed by *Phylon* in the 1940s, but apparently the editors of the new journals were not aware of it.

The "survival of the fittest" axiom finally overcame both *Soulbook* and *Black Dialogue,* after the latter had been briefly revived in 1969 with a new editorial board. *Afro-American,* with its New York orientation, proudly advertised itself in a September 1966 issue of *Liberator* as a "new magazine dedicated to you of African ancestry. . . . We feature the new young Black poets and writers; we feature your history and heritage; we feature a review of current books about Africans and Afro-Americans." The *Afro-American Woman,* an *Ebony*-type publication brought out by the Negro Book Club, issued its first number in 1967. At Terre Haute, Indiana, Englishman John F. Bayliss of Indiana State University founded the scholarly *Negro American Literature Forum* "for school and university teachers." As a quarterly, which changed its name to *Black American Literature Forum* in the mid-seventies under the editorship of Hannah Hedrick, it has been a valuable source of reviews, criticism, and poetry. Its contributors have included Upward Bound and prison poets, members of the Watts Writers Workshop, John Lovell, Benjamin McKeever, Lloyd Brown, Daryl Dance, Abraham Chapman, Turner, and Tolson. In 1972 Redmond (*Drumvoices*) edited a special poetry number that presented the work of twenty-three black poets.

The black music magazine *Cricket,* an outgrowth of *Liberator* and other journals, carried the works of Sun Ra, Askia Touré, Caldwell, Neal, Baraka, Reed, Crouch, Kgositsile, Spellman, and Norman Jordan. Spellman later helped found *Rhythm* in Atlanta. Around the time *Cricket* appeared, *Nommo* arrived as the publications arm of Chicago's well-known OBAC, founded in 1966 by Rivers, Fuller, and Gerald McWorter. It came out irregularly and usually published works by members of the OBAC Writers' Workshop. Angela Jackson (*Voodoo/Love Magic*) became editor of the journal in the mid-seventies. The indefatigable Fuller oversaw these Windy City activities from his several-pronged position of editor, organizer, and father figure. His feminine counterpart, Gwendolyn Brooks, openly and unselfishly shared her resources with the new black writers in Chicago and elsewhere. With Randall of Broadside Press (publisher of *Black Position*), Fuller and Brooks, under the ever-hovering spirit of Baraka, formed a triumvirate that literally set the course of black creative expression during the late sixties and early seventies. This was achieved by rocketing to stardom their young poet-protégé, Lee (later Haki R. Madhubuti). In the meantime, Gwendolyn Brooks made a unique contribution to little magazine history by editing *Black Position,* wherein she promised to "present the music and the muscle of contemporary black pride as an excitement, a privilege, a responsibility." Mostly done in black and white, the magazine carried the writings of Randall, Fuller, Bennett, Lee, Curtis Ellis (Chicago bookstore

entrepreneur), Neal, Francis and Val Gray Ward (of Kuumba Workshop), Carolyn Rodgers, Gayle, George Kent, and Kgositsile.

One of the most impressive literary periodicals to emerge from the Chicago and national scene, however, was Madhubuti's *Black Books Bulletin.* Though typographically imposing, with brilliant cover art and design, the journal's articles and commentaries were often of lesser quality. Part of *Bulletin's* problem was that its editor was simultaneously experiencing growing pains and occupying a vital leadership position in the Afro-American cultural sphere. Overpraised too early in his career, Madhubuti drastically simplified the most complex racial and social issues, then went on to quick-drawn conclusions. Nevertheless, the journal's service to black creativity remained invaluable, since it offered poetry contests as well as articles and essays by leading thinkers, and it became a leader in monitoring books by and about Africans. Still going strong in 1978, the *Bulletin* reflects, to use the words of poet Julius Thompson, "hopes tied up in promises."

The Black Scholar, founded in 1969 and now edited by Robert Chrisman, was established as a forum for social and political issues. However, its occasional literary criticism, book reviews, poetry, and short fiction have helped provide a platform for the new black literature. Most monthly issues have been devoted to the special concerns of black or Third World communities: Pan Africanism, black psychology, the black soldier, black women, and fund-raising for the Afro-American community. There are essay and short story contests along with irregularly appearing reviews. One important service rendered by *Scholar* is its annual *Black Books Roundup,* and it has also devoted several issues exclusively to black literature and the arts.

While *Black Scholar* was establishing its base of operations in Sausalito, *Yardbird* was launched in the early seventies by Reed, Young, and associates in Berkeley. The journal resembled *Amistad* and Mel Watkins's *Black Review* (neither of which lasted very long). *Yardbird's* inability to tangle successfully with the various conflicts among its editorial ranks led to its death after only five issues. However, in its brief life the journal was more concerned—like its predecessors *Free Lance, Dasein,* and *Umbra*—with publishing literature than with discussing or reviewing it. Brought out by the Yardbird Publishing Cooperative, *Yardbird* reflected some of the best writing being done by Afro-American and Third World authors (and occasionally carried the work of non-colored writers). This practice of including some white writers was carried over into the new *Y'bird* (Reed and Young, 1977).

Nate Mackey, Sandi Richards, Charleen Rubin, and Gloria Watkins organized the magazine *Hambone* (in the mid-seventies), which is published by the Committee for Black Performing Arts at Stanford University. It featured poetry by Barra, Watkins, Henderson, Johnnie Scott, Halifu, David Jackson, Michael Harper, Fabio, and Reed. Drawings and photographs, interviews (Anthony Braxton), articles (Eckels and John Cochran), and fiction (Wandera Ogana, Fred Johnson) helped round out one issue of the attractive publication.

Historically the major centers of black little-magazine activity have been D.C., Atlanta, Cleveland, Chicago, New York, New Orleans, and Berkeley. Oddly enough, New York City has not been able to give continuous life to a single black literary periodical, though it has seen many come and go. Recently, however, encouraging signs have been appearing on the cultural horizon, and writers hope the phoenix cycle will produce an important New York-based black journal. In other parts of the state, as well as in adjacent states, various writing and arts workshops, studios, and social organizations have often joined Afro-American studies or English departments in repeated attempts to publish little magazines. When *Liberator,* the most literary of magazines in New York during its day, was on its deathbed, *Black Theatre* was ascending. As the official periodical of the black theater movement, it was based at the New Lafayette Theatre, founded in Harlem in 1966. It had hoped to publish six times a year but soon met all the familiar adversities. During its brief existence, however, it became a valuable source of cultural news, original short plays, interviews, reviews, and poetry. Bullins and Marvin X headed the staff of editors and correspondents that represented a national range and scope: Dent, Theodore Ward, Vantile Whitfield, Adam David Miller, Goncalves, Larry Miller (*Katibu*), Caldwell, Jones, Woody King, O'Neal, and Barbara Ann Teer (founder of the National Black Theatre of Harlem).

Black Creation, the brilliant prototype of a black cultural journal, appeared in the early 1970s. As a "Quarterly Review of Black Arts and Letters," it had much of the spirit and flavor of *Liberator,* except that its editors unashamedly announced that literature and the arts would be their main focus. Veteran and beginning artists and writers were given exposure in *Creation* which—like *Liberator, Black Theatre,* and other New York magazines—had regional editors in San Francisco (Cleveland Bellows), Detroit (Melba Boyd), New Orleans (Dent), and Paris (Lillian Barlow). Editor Fred Beauford was handily assisted by James Walker, John Flateau, and playwright Buriel Clay. The following claim by *Creation* was well documented in each issue of the colorful magazine: "We are one of the few magazines around where the heart beat of Black Americans can be felt with force; where young and old, male and female, come together in a community of creative expression." The entire spectrum of black expression was repeatedly seen in the journal: film and theater criticism, creative literature (fiction, poetry, essays), art,

book reviews, in-depth interviews with authors and artists. One-time poetry editor was the gifted Elouise Loftin, who published her own poems as well as those of others. Editor Beauford published his own fiction along with that of Melvin Mitchell, Wesley Brown, Joe Johnson, Shelby Steele, King, Mignon Holland ("Gone After Jake"), and Ronnie Redd.

Bopp (earlier *BOP,* for "Blacks on paper") and *Black Works* were only two of several new magazines that showed promise in the mid-seventies. *Bopp,* originally conceived by students at Brown University, is currently edited by Kambon Obayani, who is in the graduate writing program at the University of Iowa. Associate editors are Gayl Jones, Troupe, and Cannon; contributing editors include Charles Davis, Everett Hoagland, Rhett Jones, Major, and Mustapha (included in *Jumbalaya*). The future of *Bopp* is uncertain, but its present is bright.

Black Works, which made its first impact as a literary magazine published once annually, announced in 1977 that it would come out twice a year. Based at Long Island University, the journal has been reminiscent of *Liberator* in its practice of printing photographs of everyday blacks in natural surroundings. Poetry, stories, drama, and literary criticism accompany the visuals. Editors include Cecil Lee, Patricia Nichols, Wayne Dawkins, Gibson, Patricia Lee, and Grace Corbet. Gibson is also a member of Troupe's New York poetry workshop at the Frederick Douglass Creative Arts Center.

The struggle to bridge the gap between the academy and the streets was most notably seen in journals like *Phylon, Negro Digest/Black World, Liberator,* and *Black Scholar.* Within this frame of reference, one other New York State literary magazine deserves brief consideration. Although its future was not guaranteed (and it remained in need of subscribers in early 1978) *Obsidian: Black Literature in Review* appeared at mid-decade. Its attempt to avoid the tension between the streets and the academy, and to embrace the international black literary family, was seen in its list of contributing and advisory editors: Awooner, Lloyd Brown, Clarke, Arthur P. Davis, Nick Aaron Ford, Gaines, Gayle, Harper, Blyden Jackson, Kent, Arthenia Bates, Ezekiel Mphahlele, Redding, Rowell, and Douglas Turner Ward. *Obsidian* was described as being "devoted to the study and cultivation of Black Literature, featuring critical articles, book reviews, short fiction, poetry, interviews, very short plays." It is desperately needed as a review of literature—especially in view of the abdication of this position by *CLA Journal.*

At the same time, fine new journals like *Bopp* and *Hoo-Doo* are vital and important because they specialize in creative expression. The latter's peripatetic editor

(Ahmos Zu-Bolton), who has been active on the little-magazine circuit (including the white network) for some time, made impressive strides in the mid-seventies, publishing a wide range of contemporary Afro-American poets and devoting an entire issue to women writers. A southern flavor has pervaded *Hoo-Doo,* just as it has and does in such sister journals as *Echoes from the Gumbo, Roots, Nkombo, Pound, Deep Down in My Soul,* and *The Saracen.*

The excitement caused by black and other non-white interactions and struggles has spurred the development of Third World journal publishing. Early examples were *Tropiques, Présence Africaine,* and *Black Orpheus,* but these were followed by many others: *Abbia (The Cameroon Cultural Review), African Forum* (New York), *African Arts* (UCLA), *African Literature Today* (Sierra Leone), *Journal of New African Literature and the Arts* (Joseph Okpaku, New York), *Journal of Ethnic Studies, Lotus: Afro-Asian Writings* (Cairo), *African Studies Review* (New York), *Black Images* (Ontario), *Cavite* (Barbados), *African Language Studies* (London), *Voices from the Cave, African Theatre* (Kenya), *Jamaica Journal, African Review* (Dar es Salaam), *Gumbo: A Literary Magazine* (Yusef Komunyakaa), *Mazungumzo* (Michigan State University), *Calaban, Savacou* (Jamaica), *Insight and Opinion* (Ghana), *BIM* (Barbados), *Kairi* (Trinidad and Tobago), *Ufahumu, Busara, Caribbean Quarterly, Jonala, Harambee, Neworld* (Los Angeles), *Gigibori* (Papua, New Guinea), *Copesthetic* (Harryette Mullen), *Minority Voices, African Authors,* and *African Literature Association* (Pennsylvania). This list only samples the rich productivity occurring in worldwide circles of "color." Afro-American writers have become more involved in the Pan-African and Third World little magazine movement, and a healthy reciprocity has obviously emerged.

The "black world," as many now refer to the global existence of Africans, is the stage on which the drama of the black future will be played out. *Black World,* as name and new identity, was in fact born of this urgency. *First World*—a black-derived term to counter possible negative residuals in the phrase "Third World," and to suggest black leadership instead of followership in international life—adorned the masthead of a new magazine founded by Fuller, Parks, and associates in Atlanta. "An International Journal of Black Thought," *First World* has changed its location and format. However, despite its august editorial board (Samuel Allen, Maja Angelou, Houston Baker, Brooks, Clark, Cruse, Davis, Gayle, Madhubuti, and others), not much has been done to keep the journal alive. One of the best-looking of the new magazines, it offers criticism, poetry, reviews, and political analyses, and its shoestring existence is not unlike that of other black journals. At the same time, the journal's history has been fraught with controversy. During the mid- to late sixties and into the seventies,

several writers and editors felt Fuller had allowed himself to be pushed into a myopic corner by proponents of the black aesthetic and black nationalism. This predicament, they maintained, aided in the circumvention of certain writers and their materials. So, when *Black World* folded in 1976, a number of supporters were less than eager to help Fuller develop another journal with the same editorial policies he had pursued in the last stages of *Negro Digest/Black World.* One wonders, too, why Fuller, with both a knowledge of the journal's impending death and an international network of contacts, did not act sooner to conceive and implement the *First World* project.

The black little magazine has received indirect support from the big slicks (*Ebony, Essence, Encore, The Black Collegian, Players, Unique*) which, especially in the case of *Essence* and *Collegian,* feature creative expression and literary history. In publishing the works of little-magazine contributors, these bigger ones are helping to publicize the efforts of their less stable cousins.

For the black "littles," it has indeed been a long trek from instability to an uneasy stability, aided in part by wider reading audiences and various public or private grants. The same magazine (*Umbra-Yardbird-Y-bird, Gumbo-Nkombo-Callaloo, Shrewd-Confrontation-Bopp, Free Lance-Vibrations-Black Ascensions-Juju,* or *Liberator-Cricket-Black Theatre-Black Creation*) keeps being born within the spirit and letter of the African continuum. A healthy reflection is cast by the current state of the black cultural arts: strong, flexible, multidimensional/directional, proud, controversial, and life-giving. From this robust conflict is produced the stuff of future creative expression. The individual black journals have come and gone, but the idea that they are necessitated by life (art) will never disappear. *Callaloo,* one of the newest of these magazines, is, as its editors suggested in the inaugural issue, already in "a wretched financial state"—a desperate situation, to say the least. But hope abounds in the lead-off article, in which Lelia H. Taylor, preparing to examine the survival-food recipe that became the journal's title, flings a challenge and a lifeline: "Callaloo, anyone?"

Abby Arthur Johnson and Ronald Maberry Johnson (essay date 1979)

SOURCE: Johnson, Abby Arthur and Ronald Maberry Johnson. "Black Renaissance: Little Magazines and Special Issues, 1910-1930." In *Propaganda and Aesthetics: The Literary Politics of Afro-American Magazines in the Twentieth Century,* pp. 65-96. Amherst: The University of Massachusetts Press, 1979.

[*In the essay below, the critics discuss the rise of black little magazines in early-twentieth century America, stressing their interconnectedness with political and social trends of the time.*]

The first black little magazines of the twentieth century came immediately after *Crisis* had achieved financial independence from the NAACP. In November 1915, Du Bois announced that *Crisis* was solvent. In January 1916, the journal paid his entire salary, and all other operational expenses, for the first time. Two small black journals appeared shortly thereafter, as if the success of Du Bois had bolstered the confidence of others who wanted to start periodicals. *New Era* of Boston emerged in February and *Stylus* of Washington, D.C., in June of that year. Other black little magazines followed, as did Afro-American issues of essentially white periodicals, but they arrived after the war had ended and the post-war depression had eased. *Survey Graphic,* a journal published in New York and concerned broadly with social questions, featured in 1925 a special number on Harlem, its literature and its people. Established in Guadalajara, Mexico, a little poetry magazine called *Palms* published an issue devoted to Afro-American literature in 1926. The next year saw the first Afro-American number of the *Carolina Magazine,* a student publication at the University of North Carolina. Inspired by the quality and influence of that number, the students followed with a special issue of black literature in 1928 and also in 1929. The black little magazines began in Harlem with two radical and short-lived publications, *Fire* in 1926 and *Harlem* in 1928. More conservative Afro-American journals appeared elsewhere on the East Coast, as did *Black Opals* in Philadelphia during 1927 and 1928, and the *Saturday Evening Quill* in Boston during 1928 to 1930.

Pauline Hopkins came to the fore again with *New Era.* She established the journal because she sensed the beginning of "a really new era in America," and wanted to be part of that beginning. She did not succeed in addressing the contemporary scene, however, and the magazine collapsed after its first two issues of February and March. In the opening number, she introduced her compeers, saying "the roll of the staff presents a few familiar names, but for the most part we are as young in public life as is the new year."[1] The controlling voices came out of the past, though, for Hopkins was listed as editor and Walter Wallace, her colleague on the staff at *Colored American Magazine,* as managing editor. The contributors even included Sarah Allen, or Hopkins writing under the maiden name of her mother, her previous practice when she lowered her profile.

In both issues Hopkins elaborated on the functions of *New Era.* Her commentary indicates that she envisioned the journal in three roles: as an agitator for race rights, as an historian of race progress, and as a promoter of black literature and arts. Her accents rang as of old when she placed the journal firmly within the protest tradition: "We know that there are able publications already in the field, but the pang that has set our active world a-borning is the knowledge that the colored man has lost the rights already won because he was persuaded and then bullied into lying down and ceasing his fight for civil liberty."[2] Hopkins understood the importance of journals as preservers of tradition. As editor of *New Era* she voiced sentiments reminiscent of those expressed much earlier by Max Barber. "We are," she claimed, "sparing neither time nor money to make this Magazine the most authentic historian of the race's progress." She recognized the importance of black journals in providing an outlet for Afro-American writers. She promised, then, that *New Era* would "do its utmost to assist in developing the literature, science, music, art, religion, facts, fiction and tradition of the race throughout the world." In this connection, she hoped to establish a "Race Publishing House" in Boston which would "stand as a permanent and lasting monument of race progress."[3] Undoubtedly she envisioned the publishing house along the lines of the Colored Co-operative Publishing Company which had issued the *Colored American Magazine,* as well as books by and about blacks.

In many respects, the contents of *New Era* paralleled the contents of the *Colored American Magazine* when edited by Hopkins. *New Era* emphasized biography, with each issue featuring several sketches of prominent persons. Hopkins probably wrote all the sketches, those left unsigned as well as those carrying her name, because the pieces bore her stylistic idiosyncrasies, with didactic introductions and conclusions stressing the value of individual effort. She envisioned the biographical essays as a continuation of her earlier effort, as indicated in the February issue: "The series of sketches prepared by Miss Hopkins some years since on 'Famous Men of the Negro Race,' will have a worthy sequel in this series entitled 'Men of Vision.'"[4] She likewise planned a series on "sacrificing women" of the race, including Frances Harper, Sojourner Truth, and Harriet Tubman. As in the past, her favorite subjects were New Englanders, men like John Trowbridge whom she identified as the "Last of the Famous Group of New England Authors."[5]

She continued to feature fiction and verse. The table of contents for each issue noted two short stories and one poem, and then Hopkins went ahead and included several other creative pieces which were not announced. Foremost among the poets was William Stanley Braithwaite, whose "picture adorn[ed] our cover" for the February issue, and whose lyrics appeared in prominent positions in the March issue.[6] The most significant fiction came from Pauline Hopkins, who was engaged once again with a serialized novel, this time called "Topsy Templeton." She planned her effort to "run through several issues," and consequently readers never did learn what finally happened to Topsy. The first two installments were sufficient, however, to show that Hopkins had not changed as a creative writer. Once again she concentrated on interracial relations, in this story between the white Newbury sisters and Topsy, the little black girl they adopted. She ended the first episode with much suspense and an apparently dead Topsy. In the second issue, she revived a scene which had figured significantly in *Of One Blood,* serialized in *Colored American Magazine.* A physician having psychic powers recognizes Topsy's condition as "suspended animation" and "reanimates" her before some wondering colleagues and two very grateful Newbury sisters.[7]

Not all of the journal was a look backward. Hopkins had the foresight to include a regular column, headed "Helps for Young Artists," by the sculptor, Meta Warrick-Fuller, who was art editor for the journal. In her column, Fuller urged black artists to form groups in order to experiment with suggestions advanced in the column. By so doing, she became one of the first writers in a black journal to stress the need for such organization. Only Du Bois had preceded her, with his call one year earlier for Horizon clubs dedicated to Afro-American pageantry. Hopkins recognized the merit in Fuller's comments and encouraged involvement by announcing a prize to be awarded "to the individual or group of persons . . . who will have tried out any one or more of the instructions offered in this series."[8] The journal collapsed before the plans matured, but Hopkins nevertheless anticipated Du Bois and Charles S. Johnson who later realized the value of artistic competitions and prizes.

New Era went quietly. Du Bois never alluded to its demise in *Crisis,* but then he had never announced its initial appearance. He kept a fine eye on the press, so he probably knew about *New Era.* Most likely he did not welcome the magazine because he saw it as a potential rival to *Crisis.* He would not have criticized Hopkins because she had battled long and hard in the past for a free black press and for other concerns he himself endorsed. It would have been ungracious to express satisfaction over the failure of her later attempt with a magazine rivalling his own. And so Du Bois said nothing. No one else said much about the magazine either. As a result, it slipped out of memory, forgotten by editors and literary historians.[9]

Whereas much of *New Era* echoed the past, *Stylus* looked to the future. The support for the journal came in the winter of 1915-16, when Professors Alain Locke and Montgomery Gregory organized a literary society at Howard University. Called Stylus, the group included students, to be selected from biannual competitions, and several faculty and honorary members. From the beginning, members wanted to stimulate writing based on Afro-American culture and to encourage artistic expression in the black community, especially among youth. Gregory remembered that the society had "a vision, a vision which embodied in the not too distant future a Negro literature that should secure recognition along

with that of other peoples."[10] The *Howard University Record* recalled in later years that the efforts of Stylus were not limited to Howard University, but that they extended "to the Negro race and to civilization." Benjamin Brawley noted that the organization "hoped to make a genuine contribution to racial advance."[11] To further their ends, Locke and associates issued a journal which bore the same name as the organization and which was the first purely literary magazine published at any black college. Appearing in June 1916, *Stylus* featured student efforts and special contributions by honorary members, such as Braithwaite, Brawley, and James Weldon Johnson.

World War I interrupted the work, sending Stylus members and supporters to distant parts. Efforts did not resume until peace returned and a handful of the former participants came back to campus. With that nucleus Professors Locke and Gregory attracted new student members, including Zora Neale Hurston, and additional honorary members, notably Charles W. Chesnutt, W. E. B. Du Bois, Alice Moore Dunbar, and Arthur A. Schomburg. The second number of *Stylus* appeared in May 1921.

In his "Foreword" to that issue, Montgomery Gregory voiced sentiments which would be echoed by New Negroes emerging in the latter half of the decade. "It becomes clearer daily," he stated, "that it must be through the things of the Spirit that we shall ultimately restore Ethiopia to her seat of honor among the races of the world. The Germans have amply demonstrated the futility of force to secure a place in the sun. Any individual or people must depend upon the universal appeal of art, literature, painting, and music—to secure the real respect and recognition of mankind." Gregory urged his colleagues onward with promise of better days ahead: "*The Stylus* is on the right track although like all bearers of Truth they are in a minority for a day. Theirs are the future years, rich with the promise of a fulfilment of the visions of those whose love for their race embraces humanity."[12] *Stylus* reserved further statements for future years. The third number, to be discussed later, did not appear until 1929.

Du Bois lent his name to *Stylus,* but he was not much impressed with the journal. He mentioned it only once in *Crisis,* and then with faint praise. "The poems of Otto Bohanan seem to be the only notable contributions," he asserted about the publication in 1916. Du Bois did not say so, but *Stylus* launched the careers of writers much more influential than Bohanan. Probably the most outstanding student published in the journal during its early years was Zora Hurston. In her autobiography, *Dust Tracks on a Road,* she traced her literary career from her involvement in the Howard group. She explained how Charles Johnson, who was then planning the first issue of *Opportunity,* read a short story of hers included in *Stylus* and asked her to contribute to his magazine. Hurston sent him "Drenched in Light," which he published. Later he published a second story, "Spunk," and counselled her to move to Harlem, which he considered the hub of literary activity. Hurston responded enthusiastically to his promptings: "So, beginning to feel the urge to write, I wanted to be in New York."[13] *Stylus* also served as the testing ground for Locke. From his editorial experience at Howard, he went on to involve himself in the more significant black journals of the 1920s. He related well to numerous, often conflicting groups and became the most ubiquitous Afro-American literary presence in that period.

The Harlem number of *Survey Graphic* appeared in March 1925, edited by Locke. Contemporaries applauded Locke for his role but then dickered over who gave Paul Kellogg, editor of the magazine, the idea for the issue. Du Bois claimed the credit for his own staff. At the Civic Club Dinner of March 21, 1924, he explained, Kellogg had sat next to Augustus Dill, business manager of *Crisis,* who acquainted him with those in attendance. Then "it occurred to the editor of *The Survey,*" wrote Du Bois, "that here was material for a *Survey Graphic.*" Despite his own cautions, "still he hesitated and feared the 'social uplifters' of the United States with a mighty fear," he acted on the inspiration encouraged by Dill and went ahead with plans for the special issue.[14]

Charles S. Johnson saw it differently, as indicated in a speech made in 1955 at Howard University. He explained that Locke had written a series of important essays for *Opportunity,* variously entitled "The Black Watch on the Rhine" (1921), "Apropos of Africa" (1924), and "Back Stage on European Imperialism" (1925). Johnson found the essays so insightful that he offered to share publication with *Survey Graphic* in order to find them a larger audience. Kellogg gladly published the articles at hand and requested further essays from Locke. "Thus began," declared Johnson, "an important relationship with the editor of the *Survey* and *Survey Graphic.*" At the Civic Club affair, which Johnson carefully distinguished as an *Opportunity* dinner, Kellogg asked Locke to edit an issue of *Graphic* which would "carry the entire evening's readings."[15] Johnson does deserve a large share of the credit, since ideas for the number originated during the occasion he had staged, and since the editor was the essayist he had introduced to Kellogg.

The catchword in the issue became "Harlem," with essays, stories, poems, and drawings considering life in that urban center. The cover of the number bore the designation, "Harlem: Mecca of the New Negro." In the lead editorial, entitled "Harlem," and in another article, Locke ascended the scale to near religious ecstacy, labeling the area "a race capital," "the sign and center of

the renaissance of a people," and finally, "the home of the Negro's 'Zionism.'" In Harlem, he believed, "the masses" would lead black writers toward the making of a vital folk literature. "In a real sense," he noted, "it is the rank and file who are leading, and the leaders who are following. A transformed and transforming psychology permeates the masses."[16] With such an emphasis, Locke enunciated ideas which would become increasingly prevalent throughout the decade and which would emerge, recast, as dominant in the 1930s with the pronouncements of Richard Wright and others.

Locke reinforced his ideas with an essay by James Weldon Johnson, "The Making of Harlem"; an essay by Konrad Bercovici, "The Rhythm of Harlem"; with portraits by the German artist, Winold Reiss, on "Harlem Types"; with seven well-wrought poems by Countee Cullen on "Harlem Life"; and with "The South Lingers On," sketches of life in Harlem by Rudolph Fisher. The south lingered in the new migrants, in Jake Crinshaw who came from "Jennin's Landin'," Virginia, in unsuccessful pursuit of work in Harlem, in Reverend Ezekiel Taylor who followed his congregation north—"But where were they?"—in a grandmother who thinks her Jutie has lost her soul in Harlem, "this city of Satan."[17]

Another slogan in the issue was "the New Negro." After "Harlem," the Table of Contents listed Locke's essay, "Enter the New Negro." Revised, the piece became the lead article in Locke's edition of *The New Negro.* "Enter the New Negro" illustrates the balanced prose and memorable phrases Locke used to capture the attention of his contemporaries. Gone, he declared, is the "Old Negro," who was more fiction than actuality: "The day of 'aunties,' 'uncles' and 'mammies' is equally gone. Uncle Tom and Sambo have passed on, and even the 'Colonel' and 'George' play barnstorm roles from which they escape with relief when the public spotlight is off. The popular melodrama has about played itself out, and it is time to scrap the fictions, garret the bogeys and settle down to a realistic facing of facts." The facts included a "younger generation . . . vibrant with a new psychology," a black population "awake" in a "new spirit." The awakened generation was conscious, he explained, of being "the advance-guard of the African peoples in their contact with Twentieth Century civilization."[18]

He wrote again about the New Negro in "Youth Speaks," an essay printed midway in the issue. In expanding upon his ideas, he entered headlong into the controversy over art and propaganda. He talked about literary pioneers—Du Bois, along with Chesnutt, Dunbar, James Weldon Johnson, Lucian Watkins, and others—and said they had spoken "for the Negro," meaning they had tried to interpret the race to others. The new generation wrote instead "as Negroes" and attempted to express the quality of Afro-American life to

Afro-Americans. Thus had come "the happy release from self-consciousness, rhetoric, bombast, and the hampering habit of setting artistic values with primary regard for moral effect." Among the New Negroes were Rudolph Fisher, Willis Richardson, Eric Walrond, and the young poets published on the very next pages, including Countee Cullen, Langston Hughes, Claude McKay, and Jean Toomer.[19]

The issue featured a heady sampling of those influential in interracial circles. There were essays from Melville Herskovitz, the cultural anthropologist; Arthur Schomburg, who was establishing his collection of books on black history and culture; Walter White, who was assistant secretary of the NAACP. The number also included an essay by Charles S. Johnson, on "Black Workers and the City," and a piece by Du Bois, called "The Black Man Brings His Gifts." Du Bois used an ironic style, by then familiar to *Crisis* readers. He developed a story to illustrate the pretensions of some white midwesterners who believe they have the best of everything. "We've got a pretty fine town out here in middle Indiana," the white persona declares at the beginning of the story. When told of the contributions blacks had made to American life, she and her friends become huffy and shun the speakers, who include a white professor and an educated black woman. The persona confides to the reader that the ideas of the black speaker especially "made me sick and I turned and glared right at her."[20]

The Harlem number of *Survey Graphic* was important for several reasons. The issue sold over 40,000 copies, thereby establishing a circulation record which the magazine did not match until the 1940s. The number led immediately to Locke's *The New Negro*, which was published by Boni in the fall of 1925 as an expanded form of the issue. The book was also significant, considered by Charles S. Johnson to be the "standard volume of the period," "the portal to a new world of adventure."[21] The editors of *Messenger* praised the Harlem number of the magazine for something far less tangible, for "the spirit which gave it birth." They saw in it the sign of a new day, as expressed in an editorial for April 1925: "It marks an interesting turn in the attitude of intellectual white America toward the Negroes. It was planned by black and white intellectuals. This is as it should be." Writing much later, in his study of Paul Kellogg, Clarke Chambers emphasized the uniqueness of the magazine: "In focusing on the contributions rather than the problems of the American Negro, in stressing the constructive cultural advances emerging in Harlem, in using Negro authors and critics to set forth the truths of the Negro renaissance, the *Survey Graphic* was far ahead of its time. Other journals might publish sympathetic articles now and again, but the *Graphic's* adventure stands alone as a classic account."[22]

The Harlem number was unique, but it did not stand alone in the 1920s. By its example, it encouraged other magazines to feature issues on black literature and life. In October 1926, Idella Purnell and her associate editor, Witter Bynner, published a special number of *Palms,* a poetry journal issued six times a year from Guadalajara.[23] The October table of contents carried this statement: "Countee Cullen is the editor of this issue of *Palms* which is entirely the work of Negro poets." The comment was apt in that the emphasis was on black poets rather than on black poetry. The writers included the best of the day: Lewis Alexander, Gwendolyn Bennett, Arna Bontemps, William Braithwaite, Countee Cullen, W. E. B. Du Bois, Jessie Fauset, Langston Hughes, Helene Johnson, and Bruce Nugent. Most of them wrote about love and nature, not about topics specifically pertinent to Afro-American readers. The first stanza of Du Bois's "Poem" did not, for example, run true to his customary ejaculations:

> O Star-kissed drifting from above,
> On misty moonbeams, sunshine shod,
> Dim daughter of the lips of God,
> To me and angels—Thou art Love!

Two other verses followed, one addressed to Life and the other to Truth.

There were exceptions in the issue, such as the other poem by Du Bois. In "The Song of America," Du Bois sounded a familiar theme, as a few lines from the persona, the U.S.A., indicate: "I writhe, I rave, / To chain the slave / I do the deed, I kill!" The most notable exception was "Black Madonna," by Albert Rice. The particular emphasis emerged clearly in the first two stanzas:

> Not as the white nations
>   know thee
>   O Mother!
>
> But swarthy of cheek
>   and full-lipped as the
>   child races are.[24]

Du Bois liked the composition so much that he published it, along with an announcement of the *Palms* issue, in the November 1926 *Crisis*. In the next number, he reprinted Braithwaite's "Age and Autumn," one of the best-crafted poems in the October *Palms*.

The special issue of *Palms* figures in the cultural renaissance of the 1920s. It publicized contemporary work with two timely essays: a discussion of "The Negro Renaissance" by Walter White, and a favorable review of Hughes's *The Weary Blues,* by Alain Locke.[25] It encouraged the best from young writers with two poetry contests open to anyone who cared to apply. As announced in *Palms,* Langston Hughes won the Witter Bynner Undergraduate Poetry Prize Award for 1926, as well as the John Keats Prize one year later. In her *Opportunity* column, "Ebony Flute," Gwendolyn Bennett acknowledged Hughes's award and reminded readers that they could still enter the Witter Bynner competition for 1927. In retrospect she declared that "of no small importance was the Negro issue of *Palms*."[26] The number not only provided further support for black writers, but it also indicated the widespread interest in Afro-American literature.

With their literary journal, *Carolina Magazine,* the students at the University of North Carolina gave further testimony to that interest. They published a "Negro Number" in May 1927, a "Negro Poetry Number" in May 1928, and a "Negro Play Number" in April 1929. The editors, who changed with each new year, received materials for each special issue from Lewis Alexander, a poet, an actor, and a member of both the Washington Saturday Nighters and the Quill Club of Boston. Alexander managed to include most writers who had been published in other black magazines and issues, save for Du Bois, who did not appear in any of the numbers. He clearly favored the efforts of Charles S. Johnson, whom he identified as the founder of *Opportunity,* "the ablest Negro journal in America." Johnson wrote the lead article, "The Negro Enters Literature," for the 1927 issue and one of the featured essays, "Jazz Poetry and Blues," for the 1928 number.[27] The lead article for the "Negro Poetry Number" of May 1928 was Alain Locke's "The Message of the Negro Poets."

The underlying theme in the essays of both Johnson and Locke was that New Negro poets had gained immeasurably by leaving the old propaganda emphases behind. Both men echoed statements they had made elsewhere. Locke's commentary, for example, recalled opinions he had asserted in *Survey Graphic* and made basic to *The New Negro*: "Yesterday it was the rhetorical flush of partisanship, challenged and on the defensive. This was the patriotic stage through which we had to pass. Nothing is more of a spiritual gain in the life of the Negro than the quieter assumption of his group identity and heritage; and contemporary Negro poetry registers this incalculable artistic and social gain."[28]

Some of the plays, stories, and poems included characters and situations which would not have been acceptable to Du Bois or others concerned with respectability. "The Hunch," a play by Eulalie Spence, gave a lesson in the numbers game:

MRS. REED.

Ah dream Ed an' me—Ed's mah fus husband—Ah dream Ed an' me was lyin' in bed—

MITCHELL.

Is he dead?

MRS. REED.

Bin dead five years.

MITCHELL.

That's 9.

MRS. REED.

The door opened an' in walks Joe, mah secon' husban'—Lookin' mad tuh kill.

MITCHELL.

Is he dead, too?

MRS. REED.

Yeah. Died las' year.

MITCHELL.

That's 2. Your number's 295. Play the combination an' yuh can't lose.[29]

Hughes, represented by several poems, wrote about a "Boy" who preferred to be "a sinner . . . and go to hell," about a "Boy on Beale Street" who lost his dream in "dice and women / And jazz and booze," and about an "African Dancer in Paris" who traded her native lover "for coins of gold." Waring Cuney sang the blues about "Once Bad Gal":

> Ah'd go straight if
> Ah thought Ah could,
> Say Ah'd go straight
> If Ah thought Ah could,
> But a once bad gal
> Can't never be good.[30]

Alexander put together the special issues by relying extensively on prizewinning literature from the *Crisis* and especially the *Opportunity* literary contests. The May 1927 number carried such pieces from *Opportunity* in each of the major genres: Arthur Huff Fauset's "Symphonesque" had placed first in the short story section for 1926; Helene Johnson's "Fulfillment" was first honorable mention in the poetry division for the same year; and Spence's "The Hunch" took second place in the 1927 drama competition. The editorial for the April 1929 issue identified the playwrights—Eulalie Spence, Willis Richardson, John F. Matheus, and May Miller—by their previous success: "All won prizes in *The Crisis* and *Opportunity* contests." In the same number, Alexander reflected on the meaning of those competitions, since they had by then ceased. "The contests and prizes offered reassured the race writers that it was worth while," he explained; "for some of them . . . had been writing a decade or more with little or no attention at all. The new spirit of the contests reincarnated the old writers and moved aspiring young dreamers to take up their pens and write."[31]

Crisis never acknowledged the compliment. In the November 1929 issue, Du Bois simply mentioned the drama number and then added that it included a drawing by Aaron Douglas "done for *The Crisis* and reprinted without credit." *Opportunity* responded graciously, with several laudatory reviews of the special issues. In June and July of 1927, Countee Cullen and Gwendolyn Bennett wrote in a similar vein about North Carolina University and the black number for that year. Cullen, in June, called the school and its journal "oases in that barren land," while Bennett praised the institution for its "fine liberality of thought." By July, both had recognized the number as a pioneering effort. Cullen spoke at greater length than Bennett, saying the May *Carolina Magazine* was "a number of historical importance in race relations in this country. For the first time, as it were, in the time of man, a Southern university magazine has given over one of its numbers to the work of Negro writers."[32]

Cullen was particularly impressed because he recalled an ugly episode he had written about in the December 1926 installment of "Dark Tower." He had noted that Julian Starr and R. K. Fowler, "erstwhile" editors of *Carolina Magazine,* had been "deposed" in 1926 for publishing a story having a white girl and a mulatto as principal characters. The incident had seemed, to Cullen, an immense step backward: "And this just after we had been turning double somersaults and triple handsprings because that same issue carried a sketch by Eric Walrond, along with a pronunciamento asking for contributions from people of all races, colors, creeds, and political leanings!"[33]

For some time, there had been students and teachers at North Carolina University interested in black literature and folklore. The special numbers of *Carolina Magazine* stressed this interest, describing it as part of a rich cultural legacy. The dedication to the May 1928 number called it "fitting" that the journal should feature black poetry. One of the earliest Afro-American poets, George Horton, had been a familiar figure on campus, and one of the New Negroes represented in the issue, Donald Hayes, was a native of Raleigh, North Carolina. In the April 1929 number, Lewis Alexander stated that "it is quite fitting" for the magazine to emphasize black drama, "for the University of North Carolina, thru [*sic*] its organization The Carolina Playmakers has done more for the development of the folk play in America than any other University." He urged students at North Carolina to remain true to the example set by Paul Green, a native North Carolinian who wrote *In Abraham's Bosom*; Professor Howard Odum, who edited the *Journal of Social Forces,* which was published at the University and which included several timely articles on black culture; and, among others, Newman I. White and Walter C. Jackson, editors of the *Anthology of Verse by American Negroes* published by Trinity College Press of Durham, North Carolina.[34]

Much of the excitement of the period appears in the black little magazines, which came in the second half of the 1920s, as did the special issues from journals with white management. The little magazines represented a new stage in the evolution of Afro-American culture. In the past, political and organizational concerns had dominated purely literary interests. After World War I the emerging generation sensed opportunities never seriously considered by earlier generations, partly because of the groundwork done by the NAACP and the NUL. To many New Negroes it seemed no very difficult matter to launch an entirely new type of black periodical, one concerned primarily with the arts. In November 1926, Wallace Thurman broke with tradition and issued *Fire*. As the first black magazine that was both independent and essentially literary, *Fire* deserves a place in surveys of American cultural history. It has been excluded from most studies of the 1920s, however, and mentioned only briefly in the others. Nathan Huggins, for example, took just two paragraphs to label *Fire* as a "short-lived" journal, one of "Harlem's attempts" at a little magazine.[35] One of the few to comment at length and with insight about the journal is Langston Hughes, who discussed it in *Big Sea* and in an article published later.

In his recollections he paused fondly over memories of Sugar Hill, in Harlem. At 409 Edgecombe, the address of the "tallest apartment house" on the hill, lived Walter and Gladys White, who gave frequent parties for their friends; Aaron and Alta Douglas, who "always had a bottle of ginger ale in the ice box for those who brought along refreshments"; Elmer Anderson Carter, who succeeded Charles S. Johnson as editor of *Opportunity*; and actor Ivan Sharpe and his wife Evie. Just below the hill, in the Dunbar Apartments, lived W. E. B. Du Bois as well as E. Simms Campbell, the cartoonist. Nearby was Dan Burley, a black journalist and a boogie-woogie piano player. Hughes recalled the excitement of those days: "Artists and writers were always running into each other on Sugar Hill and talking over their problems" and the ways to fellowships and grants from benevolent organizations. One evening, Hughes and six friends gathered in the Aaron Douglas apartment and made plans for a literary magazine. Hughes remembered their motives, saying generally that they wanted "to express" themselves "freely and independently—without interference from old heads, white or Negro," and specifically that they hoped "to provide . . . an outlet for publishing not existing in the hospitable but limited pages of *The Crisis* or *Opportunity*." They readily divided responsibilities for the new magazine, establishing Wallace Thurman as editor, Aaron Douglas as artist and designer, John P. Davis as business manager, and Gwendolyn Bennett, Zora Hurston, Bruce Nugent, and Hughes as the other board members.

They selected *Fire* as a title because, in Hughes's words, they desired to "*épater le bourgeois,* to burn up a lot of the old stereotyped Uncle Tom ideas of the past. . . ."[36]

Hughes did not expand further on the meaning of the name, which merits brief examination. It represented a significant contrast with the quieter labels, such as "Colored American Magazine" and "Voice of the Negro," appearing in earlier generations. It broke as well with the import of "Crisis," which suggested that a crucial moment must be met, and "Opportunity," which implied that possibilities were at hand for the observant black. *Fire!!* with two exclamation marks in the full title, sounded an alarm that the old way would be destroyed in preparation for a new world.

The group was confident, even though members had little money of their own and no benefactors in sight. They planned to share expenses, with each of the seven contributing an initial fifty dollars. The bills mounted quickly as the board selected an expensive format. Hughes noted that "only the best cream-white paper would do on which to print our poems and stories. And only a rich crimson jacket on de luxe stock would show off well the Aaron Douglas cover design." As it turned out, Thurman became responsible for the expenses since he, with a job at *World Tomorrow,* was the only one who had steady although hardly profitable employment. Thurman wrote to Hughes that "*Fire* is certainly burning me,"[37] and Hughes wondered how the number ever left the printer's office, "how Thurman was able to persuade the printer to release the entire issue to us on so small an advance payment." The available funds went to the printer, thereby leaving no money for advertising or distributing the journal. The board hoped that the magazine would quickly attract a loyal constituency who would assure solvency and a second number. They quietly asked for help on the first page of the issue: "Being a non-commercial product interested only in the arts, it is necessary that we make some appeal for aid from interested friends. For the second issue of FIRE we would appreciate having fifty people subscribe ten dollars each, and fifty more to subscribe five dollars each. We make no eloquent or rhetorical plea. FIRE speaks for itself."[38]

After November 1926, *Fire* never reappeared. "When the editorial board of *Fire* met again, we did not plan a new issue," Hughes narrated, "but emptied our pockets to help poor Thurman whose wages were being garnished weekly because he had signed for the printer's bills." Thurman's wages continued to be "garnished" for three or four more years, even after "the bulk of the whole issue" burned to ashes in the basement of the apartment in which it was stored.[39]

The end was ironic, particularly because fire had been the unifying metaphor in the periodical. Thurman autographed special copies with "Flamingly, Wallace Thurman." The "Foreword," with its provocative challenge, established the dominant motif:

FIRE . . . flaming, burning, searing, and penetrating far beneath the superficial items of the flesh to boil the sluggish blood.

FIRE . . . a cry of conquest in the night, warning those who sleep and revitalizing those who linger in the quiet places dozing.

FIRE . . . melting steel and iron bars, poking livid tongues between stone apertures and burning wooden opposition with a cackling chuckle of contempt.

FIRE . . . weaving vivid, hot designs upon an ebon bordered loom and satisfying pagan thirst for beauty unadorned . . . the flesh is sweet and real . . . the soul an inward flush of fire. . . . Beauty? . . . flesh on fire—on fire in the furnace of life blazing. . . .

> Fy-ah,
> Fy-ah, Lawd,
> Fy-ah gonna burn ma soul![40]

The poetry section announced itself with the title from Countee Cullen's poem and appeared as "Flame From The Dark Tower." The issue concluded with "A Department of Comment" by Thurman, called "Fire Burns."

Thurman indicated the literary aesthetic behind the magazine in his comments. He began by recalling his controversial review of *Nigger Heaven,* published two months earlier in *Messenger.* Instead of being honored with a statue on 135th Street and Seventh Avenue, he explained, Van Vechten had become a likely candidate for a lynching. The wheel would revolve in a few years and Van Vechten, he predicted, would then be "spoken of as a kindly gent rather than as a moral leper." For the time being, Thurman ridiculed the detractors of *Nigger Heaven* and cried freedom for black writers: "Any author preparing to write about Negroes in Harlem or anywhere else . . . should take whatever phases of their life that seem the most interesting to him, and develop them as he please."[41]

As author and editor, Thurman was primarily interested in aspects of black life generally considered disreputable by the more proper Afro-Americans, as his inclusions in *Fire* indicate. The three short stories featured characters falling far short of standards dear to the bourgeoisie, both black and white. "Cordelia the Crude: A Harlem Sketch," by Thurman, followed directly after the table of contents and Bruce Nugent's drawing of a naked African woman. The story traces the development of "a fus' class chippie," from the italicized first word of the opening sentence: "*Physically,* if not mentally, Cordelia was a potential prostitute, meaning that although she had not yet realized the moral import of her wanton promiscuity nor become mercenary, she had, nevertheless, become quite blasé and bountiful in the matter of bestowing sexual favors upon persuasive and likely young men." Later in the issue came Gwendolyn Bennett's "Wedding Day," which portrays the unsuccessful relationship between a black boxer and a white prostitute; and Zora Hurston's "Sweat," which tells the tragic end of Sykes, a loafer who loses everything, including his life, because of an obsession with fat black women: "Gawd! how Ah hates skinny wimmen!"[42]

The number also included the first part of a novel, "Smoke, Lilies and Jade," by Bruce Nugent writing under the pseudonym of Richard Bruce. In his narration, Nugent detailed the amours of bisexual black artist Alex, known to his male lover Adrian (alias Beauty) as Duce. One scene, involving an interracial relationship, particularly violated the sensibilities of the middle class on both sides of the color line: "Alex ran his hand through Beauty's hair . . . Beauty's lips pressed hard against his teeth . . . Alex trembled . . . could feel Beauty's body . . . close against his . . . hot . . . tense . . . white . . . and soft . . . soft . . . soft. . . ."[43] No other black literary magazine had previously included an explicit portrayal of a homosexual affair.

The poetry section, headed by Cullen's "From the Dark Tower," included "Elevator Boy," a controversial poem by Langston Hughes. The selection bothered many, because the protagonist showed no evidence of the American work ethic: "I been runnin' this / Elevator too long. / Guess I'll quit now." "Flame From the Dark Tower" featured other poets worthy of comment, such as Lewis Alexander, Arna Bontemps, Waring Cuney, Helene Johnson, and Edward Silvera. Alexander contributed two poems, one of them about a prostitute ironically called "Little Cinderella," a girl who did not wait for her prince:

> Look me over, kid!
> I knows I'm neat,—
> Little Cinderella from head to feet.
> Drinks all night at Club Alabam,—
> What comes next I don't give a damn! . . .[44]

Reaction to *Fire* were mixed. As Hughes noted, the white-owned press largely ignored the journal. An exception was *Bookman*, which reviewed the periodical in November 1926. In *Big Sea*, Hughes called that appraisal "excellent," an adjective he wisely removed from his subsequent discussion of the same material. The *Bookman* review shifted in tone, telling blacks first to lift themselves into the middle class by their own bootstraps and then suggesting that Afro-American writing should be separate and distinct from "American literature." The anonymous author, perhaps editor John Farrar, initially commended *Fire* for appearing "at a time when the Negro shows ominous signs of settling down to become a good American." He continued: "As the Negro begins more and more to measure up to the white yardstick of achievement, he will gain a merited position in American society." By his conclusion, the

reviewer was complimenting *Fire* for encouraging "separate but equal" in the arts: "It is to be hoped that he [the black writer] will find in this new Negro quarterly the thing he needs to keep his artistic individuality."[45]

Fire brought a greater response from black magazines and reviewers. *Opportunity* endorsed the journal enthusiastically, as it did the other black little magazines of the period. Cullen, in the January 1927 issue of "Dark Tower," suggested that the journal would offend only the unsophisticated: "There seems to have been a wish to shock in this first issue, and, though shock-proof ourselves, we imagine that the wish will be well realized among the readers of *Fire*." He called the journal "the outstanding birth of the month" and looked to the future with anticipation: "This sort of success," particularly the contributions of Hurston and Aaron Douglas, "augurs good for the development of Negro artists." Gwendolyn Bennett wrote in the same month, with the same opinion as Cullen's, but with more temperate phrasing. She undoubtedly felt constrained in using her position at *Opportunity* to trumpet her concerns elsewhere. Thus, she simply defined *Fire* as "the new literary venture of the newer Negroes," and as a quarterly which had been "hailed with enthusiasm." She kept silent about her own involvement in the journal. "To Wallace Thurman goes the praise for the editorship of this first number," she declared.[46]

Crisis did not have so much to say about *Fire*. Hughes claimed that "Dr. Du Bois in the *Crisis* roasted it," although he provided no supporting quotation. Hughes remembered inexactly, probably because he and others had wanted and expected Du Bois to respond with indignation. "As we had hoped—even though it contained no four-letter words as do today's little magazines—the Negro bourgeoisie were shocked by *Fire*," Hughes recalled. In his January 1927 review of the magazine, Du Bois showed that he was still capable of surprising contemporaries who tried to push him to the periphery of artistic circles. He graciously accepted the magazine: "We acknowledge the receipt of the first number of *Fire* 'devoted to Younger Negro Artists.'" He praised the format and the contributions by Douglas: "It is strikingly illustrated by Aaron Douglas and is a beautiful piece of printing." And he even endorsed the publication: "We bespeak for it wide support."[47]

Some unexpected criticism came later in the year from Alain Locke, who reviewed the magazine in *Survey*, August 15-September 15, 1927. Ever the diplomat, Locke commended before he corrected. He began with a statement which would please Thurman and the others, saying that with *Fire*, "the youth section of the New Negro movement has marched off in a gay and self-confident manoeuver of artistic secession." "Obvious artistic cousins" of the journal were, he observed, the *Little Review,* edited by Margaret Anderson, and the *Quill,* a magazine of Greenwich Village. Then he came to the sore point. True, *Fire* was "a charging brigade of literary revolt, especially against the bulwarks of Puritanism," but it raised the wrong standard. Simply put, *Fire* exceeded Locke's limits: "If Negro life is to provide a healthy antidote to Puritanism, and to become one of the effective instruments of sound artistic progress, its flesh values must more and more be expressed in the clean, original, primitive but fundamental terms of the senses and not, as too often in this particular issue of Fire, in hectic imitation of the 'naughty nineties' and effete echoes of contemporary decadence."[48]

The commentary appeared eight months after Hughes had sent his own bemused reactions to bourgeois readers in a note to Locke, dated December 28, 1926. He chortled over the review in the *Afro-American,* especially the part saying that at least Locke had been left out of the magazine. Under the heading, "Writer Brands Fire as Effeminate Tommyrot," Rean Graves of the Baltimore *Afro-American* had declared: "I have just tossed the first issue of Fire—into the fire, and watched the cackling flames leap and snarl as though they were trying to swallow some repulsive dose."[49]

Benjamin Brawley provided the most hostile review in "The Negro Literary Renaissance," published in the April 1927 issue of the *Southern Workman.* He did not believe black writers and artists were undergoing any especial awakening, even though promise was shown in the efforts of Claude McKay, Jean Toomer, Eric Walrond, and Walter White. The sign of the times appeared in jazz, "a perverted form of music," and in *Fire,* a magazine he considered the work of decadent loafers, not artists at all. By way of example, he quoted a passage from "Smoke, Lilies and Jade." "I certainly hope the compositor will set it up exactly as we give it to him," he added:

> he wondered why he couldn't find work . . . a job . . . when he had first come to New York he had . . . and he had only been fourteen then was it because he was nineteen now that he felt so idle . . . and contented . . . or because he was an artist . . . but was he an artist . . . was one an artist until one became known . . . of course he was an artist . . . and strangely enough so were all his friends . . . he should be ashamed that he didn't work . . . but . . . was it five years in New York . . . or the fact that he was an artist . . .

About "Cordelia the Crude," he claimed it "ought not to have been written, to say nothing of being published"; about Hughes's "Elevator Boy," he "submit[ted] simply that the running of an elevator is perfectly honorable employment and that no one with such a job should leave it until he is reasonably sure of getting

something better." The last paragraph expended on *Fire* gave his summary comment: "About this unique periodical the only thing to say is that if Uncle Sam ever finds out about it, it will be debarred from the mails."[50]

Thurman commented on the outrage over *Fire* in "Negro Artists and the Negro," an essay published in the August 1927 number of *New Republic.* He explained, essentially, that the more conservative readers had been shocked once too often, first by *Nigger Heaven* and then by *Fine Clothes to the Jew,* "a hard, realistic" volume of poems by Hughes. The latter book appeared when "Negroes were still rankling" from *Nigger Heaven* and thereby uncovered "a store of suppressed invective that not only lashed Mr. Van Vechten and Mr. Hughes, but also the editors and contributors to Fire." The magazine was "experimental," noted Thurman, who went on to define the term for those confused about the magazine: "It was not interested in sociological problems or propaganda. It was purely artistic in intent and conception. Its contributors went to the proletariat rather than to the bourgeoisie for characters and material." Unlike Jessie Fauset and Walter White, those contributors were interested in black Americans, not Negroes who were "totally white American in every respect save color of skin."[51]

As the ashes settled, some of the younger writers began to think of a new journal. And thus Zora Hurston turned to Alain Locke, whose reputation survived intact from the *Fire* controversy. In a letter to him, dated October 11, 1927, she touched on the past lightly, saying *Fire* had been a good idea which failed for lack of "better management." In surveying the present, she reiterated complaints heard previously about *Crisis* and *Opportunity,* that they were "house organ[s]" of political groups and were consequently "in literature" only "on the side." Before soliciting his aid, she asked him a rhetorical question: "Dont you think . . . that it is not good that there should be only two outlets for Negro fire?" She followed with another question, posing an intriguing triumvirate: "Why cant our triangle—Locke—Hughes—Hurston do something with you at the apex?" She concluded with a statement which flattered but which also gave testimony to Locke's influence among diverse literary circles: "I am certain that you can bind groups with more ease than any other man in America." "Will you think it over?" she added.[52]

The "triangle" never did get together. Locke had too many responsibilities with his writing and his work at Howard, which included sponsorship of *Stylus,* a magazine needing some attention. Hughes was no longer interested, for the demise of *Fire* had educated him in the ways of literary periodicals: "That taught me a lesson about little magazines. But since white folks had them, we Negroes thought we could have one, too. But we didn't have the money." And then a member outside the threesome was already setting the basis for another journal.

After the collapse of *Fire,* Thurman "laughed a long bitter laugh," Hughes remembered, and set to work again.[53] Determined to avoid problems that had ended *Fire,* he planned for a journal that both looked professional and lasted. He secured an office on Seventh Avenue and peopled it with young writers who wanted to handle the business affairs of the journal. He kept the managing board small, with himself as editor of the magazine, Aaron Douglas as art editor, and S. Pace Alexander as managing editor. He tried to repair communication with influential persons disturbed by *Fire.* In a letter of October 3, 1928, sent on *Harlem* letterhead stationery, he asked Locke to support the venture with a short article "of some kind" for the first number. He assured Locke that *Harlem* would be no *Fire.* He described the effort as a "general magazine," with all types of literature, creative and critical, and for all kinds of people: "We are not confining ourselves to any group either of age or race." The journal would, though, fill a gap left by the larger race journals: "The Crisis and The Messenger are dead. Opportunity is dying. Voila here comes Harlem, independent, fearless and general, trying to appeal to all." Thurman had not fully considered his plans, as his unlikely conjunction of "fearless" with "general" indicated. Of one matter, however, he was sure: "I am mighty glad of the chance to be able to edit a magazine and let someone else worry about the financial end, in fact, after Fire, that is the only way I would ever venture forth again."

Locke responded with a letter dated October 8. He was "committed" to the new magazine, he said, because "dear friends," whom he did not specify, were promoting it. Then, too, he agreed with Thurman over the need for an "independent journal—especially a journal that will recognize that there is more than one side to most issues." He would contribute to the first issue with an article called "Art or Propaganda,—Which?"[54]

Thurman carefully organized the one and only issue of *Harlem,* published in November 1928. He alternated the essays, which explicitly indicated the focus of the magazine, with poems, stories, and illustrations. As if to emphasize the contrast between *Harlem* and his previous little magazine, he started the issue with a political discussion he had solicited from Walter White. At the onset of his essay, "For Whom Shall the Negro Vote?" White quoted from Thurman's letter to him, which had asked for an examination of "the dilemma of Negro voters today—surveying the attitude of the old guard toward loyalty to the Republican party and the attitude of another group which is openly advocating a bolt from the traditional party of our fathers." In his analy-sis, White adopted a moderate, well-balanced tone, seemingly in keeping with Thurman's approach to his new journal. He acknowledged great inadequacies in Al Smith and Herbert Hoover, candidates for the United States presidency, but he did not call for new political parties. Seeing that black voters held a balance of power in about ten states, he urged them to "trade ballots for justice," to make white candidates listen to the needs of black people.[55]

After the political discussion came artistic considerations, including a story by Hughes, a poem by Helene Johnson, and the essay from Locke. With diplomacy, Locke considered the most debatable aesthetic matter of the times, and from the opening sentence: "Artistically it is the one fundamental question for us today,—Art or Propaganda. Which?" The query was rhetorical to anyone who had read Locke's earlier pronouncements. He asserted that "After Beauty, let Truth come into the Renaissance picture,—a later cue, but a welcome one." He distinguished between truth and propaganda, saying that the latter is monotonous and that it encourages feelings of "group inferiority even in crying out against it." Metaphors followed theory, with Locke comparing Afro-American propagandists with "too many Jeremiahs" occupying too much "drab wilderness." He likened the larger black journals to Jeremiahs and the black little magazines to David, confronting the Philistines with confidence and with "five smooth pebbles." He thought *Harlem* could be a most valuable magazine if it developed as "a sustained vehicle of free and purely artistic expression."[56]

The editorial came midway in the issue, after Locke had calmly discussed the matter of art and propaganda. Thurman considered the same issue in a basically similar way, echoing some of Locke's imagery and much of his approach. He sketched the history of black magazines, beginning with "the old propagandistic journals," such as *Crisis, Opportunity,* and *Messenger,* which had served their day but were "emotionally unprepared to serve a new day and a new generation." They had been "Jeremiahs," either "alarmed and angry," or "weeping and moaning." All they could offer the aspiring young writer was an occasional page, "but the artist was not satisfied to be squeezed between jeremiads or have his work thrown haphazardly upon a page where there was no effort to make it look beautiful as well as sound beautiful." The only recourse, until the latter 1920s, was the white press. Few blacks, though, would continually buy "white magazines" in order to read an occasional poem or story by an Afro-American writer.[57]

In 1926, *Fire* seemed to herald a new era. As Thurman remembered, it "was the pioneer of the movement. It flamed for one issue and caused a sensation the like of which had never been known in Negro journalism before." Wisely, he did not elaborate on the "sensation" but went on to credit more moderate magazines which had since developed—*Black Opals* in Philadelphia, "a more conservative yet extremely worthwhile venture," and the *Saturday Evening Quill* in Boston, published by and for members of a literary group. These little magazines had problems, however, as Thurman so well recalled: "The art magazines, unsoundly financed as they were, could not last."

With *Harlem,* Thurman thought he had the formula for success. He would lower his own profile, become relaxed, genial, tolerant. The magazine "enters the field without any preconceived editorial prejudices, without intolerance, without a reformer's cudgel," he told readers. He stated his goal with modesty, saying the journal "wants merely to be a forum in which all people's opinions may be presented intelligently and from which the Negro can gain some universal idea of what is going on in the world of thought and art."[58] He subtitled the magazine, "A Forum of Negro Life."

Thurman was not so balanced in his other contributions which appeared later in the number, after poems by Georgia Douglas Johnson, Alice Dunbar Nelson, and Effie Lee Newsome, a story by George Little, and essays by Theophilus Lewis and Bruce Nugent. When tucked into the back of the issue, Thurman felt free to be outspoken and controversial. He attacked the aesthetics of Du Bois in a review ostensibly directed towards *The Walls of Jericho,* by Rudolph Fisher, and *Quicksand,* by Nella Larsen. In the opening paragraph, he recalled that Du Bois had criticized Fisher in *Crisis* for not portraying the people he knew best, the "better class Negroes." Thurman had "chanced" upon the review, which "set my teeth on edge and sent me back to my typewriter hopping mad." He thought Du Bois ought to have known better, to have realized that "the entire universe is the writer's province." Du Bois had served his race "so well," asserted Thurman, "that the artist in him has been stifled in order that the propagandist may thrive." Thurman also came to the next novelist through a consideration first of Du Bois: "The author of *Quicksand* no doubt pleases Dr. Du Bois for she stays in her own sphere and writes about the sort of people one can invite to one's home without losing one's social prestige."[59]

Thurman was unrestrained in the "Harlem Directory: Where To Go And What To Do When in Harlem," included among the advertisements in the last pages. The initial line, with its neat parallelism, surely offended the same persons shocked by *Fire.* "There are four main attractions in Harlem," he announced with some glee: "the churches, the gin mills, the restaurants, and the night clubs," which he considered in order. He went for the exotic in churches, listing first the "largest congregations" and mentioning then "a great number of Holy Roller refuges, the most interesting of which is at 1

West 137th Street." Prohibition had made the "gin mills" more appealing, if anything: "As a clue to those of our readers who might be interested we will tell them to notice what stands on every corner on 7th, Lenox, and 8th Avenues. There are also many such comfort stations in the middle of the blocks." The most attractive night clubs, he said, were best seen in company "with some member on the staff of *Harlem.*" "Only the elect and the pure in heart are admitted to these places," he explained.[60]

Perceptive readers would have detected the old Thurman not only in the last part of *Harlem* but also in the stories and poems included throughout the issue. Hughes contributed three poems dealing with drunkenness, boredom, and jazz, and a short story called "Luani of the Jungles," which portrays the fatal attraction between a white European man and a black African woman. The other short stories offered pictures no more appealing to the black bourgeoisie. Roy de Coverly's "Holes" and George W. Little's "Two Dollars" both consider prostitution and murder. Only George Schuyler offered a respectable character in "Woof," a story about the courageous and commanding First Sergeant William Glass of Company H, Twenty-fifth U.S. Infantry.

Thurman had planned succeeding issues of *Harlem.* With this in mind, he challenged readers to support his effort. In the last page of his editorial he wrote: "It now remains to be seen whether the Negro public is as ready for such a publication as the editors and publishers of *Harlem* believe it to be."[61] He gave further evidence of his plans at the end of the journal, when he listed prominent writers who had been asked to contribute to future issues, such as Heywood Broun, a columnist for the New York *Telegram* and the *Nation*; Clarence Darrow, "noted liberal and attorney"; Eugene Gordon, editor of the *Saturday Evening Quill*; Charles Johnson, former editor of *Opportunity*; Claude McKay, author of *Home to Harlem*; H. L. Mencken, editor of the *American Mercury*; and Frank Alvah Parsons, President of the New York Schools of Fine and Applied Arts.

As a literary editor, Thurman failed once again. In part he himself was responsible, since he had not been able to develop a magazine sufficiently different from *Fire.* Thurman had a bad name with many readers, who merely shook their heads knowingly when they saw his book review, his tips on the town, and his friends sandwiched in among more respectable contributors. It was not in Thurman to edit a truly "general magazine." He had an uncontrollable urge toward controversy, of a type which readers were not buying, especially in the face of the Great Depression. In 1932, upon the appearance of Thurman's *Infants of the Spring,* Theophilus Lewis wrote that *Fire* and *Harlem* came to their end for financial reasons. "It was a lack of money," he explained, "not a dearth of merit which caused the . . .

magazines to disappear."[62] Lewis did not elaborate. Thurman lacked funds because times were hard, especially for Afro-Americans, but also because he was too outspoken to attract the type of support he needed.

Lewis was one of the few to note the demise of *Harlem*. Contemporary responses were negligible, with neither *Crisis* nor *Opportunity* venturing a comment. So many enterprises were collapsing in those days that another unsuccessful attempt by Thurman raised few eyebrows. Lewis covered essentially new ground in 1932, when he reviewed Thurman's editorial career for the New York *Journal and Guide*. The title of the piece reflects the reputation Thurman had acquired: "Wallace Thurman Adores Brown Women Who Have Beauty Mark On Shoulder; Prefers Sherry To Gin." As an editor, Thurman went from the *Outlet* in Los Angeles, to five periodicals in New York—*Looking Glass, Messenger, World Tomorrow, Fire,* and *Harlem*. The first magazine had been his most successful, wrote Lewis, because it lasted for six months. Editorial longevity remained his dream, as Lewis added: "His ambition, he says, is to be the editor of a financially secure magazine."[63]

The ambition went unmet. Disillusioned by the loss of *Harlem,* Thurman never again attempted a literary journal, and he became more and more convinced that the black renaissance had failed. In *Infants of the Spring,* he compared the 1920s to a scene at a drunken party. Raymond, who represents Thurman in this novel, describes the situation: "Whites and blacks clung passionately together as if trying to effect a permanent merger. Liquor, jazz music, and close physical contact had achieved what decades of propaganda had advocated with little success." Raymond concludes that "this . . . is the Negro renaissance, and this is about all the whole damn thing is going to amount to." Through his protagonist, Thurman also reevaluated some of the main figures of the period. He reserved gentle satire for Alain Locke, who "played mother hen to a brood of chicks, he having appointed himself guardian angel to the current set of younger Negro artists."[64] Parke appears several times in the novel, always "clucking" after a brood of scattering chicks.

The other little magazines of the period showed several "guardians" and many coteries of young writers. Arthur Huff Fauset, the brother of Jessie, and other of the "older New Negroes," developed *Black Opals* as an outlet for young Philadelphians. Arthur Fauset edited the first issue, which appeared in the spring of 1927. Two other issues followed: the Christmas 1927 number under the leadership of guest editor Gwendolyn Bennett and an editorial staff composed of Fauset, Nellie Bright, Allan Freelon, and James Young; and the June 1928 number under the control of the same editorial board, with the exception of Bennett.

The first number stated motivations clearly, indicating that *Black Opals* "is the result of the desire of older New Negroes to encourage younger members of the group who demonstrate talent and ambition." The process was more important than the product, since the editors expected to feature "embryonic outpourings of aspiring young Negroes," along with a few contributions by recognized writers. Young aspirants, who primarily wrote poetry, were students in the Philadelphia public schools and at the Philadelphia Normal Schools, Temple University, and the University of Pennsylvania. With the possible exception of Mae Cowdery, then a senior at the Philadelphia High School for Girls, most of these students did not emerge later as established poets. Identification of "older New Negroes" came on the contributors' page of issue one and included persons knowledgeable about little magazines: Lewis Alexander and Langston Hughes, "well known New Negro poet[s]," and Alain Locke, "the father of the New Negro movement."[65]

From a historical perspective, the most significant material in all three issues is "Hail Philadelphia," a short essay written by Locke and included in the initial number. The piece reinforces the picture of Locke as politician, steering cleverly between the old ways and the new, endorsing the new without a flat rejection of the old. To introduce his thesis, he criticized the elders of Philadelphia, but with humor: "Philadelphia is the shrine of the Old Negro. More even than in Charleston or New Orleans, Baltimore or Boston, what there is of the tradition of breeding and respectability in the race lingers in the old Negro families of the city that was Tory before it was Quaker. Its faded daguerotypes [*sic*] stare stiffly down at all newcomers, including the New Negro (who we admit, is an upstart)—and ask, 'who was your grandfather?' and failing a ready answer—'who freed you?'"

In his next paragraph, Locke made a gesture toward the "Old Negro" of Philadelphia and elsewhere, saying that "I was taught to sing 'Hail Philadelphia' (to the tune of the Russian anthem), to reverence my elders and fear God in my own village." After a few more conciliatory lines, he turned to the youth and remained in that direction to the end of his comments. He warned young readers about the past—"I hope Philadelphia youth will realize that the past can enslave more than the oppressor"—and came to his conclusion with a metaphor. By his references to barnyard fowl, Locke developed the very imagery Thurman would associate with him in *Infants of the Spring*: "If the birth of the New Negro among us halts in the shell of conservatism, threatens to suffocate in the close air of self complacency and snugness, then the egg shell must be smashed to pieces and the living thing freed. And more of them I hope will be ugly ducklings, children too strange for the bondage of the barnyard provincialism, who shall some day fly in the face of the sun and seek the open seas." Quieting his essay, Locke ended with a direct address to young black writers willing to experiment: "Greetings to those of you who are daring new things. I want to sing a 'Hail Philadelphia' that is less a chant for the dead and more a song for the living. For especially for the Negro, I believe in the 'life to come.'"[66]

Locke established a tone for the journal, but he did not control the publication. Arthur Fauset, the moving force behind the magazine, was more conservative than Locke, even though he could make a gesture in the philosopher's direction. Fauset was not, to use Locke's image, in a mood to smash the "egg shell . . . to pieces." Neither was he in a position to do so, publishing mostly the "embryonic outpourings" of interested students. The last number of *Opals* concluded with Fauset's review of *Quicksand*. Fauset introduced his appraisal with sentiments acceptable to Locke, among others. He praised Larsen's novel as "a step forward" in Afro-American literature. "For the first time, perhaps, a Negro author has succeeded in writing a novel about colored characters in which the propaganda motive is decidedly absent." In qualifying his comment, Fauset showed that the older New Negroes were not in complete harmony on the way to instruct youth. The propaganda novel, like the "pure" literature advanced by many contemporary black writers, had its place, Fauset asserted: "If the 'pure' artist desires to create pure art, then of course let him create pure art; but whoever set up any group of Negroes to demand that all art by Negroes must conform to such a standard?"[67] Clearly, the focus of *Opals* was to guide the young, not shock their elders. In this, it bore similarities to *Stylus* at Howard University.

The editors of *Opals* kept open the lines of communication with the larger black magazines. The Christmas 1927 number, edited by Gwendolyn Bennett, praised young Philadelphians who had distinguished themselves in the *Crisis* and *Opportunity* contests. "Pardon Us For Bragging," the older New Negroes said, as they went on to commend Nellie Bright, Mae Cowdery, Allan Freelon, James Young, and Idabelle Yeiser.[68] Du Bois was happier about *Opals* than he had been with other of the small black magazines. He liked the "little brochure," even saying that the poems were of a "high order."[69] *Opportunity* editors were just as pleased but more expansive, as they had traditionally been. Again Cullen and Bennett echoed each other in their respective columns. After applauding the journal, both looked to the larger picture. Cullen hoped the "*Black Opals* venture" would "sweep the country as the Little Theatre movement has done." Bennett, more chatty than Cullen, noted that the Philadelphia group was going to visit the Quill Club of Boston. "Mayhap some year," she dreamed, "both of these groups with one or two of New York's younger, newer Negroes will get together and go to visit the *Ink Slingers* in California."[70]

The Boston Quill Club issued the first number of the *Saturday Evening Quill* in June 1928, the very month when the Philadelphia group brought forth the last number of *Opals*. For the next two years, the *Quill* appeared annually, the second number in April 1929 and the third and final number in June 1930. The magazine included a majority of locals, but there was a scattering of writers developing national reputations. The editor was Eugene Gordon, who was on the editorial staff of the Boston *Post* and who contributed regularly to *Opportunity* and *Messenger*. Among the contributors were Waring Cuney, Helene Johnson, and Dorothy West, all prize-winners in the *Crisis* and *Opportunity* literary competitions.[71] In *Infants of the Spring*, Thurman singled West and Johnson out from among their peers for commendation. Both had "freshness and naïveté," rare among contemporary black authors, Thurman asserted, and both had skill as writers: "Surprisingly enough for Negro prodigies, they actually gave promise of possessing literary talent."[72]

With "A Statement to the Reader," printed in the first issue of the *Quill*, club members expressed their reasons for publishing a journal. As the comment indicated, they did not want to start a revolution; they did not want to make money, never offering the *Quill* for sale until the third number; and they did not want to exhibit their literary wares before a wide audience. On behalf of his colleagues, Gordon wrote: "They have not published it [the *Quill*] because they think any of it 'wonderful,' or 'remarkable,' or 'extraordinary,' or 'unusual,' or even 'promising.' They have published it because, being human, they are possessed of the very human traits of vanity and egotism." In other words, they wanted to try their work out, preferably on a close circle of friends. As explained further, they paid for the periodical out of their own pockets.[73] Evidently their pockets were more full than those of Thurman and his associates, since they were able to sustain their effort for three years.

Unlike *Opals*, which specialized in verse, the *Quill* printed fiction, drama, poetry, essays, and illustrations. Some of the selections had a decidedly conservative message, such as the poem by George Margetson, which lauded Abraham Lincoln as the black savior: "To every dark-skinned child a hope he gave, / And made four million hearts beat happily."[74] Most of the contributions, though, considered themes conventional in black magazines of the 1920s—the problems between white employer and black employee, between social worker and welfare recipient, between husband and wife, between dark-skinned blacks and "high-yaller," or those who passed as white. The same considerations had appeared in *Fire* and *Harlem*, but with different treatment. Thurman's writers employed various dialects, rural and southern, urban and northern, and a variety of terms widely considered offensive, such as "coon" and "cracker." Eugene Gordon and his colleagues depended on standard educated English, the type of language they used in their everyday professions.

In the *Quill* as elsewhere, Gordon carefully separated himself and his involvements from radical positions in literature and politics. He de-emphasized the relationship between Afro-Americans and Africa, thereby disagreeing with such contemporaries as Locke, who had no discernible role in *Quill*. In his editorial for the first issue, he urged associates to look to the ground on which they stood, not to hanker after some distant jungle. Basically, he considered the Afro-American to be as American as apple pie: "The colored artist is trained in the same schools that train the white artist, and at the hands of the same instructors. He gets the same stereotyped formulas of technique and style. He stands to the rendering of the Star Spangled Banner, and even, at times, tries to sing it. He salutes the flag throughout the farthest reaches of the land; eats baked beans and brown bread on Saturday night, in Boston; sneers, in New York, at 'the provinces'; falls in line to shake the President's hand at New Year's, in the District of Columbia; laughs at the comic strip; and he worships wealth and caste in true American fashion." Gordon realized that black writers had some rich sources unavailable to whites, but he asserted that they must use the "same method" and "the same medium," or language, available to white authors.[75]

To further his views, Gordon included an essay by William Edward Harrison, Harvard-trained journalist, in the third number of the *Quill*. Like Gordon, Harrison declared that American blacks could hardly look for inspiration to Africa, which was surely a "terra incognita" after some three hundred years. Summarizing Gordon's ideas, he claimed that black writers should use materials from their own environment in an effort to reach out to all people, black and white: "This literature must be at once profoundly racial and still universal in its appeal." He then stated opinions which were held by other club members but had not been explicitly asserted in the *Quill*. Looking to the success of the Boston and Philadelphia literary organizations, Harrison asserted that Harlem could no longer be the moving force in the black renaissance. He believed that the "Harlem theme" had grown "stale," as had writers like Thurman and George Schuyler: "Through the efforts of these and their satellites Harlem, the Negro quarter of New York, has been relegated to the place of a satrapy of Babylon or Sodom; it is the epitome of the bizarre and the unregenerate asylum of Vice in capitals, if we may trust these literati; it means somehow knowing nods and winks, and suggests forbidden *diableries*."[76]

By the turn of the decade, many reviewers agreed that the Harlem theme was indeed "stale." Writers for the New York *Amsterdam News* and the *Commonweal*, among others, called *Quill* the best of the black little magazines. A reporter for the *Amsterdam News* urged "Harlem writers" to follow the "example" of the Boston group, while the reviewer for *Commonweal* praised the journal for its "admirable absence of jazz and Harlem posturings." W. E. B. Du Bois liked the fresh beginning he saw in *Quill* and commended the journal in *Crisis*: "Of the booklets issued by young Negro writers in New York, Philadelphia and elsewhere, this collection from Boston is by far the most interesting and the best. . . . It is well presented and readable and maintains a high mark of literary excellence." Charles Johnson, in an unsolicited letter, went so far as to call the journal one of the few solid artistic achievements of the decade: "Here we have what seems to me the best evidence of a substantial deposit after the feverish activity of the last few years."[77]

As the Depression began, *Quill* came to an end, as had its predecessors. By 1930 *Stylus,* which had led the way for the others, was the only black little magazine alive. During the 1920s, *Stylus* remained dormant as Locke preoccupied himself with literary activities especially in Harlem, which he saw as the center for a great cultural awakening. The second number of *Stylus* appeared in 1921 and the third was delayed until June 1929. Then in the middle of the Depression, the magazine emerged on a more regular annual basis.[78] The journal continued, while others fell, largely because of university support.

From his perspective on the Howard campus, Locke evaluated the 1920s and presented his conclusions in "Beauty and the Provinces," an essay published in the 1929 *Stylus*. He began his remarks with definitions, calling a capital a center for creative work and a province a place empty of poets, a place "where living beauty . . . is not." Using these distinctions, Locke pointed to New York as the capital of the United States and to Harlem—"the mecca of the New Negro"—as the vitality of that capital. Washington, D.C., on the other hand, was a province, in touch only with the "nation's body." It was not, wrote Locke, "the capital of its mind or soul." Locke had endorsed the situation in the mid-1920s, but he felt some regret by the end of the decade when Harlem seemed less promising than it once had. He suggested that Washington, D.C., could have become a true capital if "Negro Washington" had dropped its "borrowed illusions" and encouraged its wealth of "intellectual and cultural talent." Had this occurred, the metropolis could have "out-distanced Harlem" and led the way in the cultural renaissance. As it was, the District "merely yielded a small exodus of genius that went out of the smug city with passports of persecution and returned with visas of metropolitan acclaim."[79]

Criticizing "Negro Washington" in general, Locke neither accepted nor apportioned any blame. He liked to issue praise and he wanted to feel comfortable about his own role in the 1920s. Thus he turned to "certain exceptions" in Washington, pointing with "collective pride" to the "pioneer work" done by *Stylus*. As Locke remembered, the Howard group was among the first to advocate an Afro-American literature rooted in racial consciousness, or on "the foundation of the folk-roots and the race tradition." Locke also remembered the many groups which had followed elsewhere, such as the Writers' Guild of New York, Krigwa of New York and other cities, the Dixwell Group of New Haven, the Scribblers of Baltimore, the Ethiopian Guild of Indianapolis, the Gilpin of Cleveland, the Ethiopian Folk Theater of Chicago, the Cube Theater of Chicago and, among others, the Dallas Players of Texas. The very enumeration of these societies irresistibly recalled the expression Locke had used in his retrospective review of 1928, published in the January 1929 issue of *Opportunity*. "The provinces are waking up," he concluded, "and a new cult of beauty stirs throughout the land."[80]

Locke's essays, particularly the two noted from 1929, give valuable insight to the 1920s. More than any other contemporary, Locke was involved in nearly every Afro-American magazine and special number of black literature issued during that period. By his publications, his correspondence, and his personal contacts, he saw better than anyone else the cultural renaissance taking place up and down the East Coast and in urban centers across the land. In the latter part of the decade, he provided the connecting link among various and frequently diverse artistic circles and became the most influential black literary critic. As such, Locke realized that the story of the 1920s was not Harlem alone. The fuller picture, the activity seen coast-to-coast, appeared in the little magazines of the day.

Notes

1. "Announcement and Prospectus of the *New Era Magazine*," and "Editorial and Publisher's Announcements," *New Era Magazine* 1 (February 1916):3, 60.

2. "Editorial and Publisher's Announcements," Ibid., p. 60.

3. "Editorial and Publisher's Announcements," *New Era Magazine* 1 (March 1916):124; "Announcement and Prospectus of the *New Era Magazine*," p. 1.

4. "Announcement and Prospectus of the *New Era Magazine*," p. 4.

5. "Editorial and Publisher's Announcements," and "John Trowbridge," *New Era Magazine* 1 (March 1916):124, 112.

6. "William Stanley Braithwaite," *New Era Magazine* 1 (February 1916):61.

7. "Announcement and Prospectus of the *New Era Magazine*," p. 2; "Topsy Templeton," *New Era Magazine* 1 (March 1916):77.

8. "Prize Contest," *New Era Magazine* 1 (March 1916):111.

9. *Crisis* acknowledged the death of Hopkins on August 23, 1930, at Cambridge, Massachusetts. The brief obituary noted only that Hopkins had been an "authoress and poetess" and that she had worked as a stenographer at the Massachusetts Institute of Technology. "Along the Color Line," *Crisis* 37 (October 1930):344.

Ann Allen Shockley says nothing of *New Era* in her brief article on Hopkins. "Pauline Elizabeth Hopkins: A Biographical Excursion into Obscurity," *Phylon* 33 (Spring 1972): 22-26.

If included anywhere, the magazine should have been mentioned in the dictionary of *Black American Writers,* compiled by Theressa Gunnels Rush, Carol Fairbanks Myers, and Esther Spring Arata. The editors did note Hopkins's association with the *Colored American Magazine,* but they made no reference to *New Era* (Metuchen, New Jersey: Scarecrow Press, 1975), vol. 1, pp. 389-90.

10. "Foreword," *Stylus* 1 (May 1921):6.

11. "The Stylus," *Howard University Record* 19 (May 1925):372; "Visions of the Dawn," *Stylus* (June 1934):1. The issues of *Stylus* following May 1921 were assigned neither a volume nor a number.

12. Gregory, "Foreword," p. 6.

13. "The Looking Glass," *Crisis* 12 (August 1916):182; *Dust Tracks on a Road* (1942: rpt. Philadelphia: Arno Press, 1969), pp. 175-76; Robert E. Hemenway, *Zora Neale Hurston* (Urbana: University of Illinois Press, 1977), pp. 18-20.

14. "Our Book Shelf," *Crisis* 31 (January 1926):141.

Within the discussion, Du Bois essentially cast Kellogg and associates as inconsistent liberals who advocated social reform for all groups save for the black. He recalled that the editors had wanted, for a 1914 issue of *Survey,* a statement concerning the aims of the NAACP. Du Bois sent back a militant, but routine comment, as his conclusion indicates: "Finally, in 1914, the Negro must demand his social rights. His right to be treated as a gentleman when he acts like one, to marry any sane, grown person who wants to marry him, and to meet and eat with his friends without being accused of undue assumption or unworthy ambition." He never expected the subsequent uproar, the calls from *Survey* editors to the NAACP office, the demand that the offending passage be excised, if the piece was to appear in the magazine. Among the NAACP leadership, Du Bois remembered, "they found easily several who did not agree with this statement and one indeed who threatened to resign if it were published." The unnamed objectors must have included those trying to intimidate Du Bois into subservience to the organization. Du Bois, stubborn from the beginning of his editorship, would not comply and thus *Survey* rejected his entire statement.

In 1923, Kellogg divided the *Survey* into two magazines: the *Survey Graphic,* which appeared on the first of each month and reached a popular audience with general information and analysis of social problems, and *Survey,* which served as a professional bulletin for the field of social work.

15. "The Negro Renaissance and its Significance," in *The New Negro Thirty Years Afterward: Papers Contributed to the Sixteenth Annual Spring Conference of the Division of the Social Sciences,* ed. Rayford W. Logan, Eugene C. Holmes, and G. Franklin Edwards (Washington, D.C.: Howard University Press, 1955), pp. 85-86. Clarke Chambers said nothing about the Civic Club Dinner but stressed Kellogg's own motivation for the Harlem number. He noted that Kellogg had always liked "folk," that he had previously published special issues on the Gypsies, the Irish, and the Mexican peasants, and that his "favorite artists were always those who worked with folk themes, especially when their styles reflected the primitive strength of the common folk." *Paul U. Kellogg and the Survey* (Minneapolis: University of Minnesota Press, 1971), pp. 112-13.

16. "Harlem," and "Enter the New Negro," *Survey Graphic* 6 (March 1925):629-30, 633.

17. "The South Lingers On," Ibid., 645, 644, 646.

18. "Enter the New Negro," Ibid., 631, 633.

19. "Youth Speaks," Ibid., 659.

20. "The Black Man Brings His Gifts," Ibid., 655, 710.

21. "The Negro Renaissance and its Significance," in *The New Negro Thirty Years Afterward,* p. 86; "The Negro Enters Literature," *Carolina Magazine* 57 (May 1927):48.

22. "Editorials," *Messenger* 7 (April 1925):156; Chambers, *Kellogg and the Survey,* p. 115.

23. The first issue of *Palms* appeared in October 1923 and the last in April 1927. Idella Purnell commented, in the last number, that *Palms* would emerge again in the fall: "The editors feel it necessary to bring forcibly to the attention of *Palms'*

readers that the magazine has continued and will continue." Despite such protestations, *Palms* never again reappeared. See "Notice," *Palms* 4 (April 1927):190.

24. "Poem," "The Song of America," and "Black Madonna," *Palms* 4 (October 1926):19, 18, 8.

25. In a letter dated September 27, 1925, Countee Cullen asked James Weldon Johnson if he would contribute a short article on black poets to the issue. Committed elsewhere, Johnson could not supply the essay; hence, the discussion by White. Cullen to Johnson, James Weldon Johnson Papers, James Weldon Johnson Collection, Yale University.

26. "Ebony Flute," *Opportunity* 5 (April 1927):123; "Ebony Flute," *Opportunity* 5 (January 1927):28.

27. "Contributors," *Carolina Magazine* 58 (May 1928): 48. Virginia Lay, acting editor of *Carolina Magazine* and also sister of Paul Green, had originally asked James Weldon Johnson either to write a survey of Afro-American literature for the May 1927 issue or to suggest someone else who could contribute the essay. Apparently, Johnson did not have time to author the piece and thus recommended Charles S. Johnson for the lead article. Lay to James Weldon Johnson, April 18, 1927, Series C, Container 83, NAACP Papers, Manuscripts Division, Library of Congress (hereafter cited as NAACP Papers).

28. "The Message of the Negro Poets," *Carolina Magazine* 58 (May 1928):11.

29. "The Hunch," *Carolina Magazine* 57 (May 1927):24.

30. "Boy," "Boy on Beale Street," "African Dancer in Paris," and "Once Bad Gal," *Carolina Magazine* 58 (May 1928):38, 36, 22.

31. "Comment," and "Plays of Negro Life," *Carolina Magazine* 59 (April 1929):4, 46.

32. "The Negro in Literature," *Crisis* 36 (November 1929):377; "Dark Tower," and "Ebony Flute," *Opportunity* 5 (June 1927):181, 183; "Dark Tower," *Opportunity* 5 (July 1927):211.

33. "Dark Tower," *Opportunity* 4 (December 1926):388. Starr and Fowler were still listed in their official capacities in the May 1927 issue of *Carolina Magazine,* even though Virginia Lay was serving as editor. In her letter to James Weldon Johnson, she indicated that Starr had to attend to business in New York for an indeterminate period. She also indicated that Starr had made plans and Lewis Alexander had gathered materials for the first special issue of black literature. Lay to Johnson, April 18, 1927, Series C, Container 83, NAACP Papers.

34. "Dedication," *Carolina Magazine* 58 (May 1928):4; Alexander, "Plays of Negro Life," p. 47.

35. *Harlem Renaissance* (New York: Oxford University Press, 1971), p. 29. John W. Blassingame called the Huggins's study "hardly definitive," saying that *Harlem Renaissance* "ignores the internal dynamics of the black community which fostered and nurtured the movement." Blassingame concluded that there still exists undiscovered "a different kind of renaissance than that which Huggins found. "The Afro-Americans: Mythology to Reality," in *The Reinterpretation of American History and Culture,* ed. William H. Cartwright and Richard L. Watson, Jr. (Washington, D.C.: National Council for the Social Studies, 1973), p. 69.

36. "The Twenties: Harlem and its Negritude," *African Forum* 1 (Spring 1966): 18-19; also see Hemenway, *Hurston,* pp. 43-50.

37. Hughes, "The Twenties," 19; Thurman to Hughes, December 8, 1927, Wallace Thurman Folder, James Weldon Johnson Collection, Yale University.

38. Hughes, "The Twenties," p. 19; *Fire* 1 (November 1926); introductory page.

39. Hughes, "The Twenties," p. 20; *Big Sea* (1940; rpt. New York: Hill and Wang, 1963), p. 237.

40. Thurman so autographed the copy of *Fire* in the Moorland-Spingarn Research Center of Howard University; "Foreword," *Fire,* p. 1.

41. "Fire Burns," Ibid., pp. 47-48.

42. "Cordelia the Crude," "Wedding Day," and "Sweat," Ibid., pp. 5, 25-28, 41.

43. "Smoke, Lilies and Jade," Ibid., p. 38.

44. "Elevator Boy" and "Little Cinderella," Ibid., pp. 20, 23.

45. Hughes, *Big Sea,* p. 237; "A Challenge to the Negro," *Bookman* 64 (November 1926):258-59.

46. "Dark Tower," and "Ebony Flute," *Opportunity* 5 (January 1927):25, 28.

47. Hughes, *Big Sea,* p. 237; Hughes, "The Twenties," pp. 19-20; "Looking Glass," *Crisis* 33 (January 1927):158.

48. "Fire: A Negro Magazine," *Survey* 58 (Aug. 15-Sept. 15, 1927):563.

49. Hughes to Locke, December 28, 1926, Literary Series, Alain Locke Collection, Howard University (hereafter cited as Locke Collection); Hughes, *Big Sea,* p. 237.

50. "The Negro Literary Renaissance," *Southern Workman* 56 (April 1927):177-79, 183.

51. "Negro Artists and the Negro," *New Republic* 52 (August 31, 1927):37.

52. Hurston to Locke, October 11, 1927, Locke Collection.

53. Hughes, *Big Sea,* p. 238.

54. Thurman to Locke, October 3, 1928, Locke Collection; Locke to Thurman, October 8, 1928, Locke Collection.

55. "For Whom Shall the Negro Vote?" *Harlem* 1 (November 1928):5, 45.

56. "Art or Propaganda?" Ibid., p. 12.

57. "Editorial," Ibid., p. 21.

58. Ibid., pp. 21-22.

59. "High, Low, Past and Present," Ibid., pp. 31-32.

60. "Harlem Directory: Where To Go And What To Do When In Harlem," Ibid., p. 43.

61. "Editorial," Ibid., p. 22.

62. "Wallace Thurman Adores Brown Women Who Have Beauty Mark On Shoulder; Prefers Sherry to Gin," New York *Journal and Guide,* March 5, 1932. The article is included in the Wallace Thurman Folder, Vertical File, Schomburg Collection of Black History, Literature and Art, New York Public Library.

63. Ibid.

64. *Infants of the Spring* (New York: Macaulay Company, 1932), pp. 186-87, 180.

65. *Black Opals* 1 (Spring 1927): n.p. In a letter to Alain Locke, dated April 2, 1927, Langston Hughes noted the appearance of *Black Opals* and declared that he would submit some poems for publication in the magazine. Hughes to Locke, Locke Collection.

66. "Hail Philadelphia," *Black Opals* 1 (Spring 1927):3.

67. "Quicksand," *Black Opals* 1 (June 1928):19.

68. "Pardon Us for Bragging," *Black Opals* 1 (Christmas 1927):16.

69. "Far Horizon," *Crisis* 34 (August 1927):130; "Browsing Reader," *Crisis* 36 (March 1929):98.

70. "Dark Tower," *Opportunity* 5 (June 1927):180; "Ebony Flute," *Opportunity* 6 (February 1928):56.

71. In 1926, Helene Johnson was executive secretary for The Colored Poetic League of the World, an organization attempting to establish itself in Bos-

ton. The league tried to found the *Poets' Journal,* a magazine which apparently never materialized. In a circular letter sent to contemporary writers Thomas Oxley, President of the league and proposed editor of the *Journal,* outlined the intentions of the organization: "Our purposes are to increase and diffuse poetic knowledge; to sell and publish books; to criticise; and to help the young poet to recognition and fame. But this is not all— *The Poet's Journal*—the organ of the League will be published according to public subscription and for those interested in poetry" (Series C, Container 83, NAACP Papers).

72. Thurman, *Infants of the Spring,* p. 231.

73. "A Statement to the Reader," *Saturday Evening Quill* 1 (June 1928): front page.

74. "Abraham Lincoln," Ibid., p. 34.

75. "A Word in Closing: On Uncritical Criticism," Ibid., p. 72. Gordon had expressed like opinions in "Group Tactics and Ideals," *Messenger* 8 (December 1926):361, and in "The Contest Winners," *Opportunity* 5 (July 1927):204.

76. "The Negro's Literary Tradition," *Saturday Evening Quill* 1 (June 1930):6, 8.

77. "Excerpts from Comments on the First Number of *The Saturday Evening Quill,*" *Saturday Evening Quill* 1 (April 1929):inside front cover; "The Browsing Reader," *Crisis* 35 (September 1928):301; "Excerpts from Comments on the Previous Numbers of the *Saturday Evening Quill,*" *Saturday Evening Quill* 1 (June 1930): inside front cover.

78. In the years following, *Stylus* appeared in 1934, 1935, 1936, 1937, 1938, and 1941, which marked the twenty-fifth anniversary of the organization and the last number of the journal.

79. "Beauty and the Provinces," *Stylus* (June 1929):3-4.

80. Ibid., p. 4. In his *Opportunity* article, Locke mentioned that he had also used the expression "elsewhere." "1928: A Retrospective Review," *Opportunity* 7 (January 1929):10.

Selected Bibliography

I PRIMARY SOURCES

A. PERIODICALS

African Forum, 1965-67

Black Opals, 1927-28

Caroline Magazine, 1927-29

Crisis, 1910-76

Fire, 1926

Harlem, 1928

Messenger, 1917-28

New Era, 1916

Opportunity, 1923-49

Palms, 1926

Phylon, 1940-76

Saturday Evening Quill, 1928-30

Stylus, 1916-41

Survey Graphic, 1925

B. MANUSCRIPT COLLECTIONS

New Haven. Yale University Library. James Weldon Johnson Memorial Collection.

New York. New York Public Library. Schomburg Collection of Black History, Literature and Art.

Washington, D.C. Howard University Library. Alain Locke Papers.

Washington, D.C. Library of Congress. National Association for the Advancement of Colored People Papers.

C. BOOKS

Du Bois, W. E. B. *The Autobiography of W. E. B. Du Bois.* Edited by Herbert Aptheker. New York: International Publishers, 1968.

Hughes, Langston. *The Big Sea.* 1940. Reprint. New York: Hill and Wang, 1963.

Hurston, Zora Neale. *Dust Tracks on the Road.* 1942. Reprint. Philadelphia: Arno, 1969.

Thurman, Wallace. *Infants of the Spring.* New York: Macaulay, 1932.

D. ARTICLES

Du Bois, W. E. B. "Editing 'The Crisis.'" *Crisis* 58 (1951):147-51, 213.

II SECONDARY SOURCES

A. BOOKS

Chambers, Clarke. *Paul U. Kellogg and the Survey.* Minneapolis: University of Minnesota Press, 1971.

Hemenway, Robert E. *Zora Neale Hurston.* Urbana: University of Illinois Press, 1977.

Huggins, Nathan I. *Harlem Renaissance.* New York: Oxford, 1971.

Logan, Rayford W., Holmes, Eugene C., and Edwards, G. Franklin, eds. *The New Negro Thirty Years Afterward.* Washington, D.C.: Howard University Press, 1955.

Rush, Theressa G., Myers, Carol F., and Arata, Esther S. *Black American Writers.* 2 vols. Metuchen, New Jersey: Scarecrow Press, 1975.

B. Articles

Blassingame, John W. "The Afro-Americans: Mythology to Reality." *The Reinterpretation of American History and Culture,* edited by William H. Cartwright and Richard L. Watson, Jr. Washington, D.C.: National Council for the Social Studies, 1973.

Joyce Durham (essay date fall-spring 1999-2001)

SOURCE: Durham, Joyce. "Dorothy West and the Importance of Black 'Little' Magazines of the 1930s: *Challenge* and *New Challenge.*" *Langston Hughes Review* 16, nos. 1 & 2 (fall-spring 1999-2001): 19-31.

[*In the following essay, Durham focuses on the role of Dorothy West and* Challenge *magazine in the history of black little magazines.*]

In an interview with Katrine Dalsgard, Robert B. Stepto stressed the importance of recovering more women writers from the Harlem Renaissance, a watershed period in African American letters. He said, "Dorothy West is another woman from the Harlem Renaissance who should be recovered in the same way Zora Neale Hurston was recovered." Stepto's observation was in tune with the renewed interest in West, who published her long awaited novel *The Wedding* in 1995. Many people have revived their interest in her current work and her Harlem Renaissance beginnings, in particular. Few would question the interest. The Harlem Renaissance of the 1920s that brought acclaim, excitement, and, above all, markets for the work of black writers and artists was an era that Langston Hughes in 1940 referred to as one "when the Negro was in vogue." In 1926, Hughes's important essay "The Negro Artist and the Racial Mountain" appeared in the magazine *Nation,* thereby becoming a manifesto for black racial pride in that decade. The year before, 1925, Alain Locke had defined the age with the title of his anthology of black writing called *The New Negro.* Today, the term "New Negro" is to most certainly a product of the 1920s, that period of the "flowering" of black American writing in America. Prominent among that assemblage, Dorothy West, according to Adelaide M. Cromwell, found herself as "the young darling of the black writers and artists who made up the Harlem Renaissance" (352). Her career was launched by winning a contest in *Opportunity,* and she

subsequently published numerous works in both that magazine and *The Messenger.* Her debt to these literary magazines as a means of encouraging and promoting the literary careers of her own and other black writers of the period was established early, and as the 1920s waned, West remained sensitive to the diminished output of black writers and the growing tensions between the older generation and the new young radical writers.

In 1934 in the aftermath of this renaissance, Dorothy West, the youngest of the Harlem Renaissance group and now the oldest living member of that period, accomplished some of her most important work. In that year she published the first volume of *Challenge* (March 1934), called at first a literary monthly. In one of the first and few black "little" magazines of the 1930s, she bravely admits, "It is our plan to bring out the prose and poetry of the newer Negroes. We who were the New Negroes challenge them to better our achievements. For we did not altogether live up to our fine promise" (39). Despite such notable contributors as James Weldon Johnson, Langston Hughes, and Arna Bontemps, however, West was disappointed with the quality of contributions from newer writers, and the next volume was published in September as "a literary quarterly." Subsequent issues appeared erratically, and in the fall of 1937, Dorothy West shared the editorial duties with Marian Minus and Richard Wright. Under the more militant leadership, the publication survived only one issue before it was discontinued.

Historians and critics alike have given diverse assessments of this particular "little" magazine, with a prominent notion being that it was, as Walter C. Daniel calls it in 1971, "an experiment that failed." Harold Cruse in *The Crisis of the Negro Intellectual* (1967) had earlier referred to it as "an anti-climactic failure—a rather feeble and half-hearted attempt to recoup lost ground given up in the 1920s without a principled struggle" (186). However, Robert Bone in his 1965 work, *The Negro Novel in America,* proclaims that "the dominant tendencies of a literary period often crystallize in its little magazines," and he further mentions *Challenge* and *New Challenge* as resuming the role that *Fire, Harlem,* and *The Messenger* had played earlier in the century. He goes on to say that as editor, Dorothy West "helped keep alive the idea of a distinctive Negro art" (187-88). Since that time, others have applauded West's efforts to provide a forum for the newer writers of the 1930s. Sandra Govan, in "Black Women as Cultural Conservators" (1988), credits West, along with Jessie Fauset, Gwendolyn Bennett, and others, as "cultural conservators, doing what they could to further the arts and careers of different artists, helping foster the idea of cultural continuity, indeed reporting upon, forming, as well as preserving African-American social and cultural history" (9). In fact, when one considers the redefinition of the work of black women writers, particularly those of this century, and the reshaping of the literary tradition by such critics as Mary Helen Washington, Farah Jasmine Griffin, Deborah E. McDowell, and others, it becomes increasingly clear why Dorothy West has begun recently to be included in important discussions of literary criticism.

Therefore, instead of concentrating on the negative aspects of Dorothy West's attempts, it is both fruitful and meaningful to analyze the positive contributions and influences this particular "little" magazine achieved in recording and advancing the contemporary black literary tradition, a tradition that historically has provided tensions and irreconcilable conflicts between art and propaganda or art and politics. In doing so, it is useful to present an overview of black literary and "little" magazines during the 1920s and 1930s, to assess the climate of black writing in the 1930s which was reflected in West's publication, and finally to note specifically the changes in the literary tradition recorded in the pages of this short-lived but important "little" magazine.

In the preface to their study, *Propaganda and Aesthetics: The Literary Politics of Afro-American Magazines in the Twentieth Century,* Abby Arthur Johnson and Ronald Maberry Johnson comment on black magazines: "The journals provide insight, not available in a comparable manner elsewhere, into the evolution of Afro-American literature," yet the authors acknowledge, "Little work has been done on individual Afro-American periodicals," those called "little" because of "a limited readership, usually numbering between 1000 for each journal." Yet, the Johnsons do mention Max Barber, editor of one of the first black magazines of the twentieth century, *Voice of the Negro,* who tried to establish the importance of these journals in his proclamation that the publication of black magazines "means that culture is taking a deep hold upon our people. It is an indication that our people are becoming an educated, a reading people" (1). The Johnsons go on to note that although the early journals, such as *Colored American Magazine, Horizon,* and *Voice of the Negro,* were involved primarily in political and social occurrences before literary concerns, they also published the work of young poets and fiction writers, most of whom had no other outlets for their efforts" (1). In fact, the Johnsons pay great homage to Pauline Hopkins, another woman editor who lost her position because of editorial disputes, in this way: "More and better fiction and poetry was published by the *Colored American Magazine* during the years Pauline Hopkins was editor than at any other time in its history" (6). Even so, it was the later journals that played a larger role in providing a forum for the writers of the 1920s.

Many Harlem Renaissance writers, finding themselves popular and marketable for the first time, found outlets for their work in major white publishing houses and in white journals, such as *Contemporary Verse, Harriet Monroe's Poetry: A Magazine of Verse,* and *Palms.* Black magazines in this period were limited primarily to three: *Crisis,* founded in 1910 by the NAACP; *The Messenger,* founded in 1917 by A. Philip Randolph and Chandler Owen; and *Opportunity: Journal of Negro Life,* founded in 1923 by The Urban League. These journals provide a fascinating account of the 1920s and their own support for the cultural renaissance, particularly the extensive literary contests they sponsored. It is also interesting to note that the controversy between art and "propaganda" continued to be recorded throughout the duration of these journals. In his chapter, "Black Journals and Negro Literature," Chidi Ikonne quotes Wallace Thurman, one of the most prominent of the New Negro Writers, as saying that "the results of the renaissance have been sad rather than satisfactory, in that critical standards have been ignored, and the measure of achievement has been racial rather than literary" (94-95). This was a legacy to be handed later to Dorothy West. Ikonne goes on to record that young writers like Claude McKay and Thurman were grateful to the three major journals for publishing their work but again quotes Thurman's dissatisfaction with being "squeezed upon a page between jeremiads or have [their] works thrown haphazardly upon a page where there was no effort to make it look beautiful as well as sound beautiful" (109).

While the history of these journals creates a fascinating picture of the 1920s, the proliferation of special issues devoted to black literature and black "little" magazines provides the immediate background for understanding the creation of Dorothy West's *Challenge* in the 1930s. A few of these publications are *New Era* and *Saturday Evening Quill* in Boston, *Stylus* in Washington, D.C., and *Black Opals* in Philadelphia. However, the most radical of the "little" magazines were the short-lived *Fire* and *Harlem,* both initiated by Wallace Thurman. Funded in 1926 by several writers, including Thurman, Langston Hughes, and Zora Neale Hurston, *Fire* achieved notoriety for one issue before it met its demise. Ikonne notes that blacks and whites alike were hostile to its uncommon and radical aims: "Yet, in spite of flaws and weaknesses of individual contributions, *Fire* achieved its artistic aim: expression of the younger writers' 'individual dark-skinned selves without fear or shame'" (111), a reference to Langston Hughes's 1926 statement in *Nation* about black artists and their parameters. In spite of its promise, however, the magazine folded, leaving Hughes to comment: "That taught me a lesson about little magazines. But since white folks had them, we Negroes thought we could have one, too. But we didn't have the money" ("Harlem Literati," 7).

Vowing to be more conservative, Thurman continued efforts to launch a successful "little" magazine. The sole issue of *Harlem* in 1928 contains some political discussion, a powerful essay by Alain Locke called "Art or Propaganda," which foreshadows Richard Wright's "Blueprint for Negro Writing" in the 1937 issue of *New Challenge,* and several poems and short stories. Yet because Thurman continued to be "outspoken and controversial," attacking DuBois, listing exotic churches in Harlem, including poems of "drunkenness and boredom," and short stories that "offered pictures no more appealing to the black bourgeoisie" (Johnson 87-88), this publication, like *Fire,* quickly collapsed. Both publications failed, the Johnsons conclude, because "he [Thurman] had an uncontrollable urge toward controversy, of a type which readers were not buying, especially in the face of the Great Depression" (88).

Of all the "little" magazines with serious literary concerns, only *Stylus,* the first black university-supported literary magazine (Howard University, Washington, D. C.), remained alive in the 1930s. Some of the larger white magazines, *Atlantic Monthly, Saturday Review,* and *Scribners,* continued to encourage the older black writers, such as Countee Cullen, Langston Hughes, and Claude McKay; only the "leftist periodicals" such as *Partisan Review, New Masses, Midland, Anvil,* and *Left Front* encouraged the newer writers, many of whom "thought the more radical publications were not sufficiently concerned with creative literature and with Afro-American culture and interests" (Johnson 98). *Opportunity* and *Crisis* continued to flourish in the 1930s, although they had limited usefulness as literary outlets for the new black writers. "Black literature became more diversified in the 1930s than it had been in the 1920s, but the market for that literature was limited in comparison with the outlets provided in the preceding decade" (Johnson 97), particularly those involving white patronage. The Johnsons maintain that the serious black writers "wanted little magazines, in the tradition of the independent journals of the 1920s but adapted to the needs of the 1930s" (111).

The needs of the proletarian 1930s did, in fact, differ markedly from the 1920s, resulting in a major shift in philosophy primarily from emphasis on race to emphasis on economic factors. As the country experienced economic depression and looked to social influences, many black writers distanced themselves from the racial concerns that dominated the earlier period. Even though historians disagree about when the Harlem Renaissance movement actually declined and the proletarian movement began, several of the tensions erupting during the 1920s blended almost immeasurably into the new proletarian issues of the 1930s. One controversy that raged in the 1920s was the conflict between the New Negro writers "who created black characters which just happened to fit the exotic stereotypes" (Young 134) and the "genteel critics" who deplored the depiction of "low life" characters. James Weldon Johnson, Alain Locke, and Langston Hughes celebrated "their dark-

skinned selves," while Benjamin Brawley, historian, critic, and academic, and W. E. B. DuBois expressed concern that these writings "were not projecting the proper image of the Negro" (Young 134). This debate was continued in the 1930s by Locke himself and such writer/critics as Sterling Brown and Richard Wright, who felt that "the characters of neither the genteel nor the New Negro writers possessed the universality and the reality which the young critics of the 1930s were desirous of stimulating" (Young 134). Social realism, not romanticized primitivism, had to be the vehicle of the new writers. Obviously the issue of art versus politics was not disappearing and continued to be debated in the pages of *Challenge* in the 1930s.

A second common aspect of the two decades of black writing is one of an apparent lack of ideology or common purpose, a factor many associate with Dorothy West's own career as editor in the 1930s. Cary D. Wintz in *Black Culture and the Harlem Renaissance* attributes the dwindling of talent to this absence of purpose: "since the [Harlem Renaissance] movement never found any common ideology to blend together its adherents other than their shared participation in this magic moment in black literature, it is not surprising that when the magic faded and the conviction gave way to doubts that the movement collapsed" (222-23). He goes on to say: "The intellectual stagnation and general lack of community cohesion that afflicted many of the former participants in the Renaissance was only one sign of a general affliction which thinned out the ranks of Harlem's literati" (224). Aware of this intellectual stagnation as well as the growing sympathy of black writers and intellectuals to Communism, Dorothy West articulated her intentions in the first issue in 1934 to "challenge" the New Negroes to supersede the achievements of the previous generation of writers. Later she was to tell Deborah McDowell in a 1987 interview: "I started it because I thought the movement was over" (271). There is no doubt in most minds that West believed she could revive the excitement and fervor that began as part of the literary tradition of the 1920s, yet her position remained somewhat ambivalent until finally Richard Wright took the less defined ideology of the early *Challenge* issues to the more clearly defined politically "leftist" leanings of the later *New Challenge.* In his commentary on the period, Robert Bone reflects some skepticism in his otherwise positive assessment of this involvement: "By thus enjoining the Negro author to explore his own tradition, the party inadvertently advanced the legitimate development of Negro art. It is not the first time in its history that the American Communist party has done the right thing for the wrong reasons" (116). Whatever the controversies, in these few but important seven issues of a new "little" magazine of primarily black writing, editor Dorothy West had become a patroness of the new writers of the 1930s and a promoter of many aspects of the African American literary tradition, however much that tradition has been debated in recent years.

The first issue of *Challenge* in March 1934 carries a foreword by James Weldon Johnson applauding West's new publication and exhorting new young writers not to be dilettantes and propagandists, but "sincere artists," who "can bring to bear a tremendous force for breaking down and wearing away the stereotyped ideas about the Negro, and for creating a higher and more enlightened opinion about the race" (2). This pioneer issue includes pieces by the "old guard," Countee Cullen, Langston Hughes, and Arna Bontemps, poetry by West's cousin Helene Johnson, as well as contributions of a few younger writers. Bontemps, who dramatizes the lower socioeconomic classes in a short story "Barrel Staves" and in a later issue, an article entitled "Saturday Night," "depended on caricatures," according to the Johnsons. They call Bontemps's stories the "best contributions" (114), yet the stories provoked criticism from others about their "low life" content. Another article typical of the debate of aesthetic standards is Harry Burleigh's "On Spirituals," which decries the commercial use of Negro spirituals. Burleigh contests the misuse of the music: "It offends the aesthetic feelings of all true musicians, white and black, and because some of us have endeavored never to sink the high standard of our art, nor commercialize the sacred heritage of our people's song, we feel, deeply, that the [wilful], persistent, superficial distortion of our folk songs is shockingly reprehensible" (26). West also includes the first of several pieces she wrote under the pen name "Mary Christopher." This particular essay recalls the trip she had made to the Soviet Union, which she remembers more for "spiritual" reasons than for political. West resists commenting on the contributions in her "Dear Reader" section of the issue, but one letter from Arna Bontemps serves as a reminder of the political climate when he mentions the "Scottsboro thing [1931 accusations against nine black men in Alabama for raping two white women] at our door" (39). Despite the inclusion of work by and letters from the older, established writers, West optimistically and adamantly concludes this first effort with an appeal to those "new voices."

The second issue of *Challenge,* now called a literary quarterly, does not appear until September 1934. Still relying on the writers of the earlier period (Hurston, Bontemps, McKay, Cullen), West expresses disappointment in the contributions received and embarrassment that she had to "fall back on the tried and true voices" (29), explaining why she moved to a quarterly: "There was little that we wanted to print. Bad writing is unbelievably bad" (29). It is evident that West, "who wrote impeccably standard English," according to Patricia Liggins Hill in *Call and Response,* is not content with these new voices. Even so, with this issue, the career of the young and exceptional Frank Yerby is launched, and

West continues to publish and praise his writing in subsequent issues. As balance, Van Vechten, Bontemps, and Hughes all send reminders that the old voices had not been entirely extinguished and were still holding their own. Continuing the debate over aesthetics, however, is a reaction to Burleigh's article on Negro spirituals in the first issue. This writer, wanting to distance himself from the "sacredness" of spirituals, denies that they are a "Negro" contribution and concludes that "Art should express Man's culture and not degradation" (Hawkins 14).

Another connection with a tradition that had been established in the earlier journals is the literary contest for young black writers. A letter from the West Virginia State College English Department indicated that *Challenge* had inspired them to conduct a poetry contest and asked if West would participate in publishing the "products of this contest" (30). Finally, appearing in this issue is a call for manuscripts to be submitted to *Challenge* by the December issue and judged by established critics. The literary competition is a tradition from which West as writer had benefitted and West as editor is obviously interested in promoting.

In the third issue, not published until May 1935 and noticeably silent about the publication's literary contest, West notes she is "rather pleased with this issue, for most of the names are new to us, and we are glad to note that not all of the voices are Negro" (45). While still containing some work by the older writers (Bontemps and Helene Johnson), many upcoming writers appear (including the young Frank Yerby) who engender West's optimism about the publication: "So *Challenge* continues to hold to its promise, and on the new voices depends its use and growth" (45). Foreshadowing some of the political issues that were to appear in later issues is a letter commenting on the previous exchange about Negro spirituals: "It seemed to me that [Hawkins] was typical of the stupidity and waste that come from too blind adherence to Marxist criticism" (45).

Appearing in January 1936, the fourth issue of *Challenge* notes many letters of praise, yet a new concern surfaces from a letter to the editor. West writes:

> Somebody [actually her friend and fellow writer, Wallace Thurman] asked us why *Challenge* was for the most part so pale pink. We said because the few red articles we did receive were not literature . . . We care a lot about style. And we think a message is doubly effective when effectively written without bombast or bad spelling . . . We would like to print more articles and stories of protest. We have daily contact with the underprivileged.
>
> (38)

This commentary reveals both West's adamant adherence to style and effective writing and her growing sympathy with the literature of social realism. With ref erence to the political ideology, Patricia Liggins Hill places West in the midst of a changing tradition, one that "despite the fine examples set by Alice Dunbar-Nelson and Angelina Grimke, broke ranks with the genteel Negro tradition of favoring a decadent romanticism" (1269). Hill continues, "By the fourth and fifth numbers of *Challenge,* West had changed her literary values a little. With Jessie Fauset and W. E. B. Du Bois, she became the third African American writer to cross the great chasm between romanticism and modernism" (1270).

West's continuing commitment to quality, art, objectivity, and balance is always evident, and as editor of one of the few black magazines of the era, Dorothy West was not alone in her dilemma. Referring to such magazines as *The Anvil* and *Partisan Review,* Frederick Hoffman, in his study, *The Little Magazine,* records: "Most interesting of all is the little magazine which tried to remain impartial and tolerant of varying ideologies in a time when one ideology made increasing demands upon the writer's conscience. The career of such a magazine is likely to be perilous, and its pilot at times bewildered about his course" (163). In this same fourth issue of *Challenge,* West goes on to castigate the potential young audience she is trying to tap by saying that the "bourgeois youth on the southern campus, who should be conscious of these things, is joining a fraternity instead of the brotherhood of serious minds" (38), but she remains hopeful that the middle-class black intelligentsia would become active contributors.

In June of 1936, the fifth issue of the journal, West includes stories and poems by older and newer writers and an article by Louis Emanuel Martin on the first National Negro Congress, one dedicated to the "liquidation of the social and economic problems which have become so vital to the welfare of colored peoples everywhere" (31). Yet a particular letter to the editor captures West's own frustrations with the quality of writing that *Challenge* is attracting, and the editor gives the "explosive" letter the entire space. The writer exclaims: "Your young writers contribute the most inept effusions you publish . . . Most disappointing are those who, young once, showed promise surpassing even your latest young'uns . . . This same basic lack of any depth of true or imaginative thought underlies nine-tenths of your contributions" (46-47).

In the sixth publication almost a year later, April 1937, in what has been called a "transitional issue" (Johnson 115), West allows that perhaps the editorial policies of *Challenge* had not been clearly stated. "Certainly we prefer a progessive magazine," she goes on to say, "But we have no intention of dictating style, choice of subject, or content" (41). She expresses disappointment in the lack of response, particularly from university students, but she also reveals her interest in the "young

Chicago group," which, of course, comprised "Leftist" writers. This apparent appeal to a different audience led the Johnsons to note that "West clearly indicated her enthusiasm for proletarian literature" (112). Referring to the earlier January and June 1936 issues, they go on: "The numbers are memorable mostly because they indicate West's evolution toward the political left" (115), particularly in her publication of Louis Martin's article on the National Negro Congress. So it is no surprise that the April issue includes an article by Marian Minus, who was to become co-editor of *New Challenge* a few months later. In it Minus argues: "No literature can approach greatness if it is not the integrated reflection of the heritage from which it springs" (9). In his search for universality, she continues, the black writer must combine his role as a creative person with that of a member of a minority group, and "His only identification with any group or school must be in terms of the fact that he is a member of a world-society" (11). The merging of the politics and aesthetics seems inevitable.

Of course, the seventh and last issue appearing later in the year called *New Challenge* would take the direction indicated above. However, it is important to note that during the course of all issues of her journal, West does capture certain "dominant tendencies of a literary period" that Bone mentions in the 1960s. She continues to publish and attract the support of the established authors of the earlier, more prolific period of writing (Hughes, McKay, Bontemps, Hurston, Cullen). Yet she also takes great risks in providing the same forum for young, inexperienced writers who both please and disappoint her. In September 1934, the white writer Carl Van Vechten writes his encouragement about the current climate of Negro writing: "If standards are higher, the talent of genius expressed is greater too. In fact, nowadays, there is no inclination on the part of the great public to say, 'Pretty good for a Negro'" (28). Likewise, West is obviously interested in fine-tuning and elevating these standards, yet she also acknowledges the changing cultural climate. Publishing accounts of social and economic debates, current reviews of books written by Hurston, Bontemps, and Du Bois, articles about blacks in Paris, Frank Yerby's poetry, and, indeed, her own chastisements about those submissions that disappoint her, West embodies the status of Negro art in the 1930s. She provides, at least for a few years, a look at the relationship between the older and newer writers, the transition from the 1920s to the 1930s reflected in her own and others' movement to proletarian interests, and a sincere effort to reconcile the differences between art and propaganda. If *Challenge* did not change the boundaries of the argument, it was certainly one of the few black journals of the 1930s that allowed critical standards to be discussed, established, and tested among black artists.

Subsequent to the April 1937 issue, it is evident that there may be some truth to the accusations that West wavered between philosophies and could not come to grips with her own aims. The Johnsons claim that West's frustrations were largely "because she could not, in the first several issues, formulate a clear and consistent editorial policy. Her difficulty emerged because of her own personal evolution, from one who could endorse the relatively conservative position of Johnson to one attracted to the more militant stands of Richard Wright" (113). An alternate view emerges in Lawrence R. Rodgers's article, "Dorothy West's *The Living Is Easy* and the Idea of Southern Folk Community," however, in which he details West's withdrawal from a reading public that became critical of her middle class values contained in her 1948 novel and the early draft of *The Wedding*. Rodgers quotes Nellie McKay's later observations about black women writers and their male counterparts: "While black men projected visions of a world in which race provided almost the only area of conflict between black and white men in the struggle for manhood and power, black women writers have always rejected such binary oppositions and created fictional worlds in which the self is in consistent interaction with a variety of issues, including race" (171). To that end, Farah Jasmine Griffin lends further insight to what may account for West's political waverings regarding the philosophy of the later *New Challenge*, published in the fall of 1937. In her study of the African American migration narrative, *"Who set you flowin'?,"* Griffin comments extensively on the radically different views of Richard Wright and Dorothy West in their novels of southern migration, *Native Son* (1940) and *The Living Is Easy* (1948). Griffin sees Wright's novel as a "vision of a bleak urban landscape" (83) and West's as "a source of inspiring resistance" (87). Citing the variant views, Griffin surmises about the earlier partnership of these two writer/editors that "it is of no surprise that there were tensions between the two at the *New Challenge*. In fact the conflict over the editorial direction of the journal is in and of itself of the different ways the two writers would approach the migration narrative" (83). West's own attempts to verbalize her conflicts with Wright appear to reflect, in part, the observations of both McKay and Griffin, particularly in West's assessment of the climate of gender in the 1930s. When asked why she gave up the journal when it was clear she financed it herself, she replies:

> *Maybe you don't realize it, but it was very hard for one little woman back then. Women of the present are a little more aggressive than I was back then. I guess you could say I was passive.*
>
> *Plus, I was small and my voice soft. So when the Chicago group started having meetings about the direction of the magazine, I remember deciding to give it up.*
>
> (McDowell 271)

That "Chicago group" was led by Richard Wright.

Few assessments of the 1920s and 1930s fail to consider the absence of women writers, women editors, and women critics from the African American tradition. In short, it was, as West herself has frequently noted, male territory. Mary Helen Washington articulately addresses the issue in "'The Darkened Eye Restored'": "Tradition. Now there's a word that nags the feminist critic. A word that has so often been used to exclude or misrepresent women" (32). If this is the case, then West's role as writer/editor was surely not squarely within the existing tradition. West was not the first black woman journal editor; she was not the last. However, despite her own disclaimer about being only "one little woman" back then, many critics have come to believe that during these four years she expanded the African American tradition to include women in the role of responsible and influential promoters of the culture.

New Challenge, the seventh and last issue of West's publication which appears in the fall of 1937 under the new editorship of West, Marian Minus, and Richard Wright, clearly shifts to the political left, although the editorial indicates it is "designed to meet the needs of writers and people interested in literature which cannot be met by those Negro magazines which are sponsored by organizations and which, therefore, cannot be purely literary" (3). Yet that same letter indicates that *New Challenge* will be "a medium of literary expression for all writers who realize the present need for the realistic depictions of life through the sharp focus of social consciousness . . . an organ of regional groups composed of writers opposed to fascism, war and general reactionary policies" (3). The journal is filled with short stories and poems supporting the new editorial policy, two articles addressing the new concerns, Allyn Keith's "A Note on Negro Nationalism," Eugene Holmes's "Problems Facing the Negro Writer Today," and a first book review by Ralph Ellison which was important in shaping this author's literary career. Nonetheless, the magazine's most significant contribution is Richard Wright's influential "Blueprint for Negro Writing." Just as Langston Hughes's essay speaks to and for the period of the 1920s, Wright's essay emerges as the crucial manifesto for the 1930s.

Referring to earlier black writers, Wright maintains that because "White America never offered these Negro writers any serious criticism," and because "Negro writing has been something external to the lives of educated Negroes themselves," Negro writing "assumed two general aspects: 1) It became a sort of conspicuous ornamentation, the hallmark of 'achievement.' 2) It became the voice of the educated Negro pleading with white America for justice" (53). He exhorts black writers to look at their folklore and their religious and social institutions, saying "Negro writers must accept the nationalist implications of their lives, not in order to encourage them, but to change and transcend" (58), accept the

"Marxist analysis of society" (59), and "learn to view the life as [a] Negro living in New York's Harlem or Chicago's South Side with the consciousness that one-sixth of the earth surface belongs to the working class" (62). Wright goes on to say that the writer does not deal solely with the social, economic, and political aspects of life, but must "struggle to regain in some form and under alien conditions of life a *whole* culture again" (63).

Walter C. Daniels, in his article "*Challenge Magazine*: An Experiment That Failed," alludes to the article Richard Wright wrote for *The Daily Worker* in 1937 in which he "further amplified his proposal that *New Challenge* should become a significant organ for proletarian literature." Thus, Daniels continues, Wright's essay has been heralded as "an important document in the development of an ethnic center for Black Writers" (501). On this basis alone *New Challenge* can be commended for printing the codification of a major black literary aesthetic of the 1930s. It is also relevant to note that in 1977 in the first issue of *First World: An International Journal of Black Thought,* Addison Gayle's "Blueprint for Black Criticism," an attempt to promote a separate theory of black aesthetics, is quite obviously modeled on Richard Wright's 1937 "Blueprint" essay. Similar to Wright, Gayle also advocates the coexistence of art and politics in literature.

Consequently, despite West's editorial differences and subsequent abandonment of the journal, her work on both *Challenge* and *New Challenge* helped to provide a forum for aesthetic and philosophical discussion that surfaced again in the 1970s and has continued even through the 1990s.

Theories abound about the degree of West's sympathies with the more radical editorialship and reasons for the demise of the new journal. The Johnsons purport that West's publication failed because it lacked financial support (120). However, most other accounts assume that the dispute was more complicated and personal, that "the journal's failure can in part be traced to a clash between West's reluctance to abandon her desire for non-political 'quality' black writing and Wright's radical agenda that privileged writing inspired 'from below rather than from above'" (Daniel 501), a viewpoint favored later by Griffin and others. Adelaide Cromwell insists that while Dorothy West's travels to the Soviet Union may have indicated a greater proclivity for communist teachings, yet in regard to her editorial stance, "[West] began to resent the pressure exerted by the 'Chicago group' to shape *New Challenge* in response to the party line. They had been part of her public, but had, she felt, moved to control the magazine because they saw the potential for influence she and others had established. But as Dorothy West had 'borned' the

Challenge, she could kill it. And so she did" (Cromwell 357). In the 1988 interview with Katrine Dalsgard, Dorothy West gives her own account: "The young people at the University of Chicago were leftists. I never was, because I was too independent for anything . . . But the minute they decided they were [going] to take over the magazine, I stopped it, and that was the end of that. I had no choice" (38).

For whatever reason Dorothy West's publication failed, one must remember that the nature of "little" magazines in this country, with few exceptions, is, as Hoffman notes, that they have had brief life spans. In addition to the financial instability which most similar publications share, Hoffman posits other reasons for this phenomenon: "Because editors were many and quarrels frequent" and because one of their values is they "usually come into being for the purpose of attacking conventional modes of expression and bringing into the open new and unorthodox literary theories and practices," they "often pursue a perilous career, steering their courses uncertainly and erratically" (4-5). If this is the case, then *Challenge* and *New Challenge* fit squarely within the tradition of the "little" magazine in America.

In many eyes, Dorothy West's efforts to keep alive a black literary tradition originating in the 1920s were feeble at best, yet the *Challenge/New Challenge* issues remained one of the longest running black literary magazines of the 1930s. In her 1988 article, Sandra Y. Govan writes about West:

> If we look at what she attempted and what she accomplished with the *Challenge* journals, it becomes apparent that here, too, was a woman conscious of the need to create and place strong, accurate, realistic and viable images of black life before the reading public; to make black writers themselves more conscious of their responsibilities and obligations to the total community.
>
> (12)

Despite the difficulties Dorothy West experienced with her publication, she is recorded in the history of American black "little" magazines as a writer/editor who kept alive for a number of years a literary tradition, however filled with controversy and conflict. Put another way, "As novelist, editor, journalist, and short story writer, she has spanned nearly three-quarters of a century, thence acting as a senior light in a newly emerging American canon that remains open to change" (Hill 1268). Last, as the literary community is placing more emphasis on revising the African American tradition and, specifically, the role of women in that tradition, it is West's publishing successes, not her failures, that scholarship in this community is acknowledging.

LITTLE MAGAZINES AND LITERARY TRENDS

John Tregenza (essay date 1964)

SOURCE: Tregenza, John. "The Twenties and *Vision.*" In *Australian Little Magazines 1923-1954: Their Role in Forming and Reflecting Literary Trends,* pp. 5-26. Adelaide: Libraries Board of South Australia, 1964.

[*In the essay, below, Tregenza discusses the importance of* Vision, *an Australian little magazine, in ushering in a renaissance of Australian literature in the 1920s.*]

Australian little magazines have only constituted something of a phenomenon since the mid thirties. There are several reasons, the most obvious being Australia's remoteness from European intellectual centres, her small population, her delayed industrialization, and the fact that she was not invaded, nor ever seriously threatened with invasion, during World War I. It was not really until the shock of the world-wide depression of the years 1930-32, that any considerable number of Australians, and more specifically of Australian writers, began to sense Australia's inescapable involvement in the rest of the world's economic, social, and spiritual problems. With the exception of the small group which gathered around Norman Lindsay in the early twenties, few Australian writers were concerned in that decade to shock the general public, or to attack its beliefs, or to gather into coteries. There was no equivalent in Australia during the twenties of that sophisticated and cynical society of American, English and European writers which formed in Paris after the war. Australia did not have her "lost generation", as Gertrude Stein described that society, consciously living in a spiritual Wasteland. Indeed it is doubtful if any more than a handful of Australians had read any of T. S. Eliot's poetry until the thirties. One of Australia's foremost contemporary poets, Kenneth Slessor, has said that he did not come into contact with Eliot's major poetry until as late as 1927![1]

Australians who had experienced the horrors of trench warfare in France tended to remain silent about their experiences. One of the little magazine *coups* in Australia in recent years was the publication in *Overland* (Spring 1958) of the script of an A.B.C. interview by John Thompson with the late Bill Harney, a veteran of World War I. In this Thompson remarked:

> I remember that when I was a schoolboy, I envied those men at the front, singing and fighting and marching about and going on leave and winning medals and ribbons and doing heroic deeds to protect their children and womenfolk thirteen thousand miles away. At the same time, I couldn't understand why my father's friends, men who came back from the war, would never talk about it. Public men talked about it constantly, but not the men who'd been in it. Bill Harney, I know now, would not speak about it for years—and Bill was one of the heroes. He was mentioned in despatches at least once—though he says that that was a mistake—and there's nobody I'd rather be with in a tight corner. Forty years had elapsed before he told me this tale of an ordinary soldier—the fears he had at the front, the peace and quiet after a week in battle.

When Harney returned to Australia after the war he set off immediately on an 800-mile ride on horse-back across northern Australia to the country he had grown up in, "to forget about it all". Few could take such action, but many returned soldiers seem to have shared his feelings, including those with literary talents.

Most of the leading Australian writers of the twenties had already reached middle-age, and most of those who were not overseas were either living in seclusion or were much occupied by non-literary affairs. Henry Handel Richardson was slowly writing the last two books of her trilogy *The Fortunes of Richard Mahony* in an upper room of a house in London. William Hay, author of the convict novel *The Escape of the Notorious Sir William Heans* (first published in England in 1919; Australian edition 1955) was living the life of a literary recluse in a suburb of Adelaide. Miles Franklin, whose "Brent of Bin Bin" novels appeared in the late twenties and early thirties, was abroad until the end of the decade, like another successful Australian woman writer of the early thirties, G. B. Lancaster. Katharine Prichard, after several years as a free-lance writer in London had settled with her husband at Greenmount, on the outskirts of Perth, in 1919.

Of the main poets, William Baylebridge was living in seclusion in Sydney. Bernard O'Dowd, whose last long poem *Alma Venus* was published in 1921, was a parliamentary draughtsman in Melbourne. "Furnley Maurice", another leading Melbourne poet, was the busy manager of the city's largest book-shop, Cole's Book Arcade. Shaw Neilson, whose *Ballad and Lyrical Poems* and *New Poems* were published in 1923 and 1927 respectively, was working as a labourer in the country districts of Victoria. Mary Gilmore was interesting herself in the work of the Roman Catholic orphanages at Goulburn, New South Wales, and in those of other religious denominations—experiences which were to lead to her volume of religious verse, *The Rue Tree* (1931). None of these poets was associated with any particular school or movement either here or overseas, and, like the novelists previously mentioned, all were at least in their forties by 1925.

What of the younger writers? The most successful of these were Miss Marjorie Barnard and Miss Flora Eldershaw, who co-operated in writing *A House is Built,* joint winner of the first *Bulletin* novel competition in

1928, and Martin Boyd, whose long novel in three parts, *The Montforts* (1928) was awarded the gold medal of the Australian Literature Society. Neither Miss Barnard nor Miss Eldershaw appears to have been associated with any literary "movement". After graduating in Arts at Sydney University in 1918, Miss Eldershaw became a teacher. Miss Barnard graduated two years later with First Class Honours in History and became librarian of the Sydney Technical College. Their prize-winning novel, like many of the successful Australian novels of the decade, is not concerned with contemporary issues but with the fortunes of an Australian family in the nineteenth century.

Martin Boyd's *The Montforts* is also a family chronicle, in his own words

> a pseudo-Galsworthian account of my mother's family over five generations, full of thinly disguised portraits.[2]

It is evident from his autobiography, however, published twenty years after he served in Flanders, that Boyd was personally much concerned about the nature and causes and consequences of the 1914-18 war, and seems to have had more in common than most Australian writers of the day with that cosmopolitan group which had settled in Paris after the war, and which was responsible for the production of so many little magazines in the twenties. During the war he had served in the English army, and was the only original officer in his battalion who had survived unscathed by the time he transferred to the Royal Flying Corps. On his return to Australia in 1919 he lived for a time in Melbourne, but felt himself in a "foreign country" outside the family circle, and soon left for Europe.

Another Australian writer who returned to Melbourne in the post-war years was Vance Palmer, and his reactions, as he has recorded them in his biography of Frank Wilmot, were not unlike Boyd's:

> Melbourne, in spite of its occasional production of artists, had a severely commercial tradition, an air of withholding itself, of keeping its ledgers balanced, and of conforming generally to the standards of its rich drapers. Those not interested in commercial pursuits lived on sufferance. What culture and dignity the town possessed (I speak in the past tense) had a distinctly philistine element. It was more respectable to lecture about books than to write them, and the most original painter in town attracted attention to his work by demonstrating its purely scientific base. . . . It was a strange world to me, for I had spent most of my adult life abroad and couldn't easily get used to the idea of a poet justifying himself by his business ability.[3]

Writers like Palmer and Louis Esson, the dramatist, were divided between their desire to remain in Australia to help create an indigenous culture and their desire for the lively discussion of ideas which could only be found in literary circles overseas. It was the second desire which caused Esson to leave Australia in 1917; the first which drew Palmer home in 1920. Esson's letters written to Vance Palmer during his visit abroad, and then after his return home, reveal the conflict in his mind very well. In March 1921, he wrote from London:

> There's no escape in Australia from useless drudgery. I don't want you to desert your post: I would like everybody to return to Australia. But at present you can do no more there than here. In fact it seems you can do less. London, after all, is not England. It is a great centre, like ancient Rome. You want to talk it over quietly with Nettie. You'll get out of touch with London and New York very quickly, for things are always changing. There is no reason why Australia should always be a generation behind. I don't want you to leave, but I don't want you to ruin yourself by attempting what can not yet be done.[4]

Esson, however, was soon home. A long talk with Yeats at Oxford, where he had been the poet's guest, encouraged him to believe in the possibilities of an Australian national theatre similar to the Irish Abbey Theatre. On his return an amateur group called The Pioneer Players was formed to produce mainly Australian plays. This group, rather than any little magazine, seems to have provided the main outlet for what *avant-garde* energy there was in Melbourne during the twenties. In a forbiddingly bleak building called the Temperance Hall, The Pioneer Players performed in 1922 and 1923 the creditable number of seventeen plays by the Australian playwrights, Louis Esson, Stewart Macky, Vance Palmer, Gerald Byrne, Frank Brown, Katherine Prichard, Alan Mulgan, Furnley Maurice, and Ernest O'Ferrall.[5] However, the heavy demands which the venture made on a small group of predominantly middle-aged players, the inability of the group to widen the small circle of their supporters, and the increasing competition of that new medium of mass entertainment, the cinema, forced the group to cease playing. Esson, on the invitation of E. J. Brady, went off to camp in the remote seaside township of Mallacoota West near the border of Victoria and New South Wales, and the movement petered out.

D. H. Lawrence, who paid a brief two-month visit to Australia in 1922, was quick to sense the intellectual barrenness of the country at this time, and the protagonist of his novel *Kangaroo,* published the following year, frequently refers to it:

He says on one occasion:

> Everything is outward—like hollow stalks of corn. The life makes this inevitable: all that struggle with bush and water and what-not, all the mad struggle with the material necessities and conveniences—the inside soul just withers and goes into the outside, and they're all just lusty robust hollow stalks of people.[6]

This was an emotional generalization, but certainly the small literary periodicals which Australia produced in the twenties—with one exception to be considered later—all markedly lacked a spirit of adventure, a sense of urgency, a lively interest in current overseas literature. Most of the contributions to *Corroboree,* the magazine of the Australian Literature Society,[7] to the poetry magazine *The Spinner* and to the latter's continuation *Verse* appear to have come from people comfortably rooted in the suburbs or in country homes. The kind of verse published in *The Spinner* is fairly clearly indicated in the editor's foreword to the first number, with its emphasis on romantic picture poetry, its use of consciously poetical diction, and reference to the "tonic" function of poetry. It runs:

> *The Spinner* comes before the public of Australasia to render them service, to sing them a song or two, to chant to them ballads and tales of all lands, to intone the philosophy of Nature, to paint in words, pictures of the city, the mountains, the plains, the farmlands, and the blue hosts of the sea. . . . Poetry is a tonic for the mind; it refreshes the individual and the community; it voices their ambitions, their loves, and their griefs; it is the language of thought but not of facts. *The Spinner* will give the best Australasia can supply of this great art of poesy . . .

Some of those represented, like "Furnley Maurice", Shaw Neilson, Mary Gilmore, Louis Lavater, were well-skilled in their craft, but their best contributions were quietly reflective or delicately lyrical in character—certainly not *avant garde* in the current European sense. And they were only a handful of the magazine's 130 contributors.

A high proportion of these were women. On this phenomenon, Elsie Cole, herself a contributor to *The Spinner,* commented in an address given to the Australian Literature Society and reported in an abridged form in the twelfth and last number of *Corroboree,* September, 1922:

> . . . in each Australian weekly or monthly paper we see an increasing quantity of verse over women's names. Most of it is for one reading only. It gives a passing pleasure with its music, a transient sentiment of agreement or disagreement with its thought; then it has served its purpose and may be forgotten. The authors themselves would make no more claim for it. . . . It seems . . . that women have not had the freedom of the Dominion of Verse long enough to take it for granted. Many of them are too much aware of their sex while they are writing, and over-stress the softly pretty note in lullabies or flowery details.

Elsie Cole's critical outlook, however, was exceptional. Much more characteristic of the critical articles, reviews, and reports of addresses printed in *Corroboree* is "Some Australian Women Poets" (a paper given by Miss Mary E. Wilkinson at a Women's Night at the Australian Literature Society and reported in *Corroboree,* January 1922). After talking of the "wonderful and arduous school" which inevitably must evolve in women "certain specific qualities of unpretentiousness, unselfishness, ungrudging labour in the performance of duty", she goes on to offer a series of comments on the work of thirteen poetesses, in the course of which she refers to the "sympathy" of ten, and the "understanding" or "insight" of seven. The article concludes:

> One, however, catches a tiny glimpse at times of a great light shining ahead, and realizes that our women poets are doing a greater work than they as yet comprehend.[8]

How closely this address corresponds with the proceedings of the pseudo-cultural Thanatopsis club of Gopher Prairie which Sinclair Lewis portrayed in *Main Street* in 1921!

A similar uncritical enthusiasm, although more informed, is evident in the review of Bernard O'Dowd's *Alma Venus* by "S.R."[9] in which he exclaims of the Australian poet:

> Read his poem and read "Urn Burial", and you will find that O'Dowd has successfully accomplished in verse, what Sir Thomas Browne did in prose.

This readiness to praise extravagantly, and to temper adverse criticism with words of encouragement, is characteristic of Australian literary men and women of the twenties awaiting the arrivals of the Great Australian Poet and the Great Australian Novelist with the undaunted optimism of the Hebrews expecting the Messiah. Unfortunately most of them were too comfortably settled in their ways either to encourage movements which might lead to such figures or to recognize them when they actually did appear. The first two volumes of Henry Handel Richardson's great trilogy, for instance, were hardly read by anyone in Australia during the twenties. *Australia Felix* indeed was dismissed by the *Bulletin* reviewer Arthur Adams as bearing

> the impress of the autobiography of a rather dull person.[10]

Vance Palmer relates[11] how he came across the volume by chance in a bargain basement, and how subsequently it became worn out through being posted so often to other writers like Katharine Prichard and Louis Esson!

In Sydney there was the *Bulletin,* but by the 1920's the *Bulletin* had very little new to say. As early as 1912, A. G. Stephens, a shrewd, if not wholly dispassionate commentator, had remarked in the *Bookfellow,* referring to the year 1900:

> *The Bulletin* at that time was important—it was a force, not a formula.[12]

Plainly a new Australian movement capable of stirring the country out of its literary torpor was urgently needed. Australian literature could not consist for ever of chronicle and convict novels, *Bulletin* ballads and the unreal Georgian verse being contributed in large quantities to the Melbourne poetry magazines.

In this outline of Australian literary activity in the twenties, one important group of writers has been omitted. This group formed around the Sydney artist Norman Lindsay in the early twenties, and in the course of a decade produced three little magazines, *Vision* (1923-24), *The London Aphrodite* (1928-29) and *The Australian Outline* (1933-34); an anthology, *Poetry in Australian: 1923*; and two books on philosophy and aesthetics, *Creative Effort* by Norman Lindsay (1924) and *Dionysos: Nietzsche contra Nietzsche, an essay in lyrical philosophy* (1928) by Jack Lindsay. At the centre of the group there were five writers, all of whom have considerable reputations in Australia today. Two of the five, Norman Lindsay and Hugh McCrae, were in their mid-forties when *Vision* appeared in 1923. The other three—Jack Lindsay (Norman's eldest son), Kenneth Slessor and R. D. FitzGerald—were in their early twenties. This group virtually formed the only *avant-garde* circle in Australia in the early twenties. But it did not have much in common with the *avant-garde* groups of post-war Europe—in fact it repudiated Joyce and the Sitwells and Eliot and Van Gogh and all manifestations of what it called "modernism". *Vision* believed, as many Australian writers had believed earlier in the century, that Australia, because of her youth and her sunny climate and her freedom from inter-racial and international hatreds, was in a position to heal the sickness of war-weary and disillusioned Europe. This view is advanced in the Foreword to the first number of the magazine published in May 1923:

> Considering the depths of devitalisation the world touched in the War—for Hatred is a febrile thing, the expression of spiritual inertia, not of strength—considering that now for the first time in history, Primitivism in the Arts has been expressed by a deliberate intellectual choice, it is clear that unless consciousness soon takes an upward turn, vitality will sink too low ever to recover. A Renaissance is a necessity, and we believe that already the stirring of wings can be felt. . . . If then we are to vindicate the possession of Youth, we must do so by responding to all other expressions of Youth, and by rejecting all that is hieroglyphic, or weary and depressed. If Australia alone in the world is doing this—and we see no evidence for any other conclusion—then the Renaissance must begin from here. . . .

In accordance with this programme *Vision* sought "primarily to provide an outlook for good poetry, or for any prose that liberates the imagination by gaiety or fantasy". The magazine also encouraged its contributors to introduce passion into their writing. The best expression of *Vision's* belief in the value of passion in life and art is contained in a passage reprinted in the fourth issue from Havelock Ellis's *Little Essays of Love and Virtue* (1922):

> . . . the ages in which ill-regulated passion exceeded— ages at least full of vitality and energy—gave place to a more anaemic society. Today, the conditions are changed; even reversed. Moral maxims that were wholesome in feudal days are deadly now. We are in no danger of suffering from too much vitality, from too much explosive splendour of our social life. We possess, moreover, knowledge in plenty and self-restraint in plenty, however wrongly they may be sometimes applied. It is passion, more passion, and fuller, that we need. For we know what happens in a world when those who ban passion have triumphed. When Love is suppressed, Hate take its place. . . .

Vision believed too, with Nietzsche, that the moral sanctions of other-worldly religion should no longer command respect. The Foreword to the fourth number begins:

> One of Nietzsche's gifts to the future might well be entitled *The Conscience for Life*. We legionaries of the new Roman effort to reconstruct earth deny utterly all that has been understood in the past by the term "conscience"—responsibility to external law, whether that be the Mosaic tables or the Kantian categorical "imperative" The old paraphernalia of contrition and remorse by means of which the animal is made to fear vengeance and repent, is likewise alien to our Hellenic world of strong and free spirits, creating their own heaven, their own responsibility, their own destiny.

In bringing about their Renaissance, the *Vision* writers did not intend to write about distinctively Australian subjects or to employ imagery drawn from their immediate environment. They believed that, as Australians, they were specially qualified to lead the world back to sanity, but they were also aware that they could not effect this end unless they dealt with subjects and used images which had meaning for all English-speaking people. Jack Lindsay, one of the editors of *Vision* and its most prolific contributor, wrote in an article entitled "Australian Poetry and Nationalism":[13]

> . . . all true poets are really of one stock. If they belong to any nationality, it is one that has no name upon the maps of this world, but lies with Pindar's Hyperboreans. . . . The old Dionysian truth rules here: blood is spirit: out of this body we must build all higher ones. If we are to give this stock of the poets. artists and musicians any name we may as well call it Hellenic, for the Greeks transmitted the whole mass of emotional imagery on which every poet has since built. . . . How then is the Greek to come to life in Australia? Not of course by merely writing hymns to the Olympians (though there is no reason why these exercises in piety should be disdained, and if Keats discovered Eros and Psyche sleeping together, Hugh McCrae has beheld the naked and deathless gods in the woods), but by a pro-

found response to life, by the expression of lyric gaiety, by a passionate sensuality, by the endless search for the image of beauty, the immortal body of desire that is Aphrodite. Thus we may found a genuine Australian literature. It is a short-sighted Nationalism that can be proud only of verse about shearers and horses, and measures the reality of a work by its local references.

The *Vision* programme certainly derived mainly from Norman Lindsay, and to a lesser extent from Hugh Mc-Crae. When *Vision* appeared in 1923, Norman Lindsay was already an artist of some standing in Australia—particularly in Sydney. He had been employed since the first years of the century as one of the leading cartoonists on the *Bulletin*, but apart from his work in this capacity of popular humorist and political commentator, he had been doing fine pen drawings and etchings, particularly as book illustrations, for over a decade. In 1909 he had illustrated Hugh McCrae's book of poems, *Satyrs and Sunlight*. In 1912 an edition of Petronius was published in London containing one hundred illustrations by him. More recently he had illustrated Mc-Crae's *Colombine* (1920) and *Idyllia* (1922) and Leon Gellert's *Songs of a Campaign* (1917) and *The Isle of San* (1919). In 1916, in an article entitled "The Modern Malady" contributed to the first number of *Art in Australia* (a strong Lindsay supporter in these years) he had begun to develop the anti-Christian, Nietzschean, "joy in life" views later to be expounded at greater length in *Vision* and in his book *Creative Effort,* published in London in 1924. He seems to have done this partly by way of protest against the horror of World War I (a protest strongly made in his illustrations to Gellert's *Songs of a Campaign*) and partly in order to explain his art, and to defend it against the charges of triviality and vulgarity which had been made against it.

It was during these years that his son Jack came under his influence. During his teens Jack and his brothers Raymond and Philip lived with their mother in Brisbane. P. R. Stephensen, who was a contemporary of Jack's at the University of Queensland, tells how periodically in 1919 Norman would send his sons, from his home in the Blue Mountains, "pulls" of his etchings and letters full of the ideas which he was then formulating—all of which naturally made deep impressions on the boys.[14] At this time Jack was aged nineteen. In 1921, very much under the influence of his father, he contributed to the first number of the University of Queensland magazine *Galomahra* an article entitled "Satyrs or Kookaburras?" in which he strongly advocated the use of imagery drawn from Greek mythology in Australian poetry. He also contributed a page of erotic verse which caused the whole issue to be suppressed by the university authorities. After taking a First in Classics[15] Jack

and his younger brothers moved to Sydney where they launched into a bohemian existence, living in garrets, and devoting themselves to the arts.

In the second volume of his lively autobiography, *The Roaring Twenties,* Jack Lindsay tells how his father had had hopes of making him literary editor of a reorganized *Art in Australia,* and how, when this scheme fell through, he himself began to organize his own literary magazine as a vehicle for Lindsay ideas. The business side was to be handled by Frank Johnson, an assistant in Dymock's bookshop, and the printing to be done by John Kirtley, an employee in a stock-exchange firm who had bought his own press and was anxious to do some fine printing. The literary side, and the writing of editorials, was to be Jack's responsibility, with Norman as adviser, and Kenneth Slessor and R. D. FitzGerald as collaborators and contributors of verse. Slessor was then already established as a journalist, FitzGerald in training as a land surveyor. The group mostly met in one of a line of coffee cellars then run by a Mr. Mockbell, where they could sit at ease on the capacious leather seats and slowly consume their fourpenny jugs of coffee on the marble-topped tables. In such circumstances was *Vision* born and fostered through its four numbers.

It can be seen, however, that the magazine's programme was not suddenly thought out by one or two young men in 1923. It was really based on the drawings and etchings which Norman Lindsay had been executing, and the poems which Hugh McCrae had been writing, for the last decade, though given a new urgency by the war of 1914-18. In fact much that was distinctive in the magazine seems to derive from the English nineties—the era of Oscar Wilde and Aubrey Beardsley and Ernest Dowson—the era when Nietzsche's writings were becoming known in England, largely owing to Havelock Ellis's study in *The Savoy* magazine in 1896. During the 1890's, both Norman Lindsay and Hugh McCrae had been in their teens, and there are many superficial resemblances between the erotic pen drawings of the former and those of Aubrey Beardsley.

In the work of the younger contributors to *Vision,* particularly of Kenneth Slessor, there can be found not only ideas derived from the nineties via Norman Lindsay, but many traces of direct inspiration from his art. *Vision* believed in gaiety and fantasy on the one hand and in passion on the other. It also disbelieved in the value of local references in art. Its contributors therefore tended, like Lindsay (and Beardsley) to find their subject matter in past ages which appealed to their imaginations, particularly the sixteenth and eighteenth centuries.[16] Kenneth Slessor's longest contribution to *Vision,* for example, a poem entitled "The Man of Sentiment", consists of two conversations between Laurence

Sterne and Catherine de Fromantel [Fourmantelle?] before and after *Tristram Shandy* had been published in London. Parts of this poem seem almost like descriptions of a Norman Lindsay etching. It opens with lines which immediately suggest one of Lindsay's old gardens:

LAURENCE:

> Nay, 'tis no Devil's walk.
> It leads to what? Some leaden Child with lips
> Blown open, spouting fountain-dew on birds
> That drowsily dive the pool—some secret Lawn
> Tight locked away in mazes, and trod by none
> Save one old crazy Gardener—aye, 'tis prick'd
> In curious inks on charts of old, I'll vow, . . .

Then how often Lindsay has depicted the kind of picturesque and passionate rogue which Slessor writes of in "Thieves' Kitchen".

> Leap, leap, fair vagabonds, your lives are short . . .
> Dance firelit in your cauldron-fumes, O thieves,
> Ram full your bellies with spiced food, gulp deep
> Those goblets of thick ale—yet, feast and sport,
> Ye Cyprian maids—lie with great, drunken rogues,
> Jump by the fire—soon, soon your flesh must crawl
> And Tyburn flap with birds, long-necked and swart![17]

There is a similar kind of escape into Havelock Ellis's "ages in which ill-regulated passion exceeded—ages at least full of vitality and energy" in Jack Lindsay's poems "Porto Bello" ("Loose-triggered Hugh with tarry thumb"),[18] "Lonely" ("All the pirates are gone, chasing under seas"),[19] and "The Death of Marlowe" ("Plague not the horn-eyed crew. Had I my way").[20] In a brief introduction to the last poem Lindsay writes:

> Whether Marlowe was killed in the street or within doors is uncertain and negligible. I have tried only to express something of that reckless daring quality which is so obvious in his work . . .

Several of the poems contributed to *Vision* could well have been written in England during the eighteen nineties. Compare for instance the following lines from Dowson's "Ad Manus Puellae" with Slessor's "New Magic".

> Oh, how shall I kiss your hands enough?
>
> They are pale with the pallor of ivories;
>   But they blush to the tips like a curled sea-shell:
> What treasure, in kingly treasuries,
>   Of gold, and spice for the thurible,
>   Is sweet as her hands to hoard and tell?[21]

The first stanza of Slessor's poem reads:

> At last I know—it's on old ivory jars,
>   Glassed with old miniatures and garnered once with musk,

I've seen those eyes like smouldering April stars
As carp might see them behind their bubbled skies
In pale green fishponds—they're as green, your eyes,
As lakes themselves, changed to green stone at dusk.[22]

In both passages, the first celebrating a woman's hands, the second a woman's eyes, there is a similar use of romantic imagery, a similar kind of sensibility. Or compare the fashion in which Dowson on the one hand, and FitzGerald on the other, lament the passing of beauty. Dowson's "To William Theodore Peters on His Renaissance Cloak" commences:

> The cherry-coloured velvet of your cloak
>   Time hath not soiled: its fair embroideries
> Gleam as when centuries ago they spoke
>   To what bright gallant of Her Daintiness,
>   Whose slender fingers, long since dust and dead,
>   For love or courtesy embroidered
> The cherry-coloured velvet of this cloak.
>
> Ah! cunning flowers of silk and silver thread,
>   That mock mortality! the broidering dame,
> The page they decked, the kings and courts are dead:[23]

R. D. FitzGerald's "The Dark Rose" commences:

> Philanion, who danced before the King—
> (Heart, have you then forgotten these broad days,
> The breathing Present and the present Earth,
> That once again you must go wandering
> Among old ages with a gift of praise
> To lay before her feet of little worth?)
> Of all past beauty of remembered Spring
> She is the most lost, the most utterly gone:
> The little dust that was Philanion
> Out, out of mind an hour after her fall. . . .
> Pale kings who watched her dancing, this was all;
> What dream could hold her longer? Crowns and swords
> Cover the broken years with litter and rust; . . .[24]

It is quite possible that Slessor and FitzGerald had not read Dowson when they wrote these poems. But the fact that they chose to write about such a subject in such a precious, romantic style suggests that they were in much the same poetic situation in Sydney in the nineteen twenties as Dowson in London during the nineties. They did not write then like their contemporary T. S. Eliot because they did not know his world. None of the main *Vision* contributors had been closely involved in the Great War—they had been too old or too young. They had not experienced the disillusion and bitterness of the post-war years in Europe, nor did they know at first hand the quality of life in a large industrial city. They rightly refused to assume a tired cynicism which they did not genuinely feel. On the other hand they knew nothing of the Great Australian Outback. The life that they did know—the respectably dull life of Sydney—oppressed them just as Victorian London had oppressed the poetic coteries of the eighteen nineties. In this context *Vision* provided a much needed stimulus to poetry at the time, just as the *Yellow Book* and *The Sa-*

voy and the Nietzschian magazine *The Eagle and the Serpent* had provided a much-needed stimulus to the literature of England three decades before. The *Vision* poets were often trivial, and they spent too much time peering through magic casements, but they did attempt to write vital, imaginative poetry which could be judged not by local but by the best English standards. The fact that they failed in 1923 does not destroy the value of the attempt. It was a decided step forward in the evolution of Australian poetry.

In *The Roaring Twenties* and *Fanfrolico and After* Jack Lindsay tells how he left Sydney for London in 1926 at the instance of *Vision*'s printer Jack Kirtley, who had suggested that they might experiment there with the printing and publishing of books by classical and contemporary authors sympathetic to the *Vision* creed. In London they took a second-floor room on Bloomsbury Square as offices for their Fanfrolic Press, and, by some skilful "financial tight-rope walking" and the use of Norman Lindsay's drawings and etchings for textual illustrations, managed to get established as publishers of limited editions. When Kirtley returned to Australia, Lindsay was joined by P. R. Stephensen, an old friend from university days in Queensland who had been at Oxford on a Rhodes scholarship, but had found that membership of the Communist Party and a record of having distributed Gandhi pamphlets to Indian students had prejudiced his chances for post-graduate employment. Stephensen had recently made the first English translation of Lenin's *Imperialism* (from the French) and had collaborated in the first English translations of poems by the Russians Blok and Mayakovsky. In 1926 he left the Communist Party, but for some time remained fairly much in sympathy with its ideals.[25]

By 1928 Lindsay and Stephensen felt the Fanfrolico Press sufficiently well established to allow them the satisfaction of producing a new magazine, to be named *The London Aphrodite*. *The London Aphrodite* was really a larger, more sophisticated *Vision*, with Norman's inevitable decorations, but with new anarchistical overtones from Stephensen, who was steadily bringing his co-editor round to his political views. In his personal Manifesto in the first number, Lindsay announced:

> We stand for a point of view which equally outrages the modernist and the reactionary. It is certain that J. C. Squire and T. S. Eliot, Wyndham Lewis and Dean Inge, Humbert Wolfe and Robert Graves, E. E. Cummings and Alfred Noyes, Maritain and James Douglas, Roger Fry and William Orpen, would, if compelled by physical force to read our magazine, heartily (or at least irritatedly) dislike it.

It was described by Lindsay as the "post-post-war" magazine—

> not at all neurotic, tortured, introspectively disgusted or christian. . . .

Like *Vision* it took a pose half serious and half flippantly gay. It announced right at the beginning that it would be

> thoroughly biased and unjust at times when to fritter analyses on minute qualifications is to sacrifice the larger justice.

and that it was being produced

> not for profit, but merely in a mood of exuberance.

It was also announced that there would be six numbers only, obtainable solely by pre-paid subscription. It was a calculated risk which seems to have succeeded, giving confidence to hesitant would-be subscribers and contributors, and providing a better chance of maintaining an even literary standard. Lindsay wrote in 1962:

> I forget how many we printed of the magazine, but it must have been round 3,500; and after the last issue P. R. Stephensen told me that he had raised the money for a full reprint of some 1,500 copies, which we sold bound.[26]

In the last-issue-but-one the editors thus shrewdly defended their policy of limiting the number of issues:

> There has never yet been a literary periodical which has not gone dull after the first half-dozen numbers. We do not intend to perpetuate the abominable habit of stabilising an impulse such as that which motivated the launching of this journal. Such impulses are only too rare. We must sit down awhile and hope for another. Consequently, after the appearance of Number Six, *The London Aphrodite* will exercise the prerogative of a goddess and disappear. We do not intend to let her become *The Cockney Venus*.

There were sufficient Australians then in England or on the Continent—having followed Louis Esson's line of reasoning and fled their homeland for the time-being—to contribute almost half the contents of the six numbers of *The London Aphrodite*. There was W. J. Turner, a poet who had left Australia before 1914 and become associated with the *New Statesman* as a music critic; Brian Penton, an old Brisbane Grammar School contemporary of Lindsay who was shortly to take over from Stephensen in the Fanfrolico Press and later to edit the *Sydney Morning Herald* and publish the novel *Landtakers*; E. J. Rupert Atkinson, a well-to-do Melbourne poet and dramatist, patron of Hugh McCrae, and self-styled decadent; Bertram Higgins, poet and essayist from Melbourne who had become a co-editor of the English journal *The Calendar of Modern Letters* after graduating at Oxford; and Philip Lindsay, who had followed his older brother Jack to London, and, true to the Lindsay tradition, was to publish a number of highly coloured and successful novels set in earlier centuries.

The dominant personality in the magazine, however, was Jack Lindsay. In addition to other articles by him, the magazine printed a long critical essay entitled, "The

Modern Consciousness; An Essay Towards an Integration" in its first number; a series of thirty-nine poems entitled collectively, "The Passionate Neatherd, A Lyric Sequence" and full of Greek gods, gay girls, sunlight, and Norman's romantic old gardens; and a long autobiography printed serially in the six numbers under the pseudonym of "Peter Meadows", and entitled "Dung of Pegasus".

In his essay on "The Modern Consciousness", Lindsay surveyed the confused literary scene of the late twenties, and remarked on the futility of attempting to create an integrated art

> by abstracting from every group or apostle that which is the central pronunciamento, to tabulate all these odds and ends faithfully and then to discover what general criteria may be evolved which will glucosely stretch over the mass with the least contradiction. . . .[27]

We can only create an integrated art, he wrote,

> by keeping our minds forever orientated towards the instinctive core of life, letting this plasmic energy soak us through and through, not perverting it by abstractly moral views of its nature.[28]

He had no patience with those who surrendered themselves to the flux of time, or with those who believed that art should mirror life exactly, so that if

> life is nothing but jazz and machinery, . . . we must produce a pastiche of lurching rhythms and angular forms,

or with those for whom

> an expression must be frankly experimental before it can be admitted to have achieved anything, and if every architectonic device does not stick alarmingly into the air out of a minimum of digested material, the work is considered amorphous, reactionary or romantic . . .[29]

When Lindsay came to expound his own views on life and art he was much inclined to lose himself and his reader in a cloud of abstractions (more than one reader must have shared the dismay of the old gentleman who wrote in to ask "what Jack Lindsay does when he is serious if he wrote *The Modern Consciousness* for fun?"[30]—alluding to the *Aphrodite*'s professed aim). Yet with all his unprofitable struggling after definitions, Lindsay did sense quite accurately a change which was then just beginning to take place in the English literary climate, and which was not altogether unsympathetic to the "Renaissance" proclaimed a few years earlier in *Vision*.

In "The Modern Consciousness", after describing W. B. Yeats's *A Vision* (first published two years before in 1926) as

the only truly profound contribution to thought since Nietzsche,

he went on to proclaim the arrival of Yeats's "Third Kingdom of the spirit", the signs of which were

> a liberation of irrational Dionysian force, and, simultaneously, a strengthening of the antithetical symbols of the intellect.[31]

Applying this formula to the stage-play, he wrote in his article "Poetry and Life":

> An effort has been made by W. B. Yeats in his *Four Plays For Dancers,* inspired by the Noh plays, to lift the drama altogether out of its stagey bog and concentrate it back to a clarity of poetic symbolism. . . . We see here a potent suggestion for escape from the realistic stage. Gordon Bottomley however has alone sought to develop this hint in *Scenes and Plays* which carry on this transfusion of lyrical blood and do away with the whole deadening mechanism of the realistic stage, its scenery, exits, entrance, and particularly its clumsy and hopelessly ineffective means of securing continuity. Here it seems to me is the seed of the formal revitalization of the drama . . .[32]

Of the creative contributions to the magazine, Lindsay's serialized "Dung of Pegasus", describing significant experiences in his life as he grew up in Australia, is certainly the longest and most valuable. It is just as evident in these first frank sketches, as in his recently-published autobiographical trilogy, that Lindsay living out his theories is far more interesting than Lindsay theorizing.

The contributions of the other Australians fall mostly into the light entertainment category, and in most cases are not examples of their authors' best work. In these contributions and in those of overseas writers, love of various kinds features prominently, no doubt as a consequence of the magazine's policy of encouraging "sexual candour" in writing. Most of the heroines of both stories and poems conform to the requirements of a Norman Lindsay "goddess". The heroine of Rhys Davies's story "A Bed of Feathers", for instance, is described as "a rose-red blooming creature of twenty-five, with wanton masses of goldish hair and a suggestion of proud abandonment about her", a description which could apply almost equally well to the heroine of Liam O'Flaherty's "Red Barbara". Either these blooming creatures are poetical nymphs gracing a traditional pastoral scene, or, in modern life, the wives of ageing, commercially-successful men who are incapable of satisfying them. In the latter case, the husbands almost invariably die or are cuckolded, their places being taken by young men possessed of an ardour as primitive and incalculable as that of their lovers. Fortunately, the magazine was able to secure contributions from such writers as Rhys Davies, Liam O'Flaherty and Philip

Owens, which, although conforming to the pattern outlined above, are at least quite well written and constructed, for most of the others of this kind are as immature in execution as they are in conception. Interestingly enough, Owens's play, "The Widow of Ephesus"—"a dramatic version of the story of the widow in Petronius, and based on the complete translation of the works by Jack Lindsay" antedates by seventeen years the use of the same story by Christopher Fry in his *A Phoenix Too Frequent,* Fry having come by it through Jeremy Taylor.

It was while he was publishing *The London Aphrodite* that Lindsay received a number of criticisms which led him to question whether the Fanfroliconean doctrines were not leading him away from reality rather than into its heart. D. H. Lawrence told him bluntly:

> Stop the love slush. Stick to your hate.

Freud insisted that he (Lindsay) had been "quite wrong' in what he had written of Nietzsche's relations with Frau Salome, while Edgell Rickword, of *The Calendar of Modern Letters,* took him to task for claiming that another of his heroes, Aristophanes, did not care for Athens as a political entity.[33] At the same time he came steadily under the influence of Stephensen, who was not at all inclined to drown his hates in love slush. The tone the magazine might increasingly have adopted, had it continued beyond the six numbers, is indicated in Stephensen's essay entitled "Bakunin". To Stephensen, Michael Bakunin was the very fore-runner postulated by Nietzsche, "the essential revolutionary, the antithesis of Baldwin". Only through the "Bakunin principle" could Baldwin's England conceivably be humanized:

> No well-intentioned person could journey in an underground tube-train full of wan faces coming in to work in the mornings from the suburbs, reading their *Daily Express,* or returning from their work in the evenings towards the suburbs, reading their *Evening Standard,* without feeling homicidal. If this massed paleness and vacuity is what civilisation has brought man to, by all means let civilisation be destroyed.[34]

After the six numbers of *The London Aphrodite* had run their prescribed course, the *Vision* movement seems to have waned. It did give birth, it is true, to two numbers of *The Australian Outline,* which was published in Sydney in 1933-34 by a former editor of *Vision,* Frank C. Johnson, but this magazine lacked the vigour and urgency of its predecessors. The second number failed to come up to the expectations aroused by the dramatic statement in the first that it would contain:

> *unusual* stories, articles, verse, reviews, hors d' oeuvres by a brilliant list of Australian writers who are not allowed to say *this kind of thing* elsewhere.

There were articles and poems by the original *Vision* contributors Norman Lindsay, R. D. FitzGerald, and

Kenneth Slessor, but there was little evidence in the magazine of the old intense desire to promulgate a new vision, a new aesthetic.

The failure of *The Australian Outline* made it clear that the time had come for other little magazines with new outlooks to lead the *avant-garde.* By the mid thirties most of the younger writers originally composing the movement were proceeding to take roads of their own, dropping the elements of the old creed which were no longer of value, and retaining those which they could successfully incorporate into their new work. On his return to Australia at this time, P. R. Stephensen, the sometime co-editor of *The London Aphrodite,* rejected forcibly the *Vision* assertion that Australian poets should avoid local references in their poetry, but still retained and promulgated with even greater vigour, social and political theories derived from Nietzsche. On the other hand, Jack Lindsay, settled now in England, and soon, in 1936, to become a Marxist, retained his early interest in the Renaissance and Classical Greece and Rome. Kenneth Slessor and R. D. FitzGerald continued to subscribe consciously or unconsciously to several tenets of the *Vision* programme through the thirties. In an article entitled "Vision of the Twenties" contributed to *Southerly* in 1952, Jack Lindsay suggested that these two writers had been, to their detriment as poets, "sucked into" what he called the "*Vision* trend". Slessor has denied this, claiming that he contributed to *Vision* just as he would have contributed to any other magazine, and that his role as co-editor with Lindsay and Frank Johnson was restricted to the practical journalism of selecting and preparing copy, writing heads and correcting proofs. Yet without claiming that *Vision* in itself had any serious effect on Slessor's poetry, it can still be said that *Vision* did make explicit a number of assumptions about art and society implicit in the works of Norman Lindsay and Hugh McCrae, and that Slessor and other *Vision* contributors were for some time involved in a trend originating in the personalities and art of these two men. It was the function of *Vision* to define this trend, and, by attracting a "large and determined audience of several thousands"[35] to help create a taste in Australia for the kind of poetry then being written by the *Vision* writers, including Slessor and FitzGerald.

In recent years Slessor has been inclined to discount the significance of his association with *Vision,* but not so R. D. FitzGerald. In 1939, when reviewing a book of poems by Hugh McCrae, he exclaimed:

> I contributed to *Vision* which I shall claim as an unshadowable distinction till earth breaks me in little pieces. It need hardly be said then, that McCrae has been a star in my firmament.

His comments on McCrae's poetry in this review, make it quite clear that in 1939 he still retained the *Vision* dislike of "modernism". He wrote:

In the regrettable state of poetry in the world today, that McCrae must be assigned a high, perhaps the highest, place among living English-speaking poets is not flattery; were he considerably less than he is it would still be only too distressingly obvious. Much more to the point is it that consistently his work has stood for soundness and sincerity and conscientious craftsmanship. That would not be enough. It has stood also for love of the fruitful earth, for simplicity, for zest, for joy of living, for that unique vitality which is Hugh McCrae.[36]

As late as 1955 he wrote the following, even more emphatically worded, "Acknowledgment to Norman Lindsay":

> Thin solvency is proud, eats weeds.
> I, being borrower yet
> whom the sun warms and turned soil feeds,
> claim there is honor in debt.
>
> Much I acknowledge owed: the sight
> of the mind quickened and stirred
> to vast realities—tremblings of light
> become a shape or a word.
>
> I own the whole attitude to the task
> derived—thence anything won
> through effort. For we take, we ask,
> we do not repay the sun.[37]

In his poetry FitzGerald has asserted again and again, usually in romantic terms, the *Vision* belief that modern man is starved of adventure and gaiety and passion. In *Moonlight Acre* (1938) he remarks:

> It is best to make provision against the rot
> of peace, which fattens harvest, but whets no stars
> in the bewildered blood, swung scimitars—
>
> to ride out with some frenzied Lancelot
> upon an exploit perilous as vain,
> and in deep woods do battle with the dark
> of passion's madness, . . .[38]

In another section he remarks ironically:

> As for this atavistic twitch
> of muscles, bricked up in the gaol of town,
> which find in collars a slave-ring, in chairs an itch,
> and start you walking up and down, up and down—
>
> Better to wear out your chain
> than greet fresh lands that dawn through veiling rain.[39]

In "Essay on Memory", written on the eve of the Second World War, he asks defiantly:

> How should we hold us from wild enterprise,
> who use the limbs of the past and its quick eyes
> and are eternally in debt to those
> who stung into the earth-dawn's turgid throes
> urge of keen life? We'll crash the trestles down
> that barricade clear laughter, take the town

> on a burst of shouting that through fissures rent
> cascades its fervid glee, magnificent.
> We'll slit gloom's gullet, oracling defeat,
> and crack great barrels of song in open street,
> free for the drinking. We'll make fabulous
> this world, in honour of them who gave it us, . . .[40]

Well over a decade before, *Vision* had been asserting the virtues of youthful gaiety and "wild enterprise", and had been encouraging Australian poets to "make fabulous" the world.

There could be no better testimony to the persistent vitality of the *Vision* trend than the publication in Sydney in 1963, forty years later, of another *Vision*, sanctioned and blessed by Norman Lindsay, and edited by that most unorthodox of estate agents, Bruce Skurray.[41] The new journal, described as a "magazine of the Arts, Science and Australiana", makes a renewed protest against the dreary uniformity of urban Australian life, and in its first issue fittingly prints reproductions of works by Albrecht Dürer, a tribute to Norman Lindsay, and poems by Kenneth Slessor, Judith Wright, W. Hart-Smith, Rosemary Dobson and Douglas Stewart.

Notes

1. *Southerly,* no. 4, 1952, p. 218.

2. *A Single Flame* [autobiography], 1939, p. 204.

3. *Frank Wilmot (Furnley Maurice),* 1942, p. 8.

4. Vance Palmer: *Louis Esson and the Australian Theatre,* Georgian House, 1948, p. 33.

5. *Ibid,* pp. 47-53.

6. *Kangaroo,* Penguin ed., p. 146.

7. Melbourne, 12 nos., 1921-22.

8. *Corroboree,* Nov. 1921, p. 5. Miss Wilkinson was the editor of *Gleanings From Australasian Verse.* (1919-1920)

9. *Corroboree,* Jan. 1922. According to a note in *Meanjin,* Summer, 1949, by Louis Lavater, this was the first review printed.

10. *Bulletin,* 6 Dec. 1917.

11. Vance Palmer, *Louis Esson and the Australian Theatre,* pp. 75-76.

12. "The Moral of Norman Lindsay", Nov. 1912.

13. *Vision,* no. 1, p. 33.

14. P. R. Stephensen, *Kookaburras and Satyrs,* 1954, p. 10.

15. Jack Lindsay kept up his classical studies and is represented by fourteen translations in *The Oxford Book of Greek Verse in Translation.*

16. The eighteenth century has always attracted Hugh McCrae. His long prose work *The Du Poissey Anecdotes,* a kind of imaginary companion to Boswell written in the latter's style, was published in 1923, the year in which *Vision* appeared.

17. *Vision* II, p. 10 (Reprinted *One Hundred Poems,* p. 28).

18. *Vision* III, p. 46.

19. Ibid IV, p. 9.

20. Ibid II, p. 23.

21. *The Poetical Works of Ernest Christopher Dowson,* Cassell. Pocket Ed., 1950, p. 50.

22. *Vision* II, p. 9.

23. Op cit, p. 110.

24. *Vision* IV, p. 7.

25. Jack Lindsay: *Franfrolico and After,* 1962, pp. 68, 102-105.

26. *Franfrolico and After,* p. 126.

27. *London Aphrodite,* p. 3.

28. Ibid, p. 8.

29. *The London Aphrodite,* p. 3.

30. *Franfrolico and After,* p. 137 (Lindsay quoting Stephensen).

31. *London Aphrodite,* p. 24.

32. *Ibid,* pp. 473-4.

33. *Fanfrolico and After,* pp. 152-4.

34. *The London Aphrodite,* p. 431.

35. *Vision,* no. 4, p. 59.

36. *The Australian Quarterly,* December 1939, p. 59.

37. *The Bulletin,* Jubilee Issue, February 2, 1955, p. 2.

38. *Moonlight Acre,* 2nd ed., p. 5.

39. Ibid, p. 9.

40. *Moonlight Acre* (2nd edn.), p. 52.

41. See Ronald McKie, "Masked Agent", in *Nation,* no. 126, August 24, 1963, pp. 15-16.

Christopher Sawyer-Lauçanno (essay date 1992)

SOURCE: Sawyer-Lauçanno, Christopher. "The Rebirth of Paris English-Language Publishing: Little Magazines, Literature, and D.B.'s." In *The Continual Pilgrimage: American Writers in Paris, 1944-1960,* pp. 125-44. New York: Grove Press, 1992.

[*In the following essay, Sawyer-Lauçanno explores the history of a number of Paris-based little magazines that promoted and published the works of emerging expatriate authors in the 1920s and 1930s.*]

During the 1920s and 1930s, twenty significant English-language publishers were turning out memorable literature in France, in response to the influx of English-speaking expatriate writers and readers. By 1940 not one of these presses was still operating. Although the war did have an impact, in reality only Obelisk Press was forced to close because of the Occupation; the others had disappeared gradually, in part as a result of the willingness of London and New York to publish a number of expatriate writers, such as Joyce, Pound, Stein, Hemingway, Kay Boyle, Djuna Barnes, and Henry Miller, who had formed the authorial nucleus of the imprints. There had been as well, by the middle to late thirties, a gradual but decided drop in the number of exiles in Paris, either through repatriation or general global scattering.

The legendary English-language literary magazines— among them *transition, Contact, The Little Review, The Transatlantic Review, This Quarter, The New Review,* and *Tambour*—had also ceased to exist, some well before the beginning of World War II, largely for the same reasons as had the publishers. For the reviews, however, it was the usual plague of little magazines, chronic lack of funds, that also contributed to their demise.[1]

After the war, with Paris once again inundated with anglophone expatriates, it naturally followed that there would be a resurgence of publishing in English. And just as the little magazines of the twenties and thirties had often served as vehicles for first-time writers, so did the literary journals that came into existence in Paris in the late forties and early fifties. In many instances, these magazines were the first to publish emerging writers who would later make significant contributions to American and international letters. Perhaps even more daring than their predecessors, the Paris-based reviews of the postwar era provided a forum for an array of talent ranging from the highly conventional to the thoroughly experimental. It was in the pages of these journals that writers tested their wings and, in many cases, ascended to full flight.

The first of the literary magazines to spring up after the war was *Points,* founded in late 1948 by Sindbad Vail, son of Peggy Guggenheim and Laurence Vail. No grandiose pretensions were behind its inception; rather, it was conceived "to give the editor or editors and his pals an outlet for their work plus an egotistical desire to acquire 'fame' or 'notoriety.'"[2] According to Vail, the idea of starting a magazine came to him in the summer of 1948 while visiting his mother in Venice. Twenty-five at the time, he was thinking he ought to find something to do. His first inclination was to open an art gallery in Paris, but as he knew "even less about art than literature," he was discouraged by the prominent collectors in his family. "What else to do," remembered Vail, "than turn to literature?"[3]

Back in Paris that fall, he decided to test the literary waters by seeking submissions through an ad in the *Herald Tribune.* Under the heading "Attention Young Writers," he proclaimed that a new review was being conceived that "welcomed young writers and ideas."[4] The response was so overwhelming that Vail was forced to cancel the original three-day ad run after just the first day. The next step was to set up business. For this, he discovered, he needed a French partner. After one false start, with a French businessman who apparently tried to cheat him, Cyril Connolly, editor of the English review *Horizon,* put Vail in touch with a young French writer and editor, Marcel Bisiaux. Bisiaux was at that time running a literary magazine, *84.* The two hit it off at once and agreed to join forces. The cognate *Points* was chosen as a title, and a decision was made to publish half of the journal in French.

Through Bisiaux, who was also connected to Les Éditions de Minuit, they set up an office at the vanguardist publishing firm and waited for quality submissions to arrive. For Vail this proved more difficult than he had imagined; while a great deal of material did arrive over the transom, little of it was publishable. (Bisiaux, who already had a number of contacts in the French literary community, did not have this problem.) Eventually, however, Vail felt he had enough English-language writing, of at least some quality, and *Points* went to press. "In our innocence," he recalled, "we printed 5000 copies of POINTS No. 1, and we feared that might not be enough. We had no advance publicity, no agent and no means of distribution. . . . Naturally we sent copies to everyone we knew, but after three or four hundred that gave out."[5] These copies amounted to nearly the entire circulation of that first issue. About ninety-nine percent of the other copies distributed to booksellers and newspaper kiosks were returned.

It was hardly a propitious start for Vail's enterprise, but he doggedly kept on with it, learning rapidly how to edit and sell a magazine. In retrospect it is easy to see why the first issue did not make much of a splash. Aside from Vail's general naiveté about the business of running and distributing a literary review, *Points* No. 1 suffered for two main reasons: first, the English-language work was of rather poor quality; and second, another magazine appeared on the scene almost simultaneously, *Zero.*

Zero's debut was far more successful than that of *Points.* Its editor, Themistocles Hoetis, not only had done far more advance work in terms of distribution but had had the foresight to include name writers among his contributors. Its premiere issue, in the spring of 1949, featured work by Christopher Isherwood, Kenneth Patchen, William Carlos Williams, and Richard Wright, as well as the controversial essay on Wright by the young James Baldwin. But what *Points* lacked in terms of good writ-

ing, *Zero* lacked in funds. Vail later admitted that a *New York Times* correspondent in Paris suggested to him quite seriously that he give Hoetis his money and let *Zero* do the work.[6] In the end, Vail's cash prevailed over Hoetis's literary acumen; after just three issues in Paris, *Zero* moved to Tangier and then Mexico, where despite an attempted revival it succumbed to its ever-mounting financial woes.

Two other, very short-lived magazines saw the light of day in the early summer of 1949, *Janus* and *ID.* Although *Janus,* a half-French, half-English poetry journal, had a stirring manifesto, the poetic contributions did not match its rhetorical flourishes. *ID* printed stories, comparably as atrocious as *Janus*'s poetry. After a few issues the two magazines merged, but then folded after just one composite number. Not everybody writing in Paris was destined for fame.

Points, meanwhile, continued for nearly a decade, noticeably improving with each number. After a few issues and the discovery that not many Frenchmen bought the journal, the French-language contributions were cut by half; eventually they were purged altogether. Vail reduced the number of issues from six to five to four a year and settled on a print run of a thousand copies, the majority of which he was actually able to sell.[7]

Curiously, *Points* got better as the competition increased, as it noticeably did in the early 1950s with the advent of two remarkable little magazines: *New-Story* and *Merlin.* Part of the reason was that many of the contributors to these magazines also sent their work to Vail. *The Paris Review* was begun around this time as well, but with its consistently high-quality, often international writing by name authors, its advertisements and capable distribution, it quickly entered a different echelon and could not really be construed as competition.

New-Story, a monthly that premiered in March 1951, although Paris-based, relied heavily on contributions from Britain and the United States. Originally edited by David Burnett, the magazine immediately distinguished itself with its eclecticism. Aside from contributions by prominent French writers (in translation), however, the majority of the work was by American writers—such as Alison Lurie, James Baldwin, Terry Southern, William Goyen, and Ray Bradbury—who were young and relatively unknown. Despite the excellence of its short stories, editorial disputes and lack of funds destined it to a short print life. By 1953 it had ceased publication.

Of all the little magazines that began during the postwar era, *Merlin* was by far the most experimental. Founded in the spring of 1952 by Scottish-born Alexander Trocchi and an American, Jane Lougee, it also included on its international editorial board Americans

Richard Seaver and Austryn Wainhouse, South African Patrick Bowles, and Englishman Christopher Logue. Besides being gifted writers and editors, they were a colorful group, as passionate about living as they were about literature. Trocchi and Logue were "true bohemians, Beats before the Beats officially existed,"[8] remembered bookstore owner George Whitman. "Christopher was the scruffy poet, quite down and out most of the time. He definitely fancied himself as Baudelaire or somebody like that. Alex was always haranguing about something or other, usually the government or puritan society. He and Jane were a real contrast: the angry young man and this sweet, pretty girl from Maine whose father was a banker."[9]

Writer Eugene Walter also recalled the group, in particular Logue: "He liked to propagate the idea that he was a somewhat shady character; he told wondrous wild tales to further the effect. . . . When Christopher's mother visited Paris, he tried to keep her under wraps, finally brought her to the [Café de] Tournon. Everybody thought she'd be at least a red-haired Polish gypsy, or a Tunisian midwife, but she was a pink-cheeked little English lady with a silk print dress and a cameo."[10] As for Seaver, Wainhouse, and Bowles, they were quite different from Logue and Trocchi. Noted Whitman, "They were more reserved, every bit as intense, but not so ostentatious about it."[11]

Merlin's inaugural issue, which hit the stands in the fall of 1952, featured a manifesto by Trocchi which proclaimed that "MERLIN will hit at all clots of rigid categories in criticism and life, and all that is unintelligently partisan. To say that MERLIN is against obscurantism in criticism is not to say that it is against obscurity in poetry. MERLIN is for innovation in creative writing which renders creative writing more expressive."[12]

Later, less bombastically, Trocchi remarked that *Merlin*'s primary objective had been to create "a vital meeting ground for the thought and work of American and English writers on the one hand and Continental writers on the other."[13] A glance at the contents of the quarterly over the three years of its erratic existence reveals that the editorial objective was clearly met. Along with numerous works by the editors, particularly Logue, Wainhouse, Trocchi, and Seaver, and other English-language authors in Paris, it also featured prominent European writing, usually in superb translations, including work by Genet, Henri Michaux, and Eugène Ionesco. The acquisition of these Continental writers was made possible by an arrangement with Sartre and Beauvoir's *Les Temps Modernes*, whereby *Merlin* was granted rights to reprint in translation any of the writing appearing in the French magazine.[14] But one name that did not appear in Sartre's journal dominated *Merlin*'s pages, in quantity if not also in quality: Samuel Beckett.

Beckett's inclusion in practically every issue of the quarterly was not coincidental. He was, at least in the minds of the *Merlin* editors, their "discovery." Actually it was Richard Seaver who first brought Beckett's work to the attention of the *Merlin* group, but they all quickly latched on to the writer as if each had personally discovered him.[15] According to Seaver, in early 1952 he came across Beckett's work in the display window of Les Éditions de Minuit: "I remember looking in the window a dozen times and reading the titles [*Molloy* and *Malone Meurt*], vaguely recalling the author's name. He was Irish and I associated him with Joyce."[16] Seaver finally bought the books. After the second reading he was convinced that *Molloy* and *Malone Meurt* were "miracles, two stunning works."[17]

Through further inquiries at Minuit he learned that the third volume in the trilogy, *L'Innommable*, was forthcoming and that an earlier novel, *Murphy*, had been published five years before by Bordas. (Although Seaver did not know it then, *Murphy* had been published in English in 1938, but to no acclaim.) Seaver, by now a Beckett fanatic, rushed to Bordas, hoping that the novel was in print. Not only was it still available, but as Seaver noted, "by the look of the stock in the back of the shop, the original printing was virtually intact."[18] At the same time he learned that French radio was about to record an unproduced play of Beckett's, *En Attendant Godot*. He managed to finagle his way into the studio in the hope of meeting the great unknown author. His wait was as much in vain as that of Vladimir and Estragon, but he did hear Roger Blin, who would later perform innumerable Beckett works, read the part of Lucky for the first time.

Meanwhile Seaver associated himself with *Merlin* and for its premiere issue wrote the first substantial essay in English on Beckett. A copy was sent to Seaver's literary hero. Silence. Then Seaver learned through Jérôme Lindon, publisher at Minuit, that Beckett had a manuscript in English that he had written during the war. Seaver wrote to Beckett asking if he could publish excerpts from the novel in *Merlin*. Again, no response. Then, one rainy afternoon, months later, "a tall, gaunt figure" appeared at Seaver's door, handed in a manuscript in a black binder, and disappeared. That same night, recalled Seaver, "a half-dozen of us—Trocchi; Jane Lougee, *Merlin*'s publisher; two English [*sic*] poets, Christopher Logue and Pat Bowles; a Canadian writer, Charles Hatcher; and I—sat up half the night and read *Watt* aloud, taking turns till our voices gave out, until we had finished it."[19]

In a note accompanying the manuscript Beckett had specified which section from *Watt* they could use in *Merlin*: Mr. Knott's inventory of his possible attire, and possible positioning of furniture in his room, hardly an easily excerptible passage. "I believe," remarked Seaver, "that Mr. Beckett was testing *Merlin*'s integrity by that demand, for he tended to denigrate all his work, we were later to learn, and perversely chose a section which, taken out of context, would, he deemed, have to be rejected."[20]

Naturally, *Merlin* published the extract. The response from the small readership was almost completely negative. "Avant-garde, all right," replied an angry reader, ". . . but let's draw the line at total absurdity."[21] Five percent of the subscriptions—that is, five—were canceled. "We knew we were on the right track," remembered Seaver. "Thereafter not an issue of *Merlin* appeared without something by Beckett."[22]

The continual inclusion of work by Beckett had other negative repercussions—this time from the French postal authorities from whom *Merlin* had been trying to obtain magazine-rate postage. After numerous requests for the cut-rate mailing privilege had been turned down, *Merlin* finally secured a personal interview with a postal bureaucrat to appeal the case. The meeting was short, the appeal denied. Mailing privileges were not given to "organs of propaganda," the postal authority explained. "We were stunned," recalled Seaver. "We pressed for a clarification. 'Messieurs, who is Samuel Beckett?' A writer, a very fine one; we have published several of his works, we said. 'And this Mr. Beckett, does he not finance your magazine? . . . Because, gentlemen, it appears to our examiners that your magazine is an organ of propaganda dedicated to furthering the fame of Mr. Beckett. I'm afraid your case is closed.'"[23]

Undaunted by reader or postal authority reception, the *Merlin* group continued to push Beckett's work. Amazed to learn that *Watt* had been rejected by a number of publishers, *Merlin* decided in the autumn of 1953 to launch a publishing house in order to issue the novel. As Seaver explained: "Having lost relatively little money on the magazine, we determined we would expand and see if we could lose more money more quickly by publishing books."[24] Beckett was paid an advance of 50,000 francs ($100), double the amount paid by Minuit for *Molloy*.[25]

The matter was not so easily settled, however. To their dismay the *Merlin* group learned that under French law they needed to form a company to go into publishing and for that they needed a French manager (*gérant*). This law, they also discovered, applied to *Merlin,* which now, having come under scrutiny by the authorities, was being threatened as well. In addition to the legal woes, there was the small problem of money. In their initial enthusiasm they had contracted for several more books, counting on getting credit from printers around Paris, only to be informed categorically that printing jobs had to be paid up front. The difficulties seemed nearly overwhelming, and serious consideration was

given to pulling out of both the magazine and book enterprises, when an unlikely angel appeared on Seaver's doorstep: the dapper and flamboyant Maurice Girodias.

Girodias, then in his mid-thirties, was no stranger to publishing. His father, Englishman Jack Kahane, had founded and run the legendary Obelisk Press in Paris, which published Henry Miller, Anaïs Nin, Lawrence Durrell, Radclyffe Hall, Frank Harris, and D. H. Lawrence. After his father's death in 1939, Girodias began his own publishing firm, Les Éditions du Chêne, specializing in art books. (Continuing Obelisk Press under German occupation would have been impossible. Girodias also deemed it wise to begin using his French mother's last name to avoid persecution as a Jew.) Since Les Éditions du Chêne did not publish work that could be construed as at all critical of the occupying forces, it actually flourished during the war.

In 1945, while continuing his French imprint, Girodias revived Obelisk Press, reissuing Miller's *Tropic of Cancer* among other titles. But the next year his legal troubles began. First he was sued for libel by Félix Gouin, French Socialist Party leader, for publishing a pamphlet by Resistance leader Yves Farge critical of collusion between the government and big business. Girodias no sooner won the case than he, along with two other French publishers, was prosecuted by the government for publishing obscene books: Miller's *Tropic of Cancer, Tropic of Capricorn,* and *Black Spring*. This was the first obscenity trial in France since the celebrated cases involving Flaubert's *Madame Bovary* and Baudelaire's *Les Fleurs du Mal* in 1857. The French intellectual establishment rallied to his defense, but for two years *l'affaire Miller* continued. Ultimately, the government dropped the case. By now Girodias was nearly broke. A short time later, through a bad business deal made with a creditor, he lost all of his publishing businesses.

For nearly three years Girodias lived in what he described as "near-complete bumhood."[26] Devastated by the loss of his publishing houses, embittered against what he saw as the government's enfranchisement of bourgeois morality, he felt desolate, unable even to contemplate rising above his circumstances. Then, in the spring of 1953, he founded Olympia Press, in order to "escape complete social and economic annihilation."[27] He reasoned that "publishing books in English, in Paris, books that would sell easily because they would belong to the 'not to be sold in USA and UK' category, appeared . . . the only possible way for me to make money and build up a new publishing business in spite of my lack of capital."[28] It was at this point that he learned from *Merlin* editor Austryn Wainhouse that Collection Merlin, as the magazine's book-publishing enterprise was called, needed a French partner. Thus his appearance in early spring 1953 at Seaver's lodgings; thus the birth of Collection Merlin-Olympia Press.

The deal Girodias offered the young expatriates was simple: He would agree to act as *gérant,* would put up the money for the books, would allow Collection Merlin total editorial autonomy. In exchange, the *Merlin* group would let Girodias publish under his own imprint several of the books, besides *Watt,* for which Collection Merlin had already contracted. These included English translations of Jean Genet's *The Thief's Journal*; the Marquis de Sade's *La Philosophie dans le Boudoir,* and Georges Bataille's *Histoire de l'Oeil.* Additionally, Girodias wanted to sign up Seaver and other bilingual Paris residents as paid translators, perhaps even as writers of erotica. "He was eloquent, suave, compelling,"[29] Seaver recalled. The arrangement was quickly concluded, both sides ecstatic. For Girodias, it meant a fixed stable of translators and writers; for the expatriates, the deal represented not only an end to *Merlin*'s legal and cash-flow difficulties, but also improvement of their generally precarious personal financial situations, because of the expected commissions for translation and writing. Amazingly, the agreement was actually what it seemed, benefiting both parties for a good long while.

Soon after the joint venture was formed, the *Merlin* group took Beckett to meet Girodias. They went en masse—Seaver, Trocchi, Logue, and other members of the *Merlin* group—parading "their writer" up the Boulevard St.-Germain, exuberantly chattering, forcing a wondrous Beckett to turn his head continually from side to side to catch the reverential, ponderous, as well as mundane, remarks being thrown his way. But once at 13 Rue Jacob, Olympia's headquarters, Beckett became silent. According to Girodias: "There was nothing you could say or do to get Beckett to enter into any conversation, to utter any opinion or to make any statement. We went ahead with the book because of the *Merlin* enthusiasm. By then I had read it, and I knew we had no hope of selling the book to tourists—they were only interested in porno."[30]

Deirdre Bair points out in her biography of Beckett that the author's reticence may have been due to concern over being published by Girodias. In 1938, Beckett had refused a commission from Girodias's father to translate Sade for Obelisk, not because he was unenthusiastic about Sade but because he did not want his name associated with a press that published primarily erotica. Now, however, he did not object. There were at least three reasons: first, he genuinely appreciated the enthusiasm of the *Merlin jeunes*; second, after several rejections, he was eager to get *Watt* in print in English, as it might result in foreign sales in Britain and the United States; and third, the book would be issued under the dual imprint Collection Merlin-Olympia Press, and thus would be separate from the main Olympia enterprise— pornography.[31]

As Beckett refused to make any changes to the text, the printing of *Watt* was accomplished promptly. In May 1953, the first Merlin-Olympia title appeared. According to Girodias, although only 2,000 copies were printed, it took five years for the first edition to sell out.[32] The publication of *Watt* ended neither the Merlin-Olympia collaboration nor the relationship with Beckett. Over the next few years Merlin-Olympia brought out a number of other works including a stunning first novel by Wainhouse, *Hedyphagetica*; a book of poems by Logue, *Wand & Quadrant*; and in the spring of 1954, *Molloy,* in an English translation by Patrick Bowles in collaboration with Beckett.

The *Merlin* group's move into translating Beckett came about simply because they wanted to publish more of his work, but as he had ceased writing in English, he would not give them anything new. As for the older work, aside from *Watt,* Beckett was disinclined to have any of it issued. Translating Beckett, however, proved to be a monumental undertaking.

According to Seaver, who took on translating Beckett's story "La Fin," the process was excruciating. Each day they would meet for about five hours at La Coupole. At the end of the first week, Seaver tallied up the number of pages brought into English and discovered that despite thirty to thirty-five hours of work they had managed to render only four or five pages of the original. "Every word, every phrase, was gone over with meticulous care," remarked Seaver. "Sam is the most polite as well as the nicest of men, so that whenever a word had to be changed, he prefaced it with how much he liked what I had done, 'but . . . ,' or else he would say of his own French, "That's impossible, it can't be translated,' as if what he had written wasn't any good." What Beckett wanted, Seaver realized, was not so much a translation as a re-creation of the work in English, but one that was wholly faithful to the French. In the end they achieved just that. The final product was, in Seaver's words, "a complete redoing of the original."[33]

With *Molloy,* Beckett decided a different approach was needed. He asked Bowles for a draft of the entire novel, which he would then revise. But he cautioned that Bowles should not merely translate the book, but "write a new book in the new language."[34] In the meantime, Beckett had been translating *En Attendant Godot* himself, as Barney Rosset, then starting up Grove Press, had offered him a contract for the book in English.

Despite Rosset's attempts to sway him to move swiftly on the translation with promises of large sales and an American production of the play, Beckett could not be persuaded to produce the re-creation quickly. He had stated to Rosset at the outset that it would take him six months to a year to reinvent *Godot* in English, and he refused to be hurried. Rosset waited.[35] As Seaver noted, the only benefit Beckett had really received from him on "La Fin" was that Seaver made the process go faster. "Otherwise he would have agonized over it."[36] But with *Waiting for Godot,* Beckett would not let anyone remove the agony. In fact, from then on he always did his own "translations," in his own time frame, his own way.

As serious as the members of the *Merlin* group were about literature, they managed to indulge themselves from time to time in the pleasures of Paris. *Paris Review* editor George Plimpton remembered going one summer with Trocchi, Lougee, Logue, and others from *Merlin* to the famous Quat'zarts Ball, the wild all-night party hosted by French art students. The Quat'zarts began with a raucous half-naked procession through the streets. Next, the revelers entered the Théâtre Wagram, where at ten the doors to the packed hall were locked, and not opened until dawn. Music and dancing started, followed at around midnight by the "spectacles." These consisted of "living statue" tableaux performed by different ateliers in the boxes and on specially rigged scaffolding in the balcony. A spotlight moved from spectacle to spectacle, illuminating the participants. A grand prize was given for the most spectacular.

Plimpton's hosts had not prepared a tableau, but only fifteen minutes before the spotlight would hit their box, Trocchi announced that he and Lougee would present a spectacle no one would ever forget. Not only that, it was guaranteed to win first prize: Trocchi and Lougee would copulate on the velvet balustrade of the box while the others would stand in attendance and fan them with palm fronds. "All of this came as somewhat of a surprise to the French student-hosts, and also to Alex's [Trocchi's] friends, especially Jane [Lougee]," recalled Plimpton. "But such was the excitement of the moment—the booming from the military bands, the frenzied movement of the dancers, the searchlight in the darkness—that the scheme seemed inspired."

Lougee undressed and got into position. The others, meanwhile, gathered up sheafs of straw to serve as palm fronds. In response to shouts from above that Trocchi needed to make his entrance, he came charging up the stairs. But in his haste he hit his head on an overhang and knocked himself out. "When the searchlight reached the 'tableau' it illuminated the back of a naked girl half-reclining on the balustrade, her head turned away looking back, as if expecting someone, into the recesses of the box where in the shadows, a single figure [Plimpton] was discernible waving a stalk-like sheaf of straw. No one knew what to make of it." They did not win the grand prize but were rumored to have been favorably mentioned for having the spectacle with the most "symbolic effect." Upon reviving, Trocchi expressed his fury: "Why didn't one of you take my place?" he queried. "No one was quite sure how to answer that,"[37] remarked Plimpton.

In between such wild antics as these, the *Merlin* group kept up its publishing enterprises. Although none of the Merlin-Olympia titles was helping Girodias pay even the printers' bills, the *Merlin* group, as translators and "d.b." (dirty book) writers—the term was Girodias's—were contributing substantially to Olympia's coffers. At the same time, the young writers profited from the arrangement, as Girodias paid them, often in advance, between $500 and $1,000 per manuscript. While by no means a sizable amount, such a sum could keep a non-extravagant expatriate in food, drink, and lodging for a good many months in the early fifties, when a room could be had for about $15 a month, a café meal for well under a dollar.

Of those associated with *Merlin,* everyone but Jane Lougee contributed to Olympia's output of d.b.'s. Richard Seaver translated Apollinaire's erotic novel *Les Exploits d'un Jeune Don Juan*; Austryn Wainhouse rendered Sade's *La Philosophie dans le Boudoir* and Bataille's *Histoire de l'Oeil.* Christopher Logue, as Count Palmiro Vicarion, authored an erotic espionage tale called simply *Lust* and another potboiler entitled *White Thighs.* Patrick Bowles, writing as Marcus van Heller, contributed *Roman Orgy.* Iris Owens, another talented writer associated with *Merlin,* as Harriet Daimler wrote a number of books, including *The Woman Thing.*

Alexander Trocchi, though, was by far the most prolific of the group. He translated Apollinaire's *Les Onze Mille Verges,* reading aloud at a café each night the parts of the translation he had completed that day. He was also turned into Frances Lengel and wrote the novel *Helen and Desire,* which according to Girodias "was to become the model of a new brand of erotic writing."[38] Later, under the pseudonym Carmencita de las Lunas, he wrote *With Open Mouth,* another profitable title. Trocchi also authored a serious novel under his own name for Olympia, *Young Adam.* No sooner had the novel been published in France than Trocchi learned it had been accepted by an established publisher in the States. To his chagrin, he had to inform the American house that it was no longer available.[39] George Plimpton also sent Olympia some sample chapters of a porn novel, but to his surprise they were rejected. Girodias "had never turned down anything anybody in the literary colony wrote for him," noted the *Paris Review* editor, "but two chapters of this thing . . . were quite enough."[40]

The contributors to Olympia, Girodias observed, "usually were genuine writers and even the most one-sided and single-minded creations of that time often reveal attractive talents."[41] They did indeed. Trocchi later wrote a startling, extremely good novel, *Cain's Book.* Logue, when he returned to poetry, produced some excellent verse. Seaver went on to become an editor at Grove

Press and other houses, where he distinguished himself as a discerning champion of the avant-garde. Another of Olympia's authors, Alfred Chester, who was also on the *Merlin* fringe, wrote the powerful and disturbing novel *The Exquisite Corpse* and a number of superb short stories.

* * *

Girodias also found talent (and profits) beyond the *Merlin* group. Henry Miller sent him *Plexus.* Through association with French publisher Jean-Jacques Pauvert, with whom Girodias shared an office for a time, he acquired the English rights to the now classic sadomasochistic novel *Histoire d'O.* Mason Hoffenberg, longtime Paris hanger-on, repeatedly tried to sell Girodias his work, convinced that "his manuscripts were glorious achievements and that they were thick enough to be converted into books," remembered Girodias, who disagreed with Hoffenberg's assessment. One day Hoffenberg appeared with his friend Terry Southern. "I had never met Terry before," Girodias recalled, "although I had heard about his wild sense of humor, and I sensed that working with Terry would help bring out the constructive aspects of Mason's submerged talents. We agreed that the story should be about sweet, blue-eyed, curvaceous Candy."[42] *Candy,* by "Maxwell Kenton," was one of Girodias's all-time hits, and a best-seller in the United States as well when it was reissued by G. P. Putnam's Sons.

Within a year or so of its founding, Olympia Press was beginning to turn rather handsome profits. Part of the reason for Girodias's early success was his publishing stratagem, which he vigorously maintained for most porn titles through the press's first five years. It was extremely simple, and extremely lucrative. Rather than publish a book first and then sell it, he would invent titles and authors, then write imaginary blurbs for the d.b.'s to stir the libidos of his subscribers (mostly in England), to whom his catalogue of new books would be sent. According to Girodias, "They immediately responded with orders and money, thanks to which we were again able to eat, drink, write, and print. I could again advance money to my authors, and they hastened to turn in manuscripts which more or less fitted the descriptions."[43]

This process was reserved solely for Olympia's pseudonymous erotica. A number of titles arrived completed, most of them unpublishable. But one manuscript in particular proved to be an exception. It was by a Russian émigré professor who taught at Cornell University, Vladimir Nabokov. The book was *Lolita.* Through Nabokov's Paris agent, Girodias learned that the book had been sent to a number of American presses but had been rejected by all of them. Girodias, "struck with wonder, carried away by this unbelievable phenom-

enon: the apparently effortless transposition of the rich Russian literary tradition into modern English fiction," signed up the book immediately.[44]

Initial reaction to *Lolita*'s publication, in September 1955, was hostile—not from the critics, who didn't even bother to review it, but from his subscribers: "Why are you publishing junk like that?" "You're giving yourself a bad name." "Trash like this is a sheer waste of time." "Any more like the last one and you can strike my name from your list."[45] Then, more than a year later, eminent English novelist Graham Greene, in an interview with the *Times Literary Supplement,* pronounced *Lolita* one of the "three best books of the year."[46] This, quite naturally, stirred up a great deal of commotion in England. Critics took sides. Public debates were held. Sales soared. Girodias thought he might have a bestseller in the making.

And he would have had, save for the intervention by the French authorities. As a result of the novel's new celebrity, *la brigade mondaine* (the worldly brigade), as the French vice squad was charmingly called, arrived at his office and seized twenty-five titles, including *Lolita,* for inspection. A couple of weeks later, all of the books seized were banned in France. Meanwhile, in an ironic turn, American customs had deemed the book not obscene, thus clearing its way for sale of rights in the United States. This was now, Girodias figured, his best shot at getting the book back in print, but in the interim he appealed the French decision. In the end, Girodias triumphed on all scores. *Lolita* was sold to G. P. Putnam's Sons in the United States and to Weidenfeld & Nicolson in Britain. The French ban was lifted. Not long after, Girodias and Nabokov finally had a bestseller.

Success, however, was still not quite as unfettered as it should have been for Girodias. He had become embroiled in a major struggle with Nabokov, who felt that the 17.5 percent due Girodias on all American sales (as called for in the Olympia-Nabokov contract) was excessive, if not dishonest. The "Lolitagation," as Nabokov termed it, dragged on for years, but Girodias prevailed, earning by some accounts more than $300,000 on the deal.[47]

This was not the last of Girodias's problems with authors. J. P. Donleavy, whose book *The Ginger Man* was published the same year as *Lolita,* and eventually to great acclaim and large sales, also sued Girodias, claiming that he had been cheated out of a portion of his royalties. He kept up litigation for fifteen years, finally winning, at least in principle, and not in the courts but by buying the press at a bankruptcy auction in 1972. Unfortunately for Donleavy, his strategy backfired. Not only did he no longer have a case, as he now owned the press he was suing, but the debts so outstripped the assets that there was no way to relaunch Olympia without a considerable investment.[48]

Nor was *l'affaire Lolita* the end of Girodias's problems with the law. *Lolita* was banned again in 1959, then unbanned after Girodias agreed to drop his suit against the government. In other cases, though, he was not so lucky. By the late fifties a concerted effort was mounted against Olympia, the charge *outrage aux bonnes mœurs par la voie du livre*—outrage to propriety by way of books. By 1965 he had been indicted and acquitted twenty-five times, had racked up fines totaling $80,000, and had been banned from publishing books in France for eighty years. He eventually won against the government, but the continual litigation, in combination with other bad business deals, including an absurd adventure in running a nightclub, culminated in financial disaster.

At the same time, the gradual lifting of restrictions on "obscene" literature in the United States and Britain resulted in greatly increased competition for Olympia; its status as premier pornography publisher was reduced and its sales adversely affected. In a sense, Girodias's mission, to attack the priggish establishment, was completed. "The first shock was over, and formerly obsessed readers had become used to the notion that their clandestine world was open to all, that the secret was a fake, that nothing was reprehensible or forbidden,"[49] Girodias commented. "Those literary orgies, those torrents of systematic bad taste were quite certainly instrumental in clearing the air, and clearing out a few mental cobwebs."[50] But as in all successful revolts, victory disarmed the revolutionary. By the early 1960s Girodias had nothing much left to fight for; in winning the war, he essentially put himself out of business.

Yet when the barricades were still up, the struggle was glorious. Not only did Girodias's enterprise make him, for a while at least, a considerable amount of money. More important, the little porn press that could also managed, as a sideline, to catapult into prominence some of the most important writers of the latter half of the century, among them Beckett and Nabokov. Others, like Trocchi, Southern, and Donleavy, were launched in their careers. And more than a handful of expatriates paid the rent thanks to Girodias's d.b. mill. In the end, Olympia's fostering of distinguished international literature in the mid-fifties set a record that any major publisher could envy.

The magazines too not only provided expatriates in Paris a forum for publishing but also brought new French writing to the attention of American editors. Barney Rosset's Grove Press, which had first published Beckett in the United States, hired Beckett's "discoverer," Richard Seaver, in the late fifties. With his arrival, the house increased even further its already substantial investment in French writing, adding Genet, Duras, Robbe-Grillet, Robert Pinget, Albertine Sarrazin, Pauline Réage, and many others to its list. Among those Grove did not publish, such as Sartre, Nathalie Sarraute, Claude Mauriac, and Claude Simon, George Braziller generally did. In Britain, John Calder performed a similar service.

A great many of these French writers had made their English-language debuts in *Merlin* or *The Paris Review*. *Evergreen Review,* in some ways *Merlin*'s logical successor, was first published in New York by Rosset in 1957 and continued to bring international writing to the American public. That an American-based review could now do what formerly was the province of the little Paris magazines reflected the growing interest in contemporary European literature and, moreover, the impact these magazines had made on discovering for English-language editors and readers new literary trends in France. This is not to say that these authors would not have eventually appeared in print in English translation, but certainly the pioneering efforts of *Merlin* and of Seaver (who also assumed a major responsibility at *Evergreen Review*) hastened their arrival on American shores. In sum, the Paris-based reviews gave opportunities to the young expatriate writers and contributed to promoting awareness of some of the most impressive and influential European literature of this part of the century.

Notes

1. CONTRIBUTED TO THEIR DEMISE: See Hugh Ford, *Published in Paris: American and British Writers, Printers and Publishers in Paris, 1920-1939* (New York: Macmillan, 1975).

2. "'FAME' OR 'NOTORIETY'": Sindbad Vail, in *Points,* no. 18 (1953-54), p. 2.

3. "TURN TO LITERATURE?": Ibid.

4. "WRITERS AND IDEAS": Ibid.

5. "HUNDRED THAT GAVE OUT": Ibid., p. 5.

6. LET *ZERO* DO THE WORK: Ibid., p. 6.

7. ACTUALLY ABLE TO SELL: Ibid., p. 7.

8. "BEATS OFFICIALLY EXISTED": George Whitman, conversation with author, July 16, 1990.

9. "FATHER WAS A BANKER": Ibid.

10. "PRINT DRESS AND A CAMEO": Eugene Walter quoted in "The *Paris Review* Sketchbook," *The Paris Review,* no. 79 (1981), p. 321.

11. "OSTENTATIOUS ABOUT IT": Whitman, conversation with author, July 16, 1990.

12. "WRITING MORE EXPRESSIVE": Alexander Trocchi, in *Merlin,* Sept. 1952, p. 2.

13. "Writers on the Other": Alexander Trocchi, in *Merlin,* March 1955, p. 2.

14. In the French Magazine: George Plimpton quoted in "The *Paris Review* Sketchbook," p. 334-35.

15. Personally Discovered Him: Whitman, conversation with author, July 16, 1990.

16. "Associated Him with Joyce": Richard Seaver, "*Watt,*" in *The Olympia Reader,* ed. Maurice Girodias (New York: Grove, 1965), p. 222.

17. "Two Stunning Works": Ibid.

18. "Virtually Intact": Ibid.

Binder, and Disappeared: Ibid., p. 223.

19. "Had Finished It": Ibid.

20. "Have to be Rejected": Ibid.

21. "Total Absurdity": Ibid.

22. "Something by Beckett": Ibid.

23. "'Your Case is Closed'": Ibid., p. 224.

24. "By Publishing Books": Ibid.

25. Minuit for*Molloy*: Jérôme Lindon, "First Meeting with Samuel Beckett," in *Beckett at 60: A Festschrift,* ed. John Calder (London: Calder & Boyars, 1967), p. 18; Seaver, "*Watt,*" p. 224.

26. "Near-Complete Bumhood": Maurice Girodias, introduction to *The Olympia Reader,* p. 11.

27. "Economic Annihilation": Ibid.

28. "Lack of Capital": Ibid., pp. 11-12.

29. "Eloquent, Suave, Compelling": Seaver, "*Watt,*" p. 225.

30. "Only Interested in Porno": Maurice Girodias quoted in Deirdre Bair, *Samuel Beckett* (New York: Harcourt Brace Jovanovich, 1978), p. 433.

31. Olympia Enterprise—Pornography: Bair, *Samuel Beckett,* pp. 433-43.

32. Edition to Sell Out: Ibid., p. 433.

33. "Redoing of the Original": Richard Seaver quoted in Bair, *Samuel Beckett,* p. 438.

34. "In the New Language": Patrick Bowles, translator's note to Friedrich Dürrenmatt, *The Visit* (New York: Grove, 1962), p. 6.

35. Rosset Waited: Bair, *Samuel Beckett,* p. 438.

36. "Agonized Over It": Richard Seaver quoted ibid.

37. "How to Answer That": George Plimpton quoted in "The *Paris Review* Sketchbook," p. 358.

38. "Brand of Erotic Writing": Girodias, introduction to *The Olympia Reader,* p. 18.

39. No Longer Available: Plimpton quoted in "The *Paris Review* Sketchbook," p. 336.

40. "Were Quite Enough": Ibid.

41. "Reveal Attractive Talents": Girodias, introduction to *The Olympia Reader,* p. 23.

42. "Blue-Eyed, Curvaceous Candy": Ibid., p. 21.

43. "Fitted the Descriptions": Ibid., p. 19.

44. Signed Up the Book Immediately: Maurice Girodias, "A Sad, Ungraceful History of *Lolita,*" in *The Olympia Reader,* p. 535.

45. "From Your List": Responses to *Lolita* quoted in Ted Morgan, *Literary Outlaw: The Life and Times of William Burroughs* (New York: Henry Holt, 1988), p. 278.

46. "Books of the Year": Graham Greene quoted in Girodias, "A Sad, Ungraceful History of *Lolita,*" p. 538.

47. $300,000 On the Deal: Morgan, *Literary Outlaw,* p. 279.

48. A Considerable Investment: Ibid., p. 280.

49. "Reprehensible or Forbidden": Girodias, introduction to *The Olympia Reader,* p. 20.

50. "A Few Mental Cobwebs": Ibid., p. 19.

R. J. Ellis (essay date 1993)

SOURCE: Ellis, R. J. "Mapping the United Kingdom Little Magazine Field." In *New British Poetries: The Scope of the Possible,* edited by Robert Hampson and Peter Barry, pp. 72-103. Manchester, England: Manchester University Press, 1993.

[*In the essay below, Ellis provides a survey of pre World War II little magazines in the United Kingdom focusing on poetry.*]

> where our present is, is, strictly speaking,
> irredeemable. terms jostle. within
> the elastic limits speeches slide collide
> bumping against the steel skull-cap it's
> undeniable the step is gone
>
> Wendy Mulford from 'Valentine'[1]

I

The field of United Kingdom little magazine publishing is large and varied: *International Directory of Little Magazines and Small Presses* lists over 100 titles in production in the United Kingdom during 1990-91 that could be reasonably described as 'little magazines', and almost cetainly at least as many more exist which remain unlisted.[2] Eventually I will become compelled to search for a definition of the term 'little magazine', but pretending for the moment that the term is self-explanatory, I will begin by making the self-evident assertion that a field which regularly in the last three decades has consisted of between one and two hundred more or less regular serial publication titles cannot be adequately described, let alone analysed, in one short article. This is why I have taken the decision to focus my attention on analysis rather than description, though acknowledging that this analysis will be both partial (incomplete) and partial (biased). What I am seeking is an analytical over-view—a species of 'mapping' which will depend on my perspective but, I hope, will not be entirely reliant on it. To this end, I wrote to twenty-four little magazine editors in 1990, enclosing a questionnaire,[3] which I will make free use of in my analysis—to provide both reinforcement of and counterpoint to my views.

I anticipated a low response rate, and that is what I got. I anticipated this for three reasons: firstly, some of the little magazines would have ceased to exist, in a field which is notoriously volatile as editors run out of cash, or patience, or interest—as they themselves report (self-deprecating humour recurrently appeared in the questionnaire replies);[4] secondly, the editors would have moved on and the questionnaires would not have reached them—this a product (in a different but complementary way to the first) of the non-commercial status of the great majority of little magazines; thirdly, and most revealingly (though already we have learned some fundamental things about the field), I believed that the editors would find filling in questionnaires about their 'aims and objectives' disconcerting, difficult or even distasteful, and would not wish to conform to my request. Some measure of validation for this belief resides in the fact that almost all of the editors who did reply declined to answer several of my questions, and many declined to answer over one-third of them. Anthony Linick, carrying out a much more comprehensive, yet not unrelated survey in the United States in 1963,[5] experienced similar problems about getting survey replies, and advanced a related set of reasons, including my third one—that editors chose deliberately to decline to conform.

The grounds on which I base my belief that this third reason is the most revealing are, to some extent, ones that derive directly from the central proposition of my analysis. I estimate that editors might find my request disconcerting because they are functioning very often, but not always, in a discursive matrix that does not encourage a systematic questioning of the rationale behind the act of (editorial) creation—a matrix representing creativity as a product of imagination, inspiration,

genius or the like, which establishes a virtually tautologous, hermetic argument and one which, since it is advanced recurrently by practising poets, bears comparison with a hermeneutic circle, excluding analysis. This also accounts in large part for why I feel some editors might find answering the questionnaire difficult: trapped in such a circle, explanations or analyses of an activity that seems 'natural' become difficult. Finally, and again relatedly, the task might seem distasteful to some editors because, precisely, assumptions about their editing activities are in some ways being affronted by the questions posed merely because the questions are posed—in a sense, because they can be posed about what seems to them to be self-explanatory.

Let me offset this by offering one other explanation for non-reply: busy-ness, perhaps related to a surfeit of surveys/questionnaires, an argument advanced by, amongst others, Martin Bax (*Ambit*).[6] Certainly, my questionnaire's demands on their time were clear, and any response would go unrewarded. In a sense, though, I could turn this excuse around on the editors: the real demand on time was perhaps made greater precisely by the lack of a framework of arguments and theories to which they could refer about the processes of little magazine production, a lack precisely stemming from my hypothesised tautologous matrix.[7]

That hardly anyone has written concertedly about little magazines in the UK (despite the expansion of the field since World War II and the acceleration in activity generated by the introduction of affordable off-set lithographic printing processes could, with a touch of irony, be attributed to the same problem—of busy-ness amongst those critics and academics who otherwise one might have expected to show at least an interest in, if not a concern about, little magazines. The few who have engaged with it have generally had a finger in the pie—as poets, as editors, or as both—and as such were often bound by the genre's convention of (almost at times a conspiracy of) critical silence: 'there are certainly some magazines which have slightly modelled themselves on *Ambit* around now, but it would embarrass them if I stated who'.[8] Here, I feel sure, Martin Bax is influenced by a sense of solidarity generated by participating in little magazine publishing and stemming from the constant disheartening sense that no one out there is actually reading what you produce—another recurrent (but not omnipresent) theme in questionnaire returns, and one which can give way to an elitist, resigned acquiescence, centreing on the idea that those who care and who, in return, need to be cared about are the ones who do, indeed, subscribe.[9] My questions asking editors to relate their magazine's position to that of others in the field were frequently avoided.[10] This is not to say some reviewing of other little magazines does not occur, and that some of this is highly critical. But it is equally true that the 'reviews' section in a little magazine is usually last to come and first to go, and many little magazines avoid it altogether; furthermore, reviews of other little magazines are, overall, surprisingly rare.

II

Thus, faced with the question, 'How would you attempt to "map out" the "landscape" of little magazine activity in the UK at present?' editors, like critics and academics, mostly fell silent. Commentators and commentaries are plainly rare, and, I am maintaining, this lack is produced by the discursive matrix investing the field. Those commentaries that do appear, in this sense, tend to be descriptive rather than analytic, following in the footsteps of Denys Val Baker, who in 1943 was almost resolutely descriptive in approach.[11] Since even such descriptive accounts are rare, they can be of real interest and value, but I try to eschew this approach because other articles I have published (mostly with Geoffrey Soar of University College, London) have described this field, not comprehensively, of course, but in some breadth.[12] These articles have also attempted to offer some analysis, but rather than use these, I will turn to an attempt at 'mapping' offered by one of the editors responding to my questionnaire, Ken Edwards (*Reality Studios*). His necessarily brief outline of how he would map the little magazine field ran as follows: 'Mainstream/Establishment/Funded on the one hand; Independent/Marginalised on the other. The latter category is very heterogeneous'.[13] In fact, it could be claimed that this apparently simple binary opposition is quite conceptually daring, linking as it does apparently disparate categorisations under the same grouping on either side of his binary divide. Thus for a little magazine to be funded (an economic distinction), is to ally it with the mainstream/establishment (a distinction based on what might be loosely described as the politics of poetry publishing), and this, by implication at least, means that if a little magazine is financially independent it is more likely be part of the heterogeneous complex 'independent/marginalised', which also includes 'the avant-garde/experimental'.[14]

A lot of issues are thus raised by Ken Edwards, and in pursuing these I shall be led steadily away from what has so far been my main argument concerning a constricting discursive matrix. But, importantly, the lines of analysis which will now develop will also come to constitute a critique of what I have so far said. The dialectic thus established will, better than anything, I believe, establish the contradictoriness of the little magazine publishing field, rendering it unstable both financially and (not coincidentally) in terms of its constituent titles' survival. In other words, I will start to argue that the grip of the discourse of artistic creativity, with its insistence on individual genius, is rendered inherently incomplete by the very dynamics and economics of the

field: little magazines stand in an inherently contradictory relationship to commercial publishing.

A way of approaching Edward's points which will lead me in this direction, I think, is to return to the problem of defining the little magazine genre: what is a 'little magazine', especially if one element of Edwards' binary divide alone can be described as 'very heterogeneous'? The simple consequence is that all generalisations about the field are going to be false, and my failure will only be one of many other, at best only partially successful, previous attempts.[15] My approach will hinge on an inclusive/exclusive system thickly hedged by a set of qualificatory conditions. To some extent, however, what follows is intended to be rank-ordered:

1. *Little magazines are generally not commercial* in terms of viability or intent, but to be a commercial success cannot in itself be sufficient to be a disqualification. A classic case to point to here is that of Bill Buford's *Granta* which, all said and done, 'evolved from a student magazine',[16] and which was, in 1982, still edited in 'the same unheated attic' as when founded in 1979,[17] however much a distribution agreement with Penguin and consequent visibility might complicate an assessment. Even if the disease most rife among little magazines is low circulation, terminally enhanced by distribution problems, little magazine editors are happy to confess that they are 'trying to get th[e] poetry [they publish] an audience',[18] and Martin Bax is happy to recognise that 'some little magazines have of course been enormous'.[19] *Granta* really should not be excluded, not least because 'we [at *Granta*] need cash', despite a print run of 10,000 as at December 1990.

2. *Little magazines primarily, or only, publish poetry and/or fiction and/or other forms of imaginative writing,* and most usually primarily publish poetry in their pages (though a significant number deliberately seek to bring the arts together). Again, a qualification must be erected to some extent, for a number of serial publications exist with very small publication runs, acute circulation problems, precarious finances, non-commercial in approach whilst seeking as many readers as possible, which rarely if ever publish imaginative writing, fiction, or poetry. These are frequently attached to pressure or single-issue groups, or seek to disseminate the ideas of groups outside of the cultural mainstream (e.g. the 'New Age' proponents of humanity's possession of sixth sense faculties or those seeking to promote or sustain the beliefs of the counter-culture). It would be easy to simply rule these exceptions out, and this essay will, indeed, entirely neglect them, but the qualification needs to be drawn up: many publish imaginative writing, fiction and poetry, if to limited extents. Thus, for example, *Writing Women,* and *Spare Rib* (the latter publishing a deal of creative writing) are not entirely unrelated, particularly if their early histories are compared.

3. *Little magazines are oriented towards publication of the experimental, and/or the avant-garde, and/or the emergent/new,* classically, they should claim to be doing at least two of the above. In practice, when survey-

ing the little magazine field, it has to be said that many, or even most, little magazines do no such thing, unless the adjectives 'new' and 'emergent' are taken merely to refer to previously unnoticed or unpublished poets and writers, or those just beginning to write (a classic role of little magazines, and one frequently and correctly emphasised, is that they provide forums for new young writers' work). This qualification, that the 'emergent' or 'new' may rarely or never also be experimental or avant-garde in some little magazines, is of critical importance, of course, and feeds directly into one element of Ken Edwards' binary system's dividing line. It is a point to which this essay will return.

4. *Little magazines are prepared to take risks.* This assertion is closely linked to my first, and also bears fundamentally on my third proposed characteristic. Recurrently non-commercial, frequently experimental in approach, little magazines can potentially enjoy an enormous flexibility in terms of format, production processes, even the medium used; *Alembic, Curtains,* Allen Fisher's *Spanner* and David Mayor's *Schmuck* spring to mind here, but one could also even name *Poetry Review* at the other extreme, for this Poetry Society organ has shown a preparedness to change format to some extent, as part of a limited recognition of the need to adapt to encompass the growing degree of formal experimentation in UK verse. This last example will seem pretty thin to some, even if I point out that the review's format change incorporated page enlargement, by which the magazine grew to a size where 'open field' compositional approaches stood more chance of adequate deployment (a point made by Peter Hodgkiss, when emphasising that, after all, most poets compose on A4 sheets of paper).[20] But this, I suppose, is my point, for one could also enter into a debate about to what extent *Poetry Review* is, really, a 'little magazine' in the sense emerging here, underpinned and limited as it is by its institutional identity. Which is why, perhaps, this point deserves some emphasis; for example, the 'risk' taken may be to endeavour to marry, merge or otherwise bring together artistic forms usually regarded as somehow distinct. Just eight editorial examples would be: Stuart Mills, in *Aggie Weston*'s interest in concrete poetry, particularly that of Ian Hamilton Finlay, Finlay's own *Poor, Old, Tired, Horse., 1983*'s (unsuccessful) attempt to establish itself as a series of performance poetry audiocassettes, Jake Tilson and Stephen Whitaker in *Cipher*'s use of colour xeroxes, stickers, hand-tinting and rubber stamps, Stephen Willats in *Control*'s use of photography linked to texts, George Maciunas in *Fluxus 1*'s use of mail art, and, less ambitiously, Martin Bax in *Ambit*'s interest in existing as a 'magazine . . . where artists appeared together, complemented each other'.[21] 'Risk' is, quite simply, here to be understood in the broadest meaning of the word but *Poetry Review* hardly qualifies.

III

By now, I believe, something of a pattern has emerged to the recurrence of cautionings built up around my definition of the term 'little magazine'. For the pattern seems to me repeatedly one concerned with the degree of risk, or let us call it radicalism, built into any little magazine publishing project. And this, I think, is pre-

cisely what systematises, conceptually, Ken Edwards' mapping, for all of its apparent categorial inconsistencies. What he is postulating is the existence of two 'camps', both of them in fact large and heterogeneous; the inherent danger, of course, is of some sort of combat between them.

Recurrently, this is in fact what commentators have claimed has existed over the last four decades or so. It is, anyway, a 'split' that could be said to pre-date this period—a split ultimately emanating from the impact of modernism upon the late Victorians and, in a different way, upon the Georgians' reactions to late Victorianism, and the unceasing variety of responses to these collisions in the United Kingdom (in poetry, via the imagists, Wyndham Lewis, Ezra Pound, David Jones, and, later, Basil Bunting, Hugh MacDiarmid and many others on the one hand and those figuring in the lineage of the Movement poets, and to a lesser extent also the Group, in their reactions against the Apocalypse, on the other; in prose, via James Joyce, Virginia Woolf, Malcolm Lowry etc.,—summary here is quite impossible) and in America (in poetry, via Pound [again], William Carlos Williams, Louis Zukofsky, George Oppen, Charles Reznikoff, Marianne Moore, H. D. and many more on the one hand and those whose lineage needs to make close reference to the Fugitives on the other; in prose, via Gertrude Stein, John Dos Passos, William Faulkner etc.,—summary again is quite impossible). It must quickly be conceded that this rapid sketch is over-schematic; the one hand/other hand divisions set up here are not simple. This can well be illustrated by mentioning a few other poetry practitioners: T. S. Eliot, W. H. Auden and the left-wing Louis MacNeice, for example, whose locations are more problematic.

However, it supplies us both with a way of illustrating *en passant* the importance of little magazines, which served throughout this period as forums for debate and definition, and, more central to my argument, with one method of understanding how I resolve my dilemmas over *Granta*'s status, for Bill Buford, despite the scale of his enterprise, has been concerned when publishing to 'develop . . . a writing that started to satisfy an appetite for a literature that engaged actively with the culture'. Thus he turns to writing of the sort which leads him to list, as his 'especially significant/ representative contributors' the writers 'Richard Ford, Raymond Carver, James Fenton . . . Ian Jack . . . John Berger, Seamus Deane and Salman Rushdie' (amongst others).[22] And yet, in the same questionnaire, Buford writes that he possesses a 'loathing for the traditional little magazine that no one buys and fewer people read'.[23] Buford is here, I believe, collapsing several issues into one statement, and a fundamental conceptual confusion exists. On the one hand, certainly, the shades of the 'split' are invoked: the adjective 'traditional' carries within it an implication that little magazines that operate within conservative parameters in terms of form and content warrant neglect and are deservedly small circulation ones. But this implication is undercut by an ambiguity lacing the statement, for another reading of his words would understand them as asserting that small circulation is a vice of little magazines—a tradition to be broken—and that what the genre needs are innovatory serials deliberately seeking large audiences. After all, almost all of the authors' names that Buford regards as being of special significance to *Granta* are ones that one could count on as also appearing on the spines of book covers in any branch of the large bookshop chains. In a sense, 'risk' in one (economic) sense is limited here, but I do not believe that Buford would wish therefore to ally himself with the sentiments of Charles Osborne, who, in a not unrelated way, attacked the whole terrain of little magazine publishing in 1975 (and in successive years) '[. . . little magazines] make no useful contribution to literature [and] generally are not worth supporting'.[24] Here, any apparent consanguinity is not real; Buford's averred intent of featuring literature that 'engaged actively in the culture' carries within it, in sharp contrast to Osborne's predilections, an implied radicalism that *Granta* recurrently bears out in its pages.

It is precisely these discursive instabilities that I am interested in, for I believe they permeate the whole level of debate concerning the field of little magazine activity and its characteristics, whenever descriptive accounts of it advance towards analysis. I find related instablities, for example, in the discussion of the 'split' in the field of poetry production in the United Kingdom, even within my own minor contributions to this debate. Osborne's astringent dismissal of little magazines, voiced when he was Director of the Arts Council's Literature Panel, ensured hard financial times for UK little magazines in the second half of the seventies (from which they have never really recovered), and well introduces the note of acerbity that was extant in a battle commencing in the fifties and sixties, raging in the seventies and lingering on into the eighties and nineties still. It proved to be a battle with a more or less clear winner emerging in economic and mainstream cultural terms, at least for a while; how else can one account for the otherwise extraordinary statement in Blake Morrison's and Andrew Motion's *The Penguin Book of Contemporary British Poetry,* that '[for] much of the sixties and seventies very little . . . seemed to be happening . . . in British poetry'.[25] The fact is that this was precisely the period when the groundwork laid down in the late Fifties in the terrain of modernist re-engagement, after the (not complete but noticeable) hiatus created by the war years and their immediate aftermath, began to bloom quite copiously within the inter-related little magazine and small press fields, as the influence of such figures as MacDiarmid, Bunting, Wyndham Lewis and Pound revived, and Surrealism, in Britain and America, attracted new practitioners. It would quite

plainly be wrong to pretend that the little magazine field in this period was wholly or even on balance dominated by the avant-garde and experimental in poetry writing, since a large number of more or less institutionally-linked serial titles continued to appear, and perhaps found main expression in the regular publication of Howard Sergeant's *Outposts,* the model to which, one could argue, many local poetry society publications or college poetry magazines aspired, consciously or not.

Nevertheless, set against the general lack of interest in little magazines as outlets amongst the Movement poets and their fellow travellers (since, as Edward Lucie-Smith put it in 1970, speaking perhaps on their behalf, 'the network of little presses and little magazines . . . has always existed . . . encouraging writers who were for some reason unfashionable'),[26] the United Kingdom modernist revival had a clear and contrasting regard for little magazines. These they saw as the correct medium for experimental development. This meant that, quite visibly, the cutting edge of little magazine activity in the fifties and sixties became dominated by writers working with new forms. These frequently were American, also, to a lesser extent, from Europe: Peter Russell's *Nine* (1949-58) and William Cookson's *Agenda* (1959-) brought together, amongst others, Ezra Pound and Basil Bunting; William Carlos Williams' influence showed clearly in the pages of *The Window* (1951-55?) and *Artisan* (1953-55); Black Mountain poetics were important to Gael Turnbulls' and Michael Shayer's *Migrant* (1959-60) amongst others; Michael Horovitz's *New Departures* (1959-?] paid close attention to US activity in general, particularly the Beats' writings, but also to European activities; Bob Cobbing's *And* (1954-?) moved towards exploring visual poetry's possibilities, and Jon Silkin's *Stand* (1952-) consistently published European poetry. This list is very partial, and only begins to usher in the Sixties (well signposted, anyway, by magazines like *New Departures* and *And*), when the list extends itself very rapidly; to name but a few, Tina Morris' and Dave Cunliffe's *Poetmeat, PM Newsletter* and *Global Tapestry Journal,* Finlay's *Poor. Old. Tired. Horse,* Jeff Nuttall's *My Own Mag,* Tom Pickard's *King Ida's Watch Chain,* Andrew Crozier's *Wivenhoe Park Review,* Lee Harwood's *Horde, Soho,* and *Tzarad,* Peter Riley's *The English Intelligencer,* Kris Hemensley's *Earthship,* and Pierre Joris' *Sixpack,* all started up in the period 1960 to 1970. This burst of activity I want to relate to the recovery of modernism, but also, of course, to the impetus provided to Sixties writers by the arguments of the counter-culture following in the wake of the decisive advances in cheap reproduction processes.

Thus it is that Eric Mottram formulated, in his essay for the 1974 Modern British Poetry Conference at the Polytechnic of Central London, the idea of a 'British Poetry

Revival' during the period 1960-74. This, of course, was the very period when, for Morrison and Motion, 'very little' was happening.[27] Mottram's use of the phrase becomes exact, and the contradiction between him and Morrison and Motion becomes largely alleviated, if we take the words of his essay title as ones that are carefully weighed: 'modern' here does not mean 'contemporary', but modernist-inspired. Whilst it cannot be said that the Morrison and Motion anthology consists of poets completely uninterested in the modernist revolution of the word, it is true to say that not one of the poet-editors of the titles listed above, and virtually no one from the long list of their little magazine's contributors, were anthologised by Morrison and Motion. The division this implies was one Mottram was precisely intent on describing, and five years later Barry MacSweeney was concerned to extend it on to 1979, in the process re-confirming that a sense of a split existed.[28] Both their positions were openly partisan, but even slightly less committed commentators, such as Douglas Dunn, showed a sharp awareness of some sort of divide.[29] By 1981, Stephen Pereira (*Angel Exhaust*), in trying to put together as exhaustive as possible a survey of contemporary United Kingdom poetry, was to speak of a total breakdown: 'The radicals have nothing to do with the Establishment and vice versa'.[30] His was one of the relatively few attempts to bridge the gap, others perhaps being made by *Palantir, Slow Dancer, Little Word Machine* and *The Wide Skirt*. That such mainstream serial titles as *Poetry Review* and, in a different, more mixed way, *PN Review* have become over the years a little more receptive to living as well as dead modernists might be in part taken as a tribute to their efforts.

All this may sound extreme, but an extraordinary, illustrative anecdote will intimate the degree of breakdown as well as anything: significantly, it returns us to the history of *Poetry Review,* the creative-writing organ of that 'establishment' institution, the Poetry Society. In 1969 *Poetry Review*'s editor, Derek Parker, chose to feature the work of a number of avant-garde/experimental post-war UK modernists and in 1970 some of these (Allen Fisher, Lee Harwood, Peter Hodgkiss, Pete Morgan, Tom Pickard, Elaine Randell, Ken Smith and Barry MacSweeney) were elected to the society's general council, Hugh MacDiarmid and Basil Bunting to the presidency and Eric Mottram took over the editing of *Poetry Review* from Parker. Mottram set about deliberately to transform it from 'a mansion of grandmotherly amateurism into the outpost of American and European modernism'.[31] To do this, however, he had to upset the sensibilities of a number of Poetry Society luminaries, not least through his use of rejection slips to make room for the work of such poets as Tom Pickard, Michael Horovitz, Andrew Crozier, F. T. Prince, and the Americans Robert Kelly and Joel Oppenheimer. What next happened is well described by Mottram in *Poetry*

Information, Number 20/21 (Winter 1979/80).[32] In brief, Charles Osborne of the Arts Council was called in to restore a 'balance' and in a heated public meeting in 1974 the Arts Council assumed effective control of the Poetry Society; subsequently, Mottram was squeezed out of the editorship of *Poetry Review.*

It would, I believe, not be much of an exaggeration to suggest that this battle, and the defeat, had long-lasting repercussions, as well as injecting a degree of rancour. For, during the coming decade, the Arts Council was fundamentally to re-assess the amount of financial subsidy it was prepared to give to 'little magazines'. Dunn's belief in 1977 that 'a little magazine's . . . prayers . . . are likely to be answered by the Arts Council' was already almost anachronistic;[33] on the contrary, in the period 1975 to 1985, and ever since, re-assessments of policy were under way that ensured that right through the Eighties grants were sharply reduced or withered away (depending on which Regional Arts organisation was involved). Whether this withdrawal of support is a good or bad thing is a matter of unresolved debate: Graham Sykes of *Kudos* sees subsidy as meretricious, since arts grants shield little magazines from their primary *raison d'être*—to get themselves out to as wide an audience as possible through 'actual grass roots sales'.[34] More fundamentally, Paul Buck argues, in typically outspoken fashion, that: 'Subsidy is the death of art. I discovered that more and more as the magazine developed. Do anything but give yourself over to government control'.[35] It perhaps needs to be recalled here that Buck is speaking from experience: his May 1978 issue of *Curtains,* named *bal:le:d curtains,* contains a labyrinthine account of a censorship intervention by Yorkshire Arts, which (predictably) centrally involved Charles Osborne and ended in the axing of *Curtain*'s grant: '. . . the prime villainy of the Osborne Mafia, with its operations room in the Arts Council Literature Department is working . . . effectively to undermine the energy of the new contemporary writing', Buck went on to claim he was 'turning [his] back' on English literature' by moving to Paris.[36]

In fact, *Curtains* virtually ceased publication from that moment, which is one way of reminding us that loss of subsidy can cut both ways for a little magazine. The real risk is of marginalisation in economic as well as literary terms, and their interaction, here quite apparent, needs always to be borne in mind. It is true to say of little magazines that their potential role is well illustrated by reference to past achievements: James Joyce's *Portrait of the Artist* was at first published serially in *The Egoist,* much of *Ulysses* in *The Egoist* and *The Little Review* and *Finnegans Wake* in *transition*; little magazines were important to the development of William Carlos Williams, Ezra Pound, T. S. Eliot, Wallace Stevens and W. B. Yeats. Pound's editing of *The Exile* and Williams' editing of *Contact* were part and parcel of their development as poets and Pound's *Cantos* and Williams' *Paterson* at least partly evolved in little magazine publication; much of Wyndham Lewis's development was enabled via his editing of *Blast,* and Robert Duncan's and Charles Olson's moves towards achieving their long-poem projects were enabled via experimentation in little magazines in America.

But the risk in adopting this approach when specifying the merits of the little magazine genre is that it looks backwards anachronistically, by failing to take account of the fundamental transformations which have beset publishing in the intervening decades. The risk of stressing the past as a means of understanding the significance of the little magazine field is that this implicitly accepts somehow the very limited audience that little magazines in particular and poetry in general commands at present. I believe that the very decision to edit and publish a little magazine carries within it an implicit (perhaps even unrecognised) or an express desire to direct more people's attention to what poetry can do in terms of producing an alertness to meaning and language, and their interaction, for poet, poets and readers. Donald Davie writes in a recent *PN Review* that 'poetry which should speak to all men at present speaks to few' and that the poets in *A Various Art* (a 1987 anthology edited by Tim Longville and Andrew Crozier and publishing such avant-garde experimentalists as J. H. Prynne, David Chaloner, Nick Totton, Roy Fisher, Veronica Forrest-Thomson, Douglas Oliver, Anthony Barnett and Peter Riley) are an 'antidote' to an 'abyss of self-regarding and cynical frivolity' into which 'English literary culture' has sunk. In saying this he is precisely, I think, legitimating my concern over the problems posed by Arts Council subsidy withdrawals.[37] Ironically, earlier in his article Davie had, quite inconsistently, argued that the poets anthologised in *A Various Art* had 'never tried' to be 'generally "on offer"',[38] a statement completely disregarding the actual struggles enacted around the split between the institutional establishment and the experimental/avant garde that the little magazine field accurately maps out—as complex, shifting, unstable but very real. The poets featured in *A Various Art,* and their fellow experimentalists, have in fact been 'on offer' in the Seventies and Eighties, in such magazines as *Spanner, Figs, And, Reality Studios, Grosseteste Review, Alembic, Ninth Decade,* and *Rock Drill,* but, quite simply, this offer has not been taken up. The evidence provided by *A Various Art* is quite plainly that, as its title implies, a very varied set of poetic practices are in full flood in the United Kingdom, though their emergence into the 'customary institutions of British poetry' is at best spasmodic and usually incomplete.[39] This can be attributed, as it is by Gavin Selerie, to attempts by the 'critical establishment . . . to reject or simply ignore the vitality of the new British poetry in its various forms', but Selerie also goes on, correctly to my mind, to stress how 'the current policies

of many grant-giving authorities [such as the] Arts Council of Great Britain . . . [by] shift[ing] the emphasis of its support away from writers in favour of secondary aid, meaning channels of distribution and direct bookselling', has meant favouring 'authors "of merit" (in some cases those who are already dead)',[40] with the result that the existing contemporary establishment 'canon' is reinforced. Selerie censoriously quotes from a Greater London Arts Council Policy Paper which suggests that: 'Publishing grants . . . have become lower and lower priorities . . . for a variety of reasons . . . [including] the constant doubt about whether such grants do more than provide a little clotted cream for the heavily jammed scones of the printing industry',[41] a policy suggestion that displays an appalling ignorance about the processes of little magazine and small press production; if an editor goes along with the maintenance of economic independence, it is precisely because of 'distrust . . . [of] the big houses' media-hype and show-casing of personalities', as Donald Davie correctly points out.[42]

IV

It is perhaps a good idea to temporarily focus here on anthology-publishing to provide some specific focus for these generalisations. In this respect *A Various Art* is plainly almost diametrically opposed to the collection edited by Morrison and Motion, *The Penguin Book of Contemporary British Poetry,* published five years earlier; they do not, nor could they, have any poets in common. An anthology following soon after *A Various Art,* and one perhaps to a minor extent capitalising on the space created by Longville's and Crozier's anthology, was *The New British Poetry* (1988), divided into four sections—black (edited by Fred D'Aguiar), feminist (edited by Gillian Allnutt) and two experimental, one edited by Eric Mottram and one ('Some Younger Poets') by Ken Edwards.[43] That it followed so closely behind *A Various Art* is in itself encouraging, as is the breadth it achieves by bringing together four different sets of poets. Less encouraging was the pasting this Paladin anthology received in many reviews. Robert Sheppard's defence of it in *Pages,* against a Peter Porter attack, clarifies well the discouraging gulf that still exists:

> So many aggressive terms in Peter Porter's review for *The Observer* could be translated from the sneering of the well-anthologised into the language of the neglected. For 'whingeing' read 'angry'; for 'Sixties Old Boys' Society' read 'poets who, since the flash of publicity in the 1960s, have been forced further underground than the "Underground" ever was'; for 'ageing experimentalist' read 'senior formalists'; for 'self-referring hagiography' read 'axiomatic reference points not normally associated with British poetry'.[44]

These 'axiomatic reference points' are mainly American, as the title 'New British Poetry' implies, with its oblique reference to *The New American Poetry* anthology edited by Donald M. Allen and published in 1960.[45] This association would have been eased by the more recent publication of a follow-up US anthology, *The Postmoderns: The New American Poetry Revisited* in 1982.[46] Thus Michael Horovitz, in a review published in *PN Review*,[47] makes the link back to the 1960 anthology, and specifically, in turn, relates the Paladin anthology to his own Penguin anthology, *Children of Albion,* published in 1969, itself intended as a UK reponse to Allen's first anthology.[48] This US orientation can in turn be reinforced by reference to Gavin Selerie's guest editing of a forty-eight page 'Selection of Contemporary British Poetry' section in *North Dakota Quarterly*.[49] This transatlantic link is mostly a matter of influence, though it has not, especially recently, been solely a one-way affair, and it has to be understood that the influence has been multi-faceted: the Beats influencing Michael Horovitz's endeavours in *New Departures* and Jim Burn's in *Palantir* to some extent; Black Mountain poets (and the earlier Objectivists) having a recurrent influence, for example on *Grosseteste Review* (especially before it developed its interest in the Cambridge school of poets) and on *Spectacular Diseases*; the New York poets (particularly Ashbery and O'Hara) proving similarly recurrent as a reference point; the $L=A=N=G=U=A=G=E$ school interacting with amongst others, *Lobby Press Newsletter* and *Reality Studios*; and *Alembic 7* (*Assemblic,* Spring 1978) borrowing Richard Kostelanetz's 'assemblage' technique.[50] If one takes these cross-seminations in sum, it is possible to see that the Beats' demand for a reappraisal of the social role of creative writing, the Black Mountain poets' insistence on open form, proprioceptive verse forms to liberate meaning from the constraints of conventional forms, and the subversions of language and syntax erected in different ways by the New York school and the $L=A=N=G=U=A=G=E$ poets can all interact with the modernist practices of Bunting, MacDiarmid, Jones and their progeny (which were in part rediscovered via the impact of US activities in Britain), particularly as these were taken up in the Fifties, to constitute a sustained, versatile and various interrogation of the politics of signification.

Indeed, if one reads back over the last several paragraphs an undercurrent of political dissent is plainly present: Buck's concern to stay clear of 'government control' interacts complexly with the Arts Council's progressive withdrawal from any preparedness to subsidise little magazine publishing activities, for example, since, as Selerie points out, the 'aim . . . of the present [Thatcher] government . . . [is] to remove support from all but the most "essential" services.[51] The interaction is complex because Donald Davie's accurate identification of the distrust the avant-garde has for the hype and personality-vaunting of the commercial publishing arena is plainly allied to unease about the discursive representations of the subject—as self-reliantly able to make his

(patriarchal) own way—erected by bourgeois individualism. Davie in fact goes on to value most the romantic strain he detects in the work of some of the contributors to *A Various Art*,[52] thereby confirming my initial contention that activity within the little magazine field constantly tends to risk collapsing the debate back into the terms of individual creativity offering transcendent insight (here by not specifying what he understands by 'romantic'), rather than setting up the possibilities of negotiated re-definition—poet to poets to reader. In this respect I believe that the best little magazines are those which seek out interactive positions through sustained critical debate (rather than short reviews), through a sense of continuity and fraternal/sororial endeavour. Choosing more or less at random, but from (unfortunately) a readily exhaustible list, one could point out the continuity set up by *Poetmeat, PM Newsletter* and *Global Tapestry,* and the way in which the newsletter served, in incidental combination with Cavan McCarthy's *Loc-Sheet,* as a composite information bank about little magazine/small press activity; how *Reality Studios* first set out to be a 'monthly newssheet . . . a supplement to *Alembic*',[53] how at first *Poetry Information,* and then subsequently *Poetry and Little Press Information* sought to function as information exchanges and debating forums for the experimental/avant-garde wing of little magazine activity, and how *Ninth Decade* brought together the editors of *Shearsman* (Tony Frazer), *The Atlantic Review* (Robert Vas Dias), and *Oasis* and *Telegram* (Ian Robinson).

This co-operative spirit suggests how the writer and reader as subjects might break out of the powerlessness of individualised subjectivity, into re-formulation—an already implicitly disruptive possibility, I would wish to maintain, set up by a little magazine's establishment of a non-commercial community in its pages. As Eric Mottram put it: 'There's a whole hidden etymological environment in the word 'private' . . . in which we are held'.[54] The little magazine field has the potential to erode this grip, but it is only a potential. It can be seen to be emergent in this statement by Allen Fisher that '. . . much of my work has included the need to carry the work process across into book production . . . partly out of a wish to *make* for oneself - to have autonomy in production—and partly to engage with the 'communities' of artists similarly involved. . . . The overall activity complex can be seen as a political one—against an established norm.'[55]

If we ally this potential to the view of the poet as someone seeking, in this sort of communal endeavour, to fracture, loosen and re-formulate the referential structure of language and language-forms, to liberate meaning for the producer (poet/poets/readers), then Kris Hemensley's apparently large claims make sense:

> In order to be a big press in a liberal-capitalist-consumer society, you have to have availed yourself of

the wherewithal of the existing value system, economic political cultural. There is a point to the littleness of the little press. . . .

It is not turned out for a market. . . .

The point is to devolve control . . . to decentralize the creative capacity of society.[56]

V

This potential, which can exist for a group of poets nationally, locally or regionally, I am therefore claiming as a specifically political one, and it is here, perhaps, that the pervasive discursive representation of creativity as essentially personal, inspirational and private, draws the 'terrain' of the little magazine into most obvious incoherence. Thus Gavin Selerie, in attempting to map out contemporary British poetry in a way akin to mine, through identifying a modernist-derived tradition which seeks to recognise the dimensions of the referent ('the crucial issues here, I think, are language and the scope of reference'), also quotes approvingly Alan Halsey's unresolved contention that 'The demand for "political" or "committed" poetry is betrayal of poetic as mode . . . Yet it is true that poetic cannot fail to be political . . . the Political completely embedded in the word'. The more than residual oscillations of meaning here are, for me, symptomatic of a mistrust of the political as being, somehow, in its essence incompatible with the sort of poetic practice that Robert Sheppard calls 'the poetry . . . of unproblematic experience'.[57] The point is that Halsey's position is itself not uncontentious, and a recurrent debate in the eighties has been, I think, the extent to which it is possible to sustain political commitment within contemporary modernist practices; this problem is one, of course, infusing debates about postmodernism as a concept and as an aesthetic, and poets and writers have been debating this as actively as critics and academics.[58] My point here will merely be that for poets and writers this debate has been one of raw necessity and often therefore of real intensity; Glenda George's guest editing of *Reality Studios* No. 7 (1985), 'The Inseam', is just one successfully provocative outcome, and as such an implicit answer to Gavin Selerie's reservations about how feminism operates within UK poetry activity.[59] Elsewhere, too, exploration predominates; Bob Perelman perhaps best sums up one dilemma these poets face: that any poetry which is alert to the referential treachery of words can become what, for him, some $L=A=N=G=U=A=G=E$ poetry becomes: so burdened by 'large supplies of surplus meaning' that it can have 'little political effect' (except, I would add, that which is contained within its consequent self-referential interrogation of language's relationship to meaning).[60] It would seem to be the belief of some poets moving within this field of poetic practice that this last—let us call it formal—mode of political engagement is in itself enough. This would seem, for example, to be both the grounds for Gavin Selerie's unease with

poetry adopting specifically feminist positions, and instructively, from my point of view, to lie behind Michelene Wandor's defence of feminist poetry by attacking Ken Edwards for what she sees as his belief that one can be 'uncommitted', a position which she feels gives rise to 'a deep-rooted philistinism across the board in British poetry, in which one must be seen either in "art" or in "politics"'.[61]

To my mind this is reminiscent of an earlier debate, in the sixties and seventies, fought out mostly in the pages of *Stand,* when Jon Silkin (primarily) and others (including Terry Eagleton, Raymond Williams, E. P. Thompson, Cairns Craig and Jim Wyatt), in argument with *P. N. Review* stalwarts Michael Schmidt, A. R. Simmons, Donald Davie, and a Movement alumnus, Robert Conquest, took up the position that in a pluralist society the search for 'common values' was a search for that hoary old ideological illusion, the apolitical, and that instead, all writing activity had to be seen as necessarily 'committed', either implicitly or explicitly.[62] I think it can be argued that this perspective of Silkin's *Stand* was assisted by the pronouncedly European orientation of its editorial attentions (in contrast to the already-noted US emphasis apparent in some other modernist-oriented little magazines' interests). Certainly, it is incorrect to over-stress this American/ European divide; *Ecuatorial, Curtains, Granta, Prospice,* Buck's guest-edited issue of *Spectacular Diseases* (No. 5, 1980) and earlier on, *Soho, Tzarad, Schmuck, Adam* and *New Departures* are just a few examples of modernist-oriented little magazines with a European orientation. Thus Eric Mottram, in attempting to speak of the fields of interest of contemporary avant-garde modernist activity in Britain, does indeed name Olson, Duncan, Zukofsky, William Carlos Williams, Pound, Oppen and Jerome Rothenberg, but he also approvingly quotes Jeff Nuttall's nomination of 'Picasso and the picture-object, Schoenberg and the serial form, Breton and automatism, Tzara and anti-art, Jarry and Duchamp and the mythic logic method, Mondrian and proportion, Braque and surface, Max Jacob and the dislocated image . . .'.[63] These interactions are seminal, but there is, nevertheless, more than a trace of a not un-American political confusion reverberating through the more recent debates about modernism and postmodernism, which cannot be readily resolved, or reconciled with the interrogation of language that otherwise is quite plainly foregrounded, in theory and in the writing produced. The important thing that *Stand* did in the middle decades of the twentieth century was attend to events in Eastern Europe, to the writing activity generated there and the censorship suffered; to drive home my point, I recall David Mayors' and Felipe Ehrenberg's production of 'The Czech *Schmuck*' in January 1974, an issue that went unchecked by its contributors because of censorship fears so real that the arrest, shortly afterwards, of many of the contributing Czechs was almost predictable. As the Iron Curtain draws back in the nineties we are, perhaps ironically, in danger of losing this simple reminder of the political potential of radical art practices evidenced by this sort of oppression. Poetry and prose at their best are able to remind us of the repressive potential of language arranged as hegemonic discourse; I find it hard to disagree, therefore, with Nicki Jackowska when (to return to the debate about the desirability of subsidising little magazines) she attacks the arguments of opponents of subsidy for recurrently reminding her of 'so much of Thatcher's peculiar and unpleasant mixture of naive philosophising and materialistic moralising'.[64] To swerve rather violently in my argument yet again, I would propose that, in the 'discourse' of poetry writing, the inherent resistance provided by the publication of little magazines (and small presses) in all parts of the British Isles to the centripetal, cosmopolitanising tendencies of commercial London publishing is, in itself, political, as the recurrent neglect of these activities in the mainstream (London) cultural debate illustrates. I am conscious here of how I have had to pass over in this essay the regional roles of the little magazines, itself another complex debate in which the 'discourse' set up by such diverse magazines as *Akros, Cencrastus, Lines Review, Poetry Wales, Anglo-Welsh Review, The Honest Ulsterman* etc. would have to be analysed.[65] John Crick is precisely right in suggesting that contemporary British poets, and I would add, their little magazines, are at their most exciting in their 'involvement with history, class, feminism and "nation"'.[66] But Crick's mistrust of contemporary modernism is less helpful; better, I feel, to stress that, as Peter Middleton puts it, 'formal experiment is not necessarily politically radical',[67] though once again with the qualification added that to recognise that the politics centreing on the lapses between signifier, signified and referent is both political and a space that the dominant ideology, or rather ideologies, seek to fill: radicalism is the remaining constituent. Perhaps an appropriate note to end on, then, is to quote a poem that cuts to the heart of the debate I am entering into here from the direction my essay has overall assumed (the politics of signification). The point of the little magazine, potentially, is to teach us how not to 'shut up'. If a little magazine (to risk a pun) *realises* this, it has succeeded:

this is thi
six a clock
news thi
man said n
thi reason
a talk wia
BBC accent
iz coz yi
widny wahnt
mi ti talk
aboot thi
trooth wia

voice lik
wanna yoo
scruff. if
a toktaboot
thi trooth
lik wanna yoo
scruff yi
widny thingk
it wuz troo.
jist wanna yoo
scruff tokn.
thirza right
way ti spell
ana right way
ti tok it. this
is me tokn yir
right way a
spellin. this
is ma trooth.
yooz doant no
thi trooth
yirsellz cawz
yi canny talk
right. this is
thi six a clock
nyooz. belt up.[68]

Notes

1. Wendy Mulford, from 'Valentine', in G. Allnutt, F. D'Aguiar, K. Edwards and E. Mottram (eds.), *The New British Poetry,* Paladin, London, 1988, p. 207.

2. Len Fulton (ed.), *The International Directory of Little Magazines and Small Presses: 26th Edition, 1990-1991 Dustbooks,* Paradise, California, 1990. I should perhaps add that this *International Directory* also lists many, but not all, of the small presses active in Britain, and that some of these run in conjuction with little magazines. In this article it has not been possible to survey both the little magazine and the small press fields, even though these are inextricably linked. Arbitrarily, but necessarily, I have therefore determined to focus solely on little magazine publishing activities. If readers are interested in exploring the small press field, they will rapidly find that hunting down the little magazines listed at the end of my article will lead them to discovery of the small press publishing universe. The annual *Small Press Yearbook,* now in its third edition, provides some details, as well as being another source of information on little magazines: E. Baxter (ed.), *Small Press Yearbook: 1991,* Small Press Group, London, 1991. Peter Finch's 'The Small Press Scene', *ARLIS Newsletter,* 11, July 1972, was, in its day, comprehensive.

3. The questionnaire was sent out to twenty-four little magazine editors in late 1990 and was answered by nine of them. The text takes care to identify, where applicable or important, which

editor in particular is referred to. The eight editors who replied were Paul Buck (*Curtains*), Bill Buford (*Granta*), Martin Bax (*Ambit*), Ken Edwards (*Reality Studios*), John Harvey (*Slow Dancer*), Peter Mortimer (*IRON*), Jon Silkin (*Stand*), Martin Stannard (*joe soap's canoe*). To make reference easy for the reader, an editor's name is usually immediately followed by his current or main little magazine's title, in brackets. The questionnaire asked seventeen interrelated questions about the editor's views concerning little magazine publishing, and was accompanied by a basic bibliographic data sheet.

4. For example Martin Stannard: 'Q: What were your aims in setting up a little magazine? / A: No idea. I guess I thought there was a gap to fill. . . . Q: Why and when did your aims evolve/change (if at all)? A: I got older. Learned more. Forgot a lot, too. The forgetting was probably more important. Now I think I'm getting younger. That means remembering a lot' (questionnaire response, December, 1990).

5. Anthony Linick, 'A History of the American Literary Avant-Garde Since World War II', unpublished dissertation, University of California, Los Angeles, 1965 Ann Arbor, Michigan, University Microfilms, 1965).

6. 'Thanks for your questionnaires. I must confess I do seem to get lots of these at the moment and what I've done is filled in the short one [the bibliographic data sheet]'. Martin Bax, questionnaire response (7 Dec. 1990).

7. The allusion to Pierre Macherey's *Theory of Literary Production,* trans. G. Wall (Routledge and Kegan Paul, London, 1978) is deliberate. An argument this essay develops is that editors' magazine production is produced—in the sense that the 'story' ['fable'] editors tell about contemporary poetry is constrained inextricably by the ideological 'project'—constraints of language as a social product, of generic conventions, and of their magazine's ['texts'] problematic. However, my allusion to Macherey will also turn out to be revisionary in two critical respects: firstly, 'production' here also alludes to the production process of publishing the magazine; secondly, I do not subscribe to a prevalent interpretation of Macherey that describes him as situating the author as passive in the face of ideology. Macherey's Althusserian view of ideology sees it as complex and contradictory, a terrain of conflict where 'ideology' encounters 'ideologies', where subjectivity is both produced and destabilised, and where, therefore, space exists for the interrogative to emerge in disturbances to the trajectory of the (in this case) little magazine publishing field—not only in gaps, lapses and silences, but also fissures, incompletenesses and, significantly, divisions of meaning. Macherey, fortunately, does not insistently follow Althusser down scientificity-loaded paths. Compare, for example, Louis Althusser's arguments in 'Ideology and the ideological state apparatuses', in *Lenin and Philosophy and Other Essays,* trans. B. Brewster, Monthly Review Press, London, 1971, pp. 127-86 and *For Marx,* trans. B. Brewster, Penguin Books, Harmondsworth, 1969. My revisionary reading, as you can see, has looming over it the shadow of Michel Foucault; see for example, his 'The order of discourse' in R. Young (ed.), *Untying the Text: A Post-Structuralist Reader,* Routledge and Kegan Paul, London, 1981.

8. Bax, questionnaire response.

9. The tendency towards elitism I will leave unillustrated; the sense of a limited readership comes across in these quotes: '. . . you won't get a very large audience through little magazines', Bax, questionnaire response; 'I started to see the magazine as a research project, not necessarily something to attract readers', Paul Buck, questionnaire response, (9 Dec 1990).

10. Martin Stannard sums up this reluctance when he baldly states that he would only attempt such a mapping 'after several drinks' (Stannard, questionnaire response).

11. Denys Val Baker, *Little Reviews 1914-1943,* Allen and Unwin, London, 1943. In contrast, Remy de Gourmont, in the preface to his bibliography, *Les Petits Revues,* Mercure de France, Paris, 1900, Ezra Pound, in his essay, Small magazines', *English Journal,* XIX, Nov. 1930, pp. 689-704 and Cyril Connolly, 'Fifty years of little magazines', *Art and Literature,* 1, August 1974, pp. 28-30 have attempted analysis; see Geoffrey Soar and David Miller, 'Little magazines and how they got that way', exhibition catalogue, Festival Hall, London, 1990, n.p. [p.4].

12. Geoffrey Soar and R. J. Ellis, 'UK little magazines: an introductory survey', *Serials Review,* VIII, 1, Spring 1982, pp. 15-28; G. Soar and R. J. Ellis, 'Little magazines in the British Isles today', *British Book News,* Dec 1983, pp. 728-33; R. J. Ellis, 'Producing the poem: UK little magazines · a second survey (Part 1)', *Serials Review,* X, 4. Winter 1984, pp. 15-23; R. J. Ellis, 'Producing the poem: UK little magazines—a second survey (Part 2)', *Serials Review,* X, 1, Spring 1985, pp. 35-44. My debts to Geoffrey Soar are substantial; the assistance of David Miller also needs acknowledgement. Any errors that appear are all my responsibility, however.

13. Ken Edwards, questionnaire response (1 Dec 1990).

14. *Ibid.*

15. See, for example, explicit or implicit attempts in M. Bradbury, 'Literary Periodicals and Little Reviews and Their Relation to Modern English Literature', unpublished Ph.D. dissertation, London University, May 1955; Anthony Linick, 'History of the American Literary Avant-Garde'; Frederick J. Hoffman, Charles Allen and Carolyn F. Ulrich, *The Little Magazine: A History and a Bibliography,* Princeton University Press, Princeton, 1967; I. Hamilton, *The Little Magazines: A Study of Six Editors,* Weidenfeld and Nicholson, London, 1976; Geoffrey Soar and R. J. Ellis, 'Little Magazines in the British Isles Today'. Other attempts to depict the little magazine field include A. Sullivan (ed.), *British Literary Magazines: The Victorian and Edwardian Age, 1837-1911,* Greenwood Press, Westport, 1984, *British Literary Magazines: The Modern Age, 1914-1984,* Greenwood Press, Westport, 1986; J. Burns, 'Little magazines', *Palantir,* 2, 1974, pp. 63-9; Thalia Knight, 'An Examination of the Bibliographical Problems Posed by the Alternative Publication of Fiction and Poetry', unpublished M.A. dissertation, University College, London, 1981; E. Stevens, 'A Study of British Literary Little Magazines 1960-1980 together with a critical analysis of their bibliographical control', unpublished Ph.D. dissertation, Polytechnic of North London, 1982; Jacob Korg, 'Language, change and experimental magazines, 1910-1930', *Contemporary Literature,* XIII, 1972, pp. 144-61; A. Wall, 'Little magazines: notes towards a methodology', Francis Barker *et al.* (eds.), *Literature, Sociology, and the Sociology of Literature: Proceedings of the Conference held at the University of Essex, July 1976,* University of Essex, Colchester, 1976, pp. 105-117. Wall's approach is of real interest; in a sense, I have adopted his approach of regarding a little magazine as a 'composite text'. I have also adapted it, however, by regarding little magazines, taken together, in groups, and as a generic whole, as both composite texts and *a* composite text, or, more exactly, as a composite 'discourse' about 'writing'.

16. Bill Buford, undated questionnaire response [December 1990].

17. Buford, quoted in R. J. Ellis, 'Producing the poem (Part 1)', p. 17.

18. Stannard, questionnaire response.

19. Bax, questionnaire response.

20. P. Hodgkiss, 'Editorial', *Poetry and Little Press Information,* 7, Dec 1981, p. 7.

21. Bax, questionnaire response.

22. Buford, questionnaire response.

23. *Ibid.*

24. Charles Osborne, quoted by Richard Tabor in *Lobby Press Newsletter,* 6, Feb 1979, reprinted in R. J. Ellis, 'Producing the Poem' (Part 2), p. 36.

25. Blake Morrison and Andrew Motion, *The Penguin Book of Contemporary British Poetry,* Penguin Books, Harmondsworth, 1982, p. 11. Geoffrey Soar and R. J. Ellis have also raised this point in their 'Little magazines in the British Isles Today'. Some of the following discussion follows the tracks laid down there. An acerbic review of the Morrison and Motion anthology is by John Ash, in *Rock Drill,* 4, 1983, p. 32.

26. Edward Lucie-Smith, *British Poetry Since 1945,* Penguin, Harmondsworth, 1970, p. 31.

27. Eric Mottram, 'The British Poetry Revival, 1960-1974', *Modern British Poetry Conference,* Polytechnic of Central London, 1974, pp. 86-117; see pp. 15-45. . . .

28. Barry MacSweeney, 'The British poetry revival, 1965-1979', *South East Arts Review,* 9, Spring 1979, pp. 33-46.

29. Douglas Dunn, 'Coteries and commitments: little magazines', *Encounter,* XXXXVIII, 6, June, 1977, pp. 58-65.

30. Stephen Pereira, untitled, *Angel Exhaust* 4, 1981.

31. Dunn, 'Coteries', p. 62.

32. Eric Mottram, 'Editing *Poetry Review*', *Poetry Information,* 20/21, Winter 1979/80, pp. 154-55. See also my account in B. Katz (ed.), *Magazines for Libraries: 5th Edition, 1986,* Bowker, New York, 1986, pp. 202-3.

33. Dunn, 'Coteries', p. 58.

34. G. Sykes, 'The state of affairs', *Kudos,* 8, 1981, p. 4.

35. Buck, questionnaire response.

36. Paul Buck, [untitled], *bal:le:d curtains,* May, 1978, p. 17.

37. D. Davie, review of *A Various Art, PN Review* XVI, 2, 1989, p. 58; A. Crozier and T. Longville (eds.), *A Various Art* Carcanet Press, Manchester, 1987.

38. Davie, p. 57.

39. Anon., publicity flier for *A Various Art,* Carcanet Press, Manchester, n.d. [1987].

40. G. Selerie, 'Introduction [to 'A selection of contemporary British poetry']', *North Dakota Quarterly,* LI 4, Fall 1983, pp. 6-7.

41. *Greater London Arts Council Policy Paper: 1982,* Greater London Arts Council, London 1982, quoted in Selerie, p. 7.

42. Davie, p. 57.

43. G. Allnutt, F. D'Aguiar, K. Edwards and E. Mottram (eds.), *The New British Poetry*; the four sections are headed, respectively, 'Black British Poetry', 'Quote Feminist Unquote Poetry', 'A Treacherous Assault on British Poetry', 'Some Younger Poets'.

44. Robert Sheppard, 'Poor fuckers: the New British Poets', *Pages,* (n.d.) [May, 1989], p. 161-63.

45. Donald M. Allen (ed.), *The New American Poetry 1945-1960,* Grove Press, New York, 1960.

46. Donald M. Allen and G. F. Butterick, *The Postmoderns; The New American Poetry Revisited,* Grove Press, New York, 1982.

47. M. Horovitz, 'More New Brits', *PN Review,* LXXVIII, Winter 1988/9, pp. 64-7.

48. M. Horovitz, *Children of Albion: Poetry of the 'Underground' in Britain,* Penguin, Harmondsworth, 1969.

49. G. Selerie (ed.), 'A selection of contemporary British poetry', *North Dakota Quarterly,* LT, 4, Fall 1983, pp. 5-67.

50. See R. J. Ellis, 'Assembling', in id. 'Accessing US little magazines', *Sow's Ear,* 1, Summer 1983, pp. 10-11.

51. Selerie, p. 7.

52. Davie, p. 58.

53. Ken Edwards, quoted in R. J. Ellis, 'Producing the poem (Part 2)', p. 39.

54. Eric Mottram, quoted by B. Morton, 'At the edge of darkness', *The Times Higher Education Supplement,* 24 March 1989, p. 13.

55. Allen Fisher, quoted in G. Soar and R. J. Ellis, 'Little Magazines' p. 732.

56. K. Hemensley, 'Up the Merri Creek or Nero', *Poetry and Little Press Information,* 3, Dec 1980, pp. 7-8.

57. G. Selerie, 'Introduction', p. 17; Alan Halsey, 'On poetics: notes in the blackout', *Rock Drill,* 4, 1983, p. 13, quoted in Gavin Selerie, p. 167; R. Sheppard, 'Poor fuckers', p. 163.

58. See, for example, successive issues of *Reality Studios* and *Rock Drill,* or, more specifically, the special issue of *Poetics Journal,* 'Postmodern?', 7, Sept 1987.

59. Selerie, pp. 16-17.

60. Bob Perelman, quoted in a review of his *Face Value,* Roof Books, New York, 1989 by Robert Sheppard, 'Meet me outside the Daily Planet', *Pages,* n.d. [1989], p. 201.

61. M. Wandor, letter to Ken Edwards, *Reality Studios,* VI 1984, p. 83.

62. See, in particular, the symposium 'Common values? An argument' in *Stand,* XX, 2, pp. 11-42 and XX, 33, 1973, pp. 8-48. See also for example interview with Anthony Thwaite in *Stand,* VI, 2, 1963, pp. 7-24 and J. Silkin, 'Introduction', *Poetry of the Committed Individual,* Gollancz, London, 1973, pp. 16ff. The title of this last anthology demonstrates, perhaps, how broadly my hypothesised 'disarray' resonates throughout the field of little magazine activity.

63. J. Nuttall, 'Why do we play to kids?', *Time Out,* 189, 5-12 Oct 1973, p. 24; Eric Mottram, 'Editing Poetry Review', *Poetry Information,* 20/21, Winter 1979-80, pp. 154-55.

64. Nicki Jackowska, letter to the editor, *Poetry and Little Press Information,* 6, Sept 1981, p. 6.

65. John Harvey (*Slow Dancer*) makes this point, in his own way, as well as I, when he writes: '. . . there's Huddersfield, then there's Tyneside, then there's Nottingham and somewhere else there's London (and in some miasma of his own making, there's Michael Blackburn's *Sunk Island*) . . . Huddersfield happened. Newcastle on Tyne continued to happen, but in a more lively way. Whatever was going on down in London or up in Manchester became even less relevant, which is a shame since they don't know that yet' (questionnaire response, 19 Dec 1990). Peter Mortimer (*IRON*) makes a related point when, like Harvey, he chooses to 'map' the little magazine field geographically, and describes 'the South' as 'pretty dull' (questionnaire response, 26 Nov 1990).

66. J. Crick, 'Spitting Image', *PN Review,* XVI, 6, 1990, p. 55.

67. P. Middleton, review of B. Andrews and C. Bernstein, *The L=A=N=G=U=A=G=E Book,* Southern Illinois University Press, Urbana 1983. *Poetics Journal,* 7, Sept 1987, p. 85.

68. T. Leonard, from *Unrelated Incidents,* in *The New British Poetry,* p. 191.

Little Magazine Select Bibliography

For ease of reference, and to provide some sort of overview, the following list incorporates all the UK little magazines mentioned in my article and footnotes, their dates of duration (so far as they are known; often no definitive termination date exists), and their chief/main/significant/indicative editor's or editors' name(s)—in this case, an intervening comma indicates editorial collaboration, a semi-colon sequential editing. The obvious omissions that show up will indicate how partial my 'map' of the little magazine field has had to be. Ultimately, to understand the role of little magazines they have to be read, for their sense of immediacy and vitality; University College London's justifiably famous little magazine library collection is, I think, the place to do this, and there my omissions will become apparent.

1983 Robert G. Sheppard, Supranormal cassettes. 1975-78

Adam Miron Grindea. 1929-?

Agenda William Cookson. 1959-

Aggie Weston's Stuart Mills. (Superseded *Tarasque*) 1973-?

Alembic Robert Hampson, Ken Edwards, Peter Barry. 1973-79

Akros Duncan Glen. 1965-82

Ambit Martin Bax. 1959-

And Bob Cobbing. 1954-?

Anglo-Welsh Review Raymond Garlick; Roland Mathias; Gillian Clark. (Superseded *Dock Leaves*) 1958?-

Angel Exhaust Stephen Pereira. 1980?-81?

Artisan Robert Cooper. 1951-55

The Atlantic Review Robert Vas Dias. 1979-80

Cencrastus Sheila Hern. 1979-

Cipher Jake Tilson, Stephen Whitaker. 1979-?

Control Stephen Willats. 1966-82

Curtains Paul Buck. 1971-78?

Dock Leaves Raymond Garlick. (Superseded by *Anglo-Welsh Review*) 1949-58?

Earth Ship Kris Hemensley, Colin T. Symes. 1970-72

Ecuatorial William Rowe, Jason Wilson, Juan A. Masoliver, Anthony Edkins. 1978-

The English Intelligencer Andrew Crozier, Peter Riley. 1966-67

Figs Tony Baker. 1980?-?

Fluxus 1 George Maciunas. 1964

Global Tapestry Journal Dave Cunliffe, Tina Morris. (Incorporated *PM Newsletter*) 1970-?

Granta Bill Buford. 1979-

Grosseteste Review Tim Longville. 1968-84?

The Honest Ulsterman Frank Ormsby. 1968-

Horde Johnny Byrne, Lee Harwood, Roger Jones. 1964

IRON Peter Mortimer. 1975-

joe soap's canoe Martin Stannard. 1978-

King Ida's Watch-Chain Tom Pickard. 1965-?

Kudos Graham Sykes. 1979-

Lines Review Alan Riddell; Robert Calder; Robin Fulton; William Montgomerie; Trevor Royale. 1952-

Little Word Machine Nick Toczek, Yann Lovelock. 1972-80

Lobby Press Newsletter Richard Tabor. 1978-82

Loc-Sheet Cavan McCarthy. 1966-68

Migrant Gael Turnbull, Michael Shayer. 1959-60

My Own Mag Jeff Nuttall. 1964?-66

New Departures Michael Horovitz. 1959-?

Nine Peter Russell. 1949-56

Ninth Decade Tony Frazer, Ian Robinson, Robert Vas Dias. (Superseded by *Tenth Decade* for the obvious reason) 1978-

Oasis Ian Robinson. (Superseded by *Telegram*) 1969-80

Outposts Howard Sergeant. 1944-

Pages Robert Sheppard. 1987-

Palantir Jim Burns, Stuart Brown. 1973-83

The Park Andrew Crozier, (Superseded *Wivenhoe Park Review*) 1968-?

PM Newsletter David Cunliffe, Tina Morris. (Superseded *Poetmeat*; superseded by *Global Tapestry Journal*) 1967-69

Poetmeat Tina Morris and David Cunliffe. (Superseded by *PM Newsletter*) 1964-67

Poetry Information Peter Hodgkiss. (Superseded by *Poetry and Little Press Information*) 1970-79

Poetry and Little Press Information Peter Hodgkiss, Bob Cobbing. (Superseded *Poetry Information*) 1980-?

Poetry Review Harold Monro; Stephen Phillips; Galloway Kyle; Muriel Spark; John Gawsworth; Thomas Moult; John Smith; Derek Parker; Eric Mottram; Roger Garfitt; Andrew Motion; Mick Imlah, Tracey Warr; Peter Forbes. 1912-

Poetry Nation (Superseded by *PN Review*) 1973-76

Poetry Wales Meic Stephens; Sam Adams; J. P. Ward; Cary Archard, 1965-

Poor. Old. Tired. Horse. Ian Hamilton Finlay. 1962-67

PN Review C. B. Cox, C. H. Sisson, Donald Davie, Michael Schmidt. (Superseded *Poetry Nation*) 1976-

Prospice J. C. R. Green, Michael Edwards. 1973-?

Reality Studios Ken Edwards. 1978-

Rock Drill Penelope Bailey, Robert G. Sheppard. 1980-

Schmuck Felipe Ehrenberg, David Mayor. 1972-76

Shearsman Tony Frazer. 1981-82

Sixpack Pierre Joris. 1972-76

Slow Dancer John Harvey. 1977-

Soho Lee Harwood, Claude Royet-Journoud. 1964-?

Spanner Allen Fisher. 1974-

Spectacular Diseases Paul Green. 1976-

Stand Jon Silkin. 1952-

Sunk Island Review Michael Blackburn. 1989-

Tarasque Stuart Mills. (Superseded by *Aggie Weston's*) 1965-71

Telegram Ian Robinson, John Stathatos. (Superseded *Oasis*) 1980-82

Tenth Decade Superseded *Ninth Decade.*

Tzarad Lee Harwood. 1965-67

The Window John Sankey. 1951-55

Wivenhoe Park Review Andrew Crozier; Thomas Clark. (Superseded by *The Park*) 1965-67

The Wide Skirt Geoff Hattersley. 1987-

Writing Women Eileen Aird, Linda Anderson, Gay Clifford, Sheila Whitaker. 1981-

Jayne E. Marek (essay date 1995)

SOURCE: Marek, Jayne E. "Making Their Ways: Women Editors of 'Little' Magazines." In *Women Editing Modernism: "Little" Magazines & Literary History,* pp. 1-22. Lexington: The University Press of Kentucky, 1995.

[*In the following essay, Marek centers on women who served as editors of little magazines and who—despite often being neglected by literary historians—aided the beginnings of the modernist era in England and America.*]

It is some kind of commentary on the [modern] period that Joyce's work and acclaim should have been fostered mainly by high-minded ladies, rather than by

men. Ezra first brought him to Miss Weaver's attention, but it was she who then supported him. The *Little Review,* Sylvia Beach, and Harriet Weaver brought Joyce into print.

—Robert McAlmon, *Being Geniuses Together*

This book so far may have given the impression that I have had no difficulty in making myself, that I sprang like a warrior out of the earth. If so, I have been unjust to my effort. . . . The causes I have fought for have invariably been causes that should have been gained by a delicate suggestion. Since they never were, I made myself into a fighter. . . . I remember periods when I have been so besieged that I had to determine on a victory a day in order to be sure of surviving.

—Margaret Anderson, *My Thirty Years' War*

These passages, quoted from two publishers who were closely associated with the foremost innovators in modernist literature, give a sense of context for discussing women's contributions to the development of modern literature, particularly in terms of publishing. In any such discussion one ought to bear in mind the climate of opinion suggested by these quotations. McAlmon's comment implicitly relies on masculinist assumptions and privileges—he characterizes women as "high-minded" and worth acknowledgment because of their promotion of Joyce's writings, although his tone carries a distinct note of regret, or surprise, that women's support was integral to Joyce's success. In the second passage, Anderson expresses her sense of constant struggle not only for acceptance and "victory" but also for bare recognition of what she was trying to do; she expresses, in short, her feeling of being limited by social attitudes and prescribed roles. If one looks past the habitual flamboyance of both Anderson's and McAlmon's writings, one may see in these quotations the indications of substantial differences between the experiences of male and female modernists. Such differences come as no surprise to scholars aware of the nature of women's history or the much higher proportion of attention that has been given to male modernists. Men, as had been usual, operated from an assumption of power and capability, looking among themselves for the important work of the new century; women, also as usual, faced exhausting struggles even to achieve passing notice. For readers who take seriously Anderson's work as an editor of the *Little Review,* or the work of dozens of other women connected with modernist publishing, it is clear that women had far more to do with the support and evolution of modernism than has been generally acknowledged. The skein of women's influence that I shall address in this book concerns the contributions made by some of the women who edited "little" literary and arts magazines.

The dynamic history of modernist publishing is embodied in the trajectories and vicissitudes of such little magazines. Many young writers, charged with the excitement of ideas and artistic perspectives that had been developing in Europe, could find neither a sympathetic audience nor a market among the generally conservative publishers of the day. Granted, the aesthetic risks of publishing experimental materials were underscored by obscenity laws that could—and did—censor publications and ruin businesses. As a consequence, scores of small journals sprang up, usually fueled more by energy than by funds or knowledge of the exigencies of publication. Nevertheless, these magazines created vigorous new connections between readers and writers who wanted to foster experimentation and challenge aesthetic traditions. George Bornstein notes a strong connection between the literature in and the editing of such new venues: "Both their astute sense of literary politics and their respect for documentary transmission led the major modernists to enmesh themselves in a wide range of editorial activities. They saw clearly that editors set the field of literary study, both by deciding what works came to the public and by determining the form in which those works appeared."[1]

Modern little magazines, as Frederick J. Hoffman, Charles Allen, and Carolyn F. Ulrich, authors of *The Little Magazine: A History and a Bibiliography,* describe them, were "designed to print artistic work which for reasons of commercial expediency [was] not acceptable to the money-minded periodicals or presses," which appealed to "a limited group of intelligent readers," and which expressed a "spirit of conscientious revolt against the guardians of public taste" (2-4). These iconoclastic publications—deliberately violating accepted principles of publishing and commercial success—afforded a particularly pertinent venue for the avant garde work that few established magazines were willing to print.[2] The precarious and idiosyncratic nature of such alternative magazines meant that a good portion of the contents was acquired through word of mouth among circles of experimental writers and was often borne on the currents of internecine squabbles, strong personal enthusiasms, and plays for power and influence. The personalities of editors, like those of the writers and artists who opened the doors of experimentation, became central to the dynamics of modernist publishing. Considering the cultural constraints upon women at that time, it is therefore particularly significant that the editors of many of the most important avant garde journals were women.

One might not at first expect this to be true. Very few literary histories treat women editors seriously. Modern historians have concentrated on the works of men, for the most part, and the act of editing itself has drawn attention mostly in terms of what happened when Ezra Pound met T. S. Eliot's draft of "The Waste Land" or when James Joyce added huge quantities of text to successive galleys of *Ulysses.* The women editors who are mentioned in such influential works as Malcolm Bradbury and James McFarlane's *Modernism* (1976) gener-

ally appear as adjuncts or foils to the men whose works they printed. As Bonnie Kime Scott notes in the introduction to her book *The Gender of Modernism* (1990), "Typically, both the authors of original manifestos and the literary historians of modernism took as their norm a small set of its male participants, who were quoted, anthologized, taught, and consecrated as geniuses. Much of what even these select men had to say about the crisis in gender identification that underlies much of modernist literature was left out or read from a limited perspective. Women writers were often deemed old-fashioned or of merely anecdotal interest" (2). As a result, Scott notes, "Modernism as we were taught it . . . was perhaps halfway to truth. It was unconsciously gendered masculine" (2). Scott's words reinforce the observations of a number of recent studies that note that in histories, biographies, compilations, critical commentaries, and memoirs, women's contributions and reputations have rarely been treated with the same depth and discernment used for men's work, which was assumed to be "universal" in scope—an assumption that affects many critical histories to this day.[3]

No compelling argument upholds such exclusion. In terms of women editors alone, for instance, most readers interested in the modernist era know that small magazines were extremely important in bringing the new literature to its public—witness the central roles played by *Poetry,* edited by Harriet Monroe and her associates, and the *Little Review,* edited by Margaret Anderson and Jane Heap. As the passage quoted from McAlmon indicates, the appearance of *Ulysses* itself depended upon the discernment and tenacity of various women, Heap and Anderson among them. Further investigation uncovers the names of a striking number of women editors active during the rise and flowering of modernism, including Monroe, Anderson, Heap, Kay Boyle, Bryher (Winifred Ellerman), Emily Clark, Caresse Crosby, Nancy Cunard, H. D. (Hilda Doolittle), Jessie Fauset, Florence Gilliam, Alice Corbin Henderson, Maria Jolas, Amy Lowell, Katherine Mansfield, Marianne Moore, Lola Ridge, Laura Riding, May Sinclair, Harriet Shaw Weaver, Rebecca West, and Virginia Woolf. The work of these women editors was extremely varied and highly influential; the incongruous paucity of scholarship about many of these women raises important issues for theorists of modernism who are willing to deconstruct the assumptions characterized by McAlmon's statements and explore the hardships and strengths characterized by Anderson's. What remains obscured in literary history that will be uncovered once women's contributions to "gatekeeping" as well as to creative work are taken seriously?

Since women's experiences, in literary as in other milieus, have differed considerably from those of men, women's writings often reflect this disparity through theme, writing style, and imagery.[4] The pervasive nature of such differences shows the need to continue studying implications of gender bias in the history and operations of literary production, criticism, and evaluation. In some cases, the poetry or fiction women wrote has received far more attention than their editorial and critical work; in other cases, women's editorial contributions have been overlooked, denigrated, or even attributed to men. Any assessment of the nature of modernism that aims to provide a sufficient overview, however, must address how women's writing, criticism, and publishing affected literary history, and how the roles these women chose had distinctive effects on what they accomplished. Such study seems especially appropriate to the modernist era, with its literature expressing considerable anxiety over the upheavals that characterized the early twentieth century.

Modernist literary experimentation arose from many aspects of life that were affected by a strong contemporary sense of cultural flux. Pertinent historical pressures of the time included the First World War, the residues of works by Darwin, Marx, and Freud, immense technological innovation, and archaeological and philological discoveries that modified ideas of human history—a set of pressures that culminated in the "disestablishing of communal reality and conventional notions of causality . . . [and] the destruction of traditional notions of the wholeness of individual character. . . . [In modernism] all realities [had] become subjective fictions."⁵ Reflecting on these momentous changes, modernist writers and artists attempted to express the flux of reality by dispensing with conventional modes of depiction and by experimenting instead with abrupt and unusual juxtapositions, sensory immediacy, linguistic play, and combinations of prosaic subject matter with idiosyncratic and esoteric allusions, all of which radically challenged aesthetic conventions.

Not surprisingly, the many aspects of modernist development have given rise to an impressive—and confusing—range of interpretations. Standard histories of modernism, particularly those predicated upon New Criticism, are currently being revised, although for the most part scholars still orient their studies toward literary and critical works written by men. Such an approach may express itself in the form of theoretical positions that do not include attention to women's history, or in a "humanism" that claims to include women's history and feminist theory but that in fact subsumes them, once again, into a presumably "universal" position.

In one discussion, for instance, historian Albert Gelpi finds that modernism, like the Enlightenment and Romanticism, was a response to "the rising sense of threat and confusion at every level of life in the West, religious and psychological, philosophic and political: a sense of crisis."⁶ This crisis developed from the decay of the Romantic notion of "the individual's intrinsic ca-

pacity to perceive and participate in the organic interrelatedness of all forms of natural life and . . . to intuit [through the imagination] the metaphysical reality from which that natural harmony proceeds" (3). Gelpi believes this decay turned into a skeptical modernism, of which the salient characteristics were "complexity and abstraction, sophisticated technical invention and spatialized form, the conception of the artist as at once supremely self-conscious and supremely impersonal" (5). The dualism of such paradoxical constructions reinscribes a good many of the qualities it seems to question, most obviously in the familiar notion that modernist dissonances expressing "crisis" necessarily undergirded a drive toward an encompassing consonance. It is also apparent that this sort of critical language itself reflects the values of a masculinist viewpoint that reinforces hierarchy.

Another way in which dualism tends to be reinscribed in conservative literary histories concerns the "break with the past" that many critics see as essential to the modernist agenda, as if the artistic expressions of the twentieth century were an abrupt and complete change from earlier traditions. In discerning and interpreting such a break, Michael Levenson decides, for instance, that the emphasis he sees on "two-ness" in the pronouncements of Eliot, Pound, Ford, and Hulme indicates a desire for "thorough historical discontinuity" (ix), which would obviously invest these men's works with pivotal significance in the development of modern thought. One kind of radical discontinuity, however, is absent from Levenson's own "genealogy" of modernism; this book, too, concentrates on the work of a few—mostly very familiar—male writers, despite its overt language of reproduction that might at least suggest the presence of women. Of course no single book can do justice to the huge range of writers and artists who might be included in a discussion of modernism, but it is particularly ironic, given Levenson's refusal even to acknowledge the influence of such women as Dorothy Richardson, Gertrude Stein, and H. D., that he writes, "Part of the difficulty of modernism is that it has suppressed its origins" (xi). Indeed.

The problems occasioned by ignoring or suppressing women's contributions must be taken seriously, since the effects infiltrate every aspect of history-making and canonization. One instance of such a "filtering" effect, as Shari Benstock terms it in *Women of the Left Bank* (27), can be found in the language of the following scenario from Hoffman, Allen, and Ulrich's *The Little Magazine: A History and a Bibliography,* in which the authors note that little reviews often served as the key to recognition for beginning or experimental writers:

> One may speak casually of an Ernest Hemingway's receiving his first half-dozen publications in little magazines and thereby gaining a reputation. . . . But let us

be more specific. Hemingway publishes his first story in *The Double Dealer* in 1922. Assume that the editor and a few other people read this story and like it. These people talk enthusiastically of the story and perhaps twice as many read the next Hemingway offering. Soon many admirers are talking—a snowball is rolling in the advance guard. A half-dozen little magazines are printing Hemingway stories and he has several thousand readers. An obscure, noncommercial press in Paris publishes his first thin volume, *Three Stories and Ten Poems*. The snowball rolls into the Scribner's office. Finally in 1926 comes *The Sun Also Rises*. A writer has been started on the road to success—by the little magazines and their readers.

[14]

One might well add, "and by their editors and sponsors." If the appearance of *Three Stories and Ten Poems* in 1923 helped Hemingway's "snowball" to gain crucial momentum (or at least to bring him to Contact Editions' affiliation with Three Mountains Press, which printed his *In Our Time* a year later), then thanks in good measure can be laid not only at publisher Robert McAlmon's door but also at the door of his wife, Bryher, whose funds and connections helped provide for the success of Contact Editions.[7] After two brief publications in *The Double Dealer,* Hemingway's next appearances were in *Poetry,* with poems and bits of literary gossip that were to become characteristic, and in the *Little Review,* with six stories that later appeared in *In Our Time* and the poem "They All Made Peace—What Is Peace?"[8] Clearly, the discernment of the women who edited little magazines and supported small publishing concerns proved essential to the "snowballing" of Hemingway's reputation.

The Little Magazine: A History and a Bibliography (1947) remains the best general introduction to the role that small magazines played in the early twentieth century, but its tendency to highlight the works of men reflects an approach that many literary histories have used. This tone particularly affects interpretations of the psychological politics behind the creation and promotion of avant garde work. If men have been expected to be bold or experimental, and women have been expected to be emotional or compliant, then post hoc discussions of the bravado that is obvious in much modernist writing will be pitched a certain way. For instance, Hoffman, Allen, and Ulrich choose to characterize Ezra Pound as "truly the 'personality as poet,'" a man whose "critical remarks are characterized by spasmodic penetration, an arbitrary and cocksure forthrightness, and an obstinate refusal to brook what he considered untimely or petty opposition," and who thereby became "one of the most effective sponsors of experimental literature in our century" (21). Their assessment of the *Little Review* notes some of the same energy and individuality but gives these qualities a distinctly different spin; the *Little Review* is characterized as a "per-

sonal" magazine that reflected Margaret Anderson's "breathless racing with life" from interest to interest (20): "It was an exciting magazine, quixotic, sometimes immature, but always radiating the blue sparks of highly charged feeling. Many were the stars that danced before Margaret Anderson's impulsive vision. . . . Inevitably, there was to come a time when she could glimpse no further horizon" (52). The style of Anderson's magazine is equated with her personality and dismissed as a limitation, and Anderson's successes in dealing with "opposition"—most notably in her and Jane Heap's attempts to publish as much of *Ulysses* as they could in the face of legal and economic sanctions—are given little credit even during the more extended discussion of the magazine found in the book. Also, Anderson is often discussed as if she stood alone in her editorship, although readers of the magazine find abundant evidence of Heap's contributions made in her own particular style. In general, the terms applied to Anderson carry heavy connotations of emotionalism, immaturity, and frivolity, which have often been used to dismiss women and their achievements, whereas Pound's strong personality quirks are treated as an important component of the era's powerful experimental urge.

Through such selective discussion of their topics, these and other literary historians often decide, for example, that Pound "took over" or managed literary magazines more ably than the actual editors, and in a broader sense base their discussions on an assumption that only men's literary work merits critical attention. Discussions of women's work are usually predicated upon the work of associated men, or upon the assumption that women's accomplishments occurred in spite of their personalities rather than because of them. Some historians, sharing the viewpoint of many male modernists, see women's literary magazines as "vessels" that carried the "creations" of male writers—an extension of the belief that women's importance rests in "serving men," a figure of speech carrying a negative sexual charge. Such attention skews and reduces the complexity that these historians claim for modernism, even as it marks the prevailing attitudes within which literary women had to work.

Fortunately, some recent scholarship has begun to correct the neglect and misunderstanding that has resulted from a masculine orientation in scholarship and criticism. When scholars decide to evade certain masculinist assumptions by returning to original data, there is much to discover. Women's influence in literary publishing has been persistent even if not immediately apparent. First books by Ernest Hemingway, Marianne Moore, Samuel Beckett, and William Carlos Williams, for instance, appeared as a result of publishing ventures managed or paid for by Bryher, Harriet Shaw Weaver, and Nancy Cunard, while other women, including Caresse Crosby and Maria Jolas, actively arranged for publication of work by Gertrude Stein, James Joyce, and D. H. Lawrence. The extensive influence even of acknowledged little reviews sometimes comes as a surprise. Perhaps the most important example is the English periodical the *New Freewoman.* Under its former identity (the *Freewoman,* started in 1911 by Dora Marsden), the paper had pursued social issues, particularly feminist and suffragist concerns; after an eight-month hiatus resulting from the publisher's bankruptcy and a distributor's boycott, the fortnightly was refunded through the initiative of Harriet Shaw Weaver, who had answered Marsden's call for assistance in the last issue of the *Freewoman* and had become a good friend, interested in supporting Marsden's socialist, feminist, and individualist ideas. In 1913 the periodical's title became the *New Freewoman,* with Rebecca West, who had both contributed to and raised funds for the paper, as assistant editor, and the paper began to print more poetry and fiction. Les Garner notes that West worked tirelessly for the paper and served as a link to the public "Discussion Circles" it had spawned (93). After a few months, she secured the additional services of Ezra Pound as literary editor, although his demanding nature was one reason she decided to resign in October 1913, with the assistant editorship going to Richard Aldington.[9]

But the magazine's most influential era lay ahead, when the *New Freewoman* became the *Egoist* in 1914, with Weaver as editor and Aldington as literary editor, a position that passed to H. D. during 1916 and then to T. S. Eliot in 1917.[10] Gillian Hanscombe and Virginia Smyers note that, under Weaver, "*The Egoist* became clearly a literary periodical" (178); Marsden had effectively withdrawn due to strain and a desire to spend more time with her own writing. The *Egoist* printed the much-discussed "Imagist number" in 1915, as well as many serializations, particularly James Joyce's *Portrait of the Artist as a Young Man* and portions of *Ulysses.* Its literary reviews provided early critical notice for H. D., Ford Madox Ford, Joyce, Wyndham Lewis, Amy Lowell, Marianne Moore, Pound, Dorothy Richardson, and many other emerging figures. In addition, Weaver developed the Egoist Press in order to publish *Portrait of the Artist* in book form, since no other publisher would do it; some extremely important by-products of the Egoist Press's existence included books by Richard Aldington, Jean Cocteau, H. D., T. S. Eliot, Moore, and Pound.[11] Weaver's propitious decision to become editor despite her inexperience not only led to the printing of significant modern writing but also served private purposes: it allowed her to provide a steady outlet for her friend Marsden's philosophical writings, it kept Marsden independent from Pound's antagonism, and it allowed Weaver to expand her skills and knowledge in new directions while still consulting with her friend through frequent correspondence (Garner 133, 135).

Marsden and Weaver's cooperation in running the *New Freewoman* and in consulting about the *Egoist* served their ambitions in mutually satisfactory ways.

At almost the same time as the *New Freewoman, Poetry: A Magazine of Verse* appeared in Chicago under the editorship of Harriet Monroe and her first coeditor, Alice Corbin Henderson. *Poetry* presented in its early years an astonishing gallery of new poetry by H. D., T. S. Eliot, Marianne Moore, Ezra Pound, Carl Sandburg, Wallace Stevens, and William Carlos Williams, among others. Although, as Ellen Williams points out, retrospect causes us to expect more from the first issues than they actually contained, the impact of that magazine upon the literary community was immediate (31-33). *Poetry* served as a forum for debate about the Imagists, free verse, international versus national identity in art, and the role of the artist's audience—all issues of considerable importance for the development of modern aesthetic ideas. The early editorial dynamics of *Poetry* included not only Monroe and Ezra Pound, as is usually pointed out, but also Henderson, who assisted Monroe during the first crucial years of the magazine's existence. The relationship between Monroe and Henderson altered and sharpened *Poetry*'s editorial policies. Henderson, for example, mediated between Monroe and Pound, discovered and promoted such figures as Sandburg, Edgar Lee Masters, and Sherwood Anderson, and engaged in vigorous defense of *vers libre.* Henderson and Monroe's interactions, like those of Weaver and Marsden at the *New Freewoman,* demonstrate the kind of cooperative work often found in women's editorial activities, which when viewed in the aggregate suggest that women's community was integral to the development of modern critical sensibility.

In addition to the pioneering work done in *Poetry* and the *Egoist,* numerous other periodicals that were edited, produced, or funded by women provided space and encouragement for new ideas. Among these, two of the most important are the *Little Review,* edited by Margaret Anderson and Jane Heap, and the *Dial,* under Marianne Moore's editorship from 1925 to 1929. The *Little Review,* founded in Chicago in 1914, carried sections of Joyce's *Ulysses* (later published in its entirety by Sylvia Beach in Paris), and pieces by Djuna Barnes, Mary Butts, H. D., Eliot, Moore, Pound, and Richardson; it also served, under Jane Heap's guidance especially in the 1920s, to introduce many avant garde visual artists and theorists. The *Dial,* which had already demonstrated a bold modern vision by printing Eliot's "The Waste Land" and work by E. E. Cummings, came under Moore's hand in 1925; she solicited and secured work from such important writers as D. H. Lawrence, Pound, and Gertrude Stein.[12]

Other women such as Ethel Moorhead and Kay Boyle (*This Quarter*), Katherine Mansfield (*Rhythm,* the *Blue Review,* the *Signature*), Florence Gilliam (*Gargoyle*), and Maria Jolas (*transition*) helped to edit and produce small magazines that extended the influence and scope of avant garde art and writing. Women were drawn to work in and support other kinds of publishing as well, most notably through independent publishing concerns founded or operated by Sylvia Beach (Shakespeare and Company), Gertrude Stein (Plain Editions), Nancy Cunard (The Hours Press), Caresse Crosby (Éditions Narcisse, At the Sign of the Sundial, and Black Sun Press), and Wyn Henderson (Aquila Press), or through financial "patronage" of fine presses by such women as Barbara Harrison (Harrison Press), Helena Rubinstein (who staked her husband, Edward Titus, for At the Sign of the Black Manikin Press), Harriet Shaw Weaver (The Egoist Press), and Annie Winifred Ellerman—known as Bryher—whose funds helped support a number of avant garde presses in England and Europe, as discussed in chapter 4. Whatever list one might compile of the "masterpieces" of the early twentieth century, it will include a high proportion of pieces for which women provided the forum for first publication, the impetus, the monetary support, or the initial critical reception, which was extremely important because so much experimental writing was going on. The more one looks, the more evidence one finds that, but for women's foresight and resourcefulness, much important modernist literature, art, and criticism might never have been printed.

As a result of this pervasive influence, it is imperative to learn more about what these women did, and how and why they chose to pursue their particular paths. A few books do address the roles of women as catalysts of literary modernism, and often decide that the connections between literary production and "authority" were addressed differently by female and male writers.[13] In their readings of modernist works, these scholars find a general sense of sexual anxiety or misogyny in many of the male writers, while they find in female writers a new sense of purpose as well as some confusion over the variety of roles that were becoming available to women at the time. These scholars also question the outspoken masculinism of certain literary men that has often been characterized as the sort of rebelliousness necessary for dismantling outmoded sensibilities in the early twentieth century. Sandra M. Gilbert and Susan Gubar, for instance, link the assumption of an intrinsic male rebelliousness to a misogynistic egotism, or fear, that refused to accept or to credit women as real contributors within the literary world.[14] Cheryl Walker points out the extreme condescension expressed later in John Crowe Ransom's 1937 essay "The Poet as Woman," in which Ransom not only dismisses the work of women poets but also "refuses to acknowledge the role of culture in shaping his own views" (5). The treatment of "women poets" as an undifferentiated mass, which Walker sees as a legacy of the popular "nightingale tradition" in nineteenth-century women's poetry, reflects the ways in which twentieth-century male critics have ignored the many different ways in which women have pursued their art (2, 7).

As may be surmised, women's methods for dealing with the male-oriented literary establishment varied widely according to individual circumstances and temperament. Studying the contributions of literary women, therefore, should not be expected to result in neat sets of reactions centered on imposed roles and prescribed behaviors. The assumption of reaction, which informs several recent studies of modernist women's work, provides one initial means of approach, although in a reductive way that can distort readings of texts. Women's work did not simply form "the underside" of modernism, as Shari Benstock suggests, or one side of a "battle of the sexes" in which women provided the "female half of the dialogue" expressing a sense of "feminine mimicry," as Sandra M. Gilbert and Susan Gubar propose.[15] Nor is it fully satisfying to decide that women who were "inheritors" of their literary and social worlds necessarily felt that they were also "outsiders," as Hanscombe and Smyers suggest.[16] Marianne DeKoven's assumption that female and male modernists reacted in two different ways to visions of social change imposes a gender-based dialectic (4), which, like the other dualistic approaches, can easily obscure the personal motivations and accomplishments of individuals and coteries.

These critics' stances are limited in presuming that women's lives and art developed only in reaction to the constrictions of prevailing social modes. Modernist women did not necessarily consider gender to be an analytic category, as scholars now do, and it is misleading to assume that a "sex war" necessarily pitted women against men in bruising struggle, or that women's achievements represent the "underside" of a modernism that must first be understood in terms of men's work and ideas. The varied nature of women's experiences, clearly, cannot be adequately theorized within such reductive pronouncements despite the cultural paradigms such pronouncements represent. The very nature of theorizing presumes the existence of commonalities as well as a privileged position that may well be unsuitable for approaching certain texts.[17]

One persistent conundrum in literary theorizing that is bolstered by feminist and new historical approaches remains the question of what to do with gender without necessarily falling into dualism. It is true that cultural language, especially earlier in the century, has made use of dualistic imagery, which offers a persuasive model to scholars returning to historical materials. From the standpoint of the current critical climate, however, dualism must be reconsidered at least in terms of the proposals of French theorists. If women are assumed to constitute or to see themselves in terms of being half of a dualism, or as some form of "Other," French feminist theories offer an obvious choice for critics trying to illuminate some of the political and psychoanalytic resemblances between literary history and women's experiences in patriarchal society. Anne Rosalind Jones notes that "French theorizing of the feminine emphasizes the extent to which the masculine subject has relegated women to the negative pole of his hierarchies, associating her with all the categories of 'not-man' that shore up his claim to centrality and his right to power," a view based upon Lacan's reading of Freud.[18] Since in Lacan's view an individual's sense of self is shifting and fictionalized according to internalization of others' views, with the symbol-pronoun "I" designating entry into public discourse through identification with the "Father," the position of women is negated; woman can "enter into the symbolic life of the unconscious only to the extent that she internalizes male desire . . . [if] she imagines herself as men imagine her" (Jones 83). Therefore Lacan's view places woman as either a male-determined fiction or a silent figure. Jones notes that French feminists' deconstruction of male-authored texts reveals "the suppression of whatever stands outside masculine norms," which may take the form of treating women as "separate, manipulable body parts" or a "surrealist view of women as childish, close to nature and irrational" (98). This oppression of women gives rise to the *différence* of women's writing, as described variously by Luce Irigaray, Monique Wittig, Hélène Cixous, and Julia Kristeva, characterized as taking a multitude of antirational and unconventional forms that are incomprehensible to readers schooled according to patriarchal traditions.[19]

Among these theorists, Luce Irigaray has been especially influential. Like many French feminists, Irigaray retains a dualistic division between "male" and "female" as a residue of psychoanalytic theory, but her approach is nevertheless useful because she refuses to place restrictions on the experiences of women or on the concept of "woman." Whereas Hélène Cixous in her well-known essay "The Laugh of the Medusa" imagines an anti-authoritarian reversal of what "woman" has meant in patriarchal ideology, Irigaray predicates her assessment of women's place upon the idea that "woman" embodies a multiplicity that cannot be understood in terms of patriarchal culture. Specifically, she uses the sexuality of the female body as an emblem for women's integrative experiences of life. The multiple and mutable forms of women's sex organs, Irigaray decides, cannot be defined within a "culture claiming to count everything, to number everything by units, to inventory everything as individualities. . . . *woman has sex organs more or less everywhere.* . . . the geography of her pleasure is far more diversified, more multiple in its differences, more complex, more subtle, than is commonly imagined—in an imaginary rather too narrowly focused on sameness" ("This Sex Which Is Not One" 26-28). In this sense a woman eludes definition

and expresses herself in the same multivalent ways she experiences the world. In order to comprehend what "the female" can be, Irigaray writes that one "would have to listen with another ear, as if hearing *an 'other meaning' always in the process of weaving itself, of embracing itself with words, but also of getting rid of words in order not to become fixed, congealed in them.* For if 'she' says something, it is not, it is already no longer, identical with what she means. . . . [A woman] enters into a ceaseless exchange of herself with the other" (29, 31).

If modernist literature is indeed characterized by its "subjective fictions" of reality, then French feminist thought not only illuminates women's language but also offers an approach for theorizing about the ways modernist subjectivity may have provoked, as well as expressed, masculine anxieties. Certainly modernism proper, like women's experimental writings, necessarily undermined a definitive worldview; to define modernism as multifarious, diffuse, and self-conscious suggests that there may be important connections between modernist innovations and qualities that have often been seen as "female" attributes. Particular aspects of modernism might serve as metaphorical equivalents to contemporary theories of women's psychology proposed, for instance, by Nancy Chodorow, Mary Belenky et al., and Carol Gilligan.[20] The so-called "break with the past" that modernism supposedly enacts might even be seen as a metaphorical equivalent of masculine anxiety, reducing the complexities of cultural developments to a coded phrase expressing loss and disjunction and creating an antagonistic "other." It is this oppositional construction of the "other" that some feminist models reject, preferring to theorize women's lives and writings in more inclusive or loosely structured ways in order at least to suggest the diversity of female experience, adapting and selecting from different critical approaches in the process.[21]

Bakhtinian dialogics, a theoretical model that has proven useful in postmodern considerations of polyvocality and of resistance to various forms of literary authority, has offered an appealing structure for feminist adaptation. In its original form, dialogics neglects to consider the function of gender. To create feminist dialogics, then, theorists must include gender in analyzing the "position" of women's responses. These can express resistance "when women negotiate, manipulate, and . . . subvert systems of domination they encounter" (Bauer and McKinstry 3), including the so-called objectivity or rationality that masculinist discourse has claimed. In the case of modernist women editors, it is clear from public and private evidence that these women were engaged in negotiation with, and manipulation of, systems of literary authority on a number of levels—the *Little Review*'s "Reader Critic" section is perhaps the most visible example. Feminist dialogic theory is concerned with gender-based redefinitions of the "answers" that Bakhtin claimed were necessarily part of the context of an utterance and that created meaning in dialogue. Whereas Bakhtin posited a "double-voicedness" ("dialogism"), however, many feminists prefer to see "multi-voicedness" or polyvocality in the ways women express themselves in language. The real question of Bakhtin's usefulness for feminist theories lies in whether a critic believes Bakhtin finally deconstructs dualism by imagining endless dialogic exchanges— through a continual modification of the speakers' contexts of meaning—or believes that dialogics reinscribes dualism in a way that continues to force women to create space for themselves as "Other," or indeed as "others."

In part, the several strategies included in this study offer a small taste of the variety of ways women have found to express themselves and shape their experiences—a variety that critical theories have only begun to address. While dualistic as well as masculinist approaches tend to obscure women's work, and although the dualism within French feminist theory provides space for women's experiences, a more open attitude is needed in order to treat fairly the variety of, and within, these materials. Michel Foucault's example of using a number of social, political, and economic aspects to rethink historical approaches as well as history "itself" demonstrates the necessity of awareness about one's own critical positionality—especially as regards power relations—which many feminist critics have found to be a crucial tool. One of the benefits of contemporary feminist theories, in fact, is that they encourage critics to see a far broader range in the expressions and effects of women's literary voices. Seeing constructions of "the other" in terms of women's collaborative writing and editing, for instance, radically revises the oppositional assumptions inherent to the term; if an "other" is a friendly and knowledgeable coworker—indeed, if "the other's" work can scarcely be distinguished from one's own—the meaning of "otherness" can become as fluid as perceptions of self.

At the very least, women editors and publishers took a variety of paths in pursuing their ambitions within a society oriented toward the work of men. It is true that a number of women who saw male dominance in literary matters acceded to it and refused to take credit for their own accomplishments; sometimes women accepted the expectation that their work was "in the service of literature" and that they should encourage the men with whom they were connected, act as mediators and comforters, and efface their own ambitions. Sylvia Beach, Harriet Monroe, Harriet Shaw Weaver, Maria Jolas, and Marianne Moore, for instance, at various points played down their own contributions and innovations, giving credit instead to the men with whom they were associated. Hanscombe and Smyers note that Katherine Mans-

field "had to encourage [John Middleton] Murry, rather than he her work, even when she was terminally ill" (245). H. D., during her early years in London while she was still closely associated with Pound, expressed uncertainty about her own abilities in her letters, even though she also helped to arrange the Imagist anthologies through solicitation, encouragement, and mediation among a group of writers.[22] The apparent internalization of "female" roles—which Mina Loy sarcastically characterized as "Parasitism, Prostitution, or Negation"[23]— seems to have carried with it some degree of reluctance to assert women's own abilities, a self-censorship that could go so far as silence.

Other women, including some of those who at times acceded to men, found more proactive ways to define their positions within the literary world, although usually at a cost. Women who did assert themselves, or who openly flouted male expectations, such as Margaret Anderson, Jane Heap, Gertrude Stein, and Nancy Cunard, have generally been characterized as intimidating, pushy, or flighty, and as having made their contributions in spite of themselves. Considering these women's extraordinary accomplishments, however, it is clear that traditional expectations did not prevent them from working or creating new lifestyles for themselves. Many of these women, in resisting patriarchal restrictions, also rejected traditional sexual roles, including motherhood and heterosexual marriage; others, for instance Nancy Cunard, Jane Heap, and Margaret Anderson, ironically manipulated the stereotypes attached to women's appearance. Of the few modernists who were mothers, some, like H. D. and Mary Butts, let their children be raised by other people. Of those who married, several—including H. D., Bryher, Dorothy Richardson, Katherine Mansfield, and Djuna Barnes—also maintained lesbian attachments that were more enduring than their marriages with men. Benstock suggests that lesbians often enjoyed much more freedom in choice and lifestyle than did women in heterosexual relationships; they could distribute their time and inheritances as they chose, and they had access to a distinct female subculture that provided a strong base for community (9). Even those women who never married and had no obvious lesbian relationships were often criticized for their failure to follow a traditional lifestyle, even though men's personal attachments did not occasion such comments. "Unattachment is, after all," note Hanscombe and Smyers, "as subversive of social expectation [for women] as is lesbianism" (246).

Such rejection of social conventions reflects a deep dissatisfaction with, or disbelief in, "male consciousness" or traditional authoritarian structures. Dorothy Richardson and Mina Loy spoke out specifically against using men as any yardstick by which to discuss women's ideas and concerns; Gertrude Stein deliberately subverted the authority of language linked with male cultural authority; Bryher protested against the restrictions placed upon young women by the English educational system. Women's frequent rejection of conventional lifestyles and of conventional literary forms, their sense of obligation to literature and their indirect as well as direct support of it, their rejection of "male consciousness" and concomitant development of female-centered systems of support—these are crucial aspects of women's experiences during the modernist era. A close examination of women's aims during the growth and maturity of modernism reveals the deeply radical nature of much of their work, breaking the "sentence" and the "sequence" of traditional language and literature the better to allow for women's experiences (DuPlessis, *Writing Beyond the Ending* x, 32).

Literary historians and theorists with a traditional orientation have treated these women as if they were anomalous—or anonymous—in the processes of canonical choice, rather than seeking out their real function as powerful and influential arbiters of modern aesthetic views. Additionally, history has neglected the cooperative work often found in women's editorial operations, a teamwork less common in men's, perhaps due to cultural training that "the other" was a threatening presence. Collaborative female relationships indicate that feelings of community between women, described by Hanscombe and Smyers as vitally important to the actual writing and production of literature, were integral to the development of modern sensibilities in other ways as well.

Modernism therefore designates not only a literary phenomenon but also a period in which women were developing alternative ways of thinking and living their lives. By upending conventions, modernist women developed their literary tastes and their lives in ways that were not necessarily predicated upon the prerogatives of men. If women participated in silencing themselves, the silence often served as a diversion so that they could work without attracting censure. If women served as mediators, the mediation need not be seen as acquiescent compromise but as a token of connection and interaction. If women openly defied tradition, this defiance may be viewed as protest through which viable new definitions of culture could arise. The possibilities of such critical reinterpretations prove the importance of reexamining modernism from the points of view of women who enacted some of its most radical tenets. New approaches to gender issues in modernism will allow critics to understand women's contributions with much more sensitivity to complexity. Whether a critic chooses to examine the "cultural poetics" of disparate material texts in the manner of new historicists, adopt a technological metaphor for diversity as proposed by Laurie Finke, or analyze the psychological or philosophical possibilities of feminist epistemologies, what is needed is a flexible framework that can accommodate

as many versions of literary creativity as there are writers—and the certainty of change within critical approaches as well.[24] My purpose is not to sketch a theory around literary data but to write a portion of women's history, as part of new historical reassessments of cultural data that affirm women's involvements in the development of modernism, a project upon which future theorists can draw.

In this study, I will recover and examine the roles seven white American and English women played in editing and producing highly influential literary magazines during the modernist era. Also, with an eye toward revising some existing sex-biased assumptions about these women's work, I will consider how these women responded to the difficulties placed before them by the male-oriented literary establishment. Both actions—of recovery and of revision—are necessary in order to restore the achievements of these women and to evaluate the overall importance of their contributions to modernist literature. Additionally, I must note that in this book I have not addressed the experiences of women of color, particularly the African-American women editors—such as Carrie Clifford, Jessie Fauset, Nora Douglas Holt, Pauline Hopkins, Paulette and Jeanne Nardal, and Dorothy West—who contributed enormously to the cultural climate that eventually fostered the Harlem Renaissance. My context, deriving as it does from a few white women of a certain social class, is not appropriate to a broader discussion of issues of race and ethnicity as they relate to modernist publication; the power relations faced by women of color in publishing show significant features of their own. There exists a great need to locate the texts of underrepresented writers and editors so as to explore further aspects of the history of modernist development. Here again my work is intended to advance critical discussion onto ground upon which later studies can build.

The two chapters following will examine in detail the crucial editorial interactions between Harriet Monroe and Alice Corbin Henderson of *Poetry* and between Margaret Anderson and Jane Heap of the *Little Review*. The fourth chapter will take up H. D. and Bryher's editorial and aesthetic interests, focusing on the Imagist anthologies of 1914-16, the *Egoist,* and *Close Up,* the film magazine founded by Bryher and Kenneth Macpherson in 1927. Collaboration and community serve as recurrent themes in examining the work of these women and others; as another chapter will illustrate, even Marianne Moore, editing the *Dial* from 1925 to 1929, created a fiction of working in concert with Scofield Thayer and J. Sibley Watson, although not quite in the way suggested by the standard *Dial* histories. After these four chapters concentrating on women's work in some of modernism's most influential little magazines, one chapter will reassess Pound's interactions with these women.

The neglect of women's critical literary work finds its paradigmatic expression in the opinions of Ezra Pound. What opinion exists about women editors has been shaped to a considerable extent by Pound, whose influence over current perceptions of twentieth-century literature is as pervasive as his pronouncements are idiosyncratic. As a catalyst of modernism, and as a figure integrally involved with the editorial dealings of many of the most important literary magazines, Pound necessarily serves as one of the focal points of this study. His responses to women editors and writers are problematic, since even as he depended upon some to provide outlets for his literary promotions, he fought with them and derided their tastes and accomplishments with language that is noticeably gender-inflected. Even as he drew upon the friendship and artistic sensitivity of H. D., he presented her with a sore trial during the Imagist years in London; his work as "foreign correspondent" for *Poetry* and the *Little Review* included bullying letters and the vainglorious assumption of his right to make policy; his acrimonious disagreements with Amy Lowell over the Imagist anthologies are popularly known. Although his relationships with other writers and publishers often display similar problems, the misogyny displayed by Pound and other people helped to create the intertexts in which these women's work took place.

The afterword to this book briefly notes some ways in which further reassessments might proceed, although my purpose clearly is not to deduce or propose a new theory of modernism but to discuss women's accomplishments that have heretofore been misrepresented or ignored. In light of the current critical climate, which has allowed many values and judgments that were formerly rigid and exclusive to be questioned, it seems crucial to continue to interweave awareness of evolving critical and theoretical approaches with solidly grounded historical research. Finding out about these women editors has been a great pleasure; so too is the hope of assuring that they, and scores of other women, secure a prominent place in the continuing development of the history of modernist literature.

Notes

Epigraphs: Robert McAlmon, *Being Geniuses Together, 1920-1930,* rev. ed. by Kay Boyle (San Francisco: North Point Press, 1984) 74; Margaret Anderson, *My Thirty Years' War* (New York: Covici, Friede, 1930) 123.

1. George Bornstein, "Introduction: Why Editing Matters," *Representing Modernist Texts: Editing as Interpretation* (Ann Arbor: U of Michigan P, 1991) 1-2.

2. See Frederick J. Hoffman, Charles Allen, and Carolyn F. Ulrich, *The Little Magazine: A History and a Bibliography* (Princeton: Princeton UP, 1947); Edward E. Chielens, ed., *The Literary Journal in America, 1900-1950,* American Literature, English Literature, and World Literature in English Information Guide Series 16 (Detroit: Gale, 1977); and Shari Benstock and Bernard Benstock, "The Role of Little Magazines in the Emergence of Modernism," *The Library Chronicle of the University of Texas at Austin* 20.4 (1991): 69-87.

3. Gillian Hanscombe and Virginia L. Smyers, in *Writing for Their Lives: The Modernist Women, 1910-1940* (Boston: Northeastern UP, 1987), point out the fallacy in this belief: "This 'universality' is an assumption implicit in men's creative writing and is explicit in their aesthetics. . . . Since a man's viewpoint has primacy and a woman's does not, it has traditionally passed unremarked that male writers have subsumed the female half of 'human' experience and that they have done so without qualification" (5).

4. Two books that have been particularly influential in proposing such differences in women's writings are Sandra M. Gilbert and Susan Gubar, *The Madwoman in the Attic: The Woman Writer and the Nineteenth-Century Literary Imagination* (New Haven: Yale UP, 1979), and Rachel Blau DuPlessis, *Writing Beyond the Ending: Narrative Strategies of Twentieth-Century Women Writers* (Bloomington: Indiana UP, 1984).

5. Malcolm Bradbury and James McFarlane, eds., *Modernism: 1890-1930* (Harmondsworth: Penguin, 1976) 27.

6. *A Coherent Splendor: The American Poetic Renaissance, 1910-1950* (Cambridge: Cambridge UP, 1987) 3. Albert Gelpi's book includes only one woman, Hilda Doolittle, as a major figure. While Gelpi claims he will "call attention, from time to time, to the ways in which elitist, individualist assumptions about gender, race, and class limit and even distort the work under discussion," his discussion is still predicated upon "what the poetry *does* rather than what it does not do" (6)—which means that the book necessarily privileges the white male purview underlying the bulk of the writing examined, responds to men's works in great part, and marginalizes "gender, race, and class" in a convenient phrase that gives just a nod to three factors that in actual life enormously shape writers' experiences and expressions.

7. This is attested to in the first of Bryher's autobiographical books, *The Heart to Artemis: A Writer's Memoirs* (New York: Harcourt, Brace, 1962) 201.

8. Nicholas Joost, *Ernest Hemingway and the Little Magazines: The Paris Years* (Barre: Barre, 1968) 19-33, 41-42.

9. Hanscombe and Smyers 169-70. See also Jane Lidderdale and Mary Nicholson, *Dear Miss Weaver: Harriet Shaw Weaver, 1876-1961* (New York: Viking, 1970), and Les Garner, *A Brave and Beautiful Spirit: Dora Marsden, 1882-1960* (Aldershot: Avebury/Gower, 1990) 114-16. Marsden and West were not particularly happy about the direction Pound seemed to want to take, but both wanted the paper to increase its literary aspects.

10. Hanscombe and Smyers quote a letter written in 1914 by Aldington to Amy Lowell in which he states, "Hilda is taking over the Egoist. I seem to be a little 'out' with Miss Weaver just now" (176). This piece of evidence suggests that, although Aldington and H. D. worked closely together on a number of literary projects through World War I, H. D. had more influence on the *Egoist* than the "official" date of her literary editorship (1916) would credit. See Cyrena N. Pondrom, ed., "Selected Letters from H. D. to F. S. Flint: A Commentary on the Imagist Period," *Contemporary Literature* 10.4 (1969): 557-86, and my discussion in [Marek, Jayne E., *Women Editing Modernism: "Little" Magazines and Literary History*. Lexington, University Press of Kentucky, 1995], chapter 4.

11. Lidderdale and Nicholson 459-65.

12. For a discussion of Moore's work for the *Dial*, see [Marek, 1995], chapter 5. I rely heavily on unpublished correspondence in the American literature collection, Beinecke Rare Book and Manuscript Library, Yale University. See also Grace Schulman, *Marianne Moore: The Poetry of Engagement* (Urbana: U of Illinois P, 1986) 9-25, and Taffy Martin, *Marianne Moore: Subversive Modernist* (Austin: U of Texas P, 1986) 48.

13. Of scholarly books, the most useful are Sandra M. Gilbert and Susan Gubar's *No Man's Land: The Place of the Woman Writer in the Twentieth Century*, in three volumes: *The War of the Words* (New Haven: Yale UP, 1988), *Sexchanges* (New Haven: Yale UP, 1989), and *Letters from the Front* (New Haven: Yale UP, 1994); Hanscombe and Smyers's *Writing for Their Lives; The Gender of Modernism* (Bloomington: Indiana UP, 1990), edited by Bonnie Kime Scott; Marianne DeKoven's *Rich and Strange: Gender, History, Modernism* (Princeton: Princeton UP, 1991); and Shari Benstock's *Women of the Left Bank: Paris, 1900-1940* (Austin: U of Texas P, 1986).

Among other books, Morrill Cody and Hugh Ford's brief *The Women of Montparnasse* (New York: Cornwall, 1984) examines the lives and contributions of certain of these women; however, the book's approach is neither scholarly nor exhaustive. The same problems arise with Hugh Ford's *Four Lives in Paris* (San Francisco: North Point, 1987), which includes biographical essays on Margaret Anderson and Kay Boyle, and *Published in Paris: American and British Writers, Printers, and Publishers in Paris, 1920-1939* (New York: Macmillan, 1975), which presents much fascinating background information without giving citations. Noel Riley Fitch's *Sylvia Beach and the Lost Generation: A History of Literary Paris in the Twenties and Thirties* (New York: Norton, 1983) provides a coherent view of this literary era by focusing on a central figure. Dale Spender's *The Writing or the Sex? Or Why You Don't Have to Read Women's Writing to Know It's No Good* (New York: Pergamon, 1989) provides a slightly different but very provocative angle on the (mis)uses made of women's literary work.

14. Gilbert and Gubar, *War of the Words* 147-56.

15. Benstock x; Gilbert and Gubar, *War of the Words* xii, 66, and *Letters from the Front,* chapter 2.

16. Hanscombe and Smyers 185.

17. See, for example, discussions about privilege and distortions in theorizing in Barbara Christian, "The Race for Theory," *Making Face, Making Soul: Haciendo Caras,* ed. Gloria Anzaldúa (San Francisco: Aunt Lute, 1990): 335-45, and in Susan Stanford Friedman, "Post/Poststructuralist Feminist Criticism: The Politics of Recuperation and Negotiation," *New Literary History* 22.2 (1991): 465-90.

18. Ann Rosalind Jones, "Inscribing Femininity: French Theories of the Feminine," *Making a Difference: Feminist Literary Criticism,* ed. Gayle Greene and Coppélia Kahn (London: Methuen, 1985) 81.

19. See, for example, Elaine Marks and Isabelle de Courtivron, eds., *New French Feminisms* (New York: Schocken, 1981); and Luce Irigaray, *This Sex Which Is Not One,* trans. Catherine Porter (1977; Ithaca: Cornell UP, 1985).

20. See, for example, Nancy J. Chodorow, *Feminism and Psychoanalytic Theory* (New Haven: Yale UP, 1989); Mary Field Belenky, Blythe McVicker Clinchy, Nancy Rule Goldberger, and Jill Mattuck Tarule, *Women's Ways of Knowing: The Development of Self, Voice, and Mind* (New York: Basic, 1986); and Carol Gilligan, *In a Different Voice: Psychological Theory and Women's Development* (Cambridge: Harvard UP, 1982).

21. DuPlessis's *Writing Beyond the Ending,* for instance, offers an approach that mediates between

positing an "otherness" on the part of women's experiences and providing space for discussion of the many differing strategies of individual writers.

22. See, for instance, her letters to Pound's mother, quoted in Hanscombe and Smyers 25-27, and her correspondence with Amy Lowell, as discussed in [Marek, 1995,] chapter 4.

23. Mina Loy, "Feminist Manifesto," *The Last Lunar Baedeker,* ed. Roger L. Conover (Highlands: Jargon Society, 1982) 269.

24. Laurie A. Finke, in *Feminist Theory, Women's Writing* (Ithaca: Cornell UP, 1992), proposes a technological paradigm based on chaos theory that would allow for polyvocality and greater inclusiveness in theoretical formulations.

LITTLE MAGAZINES AND POETRY

Ian Hamilton (essay date 1976)

SOURCE: Hamilton, Ian. "Poetry in Porkopolis." In *The Little Magazines: A Study of Six Editors,* pp. 44-66. London: Weidenfeld and Nicolson, 1976.

[*In the essay, below, Hamilton traces Harriet Monroe's editorship of* Poetry *magazine between the years 1912 and 1935.*]

'A Milton might be living in Chicago today and be unable to find an outlet for his verse.' Harriet Monroe announced this sorry truth to the Chicago *Tribune* over sixty years ago, on the eve of publishing the first issue of *Poetry*. During the course of her long editorship of the magazine (from 1912 until 1935) she may not have been able to come up with any Miltons, but she did provide the outlet—and the outlet is still there today. *Poetry* has turned out to be the most durable of all the little magazines.

If the original stimulus of *The Little Review* was flaming inspiration, it could fairly be said that *Poetry* was born of dogged indignation—indignation on behalf of the neglected bard. Harriet Monroe was involved in fashionable cultural circles in Chicago at the turn of the century, but her chief interest was in verse. And verse could hardly have been less fashionable, in Chicago as in the rest of the United States. It was the poorest of Art's poor relations. 'The minor painter or sculptor,' Miss Monroe recalled, 'was honoured with large annual awards in our great cities, while the minor poet was a joke of the paragraphers, subject to the popular preju-

dice that his art thrived best on starvation in a garret.' It was to correct this imbalance, rather than to promote a body of work or a critical theory, that *Poetry* was founded: 'An idea occurred to me: the poets needed a magazine, an organ of their own, and I would start one for them!'

On June 23rd 1911 Harriet Monroe arranged a meeting with one Hobart C. Chatfield-Taylor—'novelist, lover of the arts, man of culture, wealth and social prominence'—to enlist his advice and hopefully his practical support. Hobart turned out to be the perfect choice, and if *Poetry*'s success can be attributed to any single figure, that figure must be him: quite simply (and quite unusually, in the history of little magazines) he laid foundations that would last.

Chatfield-Taylor's simple idea was to get one hundred of his Chicago friends and contacts to donate fifty dollars a year for five years. Five thousand dollars, he predicted, would be sufficient to cover printing and office expenses, and the money from subscriptions could therefore be used to pay contributors. It was very simple, and it worked. Chatfield-Taylor undertook to make the approaches himself and it took him less than a year to raise the cash. By June 1912 Harriet Monroe (who had been spending *her* time in the local library, mugging up all the English and American poetry magazines of the previous five years) was installed in an office and preparing her introductory circular announcing *Poetry* as 'this first effort to encourage the production and appreciation of poetry, as the other arts are encouraged, by endowment'.

If, in her charitable enthusiasm, Miss Monroe had sometimes paused to wonder what she was going to put in her magazine, such worries were offset by one of the first replies her circular provoked. On September 1st, she got a letter from Ezra Pound, whose work she had come across and liked two years earlier in London; it set her pulses racing. The letter spoke, she said, 'with a fresh voice, and promised inestimable value to the magazine, for at that time he was the dynamic center of the keenest young literary group in England'. And also, had she but known it, an indefatigable colonizer of little magazines:

> Are you for American poetry or for poetry? The latter is more important, but it is important that America should boast the former, provided it don't mean a blindness to the art. The glory of any nation is to produce art that can be exported without disgrace to its origin.

> I ask because if you do want poetry from other sources than America, I may be able to be of use. I don't think it's any of an artist's business to see whether or not he circulates but I was nevertheless tempted, on the verge of starting a quarterly, and it's a great relief to know that your paper may manage what I had, without financial strength, been about to attempt rather forlornly.

I don't think we need to go to the French extreme of having four prefaces to each poem and eight schools for every dozen of poets, but you must keep an eye on Paris. Anyhow, I hope your ensign is not 'more poetry', but more interesting poetry, and *maestria*!

Pound went on to suggest that he keep Miss Monroe in touch with 'whatever is most dynamic in artistic thought, either here or in Paris'; she accepted instantly, and offered him the post of Foreign Correspondent. By September 21st the pact was sealed—just in time for Pound's name to appear on the mast-head of the first issue, which was dated October 1912. (Some of Miss Monroe's civic self-consciousness can be seen in the rush with which she got this issue out; rumours had been going around that a similar venture was being planned in Boston—but, as she later boasted, *Poetry* appeared 'nearly two months before the laggard Bostonians'.)

Pound not only got his name on the mast-head, but also managed to smuggle in his 'To Whistler, American':

> You and Abe Lincoln from that mass of dolts Show us
> there's chance at least of winning through.

Such sentiments sat oddly with Miss Monroe's other contributions (in the main, stiff, archaic poeticizings from ladies with names like Grace Howard Conkling and Emilia Stuart Lorimer) and also with the drift and tone of her first editorial pronouncement. Pound (though she was ignorant of his views at the time) was to recoil violently from her happy notion that the quality of modern poetry depended in some important measure on the size of its audience. She opens with her expected complaint about the status of the art:

> Poetry alone, of all the fine arts, has been left to shift for herself in a world unaware of its immediate and desperate need of her, a world whose great deeds, whose triumphs over matter, over the wilderness, over racial enmities and distances, require her ever-living voice to give them glory and glamor.

So far, so good, but as the rhetoric mounts, the claims get rather less banal:

> The present venture is a modest effort to give to poetry her own place, her own voice. The popular magazines can afford her but scant courtesy—a Cinderella corner in the ashes—because they seek a large public which is not here, a public which buys them not for their verse but for their stories, pictures, journalism, rarely for their literature, even in prose . . .

> We believe that there is a public for poetry, that it will grow, and that as it becomes more numerous and appreciative the work produced in this art will grow in power, in beauty, in significance.

As to criteria, *Poetry* was to be quite unprogrammatic; there would be no commitment to any single style or genre. In short, Miss Monroe breathily concludes:

We hope to offer our subscribers a place of refuge, a green isle in the sea, where beauty may plant her gardens, and Truth, austere revealer of joy and sorrow, of hidden delights and despairs, may follow her brave quest unafraid.

The immediate response to *Poetry*'s first issue registered enough amused condescension—especially in East Coast quarters—for Miss Monroe to grit her teeth. 'Poetry in Porkopolis', sneered a Philadelphia headline, 'Chicago loves poetry. It uses the proceeds of pork for the promotion of poetry', and the *New York World* rhapsodized as follows:

> From every clime Chicago will draw its poets. Not that it has too few native sons, but the most ambitious and the best shod from every corner of the earth will journey there. The highways need no longer bruise the heel as, fingering lyres, the slender wooers of the muse wend their way Chicagowards.

Rather less amused, though, was the response to Pound's 'mass of dolts' insult. Wrathful correspondents weighed in with a fair dose of patriotic indignation and Harriet Monroe had to rise—she could hardly bring herself to leap—to Pound's defence. She was able to agree with Pound that it was doltish of Americans to ignore their poets, but—and this was a division between them which was there from the start and would grow— she couldn't accept that Americans were uniquely incurable. *Poetry* was first of all an American magazine, and after Harriet Monroe found her feet she was to become less and less nervous of saying so.

In the first few issues, though, it was apparent that Harriet Monroe didn't quite know what kind of poetry she really liked or was looking for. In the second number, Richard Aldington had three mournfully Attic slices of free verse which had been sent in by Pound, but Miss Monroe's own taste seemed, if anything, to be soggily traditional. She printed Lily A. Long's 'Immured', for instance:

> Within this narrow cell that I call 'me'
> I was imprisoned ere the world began
> And all the worlds must run, as first they ran,
> In silver star-dust, ere I shall be free.
> I beat my hands against the walls and find
> It is my breast I beat, O bond and blind!

and this, from Margaret Widdemer:

> I have known great gold Sorrows;
> Majestic Griefs shall serve me watchfully
> Through the slow-pacing morrows.

Such contributions made depressing sense of Miss Monroe's second editorial, entitled 'The Open Door'. In answer to criticisms that *Poetry* could very well turn out to be a 'house of refuge for minor poets' she commented that everyone, even the poet, has to begin somewhere, and went on to reaffirm her determination to keep *Poetry* free of schools and factions. But Pound's presence was already beginning to spread itself; in addition to the Aldington poems, there was a note at the back of issue No. 1 declaring the existence of 'a group of ardent Hellenists who are pursuing interesting experiments in *vers libres*'. It could hardly be contended that Miss Monroe's own contributions had, at this stage, anything remotely experimental or interesting to set against this ardent group.

In *Poetry*'s third issue, Pound had moved even further to the centre of the stage. Not only did he provide five poems by Yeats (including 'Fallen Majesty') but it was made clear that he was beginning to win over *Poetry*'s staff. Alice Corbin Henderson, the assistant editor, gave notice that the magazine was prepared to succumb to the novel possibilities of *vers libre*. It was significant, though, that she was principally anxious to claim the new poetry as an American phenomenon. Whitman was the father of *vers libre*, Poe had influenced Baudelaire. Was it not lamentably typical, she asked, that these American geniuses had been best appreciated in Europe?

> Must we always accept American genius in this round-about fashion? Have we no true perspective that we applaud mediocrity at home and look abroad for genius, only to find it is of American origin.

Though Pound might well have been scornful of the patriotism, he would not have quarrelled with the main strictures. He, after all, had had to look abroad for *his* American genius to be acknowledged. The editorial, he must have seen, was intended as a clear gesture of goodwill.

In the fourth number of *Poetry*, H. D. made her historic first appearance, signing her poems 'H. D. Imagiste', and Pound contributed a Letter from London entitled 'Status Rerum'. It was the magazine's lengthiest and most lucid statement to date of early Imagist theory, and was to prove a turning point for the magazine. It offered the beginnings of a policy, of an allegiance which had vital possibilities. Not that Pound was beating any drums for London; on the contrary, he found 'Mr Yeats the only poet worthy of serious study' and regarded his contemporaries as 'food, sometimes very good food, for anthologies':

> The important work of the last twenty-five years has been done in Paris . . . there has been some imitation here of their manner and content. Any donkey can imitate a man's manner. There has been little serious consideration of their method. It requires an artist to analyze and apply a method.

Pound went on to pay tribute to Ford Madox Hueffer, and—incidentally—to indicate for posterity what it has not sufficiently acknowledged: the extent to which Hueffer's critical ideas were an essential influence on Imagism. 'Mr Hueffer believes in an exact rendering of things. He would strip words of all "association" for the sake of getting a precise meaning.' Hueffer's masters were said to be Gautier and Flaubert; his disciples were quite evidently the Imagists, whom Pound describes as 'the youngest school here that has the nerve to call itself a school':

> Space forbids me to set forth the program of the Imagistes at length, but one of their watchwords is Precision, and they are in opposition to the numerous and unassembled writers who busy themselves with dull and interminable effusions, and who seem to think that a man can write long poem before he learns to write a good short one, or even before he learns to produce a single good line.

Harriet Monroe's hospitality to Pound and his protégés may have been developing but there was no real sign that she had begun scrutinizing her own contributors with anything like his kind of astringency. Fulsome ladies were still allowed to get away with their 'eres' and 'yonders', and the critical section of the magazine was slack and bountiful. Edith Wyatt's review of John Masefield's *The Story of a Round House* was fairly typical:

> Wonderful, wonderful it is that in the hearing of our own generation, one great voice after another has called and sung to the world from the midst of the sea mists of England. From the poetry of Swinburne, of Rudyard Kipling, of John Masefield, immortal things still give us dream.

The magazine, like the other magazines Pound was to invade, had been split in two. On the one hand, the editor's own faltering traditionalism; on the other, the seductive energy of Pound's experimentalist unknowns.

Issue No. 6 marks the high point of Pound's influence, and is perhaps the issue of *Poetry* that has been most remembered and most quoted from. It contains F. S. Flint's note on the history of Imagism, together with his statement of the three golden rules:

1 Direct treatment of the 'thing', whether subjective or objective.

2 To use absolutely no word that does not contribute to the presentation.

3 As regarding rhythm: to compose in sequence of the musical phrase, not in sequence of a metronome.

Flint's contribution was followed by Pound's famous 'A Few Don'ts by an Imagist'. It is significant that Miss Monroe's reaction to what was to be her most historic issue was tentative and slightly baffled. 'It will be seen from these,' she ventured, 'that *Imagism* is not necessarily associated with Hellenic subjects.' She had also not yet sorted out if these new men were to be described as Imagists or Imagistes. It was to turn out to be a distinction that mattered, at any rate to Pound.

Although there had been much talk of Imagism in the magazine, there had not so far been many examples of Imagist poems, and the appearance of Pound's *Contemporania* in the issue of April 1913 provided a bolder representation of the new method than either of the earlier offerings from Aldington and H. D. In the same number, Harriet Monroe printed an article on what she called 'The New Beauty'. It marks her (theoretical) capitulation to the cause of *vers libre*. After a preamble about the need for new forms, she committed herself to the following courageous insight:

> We have printed sonnets, but always with the *arriere pensee* that the sonnet is an exhausted form, whose every possible shade of cadence has been worked out and repeated until there are no more surprises left in it.

Although it seems clear where Miss Monroe got that 'cadence' from, her own exemplar of the New Beauty was not Pound nor any of his London associates, but the Hindu poet Rabindranath Tagore. Tagore had been introduced to Pound by Yeats, who'd called him 'greater than any of us'. Pound immediately ordered Miss Monroe: 'This is *The Scoop*. Reserve space in the next number . . . he has sung Bengal into a nation.' Miss Monroe obeyed, but one doubts if Pound anticipated, or enjoyed, the terms in which she chose to greet his scoop:

> This Hindoo shows us how provincial we are; England and America are little recently annexed corners of the ancient earth, and their poets should peer out over sea walls and race walls and pride walls and learn their own littleness and the bigness of the world.

Such flickers of independence were to sustain Miss Monroe throughout the next two years, years in which Pound's hold over the magazine was such that *Poetry* came to be generally regarded as the chief organ of the New Poetry. She continued to print traditional pieces (this in spite of Pound's rebukes: 'Good God! Isn't there one of them that can write natural speech without copying clichés out of every eighteenth century poet still in the public libraries?'); and she adopted two important home-grown heroes—neither of these especially to Pound's taste. Carl Sandburg's *Chicago* poems and Vachel Lindsay's *General William Booth Enters Into Heaven* each caused a stir in America—not quite on the scale of the *vers libre* debate, but of sufficient vigour to persuade Harriet Monroe that she wasn't just Ezra's handmaiden. Pound's internationalism was all very well, but it never really excited Miss Monroe; she was a patriot, and perpetually on the look-out for some distinctively American retort to her European imports. Here she is, in the issue of October 1913, searching for 'Our Modern Epic'. She had just taken a trip to the Panama Canal:

> One who goes to Panama with eyes not too narrowly focused must see, in the making of the Canal, the proportions of a great myth. Prometheus the Fire-bringer

> Ulysses the wanderer, Seigfried the dragon slayer are not more typical of humanity than this modern piercing of the Isthmus . . .

> These men on the Isthmus, performing seven thousand labors of Hercules with their giant tools, removing mountains and uniting oceans in a mood of lyric rapture—these men, our strong compatriots, are poets, in imagination and idealistic motive, if not in words.

> Will the articulate poets prove worthy of them?

The Great American Poem. Harriet Monroe was a poet herself, or had ambitions to be one, and two issues later she printed a poem of her own called 'The Canal' which opens:

> In lazy laughing Panama—
> O flutter of ribbon twixt the seas!

The gushing expansiveness of both poem and preface was a clear signal of the direction she was moving in— scope, energy, size and American-ness were more, or more explicitly, beginning to attract her. In the same issue as her Panama praises she includes her own ecstatic review of Vachel Lindsay. She prays that 'the prairie muses' would help Lindsay to reveal his 'message, a message which his fellow countrymen would seem to be in need of'. Pound must have known that he could not live with this for very long.

The division between Pound and *Poetry* was to become an open one in 1915. Harriet Monroe had accepted pretty well everything Pound sent her, and although Tagore and Yeats were gifts to be grateful for, there must have been moments when she had her doubts about, say, Richard Aldington. But she suppressed any such misgivings and she was tolerant also of Ezra's repeated attacks on her home-grown favourites. There had been minor skirmishes, but nothing drastic. But sooner or later there had to be an issue which would bring into direct and lasting conflict the essential differences between them. Happily enough, the issue turned out to be T. S. Eliot.

Pound sent Eliot's *Prufrocke* to *Poetry* in October 1914. 'I was jolly well right about Eliot' he had written in September. 'He has sent in the best poem I have yet had or seen from an American. PRAY GOD IT BE NOT A SINGLE OR UNIQUE SUCCESS. He has taken it back to get it ready for the press and you shall have it in a few days.' When the poem was ready, Pound wrote again, describing it again as 'The most interesting contribution I've had from an American' and pleading with her to 'Get it *in* soon'. Harriet Monroe's response was less than fulsome; clearly bewildered by the work, she made suggestions for changes—in particular, she thought it went 'off at the end'. For Pound this lukewarm reception was the climax:

> No, most emphatically I will not ask Eliot to write down to any audience whatsoever. I dare say my in-

stinct was right when I volunteered to quit the magazine quietly about a year ago. Neither will I send you Eliot's address in order that he may be insulted.

In January 1915, he was still fuming. The poem had not yet been accepted, and he was having a hard time persuading Miss Monroe that it ought not to 'end on a note of triumph'. Eventually, she capitulated but managed to sustain her non-enthusiasm by taking nearly six months to put *Prufrock* in the magazine. It eventually appeared, after nagging by Pound, in the issue of June 1915. Even then, though, the squabble wasn't over. At the end of the year, Pound was asked to cast his vote for *Poetry*'s annual prize for the best poem of the year: 'I have cabled my vote for Eliot. As you might have known, I see no other possible award of the prize . . . If your committee don't make the award to Eliot, God knows what slough of ignominy they will fall into—reaction, death, silliness!!!!!!'. He must have known, however, that Eliot didn't stand a chance. Vachel Lindsay bagged the first prize and Constance Lindsay Skinner the second. Pound described the awards as 'filthy and disgusting'.

Miss Monroe's own memory of the *Prufrock* episode, as revealed in her autobiography, doesn't quite tally with the correspondence. 'The most exciting of those early introductions,' she recalled, 'after Lindsay and Sandburg, was that of a young Missourian in London, T. S. Eliot, whose 'Love Song of J. Alfred Prufrock,' printed in June 1915, although an extraordinarily finished product to begin with, was his first appearance as a poet'. It is notable, however, that whilst claiming that the poem's first lines 'nearly took our breath away' on first reading, they had done so as an instance of 'modern sophistication dealing with the tag ends of overworldly cosmopolitanism'. Even as a fond memory, *Prufrock* still managed to repel her.

Pound was to continue as *Poetry*'s Foreign Correspondent until 1919, but after the Eliot episode his involvement with the magazine was never again to be exclusive: he had involvements with *Blast* and *The Egoist* in London and, of course, he took over a large part of *The Little Review*, perhaps *Poetry*'s main rival. Harriet Monroe was particularly piqued by this attachment, and with justice—Pound supplied *The Little Review* with the best of Yeats and Eliot, reserving only his own work for *Poetry*. And he was none too tactful about his former allegiance to the magazine. This was Pound's editorial on joining *The Little Review*:

> My connection with *The Little Review* does not imply a severance of my relations with *Poetry* for which I will still remain Foreign Correspondent, and in which my poems will continue to appear until its guarantors revolt.
>
> I would say, however, in justification both of *Poetry* and myself, that *Poetry* has never been 'the instrument' of my 'radicalism' . . . my voice and vote have always been the vote and voice of a minority.

> . . . *Poetry* has done numerous things to which I could never have given my personal sanction and which could not have occurred in any magazine which had constituted itself my 'instrument'. *Poetry* has shown an unflagging courtesy to a lot of old fools and fogies whom I should have told to go to hell toute pleinement and bonnement.
>
> Had *Poetry* been in any sense my 'instrument' I should never have permitted the deletion of certain fine English words from poems where they rang well and soundly. Neither would I have felt it necessary tacitly to comply with the superstition that the Christian religion is indispensable or that it has always existed or that its existence is ubiquitous, or irrevocable, or eternal.

It says a lot for Harriet Monroe's tolerance, or pusillanimity, that Pound was not instantly relieved of his post—and, incidentally, of the small salary that went with it, a salary that Pound had serious need of at that time.

During the war years, an uneasy truce prevailed between Miss Monroe's developing provincialism and Pound's cosmopolitanism—but the combination of Chicagoan local pride with rhetoric about an international renaissance continued to seem unstable and bizarre. During the war, much of Harriet Monroe's energy went into proclaiming the poet's duties and responsibilities: she campaigned from the outset against versified patriotics, against 'war-songs and epics'. She printed Brooke's *War Sonnets* ('the draft we sent him to pay for these sonnets came back with "deceased" scrawled on the envelope') and some of Rosenberg's trench poems ('sent on ragged scraps of dirty paper') but in spite of war poetry competitions and special war numbers, *Poetry* managed little more than a monthly round-up of well-meant ephemera. D. H. Lawrence (his 'Resurrection' appeared in June 1917) wrote her that 'in a real fury I had to write my war poem, because it breaks my heart, this war. I hate, and hate and hate the glib irreverence of some of your contributors'. Perhaps the most apt footnote to these years in which Miss Monroe 'found the war excitement submerging all other interests' can be found in the story she tells of one of her favourite contributors:

> One of the saddest of the war's casualties was Gladys Cromwell. Delicately reared in a wealth-protected New York family, a poet of the finest and most austere sensibility, she and her twin sister volunteered for canteen service in France. But the contrast was too shocking, the nervous strain too severe. They remained at their post heroically to the end, but with release the inevitable collapse came with shattering power. The sisters leaped into the Seine from the ship which was to have taken them home.

For all her evident concern, Miss Monroe cannot hide the genteel, rather bland puzzlement of her response. It was all too far from home. She was more comfortable printing cosy poignancies from the girls who had been left behind. In a single issue of 1918 we find poems by Eloise Robinson, Ruth Gains, Allene Gregory, Louise Ayre Garnett, Antoinette de Coursey Patterson, Julia Wickham Greenwood and Lola Ridge; there are choice blooms to pick from here, but the following coy quatrain can be taken as thoroughly representative:

> O France's lilies are tall with pride
> Flooding the slopes of the western side.
> It comforts me they sway above
> The quiet head of one I love.

In the immediately post-war years, Harriet Monroe's patriotism became more blatant, and more simple-minded. Hymning the centenary of Illinois, she declares that the 'spirit' of Chicago is 'the spirit of active and immediate response to the need of the hour'. It was in this spirit that Chicago had invented the skyscraper and it was also in this spirit '—let me hope—that *Poetry* was founded'. Surveying the magazine's achievements to date, she says that *Poetry* had from the outset been faced with two possible courses: it could have become 'what *The Little Review* is now, the organ of a choice little London group of superintellectualized ultimates and expatriates' or it could have aimed to be 'the organ of a higher and more conscious, concentrated and independent imaginative life of this country'. The first of these courses would, Miss Monroe claimed, have been all too easy to pursue: 'I remember with what cordial kindness a poet in exile once offered to conduct from London our entire prose section.' In fact, of course, *Poetry* had chosen the second, nobler course and its new mission was announced as follows:

> If *Poetry* can help to develop and make articulate the imaginative life of the nation—as when, for example, it wrings out of a poet's over-modest reluctance the beautiful Cheppewa monologues in the present number—then its editors will be more proud than of having introduced the imagists; important as that episode was in the literary history of the period.

This was the first public statement of *Poetry*'s break with the influence of Pound. The Imagist era was over; from now on the magazine would concentrate on what was under its nose. In fact, the announcement coincided with the publication in *The Little Review* of Edgar Jepson's attack on the Americanist trend that *Poetry* had been following in recent issues. The article had been originally commissioned by *Poetry* (said Pound; Miss Monroe denied this) and had eventually appeared in London in *The English Review.* Pound had arranged for *The Little Review* reprint:

> By the reprint Mr Pound freshens up, so to speak, the article's attack on *Poetry,* a magazine which, during the past six years, he has so amicably represented in London. Evidently, this poet obeys the scriptural injunction not to let his right hand know what his left is doing.

It could hardly have been more appropriate that in the following issue (Vol. 13 No. 3) Harriet Monroe should print a poem of her own called 'America'. Slack and cliché-ridden, it celebrates:

> the iron vow of war—
> War to the end, to the death, war to the life
> War of the free, for the free, till the world is freed.

Other poems in the same issue speak of

> Mississippi, you mothered me when the child in me
>   was young

and:

> You, too, America, have seen the hugeness of days
> Break with unguessed being out of the sullen past.

It's as if, with Pound finally out of the picture, Miss Monroe could now relax. Or to use her words (from her review, in the same issue, of Edna St Vincent Millay's book): 'Almost we hear a thrush at dawn, discovering the ever-renewing splendor of the morning.'

By the end of 1919, although *Poetry* continued to print sophisticates like Yeats ('A Prayer for My Daughter' appeared in November) and Stevens, the 'prairie muses' had effectively taken over. One of Miss Monroe's proudest discoveries was a poet called Lew Sarett, who specialized in Red Indian dialogues and chants. His poems had titles like 'Chief Bear Heart Makes Talk' and lines like

> Ho!
> Hi! Plenty-big talk!
> Ho! Ho! Ho!

Sarett had an immediate impact, and the Red Indian poem became a regular ingredient. One found, in almost every other issue, a 'Hopi Sun Christening' or a 'Little Chief'. 'The wind is wearing mocassins / the wind is wearing mocassins'. It was indeed.

Miss Monroe also discovered a critic; an articulate, if somewhat wild-eyed, spokesman for the Americanist position. Emmanuel Carnevali made his first appearance in January 1920 and appropriately his first major contribution was a review of Pound's *Pavannes and Divisions.* The book itself, Carnevali said, 'has no sadness, no drunkenness, no love, no despair, no whimsicality. No human quality there, nothing but opinions and—an attitude.' As to the Poundian attitude, and in particular his attitude to America, Carnevali strikes an almost Poundian posture of reproof:

> . . . we—and I stand together with all the fools he so hopelessly curses—acknowledge that there are many things the matter with us; but we realize that he is not really interested and we consider his talk an intrusion; he irritates us.

There was much in Carnevali of Pound's own fire and intelligence, and he introduced a much-needed toughness of concern into the critical pages of *Poetry*. He was capable, it is true, of letting things get out of hand:

> Enfin, its poetry! Long live Carl Sandburg, to sing the song of his own beauty, and to tell God about Chicago, America, the world.

But he was a good deal more exciting than most of Miss Monroe's protégés. A Florentine, he had been taken up by *Poetry* on the strength of some 'captivating' poems, but his temperament—it transpired—was somewhat less attractive. He was, according to Miss Monroe, 'the limit of irresponsibility'. Or so she discovered after she made the mistake of hiring him as her assistant editor:

> He accepted with enthusiasm—forever and ever he longed to serve our beloved little magazine. But alas, the result justified my fears. He would slam into the office at chance moments, dash through a few manuscripts with violent contempt, skip all the routine work, and dash out again for more romantic explorations. His six months tenure of office proved the least useful in *Poetry*'s history, and I felt immensely relieved when he gave us up and resigned in favor of a mysterious offer from New York.

In fact, Carnevali never managed to take up the offer. He fell ill with what turned out to be a form of sleeping sickness and lingered on in Chicago in a near-vegetable condition. Eventually, relatives in Italy arranged to take him home. 'He left Chicago, to my unspeakable relief,' Miss Monroe has icily recorded. Carnevali was placed in a sanatorium and was given only a short time to live. But he was still alive, or half-alive, at the outbreak of World War Two; after that, no more was heard of him.

Once Miss Monroe had embarked on her patriotic course, there was no holding her. The proclamations became more and more dewy-eyed:

> I would be willing to put our present day poets (i.e. American poets) man for man or choir for choir, against those of any country in Christendom; because I believe, aided by such small linguistics as I possess, that no other group is doing work so vital and various and beautiful, so true to the locale and to modern life.

This gushingly uncritical note was to become characteristic of the reviewing pages of *Poetry* in the coming years, and the presence of Yvor Winters as a regular contributor (an exception to the rule) was made all the more incongruous by, say, Charlotte Mew writing about Marion Strobel (her book is 'like an apple tree burdened by an excess of its own beauty') or by Marion Strobel writing about Edna St Vincent Millay: 'If I could only sound a fanfare in words! If I could get up on some high place and blow trumpets, and shout and wave my hands and throw my hat.'

Meanwhile, good poems continued to appear, by Stevens, Williams, Frost and Marianne Moore, and *Poetry* continued to regard itself as a magazine for the rebellious and experimental. But the terms in which Miss Monroe described this kind of attachment revealed how far she was from recapturing the genuine novelties of the Pound era:

> So hail to conquering Youth—even to sacred Infancy in its mother's arms! May the newly risen or newly born solve the riddles and sing the songs of the world!

In October 1922, *Poetry* celebrated its tenth anniversary with a party in its new offices (or office; it was one room in a building owned by the American Bankers' Insurance Company whose president was one of *Poetry*'s guarantors). Poets drank prohibition punch, ate slices of *Poetry*'s ribboned birthday cake, and read their works aloud. Miss Monroe herself delivered an anthology of *Poetry*'s most famous poems—*General William Booth Enters Into Heaven, Chicago,* Joyce Kilmer's 'Trees', Rupert Brooke's 'The Soldier' and even some of Pound's *Contemporania*. (The birthday issue of *Poetry* had in fact taken pains to give Pound his proper thanks for having 'with much tumult and shouting turned the dry bones of the past and sounded the tocsin for the future'.) It was a sedate, self-satisfied occasion.

The problem was, though, where would *Poetry* go next? Miss Monroe was firmly set on her Americanist course, but her efforts to create the appearance of an Americanist movement had all seemed fairly desperate. And her attempt to produce a major American poet had been similarly unsuccessful. Both Sandburg and Lindsay were already well-established and so too was Williams (though there is nothing to suggest that Miss Monroe quite appreciated how Americanist *he* was). She needed someone new, someone Western, someone vast. In March 1923 she reviewed *The Waste Land* alongside Lew Sarett's *The Box of God*. One could hardly wish for a neater summary either of the internal conflict which had distinguished most of *Poetry*'s first decade, or of the dismal outcome of that conflict. Headed 'A Contrast', the review spoke of there being 'two immemorial types . . . the indoor and the outdoor man'. Eliot, she goes on, 'gives us, with consummate distinction, what many an indoor thinker thinks about life today', but

> to the men of science, the inventors, the engineers who are performing today's miracles, the miasma which afflicts Mr Eliot is as remote as a speculative conceit, as futile a fritter of mental confectionary as Lyly's euphemism (*sic*) must have been to Elizabethan sailors. And these men are thinkers too, dreamers of larger dreams than any group of city-closeted artists may evoke out of the circling pipesmoke of their scented talk.

Set against the shrivelled metropolitanism of Eliot, we have Sarett, a poet who would make real sense to those visionary engineers. He offers what Eliot so miserably doesn't: 'the creed of the pioneer, of the explorer, the discoverer, the inventor in whatever field'.

To compound this extraordinary philistinism, Miss Monroe goes on to tell of Sarett how 'last summer, while taking his vacation as a forest ranger of the government, he chased a pair of bandits through Glacier Park for forty-eight hours alone, and single handed brought them back to camp for trial'. Imagine Prufrock pulling off a stunt like that.

The promotion of a mediocre poet like Sarett was a mistake any editor might make, but there was little excuse for promoting him in these terms. And the crude disparagement of Eliot indicates how little Miss Monroe knew about her magazine's achievements or about how the future would estimate them. The simple-mindedness of her poetic pioneerism stood horribly revealed.

Poetry from this point on became what it still is today, a verse-printing periodical with no real policy, no special attachments, no enemies. And this was the magazine, after all, which Miss Monroe had originally set out to edit. Pound's intervention and her own wish to win free of his control had altered its course, but once Pound had gone and once Miss Monroe realized that her Americanist retort did not supply a vital new polemic, *Poetry* was free to settle back into its original Open Door complacency. Apart from a crisis during the Depression, when it did look for a time as if the magazine might have to close, *Poetry* was always financially sound and its position as poetry's friend and shopkeeper is not one to be glibly disparaged. Harriet Monroe, after all, was always more of an entrepreneur than an editor, and as such she deserves high praise. The truth is that, in 1923, she was faced with much the same choice as Margaret Anderson was faced with once it became clear that *The Little Review* had lost its vital spark. She could close it down, or accompany it into respectability. It was an easy choice because for Miss Monroe respectability had never been an enemy.

Harriet Monroe edited *Poetry* until a year before her death in 1935. In her later years she devoted less and less of her time to the magazine, and she threw herself into a series of ambitious foreign journeys. She died, dogged to the last, while attempting to cross the Andes with Norah Rowan Hamilton, the English delegate to the PEN International Congress in Buenos Aires. The altitude, it was said, proved too much for her.

The December 1936 issue of *Poetry* carried a number of tributes from friends, colleagues and contributors. Perhaps the most accurate and heartfelt tribute came from Pound—he writes in effect an obituary both for

the doomed, exciting little magazine that *Poetry* might have been and for the worthy, durable 'trade journal' that it actually became:

> The new generation of the 1930s can not measure, off-hand, the local situation of 1910. An exclusive editorial policy would not have done the work of an inclusive policy, (however much the inclusiveness may have rankled one and all factions).

> It is to Miss Monroe's credit that *Poetry* never degenerated into a factional organ. Her achievement was to set up a trade journal in the best sense of the word.

> During the twenty-four years of her editorship perhaps three periodicals made a brilliant record, perhaps five periodicals, but they were all under the sod in the autumn of 1936.

Mark Manganaro (essay date fall 1983)

SOURCE: Manganaro, Mark. "The Problem of Self Poetry in the Little Magazine." *Missouri Review* 7, no 1 (fall 1983): 249-59.

[*In the essay below, Manganaro discusses the balance between the personal and the universal in poetry published by contemporary little magazines.*]

As an editor I have noticed that there is a lot of "good" poetry about these days, perhaps more than ever before I think that much of the poetry published in magazines today remains in that dubious category simply because it follows, or I should say, falls into modes established by someone else long ago who is now residing, as one popular film has it, in a galaxy far, far away.

This essay attempts to outline one of the basic tendencies which contributes to making the all-too-familiar the only "good," in today's poetry. I decided to go to the little magazines themselves for examples, choosing twelve of the most notable "littles" as a basis, though cite only six in the essay itself. I have no wish to "rate" or evaluate the magazines themselves, and my choosing them certainly does not mean I think them mediocre Nor am I attempting to judge the poets whose works happen to choose. To insure that, I have decided to keep the names of the poets anonymous, with the exception of one whose work I find especially praiseworthy. The individual poems merely serve as examples of what is too often seen, or not seen enough, by editors.

Louise Gluck, in a recent issue of *Antaeus*, delineates two kinds of modern poems, those in which a reader is sought, which "postulate a listener" (Eliot is given as an example), and those which are "not addressed outward" but only "allowed to be overheard" (Wallace Stevens serves as an example). According to Gluck, the reader in this second type is alienated, for "to overhea is to experience exclusion." This is an interesting and useful distinction. My feeling is that since the great Modernists we have moved in great numbers toward the first type, termed by Gluck the poem of "invitation." Indeed, I think we often unwittingly go far beyond it, straining the limits of the reader's tolerance as we do not invite so much as hound the guests into our homes. Many poems sent to magazines today are of unwarranted invitation, not bothering to take into consideration the question of whether the reader would wish to enter into the particular world of the poet or persona.

This tendency is especially seen in poems containing a great deal of personal or highly circumstantial detail, enough to make it necessary for the reader to work out the tangle of the persona or poet's autobiographical complex, a task which may very well not be worth the effort. The key of course is that the poem succeed in transcending the personal detail upon which it is based. Yet even when the overly particular detail is balanced by other qualities at work in the poem, the reader, out of an often understandable lack of interest, may drop the poem before it has run its course. Are we always to lay the blame on the reader for this? Does not the poet today, as in times past, owe some consideration to audience?

One might respond that such a protest is nothing new—the same kinds of questions were raised, out of frustration, over the obscurity or complexity of Modernists such as Eliot and Pound. Yet with both Eliot and Pound the difficulties were warranted by the scope and magnitude of the efforts. We tried harder with them because we recognized them as comprehensive responses to and revisions of modern culture. The contemporary poem of circumstantial detail does not usually offer a vision broadening beyond the immediate world of the poem. Let's look at an example, from a poem entitled "Catching Eels," published in the Spring 1983 issue of *Prairie Schooner*:

> Out there,
> on the channel sea that barely ripples,
> water fit to be a mirror, he hears
> the first whimper of his dead brother,
> then the second, the third, until
> he is lost in the counting and so stops
> counting and listens and stares. He
> remembers the story of his brother treating
> typhus-ridden Partisans on the coast, how
> he slept with the sick, gave them
> his water to drink, his hand
> to write the letters saying they would come home,
> his hand to write some woman living
> inland that her husband, or son, father
> or lover was dead; how the Colonel
> saw his brother crumple under the clear sky
> that filled with the death plans of his fever,

> how they dug a separate hole, would not
> throw his body into the general ditch . . .

I feel this poem's detail is not justified by any worthwhile perception above the chronicling of the concrete. Nor does the narrative element stand out in terms of vividness or originality. I am ultimately forced to ask: What do I really care that ". . . He / remembers the story of his brother treating / typhus-ridden Partisans on the coast . . ."? This tendency towards overly circumstantial detail is much more abused, however, in poems which have a more obvious autobiographical base and are usually told through the first person. The confessional mode of the fifties and sixties had a lot to do with legitimizing this habitual use of unbridled personal detail. The result in that the magazines today are filled with poems which either ignore any sense of the audience's capacity for interest or assume that the reader is bound to be captivated by this party or that picnic, this father's breakdown or that mother's hysterectomy.

Still, the poem of circumstantial detail *can* work—see as an example this excerpt from a poem about an aging man learning to play an autoharp, published in issue 15 of *Quarterly West*:

> And always and in pain hearing the song
> precisely as it ought to be,
> the Benfields, Kirby Snow or Maybelle Carter
>
> working out the broken, sweet arpeggios and rolls,
> each note caught cleanly on the pick, fingers
> working light and fluent, quick
> work for the thumb, remembering its place,
>
> the runs that underline and never overpower
> the melody, which all the time
> plays ascending and descending joyously
> against them, and the free voice
>
> given freely over to become
> the song itself, caught and delicately
> underscored—none of which
> is possible for me, not now, my fingers
>
> stiff and tortured by the picks,
> playing artlessly against themselves . . .

Though this is not the most striking of examples, in my mind this poem succeeds precisely because its detail contributes toward the understanding of something beyond itself, and, just as importantly, getting to that comprehension is a verbally exciting experience. The persona in the poem functions not to limit the experience of the poem to an individual, but to universalize that experience—the learning of a song on the autoharp gives expression to the feeling of loss with age of the ability to create art out of the given materials.

Many of the poets today are aware at least of the need to universalize the experience of the poem, to take it beyond the matter of the individual acting or speaking in the poem. However, often the poet writing in the little magazine today achieves only a superficial broadening beyond the particular. Many times it seems as if the poet is trying to tell his own story but trying to cover the tracks. One way by which the poet gives the impression of universality while remaining particular is through the use of the second person. The following excerpt appeared in a poem published in the Winter 1983 issue of *Poet Lore*:

> You have slept too long in the sun
> dreaming of old women dying,
> their hearts deflating in your hands.
> You wake to the grind of sand
> on flesh, cold and alone,
> every swimmer gone.

Here the poet strives to give the semblance of universality while still rooting the poem in the idiosyncracies of the individual within the piece. How many of you fall asleep on the beach dreaming of old women dying? I get very tired of poets telling me what I'm doing and using that as a guise for what they, or their personae, are doing and thinking. Here's another example from the same issue of *Poet Lore*:

> When you open the door
> To a killer's room
>
> And on the wall is a photograph
> And on the table is a cereal box
> And on the floor a pair of black shoes
>
> When you know someone
> Has slept there alone
> And you see the window cracked and open . . .

Both of these poems also use another all-too-easy and overdone technique, the suspended present tense. It is as if the poets presume that if we the readers are kept continually in the present, we are bound to think the poem more immediate and hence relevant to our experience. The use of both these techniques only makes more painfully obvious to me the need for many of today's poets to break out of the mentality of "self-speak" and enter into that frame of mind in which, as Emerson might say, we ought not to stop with the mere "facts" but forge ahead toward the great universal. A poem by a rather prominent contemporary poet in the Winter 1983 *TriQuarterly* sums up well what I think an unfortunate state: "We looked at it and we saw it. / We wanted to tell the story, but could tell only / The one that included us."

Speaking of Emerson, I think it significant that more often than not the short lyric/narrative poem today moves not from the "me" to the "not me," not from the inside moving outward, but instead progresses from the external to the internal, from the objective to the subjective. This pattern certainly has something to say about the premium we put upon individual perception. But even if we accept the philosophic base upon which such a narrowing process originates, we cannot applaud the frequent and predictable versions of this pattern which often vary only in time and place. The poem usually opens with a fairly detailed description of the external scene which inexorably moves toward the application of the external or objective to the self or subject. Poets working in this pattern seem to me to be working with a kind of "slot and filler" poetry (to borrow a linguistic term). Continuous usage has created certain "slots" or habitual turns in the base poem—it is up to the individual poet to "fill" that slot with his own particulars. Let's look at an example, from the poem "Trash," in the Winter 1983 issue of *TriQuarterly*:

> Scavengers start out early to beat the garbage trucks,
>   their scabby pickups and cankered vans hacking
> at the curb while they rummage through our castoffs
>   lining the
>   street
>   like mourning friends or night women few men
> stop for.

*   *   *

> Maybe one of them will have good luck with the lamp
>   I've given up
>   for dead, and his room will shine, radiant and warm,
> while I read in mine the lessons of the past
>   or some current cry of pain or listen to news
>
> tossed on the midden of the world or think of friends
>   whose lives are collapsing or of others long ago
> chucked out from the cluttered households of the human heart that I for a time so eagerly caught up.

What we see here that *is* typical and peculiarly contemporary is the application of some part of the outside world to a specific condition of the poet or persona. In this case the poet's observation of the trash collector leads to a meditation on the details of his own, and his friends', problems. The pose of the poet-persona in this particular poem is also fairly typical—that of the worldwise and weary poet who meditates sagely from the unfortunate heights where he is destined to view the trash heap of the world. Pontificating and patronizing, yet although not without precedents in the late eighteenth and early nineteenth centuries. These latter-day poets at thirty thousand feet are less tolerable because, for at that height, the scope of their vision is really rather small.

Let us take another version of the attitude of world-wise poet, that of experienced age witnessing youth and warning of the troubled times to come. The following is from a poem in the Spring 1983 *Prairie Schooner*:

> Vigor rides here,
> a day pack over shoulders.
>
> All the girls are beautiful;
>
> The boys handsome. I watch them.
> Their sadnesses rise toward me—
>
> * * *
>
> flakes rattle the beech
> leaves, lace pine branches.
> A girl pulls off a cap, tosses
>
> her hair, thinks she possesses
> this dazzle. I remember
> such thinking. Can she foresee
>
> what is moving toward her,
> the obdurate weather?

This type certainly has its literary precedents. Thomas Gray's Eton College piece being, for me, the most memorable, and many of W. D. Snodgrass' poems being fine contemporary examples. My objection here is not so much with the type as with the unoriginal use of it. When using a traditional form or subgenre, the poet assumes an added responsibility to "make it new." This poet has treated the tradition as ready-made—again, as a pre-existing series of slots that merely require filling.

Another manifestation of the superficial universal, that tendency by which the poet uses externals for particular internal purposes, is seen in the poem of personal travel. Here the poet attempts to convey vividly a specific personal experience in a remote part of the country or world. Again, there is nothing inherently wrong with using a foreign setting for a poem, but what often happens in such a poem is that the premium is placed upon the foreignness itself rather than upon the nature of the experience. Here is the latter half of "At five the train left Nendaye," published in the recent *TriQuarterly*:

> Half the passengers dismounted,
> and doors slammed on crowds.
> That's how we knew it was Lourdes,
> that and the little fires
> carried up under the stars.
> We sat in the dark carriage,
> broke bread and drank wine,
> until we couldn't see
> what was flame and what star,
> and the train took us off to Marseilles
> in secret, as before.

I must admit this poem is lovely in its way, yet I still find it slight since the weight of the poem rests upon the remoteness of setting. Even less appealing is a work which appeared in the recent issue of *Prairie Schooner*, the latter half of which follows:

> I've had no address for a year but car and suitcase
> knowing only road, a typewriter ribbon
> spilled out over mountain and plain,
> trying to find the address of my self's country.
>
> And I've felt my life blown, tumbleweed
> before headlights in Wyoming or dust off the Colo-
>   rado flats
> and I have feared that I will be
> dust baked to the hard bricks of old mosques.
>
> I come home to hear her voice gentle
> as the eroded profiles of Persepolis whose 6,000 years
>   of
> dust is baked to the hard bricks of old mosques,
> "I have lost the address of my country."

Again, the emphasis is upon poet as great traveler. The implication of the "typewriter ribbon" as metaphor for this poet's road is that travel makes for the creative personality. Furthermore, in any poem whose form is based upon repetition, whatever is repeated must be damn good—another responsibility a writer has when adopting a fixed form—and I don't find the key lines of this poem at all compelling. (Perhaps it is an unfair comparison, but contrast these lines with Dylan Thomas's "Do not go gentle into that good night. / Rage, rage against the dying of the light," or Roethke's "I wake to sleep, and take my waking slow. / I learn by going where I have to go.")

Another version of the superficial universal, of the personal with the semblance of the universal, is the beloved-relative poem, probably the most common variety of which is the "grandma" or "grandpa" poem. Again, this is another example in which, because of an understandable emotional attachment on the part of the poet, shortcuts are often taken. God knows, no one wants to criticize a work on a dead, or dying, loved one. Nevertheless, I do feel that some pretty lackluster poems on grandparents continue to get published. The following excerpts are taken from a poem published in the Fall/Winter 1982-83 issue of *Quarterly West*:

> On a bright day in October
> I go to visit Grandma, who is so old
> Her skin looks like *lefse*. She is half bald
> But hardly unhappy. Air-conditioning, color TV,
> More than enough money saved
> To purchase her coffin,
> A stone for the grave . . .
>
> * * *
>
> I leave her alone, still hanging on,
> A tough leaf the wind left behind,
> And, driving home, I am oddly excited

By the horses grazing the green hillsides
And the velvet cattails lining the road,
The scepters that rule the other kingdom,
And the certainty that a day will come
When I, too, will get to be old and die,
And I notice the brassy aspens,
And the birches are shining like brandy,
And the lakes look as deep as the sky.

This is the same old story—upon the realization of the approaching death of a loved one, the persona realizes with intensity the value of his own life. Perhaps the overworked theme would be forgivable if the poet's use of the language were more original, startling—but alas, lines like "the lakes look as deep as the sky" and "I, too, will get to be old and die" pretty much wrap things up for me.

By now I've certainly given the impression that in my mind the bottom has dropped out of poetry in the little magazine today. To the contrary, in those same magazines I see some poets doing exciting things, taking welcome new directions, and often doing so by finding a release from the "mere" self.

Among the several positive tendencies in magazines today is the emergence of the new long poem. This is a poem whose size is not in its length but in its ambitious grappling with important aspects of man's physical, psychological, and spiritual experience. This description probably sounds pretty typical of any poetry of great scope, yet one thing that makes these new poems distinctive from those of the past is that the poets draw from an increasingly deepening body of knowledge from fields such as biology, psychology, anthropology, cosmology, etc. Through the use of such disciplines these poets are attempting to create, in varying individual styles, unities, connections, patterns of meaning out of the confluence of common phenomena. The following are excerpts from "The Psychopathology of Everyday Life," which appeared in the Autumn 1982 *Antaeus*:

Just as we were amazed to learn
that the skin itself is an organ—
I'd thought it a flexible sack,
always exact—we're stunned
to think the skimpiest mental
event, even forgetting, has meaning.
If one thinks of the sky as scenery,
like photographs of food, one stills it
by that wish and appetite,
but the placid expanse that results
is an illusion. The air is restless
everywhere inside our atmosphere,
but the higher and thinner it gets
the less it has to push around
(how else can we see air?) but itself.

It seems that the mind, too,
is like that sky, not shiftless . . .

* * *

We forget
that the trout isn't beautiful and stupid
but a system of urges that works
even when the trout's small brain is somewhere
else, watching its shadow on the streambed,
maybe, daydreaming of food.
Even when we think we're not,
we're paying attention to everything;
this may be the origin of prayer . . .

What I see happening in this and other poems is the application of the physicality of the sciences to the human condition. I find it significant that, although the focus of the poem is upon the human condition, the things compared to the human—skin, trout, and sky—do not relate merely by analogy; they all function as *examples* of the class of living things, rather than as discrete objects with no vital link to the human, conveniently used to further the image of self.

One can see that if a poet keeps these avenues to the outside world open, it is still possible to be personal in a poem while not sacrificing universality. I think that the work of Albert Goldbarth best illustrates that new poetry whose base is the self yet whose reach extends towards the stars. In the Whitmanesque tradition, the egocentricity in Goldbarth's poetry is legitimate because it works like the hub of a wheel, its spokes radiating outward to form a circle (an image Goldbarth is fond of). Goldbarth also, like few poets today, draws from all corners of lore and learning, from the physical and the social sciences to ancient religious texts and modern technology. Goldbarth's innovations in content are reflected in form, as he calls into question what is commonly assumed to be the "proper" shape of a poem. Excerpting from his longer work does make it difficult to preserve the integrity of the whole, but the following may at least give an indication of the contours of his writing:

A thighbone the length of a student of thighbones. A Stegosaurus: two metric tons. Students of thighbones convening in museums, under conventions of bones that dwarf them. There were giants in those days.

I give you Ralph von Koenigswald, in 1934, among the desiccated animal bodies, baskets of shells and pungent herbal necklaces of a Hong Kong alchemist's shop . . . "so astounded, as he later recalled, that his hair actually stood on end." A tooth, a human molar, though six times greater in size. The shock of it, almost a stone from a lake, still dripping Time off its thick black swags.

* * *

Ralph von Koenigswald dated his teeth—he had three by 1939, and a jawbone was found in Kwangsi Province—to 600,000 years ago, the Middle Pleistocene.

What does it feel like, holding the bite of our being halfway here? "The distinction between ape and man . . . seems premature. It is therefore more prudent to say no more than that the creature which von Koenigswald called Gigantopithecus was a giant ape man." Thirteen feet high. Dying out. Leading on. Surviving. A farmboy stops by the mirror, checks: no gloppy stuff in the spaces. A convention of dentists, a hallway of living nerve.

I give you leading on: I'm five-foot-seven, breathing deep tonight, how Time's swagged sweet in my lungs. I give you surviving: here, the Komodo dragon, today in the Lesser Sundra Islands, 300 lbs. and 10 feet long and living to be centenarians. "A hunting dragon lumbers and sashays, head down, its forked tongue flicking . . ." Deer fall, and boar. Descendant of the dinosaurs, truly—as are we, by a crazier line of connection. As are we, bent joining bone, by rivet, to bone, then drilling the nametags.

This is a sallow stretch of land, with a few insistent swatches of green. It's the Cretaceous, it's the moment a certain conjoining of bones—name it what you will— will lead to a dead end. Or an evolving. I give you a photo: my arm is around Elaine. The breathing deep of those days—what she gave me. My ex-fiance Elaine. I'm not even sure we understand the moment, our faces washed so bland by the camera flash, our smiles so fixed, I'm not even sure we understand we're holding on by the skin of our teeth.

Is it not self-indulgent for Goldbarth to tell us the details of his broken engagement? It would be so if the poem did not proceed outward from the self, linking the engagement to ring and ring to bone and bone to the ring that unites us all, and ending with the following stanza:

Maybe it's vague but it's what I know, tonight it's what suffices. There's a museum here, and a little thing of pieced-together bone that's been extinct for I-don't-remember-how-many epochs. Just enough to be fully fleshed by the muscles a human chest holds. Maybe it *is* the ancestor of the human breast. I doubt it, but maybe. And when the guard leaves, you can hug it, it's just that size. Believe me, it feels right. Your arms can make a circle.

Goldbarth's poetry illustrates *one* way out of the ordinary: there are many others. The key to distinctiveness, however, lies not just in *difference,* for the plethora of poetry being written today makes it all too easy for a poet to assume he has a place just because he has his own particular story to tell. Just as inviting a reader ought not to evolve into ignoring him, so making it new should not be translated into making it irrelevant. At the advent of this century the individual voice was wanting, and many found it necessary to find a way into the sanctum of self; now too often we speak from separate cells and sound the same. I think it's time we found some ways out of our differences.

FURTHER READING

Criticism

Benstock, Shari, and Bernard Benstock. "The Role of Little Magazines in the Emergence of Modernism." *The Library Chronicle of the University of Texas at Austin* 20, no. 4 (1991): 69-87.

> Chronicles the influence of such little magazines as *Poetry,* the *Egoist,* and *Contempo* on the emergence of modernism in literature.

Dean, John. "The Source of Intelligent Writing: American Little Magazines." *Revue Francaise D'Etudes Americaines* 7 (April 1979): 113-22.

> Presents an overview of little magazines in light of their influence on American Literature.

Doyle, James. "Canadian Writers & American Little Magazines in the 1890s." *Canadian Literature,* no. 110 (fall 1986): 177-83.

> Details the participation of a number of Canadian writers, notably Bliss Carman, in late nineteenth-century little magazines.

Fletcher, Ian. "Decadence and the Little Magazines." In *Decadence and the 1890s,* edited by Ian Fletcher, pp. 173-206. London: Edward Arnold, 1979.

> Discusses such late-nineteenth-century avant-garde periodicals as *The Germ, The Dial,* and *The Yellow Book* as precursors of the little magazines that flourished in the twentieth century.

Görtschacher, Wolfgang. *Little Magazines Profiles: The Little Magazines in Great Britain 1939-1993.* Salzburg, Austria: University of Salzburg, 1993, 751 p.

> Examines the features and history of little magazines between 1939 and 1993 and interviews editors, critics, and others associated with them.

Guenther, Paul, and Nicholas Joost. "Little Magazines and the Cosmopolitan Tradition." *Papers on Language & Literature* 6, no. 1 (winter 1970): 100-10.

> Explores the history of the German little magazine *Der Querschnitt* in historical context.

Monk, Craig. "Emma Goldman & the Little Magazine Impulse in Modern America." In *"The Only Efficient Instrument": American Women Writers & the Periodical, 1837-1916,* edited by Aleta Feinsod Cane and Susan Alves, pp. 113-25. Iowa City: University of Iowa Press, 2001.

> Discusses *Mother Earth,* the little magazine published by political radical Emma Goldman from 1906 to 1918, noting that it "provided durable models of idealism and activism."

Newcomb, John Timberman. *"Others, Poetry,* and Wallace Stevens: Little Magazines as Agents of Reputation." *Essays in Literature* 16, no. 2 (fall 1989): 256-70

    Assesses the role that Wallace Stevens' publishing in little magazines played in the formation of his career and reputation.

Norris, Ken. *The Little Magazine in Canada 1925-80: Its Role in the Development of Modernism and Post-Modernism in Canadian Poetry.* Toronto: ECW Press, 1984, 203 p.

    Details the history of little magazines in Canada as "alternative outlet[s] for literature."

Williams, Ellen. "Introduction: The Background." In *Harriet Monroe and the Poetry Renaissance: The First Ten Years of* Poetry, *1912-22,* pp. 3-27. Urbana: University of Illinois Press, 1977.

    Focuses on Harriet Monroe's leadership of *Poetry* magazine in its first decade of publication, her shaping of its literary sensibility, and her interactions with its contributors.

World War II Literature

INTRODUCTION

World War II literature exhibits an extraordinary variety in terms of theme, locale, point of view, and purpose. Critic Joseph J. Waldmeir has written that "World War II was perhaps the most painstakingly recorded war, in fiction at least, of all time." Novelists, poets, and playwrights explored the war's political, moral, and ethical aspects from their specific national and cultural contexts as well as through the filter of their personal experience. For example, German authors like Günter Grass, Heinrich Böll, and Klaus Mann wrote about the pivotal period leading up to World War II in Germany, as early as 1933—the year that Adolf Hitler was appointed chancellor—when Nazi ideology began penetrating ordinary citizens' lives. Many French writers, such as Vercors and Philippe Soupoult, treated the experience of daily life under German occupation in their own country, describing the efforts of the resistance movement, and time spent in Prisoner of War camps. Japanese personal narratives such as Ishikawa Tatsuzō's *Ikite iru heitai* (1945; *Living Soldiers*) and Yoshiko Uchida's *Desert Exile: The Uprooting of a Japanese-American Family* (1982) chronicle life in Japan during and after the war, as well as the ordeals of internment camps for Japanese Americans. Other works detailed military action in various phases of the war and in settings as diverse as the Pacific and North Africa. While some authors strove to convey a strict sense of realism, others presented stylized or even romantic images of the war. Stylistically influenced in part by World War I literature, World War II writers were also shaped by the disillusionment and social criticism that characterized the 1930s. Some works, such as Samuel Beckett's *The Unnamable* (1953), display a general sense of malaise or reflect the emerging Cold War struggle for ideological primacy.

Besides providing an outlet for personal reflection and documenting the political and human costs of war, World War II literature played a key motivational role in both the pro-war and anti-war movements. The United States was the last of the major powers to enter the war, and many of its citizens were reluctant even as US troops engaged in combat. Antiwar sentiment is clear in such works as James Gould Cozzens' *Guard of Honor* (1948) and Irwin Shaw's *The Young Lions* (1948). Many of the hundreds of novels, plays, and other texts written in the early years of the war consciously sought to promote the cause of the war, to encourage patriotic sentiment, and glamorize the image of the soldier fighting fascism. Examples include Moss Hart's blockbuster play *Winged Victory* (1943) and *The Army Play by Play,* a series of one-act plays about army life composed by John Golden in 1943. The U.S. government, too, engaged in forming public opinion—for instance in propagandistic army training dramas and in posters featuring racial stereotypes. As the war progressed, its literature increasingly reflected the ordinary soldier's fatigue and boredom. Writers registered their sense of outrage at the devastation produced by the war in such works as Harry Brown's *A Walk in the Sun* (1944), Lillian Hellman's *Watch on the Rhine* (1941), James Jones' *From Here to Eternity* (1951) Norman Mailer's *The Naked and the Dead* (1948), and Ernst Wiechert's *Der Totenwold* (1946; *Forest of the Dead*). With awareness of the Holocaust widespread, interest in Anne Frank's *Diary* increased,the play version, (*The Diary of Anne Frank,* 1955) by Albert Hackett was a huge success. The devastating bombing of the German city of Dresden late in the war was attacked in in Kurt Vonnegut's *Slaughterhouse Five* (1969) and Harry Mulisch's *Het stenen bruidsbed* (1959; *The Stone Bridal Bed*).

REPRESENTATIVE WORKS

Martin Abzug
Spearhead (novel) 1946

James Aldridge
The Sea Eagle (novel) 1944

Samuel Beckett
The Unnamable (novel) 1953

Heinrich Böll
Gruppenbild mit Dame [*Group Portrait with Lady*] (novel) 1971

Pierre Boulle
Le Pont de la Rivière Kwai [*The Bridge on the River Kwai*] (novel) 1952

Elizabeth Bowen
The Demon Lover and Other Stories (short stories) 1945
The Heat of the Day (novel) 1949

Harry Brown
A Walk in the Sun (novel) 1944

Alex Comfort
No Such Liberty (novel) 1941

Henri Coulonges
L'Adieu à la femme sauvage [*Farewell, Dresden*] (novel) 1979

James Gould Cozzens
Guard of Honor (novel) 1948

Arnand d'Usseau and James Gow
Deep Are the Roots (play) 1945

Anne Frank
Het Achterhuis [*Anne Frank: The Diary of a Young Girl*] (autobiography) 1947

John Golden
The Army Play by Play (plays) 1943

Günter Grass
Die Blechtrommel [*The Tin Drum*] (novel) 1959

Henry Green
Caught (novel) 1943

Albert Hackett
The Diary of Anne Frank (play) 1955

Moss Hart
Winged Victory (play) 1943

Ben Hecht
A Flag Is Born (play) 1946

Thomas Heggen
Mr. Roberts (novel) 1946

Lillian Hellman
Watch on the Rhine (play) 1941

John Hersey
A Bell for Adano (novel) 1944

James Jones
From Here to Eternity (novel) 1951

Norman Mailer
The Naked and the Dead (novel) 1948

Klaus Mann
Mephisto (novel) 1936

Harry Mulisch
Het stenen bruidsbed [*The Stone Bridal Bed*] (novel) 1959

J. B. Priestley
Out of the People (nonfiction) 1942
Daylight on Saturday (novel) 1943

Erich Maria Remarque
Zeit zu leben und Zeit zu streben [*A Time to Live and a Time to Die*] (novel) 1954

Irwin Shaw
The Young Lions (novel) 1948

Robert Sherwood
The Rugged Path (play) 1945

Philippe Soupoult
Le Temps des assassins (novel) 1945

Ishikawa Tatsuzō
Ikite iru heitai [*Living Soldiers*] (novel) 1945

Yoshiko Uchida
Desert Exile: The Uprooting of a Japanese-American Family (memoir) 1982

Vercors
Le Silence de la Mer (novel) 1942

Kurt Vonnegut
Slaughterhouse Five (novel) 1969

Evelyn Waugh
Men at Arms (novel) 1952

Ernst Wiechert
Der Totenwald [*Forest of the Dead*] (novel) 1946

Virginia Woolf
Between the Acts (novel) 1941

OVERVIEWS

Frederick J. Harris (essay date 1983)

SOURCE: Harris, Frederick J. "Germany—Life under the Nazis." In *Encounters with Darkness: French and German Writers on World War II*, pp. 97-132. New York: Oxford University Press, 1983.

[*In the following essay, Harris presents an overview of the social and cultural aspects of German life before and during World War II, focusing on literary works that depicted the period.*]

NEW REALITIES

Though daily life in France underwent a series of changes after 1940, in Germany the changes had come much earlier. Adolf Hitler, leader of the National Socialist or Nazi Party, was named chancellor by President Hindenburg on January 30, 1933, and when Hindenburg died on August 2, 1934, Hitler, according to a law enacted by the cabinet, assumed the role of president. That title itself was quickly abolished and Hitler was officially called Reich Chancellor and Führer, his old Party name. On the night of May 10, 1933, thousands of students marched in a torchlight parade to a square opposite the University of Berlin and there burned some 20,000 books. Any book that could be construed as alien to "German thought" or to the Nazi conception of Germany's future was vulnerable, as was any book that might have an undermining influence on the German home or the "driving forces" of the German people. Thomas Mann, Erich Maria Remarque, Arthur Schnitzler, Stefan Zweig, Albert Einstein, Sigmund Freud, André Gide, Marcel Proust, Emile Zola, and many others went up in flames. General reading as well as the school and university system were thenceforth more closely scrutinized. Beginning at the age of six children of both sexes were brought into various levels of the Nazi youth organizations. At fourteen a boy entered the Hitler Youth (*Hitlerjugend*), where he remained until he was eighteen and fit for the Labor Service or the Army. Girls of fourteen were placed in the BDM, the League of German Maidens (*Bund Deutscher Mädchen*), where they remained to the age of twenty-one.[1]

The press and radio were censored and exploited by the government for propaganda purposes. On October 4, 1933, the Reich Press Law stipulated that every editor had to be a German citizen of Aryan descent not married to a Jew. Journalism was declared a "public vocation" and any deviation from government policy was prohibited.[2] As is true even today in most European countries, the radio was already a state monopoly, and so the task of enlisting it in the service of the Nazi state was easily accomplished.

Hitler began his public war against the Jews soon after assuming office by issuing laws that excluded them from public service, the universities, and the professions. On April 1, 1933, he ordered a national boycott of Jewish shops. The Nürnberg Laws of September 15, 1934, deprived Jews of their citizenship and relegated them to the status of "subjects," thus incorporating into the legal system the idea that Jews could not be Germans. Marriage between Aryans and Jews was officially forbidden and so were extramarital relations. As the years went on new laws were added to outlaw the Jew even further from German society.[3]

The Christian churches fared better, certainly, for with them there was no racial issue involved. But the pulpit was another form of media, and those who "misused" it to speak against the Nazi state had to be silenced. Thousands of arrests were made.[4]

But all was not grim in Germany in the 1930s. From works such as Robert Merle's fictionalized account of the life of an Auschwitz camp commandant in *La Mort est mon métier* (1952), Klaus Mann's fictionalized rendition of the rise of actor/director Gustaf Gründgens in *Mephisto* (1936), Leni Riefenstahl's film of the 1934 Nazi Party rally in Nürnberg, *Triumph des Willens* (1935), and even Inge Scholl's *Die Weisse Rose* (1953), a documentary written in memory of her brother and sister who were put to death in 1943 for their part in an anti-Nazi student movement of the same name in Munich—from these works and others it is quite clear that for many Germans Hitler's state brought relief, hope, and joy after the economic chaos that followed World War I with its poverty, inflation, and unemployment. Germans were working once again. Once again they could look forward to relative economic security, and after the political humiliation imposed on them by the Versailles Treaty, many felt they could again take pride in their country. People of all ages, children and adults alike, were inspired with the idea of working toward a common goal, which was the betterment of life in Germany.

Not everyone, of course, had the same idea of what a better life meant, and for those who refused to obey the government or who challenged its conceptions, there were the Gestapo and the concentration camps. Gestapo is an abbreviation of Geheime Staatspolizei, the Secret State Police, which was originally established on April 26, 1933, to operate in Prussia only, but expanded one year later when Field Marshal Hermann Göring placed it under the direction of Heinrich Himmler, whom Hitler had made head of the SS or Schutzstaffel in 1929. The SS together with the SA, the Sturmabteilung of storm troopers or Brown Shirts as they were called, formed the armed military wing of the Nazi Party. A series of rulings in 1935 and 1936 placed the Gestapo above the law and beyond the reach of judicial review. This meant that if the courts, which were already reduced to a state of subservience, should, nonetheless, on occasion hand down a verdict whose decision ran counter to the wishes of the Nazi Party, the Gestapo might intervene, as it actually did in the case of Pastor Martin Niemöller. When Niemöller was acquitted by the courts after eight months of prison on charges of "underhand attacks against the State,"[5] the Gestapo hauled him off to a concentration camp.

The concentration camps mushroomed during Hitler's first year in power, and by the end of 1933 there were already some fifty of them, not yet the mass extermination camps of the war years, to be sure, but places where a prisoner could be beaten or tortured. Some prisoners were simply put to hard labor, occasionally to the point of exhaustion and death; others were murdered outright as a result of the sadistic brutality of the torturers.[6]

ADAPTING TO THE NEW REALITIES. THE NAZI PARTY.

Scholars may continue to speculate for years to come as to why the German people allowed a man like Adolf Hitler legally to come to power in Germany or to stay in a position of power once he had acquired it. Stefan Zweig, an Austrian writer who considered himself, along with Romain Rolland in France and others of their day, more of a European than a national of any particular country, offered several explanations for Hitler's extraordinary success. In a memoir-essay called *Die Welt von Gestern,* written in exile, largely in Ossining, New York, and published posthumously, first in English translation in 1943, then in German in Stockholm in 1944, he wrote: "Inflation, unemployment, the political crises and, not least, the folly of lands abroad, had made the German people restless. . . ." At every level and in every group there was a longing for order, and for the German people "order had always been more important than freedom and justice. And anyone who promised order—even Goethe said that disorder was more distasteful to him than even an injustice—could count on hundreds of thousands of supporters from the start." So much for those hundreds of thousands. But there were others who should perhaps have had the foresight to squash the Nazi movement while it was still possible to do so. Those people, Zweig objects, simply never took Hitler seriously until it was too late. "Germany has not only always been a class-conscious country, but within these class ideals she has, besides, always borne the burden of a blind overestimation and deification of 'education.'" A few generals may have gotten by without university training, but what Lloyd George had accomplished in England, Garibaldi and Mussolini in Italy, and Briand in France, that is, to rise from the ranks of the people to the highest positions in the state, was not thought possible in Germany. It was "unthinkable to Germans that a man who had not even finished high school, to say nothing of college, who had lodged in flop-houses and whose mode of life for years is a mystery to this day, should even make a pass toward a position once held by a Bismarck. . . ."[7]

Zweig left his home in Salzburg in 1934. After his house was searched under police warrant with the pretext of looking for subversive materials, he realized just how great the pressures from across the German border were becoming. From then until 1940, when he emigrated to New York, while he resided primarily in London, he traveled frequently and in the fall of 1937 flew back to Vienna to see his mother one last time before it was too late. Though by then Hitler had long since secured his base of power in Germany, and though Austria would fall under Nazi domination the following March, Zweig could not convince the Viennese that anything serious was in the offing, and he reflected sadly that those who were still wearing tuxedos to the opera and the gala social events of the city would in a few months be wearing convict attire in the concentration camps. But perhaps they were right to enjoy themselves while they could. Perhaps the "eternal light-heartedness of old Vienna" was indeed the best remedy. Those whose make-up allowed them this kind of carefree existence suffered only once, when disaster finally struck, whereas those who were too realistic and too farsighted suffered first in their imagination and a second time through the reality which in the end spared neither.[8]

Sooner or later everyone had to make some accommodation to life in the new Germany. For some this was more painful than for others, but there were those, especially in industry, for whom the adaptations were downright profitable. For Leni Pfeiffer, the central character of Heinrich Böll's *Gruppenbild mit Dame* (1971), as unpolitical a nature as there could be, adaptation primarily meant adjusting to the fortune or misfortune of friends and relatives more politically committed than she, and later, during the war, making do with whatever food supplies were available. To espouse the "forces of order" some joined the Party early, like Alfred Matzerath, the father of the midget Oskar, narrator of Günter Grass's *Die Blechtrommel* (1959), which was made into a film of the same name in 1979 by Volker Schlöndorff. Matzerath's entrance into the Nazi Party brings little change either to his own life or that of his household. Beethoven's picture is removed from its nail over the piano and replaced by that of Hitler, and Matzerath himself has to piece together a uniform consisting of a brown shirt, "shit-brown riding breeches and high boots," to go parading and drilling with his fellow Nazis on the Maiwiese in Danzig where the family live. Oskar's mother, however, is adamant that Beethoven's picture should remain somewhere in the living room, and the result is that "Hitler and the genius" have to look each other in the eye, with neither too happy about the situation. During the time between the end of World War I and the beginning of World War II, the free city of Danzig was a place where a German and a Polish population coexisted more or less harmoniously despite an increasing Nazi presence in the last years. Jan Bronski, Oskar's mother's Polish lover, for example, adapts readily to Matzerath's entry into the Party. He comes calling regularly on Sundays while Matzerath is out parading.

Some were idealistic in their adherence to the Party, others joined for purely personal advantage. In Albrecht Goes's *Das Brandopfer* (1954), the husband of the cen tral character Margarete Walker joins the Party in the hopes that it may procure him certain advantages and spare him some inconveniences. He finds, however, that it does him even less good than it does Matzerath. Herr Walker has to report for military duty on the second day of the war with Poland.[9] For some like the habitually intoxicated trumpeter Meyn in *Die Blechtrommel,* joining the Party seemed to provide at least a temporary sense of direction, straightening out a crumbling moral and emotional life. In May 1938 Meyn renounces his gin and tells everyone he meets that he is starting a new existence.[10] But when the Nazis, who have their own code of morality, discover that Meyn has half-killed his four cats, stuffed them into a sack, and then put them into a garbage can to die, he is stricken from membership in the SA for conduct unbecoming to a stormtrooper and for "inhuman cruelty to animals." This despite his "conspicuous bravery" on the night of November 9, 1938.[11] On that night, the infamous Kristallnacht, Jewish synagogues, homes, and shops throughout Germany went up in flames in what was called a "spontaneous demonstration." On November 7 the third secretary of the German embassy in Paris, Ernst vom Rath, had been murdered by a young German Jewish refugee, Herschel Grynszpan, whose father had been deported with thousands of other Jews in boxcars to Poland.[12] Meyn helps set fire to the Langfuhr synagogue in Danzig but, as Oskar notes with characteristic irony, "even his meritorious activity the following morning when a number of stores, carefully designated in advance, were closed down for the good of the nation, could not halt his expulsion from the Mounted SA."[13]

That many people, before the war had started and after, joined the Nazi Party or used their position within the Party to justify acts that can only be termed psychologically sick is incontestable, and literature abounds with examples. Erich Maria Remarque's *Zeit zu leben und Zeit zu sterben* (1954) is the tale of a German soldier, Ernst Graeber, who returns home on furlough from the Russian front in the spring of 1943 at the time of the German retreat after Stalingrad and after the first heavy bombings of German cities in the west had begun. By chance Graeber meets a former schoolmate, Alfons Binding, who has become a Nazi *Kreisleiter,* a kind of district supervisor. Clearly Alfons has done well for himself and can afford to treat a friend to a spree, especially an old classmate like Graeber whose family home has been obliterated in the bombings and who cannot even find out whether his parents are still alive. The political and social climate in Germany has deteriorated by this time to such a degree that people hardly dare say anything beyond the absolutely necessary even to their friends, and Graeber regrets the irony that has made the first person willing to help him a Party bigwig. One of the first stories Binding tells him is about an old mathematics teacher they had had, who years ago had reported Binding for some vague "business"

relating to a girl. Binding had pleaded with the teacher but to no avail: it was his moral duty to file a report. Binding's father had subsequently beaten him half to death over the incident. Now Binding has had a chance to even the score, and he had the teacher banished to a concentration camp for six months. "You should have seen him when he got out. He stood at attention and almost wet his pants when he saw me. He educated me; so I reeducated him thoroughly."[14]

A friend of Binding's, an SS officer named Heini, boasts openly of sadistically working off his anger on the inmates of a concentration camp he is helping to run.[15] And Frau Lieser, a committed Nazi who has been placed as a watchdog in the house of another of Graeber's school friends, Elisabeth Kruse, has been given part of her apartment for having denounced the girl's father and gotten him sent off to a concentration camp. To obtain control of the whole apartment she would denounce the daughter, too, if she could find an excuse for doing so. Frau Lieser is one of those fortunate ones whose personal ideals and aspirations march hand in hand with the times.

If people felt shortchanged in life for one reason or another, the Party provided a way for them to correct the balance. In Carl Zuckmayer's play *Des Teufels General* (1946), a flying ace named Harras has enjoyed both personal and professional success in life, all of which he has accomplished without the help of the Nazi Party. The Party people envy him his success, his girlfriend observes, especially his success with women. For in that area "they are way below zero."[16] For them joining the Party was a way of setting things right.

LIVING IN FEAR

Whatever may have been the motives of the Nazi leaders and however ill-equipped psychologically they may have been for the positions of prominence they assumed, they did in fact impose themselves on the German nation, and to such a degree that they affected virtually every area of German life. Fear so infiltrated daily existence that shortly before the end of the war most people could think about only one thing: how to survive. With the Americans at Germany's western flank in the fall of 1944, they knew the war could not last much longer. But worse than the war for many was the climate of fear that reigned inside Germany, especially during the last few months when, according to one of Heinrich Böll's characters in *Gruppenbild mit Dame,* "every minute someone was being hanged or shot, you weren't safe either as an old Nazi or as an anti-Nazi."[17] Some two years before the end, when the tide first began to turn against Germany, Remarque's Ernst Graeber, home on leave from Russia, found the domestic climate well nigh intolerable. It may be paradoxical though not really surprising that life on the front lines was freer than on the homefront. Under enemy fire life seems to take on a larger meaning, if the experiences created or re-created in literature, and particularly in the novels of World War I, are any guide. Then, as in World War II, the fighting man had neither the time nor the energy to concern himself with the often petty preoccupations of the society back home. Even before his west-bound train has entered German territory Graeber gets a taste of what to expect. After the soldiers are put through controls by the German MPs, they begin grumbling among themselves, as "real" soldiers will, about the army of bureaucrats who have stayed behind. They are quickly admonished by one of the older noncoms: "At the front you can talk any way you like. But from now on you'd better shut your trap if you know what's good for you." When the train arrives at the German border, all the men are ordered out into a delousing station[18] and then informed of their responsibility, under penalty of severe punishment, to utter no criticism and to reveal nothing to friends and family at home of the time they have spent at the front. This is routinely accepted. But the next announcement is of a different order. Those heading for the Rhineland, Alsace, or Hamburg are ordered to step forward, and since there is no one from Alsace or Hamburg among them, the Rhinelanders alone step up and are informed curtly and without explanation that the entire Rhineland has been closed to soldiers on furlough. One man who has a wife and child in Cologne demands some excuse, but none is forthcoming. It is not his business to ask questions. He must choose another city to visit instead. What's wrong in Cologne? he asks the others, tears in his eyes. Why can they all go home and not I? Little by little as the train proceeds into Germany, the soldiers become aware that Germany has changed in their absence, that this is no longer the land they left behind and whose memory they have carried in their imaginations, that the scenes of destruction they witnessed in Russia were not unlike what they are beginning to see at home. Already on the night of May 30, 1942, the British "had carried out their first one-thousand plane bombing of Cologne,"[19] but of such large-scale bombings the soldiers at the front had known nothing. Just as they were told to reveal nothing about the front to the folks at home, so the homefront feared to reveal anything to the soldiers that could have political implications. After all, one could be sent to a concentration camp for so much as intimating that Germany might lose the war. The soldiers, however, happy in their ignorance, were simply glad to be back home. They try to explain away what they are beginning to see. Perhaps there had been a few isolated bombs here and there. Like the French prisoners of war headed for Germany in 1940, they wave from their train to farmers in the fields, and like the French they receive no response. Insulted, a noncom on Graeber's train jerks his window shut. "Oxen . . . Village idiots and milkmaids."

The train finally arrives in Graeber's hometown, Werden, a city somewhere "in the middle of Germany" whose name ironically suggests growth or becoming. It is only thanks to a railroad official who announces the stop that he knows where he is, for there is no more sign, no more station. Uncertain, Graeber at first hesitates to alight at what appear to be the outskirts of the town since he knows the station is in the middle of the city. Confused, he steps down from the train, nonetheless, and finds that there is a bus waiting that goes on into the city. When he asks the driver why the train no longer goes through to the station, he receives a curt, matter-of-fact answer: "Because it only goes this far."

Getting through Werden to reach his house is a totally disorienting experience. Old landmarks by which he knew the layout of the city have simply vanished. His own house in the Hakenstrasse, whose remnants he finally locates after considerable ado, is a pile of ruins in a street of ruins. And the towns-folk are of little help. No one dares open his mouth. At last Graeber finds a couple who were friends of his family and whose children have all been killed in the bombings. "You don't know what it has been like here during the last year with everything getting worse and worse," says the father. "No one could trust anyone else any longer. They were all afraid of one another."[20]

With increased surveillance and brutality, fear indeed escalated as the Nazi regime began to show signs of panic after 1942; but, in effect, Germany had been living in a climate of fear for a decade. Many of her greatest writers, like Thomas Mann and Bertolt Brecht and the Austrians Stefan Zweig and Franz Werfel, had emigrated to America; Carl Zuckmayer had fled Nazi Germany for Austria, but after the Anschluss of Austria to the German Reich, he fled again, first to Switzerland, then France, and finally he, too, made his way to America. Max Reinhardt and other theater producers and directors, many of whom were Jewish, also left. Freud fled to London in 1938 after the Anschluss had made Vienna an impossible place for him to live. German cinema, which in the twenties and early thirties had occupied so prominent a position in the development of the art form, was so utterly destroyed by government manipulation that it has only in the last decade really begun to recover. The noted playwright Gerhart Hauptmann remained, however; and Leni Riefenstahl's films, whether she intended them to do so or not, embodied Nazi ideas on the function of the arts.

In 1933 Leni Riefenstahl made the film *Sieg des Glaubens* covering the fifth Nazi Party rally in Nürnberg. Though Hitler himself asked her to make the film, she later claimed she could not secure Goebbels's cooperation at the Propaganda Ministry and was dissatisfied with the footage obtained. In any event, Hitler asked her to do a film on the sixth Party congress in Nürnberg in 1934, and the famous *Triumph des Willens* was the result. Riefenstahl insisted on and apparently obtained complete artistic freedom in making this film. The following year she made *Tag der Freiheit-Unsere Wehrmacht* to placate the army which felt it had been neglected in *Triumph des Willens*.[21]

Music, the least political of the arts because it is the most abstract, was also the most firmly entrenched in German soil and suffered the least uprooting. Composer Richard Strauss and conductor Wilhelm Furtwängler among others had little difficulty continuing their careers under Nazi vigilance.

In 1936 after he and his family had emigrated, Thomas Mann's son Klaus published in Amsterdam the novel *Mephisto* adapted into a film of the same name in 1981 by Hungarian director István Szabó. Despite Klaus Mann's denials, the novel is clearly a satire on his former brother-in-law, the noted actor and director Gustaf Gründgens. Gründgens had married Mann's sister Erika, though the marriage had ended in divorce in 1929. Clearly Mann's hero, whom he calls Hendrik Höfgen, shifting the double *G* of his prototype's initials to the double *H* of his protagonist's, transcends Gründgens. A novel can never restrict itself to biography, for it carries with it its own momentum and its own dynamism. As a novelist, it is true enough, Klaus Mann maintains almost absolute control over his characters, allowing them very little freedom to develop themselves. His interventions in the guise of a third-person narrator are frequent and blatant; and when feasible, rather than allow his characters to present themselves, he controls their presentation to the reader through flashbacks and free indirect discourse (*discours indirect libre*). But despite his rigid control Klaus Mann was still enough of a novelist to have known that if it was only a portrait of Gründgens he intended, the novel would not have been the most appropriate genre. And so when he claimed that his characters represented "types" rather than "portraits,"[22] he was no doubt being sincere. The novel was published for the first time in Germany in East Berlin in 1956, but West German courts, still fearful in 1971 of injuring Gründgens's reputation, even though the director had died in 1963, upheld the ban on *Mephisto*'s publication. When Rowohlt Verlag published the book in 1980, it chose simply to ignore the injunction.

Hendrik Höfgen is one of those artists who elect to remain in Hitler's Germany. He can not see himself as an emigrant, starting from scratch in a country in which he would have to learn even the language. As the years pass he becomes more and more successful and powerful, and thanks to his co-star Lotte Lindenthal, manages to ingratiate himself with the head of the Air Ministry, a man named Männe, who is a hardly at all disguised Hermann Göring. Männe makes Höfgen head of the Prussian State Theater, but his success carries a price. He must forevermore do the bidding of the Nazis. His own youthful flirtation with communism must be eradicated as well as the sexual liaison he had enjoyed in a sadomasochistic relationship with a black African girl. She is deported, whip and boots and all, to Paris, and Höfgen has made the age-old compromise with the devil that Goethe enshrined in German culture. Not only is Höfgen identified with Mephistopheles as the book title suggests, but he has become a Faust for the Mephistopheles he so brilliantly incarnated again and again on the German stage.

Anyone who was to any degree a public figure had to exercise extreme caution. In *Der Totenwald* (1946) Ernst Wiechert created the portrait of a writer of some renown whom he calls Johannes, a name general enough, but a man whose experiences closely resemble Wiechert's own. In 1938 Wiechert's opposition to the Nazi régime cost him several months of imprisonment in Buchenwald. Early one morning at the outset of the book, Johannes is subjected to a house search by the Gestapo. For four years he has held no public conferences; but more recently, on the occasion of the Austrian Anschluss, when Hitler himself had spoken of rights and justice, Johannes felt compelled to write to the local Nazi Party leader on behalf of the wife and children of a certain unnamed clergyman. The clergyman is never identified, but, given the description of his wide-ranging career from ship commander to preacher, his long imprisonment before a court acquittal, and his subsequent kidnapping and internment in a concentration camp by the Gestapo, he can only be Pastor Martin Niemöller. It is to his letter on behalf of the Pastor's family that Johannes owes the early morning visit of the Gestapo, "whose Asiatic methods have brought more blood and tears to the German people than was possible in a hundred years of western storytelling." In this commentary on Gestapo techniques made by an omniscient third-person narrator, there is a play on the same time-hallowed expression so often evoked against Germany by the western Allies during World War I, of the barbaric East versus the civilized West. Though the narrator remains distinct from Johannes, he is clearly Johannes's spokesman, and in the context of the whole narration they are both too cultivated and intelligent to accept such a ready-made cliché about the German nation; but at the same time, who could deny that the methods of the Gestapo had gone beyond what civilized people could imagine? What the search party hopes in vain to find is a written correspondence with the clergyman or with ecclesiastical authorities, and since Johannes has collected a mound of foreign stamps, they hope to find evidence of connections with German emigrés. Finding no such evidence they have to settle for Johannes's diary and letters from unknown people who made no secret of their feelings about the times. It is of no avail to Johannes to point out to his investigators that the laws of the Reich forbade the use of diaries that had the character of private monologues as matter for indictment. Like Pastor Niemöller Johannes is sent to concentration camp.

This was not a time for justice on any level in Germany. Free elections in such a state were a myth, and Wiechert's narrator reflects that only half an hour after the elections that authorized Austria's annexation to the Reich, all those who had voted against the annexation were beaten half to death.[23]

Among the most blatant and scandalous of the injustices of the Third Reich were those against the Jews. Lutheran pastor Albrecht Goes's novella *Das Brandopfer* is the story of Margarete Walker, proprietress of the only meat market in an unnamed German city authorized to sell to Jews. In a structural technique harking back to the eighteenth century novel, she reveals much of her tale in a long letter written to the narrator after the war. It is easier for her to write this story than to tell it aloud. The time she will spend in writing her letter and the narrator in reading it give her a vague kind of assurance, furthermore, that the people of the story who are now dead can for those moments return and dwell among us.

Her Jewish clientèle are restricted to making their purchases on Friday evenings between five and seven, a time specifically chosen by the Nazis because it interferes with the Jewish Sabbath which begins Friday at six. Since all forms of public transportation are forbidden the Jews and park benches are clearly marked "Not for Jews," many from distant sections of the city have to spend an hour or two on foot to reach Frau Walker's store to buy what little they can with the ration cards they receive. The cards have different colors every month and are always stamped with a large "J".[24] Since the Jews are forced to begin their Sabbath in a butcher shop rather than in a synagogue, a Rabbi begins on one of those Fridays to lead the congregation in prayer. Out of fear, the Jews have virtually stopped talking to each other, on occasion they have even taunted one another, but henceforth in Frau Walker's store they unite briefly every week for a few moments of prayer. Frau Walker is only too happy to accommodate them. But SS patrols often select these Friday evenings to make their visits to the shop, and during one such visit a Nazi officer publicly humiliates the Rabbi, who is taken off and is never seen again. For a few days Frau Walker considers filing a legal complaint for trespassing against the Nazi, but then she abandons the idea, knowing full well that there is no chance of obtaining justice.

Thereafter there is no more public praying at the Walker meat market, but Frau Walker herself, remembering a word she learned from the Rabbi, sometimes greets her Friday evening customers with "Shalom" and thus tries to help them retain something of their Sabbath. One Friday two Nazi officers in uniform stride into the shop: in the higher ranking of the two Frau Walker recognizes the same giant of a man who had taken away the Rabbi. Even then he had seemed to her to evoke all the mindless, barbaric, and heathen terror of the giant Goliath of the Bible pitted against a frailer David. Unfortunately the biblical ending had not followed through, and now Goliath has returned, drunk and meaner than before. When he lights a cigarette and extinguishes it against the face of one of her clients, Frau Walker can hold her silence no more. Diplomatically confining herself to the facts of the situation, she draws the giant's attention to a visibly posted sign stating that smoking is legally prohibited on the premises. There are laws that even a Nazi must obey, and so he cannot find fault with her. In his drunken stupor, however, he looks at an old man in the line, a long retired judge, and, knocking his package out of his hands, tells him point blank not to eat so much lest he become too heavy to ascend "through the air" into heaven. His subordinate reminds him that he is on duty, and Goliath retorts that he is actually being rather nice to tell them that "they are soon going to go through the chimney." One younger woman, Frau Zalewsky, a musician's wife in her last months of pregnancy, has already put her bag on the floor and begun to tremble. The Nazi officer notices her and turns to his subordinate: ". . . Sara with the fat belly, she is—aren't you, Sara?—even grateful to me when I tell her that she shouldn't trouble herself about children's diapers, the sweet little shitty diapers." For Frau Zalewsky this is the last straw. Certain now that she is without recourse, she comes back later the same evening to offer Frau Walker the baby carriage that she has prepared for the child. Frau Walker has been good to her; perhaps one day she will be able to use the carriage. Frau Walker is left to reflect that if such things can happen, that "a woman who is expecting her baby must give away her baby carriage because a sentence of death has been placed without grounds on her and the unborn child," then there is no more hope of redemption, for such a wrong cannot be righted. The only remedy would be for everything to be cleansed thoroughly and purified by fire.[25]

Fire, the age-old purifier, even mightier and more dramatic than water, is not long in coming. In the British bombings that strike the city, amid the shrieking of air-raid sirens, Margarete Walker remains in her apartment, immobilized. With ironic coincidence it is a Jew wandering through the burning city that night who sees her through the shattered windows sitting at her table, engulfed in fire. When he manages to get her into the street, her face is already badly burned. He covers her with his overcoat and then leaves, as he had left his own family some time before, hoping that since he alone was Jewish the others would not be harmed. The attack is over for the time being and Frau Walker will be cared for. In a last minute reflection he returns to remove from his coat the yellow Star of David, which after 1941 all Jews in Germany were obliged to wear. Because of the star he had been denied the shelter of the city bunker. Frau Walker comes to, and recognizing him as her rescuer, begins to speak: "He did not accept it. . . . The burnt offering. . . . God did not accept it."[26]

DENUNCIATIONS

While Frau Walker's heroism and compassion were not unique, she is somewhat exceptional in the pages of literature. Far more common seems to have been the realization that the individual in Nazi Germany could do nothing and for his own sake had best attempt nothing. Anyone—friend or family, passer-by, neighbor, colleague—might make a denunciation. The narrator's mother in Heinrich Böll's *Ansichten eines Clowns* (1963) claims in all sincerity to an *ad hoc* investigating committee, hastily gotten together after her ten-year old son has had a squabble with a fourteen-year old boy in the Hitler Youth, that she would turn her back on him if she really believed he called the other boy a "Nazi swine."[27] For many the only path was that of passive resistance. Witchcraft has it, wrote socialist Luise Rinser in the third brief narrative of her *Weihnachts-Triptychon* (1963), that one can kill a person on the night of a new moon by sticking a pin through that person's photograph in the area of his heart. On the third Christmas of the war in 1941, though there is no full moon and though she has no pin and photograph at hand, she wishes death on the man responsible for the "desecration" of Christmas. Though she has been forbidden to write, the Nazis cannot forbid her to think, and in her thoughts, though she does not name him in her narrative, she would put Adolf Hitler to death.[28] But in the end Luise Rinser was too outspoken and after being denounced by an old school friend, she was arrested in October 1944 and taken for several months' internment to a prison camp in Traunstein in Bavaria near the Austrian border and Salzburg.

Some filed denunciations from idealistic motives, some because denunciations worked to their benefit. The Nazi Party fanatic, Frau Lieser, in Remarque's *Zeit zu leben und Zeit zu sterben* may have denounced Graeber's girlfriend's father out of ideological motives after he said he no longer believed Germany could win the war, but the fact remains that because of her zeal she also secured a share of his apartment for herself. Lest the same fate befall her and lest she lose to Frau Lieser the one room she has been allowed to retain and end up in a concentration camp, is it not better for Elisabeth Kruse to turn on the record player when Graeber is visiting to muffle their conversation and prevent Frau Lieser from detecting something that might serve as material for a denunciation? It is better, too, to keep lights off during the air-raid emergencies in accord with the government directives that Frau Lieser religiously enforces.[29]

Children, too, could bring denunciations, and in Günter Grass's *Hundejahre* (1963), a schoolteacher named Dr. Oswald Brunies is reported by some of the pupils in his class for chewing the lemon candy-like vitamins called Cebion tablets that, beginning in the fall of 1941, were supplied for distribution to schoolchildren. The denunciation comes as no surprise. Brunies had asked Walter Matern, one of the book's central characters, just returned to Danzig from the Russian front, wounded and unfit for combat, to read a poem to the class instead of delivering the lecture about the fighting on the eastern front that he was supposed to deliver. In court several members of the class testify that Brunies had on occasion eaten candy in class, but never Cebion tablets. Unfortunately the teacher begins pulling Cebion tablets from his pocket and sucking on them right in the middle of the hearing. The book provides little justification for Brunies's absurd action in court. The story is narrated by one of his former pupils, Harry Liebenau, who himself testified on his teacher's behalf at the time of the hearing. Even though the story is related in retrospect and Liebenau is much older at the time of the narration, it is not uncharacteristic of Günter Grass's storytelling that the *Erzählungszeit* or time of the narration should shed no light on the *erzählte Zeit* or time narrated. As a result the whole presentation is rather naïve, innocent, and childlike; the reader sees what the child saw. Whatever may have driven Dr. Brunies to eat the Cebion tablets in front of the court, the fact that he never hung out the flag on state occasions like the Führer's birthday was of no benefit to him. Both he and Herr Kruse in Remarque's book die in concentration camps of alleged heart failure. Brunies's daughter Jenny receives a telegram announcing the death and Elisabeth Kruse a mailed invitation to report to Gestapo headquarters. Graeber, who by that time has become Elisabeth's husband, takes the dreaded summons to the Gestapo for his wife. He is asked to sign for receipt of a cigar box filled with what are purported to be his father-in-law's ashes. Both he and Jenny Brunies are instructed that no mourning garb or ceremony will be tolerated: mourning tends to undermine national morale. But from the moment her father is taken away, Jenny Brunies wears black.[30]

GETTING BY ON THE HOMEFRONT

By 1943 the German homefront became almost more treacherous than the battlefields of Russia. Remarque's Ernst Graeber, on furlough in Werden, cannot at first even locate his family home. The whole street has been bombed and a local air-raid warden informs him curtly that since the whole area has been scheduled for a cleanup, Graeber will be arrested if he remains. Out on the front Graeber had felt fairly immune to the snares of petty bureaucracy, but the warden retaliates bitterly. "Do you suppose this isn't a front right here? . . . We have had six air raids here in ten days, in ten days, you front-line soldier!"[31] He clearly resents Graeber's coming home hale and hearty while his own wife lies dead under the rubble. Perhaps it is because the soldiers have done such a poor job on the front that catastrophe has befallen the homeland. Not long after this unnerving encounter shrill sirens scream out warning of yet another air attack.

The diehards, of course, remained diehards. The informer Frau Lieser sets up an altar to the Führer in her room replete with his portrait, candles, and a luxuriously bound copy of *Mein Kampf* resting on a swastika flag.[32] Her husband is serving with an army unit in Russia, and Graeber tries to reassure her that for the moment all is quiet in her husband's sector. But he has misjudged her priorities. All is not quiet out there, she snaps back. Her husband's group is in the thick of the fight and he is in the first line of fire. Graeber is only too well aware that such concepts as the front line no longer have any meaning in Russia, but to try to explain that to Frau Lieser would be futile.[33] The less one had to do with people like her the better. According to one of his old schoolmates, also home on leave, the less one had to do with anybody the better. Cynicism is becoming contagious, and the army barracks where Graeber spends his first few nights in town echo the mood. When one soldier offers him some prophylactics as a protection against disease during his leave, another interjects that since Graeber is an "Aryan stud with twelve thoroughbred ancestors . . . rubbers are a crime against the fatherland."[34]

But by 1943 some were already beyond cynicism. A couple who lost all their children in the bombings of Werden recall that the more conditions deteriorated, the more people became fearful and reticent. "Today each can think only of himself. There is too much unhappiness in the world."[35] The singer and actress Hildegard Knef, having lived through the war in Berlin, writes in her autobiography *Der geschenkte Gaul* (1970) that sooner or later everyone was bombed out and it was simply an unwritten law not to expect help from others.[36]

Angst increased, not the metaphysical *Angst* of the philosophers, but fear pure and simple, fear of the Gestapo, fear of one's neighbors, and eventually fear of the war itself. One of the characters in Zuckmayer's *Des Teufels General*, Diddo Geiss, the daughter of an opera diva, reflects: "We know no real joy. None of us. We are always uneasy—encumbered. . . . There is too much fear in everything.—And if one has no fear oneself, then there are always others who are afraid. This can't always have been this way?"[37]

As always there were a few who managed to be merry despite everything. One of them is Waltraut von Mohrungen, affectionately called Pützchen by everyone else in the Zuckmayer play. A girl from the BDM, she is a blithe spirit, or at least does her best to be. She claims that neither she nor any of the other girls intends to marry because getting married has become too much of a hassle: "all the proofs, Aryan blood down to your great-grandmother's big toe, health certificate, ability to bear offspring . . . it's all necessary on account of the race—but if you want to wait for all of this in the normal course of life, you could get old and rancid."[38] Not at all reflective by nature, she does not question the ideology. But she cannot accept the inconveniences and has decided to take whatever amusement she can find.

Not everyone could be so lighthearted, however, and not everyone could reconcile the goings-on in Nazi Germany with his own conscience. Pützchen's brother-in-law, pilot Friedrich Eilers, says that one gets used to one's job killing people, and his wife tries to support him by telling him that what he is doing is for the sake of the fatherland, the future, and a better world. But Eilers is not totally convinced. Recalling a few verses from the eighteenth-century poet Matthias Claudius, he asks: "Strange people we are, strange. Guernica—Coventry—and Matthias Claudius. How does that fit together?" His wife has a ready answer: believe and don't question. "Whoever believes will survive."

But believing was not always easy. Before the play is over Eilers is killed in a suspicious plane crash, and the Führer orders a state funeral.[39] Another air force officer, a man named Hartmann, in an apparent crisis of nervous exhaustion one day suddenly sputters to his commander, Harras: "It is all true what one hears. They are not horror rumors. I have beheld it with my own eyes. And they are the same—the same boys—the same ones who lived, dreamed, and sang with me in the Hitler Youth, spoke of ideals, of sacrifice and effort, of duty, of clean-living." In Poland Hartmann had run into one of his old school friends in the town of Lodz where he was awaiting a transport. He did not know the friend was part of an extermination squad, and when the friend invited him to come along, promising him a good time, Hartmann consented. "They shot at defenseless people—just for fun. They laughed when these people whimpered. . . . This has nothing more to do with war." Like a child in dilemma turning to his father or teacher for advice and consolation, he turns to Harras. Can everybody become like that? Could I become like that? Harras's answer is diplomatic and somewhat evasive but none the less profound because of that: for thousands of years man has tried to erect some kind of safeguard against himself, but the safeguard must not have been very sturdy since one lifetime was enough to destroy it.[40] Harras answers more definitively at the end of the play. He takes his plane up from the base in an unauthorized suicidal flight and is cut down. For Harras, too, though he could never be persuaded to join the Party, there would be a state funeral.[41]

Right or wrong, Harras chooses to die rather than stay and fight Hitler as the Luftwaffe engineer Oderbruck decides to do. Oderbruck reaches his decision the day he feels ashamed for the first time to be a German. He has no other reason, no family in a concentration camp and no ties of any kind with the Jewish community. Only shame. Others join him, some also out of shame, but others out of hatred or anger, some because they like and respect the work they had been trained for and can no longer stand by to see their work perverted, and still others because they want freedom for themselves or their brothers. Oderbruck is convinced that if Hitler wins this war, both Germany and the world will be lost. Harras encourages Oderbruck, but having himself become the devil's general (*Teufels General*) for Adolf Hitler, he has already selected his own form of resistance and reparation; his spirit is too drained to share that of his colleagues. Dramatically, the play has to end in a climax with the death of Harras. The audience knows his plane has been hit when Oderbruck intones in a low voice and with classical restraint the first phrases of the "Our Father." One can only guess what fate may await Oderbruck and his followers, who know in advance the futility of their resistance.[42]

The Call to Arms

Not all German fighting men thought themselves as glamorous as Sartre's Daniel imagines them in *La Mort dans l'âme,* watching them ride through the streets of Paris in June 1940. Many German men and boys found no more joy in the thought of mobilizing for the army than did their French counterparts. In Heinrich Böll's "Die Postkarte" (1952), one of eighteen stories written in the fifties and sixties and collected under the title *Als der Krieg ausbrach,* a young man named Bruno Schneider, early in August 1939, receives a postcard bordered in red and ordering him to report the very next day for an eight-week stint of duty. He is sitting at home in his mother's house eating a late breakfast of bread and butter when the card arrives. The food sticks in his throat, and his mother begins to cry as she had only once before in her lifetime, at the death of his father. Knowing that they are lying to each other, mother and son seek reassurance in the idea that Bruno will only be gone for eight weeks. Bruno tells his story in retrospect after the war is over, but as happens so often in Böll's writings about the postwar period, his characters cannot escape its memory. The past continues to live in the present. It refuses to be put away. One day Bruno discovers, quite by accident, a small postal receipt for registered mail bordered in red and now yellowed with age. Instantly it brings to his mind the fateful postcard that had summoned him to duty in 1939.

He remembers being unable to finish his breakfast. Instead he retreated to his room to perform a whole ritual of senseless actions like opening and closing the drawers of his desk. At the moment when he was being forced to abandon his room, he needed the assurance that he was still in complete possession and control of it. But the postcard seemed to nullify that relationship. The room simply no longer belonged to him and that was all that was to it. His train to the army camp was to leave at eight that night, and though the railroad station was only fifteen minutes away, he left home at three in the afternoon. "Mother blessed me, kissed me on the cheeks, and as the house door closed behind me, I knew that she was crying."[43]

Germany had been systematically preparing her citizens for war for quite some time, and as the war drew near, propaganda was, if anything, intensified. In the story "Als der Krieg ausbrach" (1961), which lent its name to the whole collection of Böll's war stories, the narrator, an army recruit, remembers sitting in a movie theater on the last Sunday in August 1939, watching the newsreels for the week show "very unnoble-looking Poles mistreating very noble-looking Germans. . . ."[44] But despite the propaganda and the paramilitary organizations like the *Hitlerjugend* or the BDM or the Nazi Party itself which since 1933, and in some cases even earlier, had been putting Germans into uniforms of one sort or another, the war meant changes to which some people were just not attuned. One is the thirty-three year old Greck, a character in Böll's *Wo warst du, Adam* (1951), who in 1939 goes out into the field as an ensign-sergeant. Greck is an educated person with a prosperous career to look forward to. But the war cuts everything short. He finds that it is no longer sufficient to be a doctor of law and to have a professional position. "Now they all looked at his chest when he came home. His chest was only scantily decorated."[45]

The vast majority of people who were called upon to do military service in World War II did so without seriously questioning their summons. Still, a few like the book antiquarian's apprentice in Böll's *Gruppenbild mit Dame,* identified only as B.H.T., managed to avoid it. B.H.T. feels no need to justify himself to anybody by entering military service and aspires to no ideals that are not more amply satisfied by remaining in the bookshop. To achieve his ends he decides to follow the advice of a nun named Sister Rahel from whom he learns what to eat and drink in the form of tinctures and pills in order to be classified permanently as unfit when his urine is examined at recruiting time.[46]

For some, military service was a way out of a social or judicial predicament. It provides an outlet for Michel Tournier's Abel Tiffauges in *Le Roi des aulnes,* and for Günter Grass's Walter Matern, the character around whom *Hundejahre* is loosely structured, it provides a freedom and even license he could otherwise never have obtained. During his school days Walter Matern had befriended a Jewish boy named Eddi Amsel who used to make scarecrows. When uniforms, especially the black and brown ones associated with the Nazi movement, become an ever greater part of the German street scene, Eddi develops a mania for them. Since the Party's uniforms are available only to its members, and since as a Jew Eddi cannot join the Party or any of its organizations, the only way for him to get uniforms is to have his friend Walter Matern join up. Walter is admitted to the SA but later rejected for stealing while intoxicated. Like Eddi he loves the theater, but his drunkenness even gets him a dismissal from a local theater in Schwerin.[47] Matern is subsequently arrested in Düsseldorf, though the grounds for the arrest are never clarified in the book. With characteristic irony Grass presents the entire mid-section of his text covering the critical period of the Nazi rise to power and the war through a series of "love letters" from Harry Liebenau to his cousin Tulla Pokriefke, both members of the Danzig circle of friends, relatives, and acquaintances who populate the narrative. Liebenau is not an omniscient narrator, and perhaps what was a rather dangerous and precarious time becomes less gruesome in his words because of his limitations as a person and as a narrator. His neither profound nor philosophical mind enables him to maintain an ironically matter-of-fact and sometimes even casual stance. Liebenau claims not to know why Matern was forced to spend time from May through early June 1939 in the cellar of the Düsseldorf police headquarters. In any case Matern is officially a resident of Danzig, still technically a "free city" in the aftermath of the Versailles treaties, sandwiched between Poland and Germany and supervised by the League of Nations. His Danzig passport, together with his willingness to do military service, a willingness rapidly put to the test by an induction order into the German army, save him from the Düsseldorf police.

As soon as Matern gets back to Danzig he turns up in the yard in front of the Liebenau house and begins cursing loudly at the Liebenau's big black shepherd dog Harras, calling it a "Catholic Nazi hog." "I'm twenty-two dog years old, and I still haven't done anything to earn immortality . . ." Harras is no ordinary dog, for he had sired the shepherd Prinz who was selected to be presented "in the name of the Party and the German population of the German city of Danzig . . . to the Führer and Chancellor through a delegation on the occasion of his forty-sixth birthday." The Führer had accepted Danzig's gift and henceforth kept Prinz along with other dogs of the same breed in his kennels. A letter of recognition and an autographed picture of Hitler that the Liebenaus have framed and hung in their carpentry shop inspire a number of converts to the Party from among the neighbors. And so for Matern to come home to Danzig and publicly revile Harras is no trifling

matter. In the Liebenau shop machines begin buzzing furiously, and neighbors vanish into their apartments, for no one wants to hear what Matern is saying. Some denunciations are formulated, but in the end no one turns him in.

When Harras is found poisoned in August 1939, however, it doesn't take Harry Liebenau long to associate Matern with the deed. Harry and his cousin Tulla had seen a man approach the dog one night with some meat and urge the dog to eat it. From a distance and without explanation Tulla had also urged Harras to take the meat, but to Harry's rather simplistic mind Tulla always remains something of an enigma. Her generally ambivalent and unpredictable nature may be a reflection of the times in which she was raised and is certainly suited to their ambiguity. At any rate, neither he nor Tulla testifies against Matern, although Harry's father files a complaint. Matern, however, has an alibi, and proceedings against him bog down when two days later the war begins and he marches into Poland, saved from the prospect of punishment.[48]

UNHEROIC HEROES AND AN UNHEROIC WAR

Ostensibly the war began over the city of Danzig which Hitler was determined to bring back "home to the Reich."[49] By the terms of the Versailles treaties the Poles had been allowed to maintain a post office in Danzig, and in *Die Blechtrommel* Günter Grass, himself a native of that city, uses the Polish post office as the scene for the opening of the hostilities that developed into World War II. More important for the novel, the battle of the Polish post office, described in terms of a seduction scene between the oncoming German tanks and the Polish fortress, brings about the physical undoing of whatever ties may have bound Oskar to Poland through his Polish "father," Jan Bronski. Some time before, Oskar's mother seems to have decided to end the triangle she has constructed in this city where two civilizations met, with Oskar's two "fathers," the German Alfred Matzerath and Bronski. She begins eating fish of every variety and preparation, and she continues eating from morning to night until she becomes so ill that she is taken to the hospital and dies.[50] Her lover Jan is an employee at the Polish post office, and Oskar is with him when the firing begins. They both manage just in time to get under the cover of the building. When the battle is over, Bronski and thirty other men who defended the post office against the Germans are rounded up and executed. Oskar, only about fifteen and a midget to boot, sees quickly which way the wind is blowing, and instead of protecting Bronski, points him out to the pro-German Home Guards who take him prisoner, convinced that the Pole has brutally taken this helpless innocent child into the thick of the fighting.[51] Oskar's actions and attitudes are often mysterious, as here, for he has always seemed drawn more to Bronski than to his supposedly real father Matzerath. On several occasions Oskar speaks of himself as being informed by evil or even by Satan, though this is little more than an excuse and rationalization for not facing the issues. By relating virtually the whole story of *Die Blechtrommel* through the voice of the midget drummer Oskar, Grass has achieved an effect similar to, though more spectacular and colorful than, the one attained by using Harry Liebenau and his "love letters" in *Hundejahre*. To take the comparison further, where Liebenau is at times a bit dim-witted, Oskar can be downright grotesque. Because of his apparent lack of guile he is never repulsive; yet on occasion he displays such ironic callousness that one wonders if his retardation is not more than physical. Of course, Oskar does eventually wind up in a mental hospital, and the reader knows this from the first page of the book.

The heroes Grass has chosen for these two books are not heroes in the classical sense of the term. Nor are they really the anti-heroes of modern fiction who would certainly disclaim all heroism if they ever thought about it. At the very outset of *Die Blechtrommel,* however, and in no uncertain terms, Oskar claims to be a hero in his own way,[52] and on several occasions further into the narrative he describes himself in messianic terms. In *Hundejahre* the problem of identifying a hero is further complicated by the fact that no one person dominates the narrative as Oskar does in *Die Blechtrommel*. The dogs, Harras, Prinz, and Pluto, together with the character Walter Matern can at most be said to operate as a kind of framework around which the story unfolds. "The dog stands central," Grass asserts at the beginning of the third section of the book.[53] But even this assessment is precarious, since for the most part the characters function independently of the dog or dogs "populating" their lives.

On a metaphorical level, of course, the term "dog years" used to designate the prewar, war, and postwar period in Germany is not without effect. The tin drum and its drummer Oskar, however, constitute an even richer and more powerful image. First of all, the narration is Oskar's, and for much of the story the tin drum functions as his primary vehicle of expression. Oskar received his first drum on his third birthday at which time he decided to arrest the normal growth of his body. The adults of the family later attribute his stunted physique to his having fallen down a flight of cellar stairs on the occasion of that third birthday, but Oskar consistently refuses to recognize the causal relationship. His drum, painted red and white, the colors of Poland, serves several functions: it enables Oskar to unite what he calls the two souls living in his breast, Goethe and Rasputin; it enables him to create and to destroy, to conjure up the past, to put a distance between himself and the sometimes serious adult world around him, and to free himself of responsibility to that world and ultimately

even to himself. Oskar does not grow again until, approaching the age of twenty-one in 1945, with the Russians in Danzig as well as the returning Poles, he watches his German father Matzerath's burial in sandy Saspe cemetery and throws away his drum. The Oedipal conflict has been resolved along with the war. He can now proceed to the point where his white-enameled bed at the mental hospital will become what he calls the standard or norm by which he will make all his judgments and the goal toward which he will strive. This is just as he had said it would be at the outset of the narration and—since the story is related in retrospect from Oskar's hospital bed—just as it has been all along.[54]

In some ways the heroine around whose life Heinrich Böll chose to frame his long quasi-detective novel of the war period and its aftermath, *Gruppenbild mit Dame,* is like Grass's heroes. Her name is Leni Pfeiffer and for all practical purposes she is a completely insignificant person who happens to have lived through some rather crucial years in her country's history. Occasionally the times may elicit from her a noble and even brave reaction just as they might from any other ordinary human being. On Northrop Frye's scale of literary modes Böll's characterization of Leni Pfeiffer falls within the fourth or low mimetic mode. The hero is "superior neither to other men nor to his environment" and so "is one of us." For the most part *Hundejahre* can also be classified as low mimesis, though Oskar in *Die Blechtrommel* clearly belongs with the fifth and final or ironic mode. "If inferior in power or intelligence to ourselves, so that we have the sense of looking down on a scene of bondage, frustration, and absurdity, the hero belongs to the ironic mode."[55] In describing a war in which, with a few exceptions, heroic behavior was not the order of the day in Germany or in France, either because this was not a particularly heroic war or because war itself had lost its capacity to be heroic, the ironic mode has proven to be a very useful structuring device in fictional literature. In *Die Blechtrommel* it is the sustained point of view of the narration; in many other novels it has been used more selectively but certainly not without effect.

On September 1, 1939, when German soldiers marched into Poland, there were, by and large, no celebrations on the part of the civilian population. Nor were there any later on. A few pompous vestiges of World War I remained to the end, however. In Remarque's *Zeit zu leben und Zeit zu sterben,* when Ernst Graeber is ready to return to the Russian front after his furlough in Werden, he is surprised to see the troops still being given a musical send-off as the train prepares to leave. But by that time the new recruits are very young, "vegetables" and "cannon-fodder" a lance-corporal calls them, and the four musicians sent to play the *Deutschland-Lied* and the *Horst-Wessel-Lied,* a Nazi Party song commemorating one of National Socialism's first martyrs, play both songs rapidly and perfunctorily, giving only one verse of each.[56]

Though there was little enthusiasm among the general population, there were the usual expressions of support for the men, and letters and packages from their families. Letters from home had to be increasingly cautious, however, and after the bombings in Germany began in earnest, the civilians were often in greater need of packages than were the soldiers at the "front."[57] A girl named Elisabeth in one of Böll's stories, "Die blasse Anna" (1953), writes to her boyfriend somewhere with the German army, that she is proud he is in the army and sure they are going to win; but the soldier is not proud, and when he comes home on leave does not even bother to write to her. Instead he dates another girl who lives in his building.[58] In Günter Grass's *Hundejahre* Jenny Brunies allows her girlfriend, Tulla Pokriefke, to put nine leeches on her skin in the hope of preventing the fulfillment of a childish superstition that Tulla's brother fighting in France will otherwise bleed to death. Jenny faints during her ordeal, but after Harry Liebenau pulls the leeches off her and she revives, her only concern is that Tulla's brother will now be safe.[59]

Some German civilians like some French civilians inevitably made good profits from the war effort. In Böll's *Gruppenbild mit Dame* Leni Pfeiffer's father, Herbert Gruyten, who heads a construction company, makes a fortune building the Siegfried Line, the row of German fortifications that paralleled the Maginot Line on the east side of the Rhine. Business first begins a noticeable upward trend for the Gruyten firm in 1933, and ten years later no ratio can be established to measure its growth. Unfortunately for Gruyten a tax collector nabs him for irregularities in his finances and he spends the latter part of his career first as a construction worker operating a cement mixer with a penal unit on the French Atlantic coast and later clearing rubble after the air raids on Berlin.[60]

As the new masters of Europe, the Germans, or perhaps better said, some Germans, like Ernst Graeber's old school friend, Kreisleiter Alfons Binding, were able to help themselves to the luxuries among European products: canned turtle soup from France, canned asparagus from Holland, ham from Prague, Danish cheese, and so on.[61] Even people simpler than Binding had access to such things, food as well as fine handicrafts, if they had a husband or son or brother on military duty in occupied Europe. Only in Russia, as a haunting Brecht *Lied* recalls, did the German harvest turn bitter: from Russia the Germans sent back death.[62]

In the light of the sizeable emigration of German writers and the pronouncements they made against the Hitler regime, Stefan Zweig's claim that "almost all German writers" felt it their duty to support the advancing German troops and spur their enthusiasm seems somewhat unjust. Zweig charges furthermore that "they denied overnight that an English or a French culture had ever existed," and that compared to the German character and German art, they deemed what others had to offer "scant and worthless."[63] A few writers like Gerhart Hauptmann, to be sure, did opt openly to support the Nazi Party, but within the writing community Hauptmann was, if anything, in a minority. And if we are to believe what fiction tells us, even highly placed Nazi officials such as those in the entourage of the camp commandant of Auschwitz, let alone the writing community, were quite capable of appreciating the good things that came from abroad. It was certainly not the Party line, and they may not always have had the cultural formation that would have enabled them to appreciate good literature, but as Robert Merle indicates in *La Mort est mon métier,* they could appreciate other things, speak of France as a "marvelous country," and enjoy and revere the excellent quality of French cognac.[64] From these highly placed SS men to Oskar the tin-drummer at another end of the spectrum there is a fascination with Paris and an admiration for it. Oskar's first contact with Paris comes from the shiny postcards sent or brought home by Sergeant Fritz Truczinski, the brother of Maria Truczinski who becomes Alfred Matzerath's second wife after Oskar's mother dies. Thanks to the postcards and his drum Oskar can conjure up a mild Parisian springtime, climb the Eiffel Tower, and enjoy the magnificent view of Paris as every good tourist was supposed to do.[65]

To many Germans, however, France also meant "brothels and lewdness," reports Hildegard Knef, "and a respectable German didn't even entertain the thought. . . ." A German could learn nothing decent and respectable there. Her Aunt Emma, in any case, had once been a cook in France, and that was a fact her relatives discussed only in undertones.[66] This negative moral attitude that many Germans had toward France is also visible in Robert Merle's *La Mort est mon métier,* a psychological study in fictional terms of the life of Rudolf Lang, the name of Merle's protagonist whose life roughly parallels that of Rudolf Höss, the actual commandant of the Auschwitz-Birkenau concentration camp in Poland from May 1940 to October 1943. Merle devotes the first part of the book to an examination of Rudolf's home life as a boy. His father is the stereotype of the Germanic tyrant tolerating no disorder or infraction of any kind in his household. On one of the rare occasions on which father and son have a talk of any length and substance, Rudolf's father tells him that he has decided that his son should be a priest; this, in part, to atone for the sins that he, the father, committed during a business trip to Paris before Rudolf's birth. Even now it is only with disgust that he can pronounce the names of Paris and of France. His religious fanaticism appears to date from his return from that business trip.

What actually transpired during his stay in Paris can only be assumed from the general statements he makes that Paris is the capital of all vices and that after his stay there God had visited his soul. "'I became ill,' he said in a tone of incredible disgust, 'I took care of myself and I was cured but my soul was not cured.'"[67] Rudolf does not become a priest according to his father's wishes. Perhaps he does not even love his father, but he does revere him as one might revere a god, and that reverence and obedience he later transfers to the head of the SS, Reichsführer Heinrich Himmler. The negative impression of France his father bequeaths him only sears deeper into Rudolf's flesh when Germany loses the First World War in France and finds herself plunged into economic chaos.

When the Germans marched into France in 1940 there were some who felt that they were paying back a debt that had been allowed to stand for over twenty years. In Böll's *Gruppenbild mit Dame* Alois Pfeiffer, whom Leni Gruyten eventually marries, takes part in the battle. He apparently thinks he has some talent as a writer and writes a series of descriptions for publication about the French campaign. They are overly rhetorical and pompous in nature and the narrator reserves the right not to comment on them. According to Pfeiffer it was up to the German soldier of 1940 to complete the task of those who had passed before him in World War I along the river Aisne.[68] But outside of his immediate family, no one, including his wife, seems to take anything that Alois Pfeiffer does or says very seriously. Leni, in fact, appears to have been much more attracted to her cousin Erhart Schweigert, but Erhart is timid with girls and never has time during his brief interludes from the army to make anything of that attraction. Both Erhart and Leni's brother Heinrich whose father does not want him to have to soil his hands with money and the dirty business of the family construction firm, meet their end together, facing a firing squad for trying to sell an anti-aircraft cannon for a few marks to the Danes. Heinrich was given the best humanistic education available in Germany and abroad, and, filled with lofty ideals, suddenly finds himself thrust into the often squalid reality of Hitler's war machine. "Too much Bamberg Rider and too little Peasants' War," reflects Lotte Hoyser, wife of Otto Hoyser who rises from the position of the elder Gruyten's head bookkeeper to that of his successor.

Among all the characters in Böll's book, Heinrich Gruyten remains among the most ambiguous, although he is potentially far more interesting than his sister Leni, whom the book is ostensibly about and who is at the center of the narrator's investigations. But if Böll was going to put together a fictional inquiry into the war years and their effect on the German people, he had to choose someone as ordinary as Leni Pfeiffer around whom to structure his investigation. People like Leni, unpolitical for the most part and on the whole relatively discreet, were the ones who survived. One thinks of Jean Giraudoux's Electra and Aegisthus's attempts to marry her off to a gardener in the realization that the gods do not strike the average citizen but only those who stand out from the multitude and can be distinguished from the rest. Unlike Leni, Heinrich was not meant to blend into the landscape. The letters he writes from the service to his family, without salutations or conclusions, read like military instruction manuals. Is this the revenge of an adolescent whose dreams have been shattered by the cruel reality of the world, or perhaps more to the point, the revenge of an adult son on his father who had so wanted him to be educated, his revenge on the system for which and under which his father is working and profiting? Heinrich shouts "Shit on Germany!" as he dies with his cousin Erhart, "two Bamburg riders," in the words of Lotte Hoyser, "who wanted to die together, and God knows they did. . . ." In the process and perhaps unwittingly, Erhart in his mother's eyes makes up for her husband who had failed to die in battle at Langemarck in 1914.[69]

Since Erhart cannot be for Leni, she marries in the spring of 1941 the vindictive and hawkish Alois Pfeiffer who was made a sergeant the year before when France was invaded. She refuses to wear white for the wedding ceremony. Alois has orders to report to his unit in the east on the very night of the wedding, and since he forces her to have conjugal relations with him half an hour before his departure, she writes him off as dead to herself even before he is killed a few days later in Russia and then she refuses to wear mourning.[70]

Not all Germans went to France with Pfeiffer's vengeful turn of mind. Werner von Ebrenach, a German officer billeted in a French provincial house in Vercors's *Le Silence de la mer,* reveres French culture to the point of adoration. And then there were those who did not want to be in the war at all, like the soldier-narrator of Böll's story "Entfernung von der Truppe" (1963-1964), who in his own words feels toward war as a pedestrian might feel toward cars.[71] Or novelist and short-story writer Alfred Andersch who in 1933 at nineteen years of age spent six weeks in Dachau as a communist, was subsequently drafted into the German army, and in his autobiographical *Die Kirschen der Freiheit* (1952) claims to have regretted not being able in 1940 to desert that army as it stood poised on the Rhine and ready to march into France. The river currents were too strong, and even if he had made it across, he would only have "bumped up against an army whose defeat was determined."[72]

If the Germans, in turn, encountered any real animosity in France, literature does not speak very much of it, at least not in the early stages of the Occupation. The French Résistance took time to develop, and for some time after the invasion of 1940 had been completed, relations between the German soldiers and the French population did not always turn sour. France was, of course, for the German army one of the early battles of the war, and to those Germans who had been there and who later found themselves on rail transports headed for Russia, France in retrospect seemed like paradise. On one such transport in Böll's *Der Zug war pünktlich,* rolling through what is described here and elsewhere as cheerless, unhappy Poland, a German soldier named Andreas is trying to remember the eyes of a French girl he had been smitten with and who lived on the fringes of Amiens. Andreas wound up for a time in a military hospital in Amiens, and when he got out, he went back to what he thought was the girl's house, but everything seemed to have changed. To his dismay he found a petit bourgeois Frenchman standing in front of the house, a pipe in his mouth and derision in his eyes. Everyone had fled; the Germans had plundered everything even though acts of plundering were supposedly punishable by death. The man knew nothing of the girl. The Germans had smashed his windows, burned his rug with their cigarette butts, whored on his couch. He had ample reason to resent them, but he could still feel sympathy for this German soldier trying in vain to locate his girlfriend.[73]

The spirit not only of France but of Paris itself may have been blunted by the arrival of the Germans, as Stefan Zweig says,[74] but if Paris was to become Greater Germany's amusement park as Rolf Hochhuth's play *Der Stellvertreter* (1963) indicates,[75] its spirit could not be allowed to deteriorate altogether. At least the Germans destroyed nothing in Paris, Ernst Graeber explains to his girlfriend Elisabeth.[76] But she is generally apprehensive about what the Germans have done in the occupied countries and fearful that once the war is over no one in Europe will want to receive them as visitors or tourists. She asks Ernst, who had been in the French campaign, if there is much hatred in France. "I don't know," he answers. "Perhaps. I didn't see much of it. Of course we didn't want to see it either. . . . We wanted to get the war over in a hurry and sit in the sun on the streets in front of the cafés drinking the wines of a foreign country. We were very young.'"[77]

The first soldiers who went into France seem on the whole to have been innocent enough, innocent at least to the extent that they had not yet experienced or participated in mass liquidations and other atrocities that many of them later came to know in the east and even in France itself. Events like the tragedy at Oradour-sur-Glane near Limoges came later. Most of the soldiers who marched into France in 1940 did so with a clear conscience. From Russia Graeber recalls those days with nostalgia in a kind of interior monologue in which his own voice blends almost imperceptibly with that of the narrator.

The summer of 1940 in France. The stroll to Paris. The howling of the Stukas over a disconcerted land. Roads jammed with refugees and with a disintegrating army. High June, fields, woods, a march through an unravaged landscape. And then the city, with its silvery light, its streets, its cafés, opening itself without a shot fired. Had he thought then? Had he been disturbed? No. Everything had seemed right. Germany, set upon by war-hungry enemies, had defended itself, that was all.[78]

Obviously a point of view is always relative and from the French point of view the situation was certainly less than idyllic!

Of all the Germans who made it to Paris in one capacity or another during the years of occupation one of the more colorful is Grass's Oskar Matzerath. Oskar goes to Paris not as a soldier, naturally, but as part of a troupe of midgets who have arranged to play in the Théâtre Sarah Bernhardt and the Salle Pleyel. As a child Oskar had learned to shatter glass with the high intensity and pitch of his voice, and in Danzig had tried his voice successfully on the windows of local churches and once even on Nazi Party headquarters. In Paris he proceeds to do the same with French glassware from the time of Louis XIV to the Third Republic. The audience on the whole does not grasp what Oskar calls the historical significance of his act,[79] but lest one be tempted to attach an anti-French significance to it, one should recall the scene much earlier in Oskar's career, when his father Matzerath attends the Nazi mass meetings on the Maiwiese in Danzig. Oskar, thanks to his height which enables him to hide easily and his drum which enables him to set the tone, turns Nazi martial airs into rather innocuous Viennese waltz and charleston melodies.[80] In June 1944, just before the Allied landings in Normandy, Oskar and the troupe go out to the Norman coast to tour the Atlantic Wall, a series of fortifications that the Germans built on the Channel coast to repulse precisely the kind of invasion that is in the offing. To Oskar the somber and ominous-looking German pillboxes, squatting heavily on the gentle elevations overlooking the Channel, are like big toys. He domesticates them as children do today, crawling playfully and heedlessly over the huge gray humps: "And then we had our concrete. We could admire it and even pat it to our heart's content; it didn't budge." The pillbox, "shaped like a flattened-out turtle, lay amid sand dunes, was called 'Dora Seven', and looked out upon the shifting tides through gun embrasures, observation slits and machine-gun barrels."[81] When the invasion comes Oskar and his troupe leave France and hurry back to what by now can only be called relative safety in Danzig.

Notes

1. William L. Shirer, *The Rise and Fall of the Third Reich* (New York: Simon and Schuster, 1960), pp. 226, 241, 253-54.
2. *Ibid.,* pp. 244-45.

3. *Ibid.,* pp. 203, 233.

4. *Ibid.,* pp. 234-40.

5. *Ibid.,* p. 239.

6. *Ibid.,* pp. 270-72.

7. Stefan Zweig, *Die Welt von Gestern* (Frankfurt/Main: Fischer, 1975), pp. 260-61 (orig. German ed., 1944). E. and C. Paul, trans., *The World of Yesterday* (New York: The Viking Press, 1943), pp. 361-62, 439 (orig. English ed., 1943).

8. *Ibid.,* pp. 273-90.

9. Albrecht Goes, *Das Brandopfer* (Frankfurt/Main: Fischer, 1968), pp. 10-11. Orig. ed., 1954.

10. Günter Grass, *Die Blechtrommel* (Darmstadt: Luchterhand, 1979), pp. 92-93, 140-41 (orig. ed., 1959). Ralph Manheim, trans., *The Tin Drum* (New York: Random House, 1964), pp. 115-16.

11. *Ibid.,* p. 162 (p. 201). Grass erroneously lists the date of the Kristallnacht as November 8. It actually occurred on the night of November 9.

12. Shirer, *The Rise and Fall of the Third Reich,* p. 430.

13. Grass, *Die Blechtrommel,* p. 162 (p. 201).

14. Erich Maria Remarque, *Zeit zu leben und Zeit zu sterben* (Frankfurt/Main:Ullstein, 1974), pp. 76-77 (orig. ed., 1954). Denver Lindley, trans., *A Time To Love and a Time To Die* (New York: Harcourt, Brace, 1954), p. 117.

15. *Ibid.,* pp. 105-7.

16. Carl Zuchmayer, *Des Teufels General* (Frankfurt/Main: Fischer, 1974), p. 100. Orig. ed., 1946.

17. Heinrich Böll, *Gruppenbild mit Dame* (München: DTV, 1978), p. 192 (orig. ed., 1971). Leila Vennewitz, trans., *Group Portrait with Lady* (New York: Avon, 1974), p. 224.

18. Remarque, *Zeit zu leben und Zeit zu sterben,* pp. 36, 40 (p. 54).

19. *Shirer, The Rise and Fall of the Third Reich,* p. 934.

20. Remarque, *Zeit zu leben und Zeit zu sterben,* pp. 44-47, 64 (pp. 59, 70, 72, 97). The geographical location of the actual Werden on the Ruhr just south of Essen does not fit Remarque's description.

21. Richard Meran Barsam, *Filmguide to "Triumph of the Will"* (Bloomington, Ind.: Indiana University Press, 1975), pp. 14-15.

22. Klaus Mann, *Mephisto* (Reinbek bei Hamburg: Rowohlt, 1980), pp. viii, 344. Orig. ed., 1936.

23. Ernst Wiechert, *Der Totenwald* (Frankfurt/Main: Ullstein, 1972), pp. 13, 16-18, 20. Orig. ed., 1946.

24. Goes, pp. 15-16.

25. *Ibid.,* pp. 52-53, 57-58, 60-61.

26. *Ibid.,* p. 70.

27. Böll, *Ansichten eines Clowns* (München: DTV, 1980), pp. 25-26. Orig. ed., 1963.

28. Luise Rinser, "Weihnacht hinterm Totenholz" in *Weihnachts-Triptykon* (Zürich: Peter Schifferli Verlags AG Die Arche, 1963), pp. 40-41.

29. Remarque, *Zeit zu leben und Zeit zu sterben,* pp. 66, 85-86, 91.

30. Günter Grass, *Hundejahre* (Darmstadt: Luchterhand, 1978), pp. 232-38, 271. Orig. ed., 1963. Remarque, *Zeit zu leben und Zeit zu sterben,* pp. 204-6.

31. Remarque, *Zeit zu leben und Zeit zu sterben,* pp. 50-51 (p. 77).

32. *Ibid.,* 84-85.

33. *Ibid.,* p. 146.

34. *Ibid.,* pp. 79, 88 (p. 136).

35. *Ibid.,* p. 64 (pp. 97-98).

36. Hildegard Knef, *Der geschenkte Gaul* (Frankfurt/Main: Ullstein, 1975), p. 42. Orig. ed., 1970.

37. Zuckmayer, p. 91.

38. *Ibid.,* p. 17.

39. *Ibid.,* pp. 119, 45.

40. *Ibid.,* pp. 139-40.

41. *Ibid.,* pp. 154-56.

42. *Ibid.,* pp. 149-54.

43. Heinrich Böll, "Die Postkarte" in *Als der Krieg ausbrach* (München, DTV, 1968), pp. 78-83. Orig ed. of this collection, 1965. Dates when the individual stories from the collection were written appear in the bibliography.

44. Böll, "Als der Krieg ausbrach," in *Als der Krieg ausbrach,* p. 23.

45. Böll, *Wo warst du, Adam?* (München, DTV, 1975), pp. 57-58. Orig. ed., 1951.

46. Böll, *Gruppenbild mit Dame,* pp. 37-42.

47. Scherwin is located in Mecklenburg east of Hamburg in what is now East Germany,

48. Grass, *Hundejahre,* pp. 159-60, 200, 206-10, 129-30. Ralph Manheim, trans., *Dog Years* (Greenwich, Conn.: Fawcett, 1965), pp. 251, 159.

49. *Ibid.,* p. 163 (p. 199).

50. Grass, *Die Blechtrommel,* pp. 128-30.

51. *Ibid.,* pp. 174, 200-201.

52. *Ibid.,* pp. 10-11.

53. Grass, *Hundejahre,* p. 301.

54. Grass, *Die Blechtrommel,* p. 9.

55. Northrop Frye, *Anatomy of Criticism* (Princeton, N.J.: Princeton University Press, 1971), p. 34. Orig. ed., 1957.

56. Remarque, *Zeit zu leben und Zeit zu sterben,* p. 218.

57. *Ibid.,* p. 194.

58. Böll, "Die blasse Anna," in *Als der Krieg ausbrach,* p. 138.

59. Grass, *Hundejahre,* p. 218.

60. Böll, *Gruppenbild mit Dame,* pp. 67-68, 217.

61. Remarque, *Zeit zu leben und Zeit zu sterben,* p. 127.

62. Bertolt Brecht, "Und was bekam des Soldaten Weib," in *Gedichte und Lieder aus Stücken* (Frankfurt/Main: Suhrkamp, 1976), pp. 128-29. This *Lied* is taken from the play *Schweyk im zweiten Weltkrieg* which was written in 1943 and copyrighted in 1957.

63. Zweig, pp. 169-70.

64. Robert Merle, *La Mort est mon métier* (Paris: Gallimard, 1968), p. 399. Orig. ed., 1952.

65. Grass, *Die Blechtrommel,* pp. 245-46.

66. Knef, p. 8. David Anthony Palastanga, trans., *The Gift Horse* (New York: Dell, 1972), p. 8.

67. Merle, *La Mort est mon métier,* pp. 18-20.

68. Böll, *Gruppenbild mit Dame,* p. 108.

69. *Ibid.,* pp. 54-74 (pp. 89-90). Langemarck is located in Belgium, just northeast of Ypres.

70. *Ibid.,* p. 117.

71. Böll, "Entfernung von der Truppe" in *Als der Krieg ausbrach,* p. 240.

72. Alfred Andersch, *Die Kirschen der Freiheit* (Zürich: Diogenes, 1968), pp. 89-90. Orig. ed., 1952.

73. Böll, *Der Zug war pünktlich* (München: DTV, 1975), pp. 38-40. Orig. ed., 1949.

74. Zweig, pp. 99-100.

75. Rolf Hochhuth, *Der Stellvertreter* (Reinbek bei Hamburg: Rowohlt, 1975), p. 40. Orig. ed., 1963.

76. Remarque, *Zeit zu leben und Zeit zu sterben,* p. 131.

77. *Ibid.,* pp. 130-31 (p. 204).

78. *Ibid.,* pp. 17-18 (p. 24).

79. Grass, *Die Blechtrommel,* pp. 270-71.

80. *Ibid.,* p. 97.

81. *Ibid.,* p. 273 (p. 332).

Eric Homberger (essay date 1984)

SOURCE: Homberger, Eric. "United States." In *The Second World War in Fiction,* edited by Holger Klein, with John Flower and Eric Homberger, pp. 173-205. London: Macmillan, 1984.

[*In the essay below, Homberger surveys American fiction written about World War II, noting its variety of perspectives and concluding that there is "no typical novel of the war."*]

The United States was the last of the major combatants to enter the war, and, except perhaps for the British, experienced the greatest diversity of combat. In effect, the US armed forces fought a half-dozen different wars, on two oceans as well as in five theatres, from the South Pacific to North Africa. The shape of American war literature was imposed by the variousness of war itself. There are American novels set in the Pacific (by Norman Mailer, James Jones, Thomas Heggen), in Italy (Harry Brown, John Horne Burns, John Hersey), in France and Germany (Glen Sire, Stefan Heym, Irwin Shaw), and in England (Hersey, etc.). There are war novels wholly set in America (J. G. Cozzens), and some which do not involve any Americans at all: John Steinbeck's *The Moon is Down,* about German-occupied Norway; Hersey's *The Wall,* which describes the destruction of the Warsaw ghetto; Godfrey Blunden's *The Time of the Assassins,* set in German-occupied Russia; and Albert Maltz's *The Cross and the Arrow,* about German civilian workers in 1942. There are novels of the Marine Corps (Leon Uris's *Battle Cry*), Navy (Heggen's *Mr. Roberts*), Air Force (Hersey's *The War Lover,* Heller's *Catch-22*), and of course, the infantry. There are novels about virtually every kind of military unit; there are pure combat novels (Harry Brown's *A Walk in the Sun*), and novels concerned with military administration of newly-occupied territory (Hersey's *A Bell for Adano*). At least two novels end with concentration camp scenes. There is, in other words, no typical novel of the war.

Americans were actively engaged in the war for less than four years. This was long enough for a small body of war novels to be published during the war, but conditions did not permit an active literary life by soldiers. Journalism was a more characteristic product of the war, and many distinguished writers served as war correspondents: Steinbeck for the New York *Herald Tribune,* Hemmingway for *Colliers,* Dos Passos for *Life.* Professional journalists like Ernie Pyle, who covered the war for Scripps-Howard, Vincent Sheean, who wrote for *Red Book,* and John Gunther, who went overseas as a broadcaster for the Blue Network, were joined by younger journalists and writers: Richard Tregaskis was sent to Guadalcanal by the International News Service, John Hersey was a *Time-Life* correspondent, Ira Wolfert wrote for the North American Newspaper Alliance. (Wolfert's *Battle for the Solomons* won the Pulitzer prize for journalism in 1943.) Steinbeck and Hersey were authors of early war novels, but combatant-writing generally did not begin to appear in significant quantities until the late 1940s. The high water mark was reached in 1948, when major novels appeared by Mailer, Heym, Cozzens and Shaw. War novels have continued to appear with some regularity ever since.

The cultural context for these novels is not the home front during the war, but the tensions of American culture during the Cold War, the McCarthy witch-hunts, and the 1950s. In an interview in 1948, Norman Mailer explained that he did not initially regard *The Naked and the Dead* as an anti-war book, but it became one as he responded to the mood of America after he returned home:

> every time I turned on the radio and looked in the newspapers, there was this growing hysteria, this talk of going to war again, and it made me start looking for the trend of what was happening.[1]

An unexpected consequence of this was to diminish the presence of the *specific* causes of war, and to see it as a phenomenon which was caused by man's nature: evil and fallen man's innate propensity for aggression and violence seemed responsible for the woes of mankind. There was an inclination in the early 1940s to regard war as a phenomenon transcending history which could only be understood in psychological and ethical terms. Nazism was regarded by most Americans as an unmitigated evil. (Fascism, on the other hand, was not without its devotees on the right and the liberal left.) But the growing influence of Freud's social thought in the 1940s assisted the inclination to empty the war of its political content. The "thinking classes" by and large seem to have accepted the war as a crusade. To understand the American war experience, it is necessary to understand how little this attitude was shared by the man in the street and by the enlisted men in the armed forces. In the literature of the war only a small minority of char-

acters regard the war with enthusiasm. By the late 1940s the enemy had changed, but the fixation upon the "enemy" remained a helpful way to understand the popular mind.

The clearest expression of the way the war was seen by American writers is the prevalence of stark oppositions between characters who endorse a humane and liberal viewpoint and those who either love war and killing, or whose temperament is repressive, conservative and fascistic. The latter are likely to be in positions of authority in the American military; the former to be junior officers—captains and lieutenants—torn between necessity and humane sentiment, or enlisted men like Ackerman in *The Young Lions* (1948) and Prewitt in *From Here to Eternity* (1951), bursting with individualism and conscience. In Hersey's *The War Lover* (1959) the dichotomy is suggested by the conflict between Boman and Buzz Marrow; in Martin Abzug's *Spearhead* (1946) in the conflict between Hollis and Knupfer; in Heggen's *Mr. Roberts* (1946) between Lieutenant Roberts and Captain Morton; in Alfred Coppell's *Order of Battle* (1969) between Devereux, who reads the *Oxford Book of English Verse,* and Porta, who loves to kill; in *The Naked and the Dead* (1948) between Hearn and Cummings, and Valsen and Croft. James Gould Cozzens reverses the liberal bias of the war novel in *Guard of Honor* (1948), but finds the same structure of polar opposition congenial to his purposes: the symbol of order (Colonel "Judge" Ross) is emphatically opposed to that of political and racial disorder (Lieutenant Edsell). In comparatively few American novels does the Fascist enemy actually turn out to be a cunning, brutal, wily Nazi: Pettinger in Heym's *The Crusaders* (1948) is opposed to Lieutenant Yates; Lieutenant Raeder in Glen Sire's *The Deathmakers* (1960) is opposed to Captain Brandon; and Lieutenant Hardenburg and Sergeant Diestl in Shaw's *The Young Lions* are carefully opposed to the liberal intellectual Michael Whitacre and the New York Jew Noah Ackerman. (The "enemy" first showed his face in *The Young Lions* in an army training camp in the American south: the southern racists, bigots and anti-Semites who made up the majority of Whitacre's and Ackerman's company.) These patterns are insistent; authorial loyalties are involved. Such elaborate dichotomization is less typical of the interwar years, when this patterning appealed mainly to authors of proletarian novels, than of the harsher political climate which followed the war and the opposed categories (East/West, democracy/dictatorship) which characterised Cold War thought. The very structures of the American war novel bear the stamp of the mental climate in which they were written.

There is a paradoxical point here about literary history. The generation of American writers who served in the Great War left an important legacy. Dos Passos's early novels, especially *Three Soldiers* (1921), Cummings's

The Enormous Room (1922) and Hemingway's *A Farewell to Arms* (1929), to say nothing of the minor classics of the 1930s, *Company K* by "William March" (1933) and Humphrey Cobb's *Paths of Glory* (1935), established the war novel as an important contemporary genre. To some extent these books influenced attitudes towards the army and patriotism. It would be hard not to conclude, after a reading of the American fiction of the Great War, that the army was a vicious, repressive and totalitarian microcosm of American society, that war was dehumanizing, and that heroism and patriotism were things which serious people could no longer believe in. (Such attitudes were far more likely to be found among American intellectuals, and the liberal middle-class, from which class the writers were drawn, than elsewhere in American culture.) It is striking, however, that even among the war generation there was little interest in war literature. The great European novels and poems of the First World War seem to have left no trace on American writers. Fitzgerald is in this something of an exception. Shane Leslie introduced him to Scribner's Sons in 1918 as an American prose Rupert Brooke.[2] The comparison is not wholly frivolous: Fitzgerald took the title of *This Side of Paradise* from a Brooke poem. Perhaps because he did not manage to get overseas in 1918, Fitzgerald was one of the few American writers who remained actively interested in war writing. He did a screenplay in 1937 for Erich Maria Remarque's *Three Comrades*. Those who grew up in the interwar years in Europe may have lived with the shadow of the Great War—Christopher Isherwood is an interesting example—but their American contemporaries, the writers of Second World War novels, do not seem to have much familiarity with Remarque, Sassoon, Owen and the others. American isolationism had an important cultural dimension. If anything, American writers seem to have been influenced more by movies about the Great War than by its European literature.[3]

The specific image of the war on the Western Front, whether derived from films or war literature, with its rituals, elaborate patterns and precise structures, remained in most people's minds as *the* shape of war. War meant knowing with some precision that the enemy was in trenches which closely mirrored our own. Like ourselves, they had to live underground, and follow the same daily rituals of stand-to at dawn and dusk. When they attacked, they had to go over the top and pass through nearly identical patterns of barbed wire, and face our machine guns; and the same applied to ourselves. The characteristic flavour of despair in war literature seems to have faded; what survived was a formal pattern of combat, with its own etiquette, vocabulary and mythology.[4]

Despite the overwhelmingly anti-heroic nature of the war literature of the 1920s and 1930s, writers continually felt the need to debunk the fantasies of heroism

which have for so long cast an aura around militarism. Novelists of modern warfare, certainly since Stendhal, have found something decidedly useful in romantic dreams of heroism. The conjunction of dream and reality makes available the traditional forms of irony. There is a long passage in *The Naked and the Dead* in which Wyman, Toglio and Goldstein haul a heavy anti-tank gun through the jungle. One layer of irony is revealed when we learn that the effort has gone for nothing: there never had been any chance of a Japanese counter-attack. Mailer enhances the irony by contrasting the foul-smelling and exhausting work (no other writer on war has so devastatingly caught the depths of physical tiredness) with Wyman's vague dreams of military glory: "He dreamed of himself charging across a field in the face of many machine guns; but in the dream there was no stitch in his side from running too far while bearing too much weight." Journalists, no less than novelists, felt in themselves lingering traces of romantic expectation about going into combat. "This generation", wrote the liberal journalist Ralph Ingersoll,

> has been brought up on the novels and the histories of the last war which told of weeks in the trenches under continuous fire, of 36-hour barrages and 'going over the top,' of mass charges to cut your way through wire while enemy bullets burned around you. Maybe it was like that all the time. . . . Nothing could be more violent than the most violent moments, but these moments were spaced out. Between them there were long spells of waiting, walking, and waiting.[5]

War, in other words, had its boring moments. Harry Brown, writing in *A Walk in the Sun* (1944) of the Italian campaign, said that "the soldier waits for food, for clothing, for a letter, for a battle to begin. And often the food is never served, the clothing is never issued, the letter never arrives and the battle never begins". Even though every war was mostly like this, the fact was soon forgotten. It is almost more important to study the ways war is forgotten than to study the ways it has been remembered.

Memories of the Great War hover above the war literature of 1939-45, through a selective and distorted memory, even to the point of nostalgia. The Great War seemed somehow coherent and *organized* by comparison to the jungle warfare in the Pacific, or the fighting on the deserts of North Africa. Irwin Shaw suggests such a nostalgia in *The Young Lions* when a German Sergeant, Christian Diestl, compares the irregular and fluid fighting in the desert, in a landscape which lacked definition, to the Western Front in the Great War:

> The slaughter was horrible in the trenches, but everything was organized. You got your food regularly, you had a feeling that matters were arranged in some comprehensible order, the dangers came through recognizable channels.

The jungle warfare of the Pacific seemed to American writers particularly terrifying because it lacked clear demarcations and sides. Hence Mailer's description of the initial landing and advance on Anopopei in *The Naked and the Dead*:

> There was no front line for several days at least. Little groups of men filtered through the jungle, fought minor skirmishes with still smaller groups, and then moved on again. Cumulatively there was a motion forward, but each individual unit moved in no particular direction at any given time. They were like a nest of ants wrestling and tugging at a handful of breadcrumbs in a field of grass.

Peter Bowman, in his verse novel *Beach Red,* emphasised the same point:

> In front of you is a fringe of matted vegetation, and the push slows down. There is no precision here, no formation of steadily advancing men. Just an unhealthy mixture of friend and foe stirred vigorously in seething cauldron.

At one point on Guadalcanal Richard Tregaskis heard mortar shells burst in the direction of the Tenaru river front. Someone wondered if they were theirs or ours.

> 'I don't know,' said Col. Gates, taking a puff from his long cigarette holder. 'That's the trouble with this war', he said with a smile. 'You never know.'
>
> 'In the last war we used to know where the enemy was . . .'[6]

Newsreels of the first part of the war suggested a new pattern of rapid movement, the *Blitzkrieg,* and were especially particularly effective in presenting the devastating impact of air power. But the newsreel paled in comparison to the feature film as a medium of propaganda and information.[7] Novelists who served in the war and who generally had to wait until the war ended before they could begin work, found themselves struggling against the Hollywood version of the war. It was so pervasive, and in the eyes of returning veterans, so dishonest, that "the movies" became synonymous with the falsification of war. "Instead of trying to show the distressing complexity and puzzling diffusion of war", wrote James Jones,

> they pulled everything down to the level of good guy against bad guy. Instead of showing the terrifying impersonality of modern war, they invariably pulled it down to one-on-one situation, a man-against-man, like a tennis match. At best they made it like a football game. And modern war was not men against machine. It it was industry against industry. And we had the best machines.[8]

Jones felt that the nature of popular entertainment, with its tidy and reassuring structures, was at the heart of its dishonesty. "If this were a movie", Sergeant Bell mused in *The Thin Red Line* (1962),

> this would be the end of the show, and something would be decided. In a movie or a novel they would dramatise and build to the climax of the attack. When

the attack came in the film or novel, it would decide something. It would have a semblance of meaning and a semblance of an emotion. And immediately after it would be over. The audience would go home and think about the semblance of the meaning and feel the semblance of the emotion. Even if the hero got killed, it would still make sense. Art, Bell decided, creative art—was shit . . .

> Here there was no semblance of meaning. And the emotions were so many and so mixed up that they were indecipherable, could not be untangled. Nothing had been decided, nobody had learned anything. But most important of all, nothing had ended. Even if they had captured this whole ridge nothing would have ended. Because tomorrow, or the day after, or the day after that, they would be called upon to do the same thing again—maybe under even worse circumstances. The concept was so overpowering, so numbing, that it shook Bell. Island after island, hill after hill, beachhead after beachhead, year after year. It staggered him.

The sensitive soldier-novelist might perceive the profound incomprehensibility and disorder of modern warfare, but the demands of art, and of contemporary readers, do not allow the fallacy of imitative form: even though Jones saw the meaninglessness of war, his war novel cannot be without structure or meaning. In a more complex fashion the novelist (no less, it must be said, than the Hollywood film maker) imposes coherence, meaning and structure.

Contempt for Hollywood, for its artificial tidiness, often surfaces in war novels. British films made a substantial impact in the early phase of the war, and gave a measure of the ways in which life was seen to imitate (bad) art. Sailing on an American merchant marine vessel entering a combat zone in the South Pacific, Ira Wolfert complained that the crew were "so damned casual" that "you'd think they were a bunch of limeys in some movie with Leslie Howard".[9] John Gunther, on board a British destroyer in the Mediterranean in July 1943, was mightily impressed by the calm in which the captain responded to unidentified aircraft: ". . . for a few minutes the scene was remarkably like Noel Coward's [1942] movie 'In Which We Serve'".[10] A soldier in Peter Bowman's *Beach Red* overhears Japanese soldiers singing: "What do the Japs think this is—Gilbert and Sullivan?" (There were other ways in which life imitated art: a character in John Horne Burns's *The Gallery* (1948) noted the GIs who "deliberately tried to look like Bill Mauldin cartoons".

War movies provided the war novelist with good examples of hollow, clichéd, insincere speeches, and stagey gestures. In October 1942, John Hersey noted that a Marine captain was showing excessive caution. The soldier's vigilance seemed "just a little exaggerated, like something out of an unconvincing movie".[11] In Joe David Brown's *Kings Go Forth* (1956), Major Blaine shakes his men's hands before a dangerous mission. "'Good killing, men,' he said. Major Blaine had seen too many movies." An American platoon leader in Harry Brown's *A Walk in the Sun* gets "that old Lost Patrol feeling". Memories were still fresh enough during the war to recall John Ford's 1934 film starring Victor McLaglen about an isolated British patrol under Arab attack. Reassuring his men ("We'll get through") only makes the American officer feel like a "damned fool": "This wasn't the movies." When Minetta in *The Naked and the Dead* attempts to fake madness to avoid being returned to his platoon after a minor injury, the movies show him how: "He began to tremble and allowed some spittle to form on his lips. That'll work. He had a picture of a madman he had once seen in a movie who had foamed at the mouth." Michael Whitacre in *The Young Lions* parodies the wartime spy fever on the West Coast:

> Perhaps this aged gardener in his ragged clothes was really a full commander in the Japanese Navy, cleverly awaiting the arrival of the Imperial Fleet outside San Pedro harbor before showing his hand. Michael grinned. The movies, he thought, there is no escape for the modern mind from their onslaught.

Movies powerfully reinforced romantic attitudes to war. Students of literature are apt to exaggerate the impact of anti-war novels and memoirs of the Great War, and ignore the way Hollywood between the wars contributed to the popular associations of war with personal courage, and heroism with patriotism. The isolated anti-war films represent an honourable exception to the general tendency.

The reality of war, and of the US Army, did not encourage romantic fantasies of heroism, but contemporary observers often wrote as though such expectations survived intact. "In the imagination of every soldier who expects to fight", according to Ralph Ingersoll,

> the word 'battle' grows until he expects the real thing to call for continuous heroism, unbelievable fortitude and a superman's skill at arms. He is just a little surprised then, when he finds that so much of a battle is no more strenuous than the maneuvers he's been on . . .[12]

If many die in battle, even more unheroically survive. Dr. Karandash, the tragic Ukrainian intellectual in Godfrey Blunden's *The Time of the Assassins* (1952), records in his notebook that "the truth about war is that it is never quite Homeric; that humanity survives. Though the villages are empty, and many dead are to be counted in the ruins, there is life in the country". "Never quite Homeric": a nice understatement for the war in Russia, and scarcely less appropriate for the war in the Pacific, where nothing survived of chivalric codes of conduct. Few writers have been as systematically devoted to the discrediting of romantic conceptions of war as James Jones. Consider, for example, his description of a soldier under mortar attack in *The Thin Red Line*:

Slowly he stopped weeping and his eyes cleared, but as the other emotions, the sorrow, the shame, the selfhatred seeped out of him under the pressure of self-preservation, the fourth component, terror, seeped in to replace them until he was only a vessel completely filled with cowardice, fear and gutlessness. And that was the way he lay. This was war? There was no superior test of strength here, no superb swordsmanship, no bellowing Viking heroism, no expert marksmanship. This was only numbers. He was being killed for numbers.

This would have been better prose if Jones had not simply named the emotions but tried to show them in the sequence of events, in consciousness itself. Jones's point is that the conditions of modern war do not permit exercises in heroism. The war as a whole never seems to have become an heroic or uplifting cause for American GIs. Popular wisdom decades after the war concludes that it was a Good Thing, that the defeat of Hitler redeems the war as a whole. But the war novels suggest no such conviction. "I just don't know whether our soldiers think much about causes", remarked Major Victor Joppolo in John Hersey's *A Bell for Adano* (1944): "That's one thing that worries me about this war." Liberals like Hersey and Ralph Ingersoll were bothered by a lack of serious commitment both in the army and on the home front (where Ingersoll pointed to "the thousand daily evidences of our lack of determination"). Lieutenant Roberts in Thomas Heggen's novel, who has a long record as a "frustrated anti-fascist", is the only one on board the *USS Reluctant* to be actively concerned about the war: "'I feel left out', he said to Doc. 'I wanted in that war, Doc. I wanted in it like hell'." Doc's reply comes closer to what seems the common view: "I see it as a war of unrelieved necessity—nothing more. Any ideology attaching is only incidental. Not to say accidental." Martin Abzug reverses these attitudes in *Spearhead,* in which a humane and liberal captain regards the war as ". . . nothing more or less than an unpleasant job that has to be done", while his German-born lieutenant, who hates Nazis, is perceived to be a dangerous fanatic. The reversal of attitudes, in which liberals are portrayed as both believing and not believing in the war, adds to the confusion and moral ambiguity of the war as portrayed in war novels. Warfare in the desert or jungle heightened uncertainty over where the enemy was. The failure to believe in the war as a cause left a blankness at the heart of the American involvement in the war, and, of course, in war novels.

In the missing place of public values and purpose, which Archibald MacLeish and the Office of Facts and Figures gamely tried to instil in the nation, James Jones's soldiers fought only for personal respect, for each other, and for survival. Fife, so often the voice of Jones's thoughts in *The Thin Red Line,*

> could not believe he was fighting this war for God. And he did not believe he was fighting it for freedom,

or democracy, or the dignity of the human race. When he analyzed it . . . he could find only one reason why he was here, and that was because he would be ashamed for people to think he was a coward, embarrassed to be put in jail.

In *Whistle* (1978), the third volume of Jones's war trilogy, Private Landers is asked to give a talk on the soldier's responsibilities to draftees at this hometown Elks Club:

> the soldier's first responsibility is to stay alive . . . I can't in honesty tell you that you will be fighting for freedom, and God, and your country—as all these other gentlemen have told you. In combat you don't think about any of that. But I can assure you that you will be fighting for your life. I think that's a good thing to remember. I think that's a good thing to fight for.

"Responsibility", during the war, was a code-word used in a vociferous attack on the politics of American intellectuals and writers. Archibald MacLeish's polemic in 1940, *The Irresponsibles,* and Van Wyck Brooks's lectures on contemporary letters delivered at Columbia University in 1940 and 1941, suggests the flavour of the attack on intellectuals, modernism, and avant-garde cultural attitudes. Many old scores were being settled.[13] Private Landers in *Whistle* was an "irresponsible" in MacLeish's phrase, who remained quite indifferent to the ideals and "inherited culture of the West". None of the draftees came over to thank Landers for his speech. The tough and realistic 1st/Sergeant Mart Winch, in an impulsive address at an outdoor political rally in San Francisco, shows that he, too, is an "irresponsible": ". . . I'm more like a Jap first sergeant or a German first sergeant than I am like these civilian sons of bitches."

James Gould Cozzens, who would certainly have been among the "responsibles", assumes in *Guard of Honor* that the ideals and high principles of the army were little more than a necessary fiction, useful to preserve the outward seemliness of military affairs, but which had nothing to do with people's behaviour and beliefs. Cozzens gives a further conclusion to "Judge" Ross: the war aims of the average man "was to get out as soon as possible and go home":

> Though the level of intelligence in the average man might be justly considered low, in very few of them would it be so low that they accepted notions that they fought, an embattled band of brothers, for noble 'principles'. They would howl at the idea; just as, in general, they despised and detested all their officers; hated the rules and regulations and disobeyed as many as they could; and from morning to night never stopped cursing the Army, scheming to get out of it, and hotly bitching about the slightest inconvenience, let alone hardship.

Cozzens's nihilism is even bleaker than Joseph Heller's. The change of sensibility between *Guard of Honor* and *Catch-22* is clearest in Heller's open recognition of the meaninglessness of the "official" purposes of the Air Force and the war. For Cozzens that kind of truth is best repressed in the name of military discipline, and of the public values of duty, honour and country, no matter how little one may privately believe in them. The commanding officer at an Air Force base may have been a drunk and a suicide, but a guard of honour, and all that it implies, is provided for the funeral. It is a matter of taste which of these nihilisms is preferred.

The official mind in the Pentagon recognized that morale in the armed forces was not well. The Assistant Secretary for Air noted that there was "very little idealism" in the armed forces. The general attitude towards the war was to regard it "as a job to be done and there is not much willingness to discuss what we are fighting for". John Morton Blum has pointed out that in 1942 only one American in ten could name even one provision of the Atlantic Charter, and a majority had no "clear idea what the war is all about". By 1945 only a minority remained openly puzzled by the war. America had not been bombed, except at Pearl Harbor, nor had it experienced invasion or military occupation. As Blum interestingly notes, alone among the great powers America was "fighting this war on imagination alone".[14] At certain deeper levels of national life, the war remained remote and irrelevant. War novelists showed a good understanding of the limits to the American participation in the war. Few Americans, and few novelists, exercised themselves over the question of war aims. It was simply there, and needed no further explanation. An unusual exception is Stefan Heym's *The Crusaders.* (Heym's work is also discussed in Chapter 3.) As much a political thriller as a war novel, Heym dramatizes the issue of war aims through conflicting attitudes towards a propaganda leaflet. Captain Yates believes the only credible appeal to German soldiers lay in ". . . corned beef hash, Nescafé and the beauties of the Geneva Convention". His chief interrogator of POWs, the German-born Private Bing, appreciated the need to appeal to higher principles and ideals. Bing's leaflet works, but his struggle to define American ideals, even on so limited a scale, reveals a cynicism and naïveté which Heym takes to be characteristically American. Captain Yates, with frequent prodding from Private Bing, comes to suspect that his superior officer, Major Willoughby, is actively pursuing his private financial advantage in the reconstruction of a steel cartel after the war. Willoughby's deal with the von Rentelen steel interests, which had been actively mobilized in support of the Nazi war effort, typified the cynical and corrupt capacity of the American military administration to line its own pockets at the expense of the postwar hopes of the German people. Here is another case in which the powers of selective forgetting need correction. The common assumption takes the victorious Yanks to have been generous, perhaps a little innocently so, but motivated by idealistic and humanitarian concerns. But American war novels suggest, in Malcolm Cowley's phrase, that the military administrations were "irresponsible and corrupt".[15] Hersey's *A Bell for Adano*, John Horne Burns's *The Gallery*, and Heym's novel contradict some of the basic assumptions of American character and motivation. There are in all three novels "good" characters moved by decency and integrity; but the overwhelming impression is of cynicism and self-seeking. The symbolic resolution of the issue in *The Crusaders*, in which the von Rentelen family estate was turned over to the survivors of the Paula concentration camp is not persuasive. But Heym's novel, written by a German antifascist emigrant who attended the University of Chicago and served in the psychological warfare branch of the US Army (and subsequently returned to live in East Germany), assumes that the enemy is not only on the other side, but that evil exists within the American Army and within American values.

This was not the self-image which most Americans had of themselves, or why they were in the war. John Hersey asked a group of young Marines on Guadalcanal in October 1942 why they were fighting. After a long, uneasy pause, one Marine remarked, "'Jesus, what I'd give for a piece of blueberry pie.'" Another preferred mince pies, a third apple: pie was a potent symbol of home. Other men had other symbols, but the meaning was clear. They were fighting "to get the goddam thing over and get home": "Home is where the good things are—the generosity, the good pay, the comforts, the democracy, the pie."[16] Peter Bowman assembles a different catalogue with a similar intention:

> Here's what really matters to him: a paved street lined
> with familiar trees and a grassy lawn and a car
> and a girl and a hamburger joint and a crowd
> coming out of a movie and a hot bath and
> a gay necktie and the labor of a trolley going
> uphill and a glossy pond and peanuts behind third
> base.
>
> (Beach, Red)

Normality defined itself in comfortable ways. The one class of characters in American war novels to be uncomfortable with apple pie and hamburger joints as symbols of American values were the intellectuals and liberals. There is a surprisingly large number of them: Milton Norton in *Battle Cry* (1953), Tyler Williams in *The Steel Cocoon* (1958), Jim Edsell in *Guard of Honor*, Terence Reardon in *Wolf Pack* (1960), Doug Roberts in *Mr. Roberts*, Hollis in *Spearhead*, Michael Whitacre and Noah Ackerman in *The Young Lions*, and Robert Hearn in *The Naked and the Dead*. Very few survive the war with their liberalism intact. Norton, Roberts, Ackerman and Hearn die in the war; many of the others lose their liberalism in collision with reality; Edsell, the radical in Cozzens's novel, is shown to be a liar and a loud-mouthed troublemaker. One might write the history of post-war liberalism through their fates.

Mailer's Lieutenant Hearn is the most fully-realized portrayal of a liberal in the American war novel, and will repay closer attention. Hearn does not simply embody a series of abstract propositions or political opinions. His liberalism is uneasy, and is without the destructive confidence of Lieutenant Edsell in *Guard of Honor*. Mailer roots Hearn's politics in his childhood rebellion against the philistine prosperity of his father. Marked by "guilt of birth", Hearn's rebellion extends to the Army, and to the privileges of the officer class. He has earned his commission the hard way, through Officer Candidate's School; but, as Mailer indicates, it has not been easy for Hearn to sustain his anger at the injustices of society, especially when he was himself the direct beneficiary of injustice. A partial explanation of Hearn's outburst at Lt. Col. Conn's "labial interpretation of history" (the near-universal belief among Republicans and Southerners that Roosevelt had a black mistress. In fact, she was white.) was his fear that he did not really care if such ignorant racism was openly displayed in Headquarters Company, or whether rations were unfairly distributed between officers and men. Mailer emphasizes the conflict between Hearn's objective interests (a larger meat ration, avoiding conflict with a superior officer) and his sentimental inclinations. When he is asked to leave the John Reed Society at Harvard, Hearn is reminded that "You're independent of economic considerations, and so you're without fear, without proper understanding." This emphasis on the economic paradoxes of middle-class liberalism is unsubtle; it is also necessary for the understanding of the basically frail and, in Mailer's view, undependable nature of liberalism itself. It is a nice touch on Mailer's part that those with the requisite "economic considerations" such as Martinez, Gallagher and Valsen were hardly liberals: there is nothing like Marxist orthodoxy in Mailer's criticism of liberalism.

Hearn's conversations with General Cummings are rightly felt to contain the heart of the book's politics. Cummings sees in Hearn a proper adversary and an educated man; he alone in Headquarters Company is capable of understanding the political and philosophical implications of the general's thought. Their relationship is objectively unequal, and something central to Cummings's personality is revealed in the evident pleasure he takes in baiting Hearn, and then slapping him down. The strong undercurrents of sexual tension between Cummings and Hearn have often been noted. Cummings would like to see the aloof, Harvard-educated liberal humiliated, to see him "afraid, filled with shame if only for an instant". His relationship to Hearn is a long, aggressive prelude to buggery. Hearn on the other hand knew, while attacking Lt. Col. Conn, that Cummings would intervene to save him. The general is more a father-figure, someone against whom he can safely rebel, than a real object of fear. There is another aspect of Cummings which attracts Hearn: he is a man who exercises power, whose will, at its deepest level, seeks the domination of others. Cummings's Faustian urge for power touches upon a similar impulse within Hearn; the "peculiar magnetism" of power attracts him, and dissolves the clear political difference between the two men:

> There were times when the demarcation between their minds was blurred for him. . . . Divorced of all the environmental trappings, all the confusing and misleading attitudes he had absorbed, he was basically like Cummings. . . . They were both the same, and it had produced first the intimacy, the attraction they had felt toward each other, and then the hatred.

When Hearn is sent off on a dangerous patrol by Cummings, he discovers that the experience of leading men was deeply satisfying. He recognizes in himself that he was, in the desire to lead, "just another Croft" (the sergeant who was the previous leader of the Intelligence and Reconaissance platoon). The recognition that he was like Cummings and Croft humanizes Hearn, saves him from liberal priggishness. But it does not save him from sentimentality, a far more serious failing in Mailer's eyes. Hearn struggles to reconcile his liberal instinct to be a nice guy (qualified by the "casual truth" which Hearn grants that he cared for others only in the abstract) with the objective reality (again!) that he must dominate his new platoon, and its highly competent and vicious sergeant, or lose control of the patrol altogether. The separation of Hearn and Cummings deprives *The Naked and the Dead* of some of its political energy. Croft is too instictive and inarticulate to engage in a dialogue with Hearn; all he can do is kill him. Hearn was isolated in Headquarters Company, and even more so on the patrol. His overtures are rebuffed by the men, contemptuous of officers trying to buddie up with them, and he is decieved by Croft. The odds have been stacked against Hearn, and his sentimental liberalism, but not with contempt. The political alternatives present elsewhere in Mailer's book leave room mainly for qualified pessimism. Cummings's vision of a totalitarian future ". . . the only morality of the future is a power morality . . .") is not answered by liberalism: for reasons of temperament and *force majeure,* Hearn must "crawfish" before authority. Ironically, it is the anonymous American soldiers on Anopopei who successfully resist Cummings's will. When the difficult wheeling manoeuvre to face the Toyaku line was completed, the offensive stalled. The soldiers settled down in their positions, attended to improving their creature comforts; inertia, not political principle, resisting the Faustian will:

> . . . apparently without cause [the general thought], or at least through causes too intangible for him to discover, he had lost his sensitive control. No matter how he molded them now the men always collapsed into a sodden resistent mass like dish-rags, too soft, too wet to hold any shape which might be given them.

The central drama of General Cummings's existence was the sheer exertion of power, the struggle of the will against the mass. His temporary defeat before the Toyaku line has a biological basis: however imperiously the will asserts itself, there is always that other, "intangible" limitation in man's nature which constrains his reach. As much as Hearn's liberalism was an act of will, qualified by objective interests and his "guilt of birth", Cummings's Faustian vision of a world responsive to the will of an individual arrives at its own limits. Hearn and Cummings represent opposite positions politically, but come to resemble each other in ways by now characteristic of the American novel of the war. Opposites lose their distinctness; clarity of definition fades; the grey fog of history looks more and more impenetrable.

In *Battle Cry* a trouble-maker is, after much provocation, beaten up by L.Q., Danny, Ski, Norton and the rest of the guys—but he refuses to rat on them to the drill instructor. Danny would rather flunk his radio test than leave his pals behind: "Just that you make a buddy—and, well, I think it's more important we stick together than we make it alone." Buddies look after each other when they fall ill, and when they are betrayed by women: ". . . a smile and the voice of a buddy meant something that none but us could understand". The feeling that soldiers learn to have for each other is a glowing, precious thing which flies in the face of the demoralized and cynical routine of army life. The platoon or company, the crew of a bomber or a submarine, are natural communities, dependent upon each other for survival. If the characteristic malaise of twentieth-century life is anomie and alienation, it is no wonder that, in J. Glenn Gray's phrase, the feeling soldiers have of caring and depending upon each other constitutes an important part of the "enduring appeal" of battle.[17]

"If one died," writes Alfred Coppel in *Order of Battle,* "the chances were that all would die, and so each became very precious to the others. Together they were more than the sum of their individualities. They were a team, a unit. Only war could do that to a group of men." For those who did not experience combat, the feeling of mutual dependence and solidarity was rare and to be savoured for its uniqueness. "The fresh breeze blew on the faces of the crew", writes Heggen of the *USS Reluctant* after liberty on Elysium:

> They felt good in the same way . . . that any group with the bright bond of communal achievement feels good. The crew was a unit at last, and the common artery of participation ran through and bound together such distant and diverse characters as Costello and Wiley and Ringgold and Schlemmer. They stood along the rail in little groups; but those were accidental groups with interchangeable membership, and not the tight, jealous cliques of old.

The feeling of mutual dependence is seen with greatest clarity when danger threatens. Peter Bowman writes in *Beach Red*:

> You walked through the jungle and Lindstrom and
> Egan and Whitney were in front of you and you were
> behind them, and between you there was connecting tissue.
>   It was not because of any similarity you may have
>   had in thought or behaviour or habit or belief, but
>   because you had groped for it and found it and
>   it had drawn you close. One of you fell and another
> picked him up and carried him in the simple compulsion
>   of linked survival, and that is the parallel
> transcending tribe and race in the utter need of existence.

William M. Hardy in *Wolf Pack,* a popular adventure novel about submarine warfare in the Pacific, assumes that for the crew survival was a collective instinct: "The boat must survive, and, if it did, then every man aboard had the right to expect that he would survive also." The crew of a B-17 had an identical sense of mutual dependence. "All ten of us were linked to the ship," writes John Hersey in *The War Lover,* "and to each other by those life-keeping hose lines, and we were like an unborn litter of young in the belly of our common mother. Never before had I—nor since have I—had such a feeling of being part of a brood in a plane." The "common artery of participation" (Heggen), "connecting tissue" (Bowman), "instinct" (Hardy), and the feeling of being in the belly of "our common mother" (Hersey), suggest a solidarity which transcends other kinds of shared purpose, and which is firmly rooted in a naturalistic perspective.

Mailer suggests the naturalistic lineage of *The Naked and the Dead* in similes emphasising the insignificance of human effort:

> . . . they ground the guns forward blindly, a line of ants dragging their burden back to their hole.

> They had the isolation, the insignificance of insects traversing an endless beach.

> Their minds scurried about inside their bodies like rodents in a maze . . .

Mailer was more deeply influenced by naturalism than any of the other writers of the war; at a certain fundamental level naturalism pervaded the common culture. Mailer found in the biological pessimism of Jack London political overtones which made sense in 1946-7; others may have seen in the example of the Joad family in Steinbeck's *The Grapes of Wrath* (1939) a more optimistic way of understanding the communal instinct.

Where the American novels of the Great War powerfully asserted the rights of the individual against the state, embodied in the army, and against the threatening claims of society (and in this were very *American*), by the 1940s Romantic individualism did not make sense on Anopopei or elsewhere. The gesture of a Frederic Henry, declaring a "separate peace" between himself and history, is not possible in the conditions of the Second World War. Maggio, Prewitt's friend in *From Here to Eternity* (1951), declared his own separate peace in the war between himself and the army—and received a dishonourable discharge. At one point in Jones's *The Thin Red Line,* Fife and Storm analyse the prospects for evacuation:

> It was easy to see, when you looked at it from one point of view, that all prisoners were not locked up behind bars in a stone quadrangle. Your government could just as easily imprison you on, say, a jungled island in the South Seas until you had done to its satisfaction what your government had sent you there to do. And when one considered it—as all the wounded had—this matter of evacuation might well be actually and in fact a life and death matter.

There was no convenient Switzerland for Americans fighting in the Pacific, nor the chance to play snooker with Count Greffi before escaping by rowboat at midnight. Hemingway in *For Whom the Bell Tolls* suggests a more complex understanding of the conflict of loyalties. Robert Jordan, unlike soldiers in most American war novels, had a cause to fight for: ". . . you fought that summer and that autumn [1936] for all the poor in the world, against all tyranny, for all the things that you believed and for the new world you had been educated into".[18] The "things" he believes in, as the war goes on, become meaningless; his faith in "the new world" does not remain innocent or even hopeful. (Jordan has seen too much at Gaylord's Hotel, seen too many lies and too much deception; he has even come to enjoy the machinery of deceit for its own sake.) Yet the cause, the Republic and the Spanish people, is strong enough to sustain his loyalty. However drastically the cause has been corrupted, defeating Fascism is important enough for Jordan to accept his own death. His loyalty is to an idea, a metaphysical hope, for which he is willing to sacrifice himself and everyone in El Sordo's and Pablo's band. Romantic gestures and political commitments like Robert Jordan's have little place in the mechanized and collective war in American novels.

The fate of Robert E. Lee Prewitt, a miner's son from Harlan County, Kentucky, hero of James Jones's *From Here to Eternity,* is a case in point. Prewitt enlisted in the army to escape the coalmines. (Harlan County was the scene of a desperate conflict in the early 1930s between miners and coal operators: the name was synonymous on the American left for repression and violence against workers.) He thinks of himself as a thirty-year-man who loves the army, and what he believes it stands for, with passionate conviction. He has a lonely, courageous integrity, a belief in ethical imperatives and the honourableness of institutions, which older and wiser heads among the noncoms try to bring down to earth. One old soldier tells him that a man can no longer do what he wants to do:

> 'Maybe back in the old days, back in the time of the pioneers, a man could do what he wanted to do, in peace. But he had the woods then, he could go off in the woods and live alone. He could live well off the woods. And if they followed him there for this or that, he could just move on. There was always more woods on up ahead. But a man cant do that now. He's got to play ball with them.'

Prewitt is an heir of the frontiersman and pioneer, with the integrity of someone for whom "words meant what they said".[19] He believes in the the letter of Army Regulations, and hopes that by avoiding any infringement in the law, he cannot be impelled to violate his own code of integrity:

> '. . . I don't think they got the right to order me what to do outside of duty hours.'

> 'It aint a question of right or wrong [replied Chief Choate], its a question of fack. But there is awys been a question if there is any outside duty hours for a soljer, whether the *soljer* has the right to be a man.'

Prewitt would like, in some vaguely-understood way, to change the world. He seems a "Kid Galahad" to his friend Angelo Maggio. The company commander wants Prewitt to box in the regimental tournament. Prewitt, who has killed a man in the ring, does not want to box again. The choice confronting him is stark enough: he can either go out for the boxing team, or else refuse and receive "The Treatment", a systematic and brutal Army coercion, ending as he saw with "company punishment for inefficiency plus extra duty plus restrictions plus, eventually, the Stockade". In a rueful moment of introspection Prewitt grants that he had suffered "from an overdeveloped sense of justice". Pride, even more than a belief in justice, has shaped Prewitt's character: "I can take everything they can all of them hand out, and come back for more . . ."

What sustains Prewitt through his ordeal is the comradeship of men he respects: Maggio, Jack Molloy, and, from a distance, 1st/Sgt. Warden. Each in a different way breaks through the shell of self-protective pride which Prewitt has erected about himself, and touches him as a man. In Jones's world such allegiances form isolated moments in a military system dominated by fear and violence. Brigadier Slater develops this theme in a discussion with Captain Holmes. In the past, he argues, the fear of authority was only the negative part of a moral code emphasising Honour, Patriotism and Ser-

vice. Now the world has changed, the positive code has been destroyed by "the machine": "In the Civil War they could still believe they fought for 'Honor.' Not any more. In the Civil War the machine won its first inevitable major victory over the individual. 'Honor' died." Prewitt, like Guy Crouchback in Waugh's *Men at Arms* (1952), felt the "sickening suspicion . . . that he was engaged in a war in which courage and a just cause were quite irrelevant to the issue."

After hearing a song ("The Truckdriver's Blues") Prewitt lapses into reverie on the human condition:

> he saw himself and Chief Choate, and Pop Karelson, and Clark, and Anderson, and Warden, each struggling with a different medium, each man's path running by its own secret route from the same source to the same inevitable end. And each man knowing as the long line moved as skirmishers through the night woodsey jungle down the hill that all the others were there with him, each hearing the faint rustlings and straining to communicate, each wanting to reach out and share, each wanting to be known, but each unable, as Clark's whining nasal was unable, to make it known that he was there, and so each forced to face alone whatever it was up ahead, in the unmapped alien enemy's land, in the darkness.

The whole of Jones is in this passage. Men must live their lives in an inner isolation. While hoping to make contact with other men, they must face the prospect that their efforts will fail. At one moment in *From Here to Eternity,* when Prewitt plays taps at Schofield barracks, there is a revelation of "sympathy and understanding":

> The notes rose high in the air and hung above the quadrangle. They vibrated there, caressingly, filled with an infinite sadness, an endless patience, a pointless pride, the requiem and epitaph of the common soldier, who smelled like a common soldier, as a woman once had told him. They hovered like halos over the heads of the sleeping men in the darkened barracks, turning all grossness to the beauty that is the beauty of sympathy and understanding. Here we are, they said, you made us, now see us, dont close your eyes and shudder at it; this beauty, and this sorrow, of things as they are. This is the true song, the song of the ruck, not of battle heroes.

As the notes reverberate across the quadrangle, men come to the porches "to listen in the darkness, feeling the sudden choking kinship bred of fear that supersedes all personal tastes":

> They stood in the darkness of the porches, listening, feeling suddenly very near the man beside them, who also was a soldier, who also must die. Then as silent as they had come, they filed back inside with lowered eyes, suddenly ashamed of their own emotion, and of seeing a man's naked soul.

A few such beautiful moments in *From Here to Eternity* intimate the yearning for community, and its frustration. The stark choice before Prewitt, whether to box or go to the Stockade, is no longer available when, in Jones's *The Thin Red Line,* the company lands on Guadalcanal late in 1942. Corporal Fife experiences ". . . a terror both of unimportance, his unimportance, and of power-lessness: his powerlessness. He had no control or sayso in any of it". Sergeant Bell comes to the same realisa-tion. "Free individuals?" he wonders:

> Ha! Somewhere between the time the first Marines had landed here and this battle now today, American war-fare had changed from individualist warfare to collec-tivist. . . . But free individuals? What a fucking myth? *Numbers* of free individuals, maybe; *collections* of free individuals.

Confronted by the prospect of their own death, Jones shows the soldiers appreciatively agreeing with S/Sgt. Skinny Culn, the company's folk philosopher: "What-ever they say, I'm not a cog in a machine." Jones's point, and the naturalistic perspective, contradicts this hopefulness. The more reflective men, like Fife and Bell, grasp the "total isolation and helplessness" of their situation. Their nightmares are of total entrapment. The autonomous individual of Western humanist cul-tures reaches its nadir in Jones's *The Thin Red Line.* This kind of exhausting battle turns men into unfeeling, unthinking automatons. The soldiers become indifferent to their tiredness, and this itself was an essential tool for survival:

> Exhaustion, hunger, thirst, dirt, the fatigue of perpetual fear, weakness from lack of water, bruises, danger had all taken their toll of him until somewhere within the last few minutes—Bell did not know exactly when—he had ceased to feel human.

Even fear was dulled by this emotional apathy. Bell no longer cared about anything. But Jones emphasises that this did not impair Bell's ability to function as a soldier. There is, as Jones sees it, a biological basis to this emo-tional closure:

> Their systems pumped full of adrenaline to constrict the peripheral blood vessels, elevate the blood pressure, make the heart beat more rapidly, and aid coagulation, they were about as near to automatons without courage or cowardice as flesh and blood can get. Numbly, they did the necessary.[20]

(Orwell's splendid 1940 polemic, "Inside the Whale", concludes with the advice that one must "Give yourself over to the world-process, stop fighting against it or pretending that you control it; simply accept it, endure it, record it." Other contemporary sources might be cited to similar effect: the war, whether for civilians or soldiers, was too immense an experience to be endured with anything other than the wise passivity of quietism.[21]) During combat, sympathy and concern for others narrowed: ". . . while B's middle platoon shot and were shot, fought and sobbed thirty yards away be-

yond the ledge, Gaff's group talked". (Auden in "Musée des Beaux Arts", written in December 1938, has made this point in a different context.) Combat numbness could, with experience, be recognised and even antici-pated. Private Doll welcomes the return of numbness: "It left his mind clear, and cool, suffused with a grin-ning bloodthirstiness. It spread all through him, making a solid impenetrable layer between himself and the choking fear which would not allow him to swallow as he hugged the ground." After being relieved, the "uni-versal numbness" took two or three days to go away. This kind of collective experience brought the company together; at the same time the personnel of the company changed. Some of the younger officers had been killed, the original noncoms of C-for-Charlie were dead; pro-motions and the arrival of replacements changed the old company pecking order. Fife was promoted to sergeant, Bell received a battlefield commission. "It was a totally different organisation, with a different feel altogether now." The inevitable tragedy of change was taking place.

Despite the many alterations in C-for-Charlie, the *idea* of the company remained fixed in the minds of those who, in *Whistle,* have been sent to convalesce in Army hospitals in America. Their names have changed (1st Sgt. Welsh is now Mart Winch, Witt is Bobby Prell, Mess/Sgt. Storm is now John Strange) but their group loyalty is still intense. It is the strongest thing they have left. Landers and Winch are the only ones to understand that they are alone with themselves, and their debilitat-ing wounds; they must learn to live with their isolation. Prell, whose legs had virtually been smashed by a Japa-nese machine-gun, had no other life or identity to turn to. "Without the old company, Prell did not really feel he belonged anywhere." They each fail to make contact with their old civilian selves. Strange's wife has fallen in love with another man; Landers cannot get along with his family; Winch feels nothing but contempt for his unfaithful wife. They are together in a hospital in Luxor (i.e., Memphis), Tennessee, and form a closely knit group:

> 'It's not so much that we think a lot of Prell. It's like we were investors. And each of us invested his tiny bit of capital in all the others. When we lose one of us, we all lose a little of our capital. And we none of us really had that much to invest, you see.'
>
> '"Do not ask for whom the bell tolls,"' Curran quoted.
>
> 'John Donne, sure,' Landers grinned wolfishly. 'But that's shit. And that's what it is with us. That's ab-stract. And it's poetry. That's all of humanity. We're not all of humanity. And we don't give a shit about all of humanity. We probably don't give much of a shit about each other, really. It's just that that's all the capi-tal we have.'

The allusion to Donne enables the real point of the comparison to surface: Jones is thinking of Heming-way's use of the passage from Donne as epigraph (an title) of *For Whom the Bell Tolls*. Jones opposes the personal ethic of Robert Jordan with a tragic, intensely-felt group loyalty. As news reaches them of changes in the company, each reacts differently. Sergeant Winch is a supreme realist who knows that no matter how important he once was in the company, he now must be forgotten. He has no lingering hopes of reconstructing the past. Strange regards the news from the South Pacific as a calamity. He had a secret hope ". . . that some day when the war was over they would all of them get together again somewhere". In the middle of a drunken party, Prell has an apparition. The members of his old platoon appear before him, like the sequence in Lewis Milestone's 1930 film adaptation of Remarque's *All Quiet on the Western Front*: "Slowly, each hollow-eyed face turned back to smile wistfully, sadly, before it moved on and faded."

Each in turn were inevitably drawn into their own private lives. Prell, the rebel and individualist, is awarded the Medal of Honor and tours the country selling war bonds. This is an unexpected fate for Prewitt-Witt-Prell, and a sad one. Strange is assigned to a new company, but feels no loyalty to anyone about him. Despite his physical decline, Winch is assigned to a new posting. His attempts to help Prell and Landers are rebuffed and misunderstood. His emotional decline ends in collapse and insanity. Landers cannot face life in the army or outside it, and kills himself in an accident with a car. On his way back to combat in Europe, Strange, like Jack London's Martin Eden, commits suicide by jumping off his ship. *Whistle* portrays the disintegration of the collective loyalties which held these men together. Their solidarity has faded, but there is nothing to put in its place. Strange now suffers ". . . from feeling naked and alone and orphaned with a severity he'd never experienced before". At the heart of their tragedy, as Jones sees it, is the inevitable disintegration of the feelings which these men had for each other.

As group solidarity takes on a new meaning in war novels, the perceived role of individual soldiers diminished. It was part of the accepted wisdom, in Jones's words, that an infantryman "was about as note-worthy and important as a single mosquito in an airplane-launched DDT spray campaign . . .".[22] Guerilla warfare on Leyte in the Philippines was described by Ira Wolfert in similar terms: "We are a tick in their [the Japanese] hide. All the building we do, all the work . . . is just to build ourselves up to a tick in their hide. Then the minute they feel the itch of us, they reach with their two fingers and squash."[23] The scale of war intimidated ordinary soldiers, and produced a cynicism well-expressed by Red Valsen in *The Naked and the Dead*: "No one's gonna ask you what to do. . . . They just send you out to get your ass blown off. . . . Don't kid yourself . . . a man's no more important than a goddam cow." This is a theme preoccupying General Cummings, who notes in his journals:

> in battle, men are closer to machines than humans. . . . We are not so discrete from the machine any longer. . . . A machine is worth so many men; the Navy has judged it even more finely than we.

The tendency of wartime journalism, and the Hollywood war movie, was to emphasise the individual's role in the war, and to stress that GIs were ordinary Americans with values recognisably emerging from American culture. Journalists tried to humanise the face of war.[24] Soldiers in their reports were not mosquitoes or ticks caught up in an experience that defied understanding: they were hometown boys, athletes with sweethearts, whose image of home was a compound of soda shops, tinkering with the jalopy, and blueberry pie. In the first part of the war—through 1943—novelists were competing for a contemporary audience with journalists, and it is true that some of the interest of the early war novels is more documentary and journalistic than anything else. The frequent use of details from journalism in this chapter, side by side with the fiction, has tried to emphasise their affinity. Some of the finest prose of the war is to be found in the wartime journalism of Pyle, Gunther, Tregaskis and Hersey.

It is hard not to feel that the American novel of the Second World War has passed into an almost total neglect. Mailer is still read with attentiveness, but Jones, so powerful a presence in the 1950s, scarcely exists for students of the contemporary novel; and there are few others. Two writers of undoubted promise died young (Thomas Heggen and John Horne Burns), others have become, or more precisely remained, hacks. It is perhaps too easy to exaggerate the importance of academic opinion in the current neglect of the war novel. But the shift in critical enthusiasm away from realism has helped to relegate the war novel to its present cul-de-sac. Having lost its topical interest, and belonging in literary technique to an unselfconscious realism, one might as well be exploring the popular fiction of the civil war for all the currency this literature possesses today. And yet many of these books are interesting, and some are capable of gripping a reader. A few can shock and move. With the exception of Leon Uris, no war novelist filled me with contempt. Even *Battle Cry,* with its cult of the Marine Corps, and comic thinness of characterisation, has its moments of vivid interest. Uris's description of the pursuit of the Japanese through the Tarawa atoll is, perhaps, the finest thing he has ever written.

There is a claim, however, which this literature taken as a whole makes on us. The war killed so many millions of people that the sheer numbers mean nothing, cannot be held in the mind no matter how easily they roll off the tongue. New terms such as "genocide" and "holocaust" have entered our vocabulary, but the reality of individual death, to say nothing of forty million dead, leaks out of western culture. Philippe Ariès has argued that death has been progressively alienated from our lives. People die in hospital, or nursing home, and not with their families; unlike any earlier period in history, it is possible in our society to grow into middle age and beyond without seeing a dead person or having any close relatives die. Overt displays of mourning are likely to make others uncomfortable. Ariès suggests that there is a powerful tendency in western culture towards "the almost total suppression of everything reminding us of death".[25] Ariès does not analyse popular entertainment, however. If he had done so, a puzzling contradiction would have emerged. As we very well know, the representation of death, along with violence and crime, is overwhelmingly present, but the physical reality of death is studiously avoided. The old Hollywood conventions apply with virtually unabated strength. Physical wounds are generally tasteful and people do not make an excessive fuss over their pain. No screaming or tears, and for the most part no gore or smashed limbs.

War writing is not without its own version of these conventions, as may be seen in Richard Tregaskis's account of the aftermath of the battle of Tenaru in *Guadalcanal Diary.* "I watched our men standing in a shooting-gallery line, thumping bullets into the piles of Jap carcasses. The edge of the water grew brown and muddy. Some said the blood of the Jap carcasses was staining the ocean."[26] The "Jap" was a wily and dangerous opponent. Among the dead there may have been wounded men, or those only pretending to be dead. American soldiers had died in the Pacific when Japanese suicidally rose to stab or shoot one last enemy. It was a symbol of the mental and cultural gap separating the adversaries. So the dead must be re-butchered. The erect posture of the soldiers suggests to Tregaskis a shooting-gallery, with its kewpie-doll prizes and fairground atmosphere. The dead have been transformed into "carcasses", the Japanese into "Japs", re-butchery into a shooting-gallery: each transformation subtly alters the human meaning of the scene. Tregaskis indicates that a later count of the dead revealed 871 Japanese corpses, enough for their blood to turn the edges of the river "brown and muddy". The scale of human death is transforming nature, although Tregaskis withdraws from such a conclusion. It was not he who saw the ocean stained by Japanese blood, but unnamed others.

The battle of Tenaru was over, and the American perimeter around Henderson Field on Guadalcanal was secured. A day later Tregaskis revisited the scene. By then the bodies on the spit were "puffed and glossy, like shiny sausages"; one soldier's chest had expanded and been peeled back "like the leaf of an artichoke"; another, wearing tortoise-shell glasses, lay on his back "with his chest a mass of ground meat". The truth about violent death is forced upon us, but domesticated in simile. Tregaskis's description of the Tenaru battlefield is easily among the most powerful passages in *Guadalcanal Diary.* Only Norman Mailer's description of Japanese dead on Anopopei in *The Naked and the Dead* compares with it in impact. Mailer's prose is as heavily figurative as Tregaskis's, and in part serves a similar function. The head of the driver of a Japanese halftrack, crushed, lay sodden as if "it were a beanbag". Another corpse lay with its intestines bulging out "like the congested petals of a sea flower"; a body has swollen "like a doll whose stuffing had broken forth". Japanese entrenchments, heavily bombed by the Americans, had partly caved in "like a sand hole on the beach after the children have deserted it and people tread over its edges". Beanbags, flowers, dolls, children playing on the beach: the over-whelming incongruity of the comparisons is, even more than in Tregaskis, calculated and daring. Mailer allows the resonances of violent death to mingle with a whole series of emotions introduced through simile and metaphor which pertain to peace, life, normality. He has attempted to go beyond this in re-humanising the "carcasses": the men in Sergeant Croft's platoon see Japanese dead who "lay very far from repose, their bodies frozen in the midst of an intense contortion"; another's "hands in their death throe had encircled the wound. He looked as if he were calling attention to it". The gestures remain, after death, as reminders of life unwillingly lost. When seen in narrative context (the platoon had been heavily drinking, and on Red Valsen's suggestion went to the site of a recent battle to look for souvenirs), with the brutally unsentimental comments of the platoon, the full force of Mailer's prose is abundantly clear. The tensions created by domesticating the corpses, and then restoring their human and emotional reality, touched the men in the platoon differently, and in ways which the reader can expect if not share. The effect is sombre and complex, and suggests layers of meaning not to be found in superficially similar passages in *Guadalcanal Diary.* Only writing of this quality can make the ultimate meaning of war accessible to our understanding.

Of all the many images of war in American war novels, it is not descriptions of the dead which haunt the memory, but of transformation, the passage out of life, in which war reveals its true face. The central character in Glen Sire's *The Deathmakers,* a tank commander, recalls early in the novel something he saw during the Battle of the Bulge:

> In the right-hand lane of the road stretching in toward Bastogne, and for as he could see, there were the six-by-sixes, loaded with the orderly rows of sitting men, living men, whose bodies breathed, and who were warm with life and dreams.

And in the left-hand lane, the other column of trucks, coming back out of Bastogne, and for as far as he could see—coming away from the great machine of the war, in their six-by-sixes, were the cadavers of men who, only a few hours before had been in column going up. And now, as they returned the dignity was gone out of them. They were piled high in the trucks like cordwood—no, not like cordwood; more like garbage. Tumbled, pushed, jammed, crammed, contorted; arms, legs, faces, hands jutting out the sides of the trucks—yes, like garbage, he thought, remembering. The orderliness was gone, the sitting side by side. It was a crowd of death, and the dead need no comfort.

Mechanisation has indeed taken command. There were small hints of this process embedded in the linguistic quirk of weapons being endowed with their own voice:

> machines guns cry out, 'Da-da-dat! Da-da-dat!'
> The Garand exclaims 'Kapow!' and the 4.2 mortar
> adds 'Palot!'
> while the bazooka terminates the discussion with an
> irrefutable 'Phoosh!'
>
> (*Beach Red*)

The same idea, of weapons speaking to each other, occurred to Tregaskis: "It was 11.40, and we were working our way down the beach at the fringe of the jungle, when there came a sudden splattering of sharp rifle reports. . . . Deeper-toned rifles took up the chorus, machine guns joined in, and the shower of sound became like a rainstorm."[27] The trucks roll to and fro from the battle, carrying soldiers and returning with disorderly "garbage"; guns speak out, seemingly with a volition of their own: war is carried on increasingly without the need for further intervention by soldiers. There is a bleak comedy in warfare taken over by weapons, and perhaps also a preview of a battlefield mainly consisting of computers, weapons-systems and electronic counter-measures. The transformation of the soldier from central importance in war to an adjunct of diminishing interest hints at a host of other reversals and transformations which now characterise modern warfare. The writer who grasped the ironic possibilities of such fluid meaning was Joseph Heller. *Catch-22* (1961) caught the temper of the 1960s, at a time when the other novels of the war had begun to fade from memory (and when the cycle of adaptations of major novels for the cinema had been completed).

None of the meanings of normality or sanity survives in Yossarian's world. He alone is the one who cares, who is outraged at the moral wilderness which constitutes the Air Force on Pianosa. There is no shred here of purpose, group loyalty or idealism. Every value comes under Heller's skeptical scrutiny:

> 'The hot dog, the Brooklyn Dodgers, Mom's apple pie. That's what everyone's fighting for. But who's fighting for the decent folk? Who's fighting for more votes for the decent folk? There's no patriotism, that's what it is. And no matriotism, either.'

The warrant officer on Yossarian's left was unimpressed. 'Who gives a shit?' he asked tiredly, and turning over on his side to go to sleep.[28]

The verbal energy, and Heller's openness to nonsense while in search of fresh meaning, suddenly run up against a discourse from a different novel. The warrant officer is closer to Sergeant Croft's world than Yossarian's. Heller gaily allows his considerable verbal gifts free rein, and is not afraid to negotiate the distance from tragedy to black comedy in successive paragraphs. He adores the snappy one-liner, the stand-up comedian's wisecrack, the pun and verbal misunderstanding. Heller is the first novelist to show the influence of the Marx Brothers. He seems also to have realised that there was a new audience to write for, a college-educated readership able to appreciate literary allusions of an accessible sort: the Chaplain finds himself echoing Shylock; ex-Pfc Wintergreen makes a nice joke with T. S. Eliot's name; and there is an allusion to "Raskolnikov's dream".

At a deeper level, Heller's humour is serious, indeed even political. It is firmly based upon the perception (so widely to be observed in American war novels) that the old clarity between enemy and friend, them and us, was no longer meaningful in the conditions of modern warfare. *Catch-22* submerges its bitterness in humour and irony, but its meaning is not to be mistaken: the old claims of patriotism and loyalty have, for the *Catch-22* generation, lost their power, have indeed become an obscene charade. The novel bids a plague on both sides. Indeed, in Heller's world causes are immediately recognisable as deceits and frauds. We see nothing of the Nazis in the novel, but "our" side was as blandly bureaucratic, as inhumane, as uncaring, as we know "they" were. The politics of the novel are from the Cold War, but belong more to an undercurrent of suspicion which gained ground in the 1950s that the rival states were far more akin to each other, were being reciprocally deformed by their conflict, than the proclaimed official ideologies would suggest. Heller tapped a subterannean current of feeling on the American left, which was looking for a way to escape the Cold War dichotomies. He gave brilliant comic expression to a minority, fugitive sentiment, and helped persuade a generation that they agreed. The novel ends—shades of *Huck Finn*—with flight and escape, a psychologically accurate and sympathetic response to the dilemmas it poses. The irony of ironies is that, unnoticed by the millions of young readers of *Catch-22,* anxiety was growing in the Pentagon and the State Department in Washington over the deterioration of the position in South Vietnam. A few soldiers and politicians were beginning to wonder in 1961 whether it might be necessary to send American advisers to bolster up the Saigon regime.[29] As one nightmare began to lift, another swiftly loomed upon the horizon.

Notes

1. Louise Levita, "The *Naked* are Fanatics and the *Dead* Don't Care", *New York Star Magazine,* 22 Aug. 1948, p. 3. Quoted by Robert Solotaroff, *Down Mailer's Way* (Urbana, 1974) p. 18n.

2. Matthew J. Bruccoli, *Some Sort of Epic Grandeur: The Life of F. Scott Fitzgerald* (London, 1981) p. 86.

3. Malcolm Cowley in *The Literary Situation* (New York, 1955) p. 41, writes: "In the novels of the Second War I can find very few signs that their [American] authors have been reading French, German, or even English books."

4. Of all the extensive literature on writing on the Great War Paul Fussell's *The Great War and Modern Memory* (New York, 1975) stands out for its sensitivity and insight.

5. Captain Ralph Ingersoll, *The Battle is the Pay-Off* (Washington, 1943) p. 154.

6. Richard Tregaskis, *Guadalcanal Diary* (New York, 1943) p. 132. This feeling appears to have been widespread during the war, and after. The Welsh writer Alun Lewis wrote to his parents on 2 February 1944 from India:

    . . . although the Army is supposed to have everything it requires, I'm jiggered if I can equip my boys with the odd things they need. They give us bicycles and pumps and lamps, but no connections and bulbs. And so on. So what? We learn code after code, cipher after cipher: inevitably a new replaces the old. I think I'd prefer the 1914 type of war; it was more methodical than this one—and it ended before this one has really begun—for me.

    (Alun Lewis, *In the Green Tree* [London, 1948] p. 59.)

    In the preface to a powerful memoir of the Vietnam war, Philip Caputo regretted the absence of clear, decisive battles in Vietnam:

    Writing about this kind of warfare is not a simple task. Repeatedly, I have found myself wishing that I had been the veteran of a conventional war, with dramatic campaigns and historic battles for subject matter instead of a monotonous succession of ambushes and fire-fights. But there were no Normandies or Gettysburgs for us, no epic clashes that decided the fates of armies or nations.

    (Philip Caputo, *A Rumor of War* [1977; London, 1978] p. xii.)

7. See Roger Manvell, *Films and the Second World War* (London, 1974) and Richard R. Lingeman, *Don't You Know There's a War On? The American Home Front, 1941-1945* (New York, 1971) ch. 6.

8. James Jones, *WW II* (New York, 1975) p. 150.

9. Ira Wolfert, *Battle for the Solomons* (Boston, 1943) p. 7.

10. John Gunther, *D Day* (New York, 1944) pp. 69-70.

11. John Hersey, *Into the Valley: A Skirmish of the Marines* (London, 1943) p. 43.

12. Ingersoll, *The Battle is the Pay-Off,* p. 156.

13. This debate is abundantly represented in Jack Salzman, ed., *The Survival Years: A Collection of American Writing of the 1940s* (New York, 1969) pp. 173-216.

14. John Morton Blum, *V was for Victory: Politics and American Culture During World War II* (New York, 1976) pp. 67-8, 46, 16.

15. Cowley, *The Literary Situation,* p. 27.

16. Hersey, *Into the Valley,* pp. 51-2.

17. J. Glenn Gray, *The Warriors: Reflections on Men in Battle,* with an Introduction by Hannah Arendt (New York, 1973) pp. 46-60. This is a major theme in novels of the Vietnam war. A character in one such novel, Lt. Hodges, recovering from shrapnel wounds in a hospital on Okinawa, and thinks of his old platoon:

    He missed the people in the bush, more than he had ever missed any group of people in his life. There was a purity in those relationships that could not be matched anywhere else. . . . There was a common goal, and a mutual enemy.

    And, of course, Lt. Hodges turns down the chance to remain on Okinawa as Special Services Recreation Officer in order to return to what remains of his platoon. (James Webb, *Fields of Fire* [1978; London, 1981] p. 318.)

18. Ernest Hemingway, *For Whom the Bell Tolls* (1940; Harmondsworth, 1955) p. 227.

19. John Dos Passos, *USA* (Harmondsworth, 1966) p. 353. This comment was made apropos John Reed.

20. On this theme see Gray, *The Warriors,* pp. 60-9.

21. George Orwell, *Collected Essays, Journalism and Letters,* ed. Sonia Orwell and Ian Angus (London, 1968) I, p. 526.

22. Jones, *WW II,* p. 62.

23. Ira Wolfert, *American Guerrilla in the Philippines* (New York, 1945) p. 166f.

24. See the discussion of wartime journalism in Blum, *V was for Victory,* ch. 2.

25. Philippe Ariès, *Western Attitudes toward Death: From the Middle Ages to the Present,* trans. Patricia M. Ranum (London, 1976) p. 100.

26. Tregaskis, *Guadalcanal Diary,* pp. 146-7.

27. Tregaskis, ibid., p. 69.

28. Milo Minderbender in *Catch-22,* who brings the true spirit of capitalist entrepreneurship to the conduct of war, is anticipated in detail by Corporal Soeft in Hans Hellmut Kirst's *Gunner Asch Goes to War,* trans. Robert Kee (London, 1956). Soeft is a type who would have been very much at home with the American Army in Naples (as described by John Horne Burns in *The Gallery*).

29. See *The Pentagon Papers, as published by The New York Times* (New York, 1971). In 1961 President Kennedy ordered 400 Special Forces soldiers and 100 other advisers to South Vietnam. The Joint Chiefs estimated that 40,000 US servicemen would be needed to "clean up the Vietcong threat". By 1967 the "optimum force" requested by General Westmoreland had reached 671 616.

Alan Munton (essay date 1989)

SOURCE: Munton, Alan. "Fiction and the People's War." In *English Fiction of the Second World War,* pp. 6-33. London: Faber and Faber, 1989.

[In the following essay, Munton charts the reaction of English writers to World War II.]

The term 'the People's War' became current with the publication of Angus Calder's *The People's War: Britain 1939-1945* in 1969. Describing the effect of the war on civilian life Calder argues that the social structure of Britain was altered by the mobilization of resources needed to fight a war. During 1940-1 there existed amongst a significant proportion of the British people a dissatisfaction with the way the war was being run so deep as to generate political attitudes which were, or were very nearly, revolutionary in content. Two related questions were involved: the immediate question of the conduct of the war, and long-term considerations of the kind of society that should exist in Britain after it was won. There was a widespread belief that those who had fought (or, as civilians, had undergone) the war should benefit when it was over. General agreement existed that the way forward lay through planning; and since planning was associated with the Left, this carried with it the implication that there should be post-war socialist planning. This expectation was fulfilled to the extent that in 1945 the Labour Party won the first general election for ten years.

To compile information about the People's War, Calder drew upon the reports collected by Mass-Observation, whose observers recorded the behaviour and opinions of people throughout the country; others wrote diaries describing their own experiences. Because this material was gathered by untrained and only loosely co-ordinated individuals, its reliability as an historical source has been questioned. Calder defends his use of these materials as 'an indispensable aid to tracing popular views and reactions in all kinds of fields, from aerial bombardment to greyhound racing' (Calder, 1969, p. 13).

In a critical commentary upon the term, Arthur Marwick has written that 'any snappy generalization such as "People's War" is open to all sorts of qualifications', for example that the war confirmed many traditional attitudes as well as encouraging new ones (Marwick, 1976, pp. 180-3). Marwick nevertheless finds four reasons for believing that the Second World War was genuinely a People's War:

> First, for a relatively short period during the blitz ordinary people were in the front line, bearing the direct brunt of enemy fire power; second, over the longer period of the whole war, direct participation in all aspects of the national effort by ordinary people was absolutely vital, first to survival, then to victory; third, the war for the first time gave a genuine influence to individuals who believed themselves to be spokesmen, not of the establishment, but of the people—film-makers like John Baxter and Thorold Dickinson, publicists like J. B. Priestley and Ritchie Calder . . . ; and fourth, for all the powerful resistances that remained, there was in all sections of society a movement in favour of radical social reform.
>
> (p. 180)

This is a distinctly less political interpretation of the war than Angus Calder's, but it indicates that there is agreement among historians that 'the People's War' is a valid concept.

Literary critics are likely to feel that the detailed information on people's lives assembled in *The People's War* belongs unambiguously to their area of interest, for this is the kind of detail out of which fiction is made. Further, the level of generalization achieved by organizing this material under the heading of 'the People's War' is sufficiently secure to allow a critique of war fiction to be built around it.

From the outset it was recognized that the phrase 'a People's War' belonged to the Left. The most audacious use of the term during the war was by Tom Wintringham in *New Ways of War,* completed in June 1940 when invasion seemed imminent. Wintringham's emphasis is on 'the people's *war*', however, for his book contains instructions on how the civilian population should fight and defend itself. There are diagrams illustrating how to set up crossfire (these also appeared in the popular weekly magazine *Picture Post*) and how to defend a house against attack, together with instructions for a home-made grenade that might stop a tank. Wintringham uses the classic argument for arming the people:

A government of a country that has been long accustomed to peace is naturally reluctant to put explosives and lethal weapons in the hands of its citizens. A government that represents propertied classes is always terrified by the fear of revolution. If we are to have a People's Army we must break down this reluctance and this fear, and find for ourselves a government that will entrust to the people the means for their defence.

(Wintringham, 1940, p. 85)

This passage, published in a Penguin Special, indicates the kind of thinking that took place after the retreat from Dunkirk. When Churchill told the House of Commons that the British would 'fight in the fields and in the streets', it is unlikely that he had in mind the kind of revolutionary transformation in the conduct of the war envisaged by Wintringham, but it is difficult to see how Churchill's hopes could have been fulfilled except on the basis of a people's army organized for its own defence. The political consequences of that would have been immense, and probably not to Churchill's liking.

Wintringham's experience fighting Franco's rebels in the Spanish Civil War with small, scarcely trained forces were his model for the defence of Britain. George Orwell had also fought in Spain, with the militia of POUM (Partido Obrero de Unificación Marxista), a highly political and democratized organization, and this experience encouraged him to believe that the Home Guard might become an organization with revolutionary potential. (The only fiction to take up these issues is Len Deighton's SS-GB, published in 1978, which is based on the premise that the German invasion succeeded early in 1941. The fighting during the invasion is conceived in conventional military terms, and popular resistance is shown as ineffectual to the point of being ridiculous. Deighton appears uninterested in the possibilities envisaged by Wintringham and Orwell.)

The reality of the People's War, in terms of injury and loss of life, was grim enough. It was non-combatant civilians who faced the first onslaught, not the fighting services. There were 22,428 civilian deaths due to war operations in 1940, and 22,350 in 1941, but only 3,884 in 1942; total civilian deaths due to the war were 63,689. Civilian casualties of this order are one aspect of 'total war', the complete mobilization of a country's resources for war. The army lost 144,079 killed between 1939 and 1945, the RAF 70,253.

One difficulty in using the term 'People's War' in a discussion of war fiction is that the concept is partly built up from that fiction itself. Calder quotes several times from Evelyn Waugh's novels and takes some particularly atmospheric passages from Elizabeth Bowen's The Heat of the Day (1949). In A People's War (1986), another valuable source based on Mass-Observation archive material, Peter Lewis structures his chapter on industry around the title of J. B. Priestley's aircraft-factory novel Daylight on Saturday (1943). This tendency is not sufficiently marked for the People's War concept to seem to chase its fictional tail, but it does suggest that fiction is not an autonomous activity separate from historical developments, and that under certain circumstances it can possess the same persuasive status as fact. This affects our understanding of the relationship between fiction and 'factual' autobiography, a question to which I shall return.

The relationship between fiction and fact is often an intriguing one. In his discussion of the internment of foreign nationals Calder mentions that some were detained in 'a derelict cotton factory infested by rats' (p. 152). This factory is evidently the setting for the internment camp in Alex Comfort's novel No Such Liberty (1941). The reason for this coincidence of interest is that both writers draw upon the same source, François Lafitte's The Internment of Aliens, a Penguin Special of 1940. Writers who are too young to have experienced the war as adults face a different problem of authentication. In Leslie Thomas's The Magic Army (1981) a middle-class girl exclaims, 'There are women going home with six or seven pounds a week in their pockets and they feel the war's the most wonderful thing that's ever happened' (Thomas, p. 278). The figures are rather high, but this remark is a legitimate reinterpretation of Angus Calder's account of women's wartime earnings: 'There were undoubtedly a proportion of women who earned at male rates, even the occasional girl . . . who built up earnings at piece rates which exceeded those of many men.' In 1944, the year in which the novel is set, the average wage for men in metalwork and engineering was £7, for women £3 10S (Calder, p. 465), and it was possible for women to approach the male wage. In other words, Calder's The People's War has itself become a source for writers of fiction who want to ensure that their facts are accurate.

Leslie Thomas acknowledges his debt to this and to other books in a bibliography appended to the novel. The novel which acknowledges its sources is becoming increasingly common—Penelope Lively's Moon Tiger (1987) is another example—but J. G. Farrell's The Singapore Grip has a bibliography of nearly three pages. Len Deighton's Bomber (1970) and Goodbye, Mickey Mouse (1982) are among the most heavily researched of all war novels. This development makes it possible to distinguish between 'researched' and 'experienced' war fiction. The latter category usually includes work written during or just after the war that is a reworking of personal or communal experience. James Hanley's No Directions (1943), describing a night of the Blitz, is an example, as is Alexander Baron's From the City, From the Plough (1948) or Dan Billany and David Dowie's The Cage (1949). David Holbrook's Flesh Wounds (1966) is a later example.

'Experienced' or 'felt' novels possess a sense of immediacy that brings with it fictional authority. Novelists writing in later decades attempt to establish their authority by insisting that their fictions are authentic. Through research they attempt to establish for a new readership facts and attitudes that those who lived during the war took for granted. These research activities are inevitably conducted according to certain presuppositions about what was significant in wartime, so that the 'researched' novel does not so much reproduce the period as construct a post-war view of wartime life. In practice, researched war fictions very rarely possess the same atmosphere as works written during the war itself. Reviewers frequently praise post-war war fiction for showing life 'exactly as it was'. Since these fictions often differ widely among themselves in atmosphere, subject-matter and attitude—consider Leslie Thomas, Anthony Powell and Len Deighton, all of whom have been praised in these terms—it will be apparent that what the reader is being persuaded to accept as 'authenticity' is a very particular selective reconstruction from the available research materials. Each of these fictions is the product of a particular view of the war which the author wishes to promote under the protective cover of researched 'authenticity'.

In discussing war fiction I have situated each novel as participating in a debate around the concept of the People's War. It is not my intention to produce a definition of what the People's War may have been and then to measure the war fiction against the definition. A novelist's refusal to acknowledge the existence of the concept, or a decision to write in opposition to it (as Evelyn Waugh does) may be as significant as any endorsement. On the other hand, a novelist's wish to write in People's War terms can produce writing which does little to make the concept persuasive. The following example from Jack Lindsay's novel of the campaign in Crete shows such a failure:

> Thinking of Sally—would she be on a day-shift now or cuddling up in her bed with the chintz curtains drawn, half-awake listening for the alarm-clock? Lured out at last by the thought of a cup of tea or a chat with Gladys? Or at the works kissing one of the shell-cases (as she said in her last letter), thinking how it might blow up the very German that was aiming at dear Ted? You never knew.
>
> (Lindsay, 1943, p. 80)

This is from *Beyond Terror: A Novel of the Battle of Crete,* which contains many examples of how not to write about the People's War.

Although the People's War concept can include a great deal of varied experience, it also acts as a limitation or boundary. Much that was commonplace in Europe and the Far East, notably occupation, did not occur in Britain. Alex Comfort, writing in 1948, assumes that the post-war novel will be concerned with Europe, with 'the first days of the Russian occupation of Berlin; the last days of the German occupation of Paris; Hitler and his doxy cremated in the ruins of the *Reichskanzlerei* among old petrol tins; the buffoons and charlatans of the peace conference . . .' (Comfort, 1948, p. 75). In practice, such subjects did not interest the writers of English fiction, and the question of how they might be realized never arose. English war fiction has evaded as many subjects as it has embraced.

The British mainland was neither occupied nor fought over. Britain's Jews—with the exception noted below—were not deported, as they were throughout Europe. There was no Resistance, and so no reprisals, as there were in every occupied European country. English villages and their inhabitants were not systematically destroyed as they were in the Soviet Union. Only the Channel Islands were occupied and—in an indication of what would have happened—its Jews, few in number, deported. 'Every country in this last war had its Fifth Column,' wrote Arthur Calder-Marshall in 1949; 'how large it was in Britain was never revealed because the country was never occupied' (*Our Time*, April 1949, p. 91). There were active collaborators and informers in the Channel Islands who caused the deaths and imprisonment of fellow islanders. Angus Calder believes that the population of Great Britain would have divided into resisters and collaborators, but that the Fifth Column would have been small: 'besides a no doubt tiny number of active Fifth Columnists, many reputable people, great and small, would have collaborated with the Nazis when the time came' (pp. 476 and 150). It is because that time did not come that there is no equivalent in English fiction to Vercors's occupation novel, *Le Silence de la mer* (1943), or the stories of the French Resistance, based on her own experience, in Marguerite Duras's *La Douleur* (1985, trans. 1986).

The only fictions to raise the question of collaboration and resistance in Britain are Len Deighton's *SS-GB* and Derek Robinson's *Kramer's War* (1977). The former has a police officer hero who moves from a form of 'legitimate' collaboration (criminal investigation: murderers must be caught, whatever the regime) to a form of resistance; but since German officers also participate in it for their own purposes, this is far from resembling the resistance movements that actually existed in Europe.

Despite the extent of suffering in Britain, particularly during the Blitz, British war experience was less severe than in Europe and distinctly less so than in the Soviet Union. The worst treatment suffered by British troops occurred in Burma and Malaya, particularly amongst those who were prisoners of war. It is perhaps significant that both popular memory, and fiction, have shied away from the Far East. The exceptions are J. G. Ballard's remarkable *Empire of the Sun* and J. G. Farrell's *The Singapore Grip*.

English war fiction did not have to confront such knowledge as Primo Levi had of the German concentration camps, but writers none the less had difficulty in finding an order for what they knew. The greatest problems arose amongst those writing about European resistance movements. For Stuart Hood, who spent a year with Italian partisans during 1943-4, ordering the experience has remained a permanent difficulty. He has used both fiction and autobiography (another indication of the closeness of those two forms). The novellas 'The Circle of the Minotaur' and 'The Fisherman's Daughter: a Tale' appeared under the title *The Circle of the Minotaur* in 1950. A novel, *Since the Fall,* followed in 1955. Set in the post-war years, it looks back to the period of partisan warfare. An autobiographical version of this experience appeared in 1963 as *Pebbles from My Skull,* and was reprinted in 1985 as *Carlino,* with a new Afterword showing how memory repeatedly undermines what the autobiographer believed to be the 'facts'.

If fiction deals with difficult experiences by situating them in a narrative 'out there' with an apparent logic of its own, autobiography admits that the experience is close to home, but suffers from the treacheries of memory, which unknown to the author works its own distortions, turning 'the truth' into something very little different from fiction. Again and again Hood discovers that his memory is at fault, yet the memory, not the reality, remains as truth for him. Fiction and autobiography merge and cross, two unreliable records which are for the reader varying truths rather than different genres.

Certain episodes in Hood's books occur in both forms. There is the occasion when a partisan group awaiting a parachute drop is joined by an additional man, who is immediately suspect. In *Since the Fall* Gavin Hamilton (a version of Hood) asks for him to be 'bumped off', a term in keeping with the comic-satiric tone of the book. In *Pebbles from My Skull* Stuart Hood, in his own person, tells his lieutenant: '*Bisogna che sparisca*'—he's got to disappear; and he does. It is not a question of which version is the more true, for each is true to the text in which it appears. It is rather a matter of how the truth is to be told, to what audience and for what end.

Just as people in Britain believed that never again should they suffer the social conditions of the 1920s and 1930s, so did the European Left believe that the post-war world should be transformed: for those who had actually suffered Fascism in Italy, France, Poland, Greece, Yugoslavia and the Balkan states, there was a far greater urgency than existed even in Britain. At Christmas 1943 Frank Thompson wrote from Cairo to his brother E. P. Thompson to describe what the possibilities for Europe might be:

> There is a spirit abroad in Europe which is finer and braver than anything that tired continent has known for centuries, and which cannot be withstood. You can, if you like, think of it in terms of politics, but it is broader and more generous than any dogma. It is the confident will of whole peoples, who have known the utmost humiliation and suffering and have triumphed over it, to build their own life once and for all. I like best to think of it as millions—literally millions—of people . . . completely masters of themselves, looking only forward, and liking what they see . . . There is a marvellous opportunity before us—and all that is required from Britain, America and the U.S.S.R. is imagination, help and sympathy.
>
> (Thompson, 1947, p. 169)

What, in fact, was the outcome? In *Since the Fall* Gavin reflects on what happened after the war:

> 'There was a moment when we seemed to be on the edge of something—as if everyone was going to become braver, wiser, more generous. Now there is nothing left but politics. Man makes his own best dreams impossible.'
>
> (p. 105)

During the war years it was felt all across Europe that a People's War was being fought. The post-war defeat of the parties of the Left, largely induced by the political settlements made by Britain and America at the end of the war, was a betrayal of the best dreams of the war years. The same defeat was suffered again in fiction. The success of Evelyn Waugh's *Unconditional Surrender* (1961) as the novel of partisan warfare is a success for pessimism and conservatism and for carelessness about people's hopes. Nevertheless, the sense that people had of looking forward 'and liking what they see' was extremely powerful, and in my discussion of war fiction I have made the sense of the future one of the tests of meaning.

A peculiarity of the literary history of the early part of the war period is the demoralization of the writers who had become well known during the 1930s. If any group seemed likely to thrive on a popular war, it was those writers who had built a reputation from their political radicalism, from their opposition to government measures against the poor at home, and who had supported the Spanish Republic during the Spanish Civil War. Yet this never became their war.

W. H. Auden and Christopher Isherwood, the two most prominent members of the 'Auden group', departed for the United States in January 1939, and caused a great deal of anger on the Left for doing so. War was inevitable, and they seemed to be ensuring their own safety. Isherwood's own description of their feelings during their journey shows that they felt the 1930s were over, that a break had occurred:

One morning, when they were walking on the deck, Christopher heard himself say: 'You know, it just doesn't mean anything to me any more—the Popular Front, the party line, the anti-fascist struggle. I suppose they're okay but something's wrong with me. I simply cannot swallow another mouthful'. To which Wystan answered: 'Neither can I.'

(Isherwood, 1977, pp. 247-8)

Many people on the Left felt that with difficulty they had constructed a politics appropriate to their time that was disrupted by the outbreak of war, with all its immediate chaos and future uncertainty. Others tried to find a continuity in the chaos, but refused to recognize that anything new was occurring. Stephen Spender (another member of the Auden group) argued in a booklet entitled *Life and the Poet* (1942) that the suffering caused by the war was of no greater significance than the suffering that already existed in the world. He quotes the poet Geoffrey Grigson: 'The greatest intensities of suffering or evil are always being endured somewhere by somebody in peace or war' (Spender, 1942, p. 122). This is no doubt true, but it meant that the war did not have to be understood as a war; it was just another example of suffering. In this way the war was dissolved as a subject of particular interest.

Nevertheless, many writers did feel a need to understand the new period and to make sense of the war while it was still in progress. Their difficulties in doing so can be understood by looking at successive volumes of John Lehmann's magazines *Folios of New Writing* and *New Writing and Daylight*. Lehmann had been one of the outstanding editors of the 1930s, in effect creating the Auden group in the pages of *New Writing*. Its successor *Folios of New Writing* was published in 1940 and 1941, and in 1942 became *New Writing and Daylight,* published in book form once or twice a year throughout the war.

Folios of New Writing looked back to the 1930s—here are to be found Stephen Spender, Dylan Thomas, Rex Warner, Henry Green, George Orwell, Edward Upward, William Plomer and David Gascoyne. Only in an editorial to the Autumn 1941 number, entitled 'Looking Back and Forward', does Lehmann begin the long process of examining the effect of the war on contemporary literature.

He admits that the response of the best-known 1930s writers to the war had been puzzling and confused. These writers had been anti-Fascist when the government had tended to favour the Nazis and Italian Fascists, but now that they had to line up beside the appeasers they found it difficult to do so. They were suspicious of this change of allegiance by the men of Munich (who had tried to satisfy Hitler by betraying Czechoslovakia), wondering if the leopard really had changed its spots. It is not a strong argument to justify inaction: if they were anti-Fascist in the 1930s, why should they have doubts now, when Hitler's intentions were plain to see? Why should the Left be any the less vigorously anti-Hitler because the appeasers had recognized their own errors? Some, Lehmann said, remembered the enthusiasm that greeted the conflict of 1914-18, and the horror and disillusion with which it ended; these writers' admiration for the poetry of Sassoon and Wilfred Owen forced them to recognize the suffering of both sides, and fear of a similar development on this occasion inhibited their support for an anti-Hitler war. It required Churchill to come to power in 1940 before they resumed their activities.

Lehmann's third reason for the silence of the Left shows how strongly they felt the differences between the war years and the 1930s. These writers had anticipated a catastrophe which, despite their warnings, had not been avoided: with the outbreak of war a phase in their writing lives was over. Lehmann concludes: 'there remained, cargoes washed up on the shore from the wreck, some very beautiful verse and prose of permanent value' (p. 7). The 1930s writers had been unable to anticipate a wartime function for themselves; locked into opposition, they could not adjust to a People's War. This is all the more puzzling because the strong documentary element in the writing of the 1930s had prefigured the way things were to go: the very people investigated by Orwell in *The Road to Wigan Pier,* or by Mass-Observation, or who had been celebrated in hundreds of poems and articles, were to play a central part in the war itself. Why did writers not recognize this? Their hopes wrecked by the outbreak of the war they had so long anticipated, they fell at once into a demoralized silence.

That silence can partly be explained by the difficulties created for the Left—particularly the organized Left—by the German-Soviet non-aggression pact of August 1939. This undermined the argument that the Soviet Union was the standard-bearer of opposition to Fascism in Europe, though it remained possible to say that Stalin was buying time to prepare his country against an inevitable German invasion. At the outbreak of war the Communist Party in Britain took the line that militarily this was an anti-Fascist war which should be conducted with vigour; when Douglas Springhall returned from Moscow on 24 September 1939 with the Communist International's declaration that it was an imperialist war in which the working classes could support neither side, there was confusion. In the 1930s the Communist Party had been central to the Left's idea of itself; even if one was not in the party, one nevertheless stood in a definable relationship to it. Changes of line by the Communist Party made it vulnerable to attack from a variety of positions that included the anti-Communist Left (George Orwell, for example), disillusioned fellow-travellers (the Left Book Club publisher Victor Gollancz), socialists and liberals, as well as the Right. The effect was to undermine self-confidence everywhere on the Left.

It was Rex Warner who made the most cogent case for utopia from within the war years themselves. In an essay entitled 'On Subsidising Literature' he summarized the various views of the future then current:

> All have in common the resolution that this time deeds not words are required, and that these deeds shall take the form of an organization of society that is both fair and efficient. In short it appears to be the wish of the vast majority of the people that after the war their Government should be, in some form or another, socialistic, and that the Government should, unlike those of the pre-war period, have a clear idea of what it is aiming at.

> *(Folios of New Writing,* Autumn 1941, p. 188)

This is a classic statement of the People's War position, and an early and prescient one. Warner goes on to say that the current vagueness in thinking about social and political matters was dangerous because it might lead in any direction, towards Fascism as much as towards socialism. He adds:

> I should suggest that today this thinking about ends, about ideals, about suffering and happiness, about life and death is more needed than political and economic thinking.

> (p. 190)

This implies that the important thinking of the time should be conducted in and through fiction and poetry. Warner's stress upon thinking about ends is particularly relevant to a discussion of fiction and its relation to the future, and is a theme that I shall pursue here.

Several stories published by Lehmann show writers taking as their subject the very fact that they could not make sense of their present circumstances. One, Raymond Williams's 'This Time', is a satire upon those on the Left who believed that they could understand any political situation. A soldier, drunk or dreaming, recalls the pre-war confidence:

> It was a good job they had seen through the illusions. If the war came they would understand it perfectly. And they understood themselves and the political struggle and the god fallacy. Munich, Danzig, Warsaw, Paris. 'This time we understand'.

> *(NWD,* Winter 1942-3, pp. 159-60)

A song runs through the soldier's thoughts:

> Once before / We were unaware the chance we were waiting / Was close at hand. / This time we understand.

> (p. 159)

The break in the rhythm between the second and third lines disturbs his dreams:

> It was a little frightening, the break of the rhythm. Remember how we laughed at anarchy and feared it? We are in it now. Where has the grand synthesis got to? What about the inevitable forces of history? Our movements are breaking up. Our masses scatter into thousands of frightened sheltering humans. War is tearing out our vitals . . . We are improvising, madly. Learning how to cook in fields, and make sanitary ditches. Starting from nothing, moving on to nothing again . . . It is anarchy, anarchy, anarchy.

> (p. 161)

Even the words of the Okey Pokey [*sic*] make an ironic comment on left-wing certainties: 'You do the Okey Pokey / And you turn about. / THAT'S WHAT IT'S ALL ABOUT!' The soldier finds he is nearly late for parade, where he 'turns about' with precision. But the wider meaning escapes him: he doesn't know what it's all about. In time of war fiction is forced to recognize its limitations as a means of interpretation.

In 1946 *New Writing and Daylight* published a symposium entitled 'The Future of Fiction'. Of the six contributors only one had anything substantial to say about the effect of the war on the writing of fiction. Rose Macaulay wrote that 'it has been a tragedy too vast, too gross, too ill-understood; it has clogged and stunned imagination, and intellectual activity has been paralysed' (*NWD,* 1946, p. 73). Of those young enough to fight she wrote:

> The communal living, the unsteady, chancey drug of danger, the constant keying up of nerve and sinew [*sic*], may have broken his mind into disorderly fragments, made consecutive thought, initiative and concentration difficult; if he writes he may write in spasms and fragments, without coherent pattern . . . Fragments, impressions, brief glimpses—these are, on the whole, the mode.

> (p. 73)

These remarks confirm the argument of this book, that those writing during the war were forced into constructing fragmentary texts which could not order or shape the experience of war on any significant scale. This is not a criticism of these writers, but a description of the consequences of the very real difficulties that they faced, and of their attempted solution to it.

The failure to understand these difficulties is partly responsible for the way war fiction has been treated critically. Since most of it was improvisation in the face of chaos, and is clearly not 'major', the period as a whole has been dismissed as having little significance. These are the 'lost years' of English fiction. Yet, quite obviously, a great deal happened. Everything depends upon how the years 1939-45 are defined. It is not unduly paradoxical to argue that they are significant precisely because indisputably great fiction was *not* written then. That absence is a measure of the impact public events can have upon the capacity to create. Creativity is not constant but vulnerable to difficult conditions. The authors who did go on writing during the war had to develop particular strategies in order to deal with the special nature of the period in which they were living. These strategies centre upon their conceptualization of the war as a period, and this question I shall now discuss.

Fiction written during the war was end-stopped by history. For the author, as a contriver of narrative, the climactic or concluding historical moment gave retrospective shape to a sequence of experiences which were otherwise difficult to order. The reader, reading forwards, anticipates or finds satisfying the resolution offered by a known historical moment; he may feel even more confidently situated in present time because his knowledge of the past—of how it 'worked out'—confirms his present experience of the narrative. For the author, working backwards, history can be a constraint. Unless the work is a fantasy, fictional events must be related to or must confirm actual occurrences known to the readership. This requirement reduces an author's freedom to choose the direction of a narrative, compared to the possibilities open to the writer of fiction not set in wartime. Some writers felt this constraint very heavily and abandoned the attempt to develop an unfolding narrative in favour of fragmentary structures that proceed without direction. To choose the form of the short story was also a means of avoiding the difficulties that followed upon not knowing the outcome of the war. 'Wartime' was a special kind of time; begun at a specific moment, it had—as everyone knew—to end, but the moment of its ending moved ahead of all anticipation, requiring a constant adjustment to the psychological space that still lay ahead. In these circumstances the most characteristic war fiction written during the war was short, limited in scope, intense in feeling, fragmentary in structure, and often climaxed or closed off by a known historical event.

Fiction about the war written after it was over has a quite different structure. Once the outcome is known the experience of the entire war is open to interpretation in ways not previously possible. Post-war fiction is most characteristically structured on a large scale. Writers often take the whole of the 1939-45 period as their subject, and write expansively. I have in mind the trilogies written by Anthony Powell, Evelyn Waugh, and Olivia Manning, together with the two war novels written by C. P. Snow. The scale often implies that the war can now be seen in epic terms; but heroic deeds, the usual subject of epic, do not in fact predominate. These fictions are often about disillusionment with the war, discovering in it futility or emptiness. Writers now find

a moral confusion or contradiction that contrasts with the single-mindedness supposedly felt while the war was actually taking place. Freedom from the constraints of history has released these writers into self-criticism, the reflectiveness that follows upon action. These fictions are therefore inverted epics, in which the heroic temperament is undermined or the unheroic given privileged attention.

These novels were written by authors considered 'literary' rather than 'popular'. With the exception of C. P. Snow's war novels, and the first two volumes of Waugh's trilogy, this writing appeared, after long reflection, in the 1960s and subsequently. It had been preceded, in the 1950s, by an outpouring of popular works which vigorously asserted an heroic version of events, works which were heavily fictionalized in the double sense of being both in fictional form and palpably falsified. Most of these books are still well known: Paul Brickhill's *The Dam Busters* and *The Great Escape* (both 1951), Pierre Boulle's *Bridge on the River Kwai* (1952), *The White Rabbit* by Bruce Marshall (1952), *Cockleshell Heroes* by C. E. Lucas Phillips (1956), *Safer Than a Known Way* by Ian MacHorton (1958), and many others. A genuine heroic epic in fiction, Nicholas Monsarrat's *The Cruel Sea,* appeared in 1951. This onslaught made the heroic mode impossible for literary writers, who chose instead to write understated, ironic novels of wide scope about figures who fitted only awkwardly into the war, if they fitted at all. It is from this partially detached point of view that the post-war critique of the war years is made. By writing in trilogies or as part of longer novel sequences, the novelists I have named make a particular claim upon our attention. It is the claim to a particular authority: a claim to understand the war, of being able to grasp the whole of it and to situate it within the social and political history of our times. These writers use their authority, I shall argue, to present a socially conservative account of the war years which is at variance with what most people felt was actually occurring at the time.

To organize experience whilst in the middle of it is always difficult. It was doubly difficult to do so in the middle of unprecedented events: 'wartime conditions were such that writers found it difficult to establish a point of perspective from which to view what was happening around them' (Hewison, p. 97). The major technical question that arose was: how does one end a fiction? The writer has privileged access to those formal structures and conventions that allow fictions to be resolved, but where the outcome of a war is concerned, the novelist is no more privileged than the readership. A proleptic fiction guessing at the outcome of the war would be instantly disproved, and authors naturally did not attempt this. The answer had to be found by creating a space for fiction within the events of the war itself.

In these circumstances authors chose to limit their fictions to single incidents or to short periods of time. One night in the Blitz is the choice made in James Hanley's *No Directions*. Many writers used well-known historical events as motives, climaxes or end-points in their fictions. For example, in Patrick Hamilton's *Hangover Square* (1941), George Bone commits a double murder as Chamberlain announces the declaration of war, and J. B. Priestley makes the second battle of El Alamein an inspiration for the factory workers in *Daylight on Saturday* (1943). The invasion of Crete is the subject of 'single-episode' fictions in James Aldridge's *The Sea Eagle* (1944) and Jack Lindsay's *Beyond Terror* (1943). In *There's No Home* (1951) Alexander Baron neatly solves the problem by describing an interlude in the war in Sicily, the month between arriving in Catania in August 1943 and moving on towards Italy in September. Such a strategy as this depends upon understanding the war as falling into identifiable periods.

The question of periodization is a difficult one. The years from 1939 to 1945 are, for the British, 'the war'. We mean many things when we use those words, but there exists a basic agreement as to what is meant in terms of shared experience, known facts, and extension in time. But for the Soviet Union the war ran from June 1941 to 1945, for the United States from December 1941 to the final date. For the French the war—considered as fighting between armies—was over by June 1940, and a period of occupation began, in which battle was replaced by passivity or by organized resistance. When people in these countries conceive the war years, the period known as 'the war' is thought of in an entirely different way than it is in Britain.

The years before are also different. The United States and the Soviet Union were onlookers during 1939-41, but in western Europe there was a continuity between the end of the Spanish Civil War early in 1939, and the fresh outbreak in September of that year. Such continuity is important, for the same weapons were to be used by the Germans against the British as the Germans had used against the Spanish Republicans (the 88mm anti-tank and anti-aircraft gun, and the Stuka dive-bomber). The question then was: could the British learn anything from the Spanish war? The military leadership thought not; but when the threat of invasion came in 1940-1, it was the recollection of guerrilla operations in Spain that provided Tom Wintringham and others with the model for a possible resistance in Britain. *Piece of Cake* (1983), Derek Robinson's novel about Hurricane fighter pilots, shows the importance of the Spanish experience—don't fly in formation, attack out of the sun, use back-armour in seats. Only by learning the lessons of Spain in the weeks before the Battle of Britain were they able to survive the assault itself.

There were also contemporary periodizations, ways in which those living within the years 1939-45 tried to understand the experience they were undergoing. Churchill was a shrewd periodizer, and many people came to understand the war in terms that he proposed for them. After the success at El Alamein in November 1942 he urged caution: 'Now this is not the end. It is not even the beginning of the end. But it is, perhaps, the end of the beginning' (Calder, pp. 351-2). Orwell too had a strong sense of period. He wrote a diary (unpublished) running from 10 July to 3 September 1939, his end-date suggesting that he saw the declaration of war as a final post-Munich episode rather than the beginning of something new. His next diary, from May 1940 to August 1941, was concluded because he believed that 'the quasi-revolutionary period which began with Dunkirk is finished' (Orwell, 1970b, p. 463). He begins again in March 1942 with Cripps in India and the threat of a separate peace between the Soviet Union and Germany. He ends on 15 November with a report of the church bells ringing for El Alamein, making the same choice of ending as Churchill. To periodize the war requires the political interpretation of an historical moment that is not yet complete.

There was also a form of non-historical short-term periodization. Civilians threatened by bombing or by the V1 and V2 rockets that fell in 1944-5 had to find a way of dealing with the possibility that their deaths might (or might not) occur, knowing that if they were killed it was not a matter they could do anything about. This created in many people the hedonist option of living from day to day. The 'period' was made as short as possible, so that the claim to have survived could be made again and again. Another version of short-term periodization is recorded by Naomi Mitchison in her diary. 'Jack and Helen are really frightened,' she wrote of her brother J. B. S. Haldane and his future wife, Helen Spurway, 'Helen saying how earlier it has been periodicity that got her—would she ever wash her hair again . . . I wonder how many people are scared like that' (Mitchison, 1986, p. 302). The fear that one may never again carry out a commonplace action may be a mild neurosis in peacetime, but in war it is a not unreasonable attempt to give order to a difficult situation. In a massive democratization of fear every threatened person could conceive his or her own life as a narrative, not quite completed. Everyone becomes a potential subject for fiction.

Periodization became more difficult after the end of 1942, when for the British the war ceased to be a matter of spectacular defeats or victories and became a hard and persistent struggle. The long slog through Sicily and Italy from July 1943 to May 1945 is the outstanding example of an undifferentiated period, ending only with the conclusion of the war. It is because the year 1943 lacks major events to which fiction can be attached, that novels dealing with that year face difficulties. Maureen Duffy's skilful overview of the war,

Change (1987), is strongly periodized ('So ended the period of our innocence', p. 63) around well-known episodes: but 1943, represented by the end of the North African campaign and the beginning of the invasion of Italy, is indistinct, so that D-Day in June 1944 is reached sooner than the pace of the novel leads the reader to expect. The tendency to periodize weakens when the future begins to open out more hopefully. Conversely, the difficulty of ending a novel set in 1943 is shown by Patrick Hamilton's *The Slaves of Solitude,* which was begun during the war and laid aside, completed in 1945-6 and published in 1947. The lonely but sympathetically ordinary Miss Roach is offered an unexpected night at Claridge's in the last days of 1943:

> Then Miss Roach, knowing nothing of the future, knowing nothing of the February blitz [of 1944] about to descend on London, knowing nothing of flying bombs, knowing nothing, of Normandy, of Arnhem, of the Ardennes bulge, of Berlin, of the Atom Bomb, knowing nothing and caring very little, got into her bath and lingered in it a long while.

(pp. 241-2)

Up to this point Hamilton has avoided specific historical references, partly because little 'happened' in 1943. Put into difficulties by the time that has elapsed between the events described and the date of publication, he is forced to historicize radically in order to situate the reader in relation to his ending. In passing, Hamilton mentions the atomic bomb, which ended (it is argued) the war against Japan, but which has now become, in its subsequent development, a possible ending of a particularly conclusive kind for the contemporary reader.

After 1943, fiction might be attached to D-Day or VE Day (8 May 1945). There are many novels of the battle for Normandy, few of the end of the war. Normandy is represented in my discussion by Alexander Baron's *From the City, From the Plough* and by David Holbrook's *Flesh Wounds.* These Normandy fictions bring in another factor, the possibility of a changed future. For Baron, success in Normandy is not a conclusion; it is part of a continuity that reaches forward not only 'across the map, towards Germany', in the novel's final words (Baron, 1979, p. 191), but towards a future in which the possibilities created by victory may transform the post-war world, or be betrayed by it.

From the City, From the Plough is a novel of collective experience, describing men of all ranks from private to colonel. The commonest narrative strategy for such fictions is to build up sympathy for a number of characters and engage the reader's feelings by allowing some, but not all, to die; the selection is usually made on moral grounds. Baron's novel is exceptional in that no named person survives. Men of the Wessex Regiment, already exhausted, have been asked to ambush German guns so that American tanks can proceed:

> Among the rubble, beneath the smoking ruins, the dead of the Fifth Battalion sprawled around the guns which they had silenced; dusty, crumpled and utterly without dignity; a pair of boots protruding from a roadside ditch; a body blackened and bent like a chicken burnt in the stove; a face pressed into the dirt; a hand reaching up out of a mass of brick and timbers; a rump thrust ludicrously towards the sky. The living lay among them, speechless, exhausted, beyond grief or triumph, drawing at broken cigarettes and watching with sunken eyes the tanks go by.

(p. 190)

There is hope in this indignity. If certain men had been allowed to survive, their characters would have spoken too clearly about Baron's beliefs and intentions. By reducing them to anonymity he ensures that the reader must reflect upon what this collective dying means. We are to understand that it is a commitment to the possibilities of the future.

When a novel follows this strategy, it places itself in a definite relationship with the future that it envisages. One period—that of the novel itself—is projected forwards so that another may be conceived. This future, not present in the novel itself, becomes another possible period. When the author suggests that the suffering and destruction actually shown in the novel are a preparation for better things, people's lives can be thought of as open to transformation. This is proposed at the end of Holbrook's *Flesh Wounds.*

Every war novelist stands in a particularly acute relationship with the past and with the future because in the act of writing he or she is forced to clear a space within a period already heavily defined by other means, particularly by readers' knowledge of history. The marked periodization of war fiction is consequently one of its distinctive features. It is noticeable that almost every war novelist takes care to establish as soon as possible the date and place of events. The novelist writing during wartime dare not risk working within too wide a span in time; novelists writing after the war is over have the advantage of knowing the temporal limits of 'the war', but are at the same time constrained by knowing that every reader has an idea of the war years against which his own fiction must struggle in order to define itself. It is because history asserts itself so powerfully within war fiction that in the present discussion I have placed a strong emphasis upon the precise time and place in which events occurred. When the subject is war, history imposes itself as much upon the critic as upon the novelist.

In reading war fiction we shall find that work is a recurrent theme. War transformed the conditions of work for almost everyone. Men and women could be conscripted into the armed forces and their auxiliaries, or into factories. It was Ernest Bevin, Minister of Labour from 1940 to 1945, using sweeping powers under the Emergency Powers (Defence) Act of 1939, who directed labour at home, causing at the same time some of the most far-reaching social changes of the century. A significant decision was made in December 1941, when unmarried women between the ages of twenty and thirty were called up and given a choice between entering the auxiliary services (ATS, WAAF, WRNS) or taking jobs in industry. 'By 1943', writes Angus Calder, 'it was almost impossible for a woman under forty to avoid war work unless she had heavy family responsibilities or was looking after a war worker billeted on her' (p. 383). Women were categorized as 'immobile' or 'mobile'; the latter, young and unmarried, were moved around the British Isles as the ministry required.

Conscription for the armed services began in May 1939—too late, many thought—and on 4 September all men between eighteen and forty-one became liable. The army grew from 400,000 in May to 1,128,000 in December. Reserved occupations—which included journalists but not authors—were excluded from conscription, depending on age. At the outbreak of war there were also 400,000 men in the Territorial Army and the same number of full-timers in Civil Defence, with over a million part-timers in addition. The Auxiliary Fire Service, whose members massively outnumbered the regulars, became unpopular with the public (no fires) and with the regulars, whose conditions of work they undermined (Calder, pp. 58-60, 78).

War fiction gives human substance to these changes. Henry Green's *Caught* (1943) shows the tensions between the AFS and the regulars, whilst John Strachey's lightly fictionalized *Post D* (1941) describes the work of an ARP warden. In the factories it was soon apparent that conscripted or 'diluted' female workers could do skilled work as well, and often better, than the men they replaced. The consequent difficulties are well described in J. B. Priestley's *Daylight on Saturday,* set in an aircraft factory. In the services there was an obvious distinction between 'hostilities only' recruits and experienced regulars, and this is a frequent theme in the fiction. Nevertheless, during five years of war, conscripts became experienced soldiers themselves. It is arguable that by the end of the war Britain was fighting with a people's army. This is how Dan Billany describes them in his novel *The Trap* (1950):

> Here there were, trudging through the rain [on an exercise], bricklayers, dustmen, teachers, 'bus-conductors, plumbers, ploughboys, engineers, riveters, painters, bank-clerks, journalists, butchers—fathers, sons and brothers: middle-aged men down to boys like Shaw: their personal lives abandoned in scattered corners of the country.
>
> (Billany, 1986, p. 104)

Those personal lives were abandoned in order to learn a new job, to find a new if temporary role in one of the

services. That was the predominant experience of the war years: of being trained into a new competence.

At home, most people experienced the war as deeply tiring. 'In offices, factories, ministries, shops, kitchens the hot yellow sands of each afternoon ran out slowly; fatigue was the one reality', wrote Elizabeth Bowen in *The Heat of the Day* (p. 86). The diary of John Colville, who was a Foreign Office civil servant, then Churchill's Private Secretary, and later a fighter pilot, shows how rapidly work was transformed, even before Churchill took power. On 11 September 1939 Colville arrived at the Foreign Office at 11 a.m.; in October a 9.30 a.m. start at Downing Street is 'disgustingly early', but on 26 January 1940 he is 'almost blind with overwork' (Colville, 1985, pp. 21, 43, 84). Naomi Mitchison records that on VE Day 'all but the very young looked very tired when they stopped actually smiling' (Mitchison, 1986, p. 321).

Although much extra work fell to men, who might have parttime ARP or firefighting work in addition to their regular jobs, it was women who took the full weight of the changed circumstances. This becomes apparent in one of the most remarkable of wartime diaries, that written by Nella Last for Mass-Observation. She was a working-class woman living in the shipbuilding town of Barrow-in-Furness. By September 1942 she was running a home, and a Red Cross shop, worked at the Women's Voluntary Service centre on Tuesdays and Thursdays, and at the WVS canteen on Friday afternoons. These energetic activities were carried through at considerable cost to herself in nervous stress. This is what could lie behind 'cheerfulness':

> I wonder if it's true that all women are born actors. I wonder what I'm *really* like. I know I'm often tired, beaten and afraid, yet someone at the canteen said I radiated confidence . . . I've a jester's licence at the Centre, and if I stick my bottom lip out and mutter, 'Cor lummy, you've got a blinking nerve' like [film comedian] Gordon Harker, I can often do more—no, *always* do more—than if I said icily, 'I think that was a perfectly uncalled for remark, and I'd like an apology'. What would I *really* be like if all my nonsense and pretence was taken from me? I have a sneaking feeling I'd be a very scared, ageing woman, with pitifully little. It's an odd thing to reflect: *no* one knows *any*one else, we don't even know ourselves very well (10 September 1942).
>
> (Last, 1983, p. 217)

I know of no war fiction which recognizes women's subjectivity as existing in the way described here. Nella Last's feelings are both subversive and tragic. There was a considerable propaganda investment in working-class cheerfulness; to reveal that it was *acting* would have undermined one of the main strategies used to integrate the working class into the war effort.

Nella Last must define herself by means of a shared popular culture, imitating a comedian to achieve male respect where she works. To herself, however, she scarcely exists at all. This passage shows her being defined by others, or by a popular culture that can be appropriated for her to play her part. Such a crisis ought to be the content of war fiction, making accessible the otherwise withheld experience of women. Narrative fiction would privilege and legitimize events and feelings which as diary entries are soon overwhelmed by the banal chaos of passing time. Such fictions have not been written, perhaps because realistic writing lacks the technical resources to engage with difficult mental states. Modernism, always ready to welcome the disturbed subject, had broken up by 1939. Virginia Woolf's *Between the Acts* (1941) is built around a village pageant celebrating English life; with war imminent, history must be recovered and 'Englishness' again defined. Woolf treats with irony materials that wartime propaganda was to take all too seriously, but it is at this point that the modernist subject disappears, re-emerging only in the post-war work of Samuel Beckett.

It is nevertheless possible for a reader to construct a narrative out of the diffuse materials of a diary. Nella Last can be shown redefining herself. 'A growing contempt for man in general creeps over me . . . I'm beginning to see that I'm a really clever woman in my own line, and not the "odd" or "uneducated" woman that I've had dinned into me' (1 August 1943, p. 255). 'I looked at his [her husband's] placid, blank face and marvelled at the way he had managed so to dominate me for all our married life, at how, to avoid hurting him, I had tried to keep him in a good mood, when a smacked head would have been the best treatment' (10 May 1945, p. 282). It was work, in the new circumstances caused by war, outside the home and in daily contact with other women, that gave Mrs Last this confidence.

She was undoubtedly exceptional, and it needs to be said that working for the WVS was somewhat different from working in an aircraft factory. For women in industry, working away from the home for the first time, the war years were a moment of decisive liberation from pre-war moral and social restrictions. There was a sense of worthwhile collective activity at work, and of new opportunities away from it. Nevertheless, most industrial work was repetitive and boring, whether done by men or by women. Women proved their competence, but were as likely to find work alienating, in Marx's sense, as did men. *War Factory,* a Mass-Observation study published in 1943, showed this. Alienated work implies the existence, somewhere, of fulfilling work, and for this possibility to be raised without being realized was deeply frustrating.

For men in the army there were two kinds of work: fighting and labouring. Fighting was by far the least important. 'I had the normal skills in killing', remarks Stuart Hood (Hood, 1963, pp. 12-13). Killing was the skilled aspect of army work. The majority of the army were working-class men who spent most of their time as labourers. As a former gunner puts it, army work was 'marching and drilling, constant cleaning of guns and vehicles, digging latrines, waste-pits, trenches, gun-pits and dug-outs, cooking meals, waiting on officers; a soldier's military training and skills are used periodically but work and boredom predominate' (Ronald Gray, letter to the author). Most war fiction ignores work and boredom, but there are some remarkable pages in Dan Billany's *The Trap* describing exhaustion from digging trenches into the rock of the Libyan desert. The outstanding record of work, and what soldiers felt about it, is found in Spike Milligan's war memoirs, for example the description of digging a Command Post given in *Mussolini: His Part in My Downfall* (1980, pp. 126-30).

A short story by Graham Greene, 'Men at Work' (1940) does isolate killing as work. The activities of a committee at the Ministry of Information, where nothing of any value is done, is contrasted with the German bombers on a daylight raid over London. The condensation trails 'showed where men were going home after work' (Greene, 1977, p. 68). But this recognition of war as work is most uncommon.

Unfortunately for the status of war fiction, novels about work have rarely entered the canon of received texts. Work exists as a subject in Dickens and Hardy, in Gissing and in Robert Tressell's *Ragged-Trousered Philanthropists,* and during the 1930s there had been a number of novels about mining, by Harold Heslop and others. Critical orthodoxy has marginalized this kind of writing so that the self-realizations arising from work have never been as important as the questions of manners and morals generated by women's response to male desire. For an author to take up the subject of immature young men living in a single-sex society is immediately to be at a disadvantage. Fiction describing the business of killing, and all its associated activities, must struggle to achieve the authority already granted to the novel of morals and manners. Killing is, after all, only work.

Bibliography

Where two dates of publication are given for works quoted in the text, the second refers to the edition from which the quotation is taken.

FICTION

Aldridge, James, *The Sea Eagle,* Michael Joseph, 1944

Ballard, J. G., *Empire of the Sun,* Victor Gollancz, 1984

Baron, Alexander, *From the City, From the Plough,* Jonathan Cape, 1948; Triad Mayflower, 1979

Billany, Dan, *The Trap,* Faber and Faber, 1950; reprinted 1986

Billany, Dan, and David Dowie, *The Cage,* Longmans, Green, 1949

Bowen, Elizabeth, *The Heat of the Day,* Jonathan Cape, 1949

Comfort, Alex, *No Such Liberty,* Chapman and Hall, 1941

Deighton, Len, *SS-GB: Nazi-occupied Britain 1941,* Jonathan Cape, 1978; Triad Grafton, 1980

———. *Goodbye, Mickey Mouse,* Hutchinson, 1982

———. *Bomber,* Jonathan Cape, 1970

Duffy, Maureen, *Change,* Methuen, 1987

Duras, Marguerite, *La Douleur,* POL, 1985; William Collins, 1986 (trans. under same title)

Farrell, J. G., *The Singapore Grip,* Weidenfeld and Nicolson, 1978; Fontana, 1979

Green, Henry, *Caught,* Hogarth Press, 1943

Greene, Graham, 'Men at Work' in *Twenty-One Stories,* Penguin, 1970; reprinted 1977

Hamilton, Patrick, *Hangover Square,* Constable, 1941; Penguin, 1974

———. *The Slaves of Solitude,* Constable, 1947

Hanley, James, *No Directions,* Faber and Faber, 1943

Holbrook, David, *Flesh Wounds,* Methuen, 1966; ed. G. Halson, Longmans, 1968

Hood, Stuart, *Since the Fall,* Weidenfeld and Nicolson, 1955

———. *The Circle of the Minotaur,* Routledge and Kegan Paul, 1950

Lehmann, John (ed.), *Folios of New Writing,* Hogarth Press, 1940-1

———. *New Writing and Daylight,* Hogarth Press, 1942-6

Lindsay, Jack, *Beyond Terror: A Novel of the Battle of Crete,* Andrew Dakers, 1943

Lively, Penelope, *Moon Tiger,* André Deutsch, 1987

Manning, Olivia, *The Balkan Trilogy,* Penguin, 1981; comprising *The Great Fortune,* Heinemann, 1960; *The Spoilt City,* Heinemann, 1962; *Friends and Heroes,* Heinemann, 1965

Monsarrat, Nicholas, *The Cruel Sea,* Cassell, 1951

Priestley, J. B., *Daylight on Saturday: A Novel About An Aircraft Factory,* Heinemann, 1943

Robinson, Derek. *Kramer's War,* Hamish Hamilton, 1977.

———. *Piece of Cake,* Hamish Hamilton, 1983; Pan, 1984

Snow, C. P., *Strangers and Brothers,* vol. 2, Macmillan, 1972; Penguin, 1984; including *The New Men,* Macmillan, 1954; *Homecomings,* Macmillan, 1956

Strachey, John, *Post D,* Victor Gollancz, 1941

Thomas, Leslie, *The Magic Army,* Eyre Methuen, 1981

Tressell, Robert, *The Ragged-Trousered Philanthropists,* abridged edn. 1914, full text Lawrence and Wishart 1955; Panther/Grafton, 1965

Vercors, *Le Silence de la mer,* Les Cahiers du silence, 1943; trans. as *Put Out the Light,* Macmillan, 1944

Waugh, Evelyn, *The Sword of Honour Trilogy,* Penguin, 1984; comprising *Men at Arms,* Chapman and Hall, 1952; *Officers and Gentlemen,* Chapman and Hall, 1955; *Unconditional Surrender,* Chapman and Hall, 1961

AUTOBIOGRAPHY, LETTERS, DIARIES

Colville, John. *The Fringes of Power: Downing Street Diaries 1939-1955: Volume One: September 1939-September 1941,* Hodder and Stoughton, 1985, Sceptre, 1986.

Hood, Stuart, *Pebbles from My Skull,* Hutchinson, 1963

———. *Carlino,* Carcanet, 1985 (reprints *Pebbles from my Skull* with Afterword)

Isherwood, Christopher, *Christopher and his Kind: 1929-1939,* Eyre Methuen, 1977

Last, Nella. *Nella's Last War: A Mother's Diary 1939-45,* ed. Richard Broad and Suzie Fleming, Falling Wall Press, 1981; Sphere, 1983.

Milligan, Spike. *Mussolini: His Part in My Downfall,* Michael Joseph, 1978; Penguin, 1980 (vol. 4 of war memoirs)

Mitchison, Naomi, *Among You Taking Notes . . . The Wartime Diary of Naomi Mitchison 1939-1945,* ed. Dorothy Sheridan, Victor Gollancz, 1985; Oxford 1986

Orwell, George, *The Collected Essays, Journalism and Letters of George Orwell: Volume I: An Age Like This 1920-1940,* ed. Sonia Orwell and Ian Angus, Secker and Warburg, 1968; Penguin, 1970a

———. *The Collected Essays, Journalism and Letters of George Orwell: Volume II: My Country Right or Left 1940-1943,* ed. Sonia Orwell and Ian Angus, Secker and Warburg, 1968; Penguin, 1970b

Powell, Anthony, *To Keep the Ball Rolling: The Memoirs of Anthony Powell,* Penguin, 1983 (abridgement of the four volumes published by William Heinemann, 1976-82)

T[hompson], T. J. and T[hompson], E. P. (eds.), *There is a Spirit in Europe . . . : A Memoir of Frank Thompson,* Victor Gollancz, 1947

Waugh, Evelyn, *Robbery Under Law: The Mexican Object-Lesson,* Chapman and Hall, 1939

HISTORICAL AND OTHER WORKS

Brickhill, Paul, *The Great Escape,* Faber and Faber, 1951; Arrow, 1979

Calder, Angus, *The People's War: Britain 1939-1945,* Jonathan Cape, 1969; Panther, 1972

Hewison, Robert, *Under Siege: Literary Life in London 1939-1945,* Weidenfeld and Nicolson, 1977

Lewis, Peter, *A People's War,* Thames Methuen, 1986

Marwick, Arthur, *The Home Front: The British and the Second World War,* Thames and Hudson, 1976

Wintringham, Tom, *New Ways of War,* Penguin, 1940

CRITICISM

Comfort, Alex, *The Novel and Our Time,* Phoenix House, 1948.

Spender, Stephen, *Life and the Poet,* Secker and Warburg, 1942

David Rosenfeld (essay date 2003)

SOURCE: Rosenfeld, David. "Wartime Fiction." In *The Columbia Companion to Modern East Asian Literature,* edited by Joshua S. Mostow, pp. 175-78. New York: Columbia University Press, 2003.

[*In the essay below, Rosenfeld describes two main types of writings in Japanese literature about World War II—the shihōsetsu (factual personal narrative) and the jūgunki (fictional narrative).*]

The most important fact to keep in mind about Japanese literary prose written during the war is that it was written during the war—that is to say, whether or not the war itself was the predominant subject of such works, they were written according to tenets defined by, and under the strict supervision of, the government. The Japanese government, which was dominated by the military beginning in the early 1930s, designated very specific guidelines about what could be written and published in Japan and maintained an extensive censorship regime that not only examined magazine articles and books for acceptable content before publication, but also could ban the distribution of specific books and specific issues of magazines even after they had been published and distributed to bookstores and newsstands.

This is not to say that Japanese writers resisted the government's strict regulation of literary activity. Indeed, most writers saw it as their patriotic duty to support the nation's military enterprise in their work. Almost all major writers—including those who were harshly critical of wartime collaborators after the war—participated in literary trips to China and other Japanese-occupied areas sponsored by the government and joined government-sponsored literary organizations. Only two major writers, Nagai Kafū and Tanizaki Jun'ichirō, and a few committed Communists who spent much of the wartime period in prison, are commonly recognized as having withdrawn from the war effort and refrained from supporting Japan's military activities (Keene 1971:301). But the roster of writers and intellectuals who did take part in government-sponsored activities and supported the war more or less enthusiastically included the stars of the Japanese literary establishment, such as writers Ozaki Shirō (1896-1964) and Yoshiya Nobuko (1896-1973), critics Kobayashi Hideo (1902-1983) and Hirano Ken (1907-1978), and other important figures such as editor Kikuchi Kan (1888-1948). Many writers who had been members of the Communist Party, or were at least sympathetic to leftist causes, were encouraged or coerced by the government to make public statements repudiating their leftist politics and, implicitly, endorsing the authoritarian state. This renunciation, commonly referred to as *tenkō* (conversion), was an experience shared by so many writers and intellectuals that it would be a major focus of the literary world's debates over the war experience in the postwar period.

The most notable prose literary genre practiced during the war was a form of documentary autobiographical prose that came to be called *jūgunki*, or "campaign accounts." These were first-person descriptions of the experiences of Japanese soldiers at the front, and often on the battlefield itself, in China and other places Japan's aggressive expansion reached. Many *jūgunki* were written by literary celebrities flown to the front in China for periods as short as a few days, put up in luxury accommodations and wined and dined by Japanese military escorts. But more popular credence was extended to *jūgunki* written by actual soldiers on the battlefield, the most famous of whom was Hino Ashihei (1907-1960).

Hino had been an aspiring poet and writer, studying English literature at the elite Waseda University in Tokyo, and a supporter of labor unionism in his native Kyushu, even journeying with a band of Kyushu longshoremen to support labor strikes in Shanghai in 1932. Hino was drafted as a regular soldier in 1937 and had already been sent into combat in China when a novel he had completed just before entering the army won the prestigious Akutagawa Prize. His ensuing celebrity prompted the army to transfer him from his combat unit to the Army's Information Bureau, which disseminated Japanese propaganda abroad and provided inspiring war information to the home front. After a few months with the Information Bureau, Hino published a campaign account of his experiences accompanying a Japanese platoon as it advanced through southern China. The book, *Wheat and Soldiers* (Mugi to heitai, 1937), became the best-selling volume of the war, along with the two companion volumes that formed "the Soldier Trilogy," eventually racking up sales of 1.2 million copies.

Hino's acclaim was based on his sentimental, heartwarming descriptions of individual Japanese soldiers—the *heitai* of the title, which carries the unpretentious, common-man connotations that the term *GI* does in reference to U.S. soldiers. His soldiers plodded through the vast Chinese wheat fields, usually hungry and tired, but always dedicated, devoted to the emperor, and warmly supportive of each other. They were kind to but disdainful of the Chinese farmers and refugees they encountered, considering them childish, ignorant, and dirty and in need of guidance from their "big brother," Japan. Hino presented himself as one of the *heitai,* simple and patriotic—glossing over his elite education and literary fame. His narrator loves a good beer and a good bath, and he often finds an opportunity for comradeship by sharing one or the other with fellow soldiers. He unabashedly describes incidents that demonstrate his own clumsiness or ignorance, describing with relish, for example, how his unit unwittingly used an elegant chamber pot they found in an abandoned house to cook in.

Hino's unpretentious narrative persona was quite different from another well-known soldier-writer of the period, Hibino Shirō (1903-1975), whose novella *Wusun Creek* (Wusun kurîku, 1939), described his combat experiences dramatically, but clearly from an elite perspective: Hibino carries his copies of the classical texts the *Manyōshū* and *Saikontan* with him on the battlefield, and says he would sooner abandon his rifle than his books (*Zenshū* 2:225). Equally cultured but less impressed with himself, Ibuse Masuji described his experiences as an Information Bureau officer in Japanese-occupied Singapore in the novella *City of Flowers* (Hana no machi, 1942). Other writers whose accounts of their military experiences, whether in combat or as members of an occupying force, were well received in Japan included Takami Jun (1907-1965), for works such as his short story "About Nokana" (Nokana no koto, 1943), and Satomura Kinzō (1902-1945), whose death in combat in the Philippines in 1945 cut short his literary career after he published only a few books describing his military service in China.

Not so well received was the novel *Living Soldiers* (Ikite iru heitai, 1938), by another Akutagawa Prize-winning author, Ishikawa Tatsuzō (1905-1985). Ishikawa was dispatched by the literary and intellectual magazine *Chūō kōron* to accompany a Japanese military unit that participated in the infamous siege and capture of Nanjing in December 1937. It is surprising that the editors of the magazine thought that Ishikawa's lurid depiction of the brutal killing of both enemy soldiers and civilians and the cynical attitudes of Japanese soldiers would meet the government's approval. The editors' miscalculation resulted in the recall of the entire issue and the conviction of Ishikawa and some editors for violations of the Peace Preservation Law, and the incident certainly weighed heavily in the government's decision to ban publication of the magazine in 1944. (Issued in December 1945 by the publisher Kawade shobō, *Living Soldiers* was one of the first works to be published in postwar Japan.)

Although few writers were as bold in their representation of atrocities by Japanese soldiers as Ishikawa was, careful readings of many wartime texts reveal elements that could be read as critical of or resistant to the wartime state. Ibuse's gentle but pointed descriptions of the inefficiencies and ineptitude of Japanese administration in Singapore in *City of Flowers* and Takami's criticism of racial prejudice by Japanese soldiers against darker-skinned natives in "About Nokana" are examples of this subtle resistance. And even some of the wartime writings of Hino, anathematized as a "cultural war criminal" after the war, suggest revulsion at the excesses of some Japanese soldiers. Indeed, significant portions of Hino's works depicting such war crimes as the execution of prisoners of war were cut from his wartime works by military censors.

The *jūgunki* form, as practiced by Hino, Ishikawa, and others, had much in common with the dominant prose genre of the prewar period, the *shishōsetsu,* or personal novel. Like the *shishōsetsu,* the *jūgunki* was typically narrated in the first person and could encompass both purportedly factual documentary accounts and works that seemed to be fiction. In either case, however, both the *jūgunki* and the *shishōsetsu* were conventionally read as the actual experiences of the author, who was equated with the narrator of the text. As many modern explorations of the *shishōsetsu* have revealed, they were often heavily fictionalized and mediated for literary effect, despite being presented as unmediated experience. *Jūgunki,* too, claimed authority for their narratives based on the credibility of their authors' experience in the war: much of Hino's acclaim, for instance, was based on the fact that he had been in fact a common soldier, and he consciously sought to enhance this effect by suppressing from his texts aspects of his identity as an educated man of letters.

One crucial difference between the *shishōsetsu* and the *jūgunki,* though, was the social commonality of the subject matter they depicted. *Shishōsetsu* authors moved in rarefied literary circles, and emphasized their detachment from mainstream society. Their texts emphasized the solitary and individual character of their experiences. Chronicles of the war, however, described events and experiences that millions of Japanese would share.

Bibliography

Hibino Shirō. *Wusun kurīku* (Wusun Creek). In Hirano Ken, ed., *Sensō bungaku zenshū* (Complete Works of War Literature), 2:5ff. Tokyo: Mainichi shinbunsha, 1971-72.

Hino Ashihei. *Wheat and Soldiers.* Trans. Shidzue Ishimoto. New York: Rinehart, 1939.

Ibuse Masuji. *Black Rain.* Trans. John Bester. Tokyo: Kodansha International, 1969.

Keene, Donald. *Landscapes and Portraits: Appreciations of Japanese Culture.* Tokyo: Kodansha International, 1971.

Clair Wills (essay date spring 2004)

SOURCE: Wills, Clair. "The Aesthetics of Irish Neutrality during the Second World War." *boundary 2* 31, no. 1 (spring 2004): 119-45.

[*In the following essay, Wills examines the ramifications of Ireland's neutrality during World War II on literary works of the period.*]

The neutral island facing the Atlantic,
The neutral island in the heart of man,
Are bitterly soft reminders of the beginnings
That ended before the end began.

Look into your heart, you will find a County Sligo,
A Knocknarea with for navel a cairn of stones,
You will find the shadow and sheen of a moleskin
    mountain
And a litter of chronicles and bones.

Look into your heart, you will find fermenting rivers,
Intricacies of gloom and glint,
You will find such ducats of dream and great doubloons of ceremony
As nobody today would mint.

But then look eastward from your heart, there bulks
A continent, close, dark, as archetypal sin,
While to the west off your own shores the mackerel
Are fat—on the flesh of your kin.[1]

Louis MacNeice wrote "Neutrality" in September 1942, after the death of his friend Graham Sheppard, who drowned in the Atlantic following a German U-boat attack. MacNeice is sometimes regarded as having been straightforwardly hostile to Irish neutrality—but, as the poem suggests, the real picture was far more complicated. He often finds it hard to resist the spell of Ire-

land's solipsism and self-romanticizing, even as he chides her for failing to come to terms with the demands of maturity and the modern world. In 1941, he writes, "I have no wish now to bring up the undying (though Chameleonic) Irish Question but I would ask you to remember that the feeling in Eire is now predominantly pro-British (though still opposed to participation in the War), that the pro-German minority is extremely small and de Valera's position is agonizingly difficult. Those who propose the application of the strong hand to Eire are forgetting their history."[2] The neutral island is isolationist, and MacNeice portrays Ireland's isolation as a symptom of her folie de grandeur. (He puts it here in explicitly Yeatsian terms, not only in the swipe at Sligo but in the bankrupt coupling of "ceremony" and "dream.") Modern political and ethical universalism also requires a kind of neutrality, or at the least impartiality. Indeed, some thinkers have distinguished a "cosmopolitan" strain within the political tradition of neutrality itself, jostling uneasily with a tendency toward national egoism.[3] Yet how do we distinguish impartiality—the "neutral island in the heart of man"—from indifference? We could put that line together with a sentence by Elizabeth Bowen from the postscript to her wartime collection of stories, *The Demon Lover,* where she says, "Through the particular in wartime, I felt the high-voltage current of the general pass."[4] The ambivalence of neutrality, the tension between the broader moral questions raised by the Second World War, and a sense of the uniqueness of Ireland's situation, the tug between awareness of a particular location and general European, indeed global, issues, is central to the Irish writing of the period. As the possessive, blinkered Hannah Kernahan puts it in Kate O'Brien's *The Last of Summer,* "Danzig's a long way from Drumaninch, my son."[5] Her son, Martin, however, "although his Eire citizenship would give him a just immunity,"[6] feels pledged to war nonetheless because of the moral issues at stake (though he decides to join the French army rather than fight alongside the British). This conflict between isolation and orientation toward Europe is played out not just in the writing but in the lives and identities of the writers themselves. A distinctive interplay takes place between the private sense of belonging and allegiance, and the compelling force of public issues that often results in a fracturing of the sense of self. *To Ireland, I,* the punning title of Paul Muldoon's recent book of essays on Irish writing, nicely captures this intertwining. The shifting boundary between the public and the private or intimate sphere (condensed in the title of Muldoon's book) is also, in another sense, the relation between national and global—or national and universal.

To put this another way: far from being solely an act of isolationism, the declaration of neutrality led to a fundamental rethinking of Ireland's relationship to European culture and politics and a new sense of national identity. As Bowen puts it, Irish neutrality during the Second World War was "Eire's first *free* self-assertion."[7] The issue of neutrality was intensified and took on something of the form of a personal crisis for many of the leading Irish writers of the time, however, by virtue of their wartime roles and location. Bowen was based in London during the Second World War but traveled frequently to Ireland to assess attitudes to neutrality in her work for the British Ministry of Information; MacNeice sailed for the United States in 1940 but returned to Britain within the year and worked for the BBC in London; O'Brien lived and traveled widely in Spain in the thirties; Francis Stuart went to Germany at the start of the war and broadcast propaganda from there; and Denis Johnston followed the North African campaign and the aftermath of the D-Day landings, and was one of the first civilians to enter Buchenwald in 1944 as a reporter for the BBC. Or one could instance other writers such as Samuel Beckett, who was in the French Resistance, and Hubert Butler, who traveled widely in Eastern and Central Europe in the immediate prewar and postwar periods. The wartime and postwar texts of these writers record the morally complex and sometimes traumatic exposure of an Irish sensibility to the violent politics of mid-twentieth-century Europe, an exposure that often has a disruptive impact on the sense of self.

Why should an Irish sensibility be distinctive in this regard? Some reminder of the issues at stake in the choice of neutrality may be useful. From a sober political standpoint, it would have been impossible for Eire to be anything other than neutral, given the recent history of relations with Britain, culminating in the war of independence and the establishment of the Irish Free State in 1921. Neutrality was a declaration of publicly nonaligned independence that finally demonstrated the sovereignty of Eamon de Valera's state and its break with empire. In effect, Ireland's internal political divisions in the wake of the Civil War, and the continuing problem of partition, required neutrality. Undoubtedly, too, de Valera's experience at the League of Nations played its part. It was, ironically, while Ireland had presidency of the council that the League of Nations conspicuously failed to deal with Italy's invasion of Abyssinia, an event that irrevocably tainted de Valera's faith in the politics of collective security and led him to rely on diplomacy as the only possible alternative to imperialist militarism. Assessment of Irish neutrality was complicated, however, by awareness of the pro-German feeling within certain sections of the society. Estimates of Irish support for Germany vary wildly, but certainly some republicans were in accord with Roger Casement's 1914 formulation that "God Save Ireland is another form of God Save Germany,"[8] and there were fears that IRA leader Séan Russell might become an Irish quisling (fears that were heightened during the conscription crisis in 1939 and 1940). These tensions were made more

acute by the fact that members of de Valera's own cabinet, such as former IRA Chief of Staff Frank Aiken, thought Britain a more serious threat to Ireland than Germany during the war.[9]

In 1938, Ireland reclaimed the Treaty ports at Cobh, Berehaven, and Lough Swilly, and this made neutrality an economically viable option. It also had dire political consequences for Britain, however. The most difficult test for neutrality occurred during the second half of 1940, when England wanted to use the Treaty ports as a base to coordinate the sinking of German U-boats attacking the North Atlantic convoys. It was during this period that Bowen was recruited to gather information on Irish attitudes to Ireland's status as "friendly neutral." (At around the same time, the poet John Betjeman, who was acting as British press attaché in Dublin, was recruited to plant rumors [or "sibs"] among proBritish contacts in the Irish capital, having received the required instruction in "operational whispering.")[10] Throughout the war, de Valera did try to bargain use of the ports against Irish unity, but he kept coming back to neutrality as the safer option. In effect, the border became more clearly defined during the war years, as both parts of Ireland sought to define their opposing territorial states within the context of the European conflict. Most histories of the period pay tribute to de Valera's balancing act. He managed to appease republican elements for whom the war was a further stage in Britain's imperialist warmongering rather than an antifascist crusade, while offering guarded assistance to the allies by, for example, repatriating allied planes or forwarding information about the presence of U-boats, and at the same time remaining outside the fighting. Nevertheless, Irish neutrality was possible only because the invasion of Ireland never became vital for either the Allies or the Axis powers (though Ireland continued to be haunted by the fear of invasion and by anxiety over possible aerial bombing).

One of the most striking aspects of this history, and the most damaging in the long run, was de Valera's refusal to acknowledge—publicly, at any rate—the moral dimensions of the war. He never appeared to see the war in broad terms of European morality but concentrated on Ireland's destiny within a domestic framework far removed from the struggle against Nazi Germany. In this he was aided by the extremely strict censorship in operation throughout the war, which forbade publication of any story that could be deemed partial to one side or the other, thus in effect banning any news that might create anti-Nazi (or anti-British) sentiment. As Donal Ó Drisceoil has argued, "Aiken envisaged a snowball effect if any moral judgements about the belligerents were allowed, eventuating in a civil war on the question of who Ireland should go to war against."[11] In effect, Aiken attempted to enforce a "moral neutrality" on Irish attitudes toward the war, an interpretation of neutrality that differed markedly from, for example, the Swiss version, where freedom of expression on the war was allowed, if not encouraged.[12] In fact, as Joe Lee has emphasized, censorship was vital for the sense of moral superiority that accrued distinctively to Irish neutrality—what he calls "the necessary sense of righteousness." This self-deception with regard to the nature of Ireland's stance could not be sustained "if the belligerents turned out to have been unevenly matched in the savagery stakes."[13] The most ignominious moment in the history of Irish neutrality is also the most famous—de Valera's visit to the German legation to offer condolences on the death of Hitler. We can understand this in part as born of his conviction that a rigorous adherence to diplomacy was the only way for small nations to survive, but it is fair to say it was not understood in this way at the time. Bad enough as it looked, this very public act coincided with the lifting of censorship and the sudden circulation in Ireland of stories of atrocity that had been suppressed for the duration of the war. This included pictures and newsreels of Buchenwald, which were shown in the weeks following his visit.[14]

As I have suggested, the moral politics of neutrality became the occasion for a particularly intense form of self-questioning, often amounting to a kind of fracturing of the self, on the part of the writers with whom I am concerned. In the following pages, I focus on Johnston, Stuart, and Bowen, all of whom accept the need for neutrality, given the historical context, and profess guarded support for it. At various points, their stance could be summarized in the following formula: Ireland should be neutral, but individuals don't need to be, as though public and private aspects of the self can be neatly disentangled. As Bowen puts it in one of her intelligence reports, "Eire (and I think rightly) sees her neutrality as positive, not merely negative. She has invested her self-respect in it." She goes on, "It is typical of her intense and narrow view of herself that she cannot see that her attitude must appear to England an affair of blindness, egotism, escapism, or sheer funk."[15] Bowen's particular sense of internal conflict, literally caught "between worlds," is perhaps only the most extreme example of a more general malaise. When Stuart emigrated to Berlin at the start of the war to take up an academic post, and subsequently began to broadcast propaganda to Ireland from the Nazi capital, he claimed his actions were in defense of Irish neutrality—to combat the overwhelming diet of British propaganda on the airwaves (propaganda for which MacNeice and Johnston were partly responsible). But in Stuart's radio talks, one senses a disappointment with a country that can simply withdraw from the momentous political and military struggle unfolding in Europe, a disgust with what he calls, at one point, "an Ireland that has sat out the world conflict on bacon and tea."[16]

Bowen and Stuart are, in a sense, the two extremes. Bowen strongly identifies with the British war effort, whereas Stuart's political stance shows clear affinities with European fascism. For the playwright Johnston, Irish neutrality offers a nonbelligerent status that seems to provide a platform for the writerly ideal of detachment. However, as we shall see, this detachment is put under extreme pressure and eventually breaks down. We could say that for each of these authors, the politically problematic question of Ireland's status also poses the question of their status as writers. Is their allegiance to the private but ultimately generalizable truth of the independent, imaginative witness, or must this be overridden by a public, and putatively ethical, responsibility (which in fact may depend on idiosyncrasies of personal history and location)? Each writer seeks a solution to the problem of Ireland's status, an overcoming of the dangers of parochialism, and an appropriate sense of "Europeanness," or—at least—of Ireland's relation to Europe.

This whole issue is exacerbated in wartime texts by the types of writing undertaken—the mode of public address. The task of gathering and disseminating various types of "intelligence" during the war had a profound and lasting effect on these writers' conceptions of the relationship of self to society. I am thinking here beyond the obvious examples of Bowen's intelligence-gathering activities or Stuart's wartime broadcasts, to writing that cannot simply be classified as propaganda—travel writing, reminiscence, journalism, eyewitness accounts. All complicate the relation between public and private roles, and compromise any aesthetic resolution. As MacNeice puts it in his defense of Auden's decision to go to the States in 1939:

> Whether the intelligentsia at the moment can directly affect public affairs to any extent seems to me doubtful. What they ought to do is reassess their position *as intellectuals*; it is worthwhile remembering that there are more than the two alternatives of the Ivory Tower and the political tub. If you come to analyse it, public-mindedness itself can be a form of escapism. I don't think for a moment we should all go private; what I do think is that we have been much too naive about politics. Perhaps we all need a dose of the desert, and perhaps that is just what we shall get, whether we want it or not.[17]

NEUTRALITY AS DETACHMENT

The desert stages the beginnings of the quest that lies at the heart of Denis Johnston's wartime autobiography-cum-diary, *Nine Rivers from Jordan*. Johnston came from a liberal Protestant background (his father had supported Home Rule[18]), and, despite (or because of) his education at Merchiston and Cambridge, he was well disposed to the independence of the Free State (indeed, of a united Ireland) and supportive of Ireland's neutral position. This caused him some difficulties in the early part of the war, when he was employed by the BBC in London. In 1939, Johnston worked for the BBC's fledgling television station, but this was closed down at the beginning of September, and he was moved to radio, where he feared he might become involved in anti-Irish propaganda or attacks on Ireland's neutrality. In the event the BBC sent him back to Ireland in 1940, where for two years

> he was to be enlisted in the drive to win Eire's support for the war or, if that was not possible, at least making its neutrality as pro-British as possible. His task was to investigate whether radio talks and other material could be provided from Dublin, for transmission on the BBC's Overseas Service, which could reach the tens of thousands of Irish citizens who were already serving with the British forces abroad. The thinking was that supporting Irish soldiers in the field with news and reminders of home would be a first step towards winning hearts and minds in Eire.[19]

In addition, Johnston was to supply program ideas for the BBC in Northern Ireland aimed at encouraging Ireland to enter the war, in order to fulfill the policy objectives of the British Ministry of Information. He was involved in delicate dealings with officials in the North, for whom any negotiation with the southern state amounted to appeasement. As the Northern Ireland prime minister, J. M. Andrews, puts it, in response to plans for a regular cross-border Irish magazine program, "This, in my view, would be an insidious form of propaganda which would entirely misrepresent the position of Northern Ireland in the United Kingdom and would slur over the neutral and most unhelpful attitude which Eire has taken up during the war."[20] From the very beginning of the war, then, Johnston found himself having to compromise his belief in Ireland's right to be neutral. In 1940, he joined the Local Security Force in Dublin, where his brief was the protection of Ireland from both sides in the war, and, at the same time, he was making programs designed to undermine Ireland's nonpartisan status.

In April 1942, the BBC sent Johnston to join the Middle East News Division as a correspondent. Bernard Adams notes a diary entry Johnston made at the time: "Before he said his goodbyes in Dublin he carefully explained to himself why he had chosen to go: 'it is my belief in Ireland's neutrality that has so largely sent me forth. Only those who are prepared to go into this horrible thing themselves have the right to say that Ireland must stay out.'"[21] Johnston maintains this reflection on the dilemmas of partisanship, neutrality, and detachment throughout the volumes of War Field Books, which he wrote during the next three years in three separate theaters of war and which form the basis of *Nine Rivers from Jordan*. He began reporting from Egypt with the Eighth Army; later he covered their advance through Italy. Later still he followed the advance of the Ameri-

cans through Holland and Germany. *Nine Rivers from Jordan,* published in 1953, is a highly worked version of the diaries, filtered through several generic conventions such as the bildungsroman and the quest narrative, as well as parodic versions of the Catholic liturgy, Celtic myth, Faust, *Ulysses, Finnegans Wake,* and many other works besides.[22] Two sections of the book appeared in the *Bell* in 1950 and 1951. But Johnston also deposited a three-volume typescript of the work in the British Library in 1946 or 1947. This typescript, entitled *Dionysia,* is anonymous (and undated). It is an extraordinary document—a mass of manuscript pages, sometimes double-, sometimes single-spaced, with numerous handwritten corrections, and with Johnston's own photographs included, as well as staff directives, Eighth Army directives, and German and British propaganda leaflets. A comparison of the typescript with the War Field Books and with *Nine Rivers from Jordan* reveals that it corresponds far more closely with the 1953 text, and suggests that Johnston worked on the diaries very soon after his return from Europe in 1945. What is striking, however, is the way that he seems to want us to understand the text as the unmediated presentation of his wartime experiences. His use of tense, and some odd jarring moments, sometimes gives the impression that the work is woven from raw diary material written from day to day. More often, it is clear that a considerable amount of artifice has gone into its construction—he uses composite characters, for example, and, rather bizarrely perhaps, the narrative structure of a novitiate in the Catholic Church, with bits of the mass and the catechism thrown in.

These considerations are important, because to read the narrative as a relatively straightforward presentation of Johnston's experiences requires us to believe in the naïveté of the detached observer character at the beginning of both *Dionysia* and *Nine Rivers from Jordan.*[23] His naïveté stretches credulity: "Knowing what was wanted under our system of free and objective reporting, I was not going to concern myself with propaganda. I was going to describe soberly and sensibly exactly what I saw, and give the people at home the Truth, the whole Truth, and nothing but the Truth, whether unhappy or unfavourable."[24] Johnston posits the very existence of the diary as a result of his frustration at being unable to be an impartial voice. As a spokesperson for the BBC, he wants to be neutral and objective, but he is caught in the snares of propaganda, and the journals are his response—the place he will be "truly neutral." Here, he says, he will tell the stories of "good German soldiers" and of fraternization, which are supposed to be bad for morale, to endanger the war effort. He begins his work—he would have us believe—full of idealism: "I am not in this war as a belligerent, and so long as I remain firmly fixed in my own role and refuse to carry arms, the war can do no harm to me."[25]

To this end, Johnston peppers his narrative with anecdotes that belittle the earnestness of the propaganda merchants on both sides, who come off badly in relation to the soldiers themselves. He wants to believe in an idea of war itself as heroic and decent, and this is certainly a stance he can keep up as he reports the encounters between Field Marshals Bernard Law Montgomery and Erwin Rommel in the western desert. But it is an idea that becomes increasingly strained when he comes back to Europe. With respect to his narrative of growth, Italy is the place where he loses the naïveté of youth, as he bemoans, "Too many liberated adolescents thinking of war in terms of the desert and excitement and pursuit and loot. But war isn't really like that."[26] Nonetheless, he continues to articulate his disgust with the way peace is being imposed, and this becomes his way of maintaining his moral neutrality, as he claims that one side is as bad as the other.

> I had just been given a lecture . . . on the evils of Irish neutrality—the text being that people who benefit from the blessings of justice and democracy ought to help in their preservation. Fair enough, if we really know that this is what we are fighting for. But do we know it? According to these papers, we are fighting for as vindictive and as horrible a peace as Hitler's would ever have been. What that priest on the Sangro said was true. Evil is like a Vampire. When you take arms against it and destroy it, you find in the end that you are evil too—that it is living on your own actions.[27]

Paralleling these reflections on neutrality and the existence of evil is a quest narrative of sorts, which begins in the first part of the book, after Johnston finds a packet of letters from a German woman to a soldier who has been killed on the retreat from the Battle of Alamein. He becomes obsessed with the woman, and, in April 1945, finding himself in the region of Germany where she wrote the letters, decides to look for her. He is met with stony stares and realizes that for the ordinary villagers he is not a neutral—he wears the uniform of an invading army. He has attempted to maintain this distinction between looking British and being neutral throughout his three years—primarily through being unarmed—but it breaks down at this point, just as he is given other reasons to feel himself a belligerent. An American soldier advises him to go and look at the local camp, which turns out to be Buchenwald. Importantly, he has already seen a concentration camp in Alsace, which he regards primarily as a propaganda exercise—which he reads from a neutral standpoint, if you like; Buchenwald shatters his protective "nonbelligerent status":

> —Here's the Block you want to see, said Quick. Don't come in if you don't want to.
>
> I went in. At one end lay a heap of smoking clothes amongst which a few ghouls picked and searched—for what, God only knows. As we entered the long hut the stench hit us in the face, and a queer wailing sound came to our ears. Along both sides of the shed was tier upon tier of what can only be described as shelves. And lying on these, packed tightly side by side, like knives and forks in a chest, were living creatures—some of them stirring, some of them stiff and silent, but all of them skeletons, with the skin drawn tight over their bones, with heads bulging and misshapen from emaciation, with burning eyes and sagging jaws. And as we came in, those with strength to do so turned their heads and gazed at us; and from their lips came that thin unearthly sound.
>
> Then I realized what it was. It was meant to be cheering. They were cheering the uniform that I wore. They were cheering for the hope that it brought them.
>
> We walked the length of the shed—and then through another one. From the shelves feeble arms rose and waved, like twigs in a breeze.[28]

Admittedly, this is a rather forced mechanism—he thinks he is looking for the woman, but the reality he needs to "find" is Buchenwald. Having found it, he picks up a gun; symbolically, he is no longer a nonbelligerent. Some weeks later, Johnston ends his journal—and ends it twice. In one version, he comes across a high-ranking Nazi official who has been trying to escape into Switzerland but has reached the border too late. He offers to shoot the Nazi, partly in atonement for his own neutrality, but then hands the gun to the German, who turns it on Johnston. Johnston is killed. In the other version, he passes a car with a dead German in it, obviously a Nazi official who has killed himself after failing to get across the border. This, too, is slightly forced perhaps, but it is a very clear representation of the nightmare of the split self—morally in two absolutely different places at the same time—one the murdered, another the murderer.[29]

For all the intertextual allusions and antirealist conventions, Johnston's wartime reflections are clearly intimately linked to his own experiences. Yet they can also be read as a sustained, cryptic, ironic reflection on de Valera's neutral stance. Johnston's actual diaries and wartime notebooks betray an increasing sense of irritation with the power of the Catholic hierarchy and a growing alienation from de Valera's version of Ireland.[30] Yet very little of this finds its way into *Nine Rivers from Jordan*. Instead, the Johnston character betrays certain patterns of behavior that echo de Valera's public persona to a remarkable degree. There is, for example, the obsessive observation of "protocol" with regard to the Germans and the refusal to be swayed by anything that might be propaganda (which amounts to a form of censorship). More specifically, de Valera's visit to the German legation to offer condolences on the death of Hitler is, I believe, echoed in Johnston's fictional conversation with the SS officer over war guilt in the final pages of the journal. The discovery of Buchenwald overshadows both meetings, and Johnston's death at the hands of the high-ranking Nazi official suggests a profound criticism not only of his own former idealistic championing of neutrality but of de Valera's stance. *Nine Rivers* enacts a complex interrogation of the sense of moral superiority that accrued to Irish neutrality, as the tension between the political logic of Ireland's position and its ethical obscurity finally tears the Johnston character apart.

NEUTRALITY AS IMMUNITY

One could think of Francis Stuart as a kind of parodic mirror image of Johnston. Both came from middle-class Protestant backgrounds, both were moderately successful writers in the twenties and thirties, both left Ireland during the war because of disastrous marriages, and both engaged in radio propaganda—but for opposite sides. Stuart was completely out of sympathy with the liberal view of politics and human relations that propelled Johnston through the war. He put his faith in what might be called the anarchy of the imagination, a form of extreme, antisocial, mystical romanticism. In his fictionalized autobiography, *Blacklist, Section H,* he describes his brief involvement with the anti-Treaty side during the Civil War, through his mother-in-law, Maud Gonne, and his imprisonment by the Free State government in the early twenties. Yet he presents his political commitment negatively, suggesting it has to do with revolutionary ambitions of a different sort: "He was embarked on a private war which he hoped might cause a few cracks in the walls erected by generations of pious and patriotic Irishmen around the national consciousness. Then perhaps the dawn of the imaginative and undogmatic mood, that he saw as the prerequisite of true revolution, might set in."[31] This vision of himself as a romantic outcast is not wholly retrospective. In an earlier autobiography, *Things to Live For,* published in 1934 and written while he was in his early thirties, Stuart presents himself as dis-illusioned with all available structures in Ireland—including marriage; in his self-dramatization, he lives the life of the gambler and political, social, and imaginative outcast.[32] It was this impatience with "moral righteousness" (as well as a need to earn money) that impelled him to leave Ireland in January 1940 and journey to Berlin, where he remained for the duration of the war. The move, so he claimed in retrospect, put him on the side of the condemned, where the life of the imagination was sustained by the very intensity of defeat and humiliation (although it was of course not clear in 1940 that Germany would lose the war).

The extent of Stuart's collaboration with the Nazi regime has long been a source of controversy, a controversy recently fueled by publication of transcripts of the broadcasts he made to Ireland for Irland-Redaktion, between 1942 and 1944.[33] Stuart himself insisted that his move to Germany indicated not a pro-Nazi stance but a neutral one, and that his broadcasts were in the main an attempt to combat the overwhelming stream of British propaganda on Irish airwaves. In what was possibly the first of Stuart's talks, picked up by Irish and British monitors on St. Patrick's Day 1942, Stuart declared that he was "not trying to make propaganda."[34] It was an assertion he returned to repeatedly, and he argued in later years that his broadcasts were not political, except in that they supported Irish neutrality. However, as Brendan Barrington has argued, this was hardly an impartial position given Stuart's Berlin location. The leaders of the Third Reich had no doubts that an Ireland which joined the war on the side of the Axis powers would instantly be invaded by Britain. Since neutrality forbade the use of the Treaty ports to Britain, Irish neutrality was in Germany's best interests—indeed Stuart admits as much in *Blacklist, Section H.* Here he reasons that the German authorities asked him to undertake weekly broadcasts to Ireland because they were "afraid that America's entry into the conflict would influence Ireland to abandon her neutrality, though this seemed a very slight threat in the light of the powerful forces that the Germans had managed to line up against them."[35]

Stuart viewed the war as a conflict between the "liberal materialism" of Anglo-American civilization and the culture of Europe. He repeatedly asserted the need for Ireland to connect culturally with Europe rather than with Britain. As he states in his first broadcast, "We have had too little contact with countries that have something to give us. We have on the other hand been surrounded by communities whose life is [based] on money and the power of money. Whether we turn to England or the United States we see the god of money. . . . Ireland belongs to Europe and England does not belong to it. I believe that after this war our future should be linked with the future of Europe and no other."[36] This stance generates a dilemma for Stuart, however. As the radio talks progress, defense of Irish neutrality starts to feel like a defense of Irish parochialism, and even the traditional goals of Irish republicanism begin to appear in this light: "There is no good of saying, we want our lost provinces back, we want freedom and security and then we want to be left alone. . . . No if we hope to find national fulfillment after this war, in the new world, as I believe we shall, then we must not be merely intent on taking, we must give too."[37] The vague image of a new, spiritual European order that Stuart, in 1942, could still delude himself would arise from the conflagration reflects, of course, a perverse kind of internationalism. But it is one that sits uneasily with the isolationist stance he sees in Ireland.

The ambivalence of Stuart's attitude toward neutrality is vividly played out in his postwar fiction, particularly in the group of novels *The Pillar of Cloud, Redemption, The Flowering Cross,* and *Victors and Vanquished,* which were written while Stuart was living in Freiburg,

Germany, and in Paris in the second half of the 1940s. The second of these novels imagines a return to Ireland. It is the story of the events that occur in a small Irish town to which Ezra Arrigho has returned after the war. Ezra's experience of the destructiveness of war is the basis for the "counter-civilization of the abyss," as one contemporary critic called it, which he teaches to those he meets.[38] The stories Ezra tells lead, by a complicated path, to a murder. At the same time, the characters Ezra meets learn an alternative moral code, a shared understanding that goes beyond the rectitude of small-town Ireland. They know the murderer is guilty, but they shelter him nonetheless, an experience that brings them outside the safe moral categories of the justice system. Admittedly, Stuart describes the plot in rather different terms in a 1994 postscript written for the re-publication of *Redemption*: "The narrator of the novel returns from Germany after the war to his native Ireland, an Ireland that has sat out the world conflict on bacon and tea— with the odd pint; and whom Ezra affects to despise and says so to his estranged wife, Nancy. He, as she and some others close to him realise, is the despicable one and the title of the book suggests that he is finally redeemed."[39] Stuart wrote this account nearly forty years after writing the novel, but it offers a rather skewed interpretation, not least because Ezra is the main character and not the narrator of the story. There is also very little evidence that Ezra is meant to be understood as despicable. Nonetheless, Stuart's account has the virtue of drawing attention to his ambivalent attitude to neutral Ireland (a place the central character "affects to despise"). The conflicting connotations of neutrality are captured in his term "immunity."

"Immunity" is desired or rejected by nearly all the principal characters in *Redemption,* and indeed it is a term that appears in a surprising number of wartime and postwar Irish novels and stories. Part of its meaning, of course, is resistance to infection—the disease in this case being war. In 1942, Bowen reported back to the Dominions Office that the entry of the United States into the war, and in particular the presence of American troops in the north of Ireland, was causing a wave of war panic south of the border: "There is also a heightening of the fear that Eire is on the verge of 'being dragged into the war.' I believe that with many people there is a nebulous fear that war is infectious: the more belligerents accumulate in the Six Counties, the more likely it is that the 'germ' will spread. War, in fact, is not entered but 'caught'—or picked up—just as, passively and unwillingly, one catches or picks up measles."[40] Immunity offers protection but may also act as a screen, closing one off from experience—it can become another version of insensitivity. In the end, it may harm the imagination. In Kate O'Brien's *The Last of Summer,* Jo Kernahan explains to her visiting French cousin, in the summer of 1939, "Oh yes, Eire will be neutral, which is only the clearest sense politically. But

that's beside the point. Little patches of immunity like ours are going to be small consolation for what's coming. Being neutral will be precious little help to the imagination, I should think."[41] Creative insight, on this account, is a product of practical engagement with the world and with others, not the distillation of reflective detachment. It is precisely this closed-off, aloof aspect of immunity that irritates Ezra Arrigho. A passage early in the novel sets up a contrast between the desire to be "touched" or "untouched":

> Let the heart only open wide enough and all is given to it. There are two ways to go down a street of the big city at night. There are two ways that I know, as well as all the others that I don't know. There is the way of the shut heart, gone into a glass core reflecting, registering, an exact instrument of precision like a camera, a cylinder, a vacuum-cleaner and all other small machines, carried out in highly polished glass. Then all is reflected in a blind precision, faces, stone, paper, gestures, grimaces. And there is the other way, with the heart open, dark, expanded and reflecting nothing. Being touched by what the street is and what is in it, the night in the street and the street in the night.

Perhaps, predictably, Stuart images this openness in terms of women's bodies. Ezra, for example, contrasts the perfect body of the priest's sister, Romilly, "immured in its white immunity," with the broken body of his German lover, who has been crippled in a bombing raid. Romilly's progress beyond traditional moral categories is measured by her decision to submit herself to Ezra, thus "spoiling" herself for her marriage. Her later decision to marry the murderer, Kavanagh, so that he will not be alone on the eve of his execution, marks her journey beyond convention to acceptance of shame and refusal to condemn. She escapes the deadening effects of immunity, which is characterized as a place "where walls really were walls and fences were fences, protective, sheltering, shutting out."[42] Interestingly, the isolation and detachment of immunity are also associated with Ezra, especially in his failures of duty and responsibility toward his wife. Here, it seems, neutrality is connected with moral failure, more or less conventionally understood. But for the most part, Stuart rejects such notions, suggesting that authentic response drives us beyond inherited morality.

The loss of self, or emptying out of the self, achieved by Romilly in *Redemption* is related in other novels to the suffering of imprisonment. In *The Pillar of Cloud,* for example, "openness" is linked to the ability to forgive for the brutality of the concentration camps, and once more, it is imaged in terms of a woman's body. *The Pillar of Cloud* is set in the immediate postwar period in Germany, when the main character, an Irishman called Dominic, is suspected of collaboration and imprisoned for a period. The woman he is in love with, Halka, has recently been released from a concentration camp, where she has been held for harboring a Jew. At one point, Halka is allowed to visit Dominic in prison and has sex with him, a few feet from the concentration camp guard who has previously tortured her and is locked up in the same cell. Halka then shows her compassion by refusing to testify against the guard. As Stuart makes clear, the scene is all about judgment and who has the right to judge another.

> "But, you know, I won't testify," she said.
>
> "No?"
>
> "Let them do what they like with him, but I don't want to take part in it."
>
> "Captain Renier will tell you that it is your duty to give evidence, your duty to all the other victims who can't speak, who are dead," Dominic said. "And not only to them, but to others whom, if he is not convicted and executed, might become his victims in some future war or revolution."
>
> "All the same, I won't testify," she said. "Because I forgive him."
>
> Dominic was silent. He was almost shocked at her words, as he had been almost shocked at how she had managed everything so simply and directly since she had come into the cellar. Nothing had weighed with her, neither the thought of Lisette in the sanatorium, nor the presence of Bergmann, nor the uncertain moment of the policeman's return. Yet he knew that she was right, in all she was right, without false sentiment, false shame, and without one drop of vindictiveness or malice. Hers was the innocence of which he had spoken, the unfathomable innocence that was on the earth to set over against the monstrous evil.[43]

There is an obvious sense in which this passage seems to express Stuart's need for the public to forgive him for his collaboration with the Nazi regime during the war. If the guard cannot be judged except by the truly innocent, those who have suffered blamelessly, then neither can Stuart. It is tempting to accuse Stuart of bad faith here, for there is an almost aggressively voyeuristic aspect to the sex scene in the prison. Halka's orgasm is watched as much by Dominic as by the guard who turns his back, suggesting Dominic's detachment and the vicarious nature of the suffering Dominic claims to undergo. But it is worth noting that there are other, perhaps more disingenuous ways to disclaim guilt, which Stuart conspicuously forgoes. He does not try to excuse himself, and he does not claim ignorance of the persecution of the Jews. Instead, he continues to insist on his belief in the redundancy of moral categories and moral judgments, a belief that brought him to Germany in the first place. An earlier passage in the novel gives voice to Dominic's sense of the new order, new fraternity, and way of being that might arise from the war:

> For a moment he thought he even saw how the great cataclysm had to come, how all the old pretence and the faux sublime, the false idealism, had to be swept away in blood and tears. So much blood and tears had

to flow until all that old civilization had been shaken and undermined, and he felt a bitter anger against Frau Arnheim as one of those who had played the old, insidious game, who had gone on marrying and giving in marriage, attending church services and listening to the words of the professional moralists about the idealistic God who from his secure heaven smiled down complacently on a more or less secure world.[44]

NEUTRALITY AS DISSOLUTION

We might put this refusal of the conventional moral categories of good and evil together with another passage, from Elizabeth Bowen's short story, "Summer Night," first published in 1941: "I'm torn, here, by every single pang of annihilation. But that's what I look for; that's what I want completed; that's the whole of what I want to embrace. On the far side of the nothing—my new form. Scrap 'me'; scrap my wretched identity and you'll bring some new bud to life. I *not* 'I'—I'd be the world . . ."[45] The central character in Bowen's story, Justin Cavey, is spending the summer in the Irish country town of his birth, where his father was a doctor, since the war prevents his usual continental holiday. He spends much of his time with his deaf sister, Queenie, who lives in the town, making the social rounds. Here he tries to articulate his sense of how the pressure of world historical events has hollowed out his identity.

In "Summer Night," Bowen captures with supreme skill the sense of profound unease associated with the notion of Ireland's immunity. This is a story of individuals locked in private worlds. One evening, Cavey and his sister make a casual visit to the home of a local industrialist, Robinson, with whom Justin has struck up an acquaintance. Robinson is preoccupied by the impending arrival of his mistress, but Justin holds forth nonetheless:

> Our faculties have slowed down without our knowing—they had stopped without our knowing! We know now. Now that there's enough death to challenge being alive we're facing it that, anyhow, we don't live. We're confronted by the impossibility *of* living—unless we can break through to something else. There's been a stop in our senses and in our faculties that's made everything round us so much dead matter—and dead matter we couldn't even displace. We can no longer express ourselves: what we say doesn't approximate to reality; it only approximates to what's been said. I say, this war's an awful illumination; it's destroyed our dark; we have to see where we are. Immobilized, God help us, and each so far apart that we can't even try to signal to each other.
>
> (*CS*, 590)

Justin's cri de coeur falls on deaf ears, not just those of his sister, who is present, but also those of Robinson ("'You don't think thinking gets one a bit rattled?'" [*CS*, 590]). Later, in his hotel room, having realized that Robinson had an assignation, Justin dashes off a barbed and wounded letter severing ties and character-izing his host in terms of "imperviousness" and "indif-ference." Queenie has responded to the evening's events in an entirely different way, reliving memories of a long-ago summer night with a lover, in which Robinson now plays the fantasy part. Bowen leaves us suspended between an immunity that (as in the case of Queenie) may bring quiet insight, even though it is a fantasy, and an exaggerated susceptibility that results in Justin's over-the-top letter breaking off relations with Robinson.

Part of the skill of the story lies in the element of irony in Bowen's treatment of Justin, who comes off badly by comparison with his sister: "Her deafness broke down his only defence, talk. He was exposed to the odd, im-mune, plumbing looks she was forever passing over his face" (*CS,* 587). Justin's longing to break through the general anesthesia may be genuine, but there is a hys-terical edge to his talk that, as Bowen suggests, is itself another kind of barrier: "'And our currency's worth-less—our 'ideas' and so on, so on. We've got to mint a new one. We've got to break through to a new form—it needs genius. We're precipitated, this moment, through genius and death. I tell you, we must certainly have ge-nius to live at all'" (*CS,* 590). The rhetoric of transfor-mation through catastrophe is not all that far from the language of Stuart, even though we must assume that Justin's political sympathies lie on the other side. There is a disturbing symmetry here. Stuart naively imagines he can be a "neutral" while broadcasting from the Nazi capital. Justin Cavey tries to break through the indiffer-ence of his fellow countrymen, citizens of a neutral state. Yet both end up suggesting that the horror and de-struction of the war may somehow be the prelude to spiritual renewal. It is neutrality in one form or another, we might conclude, that makes this welcoming, if not glorification, of violence possible. And such glorifica-tion is itself a trait of fascist ideology—a form of col-laboration, if you like.

It is a well-established contention by now that Bowen's concern with duplicity, betrayal, and double identity re-flects her own sense of torn allegiances. Thus, as Bill McCormack has suggested, the fascism of the spy Kelway in Bowen's wartime novel, *The Heat of the Day,* can be seen as "an Irish 'trace' in the novel."[46] In other words, had Bowen remained in North Cork throughout the war, which was one of her options, she would have become to some extent complicit with the sympathy for fascism that she detected here and there in Ireland. Perhaps this is what interests her about her character Cavey. Justin is a "European" who feels pow-erless to stop the destruction of "what had been his own intensely" (*CS,* 588). But the story as a whole suggests the difficult of "feeling" appropriately and of disentan-gling what is felt. Robinson is "immune" to Cavey. Is

he therefore culpably indifferent to the war, too? Or is he simply less susceptible to a dubious apocalyptic rhetoric dressed up as feeling?

If immunity is a key metaphor for the moral complexi-ties of neutrality, the notions of immunity and the break-down of immunity to the pressures of the surrounding world area also central to Bowen's reflections of her practice as a writer during wartime. An important text here is the postscript, which she wrote in 1945, for the American edition of her collection of short stories, *The Demon Lover.* Here Bowen suggests that the extreme conditions of the war brought about a transformation of sensibility, in which the conscious intentions of the au-thor as an experiencing individual ceased to be the de-cisive factor in artistic creation. Bowen writes, "It seems to me that during the war the overcharged subconscious-nesses of everybody overflowed and merged. It is be-cause the general subconsciousness saturates these sto-ries that they have an authority nothing to do with me." She goes on to remark, "The stories had their own mo-mentum, which I had to control. The acts in them had an authority which I could not question. Odd enough in their way—and now some seem very odd—they were flying particles of something enormous and inchoate that had been going on. They were sparks from experi-ence—an experience not necessarily my own."[47] Bowen portrays the collapse of internal reflective distance, an openness to external pressures that disempowers the in-dividual, as the condition for a new form of creativity, a new way of registering the "high-voltage current of the general," as she calls it.

I want to suggest that there are strong conceptual, and possibly verbal, echoes here of Wallace Stevens's fa-mous essay "The Noble Rider and the Sound of Words." In one sense, this would scarcely be surprising, since Stevens first read this essay as a lecture at Princeton in 1941—and published it soon after[48]—and Bowen was writing for an American audience. Both Bowen and Stevens reflect explicitly on the unprecedented events of the world war and the impact of these events on our conception of the creative writer's task. In his enor-mously complex and allusive essay, Stevens seeks to define nothing less than "the end of one era and the be-ginning of another" (*NA,* 21). What brings about these shifts, according to Stevens, is the "pressure of reality." Formally, he defines this force as "the pressure of an external event or events on the consciousness to the ex-clusion of any power of contemplation" (*NA,* 20), a definition that clearly links up with Bowen's account of her short story writing.

Stevens seems to suggest that his contemporaries were living through a transition to a state in which social and global processes could no longer be "processed" and mastered imaginatively in the way that creative artists had mastered and shaped reality in the past. The noble

rider of the title alludes to an outlook in which imagination could be given preponderance over reality, without any fear that this would lead to implausible illusions. However, Stevens stresses that "the imagination
loses its vitality as it ceases to adhere to what is real"
(*NA,* 6). In the current situation of society, the traditional idea of aesthetic nobility exists only in "degenerate forms" (*NA,* 12-13). What has brought this change
about, the "pressure of reality" that Stevens repeatedly
evokes, consists of "life in a state of violence, not physically violent yet, for us in America, but physically violent for millions of our friends and for still more millions of our enemies and spiritually violent, it may be
said, for everyone alive" (*NA,* 26-27). The overt violence of global conflict, on this account, is merely the
most lurid symptom of a world historical shift that has
collapsed existing notions of time and space, including
the private, or at least internal, space of subjectivity. As
Stevens writes, "It is not only that there are more and
more of us and that we are actually closer together. We
are close together in every way. We lie in bed and listen
to a broadcast from Cairo, and so on. There is no distance. We are intimate with people we have never seen
and, unhappily, they are intimate with us" (*NA,* 18).
The ultimate aim of Stevens's essay is to retrieve a new
sense of the purpose of poetry in this situation, which is
tantamount to a new sense of "nobility." Devised in a
world in which the traditions that situated individuals
and shaped their inwardness are being aroded, Stevens's
new account of nobility—his term for the integrity of
the aesthetic domain—is a striking and surprising one.
"Nobility," he concludes, ". . . is a violence from
within that protects us from a violence without. It is the
imagination pressing back against the pressure of reality" (*NA,* 36).

At the start of the preface to *The Demon Lover,* Bowen
writes, "Each time I sat down to write a story I opened
a door; and the pressure against the other side of the
door must have been very great, for things—ideas, images, emotions—came through with force and rapidity,
sometimes violence. . . . The stories had their own
momentum, which I had to control."[49] The verbal echoes of Stevens may be fortuitous, though this seems unlikely. What is clear is that Bowen, too, was seeking to
define the changed nature of the creative process in a
world where the bombardment of events resists the traditional acts of aesthetic shaping, and indeed reveals
such shapings—as Stevens suggests—as forms of impo-
tent, and even irresponsible, idealism. Such "immunity"
as imaginative writing confers (which Stevens describes
as a positive form of "escapism"[50]) is achieved not by
closing off oneself from events but rather by allowing
an inner violence to respond to outer violence, in effect
by allowing oneself to be contaminated.

Bowen's use of the conventions of gothic fiction and
the ghost story allows her to explore this ambiguity of
inner and outer irruptions. She is quite clear that her
ghosts can be understood more or less subjectively, and
indeed she may have had such gradations in mind when
she wrote the stories. She writes, "The hallucinations in
the stories are not a peril; nor are the stories studies of
mental peril. The hallucinations are an unconscious, in-
stinctive, saving resort on the part of the characters."[51]
In short, we would almost say that the stories represent
ordinary people engaged in the same escapist mechanisms described by Stevens:

> You may say that these resistance-fantasies are in them-
> selves frightening. I can only say that one counteracts
> fear by fear, stress by stress. In "The Happy Autumn
> Fields," one finds a woman projected from flying-
> bombed London, with its day and night eeriness, into
> the key emotional crisis of Victorian girlhood. In "Ivy
> Gripped the Steps," a man in the early '40s peers
> through the rusted fortifications and down the dusty
> empty perspectives of a seaside town at the Edwardian
> episode that has crippled his faculty for love. In "The
> Inherited Clock," a girl is led to find the key to her
> own neurosis inside a timepiece. The past, in all these
> cases, discharges its load of feeling into the anaesthe-
> tized and bewildered present. It is the "I" that is
> sought—and retrieved at the cost of no little pain. And
> the ghosts—definite in "Green Holly," questionable
> (for are they subjective purely?) in "Pink May," "The
> Cheery Soul" and "The Demon Lover"—what part do
> they play? They are the certainties. The bodiless fool-
> ish wanton, the puritan other presence, the tipsy cook
> with her religion of English fare, the ruthless young
> soldier lover unheard of since 1916: hostile or not, they
> rally, they fill the vacuum for the uncertain "I."[52]

Bowen's inversion, in which the specters of the past become the only "certainties," while the self becomes
ever more empty and elusive, is a striking one. The
boundary between life and death, past and present, becomes permeable and insecure. And it is hard to resist
the thought that the half-dead figures, the "ghouls,"
whom Johnston encounters with such traumatic results
in Buchenwald, may offer a more general image for the
state of suspension and liminality which are so commonly evoked in wartime fiction. Their wailing is an
expression of hope, but it sounds like despair. Ghosts
appear when we are fundamentally disturbed, disoriented by the enormity of events. They mark the points
where the buried, private sufferings of the past meet the
unimaginable political horrors of the present.

It is not only the relation between past and present that
becomes dislocated under the "pressure of reality." In a
closely parallel way, the relation between public and
private is reconfigured, too. I have already suggested
that the violent conflicts of the period, the tensions between moral demands, political visions, and national interests are reflected in disruptions of the writer's inwardness and sense of identity. One obvious
consequence of this is that the private and the personal
can no longer function as a place of refuge or exemp-
tion.

An interesting contrast can be drawn here between Stuart and Bowen. Apologists for Stuart's wartime activities have often suggested that his concern was with the suffering and destiny of individuals, that he did not think in essentially political terms. In his broadcast of March 29, 1942, Stuart himself remarks, "I do not know the various political currents, intrigues and secret alliances that went on between the last war and this. I am no politician and all that is quite beyond me. I'm interested in people, in individuals and their lives."[53] Bowen's assumptions are completely different, and a remarkable illustration of this fact is the family history, *Bowen's Court,* which she wrote during the early years of the Second World War at the same time that she penned her intelligence reports for the Ministry of Information. To write the history of the North Cork mansion, of which she was the first female inheritor, when the world was caught up in unprecedented violence, might appear like a withdrawal into the private sphere. But Bowen, in her afterword, written in 1963, does not portray it that way. Rather, she suggests that the private is no longer opposed to the domain of public events, just as the pressure of the present pervades the past. In a striking passage, she writes, "The war-time urgency of the present, its relentless daily challenge, seemed to communicate itself to one's view of the past, until, to the most private act or decision, there attached one's sense of its part in some campaign. Those days, either everything mattered or nothing mattered. The past—private as well as historic—seemed to me, therefore, to matter more than ever; it acquired meaning; it lost false mystery. In the savage and austere light of a burning world, details leaped out with significance."[54] *Bowen's Court,* then, is both a personal and a public document. It is an attempt by the writer to address, if not to resolve, some of her own deepest internal conflicts. On the one hand, it is a gentle assertion of the general significance of certain values of the Anglo-Irish gentry, and in particular of Bowen's own family, values that the turmoil of the world has put in doubt. Bowen writes, "I was taking the attachment of people to places as being generic to human life, at a time when the attachment was to be dreaded as a possible source of too much pain."[55] But at the same time, the book is an attempt to acknowledge the injustice of the past, from which, as she does not attempt to disguise, her own family benefited. "With the Treaty," she writes, "with which I virtually close my book, a new hopeful phase started: I believe in its promise. But we cannot afford to have ghosts on this clearing scene. I wish not to drag up the past, but to help lay it."[56]

As the subsequent course of Irish history has shown, those ghosts have not been so easy to lay. Portrayed by Bowen as a world teeming with ghosts, you can read the Big House and Anglo-Irish tradition as a kind of negative or reverse image of Irish neutrality—an island within an island, but one, as Bowen keeps saying, in-

formed by "the European idea." It prides itself on its superiority, looking beyond the narrow nationalism of the Irish island, but at the same time, it is propped up and compromised by external configurations of power.

Ambivalence continues to haunt the politics of Irish neutrality today. One plank of the opposition to the enlargement and transformation of the European Union envisaged by the Nice Treaty ostensibly focuses on the conflict between Irish neutrality and proposals for collective European security and defense, but may also be driven by regrets for the loss of Ireland's privileged marginal status. In this debate, one transnational orientation is opposed to another: the idealistic vision of a neutral Ireland devoted to the promotion of peace and human rights around the globe, versus a conception of Ireland joined in the common pursuit of a European identity and, if necessary, the defense of a common heritage. The threat posed by EU membership to Ireland's neutrality is, of course, an issue, usually dodged around, that has been simmering in Irish politics for decades. In the current world situation, however, the potential equivocations of neutrality, in the broadest sense, go much further. For, as Patrick Keatinge has pointed out, classical neutrality "depends on the existence of a clear, legally definable distinction between the condition of war and that of peace."[57] Essentially a product of the nineteenth-century European diplomatic system, it presupposed that wars were formally declared armed conflicts between states and laid down quite strict and specific obligations on countries claiming neutral status. But since 1945, at least, wars of this kind have been less and less the norm.

The simmering, inchoate conflicts that characterize the contemporary world, conflicts no longer focused on territorial disputes between nations but on claims for cultural and political recognition and the distribution of resources, make it ever more difficult to imagine an impermeable private sphere, safe from the psychic impact of global dislocation and violent disruption. Though immunity may be no more than a fantasy, as Bowen suggests, it can be a saving fantasy. That neutral island in the heart of man may connote indifference, but it can also harbor a stubborn aspiration to ethical universalism and impartial responsibility. In such a world, the images of the moral and psychological complexities of neutrality bequeathed by mid-century Irish writers are likely to continue resonating for a long time to come.

Notes

1. Louis MacNeice, "Neutrality," in *Collected Poems* (London: Faber and Faber, 1966), 202.

2. Louis MacNeice, "London Letter [3]: War Aims; The New Political Alignment," in *Selected Prose of Louis MacNeice,* ed. Alan Heuser (Oxford:

Clarendon Press, 1990), 116. Under the 1937 Constitution, the term *Free State* was dropped, and the country became known simply as *Ireland,* or, in Irish, *Éire.*

3. See Patrick Keatinge, *A Singular Stance: Irish Neutrality in the 1980s* (Dublin: Institute of Public Administration, 1984), 7.

4. *The Mulberry Tree: Writings of Elizabeth Bowen,* selected and introduced by Hermione Lee (London: Vintage, 1999), 99.

5. Kate O'Brien, *The Last of Summer* (London: Virago, 1990), 179.

6. O'Brien, *The Last of Summer,* 186.

7. Bowen, "Notes on Eire," November 9, 1940 (PRO, London), F.O. 800/310 (251-66). Also published in Jack Lane and Brendan Clifford, *Elizabeth Bowen: "Notes on Eire," Espionage Reports to Winston Churchill, 1940-2: With a Review of Irish Neutrality in World War II* (Millstreet, Co. Cork: Aubane Historical Society, 1999), 12.

8. Roger Casement, letter to his cousin, Gertrude Bannister, National Library of Ireland, 13074/9.

9. See Robert Fisk, *In Time of War: Ireland, Ulster, and the Price of Neutrality, 1939-45* (Dublin: Gill and Macmillan, 1983), 81.

10. See Eunan O'Halpin, "'Toys' and 'Whispers' in '16-land': SOE and Ireland, 1940-42," *Intelligence and National Security* 15, no. 4 (Winter 2000): 12.

11. See Donal Ó Drisceoil, *Censorship in Ireland, 1939-45: Neutrality, Politics, and Society* (Cork: Cork University Press, 1996), 294.

12. See Ó Drisceoil, *Censorship in Ireland,* 288.

13. See J. J. Lee, *Ireland, 1912-1985: Politics and Society* (Cambridge: Cambridge University Press, 1989), 266, 267.

14. Buchenwald was liberated in April, and emergency censorship was lifted on May 11, 1945. See Ó Drisceoil, *Censorship in Ireland,* 123-29, on censorship of atrocity stories.

15. Bowen, "Notes on Eire," November 9, 1940. Throughout her report on this date, Bowen pushes the argument that Ireland could (and should) lease the Treaty ports back to Britain for the duration of the war, while maintaining her neutrality.

16. Francis Stuart, afterword to *Redemption* (Dublin: New Island Books, 1994), 252.

17. MacNeice, "American Letter," in *Selected Prose,* 76-77.

18. Bernard Adams, *Denis Johnston: A Life* (Dublin: Lilliput, 2002), 14-15.

19. Adams, *Denis Johnston,* 204.

20. Rex Cathcart, *The Most Contrary Region: The BBC in Northern Ireland, 1924-1984* (Belfast: Blackstaff Press, 1984), 117. See also Adams, *Denis Johnston,* 204-5, and 209-12.

21. Adams, *Denis Johnston,* 216.

22. See Vivian Mercier, "Perfection of the Life, or of the Work?" in *Denis Johnston: A Retrospective,* ed. Joseph Ronsley (Gerrards Cross: Colin Smythe, 1981), 228-44.

23. Denis Johnston, *Nine Rivers from Jordan* (London: Derek Verschoyle, 1953). On this issue, see the contrasting views of Terry Boyle, "Denis Johnston: Neutrality and Buchenwald," in *Modern Irish Writers and the Wars,* ed. Kathleen Devine (Gerrards Cross: Colin Smythe, 1999), 205-18; and Mercier, "Perfection of the Life, or of the Work?"

24. Johnston, *Nine Rivers,* 8.

25. Denis Johnston, *Dionysia* (The Author, 1949), 138.

26. Johnston, *Dionysia,* 235.

27. Johnston, *Dionysia,* 656.

28. Johnston, *Nine Rivers,* 395-96.

29. Significantly, the War Field Books make no mention of any encounter with an SS officer, though the entry of April 29, 1945, does record the attempted suicide of an officer. On the other hand, Johnston's symbolic acceptance of belligerent status after his visit to Buchenwald is reflected in the Field Books, which mention his possession of a Luger.

30. See Adams, *Denis Johnston,* 238-44.

31. Francis Stuart, *Blacklist, Section H* (Dublin: Lilliput, 1995), 80. Stuart wrote the book, first called *We the Condemned,* in 1961 and 1962. After revision, Southern Illinois University Press published it as *Blacklist, Section H* in 1971.

32. Francis Stuart, *Things to Live For: Notes for an Autobiography* (London: Jonathan Cape, 1934).

33. Brendan Barrington, ed., *The Wartime Broadcast of Francis Stuart, 1942-44* (Dublin: Lilliput 2000).

34. Barrington, *The Wartime Broadcasts of Franci Stuart,* 69.

35. Stuart, *Blacklist, Section H,* 353. As Brendan Barrington has pointed out in *The Wartime Broadcasts of Francis Stuart,* for Stuart to describe himself as "a neutral," as he did repeatedly, was a "largely meaningless formulation" (39).

36. Barrington, *The Wartime Broadcasts of Francis Stuart,* 70.

37. Barrington, *The Wartime Broadcasts of Francis Stuart,* 71.

38. Bernard d'Astorg, "Des Ruines, Le Sacré Renaîtra," review of *Redemption* and *Le Baptême de la Nuit,* in *Aspects de la Littérature Européenne depuis 1945,* trans. Richard York and republished in *A Festschrift for Francis Stuart,* ed. W. J. Mc-Cormack (Dublin: Dolmen Editions, 1972), 29.

39. Stuart, *Redemption,* 252.

40. Bowen, "Notes on Eire," February 9, 1942, D.O. 130/28. Also published in Lane and Clifford, *Elizabeth Bowen: "Notes on Eire,"* 20.

41. O'Brien, *The Last of Summer,* 81.

42. Stuart, *Redemption,* 120.

43. Francis Stuart, *The Pillar of Cloud* (Dublin: New Island Books, 1994), 222-23.

44. Stuart, *The Pillar of Cloud,* 195-96.

45. Elizabeth Bowen, "Summer Night," in *Collected Stories* (London: Vintage, 1999), 591. Hereafter, this work is cited parenthetically as *CS.*

46. W. J. McCormack, *Dissolute Characters: Irish Literary History through Balzac, Sheridan Le Fanu, Yeats, and Bowen* (Manchester: Manchester University Press, 1993).

47. Bowen, *Mulberry Tree,* 95.

48. Wallace Stevens, "The Noble Rider and the Sound of Words," in *The Language of Poetry,* ed. Allen Tate (Princeton, N.J.: Princeton University Press, 1942), 91-125. Republished in Wallace Stevens, *The Necessary Angel: Essays on Reality and the Imagination* (London: Faber and Faber, 1960), 1-36. Hereafter, *The Necessary Angel* is cited parenthetically as *NA.*

49. Bowen, *Mulberry Tree,* 94-95.

50. "The poetic process is psychologically an escapist process" (Stevens, *NA,* 30).

51. Bowen, *Mulberry Tree,* 97.

52. Bowen, *Mulberry Tree,* 97-98.

53. Barrington, *The Wartime Broadcasts of Francis Stuart,* 72.

54. Elizabeth Bowen, *Bowen's Court* (Cork: Collins Press, 1998), 454.

55. Bowen, *Bowen's Court,* 454.

56. Bowen, *Bowen's Court,* 453.

57. Keatinge, *A Singular Stance,* 3.

THE LITERARY RESPONSE TO WAR AND VIOLENCE

William Cloonan (essay date 1999)

SOURCE: Cloonan, William. "Introduction: The Writing of War." In *The Writing of War: French and German Fiction and World War II,* pp. 1-18. Gainesville: University Press of Florida, 1999.

[*In the excerpt below, Cloonan presents a literary and theoretical framework in which to study literary responses to the holocaust.*]

> If you could lick my heart, it would poison you.
>
> Words of a Warsaw Ghetto survivor, in Langer,
> *Admitting the Holocaust,* 40

If people once thought that limits existed to human degradation, that certain moral standards, however contested, nevertheless could not be totally disregarded, World War II exposed this belief as an illusion. The debatable use of atomic weaponry against Japan, the cynical terror bombings of Dresden and Canterbury were shocking enough, but no event so pulverized traditional moral sensibility as the Final Solution. Quite aside from the historical reality of the concentration camps, delimited as they were in time and space, the Final Solution was destined to become the most prominent symbol for all the new and doubtless unwanted information about human cruelty that World War II would bequeath to its survivors.

The Final Solution permanently altered the moral, intellectual, and aesthetic climate in which French and German literary artists tried to write about World War II and its aftermath, and these authors' problems, failures, and successes are the subject of this book. Nathalie Sarraute, who aptly termed the postwar era the "Age of Suspicion," dated its birth from the moment she discovered the existence of the gas chambers, where "all feeling disappears, even scorn and hatred. All that remains is an immense and empty stupor, a total and definitive inability to understand" (*L'Ere du soupçon,* 65). The knowledge of the Final Solution challenged long-held assumptions about human decency and the possibility of progress in mutual understanding; it questioned the value of the Enlightenment heritage, and for some, it even created a caesura in history: "there was an Auschwitz, and there was an afterward . . . the two terms do not represent a chronology" (Langer, *Admitting the*

Holocaust, 18). Theodor Adorno's celebrated (and later retracted) pronouncement that writing poetry after Auschwitz would be barbaric (*Noten zur Literaturen III*, 125) may well serve as the emotional counterpart to Sarraute's "immense and empty stupor," but both statements have in common the realization that in the aftermath of the Final Solution, the production of literary artifacts could not continue as in the past, as if nothing radically different had happened.

One might object, of course, that traumatic reactions from artists and intellectuals are a common enough occurrence after any major war. In his *A War Imagined: The First World War and English Culture*, Samuel Hynes points out the sorts of upheavals created by this earlier conflict: "Even as it was being fought the war was perceived as a force of radical change in society and in consciousness. It brought to an end the life and values of Victorian and Edwardian England; but it also did something more radical than that: it added a new scale of violence and destruction to what was possible—it changed reality" (xi). With specific regard to artists, Hynes writes that they "would see that if the past were indeed dead, then the future, the world after the war, would have to have a new beginning. The continuity of history had been broken" (4). In France, World War I transformed Henri Barbusse from a little-known, vaguely decadent novelist into the world-famous author of *Under Fire* (1916), a novel replete with "subversion, hatred of war, rejection of nationalism, and an appeal for social struggle against passivity" (Relinger, *Henri Barbusee*, 87). World War I gave an impetus to Dadaism and Expressionism in Germany; it launched Surrealism in France.[1] And, according to Hynes, it constituted the guiding spirit of modernism: "Modernism means many things, but it is most fundamentally the forms that the post-war artists found for their sense of modern history: history seen as discontinuous, the past remote and unavailable, or available only as ruins of itself, and the present a formless space emptied of values" (*War Imagined*, 433).

Nobody would deny the tremendous impact of World War I on the arts, or on human consciousness in general, but in a fundamental way the trauma it induced was different from the upheaval produced by World War II. The innovation of World War I involved traditional tactical developments being pushed to levels the world had never seen, coupled with the hardening human reaction to what this weaponry could achieve. The introduction of airplanes, tanks, and poison gas, the stench of the battlefields where the dead were left to rot, the apparent indifference with which commanders on both sides sent their troops into combat—these were but some of the "advances" that gave World War I its unique place in the history of warfare:

> The immobility of trench fighting, the stunningly high casualties, which made the Duke of Wellington's fa-

mous estimate in the Napoleonic Wars—that no army could sustain more than 30 percent losses and survive— seem an antiquated irony, the new technologies of submarines, tanks, barbed wire, airplanes, machine guns, and bullets designed to wound with the maximum damage and pain, the lethal poison gas banned by mutual agreement at the meeting of nations at The Hague in 1907 and in use nonetheless—these factors defied all previous notions about what military destruction could mean.

> (Douglas, *Terrible Honesty*, 156)

World War II was certainly a development of this technology in the service of destruction; from this perspective it marked a difference in degree, but not in kind.

The heightened firepower of World War II does not distinguish it from earlier wars. It was the Nazi implementation of the Final Solution that moved World War II beyond the realm of traditional warfare; it gave a new dimension to the concept of war waged against civilian populations. Concentration camps served no military purpose and had no strategic value; they cannot even be said to have served as means of terrorizing citizens since the Nazis attempted to keep their existence largely secret. They were places where death was practiced for its own sake.

Given the understandably high emotional atmosphere that often accompanies discussions of the Final Solution and its consequences, I need, before turning to the novels I wish to analyze, to distinguish between the immediate and the more lasting ramifications of the Nazis' genocidal policies; the former were as gruesome as they were dramatic, while the latter remain more subtle but ultimately more frightening.

The discovery of places like Auschwitz shocked the postwar world. The liberation of the concentration camps, accompanied by the worldwide dissemination of their contents through photos, newsreels, radio broadcasts, and newspaper articles, added a new dimension to the meaning of the word *inhumanity*. The Final Solution quickly became the standard against which other crimes committed during World War II were judged. For instance, in the midst of the Japanese war crime trials, the president of the Tokyo tribunal, Sir William Webb, noted that "the crimes of the Germans accused were far more heinous, varied and extensive than those of the Japanese accused" (Buruma, *The Wages of Guilt: Memories of War in Germany and Japan*, 168). Also, the uniqueness of the indictments handed down at Nuremburg against the surviving perpetrators of the Final Solution for their "crimes against humanity" illustrates that the Nazi activities were sufficiently beyond the bounds of wartime hatreds and excesses as to merit a new terminology, a new category of guilt.

This wholesale condemnation of the Nazis and the implicit exculpation of the Allies' wartime strategies were not, however, without their critics. William Golding probably speaks for many of his contemporaries who refused to believe that the evil unleashed in World War II was a uniquely German phenomenon; at the same time, he sounds a prescient note concerning the difficulties the war would create for the subsequent writing of literature:

> The experiences of Hamburg and Belsen, Hiroshima and Dachau cannot be imagined. We have gone to war and beggared description all over again. These experiences are like black holes in space. Nothing can get out to let us know what was inside. It was like what it was like and on the other hand it was like nothing else whatsoever. We stand before a gap in history. We have discovered a limit to literature.
>
> (Hewison, *Under Siege,* 172)

In a similar vein, Ian Buruma, writing about the Japanese reaction to the dropping of the atomic bomb, points out that in modern Japan "Hiroshima is a symbol of absolute evil, often compared to Auschwitz" (*Wages,* 92). Yet later on in this same study, Buruma makes the sort of distinction typical of those who wish to differentiate between the dropping of the atomic bomb, as well as other alleged Allied atrocities, and the Final Solution: "the case of Hiroshima is at least open to debate, the A-bomb *might* have saved lives; it *might* have shortened the war" (105, emphasis in text). Richard Rubenstein offers a variation on this argument, one that stresses the gratuitousness of the Nazi mass murders: "The American assault ceased as soon as the Japanese surrendered. During World War II, German mass violence against enemy civilians was intensified *after* the victims surrendered" (*The Cunning of History,* emphasis in text, 7).

Distinguishing between acts of war, however debatable or downright senseless, and the unprovoked destruction of people because of their racial or ethnic origins is a common motif among commentators who feel compelled to mark the special quality of the Final Solution in the context of World War II. Alain Lercher recently published a history of the Nazi slaughter of the inhabitants of Oradour, a French village without any strategic importance. An S.S. division, Das Reich, decided to annihilate the town in response to harassment from the French Resistance. Lercher's well-researched account of this incident is particularly moving since he lost relatives in the massacre. Nevertheless, at the end of his study Lercher offers a telling reflection concerning the place of Oradour on the list of wartime horrors:

> I understood a little while ago that Oradour was not comparable to genocide, because the massacre at Oradour, as horrible as it was, can be associated with the dynamics of the war, like the bombings of Cologne and Dresden, which equal it in horror. While the genocide of a people without a homeland, who threatened nobody, from whom one had nothing to take, cannot be associated with anything one could endow with a his-

torical sense, unless it was the particular destiny of the Jewish people.
>
> (67-68)

Lercher's singling out the Jews is at once understandable and typical. Of all those the Nazis chose for destruction—gypsies, political dissenters, Slavs, homosexuals—the Jewish people were by far the largest group. Jews have traditionally been the scapegoats for Christianity's various insecurities, and anti-Semitism has long been an integral part of the fabric of Western society. Perhaps for these reasons some scholarly accounts of Nazi genocide give the impression that the Jews were the only victims. Dominick La Capra, in his *Representing the Holocaust,* cites with approval Eberhard Jäckel's frequently quoted explanation for the uniqueness of the Final Solution:

> The Nazi extermination of the Jews was unique because never before had a state, under the responsible authority of its leader, decided and announced that a specific group of human beings, including the old, the women, the children and the infants, would be killed to the very last one, and implemented this decision with every means at its disposal.
>
> (49)

Without for a moment denying the fundamental truth of Jäckel's statement that the Nazis engaged in gratuitous brutality against essentially harmless and defenseless human beings, it remains nonetheless true that placing an exclusive emphasis on the destruction of the Jews, or for that matter any other specific group, at a particular historical moment, risks obscuring the second, more far-reaching implication of the Final Solution.

The enduring ramification of the Final Solution may ultimately have less to do with the identities of the victims as Jews, homosexuals, gypsies, or political dissenters than is often supposed. The Final Solution demonstrated human beings' willingness and ability to facilitate the emplacement of a carefully developed bureaucratic structure capable of wide-ranging murderous acts, while at the same time freeing its various functionaries from any sense of personal responsibility for the activities they directed. As terrible as were the Nazis' professed aims—the annihilation of specific groups—the mindset of "persons who are permitted to commit murder without remorse by a language stripped of conscience" (Wolf, *Patterns of Childhood,* 237) is at least as daunting. Thus the Nazi genocidal policy was much more than the ugliest phenomenon of World War II; it was and remains a potent blueprint for the future, in which any group or groups can be chosen for extermination, and those who carry out the task will do so without remorse or doubts:

> The passing of time has made it increasingly evident that a hitherto unbreachable moral and political barrier in the history of Western civilization was successfully

overcome by the Nazis . . . and that henceforth the systematic, bureaucratically administered extermination of millions of citizens or subject peoples will forever be one of the capacities and temptations of government.

(Rubenstein, *Cunning,* 2)

The existence of Auschwitz, Buchenwald, and other prisons made apparent both the human capacity for massive, wanton destruction and the ease with which traditional ethical constraints could be shunted aside by relatively large numbers of people in the interest of serving the State. Extrapolating from the German experience, one comes to realize that genocide can be the potential policy of any government. When Marguerite Duras declares in *The War: A Memoir* that in order to endure the idea of a concentration camp, "we must share the crime" (50), it is easy to dismiss her statement as a reaction more emotional than rational. The Nazis ran those places and killed those people; we did not. Yet what lies behind the shock and outrage motivating Duras's words is the possibility that while we are not those Nazis, we are perfectly able to act like them. These nefarious acts could have been, or could be in the future, "committed by anyone" (Duras, *War,* 50). Christa Wolf succinctly sums up this fear: "We, the people of today, don't put anything past anybody. We think that anything is possible. This may be the most important difference between our era and the preceding one" (*Patterns,* 242).

Without mitigating the Nazis' responsibility for the events that transpired in the concentration camps during World War II, an awareness of the Final Solution's broader ramifications helps explain the puzzling reaction of some German intellectuals to the often-reiterated insistence by the Allies on their nation's guilt. When a German writer like Hans Egon Holthusen insists upon Germany's continuing responsibility and need to remember its crimes, his remarks are generally greeted with approval within the international intellectual community: "the past, as we know, has not faded or become indifferent . . . but rather stronger, more terrifying, more unbearable, and one would like to add, more incomprehensible" (in Bosmajian, *Metaphors of Evil,* 17). However, one is initially taken aback by the comments of the poet and political activist Hans Magnus Ensensberger: "the reality of Auschwitz shall be exorcised as if it were the past, specifically the national past, and not a common present or future" (in Bosmajian, *Metaphors,* 12). Or, for that matter, Heinrich Böll's insistence that the ill-treatment he received in a prisoner of war camp increased his desire to express himself not simply as a writer, but as a specifically German writer who was proud of his national identity: "When for months at a time you are treated as a fucking German Nazi, and kicked in the behind, then you think, not just kiss my ass, but also that in spite of everything I am a German, and I will write" (*Eine deutsche Erinnerung,* 102)

Neither Ensenberger nor Böll can be accused of harboring any latent Nazi sympathies, and their words and actions have never denied the historical reality of the Final Solution. Their anger, I would suggest, stems from the self-righteous condemnation of Germany by her conquerors and occupiers. These writers resent the holier-than-thou attitudes they encountered from victors whose wartime activities, however much they remain within the loosely defined category of "military strategy," contributed also to our awareness of the lengths to which human beings would go in order to intimidate and kill their fellow creatures. The atomic bombings of Japan, the terror attacks unleashed on civilians by both sides during the war, certainly are more open to debate than is the Final Solution, but they too contributed to the creation of a postwar climate characterized by extreme suspicion of any individual's or group's claims to moral authority.

The Final Solution as a historical phenomenon that can be described and dated is horrific enough; nevertheless, to limit our understanding of that experience to the events themselves constitutes a serious misreading of just how greatly the Final Solution has challenged or even destroyed moral values once considered sacrosanct in Western culture. Hannah Arendt points to the enormity of the issues raised when she argues that Nazi Germany's methods of domination and destruction "must cause social scientists and historical scholars to reconsider their hitherto unquestioned fundamental preconceptions regarding the course of the world and human behavior" (cited by Korman in "The Holocaust in American Historical Writing," 48). And Lawrence Langer goes as far as to make the Final Solution the catalyst for the twentieth century's growing disenchantment with the values that have contributed to Western society's belief in social and moral improvement:

> Textbook theories about self-actualization, the intrinsic goodness of the human spirit, moral growth, social progress, and the valuable lessons of history collapse into pretentious evasions of the grim legacies that twentieth century reality has left us: the Holocaust above all, but only as the chief example of companion forms of mass dying through war, revolution, famine, repression and genocide.
>
> (*Admitting,* 12)

Among the many casualties of the Final Solution was the time-honored notion that there existed inherent limitations to the cruelty of which people were capable, and that to transgress these boundaries was to forgo one's humanity. Just how tenacious has been that belief is illustrated in Michel Borwicz's *Ecrits des condamnés à mort.* The author cites camp inmates whose language illustrates their inability, in the face of their own imminent deaths, to ascribe what was being done to them to their fellows. These victims speak of their Nazi torturers "as bloodthirsty creatures from another planet disguised as men" (137). Such language represents a desperate and doubtless unconscious effort to hold onto the belief that there remained sane parameters to human behavior, limits that individuals, regardless of their aims or anger, could not exceed without reverting to an animal state. The truth was the opposite, and Edmond Jabès, writing in almost direct response to the prisoners' imagery, pointed out years later the error in thinking that the Nazis were "brutes descended from another planet" (*Du Désert au livre,* 93). The German novelist Martin Walser was even more specific and unyielding when he described the oppressors and their victims: "Auschwitz was not Hell, rather a German concentration camp. And the 'prisoners' were neither the damned nor the half-damned of the Christian cosmos, rather innocent Jews, Communists, and so forth. And the torturers were not fantastic devils, but men like you and me. Germans, or those who wanted to become such" ("Unser Auschwitz," 11).

Walser's comment is exemplary not simply for its content but because of its matter-of-fact tone, free of rhetorical excess. He states the truth of the situation and eschews any effort to find greater, potentially redemptive significance in what had occurred. Walser's language is atypical; most commentators find it difficult to write about the Final Solution, or matters related to it, without finding some reassuring moral meaning, or using it as a club against individuals or groups. Two controversies provide examples of this difficulty: one is of considerable semantic importance, the other indicative of the polemical power the Final Solution continues to generate. I am referring to the use of the word *holocaust,* and the argument surrounding the wartime journalism of Paul de Man.

The very word *holocaust* is controversial since it is essentially a religious term. In their *Approaches to Auschwitz: The Holocaust and Its Legacy,* Richard Rubenstein and John Roth describe the origins of the expression: "In the Septuagint, a Greek translation of the Jewish Scripture dating from the third century B.C.E. (before the common era), *holokausten* is used for the Hebrew *olah,* which literally means 'what is brought up'. In context the term refers to a sacrifice, often specifically to 'an offering made by fire unto the Lord'" (6-7). "Sacrifice" connotes a willing or willed loss for a greater purpose, and as such has been applied by both scholars and theologians most often, but not exclusively, to Jewish victims of the concentration camps (Rubenstein and Roth, *Approaches,* 4). The problem with the term is that it implies that these people's deaths have some vaguely understood redemptive or didactic quality. The use of "Holocaust" suggests that the victims' destruction serves a higher purpose, that the living will discover some moral reinforcement from their deaths. Nothing, however, indicates that this ideal is true, or that something reassuring about the human animal can be garnered from this particular slaughter of the innocent: "To speak of a 'Holocaust' is a self-serving misrepresentation, as is any reference to an archaic scapegoating mechanism. There was not the least 'sacrificial' aspect in this *operation,* in which what was calculated coldly and with maximum efficiency and economy . . . was pure and simple *elimination*" (Lacoue-Labarthe, *Heidegger,* emphasis in text, 37). Even among some scholars who continue to use the term, "Holocaust" is deprived of any redemptive implication: "the Holocaust is an event without a future— that is, nothing better for mankind grew out of it" (Langer, *Admitting,* 38). My own choice of the phrase "Final Solution" reflects my agreement with Lacoue-Labarthe and Langer on this question.

The controversy surrounding Paul de Man's wartime activities demonstrates the Final Solution's persistent ability to foster reactions that owe more to emotion than to logic. The facts are simple enough. As a young man in occupied Belgium, de Man wrote a series of newspaper articles, several of which have a clear anti-Semitic slant. Just how, if at all, this affected his subsequent work as a literary theorist is at best highly speculative. Nevertheless, Jacques Derrida's efforts in the pages of *Critical Inquiry* to exonerate his deceased friend from charges of anti-Semitism ("Like the Sound of the Sea Deep within a Shell: Paul de Man's War") created a storm in academic circles. Shoshanna Felman's impassioned plea on behalf of de Man provides a good example of the excessive rhetoric still characteristic of so many discussions related to the Final Solution:

> It is no longer possible to distinguish between heroes and knaves, regeneration and destruction, deliverance and entanglement, speeches and acts, history and faith, idealistic faith and (self)-deception, justice and totalitarianism, utmost barbarism and utmost civilized refinement, freedom of will and radical enslavement to historical manipulations and ideological coercions.
>
> ("Paul de Man's Silence," 719-20)

If Felman's strategy in championing de Man was to blur all distinctions, Derrida chose instead to be haughty and dismissive toward those who attacked his former colleague. In the end his defense of de Man became a defense of deconstruction. Apparently Derrida foresaw this literary issue, since whatever might have been latent in some of the criticisms of Paul de Man's alleged anti-Semitism during World War II became transparently clear in a subsequent publication by David Hirsch, who mangaged to extend the ramifications of the Final Solution directly into the realm of literary theory: "In fact, are we not in all honesty to say that the real-world endpoint of Heideggerian (and now Derridean and de Manian) deconstruction of the logocentric tradition is precisely Auschwitz?" (*Deconstruction,* 87).

All the arguments and controversies mentioned here attest to the ways the Final Solution has affected, and continues to affect, postwar cultural life. The implementation of the Nazi genocidal policies was the catalyst that provoked among artists and intellectuals, as well as among many ordinary citizens of different nationalities, a profound distrust in the possibility of human decency. In fact, Western intellectuals came to question the Enlightenment tradition that has so marked their own thinking over the last three centuries. The disgust created by the discovery of places like Auschwitz added a further dimension of horror to wartime activities such as the dropping of the atomic bomb, the terror bombings of cities like Dresden, and the wanton destruction of villages like Oradour. These latter phenomena, although secondary in importance to the concentration camps, in turn contributed to the creation of the postwar moral malaise, a malaise that would make the writing of fiction about World War II particularly difficult.

The elements of the malaise that would directly affect the creation of literature in the postwar context are brilliantly illustrated in a novel published a mere eight years after the end of World War II. The visceral numbness that characterized Sarraute's "Age of Suspicion" found a powerful fictional embodiment in Samuel Beckett's *The Unnamable* (1953), the final installment of a trilogy that included *Molloy* (1951) and *Malone Dies* (1952). *The Unnamable* can be read as a series of questions that allude to complex issues without ever providing anything resembling coherent answers. This novel offers no resolutions to conflicts; where a reader might expect clarification, there is only contradiction.

It is inappropriate to speak of a narrator in *The Unnamable*; instead, a constantly self-contradicting narrative voice oscillates between several real and/or imagined identities. At times the voice associates itself with Mahood, a word that seems to contain allusions to manhood, but aside from the homonymic similarity, nothing justifies such a conclusion, nor is anything gained by attempting to make this connection. Mahood, we learn, is also Basil, but Basil is as much a cipher as Mahood, except that the voice implies that Mahood lacks a foot (42). Is the absence of a foot a physical embodiment of some sort of moral crippling? Perhaps, but also perhaps not. Once again nothing permits such a conclusion, as the text flatly denies such facile symbolic relationships. The narrative also refers to someone named Worm, but Worm seems less a person than a possibility, a tentative and stillborn effort to establish a human identity.

The disembodied narrative voice that flits from one name to another suggests what remains of individual identity after the war. Certainties of any kind are suspect, and for anything the voice can utter about human beings, the opposite is equally plausible. Given this situation, to the extent that the novel progresses at all, it is through questions: "Where now? Who now? When now?" (3); and through negative assertions: "Pupil Ma-

hood, repeat after me, Man is a higher animal. I couldn't" (69).

The force of *The Unnamable,* as well as its appropriateness as a starting point for a discussion of the postwar novel, is in its negation: without being able to affirm what truths, if any, remain, it clears away the debris of false certainties, of consoling assumptions. Christian Prigent's comment about the entire trilogy is particularly germane to *The Unnamable*: "[Since] it resists the constitutions of figures and meaning, mechanically erodes and dissipates settings, and frustrates the expectation of positive endings, this literature, simultaneously frugal, denuded, and rhetorically complex, seizes in a new way on the real" ("A Descent," 11). In this instance the "real" is the postwar world.

Among the intellectual/moral casualties of World War II were the optimism about the decency of mankind and the confidence in the possibility of human progress—ideas frequently, albeit somewhat loosely, associated with the Enlightenment. The French expression for "Enlightenment" is *le siècle des lumières* (the century of lights). Light is a source of disturbance to the narrative voice in *The Unnamable,* yet typically the voice is uncertain about "complaining about the disorder of the lights, this being due simply to my insistence on regarding them always as the same lights and viewed always from the same point . . . disorder of lights perhaps an illusion, all change to be feared, incomprehensible uneasiness" (9). Yet for this voice that at one point imagines itself as "the blessed pus of reason" (92), the lights continue to be a problem. For one thing, they hiss as they go out (95), thus providing more noise than clarity. Despite their annoying features, however, the lights remain perhaps the only means of showing what progress has been made (95). In any case, as the voice remarks, "this question of lights deserves to be treated in a section apart, it is so intriguing" (95).

To the extent that light imagery constitutes an allusion to the declining, if not moribund, Enlightenment influence, it is an allusion of the slightest sort, as if to suggest that this decline may be true, but even if it is, the discussion of the matter can be deferred until "time is not so short, and the mind more composed" (115). The alleged decline of the Enlightenment's influence is discussed in chapter 2.

The Unnamable also questions the function of language. The problem is not that information is lacking but whether language in its present state can cope with what has occurred. The voice wonders if it might best proceed by "aporia pure and simple . . . or by affirmations and negations invalidated as uttered, or sooner or later" (3). It then quickly confesses that "I say aporia without knowing what it means" (4). The voice poses the possibility that to comment clearly on the present circumstances would require verbal structures (future and conditional participles) that do not exist (16), thereby implying that traditional grammatical forms are inadequate to the current situation. Reexamination of the function of language in the postwar era constitutes part of chapter 3.

Given the semantic and linguistic condition the voice describes, what role, if any, does literature play as a means of understanding postwar experience? To the degree that the voice offers any response to this question, it is largely negative. Toward the end of *The Unnamable,* there is an effort to tell a story involving a boy, a girl, a mother-in-law, and love found and lost. This attempt is quickly abandoned; the story goes nowhere and says nothing (167-68). If this fumbling narrative has any purpose, it is to suggest that literature, in its traditional formats, no longer has much validity and might best be consigned to history's junk heap. What appears to endure is typically contradictory: the impossibility of speaking, the impossibility of remaining silent, and solitude. In a novel where every statement elicits its opposite, it is worth noting that the need to speak is nonetheless asserted at the beginning (4) as well as at the end (173), even though the voice seems to imply throughout that it learns nothing from its own remarks. Although it comes as no surprise that *The Unnamable* terminates in confusion—"where I am, I don't know, I'll never know, in the silence you don't know, you must go on, I can't go on, I'll go on" (179)—a slightly earlier statement matters more for the writing of postwar fiction: "quick now and try again, with the words that remain, try what, I do not know" (178). Parts of chapter 2 deal with early attempts and failures at finding the right words.

In his discussion of *The Unnamable,* Wolfgang Iser argues that the novel's contradictions create potentially useful paradoxes: "Only by accepting incomprehensibility is it possible to see through the fictions that pretend to know the unknowable. . . . But in addition to this, it is the incomprehensibility of reality, and indeed of the ego itself, that gives rise to fiction" ("When Is the End" 57). For Iser, Beckett's endless questioning, his debunking of facile explanations and reassuring fictions, is ultimately "a great comfort for literature and a great nuisance for ideology" (57).

With regard to the present study, the abiding merit of *The Unnamable* lies in its effort to describe, as best words can, the postwar climate in its confusion and opaqueness as well as the difficulty this state of affairs presented for the writing of fiction.

Other novelists, working in the immediate aftermath of World War II, would prove less rigorous in their approach, more comforting in their intentions, and finally less aware of how greatly the war had altered the direction literature was going to take. Hence Beckett's style, his pained, precise prose would have no imitators of consequence, and other authors would eschew his bleak mindscapes. Nevertheless, the vision of a world without meaning, except for invented ones, along with the constant need to subvert the literary text, would come to characterize the best writing about World War II.

For reasons of clarity and chronology, this study is presented in two phases. The first consists of two chapters that mingle literary history and textual analysis in an attempt to explain how World War II radically affected the writing of novels in Germany and France. The second contains six chapters examining successful efforts to create fiction about the war. . . .

Note

1. It also provoked a powerful, albeit short-lived conservative reaction in the visual arts that involved a debunking of prewar Cubism as a Germanic artform ("Kubism"), and a brief flirtation by prominent artists such as Picasso with Neoclassicism. See Kenneth Silver's *Esprit de Corps.*

Bibliography

Adorno, Theodor. *Notes to Literature III*. Ed. Rolf Tiedemann, trans. Sherry Weber Nicholson. New York: Columbia University Press, 1974.

Arendt, Hannah. *Eichmann in Jerusalem: A Report on the Banality of Evil*. New York: Viking, 1963.

Beckett, Samuel. *L'Innommable*. Paris: Minuit, 1953.

Böll, Heinrich. *Eine deutsche Erinnerung: Interview mit René Wintz*. Köln: Kiepenheuer und Witsch, 1979.

Borwicz, Michel. *Ecrits des condamnés à mort sous l'occupation allemande (1939-1945)*. Paris: Presses Universitaires de France, 1954.

Bosmajian, Hamida. *Metaphors of Evil: Contemporary German Literature in the Shadows of Nazism*. Iowa City: University of Iowa Press, 1979.

Buruma, Ian. *The Wages of Guilt: Memories of War in Germany and Japan*. New York: Farrar, Strauss, Giroux, 1994.

Derrida, Jacques. "Biodegradables: Seven Diary Fragments." *Critical Inquiry* 15 (Summer 1989): 812-73.

Duras, Marguerite, *The War: A Memoir*. Trans. Barbara Bray. New York, Pantheon, 1986.

Felman, Shoshana. "Paul de Man's Silence." *Critical Inquiry* 15 (Summer 1989): 704-54.

Hewison, Robert. *Under Siege: Literary Life in London 1939-1945*. London: Weidenfeld and Nicolson, 1977.

Hirsch, David H. *The Deconstruction of Literature: Criticism after Auschwitz.* Hanover: Brown University Press, 1991.

Hynes, Samuel. *A War Imagined: The First World War and English Culture.* New York: Atheneum, 1991.

Iser, Wolfgang. "When Is the End Not the End? The Idea of Fiction in Beckett." In *On Beckett: Essays and Criticism,* ed. S. E. Gontarski. New York: Grove, 1986.

Jabès, Edmond. *Du Désert au livre. Entretiens avec Marcel Cohen.* Paris: Pierre Belfond, 1980.

Korman, Gerd. "The Holocaust in American Historical Writing." In *Holocaust: Religious and Philosophical Implications,* ed. John Roth and Michael Berenbaum. New York: Paragon House, 1989.

La Capra, Dominick. *Representing the Holocaust: History, Theory, Trauma.* Ithaca: Cornell University Press, 1994.

Lacoue-Labarthe, Philippe. *Heidegger, Art and Politics: The Fiction of the Political.* Trans. Chris Turner. Oxford: Basil Blackwell, 1990.

Langer, Lawrence. *Admitting the Holocaust: Collected Essays.* Oxford: Oxford University Press, 1995.

Lercher, Alain. *Les Fantomes d'Oradour.* Lagrasse: Editions Verdier, 1994.

Prigent, Christian. "A Descent from Clowns." Trans. Michele Sharp. *Journal of Beckett Studies* 3, no. 2 (Autumn 1993): 1-19.

Relinger, Jean. *Henri Barbusee: écrivain combattant.* Paris: Presse Universitaire de France, 1994.

Rubenstein, Richard. *The Cunning of History: Mass Death and the American Future.* New York: Harper and Row, 1975.

Rubenstein, Richard, and John Roth. *Approaches to Auschwitz: The Holocaust and Its Legacy.* Atlanta: John Knox, 1987.

Sarraute, Nathalie. *L'Ere du soupçon.* Paris: Idées, 1956.

Silver, Kenneth. *Esprit de Corps: The Art of the Parisian Avant-Garde and the First World War, 1914-1925.* Princeton: Princeton University Press, 1989.

Walser, Martin. "Unser Auschwitz." In *Heimatkunde: Aufsätze und Reden.* Frankfurt am Main: Suhrkamp, 1968.

Wolf, Christa. *Patterns of Childhood.* Trans. Ursule Molinaro and Hedwig Rappolt. New York: Farrar, Straus, Giroux, 1980.

Susanne Vees-Gulani (essay date 2003)

SOURCE: Vees-Gulani, Susanne. "International Reactions to the Bombings." In *Trauma and Guilt: Literature of Wartime Bombing in Germany,* pp. 161-90. Berlin: Walter de Gruyer, 2003.

[*In the following essay, Vees-Gulani presents the responses of three novelists to the infamous saturation bombing of Dresden, Germany, by the U.S. forces at the end of World War II.*]

The air war has not only been taken up by German writers. In particular, Dresden, which is often understood as the central symbol of the destructive powers of large-area bombings, has inspired authors from outside Germany to address the topic as well. While Kurt Vonnegut's *Slaughterhouse-Five* is the first to come to mind when thinking about literary depictions of the Dresden raids, there are also two other novel-length examples: Dutch author Harry Mulisch's *Het stenen bruidsbed* (*The Stone Bridal Bed*) and French writer Henri Coulonges' *L'Adieu à la femme sauvage* (*Farewell, Dresden*). Interestingly, even though non-German authors do not experience directly the consequences of personal shame about the Nazi past, or external pressures about collective German guilt, the texts still display similar concerns and characteristics to the German accounts. As in their German counterparts, these novels not only deal with the strong psychological effects of the bombings and the search for proper modes of representation of the events, but also with the issue of guilt. Nevertheless, their relationship to the material also differs. The choice of the novel as the form used to address the air raids is interesting, as this requires a more lengthy treatment of the events, and many Germans have shied away from it. The publication dates (Mulisch's work, for example, was published as early as 1959), also suggest that non-German writers might have been less inhibited in dealing with the sensitive and traumatizing topic than German writers generally were. This observation is shared by Günter Grass when questioned about the scarcity of German writing about the bombings: "Vielleicht ist es für ausländische Autoren, die das erlebt haben, leichter gewesen, das zum Thema zu nehmen" ("Interview" 65).[1]

6.1 KURT VONNEGUT

Kurt Vonnegut's *Slaughterhouse-Five* from 1969 is the most famous novel about the (Dresden) air raids and their effects. Similar to many of the German narratives, the work, which has been widely discussed as an anti-war novel, is based on the author's own experiences in World War II. As a German POW, Vonnegut witnessed the bombing and complete destruction of Dresden, and

Slaughterhouse-Five is the author's manifestation of what he called "a process of twenty years [. . .] of living with Dresden and the aftermath" (Allen 163). Indeed, the words that describe the war, the Dresden events, and their effect on the people who experienced them did not come easily to Vonnegut. In an interview in 1974, he commented on the difficulties of articulating his experiences: "I came home in 1945, started writing about it, and wrote about it, and *wrote about it,* and WROTE ABOUT IT" (Allen 163). This agony is echoed in the first chapter of the novel itself:

> When I got home from the Second World War twenty-three years ago, I thought it would be easy for me to write about the destruction of Dresden, since all I would have to do would be to report what I had seen [. . .].
>
> But not many words about Dresden came from my mind then. [. . .] And not many words come now, either. [. . .][2]

Vonnegut's problems with articulation are evidence of the long term consequences that the author suffered after witnessing the destruction of Dresden as a POW. However, while critics generally recognize that the war and particularly the destruction of Dresden had a traumatizing effect on Vonnegut, the nature of this trauma and how it manifests itself in the novel has yet to be explored in a more systematic manner. A fresh look at *Slaughterhouse-Five* using the psychiatric theory outlined in Chapter 2 not only offers new insight into the work, but also opens a window into the author himself. Vonnegut's writing of *Slaughterhouse-Five* can be seen as a therapeutic process that allows him to uncover and deal with his own internal trauma. By using creative means to overcome his own distress, Vonnegut makes it possible for us to trace his own path to recovery. We slowly narrow in on his condition using the novel as a conduit first to the protagonist Billy Pilgrim, then to the narrator, and finally to the author himself.

Lawrence Broer has suggested that "[p]robably no characters in contemporary fiction are more traumatized and emotionally damaged than those of Kurt Vonnegut" (3). Billy Pilgrim in *Slaughterhouse-Five* certainly confirms Broer's assumption. Even his wife Valencia, who is unaware of Billy's psychological turmoil, gets "a funny feeling" that he is "just full of secrets" (121). Attempting to define Billy's psychological state more precisely, literary scholars have frequently associated *Slaughterhouse-Five* and its protagonist with schizophrenia, assessments most likely inspired by the author's own comments on the title page characterizing the novel as "somewhat in the telegraphic schizophrenic manner of tales of the planet Tralfamadore."[3] Yet it seems that even some of the critics who describe Billy as schizophrenic are uneasy with this assessment. In the introduction to a recent collection of essays on Vonnegut, for example, Harold Bloom qualifies his descrip-

tion of Billy as suffering from schizophrenia with the parenthetical comment: "(to call it that)" (1). Symptoms of schizophrenia have to be present for at least six months before the disease can be diagnosed and it is not caused by an external event. Schizophrenics usually suffer from auditory or visual hallucinations,[4] and from social and/or occupational dysfunction (DSM-IV-TR 299). These criteria simply do not apply to Billy's situation. He does not suffer from hallucinations or delusions. Furthermore, he manages to lead, at least externally, a very functional life after he returns home from the war, exemplified by having a family, running a business, and being a respected member of society. This would be atypical for someone suffering from schizophrenia. Rather, Billy's problems are directly related to his war experiences. His fantasies seem to be the result of memories of particularly traumatic events, and a vivid imagination which he employs as a 'sense-making' tool to deal with his war trauma.[5] In contrast to the limited insight into Billy's psyche that schizophrenia provides, his symptoms and various facets of his state of mind in the novel can be more satisfactorily explained applying the criteria of posttraumatic stress disorder.

The symptoms of PTSD can be moderated or exacerbated by the response of the environment to the individual. It has been noted that the "psychosocial atmosphere in a society is clearly a factor that facilitates or hinders the process of coping with stressful life events" (Kleber, Figley, and Gersons 2). When Billy returns home, America does not provide him with the possibility of working through the traumatizing nature of his war experiences, particularly the bombing of Dresden. For a long time, the Dresden raids and their consequences were not a topic of interest in the United States. In fact when Billy, long after the events, does speak out once about Dresden, he is immediately silenced with the 'official' position towards the Dresden bombings. After his plane crash, Billy shares a room in the hospital with a retired brigadier general in the Air Force Reserve, official Air Force historian, and Harvard professor Bertram Copeland Rumfoord, who is writing a book about air battles and bombings during World War II. When Billy tells his story, Rumfoord refuses to accept Billy's suffering and negates it by refocusing on the bombers rather than the bombed:

> "It had to be done," Rumfoord told Billy, speaking of the destruction of Dresden.
>
> "I know," said Billy.
>
> "That's war."
>
> "I know. I'm not complaining."
>
> "It must have been hell on the ground."
>
> "It was," said Billy Pilgrim.
>
> "Pity the men who had to *do* it."
>
> (198)

The long-term denial of the events and the lack of understanding about or acknowledgment of the suffering Billy endured, do not allow Billy the possibility of working through his experiences. He is supposed to go straight back to his prewar life, as if nothing has happened, which ultimately leads to Billy's chronic suffering.

The most striking symptom of Billy's condition is his altered perception of time. He sees himself as having "come unstuck in time" (23):

> Billy has gone to sleep a senile widower and awakened on his wedding day. He has walked through a door in 1955 and come out another one in 1941. He has gone back through that door to find himself in 1963. He has seen his birth and death many times, he says, and pays random visits to all the events in between.
>
> He says.
>
> Billy is spastic in time, has no control over where he is going next, and the trips aren't necessarily fun.
>
> (23)

Being "spastic in time," thus, is a metaphor for Billy repeatedly reexperiencing the traumatic events he went through in the war, particularly as a POW during the Dresden bombings. Psychologically, Billy has never fully left World War II, but instead, in Jerome Klinkowitz' words, he lives in a "continual present" (55). In *Trauma and Recovery,* Judith Herman describes a similar situation with regard to former captives suffering from PTSD. While imprisoned, they "are eventually reduced to living in an endless present" (89). Yet after their release or liberation, they "may give the appearance of returning to ordinary time, while psychologically remaining bound in the timelessness of the prison" (89). It has also been observed that a former prisoner "even years after liberation, [. . .] continues to practice doublethink and to exist simultaneously in two realities, two points in time" (Herman 89-90).

Billy's situation is comparable to that of the soldiers Herman describes. While "outwardly normal" (175), the traumatic memories persistently intrude into his thoughts in ways typical of people suffering from PTSD. Billy also finds himself at times at two different points of his life at the same time, for example "simultaneously on foot in Germany in 1944 and riding in his Cadillac in 1967" (58). In many cases, Billy relives the past through his dreams. In addition, he reexperiences the trauma as distressing recollections or flashback episodes. Certain "internal or external cues that symbolize or resemble an aspect of the traumatic event" (DSM-IV-TR 468) trigger in Billy painful memories or cause him to relive the war episodes. Psychiatrists specifically point to "sensory phenomena, such as sights, sounds, and smells that are circumstantially related to the traumatic event" to "reactivate traumatic memories and

flashbacks" in PTSD sufferers (Miller 18). This symptom is readily observed in the protagonist and explains the novel's abundance of both psychological and structural "linking devices" (Klinkowitz 78) between different scenes of Billy's life. For instance, the novel repeatedly mentions certain colors (for example "ivory and blue," "orange and black") or smells ("mustard gas and roses"), which carry significance in Billy's past.

The combination "ivory and blue" appears throughout the novel, usually as a reference to bare feet and implying cold and/or death. The image originates in the war when Billy sees "corpses with bare feet that were blue and ivory" (65). The significance of the colors "orange and black," which reappear in the striped pattern of a tent put up for his daughter's wedding (72), is connected to the POW train Billy rides during the war and which was "marked with a striped banner of orange and black" (69). The recurring smell of "mustard gas and roses" is also connected to death, and its significance arises from Billy's experience of having to dig victims out from under the Dresden ruins after the raids: "They didn't smell bad at first, were wax museums. But then the bodies rotted and liquefied, and the stench was like roses and mustard gas" (214). Other examples of triggers for flashbacks and memories include certain sounds such as a siren (57, 164), which Billy associates with the Dresden air raid alarms, so that it "scared the hell out of him" (57) and "he was expecting World War Three at any time" (57). Not surprisingly, seconds later he is "back in World War Two again" (58).

In another episode, it is the sight of men physically crippled by war going from door-to-door selling magazines that immediately causes Billy, himself mentally crippled by the war, great distress:

> Billy went on weeping as he contemplated the cripples and their boss. His doorchimes clanged hellishly.
>
> He closed his eyes, and opened them again. He was still weeping, but he was back in Luxembourg again. He was marching with a lot of other prisoners. It was a winter wind that was bringing tears to his eyes.
>
> (63)

Similarly, the optometrist barbershop quartet performing at his anniversary party causes a strong response in Billy, since they remind him of the four German guards in Dresden who, when they see the destruction of their hometown, "in their astonishment and grief, resembled a barbershop quartet" (179). This memory of the German guards lies at the center of Billy's trauma, the destruction of Dresden. In this case Billy first responds with physical symptoms, looking as if "he might have been having a heart attack" (173). Finally, away from the guests, Billy "remembered it shimmeringly" (177), but does not travel back in time to this particular event. The Dresden bombings and their effect are too painful to relive, and at first even too frightening to remember. The strong physical and psychological reaction to the barbershop quartet, which even disturbs Billy's usually normal outward appearance, thus shows how deeply Billy has buried his Dresden memories.

This suppression of memories from parts of the trauma is typical of PTSD sufferers. It goes hand-in-hand with other techniques of evasion. As has been shown, individuals try to protect themselves from the painful experience by avoiding any feelings, thoughts or conversations, and activities, places or people that could cause recollections (DSM-IV-TR 468). Billy demonstrates all of these symptoms. He hardly ever talks about his experiences in the war, even eluding the topic when his wife questions him about it (121-123). This behavior is in accordance with studies of prisoners of war which "report with astonishment that the men never discussed their experiences with anyone. Often those who married after liberation never told even their wives or children that they had been prisoners" (Herman 89).

Connected with the avoidance, and also a symptom of PTSD, is another striking feature of Billy's behavior, namely his diminished general responsiveness to the world around him. His range of emotions is severely restricted throughout the novel. He is described as one who "never got mad at anything" (30) and bears everything without reaction, since "[e]verything was pretty much all right with Billy" (157). This restricted range of affect shows itself most prominently in the much repeated phrase "so it goes" with which Billy reacts passively and without emotion to tragedy and death. Billy's behavior can easily be described by the terms "psychic numbing" (115) or "psychic closing-off" (126), which Robert J. Lifton used for labeling the reactions towards death in survivors of the Hiroshima bombing.[6] For Billy, avoidance and "psychic numbing" function as a protective shield against the horror of memory and offer him the possibility of living an "outwardly normal" (175) life by suppressing his trauma. However, it is impossible for Billy to prevent completely the intrusion of his memories because the events have destroyed him on the inside which now mirrors the ruins he saw in Dresden. At first, he follows the conventional way of seeking help by committing himself to a mental hospital since he felt "that he was going crazy" (100). Yet, just as mainstream American society does not provide an atmosphere conducive to recovery from the horrors of war, Billy is also failed by the psychiatric establishment of the time.[7] Neither providing an accurate diagnosis nor offering any coping mechanisms, it proves itself to be completely separated from true world experience. When Billy checks himself in, "the doctors agreed: He *was* going crazy" (100), but "[t]hey didn't think it had

anything to do with the war. They were sure Billy was going to pieces because his father had thrown him into the deep end of the Y.M.C.A. swimming pool when he was a little boy, and had then taken him to the rim of the Grand Canyon" (100). Billy thus falls victim to the previous tendency in psychiatry to underestimate the role of "an external factor, something outside the person" (Kleber, Figley, and Gersons 11) in causing trauma and instead to focus only on one's "individual vulnerability as the reason for people's suffering" (Kleber, Figley, and Gersons 13).

Billy and his roommate and fellow war veteran Rosewater thus embark on their own path of "trying to reinvent themselves and their universe" (101) in order to cope with the war events. Specifically, in what has been referred to as "a desperate attempt to rationalize chaos" (Merrill and Scholl 69), they resort to science fiction. Billy thus claims that he was kidnapped by aliens from the planet Tralfamadore, where he was then displayed in a zoo. Tralfamadorian philosophy helps Billy deal with the horrible events and their consequences by reinterpreting their meaning, since the philosophy opposes the quest for making sense out of the occurrences. When he asks the Tralfamadorians why they picked him to be abducted, they tell him: "'Why you? Why us for that matter? Why anything? Because this moment simply is. [. . .] There is no why'" (76-77). These beliefs also enable Billy to avoid some of the distress he feels when facing death:

> "When a Tralfamadorian sees a corpse, all he thinks is that the dead person is in bad condition in that particular moment, but that the same person is just fine in plenty of other moments. Now, when I myself hear that somebody is dead, I simply shrug and say what the Tralfamadorians say about dead people, which is 'So it goes.'"
>
> (27)

While the idea of Tralfamadore as a coping mechanism at first strikes one as bizarre, it nevertheless seems to be Billy's only option in a world clearly failing to provide him with a different path. As Leonard Mustazza points out, by indirectly identifying Kilgore Trout's science fiction novels as the source of Billy's ideas, "Vonnegut takes pains to show whence Billy's fantasy derives, and, in this regard, the novel proves to be quite realistic, a portrait of one of life's (especially war's) victims" (302). With the help of his Tralfamadorian fantasy and his idea of time travel, Billy conquers the effects of his trauma in a way that enables him to function. He controls his anxiety, so that nothing can surprise or scare him, and his symptoms of arousal are confined to his trouble in sleeping and his occasional bouts of weeping (61). However, as Herman points out, "the appearance of normal functioning [. . .] should not be mistaken for full recovery, for the integration of the trauma has not been accomplished" (165). The price Billy pays for appearing normal is high. Not only is he bound to a life of indifference, passivity, and a science fiction fantasy, but he can also never fully escape from his trauma which continues to intrude into his life.

Billy's trauma story is not the only one in the novel, but it is framed by that of the narrator, who is a fictionalized version of Vonnegut himself. While separated from Billy's story, the first chapter provides some of the "linking devices" (Klinkowitz 78); the Tralfamadorian "so it goes," the smell of "mustard gas and roses" (4, 7), and even a "Three Musketeers Candy Bar" (9), all of which appear again later in the text.[8] At the same time, the narrator interrupts Billy's story at several occasions to authenticate the events. The text implies that, because the horrible consequences of the bombing of Dresden are too far removed from normal experience to be easily reported, yet nevertheless truly happened, they can neither be completely fictionalized nor simply repeated through an eyewitness account. The novel thus becomes a mixture of autobiography and fiction, that simultaneously binds Vonnegut to, and distances him from, the text and its implications.

This need to develop new techniques to describe war experiences and particularly the bombing of Dresden, lies at the core of the trauma. As described previously, traumatic memories are usually not verbal, but surface as visual images (de Silva and Marks 166). Before they can be shared with others, they first have to be translated into language, a task that, difficult in itself, is complicated by processes of avoidance and denial. PTSD sufferers are often unable to recall important aspects of the trauma (DSM-IV-TR 468). This is a problem that the narrator faces when he simply cannot remember much about the war (14). Thus, even though he continuously tries to write the novel, he nevertheless feels unable to do so. Even after finally finishing the book after nearly a quarter of a century, he considers it "a failure" (22). In fact, as Peter Freese points out, "the thematic center of his novel [Dresden] is endlessly circumnavigated but never fully encountered" (221). This aspect of the novel is thus exactly what Herman understands as "the central dialectic of psychological trauma": the conflict between wanting to deny horrible events and at the same time wishing to share them (1).

This difficulty in expressing the events is enhanced by the political and societal denial surrounding them. The narrator shares Billy's experience that America does not offer an atmosphere that easily allows recovery, since there is no forum for a discussion of the events:

> I wrote the Air Force back then, asking for details about the raid on Dresden, who ordered it, how many planes did it, why they did it, what desirable results there had been and so on. I was answered by a man who, like

myself, was in public relations. He said that he was sorry, but that the information was top secret still.

(11)

Just as there is no public discussion of the events, there is also no discussion of them in private conversation. Since most of the victims of the air raids were Germans, the aggressors and major perpetrators of the war, the question of whether it is even legitimate to talk about the horrible and traumatizing aspects of the bombings is part of every discussion of them:

> I happened to tell a University of Chicago professor at a cocktail party about the raid as I had seen it, about the book I would write. He was a member of a thing called The Committee on Social Thought. And he told me about the concentration camps, and about how the Germans had made soap and candles out of the fat of dead Jews and so on.
>
> All I could say was, "I know, I know. I *know*."

(10)

The desperate "'I know, I know. I *know*'" seems by no means Vonnegut's "expression of his exasperation at having to hear, once again, about the horror of the death camps" (275), as Philip Watts contends. Rather it is an acknowledgment of the difficulty and inability to talk or write about a topic which deeply affected one's psychology, but which at the same time cannot be separated from questions of guilt, since it necessarily includes portraying the perpetrators of the war, the Germans, as suffering. Consequently one needs to design one's own coping strategies and path of healing in order to deal with the horror of the Dresden air raids.

As has been shown earlier, writing can be an integral part of the treatment of posttraumatic stress. For Vonnegut, the recovery process is bound to literary production, and he himself views his work as "therapy" (Allen 109). His war, and particularly his Dresden, experience has not left him scarless. What we learn in the novel is corroborated by comments that the author has made in interviews, and together these point to an underlying trauma. Vonnegut especially emphasizes his amnesia with regards to Dresden:

> [T]he book was largely a found object. It was what was in my head, and I was able to get it out, but one of the characteristics about this object was that there was a complete blank where the bombing of Dresden took place, because I don't remember. And I looked up several of my war buddies and they didn't remember, either. They didn't want to talk about it. There was a complete forgetting of what it was like. There was all kinds of information surrounding the event, but as far as my memory bank was concerned, the center had been pulled right out of the story.

(Allen 94)

Writing *Slaughterhouse-Five* thus meant the long and painful process of uncovering what Vonnegut had pushed out of his consciousness. Even though it is painful "to come face-to-face with the horrors on the other side of the amnesiac barrier" (Herman 184), it is a necessary step in recovery. However, the subject has to be approached with care, since successful recovery requires a balancing act: "[a]voiding the traumatic memories leads to stagnation in the recovery process, while approaching them too precipitately leads to a fruitless and damaging reliving of the trauma" (Herman 176). Vonnegut also does not face his suppressed memories directly, but slowly uncovers layer after layer to get to their core. The novel reflects this process of narrowing in on himself through the two trauma stories. Billy's story allows an indirect and detached exploration of the effects of the Dresden bombing, since the character is mostly fictional. The narrator's story, while on one level parallel to Vonnegut's, is on another level an integral part of a work of fiction. Moving himself from the factual to the fictional plane by creating the narrator thus still allows Vonnegut a degree of distance from himself and his experiences, a similar technique that Pennebaker and Greenberg, Wortman, and Stone found to be successful in their experiments on writing and healing (see Chapter 2). Consequently, the final point of recovery in this process of self-therapy is not achieved in the novel but rather comes with its completion:

> I felt after I finished *Slaughterhouse-Five* that I didn't have to write at all anymore if I didn't want to. It was the end of some sort of career. I don't know why, exactly. I suppose that flowers, when they're through blooming, have some sort of awareness of some purpose having been served. Flowers didn't ask to be flowers and I didn't ask to be me. At the end of *Slaughterhouse-Five*, [. . .] I had a shutting-off feeling, [. . .] that I had done what I was supposed to do and everything was OK.
>
> (Allen 107)

However, while *Slaughterhouse-Five* is the result of a successful self-treatment, telling the story does not mean that the trauma can then be forgotten. As in psychotherapy, which aims at "integration, not exorcism" (Herman 181) of the trauma, the Dresden experience does not lose its important position in Vonnegut's life after he completes the novel, but it can now be adequately integrated into the author's past. While the events no longer paralyze the writer, they are still available for further creative exploration, thus continuing as "the informing structure of all his novels" (Leeds 92). Yet Vonnegut has done more than heal himself. By publishing *Slaughterhouse-Five* and drawing the reader into his path of recovery, the stories of Billy, the narrator, and consequently Vonnegut take on a public dimension. Creating a story that mixes autobiography with fiction helps to turn the overwhelming and hard-to-grasp experience into a structured and controllable one, without concurrently sacrificing detail and complexity. While the story is different from the one experienced, it is not simplified, as these narratives of personal trauma usu-

ally become when translated into language, because the fictional layer returns the complexity into the text. In particular, the use of modern structural techniques, such as the following of Billy's wandering mind, gives the readers more immediate access to what it is like to live through such a traumatic experience as the Dresden bombings. The impact on the reader of a text such as *Slaughterhouse-Five* can thus be potent and surpass the limits of the concern for only an individual destiny. It draws attention to what we often need to suppress or deny when it is most important to remember; namely, the crippling nature of war and the terrible toll that modern warfare exacts on those forced to live through it.

6.2 HARRY MULISCH

Not as well-known internationally as Vonnegut's *Slaughterhouse-Five,* but a bestseller in the Netherlands, and recently reissued in a new German translation, Harry Mulisch's *Het stenen bruidsbed* (*The Stone Bridal Bed*) offers another impressive attempt to deal through literature with the inner and outer destruction caused by the large area bombings in World War II. Mulisch's *Het stenen bruidsbed* was published in 1959, the key year in German postwar literature in which Böll, Grass, and Johnson shattered the silence surrounding the German past in their respective important novels, by establishing the Nazi years and German guilt as dominant topics of German literary production. Yet they did not much discuss the bombings and their psychological consequences in their works even though, as the previous chapters have shown, the bombings had deeply scarred German society. So, while German literature, caught up in guilt, trauma, and fear, remained largely silent about this part of World War II, Mulisch was able to fill this gap with his novel because of his position as a Dutch-language author. He could thus add yet another view to the multiple perspectives in dealing with the war offered by the three German authors in 1959. Not surprisingly though, the novel, which after its success in the Netherlands was translated into German for the first time in 1960, did not receive any attention in the country of its setting. In an interview, Mulisch recently uttered the suspicion that the lack of success was due to the fact that Germans in the Adenauer era did not care to have a Dutchman tell them about Dresden (*NZZ* 41). However, the lack of interest in Gert Ledig's *Vergeltung* a few years before the publication of *Das steinerne Brautbett,* as well as the previously described societal and cultural situation in Germany in the 1950s and early 1960s, suggest rather that the German public at this point was not yet ready to face the complex issue of the bombings regardless of who was writing about them.

Unlike Vonnegut, Mulisch was not a witness to the Dresden raids in 1945. His novel is thus not in part the working through of a personal bombing trauma as

Slaughterhouse-Five. Mulisch did observe Dresden in its destruction eleven years after the war when he was attending a Heine conference in the German Democratic Republic. He later described his experience in an interview:

> Eigentlich hatte ich vor, ein Buch über einen hohen Naziverbrecher zu schreiben. Aber dann sah ich die öden Ruinenhaufen, wo tatsächlich Menschen lebten und immer noch Steine klopften wie die Nibelungen bei Wagner. Da wusste ich, dass ich dieser totalen Gestaltlosigkeit etwas Geformtes entgegenzusetzen hatte. [. . .] Eines Nachts stieg ich aus einem Jazzclub, der in irgendeinem Ruinenkeller eingerichtet war, und ich fand mich völlig verlassen in der Luft. Es gab hier keine Häuser, keine Straßen, keine Topographie mehr. Ich musste mich buchstäblich am Sternenhimmel orientieren, um wieder in meine Unterkunft zu finden.
>
> (dsch 29)[9]

However, Mulisch's perception of the destruction of Dresden does not seem to be the only reason why he felt the Dresden bombings and their effects to be a fitting subject matter for his novel. Indeed, Mulisch over and over again returns to different aspects of the Second World War in his texts, suggesting that he is trying to understand and work through his experiences of the war with his writing. The author's obsession with World War II is not surprising. His biography reveals that the war has left him scarred similarly to his key character of *Het stenen bruidsbed,* the American bomber pilot Corinth, whose face after a war injury resembles the ruins of Dresden, the city he had bombed just before his accident. The son of an Austrian father who collaborated with the Nazis and a Jewish mother, most of whose relatives were killed in concentration camps, Mulisch spent his childhood torn between victim and perpetrator. While hating his father for his involvement with the Nazis, he was also aware that it was his collaboration that saved his mother's life. Mulisch once fittingly summarized his paradoxical background as "more than having 'lived through' the war, I *am* the Second World War" (van der Paardt 204). It is thus not surprising that Mulisch chose a setting such as Dresden to explore further questions of guilt and responsibility and outer and inner destruction as a consequence of conflict and war. In Mulisch's words:

> Alles ist so ironisch [. . .]. Wenn mein Vater nicht bei den Deutschen mitgemacht hätte, hätte meine Mutter nicht überlebt. Denn als die mal verhaftet wurde, hat mein Vater seine hohen Freunde eingeschaltet, und sie wurde freigelassen. Was soll man darüber denken? Als Schriftsteller schreibt man dann eben über Schuld und Verantwortung.
>
> (Lebert and Weber)[10]

Het stenen bruidsbed is set in Dresden in 1958, where the protagonist of the novel, American dentist and former bomber pilot Norman Corinth takes part in a

dental conference. However, his true motives for the trip to Dresden in the middle of the Cold War can be found in his war experiences which are interjected into the text as three flashbacks. Here it is revealed that Corinth is actually returning to Dresden because he was involved in the bombing of the city in February of 1945 and personally committed a particularly cruel act when shooting at civilians who were trying to protect themselves from the raging fires in the Elbe river. Shortly afterwards, he was seriously wounded when his plane went down. Corinth is presented as deeply injured by his experiences, both internally and externally. The novel's point of view is limited mainly to Corinth's own perspective and his confrontation with the past is mediated through his interaction with several characters. He starts an affair with the attractive organizer of the conference, Hella Viebahn, who had been imprisoned in a concentration camp during the Nazi years. He also spends much time with his West German colleague Schneiderhahn whose puzzling background and intentions Corinth tries to decipher throughout most of the novel. In addition, the plot is interspersed with short conversations with his chauffeur Günther and the hotel manager Ludwig. The book ends with another act of (self-)destruction by Corinth who crashes a car into the ruins and then, seriously injured, sets it on fire.

Vonnegut's passive protagonist Billy Pilgrim is a strikingly different personality than the older, harsh, and somewhat rough Norman Corinth (who, incidentally, is hardly ever mentioned by his first name). While Billy is somewhat naive and a completely innocent victim of the bombings and war in general, Corinth is a man of action, but also ripped apart by guilt. He was an active participant in the destruction of Dresden and went beyond any call of duty as a soldier, purposefully shooting at and murdering the women, children, and old people who had found protection in the river. Still, the two men are in many ways similarly affected by their respective war experiences. Billy is completely emotionally detached from his surroundings, his life, and his past; Corinth blocks out all emotional reactions. Corinth's detachment clearly reveals itself in the first section of the novel, which introduces and describes the protagonist. It is fittingly entitled: "(But Without Feeling)" and portrays a man marked by internal and external destruction.[11] Corinth's face is so severely scarred that it is similar to the broken landscape surrounding him in Dresden and for which he was partially responsible as a bomber pilot. He looks almost animal-like, his face is a patchwork of pieces of dead blue and white skin (10) without hair or eyelashes (11). The scars prevent him from forming most natural facial expressions that would normally accompany any emotional state. Like many who suffer from the effects of trauma, while able to build an outwardly normal life with a dental practice, marriage, and friends, he is unable to form any close and meaningful bonds with other people. The relationship to his wife is cold and distant, and harmony is maintained mainly through her consumption of a large number of medications (12). Similarly, when he starts an affair with Hella in Dresden, it is based solely on his near-animalistic sexual desires, but not on any emotional involvement: "[. . .] he felt his body. Saliva shot into his mouth, and he had to swallow. His horniness barked dutifully: a cold animal, and he thought: Of course, of course, I want her" (18-19).[12]

Corinth's feelings of detachment and alienation do not only play out with regards to others, but also to himself. Several times, Corinth perceives his body and mind/soul as being two separate entities. The schisms between body and mind are immediate reactions to situations that remind him of the past. For example, after he arrives in Dresden and is led into his room, he finds that his window overlooks the destroyed city. He also becomes a witness to a large number of dead, and nearly dead, flies struggling at this very window. As the hotel manager Ludwig explains: "Every year the same. They escape from the wind into the houses. What can you do? It is a tradition in Dresden to die on a large scale" (27-28).[13] Corinth's reaction indicates that the statement reminds him of his past involvement in the mass killing, specifically his horrific deed of shooting innocent civilians who were trying to escape from the deadly fire by resting in the river—a memory he clearly tries to suppress. Corinth's mind cannot handle the return to the place of his terrible actions and the schism occurs:

> He saw himself, lying there on the bed, in a tower, in Dresden . . . smoking and constantly drinking and looking at the ceiling. [. . .] He thought, if I am not conscious of being in Dresden where am I then? [. . .] He remembered something he had read somewhere (or had he made it up himself?): *The soul travels by horse.* [. . .] At this point it was sailing a few hundred kilometers off the coast of Long Island [. . .]. It would only arrive when he would be long since back in Baltimore—months later, when he, with bare underarms sticking out of his white coat and a piece of plastic in front of his mouth, would be bending over a woman whose open mouth full of gold was facing the sky, filled with gray mountains of lead—*Dresden.* Only then would his soul go up the stairs with Ludwig and watch the dying flies.
>
> (30-31)[14]

This dissociation between body and mind is typical of Corinth's pychological adaptation. The reader is told that "after the war he made do without himself for years" (31).[15] Like so many others who experienced the war and the bombings, Corinth is lost, his experiences have fragmented him and shaken the constants that usually give orientation to life. What are left are individual pieces that cannot form a whole any longer, a condition shared by the fields of ruins of the destroyed cities.[16] Not surprisingly, Corinth directly identifies with them

when trying to reflect on his state: "[. . .] he had the feeling of being broken down. His kidneys were two collapsed villas in ravaged gardens, his back was the burnt-out church from the street corner" (56).[17]

The split between body and soul also indicates the changed view of two other points of orientation, time and space. Like Billy, Corinth can think of himself as being in two different places in time at the same time, so that temporarlity loses its linear function in his perception. Sometimes the war appears to him so unreal that he thinks it had never happened, or occurred three thousand years ago (105). Then when he successfully blocks out his memories, he finds himself immediately back in the war through flashbacks and reliving the events in his thoughts as soon as he is reminded of them. The Dresden experience was thus so extreme that he perceives it as having been "outside of history," which at the same time makes it always present for him (82).[18] The constant struggle between suppression and intrusion causes him not only to feel lost in time, but also in space. It is as if he has ceased to exist: "Already while I experience something, I have never experienced it. Never have I been anywhere. [. . .] I am nowhere. When I die, they will bury an empty coffin" (74-75).[19]

While Billy's response to the events is one of passivity, similar to the role he was forced to take during the bombings as a victim on the ground, Corinth finally continues his role as the man of action and returns to Dresden in an attempt to face himself and his guilt. His state of confusion is symbolized by the structure of the hotel he stays in, which is a labyrinth of strange rooms and towers that are accessible only through odd paths. The house seems almost organically grown and is mysteriously organized around a "mother cell," a room with glass walls in which an old woman lies in a bed, and which is located within another room. Access to Corinth's room is difficult not only because he has to climb through many others in order to get to it, but also because the key to it is in a locked box whose key is inside of the box itself:

> "Where is the key to this closet, Eugène?"
>
> "I don't know," Eugène laughed, looking at Corinth.
>
> "Huh, always this nonsense," Ludwig said. "Of course, it is *in* the closet again."
>
> "Yes!" Eugène laughed.
>
> (25)[20]

This scene is symbolic of Corinth's psychological condition. He returned to Dresden, to the center of his trauma and his guilt in order to confront his inner turmoil and destruction. He tries to find access to himself and hopes to overcome his guilt and to become whole again and reestablish his place in the world. He is thus striving for humanity and life (46), more instinctively than consciously, hoping that the resolution for his despair would be located at the source. This is symbolized by the "green whispering" (16) he starts to hear immediately after he arrives in Dresden, and which seems to come from the city, but which he cannot decipher.[21] Just as the key to the closet, being inside the closet itself, is hard to obtain, resolution is similarly difficult to achieve. While Dresden could be a place to make peace with the past, it also worsens his condition because it is full of reminders of this past.

Unfortunately, Corinth's hope for a return to wholeness is only an illusion. To Philippe Noble, Corinth "is a criminal of a 'modern' anonymous war, hidden in a big crowd of many. But he is also a criminal in the 'ancient' sense" (350), because he perpetrates senseless murder of innocents. After the bomb is dropped by his battle friend, the "eraser of cities" (111),[22] Corinth also wants to have a direct part in the battle:

> *"Look! Look!" In the black water in the flickering shine of the flames the blue-eyed Corinth sees them: heads, skulls, melons, motionless. And then he laughs in the laugh of the victor and yells: "Shall I serenade them?" And everyone laughs, all the pilots [. . .], and then he ejects the bullets into the water in front of him, where skulls crack, sway, burst, come apart, jump around, sink, and everyone laughs, all the pilots, everyone laughs into the night and sings:*
>
> *"Adieu, mein kleiner Gardeoffizier, Adieu. Adieu, und vergiss mich nicht, und vergiss mich nicht."*
>
> (112)[23]

Corinth's later feelings of profound guilt about these brutal murders lie at the center of his traumatized state. These feelings of responsibility and shame start to arise when he sees the burning city again from the plane shortly before going down, and suddenly gains some understanding that this was not a game, but that his acts had real consequences: *"Slowly the bowl of fire disappeared beneath him, and he felt that there was something changing in him, not much, but deep inside of him. [. . .] with a feeling of being drained, he turned his gaze away and stared into the night. It had really happened"* (194-195).[24] By having Corinth's plane crash right after this incident, an accident in which he is badly injured by fire, Mulisch also etches this knowledge, like a mark of Cain, permanently on Corinth's face.

Back in Dresden over a decade after the incident, Corinth, when trying to deal with his guilt, continuously emphasizes to himself and others that the war against Germany and his role in it as a bomber pilot was justified, particularly also because he is Jewish. After seeing the depressing sight of the destroyed city of Berlin, but also the Hitler bunker when he arrives in Germany, he reminds himself of the cruelty of the Nazi regime:

> Here they had hurried around with their files [. . .] to a spider who was dragging a leg and lay in bed with a film star, sent by a pig full of medals in front of a mirror, in the name of a cockroach; here they had celebrated their blood wedding while their country was engulfed in the smoke coming from burning human flesh, killing others, they had rampaged over the planet. He thought, *shouldn't* we have come here, to bomb this nest into dust and ashes?
>
> (33)[25]

While one can hardly disagree with Corinth's standpoint in this matter, the situation becomes more complex for him in Dresden. Here, he is not only confronted with the ruins, but with the victims of his own depravity. In a bar he meets a couple who tell their story of escape from the fires. The woman turns out to have been a possible victim of Corinth's shooting since she lost her leg as well as her baby in such an incident. Throughout the novel, Corinth hopes to come to an understanding of himself and his situation by evaluating these different facets of guilt. As no other author who wrote about the bombings, Mulisch thus explores through his main character the issue of guilt involved in destruction and the large area bombings. Corinth, as a fighter for the victors, the liberators, and as a Jew is looking for justification of his past acts by exploring the cruelty of the German past. In the secret service man Schneiderhahn, whom Corinth watches intently throughout his stay, he finally (erroneously) thinks that he has found the personification of this evil since, because of some remarks by Schneiderhahn, Corinth believes that he had been an SS-dentist in a concentration camp. When he confronts him about it, Corinth tries to justify his involvement in the bombings by Schneiderhahn's guilt, portraying the pilots of the air raids as bringing deserved punishments for the committed crimes:

> "In Auschwitz," Corinth said quietly, "dentists are waiting at the exits of the gas chambers. When the doors open, dead naked bodies stand closely pressed together in the chamber, because there is no room for them to fall down. [. . .] While workers search for gold and diamonds in the anus and the genitalia, SS-dentists use hooks and tongs to break gold teeth and crowns out of gums. [. . .] Wasn't it just like that? Correct me if I am wrong, *Herr Doktor*"
>
> [. . .] As a participant of ten to twelve bombing attacks on Berlin, four on Hamburg, and, let's say, thirty on Mannheim, Cologne, Essen, Hannover and more, I could make accusations against you. I hope I was at least lucky enough to kill your father, your wife, and your child."
>
> (155-157)[26]

After this episode, Corinth feels "triumphant," as if he has got closer to what he was searching for in Dresden (160-161). However, his feelings of success are an illusion. Not only because Schneiderhahn was anything but an SS-dentist, on the contrary he worked for a foreign secret service throughout the Nazi period, but also because his idea that one's own past behavior and personal guilt can be erased by that of others simply cannot hold up. Both Dresden and Auschwitz are part of what the novel describes as an anti-history of deeds without reason or purpose:

> Between the mass murders of the Huns and Hitler's concentration camps no time has passed. They lie next to each other at the bottom of eternity. *And Dresden lies there as well,* he thought. [. . .] We destroyed Dresden because it was Dresden, just like the Jews were butchered because they were Jews, there is nothing more to it. [. . .] The bombing of Dresden is part of Hilter, of Attila, of Timur-Leng.
>
> (130)[27]

However, these comments should not be misunderstood as an equating of the victimhood of the Jews who died in Auschwitz and of the Germans who lost their lives in the bombings of German cities, at least this is what Mulisch claims later in an interview. According to Mulisch, what he looks at is the comparability of the "Techniken des Tötens, die eine Kultur anwendet" (dsch 29):

> Und ich habe mich schon gefragt, welcher Mord unmenschlicher ist: die Selektion an der Rampe, bei der die Täter—wenn man so will auf altmodische Weise den Opfern direkt ins Gesicht sehen, oder der Mord aus einer fliegenden Maschine, bei der die Täter, junge Menschen auch sie, gar nicht mitbekommen, was sie anrichten. Ich habe dann geschrieben, dass jeder unmenschlicher ist als der jeweils andere.
>
> (dsch 29)[28]

Corinth feels personal guilt because he did kill and he did so with pleasure. When drunk with the feeling of victory, he shoots the civilians in the river, committing a direct and individually terrible crime. The novel shows that the consequences of his actions and subsequent personal guilt cannot be erased by the knowledge that overall he was fighting for the right side.

The more Corinth wants to believe that his guilt can be, or has been, erased and that he is whole again, suppressing the knowledge that it will never leave him, the stronger his physical reactions become to stimuli in the environment. Not only is it common in people suffering from trauma experiences to have physical reactions to stressors connected with the events, but the connection of psychological condition and physical reaction is used effectively throughout the work to describe Corinth's inner state. Just as with Corinth's face, Mulisch again employs the physical to mirror the true psychological condition, showing that Corinth is increasingly losing control. When talking to Hella about his role in the bombings, he denies that he ever thinks about the events, but his body's reaction reveals his true inner state:

> "Hella, something is happening to me . . ." Frightened she was looking at the pearls of sweat on his forehead and around his nose that became larger and larger. His eyes attached themselves to the room. Still, it became worse and worse, invisible: a vibration in the night in the deathlike objects, as they were not themselves any longer, an opening-up that in horrible ways was threatening him. Light, light, he thought, but he was unable to speak; he felt that he had to use all his strength. But what strength? How? Against what? Then he felt that it became weaker, as if a storm had suddenly died down, and it disappeared.
>
> (106)[29]

These attacks become worse throughout his stay in Dresden and the more he tries to suppress his guilty conscience.

In order not to lose control completely Corinth, instead of slowly leaving his artificial coping constructs behind and facing reality, gets more deeply involved in them. While Billy Pilgrim flees into the realm of fantasy and science fiction in order to deal with the effects of the war, Corinth looks for support in the distant past of ancient mythology. By limiting himself to the stereotypical characteristics of a Homeric hero, bound to the fate determined for him, he tries to explain his own actions within the framework of myth. The bombings and his killing of the people in the Elbe are thus translated into Homeric terms. The airplane was the warship on the way to Dresden or Troy, and the "blue-eyed Corinth" (35) was on a mission to conquer it. The shooting of the people in the river, in particular, shows Corinth fully embracing the role of the victor and thus of the destroyer. In Dresden he increasingly interprets the world and himself through myth. He reenacts his character, the destroyer, over and over again. In his essay "Erinnern, Wiederholen und Durcharbeiten" ("Remembering, Repeating, and Working-Through"), Freud had already pointed out the connection between repetition, or acting out, and the suppression of certain childhood events. Freud contends that "je größer der Widerstand ist, desto ausgiebiger wird das Erinnern durch das Agieren (Wiederholen) ersetzt sein" (*Gesammelte Werke* V. 10 130).[30] In this case this idea can be applied to the traumatic event as well. Freud views acting out as a way to remember the suppressed event from the past. Mulisch himself goes even farther and sees this repeated reenactment of the past as a typically human characteristic: "Es scheint so, als ob sich die Vergangenheit immer wiederhole. [. . .] Ich glaube der Mensch wiederholt immer. So sind die Menschen einfach. Man hat oft gedacht, dass man sie ändern kann. Das scheint nicht der Fall zu sein" (Kleinschmidt 17).[31] This path of reenacting the past is, as is typical for people suffering from trauma, a vicious circle. The more Corinth tries to rid his deeds from consciousness, the more violently he acts out his past role of the destroyer, which leads over and over again to new reminders of his actions and his personal guilt.

The reenactment of the role of the destroyer manifests itself in several ways. One is through the association of destruction with sex, that leads like a thread through the novel. The reference to a bridal bed in the title already points to this connection between the sexual and destruction. Right from the beginning, the destroyed Dresden looks to Corinth like "a bride, who, when she sees the groom, has ripped her veil in pieces" (16).[32] In the first flashback about the bombing of Dresden, Corinth connects the destruction of the city more directly with male sexual arousal: *The bombing had already started, up above the first machines were returning: Lancasters, those were the British. He felt the beginning of an erection and put himself, sweating, in position behind his canon* (37-38).[33] The "ejaculation" finally occurs when Corinth shoots his bullets at the people standing in the river in the second flashback, feeling victorious and in complete control. Incidentally, this second flashback occurs at the same moment that Corinth has intercourse with Hella, whom he had been obsessed about "conquering" sexually from the first moment he saw her. Just as his killing in the past is perceived to be a sexual encounter, by having sex with Hella he kills again in the present. Hella, already a victim of the Nazis, now also becomes one of Corinth's since she is emotionally destroyed by his lack of interest in her after she sleeps with him. Sexuality for Corinth is thus inherently linked to causing destruction, the actual opposite of its biological purpose of procreation. He embraces the archetype of the destroyer vigorously, as if it were his biological function.

Also significant and connected with the issue of power, sex, and destruction is the symbol of fire that is associated with Corinth and Dresden. It is through fire that Corinth is eternally bound to Dresden and fire has made him the broken person he is when he returns. As a bomber pilot, Corinth is one of the people who unleashed the firestorm and the devastation that followed it. He then is injured and marked for life by fire immediately after the attacks. After he returns to Dresden, different kinds of "fire" are continuously mentioned around him, and each time, Corinth is immediately reminded of his past.[34] At the same time, he is continuously directly involved with fire as well. He again is in the position of the fire-starter. At first, this role is involuntary. Early on, he nearly burns his room down with his cigarette: "He burnt his fingers and immediately stood next to his bed while beating on his clothes, the cigarette butt was smoldering on the bedside rug. Fire, he thought, treading out the butt; swaying he walked to the window" (33).[35] Similarly, at the first reception of the conference, Corinth, deep in thought, nearly burns his fingers with his cigarette before someone extinguishes it. In the final scene of the novel, however, Corinth again consciously acts out the role of the destroyer and fire-starter. He repeats his destructive act and the consequences of the past by crashing a car like

a bomb into the ruins and then setting it on fire. The reader is left with the final image of a badly hurt, broken man, bleeding from his old injuries, caught up in a war that never ends and who continues to perpetuate destruction.

The last chapter of the novel thus skillfully brings together all the earlier motives and symbols and ultimately confirms Hella's assessment that "'[t]he war is only over, when the last, who has lived through it, has died'" (95).[36] It starts out with Hella, Corinth's victim through sexual destruction, who now finds herself also caught in a repetitive cycle but, contrary to Corinth, as the ultimate victim. Schneiderhahn, the other important character in the novel, also becomes a victim of Corinth's destructive force. Enraged, Corinth tracks him down to his hotel and beats him up. While Schneiderhahn thinks this happens because Corinth still believes that he was a Nazi criminal and wants to punish him for it, he is actually beaten up because Corinth has learned that he lied about his past. While it seems strange at first that this would be the reason for Corinth to attack Schneiderhahn, the act becomes more understandable when one considers the role Schneiderhahn played in the eyes of the former bomber pilot. As has been pointed out Corinth, by projecting all his guilt onto Schneiderhahn, tries to relieve himself of his own personal guilt. While his physical reactions from the start reveal this strategy to be nothing but an illusion, Corinth has to face the truth when he finds out that Schneiderhahn had indeed lied, and had instead been working against the Nazis. Corinth's destructive rage is caused by his knowledge that the personal guilt he has brought onto himself cannot be redeemed and will never disappear; his self-destructive act and nearly complete repetition of the past events in the final pages of the novel confirm this acknowledgement.

With *Het stenen bruidsbed* Mulisch offers an impressive description of the psychological consequences of the bombings, not only for the people on the ground, but also for the pilots above. It is not a work of therapy in the sense that *Slaughterhouse-Five* was ten years later for Vonnegut, who had actually experienced the air raids. The fact that Mulisch was not directly involved in the bombings might also explain why he had little trouble writing about Dresden so soon after the war and immediately after he observed the destruction in the city in the 1950s. Still, while not therapeutic in the direct sense, the topic enabled Mulisch, whom critics have described as a moralist (Pelt 168), to explore better his difficult relationship to the past caused by his unique background and the questions of responsibility and guilt he has been struggling with ever since the war. By restricting the perspective predominantly to that of an American pilot, he offers a unique angle by which to analyze the various guilt issues involved in the Dresden bombing as well as in the Second World

War in general. Mulisch's deep insight into the two poles of the war conflict, the victim and the perpetrator and the complexities that can complicate this relationship, as well as his perspective from the outside as a Dutch writer, seemed to have allowed him to explore these issues of guilt surrounding the bombings in more depth than any other author. His approach is similar to the understanding of guilt that Jaspers developed in his lectures on *Die Schuldfrage.* Mulisch, like Jaspers, shows that guilt can arise in many different ways, but never can one kind of guilt be erased by another. In addition, Mulisch warns against the idea of collective guilt as absolving personal guilt, just as Jaspers disqualifies it in his text. When Corinth tries to see Schneiderhahn as the representative of all of German guilt, actually projecting all war guilt, no matter by whom it was committed, onto him he effectively negates all individual guilt. It helps him to try to diffuse his personal act of horror in an unspecific collective. Schneiderhahn for him is not a person, but simply a figure representing an unspecified whole. Yet Mulisch makes clear that this is, at least for the individual, the wrong strategy. Schneiderhahn indeed is an individual with his own personal characteristics and an individual past. Mulisch stresses that both trying to minimize one's own guilt by seeing it erased by acts committed by others as well as hoping to hide one's own acts of horror behind the idea of collective guilt are not acceptable ways of dealing with one's past deeds.

Choosing an American pilot as his protagonist, Mulisch does not minimize German guilt and does not compare Dresden bombing victims to the victims of the Holocaust. The novel leaves plenty of room to explore German atrocities and makes clear that the horror created by Germans to which Corinth refers is completely real. Mulisch sends a message that Germans should not think that their own guilt is atoned for because they suffered from the bombings and horrors committed by others. They should not hide behind a collective guilt that would effectively take away responsibility from each individual. Yet by making Corinth, an American, a protagonist who has committed a cruel act, albeit against Germans, and who now breaks apart because of its consequences, Mulisch widens the perspective to be truly an international one. Modern war situations, he points out, even if mainly characterized by their anonymity and lack of emphasis on the individual fighter, still lead to acts that cause personal guilt. In the example of World War II, Mulisch shows that while many of these acts are committed by the original culprits, the Germans, they are not necessarily restricted to them. Personal guilt can arise in many situations and due to many different people—be it, as in Corinth's case, the needless killing of civilians on his bomber missions or, as in Mulisch's father's case, collaboration with the Nazis. War leaves behind many victims, perpetrators and some who fall somewhere between these two extreme poles.

According to Mulisch, one way or another all of them have to carry the burden of an endless presence of their past experiences and deeds. By writing this novel, Mulisch also indicates that this state is not only limited to the people concerned directly, but can affect future generations who have to live with the deeds and destinies of their fathers and mothers and somehow have to try to make sense of them.

6.3 HENRI COULONGES

The French novel *L'Adieu à la femme sauvage* (*Farewell, Dresden*) by Henri Coulonges was published in 1979 and is the story of Johanna, a twelve year old girl from Dresden, who barely survives the 1945 firestorm, and her later wanderings in search of a place of safety. In the bombings, she loses her friend Hella, her sister Grete, and effectively her mother Leni who is left almost speechless and passive after suffering a mental breakdown in response to the attacks and her other daughter's death. Narrated mostly through Johanna's eyes the author, using the innocence of the child's perspective, tries to convey a picture of the collapse of world order at the end of the war, characterized by destruction, the breakdown of bonds and family structures, displacement, and uncertainty.

When the bombing of Dresden starts, Johanna and her friend Hella are enjoying themselves at the circus across the river from the Old City. Instead of staying there until the alarm is over, Johanna and Hella try to make it home to the other side of the Elbe, thus entering directly into the chaos of flames and death that is raging through the town. Here, houses explode around them and whole streets are engulfed in flames, so they need to move constantly to escape the all-consuming fires. Their wanderings in the chaos leave them completely disoriented, both in space and time. Since most streets are blocked off by fires and smoke, they cannot follow any known path that would lead to their homes. Instead, they move about in circles, in need of finding shelter. Just as their knowledge of the city streets cannot help them to find the right way, time has lost its organizing function and becomes meaningless in the horror of the bombings:

> "There's no use running, Hella," she said matter-of-factly. "We won't have time to get home."
>
> [. . .] "Why are you sitting there," [said Hella.] "We have to find shelter! Hurry!"
>
> Johanna shook off her torpor, stood up and looked at her watch. It was ten past one. When had it begun? Three hours ago? Four?[37]

When the two girls get separated in the chaos, Johanna is ready to give up, not caring any longer what will happen to her without the support of her companion: "Before she had time to wonder what was happening, the blast knocked her down. [. . .] She had no pain anywhere, not even where she had been burned on her forehead. At last she felt good again. *I'll just go on lying here,* she thought. *It would have been senseless to run like that all night*" (35).[38] However, the horror of wild screams by burned victims around her drive her away, and immediately start haunting her: "The scream she had heard resounded again in her" (36).[39]

Miraculously, she finds her friend again, which gives Johanna new strength, but Hella herself has been severely affected by the events around her. After seeing people flattened into the pavement, as she tells Johanna, she is wrapped in "bewilderment" and "indifference," a state that finally leads to her death in the firestorm by a collapsing glass roof, in front of Johanna's eyes.

When Johanna makes it home the next morning, she hopes for comfort and guidance from her mother. Instead, her family structure is completely destroyed because of the bombings. Her sister is dead, their house a ruin and her mother is left almost infant-like from the shock:

> Johanna looked at her, overwhelmed. Her mother's expressive face, once full of dimples, smiles and mischievous winks, [. . .] was now ashen and lifeless. Johanna sat down beside her and pressed her cheek against hers.
>
> "I'm here, Mutti," she said softly. "I'm with you."
>
> Leni didn't answer. [. . .] Not knowing what to do, Johanna scrutinized her face, watching for a quiver of her lips or a flicker of her eyes. But she saw nothing. It was as if she found a landscape she had known and loved darkened by fog, unrecognizable.
>
> (54)[40]

It is now up to Johanna to take over the adult role of the guide, setting the two off on wanderings in a world that has completely lost any order. The search for safety and comfort that had started with the bombings thus continues throughout the whole novel. They first end up in the house of the leader of the Dresden children's choir outside the city, who Johanna had met after she had found her way out from the firestorm and who coincidentally knows her mother and is in love with her. Since this state of affairs creates conflicts between the child and the choir master, and Johanna's mother needs psychological treatment, Johanna and Leni move on to Prague to stay with an old friend of the family. Here, Johanna experiences the collapse of Hitler-Germany, the passing of their family friend and her mother's violent death.

At the same time, Prague citizens are starting to take revenge on the Germans and collaborators on the streets. There is no place for Johanna any longer in this world. After everything around her has collapsed, Johanna fi-

nally becomes completely indifferent to her destiny. She can only identify with others who have now lost their place in society and joins a group of women who had worked for the Germans and were now being punished by the crowds. Yet this is not a political statement for Germany on Johanna's part. She remains the innocent victim, but now embraces this role instead of fighting it:

> Something strange was happening: she felt lighter with every step she took. [. . .] Johanna saw a group of terrified women huddled beside an overturned truck. All their hair had been cut off and they had been beaten. Two men took one of them by the arms and dragged her through the frenzied crowd. [. . .] Johanna darted through the crowd. Before the men could stop her, she reached the woman and said in German, "Give me your hand."
>
> [. . .] It seemed to Johanna that the onlookers had all fallen silent, because their shouts didn't concern her anymore. She squeezed the woman's hand harder and raised it, with their fingers intertwined, toward the sun. It was as if she had been reunited with Leni and, hand in hand, they were entering eternity together.
>
> (284-285)[41]

The novel contains strong scenes about the horror of the bombing war and manages to evoke touching and graphic descriptions of the Dresden air raids. It convincingly depicts the breakdown of order which came both with the destruction of the city and the end of the Third Reich, affecting all areas of one's own life and of society in general. Yet overall the novel is not as convincing as it could be in its approach to the bombing experience and its consequences. Apart from some rather far-fetched coincidences in plot (for example the relationship between Leni and the choir leader), there are two issues which weaken the novel. One is the neglect of a more complex discussion of (German) guilt, the other a lack of psychological depth in the characters.

"There are no gratuitous descriptions of carnage and violence, no talk about politics and Nazis, and most of all, no judgment. Johanna could be any girl in any country" (Reichel 13). With these words a reviewer in the Los Angeles Times praised Coulonges' book when it appeared in English translation (*Farewell, Dresden*) in 1989. However, does this really strengthen the novel as the reviewer implies? Choosing Johanna's naive child perspective, Coulonges indeed seems to try to minimize the need to address the political background of the events. Many times, he emphasizes the innocence of the child. As Annette, one of Johanna's friends puts it: "We're paying for something we didn't do. By 'we' I mean people our age, and even little children. You, your poor friend, Franz, me—look at what's happened to us. We didn't deserve this" (113).[42] While it is of course valid that the children were innocent, one of the problems of Coulonges' text is that this state has been expanded to almost every character in the novel. No one seems to carry any responsibility, everyone is good and decent. There is some evil lurking in the background, concentration camps are mentioned once or twice and one of the children thinks "we all had it coming" (113),[43] but the only time this evil really breaks out is when a group of deserters from Vlasov's army hit and rape Johanna's mother Leni. Yet is it an accident that they are, while fighting for Germany, actually Russian soldiers? Otherwise, one is almost always only confronted with the evil of others, the bombings and later the revenge killings in Prague. By almost completely denying the political background of the story he tells, Coulonges oversimplifies his plot. It would have been wise to consider and present the fact that politics and guilt are part of any war. When writing about World War II in Germany, one necessarily also writes about the Nazi past—particularly if one leaves it out of the text. The complexity of the issue of the bombings cannot be completely understood if questions of guilt and responsibility are ignored since these feelings influence strongly the reaction to the air raids.

Andrea Barnet in her review of the novel pinpoints another problem in the work when she talks about the lack of psychological depth of the text in which Coulonges "too often [. . .] remains outside his characters, instead of illuminating their inner lives or giving us more insight into the psychic dislocations they suffer as all order around them crumbles" (Barnet 19). Indeed, Coulonges often seems to be unclear about how to represent his characters' reactions to the experience of trauma. Just like the invented trauma stories produced during the experiments about trauma, writing, and healing that were discussed previously (see Chapter 2), his novel appears too contrived and regularly slips into the melodramatic. Part of the problem is a discrepancy between the content of the work and its form. The novel deals with chaos and disorder, the breaking down of structures and constants in Johanna's life such as place, status, and time. She loses her house and becomes a wanderer. In addition, the family dynamics are broken apart because she suddenly finds herself in the role of the caregiver and provider. This causes the biggest change in her life since, while still a child, she also has to be an adult, which throws her out of the linear natural development of growing up. However, the form does not reflect these changes in Johanna's life, as the book follows a strictly chronological order of events and uses a completely traditional style of narration. The discrepancy between a content completely out of the ordinary and a form following traditional story-telling patterns is one reason why Coulonges' work is much less impressive and convincing for the reader than the other two Dresden novels by Mulisch and Vonnegut. In contrast to Coulonges, both these authors try to implement postmodern techniques in their novels in order to recreate

the destruction, fragmentation, and chaos they are depicting in their contents.

Mulisch, for example, replicates the fragmented inner state of his protagonist and that of his environment by creating a montage of "regular text" dealing with the stay in Dresden in the 1950s, and which itself is a mixture of interior monologues (both in third and first person), stream of consciousness, conversations, and authorial descriptions, with quotations and flashback episodes from the past. Since Corinth embraces antiquity in order to deal with his situation and also to express his relationship to the past, Mulisch uses a Homeric style in the flashback episodes. He also sets off the different parts visually, through regular and cursive type, so that *Het stenen bruidsbed* achieves an image of fragmentation on all levels of the text. At the same time, the recurrence of certain symbols, such as fire and sex, make clear that the present state is a consequence of past events and this gives the novel a sense of unity.

Vonnegut, like Mulisch, uses the same combination of coherence, achieved with his "linking devices," and fragmentation, caused by breaking up any chronology by simply following Billy's "time travel." Furthermore, he interrupts the illusion by adding self-reflections and narrative comments and by blurring the distinction between fact and fiction. He also mixes different genres. As ancient Greek literature enters Mulisch's novel, so does science fiction become part of Vonnegut's. In the spirit of this genre, Vonnegut uses comedy, irony, and fantasy to try to approach the outrageous events. Employing these new techniques and devices, both works create a form that complements the experiences they describe, giving the readers real insight into the inner and outer consequences of otherwise incomprehensible traumatic events—a quality Coulonges' *L'Adieu à la femme sauvage* never fully achieves.

The shortcomings in Coulonges' approach illustrate how difficult it is to depict traumatic events successfully through literature. In the case of the air raids against Germany during World War II, it is particularly challenging since there are complex relationships to politics and guilt to consider. The international treatment of the bombings as exemplified in these three novels about Dresden shows that the air raids are not only a specifically German topic, but can hold powerful messages about the realities and effects of war for an international audience. Their successes and failures also make clear that it is and will always be difficult to create convincing and appropriate literary narratives about the air war in Germany. Making the bombings a topic of literature opens up the opportunity to explore history from a different angle and points to many difficult issues involved in the war, yet it also combines two challenging tasks. The first is that one needs to describe events that are located far outside normal human experience and that can have incomprehensible shattering consequences both internally and externally. The second is that it is impossible to talk about the air raids without also exploring issues of guilt and responsibility.

The three novels on Dresden discussed here reveal that, while authors need to address similar issues to produce a successful text, writers from outside Germany can confront the bombing experience more directly than their German counterparts. Obviously the fact that a novel like *L'Adieu à la femme sauvage* which hardly deals with the guilt issues involved, can appear and not cause a scandal, would not have been possible if the author had been German. While Coulonges' failure to include the complex guilt issues in his text can simply be understood as resulting in a weaker novel or a failed attempt to try something new, for a German writer the book would be seen as a political statement and could mark him forever as an author with revisionist tendencies. The novels described here and the experiments their writers are willing to undertake in their books, as compared to the uneasy treatment the bombings receive in most German literature, illuminate once more the problematic relationship of German literature to this part of the German past. The difficult psychological situation in response to the air raids that German authors faced when trying to write about them was accompanied by enormous political pressures, much stronger than those that non-German authors experienced. Even though these forces have been weakening over time, they still seem largely responsible for the fact that up to this date some of the most gripping and artistically boldest literary writing on the air war and its consequences has been provided by a Dutch and an American author.

Notes

1. "Maybe foreign authors who went through this had an easier time in turning this into a literary topic."

2. Kurt Vonnegut, *Slaughterhouse-Five* (New York, Laurel, 1969) 2. Subsequent references appear parenthetically in the text.

3. A few of the many examples include Leonard Mustazza in "Vonnegut's Tralfamadore and Milton's Eden" who refers to Billy as "schizophrenic" (302). Similarly, in *Sanity Plea,* Lawrence R. Broer characterizes Billy's state as "schizophrenic deterioration" (91) and in "*Slaughterhouse-Five* or, How to Storify an Atrocity," Peter Freese describes Billy's story as sounding "suspiciously like the biography of a man who develops schizophrenia" (212).

4. Hallucination is defined as "a *sensory* perception that has the compelling sense of reality of a true perception but that occurs without external stimu-

lation of the relevant sensory organ" (DSM-IV-TR 823, emphasis added).

5. Billy's more externally observable erratic behavior after the plane crash and his wife's death by carbon-monoxide poisoning also does not comply with the criteria for the diagnosis of schizophrenia. Rather, it seems consistent with the consequences of a head trauma he might have suffered in the crash, possibly adding to Billy's traumatized state by worsening his psychic condition even further.

6. Donald Greiner was first to note the applicability of Lifton's ideas to Vonnegut's text. For further details see Donald Greiner's essay "Vonnegut's *Slaughterhouse-Five* and the Fiction of Atrocity" from 1973.

7. At the time that Vonnegut wrote *Slaughterhouse-Five,* ostensibly about his own World War II experiences, PTSD was not an established diagnosis. One is left to wonder whether Billy (and/or Vonnegut?) would receive better psychiatric care today.

8. The "Three Musketeers Candy Bar" is directly related to a scene in which Billy's wife Valencia visits Billy in the mental hospital a few years after the war and eats a "Three Musketeer Candy Bar" (107). The significance of the image, however, lies in the time of the war. After the Battle of the Bulge, Billy is part of a group of soldiers called by one of them, Weary, "the Three Musketeers" (48). Weary later blames Billy for breaking up the (completely imagined) great union of the Three Musketeers and becomes obsessed with wanting Billy dead.

9. "Originally I was planning to write a book about a Nazi high criminal. But then I saw the bleak piles of ruins where people were actually living and still hammered stones just like the Nibelungen in Wagner. Then I knew that I had to counter this complete shapelessness with something formed and ordered. [. . .] One night I climbed up out of a jazz club, which had been set up somewhere in one of the cellars under the ruins and I found myself completely alone in the air. There were no houses, no streets, no topography. I literally had to use the stars in the sky for orientation in order to find my accommodations again."

10. "Everything is so ironic [. . .]. If my father hadn't collaborated with the Germans, my mother wouldn't have survived. Once, when she was arrested, my father informed his friends in high places and she was let go. What should one think about that? As a writer the consequence is that one writes about guilt and responsibility."

11. Harry Mulisch, *Het stenen bruidsbed* (Amsterdam: de bezige bij, 1959) 9. Translation by the author based on the German translation by Gregor Seferens: Harry Mulisch, *Das steinerne Brautbett* (Frankfurt a. M.: Suhrkamp 1995). Subsequent references appear parenthetically in the text and refer to the Dutch edition of the work. The original text is provided in footnotes. "(Maar zonder emotie)"

12. "[. . .] hij voelde zijn lichaam. Water liep in zijn keel. Zijn geilheid blafte, een koud dier van plicht, en hij dacht, natuurlijk, natuurlijk, ik wil haar hebben."

13. "Ieder jaar hetzelfde. Ze vluchten voor de wind de huizen in. Wat wilt u? Het is traditie in Dresden, op grote schaal te sterven."

14. Hij zag zichzelf liggen, op een bed in een torentje, in Dresden . . . rokend en onafgebroken drinkend keek hij naar het plafond. [. . .] Hij dacht, als ik niet het besef heb dat ik in Dresden ben, waar ben ik dan? [. . .] Hij herinnerde zich iets, dat hij ergens gelezen had (of had hij het zelf bedacht?): *De ziel gaat te paard.* [. . .] Op het ogenblik voer zij een paar honderd kilometer uit de kust van Long Island [. . .]. Zij zou pas aankomen, wanneer hij allang terug was in Baltimore,—maanden later, als hij met blote onderarmen uit zijn witte kiel en een stukje plastic voor zijn mond over een vrouw gebogen stond, die haar mond vol goud opensperde naar de hemel buiten, waarin grauwe bergen lood stonden:—*Dresden.* Dan pas zou zijn ziel met Ludwig de trap opkomen en naar de stervende vliegen kijken."

15. "hij het na de oorlog jarenlang zonder zichzelf had gedaan."

16. The way his driver Günther reacts when they are lost in Dresden can be used to describe Corinth's own confused state: "Everywhere I recognize individual things, and then something else again, but I don't know how everything fits together" (41) ("Overal herken ik iets, en dan weer iets anders, maar hoe het in elkaar past, weet ik niet.")

17. "[. . .] het was een gevoel van afbraak. Zijn nieren waren twee ingestorte villa's in woeste tuinen, zijn rug was de verkoolde kerk op het kruispunt."

18. "het was buiten de geschiedenis"

19. "Terwijl ik iets meemaak, heb ik het nooit meegemaakt. Nooit ben ik ergens geweest. [. . .] Ik ben nergens. Als ik sterf, is mijn kist leeg."

20. "'Waar is de sleutel van het kastje, Eugène?' 'Weet ik niet,' lachte Eugène naar Corinth. 'O, het is zo'n grappemaker,' zei Ludwig. '*In* het kastje natuurlijk weer.' 'Ja!' lachte Eugène."

21. "groene gefluister"

22. "de stedenverdelger"

23. "'*Kÿk! Kÿk!*' In het zwarte water ziet hen onder het bevend schÿnsel van de overwinnaar en schreeuwt: 'Zal ik ze eens serenade geven?' En allen lachen, alle vliegers [. . .], en dan jaagt hÿ de kogels voor zich uit het water in, waar de hoofden spatten, tuimelen, botsen, springen, keilen, verzinken, en lacht, alle vliegers, allen lachen in de nacht, en zingen: 'Adieu, mein kleiner Gardeoffizier, Adieu, Adieu, und vergiss mich nicht, und vergiss mich nicht.'"

24. "*Langzaam gleed de schotel vuur voorbÿ en hÿ voelde, dat er iets in hem veranderde: haast niets, maar precies in het midden. [. . .] met een gevoel of hÿ hol werd, wendde hÿ zÿn ogen af en keek voor zich in de nacht. Het was waar gebeurd.*"

25. "Hier hadden ze haastig rondgelopen met hun papieren [. . .] naar een manke spin die met een filmster in bed lag, van een dekoreerd zwijn voor een spiegel, namens een kakkerlak; hier hadden zij hun bloedbruiloft gevierd, hun land walmend van brandend mensenvlees, moordend over de planeet tuimelend. Hij dacht, hadden wij soms *niet* aan moeten komen vliegen om het nest in puin te gooien?"

26. "'Tandartsen in Auschwitz,' zei Corinth zacht, 'wachten bij de uitgangen van de gaskamers. Als de deuren opengaan, staan de naakte doden stijf op elkaar geperst, want er is geen plaats om the vallen. [. . .] Terwijl arbeiders goud en briljanten uit de aarzen en geslachtsdelen halen, breken SS-tandartsen met haken en tangen en hamers de gouden kiezen en kronen uit de kaken.' [. . .] 'Was het zo niet? korrigeert u mij eens. Korrigeert u mij eens, *Herr Doktor*.' [. . .] 'Ik zou het u kunnen verwijten als deelnemer aan tien of twaalf bombardementen op Berlijn, vier op Hamburg en een stuk of dertig op Mannheim, Keulen, Essen, Hannover en weet ik veel. Hopelijk heb ik het geluk gehad, daarbij uw vader, vrouw en kind te raken.'"

27. "Tussen de massacres van de Hunnen en de koncentratiekampen van Hitler is geen tijd verstreken. Zij liggen naast elkaar op de bodem van de eeuwigheid. Hij dacht, *en daar ligt Dresden.* [. . .] Wij gooiden Dresden kapot omdat het Dresden was, zoals de joden geslacht werden omdat het joden waren. Verder geen boodschap. [. . .] Het bombardement van Dresden is van Hitler, en van Attila, en van Timoer Lenk."

28. "[. . .] the comparability of the techniques of killing which a culture employs: And I did ask myself, which type of murder was more inhuman: se-

lection at the ramp, where the murderers—in traditional style, if you want, look directly into the faces of their victims, or murder from a flying aircraft, in which the killers, also young people, don't even realize what they are causing. I then wrote that each acts more inhuman than the other.'"

While it is true that Mulisch does not seem to equate the victims of the bombings and of the Holocaust in the novel or in his comments, but is more interested in the killers, it is questionable whether such a comparison between the pilots and German Nazi criminals is really necessary. Since Mulisch also emphasizes the importance of dealing with one's personal guilt, it seems counterproductive to explore such "rankings" in brutality as for each person the personal guilt weighs heaviest.

29. "'Hella, er is iets met me . . .' Angstig keek zij naar de groeiende zweetdroppels op sijn voorhoofd, naast zijn neus. Zijn ogen vraten zich vast in de kamer. Nog steeds werd het erger, onzichtbaar: een nachtelijk sidderen in de doodstille dingen, alsof zij zichzelf niet meer waren, een opengaan, dat hem walglijk bedgreigde. Hijt dacht, licht, licht, maar kon niet spreken; hij voelde dat hij zijn krachten onmenselijk inspande maar welke? hoe? waartegen? Toen merkte hij dat het afnam, alsof een storm plotseling ging liggen, en het verdween."

30. "the greater the resistance, the more extensively will acting out (repetition) replace remembering" (trans. 151).

31. "It seems as if the past will always repeat itself. [. . .] I believe that humans always repeat themselves. That's how humans are. Often one has hoped that one can change them. This does not seem to be possible."

32. By applying the symbol of the wedding to Dresden and the Nazis and their crimes, the "blood wedding" (33), Mulisch also establishes a connection between them and shows that the destruction of Dresden ultimately was a consequence of these devious acts.

33. *"De bombardementen moesten al begonnen zÿn, hoger keerden de eerste machines terug: Lancasters; dat waren de engelsen. Hÿ kreeg een begin van een erektie en ging zwetend in positie liggen achter zÿn kanon."*

34. Apart from the Dresden firestorm in 1945, the most extensive description of which is centrally located in the third chapter of the drama-like structure of the novel, Ludwig talks about the recent fire in a neighboring hotel. In addition, the text also frequently refers to lighting cigarettes, lighted cigarettes, cigarette smoke, and damage caused by cigarette burns.

35. "Hij brande zijn vingers en stond meteen op zijn kleren slaand naast het bed, het peukje smeulde in de mat. Brand, dacht hij, trapte het uit, wankelde en ging voor het raam staan."

36. "'De oorlog is pas afgelopen, wanneer de laatste die hem mee heeft gemaakt, is gestorven.'"

37. Henri Coulonges, *Farewell, Dresden* (New York: Summit, 1989) 25. Subsequent references appear parenthetically in the text. The original French passages and page numbers are provided in the footnotes.

"'Hella, dit-elle d'un ton détaché. Ce n'est pas la peine. On n'aura pas le temps de rentrer de toute façon.' [. . .] 'Pourquoi tu ne bouche pas? Il faut trouver un abri tout de suite . . .' Son ton pathétique eut pour mérite de sortir Johanna de sa torpeur. Elle se leva et regarda l'heure à sa montre. Il était une heure dix. Cela faisait trois heures, ou quatre heures, que tout avait commencé?" (37)

38. "Avant qu'elle ait eu le temps de se demander ce qui se passait, le souffle d'une détonation violente l'avait précipitée à terre. [. . .] Elle n'avait mal nulle part, même plus à son front. Enfin elle se sentait bien. 'Je vais rester là tranquille, se dit-elle. J'allais quand même pas courir comme ça toute la nuit'" (55-56).

39. "il y eut un cri [. . .] qui se propagea soudain dans son crâne comme dans une chambre d'écho" (56).

40. "Johanna la regarda, anéantie. Cette oasis de fossettes, de sourires furtifs et de clins d'oeil malicieux qu'était le visage mobile et pétillant de sa mère [. . .], ce visage béni était devenu d'une fixité livide et tragique. Johanna s'accroupit à coté d'elle et posa sa joue contre la sienne. 'Je suis là, Mutti, lui murmura-t-elle tendrement à l'oreille. Je suis là avec toi . . .' Léni ne répondit pas [. . .]. Indécise sur ce qu'il convenait de faire, Johanna scruta le visage de sa mère avec anxiété, à l'affût d'une lueur passagère dans ses yeux ou d'une crispation fugitive de ses lèvres. Mais rien, rien. C'était comme si, revenant après un cataclysme dans un paysage qu'elle avait jadis aimé [. . .], elle le retrouvait, assombri par le brouillard, impracticable, méconnaissable" (91).

41. "elle se sentait à chaque pas plus légère. [. . .] Elle vit un groupe de femmes terrifiées qui se trouvaient là, serrées les unes contre les autres, à côté d'une camionnette renversée. [. . .] Deux hommes la [une femme] prirent chacun par le bras et elle se débattit. Ils l'entraînèrent. [. . .] Johanna subitement se mit à courir, traversa la foule d'un seul élan et, avant que les hommes en brassard aient pu intervenir, s'approacha de la femme. 'Ta

main', lui demande-t-elle. [. . .] Johanna eut l'impression que la foule s'était tue, ou que leurs cris s'étaient perdus dans des contrées inconnues qui ne la concernaient plus. Elle serra plus fort la main de la femme et la leva bien haut, enlacée dans la sienne, vers le soleil. C'était comme si elle entrait lentement, au bras de Léni retrouvée, dans l'éternité" (567-569).

42. "On a payé alors qu'on n'avait rien fait. Nous, les enfants. Toi, ta copine, Franz, moi, tous on a payé plus ou moins cher alors qu'on ne le méritait pas" (199).

43. "Que ça devait arriver. Qu'on l'a bien mérité" (199).

Works Cited

Allen, William Rodney, editor. *Conversations with Kurt Vonnegut*. Literary Conversation Series. Jackson: UP of Mississippi, 1988.

Beseler, Hartwig and Niels Gutschow. *Kriegsschicksale Deutscher Architektur*. Neumünster: Wachholtz, 1988.

Biller, Maxim. "Unschuld mit Grünspan. Wie die Lüge in die deutsche Literatur kam." *Deutsche Literatur 1998*. Ed. Volker Hage. Stuttgart: Reclam, 1999. 278-283.

Bloom, Harold. Introduction. *Kurt Vonnegut*. Ed. Harold Bloom. Modern Critical Views. Broomall: Chelsea, 2000. 1-2.

Broer, Lawrence R. *Sanity Plea: Schizophrenia in the Novels of Kurt Vonnegut*. Revised edition. Tuscaloosa: U of Alabama P, 1994.

Connelly, Mark. *Reaching for the Stars. A New History of Bomber Command in World War II*. New York: Tauris, 2001.

Coulonges, Henri. *Farewell, Dresden*. New York: Summit, 1989.

Coulonges, Henri. *L'Adieu á la femme sauvage*. Paris: Stock, 1979.

Forte, Dieter. *Der Junge mit den blutigen Schuhen*. Frankfurt a. M.: Fischer, 1995.

Freese, Peter. "Kurt Vonnegut's *Slaughterhouse-Five* and the Fiction of Atrocity." *Historiographic Metafiction in Modern American and Canadian Literature*. Ed. Bernd Engler and Kurt Müller. Beiträge zur englischen und amerikanischen Literatur. Paderborn: Schöningh, 1994. 209-222.

Friedrich, Jürgen. *Der Brand: Deutschland im Bombenkrieg 1940-1945*. München: Propyläen, 2002.

Grass, Günter. "'. . . dass ich ein Instrument bin'; Ein Gespräch mit dem Schriftsteller Günter Grass." *Neue Zuercher Zeitung* 16 May 1998: 65.

Greiner, Donald. "Vonnegut's *Slaughterhouse-Five* and the Fiction of Atrocity." *Critique* 14 (1973): 38-51.

Güntner, Joachim. "Der Luftkrieg fand im Osten statt." *Deutsche Literatur 1998*. Ed. Volker Hage. Stuttgart: Reclam, 1999. 271-275.

Hage, Volker. "Feuer vom Himmel." *Der Spiegel* 12 Jan. 1998: 138-141.

Harpprecht, Klaus. "Stille, schicksallose." *Deutsche Literatur 1998*. Ed. Volker Hage. Stuttgart: Reclam, 1999. 267-269.

Herman, Judith. *Trauma and Recovery*. New York: Plenum, 1997.

Kempowski, Walter. *Das Echolot: Fuga furiosa*. Volume 4. München: Knaus, 1999.

Kleber, Rolf J., Charles A. Figley, and Berthold P. R. Gersons, editors. *Beyond Trauma: Cultural and Societal Dynamics*. The Plenum Series on Stress and Coping. New York: Plenum, 1995.

Klinkowitz, Jerome. *Slaughterhouse-Five: Reinventing the Novel and the World*. Twayne's Masterworks Studies. Boston: Twayne, 1990.

Kunert, Günter. *Erwachsenenspiele: Erinnerungen*. 1997. München: dtv, 1999.

Kurowski, Franz. *Der Luftkrieg über Deutschland*. Düsseldorf: Econ, 1977.

Leeds, Marc. "Beyond the Slaughterhouse: Tralfamadorian Reading Theory in the Novels of Kurt Vonnegut." *The Vonnegut Chronicles: Interviews and Essays*. Ed. Peter J. Reed and Marc Leeds. Contributions to the Study of World Literature. Westport: Greenwood, 1996. 91-102.

Martin, Russell. *Picasso's War*. New York: Dutton, 2002.

Merrill, Robert, and Peter A. Scholl. "Vonnegut's *Slaughterhouse-Five*: The Requirements of Chaos." *Studies in American Fiction* 6 (1978): 65-76.

Miller, Laurence. *Shocks to the System: Psychotherapy of Traumatic Disability Syndromes*. New York: Norton, 1998.

Mulisch, Harry. *Het stenen bruidsbed*. Amsterdam: De bezige bij, 1959.

Mustazza, Leonard. "Vonnegut's Tralfamadore and Milton's Eden." *Essays in Literature* 13 (1986): 299-312.

Niven, Bill. *Facing the Nazi Past: United Germany and the Legacy of the Third Reich*. New York: Routledge, 2002.

Nossack, Hans Erich. *Der Untergang*. 1948. Frankfurt a. M.: Suhrkamp, 1996.

Sebald, W. G. *Luftkrieg und Literatur.* München: Hanser, 1999.

Nicole Thatcher (essay date 2006)

SOURCE: Thatcher, Nicole. Introduction to *Six Authors in Captivity: Literary Responses to the Occupation of France during World War II,* edited by Nicole Thatcher and Ethel Tolansky, pp. 13-26. Oxford: Peter Lang, 2006.

[*In the essay below, Thatcher surveys the writings of French authors who wrote during the German occupation of France.*]

One of the tragic events of the Second World War for France was the Occupation by the Germans of part and then the whole of the country. This traumatic defeat recalled other invasions by the same enemy within the past seventy years, and revived fears and feelings still latent in the population. It was compounded by one of the conditions of the armistice under which captured French soldiers were held in German camps—an imprisonment which for most of them lasted for the whole of the war. An understanding of this period of history requires knowledge not only of facts gained through historical research but of people's views as expressed in personal testimony. Since the end of the war, all kinds of documents have been examined to establish the sequence of events or details of particular incidents; innumerable books and films have studied, analysed and represented the many aspects of people's experience, but the most reliable evidence of personal reactions is to be found in what people wrote at the time or immediately after. Not every witness or participant had recourse to the written word, but one would expect 'professional' writers to do so in order to share with readers their outlook on the action and events they have taken part in, and to reflect on their own values. This is the path followed by the six authors whose work is the focus of this book.

For our authors writing became the essential tool for their resistance—and in some cases their survival—and after the war, their literary contribution was readily acknowledged. Their common ground is to have written at one stage in their lives from the particular position of incarceration: they responded to their imprisonment by turning to literature, more especially to poetry, to the world of imagination.

The works these six authors produced in prison represent a climax in their development. They are communications by witnesses of, or actors in an event and thus help us to understand and empathise with their situation; they reveal how the writer saw herself or himself, or the reasons for the path followed and the actions taken; they are the expression of an identity, of the social and cultural factors at work in the thinking and behaviour of the writer faced with the effects of war on her or his life. These aspects are examined . . . in conjunction with their literary output.

While the fact that they all turned to writing in a difficult time unites these six writers, they display a diversity at various levels which is reflected in their works. It is worth noting the range of their identities which stand as paradigms for the variety of people in France who opposed the war situation. We have a sixty-four year old well known writer, poet, painter, old rebel, and convert to Catholicism from Judaism, Max Jacob; a forty-two year old writer interested in art, civil servant, and *résistant* from the start of the Occupation, Jean Cassou; also aged forty-two, a non-conformist, poet and reporter, Philippe Soupault; a thirty-six year old academic and Catholic writer from a middle-class background, enlisted as an officer in the army, Pierre-Henri Simon; a twenty-eight year old who turned to writing after law studies, Jean Cayrol; and an eighteen year old, Madeleine Riffaud, full of anger and idealism that she expressed in poems noted in her diary.

The variations in the social background and individuality of these six authors is compounded by the circumstances of their arrest and imprisonment. Pierre-Henri Simon, made prisoner by the Germans in 1940, in Nantes where he was serving as a reserve officer, was sent to different Oflags in Germany. Jean Cayrol, Jean Cassou and Madeleine Riffaud had other fates as *résistants*: Cayrol was sent to Mauthausen concentration camp after having first spent some time in solitary confinement in Fresnes; Cassou escaped a first arrest from the Nazi occupiers in Paris and was then imprisoned in the south of France by the French authorities; Madeleine Riffaud was sent to the Gestapo centre in Rue des Saussaies and then to Fresnes prison near Paris. Philippe Soupault was imprisoned in Tunis before being freed and escaping to liberated Algeria. Max Jacob was first confined to his village Saint-Benoît-sur-Loire in the Loiret, before being sent to the Drancy camp in Paris, where he died.

Notwithstanding their different experiences of the war, our six authors are united in opposing the loss of freedom, a reaction shared by the population at large. The traumatism of the Occupation for the ordinary French person, or of the speed of defeat and subsequent imprisonment for French soldiers, started as a stupor which was followed by resentment at the constraints put on their freedom. For a great number, resentment became a conscious refusal of the *status quo* and also of Nazi propaganda, refusal which took several forms that Jacques Sémelin calls "'la résistance civile" définie comme le processus spontané de lutte de la société civile par des moyens non-armés'.[1] For a smaller number, this civil resistance became more concerted and also led to armed action. What has been called 'the Resistance' covers all these stages, which Dominique Veillon depicts as an evolution:

> La Résistance, c'est une attitude consciente, volontaire, patriotique ou morale, qui conduit une personne, puis une minorité à refuser concrètement la défaite et l'occupation ennemie. Mais c'est aussi une lutte clandestine contre l'idéologie nazie et un combat pour le maintien des libertés et de la démocratie.[2]

Writing became an essential tool in this fight as a channel for communication, as a way to establish a network of people with whom ideas can be shared:

> To assess the contribution of the Resistance to the war effort in primarily military terms entails a fundamental misrecognition of the value to be accorded to the ideological and the discursive at this time; it is difficult to see how, without public expression, there could have been a Resistance.[3]

The works of our six authors fit into this perspective and raise issues regarding the status, importance and role of writers during the Occupation.

The written word, and for most writers this generally means the published one, can exert an important influence on society by shaping opinion. It has the possibility of reaching a large readership, and thus 'de répandre des convictions susceptibles de faire des adeptes et, partant, d'engager d'autres destins que les leurs'.[4] This was well understood by the German occupiers, who monitored and censored French literary outputs as well as journalistic ones. Although some press censorship had already existed before Vichy, now the occupiers 'made it necessary for all newspapers to submit to government control or to cease publication altogether'.[5] Furthermore, they also strictly monitored literary, philosophical and critical writings and produced 'the [. . .] *Liste Otto,* a list of prohibited authors [which] was periodically updated and [to which] names were added in increasing profusion'.[6] Commenting on the political situation, whether in fictional or nonfictional writings, was becoming dangerous unless you were living abroad. Such was the position of Bernanos, for example, who had gone into self-imposed exile in Brazil in 1938 and remained there for seven years; he published numerous articles in Brazilian newspapers, contemporary with the events unfolding, and later collected in *Le Chemin de la Croix-des-Âmes* (Paris: Gallimard, 1948). For authors living in France, manuscripts had to use allusions or disguise to convey comments on the actual situation to pass the censorship established by the Germans, or had to be printed and published clandestinely, a notable example being Vercors's *Le Silence de la mer* (1942). Recent research shows that the Nazi occupiers maintained 'un équilibre compliqué et dosé de laisser-faire, de contrôle permanent et de répresions occasionnelles, un système brouillé et impénétrable pour ceux qui avaient à y faire face'.[7] Confronted with this ambiguity, many writers chose the freedom of expression afforded by the clandestine press, in spite of the inherent dangers: 'La littérature naissant hors de la vie culturelle tolérée et encadrée par l'Occupant, celle qui pour exister n'a pas demandé qu'on ferme les yeux en haut-lieu, a été aussi, pour parler avec Éluard, un effort pour "que la clarté se décide à porter tout le poids du monde".'[8]

The situation for publication varied between early or late Occupation, between the unoccupied and occupied parts of the country, and between Paris and the provinces, but publishing clandestinely was an important means of opposing the Nazi or Vichy ideas and propaganda. Such a decision was taken very early by some journalists such as Jean Texier, who wrote 'Conseils à l'inconnu occupé' on 14 July 1940,[9] and by University intellectuals like the researchers of the group *Le Musée de l'Homme,* who, in December 1940, produced '*Résistance,* bulletin officiel du Comité national de salut public';[10] it was one of the first new resistance journals to come into existence and it included contributions from 'Jean Cassou, poète, critique d'art, ancien ministre de l'Éducation nationale et des Beaux-Arts de Léon Blum'.[11] Jean Cayrol also chose to publish poems which appeared in the clandestine press as well as journals of the 'free' zone. The moral protest that such writings represented was of the utmost importance for adolescents and young adults, such as Madeleine Riffaud, to whom they brought hope and comfort. Pierre-Henri Simon pursued the same goal in the German Oflag by publishing a clandestine information bulletin for his fellow prisoners. Max Jacob and Philippe Soupault did not publish clandestinely: the former expressed his condemnation of Hitler and Nazism in letters to friends like Marcel Béalu, Roger Toulouse and Cocteau; the latter continued his anti-fascist stance as a journalist from before the war, and openly expressed it when he was in charge of Radio-Tunis until 1940. Thus, writing to rebel against the Occupation or repudiate Nazi ideas, and to encourage readers to behave in whatever small ways they could to express these points of view, justifies a wider definition of the Resistance than the one usually associated with organised networks or armed combat: 'Le dénominateur commun, pour la plupart [des gens qui résistaient], c'était l'esprit républicain, l'absence de servilité, la haine de l'oppresseur, le goût passionné de la liberté et de la justice.'[12] The resistance of intellectuals such as Soupault and Cassou led to their imprisonment.

The situation was different for PoWs in Germany. For Pierre-Henri Simon, writing was a way of maintaining an uncrushed spirit: '[Il s'agit] de faire face au danger d'engourdissement intellectuel et moral',[13] as well as resisting Nazi and Vichy propaganda:

> La prise en charge idéologique des prisonniers de guerre par les Allemands s'exerce depuis le début de la captivité [. . .] Information et propagande allemandes s'y mêlent aux informations et aux prises de position de Vichy.[14]

In spite of the danger to prisoners, some manuscripts went to France via the 'Service diplomatique des prisonniers de guerre', and once there, they were published in defiance of censorship. Pierre Seghers confirms the importance of the written word for prisoners:

> J'ai réuni des anthologies de poètes déportés: elles sont bouleversantes. J'ai publié, pendant la guerre, en dépit de la censure [. . .] deux recueils de prisonniers [. . .] Dans ces camps, ces hommes ont parfois écrit d'admirables poèmes [. . .] Cette sorte de poésie collective, vivante, cette sorte de respiration, de mouvement de colère ou d'espoir, animait tout un peuple.[15]

Once in prison, the word, written or memorised, was the most important channel of communication for our six authors, and more particularly in the shape of poetry. The writing of poetry was especially considered with suspicion by the Vichy authorities and by the German occupiers: it had the potential of serving as 'a crystallization of [. . .] suffering and grief [. . .] Rhythm and rhyme implant [it] more easily in the memory [and can present a] combination of legality with subversiveness.'[16] Before he was arrested, Soupault was dismissed from his post as director of information at Radio-Tunis, by Jean-Louis Tixier-Vignancourt: 'Motif: "En étant poète, il est responsable de la défaite de l'armée française" [sic].'[17] The wide use of poetry in the writings of the Resistance can have several explanations. Firstly poetry seems to convey above all feelings. People in the occupied part of France experienced the demeaning effects of the Occupation in their daily life and reacted emotionally before invoking moral values:

> Dans la France envahie, l'esprit de résistance fut presque immédiat [. . .] Il suffiait d'être obligé de descendre d'un trottoir parce qu'un soldat allemand venait en face; d'entrer dans un magasin rempli de soldats allemands qui achetaient tout ce qu'ils voulaient parce qu'ils disposaient de sommes d'argent prélevées sur le trésor français.[18]

In this way, humiliation triggered Riffaud's determination to find ways of liberating her country. Whatever values formed the basis of resistance, 'they were expressed in the language of the emotions rather than the language of the intellect and, as a result of this, they were embodied more easily in the imagery of a poem than in the arguments of a political treatise.'[19]

A second reason for the primacy of poetry in expressing resisance is its very nature. Poetical language uses allusions, word play and striking metaphors; the rhythmic and phonetic links of verse allow an emphasis on ideas as well as the expression of emotion. Poetry lends itself to subversion through layers of meaning and thus to hidden communication: 'Ainsi peuvent se lire les poèmes. Le mot à mot ne sert de rien si l'imagination, la réflexion, la connivence du lecteur ne rejoignent le secret vivant caché sous chaque virgule.'[20] Aragon and Éluard, among others, were very adept at using this kind of language or stories of past times to allude to their contemporary situation. Cayrol and Cassou, drawing on symbolic imagery familiar to them—Cayrol from Catholicism and Cassou from Greek mythology—also display this art of ambivalence and inference.

One could add a third reason for the choice of poetry as a means of communication, particularly relevant to the situation of our authors, which is the fact that poems can be short and, with the help of rhythmmic accents and rhymes or assonances, easy to memorise. Thus the works that were composed in prison—Soupault's *Ode à Londres bombardée* and Cassou's *33 Sonnets*—were not in fact written there but memorised, and only put on paper once the writers were free, and then subsequently published.

Written works considered after the event possess another function, that of testimony. By testimony, we mean here not a legal, factual and dialogic text produced for a particular body of experts, but writing which expresses, whether in a fictional or non-fictional way, what the author saw, felt and participated in at the time, what he or she wanted to communicate; in this perspective, writers assume the role of witnesses. What has been said about concentration camp survivors' testimony can apply to the writings of our authors:

> La parole du témoin [. . .] marque indélébile du passé [. . .] réclame un retour sur l'action historique, une élucidation des conjonctures, un procès des idéologies, une révision des préjugés sur les structures socio-économiques.[21]

Whether any of the six writers examined in this volume aimed at rectifying the public perceptions of the war or whether they were aware of the influence of their writings, is examined in the different contributions. Questions are raised about the function and nature of the written word: considering the difficulty and dangers of writing in prison, of publication at the time, and the uncertainty of the future, what did they want to communicate? Did they turn to writing as support? as a pedagogical or influential means of spreading ideas? as coming to terms with their ordeal? In other words, why did they use the written word and what do they testify to? The variety of answers is connected with the personal make-up, social standing and, to some extent, with the circumstances of each author.

Jenny Ross situates Cassou's *33 Sonnets composés au secret* in relation to his writings and his life, and analyses his ways of expressing his passionate attachment to values such as freedom. She shows how imprisonment, while interrupting his active resistance, is a turning point which allows him to discover a new world, not just in solitary confinement but also within his own self:

> Que le poète soit ou non en prison, il contient lui-même une prison. Déjà Hugo, Musset, avaient, dans une image romantique, assimilé le crâne et le cachot. On retrouve la même assimilation chez Cassou, mais tandis qu'elle symbolisait pour eux le supplice de l'esprit contraint, elle figure pour lui un espace protégé et indéfini où l'imagination peut se perdre.[22]

This exploration of his own personal depths finds expression in the sonnet, a new form for him, which came to embody, as Aragon wrote in the preface, the reality of the time:

> Les quatorze vers du sonnet, leur perfection d'enchaînement, la valeur mnémo-technique de leurs rimes, tout cela [. . .] imposait au poète [. . .] le cadre nécessaire où se combinent à la vie intérieure les circonstances historiques de la pensée. Désormais il sera presque impossible de ne pas voir dans le sonnet l'expression de la liberté contrainte.[23]

In the sonnets, Cassou says nothing about his physical situation or state but rather dwells on his thoughts and an evocation of the past and future. For him 'poetry [is] something essentially private, a creative exploration of the interdependence of self and outside world. The sonnets exemplify the problem of the relation between poetry and "circumstance".'[24]

Being deprived of liberty is also at the heart of Jean Cayrol's poetry. Recalling the various degrees of this deprivation and the accompanying changes in Cayrol's physical treatment, Ethel Tolansky shows how this is reflected in his poems. From the call to fight and resist subjugation, when he is 'free' in occupied France, Cayrol turns to personal but at the same time universal themes, such as the meaning of life, and to sacrifice when he is faced with torture and solitary confinement; and finally, in the dehumanising world of Mauthausen, he summons his imagination to re-create himself, bringing back the past and at the same time conveying the desolation of his situation; he was unable to talk about this experience except through poetry: 'Il a vécu une épreuve dont la profondeur a crevé les fondements de la conscience humaine. Épreuve [. . .] dont il n'a, à son retour, livré témoignage qu'indirectement sur le plan tranposé de la poésie.'[25] As with Jean Cassou, the concentrationary world forced Cayrol to explore his own depths: 'La rencontre de Jean Cayrol avec le phénomène concentrationnaire [. . .] a inspiré et fait fructifier un talent de romancier qui s'est découvert par elle, à travers elle.'[26]

Olga Rosenbaum illuminates Max Jacob's literary output. His letters, essays or poetry written while he was forcibly confined in Saint-Benoît-sur-Loire, become for the recipients and for us a precious document, both at the mundane level of the problems of daily life under German surveillance, and at the higher level of the irrepressible creativity of Jacob's mind. Writing represents for the author a way of counteracting his physical powerlessness by putting his talent at the service of others, in corresponding with soldiers at the front or encouraging young poets. His letters are a contemporary and vivid testimony to the coercive treatment of Jews, even well-known figures like him, and give us an insight into the reality of life as experienced by a *de facto* prisoner; a reality which includes boredom, fear, anguish, solitude and a lack of freedom of movement.

As illustrated in Nicole Thatcher's contribution, Riffaud's poetry touches us by the idealism it displays; it epitomises the stand of many people who had decided to resist, a stand which meant

> un engagement de principe, opéré au nom de valeurs et non par calcul ou bon sens, comme ce sera souvent le cas en 1943 et 1944. Il est héroïque, isolé [. . .] Les premiers résistants s'accordent à signifier par leurs actions même dérisoires ou désespérées, que la 'reconstruction' de la France prônée par Vichy ne doit pas être à l'ordre du jour tant que l'objectif prioritaire—chasser l'occupant—n'est pas atteint.[27]

So when Riffaud claims today the absence of calculation and the purity of intention of the resistance workers, her writings from that time testify to her assertion, and counterbalance some contemporary interpretations of the Resistance movement. Writing for her is a means of dealing with her conflicting emotions—hope, fear, loneliness, love. The poetry she wrote in prison refers much more overtly to her surroundings and the chains which tie her to her cell; it does not mention the tortures she went through, but draws our attention to traces of the sufferings of others—on the walls, or in sounds coming through the walls—and to the thoughts and feelings she is experiencing.

In considering Pierre-Henri Simon's literary output in prison, Bernard Baritaud underlines the importance of beliefs and values in sustaining a prisoner and shaping his behaviour. Simon saw himself as responsible for the morale of his companions; this was reflected in the content and the tone of the bulletins he produced in captivity with news obtained from clandestine radio. On the other hand, prison made him discover new forms of expression, such as fairy tales, poetry and the novel. Interestingly, he does not use them to give details of the physical conditions of detention; the poems which he managed to get out and which were published while he was in prison, and the other works he wrote then, display hope rather than despair, and express feelings of sorrow, loneliness, and nostalgia, but under the cover of the genre's conventions.

The interaction between one's personality and experience before entering prison and one's state of mind during incarceration is also illustrated by the other authors. Retracing the origin of Soupault's love for London, Debra Kelly analyses the parallel he establishes between his situation and London under bombing, and the means he used to express it: the city becomes the beacon of hope for him and his fellow prisoners; there is no mention of their sufferings but only of those of Londoners. Soupault's description of his physical environment, of his being tortured twice, and of his state of mind when he was warned that he was considered a hostage soon to be executed, appeared only in works published after his detention, in poems such as *Message de l'île déserte*[28] and particularly in *Le Temps des assassins.*[29] It is worth noting that he refused, then, to have this last book distributed in France: 'Pourquoi? Dès lors qu'il apprit les millions de morts en camps de concentration, il eut honte de sembler se plaindre de six mois de prison. Finalement il en était sorti indemne.'[30]

An interesting issue raised by these six analyses is the effect of war on the development of one's identity. For our six authors, imprisonment was a momentous event and reverberated in the works they produced in prison and afterwards; it also led them, after the war, to decisions which changed their lives and even modified their identities. Imprisonment was a moment of rupture, of discontinuity in their existence which found expression in their writings. The time in prison allowed our six authors to experience a kind of detachment from life and from the world. For all of them, space and time lost their ordinary meaning, and this encouraged introspection: 'C'est pour des hommes mûrs, un temps étrange à vivre [. . .] Dans ce vide il nous devient loisible et presque nécessaire de plonger au fond de nous-mêmes, de rejoindre nos jeunesses et nos enfances.'[31] They also dwelt on thoughts and feelings that have a more universal scope, such as life, death, courage, human nature or liberty. These reflections were supported by varying religious or philosophical bases. Jacob turned towards his Jewish biblical heritage and drew upon his Christian faith, combining them with classical traditions in his writings. Time to think meant for Simon the deepening of his Christian values which he expressed in his novels, reinforcing his vocation as a moralist writer, for example, in the essays written after the war. But he also discovered that poetry is the appropriate means for channelling one's emotions. This is also the belief of Cassou who, in prison, rediscovered the tradition of the sonnet; he saw escaping death as giving him more time to devote to composing poems. On his return from deportation, Cayrol devoted himself to writing which included novels as well as essays and poetry, but was marked by his experience, as Philippe Sollers noticed: 'J'ai toujours été frappé par sa curieuse solitude. C'était une sorte de marginal inspiré, marqué par une expérience concentrationnaire dont il ne parlait jamais.'[32] As he revealed in *Le Temps des assassins,* written after the war, the threat of death led Soupault to examine his

life, and he confessed that his regrets were not about leaving life but about abandoning poetry. His experience of prison emphasised his non-conformity: after the war he had problems fitting in with life, with his old friends, he felt lonely, unable to adapt to a job in France, preferring to travel all over the world.[33] The same inability to adapt to the post-war period marked Riffaud. However, in her case, we must also take into account other problems linked to her gender: it is not only as an ex-prisoner that she experienced problems of adaptation to society after the war but also as a woman. Her time in prison determined her vocation: that of being a writer and more specifically a reporter. Like Soupault she felt driven to travel, to face new challenges and dangers, but always with her ideal of bringing to our attention the oppression and ill-treatment of human beings, using prose as well as poetry.

Writing while deprived of freedom of movement points to a common aim for these writers:

> Leurs voix s'élèvent avec des milliers d'autres, insoupçonnées, peut-être à jamais interdites/bâillonnées, reconduisant, sans lassitude, 'l'utopie de l'humain'— i.e. l'invention toujours sollicitée de nouvelles formes de liberté.[34]

It is this ideal of freedom, freedom to express oneself but also freedom for one's country, which is so much part of our six authors' legacy.

Notes

1. Jacques Sémelin, *Sans armes face à Hitler. La résistance civile en Europe 1939-1943,* Paris: Payot, 1989, p. 8.

2. Dominique Veillon, 'Les Femmes dans la guerre: anonymes et résistantes' (pp. 64-81), in Évelyne Morin-Rotureau (ed.), *Combats de femmes: 1939-1945. Françaises et Allemandes, les oubliées de l'histoire,* Paris: Éditions Autrement, (coll. Mémoires N° 74), 2001, p. 64.

3. Margaret Atack, *Literature and the French Resistance. Cultural Politics and Narrative Forms, 1940-1950,* Manchester and New York: Manchester University Press, 1989, p. 4.

4. Pierre Assouline, *L'Épuration des intellectuels,* Brussels: Éditions Complexe, 1985, p. 9.

5. H. Roderick Kedward, *Resistance in Vichy France,* Oxford: Oxford University Press, 1978, p. 188.

6. Kedward, op. cit., pp. 188-9.

7. Manfred Flügge, 'Contrôle allemand et production littéraire' (pp. 243-51), in (no author or editor) *La Littérature française sous l'Occupation,* Actes du Colloque de Reims, Presses Universitaires de Reims et Centre Régional du Livre de Champagne-Ardenne, 1989, p. 250.

8. Flügge, op. cit., p. 251.

9. François-Georges Dreyfus, *Histoire de la Résistance, 1940-1945,* Paris: Editions de Fallois, 1996, pp. 56-7.

10. Dreyfus, op. cit., pp. 58-9.

11. Jacques Baumel, *Résister. Histoire secrète des années d'Occupation,* Paris: Albin Michel, 1999, p. 67.

12. Claude Bourdet, *L'Aventure incertaine. De la Résistance à la Restauration,* Paris: Stock, 1975, p. 69.

13. Yves Durand, 'Les prisonniers' (pp. 261-79), in Jean-Pierre Azéma and François Bédarida, *La France des années noires,* Tome 1, Paris: Seuil, 1993 and 2000, coll. Points Histoire, p. 264.

14. Durand, op. cit., p. 273.

15. Pierre Seghers, 'La Poésie et la Résistance' (pp. 137-42), in *La Littérature française sous l'Occupation,* op. cit., p. 139.

16. Ian Higgins (ed.), *Anthology of Second World War French Poetry,* London: Methuen, 1982, p. 7.

17. Bernard Morlino, *Philippe Soupault. Qui êtes-vous?* Lyon: La Manufacture, 1987, p. 206.

18. Jean Mattéoli, in Bernard Fillaire (ed.), *Jusqu'au bout de la résistance,* FNDIR et UNADIF, Paris: Stock, 1997, p. 26.

19. Kedward, op. cit., p. 186.

20. Pierre Seghers, *La Résistance et ses poètes (France 1940-1945),* Paris: Editions Seghers, 1974 (2nd edition), p. 44.

21. Renaud Dulong, *Le Témoin oculaire. Les conditions sociales de l'attestation personnelle,* Paris: Éditions de l'École des Hautes Études en Sciences Sociales, 1998, p. 16.

22. Pierre Georgel (ed.), *Jean Cassou, choix de textes,* Paris: Editions Pierre Seghers, 1967, p. 29.

23. Louis Aragon, Introduction, *33 sonnets composés au secret,* Jean Cassou, Neuchâtel: Éditions de la Baconnière, 1946, p. 23.

24. Higgins, op. cit., p. 188.

25. Daniel Oster, *Jean Cayrol et son œuvre,* Paris: Seuil, 1967, pp. 26-7.

26. Maurice Nadeau, *Le Roman français depuis la guerre,* Paris: Éditions Le Passeur, 1970, p. 39.

27. Eric Conan and Henry Rousso, *Vichy, un passé qui ne passe pas,* Paris: Fayard, 1994, p. 232.

28. Philippe Soupault, *Message de l'île déserte,* La Haye: Stols, 1947.

29. Philippe Soupault, *Le Temps des assassins,* New York: La Maison française, 1945.

30. Morlino, op. cit., p. 217.

31. Pierre-Henri Simon, *Recours au poème. Chants du captif,* Neuchâtel: Editions de la Baconnière, 1943, p. 9.

32. Philippe Sollers, 'Une influence morale', *Le Nouvel Observateur,* 11-22 janvier 1997.

33. Morlino, op. cit., pp. 217-22.

34. Georges-Élia Sarfati, 'Pragmatique de l'écriture et pratique de la résistance', in Ruth Reichelberg and Judith Kauffmann (eds), *Littérature et Résistance,* Ardennes: Presses Universitaires de Reims, 2000, p. 249.

WARTIME PROPAGANDA

Erin E. Sapre (essay date 2004)

SOURCE: Sapre, Erin E. "Wartime Propaganda: Enemies Defined by Race." *Philological Papers* 51 (2004): 91-103.

[*In the following essay, Sapre chonicles different types of wartime propaganda employed by the U.S. government, focusing on the aspect of race.*]

Propaganda is an expression of a particular doctrine, whether through the use of visual image, statements and other verbal methods, or persistent policies. But more than just an expression, propaganda has a purpose: an attempt or "scheme" intended "for propagating a doctrine or practice" (Brown 10). In fact, the Latin root of the word is *propagare,* which describes the act of transplanting young plant shoots "in order to reproduce new plants which will later take on a life of their own" (Brown 10). In the same way, the authors of wartime propaganda plant an idea in the minds of the audience so that the idea becomes a part of the audience's own mind and ideology, thereby influencing not only their attitudes but also their actions.

Despite the abundance of World War II propaganda on television documentaries, in books, and on the Internet, the effect of propaganda is a little-explored topic. The small amount of propaganda analysis in existence leans heavily upon the work done by John Dower (*War Without Mercy: Race and Power in the Pacific War,* 1986). The theme of his book is that war propaganda portrays the enemy as "the other" (they are not like us), inferior (incompetent: we are capable of defeating them militarily), sub-human (there is nothing morally objectionable to killing something that is not human), and evil (therefore, it is our duty to eliminate them). The sources and the *effects* of this propaganda effort, however, are left largely unexplored.

My interest is the realm of human persuasion: the use of wartime propaganda, intensifying and focusing the racist attitudes that already existed in pre-war American society, to influence the attitudes and actions of soldiers. I will focus on the perspective of the American soldier toward his Japanese enemy during World War II.

Dower noted that policymakers were well aware of the stakes involved in World War II: nations were waging war in the name of good versus evil, and national survival literally depended upon retention of territory and resources (3). Such high stakes may have given nations the incentive to manipulate their populations toward the will to eliminate the enemy. The case for intentional persuasion of populations was more explicitly stated by J. Glenn Gray, a U.S. soldier in Germany during World War II who wrote that

> All forward-looking governments have learned to rate psychological preparations for war as of equal importance, at least, with the physical training of citizens and soldiers. As a consequence, the image of the enemy a contemporary soldier takes with him to the front is certain to be a synthetic product of the mass media, more or less consciously instilled in him by his government to make him a better fighter.

(Gray 133)

In other words, soldiers often enter battle with distorted views of the enemy because of intentional propagandistic influence. This distorted view assisted the soldier as an aggressor and met his need to justify his actions against the enemy. The view of the enemy endorsed by this propaganda served to persuade soldiers—and society—that the enemy can be and must be eliminated: individual men must be convinced to kill other men on a large scale, and societies must be convinced to support this aggression.

In this type of propaganda, it is common to highlight race as a very visual and very concrete means of distinguishing friendly from enemy. In fact, using wartime propaganda to highlight racial features as a characteristic of the enemy seems to play on man's natural racist inclinations and seems to increase the already-present tendency to pair violence with racial hatred. It must be noted however, that Americans were not unique in their wartime hatred for an enemy of distinct race: the World War II commander of Britain's 14th Army, Sir William Slim, treated Japanese prisoners with contempt and aimed to destroy the Japanese army, "an evil thing"

(Holmes 277). Grouping according to racial characteristics and discriminating against people with different racial characteristics from our own is a human trait, not a uniquely American trait. Seemingly "hardwired into the human psyche" (Monteith 46), xenophobia is the fear of people who are not like us and this fear is more pronounced when we are under stress. A human tends to define the "in" group, or the good group, as comprised of members who share his own characteristics, including race (Montieth 48). Therefore, the "out" group, the "other," is a group comprised of people who do not share the in-group's characteristics—and this out-group is necessarily "bad" in contrast to the definitive goodness of the in-group.

While a focus on the enemy's race is typical of wartime propaganda, this focus sometimes produces extreme and negative results. If hatred is aroused against a racial group, noncombatant members of that race may be targeted in addition to the military members. Additionally, in a situation that involves justifiable military violence, demonization of the enemy's race can magnify and distort a soldier's actions into tragic atrocities and barbaric behavior.

Two common wartime conditions make apparent the fact that propaganda is often inaccurate and misleading and that it influences soldiers' beliefs about, and actions against, the enemy. First, it is sometimes the case that soldiers nearer the front line and in more direct contact with the enemy become less barbaric toward the enemy than are soldiers in rear support positions. The officers and higher command headquarters who create this propaganda and transmit it to the troops are usually far removed from the front line, and the units that produce and distribute propaganda to the frontline troops are often rear support units comprised of soldiers who have never seen combat or been employed in combat-related jobs. In contrast, frontline troops have the rare position of personal contact with the enemy. Through first-hand experience they sometimes discover an enemy's human qualities in contrast to propaganda they have come to believe: they sometimes experience a reversal in their perception of the enemy in response to personal experience to the extent that they often treat a new prisoner to cigarettes, food, and medical care of the same quality provided to friendly troops. The rare position in personal contact with the enemy seems to give the frontline soldier the opportunity to gain experience which to some degree counter-acts the effects of propaganda. In contrast, rear echelon troops have been known to steal even the coats off the backs of prisoners. (It is interesting, however, that this phenomenon occurred more often during World War II, and occurred progressively less often from the time of World War II to the Vietnam war.)

The second condition provides testimony to the inaccuracy of propaganda: Friendly soldiers begin to commi the very acts that they have previously been highlighted to demonstrate the primitiveness or evilness of the enemy, which demonstrates the inaccuracy of propaganda because it portrays the practice of evil activities as a behavior solely characteristic of the enemy. In reality, not only is the severity of these activities often exaggerated, but the same activities are conducted by friendly forces. It may be true that soldiers might only commit these evil deeds as an intended response in kind to the deeds committed by the enemy, but I will show that friendly soldiers nonetheless tend to commit the type of activities they attribute to the enemy. Therefore, propaganda is inaccurate if it uses barbarian behavior as a characterization of the enemy.

Incidentally, when this propaganda-influenced hatred and violence occurs, it is rarely the fault of the footsoldiers, as evidenced by the reversal of feelings in the combat troops, who change their minds about the enemy in response to experience. Rather, the responsibility lies with the managers and leaders of these men— the officers, higher command headquarters, and even political leaders. These men are in positions of respect and power and have the ability to not only to influence the opinions, but also control the actions, of their subordinates.

Using propaganda collections, personal interviews with veterans, vintage cartoons and comics, war movies, and combat testimonies, my research will utilize Dower's thesis regarding the racial nature of war propaganda as a springboard from which to explore the realm of human persuasion. I will focus on the perspective of the American soldier toward his Japanese enemy during World War II. Within this historical context, I will demonstrate that racist propaganda was a manifestation of the emotions already present in the population and that the increased racial hatred caused by this propaganda influenced soldiers to target members of racial groups rather than only official enemies. Moreover, while the footsoldier ultimately translated these attitudes into angry, violent actions, it was the political and military command who hold primary responsibility for creating and transmitting these attitudes to their subordinates.

I must emphasize that it is not my intent to criticize the United States or its military. It is my intent to use the perception of the American soldier toward his Japanese enemy to illustrate a basic human condition: that xenophobia is a natural human tendency. Whether due to fear of the unknown "other" or due to dislike of anything not similar to ourselves or due to the need to find identity in community, inaccurate and negative perceptions of racial difference are inherent in all men and all societies. Further, it is not my intent to judge the necessity or morality of war or violence in the context of the modern international system. But when war does happen, men must be convinced to fight the enemy. Propaganda which demonizes the enemy is very useful in this regard, but this type of propaganda also introduces grave dangers, which will be demonstrated throughout my paper.

The length of this discussion prevents a full exploration of this topic, but the Japanese also produced propaganda depicting Americans in much the same way Americans depicted the Japanese, as a demonized "other": one Japanese drawing of President Roosevelt in 1941 actually depicted him with fangs and green skin (Devaux 54; see McClelland).

Japan brought America into World War II suddenly at Pearl Harbor. The United States had retained its isolationism for the first almost two years of World War II but could not resist reacting to Japan's surprise aerial attack on Pearl Harbor on December 7, 1941. This abrupt exposure to the Japanese presented the American people with a very foreign picture of the Japanese man that involved not only ferocity and barbarity, but sneakiness. This perception was pictorially represented in a naval recruiting poster in order to increase the perception of the Japanese as sneaky-an American naval man grasps the American flag after he has succumbed to a Japanese sword in the back (McClelland . . .).

Along this same theme, to inflame feelings of victimization at the hands of a treacherous foe, the cartoonist D. R. Fitzpatrick published in a newspaper an image of a hand emerging from obscurity, wearing the Rising Sun of Japan on its sleeve, and clutching a freshly bloodied dagger. . . .

This image is very similar to an image found in a movie entitled "Appointment in Tokyo" (Hively). The film opens with a hand emerging from a curtain of mist, wearing a Rising Sun pinky ring, clutching a dagger that has Japanese characters on the handle. As the narrator describes specific Pacific islands invaded by the Japanese, the film image is of that dagger and hand stabbing those islands labeled on a map. (This film was released in 1945: therefore, it did not influence the attitudes of people during World War II, but it surely reflected those contemporary attitudes.)

The evilness depicted by these images supported the perception produced by America's experience at Pearl Harbor: the Japanese were evil. But the perception of an evil Japanese enemy depended upon the idea that the Japanese man was somehow different from the American man. The American people were able to view the Japanese man as fundamentally different, as the "other," because the alleged dichotomy between "East" and "West" had already been established in American minds prior to the advent of World War II. Small-scale interactions in China between American priests and businessmen prior to World War II had produced stories involving an unfamiliar and sometimes mysterious Chinese stereotype. The only contact most Americans had with Asian people were the few so-called coolies who came to find work on American railroads and mines, and eventually the stereotypical laundry facilities. These menial positions held by Chinese gave Americans reason to consider Asians not only as distinctly different, but also as an inferior race. This stereotype of a strange, inferior Chinese man became the definitive American view of all Asians, and in opposition to America's own perceived moral uprightness in World War II, Japan became the *evil* "other," thereby strengthening the dichotomy which resulted in the extremely racial stereotype used in propaganda of that time. In fact, the stereotyping and hatred of the Japanese commonly emphasized the racial qualities of the enemy, focusing more along the lines of race than along lines of "enemy" versus "friend." The result of this blurred line between "enemy" and "*other* race" was that the soldier tended to target all members of that racial group rather than simply targeting enemy combatants. As an example of this blurred line, when asked about his role in the war, the American soldier did not say that it was to "defeat Japan," but to "kill as many Japanese as possible." This hatred, and the responding hatred from the Japanese, resulted in a war unlike most others: it "resulted in savage, ferocious fighting with no holds barred. This was not the dispassionate killing seen on other fronts or in other wars. This was a brutish, primitive hatred, as characteristic of the horror of war in the Pacific as the palm trees and the islands" (Sledge xiii).

This racial hate manifested itself in many forms. One manifestation was the lexicon used to refer to Japanese people. It was the most common communication of hatred and derision of the Japanese, used by people from all walks of life, thereby illustrating the pervasiveness throughout American society of this racial perception of the enemy. These offensive words usually refer to the race of the enemy, not the enemy himself, and therefore reflected a hatred directed against the race, and not the enemy forces. "Damn slant eyes,"[1] "slimy, creepy little Japs,"[2] "Jap," and "Nip"[3] were not references toward military soldiers; they were references to the race of the Japanese soldiers and people. One young navy man, upon seeing the ruins of Nagasaki, went so far as to "wish they [the Japanese people] could be made to suffer a tenth of the atrocities that they performed on our men whom they held prisoner." His justification for including Japanese civilians in the scope of his hatred was that "a nation cannot wage war as they have without the backing of the majority of their people."[4] The 1944 cartoon "Bugs Bunny Nips the Nips" not only uses the reference "Nip," but Bugs Bunny becomes more creative in his influence on every theater-goer in America: he calls the Japanese soldiers "bow-legs," "monkey face," and "slant-eyes" (Freleng).

A more visible form of the manifestation of this race-focused hate was the image popular media maintained of the Japanese enemy. This very racially stereotyped image was exaggerated to portray the Japanese as very different from Americans: not only different in his appearance and culture, but also different in his abilities—while Americans are smart and capable, Japanese were portrayed as backward and militarily, culturally, and intellectually inferior. Bugs Bunny, Popeye, and Donald Duck all starred in opposition to Japanese portrayed with slanted, slit eyes; round glasses; and buck teeth. This image, emphasizing visual difference, is similar to the image on a poster published by Texaco to encourage Americans to work hard for the war effort (Texaco Oil . . .).

The cultural differences were emphasized by featuring elements of the Japanese culture that Americans found difficult to understand. Because Americans could not come to grips with the perceived willingness of the Japanese man to give his life in battle, Americans believed that to the Japanese, "life is held less sacred than is customary in occidental lands," as reported by a bubble-gum trading card produced in 1938 (Gum Inc.; . . .).

The visual depiction of this sentiment emphasized the inconceivable cultural practice of hara kiri, as demonstrated by a 1942 postcard in which a Japanese soldier is eager to provide the short sword for his superior officer to commit suicide (Manning; . . .).

The other difference often illustrated in media portraying the Japanese is that they were inferior to the Americans—especially militarily. The 1943 cartoon "Tokio Jokio" featured a cartoon version of the military defenses supposedly found in Japan. The air raid siren is a Japanese man yelling through a megaphone "Woooooo!!!" because he has been stuck with a pin by another Japanese man (and again emphasizing exaggerated cultural difference, the two men bow to each other and smile as they trade places). A character labeled "plane spotter" is a Japanese man painting spots on a plane. The film goes on to show how "General Ham demonstrates coolness and calmness of Japanese officer during air raid," as a Japanese man with buck teeth, slanted slit eyes, and round glasses runs around chaotically and repeatedly bumps into trees (McCabe). This mocking representation portraying a highly ridiculous military could only produce a feeling in the American public that Japan was a nation of silly, backward people who were very different from Americans and who could pose no military threat.

Wartime media such as movies very explicitly endorse racially-focused hatred rather than enemy-focused hatred. It is helpful to analyze movies because in addition to influencing large numbers of people, movies tend to reflect contemporary attitudes: the aim of the movie producer, after all, is to generate revenue-his movie must appeal to the widest audience possible in order to sell the highest possible number of tickets. But the influential aspect of movies must not be ignored, especially in a time before TV at home. In fact, in 1941, each week one out of every five Americans saw a movie directly related to World War II.[5] The endorsement of racially-focused rather than enemy-focused hatred is obvious because, although both the Germans and the Japanese were America's enemies during World War II, many more anti-Japanese movies were made in America from 1942 to 1945 than anti-German movies. Additionally, many more negative references were made toward the Asian (Japanese) enemy than the white (German) enemy: among anti-Nazi movies, an average of eight negative references were made per movie whereas among anti-Japan movies, an average of twelve negative references were made per movie (Shull 297). Visual depictions of the enemy in film, cartoons, and illustrations tended to emphasize the racial features of the Asian enemy (features that were, of course, shared by the civilian population). The Japanese enemy included all Japanese people; in contrast, perception of the German enemy was very closely focused on specific people within the Nazi leadership. For example, in "Seein' Red, White 'n' Blue," a Popeye cartoon released in the theaters in 1943, the Japanese enemy was portrayed by four Japanese spies, but the German enemy was portrayed only by Hitler and Goebbels (Gordon).

This very derogatory image of the Japanese was even reinforced to new soldiers during their training-they were taught that the Japanese were different from Americans and unwilling to behave ethically. When E.B. Sledge attended basic training, his instructor told him, "Don't hesitate to fight the Japs dirty. Most Americans, from the time they are kids, are taught not to hit below the belt. It's not sportsmanlike. Well, nobody has taught the Japs that, and war ain't sport. Kick him in the balls before he kicks you in yours" (Sledge 18). The extreme image of the Japanese was simply a reinforcement of the age-old American image of the Asian. This image—which involved mystery, foreignness, inferiority, and evilness—influenced American attitudes and actions toward the Japanese enemy. The low regard for Japanese was demonstrated by the manner in which American soldiers treated Japanese dead, in which American soldiers treated living Japanese soldiers and civilians, and in which American soldiers targeted civilians.

First, treatment of the Japanese dead demonstrated that Americans believed Japanese dead just did not deserve the same respect given to the American dead. E. B. Sledge described the difference in respect for Japanese dead and American dead. Since the island of Peleliu

was solid coral, it was nearly impossible to bury the dead, but "it seemed indecent" to leave American dead exposed and uncovered. These American dead were covered with a poncho; but the Japanese dead were left where they fell, distorted among the rocks and hills,[6] eaten by flies, rotting, a few even pressed flat in the roadway by American truck after truck running over them (Khan 147). Sledge admits: I "never could bear the sight of American dead neglected on the battlefield. In contrast, the sight of Japanese corpses bothered me little aside from the stench and the flies they nourished" (148). The indifference felt toward Japanese dead was so deep that one dead Japanese machine gunner had been left until his skull was open and collected rainwater. A Marine passed the time by tossing coral pebbles into the skull (Sledge 122). Another Marine used a Japanese skull to decorate the front of his truck (Khan 68), and World War II Marine Sy M. Kahn used a Japanese skull as a candle-holder in his foxhole (82). American soldiers would even dig up Japanese corpses in order to take a skull or teeth as souvenirs (Khan 68). In addition, the dead Japanese soldiers' personal belongings were often taken for souvenirs, and gold teeth were pried out of their mouths (Sledge 118).

Second, poor treatment of the living Japanese soldiers demonstrated that Japanese life had much less value than American life. Very often soldiers contradicted the Geneva Conventions and America's own ideas of ethical behavior by shooting the Japanese as they tried to surrender. Kahn heard from another Marine that an English-speaking Japanese soldier told the Marine that he wanted to surrender because he had a wife and three children. After shooting him, the Marine said, "Now he has a widow and three orphans" (58). And Americans were very cruel to wounded Japanese: one Marine wanted the gold caps out of the mouth of a still-living, though badly wounded Japanese soldier. The Japanese soldier's writhing about made it so difficult to retrieve the caps that the Marine slashed the soldier's cheeks on both sides from the mouth to the ear, put his boot on the soldier's lower jaw as leverage, and pried the caps out with his knife (Sledge 118).

Third, perceiving the enemy in terms of race resulted in a relaxed attitude in regard to civilian casualties. It is clear that German cities were also bombed, but the targets were primarily military and industrial in nature, and those damaged by American bombing were on a smaller relative scale than the cities targeted in Japan. The United States joined the British in the skies over Germany in February 1945, and the United States actually encouraged the British to focus on military targets instead of area bombing, as British Air Marshall Arthur Harris preferred (Doughty 777). The most infamous example of civilian deaths as a result of Allied aerial bombardment over Germany was the city of Dresden in February 1945, resulting in 25,000 deaths (USAF), including military, workers in the targeted factories and industrial centers, and civilians. This is a large number, but it is a fraction of the civilian deaths resulting from American bombing of Japanese cities, and the scope of civilian deaths in Dresden was not typical of the American air effort over Germany, nor was it an American policy to target civilian centers in Germany, while targeting civilian centers in Japan was typical of the American policy there. Because of the difficulty of targeting small, decentralized military production factories, Major General Curtis E. LeMay decided in February 1945 instead to target Japanese cities: the firestorm his bombs created killed 83,000 and injured 41,000 Japanese civilians in Tokyo alone (Doughty 837). In the following incendiary attacks on all of Japan's industrial cities, hundreds of thousands of civilians died (Doughty 837). One veteran who was a tail gunner during the raids over Japan said that returning from bombing missions at night, the fires from American bombs in each city were so great that he could determine which cities they were from their position in respect to each other, and he could read them like a map (Herbert). Additionally, over 90,000 civilians died in the atomic attack on Hiroshima, and 35,000 in Nagasaki (Doughty 838).

Worse than a relaxed attitude toward civilian casualties was the intentional targeting of civilians through the soldiers' race-based perception that the enemy included Japanese civilians. As his unit was waiting to go to the front line, Kahn heard stories from other Marines. One story described how a Marine unit, after having found some comrades dead and mutilated, surrounded a group of Japanese. Several Japanese nurses came running from that group toward the Marines, trying to surrender, mostly unclothed so that it was apparent they were female. The Marines "cut them down unmercifully, claiming revenge for Bataan" (58).

Though more an evidence of homefront attitudes than military attitudes, it is also possible to see racial discrimination when the treatment of Japanese in America is examined: Japan and Germany were both enemies, but Japanese in America were treated much worse than Germans in America. This is true for both Japanese and German citizens, Japanese and German nationals living in America, and Japanese and German prisoners of war in America. The 1942 internment of approximately 120,000 Japanese in America is well documented—over two-thirds of these Japanese people were American citizens (Carroll 223). What remains undocumented is internment of any German Americans. In contrast, German prisoners of war, enemy soldiers who had been captured during combat against American soldiers, were served in American diners (Carroll 315) and given freedom from prisoner camps to do agricultural outdoor work.[7]

It must be made clear that these actions based on racial hate were not a response to actual conditions such as Japanese-American spies or any other suspicious un-American activity. In fact, many of the Japanese Americans were respected business owners or farmers, and some were even distinguished World War I veterans. As well, most members of the highly decorated 100th Infantry battalion and 422nd Regimental Combat Team during World War II were Japanese Americans (Carroll 224). Despite this reality, the common perception of the Japanese in America was that they were a "5th column" that performed "dirty inside work" to aid the Japanese military effort, as depicted in a poster encouraging Americans to report suspicious activity (Zbynek 52 . . .).

The perception was that all Japanese were spies disguised as tourists taking pictures, hair stylists on American military bases passing information they overheard to Japanese authorities, and undercover Japanese soldiers integrating themselves into American society in order later to aid the Japanese takeover (Capra). This is the view explicitly stated in the film "Know Your Enemy—Japan" and reflected in the 1943 cartoon "Seein' Red, White 'n' Blue," in which active Japanese spies are found by Popeye to be masquerading as babies in an American orphanage (Gordon). "Know Your Enemy—Japan" also instructs that all Japanese are the same, civilians included, because the Japanese government was a "vicious system of political and religious regimentation that hammers, kneads, and molds the whole population until it becomes an obedient mass with but a single mind." The necessity of eliminating the Japanese threat is expressed by the image of an American soldier in the act of firing a rifle, accompanied by the dehumanizing narration, "Defeating this nation is as necessary as shooting down a mad dog in your neighborhood." Although this film did not arrive in American theaters until after the war ended, it reflected the contemporary perception Americans held of Japanese people; for example, the very first spoken words in the film are: "We shall never completely understand the Japanese mind. But then, they don't understand ours, either." A similar commentary on the Asian mind as different from ours was expressed during an interview with a World War II veteran when he said that the Japanese "weren't as good military-wise thinking, they" were deficient in comparison to the American ability to perceive military situations (Gayle). And while the film may have come out too late to influence attitudes toward the Japanese, it established the Japanese as a distinct racial and cultural "other,"[8] which no doubt extended to the Koreans and Chinese a few years later during the Korean War.

There is a distinct difference between promoting an attitude of duty which will convince a soldier to fight the enemy, and promoting an extreme, distorted view of the enemy which is so racially negative and dehumanizing that it decreases a soldier's ability to differentiate between enemy and non-combatant and removes a soldier's reluctance to engage in extreme violence. Often propaganda used to encourage men to fight the enemy is so extreme that it does not reflect reality, and instead distorts the character of the enemy into a racial stereotype. This demonization of the enemy's race can affect a soldier's perception in such a way that necessary military violence against the enemy sometimes deteriorates into extreme violence and atrocities against a hated racial group. The other danger of using racially focused propaganda to convince men of the necessity and morality of killing the enemy is that very often there are civilians near the front who share the racial features of the enemy. If hatred is aroused against a racial group, soldiers tend to perceive the enemy in racial terms, and noncombatant members of that racial group may become targets of those influenced by the propaganda.

It is clear that representation of the Asian enemy in film and popular media consistently emphasized race, and that the American soldier's perception of the image of the Japanese enemy was consistent as the "other." It is also clear that these representations of the Japanese enemy had the power to influence action—the emphasis on race resulted in unnecessary atrocities and civilian casualties. Surely most commanders and most soldiers behaved appropriately toward civilians and enemy soldiers. But an environment that promotes a characterization of the enemy in extremely negative racial terms creates a tendency to indulge in racially-focused violence.

Notes

1. Lt. Cdr. Paul E. Spangler, M.D., a surgeon stationed at Pearl Harbor, in a letter to his buddies (Carroll, 186).

2. And "japbastards" (Lince 80).

3. 20-year old Pfc. Richard King of the 27th Infantry Division, in a September 8, 1945 letter from Okinawa to his parents (Carroll 302).

4. 19-year-old seaman Keith Lynch in a September 23, 1945 letter to his parents (Carroll 312).

5. According to Shull, "during 1942 . . . 85 million Americans attended the movies each week." This is 64% of the 1942 U.S. population. Also according to Shull, "by the end of 1941 almost a third . . . of American motion picture productions related in some way to the Second World War" (Shull 1, 17).

6. (Sledge 142) This was confirmed by World War II veteran R. Bruce Watkins, who wrote, "Our Graves Registration Troops worked valiantly to remove our dead, while the Japanese were left where they fell until the lines advanced and they could be buried in mass graves."

7. From a letter by Al Loveless, who witnessed German POWs walking down the road in front of his house en route to pick peaches in his community in Albany, Georgia (Brokaw 233).

8. The "otherness" coupled with the "Asian-ness" of this enemy was repeatedly emphasized in this film. Even the opening sequence pictures the words "Ri Ben," which means "Japan," then there is a newspaper picture of a sword execution, the background is Japanese music (which seems very discordant to American ears), and the imagery dwells on a tribal dance which seems very foreign, of the type usually associated with native peoples.

Works Cited

Brokaw, Tom. *An Album of Memories: Personal Histories from the Greatest Generation.* New York: Random, 2001.

Brown, James. *Techniques of Persuasion: From Propaganda to Brainwashing.* Baltimore: Penguin, 1963.

Capra, Frank. *Know Your Enemy—Japan.* Army Pictorial Service, 1945. Available as *Frank Capra's The War Years, Know Your Enemy: Japan.* Burbank: RCA/Columbia Pictures Home Video, 1990.

Carroll, Andrew, ed. *War Letters: Extraordinary Correspondence from American Wars.* New York: Simon, 2001.

Doughty, Robert. *Warfare in the Western World, Volume II: Military Operations Since 1871.* Lexington: Heath, 1996.

Dower, John. *War Without Mercy: Race and Power in the Pacific War.* New York: Pantheon, 1986.

Fitzpatrick, Daniel. "The Assassin Strikes." *St. Louis Dispatch.* 8 December 1941. In *As I Saw It: A Review of Our Times.* New York: Simon, 1953.

Freleng, Isadore, dir. *Bugs Bunny Nips the Nips.* Hollywood: Paramount Studios, 1944.

Gayle, Merlin (WWII Navy). Louisville: Face-to-face interview by Erin Sapre (Kilgore), May 2001.

Gordon, Dan, dir. *Seein 'Red, White 'n' Blue.* Hollywood: Paramount Studios, 1943.

Gray, J. *The Warriors: Reflections on Men in Battle.* New York: Harper, 1959.

Herbert, Kevin (WWII bombardier over Japan). St. Louis: Face-to-Face interview by Erin Spare (Kilgore), 4 June 2002.

Hively, Jack, dir. *Appointment in Tokyo.* Army Pictorial Service, 1945. Available as *Pearl Harbor Payback/Appointment in Tokyo.* Hong Kong: GoodTimes Home Video Corp., 2001.

Holmes, Richard. *Acts of War: The Behavior of Men in Battle*. New York: The Free Press, 1985.

"Japanese Soldiers Bury Their Dead." Horrors of War card #57. Philadelphia: Gum, 1938.

Kahn, Sy. *A Soldier's World War II Diary 1943-45: Between Tedium and Terror*. Chicago: U of Illinois P, 1993.

Lince, George. *Too Young the Heroes: A World War II Marine's Account of Facing a Veteran Enemey at Guadalcanal, the Solomons and Okinawa*. Jefferson: McFarland, 1997.

Manning, Reg. "The Yanks are Coming." Travelcard #19. Chicago: Curteich, 1942. Published in Menchine, Ron. *Propaganda Postcards of World War II*. Iola: Krause, 2000. 39.

McCabe, Norman, producer. *Tokio Jokio*. Burbank: Warner, 1943.

McClelland, Barclay. (poster of sword in back of seaman). Published in Devaux, Simone. *La Dernière Guerre: Vue à Travers Les Affiches*. Paris: Grange Batelier, 1976.

Montieth, Margo. "Why We Hate." *Psychology Today*. June 2002: 44-50, 87.

Shull, Michael. *Hollywood War Films: 1937-1945*. Jefferson: McFarland, 1996.

Sledge, E. *With the Old Breed: At Peleliu and Okinawa*. New York: Oxford UP, 1981.

Texaco Oil Company. (poster "You think war end soon?"). Published in Gregory, G. *Posters of World War II*. Avenel: Random, 1996.

USAF Historical Division. "Historical Analysis of the 14-15 February 1945 Bombings of Dresden." Air Force Historical Studies Office. 28 February 2005. < http://www.airforcehistory.hq.af.mil/PopTopics/dresden.htm.

Zeman, Zbynek. *Selling the War: Art and Propaganda in World War II*. New York: Simon, 1978.

Robert Calder (essay date 2004)

SOURCE: Calder, Robert. "The Magic of the Word: Mobilizing Authors for War." In *Beware the British Serpent: The Role of Writers in British Propaganda in the United States, 1939-1945*, pp. 39-55. Montreal: McGill-Queen's University Press, 2004.

[*In the essay below, Calder discusses responses by various English writers recruited to participate in wartime propaganda, including H. G. Wells, Vera Brittain, and J. B. Priestley.*]

From the middle of the 1930s until the end of the Second World War, British attempts to combat anglophobia in the United States were confronted by an enormous problem: the Americans had seen it all before. If this war was indeed no more than the second act of a bloody modern tragedy, many Americans had learned from the first act. Writing in 1940, Harold Lavine and James Wechsler observed: "The greatest obstacle to Allied propagandists in World War II was the propaganda that preceded American entry into World War I."[1]

Although propaganda had been a relatively new technique of warfare in 1914, it had not taken the British long to use it effectively. A month after war broke out, C. F. G. Masterman, a member of the cabinet, was secretly appointed director of propaganda, and for three years he guided operations covertly from the offices of the Insurance Commission at Wellington House. Only in 1917, when Lloyd George's government created the Department of Information, was the public made aware of British propaganda activities; and a year later the department was elevated to the Ministry of Information under Lord Beaverbrook.

Much of the propaganda generated by Masterman's agency was directed toward neutral countries, the most important of which was the United States. In Peter Buitenhuis's words, "The most complex and important role of Wellington House was to persuade the people of the United States that the Allied cause was just and necessary, that they should support the Allied war effort and, ultimately, that they should join the war on the allied side."[2]

Wellington House influenced American public opinion in a number of ways. It encouraged the flow of favourable news and comments by providing American correspondents with interviews, tours, and visits to the front. It provided a newsletter to American papers, many of which were grateful for the free copy, and it sent out millions of pamphlets on various wartime subjects, some written by private people on their own initiative and many commissioned from well-known public figures.[3] Even American authors were encouraged to write for the Allied cause.

Until the United States entered the war in 1917, the American activities of Wellington House were disguised. These operations were controlled by Sir Gilbert Parker, an author well known on both sides of the Atlantic for his historical romance novels. Supposedly merely a concerned private citizen, he operated from his home in London, sending thousands of letters and pamphlets to influential Americans. When the entry of the United States into the war removed the need for secrecy, Parker retired, and the British Bureau of Information was set up in New York.

In the years following the First World War, the full propaganda activities of Wellington House were gradually revealed through memoirs and historical research, and many Americans became convinced that the primary cause of American intervention had been British propaganda. As early as 1920, H. L. Mencken wrote: "When he recalls the amazing feats of the British war propagandists between 1914 and 1917—and then even more amazing confessions of method since—[the American] is apt to ask himself quite gravely if he belongs to a free nation or a crown colony."[4] When the 1930s became increasingly politically unstable, this anger over the past became mixed with apprehension for the future. In April 1936, Representative William T. Schulte warned against "the same propagandists that lit the torch that led the way for the god of war into America in 1917."[5] Similarly, in July 1937, M. J. Hillenbrand of Dayton University predicted that England would "again hamstring American public opinion with its propaganda machine."[6]

Such suspicions were given credence by a number of scholarly studies published in the 1930s, in particular two books written to warn Americans about the danger of being manipulated into another war. In 1935 James D. Squires, a professor at Colby College, published *British Propaganda at Home and in the United States from 1914 to 1917,* in which he argued that British propaganda had been instrumental in leading the United States into the conflict. Four years later, when a European war had become inevitable, this thesis was presented more directly and emphatically by H. C. Peterson in his *Propaganda for War: The Campaign against American Neutrality, 1914-17.* The United States, he said, had been forced to declare war on Germany in 1917 because, in response to British propaganda, it had already abandoned strict neutrality and given the Allies material and diplomatic and moral support. The lesson for Americans, he concluded, was that "it is impossible to be unneutral and keep out of war."[7]

If these revelations of the past alerted some Americans, one prediction of the future alarmed others. In 1938 British publicist Sidney Rogerson brought out a book entitled *Propaganda in the Next War* in Basil Liddell Hart's series "The Next War." In any future war, as in the last, he declared, the result would depend "upon the way in which the United States acts, and her attitude will reflect the reaction of her public to propaganda properly applied."[8] Britain would have to do "much propaganda" to keep the United States even benevolently neutral, he averred: "It will need a definite threat to America, a threat, moreover, which will have to be brought home by propaganda to every citizen, before the republic will again take arms in an external quarrel."[9]

Germany wasted little time in referring to Rogerson's book in its overseas radio broadcasts, and it was the main source of Dr Wilhelm von Kries's *Strategy and Tactics of the British War Propaganda,* published in

1941 by the German Information Service in its "Britain Unmasked" series directed toward American readers. Rogerson also became a favourite bogeyman of American isolationists, being cited, for example, by John T. Flynn in a speech at an America First rally in Chicago in December 1940. As well, excerpts from his book were read into the *Congressional Record* by Gerald Nye in May 1939. Even on the day that Pearl Harbor was bombed, Senator Nye reminded an America First rally in Pittsburgh that Rogerson had suggested that the threat which might bring the United States into the next war was Japan.[10]

The cumulative effect of the work of Squires, Peterson, Rogerson, and others was to instill in many Americans a supersensitivity to British propaganda which verged on paranoia. Writing in the *American Mercury* in December 1937, for example, Albert Jay Nock complained that the United States was "infested and itchy with foreign propagandists, especially those of the British persuasion." Whenever international affairs took a turn unfavourable to British interests, he suggested, people should study the lists of passengers arriving in New York by ship. There, they would be "astonished to see the volume of infiltration by first-string British panhandlers"—politicians, dignitaries, lecturers, writers, and many others over to push the British cause.[11] Nock's point seemed proven one October day in 1939 when British politician Duff Cooper, writers Cecil Roberts, S. K. Ratcliffe, Phyllis Bottome, critic Ellis Roberts, and scholar I. A. Richards all arrived on the ss *Manhattan.* On the following day, one newspaper headline proclaimed: "The British Are Here to Get Us In."[12] Lecturing in the United States a few months later, Roberts saw a sign on an auditorium marquee calling him "the foremost British propagandist," and he won his audience over only by playing along with the claim.

The English literary critic William Empson, returning to Britain by way of the United States in the winter of 1939-40, also found himself the object of American suspicions. "There were times," he wrote, "when I felt quite sure that if I had stood on my head and sung 'Three Blind Mice' [my American hosts] would have wondered placidly why the British Government had paid me to do *that.*"[13] Journalist and lecturer Jay Allen, alluding to some of the more lurid propaganda stories of the First World War, commented after a tour: "In the Midwest one gets the feeling that men are waiting with shotguns to shoot down the first propagandist who mentions Belgian babies."[14] In June 1940 British correspondent Alistair Cooke reported that "for an active variety of reasons, fears and memories, which probably no living neurologist could hope to classify," Americans had not been reassured by the British government's announcement that it was not conducting propaganda in the United States.[15]

Cooke's conclusion that there was no evidence of any organized British propaganda in the United States did not persuade isolationist Americans. In an article in *Scribner's Commentator* in November 1940, for example, Kenneth Monroe cited Minnesota Senator Ernest Lundeen's comment that there had "been in recent years appropriated for [British] propaganda in this country the sum of ONE HUNDRED SIXTY-FIVE MILLION DOLLARS." So effective was the British propaganda, said Monroe, that anyone who spoke in favour of isolationism was at once "smeared by the press as a 'Fifth Columnist,' 'Nazi,' 'Fascist,' 'traitor.'"[16] Porter Sargent, an education specialist whose letterhead proclaimed him an "adviser to parents and schools," published a weekly bulletin monitoring anything that remotely smacked of British propaganda. Sent to faculty members of private schools, colleges, and universities, as well as to selected members of the general population, a hundred or so of these appeared in book form as *Getting Us Into War* in 1941.

Perhaps nowhere was the fear of British war propaganda more luridly expressed than in the isolationist posters demanding "absolute neutrality—now and forever!":

> BEWARE THE BRITISH SERPENT!! Once more a boa constrictor—"Perfidious Albion"—is crawling across the American landscape, spewing forth its unctuous lies. Its purpose is to lure this nation into the lair of war to make the world safe for international plunder. More than ever we Americans must now evaluate this intruder into our garden of Eden, appraising Britain down to the last pennyweight of truth.[17]

In the face of such acute sensitivity to foreign propaganda in the United States, the British Foreign Office and the Ministry of Information approached the problem of influencing American public opinion in the late 1930s and early war years with extreme caution. Inactive since the end of the First World War, the ministry was brought to life again in September 1936 to "present the national case to the public at home and abroad in time of war."[18] In reality, as Ian McLaine has demonstrated in *Ministry of Morale: Home Front Morale and the Ministry of Information in World War II,* a much greater emphasis was placed on shaping opinion within Britain than in other countries.

Although in the early years of the war the Ministry of Information was much ridiculed as an elephantine bureaucracy, the American Division was small. Its first director was Sir Frederick Whyte, who had variously been the president of the Legislative Assembly of India, political adviser to Chiang Kai-shek, and director general of the English Speaking Union. Having also travelled widely throughout the United States, he had some familiarity with the American view of foreign affairs.

In a paper prepared even before his appointment on 26 August 1939, Whyte outlined his position on British attempts to shape public opinion in the United States. "The less the British Government attempts by direct propaganda to justify themselves," he argued, "the better."[19] To the American public, through an interview published in the *New York Sun* in October 1939, he was unequivocal: "We are not competing [with the Axis powers] with visiting lecturers, paid propagandists or professional partisans this time. Some people tell us in fact that we are leaning over backward in our efforts to lose this war of propaganda."[20] By late January 1940 this position had not changed. "All evidence available," he wrote to the director general of the Ministry of Information, "confirms the wisdom of continuing the policy of no overt propaganda in the United States of America."[21]

Whyte's strategy of "no propaganda" reflected the position of the Chamberlain government and Foreign Office officials in the early years of the war, but it would be a mistake to conclude that "no propaganda" meant no effort to shape American public opinion. Whyte's warning, after all, was against "*direct* propaganda" and "*overt* propaganda" (emphases mine), not against propaganda itself. In fact, from the beginning of the war, and especially after Churchill became prime minister, the Ministry of Information and the Foreign Office maintained a program of indirect and covert propaganda, though they preferred to use the less pejorative term, "publicity." Whyte's original mandate thus was to work through cultural groups such as the English Speaking Union, an Anglo-American organization which sponsored visiting speakers and published material, and to encourage the making of films and pamphlets directed toward the United States.

Shortly after the outbreak of war, the British ambassador in Washington, Lord Lothian, urged his government to expand the cultural initiative to include the use of established British authors. Writing to the Foreign Office on 28 September, he argued that there was no need for fundamental explanations of the Allied cause because Americans were already familiar with it. "But," he added, "articles about what British war aims are or ought to be by well-known authors like H. G. Wells, Hugh Walpole or about the ideological conflict, eg. like Rauschning's book, are extremely valuable. What we most need is to induce the Americans to think deeply about the war, its causes and its cure."[22]

Lothian's call for greater use of British writers clearly had its effect on British policy. In April 1940 the Foreign Office proposed to transfer F. R. Cowell to the American Division of the Ministry of Information. Commenting on the move, Cowell noted that his Foreign Office background gave him a prestige which could help in dealing with people who were suspicious of the ministry. "This," he said, "applies particularly to authors (who were outraged at the beginning of the war by a 'warning' to hold themselves in readiness to help the M. of I.—H. G. Wells for instance) . . . The M. of I. is predominantly *political*. For the U.S.A. culture is quite as strong a card as politics especially in books and films. It would be fatal to have a *merely* M. of I. approach."[23]

Whyte's response to the Foreign Office was to welcome the addition of Cowell. It would, he observed, "help us perform even more effectively in the future the two tasks to which you refer as being regarded by the Ambassador as of special importance: of stimulating articles in the British Press suitable for reproduction in America [and] of inspiring articles by British authors for publication, through commercial channels, in the United States."[24]

Although British authors came to be employed extensively during the Second World War, early attempts to involve them administratively nearly sank under the weight of bureaucratic procedure. It was, in fact, the authors themselves who first suggested their usefulness in a wartime propaganda campaign through their professional organization, the Society of Authors, Playwrights and Composers. Seven months before the war, its secretary, Denys Kilham Roberts, wrote to Humbert Wolfe—a minor poet and man of letters who was at the time a civil servant in the Ministry of Labour—regarding a central bureau that was being established by the ministry to coordinate the participation of members of learned societies and creative bodies in a National Service scheme. Kilham Roberts pointed out that the society was the official representative of roughly four thousand authors in the country and had close contacts with other writers' societies throughout the world. "In my capacity as Secretary," he added, "I have at the Society's headquarters an efficient and well-trained staff of ten whose experience would render them, in the event of a national emergency, invaluable to the Government in the spheres of Propaganda or Censorship, and I imagine that it is in one or both of these spheres that the Society and its organisation would be likely to be most of service to the country."[25]

In late February 1939 the National Service Department of the Ministry of Labour informed Kilham Roberts that the Central Registry Advisory Council, which was set up to advise the government on the use of people with scientific, technical, professional, and higher administrative qualifications, had established committees to deal with the individual professions. He would be contacted soon. At a meeting with Wolfe, Kilham Roberts was told that the Ministry of Labour would have problems in creating a register of authors, and the Society was invited to set up its own committee to do two things. First, it could consider the most appropriate employment in non-combatant duties of authors over thirty years of age; and, second, it could prepare a list of names of authors and their particular qualifications for wartime service. "I should add," Wolfe concluded somewhat dismissively, "that in any circumstances all authors of 30 or over, like other citizens, might well consider undertaking part-time duties in connection with the A.R.P. [air raid precautions]."[26]

Following this meeting, Wolfe joined the society and was elected to its council so that he could work more closely with it. Kilham Roberts wrote to a dozen prominent authors asking whether they would be prepared to speak in a National Service scheme. He received replies from Ernest Raymond, Ashley Dukes, J. B. Priestley, Philip Guedalla, R. C. Sherriff, Rex Mottram, Compton Mackenzie, Owen Rutter, and St John Ervine. Most were prepared to help, but Mackenzie offered only a "provisional promise," and Ervine wanted to know more specifically what was expected of him. "Priestley," reported Kilham Roberts, "has refused to take any part, partly on the ground of overtiredness and partly, as he says, because 'I need to know more than I do now about the policy of the present Government before I am prepared to go touting them!'"[27] Despite this early reluctance, Priestley went on to become one of the most important literary figures in the British war effort, though he remained one of the government's most outspoken critics.

By the middle of April 1939 a committee made up of Wolfe, Kilham Roberts, and L. A. G. Strong had been struck to collect and classify information about writers in a form that would be useful in time of war. When Wolfe was too busy to participate, the other two sent out a questionnaire of their own devising and, to their surprise, found it to be the subject of a question in the House of Commons. At one point in the questionnaire, authors were invited to describe their political views and their attitude to conscription and military service. Mr Mander, MP for Wolverhampton, concerned apparently that the Ministry of Labour was collaborating in an attempt to weed out writers because of their political beliefs, rose to challenge the legality of the questionnaire. In an effort to defuse the situation, Wolfe promised to raise the matter with the society, and when Kilham Roberts sent its members a letter of explanation, Mander agreed to withdraw his question.

According to Kilham Roberts, he received only about six complaints from the more than three thousand authors who had received the questionnaire. Those few complaints and Mr Mander's concern, however, touch on a fundamental problem which British officials faced throughout the war whenever they utilized authors. Like the population as a whole, the writing community covered the political spectrum, from extreme left to extreme right, but unlike the general population, the writers expected to have the freedom to express their views. Many, in fact, would have argued that their role was to remain outside the political establishment and retain their freedom to function as critics of society and of the war.

The difficulty for the government lay in co-opting authors for the cultural impact of their pens without either giving them a blank cheque to perhaps voice damaging criticism or being seen to stifle them. As the war progressed, Priestley became one of the co-opted whose political opinions disturbed those in power, while H. G. Wells, having declined an early invitation to do war work, embarrassed the government with frequent and outspoken public statements. George Bernard Shaw was deliberately excluded from radio broadcasts, and Vera Brittain was repeatedly denied permission to leave the country. Michael Arlen was forced to resign his position as civil defence public relations officer for the East Midlands when questions were raised in the House of Commons about his Bulgarian background and whether "the general tone of his writing made him a fit individual to hold the important position."[28]

Such questions about the political beliefs of writers became more directly the concern of the Ministry of Information in July 1939, when the Society of Authors' initiative became subsumed by the ministry's Authors' Planning Committee, chaired by Raymond Needham. A. D. Peters, the prominent literary agent, was the committee secretary, and Strong and Kilham Roberts joined R. H. S. Crossman, Dorothy Sayers, A. P. Herbert, and Professor John Hilton as members. Another list of potentially useful authors was devised, but as Kilham Roberts warned Cecil Day Lewis on 31 August, no official employment of authors could take place until the outbreak of war: "Until the Ministry becomes a thing of substance instead of a shadow, which it is unlikely to do until War actually breaks out, anything definite in the way of officially reserving services of authors is apparently impossible. All I can do is to say, quite unofficially, that it is likely the Ministry will in fact have use for your services and I suggest that you not at present attach yourself to any other branch of National Service."[29]

On 5 September, only two days after the declaration of war, the ministry spoke officially when Peters sent the following letter—which Kilham Roberts had obviously paraphrased—to about seventy writers:

> I am directed by the Minister of Information to inform you that your name has been entered on a list of authors whose services are likely to be valuable to the Ministry of Information in time of war.
>
> The Minister will be grateful, therefore, if you refrain from engaging yourself in any other form of national service without previously communicating with the Ministry of Information. He would also be glad to have any particulars that you may care to supply about your

specialized knowledge in any field likely to be of interest to the Ministry and of your acquaintance with foreign countries and languages.

> Please send particulars of any change of address, and all communications to me at Room 133, at the above address.
>
> Yours faithfully,
>
> A. D. Peters[30]

Some writers found Peters' letter high-handed and patronizing. To the request for a list of qualifications, the well-known writer and former diplomat Robert Bruce Lockhart snorted: "If this is the way the Ministry works in regard to British authors, what on earth will its knowledge be of foreign countries?"[31] On the same day, Sir Hugh Walpole had written directly to the minister of information, Lord Macmillan, to offer his services, grandly pointing out that he had been in charge of propaganda in Russia in the Great War and later had worked under Beaverbrook in the earlier incarnation of the ministry. Furthermore, he knew all the British writers and their works as well as anyone. However, he added: "I suggest that I would be of especial use with regard to America. I was there as a child and have been on lecture tours there constantly and my name is widely known there."[32] Having thus displayed his credentials, Walpole was indignant at having to answer to Peters, but he was nonetheless eager to accept the ministry's invitation.

Other writers responded differently. Vera Brittain, who had been an ardent pacifist for twenty years, replied that she would cooperate only if her work contributed to peace and not to national hatreds. H. G. Wells, a prominent figure in the propaganda campaign in the Great War, reacted angrily. Writing in the *New Statesman and Nation* two months later, he confessed: "I have been approached, and I suppose quite a number of us have been approached, more or less officially, to do propaganda in Europe and America. [But] I am not going to be a stalking horse for the Foreign Office again."[33]

Many writers, however, were anxious to join the war effort—some for patriotic reasons and some for financial ones—but were ignored or rejected. Ernest Raymond, having received a dismissive reply from the Ministry of Labour in April, waited in vain to hear from the Ministry of Information. In the end, he served, in his words, only as "a hopelessly confused lance-corporal in the Home Guard."[34] Evelyn Waugh personally telephoned Peters in an attempt to join the Ministry of Information, but after several months of frustration he eventually joined the Royal Marines. Francis Brett Young, who believed that his reputation in the United States would make him a valuable propagandist, was not taken on by the ministry, though in 1941 it asked him to write a pamphlet on the British Empire. "It appears to me ridiculous," he complained to Charles Evans, "that men like myself and Priestley, among the leaders of our profession, should be excluded from performing the work which we are best qualified to do."[35] Similarly, William Gerhardie approached the Ministry of Information and a number of other government offices but ended up becoming a fire guard before joining the BBC's European Productions department.

Although a number of writers took their lack of employment by the Ministry of Information as a personal slight, the truth is that beyond asking the writers to be prepared to serve, the ministry still had not formulated a clear and comprehensive scheme for their use. Even as the Peters letter was in the post, Raymond Needham was proposing that the Authors' Planning Committee be replaced by an Authors' Advisory Panel, a representative group of writers who would be individually called upon for advice or suggestions. In addition to three members of the original committee—Sayers, Strong, and Herbert—he suggested Helen Simpson, Lord Elton, Sir Hugh Walpole, J. B. Priestley, Charles Morgan, Sir Edward Grigg, Osbert Sitwell, J. M. Keynes, Noel Coward, E. M. Delafield, R. C. Sherriff, Harold Nicolson, P. G. Wodehouse, Rebecca West, and Mary Agnes Hamilton.[36]

The proposal for an Authors' Advisory Panel was postponed while the deputy director general, A. P. Waterfield, tried to appoint a director of literary publicity, who would be in charge of a Literary Division with Peters as assistant director and Kilham Roberts as consultant. Then, Waterfield suggested, when the American, Home, or European division wanted the services of an author, the Literary Division would provide an appropriate one. "The author," he said, "will be then told what we want and asked if he will be willing to undertake the job with—in nine cases out of ten—a pretty free hand to express his views on the subject in his own words and along his own lines of thought." The director would need to be able to "persuade the reluctant and placate the indignant if necessary."[37]

Anxious to find a female director in order to place a woman on the ministry's council, Waterfield considered Dorothy Sayers, Mary Agnes Hamilton, Helen Simpson, and Margaret Storm Jameson. When Sayers sensibly responded, "Why should a good writer be turned into a bad administrator?" he offered the position to Jameson, the current president of PEN (Poets, Playwrights, Essayists, Novelists). In doing so, he was following the advice of Humbert Wolfe, who had written: "I have found her very clear-minded, sensible and unemotional. She stands deservedly high in the literary world and does not belong to any particular faction."[38]

Jameson responded favourably to the invitation, but within a week Waterfield had changed his mind and recommended the appointment of Surrey Dane, who was in charge of publicity material in the form of pamphlets and periodicals. In gracefully accepting the change of plans, Jameson offered to help in any way, pointing out that PEN had close relations with writers in the United States and South America: "It is possible that our relations with these countries, and our special knowledge and experience, can be useful to you in some way. It is freely at your disposal."[39]

Amid these visions and revisions, A. D. Peters resigned from the ministry, writing to Waterfield on 29 September: "Work has not developed in the way I had anticipated."[40] Two weeks later his criticisms were more specific:

> Existing here in the void as I do, with no means of contact with my superiors except memos whose ultimate fate is unknown to me, it is obviously impossible for me to be of any service, even in matters of which I have some knowledge and experience. But I should like to put on record my opinion that the whole method of dealing with the printed word in the Ministry is wrong. The work at present is spread all over the departments, in some cases in the hands of people whose qualifications for it are by no means apparent.[41]

Peters' disenchantment with his role at the ministry appears to have been aggravated by the intrusion of Sir Hugh Walpole into the process. At the suggestion of Lord Macmillan, Walpole had contacted John Hilton, director of home publicity, and by early October was offering his own suggestion for an authors' committee, including the addition to the membership of Sir Ronald Storrs, Alan Bott, Mrs Robert Lynd, J. B. Priestley, and C. S. Forester ("a novelist immensely popular in America as well as in this country"). The unsalaried committee, he said, should be independent and advisory, attached to the ministry but not on staff, and its purpose would be "to bring the whole force of British culture to the aid of the British Government."[42]

When Waterfield suggested to Walpole that Peters should join their discussions, Walpole "was *much* averse to that!"[43] For his part, Peters saw the Walpole scheme as a backward step. "We are back where we started," he wrote Waterfield, "but with this difference: that authors and publishers are criticising the whole conduct of literary affairs inside the Ministry with a bitterness which I consider wholly justified."[44]

Peters' criticisms of the Walpole plan was echoed even more strongly by Humbert Wolfe, whose advice Waterfield sought. Wolfe agreed with Peters that authors believed that they were not being used effectively and that they had a very real contribution to make if properly organized. But, he added, "I cannot feel that the appointment of a Committee of Authors would not lead to anything but continuous bickering and would not be of real help to the Department. After many years' experience in working on committees with authors, I have found them, apart from their special gifts, extraordinarily ignorant and ill-informed people on most topics. The reason for this is the obvious one: that their contacts with the outside world are often limited and that they tend to live in a small and separate universe."

Wolfe went on to complain about Walpole's revised list of authors, noting the exclusion of Compton Mackenzie, Michael Arlen, Sylvia Townsend-Warner, Daphne du Maurier, and Rosamond Lehmann. These omissions, he argued, indicated how difficult it was to compile a list that was truly representative, and a truly representative committee would be so large and controversial that it would be nearly impossible to get any guidance from it. A better alternative, he went on, would be to appoint a publisher—A. S. Frere, of William Heinemann Ltd, for example—to solicit the appropriate work from writers.[45]

Waterfield remained committed to the idea of an authors' committee, and early in November Walpole confided to his diary that there was a "great meeting at M. of I. about my committee. Had things all my way. Everybody charming."[46] In late November, however, W. H. Stevenson, the head of the Literary and Editorial Unit, voiced his opposition. "So many diverse views will be represented," he argued, "that there will be endless discussions and, I fear, minor results. If, on the other hand, they are only called together at lengthy intervals, they will grumble about having nothing to do." The best results, he concluded, could be obtained by ministry contact with individual authors according to a general policy: "To ask every author to use every opportunity of addressing his public—whether by the written or spoken word—through all the many channels which are available to him. It is believed that their influence will be greater if their words reach the public in this way as the expression of their own personality, than would be the case if they were merely a mouthpiece for the Ministry. Each author is asked to keep in touch with the Ministry."

To bolster his argument, Stevenson pointed to a number of authors—for example, E. M. Delafield, F. Tennyson Jesse, Naomi Jacob, Helen Simpson, and Sacheverell Sitwell—who had already indicated what they might be able to write for the war effort. Ann Bridge was writing a book on England before and after the outbreak of war for publication in the United States. A. A. Milne was considering a booklet treating the moral problems of those who were uncomfortable supporting the war effort. On the other hand, warned Stevenson, "My prewar contact with Jack Priestley does not lead me to think that he will be amenable to outside suggestion of any kind."[47]

Unconvinced by Stevenson's arguments, Waterfield suggested that the problem of unwiedly size could be countered by creating a number of subcommittees—for example, Fiction, General, Political, Home Morale, with an American list to be devised by Sir Frederick Whyte. Waterfield, however, accepted Wolfe's suggestion of consulting a publisher and brought in Geoffrey Faber, who was told that most of the books sought by the ministry would be for circulation in other countries—especially France and the United States. Faber was even more skeptical about the effectiveness of authors in committee. "Authors are," he said, "with rare exceptions, egocentric persons. They are not cohesive; they are not good at collectively tackling an impersonal problem." Publishers, on the other hand, are skilled at knowing the subjects on which books should be written and at finding the authors to write them. They are, concluded Faber modestly, "better able to give informed advice than any other class of persons."[48]

Faber's commentary finally convinced Waterfield that an authors' committee was unworkable and he so advised the director general and the minister on 21 December. A week later, Waterfield informed all parties that Macmillan had abandoned the idea of an authors' committee, though he was "anxious that more direct and immediate action should be taken to enlist the help of certain of the leading writers of the day in the production of pamphlets and other propaganda material of the more ephemeral type."[49]

Despite Macmillan's decision, the Society of Authors continued to pursue the idea of an authors' planning committee. Its president, John Masefield, wrote to the ministry to object, and in the spring of 1940 the society's periodical, the *Author,* published the comments of a number of writers in a symposium on the role of authors in the war. Although some agreed with Margaret Kennedy that wars are won through physical violence, not pens, the predominant view was that expressed by Ernest Raymond. Despite his several rebuffs, Raymond argued that the Ministry of Information was the most important ministry and that authors were the most important members of the community. He referred his readers to Kipling's story "The Man with the Magic of the Word," in which a tribe under attack immediately elevated a wordsmith to a great position because he could stir and stiffen the hearts of the people to perform great fighting deeds.[50]

In the summer of 1940 the Society of Authors' campaign to be officially involved in the war effort was taken over by J. B. Priestley, who although considered difficult by the Ministry of Information, was by then a very popular radio broadcaster both in Britain and abroad. Priestley chaired a new body called the Authors' National Committee, with Denys Kilham Roberts as secretary and Margaret Storm Jameson and John MacMurray on the editorial board. George Bernard Shaw was invited to join the group, but his opinion of writers in committee echoed those of Wolfe and Faber. "Evidently," he wrote Priestley, "you have never been on a Committee of Authors. I had ten years of it in the Society of Authors. In their books they are more or less delightful creatures according to taste. In committee, to call them hogs would be an insult to a comparatively co-operative animal."[51]

Storm Jameson participated in the formation of the Authors' National Committee, along with the ubiquitous Hugh Walpole, but she had little more confidence in its success did than Shaw. Priestley was overbearing ("Does he want to be our first Minister of Culture?" she wrote in her journal) and was dismissive of her suggestions. "Nothing will come of it," she noted. "Furious with myself for wasting time on a discussion of no interest to me. Shall I ever have the courage to say No to these music-hall turns?"[52]

More eager to do a music-hall turn was Hugh Walpole, who helped Kilham Roberts devise yet another list of "eminent" suitable authors at the end of August 1940. By the following February, Kilham Roberts was able to canvass nearly a hundred well-known writers, most of whom responded positively. Priestley wanted the new minister of information, Walter Monckton, to attach writers to the various armed services, much as artists were accompanying many units in battle. When Monckton rejected this suggestion, William Collins, the publisher, was asked to produce a series of books about the problems of reconstruction after the war, and the result was Priestley's own *Out of the People,* which appeared in February 1942.

Out of the People was the only book published in the proposed series. The wartime paper shortage and Priestley's insistence that reconstruction of British society could be done only along socialist lines—a view not shared by his editorial board or the publisher—ended the project. At the same time, the Authors' National Committee, deprived of Priestley's energy while he was heavily involved in broadcasting, lecturing, and writing, faded away.

The quiet death of the committee ended any attempt to give writers a formal, structured role in the war effort. It did not, however, stop the employment of authors as individuals, either within government agencies or as loosely attached freelance writers. The Society of Authors continued to encourage its members to write articles and books that would further the British cause. The spring 1942 issue of the *Author* contained an anonymous article describing the kind of literature wanted in the United States and outlining how to get it published. Such writing, concluded the author, is "of great value politically. This nation can only be reached and swung through its emotions."[53] In the autumn of 1943 Phyllis Bentley, having recently returned from a three-month tour of the United States, wrote in the *Author*: "It is clearly important that British ideas and ways of life should be known to the Americans . . . If one really believes in the value (and I use this word in the moral not the mercenary sense) of one's ideas, the opportunity of presenting them to two or three million American readers is worth some preliminary labour of explanation."[54]

According to Peter Buitenhuis, the Ministry of Information's decision to abandon the idea of a writers' committee signalled the end of influential participation by British writers in official propaganda. Thereafter, Buitenhuis concluded, authors were generally used only in minor roles in various government departments. However, while it is true that fewer writers of the stature of Rudyard Kipling, John Galsworthy, Arnold Bennett, Ford Madox Ford, and James M. Barrie—who all wrote propaganda in the First World War—were officially employed in the Second World War, it is untrue that authors were not used extensively in the war of words. Many were employed in government departments—Malcolm Muggeridge, Graham Greene, V. S. Pritchett, John Betjeman, Cecil Day Lewis, Laurie Lee, and Phyllis Bentley in the Ministry of Information— and many more were supported, encouraged, and directed in propaganda work in semi-official ways. The Wolfe/Stevenson proposal to employ a publisher who would have an overview of the British writing community led to the appointment of Hamish Hamilton to the American Division in 1941. Moreover, their suggestion that the ministry solicit propaganda material from individual authors became the practice of the Ministry of Information and the Foreign Office for the duration of the war. Selected lecturers were sent to the United States, books, pamphlets, and newspaper and magazine articles were suggested, broadcasts to North America were developed, and film scriptwriters and producers were encouraged. The result was a considerable army of British writers whose words became weapons in the battle for American commitment to the war.

Notes

1. Lavine and Wechsler, *War Propaganda and the United States,* 89.

2. Buitenhuis, *The Great War of Words,* 54.

3. Marett, *Through the Back Door,* 89.

4. As quoted by Buitenhuis, *The Great War of Words,* 67.

5. As quoted by Jonas, *Isolationism in America 1935-1941,* 136-7.

6. Hillenbrand, "If War Comes Will Moscow Be Our Ally?" 294.

7. Peterson, *Propaganda for War,* 330.

8. As quoted by von Kries, *Strategy and Tactics of the British War Propaganda,* 88.

9. Ibid., 91.

10. Cole, *Roosevelt and the Isolationists,* 501-2.

11. Nock, "A New Dose of British Propaganda," 482-3.

12. Roberts, *Sunshine and Shadow,* 257.

13. Empson, "Passing through the U.S.A.," 426.

14. As quoted by Lavine and Wechsler, *War Propaganda and the United States,* 92.

15. Cooke, "British Propaganda in the United States," 605.

16. Monroe, "British Propaganda," 51.

17. As quoted by Cull, *Selling War,* 35.

18. As quoted by McLaine, *Ministry of Morale,* 12.

19. PRO, FO 395/648, P3227/105/150, "Report on the British Service of Information in the U.S. in Time of War," 20 July 1939.

20. Macgowan, "Fights for the U.S. on News Front," 12.

21. PRO, INF 1/848, "Publicity in the United States," Policy Committee Paper no. 2, 22 January 1940.

22. PRO, FO 371/22839, "British Publicity in the United States."

23. PRO, FO 371/24228, "British Publicity in the United States," 8 April 1940.

24. Ibid.

25. British Library, Add. Ms 63351, Society of Authors, Kilham Roberts to Wolfe, 27 January 1939.

26. Ibid., Wolfe to Kilham Roberts, 9 March 1939.

27. Ibid., Kilham Roberts to Wolfe, 13 March 1939.

28. Keyishian, *Michael Arlen,* 118.

29. As quoted by Day-Lewis, in *C. Day-Lewis,* 124.

30. William Ready Division of Archives, McMaster University, Vera Brittain Papers.

31. Lockhart, *Diaries,* 2:41.

32. PRO, INF 1/229, 1939 Committee on Authors, Walpole to Macmillan, 5 September 1939.

33. Wells, "The Honour and Dignity of the Free Mind," 607.

34. Raymond, *Please You Draw Near,* 69.

35. Young, *Francis Brett Young: A Biography,* 242.

36. PRO, INF 1/229, 1939 Committee on Authors, R. Needham, "Proposes Substitution of Authors Advisory Panel for Existing Authors Planning Committee."

37. PRO, INF 1/32, "Staff Organisation: Literature and Art Division," Waterfield to Wolfe, 8 September 1939.

38. Ibid., Wolfe to Waterfield, 11 September 1939.

39. PRO, INF 1/32, Storm Jameson to Macmillan, 29 September 1939.

40. Ibid., Peters to Waterfield, 29 September 1939.

41. Ibid., Peters to Waterfield, 10 October 1939.

42. PRO, INF 1/229, memorandum from H. Walpole.

43. Ibid., Waterfield to Hilton, 11 October 1939.

44. PRO, INF 1/32, "Staff Organisation: Literature and Art Division," Peters to Waterfield, 10 October 1939.

45. PRO, INF 1/229, Wolfe to Waterfield, 14 November 1939.

46. As quoted by Hart-Davis, *Hugh Walpole,* 415.

47. PRO, INF 1/229, Stevenson to Waterfield, 22 November 1939.

48. Ibid., Faber to Waterfield, 13 December 1939.

49. Ibid., Waterfield to Hilton, Carr, Hodson, Bevan and Stevenson, 27 December 1939.

50. "Authors and the War," *Author,* Summer 1940, 93

51. As quoted by Brome, *J. B. Priestley,* 257.

52. Jameson, *Journey from the North,* 80.

53. "Brevities," *Author,* Spring 1942, 59.

54. Letter to the *Author,* Autumn 1943, 57.

Bibliography

UNPUBLISHED AND ARCHIVAL SOURCES

British Library, London, Society of Authors Papers

Public Record Office, Kew, London

    INF 1, General correspondence and records of the Ministry of Information, 1939-45

    FO 395, News Department

    FO 371, Foreign Office correspondence and records, British publicity in the United States

Society of Authors, London. Archives

William Ready Division of Archives and Research Collections, McMaster University, Hamilton, Ontario. Vera Brittain Papers

PUBLISHED SOURCES

Brome, Vincent. *J. B. Priestley.* London: Hamish Hamilton 1988

Buitenhuis, Peter. *The Great War of Words.* Vancouver: University of British Columbia Press 1987

Cole, Wayne. *Roosevelt and the Isolationists: 1932-1945.* Lincoln: University of Nebraska Press 1983

Cooke, Alistair. "British Propaganda in the United States." *Fortnightly* 153, ns 147 (June 1940): 605-13

Cull, Nicholas John. *Selling War: The British Propaganda Campaign against American "Neutrality" in World War II.* Oxford: Oxford University Press 1995

Day-Lewis, Sean. *C. Day-Lewis: An English Literary Life.* London: Weidenfeld and Nicolson 1980

Empson, William. "Passing through the U.S.A." *Horizon,* June 1940: 425-30

Hart-Davis, Rupert. *Hugh Walpole: A Biography.* London: Macmillan 1952

Hillenbrand, M. J. "If War Comes Will Moscow Be Our Ally?" *America* 57 (July 1937): 294-5

Jameson, Storm. *Journey from the North.* London: Collins and Harvill 1970

Jonas, Manfred. *Isolationism in America 1935-1941.* New York: Cornell University Press 1966

Keyishian, Harry. *Michael Arlen.* Boston: Twayne 1975

Kries, Wilhelm Von. *Strategy and Tactics of the British War Propaganda.* Berlin: German Information Service 1941

Lavine, Harold, and James Wechsler. *War Propaganda and the United States.* New Haven: Yale University Press 1940

Lockhart, Robert Bruce. *Diaries.* Vol. 2: *1939-1965,* ed. Kenneth Young. London: Macmillan, 1980

Macgowan, Gault. "Fights for the U.S. on News Front." *New York Sun,* 9 October 1939

McLaine, Ian. *Ministry of Morale: Home Front Morale and the Ministry of Information in World War II.* London: Allen and Unwin 1979

Marett, Robert. *Through the Back Door.* London: Pergamon Press 1968

Monroe, Kenneth. "British Propaganda: 1940 Version." *Scribner's Commentator,* 9 November 1940

Nock, Albert Jay. "A New Dose of British Propaganda." *American Mercury* 42 (December 1937): 482-6

Peterson, H. C. *Propaganda for War: The Campaign against American Neutrality, 1914-1917.* Norman: Oklahoma University Press 1939

Raymond, Ernest. *Please You Draw Near.* London: Cassell 1969

Roberts, Cecil. *Sunshine and Shadow.* London: Hodder and Stoughton 1972

Wells, H. G. "The Honour and Dignity of the Free Mind." *New Statesman and Nation,* 28 October 1939

Young, Jessica Brett. *Francis Brett Young: A Biography.* London: Heinemann 1962

WRITING FROM EXILE

M. Paul Holsinger (essay date 1992)

SOURCE: Holsinger, M. Paul. "Told without Bitterness: Autobiographical Accounts of the Relocation of Japanese-Americans and Canadians during World War II." In *Visions of War: World War II in Popular Literature and Culture,* edited by M. Paul Holsinger and Mary Anne Schofield, pp. 149-59. Bowling Green, Ohio: Bowling Green State University Popular Press, 1992.

[*In the following essay, Holsinger presents an overview of the writings of Japanese-Americans and Japanese-Canadians about their experiences in internment camps during the war.*]

Japanese bombs had barely stopped falling on Pearl Harbor, Manila or Hong Kong before the governments of the United States and Canada began the process which would result in the forceful removal of nearly 135,000 Japanese residents from homes up and down the Pacific Coast.[1] It made little difference to most officials whether these persons were citizens or not;[2] what primarily determined the decision of who would move and who would not was skin coloration. As the armies of Japan roared victoriously through the Pacific theater, both nations slipped into what, some years later, a perceptive justice of the United States Supreme Court was to call "the ugly abyss of racism."[3]

Thanks to President Franklin Roosevelt's infamous Executive Order 9066 and the belief of the Army commander in charge of the West Coast that "a Jap's a Jap" irrespective of citizenship, orders were soon issued to remove from their homes and businesses all of California's, Oregon's and Washington's Japanese-American settlers. Canada was not far behind. Reacting to the fear and intemperate bigotry expressed by many of the province of British Columbia's white leaders, Prime Minister W. L. Mackenzie King soon put the Royal Canadian

Mounted Police in charge of removing, and relocating, the huge number of Japanese-Canadians living in Vancouver and the southern coast of that area.

The two neighbors differed only in degree in the approaches they took. In the United States, all Japanese were first moved to huge assembly sites, including many unused race tracks, and then to ten newly built "relocation centers"—the name euphemistically given for this nation's concentration camps. There, for the next three years (1942-1945), the bulk of Japanese-Americans were kept behind barbed wire under Army guard.[4] Canadians had a slightly different response. While they imprisoned those many young men whom they felt, justly or unjustly, to be disloyal, the majority of the country's Japanese were sent to the foothills of the Rockies nearly seven hundred miles from their former homes. Like their American counterparts, the R.C.M.P. held its evacuees as virtual prisoners for the duration of the war.[5]

Long before the last residents of these various centers returned to the freedom of the "outside," government officials on both sides of the 49th parallel were already publishing book-length justifications for their actions. The end of the war accelerated this publication record, nearly all of which pictured the relocation process in a positive light.[6] Few publishers, on the other hand, seemed willing to hear the side of those persons most intimately affected—the Japanese. One brief, heavily illustrated volume, Mine Okubo's *Citizen 13660,* a memoir of her days at both the Tanforan Race Track and the Topaz, Utah relocation center, *was* published in 1946, but the majority of American or Canadian publishers showed little interest in bringing the day-by-day details of Japanese relocation to their readers.

In 1953, Boston's Little Brown and Company issued Monica Sone's *Nisei Daughter,* one of the first serious autobiographies of a second-generation Japanese young woman, but it was not until the early 1970s, in the midst of the Vietnam War, and later that readers were able to study in any depth Japanese relocation from the participants' point-of-view. Some of the new volumes, notably Yoshiko Uchida's children's book, *Journey to Topaz,* and Jeanne Wakatsuki Houston's *Farewell to Manzanar* were widely circulated and drew much praise from their reviewers. Others, like Estelle Ishigo's emotionally written *Lone Heart Mountain,* an excellent—but privately published—volume, were barely noticed.

In Canada, a similar phenomenon was occurring. Beginning in 1971 with a children's book, Shizuye Takashima's almost lyrical semi-fictional autobiography, *A Child in Prison Camp,* Canadian readers were also slowly able to see the other side of their government's policies toward the japanese during World War II. Takashima's book was followed by the published

wartime diary of Takeo Ujo Nakano, *Within the Barbed Wire Fence* (1980) and then by Joy Kogawa's powerful autobiographical novel, *Obasan* (1981), based in part on the real-life experiences of Muriel Kitagawa. These various books, along with Uchida's later *Desert Exile: The Uprooting of a Japanese-American Family* and Kogawa's small children's book, *Naomi's Road,* provide the basis for this study.

The authors of these ten volumes offer a wide cross-section of backgrounds. Okubo, Sone, Uchida and Wakatsuki were all citizens of the United States at the time they were forced into the relocation centers. Takashima, Kitagawa and Kogawa's heroine, "Naomi Nakane," held Canadian citizenship. Okubo and Kitagawa were both young adults at the beginning of the war; Sone was a teenager just recovering from a bout of tuberculosis. Uchida was eleven; Wakatuski, seven and Nakane, only five. At the other end of the spectrum was Nakano, an already middle-aged laborer in the lumber industry just north of Vancouver. Even more unique was Ishigo. A Caucasian and the daughter of a Union Army veteran of the Civil War, she had married a Japanese-Californian in 1928, and, when his evacuation was ordered at the start of the war, she willingly went to suffer with him. Hers is the only "white" vision of the life of a prisoner, but it offers a fascinating point-counterpoint to ethnic Japanese views.

Even before the first Japanese-Americans were sent to the first assembly center, the United States Army quickly moved to depersonalize all the evacuees by assigning each family a separate identification number—a number which, for the rest of their incarcerations, became the family "name" as far as the government was concerned. Mine Okubo became Citizen 13660—the title of her memoirs; Yoshiko Uchida and her family, 13453; Monica Sone, 10710 and so on. As groups gathered with the few belongings that they were allowed to take with them to camp, everyone and everything was required to have one white pasteboard label with the assigned number on it for all to see. Even now, nearly fifty years after the war's conclusion, the image of being forced to become a "number" remains to haunt each and every American Japanese writer in exactly the same way as Nazi S.S. tattoos on Jewish arms bring back vividly the horrors of those camps throughout Europe.[7]

Because of the maddening rush to move Japanese families away from the Pacific Coast, both countries hurried them into the largest assembly areas possible—areas behind well-structured fences that could be carefully guarded to prevent the sabotage that officials illogically assumed would break out at any minute. Race tracks and state fairgrounds were "naturals" for such sites. The Santa Anita race track outside Los Angeles housed more than 18,000 Japanese residents for almost six months in early 1942; thousands of others were at the Tanforan track in San Bruno just south of San Francisco. In Washington State, officials requisitioned the state fairgrounds in Puyallup, and, in British Columbia, the Canadian government took over the huge Pacific Exposition grounds in Vancouver's Hastings Park and moved in thousands of single men over the age of 18 as well as various families and older adults unable to take care of themselves.

In every case, authorities seemed unwilling to consider whether "Japs" ought to be granted a decent standard of living. It was a common sight for entire families to be moved into just recently vacated horse stalls, the smell of rotting manure still permeating everything. Occasionally, there had been a crude attempt to paint the stall but, because of the rush, little could be done to disguise the obvious. Mine Okubo, arriving at Tanforan with her brother, found their new home, "Stall 50." "Spider webs, horse hair, and hay had been white-washed with the walls. . . . A two-inch layer of dust covered the floor, but on removing it we discovered that linoleum the color of redwood had been placed over the rough manure-covered boards" (35). Yoshiko Uchida's family, also at Tanforan, had the same experience. Assigned to "Barrack 16, Apartment 40," they finally found, after much searching, that they were to live in a stable reached only by way of "a broad ramp the horses had used to reach the stalls. Each stall was now numbered and ours was number 40. That the stalls should have been called *apartments* was a euphemism so ludicrous it was comical" (*Desert Exile* 70). Monica Sone's entire family from Seattle found dandelions pushing up between the cracks in the floor boards of their new home at the Puyallup fairgrounds. Monica's mother, refusing to be discouraged by the incongruity of the strange setting, ordered her husband and children to let the flowers grow, since they were one of the few beautiful things remaining in an increasingly ugly world (174).

The Canadian setting was not much better. Japanese families and other individuals were so rapidly pushed into the exposition grounds' Livestock Building that piles of manure had not even been cleaned from the animals' stalls. Wood planking had simply been placed over the debris with no thought for sanitation. When some of these boards were removed, "it was the most stomach-turning, nauseating thing [with] maggots . . . still breeding" throughout the manure (Kogawa, *Obasan* 99). When eleven-year old Shizuye Takashima and her mother visited friends on the grounds "a strong odor hit us as we enter[ed]: the unmistakable foul smell of cattle, a mixture of their waste and sweat. The animals were removed, but their stink remain[ed]. . . . It seemed as if we [were] visiting the hellhole my Sunday School teacher spoke of with such earnestness" (7). And Takeo Ujo Nakano, confined to the same stables and unable, even with his head under the bedclothes, to escape the

all-pervasive smell, found himself putting into classical Japanese *tanka* his feelings:

> Reek of manure,
> Stench of livestock,
> and we are herded,
> Milling—
> Jumble of the battlefield.

(13)

Everyone understood, however, that, no matter how inadequate or disgusting the various stalls, stables or other small shacks were in the spring and early summer of 1942, they were temporary. Both American and Canadian governments were determined to move their Japanese residents away from the coastal areas as soon as "permanent" locations could be provided. In British Columbia, the government designated a number of old mining "ghost towns" for Japanese family relocation. Single men as well as most Japanese alien male heads of households were at first not allowed to join their families but were assigned to work on various road gangs building highways and bridges through the eastern sections of the province. "Disloyal" men—and the Canadian government used a perverse standard to determine such designation—were sent to a former P.O.W. camp north of Lake Superior in Angler, Ontario. Takeo Nakano was one of the latter. Though his only concern was to be reunited with his wife and small daughter, Nakano was to spend twenty-one months apart from them. Not until December, 1943, were they able to live together as a family.[8] Six year-old Naomi Nakane, the heroine of both Joy Kogawa's adult novel *Obasan* and her children's book *Naomi's Road,* got to see her father for only a few days after early 1942. Even when, three years later, she and the rest of her family were moved to the southern Albertan sugar beet fields to work, Naomi's father was not allowed to join them. Not until 1950 did the family, via a coldly impersonal bureaucratic letter, discover that he had died some years before while undergoing an operation.

For those who were sent to eastern British Columbia, however, the government did attempt to make the move at least sound appealing. The Takashima family went to New Denver, with all the promise of a bright future "in one of the most beautiful spots in British Columbia" (9). To their horror, they discovered that none of the buildings had running water, electricity or adequate heating facilities. Mr. Takashima, who, as a naturalized citizen, was able to be with his family, constantly complained to authorities but to no avail. His increasing bitterness at this and his relatives' treatment came close to convincing him to renounce Canada and return to Japan.

The United States Army, in selecting the sites for its relocation centers, took the opposite approach to the matter. Far from looking for scenery that could be called "beautiful," government officials selected the most desolate, isolated locations that it could find. When they remember their days of imprisonment, all writers include the vividly depressing initial image of their future homes. Yoshiko Uchida and her family were, at first, temporarily lulled by the government's assignment to Topaz, Utah. "Such a beautiful golden name," Yoshiko's mother said. As the busses sent to the train station in Delta to pick them up neared the site of the center, however, the reality proved shocking.

> Gradually the trees and the grass and the flowers began to disappear. Soon there was no vegetation at all and they were surrounded by a gray-white desert where nothing grew except dry clumps of greasewood. . . . And [then] there in the midst of the desert, they came upon rows and rows of squat tar-paper barracks sitting in a pool of white dust that had once been the bottom of a lake. They had arrived at . . . their new home.
>
> (*Journey to Topaz* 94, 96)

Okubo, sent to the same camp, and not nearly so naive as to believe the government designation of Topaz as the "Jewel of the Desert," still confessed her depression at viewing the "desolate scene" of the camp from the bus window (121-122).

To the north, at Minidoka, Idaho, conditions were virtually the same for Monica Sone and her family. Approaching the camp north of the Snake River, "I could see nothing," she remembered ten years later, "but flat prairies, clumps of greasewood and . . . jack rabbits" (192). For self-imposed exile, Estelle Ishigo, Heart Mountain, Wyoming "stood in cactus-covered sand on ancient, weirdly jagged wasteland that spread far into the wide horizon" (19), and in the barren Owens Valley of California, Manzanar seemed to young Jeanne Wakatsuki to spread for miles across a plain of sand (14).[9]

Such inhospitable natural settings boded ill for the thousands of Japanese families from lush regions along the Pacific Coast. The Army Corps of Engineers, responsible for the construction of the ten centers, had systematically bulldozed down all trees and most vegetation in the regions around the new barracks. The result was swirling, often blinding, dust storms which seemed to blow up at any time of the day or month. Okubo remembered it looked "as if we had fallen into a flour barrel" after one such storm (123). Uchida, who had thought the dust in the early weeks after she arrived in Topaz bad, was unprepared for the "ominous strength" of one storm which

> swept around us in great thrusting gusts, flinging swirling masses of sand in the air and engulfing us in a thick cloud that eclipsed barracks only ten feet away. . . . [E]ven inside, the air was thick with dust. . . . We waited more than an hour, silent and rigid with fear, but the storm didn't let up.
>
> (*Desert Exile* 112)

In Minidoka, Sone remembers feeling "as if we were standing in a gigantic sand-mixing machine as the sixty-mile gale lifted the loose earth up into the sky, obliterating everything. Sand filled our mouths and nostrils and stung our faces and hands like a thousand darting needles" (192).[10]

Evacuees arrived at camps which were poorly constructed and, in nearly every case, unfinished. Though tar paper had been nailed on the outside walls of the various barracks, life in the camps, as Jeanne Wakatsuki notes, "was pure chaos. . . . The evacuation had been so hurriedly planned, the camps so hastily thrown together, nothing was completed when we got there, and almost nothing worked" (21). At Topaz, "many internees found themselves occupying barracks where hammering, tarring, and roofing was still in progress, and one unfortunate woman received second-degree burns on her face when boiling tar seeped through the roof onto the bed where she was asleep" (*Desert Exile* 111).

> No inner sheetrock walls or ceilings had been installed [Uchida remembered years later], nor had the black pot-bellied stove that stood outside our door. Cracks were visible everywhere in the siding and around the windows, and although our friends had swept out our room before we arrived, the dust was already seeping into it again from all sides.
>
> (*Desert Exile* 109)

Not until winter in all its fury hit Idaho did the government make any attempt to cover the inside walls of the barracks apartments at Minidoka. "Until then," Sone notes, "our four walls had looked like skeletons with their ribs of two by fours bare and exposed" (196).

At both assembly camp and relocation center, no one gave much thought to the physical comforts of the evacuees. Mattresses often consisted of bags of ticking and all the straw residents wished to stuff into them. No blankets or sheets were furnished, and many families found themselves forced to improvise with anything they could find in order to stay warm (Okubo 44-47). Partitions between the stable stalls in the camps usually did not reach to the ceilings, so the possibility of privacy was virtually non-existent. Even after residents came to the relocation centers, walls between the barrack rooms were almost paperthin creating similar situations. Indeed, privacy was at the bottom of the Army's priorities. "Men's and women's latrines were ranged in fully exposed rows, shocking the decency of everyone" (Ishigo 9). Communal showers were built back-to-back, and, though they were, of course, segregated by sex, many women were especially "very self-conscious and timid about using [them]" (Okubo 75).

Food, too, was at first poorly planned and haphazard. Early in the relocation period, "the diet was mostly cereal, rice, bread, bread-pudding, beans and hot dogs with canned tomatoes. Once in a while there was stew with an extremely small amount of meat" (Ishigo 10). Though food unquestionably did get better as the years passed, no one remembers it as anything more than adequate. Lines were everywhere and became a part of every evacuee's daily life. "We lined up for mail, for checks, for meals, for showers, for washrooms, for laundry tubs, for toilets, for church services, for movies. We lined up for everything," remembered Mine Okubo (86).

Though to the north Japanese-Canadian evacuees could, and frequently did, comment on the singular beauty of the mountains and lakes of eastern British Columbia, most rapidly realized that Canada had forced them into that region to appease the racist fears of their white neighbors in the west. Kogawa quotes "Emily Kato" (Muriel Kitagawa): "We were therefore relegated to the cesspools . . . just plopped here in the wilderness. Flushed out of Vancouver like dung drops. Maggot bait . . ." (*Obasan,* 118). Without adequate public services, most evacuees suffered endlessly. When Shizuye Takashima's father finally exploded in anger at one government official because of his family's treatment, he was bluntly told: "You are in camps. Therefore you are considered enemies. You have no rights" (40).

All the Japanese, on both sides of the border, were, from time to time, depressed at the treatment they received. Estelle Ishigo remembers "the horror of exile," the despair "of being excluded, isolated, forced out from the rest of humanity into lonely imprisonment" (16). To Jeanne Wakatsuki, even years after the war, there remained the "shame for being a person guilty of something enormous enough to deserve [incarceration, a] sense of unworthiness" (133, 140). Uchida remembered "the general sense of malaise and despair" which governed the lives of most of the evacuees (*Desert Exile* 111), and Monica Sone could not forget the "pall of gloom" that enshrouded her family at various times (158).

Canada's Japanese experienced the same feelings. "Emily Kato" writes about the "humiliation" of being forcibly relocated, a humiliation that ultimately turns to "helpless panic . . . not the hysterical kind but the kind that churns round and round going nowhere" (*Obasan* 93). Takeo Nakano repeatedly notes in his diary how the "uncertainty and irritability" at being rounded up and treated like the enemy eventually brought him and others "to the point of pondering death" (13, 21). After being sent to Angler, Ontario, he added that he and his fellow prisoners were

> stripped of all that determines [a] positive self-image. I myself had a taste of the lowest point of human existence, the powerlessness and the shame. . . . I was able, for the first time, to empathize with people who live life at the rock bottom.
>
> (48)

Takashima also remembers her father's outspoken, bitter (and useless) protests at being "treated like dogs" and at having been stripped of all "human dignity" by white Canadian officials (29, 14).

It was very hard for many traditional Japanese families to remain together emotionally as units during the evacuation period. The communal life-style in all the camps as well as the absence, in many instances, of a strong father-figure tended to destroy the role played by elderly parents or grandparents. Many young, second-generation *Nisei* took out their anger at being relocated on their parents' "Japaneseness." They refused to consider themselves Japanese at all, reserving such a designation only to those minorities who were resident aliens. Monica Sone was one such person. Rejecting her ancestry, she jumped at the opportunity to leave Minidoka and take a job in Chicago, putting her past behind her. Only after two years away from her parents, who remained in the center, did she come to see how foolish such an exclusionary attitude was. Returning for a visit early in 1945, she was finally able to say: "It's really nice to be born into two cultures, like getting a real bargain in life, two for the price of one. . . . I used to feel like a two-headed monstrosity, but now I find that two heads are better than one" (236). Jeanne Wakatsuki buried her memories of Manzanar, married a Caucasian and tried desperately "to live agreeably in Anglo-American society" for almost thirty years before finally coming to grips with her Japanese heritage (133-145).

Japanese-Canadians also rejected their ancestry, often straining family relations to the breaking point. Takashima, realizing on one occasion that she and her family were doomed to exile as long as the war continued, suddenly said: "Damn Japs! Why don't they stop fighting?" Her father, overhearing her, screamed back: "What do you mean 'Japs'? You think you're not a Jap? If I hear you say that again, I'll throttle you" (46). Years later, that same alienation had not gone completely away.

Both governments, despite overwhelming evidence to the contrary, always doubted the loyalty of their Japanese residents and encouraged the evacuees to consider repatriating to Japan whenever possible. In the United States, even as late as 1944, the government insisted on getting signed loyalty oaths from everyone. All evacuees still in the camps were required to pledge to fight for the country if called on *and* to forswear all allegiance to the Emperor of Japan or any other foreign leader. Any one who refused to provide immediate "Yes, Yes" responses was segregated as disloyal and shipped to the Tule Lake, California center for eventual repatriation. Looking back on this experience years after the event, many Japanese-American authors still remain bitter at having to demonstrate their love for America again and again.

Eventually, both the American and Canadian governments did allow the evacuees in the various camps to return to the "outside" world as long as it was away from the Pacific Coast. Okubo, Uchida and her sister, and others made the move to New York City; Sone went to Chicago; Nakano, to Toronto; the Takashimas, to northern Ontario. Authorities on both sides of the 49th parallel championed their ability to help create these and similar moves, but the patina of happy, enthusiastic evacuees willingly selecting new homes for themselves in other parts of their nations, obscures the truth. Many older, first-generation *Issei* felt trapped in the camps, rootless, yet unable to move until government officials required it. The Nakane family, featured in Kogawa's two books, were forced out of their home in Slocan, British Columbia and forcibly sent to Granton, Alberta, "a dusty, lonely place" with almost no trees, dust and endless flies. "I hate it here," little Naomi wrote to a Caucasian friend back in British Columbia, "I hate it here so much I want to run away" (*Naomi's Road* 63-64). But she did not, and, as Kogawa noted in her adult *Obasan,* Granton, for better or worse, became the family's "exile from our place of exile" (197).

Perhaps Estelle Ishigo and her husband, Shigeharu, more closely typified the "real" evacuee as the camps began to close down. When neither was willing to leave Heart Mountain to take domestic or farm jobs (Shigeharu had worked for the Hollywood movie industry before the war; Estelle had been an artist), they were placed under tremendous pressure to relocate on their own. When they chose to remain in Wyoming with others reluctant to reenter "society" with little to their name, the War Relocation Authority threatened all sorts of dire consequences. Their barracks were allowed to deteriorate and, even after winter storms had ripped off tar-paper sheathing, nothing was done to repair the damage. Heating fuel was kept to a minimum, and, finally, when even this failed to budge them, the Ishigos and others were given twenty-five dollars each, transportation to any site of their choosing, and the government's assurance that its mission was complete. "Most of us had no place to go," Estelle wrote in her memoirs thirty years later. All our personal property "had been stolen or destroyed. The twenty-five dollars we had received upon leaving camp was not enough to get a place to live and provide food and clothes" (92-94). Not until 1947, after living in crowded trailer parks and working in a fish cannery, was Shigeharu able to find permanent work.

Even those many Japanese who "successfully" made the transition from prisoner to citizen suffered in other ways. Jeanne Wakatsuki's father was "too old to start over, too afraid of rejection . . . too stubborn and too tired to travel [far] and finally too proud to do piece-work on an assembly line."

Papa did not know which way to turn. In the government's eyes a free man now, he sat, like those black slaves you hear about who, when they got word of their freedom at the end of the Civil War, just did not know where else to go or what else to do and ended up back on the plantation, rooted there out of habit or lethargy or fear.

(95-96)

Wakatsuki returned to southern California, but, as one business venture after another failed, he began to drink heavily. Before the war, though "not a great man, . . . he had held onto his self-respect, he dreamed great dreams, and . . . whatever he did had flourish" (42). But no more. When he died several years later, he had never been able to make the abrupt transition expected of him. The same story could be written again and again for hundreds of others.

Yet, surprisingly, despite the denial of their rights, the lost property and the often shattered lives,[11] the majority of the Japanese evacuees "endured the hardship of the evacuation with dignity, stoic composure, disciplined patience and an amazing resiliency of spirit. I think they displayed a level of strength, grace, and courage," Uchida writes, "that is truly remarkable" (*Desert Exile* 148).

All of the personal accounts of Japanese relocation express neither rancor nor bitterness. In many ways, each is a catharsis, a cleansing of the past, for the participants. "It has taken me twenty-five years to reach the point where I could talk openly about Manzanar," wrote Wakatsuki in the forward to her best-selling memoir (ix). For others, it was even longer, but, in putting down the truth as they remembered it, every person has been able to deal finally with his or her own personal suffering.

On the other hand, nearly all the autobiographers stress a deep personal commitment to telling the story in the hope that it may guarantee an end to such bigotry in the years ahead. Uchida, for instance, in her role as a renowned writer of children's stories, often encounters youngsters who have never heard of "America's Concentration Camps." Her books on relocation, then, have been written because, "as painful as it may be to hear, [the story] needs to be told and retold and never forgotten by succeeding generations of Americans" (*Desert Exile* 154). Mine Okubo says essentially the same thing. "I am not bitter," she writes in a 1983 reissue of *Citizen 13660,* but "I hope that things can be learned from this tragic episode" so it cannot happen again (xii, U of Washington P, 1983).

Far from bitterness, indeed, nearly all the Japanese-American/Canadian reminiscences of the war preach a theology of forgiveness. Joy Kogawa, perhaps, captures that spirit best when, in *Obasan*, she has one of her characters pray: "Father . . . we are abandoned yet we are not abandoned. You are present in every hell. Teach us to see Love's presence in abandonment. Teach us to forgive" (243). Such a prayer is a coda that repeats itself in every one of the autobiographies or autobiographical fictions written by, or about, Japanese-Americans or Canadians and the terrible days they spent as enemies of their own land.

Notes

1. There were, according to United States Army records, just over 110,000 persons of Japanese ancestry removed from the three Pacific Coast states during the war years. Canadian statistics show that country removed 21,975 persons from western British Columbia.

2. In Canada, according to the 1941 census, 13,600 of the 23,450 persons of Japanese ancestry (58%) were native-born citizens. Another 3,650 were naturalized—a total of 73.6% in all. In the United States, where, under law, naturalization was forbidden, 79,642 of 126,947—62.7% were native born citizens. Combining the two countries' statistics, 64.4% of the "Japanese" were citizens of their respective nation, though this did not prevent their deportation.

3. *Korematsu v. United States*, 323 U.S. 214, at 242 (1944).

4. There have been dozens of books written about the relocation of the Japanese in the United States. Among the best are Roger Daniels, *Concentration Camps, U.S.A. Japanese Americans and World War II* (Hinsdale, IL: Dryden, 1971); Audrie Girdner and Anne Loftus, *The Great Betrayal: The Evacuation of the Japanese-Americans during World War II* (New York: Macmillan, 1969); Morton Grodzins, *American Betrayed: Politics and the Japanese Evacuation* (Chicago: U of Chicago P, 1949).

5. Among the best comprehensive studies of the removal of Japanese Canadians are Ann Gomer Sunahara, *The Politics of Racism: The Uprooting of Japanese-Canadians during the Second World War* (Toronto: Lorimar, 1981); Patricia Roy, et al., *Mutual Hostages: Canadians and Japanese during the Second World War* (Toronto: U of Toronto P, 1990).

6. See, among many, United States, Department of Interior, *W.R.A.: A Story of Human Conservation* (Washington: GPO, 1946) or United States, Department of the Army, Western Defense Command, *Final Report. Japanese Evacuation from the West Coast, 1942* (Washington: GPO, 1943). Two popular children's books of the era: Robert L. McLean,

Tommy Two Wheels (New York: Friendship, 1943) and Florence Crandell Means, *The Moved-Outers* (Boston: Houghton, 1945) also offered justification for the evacuation by having Japanese-American characters express their willingness to be moved for the sake of America.

7. All the various authors, though more than willing to talk in terms of "concentration camps" in the American west, are very careful to emphasize that in no way were the United States camps comparable to those in eastern Europe or Asia. For all its failings, the United States did try to make life in the relocation centers as bearable as it could.

8. Nakano was placed in the Angler camp along with a huge majority of Japanese nationals whose loyalty was with Japan. When he eventually got permission to leave and work in Toronto for a packing firm, he was treated as a traitor by his fellow Japanese. Many years after the war, Nakano applied for and received Canadian citizenship.

9. Florence Means' fictional heroine, Sumiko Ohara, on seeing the center at Amache, Colorado just west of the Kansas border, has the same reaction. "This is the worst moment of all," she notes. "It's so ugly, so dull, so dry." To a Californian friend she writes: "I never dreamed how it would be. To have everything drab, even the air, with the sand in it, why it's like a dead world. No green; no fragrance" (*The Moved-Outers* 89, 93).

10. As a common theme, Means also has the Oharas experience the same problems with sand and dust everywhere and on every thing.

11. The Canadian government has never seen fit to apologize to its Japanese residents for their relocation and mistreatment during the war years though in 1964 former Prime Minister Lester Pearson did personally express regret at what had transpired. For years, the United States also tried to avoid its responsibilities. It did agree to pay minimal amounts for destroyed personal property—Uchica received the grand sum of $386.25 (*Desert Exile* 150)—but, not until 1990, did Congress finally approve a monetary sum of $20,000 for each remaining evacuee as a belated apology for the Government's actions nearly fifty years ago.

Works Cited

Houston, Jeanne Wakatsuki, and James D. Houston. *Farewell to Manzanar*. Boston: Houghton, 1973.

Ishigo, Estelle. *Lone Heart Mountain*. Los Angeles: n.p., 1972.

Kogawa, Joy. *Naomi's Road*. Toronto: Oxford UP, 1986.

———. *Obasan*. Toronto: Lester, 1981.

Nakano, Takeo Ujo, with Leatrice Nakano. *Within the Barbed Wire Fence: A Japanese Man's Account of His Internment in Canada.* Toronto: U of Toronto P, 1980.

Okubo, Mine. *Citizen 13660.* New York: Columbia UP, 1946. Reissued Seattle: U of Washington P, 1983.

Sone, Monica. *Nisei Daughter.* Boston: Little, 1953.

Takashima, [Shizuye]. *A Child in Prison Camp.* Montreal: Tundra, 1971.

Uchida, Yoshiko. *Desert Exile: The Uprooting of a Japanese-American Family.* Seattle: U of Washington P, 1982.

———. *Journey to Topaz: A Story of Japanese-American Evacuation.* New York: Scribner's, 1971.

Nicole M. T. Brunnhuber (essay date 2005)

SOURCE: Brunnhuber, Nicole M. T. "After the Prison Ships: Internment Narratives in Canada." In *"Totally Un-English?" Britain's Internment of "Enemy Aliens" in Two World Wars,* edited by Richard Dove, pp. 165-78. Amsterdam: Rodopi, 2005.

[*In the essay below, Brunnhuber discusses works by German-speaking refugees who were moved from England to internment camps in Canada during the war.*]

By the end of July 1940, approximately 4400[1] German and Austrian internees had survived hazardous and unpleasant Atlantic crossings only to find themselves imprisoned in specially allocated camps in Canada's eastern provinces. For the vast numbers who had hoped that deportation would bring adventure or lead to emigration to the USA, the following months, in some cases, the next two years, could only have been a frustrating disappointment. Deportees were branded class 2 Prisoners of War and were denied refugee status until 1 July 1941. Nevertheless, retrospective accounts, particularly by those amongst the roughly 1000 who chose to stay in Canada,[2] tend to emphasize the experience as ultimately positive, extolling Canada as a generous nation of freedom and opportunity. A letter by H. F. Reichenfeld to the editor of *To-Day Magazine,* which had published an extract from Eric Koch's seminal *Deemed Suspect: A Wartime Blunder,*[3] illustrates the depth of feelings of gratitude to Canada, and the reluctance to criticize the Canadian role in the treatment of deported internees. Reichenfeld, psychiatrist in charge at the Royal Ottawa Hospital, insists that he 'was not exposed to the humiliating experiences described by Eric Koch', and condemns the book as a biased contribution to the 'kick Canada cult'.[4]

Reichenfeld's sentiments are not singular and become still more understandable with the benefit of hindsight. However, since, as the conflicting representations of Koch and Reichenfeld illustrate, memory clearly diverges from individual to individual, *ex post facto* accounts are not necessarily entirely reliable in ascertaining authentic responses to historical events. As early as May 1941, H. M. Prison Officer, Alexander Paterson, after months of visiting camps and conducting interviews with internees and authorities alike, recognized the gaps and ambiguities of the Canadian deportation experience, and commented in his official report: 'After a whole year of self-pity and exchange of grievances, it is impossible to reconstruct the true story of what happened in all its unhappy details.'[5] An examination of internment accounts, including texts not originally intended for the public eye or the relevant authorities, sheds some light on the actual responses to internment in Canada.

Insecurity and uncertainty are key features of the collective textual production by internees in Canadian camps, and the entire Canadian experience is commonly depicted as an endless journey into the unknown. This is not surprising, since deportees only learnt of their destination during the final stages of the crossings. Even if dressed up in a jovial tone, a common feature of internment verse, a poem by an anonymous author in camp B, New Brunswick, emphasizes this point:

> One day the order comes to go
> to an unknown destination.
> We had to go, we could not know
> Of our deportation.[6]

This sense of the unknown was not, however, assuaged once the deportees found themselves on solid, Quebec ground. By all accounts, Canada was not an option for those fleeing the Nazi regime. During the inter-war years, Canada had pursued a strict immigration policy, and, with a few exceptions, the roughly four thousand Jewish refugees who were admitted had demonstrated that they had access to capital or could be employed in agriculture.[7] Thoughts of North America as the home of freedom and opportunity remained strictly associated with the USA even months after arrival in Canada. In 'Internee Julius Caesar', one of several short stories written by Carl Weiselberger during his Canadian internment, the path to freedom lies not in Canada, or even in release back to England, but 'nach Amerika hinüber, geradewegs bis an den Fuß der Freiheitsstatue von New York'.[8]

Besides being perceived as merely a transit venue by the thousand or so deportees who hoped to emigrate to the USA,[9] Canada appears to have featured only marginally in the European consciousness, and was, in the words of Henry Kreisel, 'a country that I barely knew by name and that was only a large red stretch on the school maps we had used in Vienna in our geography lessons.'[10] Several deportees support Kreisel's admitted ignorance of Canada, such as the concert pianist, John Newmark, who explains, 'Geography lessons in Bremen, Lower Saxony, Germany did not deal too much with such a faraway British colony.'[11] Even if Koch's claim that the summer uniforms of the Canadian guards led some of the new arrivals to believe that they had landed in India seems somewhat exaggerated,[12] the lack of knowledge of Canada could only have fuelled the sense of disorientation on the part of the European newcomers.

Feelings of isolation and abandonment, exacerbated by acute unfamiliarity with the country to which they had been deported, are often articulated in terms of an alienating vastness of the Canadian landscape. Noting his first impressions in his diary in camp L, Quebec City, Heinz Warschauer describes the St. Lawrence river and the summer scenery with the desultory conclusion: 'Es gibt keine Beziehung zwischen Mensch und die Natur um ihn. Das ist Traum, Romantik, Einbildung.'[13] Even after months in the camps, primary texts indicate that the deportees had not found any closer connection with the 'host' country. 'Herbst Neunzehnhundertvierzig', a poem by Robert Lamprecht, written in camp Q in Monteith, is suggestive of a profound sense of displacement couched in a deadly despondency:

> Es rinnt der Regen ins herbstgraue Land,
> der Himmel ist fahl wie Totenhand
> und die Erde ist kahl und leer.
> Meine Seele ist stumpf und grau ist ihr Pfad
> Und naht sich dem Ende.[14]

The overwhelming and enduring sense of alienation seems not to have been simply a result of the 'doppelte Heimatlosigkeit'[15] of the deportees, who had already suffered the humiliations and confines of internment in Britain, and often German concentration camps prior to their flight into exile. In Canada, the uncertainty and repeated upheavals forced upon the internees, as hopes for release or emigration dissipated amidst numerous relocations to camps elsewhere, augmented feelings of helplessness and a lack of autonomy. Ernest Pollak recorded his anxieties upon learning that Jews and gentiles were to be separated, and that he was to be moved from Monteith to camp L in October 1940:

> What will tomorrow bring? Will the new camp be better? Will there be work or is it a step towards the final release? In any event, tomorrow we shall be sitting in the train again travelling ten, twenty or thirty hours towards the unknown.[16]

Ernest Borneman's response to the decision to separate Jews and gentiles is considerably more acerbic and draws a clear distinction between the internment experience in Britain and Canada: 'The racial principle was one which would never have been accepted in England.'[17]

In spite of strict censorship rules, such concerns were not limited to private expression, but occasionally emerged as collective public protest in camp newspapers. 'Good Bye Camp L', an article in the *Camp L Chronicle,* articulates the concerns of Pollak and his voiceless peers, arguing: 'We know each other by now, we have lived, suffered, laughed and worked together. We have built up a sound and efficient community.'[18] More vehement is the front page article, which clearly seeks to make a public appeal against the perceived insensitivity of the Canadian authorities: 'Let us say: it is a most unfortunate thing we are suffering from. This disease is called: lack of organization and lack of psychology.'[19] Such complaints are corroborated by Paterson's report, which sympathizes with the deportees, and alludes further to a fundamental conflict between Canadian and European psyches: 'The Canadian tends to be a man of rigid and unimaginative mind, and therefore not well-suited to taking care of sensitive and temperamental human beings.'[20]

Even if such reasoning appears grossly unjust and suggestive of a cultural European elitism vis-à-vis the Canadians, several accounts describe thick barbed wire, armed machine gun turrets and extremely strict discipline in the camps. The fact that such harsh treatment had its origins in Britain's original declaration that the deportees were individuals 'whose removal from this country it is desired to secure on the ground that their continued presence in this country is bound to be a source of the most serious risk,'[21] seems to have been overlooked or simply not known by some deportees. Instead, texts often focus on the injustice of their situation at the hands of the Canadians, and indicate the profound sense of victimization of the authors. Borneman's internment diary illustrates a preoccupation with unjust treatment and his report, 'Transport on M. S. Ettrick and Internment in Canada', records a litany of offences by camp authorities, even claiming that articles of the Geneva Convention were deliberately ignored in the treatment of internees.[22] He describes robberies by guards on arrival in camp L, and states that a mentally disturbed man, isolated in a separate hut was shot as he tore at the barbed wire on his window.[23] Writing in his diary in Sherbrooke, camp N, Borneman even claims that guards would come in and pull away blankets in the night '"to see if internees are undressed". (Homosexuality running high among soldiers. New Years' Eve drunk guards coming into dormitory to rape internees)' [*sic*].[24] Borneman's latter claim is not corroborated in other primary documentation researched for this paper, but is cited in Koch's *Deemed Suspect.*[25] (Interestingly enough, Koch dedicates an entire section to the 'Gay Life' amongst the internees.)[26]

It should be stated that even Borneman was eventually appeased as conditions and treatment improved,[27] but the predominant grimness of his accounts constitutes a remarkable concentration on the negative aspects of the Canadian treatment of deportees. Nevertheless, the extent of universal outrage at being labelled Prisoners of War is evident in numerous letters and diaries, which often dwell on the POW uniforms as symbolic of the unjust humiliation of their mistaken identity. According to Henry Kreisel, the arrival of such attire at camp B caused an 'internal crisis'.[28] The significance of their POW status as an insult and a further hindrance to contact with the Canadian world outside the camps also manifests itself in Weiselberger's internment fiction. In 'Die Geschichte von der Geige', a young internee longs for nothing other than the arrival of his much beloved violin. At night, he dreams of giving a concert before a Canadian audience, but on realizing that he is clad in POW uniform, the dream quickly becomes a nightmare: 'Schweiß stand auf seiner Stirn, er schämte sich furchtbar vor den Damen und Herren im Parterre.'[29]

Represented as a deep source of shame in Weiselberger's story, for Ernest Pollak, the issue of POW status is the ultimate paradigm of the Canadian, as opposed to British, internment experience. As he recorded in his diary, his reply to the question of what was the greatest difference between internment in Britain and Canada in an interview with the authorities, emphasizes their POW status as central to the internees' resentment of the Canadian administration: 'How can we trust you when you treat us here like prisoners-of-war?'[30] Clearly in the case of Pollak, Canada was to remain associated with harsh treatment and the ignominy of the POW label. Returning to England in February 1941, he sardonically remarks: 'The journey home to England proves to be the only enjoyable part of the Canadian adventure. There are no more guards on board the ship.'[31]

Even documents testifying to a less virulent and more objective attitude to the Canadian authorities indicate dismay at the camp regimes, and are suggestive of a nostalgia for Britain. Undoubtedly, letters such as Andreas Göritz's report from Douglas on the Isle of Man to Eric Koch could not have helped: 'I do not know whether it is cruel if I write you that this camp is so comfortable that I would not mind to spend the summer here providing we had access to the weaker sex. The treatment is infinitely better than what we have been used to.'[32]

Nostalgia for Britain could only have been intensified by the deportee's initial ignorance of Canadian culture, which, in turn, had little chance of dissipating within the strict confinement in the camps. Such exclusion from the outside world, compounded by the mislabelling of internees as POWs, seems to have lead to a profound identity crisis, which finds clearest expression in Weiselberger's internment fiction. Particularly for those who strove to abandon their German-speaking origins, but found no commonality with their North American environment, assuming a British cultural identity may have provided one means of asserting their ideological beliefs and maintaining a sense of personal stability. This response is articulated in Weiselberger's 'Der Mann mit den tausend Gesichtern', which begins by describing rehearsals for a camp cabaret. One of the performers, a former Cambridge student, is singled out for his manifest 'Englishness'. Not only is he to sing English songs, 'englischer natürlich als der englischste Engländer', but his entire survival mechanism and the means of preserving his dignity depend on his acquired British identity:

> Alles konnte man diesem Jungen nehmen: die Freiheit, die alte Heimat, die Eltern und Geschwister, nur an seinem englischen Akzent durfte man nicht rütteln und an der Pfeife, die er bald in den rechten, bald in den linken Mundwinkel schob.[33]

The narrative itself thematizes a loss of individual identity in the face of a seemingly inaccessible Canadian culture. The central protagonist, Hoffmann-Chameleoni, formerly a successful impressionist, now 'ein leeres Gefäß' (p. 87), succeeds in escaping to the outside world in his costume as the camp's Canadian carpenter. However, his adventure into freedom is far from liberating, as he quickly realizes that the Canadian world is 'nicht meine Welt', and even cars, houses and people seem alien and threatening (p. 94). The narrative makes it clear that the protagonist's unease in the outside world is not a result of a fear of being caught, since each individual encountered amicably greets the disguised escapee without a second glance. Rather, it is the successful assumption of a Canadian identity which terrifies Hoffmann, as he interacts with each passer-by: 'Vielleicht bin ich es bereits, der Kanadier, und weiß es nicht, erschrak er einen Augenblick' (p. 96). Only once he has voluntarily identified himself to the camp guards driving by, and is sitting on the floor of the truck 'war er wieder ganz zu sich selbst geraten!' (p. 98). For Weiselberger's 'Chameleoni', physical liberation entails utter self-alienation; a German-speaking internee simply has no place in Canadian life, which, as the story concludes, remains 'sehr fern und unwirklich' (p. 100).

In the midst of the 'unreal' Canadian world, some deportees seem to have developed a tendency to withdraw into idealizations of pre-exile existences and memories of pre-Nazi European culture. In Weiselberger's unpublished 'Die Pantoffeln des Generals', such retreat from reality is precarious, even self-effacing, and reduces life in the camps to a 'Gespensterdasein'.[34] As the narrator shows a new arrival around the camp, he points out the 'Sonderfälle' (p. 3) of the camp. For the most part, these eccentrics are fixated with features of European culture. One elderly gentleman spends his time lying on the ground, drawing masterpieces in the air with his hands, 'naturalistisch, klassizistisch, impressionistisch, expressionistisch, surrealistisch, wie du nur willst' (p.

4). Even if the 'painter' succeeds in warding off the disenchantment of his fellow internees by means of his bizarre antics, his behaviour is to be seen as 'unheimlich', even 'gespenstisch' (p. 5). Similarly, the 'Typologe', a former academic psychologist, obsessed with the desire to discover 'etwas Epochemachendes' (p. 5), and the 'Geigenmacher' submerge themselves into constructs of a bygone cultural reality in an effort to escape the anonymity and futility of their actual existence. Their acute rejection of contemporary truth is made manifest in the violin-maker's refusal to let anyone in the camp play his meticulously crafted instruments simply because 'Menschen von heute dürfen nicht darauf spielen' (p. 8).

The moral of the story, however, is crystallized in the fate of the 'General', who parades around the camp in a Napoleonic pose. On one occasion, during roll call, he demands to be recognized as an officer, only to stumble ignominiously and lose his slippers, much to the hilarity of guards and prisoners alike. His modus vivendi at the end of the story drives home two perceptions of the Canadian internment experience: as a grotesque absurdity on the one hand, as symbolized by the whirling merry-go-round on the other side of the barbed wire (p. 21), and as a challenge to accept the situation and maintain contact with the real world, no matter how unpleasant in the midst of war, on the other. When the 'General' re-emerges from his humiliating performance during roll call, his voice sounds different: 'Irgendwie wahrer [. . .] als ob man einen Vorhang von ihr [der Stimme] gezogen' [sic] (p. 21). For the first time, he recognizes reality, and admits the preposterousness of his former posturings (p. 21). Weiselberger's tale illustrates, albeit to an extreme, some of the responses to the Canadian dilemma. As much as clinging to the past or some constructed identity seems understandable, particularly given the degradation and irony of the identity imposed upon them, Weiselberger urges his peers to acknowledge the true situation, no matter how grim, injurious or even absurd it may be.

The difficulty of accepting one's lot in Canadian internment was, however, not merely a question of tolerating personal degradation or material discomfort, but aggravated by the physical distance from war-torn Europe. Whilst family members, especially of younger deportees, may have found solace in the fact that at least those interned in Canada were safe from German bombs,[35] for the deportees themselves the distance from the war exacerbated anxieties and feelings of futility. Such sentiments were, of course, shared by internees in Britain. However, internees on the Isle of Man enjoyed comparatively prompt correspondence with the outside world, and could reassure themselves of the safety of friends and family. Moreover, internees in Britain who had volunteered for the Pioneer Corps were released in October 1940,[36] whereas even those who had also volunteered in Canada had to wait longer, and returns proceeded at a much lower rate.[37] The pragmatism of Pollak's comment on being excluded from the war is charged with a collective sense of inutility:

> In the meantime the first bombs have been dropped on London and the Battle of Britain has begun in earnest. And we are here in Canada behind barbed wire. Perhaps we should be pleased to be safe and not complain? We find that hard to swallow.[38]

Such concerns also made their way into more literary endeavours, such as 'Nach Heinrich Heine' by an anonymous author:

> Ich weiß nicht was soll es bedeuten,
> Dass ich in Kanada bin.
> Es kommt auch anderen Leuten
> So vor, als hätts keinen Sinn.
> Man sollte doch tatsächlich meinen,
> Man könnte was für England tun.
> Stattdessen zwingen sie einen
> Auf Staatskosten auszuruhen [sic].[39]

At first glance, this text seems to be a nostalgic recourse to Germany's cultural legacies, as already discussed. However, the poem is not merely a parody of the German lyrical classic, but assumes anti-Fascist dimensions as homage to a poem whose authorship the Nazis categorically denied. The political framework reinforces the political statement of the content and strives for association with a prominent German, who had literally experienced exile himself, and been ousted from his rightful place in the German literary canon by the National Socialists.

Recourse to the lyrical form, as opposed to simply recording personal grievances in a diary, further suggests a public political motive in exposing the internees' plight and their anti-Fascist position, even if, for the time being, the public was restricted to the camp audience. This helps explain the proportionally high number of poems dealing with exclusion from the war, as correspondence from Britain increasingly detailed the horrors of the Blitz and the sacrifices of life on the home front. In response, a number of poems indicate a desire to bridge the geographical and circumstantial barriers between the Canadian internment experience and life in wartime Britain. The untitled poem already referred to above (p. 166) concludes its comedic account of deportation with an explicit declaration of universality:

> You are with us
> And we with you.
> We are today and tomorrow too
> All of us—we and you [sic].[40]

Alfred Becker's 'Song vom verwischten Unterschied', written in 1940, and addressed to a partner in England is more specific. As the title indicates, Becker's text is a lyrical attempt to equate the restrictions and censorship of the Canadian camp experience with the constraints of wartime Britain:

> So lebst Du. In Freiheit, sollte man denken,
> und bist genau betrachtet nicht freier als ich,
> denn alles, womit sie mich hier bedenken,
> serviert zu Hause der Krieg für Dich.[41]

Such expressions of association with those directly confronted with the war are indicative of more than a desire to declare solidarity with the anti-Fascist cause, but betray a personal sense of shame for seemingly sitting out the war in far-off Canada. Furthermore, it is highly likely that such texts were also a means of avoiding succumbing entirely to the banalities of life in internment and adopting a 'camp mentality', as the months passed by with no clear end in sight. Kreisel's description of the poor conditions found on arrival at camp I, Isle aux Noix, implies that by June 1941, seemingly endless imprisonment in Canada had reduced the psychological horizons of the majority of internees: 'It is remarkable that most of us don't say: I wish I were free again but most say: O, were we back in camp B.'[42]

The importance of finding some meaning in the Canadian camps is the central theme of Weiselberger's 'Kain und Abel in Kanada'. The camp itself is introduced as a static, even deadly environment, where the posts supporting the barbed wire are '483 Galgen', each bearing an invisible corpse.[43] The two title figures are both writers who have lost their life's work, for each, 'der Sinn seines Lebens' (p. 65). The ensuing juxtaposition between the two men clearly outlines two contrasting responses to internment in Canada. Whilst Kain, characterized by 'Unrast' (p. 65), is devoured by resentment, Abel succeeds in finding inspiration even amidst the stasis of a Canadian camp and, after having lost everything, sees confinement in North America as an opportunity 'sein Leben wieder anzufangen' (p. 65).

Admittedly, the spirited attitude of Weiselberger's Abel seems somewhat heroic, even implausible, particularly in the context of the predominantly despondent accounts and the conditions endured. Consequently, in spite of its documentary value, this narrative by Weiselberger betrays the author's own struggle to attribute some sense of purpose to the languor of the Canadian experience and motivate his fellow internees. Whether Weiselberger's peers actually adopted Abel's positive attitude remains unlikely, for even the more encouraging aspects of Canadian internment frequently receive ambivalent treatment in primary accounts, and, on close analysis, often in Weiselberger's own fiction.

One positive feature of Canadian camp life was the opportunity to work, mostly in the forests cutting wood for 20 cents a day, and, occasionally unaccompanied by guards. The crucial factor of this development, was not, however, the financial remuneration, but release from confinement within the camp, which as Henry Kreisel declared, meant that 'one almost feels free.'[44] For Weiselberger's 'Rabbi mit der Axt',[45] the opportunity of physical labour prompts a theological dilemma, which is, however, typically resolved as a positive opportunity provided by the Canadian experience. However, in 'Die Pantoffeln des Generals', there is markedly less emphatic endorsement of such work, which rendered existence in the camps only 'ein wenig besser, ein wenig lebendiger' (p. 1).

A close analysis of Weiselberger's internment narratives exposes further elements of ambiguity on the part of the author. Although food in the Canadian camps was ample and nourishing, the narrator of 'Die Pantoffeln des Generals' betrays a distinctly cynical response: 'Manchmal hat man das Gefühl, sie füttern uns, sie füttern uns fett, damit wir nur ruhiger bleiben' (p. 1). Such discontent, however, is not an indication of Weiselberger's personal ingratitude, but finds a degree of corroboration in Paterson's report. Nutritional excess had a distinctly detrimental effect on the younger internees, whom Paterson declared 'grossly over-fed and under-exercised'.[46]

Paterson's concern for the well-being of the boys and young men amongst the internees is not merely a manifestation of philanthropic concern for juveniles, but refers to another fundamental feature of the Canadian internment experience: namely, the high proportion of young men and boys. Aside from the fact that young, unmarried men had been encouraged to 'volunteer' for deportation, according to Paterson, 'hundreds' of schoolboys, who had barely turned sixteen, found themselves onboard the ships headed for Canada.[47] According to a report by Canada's Central Committee for Interned Refugees, an analysis of camp N, the largest camp for 'B' and 'C' internees, and deemed demographically 'typical', concludes that 45% were under the age of 25.[48]

Retrospective accounts by those who had been deported to Canada at a young age tend to emphasize the educational opportunities Canada provided once McGill University opened its doors to allow internees to matriculate in the summer of 1941. Conversely, at the time, Paterson was convinced that 'the general effect on all of them [boys and students] after a year in Canada is bad'.[49] The written testimonies by younger internees themselves betray a growing melancholy, occasionally fulminating in wrathful frustration or an abject loss of faith. Concluding his account of the heavily armed transfer to camp I in the early summer of 1941, Henry Kreisel, who had just turned eighteen, is reduced to an expression of utter disillusionment: 'It is enough to make anybody lose faith in the world and in mankind.'[50]

In spite of such acute despondency, Kreisel's Canadian internment was triumphantly resolved. In November 1941, he was released to prepare for the senior matriculation exam, and went on to win a four-year scholarship to read English at the University of Toronto, and become a Lecturer of English and Comparative Literature at the University of Alberta and successful English-language novelist. Whilst Kreisel's academic achievements and the realization of his decision during internment to become an English-language writer would seem to promote the educational possibilities of the camp schools and the wealth of time available for intellectual pursuits as a distinct bonus of internment in Canada, a closer consideration of these aspects paints a less unilateral picture.

Undeniably, the facility to study in Canada was an outstanding gesture, offering a fresh start and an invaluable education to the young men who had frequently been forced to abandon their schooling in Europe. However, the uncertainty and conditions of their situation in the camps cast a dark shadow on intellectual endeavours in preparing for matriculation. The diary of Heinz Warschauer, who had been writing his doctoral thesis in history before fleeing to Britain, illustrates the psychological burden of camp life. In August 1940, Warschauer recorded that he had begun reading part two of Goethe's *Faust* for the first time, only to comment 'dabei gemerkt wie nun Nervosität und mangelnde Konzentrationsfähigkeit eine Dauererscheinung geworden sind in mir'.[51]

In addition to intense anxiety provoked by the external factors of Canadian internment, younger internees seem to have suffered, as much as benefited, from the demographic diversity of the camps. In fact, the cramped living conditions seem to have launched a generation conflict to the extent that Weiselberger took up the issue as a theme for his story, 'Die Wette'.[52]

The two young protagonists of the narrative challenge each other to throw a bowl of vegetables at the pompous camp cook. Besides boredom, they are motivated by a profound disillusionment with the older generation. As Heinz prepares for lunch, he strikes a pose which represents

> eine ihm unbewusste Kampfansage gegen die Würde des Alters, gegen Titel, gegen diese alte Generation, die ihre Sache so schlecht gemacht und das Leben in den Dreck geführt hatte [. . .] Wer waren sie denn, diese Alten, die genau so interniert waren und auf demselben Scheißhaus, Arsch an Arsch, neben einem saßen?
>
> (p. 3).

Although somewhat less graphic than Weiselberger, Kreisel provides the same reasons for conflict between the generations. In his diary, he recorded a complaint by an older gentleman regarding the disrespect of the younger internees. Kreisel does not deny the accusation, but explains that in the close confinement of the camps, the human fallibilities of the elderly, normally concealed beneath a 'mantle of dignity', are exposed.[53]

With the rupture of such social norms, the conditions and duration of internment in Canada entailed both exposure to and exclusion from an entirely new way of life. Certainly, primary documentation paints a grim picture of Canadian internment, characterized by isolation, mistaken identity and uncertainty. Whilst on the whole, internees had no choice but to adapt to camp life, the original cultural cleft between Europe and Canada could only be overcome by those who chose to stay, and only once they were released. For the majority, it appears that deportation to Canada only strengthened their European identities. The high proportion of academics and successful entrepreneurs amongst those released into Canada, and the success stories of Kreisel and Weiselberger as Canadian writers would suggest that Canada was a generous country of exile. Nevertheless, Canada's overall role in the history of refugees fleeing Nazi terror hardly suggests a positive assessment. Perhaps a ray of light can be gleaned from the fate of those amongst the initially undesirable deportees who chose to stay, and for whom Canada finally emerged as a unique venue for re-birth, opportunity and reconciliation between Canadian and European cultures.

Notes

1. Largely due to the haste with which the British government implemented its deportation policy, there is considerable conflict in the statistics provided by British and Canadian records and subsequent publications on the subject. In his 1941 'Report on Civilian Internees sent from the United Kingdom to Canada during the Unusually Fine Summer of 1940', Alexander Paterson states that a 'total of 4799 men and boys were within a fortnight transported across the Atlantic', (The National Archives, PO35 996 HP00147; National Archives of Canada, Eric Koch fonds, MG30-C192, vol.2), p. 2. The figure of 4400 is an estimate based on the statistics provided for each of the three deportation ships which reached Canada provided in Peter and Leni Gillman, *Collar the Lot! How Britain Interned and Expelled its Wartime Refugees* (London: Quartet, 1980), pp. 169, 182, 204, 244, and Ronald Stent, *A Bespattered Page: The Internment of His Majesty's Most Loyal Enemy Aliens* (London: Deutsch, 1980), p.96. On p. 205, Peter and Leni Gillman state that 1700 merchant seamen and other category 'A' internees and 2700 category 'B' and 'C' internees were transported to Canada. It should be kept in mind that several individuals had been falsely classified as

category 'A': Although all Germans on board the ill-fated *Arandora Star* were 'A' class, Judex argues that approximately 150 had been wrongly classified, since included were those who had entered illegally, overstayed their original permit or been falsely judged at their tribunals. See Judex [Herbert Delauney Hughes], *Anderson's Prisoners* (London: Victor Gollancz, 1940) p. 83. Stent also talks of a 'number of mislabelled refugees' aboard the *Arandora Star* (p. 101). For example, two German trade union leaders, Valentin Witte and Louis Weber, were drowned, as was Karl Olbrysch, former KPD Reichstag member, who had already endured three years imprisonment and one year in a concentration camp in Germany.

2. Peter and Leni Gillman state (p. 276) that 972 deportees chose to remain in Canada.

3. Eric Koch, *Deemed Suspect: A Wartime Blunder* (Halifax: Goodread Biographies, 1985). (Originally published New York: Methuen, 1980).

4. Letter from H. F. Reichenfeld to the editor of *To-Day Magazine* (Toronto), 31 October 1980, in the National Archives of Canada, Eric Koch fonds, MG30-C192, vol. 1, pp. 1-4, p. 4.

5. Paterson report, p. 2.

6. The poem is in the National Archives of Canada, Eric Koch fonds, MG30-C192, vol. 1, 'Correspondence between Eric Koch and other internees, A-F', p. 2.

7. Koch, *Deemed Suspect*, p. ix.

8. Carl Weiselberger, 'Internee Julius Caesar', in *Carl Weiselberger: Eine Auswahl seiner Schriften,* ed. by Peter Liddell and Walter Riedel (Toronto: German-Canadian Historical Association, 1981), pp. 74-83, p. 74.

9. In his report, Paterson stated (p. 9) that over a thousand deportees had registered for emigration to the USA. These hopes were ultimately dashed when after several attempts by Paterson, including plans to send internees to the USA via Newfoundland or Cuba, he was informed on 15 April 1941 that the American authorities would not accept former internees. The subsequent US Immigration Act of June 1941, authorizing 'the refusal of visas to aliens whose admission into the United States would endanger the public safety', made it definitively clear that internees in Canada would not be able to realize their dream of freedom in the United States. Quoted in Gillman, *Collar the Lot,* p. 274.

10. Henry Kreisel, Introduction, 'Diary of an Internment', in *Another Country: Writings by and about Henry Kreisel,* ed. by Shirley Neumann (Edmonton: NeWest Press, 1981), pp. 18-44, p. 20.

11. Account by John Newmark in the National Archives of Canada, Eric Koch fonds, MG30-C192, vol. 1, 'Correspondence, report & other material re. his internment, 1939-1941', p. 102.

12. Eric Koch, 'The Reunion of Internees 1980 in Montreal' in the National Archives of Canada, Eric Koch fonds, MG30-C192, vol. 2, 'To the Spies who Never Were' by Harry Rasky', pp. 1-36, p. 27.

13. Heinz Warschauer, entry for 29 July 1940 in his 'Diary, July-September 1940' in the National Archives of Canada, Warschauer fonds, MG30-D129, pp. 1-29, p. 2.

14. Robert Lamprecht, 'Herbst Neunzehnhundertvierzig' in the National Archives of Canada, Eric Koch fonds, MG30-C192, vol. 1, 'Lamprecht, Robert. Poetry 1938-1940'.

15. Walter Riedel, 'Im großen Menschenkäfig: Zu Carl Weiselberger's Erzählungen aus der kanadischen Internierung', *Seminar,* XIX 2 (1998), pp. 136-49, p. 139.

16. Ernest Pollak, *Departure to Freedom Curtailed* (Lewes: Ernest Pollak, [n. d.]), p. 43.

17. Ernest Borneman, 'Transport on M. S. *Ettrick* and Internment in Canada' in the National Archives of Canada, Eric Koch fonds, MG30-C192, vol. 1, pp. 1-7, p. 3.

18. 'Good Bye Camp L', *Camp L Chronicle,* 2 October 1940, p. 4.

19. *Ibid.,* p. 1.

20. Paterson report, p. 6.

21. Viscount Caldecott, Secretary of State for the Dominions, to Vincent Massey, High Commissioner for the Canadian government in London. Ottawa, PAC Dept. of National Defence, RG 24 c4, quoted in Gillman, *Collar the Lot,* p. 164.

22. Borneman, 'Transport', p. 4.

23. *Ibid.,* p. 4.

24. Ernest Borneman, Internment Diary, National Archives of Canada, Eric Koch fonds, MG30-C192, vol.1, pp. 1-39, p. 13.

25. Koch, *Deemed Suspect,* p. 139.

26. *Ibid.,* pp. 157-59.

27. Borneman, 'Transport', p. 6.

28. Kreisel, 'Diary', p. 26.

29. Carl Weiselberger, 'Die Geschichte von der Geige', in *Weiselberger, Auswahl,* p. 105.

30. Pollak, *Departure*, p. 53.

31. *Ibid.*, p. 56.

32. Andreas Göritz to Eric Koch, 24 March 1941, in the National Archives of Canada, MG30-C192, vol. 1, 'Correspondence to Otto Koch May 1941'.

33. Carl Weiselberger, 'Der Mann mit den tausend Gesichtern', in *Weiselberger, Auswahl,* p. 84. Further page references appear in the text.

34. Carl Weiselberger, 'Die Pantoffeln des Generals', dated 25 July 1941, National Archives of Ottawa, Weiselberger fonds, MG30-D191, vol. 1, pp. 1-21, p. 1. Further page references appear in the text.

35. Margaret Mayer, for example, repeatedly expressed relief at the deportation of her younger brother, Eric (Otto) Koch in their correspondence during the summer of 1940, held at the National Archives of Canada, Eric Koch fonds, MG30-C192, vol.1, 'Correspondence to Otto Koch, June 1940'.

36. Stent, *Bespattered,* p. 243.

37. In his report, Paterson states (p. 12) that 287 men returned to England on 26 December 1940, followed by 274 men on 24 February 1941 and 330 on 26 June 1941. By the time the last Canadian internment camp was closed in September 1943, 1537 internees had been returned to Great Britain, see Michael Seyfert, *Deutsche Exilliteratur in Britischer Internierung: Ein unbekanntes Kapitel der Kulturgeschichte des Zweiten Weltkriegs* (Berlin: Arsenal, 1984), p. 35.

38. Pollak, *Departure,* p. 37.

39. The poem is held in the National Archives of Canada, Eric Koch fonds, MG30-C192, vol.2, 'Behind Barbed Wire: Poetry, Sketches etc. 1940-1941'.

40. See Note 6 above. . . .

41. Alfred Becker, 'Song vom verwichsten Unterschied' in the National Archives of Canada, Eric Koch fonds, MG30-C192, vol. 2, 'Behind Barbed Wire: Poetry, sketches, etc. 1940-1941', p. 2.

42. Kreisel, 'Diary', p. 37, entry for 24 June 1941.

43. Carl Weiselberger, 'Kain und Abel in Kanada', in *Weiselberger, Auswahl.* Further page references appear in the text.

44. Kreisel, 'Diary', p. 28, entry for 2 January 1941.

45. Carl Weiselberger, *Der Rabbi mit der Axt. Dreißig Geschichten,* ed. by Herta Hartmanshenn and Frederick Kriegel (Victoria B. C.: University of Victoria 1973). Translated into English for publication in Koch (see Note 3 above), pp. 104-10.

46. Paterson report, p. 16.

47. *Ibid.*, p. 16.

48. 'Central Committee for Interned Refugees Report on Emigration of Interned Refugees' of 24 June 1941 by C. Raphael in the National Archives of Canada, Eric Koch fonds, MG30-C192, vol. 2, p.1

49. Paterson report, p. 15.

50. Kreisel, 'Diary', p. 36, entry for 21 June 1941.

51. Warschauer, 'Diary', p.13, entry for 4 August 1940.

52. Carl Weiselberger, 'Die Wette', dated 22 June 1941, National Archives of Ottawa, Weiselberger fonds, MG30-D191, vol. 1, pp. 1-8, p. 1. Further page references appear in the text.

53. Kreisel, 'Diary', p. 30, entry for 3 January 1941.

WORLD WAR II DRAMA

Richard G. Scharine (essay date 1991)

SOURCE: Scharine, Richard G. "World War II—Theatrical Themes from Antiwar to Prowar to Postwar." In *From CLASS to CASTE in American Drama: Political and Social Themes since the 1930s,* pp. 29-66. New York: Greenwood Press, 1991.

[*In the following essay, Scharine discusses theater in America before, during, and after the war, focusing especially on antiwar drama and plays that deal with race relations following the war.*]

> Fifteen years ago came the Armistice and we all thought it was to be a new world. It is! But a lot worse than it was before. Ten million men were killed and many more maimed, fifty billion dollars worth of property destroyed, and the world saddled with debts. And what for? Would it have been any worse if Germany had won? Ask yourself honestly. No one knows.[1]
>
> —William Allen White (November 11, 1933)

In America, periods of self-sacrifice and disillusionment follow one another with cyclic regularity. The 1920s probably would have reacted cynically to the "War to Make the World Safe for Democracy"—a claim which must have puzzled allies like the Czar of Russia and the Mikado of Japan—even if it had attained its aims. But clearly it had not.

Woodrow Wilson's "Fourteen Points" encouraged the Central Powers to sue for a "peace without victory." However, at the 1919 Peace Conference, Wilson was unable to forbid secret treaties and war reparations, or initiate freedom of the seas, universal disarmament, and self-determination by nationalities. He did achieve Point 14—the formation of a League of Nations.[2]

The rejection of the League by the isolationist Right (as embodied in the Republican-controlled Senate) was predictable. Article 10 of the League's charter made it necessary for every member to take part in the common defense of the victim of an aggressive act. Article 11 made a war or the threat of war "a matter of concern" to all League members, whether directly involved or not. Finally, Article 16 defined any war begun in violation of the League's convenant as a war against all members of the League.[3] A people torn equally between the desire to return to nineteenth-century "normalcy" and the pleasure of flexing their newly acquired economic muscle were not about to yield international autonomy to any non-American deliberative body. That included the League's most important creation, the Permanent Court of International Justice (the World Court). When the United States did apply for membership in 1926, it attached such reservations as to force a rejection. A compromise was worked out in 1929, but Senate opponents of the Court blocked its consideration until 1935. That January the application finally seemed destined for victory, but a flood of letters, telegrams, and petitions inspired by the Hearst newspapers and Father Coughlin, the radio priest, prevented the required two-thirds majority.[4]

Nevertheless, as Depression desperation drove country after country to find military solutions to their economic problems, it was obvious that America had to adopt some legal policy toward acts of international belligerency. Japan invaded Manchuria in 1931, and in 1933 Hitler withdrew Germany from the Geneva Arms Limitation Conference and the League of Nations, reinstated the draft, and began to build up the air force. But it was Italy that inspired the First Neutrality Act by threatening to invade Ethiopia over an incident at Walwel, a fort on the Ethiopia-Italian Somaliland border, in December 1934.

The policy was suggested by Charles Warren, Wilson's World War I assistant attorney general, in the April 1934 *Foreign Affairs* magazine, and the president signed it into law on August 31, 1935. It forbade arms sales and private loans to all belligerents and forbade American citizens to travel on ships of warring countries.[5]

The shortcomings of the First Neutrality Act were many. Most notably, it made no distinction according to blame. No matter who started the war or for what purpose, the sale of arms was forbidden to both sides. Nevertheless, it offered Roosevelt the perfect political compromise: (1) Italy, the obvious aggressor, was denied arms which landlocked Ethiopia couldn't purchase anyway; (2)

Italian-American voter support was spared; (3) in this year of the WPA, the legislative deck was cleared for social programs; and (4) the bill was only for six months.

Hidden in the language of the Neutrality Act is a common assumption of the 1930s which was shared by the isolationist Right and the internationalist Left alike: that our military involvement in the Great War was a direct result of our economic involvement.

As the prestige of the capitalist dissolved with the stock market, he was retroactively tried and convicted of war crimes in the public consciousness. In 1934 and 1935, a series of books and articles about the international arms trade popularized the phrases "merchants of death" and "blood brotherhood." An anonymous article in the March 1934 *Fortune* presented the industry's axiom: "When there are wars, prolong them; when there is peace, disturb it."[6] *Merchants of Death,* by H. C. Engelbrecht and F. C. Hanighen, described arms-makers as "one of the most dangerous factors in world affairs—a hindrance to peace, a promoter of war."[7] George Seldes's *Iron, Blood, and Profits* depicted them as "organized into the greatest and most profitable secret international of our time—the international of bloodshed for profits."[8] Walter Millis's *Road to War: America 1914-1917* showed Allied war purchases as both ending America's 1914 business slump and aligning us so completely with the Allies as to provoke the German submarine attacks which brought us into the war.[9]

In 1935, South Dakota senator Gerald Nye began investigating the World War I munitions industry, eventually documenting the huge war profits by such firms as Remington Arms, Bethlehem Steel, and DuPont (whose earnings increased sixteenfold between 1914 and 1916), close ties between arms makers and the Army and Navy Departments, and questionable techniques by which sales were made to Latin America and China.[10]

Many Depression-era analysts saw World War I and the interim period which followed it as a struggle between rival imperialisms for colonies, trade, raw materials, and world markets of all descriptions. The rise of Hitler was, therefore, a product of the reparations imposed on Germany by the treaty of Versailles. The annexation of Manchuria by Japan and the Italian Ethiopian invasion could be similarly explained.[11]

Viewing the events of 1936, the Council on Foreign Relations's annual survey concluded that the American people now feared "that another general war was in the making, more destructive than the last, and its Day was not far off."[12] Nevertheless, from Congress to classroom to church, Americans were far from resigned to the war's inevitability.

The 1933 Commission on the Coordination of Efforts for Peace listed 12 international, 28 national, and 17 local peace societies in the United States.[13] A November 1935 poll showed that 75 percent of Americans favored a national referendum before war could be declared. That year Congressman Ludlum of Indiana introduced a constitutional amendment requiring such a referendum. When the Japanese bombed an American gunboat on a Chinese river late in 1937, the amendment suddenly had 218 cosigners.[14]

On April 13, 1934, 25,000 college students left their classrooms in a "Student Strike Against the War." In 1935, when 130 colleges and universities participated nationwide, the number increased to 150,000.[15] In 1935, about 81 percent of 65,000 college students polled by the *Literary Digest* said that they would not bear arms for the United States if it invaded another country. One-sixth refused to fight even if the United States were invaded.[16]

The most imaginative student antiwar group, the "Veterans of Future Wars," was created at Princeton University and spread rapidly to three-hundred college campuses. This "VFW" demanded a $1,000 bonus paid on June 1, 1935 (plus 3 percent interest compounded semi-annually for thirty years) on the grounds that there would be no "postwar" for the soldiers of the next apocalypse. They also asked that their mothers, the Future Gray Ladies of America, be sent to Europe to visit the potential gravesites of their sons. An aptly named Texas representative, Maury Maverick, got this group a congressional hearing, but to no avail.[17]

In replay to a 1931 poll by *The World Tomorrow* magazine, 54 percent of the Protestant ministers responding said they planned "not to sanction any future war or participate as an armed combatant." Sixty-two percent wanted their church to state formally its opposition to war. When the poll (now including Jewish rabbis) was retaken in 1934, 62 percent refused to support wars as individuals and 67 percent wanted their church to take the same stand. Even Catholics argued that no modern war could fulfill St. Augustine and Thomas Aquinas's concept of a "just war."[18]

AMERICAN ANTIWAR DRAMA IN THE 1930s

All night they marched, the infantrymen under pack
But the hands gripping the rifles were naked bone
And the hollow pits of the eyes stared, vacant and
  black,
When the moonlight shone.
"It is eighteen years," I cried. "You must come no
  more.

We know your names. We know you are the dead.
Must you march forever from France and the last,
  blind war?"
"Fool! From the next!" they said.[19]

—"1936," by Stephen Vincent Binét

Nowhere was the concern over the "War to Come" more vividly expressed than on the New York stage, where, from 1932 to 1937, no fewer than seven plays depicted the beginning of World War II, illustrated its causes, and, in doing so, suggested ways by which it might be avoided. They were *Men Must Fight* by Reginald Lawrence and S. K. Lauren (1932), *Peace on Earth* by George Sklar and Albert Maltz (1933), *If This Be Treason* by John Haynes Holmes and Reginald Lawrence (1935), *Idiot's Delight* by Robert Sherwood (the Pulitzer Prize winner for 1936), *Bury the Dead* (1936), *Johnny Johnson* by Paul Green and Kurt Weill (1936), and *The Ghost of Yankee Doodle* by Sidney Howard (1937). Read today, they are monuments to futility, their bad reviews etched on millions of tombstones. Yet they often show remarkable prescience, and, although their targets are America's most cherished institutions, their attacks reveal a belief in the ideals of those institutions that revisionist historians may well envy.

The first of these targets is national honor, with its attendant surrender of individual conscience, often to an economically self-serving, jingoistic propaganda machine which promotes concepts of heroism and masculinity that justify the expense of human life in the name of abstractions. Only second comes capitalism, whose warfare is seen as class-based, with its dividends earned by those who work and fight, and paid to those for whom war is good business. The plays see nationalism as a carrier for capitalism, made palatable by appeals to a religion inextricably linked to messianic xenophobia.

In most of the plays, the experiences of characters in the Great War are cited as documentation. In *Men Must Fight,* the father of Laura Seward's son allows himself to be sacrificed in an air mission he knows is suicidal in order to fulfill what he sees as his duty as a man. The philosophy professor hero of *Peace on Earth* is aware from his service in a World War I propaganda unit of how the beliefs of a country are conditioned. The pacifistic U.S. president of *If This Be Treason* speaks of one of World War I's most moving symbols: "They are all unknown soldiers tonight, waiting for the tombs that I am asked to build."[20] The heroine of *The Ghost of Yankee Doodle* lost her husband in the war, and her wealthy, liberal brothers-in-law have devoted their fortunes to antiwar movements. Robert Sherwood, himself a veteran of the Canadian Black Watch, chose to use his only identified ex-soldier in *Idiot's Delight* to comment on the folly of nationalism. A border resident, he lost not only the war but his country when the Versailles Treaty ceded his Austrian hometown to Italy. At the end of the play, he is in uniform again for his "new country." Only *Bury the Dead,* set in the second year of "the War that is to begin tomorrow night,"[21] avoids direct reference to World War I.

Bury the Dead is also the only play to give no hint of America's new adversaries, whose diversity in the other plays is startling. *Peace on Earth* presumes a lineup much like World War I. *If This Be Treason* is closer to the mark, predicting a Japanese air attack on Manilla more than six years before Pearl Harbor. *Idiot's Delight* also begins with an air attack, this time by Italy on France, with Germany and England drawn into the war by treaty commitments. Most imaginative are *Men Must Fight,* which depicts a 1940 U.S. war with a united South America, fighting with Japanese support, and *The Ghost of Yankee Doodle,* in which the sinking of a cargo ship in the act of carrying war materials to Italy plunges us into war with France.

In the end, however, it does not matter who our opponents are. All the plays find that the seeds of war are self-planted. Once the killing starts, it is national honor that demands it continue. In *Men Must Fight,* an ambassador to Uruguay, politically appointed for his billions, insults the government and is shot by a revolutionary, triggering the Atlantic fleet. It is the Pacific fleet in *If This Be Treason* whose aggressive posture (unreported to the American people) forces Japan to seize Manilla as a defensive buffer zone.

Honor-inspired war is a crime in which the victims create themselves. Even the most articulate of internationalists, a Leninist who has been attending a United Front workers conference in *Idiot's Delight,* protests the bombing of his native France in tones so strident that they lead him to a firing squad. As a jailed worker ruefully notes while enlistments mount in *Peace on Earth*: "They're products of a system. The system goes to war and they go along with it."[22]

Nor is it sufficient that soldiers die for their country. They must be stripped of their individual humanity in order to serve as a mass abstraction in whose name others must die. In *Bury the Dead,* a panicked general realizes the consequences of the living's contact with the discontented dead: "Wars can be fought and won only when the dead are buried and forgotten. How can we forget the dead who refuse to be buried?" (*Bury the Dead,* 149) Perhaps the ultimate example occurs at the end of *The Ghost of Yankee Doodle* when a corrupt newspaper tycoon loses his about-to-enlist son in a plane crash: "My son and the first hero of the new war. . . . I've found a way to tie Steve's death in with national honor."[23]

If the war dead are to be exploited as a mass symbol, the living are to be drummed into lockstep by the mass media. The popular wisdom is expressed by Edwin

Seward, the secretary of state, who sees his peace treaty destroyed in *Men Must Fight*: "After war is declared, it is the duty of every American to surrender his life, his goods, and even his conscience to the command of his country, so that we may face the common enemy with an unbroken and united front."[24] However, his adopted son is closer to the truth when he responds to a similar statement by his fiancée: "Cut it, Peg! Don't talk like the newspapers." (*Men Must Fight,* II, 65) In *Peace on Earth,* a blues singer sways her hips to a throaty "I wanna man with a uniform on" (*Peace on Earth,* III, 116), and when a ship running contraband arms to Italy is sunk by France in *The Ghost of Yankee Doodle,* the subsequent war is sold through the cinema: "They're making a movie called 'The Farragut's Daughter.' It seems the captain of the *Farragut* did have a daughter. She's been through two divorces and runs a pet shop in Atlantic City, but she's going to be Shirley Temple on the screen!" (*The Ghost of Yankee Doodle,* v, 108)

It is in the name of religion that the women of *Bury the Dead* are urged to convince their men to lie down. In *Peace on Earth* (to a chorus of "Onward, Christian Soldiers") a minister calls upon his parishioners to "smite down the Heathen, smite down the barbarian hordes. I say to you that if Jesus walked the earth today he would be the first to join the fight." (*Peace on Earth,* III, 117)

But no matter the means of manipulation, the motivation is money. If "the first casualty of war is truth," the 1930s believed that business collected the life insurance. In *If This Be Treason,* the presidential press secretary cheerily congratulates a steel magnate turned hawkish congressman: "That was a nice jump Jennings Steel took this morning—90 to 110. Broke the amateur record, the boys tell me." (*If This Be Treason,* II, 81) When war news is desired in *Idiot's Delight,* a finger is pointed at a vacationing arms-dealer: "Because he *made* it. . . . Because he is a master of the one *real* League of Nations . . . the League of Schneider-Creusot, and Krupp, and Skoda, and Vickers and Dupont. The League of Death! And the workers of the world are expected to pay him for it, with their sweat, and their life's blood."[25] As a reporter puts it in *Peace on Earth,* "Why do you think they converted your mills, because the world stopped wearing underwear?" (*Peace on Earth,* I, 27)

As the scenes above suggest, the plays see internationalism and class consciousness as the logical alternative to economically mandated murder. *If This Be Treason* invokes international law in the form of the Kellogg-Briand antiwar pact of 1928, and its final scene was inspired by the Russian army's refusal to fire on Petrograd revolutionaries in 1917. *Peace on Earth's* German sailors, upon discovering that they are loading guncotton instead of soap, join with striking longshoremen to throw it in the sea. In *Bury the Dead,* a woman from the slums realizes that her husband's mistake is not in refusing to be buried at the Front, but rather is not standing up to his boss at home. Among the young, Robert Seward of *Men Must Fight* struck a responsive chord: "Wars may be started by old men, but they have to be fought by fellows our own age. If enough of us refuse to take any part in it—and continue to refuse—there won't be any war." (*Men Must Fight*, II, 62)

Nevertheless, of the seven plays, only *If This Be Treason* can truly be said to end happily. On the stage, as in life, the war could not be avoided. Robert Seward was given an "international" education for the purpose of training him as an antiwar diplomat. Yet, at the play's end, he flies off to meet a death as certain as his father's in the last war. In *Peace on Earth,* a character leads his country in joining the League of Nations. But the proposal is only the dream of a man about to be executed, not for the murder with which he is charged, but for his opposition to the war. The four countries one can see from the high window above the staircase in the ski resort of *Idiot's Delight* are interchangeable in their snowy mountain beauty. But that does not prevent the guests who share the resort so amicably from heeding their countries' call to war. Nationalistic paranoia, propaganda, and profits have their way. Nowhere is that unholy trio more prominent than in the group's one antiwar musical.

JOHNNY JOHNSON

> About this time there had arrived from abroad the composer whose *Three-Penny Opera* (on records) might have been described as a Group [Theatre] pastime. We befriended Kurt Weill, and Stella Adler insisted that he must do a musical play for us along lines he had made known in Germany. Weill suggested one day he would like to do an American equivalent of the comic Czech war novel *The Good Soldier Schweik,* which had been dramatized and produced with success in Berlin. . . .
>
> On a visit to Chapel Hill to discuss a play about college life that Paul Green had submitted to us, I learned something about Paul's past that he had never before mentioned. He had fought overseas in the last war and had an intimate acquaintance with the American soldier of that day. I mentioned Kurt Weill's suggestion, particularly since Paul was fascinated with the element of music in the theatre.[26]

Johnny Johnson owes a great deal to *Schweik,* as it does to the picaresque novel and the medieval morality play. Its central character is an Everyman ("John Johnson" was the most common name among American soldiers in World War I) whose pilgrimage through the world changes his perception of it. The play is international and class-conscious (without ever using those terms), suggesting both the necessity for world government based on mediation and the guilt of political/economic leaderships who manipulate nationalist aims for their own benefit without ever facing the conse-

quences personally. *Johnny Johnson* may be unique among American musical comedies in that it denigrates patriotism, questions that any country may have a special relationship with God, and undercuts any comfortable assumptions we may have about love.

The play begins on April 6, 1917, the day the United States entered World War I, and ends on the eve of a new war. Johnny's pilgrimage can be divided into four movements or levels of political awareness. In the first, he searches for a justification of the newly declared conflict and finds it in the idea of a "war to end all wars." In the second, he enlists, planning to stop the fighting by winning the German people away from the warlords who are misusing their loyalty. In the third section, Johnny discovers that his own leaders are as inhuman as those of the Germans and is arrested for trying to end the war. Finally, Johnny realizes that belief in peace is considered as insanity, but continues the increasingly hopeless struggle.

Johnny Johnson opens in a small American town's cemetery at one of those appropriately ambiguous ceremonies of mourning and rededication called a memorial service. The two hundredth anniversary of a treaty with the local Indians provides an occasion for dignitaries to pontificate upon the importance of peace and the horrors of the current European war. The speeches are to be followed by a poem, "Democracy Advancing," recited by Minny Belle Tompkins, the town's prettiest girl, and the unveiling of a statue carved by Johnny Johnson, the town's artisan/artist and tombstone maker. Where this democracy will "advance" is hinted at early when a stirring reminiscence by Civil War veteran Grandpa Joe Tompkins of the charge up Chikamauga Hill turns the crowd into a bloodthirsty, chauvinist mob. Indeed, when word arrives of the declaration of war, the town's citizens, with Minny Belle in the lead, immediately march off to the courthouse to volunteer.

Only Johnny hesitates, unable to comprehend how he and his idol, Woodrow Wilson, came to such radically different conclusions. In frustration he yanks the drawstring hanging down from the monument: "The drape rolls up and reveals the deep-cut bas-relief of a plump-breasted dove with a leaf in its mouth, its wings outspread in flight. Engraved above this in large and wide-spaced letters is the single word, 'Peace'"[27] As the scene ends with the courthouse bell tolling in the distance, the play is provided with the first of its many striking images, and the American peace movement with a fitting symbol: a tombstone.

Minny Belle, Johnny's beloved, is also being wooed by Anguish Howington, a rising young capitalist and manufacturer of rotten mineral water. Eventually, he will become mayor, governor, and a leading supporter of national defense, but at the moment, he is running an understandably distant second in Minny Belle's affections. For her part, Minny Belle calls on both men to enlist, assuming the role of "The Girl He Left Behind," smiling through her tears as she sends her man off to do or die for God and country. A large part of her subsequent communication with Johnny is an oft-repeated "How many Germans did you kill?"—a reminder of how often in wartime a lovely image is used to sell death.

However, Anguish Howington will never see action. Aggie Tompkins, Minny Belle's mother, afraid that Johnny will never "amount to a row of pins (too good—wishy-washy—no backbone)," introduces Anguish to a time-honored Tompkins tradition: self-mutilation in place of service.

Despite *his* lack of physical disabilities, Johnny resists Minny Bell's proddings to enlist: "Like if by going I could help—well . . . put an end to—sort of like the idea of—say, a war to put down war. . . . Then I'd feel the cause was worth it, and I'd go as quick as scat. When it was over the democratic nations maybe could league up and unite for peace." (*Johnny Johnson,* I, ii, 24-25) With the printing of the full text of Wilson's War Address in the evening newspaper, Johnny is naturally off to the recruiting office.

On the troop ship to France, another startling visual image reinforces one of the play's themes—the futility of dying for an abstraction. Before he lies down, Johnny swears an oath to the Statue of Liberty that he will find a way to halt the war. As he sleeps, the statue comes to life and sings the trenody of the dead, in wondering contempt of creatures who will use inanimate idols to justify their actions. (*Johnny Johnson,* I, iv, 44-45)

> A million years I dreamless lay,
> Insensate in the quiet earth,
> Unformed and will-less till the day
> Men rived me forth and gave me birth
> And set me up with queer intent
> To swear their pride and folly by,
> And I who never nothing meant
> Am used to send men forth to die.
>
> (*Johnny Johnson,* I, iv, 44-45)

Time passes slowly in the French trenches, and the soldiers hope for peace. "With genial cruelty," the English sergeant propounds the "merchants of death" theory to explain why it won't come: "This war will last ten years. The big blighters back home don't want it to end. Who'd they sell their munitions to if we have peace? Ten years? It might last twenty." (*Johnny Johnson,* I, vi, 49) Johnny spends his spare time writing letters addressed to the common German soldiers. When others laugh at his belief that the war can be ended with words, he snaps back: "Well, we don't seem to be able to end it with guns." (*Johnny Johnson,* I, vi, 54) A vet-

eran English soldier describes the Christmas of 1914, when the two armies sang carols to one another, played a soccer game between the trenches, and exchanged gifts. An American private—a Chicago gangster in civilian life—reads John 3:16 from his Bible, prompting a chuckle from Johnny: "I was just thinking the Germans are praying to the same God on their side too. Human begins are a funny race, ain't they?" (*Johnny Johnson,* I, vi, 57)

The Bible of Private Fairfax is not the only religious artifact used to prop up questionable actions. Amidst the shattered tombstones of a shell-torn churchyard, Johnny encounters the enemy in the form of a cleverly hidden sniper: "a huge black wooden statue of Christ, leaning a bit awry and showing in its posture something of the beaten and agonized torture of an El Greco figure. . . . And now, through a great wounded hole in the breast of Christ where the heart should be, is pushed the ugly muzzle of a telescopic rifle with a silencer attached. The muzzle comes to rest on the outstretched hand of the Redeemer." (*Johnny Johnson,* I, vii, 62)

When Johnny captures the sniper, he finds under the false mustache and Kaiser Wilhelm helmet only a sixteen-year-old, terrified by stories about the monsters he must fight. The boy's name is Johann (Johnny in German) and his sergeant, who was formerly his teacher, also believes that the ordinary soldiers are being sacrificed for "Faterland und Kaiser."

Johnny releases Johann, sending him back to his own troops with the speeches of Woodrow Wilson and some of his own, "which come to the point quicker," and accidentally picks up a posterior wound in the process. While in the hospital, Johnny learns that his efforts are bearing fruit and general discontent is developing in the German lines. He also learns that the Allied High Command plans to capitalize on this discontent with a new offensive rather than a peace plan.

Seated in the luxury far from the front on the eve of battle, "these mighty keepers of men's destiny speak forth their arguments and plans with puppet pomp and solemn precision," playing out a high-stakes poker game with the lives of their men. The goal is not peace, or even victory, but national honor—with tiny Belgium struggling to earn respect by raising its pledge of dead from 30,000 to 50,000 and exhausted France risking revolution by striving to meet the English bid of 100,000 dead. As he listens, Johnny realizes that he has even more in common with the ordinary German soldier than he had supposed.

During the great battle that Johnny fails to prevent, an organ plays "the stately chant music of a church prayer" while on opposite sides of a stage-rear backdrop the projections of a German and an American priest pray the same prayer for deliverance from the enemy in their respective languages. Johnny finds the body of Johann beside the shattered and mutilated statue of Christ. Kneeling in the mud, Johnny holds the dead Johann, "naked save for a piece of torn cloth tied around his middle, his body marked with sweat and powder burns"—a pietà of waste, rather than redemption: "I had this war stopped once. Maybe there's no sense in that. They said so. But you wouldn't say so—no, you wouldn't. . . . Would you!" (*Johnny Johnson,* II, iii, 96)

Johnny returns to America and the confines of an insane asylum, where he is incarcerated as a "peace monomaniac." Late in the play, we are shown an assembly of elderly men, many of whom have the appearance of well-known U.S. senators and other dignitaries. A man resembling Thomas R. Marshall, Woodrow Wilson's vice president, presides over them, and for a moment it seems that we are listening again to the debate over the establishment of the League of Nations: "The disorganized countries of the earth, frightened, suspicious, jealous of one another—loaded with the ever-increasing weight of vast armaments—sufficient already to destroy every human being under the sun—are praying to someone to show them the way out of their dilemma. . . . And in this covenant of a united world we show them." (*Johnny Johnson,* II, vi, 110)

The timelessness of this argument—more relevant today than it was in 1936—cannot be denied, and after heated discussion, the League is this time approved. The assembly is then quieted for an appearance by the new chairman of the hospital board, Anguish Howington (now married to Minny Belle), and we realize that we are still in the asylum, where to make peace the first order of business is the mark of insanity.

At the play's end, Johnny, now freed from the asylum, stands on a street corner selling wooden toys he has carved in the shape of living things. A Boy Scout—accompanied at a distance by his mother (Minny Belle)—tries to buy a toy soldier from Johnny, an item he does not make:

> "I'm named after my father. He's mayor of the town, you know. And he's going to be governor. . . . Daddy says that we're in for another big war and all the people have got to be ready to keep the enemy from destroying us." [*From the distant stadium where the people are gathering, cheering is heard and then the soaring, somewhat hysterical voice of a political rabble rouser in a splurge of raspy, indistinguishable words—even as Gog Magog from the Bible or a Tower of Bable madness.*]
>
> (*Johnny Johnson,* II, vii, 119-20)

We have come full circle to a new memorial service. Alone, Johnny continues to sing his song of hope, refusing to be drowned out by a brass band blaring the "Democracy March."

FROM ISOLATIONISM TO INTERNATIONALISM

In the presidential-election year of 1936, the foreign policy plank of the Republican Party platform pledged "to promote and maintain peace by all honorable means not leading to foreign alliances in foreign affairs." The Democrats (whose candidate won a landslide 46 out of 48 states) went even further in their platform, promising to "work for peace and to take the profits out of war; to guard against being drawn, by political commitments, international banking or private trading, into any war which may develop anywhere."[28]

Given the realities of American political parties, it can be safely assumed that antiwar isolationism was what the American voter wanted. Yet five years later, on December 10, 1941 (thirteen months after electing the same presidential candidate to an unprecedented third term, and three days after the Japanese bombing of Pearl Harbor), a poll found that the nation had approved Congress's declaration of war by 96 percent in favor to 2 percent opposed.[29] What happened to change our minds?

A plausible answer might be "Nothing." Our war with Japan began when Japan attacked us. At the time when the poll was taken, we were not yet at war with Germany and Italy. That would come the next day, when they declared war on us. In this scenario, our participation was an act of pure self-defense of our lives and our national honor.

Such an analysis, however accurate, falls somewhat short of the whole truth. Until well into the twentieth century, the United States had maintained a traditional neutrality, partly derived from geography and partly from our view of ourselves. In the 1930s, the neutrality was reinforced by our economic circumstances, revisionist views of our involvement in World War I, our always ambivalent relationship with communism, and a very real concern with the military might of Germany.

NEUTRALITY AND THE 1930S

George Washington's farewell address may have warned his countrymen "to steer clear of permanent alliances," but he was neither the first nor the last of the Founding Fathers to give that advice. Between the world wars, it was common to imagine that our two-ocean cushion could effectively quarantine us from any undesirable foreign contract. Perhaps we were close enough in time to remember that the United States had devoted the whole first half of the nineteenth century to extending its geographic borders against the British, French, and Spanish influences that surrounded it. The Louisiana Purchase, the War of 1812, the annexations of Florida and Texas, the War with Mexico, the Gadsden Purchase, the division of Oregon, and even the Civil War were in part attempts to define a continent free of European pressures. By the end of the nineteenth century, Americans were calling this process Manifest Destiny. Still later, revisionists called it the beginning of imperialism. It was really self-preservation.

This is not to suggest that American expansion had no connection to an idealistic philosophy. The American Revolution marks the beginning of the Age of Revolution (roughly 1775-1850), the political parallel to the Age of Romanticism. The United States is largely a Romantic country. Its early leaders were the intellectual children of Jean-Jacques Rousseau and John Locke. The likelinesses of their fathers are stamped on its institutions and documents, of which Thomas Jefferson's *The Declaration of Independence* is only the most obvious example. America saw itself as the haven of individual accomplishment, in harmony with nature, and in opposition to older, man-structured societies which Romantic philosophy saw as a corruption of God's original creation. As historian Paul Seabury put it:

> In conventional American folklore, populistic nationalism has rested upon certain assessments of America's novel relationship to world politics. The New World, which the nation represented, was pervaded by an individualistic and egalitarian ethos. It was juxtaposed to an Old World; its newness arose from the fact of America's recent birth and settlement (which rendered it in a certain sense "historyless"); its newness depended upon the newness of applied principles. The *novus ordo seculorum* was not simply the antithesis of the Old World. It was a qualitatively new and better system of politics.[30]

Our traditional neutrality, then, has been a fortunate blend of realpolitik and religion. The Depression probably reinforced both. The classic horror films of the times are thinly disguised metaphors depicting the dangers of departing from God's (and the American) Way. *Dracula* (1931) with its suave European aristocrat sucking the lifeblood out of innocent American beauty, clearly warned against involvement with Continental decadence. Only the Cross and the shining light of the sun can protect us against the undead children of the European night. On the level of practical politics, any officeholder publicly more concerned with international affairs than the day-to-day survival of his constituents would have had a short political life. The quotes from the 1936 foreign policy planks are easy to excerpt because the originals were so short.

Earlier in the chapter, we took note of the "merchants of death" theory—the supposition that our entry into World War I was engineered by industrialists who traded American blood for inflated profits. Another widely advanced revisionist theory was that we had become, during the war, a pawn of British foreign policy. Under this hypothesis, Great Britain always follows a strategy of "divide and rule," supporting the second military power on the Continent as a means of checking the ambitions of the most powerful. Prior to World War I, it was not German militarism that threatened democratic freedoms, but rather German mercantilism that threatened British imperialism. After the war, however, Germany was bereft of all armaments and curbed by huge war reparations, while France maintained a large standing army and (after 1932) a military alliance with Russia. To counter France, Great Britain supported Germany's rebuilding of its navy. Even as late as 1934, Montagu Norman arranged for the Bank of England to loan Hitler 750,000 pounds.[31]

In World War I, the path America had followed to "save democracy" had been greased by British indoctrination—a mechanism amply documented in such books as Harold Lasswell's *Propaganda Technique in the World War* (1927), James Squires's *British Propaganda at Home and in the United States from 1914 to 1917* (1935), and Horace Peterson's *Propaganda for War: The Campaign Against American Neutrality, 1914 to 1917* (1939).[32] As a second world war began, Hitler was just another British-created Frankenstein monster to many Americans, and the idea that we should defend Great Britain again seemed cruelly absurd.

Furthermore, many Americans and Britains believed that a strong Germany would be a stabilizing factor in Europe. In 1937, Lord Lothian, later Great Britain's ambassador to the United States and its most effective propagandist in the period between their respective entries into World War II, expressed the idea that German control could end the Depression in Central Europe: "Germany and the smaller countries to the east and south are largely economically correlative, and the present economic sub-division of Eastern Europe cannot be permanent."[33] When, on March 12, 1938, Austria yielded to German military pressure and allowed itself to be incorporated into greater Germany, Senator William E. Borah of Idaho, the author of the 1936 Republican foreign policy platform, wrote a constituent: "Austria was really a German state and the Versailles peacemakers had ruined, crippled and dismembered it, and [it] could not stand alone."[34]

As it happened, neither could Czechoslovakia. In September, Germany demanded that that country (itself a polyglot product of the Versailles Treaty) surrender the Sudetenland, Czechoslovakia's German-speaking western border. Great Britain and France, nominal allies to the Czechs, vacillated and appealed to the United States. On September 26, President Roosevelt sent telegrams urging peace to the heads of all the states involved. At the same time, he refused a French request that he offer to mediate the dispute and Chamberlain's request for radio time to explain British policy. The following day, Roosevelt sent two more telegrams: one to Hitler, assuring him that the United States took no responsibility for ensuing negotiations, and one to Mussolini, asking him to influence Germany toward peace. At the Munich conference on September 29-30, Hitler offered a choice: appeasement or war. Without American support and without consulting the Czechoslovakian government, Great Britain and France yielded. Hitler declared himself satisfied. Germany would require no further acquisitions of land in Europe. In a radio address, American under secretary of state Sumner Welles was delighted, seeing the post-Munich era as presenting the best opportunity since Versailles to establish "a new world order based upon justice . . . and law."[35] Late the following March, Germany occupied the remainder of Czechoslovakia, and two weeks later Italy annexed Albania without opposition.

Thirty days after Munich, Orson Welles and the Mercury Theatre of the Air broadcast their version of H. G. Wells's *War of the Worlds* over CBS radio. It was told in the form of radio news bulletins interrupting regularly scheduled programming—such as those with which the public had become very familiar during the year's European crises. Of the six million people listening, approximately 20 percent believed America was actually being invaded. Follow-up questionnaires, however, showed that many believed the attackers were not actually Martians, but rather German airships in disguise.[36]

The Spanish Civil War

At Munich, England and America embarked on similar courses for different reasons. In Spain, often cited as the classic case of appeasement, their motives were very similar: a sense that they had more to fear from Communist Russia than from Fascist Germany. As George Orwell asserted: "In essence it was a class war. If it had been won, the cause of the common people everywhere would have been strengthened. It was lost, and the dividend-drawers all over the world rubbed their hands. That was the real issue; all else was froth on its surface."[37]

That there was an uprising in Spain surprised no one. By the twentieth century, Spain's two most venerable institutions, the Crown and the Church, had declined greatly in popular support. A military dictatorship was in force for much of the twenties, and King Alfonso XIII fled the country in 1931. Coalitions of first the Left and next the Right ruled the following five years, until the elections of February 1936, when a Left-Center alliance was victorious. Months of unrest followed, and on July 17 a faction of the military, primarily led by General Francisco Franco in Spanish Morocco, went into open revolt. The immediate availability of German transports to ferry Franco's troops from Morocco clearly established the ideology of his rebellion.

On August 15, 1936, Great Britain and France pledged to "rigorously abstain from all interference, direct or indirect, in the internal affairs of Spain." Within two weeks, nearly two dozen other nations, including Italy, Germany, and the Soviet Union, pledged nonintervention and agreed to establish an international committee to enforce an embargo on all arms sales. Nevertheless, within six weeks, Germany and Italy had supplied Franco with dozens of tanks, nearly 200 warplanes, and 10,000 rifles and machine guns. By January, 20,000 Italian "volunteers" (one-fifth of the eventual total) would be in the rebel zone.[38]

For the Western democracies, however, it was "eyes left." As early as January 1925, the State Department was checking rumors of an impending Comintern-guided revolution against Spain's military dictatorship. In December 1930, when a Republican overthrow of the monarchy misfired, American charge d'affaires Sheldon L. Crosby attributed the insurrection to "very decided left and Comuno-Bolshevist influences in this country doubtlessly directly inspired from Moscow."[39]

Equipment from Soviet Russia did bolster the defenses of the Republican government. However, Italian troops and armor, fresh from their conquest of Ethiopia, and German air power and the Condor Legion, which had recently occupied the Rhineland, made up much of the Fascist military force in Spain.[40] Modern air warfare began with terror bombings of civilians in Madrid, and then in April 1937, in Guernica—the inspiration for Pablo Picasso's impression of his birthplace's destruction.

The Spanish Civil War was replete with ugly ironies. On August 2, 1936, Admiral Jean Darlan—later to become infamous as a Fascist collaborator in German-occupied France—warned an international group about "the establishment of a Francist regime in Spain allied with Italy and Germany." Sir Samuel Hoare, the first lord of the British Admiralty, scoffed at Darlan: "On no account must we do anything to bolster up Communism in Spain, particularly when it is remembered that Communism in Portugal, to which it would probably spread, . . . would be a grave danger to the British Empire."[41] As late as 1938, Lord Londonderry, former British air minister, wrote: "The robust attitude of Germany, Italy and Japan, which whole-heartedly condemn communism and bolshevism . . . is an attitude of mind which is not properly appreciated in this country."[42]

As was already suggested in Chapter 1, America's relationship with communism was slightly more complex. Its promise of hegemony to industrial workers was less of a physical threat than a threat to our ideological identity. Abroad, however, it was a menace to our multinational corporations, and we sensed its shadow on every trade agreement with a country with marginal standards of living.

Furthermore, if American politicians had no reason to worry about Spanish communism, they did have to be concerned with Catholic voters in the United States. In the early weeks of the war, hundreds of priests and nuns were indiscriminately slaughtered as "Fascist fifth communists," and although anticlerical feelings were not limited to the Communists, their professed ideology did provide fuel for yet one more stand against "godless atheism." Even Pope Pius XI openly supported the Fascists.

Unfortunately for the Republican government (which tried seriously to limit its excesses), the working-class Left also provided the most effective military defense against Franco's rebels. The International Brigade, which provided 40,000 anti-Fascist volunteers (including 3,000 Americans in the Abrahm Lincoln Brigade) was also recruited largely from Communists. In addition, whatever Russia cost in goodwill, she was not always able to make up in support. Initially generous in goods and equipment, Russia was within the year bogged down in a major civil disturbance of its own—the Great Purge Trials. Between 1937 and 1939, the Communist Party was expunged of one-third of its membership, including 214 of its top army commanders. The decimation was even higher in the navy.[43] Other than a few advisors, Russian participation in the Spanish Civil War was limited by necessity.

Stalin ceased support of the Republican government in the summer of 1938, but by then many non-Russian participants, including Orwell and Arthur Koestler, had become disillusioned by the men of the NKVD (People's Commissariat of Internal Affairs) among the Soviet advisors, who were more concerned with enforcing Party conformity than preserving Spanish democracy.

America's Neutrality Act, which had been extended on February 29 until May 1, 1937, did not cover civil wars. Therefore, on August 7, the State Department declared a moral embargo, requesting that American companies treat the Spanish situation like a war between two national belligerents. When a New Jersey scrap dealer insisted that business superseded morality and tried to sell airplane parts to the Republican Loyalists, Congress passed special legislation blocking the sale of war materials to Spain. The legislation went into effect on January 8, 1937, and was lifted immediately after the fall of Madrid on March 28, 1939, signalled Franco's victory.[44] When the skies over Madrid became quiet, the blitzkrieg of Poland was only five months away.

In February 1937, Joseph E. Davies, the American ambassador to Moscow, was surprised to find that European diplomats in the U.S.S.R. believed that an understanding between Hitler and Stalin was not beyond possibility. In the following two years, Russia sought in vain for Western help in Spain. On May 3, 1939, Foreign Commissar Maxim Litvinov, the architect of the Popular Front Movement, was dismissed from office and replaced by V. I. Molotov.[45] On August 18, 1939, Germany and Russia concluded a trade treaty, and five days later, Hitler announced a Nazi-Soviet non-aggression pact. Freed of the fear of a two-front war, on September 1 Germany invaded Poland. Unable to vacillate any longer, Great Britain and France declared war on September 3. "Fascism," said Molotov, "is a question of point of view."[46]

In the end, it is impossible to disagree with the assessment of Julio Alvarez del Vayo, Republican Spain's last foreign minister: "Today, no one should be able to deny that the collapse of the Spanish Republic was due to Non-Intervention. . . . [Events] have confirmed our contention that appeasement, which reached the limits of folly in Spain, would lead inevitably to war."[47]

THE CURTAIN RISES ON INTERVENTIONISM

For twenty years, I've devoted myself to decrying war and the war makers, agitating for disarmament, for a world commonwealth. But more and more, I began discovering to my horror that my facts and my arguments were being used in ways that I never intended, by rabid isolationists, by critics of democracy, even by Nazi propagandists. And . . . it's knocked the props from under me.[48]

—*Flight to the West* by Elmer Rice (1940)

Anti-Fascist drama was neither frequent nor unheard of between Hitler's ascendancy to the German chancellorship in 1933 and Pearl Harbor. S. N. Behrman's Comedy of Manners suffered under the strain of his protest against anti-Semitism in *Rain from Heaven* as early as 1934. The story that a German-Jewish music critic tells about the annihilation of the Last Jew was a parable then, but the Third Reich was already planning how to turn it into a reality. Georgi Dimitroff, the Bulgarian Communist falsely tried for setting fire to the Reichstag, provided a hero for two plays of 1934: *Dimitroff,* a (Marxist) New Theatre League agitprop piece written by Group Theatre moonlighters Art Smith and Elia Kazan; and *Judgment Day,* a thinly disguised full-length treatment by Elmer Rice. The same story inspired *Till the Day I Die,* a more imaginative one-act play which Clifford Odets wrote as a companion piece for the Broadway production of *Waiting for Lefty* in 1935. Sinclair Lewis's novel *It Can't Happen Here,* as dramatized by the author and John Moffit in 1936, provided an occasion for the Federal Theatre's most heroic production effort—the opening of twenty-one separate performances in seventeen different cities on the same day[49]—but not its finest play. The subject was a Fascist overthrow in the United States, a possibility also warned against by Elmer Rice in *American Landscape* (1938). That same year, *Kiss the Boys Goodbye* by Claire

Boothe (Luce) hid an allegory of a Fascist takeover so well that those who did not read the preface to the published version could be excused for missing the point. More interesting from our thematic standpoint, and, ultimately, from the standpoint of drama as well, were the agonizing reappraisals of authors who had earlier opposed wars of any kind. The farce of "neutrality" in Spain and the 1938 Nazi annexations of Austria and the Sudetenland resolved their conflict. At the beginning of 1937, Maxwell Anderson's *A Masque of Kings* suggested that any overthrow of tyranny could only bring about a counter-tyranny, and the hero of his *High Tor* decided that nothing was worth fighting for and headed west. However, by *Knickerbocker Holiday* (1938), Anderson's protagonist decides in favor of a democracy which is less efficient in removing freedom than the corporate state, and in *Key Largo* (1939), King Mc-Cloud finally concludes that it is more important for values to survive than individuals. During the Spanish Civil War, McCloud abandoned his men when they refused to retreat from a military position which was untenable in a war that was already lost. Given a second chance, he sacrifices himself to destroy a more personalized fascism in the form of the gangster, Murillo: "A man must die for what he believes—if he's unfortunate enough to have to face it in his time—and if he won't, then he'll end up believing in nothing at all—and that's death too."[50]

Irwin Shaw, the author of *Bury the Dead,* also wrote about ordinary men fighting back against gangsters in *The Gentle People* (1939), a Group Theatre-produced allegory about the necessity for peace lovers to resist fascism. The same year the Group produced *Thunder Rock* by Robert Ardrey (of whom we shall hear later). In conversations with ghosts from the past, the play's lighthouse-bound hero decides that the progress of mankind is inevitable, and he cannot withdraw from the world simply because the evil that opposes it is just as inevitable.

In the postscript to the published version of his 1936 Pulitzer Prize winner, *Idiot's Delight,* Robert Sherwood, who had fought with the Canadian Black Watch in World War I, predicted the effect of a second world war: "The world will soon resolve itself into the semblance of an ant hill, governed by commissars who owe their power to the profundity of their contempt for the individual members of their own species."[51] In 1938, however, he won his second Pulitzer for *Abe Lincoln in Illinois,* about "a man of peace who had to face the issue of appeasement or war."[52] His Lincoln decides to oppose slavery even if it divides the Union. Following the Russian invasion of Finland, Sherwood won his third Pulitzer in 1940 for *There Shall Be No Night,* in which a scientist who has spent his life investigating the causes of insanity suddenly finds his country and family trapped by the madness of war. Ironically, by

1943, when Alfred Lunt and Lynn Fontanne took the play to London, Russia was again an ally of the Western democracies, and Sherwood was forced to reset the action during the Italian invasion of Greece.[53] In *Watch On The Rhine* (premiering April 1941), Lillian Hellman could have faced a similar problem with a hero who was both German and Communist.

WATCH ON THE RHINE

Lillian Hellman's *Watch on the Rhine* is the perfect American political drama. It has a very specific political purpose, but very little political theory. What theory exists in the play is spoken by a child. The values of the adult world are embodied in action, and, as in any good political drama, there is one action to which the audience can contribute after the curtain is down. Although we are presented with logical arguments in support of that action, it is the emotional appeal of the situation and the characters with whom we identify that motivates us. Even the setting has made its peace with the realities of American commercial theatre production, and every incident in this advocate of interventionism takes place in the living room of a well-to-do American family, not far from Washington, D.C.

In its early nineteenth-century origins, its space, its simplicity, and above all, its eclecticism, the Farrelly living room is a metaphor for America. It has its own traditions and has encompassed many visions that have co-existed without losing their individuality. The front door is unlocked, and always has been. On the wall is a portrait of Joshua Farrelly, who, without every appearing, will be in some ways the most important character in the play. It is he who gives this family/nation its particular flavor, and it is his values that must be perpetuated. It is Hellman's particular genius that without ever leaving this living room or introducing a single bona fide Nazi into it, she brings home to America the realities of the war and makes the best possible case for our participation in it.

The house is owned by Fanny Farrelly. An old-line Washington aristocrat, she is consciously imperious, demanding, unreasonable, manipulative, and charming. One of the chief targets of all these qualities is her son, David, a Washington bachelor and lawyer whose actions, ideas, and taste in women Fanny compares unfavorably with those of his father. Joshua Farrelly was a diplomat, Renaissance man, and the sole architect of Fanny's standard of values. Extended guests in the household are Teck de Brancovis, a Romanian count whose current American exile is the result of a wrong guess taken when the Nazis came to power, and his wife, Marthe, an American heiress whose fortune and affections the count long ago dissipated. Marthe is now in love with David, and in-house relationships are becoming strained.

Watch on the Rhine is set late in the spring of 1940, at a time when German forces are knifing their way through Belgium on their way to Paris. But this action is never referred to. The uproar in the house is because Sara, Fanny and Joshua's other child, is returning home for the first time in twenty years. Shortly after World War I, Sara married Kurt Muller, a German engineer, and they settled (much against her mother's wishes) in his homeland where they raised three children. In recent years, however, Sara's letters have carried frequently changing postmarks, both from within Germany and from the countries on its borders, and have been increasingly less specific about the family's daily life. When they arrive, it is on an earlier-than-expected, cheaper, train. They have had no breakfast and Sara's dress is obviously outdated. The children show extraordinary discipline, but are amazed at the house's luxury and, especially, its unlocked front door. The real enigma, however, is Sara's husband, Kurt, who is outside of the family's frame of reference, but who strikes a chord of recognition in the more worldly, opportunistic Teck de Brancovis.

Kurt's task in America is to pick up money donated to the anti-Fascist cause. Hellman's task is to take this German national, World War I American opponent, and likely Communist, and create a hero with whom American audiences can identify. To do this, she invests him with typical American heroic virtues.

To begin with, Kurt is a man of action, not talk. Because opportunities to demonstrate anti-Fascist heroism in an upper-class living room are necessarily limited, Hellman assigns the task of explaining Kurt's attitudes to others.

When we want to know what Kurt's beliefs are, we need only listen to his children. What would seem priggish in the speech of a grown man is precocious and endearing when baldly stated or even slightly garbled by nine-year-old Bodo. And yet we are fully aware that the children, who have been constantly on the move under ideologically hostile circumstances, could only have learned their ideals from their father and mother. As ever, well-disciplined, intelligent children with good sets of values reflect with favor on their parents.

In addition, who could be a more convincing witness to a man's quality than an enemy. Desperate to obtain the reentry into the Nazi political sphere that the exposure of a major underground anti-Fascist would get him, Teck borrows a "most-wanted" list from the German embassy. Reviewing Kurt's record as a courier, a soldier in Spain, a spy, and a pirate radio operator, even the count expresses admiration for Kurt's skill and bravery.

When Kurt finally is moved to action, it is to return to Germany to save fellow agents captured by the Gestapo. With him he intends to take the money raised in America to fight fascism—money that Teck demands for not identifying Kurt to German intelligence.

Teck is presented as the antithesis to Kurt. The image of a Central European count who achieved his sustenance through blood money is too tempting to resist. Teck is a Dracula challenging Kurt's Parsifal, acknowledging no commitment beyond himself. He is not even a true Nazi, as power is his only ideology. Both Teck and Kurt made judgments about National Socialism in 1931. Kurt correctly evaluated its evil and enlisted in the fight against it. Teck underestimated Nazi strength, and found himself dealt out of a game more important to him than the principles of those who control the deal. The ability to deliver Kurt might earn Teck another hand, but for political gamblers—like actors—timing is everything: "[Some Fascists] came late: some because they did not jump in time, some because they were stupid, some because they were shocked at the crudity of the German evil, and preferred their own evil, and some because they were fastidious men. For those last, we may well some day have pity. They are lost men, their spoils are small, their day is past."[54] But Teck is clever, patient, and ruthless. He wants only to be on the winning side, and he will not play his hand recklessly. To see the Tecks of the world on the other side is to see that the odds are not in your favor.

If Teck and Kurt represent the extremes of Europe, Fanny, David and Marthe stand in for uncommitted America. Marthe married Teck at seventeen to fulfill her mother's fantasies. Now only Teck's threats hold this marriage together. The count and countess are the beneficiaries of the Farrellys' "unlocked front door" and unsuspicious natures. The family now must pass through the classic pattern of American involvement with European fascism: first, failure to recognize its existence; second, failure to see it as a personal threat; and third, appeasement.

When Fanny and David realize that Kurt will not give up the underground's money and that Teck is equally determined to betray Kurt to German intelligence, they agree to protect Kurt by meeting Teck's price. However, Teck's true aim is power, not wealth, and Kurt is aware that such ambitions cannot be bought off: "If they are willing to try you on this fantasy, I am not. What ever made you think I would take such a chance? Or *any* chance? You are a gambler. But you should not gamble with your life." (*Watch on the Rhine*, III, 387-88)

Once again, Teck has underestimated commitment, and Kurt kills him (overpowering him, by the way, not with a perfectly convenient Luger, but in true American fashion with his bare hands). It is now time for the Farrellys to make their commitment. They can either call the police and retain their isolationism, or they can give Kurt the car and the two days he needs to hide the body and get a head start, and become accomplices to a murder. Two factors will influence their decision.

The first is Fanny's late husband, Joshua Farrelly, by whose standards she measures everything. In a key early exchange, the connection is made between Joshua and Kurt when Fanny reminds her eldest grandchild (and her husband's namesake) that he bears a great name. "My name is Muller," the boy replies. (*Watch on the Rhine,* I, 341) After Teck's murder, Fanny reflects on one of Joshua's last statements: "A Renaissance man . . . is a man who wants to know. He wants to know how fast a bird will fly, how thick is the crust of the earth, what makes Iago evil, how to plow a field. He knows there is no dignity to a mountain, if there is no dignity to man. You can't put that in a man, but when it's *really* there, and he will fight for it, put your trust in him." (*Watch on the Rhine,* III, 392)

Nine-year-old Bodo provides an early description of Kurt: "He likes to know how each thing of everything is put together." (*Watch on the Rhine,* I, 349) By the time Fanny remembers the discussion above, we have already seen Kurt as a loving husband and father and as a musician, are aware of his past as an engineer and a farmer, and have been shown documentation of the exceptional range of his anti-Fascist activities. We know that he is willing to give his own life and to kill in the service of his beliefs. We are also able to anticipate Fanny's decision.

But then how could she decide otherwise? For if Kurt is anti-Fascist Europe and the Farrellys are America, it must be concluded that Joshua, Babette, and Bodo belong to both. In 1941, Hellman has revived the concept of the Popular Front by embodying it in the international family. In *Watch on the Rhine,* we are urged to fight, not for abstractions or foreigners, but for children whom we have come to love and look upon as our own. In a moving farewell to his children, Kurt recalls a family reading and discussion of *Les Misérables:*

> The world is out of shape, we said, when there are hungry men. And until it gets in shape, men will steal and lie and . . . kill. But for whatever reason it is done, and whoever does it—you understand me—it is all bad. . . . But you will live to see the day when it will not have to be. All over the world, in every place and every town, there are men who are going to make sure it will not have to be. They want what I want: a childhood for every child. For my children, and I for theirs.
>
> (*Watch on the Rhine,* III, 394-95)

With this evocation of the World Family, Kurt returns to Germany, leaving Sara and his children in the Farrelly house, taking with him Fanny and David's commitment and the money they had raised to bribe Teck, soon to be followed by other Americans who believe they might turn Kurt's dream into a reality.

WAR AND THE REVELATIONS OF CASTE

> The Negro is a born anti-fascist. Long before Hitler walked across the face of the earth we knew him. For three centuries, we tasted the bitterness of Nazism under the name of lynchocracy. . . . Yet we love America.[55]
>
> —Adam Clayton Powell, Jr. (1945)

It was W. E. B. Du Bois who predicted in 1903 that, for America, "the problem of the Twentieth Century is the problem of the color line."[56] At no time has that problem been more obvious than during wartime. George Washington was but the first of many American commanders to reverse himself on the policy of using black troops, but only because he had been outflanked by Lord Dunamore, the royal governor of Virginia, who promised freedom to any slave who would join the British army. By April 1776, the British tactic was so successful that South Carolina instituted the death penalty for blacks who fled to the enemy side or persuaded others to do so.[57]

Nine months after the declaration of the War of 1812, blacks were permitted to enlist in the navy, and eventually formed nearly 20 percent of what were integrated crews. At least 600 black troops at the Battle of New Orleans contributed to the worst British defeat since Yorktown.[58]

The North was widely perceived as losing the Civil War before Lincoln's Emancipation Proclamation, followed by War Department Order G0143 on May 22, 1863, allowing Negro enlistment. In the war against the Gray, 180,000 of those who fought for the Blue were black. They received fourteen Congressional Medals of Honor; the casualty rate of their units was 40 percent higher than white units; and their pay was 40 percent lower.[59] The fact that black troops were segregated for the first time did not seem to dampen their enthusiasm for battle.

When the peacetime army was reorganized in 1866, four black regiments were established as a permanent part of the nation's armed forces. The Ninth and Tenth Cavalry regiments—called "Buffalo soldiers" by the Indians—fought the Plains Wars, and "Smoked Yankees" (as the Spanish called them) preceded Teddy Roosevelt's Rough Riders up San Juan Hill during the Spanish-American War. But even before "Black-Jack" Pershing (given his nickname because he commanded black troops) led the Tenth Cavalry across the Mexican border in pursuit of Pancho Villa, Woodrow Wilson's administration was preparing for World War I by reducing the black role in the military.[60]

In January 1913, a House of Representatives bill called for repeal of the statutes authorizing the four black regiments. In July 1914, Representative Frank Park of Georgia introduced a bill to prevent blacks from serving as commissioned or noncommissioned officers. Two years later, southern congressmen sponsored a bill against the enlistment or reenlistment of "any person of the Negro or colored race," in the U.S. military service.[61] In July 1917, Colonel Charles Young, one of only three black line officers at the onset of the war, was "invalided" out of service, lest his next promotion give the United States its first black general.

Only one out of every nine black draftees was assigned to a (segregated) combat unit.[62] The Ninety-second Infantry Division was commanded by white American officers, who characterized their men as cowardly, stupid, and sexually brutal. The Ninety-third served under the French, spending 191 consecutive days in a frontline position without ever losing a foot of ground. The French awarded the Ninety-third the Croix de Guerre and requested that the United States send to France all black units which could be spared. A French liaison officer serving in General Pershing's headquarters sent to the French Military Mission a memo entitled "Secret Information Concerning Black Troops": "We cannot deal with them on the same plane as with white American officers without deeply wounding the latter. We must not eat with them, must not shake hands or seek to meet with them outside the requirements of military service. We must not commend too highly the black American troops."[63]

In 1917, the first year of American participation in World War I, the number of lynchings at home doubled to thirty-eight. In 1918 there were sixty-two lynchings of blacks, and in 1919—the first full year of "peace"— seventy-seven Negroes were lynched, including ten veterans, several still in uniform.[64] This was the year that the American Legion segregated black members, and that on France's Bastille Day march, the British and the French included black troops, and the Americans did not. In 1924, when a federal bureau dedicated a plaque inscribed with the names of servicemen killed during the war, the black dead were immortalized on a separate tablet. In 1930, when Gold Star mothers and widows were invited to visit the European graves of their loved ones dead in the war, black women were sent on a separate ship.[65] In 1935, when the Lincoln Memorial was dedicated in Washington, D.C., no blacks were included in the ceremonies honoring the Great Emancipator, and those attending were not allowed to sit in front.

With the approach of World War II, the past was prelude for the Negro serviceman. The first Navy Cross winner of World War II was Dorie Miller, a mess steward aboard the USS *West Virginia* at Pearl Harbor, who pulled his wounded captain to safety and, taking over a machine gun, brought down four Japanese planes. In 1944, Dorie Miller died on a ship sunk by Japanese torpedoes. He was still a messman, the only position in which the Navy accepted blacks when he enlisted.[66]

> Everything in the beginning was aimed at making World War II a race war. It was proclaimed as "a white man's war"—against "those yellow rats," the Japs. We were formally at war with Germany and Italy but we set up concentration camps for Japanese only, even when they were American born. . . . While we, the colossus of the West, slumbered, the Japanese slaughtered millions of Chinese with our scrap iron and our gasoline. Yet, we included Chinese from our shores. Even after we had been at war for some time, the yellow men, good enough to fight our enemy, were not considered good enough to emigrate to America.[67]

It is a record of racism that Hiroshima and Nagasaki did little to alleviate.

On the Western Front we faced an opponent whose goal of world domination was stated in terms of racial superiority so marked that it justified genocide. Hitler, the architect of this policy, was clearly a monster and a madman. The comparison with our own racial policies should have embarrassed us, but it was an embarrassment we concealed remarkably well. As Alabama's senator William B. Bankhead (the father of Tallulah) put it when he was asked if a Nazi was superior to a Negro: "He's white, isn't he?"[68]

Nevertheless, the value systems of all combatants are early casualties in wartime, and war's most fortunate side effect is that the less sustenance a value has, the sooner a survival-minded society will jettison it. During World War II, blacks made inroads, not only in the military, but in the economy as well. In the autumn of 1940, the disappointment of blacks in the position they had been given in the country's burgeoning wartime economy and expanding military began to be heard from the NAACP (National Association for the Advancement of Colored People), the National Urban League, and newer organizations like the Allied Committees on National Defense. The proposal which most caught the public's imagination was that of A. Philip Randolph of the Brotherhood of Sleeping Car Porters calling for 50,000 blacks to march on Washington, D.C. on July 1, 1941. On June 24, the president issued Executive Order 8802, prohibiting discrimination in defense production industries and establishing the President's Committee on Fair Employment Practice (FEPC) to enforce this policy. The percentage of black workers in skilled, semiskilled, and single-skilled jobs increased by two-thirds between 1940 and 1944. The percentage of black-filled federal jobs in Washington, D.C. doubled, with most of the gains made in positions from which blacks had previously been barred.[69]

In the spring of 1946, with the war safely over, Congress cancelled the FEPC, not to reactivate it until new civil rights pressures were felt in 1957. About the March on Washington's second demand, desegregation of the armed forces, EO-8802 said nothing.[70] The implications of that segregation were found in other than duty situations. In defiance of all science, the Red Cross "Jim-Crowed" blood donations—at a time when the blood blank of England was under the direction of a black American doctor, Charles Drew of Howard University.[71] The white officers of a black artillery company in Pennsylvania determined that "any association between the colored soldiers and white women, whether voluntary or not, [will] be considered rape," and authorized the death penalty.[72] Particularly galling to the average black soldier were privileges and hospitalities accorded to German prisoners of war—as recorded by poet Wittner Bynner.

> On a train in Texas German prisoners eat
> With white American soldiers, seat by seat,
> While black American soldiers sit apart—
> The white men eating meat, the black men heart.[73]

In *The Fire Next Time,* James Baldwin expressed the feelings of many black Americans: "The treatment accorded the Negro during the Second World War marks, for me, a turning point in the Negro's relation to America. To put it briefly, and somewhat too simply, a certain hope died."[74]

Nevertheless, blacks in the armed forces became a presence to be reckoned with by friend and foe alike during the war. The air corps began to accept black applications in March 1942. The navy opened up branches other than messman in April. The Coast Guard began accepting blacks in May, followed by the marines in June. By the end of 1944, there were 40 percent more black officers in the military than there were enlisted men in 1939. Except in the air corps, the training of officers was integrated from the beginning of the war. In August 1944, the navy began to experiment with integrated ships. The need for infantry replacements during the Battle of the Bulge forced the first army modification of segregation. Negro enlisted men who were willing to sacrifice all rank were allowed to volunteer for all-black platoons within white companies. A survey taken in seven of the eleven divisions where this policy was tried found that 84 percent of the white officers and 81 percent of the white enlisted men found that black soldiers performed "very well" in combat, while the 16 percent of the officers and 17 percent of the enlisted men thought blacks did "fairly well." Performance ratings were highest where combat was the most severe.[75]

Given a taste of equality and success, how would the black soldier react to a South determined to maintain its traditions? According to the National Opinion Research Center of the University of Denver in August 1944, four out of five white Southerners expected race relations to grow worse after the war.[76] "You know what my main job in the Army was? It was to make my men believe they were fighting for a better world for themselves, as well as for you. . . . All through this war we've been living on promises—we've had to fight on faith. Now the promises have to be made good, even if we have to begin at the beginning."[77]

Shortly before the end of World War II, Gunnar Myrdal, the Swedish sociologist, published the classic treatise on white racism, *An American Dilemma,* One of its features that was to have great significance in the postwar mutual readjustment between blacks and the South was the "White Southerner's Rank Order of Discrimination"—a listing of privileges whites were least likely to yield to blacks: (1) interracial sex, (2) social equality, (3) desegregated public facilities, (4) the right to vote, (5) equality before the law, and (6) economic opportunity.[78]

DEEP ARE THE ROOTS

The major thematic points of *Deep Are the Roots* (opening September 26, 1945, and set the preceding spring) are probes of the "Rank Order of Discrimination," tests of its flexibility and response risk. The plot, however, creaks along on such readily recognizable elements as a linen-suited, silver-haired southern senator, a missing family heirloom, a conveniently remembered lynching, and a porcine southern sheriff. Arnaud d'Usseau and James Gow take no chances with their protagonist—a college graduate, academic enough to be offered a Ph.D. scholarship in biochemistry from the University of Chicago, and altruistic enough to reject it for the principalship at the local "colored" school; sensitive enough to play Othello at fourteen, and sensible enough to reject the grown-up Desdemona when she offers herself; and, in addition, an officer and gentleman with six Battle Stars, seventeen pieces of shrapnel in one leg, and a Distinguished Service Cross. Aligned with First Lieutenant Brett Charles and the winds of change are Genevra ("Nevvy") Langdon, his childhood friend, and Howard Merrick, a liberal northern novelist, unnecessary *raisonneur,* and fiancé of Nevvy's sister, Alice. Preservers of tradition are Alice Langdon, Senator Ellsworth Langdon (the girls' father), and Bella Charles (Brett's mother and a longtime family servant). Two other characters, Honey (a maid scorned by Brett) and Roy Maxwell (a cousin of the family and a congressional candidate) are important because they have no fixed ideological position and, thus, are indicators of the flow of public opinion. It is Honey who yields to the senator's pressure to help frame Brett for the theft of a watch, and who later recants when she comes to understand the temper of the black community. And it is Cousin Roy who, like any good politician, senses that a change is coming in the power structure and wants desperately to gauge its direction so that he can get out in front and lead it.

As the son of Senator Langdon's trusted housekeeper, Brett Charles grew up with the senator's two daughters. Alice was his teacher and mentor, guiding him through Fisk University, and obtaining for him the University of Chicago scholarship. Nevvy was his playmate until Alice caught then rehearsing the murder scene from *Othello* when Brett was fourteen and Nevvy twelve. Brett's independence in choosing the local principalship over the northern scholarship distresses Alice. Reluctantly, she supports him to the extent of insuring that a new (segregated) schoolhouse will be built, but presumes that other past niceties will continue to be observed: for example, that this ex-officer and decorated war hero will continue to enter from the side door, and that this school principal will get a note from her permitting his withdrawal of a book from the public library. He will not attempt to travel on a "whites only" Pullman car to an Atlanta conference which she considers Communist-infiltrated, and he will not—literally on pain of death—lay hands on her younger sister.

For his part, Senator Langdon dislikes Alice's championship of Brett, not realizing that her patronizing is merely the flipside of his contempt. He glowers when his daughter's fiancé dares to shake hands with Brett, and disputes Merrick's eyewitness account of Brett's conduct in the public library. The senator senses that Brett is the vanguard of change, and his suspicions are especially aroused when Brett chooses to take the school-master job: "Sounds innocent enough; but I can see through you. Get hold of the colored folk around here and make them dissatisfied—put ideas in their heads—stir up trouble. . . . If he told you the truth, you'd probably find that over there he slept with white women!" (*Deep Are the Roots,* I, 61)

For all his stereotypical ravings, the senator is closer to the truth than any other white in the household. Brett's collisions with tradition are not those of a native son with a bad memory. They reflect a specific political agenda. The black community did not just offer him the principalship. He actively campaigned for it by letter before even arriving home. His speech of acceptance is designed to confront rather than conciliate: "telling our good-hearted darkies that segregation *is morally wrong* and that it won't always exist." (*Deep Are the Roots,* II, 102) Before going into the library, Brett makes sure there is "no written law or regulation prohibiting colored folk entering that front door." (*Deep Are the Roots,* II, 109) The Atlanta conference on racial problems gives him a double opportunity for challenge: The subjects to be discussed—education, job opportunities for returning servicemen, the poll tax, and so on—are important, but so is the method of getting there. Brett has Nevvy buy him a Pullman car ticket to see if they will turn him away while he is wearing his country's uniform. Inasmuch as interstate transportation was the issue upon which the Supreme court made its "separate but equal"

decision in *Plessy vs. Ferguson* (1896), Brett is disputing constitutional law as well as local tradition. Whatever his actions, Brett's motivations are clear: "In Italy I was an American officer. Here I'm a nigger. I had forgotten some of the things that means."[79] (*Deep Are the Roots,* II, 84)

It could be said that Brett's relationship with Nevvy is his only nondeliberate flouting of the "Rank Order of Discrimination." While Howard Merrick (Alice's fiancé) sees Brett as the New South, someone with whom he can "connect" without having to endure the embarrassing obsequiousness with which many southern blacks "get over" on whites, Nevvy's emotions are more complex.

On one level, Brett is her first love, now grown tall and heroic. On the other, she is moved to expiate white southern guilt. When Brett is arrested falsely for the theft of a family watch, inscribed, ironically, "Honor Above All," Nevvy sees in the face of her father the sick ecstasy she witnessed as a child on the faces of a lynch mob: "There will be men sitting on the porch of the Country Club, and they'll talk about what a problem the 'niggers' are getting to be, and there'll be a little bit of that look on their faces. . . . When [my father] searches Brett's room it's a tiny little lynching. It's an act of cruelty and he's enjoying it." (*Deep Are the Roots,* II, 118-19)

In her way, Bella is as much of a traditionalist as Langdon and Alice. However, her motivations are far different. Bella is fully aware that the sincerity of Nevvy and Brett's feelings will not keep Brett alive if the rest of the white community realizes that there is a relationship between them. The South of 1945 has upper and lower classes, but it lives and dies according to caste. Bella's standing as the senator's housekeeper and Brett's education and military record place them high in the class system of the black community, but it cannot give them the rights and privileges which are reserved for whites, many of whom are their inferiors in all other measurable factors. The penalty for attempting to cross the caste line would be death for Brett and ostracism for Nevvy—a bitter irony for Bella, who knows that racial sexual barriers are quite permeable from the top: "No we ain't good enough to claim a place among the chosen people. But we're good enough to share the white man's bed. And when we do, God punishes us as he sees fit—but nobody calls the sheriff." (*Deep Are the Roots,* III, 184-85)

It is Alice who calls the sheriff when a letter from an anonymous redneck accuses her of walking late at night with Brett. Realizing that Nevvy has been mistaken for her, Alice reveals how "deep are the roots" of her prejudice: "I have to do what I know is right." (*Deep Are the Roots,* II, 144)

Alice's betrayal challenges the widespread myth that it is the aristocracy, the "quality folk," who will bring abut equality for blacks. Booker T. Washington inaugurated the policy of "courting the best people," believing that as Negroes increased in thrift, education, and efficiency, whites would gradually admit them to full citizenship. This doctrine of conciliation, expediency, and gradualism was adopted without substantial change by a whole generation of southern black leaders. The flaw of the doctrine lay not in the sensibility of its actions, but in that it encouraged an "inferior caste" mind-set. Since Negroes were discriminated against for their "blackness," visible evidence of white ancestry—first courted for its social and economic value—came to be seen as a good in itself, creating a caste within a caste.[80] The cry of the sixties, "Black is beautiful," is a political affirmation as well as an aesthetic one. Aligning the black cause with white values and white upper-class interests was a "double whammy," ignoring the possibilities of both racial solidarity and class solidarity across the caste line.

The racial solidarity does come. Like many another political hero, Brett achieves more as a martyr than as a crusader. Not only does Bella denounce the senator and Alice in blistering terms, the rest of the help quits in protest of the family's breach of faith. Honey returns the "Judas money" the senator gave her to lie about the watch because of "colored town" pressure. Even in the white community, there are those who understand that such blatant discrimination has repercussions. Cousin Roy Maxwell is terrified by the fact that returning veterans will actually make blacks the majority in the country, but his sense of injustice is touched as well: "I'm told he was beaten up while wearing his uniform. There are a lot of people who don't like that. And you know something? I'm one of them." (*Deep Are the Roots,* III, 164)

Brett is released and put on a train to the North. He leaves it, however, and returns to the Langdon house for a final confrontation: "My men were right. . . . They knew when it comes right down to it, it's white against black—the black underneath. They had the satisfaction of hating—hating all white people." (*Deep Are the Roots,* III, 195)

As Merrick points out, this is an unworkable conclusion for Brett. To hate all white people, he would have to hate Nevvy too. For her part, Alice admits the nature of her prejudice and asks for forgiveness. Nevertheless, it is not until she allows Nevvy and Brett to make their own decision concerning marriage that we discern any real progress in her attitude.

Actually, the progress asked for has been moderate, even by 1945 standards. The code that the play finally affirms could be described as the "White *Northerner's*

Rank Order of Discrimination," in that economic, political, and legal equality are upheld, but except for the abandonment of certain social forms, separateness is never seriously challenged. Housing is never discussed, and as a school principal, Brett is concerned with a new building, not integration. Even miscegenation is a tantalizing red herring, as Brett twice turns down offers of marriage which Nevvy makes without so much as on-stage hand-holding. At the final curtain, race relations have extended only to the point of Brett dropping the obligatory "Miss" in speaking to Alice, who is moved to spontaneously shake his hand.[81]

CASTE LISTS IN THE POSTWAR THEATRE

Deep Are the Roots was the earliest and most successful of four plays by white authors dealing with the problems of the returning minority veteran during the 1945-1946 New York theatre season. Robert Ardrey's *Jeb* had a similar story: a disabled Silver Star winner gets a job running an adding machine in the mill of his Louisiana hometown, only to lose it because running an adding machine is a white man's job. Later, he is driven out of the South on a fabricated charge of dating a white woman. As his would-be employer explains it, "When we say a nigra wants a white man's girl, what we mean it's a nigra wants a white man's job."[82] Despite the presence of Ozzie Davis and Ruby Dee in the cast, *Jeb* failed. Maxine Wood's *On Whitman Avenue* (produced by and starring Canada Lee) centered on a white liberal college girl's attempt to rent an apartment in a restricted suburb to a Negro veteran and his wife, and was slightly more successful.

In the long run, a play in which no blacks appear probably had a greater affect on race relations in the United States than any of the preceding three. Arthur Laurents's *Home of the Brave* explored the guilt of a Jewish soldier who survives the ambush in which his gentile best friend dies. The play ran only sixty-seven performances in 1945-1946, but as a film with the Jewish character replaced by a black, *Home of the Brave* was one of the top motion pictures of 1949.[83]

We should also note a play that focused on another aspect of black/white relationships that war seemed to exacerbate in the United States: lynching. In 1944, Lillian Smith published a novel entitled *Strange Fruit,* taking her title from the Lewis Allan song which Billie Holiday made so unforgettably her own, and in 1945, Ms. Smith and her sister, Esther, dramatized the story. Late the following year, even before *Deep Are the Roots* had finished its Broadway run, President Truman was listening to national black anger over postwar lynchings. His Civil Rights Commission, appointed that December, took only ten months to produce a report entitled *To Secure These Rights,* a blueprint for many of the court decisions of the fifties and for the congressional civil rights acts of the mid-sixties.

As the forties waned, America was becoming increasingly aware that her internal affairs could not be separated from the impression she had upon the rest of the world.

> A lynching in Georgia is not ignored by textile workers in Bombay. A race riot in Detroit does not escape the notice of the dock worker in Shanghai. The existence of our Negro ghettos is known to the Chinese peasant and the South African mine worker even though many Americans continue to ignore it. . . . During World War II we appealed to such people for support against a regime that posed a theory of racial superiority as part and parcel of a program of world domination. We are appealing to them now in our world wide opposition to what many regard as an equally repugnant ideology; we seek their support against a dire threat to our national interest and to the democratic potentials of other countries. . . . The colored races over the world are likely, however, to judge us by what we do and not by what we say. . . . As the world becomes smaller, our neighbors not only can look over our back fence; but they also can examine the contents of our closet. Many of them—black or yellow or of some other hue—will not like what they see.[84]

For good or for ill, civil rights was now a battlefield in the Cold War, and the two would never be separated again.

Notes

1. Quoted by Lawrence S. Wittner, in *Rebels Against War: The American Peace Movement, 1941-1960* (New York: Columbia University Press, 1969), 3.

2. The idea of a League of Nations (referred to in the 1917 War Address as a "League of Honor") evolved from a suggestion made to Wilson by Charles William Eliot, the former president of Harvard, on August 6, 1914. Edwin Borchard and William Lage, *Neutrality for the United States* (New Haven: Yale University Press, 1937), 236-37.

3. Charles G. Fenwick, *American Neutrality: Trial and Failure* (New York: New York University Press, 1940), 17.

4. Robert A. Divine, *The Illusion of Neutrality* (Chicago: University of Chicago Press, 1962), 83.

5. Divine, *The Illusion of Neutrality,* 68-72.

6. Divine, *The Illusion of Neutrality,* 65-66.

7. H. C. Engelbrecht and F. C. Hanighen, *Merchants of Death: A Study of the International Armament Industry* (New York: Dodd, Mead, 1934), 9.

8. George Seldes, *Iron, Blood, and Profits* (New York: Harper & Brothers, 1934), 13.

9. Walter Millis, *Road to War: America 1914-1917* (Boston: Houghton Mifflin, 1935), 82-102.

10. Robert A. Divine, *The Reluctant Belligerent* (Chicago: University of Chicago Press, 1965), 9.

11. John K. Nelson, "The Peace Prophets: American Pacifist Thought, 1919-1941," in *The James Sprunt Studies in History and Political Science,* Vol. 49 (Chapel Hill: University of North Carolina Press, 1967), 60-61.

12. Divine, *The Reluctant Belligerent,* 9.

13. Charles Chatfield, *For Peace and Justice: Pacifism in America 1914-1941* (Knoxville: University of Tennessee Press, 1971), 94-97.

14. Wittner, *Rebels Against War,* 29.

15. Hal Draper, "The Student Movement of the Thirties: A Political History," in *As We Saw the Thirties,* ed. Rita James Simon (Urbana: University of Illinois Press, 1967), 168-72.

16. Chatfield, *For Peace and Justice,* 259-60.

17. Nelson, "Peace Prophets," 32-33.

18. Nelson, "Peace Prophets," 24-26.

19. Stephen Vincent Benét, "1936," in *Selected Works of Stephen Vincent Benét, Vol. 1: Poetry* (New York: Farrar & Rhinehart, 1942), 454-55.

20. John Haynes Holmes and Reginal Lawrence, *If This Be Treason* (New York: Macmillan, 1935), I, 53. Subsequent references to this play will be included within the text.

21. Irwin Shaw, *Bury the Dead,* in *New Theatre and Film, 1934 to 1937,* ed. Herbert Kline (San Diego: Harcourt, Brace, and Jovanovitch, 1985), 130. Subsequent references to this play will be included within the text.

22. George Sklar and Albert Maltz, *Peace on Earth* (New York: Samuel French, 1936), III, 92. Subsequent references to this play will be included within the text.

23. Sidney Howard, *The Ghost of Yankee Doodle* (New York: Charles Scribner's Sons, 1938), vii. 152. Subsequent references to this play will be included within the text.

24. Reginald Lawrence and S. K. Lauren, *Men Must Fight* (New York: Samuel French, 1933), II, 58. Subsequent references to this play will be included within the text.

25. Robert E. Sherwood, *Idiot's Delight* (New York: Charles Scribner's Sons, 1936), II, i, 79-80. Subsequent references to this play will be included within the text.

26. Harold Clurman, *The Fervent Years* (New York: Hill and Wang, 1945), 172.

27. Paul Green, *Johnny Johnson* (New York: Samuel French, 1936), I, i, 14. Copies of this play, in individual paper covered acting editions, are available from Samuel French, Inc., 25 W. 45th St., New York, N.Y. 10036 or 7623 Sunset Blvd., Hollywood, Calif. 90046, or from Samuel French, (Canada) Ltd., 80 Richmond Street East, Toronto M5C, 1P1, Canada. Other references to the play are in the text.

28. Wayne S. Cole, *Roosevelt and the Isolationists* (Lincoln: University of Nebraska Press, 1983), 199.

29. Wittner, *Rebels Against War,* 34.

30. Paul Seabury, *The Rise and Decline of the Cold War* (New York: Basic Books, 1967), 88-89.

31. Porter Sargent, *Getting US into War* (Boston: Porter Sargent, 1941), 20-21.

32. Donald Drummond, *The Passing of American Neutrality, 1937-1941* (New York: Greenwood Press, 1968), 40-41.

33. Sargent, *Getting US into War,* 29.

34. Cole, *Roosevelt and the Isolationists,* 278.

35. Drummond, *Passing of American Neutrality,* 77-78.

36. Howard Koch, *The Panic Broadcast* (Boston: Little, Brown, 1970), 103.

37. George Orwell, "Looking Back on the Spanish War," in *A Collection of Essays by George Orwell* (San Diego: Harcourt Brace Jovanovich, 1946), 203.

38. Douglas Little, *Malevolent Neutrality: The United States, Great Britain, and the Origins of the Spanish Civil War* (Ithaca, N.Y.: Cornell University Press, 1985), 246-48.

39. Little, *Malevolent Neutrality,* 50-53.

40. During World War II, Hitler was to present a neutral Spain with a 374-million-reichsmark bill for services rendered.

41. Little, *Malevolent Neutrality,* 240-41.

42. Sargent, *Getting US into War,* 26, 28.

43. M. K. Dzienwanowski, *A History of Soviet Russia* (Englewood Cliffs, N.J.: Prentice-Hall, 1979), 130-31.

44. Divine, *The Illusion of Neutrality,* 170-71.

45. Drummond, *Passing of American Neutrality,* 49, 87.

46. Quoted by Alan Landsburg, in *Between the Wars: The Spanish Civil War* (Wilmette, Ill.: Films Incorporated, 1978).

47. Little, *Malevolent Neutrality,* 17.

48. Elmer Rice, *Flight to the West* (New York: Coward-McCann, 1941), I, 22-23.

49. John O'Connor and Lorraine Brown, *Free, Adult, Uncensored* (Washington, D.C.: New Republic Books, 1978), 59.

50. Maxwell Anderson, *Key Largo* (Washington, D.C.: Anderson House, 1939), II, 118.

51. Robert E. Sherwood, "Postscript," *Idiot's Delight* (New York: Charles Scribner's Sons, 1936), 189-90.

52. Quoted by Gerald Rabkin, in *Drama and Commitment: Politics in the American Theatre of the Thirties* (Bloomington: Indiana University Press, 1964), 110.

53. Malcolm Goldstein, *The Political Stage: American Drama and Theater of the Great Depression* (New York: Oxford University Press, 1974), 352.

54. Lillian Hellman, *Watch on the Rhine,* in *Modern American Plays,* ed. Frederic G. Cassidy (Freeport, N.Y.: Books for Libraries Press, 1970), III, 383. Subsequent references to this play will be included within the text.

55. Adam Clayton Powell, Jr., *Marching Blacks* (New York: Dial Press, 1945), 4-5.

56. W. E. B. DuBois, *The Souls of Black Folk* (New York: New American Library, 1969), ix.

57. Jack D. Foner, *Blacks and the Military in American History* (New York: Praeger Publishers, 1974), 6-15.

58. Foner, *Blacks and the Military,* 22-25.

59. John S. Butler, *Inequality in the Military: The Black Experience* (Saratoga, Calif.: Century Twenty-One Publishing, 1980), 23.

60. Foner, *Blacks and the Military,* 106-7.

61. Butler, *Inequality in the Military,* 24-25.

62. Richard M. Dalfiume, *Desegregation of the Armed Forces* (Columbia: University of Missouri Press, 1969), 13-14.

63. Butler, *Inequality in the Military,* 25-26.

64. Arthur Waskow, *From Race Riots to Sit-in, 1919 and the 1960's* (Garden City, N.Y.: Doubleday, 1966), 9-12.

65. Foner, *Blacks and the Military,* 124-27.

66. Foner, *Blacks and the Military,* 173-74.

67. Powell, *Marching Blacks,* 126.

68. Powell, *Marching Blacks,* 32.

69. Arnold Rose, *The Negro in America* (New York: Harper & Brothers, 1948), 134-35.

70. Dalfiume, *Desegregation of the Armed Forces,* 115-22.

71. Powell, *Marching Blacks,* 127.

72. Dalfiume, *Desegregation of the Armed Forces,* 69.

73. Foner, *Blacks and the Military,* 153.

74. James Baldwin, *The Fire Next Time* (New York: Dell Publishing Co., 1964), 76.

75. David G. Mandelbaum, *Soldier Groups/and Negro Soldiers* (Berkeley: University of California Press, 1952), 103-4.

76. Powell, *Marching Blacks,* 6-7.

77. Arnaud d'Usseau and James Gow, *Deep Are the Roots* (New York: Random House, 1945), I, 63-64. All subsequent references to this play will be noted in the text.

78. Rose, *The Negro in America,* 24.

79. Brett's experience in the post office was typical. After World War II many black veterans in the South were unable to take advantage of the GI Bill of Rights, because post offices would not give them the necessary applications. Rose, *The Negro in America,* 178.

80. Adam Clayton Powell, Jr., called self-hatred, which resulted from blacks valuing a white skin "one of the most disastrous forces retarding the progress of the race." Powell, *Marching Blacks,* 12-13.

81. The fates, which subsequently befell some of those people involved with the original production of *Deep Are the Roots,* were scarcely encouraging. On the tour of the play through the South, the original Brett Charles (Gordon Heath) became so depressed from the discrimination he faced that he quit the show and moved to Paris, from where he never returned. Arnaud d'Usseau and the play's director, Elia Kazan, found themselves accused of being Communists before the House Un-American Activities Committee in the 1950s. The original Nevvy (Barbara Bel Geddes) wound up on *Dallas.*

82. Robert Ardrey, *Jeb,* in *Plays of Three Decades* (New York: Atheneum, 1968), II, 149.

83. Rob Edelman, *"Home of the Brave,"* in *Magill's Survey of Cinema, Second Series* 3, ed. Frank M. Magill. (Englewood Cliffs, N.J.: Salem Press, 1981), 1047.

84. Wilson Record, *The Negro and the Communist Party* (Chapel Hill: University of North Carolina Press, 1951), 2-3.

Albert Wertheim (essay date winter 2004)

SOURCE: Wertheim, Albert. "The Dramatic Art of Uncle Sam: The Government, Drama, and World War II." *American Drama* 13, no. 1 (winter 2004): 86-119.

[*In the essay below, Wertheim surveys wartime drama, emphasizing examples of didactic plays written to support the war effort.*]

On 14 June 1943, the reigning glitterati of the day—Eleanor Roosevelt, Mayor LaGuardia, the Duke and Duchess of Windsor—were at the 46th Street Theatre in New York to witness the Broadway Production of five one-act plays written and enacted by enlisted men. The performance, called *The Army Play by Play,* was the remarkable product of the U.S. Army and the genius of famed producer John Golden. In his introduction to published version of the plays, Golden explains how, working with the Army Special Service Staff, he created the John Golden-Second Service Command One-Act Prize Play Contest, which garnered 115 original playscripts from American soldiers at Army camps around the nation (x-xii).[1] A selection committee that included Elmer Rice and Russel Crouse chose the five best scripts. Golden asserted that staging the plays "became my patriotic duty" (xii-xiii). The five scripts chosen were mounted and presented on Broadway to raise funds for the Soldiers and Sailors Club. The opening performance earned $100,000, and the plays were subsequently staged for President Roosevelt at Hyde Park. They officially opened on 2 August 1943 at the Martin Beck Theatre in New York, where they ran for 40 performances; and later were produced at theatres and army bases around the country.

One wonders what sort of instructions Crouse, Rice, and the others on the selection panel might have given about the desired criteria for choosing scripts. One also wonders about the 110 scripts not chosen. Their whereabouts are not known; and it would be illuminating to know what issues they raised. But the five surviving and published scripts that comprise *The Army Play by Play* were written and performed, for the most part, by first time playwrights and by inexperienced, non-professional actors all drawn from the military. The five one-acters of *The Army Play by Play* thus provide a unique glimpse of wartime military life and the war effort as it is seen and dramatized by servicemen. In part, Golden's enthusiastic and somewhat magniloquent praise is apt. He writes:

> The plays that you are about to read are, in a sense, folk-plays, for they express with disarming simplicity, the sentiments, the expressions spoken, listened to and

lived through by our boys in the service—gleaned from their experiences as characters participating in the greatest drama the world has ever known. And so it is that these "little plays," born of this great Drama, tell the story, not of death, but of living calmly, alongside death, and laughing at it.

(xiii).

What is interesting about the five plays are the topics they cover and those they do not. Did the selection committee favor particular issues? Is there a reason the atrocities being committed in Europe and Asia were barely mentioned or that the cultural diversity among the troops arises often? We are not likely to know the answers to these questions. It is important to recognize that what we do have in *The Army Play by Play* is a government initiative to use drama in shaping both civilian and troop attitudes toward World War II and American involvement in that war. It is also important as well to value *The Army Play by Play* as five dramatic artifacts that register in fairly undiluted ways the feelings, issues, and points of view of not untalented enlisted men who were encouraged by the military to express themselves through playwriting and whose plays were subsequently performed by ordinary soldiers rather than professional actors. Filled as they are with personal and patriotic feelings of American soldiers, the plays were highly effecive vehicles for boosting the morale of both military and civilian audiences because performances would seem to present truth unvarnished by any professional training or prior agendas by either playwrights or performers.

Three of the five plays contained in *The Army Play by Play* center on barracks life. *Where E'er We Go* by Pfc. John B. O'Dea of Fort Lewis, Washington, is a light-hearted portrayal of restless soldiers waiting for furloughs and battle action while cooped up at dull, rain-soaked Fort Lewis outside Seattle. *Button Your Lip,* subtitled *A Farce in One Act,* by Cpl. Irving Gaynor Neiman stationed in Chanute Fields, Illinois, is a comedy of mishaps and misadventures stemming from misplaced military records and the appearance of 1940s film star Dorothy Lamour in a USO entertainment being performed at the army camp. The third play, *Mail Call,* written by Aviation Cadet Ralph Nelson stationed in Americus, Georgia, is a more serious play located abroad *"somewhere in the Theatre of Operations"* (101) and is centered around the decision of whether or not to open a package of food from home addressed to a deceased comrade and then whether to devour its contents.[2]

What is common to these plays and to others in the volume (as well as to the many plays and films of the period set in army barracks) is the portrayal of a military unity as an American microcosm, an American cross-cultural snapshot. Of course, it is important to interject

that, during World War II, African-Americans were segregated into their own units; and thus the supposed American cross-section is not racial. It is always purely white, devoid not only of African-Americans, but also of Asian-Americans, Hispanics and other persons of color. In *Mail Call,* for example, Johnson is from Oklahoma, Spider from Alabama, Abe Meitelbaum is "a wiry little New York Jew" and the son of a Jewish tailor, Minnick is said to be "representing New Jersey" but with a girlfriend in Montana, and Luckadoo is from Tennessee. The deceased McKinley's family is sketched as a generic American family straight from a Norman Rockwell scene on the cover of *The Saturday Evening Post.* Here, as in so many wartime plays, is the strong message that this is a war that bonds all Americans from all walks of life to face a common enemy, one that threatens American democracy, The American Way of life, and an ineffable American spirit that is, paradoxically, comprised of a national unity that is engendered by the country's very diversity. In many ways the dramas like those in *The Army Play by Play,* scripted an American cross cultural comradeship and worked to dismantle the regionalism and ethnic divisions that were a legacy of the Civil War and that continued to be a force in pre-World War II America. The cultural diversity valorized in these plays, moreover, set the stage as well for the breaking of barriers that took place in the post-war period and continues to this day.

While the Army's playwriting competition was going on and drawing its material from the pens and acting of ordinary servicemen, the Army Air Forces committed themselves to a much larger, splashier project that pulled out all the stops in an attempt to employ the drama for conveying to the American public an image of life in the Air Forces and the commitment of those who serve in that branch of the military. Early in 1943, General H(enry). H(arley). "Hap" Arnold, the Chief of the Army Air Forces (1941-1946), summoned the popular playwright Moss Hart to Washington. Hart had by then made his reputation as the co-author, with George S. Kaufman, of three zany American comedies that had by then become—and are still—classics of American theatre: *Once in a Lifetime* (1930), *You Can't Take It With You* (1936), and *The Man Who Came to Dinner* (1939). He had also written with Kaufman *The American Way* (1939), the serious, patriotic runway hit play dramatizing the history of a German immigrant from his arrival at Ellis Island in 1896, to his life in Mapleton, Ohio, through the loss of his son in World War I, and his own final moments protesting against Fascist elements in his community.

It seems likely that *The American Way* inspired General Arnold to tap Hart for the job of writing what was an enormously ambitious government-sponsored patriotic and theatrical World War II undertaking: *Winged Victory: The Army Air Forces Play* (1943).[3] What the Army wanted was a play, ready for production in fall of 1943, which would extol and promote the Army Air Forces, while reaping profits to support the Army Emergency Relief Fund. To this end, the manpower of the Army was put at Hart's disposal. All he had to do was come up with a winning, patriotic play about the Air Forces. Burns Mantle and Steven Bach both relate how Hart then traveled on a research trip to scores of Air Forces training camps to learn firsthand what life in the Air Corps was like. It then took Hart three weeks to write a *Winged Victory* and seventeen days to stage it (32-33).[4] Or, as one writer put it, "From blue print to happy landing on Broadway, *Winged Victory* was produced in the manner of a new superbomber."[5]

In *Winged Victory,* Hart returned to his fictional town of Mapleton, Ohio, where he had set *The American Way* and which by then was almost as well known to the theatre-going public as Grovers Corners, New Hampshire, in order to create another powerful, moving, patriotic play this time about the young men who eagerly join the Air Forces; their loyal families, spouses and girlfriends; the pleasures and pains of serving one's country in a time of need. *Winged Victory* calls for very few female parts, but there are scores of male parts and an oversized orchestra and chorus, which were all filled by men in uniform. Indeed, over 300 military personnel on stage and an oversized military band in the orchestra pit surely created in the audience a sense of national strength, patriotism, and the will to victory.[6] Several of the actors were already well known stars then serving under the Stars and Stripes; others were on the brink of making their mark as celebrities; and still others, who were drafted for the production but would not go on to post-war careers in the entertainment industry, would remember *Winged Victory* as their one glorious wartime moment in front of the footlights. When *Winged Victory* opened at New York's 44th Street Theatre on 20 November 1943, among the large cast could be found, such names as Cpl. Mark Daniels, Pvt. Red Buttons, Sgt. Kevin McCarthy, Pvt. Barry Nelson, Pfc. Edmond O'Brien, Sgt. George Reeves (in the 1950s to become television's first Superman), Sgt. Ray Middleton, Pvt. Karl Malden, S/Sgt. Peter Lind Hayes, Pvt. Alfred Cocozza (alias Mario Lanza), and Pvt. Lee J. Cobb.[7] Even before it arrived in New York, *Winged Victory* was a smashing success in Boston during its pre-Broadway run; and Burns Mantle recalls the long lines that formed for tickets at the New York box office.[8]

Writing at the heart of World War II in 1943, Moss Hart enunciated not merely America's sense of the war's meaning, but the dawning of a global mission that later dominated the American national agenda during the second half of the twentieth century. Gerald Bordman reports that, "The play ran for six months, then toured widely, earning millions of dollars for the Army Emergency Relief Fund."[9] It is easy now, decades later, to

fault, as Steven Bach does, *Winged Victory* for its sentimentality and unabashed patriotism.[10] But the U.S. was two years into the war. Families were in mourning for sons dead or missing, men were returning from the battlefields wounded and maimed, there seemed to be no end in sight. What could be more appropriate or welcome to mount, on a large stage and with scores of actors and musicians, the undiluted, uplifting patriotism of *Winged Victory,* which foregrounded the physical and moral strength of American troops, suggested in its very title that victory was imminent, and encouraged a war-weary populace to rededicate itself to the struggle? Karl Malden, who was one of the actors, recalls in his memoir, "Civilians thrilled to sight of three hundred young men in uniform."[11] *Winged Victory* may not be the most sophisticated of dramas, but were it judged solely in terms of its national impact and popularity, it would, like Hart and Kaufman's earlier *The American Way,* surely be considered a strong contender for the 'the great American play.'

The Army Play by Play and *Winged Victory* were directed by the government toward both military and civilian audiences. They were produced in New York and traveled elsewhere with a consistent cast of professional and non-professional actors. The War Department and other government branches, however, also and importantly provided dramatic entertainment aimed exclusively at American troops and not at civilian theatre audiences. These entertainments were to be staged at army camps not by a designated, well-rehearsed cast, but by servicemen themselves for their own local diversion and amusement. The government merely provided the scripts and in some cases, instructions for production and advertisement. In 1942, for example, soon after the bombing of Pearl Harbor and American entry into World War II and during the course of the war, the U.S. military issued a series of *Soldier Shows,* which were largely scripts and ideas for troops to entertain themselves with skits, quiz shows, blackouts, reviews, and games.[12] Two of these volumes were USO-Camp Shows entitled "At Ease." The first of these was a collection of comedy sketches and blackouts "For use," as the title page reads, "exclusively in MILITARY AND NAVAL ESTABLISHMENTS By the personnel of the ARMED FORCES OF THE UNITED STATES." The open-ended exclusive copyright for these volumes was not to expire until "six months after the cessation of hostilities" whenever that might be. The USO (United Service Organization), founded in 1941 by President Roosevelt, not only brought professional entertainers to American troops stationed at home and abroad, but provided material, such as that in the "At Ease" volumes, for performance by the troops themselves for the ir own entertainment. A commentator in *Theatre Arts* astutely wrote:

> To soldiers, a show written by their buddies takes on a
> much deeper meaning than the artistic or entertainment
> value of the show itself. It is their show, written for

them, produced for them, and applauded by them. It's a wonderful feeling to sing a song that your pal in the next barracks has written especially for you and your buddies. It's a personal thing, not something that's come to you third hand. It's a personal thing because the chances are that it concerns a subject which only the soldiers know about. In other words, it 'belongs', whereas similar material from the 'outside' is, at best, a good imitation.[13]

The government, in issuing dramatic material to the troops obviously also understood the truth of this statement.

The first USO volume is titled *Comedy Sketches* and is largely comprised of blackouts reprints of comedy sketches from 1930s radio shows like *Baby Snooks* and *Morey Amsterdam*.[14] What seems important is that almost no sketch bears on the war or wartime issues. Rather, they lead the soldier-actors back to a peacetime world when laughing at the follies and errors of others either provided a sense that all was well or offered healthy comic relief from the often grim realities of a country in the midst of a Depression. Most of the sketches are innocuous, though one does wonder about the inclusion of George S. Kaufman's well known one-acter, *If Men Played Cards as Women Do*, and five other imitations of the Kaufman model written by Morey Amsterdam, *If Men Acted in Barbershops as Women Do in Beauty Parlors*, *If Men Attended Fashion Shows as Women Do*, *If Men Gave Showers for Grooms as Women Do for Brides*, *If Men Went Apartment Hunting as Women Do*, and *If Men Went Christmas Shopping as Women Do*. In all these, men satirize women by taking a traditionally gender-coded masculine situation and comically italicizing gender differences using risible feminized language. This in that very male preserve, the barbershop, we have the following feminized dialogue among the men:

WILLSON:

(*sits up beaming*) Hello, men. My, but you two look stunning!

MORGAN:

How can you say that? You know my hair is a sight. (*Takes off his hat to prove his point*) But yours! Stafford and I were just saying how—er—unusual you look in your new windblown.

WILLSON:

(*Flashing a big smile*) It is striking, isn't it? But I'm letting it grow out. (*Runs a hand through it*) I'm sure I'll look better with it "page-boy."

TAYLOR:

Don't you dare touch it. (*Combs it again*) Your hair looks just darling as it is. . . . Now, how about your eye-brows? Think they need a little arching?

(94-95).

The opening stage directions note for *If Men Attended Fashion Shows as Women Do* give an indication of how these sketches were intended to be played. It reads "*All characters play the sketch in a normal, manly manner. The humor results from the fact that men are speaking words and thinking along the lines of women and not from burlesquing their actions or voice inflections*" (98). Still, in light of Allan Bérubé's research and of the anecdote Arthur Laurents relates in his autobiography concerning the all-male production of Claire Boothe's *The Women* at Fort Aberdeen, Maryland, one can but speculate about gay subtexts and revelations may have emerged when these USO-promulgated *If Men . . .* sketches were produced.[15]

It is the second of the two USO volumes that is startling to the contemporary reader; titled *Minstrel Shows*, it contains two full scripts for minstrel entertainment.[16] The tacit assumption is that USO entertainment is meant only for white soldiers in the then segregated U.S. military. This minstrel show volume includes not only script material, but instructions on how to create blackface make-up and how to apply it (10-11). It includes the descriptions of the four comedians or "end men" who play the black roles: Ephus, Asbestos, Chinchilla, and Macbeth. The descriptions of the four men represent what one now recognizes as unsettling racist portraits. The description of Ephus, for example, reads as follows:

End Man #1, whom we have called 'Ephus,' is the small, meek, nervous type. His nervousness manifests itself in many ways, such as: occasional stuttering and stammering; quivering of the lower lip; rolling of the eye-balls; trembling of the body; and difficulty in having his vocal chords function when he is especially frightened.

(9)

Inflected with the markings of racial inferiority, these USO minstrel 'entertainments' for white troops draw upon the mannerisms and language employed by characters in the then popular *Amos and Andy* radio show.

A mixture of song and dance, the scripts derive their humor by enacting a comedy based on the presumed naiveté and inferior intelligence of dark-skinned subalterns. In one monologue, for example, a blackfaced minstrel, telephones Heaven to speak with Uncle Tom. The conversation closes on the following note:

Well, it must be awful nice up there, just sitting around all day, listening to those comics like me and eating fried poultry—(*Listens*) Huh? (*Registers surprise*) You don't eat poultry?? (*He is horrified*) You're not allowed to eat chicken up there? (*Almost pleading*) Not even one innocent little drumstick? (*A look of bewilderment covers his face for an instant*) Uncle Tom, are you sure you're in Heaven??? *CHORD BY ORCHESTRA*

(p. 50)

In another comic routine, a black soldier explains why he has just spent time in the guardhouse, "We wuz in a mock battle and the enemy was coming toward us and our captain yells at us, 'Shoot at will!' And I don't know which one was 'Will', so I shot our top sergeant!" (77). When the mirth subsides, the white soldiers who have laughed at this routine have had reinforced through comedy the reasons that the very thought of having black soldiers in their unit would be not just ludicrous, but dangerous. The texts of these army minstrel shows are not hard to deconstruct; and their implicit message is that blacks are inferior, and that it is good for the safety of all that they are remanded to segregated units.

Evidently, in 1942, the government sanctioned use of minstrel material in a way that validated and enshrined racist archetypes and implicitly endorsed a belief in both the inferiority of African Americans and the need for keeping them segregated. After the war, on 28 July 1948, President Truman issued Executive Order 9981, which brought an end to racial segregation in the American armed forces.

More impressive, however, for both their length and their pointed material, than the USO volumes and the other *Soldier Shows* volumes are the government-issued scripts of three War Department original musicals designed for production by the troops themselves at army camps around the nation: *Hi, Yank; P.F.C. Mary Brown*; and *About Face!*.[17] The music (and possibly some of the lyrics) for all three of these now little-known musicals were written by Pvt Frank Loesser, who was to achieve renown after the war for *Guys and Dolls, The Most Happy Fella, Where's Charlie?*, and *How to Succeed in Business*. Suprisingly, *Hi, Yank* and *P.F.C. Mary Brown* have been lost to the annals of American musical comedy; even Susan Loesser fails to mention them in her biography of her father.

Irving Berlin's World War II revue *This is the Army*, a revision of the one he wrote during World War I, is well known, especially in its 1943 film version, but the three original Frank Loesser shows for the armed forces have more than mere entertainment value. The *Soldier Show* "Blueprint Special" of *About Face!* is the product of a collaboration of remarkably talented individuals. Graced by a comical cover drawing from the pen of then already well-known cartoonist Al Hirschfeld, *About Face!* contains music and lyrics by Frank Loesser assisted by Pvt Hy Zaret, T/Sgt Peter Lind Hayes, Pvt Jerry Livingston and Lou Singer. Many of the sketches are by the gifted comedy writer Pvt Arnold Auerbach. The talent collected for this show is truly impressive. Hayes (1915-1998), who had appeared in *Winged Victory*, was an actor, comedian, and singer, who became a celebrity (often appearing with his wife Mary Healy) in the 1950s and 1960s through popularity of his long running weekly television show, *The Peter Lind Hayes*

Show. Jerry Livingston (1909-1987) is one of the great twentieth-century American popular song writers. His "Mairzy Doats" (1943), written approximately the same time as *About Face!*, was a runaway hit as was his "Fuzzy Wuzzy." He went on after the war to write the musical score for Walt Disney's *Cinderella,* the theme music for the television series 77 *Sunset Strip,* and the popular song "The Twelfth of Never" (1956). In the decades after the war, Hy Zaret and Lou Singer frequently teamed up as lyricist and composer respectively. Together in the late 1950s and early 1960s, they composed a series of recordings called *Ballads for the Age of Science,* which were sung by Tom Glazer, Dorothy Collins, and Marais and Miranda. They wrote the score, in 1947, for *Patrick Henry and the Frigate's Keel: A Musical Legend* by Howard Fast (Decca No.DA-522), and the popular song "Young and Warm and Wonderful" (1958). Zaret is best known as the lyricist for the often recorded song, "Unchained Melody." Arnold Auerbach (1912-1998), who wrote many of the sketches in *About Face!* had already written some of the script for George Gershwin film musical *Lady Be Good* (1941). In the course of his career, Auerbach wrote comedy sketches for Milton Berle, Fred Allen and Al Jolson; with Arnold Howitt he wrote the script for the Harold Rome musical *Call Me Mister* (1946) and together with Howitt and Moss Hart he produced sketches for the musical revue *Inside USA* (1948). He was also a writer for the *Sgt. Bilko* television comedy series, and in 1955 was one of a group of writers who garnered an Emmy for the comedy series *You'll Never Get Rich.*

Together, these talented men were largely responsible for the series of sketches that comprise *About Face!*. The sketches spoof army life and include very funny scenes about an army psychological examination (22-24) and a lecture for soldiers on sex (27-28). The high point of *About Face!* is the satiric scene in which a soldier receives his notice from the Civilian Selective Service, which threatens to draft him back into civilian life. In a comic reversal of those who challenged their draft notices for the military, the soldier here protests his civilian draft notice; and as a result is given some tests. First he is shown "a loud checked suit on a hanger" and asked to identify it. Studying the suit, he pleads, "Gee, it looks familiar, I could swear I've seen it before" (35). Shown "a tray with dishes and a large folded napkin," he again says he remembers them vaguely from his past, but cannot identify them. When "A GIRL IN A SARONG ENTERS," "JOE LOOKS AT HER. HE IS PUZZLED. HE WALKS AROUND HER, LOOKS HER UP AND DOWN, TOUCHES HER CHEEK, THEN HER SHOULDER, THEN HE LOOKS HOPELESSLY AT THE MAJOR." This scene ends with his saying to the Major, "But Major! I've been the Army for two years (POINTS AT THE GIRL) What is it?," to which, before the blackout and curtain, the Major replies, "How the heck do I know? I've been in for twenty!!" (35-36). Once more the government and the writers created a theatrical venue that allowed the enlisted men both in the cast and in the audience to release their tensions by having a laugh at the army and its bureaucracy, even as it took their minds off the bloodshed that spanned two oceans. And as part of the aim of pointing out the comical side of military life, Loesser and his associates wrote for the show "Gee But It's Great to Be in the Army," the humorous song that was to gain national hit status (14-15).

For *Hi, Yank,* Frank Loesser was joined by the talented Lt. Alex North, who became one of Hollywood's most distinguished and sought-after composers, creating the music for such films as *Streetcar Named Desire, Viva Zapata!, Spartacus, The Agony from the Ecstasy, Cleopatra, Shoes of the Fisherman, 2001: A Space Odyssey, The Rose Tattoo, Who's Afraid of Virginia Woolf?,* and *Prizzi's Honor.*[18] The choreography for *Hi, Yank* was provided by none other than Pvt. Jose Limon, whose reputation as a dancer had already been established and who was, of course, to become after the war one of the truly great choreographers in American dance history. Arnold Auerbach was the primary writer of *Hi, Yank*'s sketches.

Although *Hi, Yank* has no real plot, it centers around the figure of the Sad Sack, drawn by cartoonist George Baker, who first appeared in the Army magazine *Yank,* Decades after the war, Baker's *Sad Sack* was a regularly syndicated newspaper cartoon. Baker provided the comical cover with his well-known character and Sad Sack's equally well-known abusive sergeant for the script of *Hi, Yank,* and his wonderful cartoons graced the pages of the published playtext. The *Hi, Yank* volume contains the script, Loesser and North's full musical score, Limon's precise choreography directions, set designs, instructions for set construction, costume designs, lighting designs, and an audience evaluation form.

Soon after *Hi, Yank,* Pvt. Frank Loesser teamed up with Capt. Ruby Jane Douglass, Pvt. Hy Zaret, and Arthur Altman to write *P.F.C. Mary Brown: A WAC Musical Review.*[19] In addition to its entertainment value, *P.F.C. Mary Brown* is an important work because it is one of the very few wartime stage works to focus on American women in the military.[20] Once again, the volume for the revue included not merely the playtext but a full musical score, lighting designs, set designs, a sample program, and Mary Schenk's imaginative costume design.[21] In part, *P.F.C. Mary Brown* seems inspired by the "First Class Private Mary Brown" song that featured in *About Face!* and which reappears in *P.F.C. Mary Brown.* Moreover, one of the comic scenes in *P.F.C. Mary Brown* about issuing regulation WAC uniforms was likewise lifted from *Hi, Yank.* Although its disparate scenes are loosely connected, *P.F.C. Mary Brown* is less a revue and boasts far more plot line than other musi-

cals; it shows some of the concerns that brought women into the military even as it provides a modest window into their life in the WACs. The subject was a timely one, since the WACs was a new organization formed in 1943 to replace the WAACs (Women's Auxillary Army Corps).

The image of Pallas Athena, the Greek goddess whose statues often depict her wearing a military helmet, had been used as the image on the WAC lapel pin. In *P.F.C. Mary Brown,* the writers, a bit weak on their Greek mythology, begin with Pallas Athena's leaving Mt. Olympus and walking out on Jupiter (incorrectly portrayed as her philandering and preoccupied husband), to join the WACs. Since *P.F.C. Mary Brown* was directed by the government to servicemen and service women, it affirmed for the former the place of women in the military and valorized for the latter their commitment to their country's wartime cause.

It is not surprising that the U.S. Army should underwrite entertaining plays designed to inspire patriotism and positive images of armed forces aimed at both the general public and at the G.I.s. Nor is the endorsement and sponsorship of dramatic vehicles and musicals for the entertainment of the troops. It is striking, however, that the Army also used theatre in a more consciously focused way, sponsoring drama designed not for entertainment but for didactic purposes. The Military Training Division of the Second Service Command at Governors Island, New York, prepared dramatic training scripts that were released in mimeographed typescript form and presumably employed around the country. These were used to train military personnel and educate them about preparedness, vigilance, and proper behavior. No authors are cited for these plays, and one wonders who wrote them, for several of them show effective dramatic techniques that inform a heavily didactic tone. What these scripts reflect, moreover, is an impressive trust by the military in the power of drama as an effective way of shaping attitudes and behavior of both officers and enlisted men.

One such script that is particularly poignant is *Death Without Battle,* which was employed to warn of the need to use the army issued anti-malaria cream and mosquito netting.[22] In that play, soldiers have either skipped a training lecture on malaria entirely or have attended and now scoff at the mosquito cream they have been given. By acknowledging the skepticism of the audience and their resistance to the training sessions in general, the script uses its didactic techniques to convert its military audience from skeptics to believers. Under the guidance of Dave, who is distressed by the flippancy of his pals, there are flashbacks Battista Grassi, the nineteenth-century Italian physician who did the pioneering work on malaria and the anopheles mosquito. With his friends still resistant, Dave ends the play with a powerful parting shot: a letter telling him that his brother and several others became ill and died of malaria:

> WHAT DO WE HEAR BUT THAT THE REASON THERE WAS NO RELIEF FOR US WAS THAT AT LEAST HALF THE MEN THAT WERE TO RELIEVE US HAD COME DOWN WITH MALARIA, TOO. AND ON THAT ACCOUNT OF WHAT DO YOU THINK??? ON ACCOUNT OF THE FACT THAT THEY WOULDN'T USE THAT MOSQUITO CREAM OR THOSE NETS.
>
> (11)

The drama and acting work in *Death Without Battle* to render the pathos of Dave's letter and the fortitude of Grassi meaningful to an initially skeptical or hostile audience. The play not only casts the heedless characters in the role of villains but, more importantly moves an audience of recruits to take their mosquito netting and anti-bacterial salve seriously. Clearly the Army recognized that the magic of theatre can be more effective than lectures in a classroom setting.

Other plays in this didactic genre include *Stripes,* which is directed to military officers, and meant to remind them of their responsibility as care-givers to the men who serve under them; and *The Eternal Weapon,* which unsubtlely drives home the point that soldiers must recognize and value the importance of training regardless of how may sometimes appear to seem like purposeless drudgery.[23] In the latter play, a soldier goes back in time and discovers the importance of preparedness and training in past wars. He is then projected into the future to discover his own death and those of seventeen others stemming from his cavalier attitude toward training and his consequent lack of preparedness in battle. A Pfc gives a didactic eulogy:

> No, these men here will not speak. How can they, when in the heat of battle, his chance came to do the things he should have learned—when upon HIS knowledge of the arts of war his company in that vital moment fully depended—and he failed and dragged them with him. Seventeen men—seventeen good soldiers—seventeen futures now lie soundless—and in seventeen parts of America, seventeen families hang the death crepe over their hearts forever . . . here lies the untrained soldier and around him lies his murderous work.
>
> (IV - 2)

Like many of the other training plays, *The Eternal Weapon* depicts soldiers questioning their chores and training and slacking off their responsibilities or cutting corners. This is followed by a projection into a future in which the dire consequences of such behavior are made manifest.

Another forceful and moving example of these training dramas is *Ghost Column,* set on an island in the Pacific.[24] A battle which should have been an easy Ameri-

can win has been lost to the Japanese at a great expense of human lives. Soldiers in the play waste resources, refuse medical treatment, and ignore nutritionally sound meals in favor of junk food, causing them to lose the battle due to unpreparedness, illness, and lack of nutrition. The theme of squandering and waste versus prudent conservation and sound health practices is the powerful lesson of *Ghost Column,* a theme strongly pushed by the government in plays, publications, advertising, and domestic propaganda.

One training play, *This Is Your Enemy,* stands out for it reveals the hand of a rather skilled anonymous propagandist playwright.[25] It opens with force and panache as the stage directions tell us, "THEATRE IS COMPLETELY BLACKED OUT. THE SOUND OF MARCHING FEET SLOWLY INCREASING IS HEARD OVER THE LOUDSPEAKER" (1). This is followed by the command "halt" in German, and then a spotlight suddenly shines upon a young Nazi boy in uniform on a pedestal marked with a swastika. In the strongest terms, he touts the strength of the Third Reich and the weakness of America and American democracy. His speech, replete with exclamation points, is clearly meant to set the audience's teeth on edge:

> The Third Reich—does that mean anything to you idiots?? We have conquered half the world and enslaved its populations! We have torn up your books, your religion, your culture and your ideology! Everything that your American democracy represents we are destroying, and next we will destroy YOU! . . . You driveling fools do not know importance of perfect discipline in maintaining a fine machine of war. You call yourselves an Army! You <u>are</u> an Army! An Army of mongrels! A mixture of black, white, Protestant, Catholic, and Jew! An Army that has risen from the cesspools of the world! . . . Since I was old enough to walk I have held a gun ready to destroy your putrid democracy! There are millions like me, and you idiotic Americans have the audacity to think you're a match for our superior force!
>
> (1)

This is followed by the showing of actual film footage showing Nazi soldiers on parade, close-ups of their enthralled faces as they listen to the impassioned sounds of Hitler, scenes of the destruction of homes and churches, images of women's dead bodies, corpses sprayed with gasoline and set afire, the theft of clothing from the corpses, and the capture of Allied equipment. These film clips are accompanied by continued inflammatory narration by the Nazi youth.

The playwright follows this potent preface with realistic scenes of discontented soldiers who yearn for action on the battlefront and find the seemingly unsoldierly tasks they have been assigned demeaning. They grumble and feel like mere clerks in uniform because they are stationed stateside, are far from the glories of combat, and carry out such mindless tasks as shipping paper dolls and pinwheels to the troops. The playwright renders the American soldiers with a remarkable feel for the language, slanguage, and speech rhythms as the dispirited men shirk their responsibilities, goldbrick, and malinger. The scenes of G.I. discontent are sneeringly punctuated by the Nazi boy's cynical, scornful, and triumphant remarks:

> Yah! You will never see combat! You are stationed in America doing work no different from civilians! You are not in the Army! You are underpaid civilians doing the work of a civilian without the freedom of a civilian! Isn't that the way you see it? Good! That is the Fuehrer wants you to see it, too! . . . Do you not watch the clock to be ready to leave your work exactly at quitting time? . . . Why should you drill? Why should you go on long marches—? Why should you take refresher courses in marksmanship and gas drill—? . . . What can you lose if the requisition is late? . . . No one but the Fuehrer! Delay! He pleads with you! He knows what you are too stupid to see. He knows the combat forces completely depend on you Service Force soldiers to supply them with trained men and the necessary material.

(13)

In the course of the play, this is countered by patriotic and didactic speeches in which the goldbricking soldiers are reviled, the importance of the service division extolled, and the fact that this is the war to preserve American democracy remembered (21-22, 28-29). The play ends, however, with a return to its frame and the Nazi boy telling the audience, "What you have just seen is, of course, your own propaganda," reminds them America is a country of loafers and that "your lazy spirit is part of your American tradition . . . [and that] your nature is to delay!—to complain about everything that will speed up your victory!" (30). *This Is Your Enemy* is indeed unabashed propaganda leveled at servicemen to instill pride in working for the military at domestic supply posts instead of on the battlefield, as well as a sense of responsibility, urgency, and pride in one's work. The inflammatory figure of the Nazi youth and the anonymous playwright's firm grip on the dramatic medium ensure a powerful awareness among this training play's military audience that the war against the Third Reich is being fought at home as well as in Europe.

The U.S. Army was by no means the only branch of the government that recognized drama as a powerful weapon for shaping the attitudes of Americans about the war and wartime issues. The staff of the Treasury Department during the war years commissioned and created dozens of plays for elementary school children, junior high school and high school students, and adults. The ultimate aim of all of the Treasury Department plays was the promotion of War Stamps and War Bond sales and the curtailment of American monetary squandering.

One must remember that during the Depression of the 1930s many had lost their savings and financial instruments had gone bust. With this still very fresh in the minds of Americans in the 1940s, asking citizens to invest in War Bonds was often a hard sell. The war also brought with it jobs and new prosperity; and after a decade of Depression austerity and a time when savings had been lost, some were in search of immediate consumer gratification and loathe to defer that gratification by allocating part of their earnings for the purchase of War Bonds. The war years also brought the rationing of staple foods and the scarcity of material goods. Consequently, there were those ready to dedicate their discretionary money not to War Bonds but to hoarding clothes, meats, soap, razor blades, and other consumer goods or to obtaining scarce goods on the black market. Others felt that, with the entrance of the U.S. into the fray, the Allies would prevail and conquer quickly and handily, and the war would soon be over. Why, then, should they stint on luxury items, save scrap metal, or buy War Bonds? The Treasury Department was worried that such attitudes posed a serious threat of inflation if Americans were willing to pay higher and higher prices for foods and other material goods that they suspected might be rationed or become unavailable altogether. The great fear was that at a time when the U.S. was vulnerable as it fought a bloody war across two oceans, it would be further endangered if it also had to fight runaway inflation on the domestic front. Thus, in response to the monetary needs of a nation at war and to the fear of a new inflationary post-Depression economic instability, the Treasury Department propagandized the responsibility of every American to save money, curb inflation, and help the war effort by investing in U.S. War Bonds and War Stamps. Drama was one of the principal instruments of that propaganda effort.

Looking at these Department of Treasury plays, it is revealing to see how particular groups are targeted, and in each case what propaganda strategies are employed, and which issues are stressed. Cleverly, the Treasury Department targets American schools by creating a "Schools-At-War" program, complete with pamphlets, classroom activities, and drama programs for American youngsters from kindergarten through high school. The authors of the plays surely knew that the messages of wartime thrift and bond purchase would become daily issues for the students as they read the play, rehearsed their parts over the course of some weeks, and then performed the play. They knew, too, that the audience for the plays would be not only the other students and teachers in the school but also the parents who heard their children rehearsing each day; after all, it was those parents who formed the adult and money-possessing mainstay audience for the children's plays.

The Treasury Department playwrights began at the ground level, with the primary school grades. Indicative of the War Stamps and War Bond drama authored for these pupils in *Squanderbug's Mother Goose,* which features Everyboy and Everygirl figures, Phil and Lis, who are led by a kindly neighbor, Miss Moppity, through the world of a modernized, wartime Mother Goose where they meet nursery rhyme characters and the villain of the piece, Squanderbug, who is the allegorical image of spendthrift, inflation prone America.[26] In *Squanderbug's Mother Goose,* Lis and Phil first encounter Old Mother Hubbard, and one quickly sees where the play is headed:

MISS M:

> Old Mother Hubbard
> Went to the cupboard
> For an Album of which she was fond.
> And when she got there
> She said,

OLD M.H.:

> I declare! I've got enough
> Stamps for a Bond!

(5)

Along the way in Mother Goose Land, Lis and Phil encounter the Squanderbug, who grows fat on the money when people squander when they could be investing it in War Bonds and War Stamps. Squanderbug is not merely the villain of this playlet but a figure who reappears in several other Treasury Department dramas.

The propaganda of a play like *Squanderbug's Mother Goose* continues to be transparent when the Squanderbug is rejected, and when as Lis and Phil take their leave of Jack and Jill, those nursery rhyme characters bid them farewell with, "See you at the victory parade. Cheerio!" (12). At the conclusion of the play, Lis and Phil recapitulate the lessons of the didactic play for their audience of schoolchildren and parents:

LIS:

> You know, Phil, I feel all different about everything now.

PHIL:

> Me, too. As long as the war lasts I won't care a peanut about driving out to the lake for a picnic.

LIS:

> Let's start planning a Victory Garden, Phil . . . right away. . . . I haven't felt so good in a long while or had so much fun. . . . Why, I bet I could even write an up-to-date nursery rhyme. . . .
> Sing a song of sixpence . . .
> A pocket full of rhymes . . .
> We used to waste our money,

PHIL:

> Our quarters and our dimes.

LIS:

> But now . . .

BOTH:

> We'll both buy War Stamps, AND KEEP UP WITH THE TIMES (*THE CURTAIN FALLS*)

(13)

Victory, savings and the purchase of financial instrument, War Stamps, unite in an amalgam of patriotism and economic good sense.

In a slightly different key, Sally Miller Brash's *The Magic Bond* creates a children's allegory in which a sad and troubled princess is saved by and then betrothed to a palace page who lifts her spirits and makes her smile by fetching her a War Bond from across the sea in America. In the concluding words of the play, the lucky young page exults:

> My princess has her Bond safe in her hand,
> And I've had a chance to visit a glorious land
> A land with people determined to fight
> To keep love and liberty and all that is right,
> Let us all honor these Americans so true,
> Love wave their Flag . . . the Red, White and Blue!

(7)[27]

The rescued princess is obviously a grim Europe rescued by an America devoted to liberty and freedom, and willing to place its economic power in War Bonds which will at once ensure the rescue of Europeans and applaud American patriotism.

In one elementary-school-level play by Mildred Hank and Noel McQueen, *We Will Do Our Share,* coins and Bank-Roll lying around the house combine to help children buy War Stamps.[28] In their far more sophisticated *Citizens of Tomorrow,* likely aimed at the higher elementary-school grades, Hank and McQueen begin to spell out not merely the propaganda for buying War Bonds but appropriate wartime gender roles.[29] *Citizens of Tomorrow* is about 5 boys who, realizing that V is the Roman numeral for 5, for a V for a Victory club in the empty garage of a father who has sold the family automobile in order to buy War Bonds. With the help of older brother, Bill, home on furlough, the boys organize to engage in their own form of wartime combat as brother Bill tells them, "collecting junk and paper and stuff to make guns and supplies is fighting, too" (74). The boys reluctantly allow girls to join their club, after the girls complain of their exclusion and then offer to fulfill their gender roles, "We want to join the Victory Club . . . and [you] won't let us. Why, girls can do a lot—sew and knit and work for the Red Cross—and we can buy as many War Stamps as they can?" (75).

Elementary school children were only one target of the Treasury Department's propaganda plays. The tone of these government-sponsored plays becomes more imperative and the messages more direct when the works are directed toward high school students, who will soon be eligible for enlistment and the draft, and who will enter their adult lives upon high school graduation. One can quickly see the change of tone by realizing how Sally Miller Brash moves from the fairy tale mode of her elementary school play *The Magic Bond* to her high school musical, *Star for a Day*.[30] In this play, high school students await a movie star who is to make her appearance in order to help sell War Bonds and War Stamps. A show about the war effort on the home front is created in honor of the star's arrival. The high school girls prepare to sing a number to the tune of "Sleepy Time Gal":

> We're wide awake gals,
> And when this World War is thru'
> We stay-awake gals will all be singing to you.
> We hope Hitler will hang
> And all the rest of his gang,
> That's why we're stay-at-home, work-at-home, knit-
>   at-home,
> Wide-awake gals!

To the sentiments embodied in the song, the girls' teacher, Miss Bennett, exclaims, "That's an excellent spirit . . . You are truly ALL-AMERICAN girls!" (7). Clearly, even during the war a woman's place was in the home.

Far more serious in tone are two other rather moving Treasury Department plays for high school students, Walter Hackett's *For The Duration* and Howard Tooley and Carolyn Wood's *A Letter From Bob*.[31] Both plays raise the conflict between materialism and economic self-indulgence and abjuring personal desires and gain in order to support the war effort. *For The Duration* is specifically focused on high school students. It uses as its main character, sixteen year old Tom Hill, who is eager to spend his savings on skis and skiing lessons when his family takes their planned vacation in the mountains. By contrast, Tom's friends are investing their savings in War Bonds, and Ronald Batty, an English boy dating Tom's sister, is putting aside $18.75 of his weekly $20 allowance in order to buy War Bonds and thereby gives his thanks and support to the country offering him sanctuary while his father serves in the RAF. Likewise, Curt Hansen, the Norwegian newspaper boy sells War Savings Stamps to the customers on his route, and Mother buys some. Father, who works in the shipyard, returns home and announces the vacation is off because his working on Sundays from now on to build Liberty ships. The family takes its vacation money, and Tom takes his earnings, and they apply the money to War Bonds.

Perhaps the most dramatically effective and hard-hitting of all the plays produced by the Department of Treasury is Tooley and Woods' *A Letter From Bob*. In this play Mother is the only sensible one in the family; she writes regularly to her son Bob stationed in the Pacific, where he flies a B-24. Bob's younger brother, Dan, the narrator of the play, looks back into his recent past, and recognizes that he has been a feckless high school student bent on spending money foolishly. His sister Jean is angry with her boyfriend who purchases War Stamps instead of spending his money to take her to the school dance. Dad is annoyed because he has been repeatedly asked—or, as he sees it, badgered—to enroll his employees in the Payroll War Bond Plan.

Everything within the selfish, solipsistic family changes when a letter from their son Bob arrives, which spells out pellucidly the agenda of the play and of the Treasury Department:

> Seems like the whole family, except maybe mother isn't even trying to do what they can to help me and my buddies out. I wonder if it's worth it all. . . . Ask a man who's been adrift on a little rubber raft, how the lives of all his shipmates could have been saved. He'll tell you . . . by having enough protection to make it safe for them to man that ship!! . . . I don't know what you're doing over there. You think must think this war is the latest in outdoor sports. But let me tell you . . . this is no game! When the fellow you ate dinner with last night doesn't show up for breakfast after a raid . . . you don't have much patience with someone at home who couldn't give up a movie, or a new coat, or part of their salary. . . . I don't say this because we aren't willing to do our job . . . I'm telling you this because you aren't willing to do yours.
>
> (9-10).

The image of young soldiers and sailors dying valiantly for their country when they might have been spared had only the folks at home sacrificed some of their vanities is powerful and effective.

A Letter From Bob is clearly directed to both a teenage and an adult wage earning population. It is unabashedly didactic from beginning to end, but the sentimentality of Bob's letter, the reasoned replies to Dad's skepticism, and the familiarity of each family member's selfish desires combine to make *A Letter From Bob* rather effective propagandistic drama. It is hardly surprising that it was reprinted in one of the Treasury Department's anthologies of plays specifically directed to an adult audience and meant for production at community centers and churches.[32]

Perhaps *A Letter From Bob* suggested to playwright Bernard J. Reins an effective dramatic technique, for the anthology contains two powerful, moving, and better than mere government-issue plays by him—*Message From Bataan* and *Letter to Private Smith*—that both employ the message home as their central dramatic device.[33] *Message From Bataan* shows the hand of a skilled dramatist rather than a government playmaker. Almost every government-sponsored play has an aura of a triumph, celebrating what it sees as American values, American heroism, American moral right, and imminent American military victory. These plays usually have a domestic setting, often somewhere in mid-America. *Message From Bataan* approaches matters from a very different standpoint using as its setting Bataan, one of the war's most significant and bloody defeats for this country. Bernard Reins focuses his drama in the heroism of Bill, his military Everyman character, whose bravery among the starving, dying men on Bataan is poignantly conveyed. During his final day on Bataan, Bill writes a last letter to his younger brother Johnny back home and entrusts it to a friend who is leaving the area. The letter reads:

> All I want to say to you is, we're doing our best, here on Bataan. But the odds are terrific . . . and we can't expect help from the States in time to save our position. We can't expect help because our country was not well enough prepared, and has to fight across the Atlantic as well as the Pacific, and hasn't yet turned out enough weapons and trained men to break through the Japanese forces. (Pause) Which means there's a big job for you back home to do . . . a job for every one of you, man and woman, boy and girl. For our workers there's the job of turning out the finest planes, tanks, guns . . . turning out more of them, turning them out faster, better. For our farmers there's the job of raising more food. For everybody, and especially for fellows and girls too young to fight or do heavy work, there's the job of collecting all the scrap metal that's lying around, all the old rubber, and the rags, and tin, and turning it in to be made into weapons . . . but whatever else you do, you can buy War Savings Stamps and Bonds, and keep on buying, and buying, and buying . . . and so lend your country the money it needs to pay for so many planes and ships and tanks and guns that we soldiers and sailors and flyers will never again be caught short by our enemies.

(51-52)

The didacticism is obvious, but the Bataan setting and the feelings that the recent defeat on Bataan roused in the American public give *Message From Bataan* just the fillip it needs to render dramatic what might otherwise be doggedly didactic.

The keynote piece in the collection is a hard-hitting short play by the already well-known Broadway playwright Bella Spewack, who, together with her husband Sam, had written *The Solitaire Man* (1926); *The War Song* (1928); *The Ambulance Chaser* (1931); *Boy Meets Girl* (1935), and *Clear All Wires* (1932) which was based on her experiences in Russia.[34] They were later to achieve celebrity by writing the book for Cole Porter's *Kiss Me, Kate* (1948).[35] In the 1950s, they worked with Cole Porter on *Boy Meets Girl,* a show meant to feature

Ray Bolger but that was aborted and never completed.[36] In 1953, they also wrote the very successful *My Three Angels* (1953).

Bella Spewack's script for the Treasury Department volume is *Invitation to Inflation,* which presents the chastising and education of Carol Larrabee, a frivolous, capricious married woman who, when she keeps an appointment to meet a friend, totes a load of parcels containing patently non-essential luxury items and black market purchases. When she is told by her friend Bess that her husband is angry with her extravagances, that her marriage is in jeopardy, and that he would like her to spend her money on bonds, she exclaims:

> You mean War Bonds? I bought a War Bond. I can't buy one a month, the way Jim wants me to—and run a house too! Do you know what beef costs? I paid a dollar a pound at—well, Jim doesn't know I spent that much—I had to tell him it was ceiling price and show him the the [sic] receipt and my stamp book—before he'd even eat it! But he certainly enjoyed every mouthful! Buying War Bonds is all right—but how are you going to buy them with things so high—not just beef you know!

(6)

Spewack, like other Treasury playwrights, has seemingly learned her technique from the agitprop plays of the 1930s. Indeed, Spewack *Invitation to Inflation* has something of Clifford Odet's tone in *Waiting for Lefty*'s "Young Actor" episode. The entire collection of scripts reflects the ways in which the often politically critical and leftist agitprop playwrights of the 1930s provided the models for successful, politically conservative, pro patria warprop in the 1940s.

The plays that follow Spewack's are all (with one exception) by women writers either presumably in the employ of the Treasury Department or the winners of a college playwriting contest sponsored by the War Bond wing of the Department. In the first of June Bingham's two contributions to the volume, *Trial By Fury* (15-19), the allegorical Squanderbug, reappears in this adult play. Squanderbugs's mission is to convince women to be vain and spend their salaries on foolish trifles instead of buying War Bonds. In the Prologue, we learn that Squanderbug is in direct contact with Hitler and is one of his operatives in the U.S. In Bingham's other play, *Cry Uncle* (20-24), a "15-minute play was written expressly for women's colleges" (20), the economic didaction of Spewack's *Invitation to Inflation* is reiterated when college co-ed Mary explains to a frivolous classmate the realities of wartime economics and that War Bonds are needed "to foot the bill for all the Flying Fortresses and little things like that" (21) and to curb inflation. Furthermore, she adds, "the Government wants you to invest in bonds, so you'll have money to spend after the war. That's when there'll be beautiful new cars and heavenly clothes—and then you'll be doing the patriotic thing by spending. Because the money you spend will help get our businesses back on a peacetime basis and reemploy soldiers" (22). Like many other Treasury plays, the argument to a populace emerging from the deprivations of the 1930s is to delay gratification just a little longer, until the war is won. Then spending and vanity will not merely be allowed but will boost the post-war economy, provide jobs for ex-G.I.s, and be part of a patriotic gesture to put peacetime America back on track.

The only piece in the collection written by a man is Phillips Brooks Keller's *Now Is the Time* (30-32). As the preface to the play tells us, "This 10-minute play was one of the five winners in a college play-writing contest sponsored by the National War Savings Staff in the Spring of 1943" (30). In it, two reporters interview John Polifka, an immigrant from Poland who has become a millionaire and who is investing money in War Bonds. His reasons are both economic and patriotic. First, he argues, "Speaking cold-bloodedly, I can't afford not to buy War Bonds. At present, interest rates they're just about the best and safest investment that I could make in times like these" (31). He sees as well that War Bonds will help the U.S. and the Allies invade Europe and restore his native Poland, "The quicker this country and her fighting allies are able to invade continental Europe, the sooner will my kinsmen and my countrymen be free to recover the heritage of living without fear and, as Mr. Roosevelt has said, living without want" (32). Looking at *Invitation to Inflation* and *Now Is the Time* side by side, one can see the disparate and gendered ways in which the Treasury Department sought to pitch similar material to female and male audiences.

A *Letter From Bob* and *Message From Bataan* paradigm is used once more and flavored with a soupçon of the supernatural in Ensign Elsie Mary White, U.S.N.R.'s *One Bullet* (56-60). The stage directions instruct prospective producers, "The plot is concerned with a farmer-father who feels that he is doing his share by raising food for the war, and sees no reason to buy War Bonds. Meanwhile his soldier-son dies for want of ammunition in the Southwest Pacific. The play can be made more timely by changing the war area mentioned to coincide with war action going on when the play is given, Southwest Pacific can become Europe, Japs-Nazis" (56). The ghost of the dead soldier-son appears and in a poignant, melodramatic moment, haunts the niggardly father with a reenactment of the son's dying moments:

JIM:

> (*As is giving up the struggle*). I-I've no bullets left—(*turning to his father*) Dad-Dad-why won't you help me? I can't—(*sound of a loud gun report. Then Jim*

> *sinks to the floor holding his middle. He is in great pain and can hardly talk but he manages to gasp out*) Dad—I needed you and you didn't help—One bullet would have sa—(*His father kneels down beside him. His words die away and as he makes a last effort to rise, he pulls a chair over. At this moment the fire goes out leaving the entire stage in darkness.*)

(58)

With a shrewdly passive-aggressive tactic, the play directs guilt feelings squarely toward those in the audiences who have not invested generously in War Bonds.

Certainly the most unusual and imaginative of all the Treasury Department plays is another of the 5 winners of the college playwriting contest sponsored by the National War Savings Staff in the Spring of 1943: Mary Moore's brief *American Curiosities* (49-51). This rather strange piece set in a dystopian future seeks to fan the flames of America's worst wartime paranoid fantasies of a post-war period in which the U.S. is ruled by the conquering Germans and Japanese. The principal characters, an archaeology professor and his wife, did not heed the call to buy War Bonds. Now they are fugitives on the run from the Germans, dressed in animal skins and hiding out for the past ten years in a cave somewhere in deepest Michigan. They are chided by their loyal American sister-in-law, Hattie, now also a fugitive and dressed like a huntress. Hattie scolds the professor and his wife because they refused to buy War Bonds, support their country or believe "that the Japanese and the Germans could make a battlefield of this country for 10 years so that the only Americans left would be living in hills like savages. You never believe that anything can happen to upset your own peace and comfort" (50). The fantasy of *American Curiosities,* which looks back to Huxley's *Brave New World* and ahead to Orwell's *1984,* expressed the deep-seated fears of Americans, encouraging or bullying them into War Bond purchases to avert the future outlined in the play.

The Treasury Department plays are far from being either masterpieces of the drama or of subtlety, but do represent significant artifacts of American wartime culture, revealing as they do the ways in which a non-military wing of the government sought to employ drama as a means of persuasion and propaganda.

Looking back at the wide array of government-issued and government-sponsored theatrical material, it becomes remarkably clear how great was the confidence of the U.S. officials that theatre and performance could help Americans win the war. In addition to the government stage material discussed here, there was also government drama conveyed through radio. Americans across the country listened to the scripts presented on radio series such as *The Treasury Star Parade, The Freedom Company Presents,* and *This Is War.*[37] Clearly the dramatic techniques employed by the pro patria government-sponsored dramatists of the 1940s were learned from the largely agitprop, anti-establishment playwrights of the decade. Writing of American theatre during the Depression era, Morgan Y. Himelstein titles his study *Drama Was a Weapon*. In the hands of the U.S. government, drama was also a weapon during the wartime years of the 1940s.

Notes

1. Numbers in parentheses following quotations refer to Golden's edition.

2. Ralph Nelson had done some acting in Los Angeles and had been married briefly to actress Celeste Holm before the war. *Mail Call* is his first play, but in June 1945, his play *The Wind Is Ninety* was produced at the Booth theatre in New York. The cast included Wendell Corey and Kirk Douglas. Nelson went on to become a distinguished television director (including the *I Remember Mama* series and *Requiem for a Heavyweight*).

3. Steven Bach, however, claims that "Arnold later admitted he had never heard of Moss Hart."

4. Burns Mantle 32-33. Bach 239-240. Rosamund Gilder 98.

5. "Winged Victory in Production." This 4-page inset on how *Winged Victory* came to be is graced with comic drawings by Sgt. Harry Horner, who had recently been the scene designer for Hart's *Lady in the Dark*.

6. See 226-227. Bach records a cast of 210, and orchestra of 45, and a choral group of 50 as well as a stage crew of 70.

7. See Bach 243-244

8. Burns Mantle 32-33.

9. Bordman 227.

10. Bach 243.

11. Karl Malden 137.

12. See for example, *Soldier Shows* (Washington: Special Services Division, Army Service Forces, USGPO, 1944) W109.102: So4; *Soldier Shows* (Washington: War Department, USGPO, 1945) W1.43:28-15c; and *Soldier Shows* (Washington: Special Services Division, Army Service Forces [Entertainment Section], USGPO, 1945) W109.116:28. The last contains, among other materials, copies of John Patrick's *The Hasty Heart* and George S. Kaufman's *Freedom of the Air.*

13. Bob Stuart McKnight 427.

14. The Writers and Material Committee of Camp Shows, Inc., eds., *"At Ease," Volume I: Comedy Sketches* (New York: USO-Camp Shows, 1942).

15. An incisive account of gay men and government-sponsored theatre in the armed forces is given in Allan Bérubé, *Coming Out Under Fire: The History of Gay Men and Women in World War Two* (New York: Penguin Books, 1990), pp. 67-97. See also Arthur Laurents, *Original Story By* (New York: Alfred A. Knopf, 2000), pp. 25-26 and Charles Kaiser, *The Gay Metropolis 1940-1996* (Boston and New York: Houghton Mifflin, 1997), pp.37-38.

16. The Writers and Material Committee of Camp Shows, Inc., eds., *"At Ease," Volume II: Minstrel Shows* (New York: USO-Camp Shows, 1942). Page references given in parentheses refer to this edition.

17. *About Face!* (Washington: Army Service Forces, Special Services Division, n.d. [c.1943-1944]); *Hi, Yank* (Washington Army Service Forces, Special Services Division, n.d.[c.1943-1944]); *P.F.C. Mary Brown: A WAC Musical Revue* (Washington: Army Service Forces, Special Services Division, n.d. [c.1944]).

18. The scripts have no dates, but *About Face!* presumably pre-dates *Hi, Yank,* since it is advertised on the inside front cover of the latter.

19. *P.F.C. Mary Brown* follows *About Face!* and *Hi, Yank,* since these shows are advertised on the back page of the *P.F.C. Mary Brown* volume. There seems to be no records revealing the identity of Capt. Ruby Jane Douglass, but Arthur Altman had already written the music for a pop tune "All or Nothing At All" (1940) recorded by Billie Holiday and in later years (1956?) by Frank Sinatra. After the war, he also wrote the music for "American Beauty Rose" recorded by Sinatra (1950) and "I Wish I Had a Record (Of the Promises You Made)" recorded by Perry Como (1949).

20. An exception here is Allan R. Kenward's *Cry Havoc,* sometimes staged as *Proof Through the Night* (1943).

21. Mary Percy Schenk was later recognized with a 1948 Tony Award for her costume designs for *The Heiress.*

22. *Death Without Battle* (Governor's Island, NY: Military Training Division Headquarters, Second Service Command, 1944).

23. *Stripes* (Governor's Island, NY: Military Training Division Headquarters, Second Service Command, 9 May 1944); *The Eternal Weapon* (Governor's Island, NY: Military Training Division Headquarters, Second Service Command, 13 September 1944).

24. *Ghost Column* (Governor's Island, NY: Military Training Division Headquarters, Second Service Command, 1944).

25. *This Is Your Enemy* (Governor's Island, NY: Military Training Division Headquarters, Second Service Command, 1944).

26. Aileen L. Fisher, *The Squanderbug's Mother Goose,* Education Section, War Finance Division, U.S. Treasury. U.S. GPO, 1944. (T66.2: Sq 20).

27. Sally Miller Brash, T*he Magic Bond, A Short Timely Play for Children of Nine to Twelve Years of Age,* "Plays for Schools-At-War" U.S. Treasury Department, USGPO, 1944 (T66.2: P69/4).

28. *War Savings Programs: A Handbook of Dramatic Material,* Treasury Department, Education Division (Washington: USGPO, 1943) (T66.6: P94), pp. 61-69.

29. Ibid., pp. 70-76.

30. Sally Miller Brash, *Star for a Day: A Musical Play for High School Students,* "Plays for Schools-At-War." Education Section, War Finance Division, U.S. Treasury Department. USGPO, 1944. (T66.2: P69/5).

31. Walter Hackett, *For The Duration: A Play for Junior and Senior High Schools,* "Plays for Schools-At-War", U.S. Department of Treasury, USGPO, 1944. (T66.2: P69/2); and Howard Tooley and Carolyn Wood, *A Letter From Bob: A War Savings Play for Junior and Senior High Schools,* "Plays for Schools-At-War," U.S. Treasury Department, USGPO, 1945. (T66.2: P69/3 1945).

32. *War Savings Programs: A Handbook of Dramatic Material,* Treasury Department, Education Division (Washington: USGPO, 1943) (T66.6: P94).

33. Ibid., Bernard J. Reins, *Message From Bataan,* pp.38-52 and *Letter to Private Smith,* pp. 77-85.

34. A useful sketch of Bella and Sam Spewack's careers is given in Jean Gould 135-140.

35. William McBrien, *Cole Porter: A Biography* (New York: Alfred A. Knopf, 1998), p. 303-309.

36. McBrien, p. 333.

37. Representative scripts appear in a William A. Bacher, James Boyd, and Norman Corwin.

Works Cited

Bach, Steven. *Dazzler: The Life and Times of Moss Hart.* New York: Alfred A. Knopf, 2001.

Bacher, William A., ed. *The Treasury Star Parade.* New York and Toronto: Farrar & Rinehart, 1942.

Berube. Allan. *Coming Out Under Fire: The History of Gay Men and Women in World War Two.* New York: Penguin, 1990.

Bordman, Gerald. *American Theatre: A Chronicle of Comedy and Drama, 1930-1969.* New York: Oxford UP, 1996.

Boyd, James, ed. *The Freedom Company Presents.* New York: Dodd, Mead, 1941.

Corwin, Norman, et al, eds. *This is War! A Collection of Plays about America on the March.* New York: Dodd, Mead, 1942.

Gilder, Rosamund. "The Fabulous Hart." *Theatre Arts Monthly* 28 (February 1944): 98.

Golden, John. *The Army Play by Play: Five One-Act Plays.* New York: Random House, 1943.

Gould, Jean. *Modern American Playwrights.* New York: Dodd, Mead, 1966.

Himelstein, Morgan Y. *Drama Was a Weapon: The Left-Wing Theatre in New York, 1929-1941.* Westport, CT: Greenwood P, 1976.

Kaiser, Charles. *The Gay Metropolis 1940-1996.* Boston and New York: Houghton Mifflin, 1997.

Laurents, Arthur. *Original Story By.* New York: Alfred A. Knopf, 2000.

Malden, Karl. *When Do I Start: A Memoir.* New York: Simon & Schuster, 1997.

Loesser, Susan. *A Most Remarkable Fella: Frank Loesser and the Guys and Dolls in His Life.* New York: D. I. Fine, 1993.

Mantle, Burns, ed. *The Best Plays of 1943-44.* New York: Dodd, Mead, 1944.

McBrien, William. *Cole Porter: A Biography.* New York: Alfred A. Knopf, 1998.

McKnight, Bob Stuart, "Original Army Shows." *Theatre Arts Monthly* 27 (July 1943): 427.

"Winged Victory in Production." *Theatre Arts Monthly* 28 (February 1944).

Albert Wertheim (essay date 2004)

SOURCE: Wertheim, Albert. Introduction to *Staging the War: American Drama and World War II,* pp. ix-xviii. Bloomington: Indiana University Press, 2004.

[*In the following excerpt, Wertheim presents an overview of the U.S. theater scene between 1934 and 1955.*]

What happened in American drama in the years between the Depression and the conclusion of World War II? How did the war make its impact on the drama? And more important, how was the drama used during the war years to shape American attitudes about U.S.

participation in the combat, who the enemy was, and the proper role of citizens both at home and in the service? Studies of American drama and anthologies of American plays for the most part skip cavalierly from the 1930s Depression-era plays of Clifford Odets and the Group Theatre to Tennessee Williams's *The Glass Menagerie,* which opened six weeks before V-E Day in 1945, or to Arthur Miller's *All My Sons* in 1947. With the exception of Thornton Wilder's *Our Town,* and perhaps Robert Sherwood's *Abe Lincoln in Illinois* and Lillian Hellman's *Watch on the Rhine,* little is said about the decade between the heyday of Odets and the first successes of Miller and Williams. Yet that very decade is the decade of World War II, arguably the most important of the twentieth century. Although there are studies of wartime film, like the two books both called *Hollywood Goes to War,* inexplicably, no one has paid much attention to the playwriting and theatre of the period.[1]

From the period of Hitler's rise in the 1930s to the decade following the end of World War II, there are many fine plays about the war and the issues surrounding it. Some of these plays were later made into films. But the films, often made months or years after the Broadway production, usually lacked the currency and immediacy of the plays, which had been staged at a particular moment in the war era. The plays examined in this study deserve close attention both for their excellence as works of drama and for the things they reveal about American society during the war. Many of the plays are still vibrant and stage-worthy, but there is much to learn as well about wartime issues from other plays that now seem dated, and from those that did not have long runs on Broadway either because they were not well crafted or because they were raising issues that audiences would rather not have had raised. With great perspicacity, Hamlet instructs the actors who have come to Elsinore Castle that "the purpose of playing, whose end, both at the first and now, was and is, to hold, as 'twere, the mirror up to nature." And so it is that the drama during the World War II period holds the mirror up to life and thought in America, registering the dominant feelings of its citizens as well as the social changes that were occurring.

The years covered by this study, approximately 1934 to 1955, are among the most critical years of the twentieth century. Certainly the combat across the Atlantic and the Pacific as well as the political issues that sparked that combat are at the vibrant heart of those years, but just as important are the changes in the American way of life. These include a renewed endorsement for the freedoms Americans had come to take for granted, for these were suddenly under attack from fascist ideologies abroad and fascist subversives at home. The war brought with it a change in the American economic picture. Big business garnered new profits from wartime

industry, and business moved from the slump of the Depression to new prosperity. The unemployment of the 1930s began to be reversed by the war of the 1940s. And wartime brought with it important changes as well for the civic and ethical responsibilities of American businessmen, who were often producing goods that would be used by the armed forces and by the fighting men overseas. World War II saw new roles for women in the workplace. As able-bodied men went overseas to serve their country, women left their traditional places at the kitchen sink and scrubbing board to take over the jobs men had left behind. They worked on assembly lines and even in heavy industry, revising a nation's idea of what roles women could assume in the work force. These things the plays of the period register.

The plays register, too, a variety of American demographic dislocations. Servicemen from around the country found themselves in boot camps far away from home, often in small towns and in new geographies. There they met, as their fathers had before them in World War I, other men from every corner of the nation. The small-town boy from Iowa became friends with the urban recruit from New York, the Southerner from North Carolina with the erstwhile logger from Oregon. Protestants mingled with Jews and Catholics, Italian Americans with Swedish Americans, the rich with the poor, the educated with the under-educated. Hitler had cited the weakness of America because it was a nation of mongrel races. Americans were themselves learning and then proving to the world that the United States embodies a strength that emanates from diversity united, even though that diversity did not extend to America's populations of color: African Americans, Asian Americans, Hispanics, and Native Americans.

As several wartime dramas reflect, a mingling of another kind took place in the towns and port cities where army and naval bases were located. Small towns found themselves changed overnight when they became the sites of sizable army camps containing a multitude of servicemen. The flood of those young men coming to town on their weekend passes radically changed the life of once conservative communities. Liquor flowed, and recruits who had lived under the military strictures for weeks came in search of pleasure. Local young women forged relationships, licit and illicit, with the GIs stationed nearby. Josephine Bentham and Herschel Williams's 1942 play, *Janie,* projects the change in comic terms. Shortly after the war, Tennessee Williams, by contrast, in *A Streetcar Named Desire,* remembers the influx of troops to the army camp near Belle Reve as a wellspring of debauchery and a major contributor to the tragic ruin of Blanche Dubois. Furthermore, as the plays show—for example, Maxwell Anderson's *The Eve of St. Mark*—men who were leaving home to serve their country often hastily married women they had but recently met, or simply short-circuited the usual courtship ritual with a girl back home. Men on leave also came to new cities, usually port cities, and before a week was up had sexual experiences and sometimes married women they had just met. The musical *On the Town*, which Leonard Bernstein wrote with Betty Comden, Adolph Green, and Jerome Robbins, offers a light-hearted insight into that situation. Edward Chodorov's important comedy *Those Endearing Young Charms* looks at the situation in thoughtful and incisive ways. Not only did the press of war give little time for extended romance, courtship, and engagements, but men died, leaving behind grieving parents, young wives suddenly made widows, and children who never would see their fathers. Lads who had lustily gone off to war saw terrible things in combat or were themselves wounded, returning home to wives and families as scarred men, physically crippled and psychologically damaged. Plays such as Lillian Hellman's *The Searching Wind*, Arthur Laurents's *Home of the Brave*, and Elsa Shelly's *Foxhole in the Parlor* made Broadway audiences aware of the war's casualties among its survivors.

Before Pearl Harbor, American plays provide eloquent evidence for the national conflict between American post-World War I isolationism and the voices of those warning that the U.S. must take a stand to stem the aggression and the ideologies of Hitler and Mussolini. And after Pearl Harbor, the drama cues the nation about the nature of American patriotism, why the United States is at war and over what issues. It speaks as well about the lives of servicemen and the lives of their families, and the need for all Americans, in the military or at home, to pull their individual oars so the war can be concluded quickly, with victory for the Allies and for the survival of (American) democracy.

During the 1930s and in the years immediately after Pearl Harbor, almost every American playwright of any note addressed the war and its issues. Some of these playwrights were more eloquent and adept at writing about political topics than others. Wartime dramatic contributions of much interest emerged from the pens of Clifford Odets, Thornton Wilder, William Saroyan, Claire Boothe, Robert Sherwood, S. N. Behrman, Sidney Kingsley, Sidney Howard, Maxwell Anderson, Lillian Hellman, George S. Kaufman, Moss Hart, Howard Lindsay and Russel Crouse, Rose Franken, Robert Ardrey, Archibald MacLeish, Philip Barry, and Elmer Rice. The one playwright notable for his absence and silence during this period is Eugene O'Neill, who had received the Nobel Prize for literature in 1936 and who remains the only American playwright ever to be awarded that honor. Nobel Prize in hand, O'Neill was ideally situated to pen an attention-getting drama or statement about World War II issues. What O'Neill produced, however, was the curiously irrelevant *The Iceman Cometh*, certainly one of his masterpieces but one that closed quickly, probably because it was so vastly removed from the concerns of the day. Why was O'Neill so remarkably silent about the war and the burning issues of the time? Was he uninterested in the world events or incapable of writing about them, beset by illness or obsessed with his own demons? Whatever the answer, his is the one voice glaringly absent from this study.

But not every American playwright was writing for the Broadway stage. Indeed, although this study considers in some detail war issues and American plays presented in the New York theatres, other important developments using drama and dramatic material were taking place in other venues. Perhaps the most illuminating and original material discussed in this study is the wealth of dramatic material issued by and performed under the auspices of the U.S. government. During the Depression the successes and strong audience effect of the Federal Theatre Project and the Group Theatre and of playwrights like Clifford Odets, John Howard Lawson, or George Sklar had shown how theatre could pack a political punch and serve to rally audiences behind causes—often leftist causes—or to support social issues. After the U.S. declared war and entered the fray, Washington seemed to remember how those very dramaturgical techniques used so effectively by the Group Theatre and its playwrights could productively be used in the service of wartime patriotic, pro-government propaganda.

The U.S. military found itself after Pearl Harbor fighting in what were called the European and the Pacific theatres of the war. But it became engaged as well in the more traditional definition of theatre, in the production of dramatic material for the stage. The U.S. Army conducted, of all things, a playwriting competition among the troops and selected, for production in New York and around the country, the five best one-act play submissions. The Air Forces (as that division of the military was then called) for its part commissioned distinguished playwright Moss Hart to write *Winged Victory*, a dramatic production that employed scores of servicemen as actors and musicians in an extraordinarily extravagant production that touted the excellence of the Air Forces, promoted the desirability of enlisting in that branch of the military, and inspired audience confidence in American air power. The U.S.O. disseminated to American military bases at home and abroad scripts of skits, entertainments, and musicals, including three written largely by Pvt. Frank Loesser. The Military Training Division also took to playwriting. It issued didactic dramas to training sites. These were largely aimed at alerting recruits to good eating habits, personal hygiene, and the insidiousness of the enemy.

An unlikely theatrical "angel" and artistic sponsor, the Treasury Department during the war issued scores of play scripts for schoolchildren, young adults, college students, and community groups. The aim of those scripts was twofold. Americans were urged to support the war effort by purchasing War Bonds and War Stamps: not an easy sell immediately after the Depression, which had so seriously compromised American faith in financial instruments. The Treasury plays also sought to address economists' concerns that wartime prosperity, coming as it did on the heels of the Depression, would encourage reckless spending on the part of American consumers. The danger the Treasury Department envisioned was that while the U.S. was fighting a war across both the Atlantic and the Pacific, it would have to fight another war against black-market buying and runaway inflation at home. The Treasury plays sought to teach citizens, from schoolchildren to adults, that if America was to win the war, its citizens would have to play their part in the war effort by curbing wayward spending, stemming inflation, and investing in the government through the purchase of War Bonds and War Stamps.

The theatrical stage was not the only dramatic vehicle that played a role in wartime awareness and propaganda efforts. Every evening during the war, Americans were tuned to their radios for the latest battlefront reports. And when they weren't hearing those, they could listen to some truly remarkable wartime drama. Even before the United States entered the war, radio was discovered as not merely a conveyor of news and light entertainment but as a powerful medium—political and otherwise—that could create a drama of words and sounds to sway audiences. Perhaps the most persuasive testimony to the power of radio, particularly in a time of global uncertainty, was Orson Welles's famous 30 October 1938 radio dramatization of *The War of the Worlds.* The success of Archibald MacLeish's two brilliant, poetic, immediately prewar radio plays, *The Fall of the City* and *Air Raid,* was likewise remarkable and eye-opening about the power of radio as a medium for drama. Not only individual plays but also drama series began to appear on radio. In the months before Pearl Harbor, a radio drama series called *The Free Company* and using playwrights like William Saroyan, Marc Connelly, Paul Green, Stephen Vincent Benét, and Maxwell Anderson bolstered American morale and helped Americans get their patriotic priorities in order in the face of the inevitable American entry into the war. Within eight days after the U.S. entered the war, radio playwright Norman Corwin aired his now famous *We Hold These Truths,* a play about the Bill of Rights and the freedoms American troops were being called on to protect. An estimated sixty million people, nearly half the American population, listened to that broadcast.

Almost immediately after Corwin's broadcast, playwrights, producers, and the government all realized that America had a whole new and incredibly vast audience for theatre: the American radio public, which numbered literally in the millions. A plethora of patriotic radio dramas and drama series resulted. And with scripts needed on a weekly basis, able playwrights were in demand. Both aspiring and seasoned playwrights were snapped up and employed by the radio networks. Those playwrights—such as Arthur Laurents, Arthur Miller, Maxwell Anderson, Morton Wishengrad, Stephen Vincent Benét, and Archibald MacLeish—wrote a spate of effective thirty-minute plays about war. Those plays were often acted by the greatest talents from Broadway and Hollywood who performed pro bono as their contribution to the war effort. Radio theatre during the war years was an often fruitful, though sometimes contentious, ménage à trois composed of talented playwrights, major radio broadcasting companies, and the U.S. government. For the playwrights, this provided the unusual job opportunity not only of writing scripts on a regular or frequent basis but of writing scripts that would be heard by an audience vastly greater than any Broadway theatre could ever deliver, and acted by the most celebrated performers. For example, a then completely unknown playwright named Arthur Miller, who wrote radio scripts during the war for the *Cavalcade of America* series, had his scripts performed by such stars as Jean Hersholt, Orson Welles, Madeleine Carroll, and Paul Muni.

Once the war was over and victory attained, once the confetti of V-E Day and V-J Day had been swept aside, drama was employed to help Americans understand what had happened and why and, more important, to script what winning the war should mean for the American future. The plays of the postwar period move Americans boldly forward toward a new era of internationalism and toward a recognition that America—which had rejected membership in the League of Nations after World War I—must now not merely become a member of the United Nations but take on a leadership role in that body. Plays like Howard Lindsay and Russel Crouse's *State of the Union* and Robert Sherwood's *The Rugged Path* were among those making an eloquent case for a new American international presence.

While the war was being waged, little was known of what was taking place in the Nazi death camps. Only when those camps were liberated at the close of the war did the full horror come into view. The postwar plays begin to help Americans come to grips with the unspeakable, with what has since come to be known as the Holocaust. Postwar dramas such as Frances Goodrich and Albert Hackett's *The Diary of Anne Frank* and Ben Hecht's *A Flag Is Born* were the first steps in helping Americans face and understand the human tragedy that was the war in Europe. And the racial matter so central to the Holocaust and the German ideals of racial purity also play themselves out in other important ways on the American postwar stage. How could Americans damn Hitler's master race politics that sent Jews and other minorities to the gas chambers and ovens, yet continue in good conscience to practice and affirm racism at home? Should Negro servicemen, who had served the U.S. so loyally during the war, albeit in segregated units, return home to be second-class citizens confined in the future to service in segregated military units, and should they continue to have racial segregation imposed upon them in their hometowns? Groundbreaking postwar plays by white playwrights depicting African-American soldiers returning home, such as Arnaud d'Usseau and James Gow's *Deep Are the Roots,* Robert Ardrey's *Jeb,* and Maxine Wood's *On Whitman Avenue,* poignantly raise the issues of racial discrimination even as they seem to prepare the way for African-American playwrights like Lorraine Hansberry, LeRoi Jones, Ed Bullins, and Loften Mitchell to soar into flight a decade later.

This study is, in part, an attempt to fill in a very significant gap in the history of American drama. More important, however, it seeks to explore the complex interrelationship between the drama and the most central and significant historical, political, and social event of the twentieth century. How did the prewar events in Europe, American participation in the war, and war's aftermath make their indelible mark on American playwriting? And how, at the same time, did playwrights use the drama and dramaturgy as an effective means for shaping the American public's understanding of why the U.S. should enter the conflict in Europe? And later, why the war was being fought? What basic freedoms had American troops committed themselves to protect? And what responsibilities were required of the American populace, first during the war and then after victory? When one examines over 150 plays in the course of a twenty-year period, as this study does, repeated patterns, central issues, and reiterated messages begin lucidly to emerge. Indeed, this study has both the advantages and disadvantages inherent in a macroproject: it shows clearly and vividly the shape of the connection between the drama and World War II, even as it will seem to some to be a discussion of too many plays. Writing this study has, however, for me been a personal pleasure because as I explored the drama from the mid-1930s to the mid-1950s, the face of the war became increasingly clear as did the power of theatre to "hold, as 'twere, the mirror up to nature."

When I began to undertake this study, I had a sketchy idea about which well-known plays I ought to examine, but I quickly discovered scores of plays—some of them quite wonderful—about which I had no previous knowledge. In unexpected ways, writing this book proved an adventure that led to the discovery of hitherto almost unrecognized dramatic material. I was amazed to discover three U.S.O. musicals written primarily by Pvt. Frank Loesser before he became famous for *Guys and Dolls, Where's Charley, Most Happy Fella,* and *How to Succeed in Business.* Even his biography, written by his daughter, fails to mention the U.S.O. musicals, one of which is graced with a cover drawn by Al Hirschfeld and another of which contains choreography notations by Pvt. José Limon.

Likewise, I happened on one treasure trove of dramatic materials issued by the U.S. Treasury Department, and another issued by the Military Training Division of the Second Service Command. In the course of writing the chapter on wartime radio plays, I was pleased to discover the almost unknown and largely unpublished radio drama that Arthur Miller wrote before his postwar Broadway success, *All My Sons,* skyrocketed him to fame. It was also a pleasure to read and discuss illuminating but now nearly unremembered plays such as Maxine Woods's *On Whitman Avenue,* Elsa Shelley's *Foxhole in the Parlor,* Dan James's *Winter Soldiers,* Ben Hecht's *We Will Never Die* and *A Flag Is Born,* and Rose Franken's *Soldier's Wife.* I was gratified, too, to discover the largely unrecognized playwriting excellence of Edward Chodorov, whose plays have never received the attention they justly deserve. If this study restores some of these plays and playwrights to life and brings them to the attention of readers, I shall be very pleased.

A discovery of another kind that I made came from reading dramas that did not seem at first glance to be about World War II. Reading those dramas in a wartime context, however, nuanced them in unanticipated ways. Suddenly Thornton Wilder's *Our Town,* William Saroyan's *The Time of Your Life,* Sidney Kingsley's *Patriots,* and Tennessee Williams's *A Streetcar Named Desire* showed new facets of meaning that I had missed when I saw or read them without the date of their original performance in mind. In short, writing this book was something of an education for me and may be one, I trust, for readers as well.

On a more personal level, writing this study has been an unusually satisfying and even sometimes cathartic experience for me. I am a child of World War II and my life was markedly shaped by its events. The plays I discuss were written and performed in the years just prior to my birth and during those of my very early childhood. In a sense, they articulate the tensions and events going on around me in the 1940s, the meaning of which I was not capable of understanding at the time. The legacy of the war and the uncertainties of wartime were already mine at my birth. My parents, both born and raised in Germany, came to America as refugees in 1937, fleeing from Nazi persecution. They arrived speaking German and brought with them little in the way of worldly possessions. Even as a toddler during the war, I sensed their feelings of profound hatred for the Third Reich as well as their enormous feelings of patriotism and love for the country that had succored them. With some strain on a meager family budget, I was proudly dressed in a child's Sunday best of the day: a wartime child-sized sailor suit. Before I was two years old, I was taught by my father and mother to recognize the photos of Hitler, Mussolini, and Hirohito in the newspapers and to spit at them. I remember the snatches of adult conversation etched with names and words like Roosevelt, Theresienstadt, sugar ration, *Judenstern*, Himmler, and later *umgekommen* (killed). And there were those two oft-repeated words, *ausgewandert nach,* which means "emigrated to," followed such words as *Brasilien, Süd Afrika, Australien, Palestina, Kuba, Bolivien, Kanada, Argentinien, England, Shanghai,* and *Nyassaland.* Those sounds of wartime diaspora were among the first I knew.

At the war's end, I found myself, then a five-year old, swept along by the crowds on a New York pier. My mother's seventy-year-old aunt was about to disembark from a ship containing one of the first boatloads of prisoners released from Theresienstadt concentration camp, where she had spent most the war. The look of the gaunt and frightened people who emerged from that ship haunts me to this day. In subsequent years, I was—and continue to be—stunned by the realization that had I been born in Germany instead of in New York, my parents and I would surely have died in Theresienstadt, Auschwitz, Gurz, Riga, or one of the other camps to which relatives were sent and from which they never returned. I understand, too, the depth of my parents' feelings of love for America. In what other land could they have arrived with no English and few belongings, and twenty years later been able to see their son attend Columbia and Yale or to have him become a university professor? If there are strains of my own patriotism in this study, they are ones that come to me naturally. In many ways, writing this study has meant for me writing the history of my origins and of my childhood and giving thanks that I was born in the U.S. and survived the war. . . .

Note

1. Clayton R. Koppes and Gregory D. Black, *Hollywood Goes to War: How Politics, Profits and Propaganda Shaped World War II Movies* (Berkeley and Los Angeles: University of California Press, 1987); Colin Shindler, *Hollywood Goes to War: Films and American Society, 1939-1952* (London and Boston: Routledge and Kegan Paul, 1979).

Bibliography

PRIMARY TEXTS

Anderson, Maxwell. *The Eve of St. Mark.* Washington, D.C.: Anderson House, 1942.

Anderson, Sherwood. *Above Suspicion.* In James Boyd, ed., *The Free Company Presents . . . : A Collection of Plays about the Meaning of America.* New York: Dodd, Mead and Co., 1941.

Ardrey, Robert. *Plays of Three Decades.* New York: Atheneum, 1968.

Benét, Stephen Vincent. *"We Stand United" and Other Radio Scripts.* New York and Toronto: Farrar and Rinehart, 1944.

Bentham, Josephine, and Herschel Williams. *Janie: A Comedy in Three Acts.* New York: Samuel French, 1943.

Chodorov, Edward. *Those Endearing Young Charms.* New York: Samuel French, 1943.

Connelly, Marc. *The Mole on Lincoln's Cheek.* In James Boyd, ed., *The Free Company Presents . . . : A Collection of Plays about the Meaning of America.* New York: Dodd, Mead and Co., 1941.

Corwin, Norman. *We Hold These Truths.* Recorded 15 December 1941, audio cassette CORW007 and compact disc CORW027, LodeStone, n.d.

d'Usseau, Arnaud, and James Gow. *Deep Are the Roots.* New York: Charles Scribner's Sons, 1946.

Franken, Rose. *Soldier's Wife.* New York: Samuel French, 1944.

Goodrich, Frances, and Albert Hackett. *The Diary of Anne Frank.* New York: Random House, 1956.

Hart, Moss. *Winged Victory: The Air Force Play.* New York: Random House, 1943.

Hecht, Ben. *A Flag Is Born.* New York: American League for a Free Palestine, 1946.

———. *We Will Never Die.* Typescript, 1943.

Hellman, Lillian. *The Searching Wind.* New York: Viking Press, 1944.

———. *Six Plays by Lillian Hellman.* New York: Vintage Books, 1979.

James, Dan. *Winter Soldiers.* Typescript, 1942.

Kingsley, Sidney. *The Patriots.* New York, 1943.

Laurents, Arthur. *Home of the Brave.* New York: Random House, 1946.

Lindsay, Howard, and Russel Crouse. *State of the Union* New York: Random House, 1945.

MacLeish, Archibald. *Air Raid.* New York: Harcourt Brace and Co., 1938.

———. *The Fall of the City.* New York: Farrar and Rinehart, 1937.

Miller, Arthur. *All My Sons.* New York: Penguin Books 1947.

Saroyan, William. *The People with Light Coming out of Them.* In James Boyd, ed., *The Free Company Presents . . . : A Collection of Plays about the Meaning of America.* New York: Dodd, Mead and Co., 1941.

The Time of Your Life. New York: Harcourt, Brace and Company, 1939.

Schiff, Ellen. *Awake and Singing: 7 Classic Plays from the American Jewish Repertoire.* New York: Mentor Books, 1995.

Shelley, Elsa. *Foxhole in the Parlor.* New York: Dramatists Play Service, 1946.

Sherwood, Robert E. *Abe Lincoln in Illinois.* New York: Charles Scribner's Sons, 1937.

Welles, Orson. His Honor, the Mayor. In James Boyd, ed., *The Free Company Presents . . . : A Collection of Plays about the Meaning of America.* New York: Dodd, Mead and Co., 1941.

Wilder, Thornton. *Our Town.* 1938. Reprint, New York: Harper and Row, 1957.

Williams, Tennessee. *A Streetcar Named Desire.* New York: New Directions, 1947.

Wood, Maxine. *On Whitman Avenue.* New York: Dramatists Play Service, 1948.

FURTHER READING

Criticism

Jarvis, Christina S. *The Male Body at War: American Masculinity during World War II.* DeKalb: Northern Illinois University Press, 2004, 243 p.

    Explores popular representation and perception of the male physique just before, during, and just after World War II.

Waldmeir, Joseph J. *American Novels of the Second World War.* The Hague: Mouton, 1969, 180 p.

    Discusses several World War II novels, treating such aspects as representation of the enemy, dissent, and commitment.

How to Use This Index

The main references

> **Calvino, Italo**
> 1923-1985 .... **CLC 5, 8, 11, 22, 33, 39,**
> **73; SSC 3, 48**

list all author entries in the following Thomson Gale Literary Criticism series:

AAL = *Asian American Literature*
BG = *The Beat Generation: A Gale Critical Companion*
BLC = *Black Literature Criticism*
BLCS = *Black Literature Criticism Supplement*
CLC = *Contemporary Literary Criticism*
CLR = *Children's Literature Review*
CMLC = *Classical and Medieval Literature Criticism*
DC = *Drama Criticism*
FL = *Feminism in Literature: A Gale Critical Companion*
GL = *Gothic Literature: A Gale Critical Companion*
HLC = *Hispanic Literature Criticism*
HLCS = *Hispanic Literature Criticism Supplement*
HR = *Harlem Renaissance: A Gale Critical Companion*
LC = *Literature Criticism from 1400 to 1800*
NCLC = *Nineteenth-Century Literature Criticism*
NNAL = *Native North American Literature*
PC = *Poetry Criticism*
SSC = *Short Story Criticism*
TCLC = *Twentieth-Century Literary Criticism*
WLC = *World Literature Criticism, 1500 to the Present*
WLCS = *World Literature Criticism Supplement*

The cross-references

> See also CA 85-88, 116; CANR 23, 61;
> DAM NOV; DLB 196; EW 13; MTCW 1, 2;
> RGSF 2; RGWL 2; SFW 4; SSFS 12

list all author entries in the following Thomson Gale biographical and literary sources:

AAYA = *Authors & Artists for Young Adults*
AFAW = *African American Writers*
AFW = *African Writers*
AITN = *Authors in the News*
AMW = *American Writers*
AMWR = *American Writers Retrospective Supplement*
AMWS = *American Writers Supplement*
ANW = *American Nature Writers*
AW = *Ancient Writers*
BEST = *Bestsellers*
BPFB = *Beacham's Encyclopedia of Popular Fiction: Biography and Resources*
BRW = *British Writers*
BRWS = *British Writers Supplement*
BW = *Black Writers*
BYA = *Beacham's Guide to Literature for Young Adults*
CA = *Contemporary Authors*
CAAS = *Contemporary Authors Autobiography Series*
CABS = *Contemporary Authors Bibliographical Series*
CAD = *Contemporary American Dramatists*
CANR = *Contemporary Authors New Revision Series*
CAP = *Contemporary Authors Permanent Series*
CBD = *Contemporary British Dramatists*
CCA = *Contemporary Canadian Authors*
CD = *Contemporary Dramatists*
CDALB = *Concise Dictionary of American Literary Biography*

CDALBS = *Concise Dictionary of American Literary Biography Supplement*
CDBLB = *Concise Dictionary of British Literary Biography*
CMW = *St. James Guide to Crime & Mystery Writers*
CN = *Contemporary Novelists*
CP = *Contemporary Poets*
CPW = *Contemporary Popular Writers*
CSW = *Contemporary Southern Writers*
CWD = *Contemporary Women Dramatists*
CWP = *Contemporary Women Poets*
CWRI = *St. James Guide to Children's Writers*
CWW = *Contemporary World Writers*
DA = *DISCovering Authors*
DA3 = *DISCovering Authors 3.0*
DAB = *DISCovering Authors: British Edition*
DAC = *DISCovering Authors: Canadian Edition*
DAM = *DISCovering Authors: Modules*
   DRAM: *Dramatists Module;* **MST:** *Most-studied Authors Module;*
   MULT: *Multicultural Authors Module;* **NOV:** *Novelists Module;*
   POET: *Poets Module;* **POP:** *Popular Fiction and Genre Authors Module*
DFS = *Drama for Students*
DLB = *Dictionary of Literary Biography*
DLBD = *Dictionary of Literary Biography Documentary Series*
DLBY = *Dictionary of Literary Biography Yearbook*
DNFS = *Literature of Developing Nations for Students*
EFS = *Epics for Students*
EXPN = *Exploring Novels*
EXPP = *Exploring Poetry*
EXPS = *Exploring Short Stories*
EW = *European Writers*
FANT = *St. James Guide to Fantasy Writers*
FW = *Feminist Writers*
GFL = *Guide to French Literature,* Beginnings to 1789, 1798 to the Present
GLL = *Gay and Lesbian Literature*
HGG = *St. James Guide to Horror, Ghost & Gothic Writers*
HW = *Hispanic Writers*
IDFW = *International Dictionary of Films and Filmmakers: Writers and Production Artists*
IDTP = *International Dictionary of Theatre: Playwrights*
LAIT = *Literature and Its Times*
LAW = *Latin American Writers*
JRDA = *Junior DISCovering Authors*
MAICYA = *Major Authors and Illustrators for Children and Young Adults*
MAICYAS = *Major Authors and Illustrators for Children and Young Adults Supplement*
MAWW = *Modern American Women Writers*
MJW = *Modern Japanese Writers*
MTCW = *Major 20th-Century Writers*
NCFS = *Nonfiction Classics for Students*
NFS = *Novels for Students*
PAB = *Poets: American and British*
PFS = *Poetry for Students*
RGAL = *Reference Guide to American Literature*
RGEL = *Reference Guide to English Literature*
RGSF = *Reference Guide to Short Fiction*
RGWL = *Reference Guide to World Literature*
RHW = *Twentieth-Century Romance and Historical Writers*
SAAS = *Something about the Author Autobiography Series*
SATA = *Something about the Author*
SFW = *St. James Guide to Science Fiction Writers*
SSFS = *Short Stories for Students*
TCWW = *Twentieth-Century Western Writers*
WLIT = *World Literature and Its Times*
WP = *World Poets*
YABC = *Yesterday's Authors of Books for Children*
YAW = *St. James Guide to Young Adult Writers*

Literary Criticism Series
Cumulative Author Index

Ammons, A.R. 1926-2001 .. **CLC 2, 3, 5, 8, 9, 25, 57, 108; PC 16**
See also AITN 1; AMWS 7; CA 9-12R; CAAS 193; CANR 6, 36, 51, 73, 107, 156; CP 1, 2, 3, 4, 5, 6, 7; CSW; DAM POET; DLB 5, 165; EWL 3; MAL 5; MTCW 1, 2; PFS 19; RGAL 4; TCLE 1:1

Ammons, Archie Randolph
See Ammons, A.R.

Amo, Tauraatua i
See Adams, Henry (Brooks)

Amory, Thomas 1691(?)-1788 .... **LC 48**
See also DLB 39

Anand, Mulk Raj 1905-2004 ..... **CLC 23, 93, 237**
See also CA 65-68; CAAS 231; CANR 32, 64; CN 1, 2, 3, 4, 5, 6, 7; DAM NOV; DLB 323; EWL 3; MTCW 1, 2; MTFW 2005; RGSF 2

Anatol
See Schnitzler, Arthur

Anaximander c. 611B.C.-c. 546B.C. .... **CMLC 22**

Anaya, Rudolfo A. 1937- .... **CLC 23, 148; HLC 1**
See also AAYA 20; BYA 13; CA 45-48; 4; CANR 1, 32, 51, 124; CN 4, 5, 6, 7; DAM MULT, NOV; DLB 82, 206, 278; HW 1; LAIT 4; LLW; MAL 5; MTCW 1, 2; MTFW 2005; NFS 12; RGAL 4; RGSF 2; TCWW 2; WLIT 1

Andersen, Hans Christian 1805-1875 .... **NCLC 7, 79; SSC 6, 56; WLC 1**
See also AAYA 57; CLR 6, 113; DA; DA3; DAB; DAC; DAM MST, POP; EW 6; MAICYA 1, 2; RGSF 2; RGWL 2, 3; SATA 100; TWA; WCH; YABC 1

Anderson, C. Farley
See Mencken, H(enry) L(ouis); Nathan, George Jean

Anderson, Jessica (Margaret) Queale 1916- .... **CLC 37**
See also CA 9-12R; CANR 4, 62; CN 4, 5, 6, 7; DLB 325

Anderson, Jon (Victor) 1940- .... **CLC 9**
See also CA 25-28R; CANR 20; CP 1, 3, 4, 5; DAM POET

Anderson, Lindsay (Gordon) 1923-1994 .... **CLC 20**
See also CA 128; CAAE 125; CAAS 146; CANR 77

Anderson, Maxwell 1888-1959 .... **TCLC 2, 144**
See also CA 152; CAAE 105; DAM DRAM; DFS 16, 20; DLB 7, 228; MAL 5; MTCW 2; MTFW 2005; RGAL 4

Anderson, Poul 1926-2001 .... **CLC 15**
See also AAYA 5, 34; BPFB 1; BYA 6, 8, 9; CA 181; 1-4R, 181; 2; CAAS 199; CANR 2, 15, 34, 64, 110; CLR 58; DLB 8; FANT; INT CANR-15; MTCW 1, 2; MTFW 2005; SATA 90; SATA-Brief 39; SATA-Essay 106; SCFW 1, 2; SFW 4; SUFW 1, 2

Anderson, Robert (Woodruff) 1917- .... **CLC 23**
See also AITN 1; CA 21-24R; CANR 32; CD 6; DAM DRAM; DLB 7; LAIT 5

Anderson, Roberta Joan
See Mitchell, Joni

Anderson, Sherwood 1876-1941 ... **SSC 1, 46, 91; TCLC 1, 10, 24, 123; WLC 1**
See also AAYA 30; AMW; AMWC 2; BPFB 1; CA 121; CAAE 104; CANR 61; CDALB 1917-1929; DA; DA3; DAB; DAC; DAM MST, NOV; DLB 4, 9, 86; DLBD 1; EWL 3; EXPS; GLL 2; MAL 5; MTCW 1, 2; MTFW 2005; NFS 4; RGAL 4; RGSF 2; SSFS 4, 10, 11; TUS

Anderson, Wes 1969- .... **CLC 227**
See also CA 214

Andier, Pierre
See Desnos, Robert

Andouard
See Giraudoux, Jean(-Hippolyte)

Andrade, Carlos Drummond de ..... **CLC 18**
See Drummond de Andrade, Carlos
See also EWL 3; RGWL 2, 3

Andrade, Mario de .... **TCLC 43**
See de Andrade, Mario
See also DLB 307; EWL 3; LAW; RGWL 2, 3; WLIT 1

Andreae, Johann V(alentin) 1586-1654 .... **LC 32**
See also DLB 164

Andreas Capellanus fl. c. 1185- .... **CMLC 45**
See also DLB 208

Andreas-Salome, Lou 1861-1937 ... **TCLC 56**
See also CA 178; DLB 66

Andreev, Leonid
See Andreyev, Leonid (Nikolaevich)
See also DLB 295; EWL 3

Andress, Lesley
See Sanders, Lawrence

Andrewes, Lancelot 1555-1626 .... **LC 5**
See also DLB 151, 172

Andrews, Cicily Fairfield
See West, Rebecca

Andrews, Elton V.
See Pohl, Frederik

Andrews, Peter
See Soderbergh, Steven

Andreyev, Leonid (Nikolaevich) 1871-1919 .... **TCLC 3**
See Andreev, Leonid
See also CA 185; CAAE 104

Andric, Ivo 1892-1975 .... **CLC 8; SSC 36; TCLC 135**
See also CA 81-84; CAAS 57-60; CANR 43, 60; CDWLB 4; DLB 147, 329; EW 11; EWL 3; MTCW 1; RGSF 2; RGWL 2, 3

Androvar
See Prado (Calvo), Pedro

Angela of Foligno 1248(?)-1309 .... **CMLC 76**

Angelique, Pierre
See Bataille, Georges

Angell, Roger 1920- .... **CLC 26**
See also CA 57-60; CANR 13, 44, 70, 144; DLB 171, 185

Angelou, Maya 1928- ... **BLC 1; CLC 12, 35, 64, 77, 155; PC 32; WLCS**
See also AAYA 7, 20; AMWS 4; BPFB 1; BW 2, 3; BYA 2; CA 65-68; CANR 19, 42, 65, 111, 133; CDALBS; CLR 53; CP 4, 5, 6, 7; CPW; CSW; CWP; DA; DA3; DAB; DAC; DAM MST, MULT, POET, POP; DLB 38; EWL 3; EXPN; EXPP; FL 1:5; LAIT 4; MAICYA 2; MAICYAS 1; MAL 5; MBL; MTCW 1, 2; MTFW 2005; NCFS 2; NFS 2; PFS 2, 3; RGAL 4; SATA 49, 136; TCLE 1:1; WYA; YAW

Angouleme, Marguerite d'
See de Navarre, Marguerite

Anna Comnena 1083-1153 .... **CMLC 25**

Annensky, Innokentii Fedorovich
See Annensky, Innokenty (Fyodorovich)
See also DLB 295

Annensky, Innokenty (Fyodorovich) 1856-1909 .... **TCLC 14**
See also CA 155; CAAE 110; EWL 3

Annunzio, Gabriele d'
See D'Annunzio, Gabriele

Anodos
See Coleridge, Mary E(lizabeth)

Anon, Charles Robert
See Pessoa, Fernando (Antonio Nogueira)

Anouilh, Jean 1910-1987 ..... **CLC 1, 3, 8, 13, 40, 50; DC 8, 21**
See also AAYA 67; CA 17-20R; CAAS 123; CANR 32; DAM DRAM; DFS 9, 10, 19; DLB 321; EW 13; EWL 3; GFL 1789 to the Present; MTCW 1, 2; MTFW 2005; RGWL 2, 3; TWA

Anselm of Canterbury 1033(?)-1109 .... **CMLC 67**
See also DLB 115

Anthony, Florence
See Ai

Anthony, John
See Ciardi, John (Anthony)

Anthony, Peter
See Shaffer, Anthony; Shaffer, Peter

Anthony, Piers 1934- .... **CLC 35**
See also AAYA 11, 48; BYA 7; CA 200; 200; CANR 28, 56, 73, 102, 133; CLR 118; CPW; DAM POP; DLB 8; FANT; MAICYA 2; MAICYAS 1; MTCW 1, 2; MTFW 2005; SAAS 22; SATA 84, 129; SATA-Essay 129; SFW 4; SUFW 1, 2; YAW

Anthony, Susan B(rownell) 1820-1906 .... **TCLC 84**
See also CA 211; FW

Antiphon c. 480B.C.-c. 411B.C. .... **CMLC 55**

Antoine, Marc
See Proust, (Valentin-Louis-George-Eugene) Marcel

Antoninus, Brother
See Everson, William (Oliver)
See also CP 1

Antonioni, Michelangelo 1912-2007 .... **CLC 20, 144**
See also CA 73-76; CANR 45, 77

Antschel, Paul 1920-1970
See Celan, Paul
See also CA 85-88; CANR 33, 61; MTCW 1; PFS 21

Anwar, Chairil 1922-1949 .... **TCLC 22**
See Chairil Anwar
See also CA 219; CAAE 121; RGWL 3

Anzaldua, Gloria (Evanjelina) 1942-2004 .... **CLC 200; HLCS 1**
See also CA 175; CAAS 227; CSW; CWP; DLB 122; FW; LLW; RGAL 4; SATA-Obit 154

Apess, William 1798-1839(?) .... **NCLC 73; NNAL**
See also DAM MULT; DLB 175, 243

Apollinaire, Guillaume 1880-1918 .... **PC 7; TCLC 3, 8, 51**
See Kostrowitzki, Wilhelm Apollinaris de
See also CA 152; DAM POET; DLB 258, 321; EW 9; EWL 3; GFL 1789 to the Present; MTCW 2; PFS 24; RGWL 2, 3; TWA; WP

Apollonius of Rhodes
See Apollonius Rhodius
See also AW 1; RGWL 2, 3

Apollonius Rhodius c. 300B.C.-c. 220B.C. .... **CMLC 28**
See Apollonius of Rhodes
See also DLB 176

Appelfeld, Aharon 1932- ... **CLC 23, 47; SSC 42**
See also CA 133; CAAE 112; CANR 86, 160; CWW 2; DLB 299; EWL 3; RGHL; RGSF 2; WLIT 6

Appelfeld, Aron
See Appelfeld, Aharon

Apple, Max (Isaac) 1941- .... **CLC 9, 33; SSC 50**
See also AMWS 17; CA 81-84; CANR 19, 54; DLB 130

Appleman, Philip (Dean) 1926- .... **CLC 51**
See also CA 13-16R; 18; CANR 6, 29, 56

Appleton, Lawrence
See Lovecraft, H. P.

Apteryx
See Eliot, T(homas) S(tearns)

Apuleius, (Lucius Madaurensis) c. 125-c. 164 .... **CMLC 1, 84**
See also AW 2; CDWLB 1; DLB 211; RGWL 2, 3; SUFW; WLIT 8

Aquin, Hubert 1929-1977 .... **CLC 15**
See also CA 105; DLB 53; EWL 3

Aquinas, Thomas 1224(?)-1274 ..... **CMLC 33**
See also DLB 115; EW 1; TWA

Aragon, Louis 1897-1982 .... **CLC 3, 22; TCLC 123**
See also CA 69-72; CAAS 108; CANR 28, 71; DAM NOV, POET; DLB 72, 258; EW 11; EWL 3; GFL 1789 to the Present; GLL 2; LMFS 2; MTCW 1, 2; RGWL 2, 3

Arany, Janos 1817-1882 .... **NCLC 34**

Aranyos, Kakay 1847-1910
See Mikszath, Kalman

Aratus of Soli c. 315B.C.-c. 240B.C. .... **CMLC 64**
See also DLB 176

Arbuthnot, John 1667-1735 .... **LC 1**
See also DLB 101

Archer, Herbert Winslow
See Mencken, H(enry) L(ouis)

Archer, Jeffrey 1940- .... **CLC 28**
See also AAYA 16; BEST 89:3; BPFB 1; CA 77-80; CANR 22, 52, 95, 136; CPW; DA3; DAM POP; INT CANR-22; MTFW 2005

Archer, Jeffrey Howard
See Archer, Jeffrey

Archer, Jules 1915- .... **CLC 12**
See also CA 9-12R; CANR 6, 69; SAAS 5; SATA 4, 85

Archer, Lee
See Ellison, Harlan

Archilochus c. 7th cent. B.C.- .... **CMLC 44**
See also DLB 176

Arden, John 1930- .... **CLC 6, 13, 15**
See also BRWS 2; CA 13-16R; 4; CANR 31, 65, 67, 124; CBD; CD 5, 6; DAM DRAM; DFS 9; DLB 13, 245; EWL 3; MTCW 1

Arenas, Reinaldo 1943-1990 .. **CLC 41; HLC 1; TCLC 191**
See also CA 128; CAAE 124; CAAS 133; CANR 73, 106; DAM MULT; DLB 145; EWL 3; GLL 2; HW 1; LAW; LAWS 1; MTCW 2; MTFW 2005; RGSF 2; RGWL 3; WLIT 1

Arendt, Hannah 1906-1975 .... **CLC 66, 98; TCLC 193**
See also CA 17-20R; CAAS 61-64; CANR 26, 60; DLB 242; MTCW 1, 2

Aretino, Pietro 1492-1556 .... **LC 12**
See also RGWL 2, 3

Arghezi, Tudor .... **CLC 80**
See Theodorescu, Ion N.
See also CA 167; CDWLB 4; DLB 220; EWL 3

Arguedas, Jose Maria 1911-1969 .... **CLC 10, 18; HLCS 1; TCLC 147**
See also CA 89-92; CANR 73; DLB 113; EWL 3; HW 1; LAW; RGWL 2, 3; WLIT 1

Argueta, Manlio 1936- .... **CLC 31**
See also CA 131; CANR 73; CWW 2; DLB 145; EWL 3; HW 1; RGWL 3

Arias, Ron 1941- .... **HLC 1**
See also CA 131; CANR 81, 136; DAM MULT; DLB 82; HW 1, 2; MTCW 2; MTFW 2005

Ariosto, Lodovico
See Ariosto, Ludovico
See also WLIT 7

Ariosto, Ludovico 1474-1533 ... **LC 6, 87; PC 42**
See Ariosto, Lodovico
See also EW 2; RGWL 2, 3

Aristides
See Epstein, Joseph

Aristophanes 450B.C.-385B.C. .... **CMLC 4, 51; DC 2; WLCS**
See also AW 1; CDWLB 1; DA; DA3; DAB; DAC; DAM DRAM, MST; DFS 10; DLB 176; LMFS 1; RGWL 2, 3; TWA; WLIT 8

Aristotle 384B.C.-322B.C. .... **CMLC 31; WLCS**
See also AW 1; CDWLB 1; DA; DA3; DAB; DAC; DAM MST; DLB 176; RGWL 2, 3; TWA; WLIT 8

Arlt, Roberto (Godofredo Christophersen) 1900-1942 .... **HLC 1; TCLC 29**
See also CA 131; CAAE 123; CANR 67; DAM MULT; DLB 305; EWL 3; HW 1, 2; IDTP; LAW

Armah, Ayi Kwei 1939- . **BLC 1; CLC 5, 33, 136**
See also AFW; BRWS 10; BW 1; CA 61-64; CANR 21, 64; CDWLB 3; CN 1, 2, 3, 4, 5, 6, 7; DAM MULT, POET; DLB 117; EWL 3; MTCW 1; WLIT 2

Armatrading, Joan 1950- .... **CLC 17**
See also CA 186; CAAE 114

Armin, Robert 1568(?)-1615(?) .... **LC 120**

Armitage, Frank
See Carpenter, John (Howard)

Armstrong, Jeannette (C.) 1948- .... **NNAL**
See also CA 149; CCA 1; CN 6, 7; DAC; DLB 334; SATA 102

Arnette, Robert
See Silverberg, Robert

Arnim, Achim von (Ludwig Joachim von Arnim) 1781-1831 .. **NCLC 5, 159; SSC 29**
See also DLB 90

Arnim, Bettina von 1785-1859 ...... **NCLC 38, 123**
See also DLB 90; RGWL 2, 3

Arnold, Matthew 1822-1888 ..... **NCLC 6, 29, 89, 126; PC 5; WLC 1**
See also BRW 5; CDBLB 1832-1890; DA; DAB; DAC; DAM MST, POET; DLB 32, 57; EXPP; PAB; PFS 2; TEA; WP

Arnold, Thomas 1795-1842 .... **NCLC 18**
See also DLB 55

Arnow, Harriette (Louisa) Simpson 1908-1986 .... **CLC 2, 7, 18**
See also BPFB 1; CA 9-12R; CAAS 118; CANR 14; CN 2, 3, 4; DLB 6; FW; MTCW 1, 2; RHW; SATA 42; SATA-Obit 47

Arouet, Francois-Marie
See Voltaire

Arp, Hans
See Arp, Jean

Arp, Jean 1887-1966 .... **CLC 5; TCLC 115**
See also CA 81-84; CAAS 25-28R; CANR 42, 77; EW 10

Arrabal
See Arrabal, Fernando

Arrabal (Teran), Fernando
See Arrabal, Fernando
See also CWW 2

Arrabal, Fernando 1932- ... **CLC 2, 9, 18, 58**
See Arrabal (Teran), Fernando
See also CA 9-12R; CANR 15; DLB 321; EWL 3; LMFS 2

Arreola, Juan Jose 1918-2001 .... **CLC 147; HLC 1; SSC 38**
See also CA 131; CAAE 113; CAAS 200; CANR 81; CWW 2; DAM MULT; DLB 113; DNFS 2; EWL 3; HW 1, 2; LAW; RGSF 2

Arrian c. 89(?)-c. 155(?) .... **CMLC 43**
See also DLB 176

Arrick, Fran .... **CLC 30**
See Gaberman, Judie Angell
See also BYA 6

Arrley, Richmond
See Delany, Samuel R., Jr.

Artaud, Antonin (Marie Joseph) 1896-1948 .... **DC 14; TCLC 3, 36**
See also CA 149; CAAE 104; DA3; DAM DRAM; DFS 22; DLB 258, 321; EW 11; EWL 3; GFL 1789 to the Present; MTCW 2; MTFW 2005; RGWL 2, 3

Arthur, Ruth M(abel) 1905-1979 ..... **CLC 12**
See also CA 9-12R; CAAS 85-88; CANR 4; CWRI 5; SATA 7, 26

Artsybashev, Mikhail (Petrovich) 1878-1927 .... **TCLC 31**
See also CA 170; DLB 295

Arundel, Honor (Morfydd) 1919-1973 .... **CLC 17**
See also CA 21-22; CAAS 41-44R; CAP 2; CLR 35; CWRI 5; SATA 4; SATA-Obit 24

Arzner, Dorothy 1900-1979 .... **CLC 98**

Asch, Sholem 1880-1957 .... **TCLC 3**
See also CAAE 105; DLB 333; EWL 3; GLL 2; RGHL

Ascham, Roger 1516(?)-1568 .... **LC 101**
See also DLB 236

Ash, Shalom
See Asch, Sholem

Ashbery, John 1927- ... **CLC 2, 3, 4, 6, 9, 13, 15, 25, 41, 77, 125, 221; PC 26**
See Berry, Jonas
See also AMWS 3; CA 5-8R; CANR 9, 37, 66, 102, 132; CP 1, 2, 3, 4, 5, 6, 7; DA3; DAM POET; DLB 5, 165; DLBY 1981; EWL 3; INT CANR-9; MAL 5; MTCW 1, 2; MTFW 2005; PAB; PFS 11; RGAL 4; TCLE 1:1; WP

Ashbery, John Lawrence
See Ashbery, John

Ashdown, Clifford
See Freeman, R(ichard) Austin

Ashe, Gordon
See Creasey, John

Ashton-Warner, Sylvia (Constance) 1908-1984 .... **CLC 19**
See also CA 69-72; CAAS 112; CANR 29; CN 1, 2, 3; MTCW 1, 2

Asimov, Isaac 1920-1992 ..... **CLC 1, 3, 9, 19, 26, 76, 92**
See also AAYA 13; BEST 90:2; BPFB 1; BYA 4, 6, 7, 9; CA 1-4R; CAAS 137; CANR 2, 19, 36, 60, 125; CLR 12, 79; CMW 4; CN 1, 2, 3, 4, 5; CPW; DA3; DAM POP; DLB 8; DLBY 1992; INT CANR-19; JRDA; LAIT 5; LMFS 2; MAICYA 1, 2; MAL 5; MTCW 1, 2; MTFW 2005; RGAL 4; SATA 1, 26, 74; SCFW 1, 2; SFW 4; SSFS 17; TUS; YAW

Askew, Anne 1521(?)-1546 .... **LC 81**
See also DLB 136

Assis, Joaquim Maria Machado de
See Machado de Assis, Joaquim Maria

Astell, Mary 1666-1731 .... **LC 68**
See also DLB 252, 336; FW

Astley, Thea (Beatrice May) 1925-2004 .... **CLC 41**
See also CA 65-68; CAAS 229; CANR 11, 43, 78; CN 1, 2, 3, 4, 5, 6, 7; DLB 289; EWL 3

Benda, Julien 1867-1956 .... **TCLC 60**
See also CA 154; CAAE 120; GFL 1789 to
the Present
Benedict, Ruth 1887-1948 .... **TCLC 60**
See also CA 158; CANR 146; DLB 246
Benedict, Ruth Fulton
See Benedict, Ruth
Benedikt, Michael 1935- .... **CLC 4, 14**
See also CA 13-16R; CANR 7; CP 1, 2, 3,
4, 5, 6, 7; DLB 5
Benet, Juan 1927-1993 .... **CLC 28**
See also CA 143; EWL 3
Benet, Stephen Vincent 1898-1943 ..... **PC 64;
SSC 10, 86; TCLC 7**
See also AMWS 11; CA 152; CAAE 104;
DA3; DAM POET; DLB 4, 48, 102, 249,
284; DLBY 1997; EWL 3; HGG; MAL 5;
MTCW 2; MTFW 2005; RGAL 4; RGSF
2; SSFS 22; SUFW; WP; YABC 1
Benet, William Rose 1886-1950 ..... **TCLC 28**
See also CA 152; CAAE 118; DAM POET;
DLB 45; RGAL 4
Benford, Gregory 1941- .... **CLC 52**
See also BPFB 1; CA 175; 69-72, 175; 27;
CANR 12, 24, 49, 95, 134; CN 7; CSW;
DLBY 1982; MTFW 2005; SCFW 2;
SFW 4
Benford, Gregory Albert
See Benford, Gregory
Bengtsson, Frans (Gunnar)
1894-1954 .... **TCLC 48**
See also CA 170; EWL 3
Benjamin, David
See Slavitt, David R.
Benjamin, Lois
See Gould, Lois
Benjamin, Walter 1892-1940 .... **TCLC 39**
See also CA 164; DLB 242; EW 11; EWL
3
Ben Jelloun, Tahar 1944- .... **CLC 180**
See also CA 135, 162; CANR 100, 166;
CWW 2; EWL 3; RGWL 3; WLIT 2
Benn, Gottfried 1886-1956 .. **PC 35; TCLC 3**
See also CA 153; CAAE 106; DLB 56;
EWL 3; RGWL 2, 3
Bennett, Alan 1934- .... **CLC 45, 77**
See also BRWS 8; CA 103; CANR 35, 55,
106, 157; CBD; CD 5, 6; DAB; DAM
MST; DLB 310; MTCW 1, 2; MTFW
2005
Bennett, (Enoch) Arnold
1867-1931 .... **TCLC 5, 20**
See also BRW 6; CA 155; CAAE 106; CD-
BLB 1890-1914; DLB 10, 34, 98, 135;
EWL 3; MTCW 2
Bennett, Elizabeth
See Mitchell, Margaret (Munnerlyn)
Bennett, George Harold 1930-
See Bennett, Hal
See also BW 1; CA 97-100; CANR 87
Bennett, Gwendolyn B. 1902-1981 .... **HR 1:2**
See also BW 1; CA 125; DLB 51; WP
Bennett, Hal .... **CLC 5**
See Bennett, George Harold
See also CA 13; DLB 33
Bennett, Jay 1912- .... **CLC 35**
See also AAYA 10, 73; CA 69-72; CANR
11, 42, 79; JRDA; SAAS 4; SATA 41, 87;
SATA-Brief 27; WYA; YAW
Bennett, Louise 1919-2006 .. **BLC 1; CLC 28**
See also BW 2, 3; CA 151; CAAS 252; CD-
WLB 3; CP 1, 2, 3, 4, 5, 6, 7; DAM
MULT; DLB 117; EWL 3
Bennett, Louise Simone
See Bennett, Louise
Bennett-Coverley, Louise
See Bennett, Louise

Benoit de Sainte-Maure fl. 12th cent.
- .... **CMLC 90**
Benson, A. C. 1862-1925 .... **TCLC 123**
See also DLB 98
Benson, E(dward) F(rederic)
1867-1940 .... **TCLC 27**
See also CA 157; CAAE 114; DLB 135,
153; HGG; SUFW 1
Benson, Jackson J. 1930- .... **CLC 34**
See also CA 25-28R; DLB 111
Benson, Sally 1900-1972 .... **CLC 17**
See also CA 19-20; CAAS 37-40R; CAP 1;
SATA 1, 35; SATA-Obit 27
Benson, Stella 1892-1933 .... **TCLC 17**
See also CA 154, 155; CAAE 117; DLB
36, 162; FANT; TEA
Bentham, Jeremy 1748-1832 .... **NCLC 38**
See also DLB 107, 158, 252
Bentley, E(dmund) C(lerihew)
1875-1956 .... **TCLC 12**
See also CA 232; CAAE 108; DLB 70;
MSW
Bentley, Eric 1916- .... **CLC 24**
See also CA 5-8R; CAD; CANR 6, 67;
CBD; CD 5, 6; INT CANR-6
Bentley, Eric Russell
See Bentley, Eric
ben Uzair, Salem
See Horne, Richard Henry Hengist
Beolco, Angelo 1496-1542 .... **LC 139**
Beranger, Pierre Jean de
1780-1857 .... **NCLC 34**
Berdyaev, Nicolas
See Berdyaev, Nikolai (Aleksandrovich)
Berdyaev, Nikolai (Aleksandrovich)
1874-1948 .... **TCLC 67**
See also CA 157; CAAE 120
Berdyayev, Nikolai (Aleksandrovich)
See Berdyaev, Nikolai (Aleksandrovich)
Berendt, John 1939- .... **CLC 86**
See also CA 146; CANR 75, 83, 151
Berendt, John Lawrence
See Berendt, John
Beresford, J(ohn) D(avys)
1873-1947 .... **TCLC 81**
See also CA 155; CAAE 112; DLB 162,
178, 197; SFW 4; SUFW 1
Bergelson, David (Rafailovich)
1884-1952 .... **TCLC 81**
See Bergelson, Dovid
See also CA 220; DLB 333
Bergelson, Dovid
See Bergelson, David (Rafailovich)
See also EWL 3
Berger, Colonel
See Malraux, (Georges-)Andre
Berger, John 1926- .... **CLC 2, 19**
See also BRWS 4; CA 81-84; CANR 51,
78, 117, 163; CN 1, 2, 3, 4, 5, 6, 7; DLB
14, 207, 319, 326
Berger, John Peter
See Berger, John
Berger, Melvin H. 1927- .... **CLC 12**
See also CA 5-8R; CANR 4, 142; CLR 32;
SAAS 2; SATA 5, 88, 158; SATA-Essay
124
Berger, Thomas 1924- .... **CLC 3, 5, 8, 11, 18,
38**
See also BPFB 1; CA 1-4R; CANR 5, 28,
51, 128; CN 1, 2, 3, 4, 5, 6, 7; DAM
NOV; DLB 2; DLBY 1980; EWL 3;
FANT; INT CANR-28; MAL 5; MTCW
1, 2; MTFW 2005; RHW; TCLE 1:1;
TCWW 1, 2
Bergman, Ingmar 1918-2007 ..... **CLC 16, 72,
210**
See also AAYA 61; CA 81-84; CANR 33,
70; CWW 2; DLB 257; MTCW 2; MTFW
2005

Bergson, Henri(-Louis) 1859-1941 . **TCLC 32**
See also CA 164; DLB 329; EW 8; EWL 3;
GFL 1789 to the Present
Bergstein, Eleanor 1938- .... **CLC 4**
See also CA 53-56; CANR 5
Berkeley, George 1685-1753 .... **LC 65**
See also DLB 31, 101, 252
Berkoff, Steven 1937- .... **CLC 56**
See also CA 104; CANR 72; CBD; CD 5, 6
Berlin, Isaiah 1909-1997 .... **TCLC 105**
See also CA 85-88; CAAS 162
Bermant, Chaim (Icyk) 1929-1998 ... **CLC 40**
See also CA 57-60; CANR 6, 31, 57, 105;
CN 2, 3, 4, 5, 6
Bern, Victoria
See Fisher, M(ary) F(rances) K(ennedy)
Bernanos, (Paul Louis) Georges
1888-1948 .... **TCLC 3**
See also CA 130; CAAE 104; CANR 94;
DLB 72; EWL 3; GFL 1789 to the
Present; RGWL 2, 3
Bernard, April 1956- .... **CLC 59**
See also CA 131; CANR 144
Bernard, Mary Ann
See Soderbergh, Steven
Bernard of Clairvaux 1090-1153 .. **CMLC 71**
See also DLB 208
Bernard Silvestris fl. c. 1130-fl. c.
1160 .... **CMLC 87**
See also DLB 208
Berne, Victoria
See Fisher, M(ary) F(rances) K(ennedy)
Bernhard, Thomas 1931-1989 ..... **CLC 3, 32,
61; DC 14; TCLC 165**
See also CA 85-88; CAAS 127; CANR 32,
57; CDWLB 2; DLB 85, 124; EWL 3;
MTCW 1; RGHL; RGWL 2, 3
Bernhardt, Sarah (Henriette Rosine)
1844-1923 .... **TCLC 75**
See also CA 157
Bernstein, Charles 1950- .... **CLC 142,**
See also CA 129; 24; CANR 90; CP 4, 5, 6,
7; DLB 169
Bernstein, Ingrid
See Kirsch, Sarah
Beroul fl. c. 12th cent. - .... **CMLC 75**
Berriault, Gina 1926-1999 .... **CLC 54, 109;
SSC 30**
See also CA 129; CAAE 116; CAAS 185;
CANR 66; DLB 130; SSFS 7,11
Berrigan, Daniel 1921- .... **CLC 4**
See also CA 187; 33-36R, 187; 1; CANR
11, 43, 78; CP 1, 2, 3, 4, 5, 6, 7; DLB 5
Berrigan, Edmund Joseph Michael, Jr.
1934-1983
See Berrigan, Ted
See also CA 61-64; CAAS 110; CANR 14,
102
Berrigan, Ted .... **CLC 37**
See Berrigan, Edmund Joseph Michael, Jr.
See also CP 1, 2, 3; DLB 5, 169; WP
Berry, Charles Edward Anderson 1931-
See Berry, Chuck
See also CA 115
Berry, Chuck .... **CLC 17**
See Berry, Charles Edward Anderson
Berry, Jonas
See Ashbery, John
See also GLL 1
Berry, Wendell 1934- .... **CLC 4, 6, 8, 27, 46;
PC 28**
See also AITN 1; AMWS 10; ANW; CA
73-76; CANR 50, 73, 101, 132; CP 1, 2,
3, 4, 5, 6, 7; CSW; DAM POET; DLB 5,
6, 234, 275; MTCW 2; MTFW 2005;
TCLE 1:1

LITERARY CRITICISM SERIES

BUCKLEY

Author Index

Brooks, Gwendolyn 1917-2000 .... **BLC 1; CLC 1, 2, 4, 5, 15, 49, 125; PC 7; WLC 1**
See also AAYA 20; AFAW 1, 2; AITN 1; AMWS 3; BW 2, 3; CA 1-4R; CAAS 190; CANR 1, 27, 52, 75, 132; CDALB 1941-1968; CLR 27; CP 1, 2, 3, 4, 5, 6, 7; CWP; DA; DA3; DAC; DAM MST, MULT, POET; DLB 5, 76, 165; EWL 3; EXPP; FL 1:5; MAL 5; MBL; MTCW 1, 2; MTFW 2005; PFS 1, 2, 4, 6; RGAL 4; SATA 6; SATA-Obit 123; TUS; WP

Brooks, Mel 1926-
See Kaminsky, Melvin
See also CA 65-68; CANR 16; DFS 21

Brooks, Peter (Preston) 1938- .... **CLC 34**
See also CA 45-48; CANR 1, 107

Brooks, Van Wyck 1886-1963 .... **CLC 29**
See also AMW; CA 1-4R; CANR 6; DLB 45, 63, 103; MAL 5; TUS

Brophy, Brigid (Antonia) 1929-1995 .... **CLC 6, 11, 29, 105**
See also CA 5-8R; 4; CAAS 149; CANR 25, 53; CBD; CN 1, 2, 3, 4, 5, 6; CWD; DA3; DLB 14, 271; EWL 3; MTCW 1, 2

Brosman, Catharine Savage 1934- ..... **CLC 9**
See also CA 61-64; CANR 21, 46, 149

Brossard, Nicole 1943- .... **CLC 115, 169**
See also CA 122; 16; CANR 140; CCA 1; CWP; CWW 2; DLB 53; EWL 3; FW; GLL 2; RGWL 3

Brother Antoninus
See Everson, William (Oliver)

Brothers Grimm
See Grimm, Jacob Ludwig Karl; Grimm, Wilhelm Karl

The Brothers Quay
See Quay, Stephen; Quay, Timothy

Broughton, T(homas) Alan 1936- ..... **CLC 19**
See also CA 45-48; CANR 2, 23, 48, 111

Broumas, Olga 1949- .... **CLC 10, 73**
See also CA 85-88; CANR 20, 69, 110; CP 5, 6, 7; CWP; GLL 2

Broun, Heywood 1888-1939 .... **TCLC 104**
See also DLB 29, 171

Brown, Alan 1950- .... **CLC 99**
See also CA 156

Brown, Charles Brockden 1771-1810 .... **NCLC 22, 74, 122**
See also AMWS 1; CDALB 1640-1865; DLB 37, 59, 73; FW; GL 2; HGG; LMFS 1; RGAL 4; TUS

Brown, Christy 1932-1981 .... **CLC 63**
See also BYA 13; CA 105; CAAS 104; CANR 72; DLB 14

Brown, Claude 1937-2002 ... **BLC 1; CLC 30**
See also AAYA 7; BW 1, 3; CA 73-76; CAAS 205; CANR 81; DAM MULT

Brown, Dan 1964- .... **CLC 209**
See also AAYA 55; CA 217; MTFW 2005

Brown, Dee 1908-2002 .... **CLC 18, 47**
See also AAYA 30; CA 13-16R; 6; CAAS 212; CANR 11, 45, 60, 150; CPW; CSW; DA3; DAM POP; DLBY 1980; LAIT 2; MTCW 1, 2; MTFW 2005; NCFS 5; SATA 5, 110; SATA-Obit 141; TCWW 1, 2

Brown, Dee Alexander
See Brown, Dee

Brown, George
See Wertmueller, Lina

Brown, George Douglas 1869-1902 .... **TCLC 28**
See Douglas, George
See also CA 162

Brown, George Mackay 1921-1996 ... **CLC 5, 48, 100**
See also BRWS 6; CA 21-24R; 6; CAAS 151; CANR 12, 37, 67; CN 1, 2, 3, 4, 5, 6; CP 1, 2, 3, 4, 5, 6; DLB 14, 27, 139, 271; MTCW 1; RGSF 2; SATA 35

Brown, James Wllie
See Komunyakaa, Yusef

Brown, James Wllie, Jr.
See Komunyakaa, Yusef

Brown, Larry 1951-2004 .... **CLC 73**
See also CA 134; CAAE 130; CAAS 233; CANR 117, 145; CSW; DLB 234; INT CA-134

Brown, Moses
See Barrett, William (Christopher)

Brown, Rita Mae 1944- .... **CLC 18, 43, 79**
See also BPFB 1; CA 45-48; CANR 2, 11, 35, 62, 95, 138; CN 5, 6, 7; CPW; CSW; DA3; DAM NOV, POP; FW; INT CANR-11; MAL 5; MTCW 1, 2; MTFW 2005; NFS 9; RGAL 4; TUS

Brown, Roderick (Langmere) Haig-
See Haig-Brown, Roderick (Langmere)

Brown, Rosellen 1939- .... **CLC 32, 170**
See also CA 77-80; 10; CANR 14, 44, 98; CN 6, 7

Brown, Sterling Allen 1901-1989 ...... **BLC 1; CLC 1, 23, 59; HR 1:2; PC 55**
See also AFAW 1, 2; BW 1, 3; CA 85-88; CAAS 127; CANR 26; CP 3, 4; DA3; DAM MULT, POET; DLB 48, 51, 63; MAL 5; MTCW 1, 2; MTFW 2005; RGAL 4; WP

Brown, Will
See Ainsworth, William Harrison

Brown, William Hill 1765-1793 .... **LC 93**
See also DLB 37

Brown, William Larry
See Brown, Larry

Brown, William Wells 1815-1884 ...... **BLC 1; DC 1; NCLC 2, 89**
See also DAM MULT; DLB 3, 50, 183, 248; RGAL 4

Browne, Clyde Jackson
See Browne, Jackson

Browne, Jackson 1948(?)- .... **CLC 21**
See also CA 120

Browne, Sir Thomas 1605-1682 .... **LC 111**
See also BRW 2; DLB 151

Browning, Robert 1812-1889 . **NCLC 19, 79; PC 2, 61; WLCS**
See also BRW 4; BRWC 2; BRWR 2; CD-BLB 1832-1890; CLR 97; DA; DA3; DAB; DAC; DAM MST, POET; DLB 32, 163; EXPP; LATS 1:1; PAB; PFS 1, 15; RGEL 2; TEA; WLIT 4; WP; YABC 1

Browning, Tod 1882-1962 .... **CLC 16**
See also CA 141; CAAS 117

Brownmiller, Susan 1935- .... **CLC 159**
See also CA 103; CANR 35, 75, 137; DAM NOV; FW; MTCW 1, 2; MTFW 2005

Brownson, Orestes Augustus 1803-1876 .... **NCLC 50**
See also DLB 1, 59, 73, 243

Bruccoli, Matthew J(oseph) 1931- ... **CLC 34**
See also CA 9-12R; CANR 7, 87; DLB 103

Bruce, Lenny .... **CLC 21**
See Schneider, Leonard Alfred

Bruchac, Joseph 1942- .... **NNAL**
See also AAYA 19; CA 256; 33-36R, 256; CANR 13, 47, 75, 94, 137, 161; CLR 46; CWRI 5; DAM MULT; JRDA; MAICYA 2; MAICYAS 1; MTCW 2; MTFW 2005; SATA 42, 89, 131, 176; SATA-Essay 176

Bruin, John
See Brutus, Dennis

Brulard, Henri
See Stendhal

Brulls, Christian
See Simenon, Georges (Jacques Christian)

Brunetto Latini c. 1220-1294 .... **CMLC 73**

Brunner, John (Kilian Houston) 1934-1995 .... **CLC 8, 10**
See also CA 1-4R; 8; CAAS 149; CANR 2, 37; CPW; DAM POP; DLB 261; MTCW 1, 2; SCFW 1, 2; SFW 4

Bruno, Giordano 1548-1600 .... **LC 27**
See also RGWL 2, 3

Brutus, Dennis 1924- ... **BLC 1; CLC 43; PC 24**
See also AFW; BW 2, 3; CA 49-52; 14; CANR 2, 27, 42, 81; CDWLB 3; CP 1, 2, 3, 4, 5, 6, 7; DAM MULT, POET; DLB 117, 225; EWL 3

Bryan, C(ourtlandt) D(ixon) B(arnes) 1936- .... **CLC 29**
See also CA 73-76; CANR 13, 68; DLB 185; INT CANR-13

Bryan, Michael
See Moore, Brian
See also CCA 1

Bryan, William Jennings 1860-1925 .... **TCLC 99**
See also DLB 303

Bryant, William Cullen 1794-1878 . **NCLC 6, 46; PC 20**
See also AMWS 1; CDALB 1640-1865; DA; DAB; DAC; DAM MST, POET; DLB 3, 43, 59, 189, 250; EXPP; PAB; RGAL 4; TUS

Bryusov, Valery Yakovlevich 1873-1924 .... **TCLC 10**
See also CA 155; CAAE 107; EWL 3; SFW 4

Buchan, John 1875-1940 .... **TCLC 41**
See also CA 145; CAAE 108; CMW 4; DAB; DAM POP; DLB 34, 70, 156; HGG; MSW; MTCW 2; RGEL 2; RHW; YABC 2

Buchanan, George 1506-1582 .... **LC 4**
See also DLB 132

Buchanan, Robert 1841-1901 .... **TCLC 107**
See also CA 179; DLB 18, 35

Buchheim, Lothar-Guenther 1918-2007 .... **CLC 6**
See also CA 85-88; CAAS 257

Buchner, (Karl) Georg 1813-1837 .... **NCLC 26, 146**
See also CDWLB 2; DLB 133; EW 6; RGSF 2; RGWL 2, 3; TWA

Buchwald, Art 1925-2007 .... **CLC 33**
See also AITN 1; CA 5-8R; CAAS 256; CANR 21, 67, 107; MTCW 1, 2; SATA 10

Buchwald, Arthur
See Buchwald, Art

Buck, Pearl S(ydenstricker) 1892-1973 .... **CLC 7, 11, 18, 127**
See also AAYA 42; AITN 1; AMWS 2; BPFB 1; CA 1-4R; CAAS 41-44R; CANR 1, 34; CDALBS; CN 1; DA; DA3; DAB; DAC; DAM MST, NOV; DLB 9, 102, 329; EWL 3; LAIT 3; MAL 5; MTCW 1, 2; MTFW 2005; NFS 25; RGAL 4; RHW; SATA 1, 25; TUS

Buckler, Ernest 1908-1984 .... **CLC 13**
See also CA 11-12; CAAS 114; CAP 1; CCA 1; CN 1, 2, 3; DAC; DAM MST; DLB 68; SATA 47

Buckley, Christopher 1952- .... **CLC 165**
See also CA 139; CANR 119

Buckley, Christopher Taylor
See Buckley, Christopher

Buckley, Vincent (Thomas) 1925-1988 .... **CLC 57**
See also CA 101; CP 1, 2, 3, 4; DLB 289

Capek, Karel 1890-1938 .... **DC 1; SSC 36; TCLC 6, 37, 192; WLC 1**
See also CA 140; CAAE 104; CDWLB 4; DA; DA3; DAB; DAC; DAM DRAM, MST, NOV; DFS 7, 11; DLB 215; EW 10; EWL 3; MTCW 2; MTFW 2005; RGSF 2; RGWL 2, 3; SCFW 1, 2; SFW 4

Capella, Martianus fl. 4th cent. - .. **CMLC 84**

Capote, Truman 1924-1984 . **CLC 1, 3, 8, 13, 19, 34, 38, 58; SSC 2, 47, 93; TCLC 164; WLC 1**
See also AAYA 61; AMWS 3; BPFB 1; CA 5-8R; CAAS 113; CANR 18, 62; CDALB 1941-1968; CN 1, 2, 3; CPW; DA; DA3; DAB; DAC; DAM MST, NOV, POP; DLB 2, 185, 227; DLBY 1980, 1984; EWL 3; EXPS; GLL 1; LAIT 3; MAL 5; MTCW 1, 2; MTFW 2005; NCFS 2; RGAL 4; RGSF 2; SATA 91; SSFS 2; TUS

Capra, Frank 1897-1991 .... **CLC 16**
See also AAYA 52; CA 61-64; CAAS 135

Caputo, Philip 1941- .... **CLC 32**
See also AAYA 60; CA 73-76; CANR 40, 135; YAW

Caragiale, Ion Luca 1852-1912 ...... **TCLC 76**
See also CA 157

Card, Orson Scott 1951- .... **CLC 44, 47, 50**
See also AAYA 11, 42; BPFB 1; BYA 5, 8; CA 102; CANR 27, 47, 73, 102, 106, 133; CLR 116; CPW; DA3; DAM POP; FANT; INT CANR-27; MTCW 1, 2; MTFW 2005; NFS 5; SATA 83, 127; SCFW 2; SFW 4; SUFW 2; YAW

Cardenal, Ernesto 1925- .... **CLC 31, 161; HLC 1; PC 22**
See also CA 49-52; CANR 2, 32, 66, 138; CWW 2; DAM MULT, POET; DLB 290; EWL 3; HW 1, 2; LAWS 1; MTCW 1, 2; MTFW 2005; RGWL 2, 3

Cardinal, Marie 1929-2001 .... **CLC 189**
See also CA 177; CWW 2; DLB 83; FW

Cardozo, Benjamin N(athan) 1870-1938 .... **TCLC 65**
See also CA 164; CAAE 117

Carducci, Giosue (Alessandro Giuseppe) 1835-1907 .... **PC 46; TCLC 32**
See also CA 163; DLB 329; EW 7; RGWL 2, 3

Carew, Thomas 1595(?)-1640 . **LC 13; PC 29**
See also BRW 2; DLB 126; PAB; RGEL 2

Carey, Ernestine Gilbreth 1908-2006 .... **CLC 17**
See also CA 5-8R; CAAS 254; CANR 71; SATA 2; SATA-Obit 177

Carey, Peter 1943- .... **CLC 40, 55, 96, 183**
See also BRWS 12; CA 127; CAAE 123; CANR 53, 76, 117, 157; CN 4, 5, 6, 7; DLB 289, 326; EWL 3; INT CA-127; MTCW 1, 2; MTFW 2005; RGSF 2; SATA 94

Carleton, William 1794-1869 .... **NCLC 3**
See also DLB 159; RGEL 2; RGSF 2

Carlisle, Henry (Coffin) 1926- .... **CLC 33**
See also CA 13-16R; CANR 15, 85

Carlsen, Chris
See Holdstock, Robert

Carlson, Ron 1947- .... **CLC 54**
See also CA 189; 105, 189; CANR 27, 155; DLB 244

Carlson, Ronald F.
See Carlson, Ron

Carlyle, Jane Welsh 1801-1866 ... **NCLC 181**
See also DLB 55

Carlyle, Thomas 1795-1881 ..... **NCLC 22, 70**
See also BRW 4; CDBLB 1789-1832; DA; DAB; DAC; DAM MST; DLB 55, 144, 254; RGEL 2; TEA

Carman, (William) Bliss 1861-1929 ... **PC 34; TCLC 7**
See also CA 152; CAAE 104; DAC; DLB 92; RGEL 2

Carnegie, Dale 1888-1955 .... **TCLC 53**
See also CA 218

Carossa, Hans 1878-1956 .... **TCLC 48**
See also CA 170; DLB 66; EWL 3

Carpenter, Don(ald Richard) 1931-1995 .... **CLC 41**
See also CA 45-48; CAAS 149; CANR 1, 71

Carpenter, Edward 1844-1929 .... **TCLC 88**
See also BRWS 13; CA 163; GLL 1

Carpenter, John (Howard) 1948- ... **CLC 161**
See also AAYA 2, 73; CA 134; SATA 58

Carpenter, Johnny
See Carpenter, John (Howard)

Carpentier (y Valmont), Alejo 1904-1980 . **CLC 8, 11, 38, 110; HLC 1; SSC 35**
See also CA 65-68; CAAS 97-100; CANR 11, 70; CDWLB 3; DAM MULT; DLB 113; EWL 3; HW 1, 2; LAW; LMFS 2; RGSF 2; RGWL 2, 3; WLIT 1

Carr, Caleb 1955- .... **CLC 86**
See also CA 147; CANR 73, 134; DA3

Carr, Emily 1871-1945 .... **TCLC 32**
See also CA 159; DLB 68; FW; GLL 2

Carr, John Dickson 1906-1977 .... **CLC 3**
See Fairbairn, Roger
See also CA 49-52; CAAS 69-72; CANR 3, 33, 60; CMW 4; DLB 306; MSW; MTCW 1, 2

Carr, Philippa
See Hibbert, Eleanor Alice Burford

Carr, Virginia Spencer 1929- .... **CLC 34**
See also CA 61-64; DLB 111

Carrere, Emmanuel 1957- .... **CLC 89**
See also CA 200

Carrier, Roch 1937- .... **CLC 13, 78**
See also CA 130; CANR 61, 152; CCA 1; DAC; DAM MST; DLB 53; SATA 105, 166

Carroll, James Dennis
See Carroll, Jim

Carroll, James P. 1943(?)- .... **CLC 38**
See also CA 81-84; CANR 73, 139; MTCW 2; MTFW 2005

Carroll, Jim 1951- .... **CLC 35, 143**
See also AAYA 17; CA 45-48; CANR 42, 115; NCFS 5

Carroll, Lewis ...... **NCLC 2, 53, 139; PC 18, 74; WLC 1**
See Dodgson, Charles L(utwidge)
See also AAYA 39; BRW 5; BYA 5, 13; CD-BLB 1832-1890; CLR 2, 18, 108; DLB 18, 163, 178; DLBY 1998; EXPN; EXPP; FANT; JRDA; LAIT 1; NFS 7; PFS 11; RGEL 2; SUFW 1; TEA; WCH

Carroll, Paul Vincent 1900-1968 ...... **CLC 10**
See also CA 9-12R; CAAS 25-28R; DLB 10; EWL 3; RGEL 2

Carruth, Hayden 1921- ..... **CLC 4, 7, 10, 18, 84; PC 10**
See also AMWS 16; CA 9-12R; CANR 4, 38, 59, 110; CP 1, 2, 3, 4, 5, 6, 7; DLB 5, 165; INT CANR-4; MTCW 1, 2; MTFW 2005; PFS 26; SATA 47

Carson, Anne 1950- .... **CLC 185; PC 64**
See also AMWS 12; CA 203; CP 7; DLB 193; PFS 18; TCLE 1:1

Carson, Ciaran 1948- .... **CLC 201**
See also BRWS 13; CA 153; CAAE 112; CANR 113; CP 6, 7; PFS 26

Carson, Rachel
See Carson, Rachel Louise
See also AAYA 49; DLB 275

Carson, Rachel Louise 1907-1964 .... **CLC 71**
See Carson, Rachel
See also AMWS 9; ANW; CA 77-80; CANR 35; DA3; DAM POP; FW; LAIT 4; MAL 5; MTCW 1, 2; MTFW 2005; NCFS 1; SATA 23

Carter, Angela 1940-1992 ...... **CLC 5, 41, 76; SSC 13, 85; TCLC 139**
See also BRWS 3; CA 53-56; CAAS 136; CANR 12, 36, 61, 106; CN 3, 4, 5; DA3; DLB 14, 207, 261, 319; EXPS; FANT; FW; GL 2; MTCW 1, 2; MTFW 2005; RGSF 2; SATA 66; SATA-Obit 70; SFW 4; SSFS 4, 12; SUFW 2; WLIT 4

Carter, Angela Olive
See Carter, Angela

Carter, Nick
See Smith, Martin Cruz

Carver, Raymond 1938-1988 ..... **CLC 22, 36, 53, 55, 126; PC 54; SSC 8, 51, 104**
See also AAYA 44; AMWS 3; BPFB 1; CA 33-36R; CAAS 126; CANR 17, 34, 61, 103; CN 4; CPW; DA3; DAM NOV; DLB 130; DLBY 1984, 1988; EWL 3; MAL 5; MTCW 1, 2; MTFW 2005; PFS 17; RGAL 4; RGSF 2; SSFS 3, 6, 12, 13, 23; TCLE 1:1; TCWW 2; TUS

Cary, Elizabeth, Lady Falkland 1585-1639 .... **LC 30, 141**

Cary, (Arthur) Joyce (Lunel) 1888-1957 .... **TCLC 1, 29**
See also BRW 7; CA 164; CAAE 104; CD-BLB 1914-1945; DLB 15, 100; EWL 3; MTCW 2; RGEL 2; TEA

Casal, Julian del 1863-1893 .... **NCLC 131**
See also DLB 283; LAW

Casanova, Giacomo
See Casanova de Seingalt, Giovanni Jacopo
See also WLIT 7

Casanova de Seingalt, Giovanni Jacopo 1725-1798 .... **LC 13**
See Casanova, Giacomo

Casares, Adolfo Bioy
See Bioy Casares, Adolfo
See also RGSF 2

Casas, Bartolome de las 1474-1566
See Las Casas, Bartolome de
See also WLIT 1

Case, John
See Hougan, Carolyn

Casely-Hayford, J(oseph) E(phraim) 1866-1903 .... **BLC 1; TCLC 24**
See also BW 2; CA 152; CAAE 123; DAM MULT

Casey, John (Dudley) 1939- .... **CLC 59**
See also BEST 90:2; CA 69-72; CANR 23, 100

Casey, Michael 1947- .... **CLC 2**
See also CA 65-68; CANR 109; CP 2, 3; DLB 5

Casey, Patrick
See Thurman, Wallace (Henry)

Casey, Warren (Peter) 1935-1988 .... **CLC 12**
See also CA 101; CAAS 127; INT CA-101

Casona, Alejandro .... **CLC 49**
See Alvarez, Alejandro Rodriguez
See also EWL 3

Cassavetes, John 1929-1989 .... **CLC 20**
See also CA 85-88; CAAS 127; CANR 82

Cassian, Nina 1924- .... **PC 17**
See also CWP; CWW 2

Cassill, R(onald) V(erlin) 1919-2002 .... **CLC 4, 23**
See also CA 9-12R; 1; CAAS 208; CANR 7, 45; CN 1, 2, 3, 4, 5, 6, 7; DLB 6, 218; DLBY 2002

Chapman, George 1559(?)-1634 . **DC 19; LC 22, 116**
See also BRW 1; DAM DRAM; DLB 62, 121; LMFS 1; RGEL 2

Chapman, Graham 1941-1989 .... **CLC 21**
See Monty Python
See also CA 116; CAAS 129; CANR 35, 95

Chapman, John Jay 1862-1933 .... **TCLC 7**
See also AMWS 14; CA 191; CAAE 104

Chapman, Lee
See Bradley, Marion Zimmer
See also GLL 1

Chapman, Walker
See Silverberg, Robert

Chappell, Fred (Davis) 1936- .... **CLC 40, 78, 162**
See also CA 198; 5-8R, 198; 4; CANR 8, 33, 67, 110; CN 6; CP 6, 7; CSW; DLB 6, 105; HGG

Char, Rene(-Emile) 1907-1988 .... **CLC 9, 11, 14, 55; PC 56**
See also CA 13-16R; CAAS 124; CANR 32; DAM POET; DLB 258; EWL 3; GFL 1789 to the Present; MTCW 1, 2; RGWL 2, 3

Charby, Jay
See Ellison, Harlan

Chardin, Pierre Teilhard de
See Teilhard de Chardin, (Marie Joseph) Pierre

Chariton fl. 1st cent. (?)- .... **CMLC 49**

Charlemagne 742-814 .... **CMLC 37**

Charles I 1600-1649 .... **LC 13**

Charriere, Isabelle de 1740-1805 .. **NCLC 66**
See also DLB 313

Chartier, Alain c. 1392-1430 .... **LC 94**
See also DLB 208

Chartier, Emile-Auguste
See Alain

Charyn, Jerome 1937- .... **CLC 5, 8, 18**
See also CA 5-8R; 1; CANR 7, 61, 101, 158; CMW 4; CN 1, 2, 3, 4, 5, 6, 7; DLBY 1983; MTCW 1

Chase, Adam
See Marlowe, Stephen

Chase, Mary (Coyle) 1907-1981 .... **DC 1**
See also CA 77-80; CAAS 105; CAD; CWD; DFS 11; DLB 228; SATA 17; SATA-Obit 29

Chase, Mary Ellen 1887-1973 .... **CLC 2; TCLC 124**
See also CA 13-16; CAAS 41-44R; CAP 1; SATA 10

Chase, Nicholas
See Hyde, Anthony
See also CCA 1

Chateaubriand, Francois Rene de 1768-1848 .... **NCLC 3, 134**
See also DLB 119; EW 5; GFL 1789 to the Present; RGWL 2, 3; TWA

Chatelet, Gabrielle-Emilie Du
See du Chatelet, Emilie
See also DLB 313

Chatterje, Sarat Chandra 1876-1936(?)
See Chatterji, Saratchandra
See also CAAE 109

Chatterji, Bankim Chandra 1838-1894 .... **NCLC 19**

Chatterji, Saratchandra .... **TCLC 13**
See Chatterje, Sarat Chandra
See also CA 186; EWL 3

Chatterton, Thomas 1752-1770 .... **LC 3, 54**
See also DAM POET; DLB 109; RGEL 2

Chatwin, (Charles) Bruce 1940-1989 .... **CLC 28, 57, 59**
See also AAYA 4; BEST 90:1; BRWS 4; CA 85-88; CAAS 127; CPW; DAM POP; DLB 194, 204; EWL 3; MTFW 2005

Chaucer, Daniel
See Ford, Ford Madox
See also RHW

Chaucer, Geoffrey 1340(?)-1400 .. **LC 17, 56; PC 19, 58; WLCS**
See also BRW 1; BRWC 1; BRWR 2; CD-BLB Before 1660; DA; DA3; DAB; DAC; DAM MST, POET; DLB 146; LAIT 1; PAB; PFS 14; RGEL 2; TEA; WLIT 3; WP

Chavez, Denise 1948- .... **HLC 1**
See also CA 131; CANR 56, 81, 137; DAM MULT; DLB 122; FW; HW 1, 2; LLW; MAL 5; MTCW 2; MTFW 2005

Chaviaras, Strates 1935-
See Haviaras, Stratis
See also CA 105

Chayefsky, Paddy .... **CLC 23**
See Chayefsky, Sidney
See also CAD; DLB 7, 44; DLBY 1981; RGAL 4

Chayefsky, Sidney 1923-1981
See Chayefsky, Paddy
See also CA 9-12R; CAAS 104; CANR 18; DAM DRAM

Chedid, Andree 1920- .... **CLC 47**
See also CA 145; CANR 95; EWL 3

Cheever, John 1912-1982 ..... **CLC 3, 7, 8, 11, 15, 25, 64; SSC 1, 38, 57; WLC 2**
See also AAYA 65; AMWS 1; BPFB 1; CA 5-8R; CAAS 106; CABS 1; CANR 5, 27, 76; CDALB 1941-1968; CN 1, 2, 3; CPW; DA; DA3; DAB; DAC; DAM MST, NOV, POP; DLB 2, 102, 227; DLBY 1980, 1982; EWL 3; EXPS; INT CANR-5; MAL 5; MTCW 1, 2; MTFW 2005; RGAL 4; RGSF 2; SSFS 2, 14; TUS

Cheever, Susan 1943- .... **CLC 18, 48**
See also CA 103; CANR 27, 51, 92, 157; DLBY 1982; INT CANR-27

Chekhonte, Antosha
See Chekhov, Anton (Pavlovich)

Chekhov, Anton (Pavlovich) 1860-1904 .... **DC 9; SSC 2, 28, 41, 51, 85, 102; TCLC 3, 10, 31, 55, 96, 163; WLC 2**
See also AAYA 68; BYA 14; CA 124; CAAE 104; DA; DA3; DAB; DAC; DAM DRAM, MST; DFS 1, 5, 10, 12; DLB 277; EW 7; EWL 3; EXPS; LAIT 3; LATS 1:1; RGSF 2; RGWL 2, 3; SATA 90; SSFS 5, 13, 14; TWA

Cheney, Lynne V. 1941- .... **CLC 70**
See also CA 89-92; CANR 58, 117; SATA 152

Chernyshevsky, Nikolai Gavrilovich
See Chernyshevsky, Nikolay Gavrilovich
See also DLB 238

Chernyshevsky, Nikolay Gavrilovich 1828-1889 .... **NCLC 1**
See Chernyshevsky, Nikolai Gavrilovich

Cherry, Carolyn Janice .... **CLC 35**
See Cherryh, C.J.
See also AAYA 24; BPFB 1; DLBY 1980; FANT; SATA 93; SCFW 2; SFW 4; YAW

Cherryh, C.J. 1942-
See Cherry, Carolyn Janice
See also CA 65-68; CANR 10, 147; SATA 172

Chesnutt, Charles W(addell) 1858-1932 .... **BLC 1; SSC 7, 54; TCLC 5, 39**
See also AFAW 1, 2; AMWS 14; BW 1, 3; CA 125; CAAE 106; CANR 76; DAM MULT; DLB 12, 50, 78; EWL 3; MAL 5; MTCW 1, 2; MTFW 2005; RGAL 4; RGSF 2; SSFS 11

Chester, Alfred 1929(?)-1971 .... **CLC 49**
See also CA 196; CAAS 33-36R; DLB 130; MAL 5

Chesterton, G(ilbert) K(eith) 1874-1936 . **PC 28; SSC 1, 46; TCLC 1, 6, 64**
See also AAYA 57; BRW 6; CA 132; CAAE 104; CANR 73, 131; CDBLB 1914-1945; CMW 4; DAM NOV, POET; DLB 10, 19, 34, 70, 98, 149, 178; EWL 3; FANT; MSW; MTCW 1, 2; MTFW 2005; RGEL 2; RGSF 2; SATA 27; SUFW 1

Chettle, Henry 1560-1607(?) .... **LC 112**
See also DLB 136; RGEL 2

Chiang, Pin-chin 1904-1986
See Ding Ling
See also CAAS 118

Chief Joseph 1840-1904 .... **NNAL**
See also CA 152; DA3; DAM MULT

Chief Seattle 1786(?)-1866 .... **NNAL**
See also DA3; DAM MULT

Ch'ien, Chung-shu 1910-1998 .... **CLC 22**
See Qian Zhongshu
See also CA 130; CANR 73; MTCW 1, 2

Chikamatsu Monzaemon 1653-1724 ... **LC 66**
See also RGWL 2, 3

Child, Francis James 1825-1896 . **NCLC 173**
See also DLB 1, 64, 235

Child, L. Maria
See Child, Lydia Maria

Child, Lydia Maria 1802-1880 .. **NCLC 6, 73**
See also DLB 1, 74, 243; RGAL 4; SATA 67

Child, Mrs.
See Child, Lydia Maria

Child, Philip 1898-1978 .... **CLC 19, 68**
See also CA 13-14; CAP 1; CP 1; DLB 68; RHW; SATA 47

Childers, (Robert) Erskine 1870-1922 .... **TCLC 65**
See also CA 153; CAAE 113; DLB 70

Childress, Alice 1920-1994 . **BLC 1; CLC 12, 15, 86, 96; DC 4; TCLC 116**
See also AAYA 8; BW 2, 3; BYA 2; CA 45-48; CAAS 146; CAD; CANR 3, 27, 50, 74; CLR 14; CWD; DA3; DAM DRAM, MULT, NOV; DFS 2, 8, 14; DLB 7, 38, 249; JRDA; LAIT 5; MAICYA 1, 2; MAI-CYAS 1; MAL 5; MTCW 1, 2; MTFW 2005; RGAL 4; SATA 7, 48, 81; TUS; WYA; YAW

Chin, Frank (Chew, Jr.) 1940- .... **AAL; CLC 135; DC 7**
See also CA 33-36R; CAD; CANR 71; CD 5, 6; DAM MULT; DLB 206, 312; LAIT 5; RGAL 4

Chin, Marilyn (Mei Ling) 1955- .... **PC 40**
See also CA 129; CANR 70, 113; CWP; DLB 312

Chislett, (Margaret) Anne 1943- ...... **CLC 34**
See also CA 151

Chitty, Thomas Willes 1926- .... **CLC 11**
See Hinde, Thomas
See also CA 5-8R; CN 7

Chivers, Thomas Holley 1809-1858 .... **NCLC 49**
See also DLB 3, 248; RGAL 4

Choi, Susan 1969- .... **CLC 119**
See also CA 223

Chomette, Rene Lucien 1898-1981
See Clair, Rene
See also CAAS 103

Chomsky, Avram Noam
See Chomsky, Noam

Chomsky, Noam 1928- .... **CLC 132**
See also CA 17-20R; CANR 28, 62, 110, 132; DA3; DLB 246; MTCW 1, 2; MTFW 2005

Chona, Maria 1845(?)-1936 .... **NNAL**
See also CA 144

Condorcet .... **LC 104**
    See Condorcet, marquis de Marie-Jean-
        Antoine-Nicolas Caritat
    See also GFL Beginnings to 1789
Condorcet, marquis de
    Marie-Jean-Antoine-Nicolas Caritat
    1743-1794
    See Condorcet
    See also DLB 313
Confucius 551B.C.-479B.C. .... **CMLC 19, 65;**
    WLCS
    See also DA; DA3; DAB; DAC; DAM
        MST
Congreve, William 1670-1729 ... **DC 2; LC 5,**
    21; WLC 2
    See also BRW 2; CDBLB 1660-1789; DA;
        DAB; DAC; DAM DRAM, MST, POET;
        DFS 15; DLB 39, 84; RGEL 2; WLIT 3
Conley, Robert J(ackson) 1940- .... **NNAL**
    See also CA 41-44R; CANR 15, 34, 45, 96;
        DAM MULT; TCWW 2
Connell, Evan S., Jr. 1924- .... **CLC 4, 6, 45**
    See also AAYA 7; AMWS 14; CA 1-4R; 2;
        CANR 2, 39, 76, 97, 140; CN 1, 2, 3, 4,
        5, 6; DAM NOV; DLB 2, 335; DLBY
        1981; MAL 5; MTCW 1, 2; MTFW 2005
Connelly, Marc(us Cook) 1890-1980 . **CLC 7**
    See also CA 85-88; CAAS 102; CAD;
        CANR 30; DFS 12; DLB 7; DLBY 1980;
        MAL 5; RGAL 4; SATA-Obit 25
Connor, Ralph .... **TCLC 31**
    See Gordon, Charles William
    See also DLB 92; TCWW 1, 2
Conrad, Joseph 1857-1924 ..... **SSC 9, 67, 69,**
    71; TCLC 1, 6, 13, 25, 43, 57; WLC 2
    See also AAYA 26; BPFB 1; BRW 6;
        BRWC 1; BRWR 2; BYA 2; CA 131;
        CAAE 104; CANR 60; CDBLB 1890-
        1914; DA; DA3; DAB; DAC; DAM MST,
        NOV; DLB 10, 34, 98, 156; EWL 3;
        EXPN; EXPS; LAIT 2; LATS 1:1; LMFS
        1; MTCW 1, 2; MTFW 2005; NFS 2, 16;
        RGEL 2; RGSF 2; SATA 27; SSFS 1, 12;
        TEA; WLIT 4
Conrad, Robert Arnold
    See Hart, Moss
Conroy, Pat 1945- .... **CLC 30, 74**
    See also AAYA 8, 52; AITN 1; BPFB 1;
        CA 85-88; CANR 24, 53, 129; CN 7;
        CPW; CSW; DA3; DAM NOV, POP;
        DLB 6; LAIT 5; MAL 5; MTCW 1, 2;
        MTFW 2005
Constant (de Rebecque), (Henri) Benjamin
    1767-1830 .... **NCLC 6, 182**
    See also DLB 119; EW 4; GFL 1789 to the
        Present
Conway, Jill K(er) 1934- .... **CLC 152**
    See also CA 130; CANR 94
Conybeare, Charles Augustus
    See Eliot, T(homas) S(tearns)
Cook, Michael 1933-1994 .... **CLC 58**
    See also CA 93-96; CANR 68; DLB 53
Cook, Robin 1940- .... **CLC 14**
    See also AAYA 32; BEST 90:2; BPFB 1;
        CA 111; CAAE 108; CANR 41, 90, 109;
        CPW; DA3; DAM POP; HGG; INT CA-
        111
Cook, Roy
    See Silverberg, Robert
Cooke, Elizabeth 1948- .... **CLC 55**
    See also CA 129
Cooke, John Esten 1830-1886 .... **NCLC 5**
    See also DLB 3, 248; RGAL 4
Cooke, John Estes
    See Baum, L(yman) Frank
Cooke, M. E.
    See Creasey, John
Cooke, Margaret
    See Creasey, John

Cooke, Rose Terry 1827-1892 ...... **NCLC 110**
    See also DLB 12, 74
Cook-Lynn, Elizabeth 1930- .... **CLC 93;**
    NNAL
    See also CA 133; DAM MULT; DLB 175
Cooney, Ray .... **CLC 62**
    See also CBD
Cooper, Anthony Ashley 1671-1713 .. **LC 107**
    See also DLB 101, 336
Cooper, Dennis 1953- .... **CLC 203**
    See also CA 133; CANR 72, 86; GLL 1;
        HGG
Cooper, Douglas 1960- .... **CLC 86**
Cooper, Henry St. John
    See Creasey, John
Cooper, J. California (?)- .... **CLC 56**
    See also AAYA 12; BW 1; CA 125; CANR
        55; DAM MULT; DLB 212
Cooper, James Fenimore
    1789-1851 .... **NCLC 1, 27, 54**
    See also AAYA 22; AMW; BPFB 1;
        CDALB 1640-1865; CLR 105; DA3;
        DLB 3, 183, 250, 254; LAIT 1; NFS 25;
        RGAL 4; SATA 19; TUS; WCH
Cooper, Susan Fenimore
    1813-1894 .... **NCLC 129**
    See also ANW; DLB 239, 254
Coover, Robert 1932- .. **CLC 3, 7, 15, 32, 46,**
    87, 161; SSC 15, 101
    See also AMWS 5; BPFB 1; CA 45-48;
        CANR 3, 37, 58, 115; CN 1, 2, 3, 4, 5, 6,
        7; DAM NOV; DLB 2, 227; DLBY 1981;
        EWL 3; MAL 5; MTCW 1, 2; MTFW
        2005; RGAL 4; RGSF 2
Copeland, Stewart (Armstrong)
    1952- .... **CLC 26**
Copernicus, Nicolaus 1473-1543 .... **LC 45**
Coppard, A(lfred) E(dgar)
    1878-1957 .... **SSC 21; TCLC 5**
    See also BRWS 8; CA 167; CAAE 114;
        DLB 162; EWL 3; HGG; RGEL 2; RGSF
        2; SUFW 1; YABC 1
Coppee, Francois 1842-1908 .... **TCLC 25**
    See also CA 170; DLB 217
Coppola, Francis Ford 1939- ... **CLC 16, 126**
    See also AAYA 39; CA 77-80; CANR 40,
        78; DLB 44
Copway, George 1818-1869 .... **NNAL**
    See also DAM MULT; DLB 175, 183
Corbiere, Tristan 1845-1875 .... **NCLC 43**
    See also DLB 217; GFL 1789 to the Present
Corcoran, Barbara (Asenath)
    1911- .... **CLC 17**
    See also AAYA 14; CA 191; 21-24R, 191;
        2; CANR 11, 28, 48; CLR 50; DLB 52;
        JRDA; MAICYA 2; MAICYAS 1; RHW;
        SAAS 20; SATA 3, 77; SATA-Essay 125
Cordelier, Maurice
    See Giraudoux, Jean(-Hippolyte)
Corelli, Marie .... **TCLC 51**
    See Mackay, Mary
    See also DLB 34, 156; RGEL 2; SUFW 1
Corinna c. 225B.C.-c. 305B.C. ...... **CMLC 72**
Corman, Cid .... **CLC 9**
    See Corman, Sidney
    See also CA 2; CP 1, 2, 3, 4, 5, 6, 7; DLB
        5, 193
Corman, Sidney 1924-2004
    See Corman, Cid
    See also CA 85-88; CAAS 225; CANR 44;
        DAM POET
Cormier, Robert 1925-2000 .... **CLC 12, 30**
    See also AAYA 3, 19; BYA 1, 2, 6, 8, 9;
        CA 1-4R; CANR 5, 23, 76, 93; CDALB
        1968-1988; CLR 12, 55; DA; DAB; DAC;
        DAM MST, NOV; DLB 52; EXPN; INT

CANR-23; JRDA; LAIT 5; MAICYA 1,
        2; MTCW 1, 2; MTFW 2005; NFS 2, 18;
        SATA 10, 45, 83; SATA-Obit 122; WYA;
        YAW
Corn, Alfred (DeWitt III) 1943- .... **CLC 33**
    See also CA 179; 179; 25; CANR 44; CP 3,
        4, 5, 6, 7; CSW; DLB 120, 282; DLBY
        1980
Corneille, Pierre 1606-1684 .. **DC 21; LC 28,**
    135
    See also DAB; DAM MST; DFS 21; DLB
        268; EW 3; GFL Beginnings to 1789;
        RGWL 2, 3; TWA
Cornwell, David
    See le Carre, John
Cornwell, Patricia 1956- .... **CLC 155**
    See also AAYA 16, 56; BPFB 1; CA 134;
        CANR 53, 131; CMW 4; CPW; CSW;
        DAM POP; DLB 306; MSW; MTCW 2;
        MTFW 2005
Cornwell, Patricia Daniels
    See Cornwell, Patricia
Corso, Gregory 1930-2001 .... **CLC 1, 11; PC**
    33
    See also AMWS 12; BG 1:2; CA 5-8R;
        CAAS 193; CANR 41, 76, 132; CP 1, 2,
        3, 4, 5, 6, 7; DA3; DLB 5, 16, 237; LMFS
        2; MAL 5; MTCW 1, 2; MTFW 2005; WP
Cortazar, Julio 1914-1984 ... **CLC 2, 3, 5, 10,**
    13, 15, 33, 34, 92; HLC 1; SSC 7, 76
    See also BPFB 1; CA 21-24R; CANR 12,
        32, 81; CDWLB 3; DA3; DAM MULT,
        NOV; DLB 113; EWL 3; EXPS; HW 1,
        2; LAW; MTCW 1, 2; MTFW 2005;
        RGSF 2; RGWL 2, 3; SSFS 3, 20; TWA;
        WLIT 1
Cortes, Hernan 1485-1547 .... **LC 31**
Corvinus, Jakob
    See Raabe, Wilhelm (Karl)
Corwin, Cecil
    See Kornbluth, C(yril) M.
Cosic, Dobrica 1921- .... **CLC 14**
    See also CA 138; CAAE 122; CDWLB 4;
        CWW 2; DLB 181; EWL 3
Costain, Thomas B(ertram)
    1885-1965 .... **CLC 30**
    See also BYA 3; CA 5-8R; CAAS 25-28R;
        DLB 9; RHW
Costantini, Humberto 1924(?)-1987 . **CLC 49**
    See also CA 131; CAAS 122; EWL 3; HW
        1
Costello, Elvis 1954- .... **CLC 21**
    See also CA 204
Costenoble, Philostene
    See Ghelderode, Michel de
Cotes, Cecil V.
    See Duncan, Sara Jeannette
Cotter, Joseph Seamon Sr.
    1861-1949 .... **BLC 1; TCLC 28**
    See also BW 1; CA 124; DAM MULT; DLB
        50
Couch, Arthur Thomas Quiller
    See Quiller-Couch, Sir Arthur (Thomas)
Coulton, James
    See Hansen, Joseph
Couperus, Louis (Marie Anne)
    1863-1923 .... **TCLC 15**
    See also CAAE 115; EWL 3; RGWL 2, 3
Coupland, Douglas 1961- .... **CLC 85, 133**
    See also AAYA 34; CA 142; CANR 57, 90,
        130; CCA 1; CN 7; CPW; DAC; DAM
        POP; DLB 334
Court, Wesli
    See Turco, Lewis (Putnam)
Courtenay, Bryce 1933- .... **CLC 59**
    See also CA 138; CPW
Courtney, Robert
    See Ellison, Harlan

e La Salle, Innocent
See Hartmann, Sadakichi

Laureamont, Comte
See Lautreamont

elbanco, Nicholas 1942- ..... **CLC 6, 13, 167**
See also CA 189; 17-20R, 189; 2; CANR 29, 55, 116, 150; CN 7; DLB 6, 234

elbanco, Nicholas Franklin
See Delbanco, Nicholas

l Castillo, Michel 1933- .... **CLC 38**
See also CA 109; CANR 77

eledda, Grazia (Cosima)
1875(?)-1936 .... **TCLC 23**
See also CA 205; CAAE 123; DLB 264, 329; EWL 3; RGWL 2, 3; WLIT 7

eleuze, Gilles 1925-1995 .... **TCLC 116**
See also DLB 296

elgado, Abelardo (Lalo) B(arrientos)
1930-2004 .... **HLC 1**
See also CA 131; 15; CAAS 230; CANR 90; DAM MST, MULT; DLB 82; HW 1, 2

elibes, Miguel .... **CLC 8, 18**
See Delibes Setien, Miguel
See also DLB 322; EWL 3

elibes Setien, Miguel 1920-
See Delibes, Miguel
See also CA 45-48; CANR 1, 32; CWW 2; HW 1; MTCW 1

eLillo, Don 1936- ..... **CLC 8, 10, 13, 27, 39, 54, 76, 143, 210, 213**
See also AMWC 2; AMWS 6; BEST 89:1; BPFB 1; CA 81-84; CANR 21, 76, 92, 133; CN 3, 4, 5, 6, 7; CPW; DA3; DAM NOV, POP; DLB 6, 173; EWL 3; MAL 5; MTCW 1, 2; MTFW 2005; RGAL 4; TUS

Lisser, H. G.
See De Lisser, H(erbert) G(eorge)
See also DLB 117

Lisser, H(erbert) G(eorge)
1878-1944 .... **TCLC 12**
See de Lisser, H. G.
See also BW 2; CA 152; CAAE 109

eloire, Pierre
See Peguy, Charles (Pierre)

eloney, Thomas 1543(?)-1600 .... **LC 41; PC 79**
See also DLB 167; RGEL 2

loria, Ella (Cara) 1889-1971(?) ..... **NNAL**
See also CA 152; DAM MULT; DLB 175

loria, Vine, Jr. 1933-2005 .... **CLC 21, 122; NNAL**
See also CA 53-56; CAAS 245; CANR 5, 20, 48, 98; DAM MULT; DLB 175; MTCW 1; SATA 21; SATA-Obit 171

loria, Vine Victor, Jr.
See Deloria, Vine, Jr.

l Valle-Inclan, Ramon (Maria)
See Valle-Inclan, Ramon (Maria) del
See also DLB 322

l Vecchio, John M(ichael) 1947- .. **CLC 29**
See also CA 110; DLBD 9

Man, Paul (Adolph Michel)
1919-1983 .... **CLC 55**
See also CA 128; CAAS 111; CANR 61; DLB 67; MTCW 1, 2

Marinis, Rick 1934- .... **CLC 54**
See also CA 184; 57-60, 184; 24; CANR 9, 25, 50, 160; DLB 218; TCWW 2

Maupassant, (Henri Rene Albert) Guy
See Maupassant, (Henri Rene Albert) Guy de

embry, R. Emmet
See Murfree, Mary Noailles

mby, William 1922- .... **BLC 1; CLC 53**
See also BW 1, 3; CA 81-84; CANR 81; DAM MULT; DLB 33

Menton, Francisco
See Chin, Frank (Chew, Jr.)

Demetrius of Phalerum c.
307B.C.- .... **CMLC 34**

Demijohn, Thom
See Disch, Thomas M.

De Mille, James 1833-1880 .... **NCLC 123**
See also DLB 99, 251

Deming, Richard 1915-1983
See Queen, Ellery
See also CA 9-12R; CANR 3, 94; SATA 24

Democritus c. 460B.C.-c. 370B.C. . **CMLC 47**

de Montaigne, Michel (Eyquem)
See Montaigne, Michel (Eyquem) de

de Montherlant, Henry (Milon)
See Montherlant, Henry (Milon) de

Demosthenes 384B.C.-322B.C. ...... **CMLC 13**
See also AW 1; DLB 176; RGWL 2, 3; WLIT 8

de Musset, (Louis Charles) Alfred
See Musset, Alfred de

de Natale, Francine
See Malzberg, Barry N(athaniel)

de Navarre, Marguerite 1492-1549 ... **LC 61; SSC 85**
See Marguerite d'Angouleme; Marguerite de Navarre
See also DLB 327

Denby, Edwin (Orr) 1903-1983 .... **CLC 48**
See also CA 138; CAAS 110; CP 1

de Nerval, Gerard
See Nerval, Gerard de

Denham, John 1615-1669 .... **LC 73**
See also DLB 58, 126; RGEL 2

Denis, Julio
See Cortazar, Julio

Denmark, Harrison
See Zelazny, Roger

Dennis, John 1658-1734 .... **LC 11**
See also DLB 101; RGEL 2

Dennis, Nigel (Forbes) 1912-1989 ...... **CLC 8**
See also CA 25-28R; CAAS 129; CN 1, 2, 3, 4; DLB 13, 15, 233; EWL 3; MTCW 1

Dent, Lester 1904-1959 .... **TCLC 72**
See also CA 161; CAAE 112; CMW 4; DLB 306; SFW 4

De Palma, Brian 1940- .... **CLC 20**
See also CA 109

De Palma, Brian Russell
See De Palma, Brian

de Pizan, Christine
See Christine de Pizan
See also FL 1:1

De Quincey, Thomas 1785-1859 ..... **NCLC 4, 87**
See also BRW 4; CDBLB 1789-1832; DLB 110, 144; RGEL 2

Deren, Eleanora 1908(?)-1961
See Deren, Maya
See also CA 192; CAAS 111

Deren, Maya .... **CLC 16, 102**
See Deren, Eleanora

Derleth, August (William)
1909-1971 .... **CLC 31**
See also BPFB 1; BYA 9, 10; CA 1-4R; CAAS 29-32R; CANR 4; CMW 4; CN 1; DLB 9; DLBD 17; HGG; SATA 5; SUFW 1

Der Nister 1884-1950 .... **TCLC 56**
See Nister, Der

de Routisie, Albert
See Aragon, Louis

Derrida, Jacques 1930-2004 ...... **CLC 24, 87, 225**
See also CA 127; CAAE 124; CAAS 232; CANR 76, 98, 133; DLB 242; EWL 3; LMFS 2; MTCW 2; TWA

Derry Down Derry
See Lear, Edward

Dersonnes, Jacques
See Simenon, Georges (Jacques Christian)

Der Stricker c. 1190-c. 1250 .... **CMLC 75**
See also DLB 138

Desai, Anita 1937- .... **CLC 19, 37, 97, 175**
See also BRWS 5; CA 81-84; CANR 33, 53, 95, 133; CN 1, 2, 3, 4, 5, 6, 7; CWRI 5; DA3; DAB; DAM NOV; DLB 271, 323; DNFS 2; EWL 3; FW; MTCW 1, 2; MTFW 2005; SATA 63, 126

Desai, Kiran 1971- .... **CLC 119**
See also BYA 16; CA 171; CANR 127

de Saint-Luc, Jean
See Glassco, John

de Saint Roman, Arnaud
See Aragon, Louis

Desbordes-Valmore, Marceline
1786-1859 .... **NCLC 97**
See also DLB 217

Descartes, Rene 1596-1650 .... **LC 20, 35**
See also DLB 268; EW 3; GFL Beginnings to 1789

Deschamps, Eustache 1340(?)-1404 .. **LC 103**
See also DLB 208

De Sica, Vittorio 1901(?)-1974 .... **CLC 20**
See also CAAS 117

Desnos, Robert 1900-1945 .... **TCLC 22**
See also CA 151; CAAE 121; CANR 107; DLB 258; EWL 3; LMFS 2

Destouches, Louis-Ferdinand
1894-1961 .... **CLC 9, 15**
See Celine, Louis-Ferdinand
See also CA 85-88; CANR 28; MTCW 1

de Tolignac, Gaston
See Griffith, D(avid Lewelyn) W(ark)

Deutsch, Babette 1895-1982 .... **CLC 18**
See also BYA 3; CA 1-4R; CAAS 108; CANR 4, 79; CP 1, 2, 3; DLB 45; SATA 1; SATA-Obit 33

Devenant, William 1606-1649 .... **LC 13**

Devkota, Laxmiprasad 1909-1959 . **TCLC 23**
See also CAAE 123

De Voto, Bernard (Augustine)
1897-1955 .... **TCLC 29**
See also CA 160; CAAE 113; DLB 9, 256; MAL 5; TCWW 1, 2

De Vries, Peter 1910-1993 ..... **CLC 1, 2, 3, 7, 10, 28, 46**
See also CA 17-20R; CAAS 142; CANR 41; CN 1, 2, 3, 4, 5; DAM NOV; DLB 6; DLBY 1982; MAL 5; MTCW 1, 2; MTFW 2005

Dewey, John 1859-1952 .... **TCLC 95**
See also CA 170; CAAE 114; CANR 144; DLB 246, 270; RGAL 4

Dexter, John
See Bradley, Marion Zimmer
See also GLL 1

Dexter, Martin
See Faust, Frederick (Schiller)

Dexter, Pete 1943- .... **CLC 34, 55**
See also BEST 89:2; CA 131; CAAE 127; CANR 129; CPW; DAM POP; INT CA-131; MAL 5; MTCW 1; MTFW 2005

Diamano, Silmang
See Senghor, Leopold Sedar

Diamant, Anita 1951- .... **CLC 239**
See also CA 145; CANR 126

Diamond, Neil 1941- .... **CLC 30**
See also CA 108

Diaz del Castillo, Bernal c.
1496-1584 .... **HLCS 1; LC 31**
See also DLB 318; LAW

di Bassetto, Corno
See Shaw, George Bernard

Dick, Philip K. 1928-1982 ... **CLC 10, 30, 72; SSC 57**
See also AAYA 24; BPFB 1; BYA 11; CA 49-52; CAAS 106; CANR 2, 16, 132; CN 2, 3; CPW; DA3; DAM NOV, POP; DLB 8; MTCW 1, 2; MTFW 2005; NFS 5; SCFW 1, 2; SFW 4

Dick, Philip Kindred
See Dick, Philip K.

Dickens, Charles (John Huffam)
1812-1870 .... **NCLC 3, 8, 18, 26, 37, 50, 86, 105, 113, 161, 187; SSC 17, 49, 88; WLC 2**
See also AAYA 23; BRW 5; BRWC 1, 2; BYA 1, 2, 3, 13, 14; CDBLB 1832-1890; CLR 95; CMW 4; DA; DA3; DAB; DAC; DAM MST, NOV; DLB 21, 55, 70, 159, 166; EXPN; GL 2; HGG; JRDA; LAIT 1, 2; LATS 1:1; LMFS 1; MAICYA 1, 2; NFS 4, 5, 10, 14, 20, 25; RGEL 2; RGSF 2; SATA 15; SUFW 1; TEA; WCH; WLIT 4; WYA

Dickey, James (Lafayette)
1923-1997 .... **CLC 1, 2, 4, 7, 10, 15, 47, 109; PC 40; TCLC 151**
See also AAYA 50; AITN 1, 2; AMWS 4; BPFB 1; CA 9-12R; CAAS 156; CABS 2; CANR 10, 48, 61, 105; CDALB 1968-1988; CP 1, 2, 3, 4, 5, 6; CPW; CSW; DA3; DAM NOV, POET, POP; DLB 5, 193; DLBD 7; DLBY 1982, 1993, 1996, 1997, 1998; EWL 3; INT CANR-10; MAL 5; MTCW 1, 2; NFS 9; PFS 6, 11; RGAL 4; TUS

Dickey, William 1928-1994 .... **CLC 3, 28**
See also CA 9-12R; CAAS 145; CANR 24, 79; CP 1, 2, 3, 4; DLB 5

Dickinson, Charles 1951- .... **CLC 49**
See also CA 128; CANR 141

Dickinson, Emily (Elizabeth)
1830-1886 ..... **NCLC 21, 77, 171; PC 1; WLC 2**
See also AAYA 22; AMW; AMWR 1; CDALB 1865-1917; DA; DA3; DAB; DAC; DAM MST, POET; DLB 1, 243; EXPP; FL 1:3; MBL; PAB; PFS 1, 2, 3, 4, 5, 6, 8, 10, 11, 13, 16; RGAL 4; SATA 29; TUS; WP; WYA

Dickinson, Mrs. Herbert Ward
See Phelps, Elizabeth Stuart

Dickinson, Peter (Malcolm de Brissac)
1927- .... **CLC 12, 35**
See also AAYA 9, 49; BYA 5; CA 41-44R; CANR 31, 58, 88, 134; CLR 29; CMW 4; DLB 87, 161, 276; JRDA; MAICYA 1, 2; SATA 5, 62, 95, 150; SFW 4; WYA; YAW

Dickson, Carr
See Carr, John Dickson

Dickson, Carter
See Carr, John Dickson

Diderot, Denis 1713-1784 .... **LC 26, 126**
See also DLB 313; EW 4; GFL Beginnings to 1789; LMFS 1; RGWL 2, 3

Didion, Joan 1934- . **CLC 1, 3, 8, 14, 32, 129**
See also AITN 1; AMWS 4; CA 5-8R; CANR 14, 52, 76, 125; CDALB 1968-1988; CN 2, 3, 4, 5, 6, 7; DA3; DAM NOV; DLB 2, 173, 185; DLBY 1981, 1986; EWL 3; MAL 5; MBL; MTCW 1, 2; MTFW 2005; NFS 3; RGAL 4; TCLE 1:1; TCWW 2; TUS

di Donato, Pietro 1911-1992 .... **TCLC 159**
See also CA 101; CAAS 136; DLB 9

Dietrich, Robert
See Hunt, E. Howard

Difusa, Pati
See Almodovar, Pedro

Dillard, Annie 1945- ...... **CLC 9, 60, 115, 216**
See also AAYA 6, 43; AMWS 6; ANW; CA 49-52; CANR 3, 43, 62, 90, 125; DA3; DAM NOV; DLB 275, 278; DLBY 1980; LAIT 4, 5; MAL 5; MTCW 1, 2; MTFW 2005; NCFS 1; RGAL 4; SATA 10, 140; TCLE 1:1; TUS

Dillard, R(ichard) H(enry) W(ilde)
1937- .... **CLC 5**
See also CA 21-24R; 7; CANR 10; CP 2, 3, 4, 5, 6, 7; CSW; DLB 5, 244

Dillon, Eilis 1920-1994 .... **CLC 17**
See also CA 182; 9-12R, 182; 3; CAAS 147; CANR 4, 38, 78; CLR 26; MAICYA 1, 2; MAICYAS 1; SATA 2, 74; SATA-Essay 105; SATA-Obit 83; YAW

Dimont, Penelope
See Mortimer, Penelope (Ruth)

Dinesen, Isak ..... **CLC 10, 29, 95; SSC 7, 75**
See Blixen, Karen (Christentze Dinesen)
See also EW 10; EWL 3; EXPS; FW; GL 2; HGG; LAIT 3; MTCW 1; NCFS 2; NFS 9; RGSF 2; RGWL 2, 3; SSFS 3, 6, 13; WLIT 2

Ding Ling .... **CLC 68**
See Chiang, Pin-chin
See also DLB 328; RGWL 3

Diodorus Siculus c. 90B.C.-c. 31B.C. .... **CMLC 88**

Diphusa, Patty
See Almodovar, Pedro

Disch, Thomas M. 1940- .... **CLC 7, 36**
See Disch, Tom
See also AAYA 17; BPFB 1; CA 21-24R; 4; CANR 17, 36, 54, 89; CLR 18; CP 5, 6, 7; DA3; DLB 8; HGG; MAICYA 1, 2; MTCW 1, 2; MTFW 2005; SAAS 15; SATA 92; SCFW 1, 2; SFW 4; SUFW 2

Disch, Tom
See Disch, Thomas M.
See also DLB 282

d'Isly, Georges
See Simenon, Georges (Jacques Christian)

Disraeli, Benjamin 1804-1881 ... **NCLC 2, 39, 79**
See also BRW 4; DLB 21, 55; RGEL 2

Ditcum, Steve
See Crumb, R.

Dixon, Paige
See Corcoran, Barbara (Asenath)

Dixon, Stephen 1936- .... **CLC 52; SSC 16**
See also AMWS 12; CA 89-92; CANR 17, 40, 54, 91; CN 4, 5, 6, 7; DLB 130; MAL 5

Dixon, Thomas, Jr. 1864-1946 ..... **TCLC 163**
See also RHW

Djebar, Assia 1936- .... **CLC 182**
See also CA 188; EWL 3; RGWL 3; WLIT 2

Doak, Annie
See Dillard, Annie

Dobell, Sydney Thompson
1824-1874 .... **NCLC 43**
See also DLB 32; RGEL 2

Doblin, Alfred .... **TCLC 13**
See Doeblin, Alfred
See also CDWLB 2; EWL 3; RGWL 2, 3

Dobroliubov, Nikolai Aleksandrovich
See Dobrolyubov, Nikolai Alexandrovich
See also DLB 277

Dobrolyubov, Nikolai Alexandrovich
1836-1861 .... **NCLC 5**
See Dobroliubov, Nikolai Aleksandrovich

Dobson, Austin 1840-1921 .... **TCLC 79**
See also DLB 35, 144

Dobyns, Stephen 1941- .... **CLC 37, 233**
See also AMWS 13; CA 45-48; CANR 2, 18, 99; CMW 4; CP 4, 5, 6, 7; PFS 23

Doctorow, Edgar Laurence
See Doctorow, E.L.

Doctorow, E.L. 1931- . **CLC 6, 11, 15, 18, 37, 44, 65, 113, 214**
See also AAYA 22; AITN 2; AMWS 4; BEST 89:3; BPFB 1; CA 45-48; CANR 2, 33, 51, 76, 97, 133; CDALB 1968-1988; CN 3, 4, 5, 6, 7; CPW; DA3; DAM NOV, POP; DLB 2, 28, 173; DLBY 1980; EWL 3; LAIT 3; MAL 5; MTCW 1, 2; MTFW 2005; NFS 6; RGAL 4; RGHL; RHW; TCLE 1:1; TCWW 1, 2; TUS

Dodgson, Charles L(utwidge) 1832-1898
See Carroll, Lewis
See also CLR 2; DA; DA3; DAB; DAC; DAM MST, NOV, POET; MAICYA 1, 2; SATA 100; YABC 2

Dodsley, Robert 1703-1764 .... **LC 97**
See also DLB 95; RGEL 2

Dodson, Owen (Vincent) 1914-1983 .. **BLC 1; CLC 79**
See also BW 1; CA 65-68; CAAS 110; CANR 24; DAM MULT; DLB 76

Doeblin, Alfred 1878-1957 .... **TCLC 13**
See Doblin, Alfred
See also CA 141; CAAE 110; DLB 66

Doerr, Harriet 1910-2002 .... **CLC 34**
See also CA 122; CAAE 117; CAAS 213; CANR 47; INT CA-122; LATS 1:2

Domecq, H(onorio Bustos)
See Bioy Casares, Adolfo

Domecq, H(onorio) Bustos
See Bioy Casares, Adolfo; Borges, Jorge Luis

Domini, Rey
See Lorde, Audre
See also GLL 1

Dominique
See Proust, (Valentin-Louis-George-Eugene) Marcel

Don, A
See Stephen, Sir Leslie

Donaldson, Stephen R(eeder)
1947- .... **CLC 46, 138**
See also AAYA 36; BPFB 1; CA 89-92; CANR 13, 55, 99; CPW; DAM POP; FANT; INT CANR-13; SATA 121; SFW 4; SUFW 1, 2

Donleavy, J(ames) P(atrick) 1926- .... **CLC 1, 4, 6, 10, 45**
See also AITN 2; BPFB 1; CA 9-12R; CANR 24, 49, 62, 80, 124; CBD; CD 5, 6; CN 1, 2, 3, 4, 5, 6, 7; DLB 6, 173; INT CANR-24; MAL 5; MTCW 1, 2; MTFW 2005; RGAL 4

Donnadieu, Marguerite
See Duras, Marguerite

Donne, John 1572-1631 ... **LC 10, 24, 91; PC 1, 43; WLC 2**
See also AAYA 67; BRW 1; BRWC 1; BRWR 2; CDBLB Before 1660; DA; DAB; DAC; DAM MST, POET; DLB 121, 151; EXPP; PAB; PFS 2, 11; RGEL 3; TEA; WLIT 3; WP

Donnell, David 1939(?)- .... **CLC 34**
See also CA 197

Donoghue, Denis 1928- .... **CLC 209**
See also CA 17-20R; CANR 16, 102

Donoghue, Emma 1969- .... **CLC 239**
See also CA 155; CANR 103, 152; DLB 267; GLL 2; SATA 101

Donoghue, P.S.
See Hunt, E. Howard

Donoso (Yanez), Jose 1924-1996 ... **CLC 4, 8, 11, 32, 99; HLC 1; SSC 34; TCLC 133**
See also CA 81-84; CAAS 155; CANR 32, 73; CDWLB 3; CWW 2; DAM MULT; DLB 113; EWL 3; HW 1, 2; LAW; LAWS 1; MTCW 1, 2; MTFW 2005; RGSF 2; WLIT 1

Donovan, John 1928-1992 .... **CLC 35**
    See also AAYA 20; CA 97-100; CAAS 137;
    CLR 3; MAICYA 1, 2; SATA 72; SATA-
    Brief 29; YAW
Don Roberto
    See Cunninghame Graham, Robert
    (Gallnigad) Bontine
Doolittle, Hilda 1886-1961 . **CLC 3, 8, 14, 31,**
    34, 73; PC 5; WLC 3
    See H. D.
    See also AAYA 66; AMWS 1; CA 97-100;
    CANR 35, 131; DA; DAC; DAM MST,
    POET; DLB 4, 45; EWL 3; FW; GLL 1;
    LMFS 2; MAL 5; MBL; MTCW 1, 2;
    MTFW 2005; PFS 6; RGAL 4
Doppo, Kunikida .... **TCLC 99**
    See Kunikida Doppo
Dorfman, Ariel 1942- .... **CLC 48, 77, 189;**
    HLC 1
    See also CA 130; CAAE 124; CANR 67,
    70, 135; CWW 2; DAM MULT; DFS 4;
    EWL 3; HW 1, 2; INT CA-130; WLIT 1
Dorn, Edward (Merton)
    1929-1999 .... **CLC 10, 18**
    See also CA 93-96; CAAS 187; CANR 42,
    79; CP 1, 2, 3, 4, 5, 6, 7; DLB 5; INT
    CA-93-96; WP
Dor-Ner, Zvi .... **CLC 70**
Dorris, Michael 1945-1997 .... **CLC 109;**
    NNAL
    See also AAYA 20; BEST 90:1; BYA 12;
    CA 102; CAAS 157; CANR 19, 46, 75;
    CLR 58; DA3; DAM MULT; NOW; DLB
    175; LAIT 5; MTCW 2; MTFW 2005;
    NFS 3; RGAL 4; SATA 75; SATA-Obit
    94; TCWW 2; YAW
Dorris, Michael A.
    See Dorris, Michael
Dorsan, Luc
    See Simenon, Georges (Jacques Christian)
Dorsange, Jean
    See Simenon, Georges (Jacques Christian)
Dorset
    See Sackville, Thomas
Dos Passos, John (Roderigo)
    1896-1970 ... **CLC 1, 4, 8, 11, 15, 25, 34,**
    82; WLC 2
    See also AMW; BPFB 1; CA 1-4R; CAAS
    29-32R; CANR 3; CDALB 1929-1941;
    DA; DA3; DAB; DAC; DAM MST, NOV;
    DLB 4, 9, 274, 316; DLBD 1, 15; DLBY
    1996; EWL 3; MAL 5; MTCW 1, 2;
    MTFW 2005; NFS 14; RGAL 4; TUS
Dossage, Jean
    See Simenon, Georges (Jacques Christian)
Dostoevsky, Fedor Mikhailovich
    1821-1881 .. **NCLC 2, 7, 21, 33, 43, 119,**
    167; SSC 2, 33, 44; WLC 2
    See Dostoevsky, Fyodor
    See also AAYA 40; DA; DA3; DAB; DAC;
    DAM MST, NOV; EW 7; EXPN; NFS 3,
    8; RGSF 2; RGWL 2, 3; SSFS 8; TWA
Dostoevsky, Fyodor
    See Dostoevsky, Fedor Mikhailovich
    See also DLB 238; LATS 1:1; LMFS 1, 2
Doty, M. R.
    See Doty, Mark
Doty, Mark 1953(?)- .... **CLC 176; PC 53**
    See also AMWS 11; CA 183; 161, 183;
    CANR 110; CP 7
Doty, Mark A.
    See Doty, Mark
Doty, Mark Alan
    See Doty, Mark
Doughty, Charles M(ontagu)
    1843-1926 .... **TCLC 27**
    See also CA 178; CAAE 115; DLB 19, 57,
    174

Douglas, Ellen .... **CLC 73**
    See Haxton, Josephine Ayres; Williamson,
    Ellen Douglas
    See also CN 5, 6, 7; CSW; DLB 292
Douglas, Gavin 1475(?)-1522 .... **LC 20**
    See also DLB 132; RGEL 2
Douglas, George
    See Brown, George Douglas
    See also RGEL 2
Douglas, Keith (Castellain)
    1920-1944 .... **TCLC 40**
    See also BRW 7; CA 160; DLB 27; EWL
    3; PAB; RGEL 2
Douglas, Leonard
    See Bradbury, Ray
Douglas, Michael
    See Crichton, Michael
Douglas, (George) Norman
    1868-1952 .... **TCLC 68**
    See also BRW 6; CA 157; CAAE 119; DLB
    34, 195; RGEL 2
Douglas, William
    See Brown, George Douglas
Douglass, Frederick 1817(?)-1895 ..... **BLC 1;**
    NCLC 7, 55, 141; WLC 2
    See also AAYA 48; AFAW 1, 2; AMWC 1;
    AMWS 3; CDALB 1640-1865; DA; DA3;
    DAC; DAM MST, MULT; DLB 1, 43, 50,
    79, 243; FW; LAIT 2; NCFS 2; RGAL 4;
    SATA 29
Dourado, (Waldomiro Freitas) Autran
    1926- .... **CLC 23, 60**
    See also CA 25-28R, 179; CANR 34, 81;
    DLB 145, 307; HW 2
Dourado, Waldomiro Freitas Autran
    See Dourado, (Waldomiro Freitas) Autran
Dove, Rita 1952- .. **BLCS; CLC 50, 81; PC 6**
    See also AAYA 46; AMWS 4; BW 2; CA
    109; 19; CANR 27, 42, 68, 76, 97, 132;
    CDALBS; CP 5, 6, 7; CSW; CWP; DA3;
    DAM MULT, POET; DLB 120; EWL 3;
    EXPP; MAL 5; MTCW 2; MTFW 2005;
    PFS 1, 15; RGAL 4
Dove, Rita Frances
    See Dove, Rita
Doveglion
    See Villa, Jose Garcia
Dowell, Coleman 1925-1985 .... **CLC 60**
    See also CA 25-28R; CAAS 117; CANR
    10; DLB 130; GLL 2
Downing, Major Jack
    See Smith, Seba
Dowson, Ernest (Christopher)
    1867-1900 .... **TCLC 4**
    See also CA 150; CAAE 105; DLB 19, 135;
    RGEL 2
Doyle, A. Conan
    See Doyle, Sir Arthur Conan
Doyle, Sir Arthur Conan
    1859-1930 ..... **SSC 12, 83, 95; TCLC 7;**
    WLC 2
    See Conan Doyle, Arthur
    See also AAYA 14; BRWS 2; CA 122;
    CAAE 104; CANR 131; CDBLB 1890-
    1914; CLR 106; CMW 4; DA; DA3;
    DAB; DAC; DAM MST, NOV; DLB 18,
    70, 156, 178; EXPS; HGG; LAIT 2;
    MSW; MTCW 1, 2; MTFW 2005; RGEL
    2; RGSF 2; RHW; SATA 24; SCFW 1, 2;
    SFW 4; SSFS 2; TEA; WCH; WLIT 4;
    WYA; YAW
Doyle, Conan
    See Doyle, Sir Arthur Conan
Doyle, John
    See Graves, Robert
Doyle, Roddy 1958- .... **CLC 81, 178**
    See also AAYA 14; BRWS 5; CA 143;
    CANR 73, 128; CN 6, 7; DA3; DLB 194,
    326; MTCW 2; MTFW 2005

Doyle, Sir A. Conan
    See Doyle, Sir Arthur Conan
Dr. A
    See Asimov, Isaac; Silverstein, Alvin; Sil-
    verstein, Virginia B(arbara Opshelor)
Drabble, Margaret 1939- ...... **CLC 2, 3, 5, 8,**
    10, 22, 53, 129
    See also BRWS 4; CA 13-16R; CANR 18,
    35, 63, 112, 131; CDBLB 1960 to Present;
    CN 1, 2, 3, 4, 5, 6, 7; CPW; DA3; DAB;
    DAC; DAM MST, NOV, POP; DLB 14,
    155, 231; EWL 3; FW; MTCW 1, 2;
    MTFW 2005; RGEL 2; SATA 48; TEA
Drakulic, Slavenka 1949- .... **CLC 173**
    See also CA 144; CANR 92
Drakulic-Ilic, Slavenka
    See Drakulic, Slavenka
Drapier, M. B.
    See Swift, Jonathan
Drayham, James
    See Mencken, H(enry) L(ouis)
Drayton, Michael 1563-1631 .... **LC 8**
    See also DAM POET; DLB 121; RGEL 2
Dreadstone, Carl
    See Campbell, (John) Ramsey
Dreiser, Theodore 1871-1945 .... **SSC 30;**
    TCLC 10, 18, 35, 83; WLC 2
    See also AMW; AMWC 2; AMWR 2; BYA
    15, 16; CA 132; CAAE 106; CDALB
    1865-1917; DA; DA3; DAC; DAM MST,
    NOV; DLB 9, 12, 102, 137; DLBD 1;
    EWL 3; LAIT 2; LMFS 2; MAL 5;
    MTCW 1, 2; MTFW 2005; NFS 8, 17;
    RGAL 4; TUS
Dreiser, Theodore Herman Albert
    See Dreiser, Theodore
Drexler, Rosalyn 1926- .... **CLC 2, 6**
    See also CA 81-84; CAD; CANR 68, 124;
    CD 5, 6; CWD; MAL 5
Dreyer, Carl Theodor 1889-1968 ...... **CLC 16**
    See also CAAS 116
Drieu la Rochelle, Pierre
    1893-1945 .... **TCLC 21**
    See also CA 250; CAAE 117; DLB 72;
    EWL 3; GFL 1789 to the Present
Drieu la Rochelle, Pierre-Eugene 1893-1945
    See Drieu la Rochelle, Pierre
Drinkwater, John 1882-1937 .... **TCLC 57**
    See also CA 149; CAAE 109; DLB 10, 19,
    149; RGEL 2
Drop Shot
    See Cable, George Washington
Droste-Hulshoff, Annette Freiin von
    1797-1848 .... **NCLC 3, 133**
    See also CDWLB 2; DLB 133; RGSF 2;
    RGWL 2, 3
Drummond, Walter
    See Silverberg, Robert
Drummond, William Henry
    1854-1907 .... **TCLC 25**
    See also CA 160; DLB 92
Drummond de Andrade, Carlos
    1902-1987 .... **CLC 18; TCLC 139**
    See Andrade, Carlos Drummond de
    See also CA 132; CAAS 123; DLB 307;
    LAW
Drummond of Hawthornden, William
    1585-1649 .... **LC 83**
    See also DLB 121, 213; RGEL 2
Drury, Allen (Stuart) 1918-1998 .... **CLC 37**
    See also CA 57-60; CAAS 170; CANR 18,
    52; CN 1, 2, 3, 4, 5, 6; INT CANR-18
Druse, Eleanor
    See King, Stephen

FL 1:5; LAIT 5; LATS 1:2; MAL 5;
MTCW 1, 2; MTFW 2005; NFS 5; PFS
14; RGAL 4; SATA 94, 141; SSFS 14,
22; TCWW 2

Erenburg, Ilya (Grigoryevich)
See Ehrenburg, Ilya (Grigoryevich)

Erickson, Stephen Michael
See Erickson, Steve

Erickson, Steve 1950- .... **CLC 64**
See also CA 129; CANR 60, 68, 136;
MTFW 2005; SFW 4; SUFW 2

Erickson, Walter
See Fast, Howard

Ericson, Walter
See Fast, Howard

Eriksson, Buntel
See Bergman, Ingmar

Eriugena, John Scottus c.
810-877 .... **CMLC 65**
See also DLB 115

Ernaux, Annie 1940- .... **CLC 88, 184**
See also CA 147; CANR 93; MTFW 2005;
NCFS 3, 5

Erskine, John 1879-1951 .... **TCLC 84**
See also CA 159; CAAE 112; DLB 9, 102;
FANT

Erwin, Will
See Eisner, Will

Eschenbach, Wolfram von
See von Eschenbach, Wolfram
See also RGWL 3

Eseki, Bruno
See Mphahlele, Ezekiel

Esenin, S.A.
See Esenin, Sergei
See also EWL 3

Esenin, Sergei 1895-1925 .... **TCLC 4**
See Esenin, S.A.
See also CAAE 104; RGWL 2, 3

Esenin, Sergei Aleksandrovich
See Esenin, Sergei

Eshleman, Clayton 1935- .... **CLC 7**
See also CA 212; 33-36R, 212; 6; CANR
93; CP 1, 2, 3, 4, 5, 6, 7; DLB 5

Espada, Martin 1957- .... **PC 74**
See also CA 159; CANR 80; CP 7; EXPP;
LLW; MAL 5; PFS 13, 16

Espriella, Don Manuel Alvarez
See Southey, Robert

Espriu, Salvador 1913-1985 .... **CLC 9**
See also CA 154; CAAS 115; DLB 134;
EWL 3

Espronceda, Jose de 1808-1842 ..... **NCLC 39**

Esquivel, Laura 1950(?)- ... **CLC 141; HLCS
1**
See also AAYA 29; CA 143; CANR 68, 113,
161; DA3; DNFS 2; LAIT 3; LMFS 2;
MTCW 2; MTFW 2005; NFS 5; WLIT 1

Esse, James
See Stephens, James

Esterbrook, Tom
See Hubbard, L. Ron

Estleman, Loren D. 1952- .... **CLC 48**
See also AAYA 27; CA 85-88; CANR 27,
74, 139; CMW 4; CPW; DA3; DAM
NOV, POP; DLB 226; INT CANR-27;
MTCW 1, 2; MTFW 2005; TCWW 1, 2

Etherege, Sir George 1636-1692 . **DC 23; LC
78**
See also BRW 2; DAM DRAM; DLB 80;
PAB; RGEL 2

Euclid 306B.C.-283B.C. .... **CMLC 25**

Eugenides, Jeffrey 1960(?)- .... **CLC 81, 212**
See also AAYA 51; CA 144; CANR 120;
MTFW 2005; NFS 24

Euripides c. 484B.C.-406B.C. .... **CMLC 23,
51; DC 4; WLCS**
See also AW 1; CDWLB 1; DA; DA3;
DAB; DAC; DAM DRAM, MST; DFS 1,
4, 6; DLB 176; LAIT 1; LMFS 1; RGWL
2, 3; WLIT 8

Evan, Evin
See Faust, Frederick (Schiller)

Evans, Caradoc 1878-1945 ... **SSC 43; TCLC
85**
See also DLB 162

Evans, Evan
See Faust, Frederick (Schiller)

Evans, Marian
See Eliot, George

Evans, Mary Ann
See Eliot, George
See also NFS 20

Evarts, Esther
See Benson, Sally

Everett, Percival
See Everett, Percival L.
See also CSW

Everett, Percival L. 1956- .... **CLC 57**
See Everett, Percival
See also BW 2; CA 129; CANR 94, 134;
CN 7; MTFW 2005

Everson, R(onald) G(ilmour)
1903-1992 .... **CLC 27**
See also CA 17-20R; CP 1, 2, 3, 4; DLB 88

Everson, William (Oliver)
1912-1994 .... **CLC 1, 5, 14**
See Antoninus, Brother
See also BG 1:2; CA 9-12R; CAAS 145;
CANR 20; CP 2, 3, 4, 5; DLB 5, 16, 212;
MTCW 1

Evtushenko, Evgenii Aleksandrovich
See Yevtushenko, Yevgeny (Alexandrovich)
See also CWW 2; RGWL 2, 3

Ewart, Gavin (Buchanan)
1916-1995 .... **CLC 13, 46**
See also BRWS 7; CA 89-92; CAAS 150;
CANR 17, 46; CP 1, 2, 3, 4, 5, 6; DLB
40; MTCW 1

Ewers, Hanns Heinz 1871-1943 ..... **TCLC 12**
See also CA 149; CAAE 109

Ewing, Frederick R.
See Sturgeon, Theodore (Hamilton)

Exley, Frederick (Earl) 1929-1992 .... **CLC 6,
11**
See also AITN 2; BPFB 1; CA 81-84;
CAAS 138; CANR 117; DLB 143; DLBY
1981

Eynhardt, Guillermo
See Quiroga, Horacio (Sylvestre)

Ezekiel, Nissim (Moses) 1924-2004 .. **CLC 61**
See also CA 61-64; CAAS 223; CP 1, 2, 3,
4, 5, 6, 7; DLB 323; EWL 3

Ezekiel, Tish O'Dowd 1943- .... **CLC 34**
See also CA 129

Fadeev, Aleksandr Aleksandrovich
See Bulgya, Alexander Alexandrovich
See also DLB 272

Fadeev, Alexandr Alexandrovich
See Bulgya, Alexander Alexandrovich
See also EWL 3

Fadeyev, A.
See Bulgya, Alexander Alexandrovich

Fadeyev, Alexander .... **TCLC 53**
See Bulgya, Alexander Alexandrovich

Fagen, Donald 1948- .... **CLC 26**

Fainzil'berg, Il'ia Arnol'dovich
See Fainzilberg, Ilya Arnoldovich

Fainzilberg, Ilya Arnoldovich
1897-1937 .... **TCLC 21**
See Il'f, Il'ia
See also CA 165; CAAE 120; EWL 3

Fair, Ronald L. 1932- .... **CLC 18**
See also BW 1; CA 69-72; CANR 25; DLB
33

Fairbairn, Roger
See Carr, John Dickson

Fairbairns, Zoe (Ann) 1948- .... **CLC 32**
See also CA 103; CANR 21, 85; CN 4, 5,
6, 7

Fairfield, Flora
See Alcott, Louisa May

Fairman, Paul W. 1916-1977
See Queen, Ellery
See also CAAS 114; SFW 4

Falco, Gian
See Papini, Giovanni

Falconer, James
See Kirkup, James

Falconer, Kenneth
See Kornbluth, C(yril) M.

Falkland, Samuel
See Heijermans, Herman

Fallaci, Oriana 1930-2006 .... **CLC 11, 110**
See also CA 77-80; CAAS 253; CANR 15,
58, 134; FW; MTCW 1

Faludi, Susan 1959- .... **CLC 140**
See also CA 138; CANR 126; FW; MTCW
2; MTFW 2005; NCFS 3

Faludy, George 1913- .... **CLC 42**
See also CA 21-24R

Faludy, Gyoergy
See Faludy, George

Fanon, Frantz 1925-1961 ... **BLC 2; CLC 74;
TCLC 188**
See also BW 1; CA 116; CAAS 89-92;
DAM MULT; DLB 296; LMFS 2; WLIT
2

Fanshawe, Ann 1625-1680 .... **LC 11**

Fante, John (Thomas) 1911-1983 .... **CLC 60;
SSC 65**
See also AMWS 11; CA 69-72; CAAS 109;
CANR 23, 104; DLB 130; DLBY 1983

Far, Sui Sin .... **SSC 62**
See Eaton, Edith Maude
See also SSFS 4

Farah, Nuruddin 1945- ...... **BLC 2; CLC 53,
137**
See also AFW; BW 2, 3; CA 106; CANR
81, 148; CDWLB 3; CN 4, 5, 6, 7; DAM
MULT; DLB 125; EWL 3; WLIT 2

Fargue, Leon-Paul 1876(?)-1947 .... **TCLC 11**
See also CAAE 109; CANR 107; DLB 258;
EWL 3

Farigoule, Louis
See Romains, Jules

Farina, Richard 1936(?)-1966 .... **CLC 9**
See also CA 81-84; CAAS 25-28R

Farley, Walter (Lorimer)
1915-1989 .... **CLC 17**
See also AAYA 58; BYA 14; CA 17-20R;
CANR 8, 29, 84; DLB 22; JRDA; MAI-
CYA 1, 2; SATA 2, 43, 132; YAW

Farmer, Philip Jose 1918- .... **CLC 1, 19**
See also AAYA 28; BPFB 1; CA 1-4R;
CANR 4, 35, 111; DLB 8; MTCW 1;
SATA 93; SCFW 1, 2; SFW 4

Farquhar, George 1677-1707 .... **LC 21**
See also BRW 2; DAM DRAM; DLB 84;
RGEL 2

Farrell, J(ames) G(ordon)
1935-1979 .... **CLC 6**
See also CA 73-76; CAAS 89-92; CANR
36; CN 1, 2; DLB 14, 271, 326; MTCW
1; RGEL 2; RHW; WLIT 4

Farrell, James T(homas) 1904-1979 . **CLC 1,
4, 8, 11, 66; SSC 28**
See also AMW; BPFB 1; CA 5-8R; CAAS
89-92; CANR 9, 61; CN 1, 2; DLB 4, 9,
86; DLBD 2; EWL 3; MAL 5; MTCW 1,
2; MTFW 2005; RGAL 4

Freud, Sigmund 1856-1939 .... **TCLC 52**
See also CA 133; CAAE 115; CANR 69; DLB 296; EW 8; EWL 3; LATS 1:1; MTCW 1, 2; MTFW 2005; NCFS 3; TWA

Freytag, Gustav 1816-1895 .... **NCLC 109**
See also DLB 129

Friedan, Betty 1921-2006 .... **CLC 74**
See also CA 65-68; CAAS 248; CANR 18, 45, 74; DLB 246; FW; MTCW 1, 2; MTFW 2005; NCFS 5

Friedan, Betty Naomi
See Friedan, Betty

Friedlander, Saul 1932- .... **CLC 90**
See also CA 130; CAAE 117; CANR 72; RGHL

Friedman, B(ernard) H(arper)
1926- .... **CLC 7**
See also CA 1-4R; CANR 3, 48

Friedman, Bruce Jay 1930- ...... **CLC 3, 5, 56**
See also CA 9-12R; CAD; CANR 25, 52, 101; CD 5, 6; CN 1, 2, 3, 4, 5, 6, 7; DLB 2, 28, 244; INT CANR-25; MAL 5; SSFS 18

Friel, Brian 1929- .... **CLC 5, 42, 59, 115; DC 8; SSC 76**
See also BRWS 5; CA 21-24R; CANR 33, 69, 131; CBD; CD 5, 6; DFS 11; DLB 13, 319; EWL 3; MTCW 1; RGEL 2; TEA

Friis-Baastad, Babbis Ellinor
1921-1970 .... **CLC 12**
See also CA 17-20R; CAAS 134; SATA 7

Frisch, Max 1911-1991 ...... **CLC 3, 9, 14, 18, 32, 44; TCLC 121**
See also CA 85-88; CAAS 134; CANR 32, 74; CDWLB 2; DAM DRAM, NOV; DLB 69, 124; EW 13; EWL 3; MTCW 1, 2; MTFW 2005; RGHL; RGWL 2, 3

Fromentin, Eugene (Samuel Auguste)
1820-1876 .... **NCLC 10, 125**
See also DLB 123; GFL 1789 to the Present

Frost, Frederick
See Faust, Frederick (Schiller)

Frost, Robert 1874-1963 . **CLC 1, 3, 4, 9, 10, 13, 15, 26, 34, 44; PC 1, 39, 71; WLC 2**
See also AAYA 21; AMW; AMWR 1; CA 89-92; CANR 33; CDALB 1917-1929; CLR 67; DA; DA3; DAB; DAC; DAM MST, POET; DLB 54, 284; DLBD 7; EWL 3; EXPP; MAL 5; MTCW 1, 2; MTFW 2005; PAB; PFS 1, 2, 3, 4, 5, 6, 7, 10, 13; RGAL 4; SATA 14; TUS; WP; WYA

Frost, Robert Lee
See Frost, Robert

Froude, James Anthony
1818-1894 .... **NCLC 43**
See also DLB 18, 57, 144

Froy, Herald
See Waterhouse, Keith (Spencer)

Fry, Christopher 1907-2005 ... **CLC 2, 10, 14**
See also BRWS 3; CA 17-20R; 23; CAAS 240; CANR 9, 30, 74, 132; CBD; CD 5, 6; CP 1, 2, 3, 4, 5, 6, 7; DAM DRAM; DLB 13; EWL 3; MTCW 1, 2; MTFW 2005; RGEL 2; SATA 66; TEA

Frye, (Herman) Northrop
1912-1991 .... **CLC 24, 70; TCLC 165**
See also CA 5-8R; CAAS 133; CANR 8, 37; DLB 67, 68, 246; EWL 3; MTCW 1, 2; MTFW 2005; RGAL 4; TWA

Fuchs, Daniel 1909-1993 .... **CLC 8, 22**
See also CA 81-84; 5; CAAS 142; CANR 40; CN 1, 2, 3, 4, 5; DLB 9, 26, 28; DLBY 1993; MAL 5

Fuchs, Daniel 1934- .... **CLC 34**
See also CA 37-40R; CANR 14, 48

Fuentes, Carlos 1928- .. **CLC 3, 8, 10, 13, 22, 41, 60, 113; HLC 1; SSC 24; WLC 2**
See also AAYA 4, 45; AITN 2; BPFB 1; CA 69-72; CANR 10, 32, 68, 104, 138; CDWLB 3; CWW 2; DA; DA3; DAB; DAC; DAM MST, MULT, NOV; DLB 113; DNFS 2; EWL 3; HW 1, 2; LAIT 3; LATS 1:2; LAW; LAWS 1; LMFS 2; MTCW 1, 2; MTFW 2005; NFS 8; RGSF 2; RGWL 2, 3; TWA; WLIT 1

Fuentes, Gregorio Lopez y
See Lopez y Fuentes, Gregorio

Fuertes, Gloria 1918-1998 .... **PC 27**
See also CA 178, 180; DLB 108; HW 2; SATA 115

Fugard, (Harold) Athol 1932- . **CLC 5, 9, 14, 25, 40, 80, 211; DC 3**
See also AAYA 17; AFW; CA 85-88; CANR 32, 54, 118; CD 5, 6; DAM DRAM; DFS 3, 6, 10, 24; DLB 225; DNFS 1, 2; EWL 3; LATS 1:2; MTCW 1; MTFW 2005; RGEL 2; WLIT 2

Fugard, Sheila 1932- .... **CLC 48**
See also CA 125

Fujiwara no Teika 1162-1241 .... **CMLC 73**
See also DLB 203

Fukuyama, Francis 1952- .... **CLC 131**
See also CA 140; CANR 72, 125

Fuller, Charles (H.), (Jr.) 1939- .... **BLC 2; CLC 25; DC 1**
See also BW 2; CA 112; CAAE 108; CAD; CANR 87; CD 5, 6; DAM DRAM, MULT; DFS 8; DLB 38, 266; EWL 3; INT CA-112; MAL 5; MTCW 1

Fuller, Henry Blake 1857-1929 .... **TCLC 103**
See also CA 177; CAAE 108; DLB 12; RGAL 4

Fuller, John (Leopold) 1937- .... **CLC 62**
See also CA 21-24R; CANR 9, 44; CP 1, 2, 3, 4, 5, 6, 7; DLB 40

Fuller, Margaret
See Ossoli, Sarah Margaret (Fuller)
See also AMWS 2; DLB 183, 223, 239; FL 1:3

Fuller, Roy (Broadbent) 1912-1991 ... **CLC 4, 28**
See also BRWS 7; CA 5-8R; 10; CAAS 135; CANR 53, 83; CN 1, 2, 3, 4, 5; CP 1, 2, 3, 4, 5; CWRI 5; DLB 15, 20; EWL 3; RGEL 2; SATA 87

Fuller, Sarah Margaret
See Ossoli, Sarah Margaret (Fuller)

Fuller, Sarah Margaret
See Ossoli, Sarah Margaret (Fuller)
See also DLB 1, 59, 73

Fuller, Thomas 1608-1661 .... **LC 111**
See also DLB 151

Fulton, Alice 1952- .... **CLC 52**
See also CA 116; CANR 57, 88; CP 5, 6, 7; CWP; DLB 193; PFS 25

Furphy, Joseph 1843-1912 .... **TCLC 25**
See Collins, Tom
See also CA 163; DLB 230; EWL 3; RGEL 2

Fuson, Robert H(enderson) 1927- .... **CLC 70**
See also CA 89-92; CANR 103

Fussell, Paul 1924- .... **CLC 74**
See also BEST 90:1; CA 17-20R; CANR 8, 21, 35, 69, 135; INT CANR-21; MTCW 1, 2; MTFW 2005

Futabatei, Shimei 1864-1909 .... **TCLC 44**
See Futabatei Shimei
See also CA 162; MJW

Futabatei Shimei
See Futabatei, Shimei
See also DLB 180; EWL 3

Futrelle, Jacques 1875-1912 .... **TCLC 19**
See also CA 155; CAAE 113; CMW 4

Gaboriau, Emile 1835-1873 .... **NCLC 14**
See also CMW 4; MSW

Gadda, Carlo Emilio 1893-1973 ...... **CLC 11; TCLC 144**
See also CA 89-92; DLB 177; EWL 3; WLIT 7

Gaddis, William 1922-1998 ... **CLC 1, 3, 6, 8, 10, 19, 43, 86**
See also AMWS 4; BPFB 1; CA 17-20R; CAAS 172; CANR 21, 48, 148; CN 1, 2, 3, 4, 5, 6; DLB 2, 278; EWL 3; MAL 5; MTCW 1, 2; MTFW 2005; RGAL 4

Gage, Walter
See Inge, William (Motter)

Gaiman, Neil 1960- .... **CLC 195**
See also AAYA 19, 42; CA 133; CANR 81, 129; CLR 109; DLB 261; HGG; MTFW 2005; SATA 85, 146; SFW 4; SUFW 2

Gaiman, Neil Richard
See Gaiman, Neil

Gaines, Ernest J. 1933- .. **BLC 2; CLC 3, 11, 18, 86, 181; SSC 68**
See also AAYA 18; AFAW 1, 2; AITN 1; BPFB 2; BW 2, 3; BYA 6; CA 9-12R; CANR 6, 24, 42, 75, 126; CDALB 1968-1988; CLR 62; CN 1, 2, 3, 4, 5, 6, 7; CSW; DA3; DAM MULT; DLB 2, 33, 152; DLBY 1980; EWL 3; EXPN; LAIT 5; LATS 1:2; MAL 5; MTCW 1, 2; MTFW 2005; NFS 5, 7, 16; RGAL 4; RGSF 2; RHW; SATA 86; SSFS 5; YAW

Gaitskill, Mary 1954- .... **CLC 69**
See also CA 128; CANR 61, 152; DLB 244; TCLE 1:1

Gaitskill, Mary Lawrence
See Gaitskill, Mary

Gaius Suetonius Tranquillus
See Suetonius

Galdos, Benito Perez
See Perez Galdos, Benito
See also EW 7

Gale, Zona 1874-1938 .... **TCLC 7**
See also CA 153; CAAE 105; CANR 84; DAM DRAM; DFS 17; DLB 9, 78, 228; RGAL 4

Galeano, Eduardo 1940- ... **CLC 72; HLCS 1**
See also CA 29-32R; CANR 13, 32, 100, 163; HW 1

Galeano, Eduardo Hughes
See Galeano, Eduardo

Galiano, Juan Valera y Alcala
See Valera y Alcala-Galiano, Juan

Galilei, Galileo 1564-1642 .... **LC 45**

Gallagher, Tess 1943- .... **CLC 18, 63; PC 9**
See also CA 106; CP 3, 4, 5, 6, 7; CWP; DAM POET; DLB 120, 212, 244; PFS 16

Gallant, Mavis 1922- ..... **CLC 7, 18, 38, 172; SSC 5, 78**
See also CA 69-72; CANR 29, 69, 117; CCA 1; CN 1, 2, 3, 4, 5, 6, 7; DAC; DAM MST; DLB 53; EWL 3; MTCW 1, 2; MTFW 2005; RGEL 2; RGSF 2

Gallant, Roy A(rthur) 1924- .... **CLC 17**
See also CA 5-8R; CANR 4, 29, 54, 117; CLR 30; MAICYA 1, 2; SATA 4, 68, 110

Gallico, Paul (William) 1897-1976 ..... **CLC 2**
See also AITN 1; CA 5-8R; CAAS 69-72; CANR 23; CN 1, 2; DLB 9, 171; FANT; MAICYA 1, 2; SATA 13

Gallo, Max Louis 1932- .... **CLC 95**
See also CA 85-88

Gallois, Lucien
See Desnos, Robert

Gallup, Ralph
See Whitemore, Hugh (John)

Gellhorn, Martha (Ellis)
1908-1998 .... **CLC 14, 60**
See also CA 77-80; CAAS 164; CANR 44;
CN 1, 2, 3, 4, 5, 6 7; DLBY 1982, 1998

Genet, Jean 1910-1986 .. **CLC 1, 2, 5, 10, 14,**
44, 46; DC 25; TCLC 128
See also CA 13-16R; CANR 18; DA3;
DAM DRAM; DFS 10; DLB 72, 321;
DLBY 1986; EW 13; EWL 3; GFL 1789
to the Present; GLL 1; LMFS 2; MTCW
1, 2; MTFW 2005; RGWL 2, 3; TWA

Genlis, Stephanie-Felicite Ducrest
1746-1830 .... **NCLC 166**
See also DLB 313

Gent, Peter 1942- .... **CLC 29**
See also AITN 1; CA 89-92; DLBY 1982

Gentile, Giovanni 1875-1944 .... **TCLC 96**
See also CAAE 119

Geoffrey of Monmouth c.
1100-1155 .... **CMLC 44**
See also DLB 146; TEA

George, Jean
See George, Jean Craighead

George, Jean Craighead 1919- .... **CLC 35**
See also AAYA 8, 69; BYA 2, 4; CA 5-8R;
CANR 25; CLR 1; 80; DLB 52; JRDA;
MAICYA 1, 2; SATA 2, 68, 124, 170;
WYA; YAW

George, Stefan (Anton) 1868-1933 . **TCLC 2,**
14
See also CA 193; CAAE 104; EW 8; EWL
3

Georges, Georges Martin
See Simenon, Georges (Jacques Christian)

Gerald of Wales c. 1146-c. 1223 ... **CMLC 60**

Gerhardi, William Alexander
See Gerhardie, William Alexander

Gerhardie, William Alexander
1895-1977 .... **CLC 5**
See also CA 25-28R; CAAS 73-76; CANR
18; CN 1, 2; DLB 36; RGEL 2

Gerson, Jean 1363-1429 .... **LC 77**
See also DLB 208

Gersonides 1288-1344 .... **CMLC 49**
See also DLB 115

Gerstler, Amy 1956- .... **CLC 70**
See also CA 146; CANR 99

Gertler, T. .... **CLC 34**
See also CA 121; CAAE 116

Gertsen, Aleksandr Ivanovich
See Herzen, Aleksandr Ivanovich

Ghalib .... **NCLC 39, 78**
See Ghalib, Asadullah Khan

Ghalib, Asadullah Khan 1797-1869
See Ghalib
See also DAM POET; RGWL 2, 3

Ghelderode, Michel de 1898-1962 ..... **CLC 6,**
11; DC 15; TCLC 187
See also CA 85-88; CANR 40, 77; DAM
DRAM; DLB 321; EW 11; EWL 3; TWA

Ghiselin, Brewster 1903-2001 .... **CLC 23**
See also CA 13-16R; 10; CANR 13; CP 1,
2, 3, 4, 5, 6, 7

Ghose, Aurabinda 1872-1950 .... **TCLC 63**
See Ghose, Aurobindo
See also CA 163

Ghose, Aurobindo
See Ghose, Aurabinda
See also EWL 3

Ghose, Zulfikar 1935- .... **CLC 42, 200**
See also CA 65-68; CANR 67; CN 1, 2, 3,
4, 5, 6, 7; CP 1, 2, 3, 4, 5, 6, 7; DLB 323;
EWL 3

Ghosh, Amitav 1956- .... **CLC 44, 153**
See also CA 147; CANR 80, 158; CN 6, 7;
DLB 323; WWE 1

Giacosa, Giuseppe 1847-1906 .... **TCLC 7**
See also CAAE 104

Gibb, Lee
See Waterhouse, Keith (Spencer)

Gibbon, Edward 1737-1794 .... **LC 97**
See also BRW 3; DLB 104, 336; RGEL 2

Gibbon, Lewis Grassic .... **TCLC 4**
See Mitchell, James Leslie
See also RGEL 2

Gibbons, Kaye 1960- .... **CLC 50, 88, 145**
See also AAYA 34; AMWS 10; CA 151;
CANR 75, 127; CN 7; CSW; DA3; DAM
POP; DLB 292; MTCW 2; MTFW 2005;
NFS 3; RGAL 4; SATA 117

Gibran, Kahlil 1883-1931 . **PC 9; TCLC 1, 9**
See also CA 150; CAAE 104; DA3; DAM
POET, POP; EWL 3; MTCW 2; WLIT 6

Gibran, Khalil
See Gibran, Kahlil

Gibson, Mel 1956- .... **CLC 215**

Gibson, William 1914- .... **CLC 23**
See also CA 9-12R; CAD; CANR 9, 42, 75,
125; CD 5, 6; DA; DAB; DAC; DAM
DRAM, MST; DFS 2; DLB 7; LAIT 2;
MAL 5; MTCW 2; MTFW 2005; SATA
66; YAW

Gibson, William 1948- .... **CLC 39, 63, 186,**
192; SSC 52
See also AAYA 12, 59; AMWS 16; BPFB
2; CA 133; CAAE 126; CANR 52, 90,
106; CN 6, 7; CPW; DA3; DAM POP;
DLB 251; MTCW 2; MTFW 2005; SCFW
2; SFW 4

Gibson, William Ford
See Gibson, William

Gide, Andre (Paul Guillaume)
1869-1951 ...... **SSC 13; TCLC 5, 12, 36,**
177; WLC 3
See also CA 124; CAAE 104; DA; DA3;
DAB; DAC; DAM MST, NOV; DLB 65,
321, 330; EW 8; EWL 3; GFL 1789 to
the Present; MTCW 1, 2; MTFW 2005;
NFS 21; RGSF 2; RGWL 2, 3; TWA

Gifford, Barry (Colby) 1946- .... **CLC 34**
See also CA 65-68; CANR 9, 30, 40, 90

Gilbert, Frank
See De Voto, Bernard (Augustine)

Gilbert, W(illiam) S(chwenck)
1836-1911 .... **TCLC 3**
See also CA 173; CAAE 104; DAM DRAM,
POET; RGEL 2; SATA 36

Gilbert of Poitiers c. 1085-1154 .... **CMLC 85**

Gilbreth, Frank B(unker), Jr.
1911-2001 .... **CLC 17**
See also CA 9-12R; SATA 2

Gilchrist, Ellen (Louise) 1935- .. **CLC 34, 48,**
143; SSC 14, 63
See also BPFB 2; CA 116; CAAE 113;
CANR 41, 61, 104; CN 4, 5, 6, 7; CPW;
CSW; DAM POP; DLB 130; EWL 3;
EXPS; MTCW 1, 2; MTFW 2005; RGAL
4; RGSF 2; SSFS 9

Giles, Molly 1942- .... **CLC 39**
See also CA 126; CANR 98

Gill, Eric .... **TCLC 85**
See Gill, (Arthur) Eric (Rowton Peter
Joseph)

Gill, (Arthur) Eric (Rowton Peter Joseph)
1882-1940
See Gill, Eric
See also CAAE 120; DLB 98

Gill, Patrick
See Creasey, John

Gillette, Douglas .... **CLC 70**

Gilliam, Terry 1940- .... **CLC 21, 141**
See Monty Python
See also AAYA 19, 59; CA 113; CAAE 108;
CANR 35; INT CA-113

Gilliam, Terry Vance
See Gilliam, Terry

Gillian, Jerry
See Gilliam, Terry

Gilliatt, Penelope (Ann Douglass)
1932-1993 .... **CLC 2, 10, 13, 53**
See also AITN 2; CA 13-16R; CAAS 141;
CANR 49; CN 1, 2, 3, 4, 5; DLB 14

Gilligan, Carol 1936- .... **CLC 208**
See also CA 142; CANR 121; FW

Gilman, Charlotte (Anna) Perkins (Stetson)
1860-1935 ...... **SSC 13, 62; TCLC 9, 37,**
117
See also AAYA 75; AMWS 11; BYA 11;
CA 150; CAAE 106; DLB 221; EXPS;
FL 1:5; FW; HGG; LAIT 2; MBL; MTCW
2; MTFW 2005; RGAL 4; RGSF 2; SFW
4; SSFS 1, 18

Gilmour, David 1946- .... **CLC 35**

Gilpin, William 1724-1804 .... **NCLC 30**

Gilray, J. D.
See Mencken, H(enry) L(ouis)

Gilroy, Frank D(aniel) 1925- .... **CLC 2**
See also CA 81-84; CAD; CANR 32, 64,
86; CD 5, 6; DFS 17; DLB 7

Gilstrap, John 1957(?)- .... **CLC 99**
See also AAYA 67; CA 160; CANR 101

Ginsberg, Allen 1926-1997 .... **CLC 1, 2, 3, 4,**
6, 13, 36, 69, 109; PC 4, 47; TCLC
120; WLC 3
See also AAYA 33; AITN 1; AMWC 1;
AMWS 2; BG 1:2; CA 1-4R; CAAS 157;
CANR 2, 41, 63, 95; CDALB 1941-1968;
CP 1, 2, 3, 4, 5, 6; DA; DA3; DAB; DAC;
DAM MST, POET; DLB 5, 16, 169, 237;
EWL 3; GLL 1; LMFS 2; MAL 5; MTCW
1, 2; MTFW 2005; PAB; PFS 5; RGAL 4;
TUS; WP

Ginzburg, Eugenia .... **CLC 59**
See Ginzburg, Evgeniia

Ginzburg, Evgeniia 1904-1977
See Ginzburg, Eugenia
See also DLB 302

Ginzburg, Natalia 1916-1991 .... **CLC 5, 11,**
54, 70; SSC 65; TCLC 156
See also CA 85-88; CAAS 135; CANR 33;
DFS 14; DLB 177; EW 13; EWL 3;
MTCW 1, 2; MTFW 2005; RGHL;
RGWL 2, 3

Giono, Jean 1895-1970 .... **CLC 4, 11; TCLC**
124
See also CA 45-48; CAAS 29-32R; CANR
2, 35; DLB 72, 321; EWL 3; GFL 1789
to the Present; MTCW 1; RGWL 2, 3

Giovanni, Nikki 1943- ...... **BLC 2; CLC 2, 4,**
19, 64, 117; PC 19; WLCS
See also AAYA 22; AITN 1; BW 2, 3; CA
29-32R; 6; CANR 18, 41, 60, 91, 130;
CDALBS; CLR 6, 73; CP 2, 3, 4, 5, 6, 7;
CSW; CWP; CWRI 5; DA; DA3; DAB;
DAC; DAM MST, MULT, POET; DLB 5,
41; EWL 3; EXPP; INT CANR-18; MAI-
CYA 1, 2; MAL 5; MTCW 1, 2; MTFW
2005; PFS 17; RGAL 4; SATA 24, 107;
TUS; YAW

Giovene, Andrea 1904-1998 .... **CLC 7**
See also CA 85-88

Gippius, Zinaida (Nikolaevna) 1869-1945
See Hippius, Zinaida (Nikolaevna)
See also CA 212; CAAE 106

Giraudoux, Jean(-Hippolyte)
1882-1944 .... **TCLC 2, 7**
See also CA 196; CAAE 104; DAM
DRAM; DLB 65, 321; EW 9; EWL 3;
GFL 1789 to the Present; RGWL 2, 3;
TWA

Gironella, Jose Maria (Pous)
1917-2003 .... **CLC 11**
See also CA 101; CAAS 212; EWL 3;
RGWL 2, 3

Grove, Frederick Philip .... **TCLC 4**
See Greve, Felix Paul (Berthold Friedrich)
See also DLB 92; RGEL 2; TCWW 1, 2

Grubb
See Crumb, R.

Grumbach, Doris 1918- .... **CLC 13, 22, 64**
See also CA 5-8R; 2; CANR 9, 42, 70, 127;
CN 6, 7; INT CANR-9; MTCW 2; MTFW
2005

Grundtvig, Nikolai Frederik Severin
1783-1872 .... **NCLC 1, 158**
See also DLB 300

Grunge
See Crumb, R.

Grunwald, Lisa 1959- .... **CLC 44**
See also CA 120; CANR 148

Gryphius, Andreas 1616-1664 .... **LC 89**
See also CDWLB 2; DLB 164; RGWL 2, 3

Guare, John 1938- .... **CLC 8, 14, 29, 67; DC 20**
See also CA 73-76; CAD; CANR 21, 69,
118; CD 5, 6; DAM DRAM; DFS 8, 13;
DLB 7, 249; EWL 3; MAL 5; MTCW 1,
2; RGAL 4

Guarini, Battista 1537-1612 .... **LC 102**

Gubar, Susan (David) 1944- .... **CLC 145**
See also CA 108; CANR 45, 70, 139; FW;
MTCW 1; RGAL 4

Gudjonsson, Halldor Kiljan 1902-1998
See Halldor Laxness
See also CA 103; CAAS 164

Guenter, Erich
See Eich, Gunter

Guest, Barbara 1920-2006 ... **CLC 34; PC 55**
See also BG 1:2; CA 25-28R; CAAS 248;
CANR 11, 44, 84; CP 1, 2, 3, 4, 5, 6, 7;
CWP; DLB 5, 193

Guest, Edgar A(lbert) 1881-1959 ... **TCLC 95**
See also CA 168; CAAE 112

Guest, Judith 1936- .... **CLC 8, 30**
See also AAYA 7, 66; CA 77-80; CANR
15, 75, 138; DA3; DAM NOV, POP;
EXPN; INT CANR-15; LAIT 5; MTCW
1, 2; MTFW 2005; NFS 1

Guevara, Che .... **CLC 87; HLC 1**
See Guevara (Serna), Ernesto

Guevara (Serna), Ernesto
1928-1967 .... **CLC 87; HLC 1**
See Guevara, Che
See also CA 127; CAAS 111; CANR 56;
DAM MULT; HW 1

Guicciardini, Francesco 1483-1540 ..... **LC 49**

Guido delle Colonne c. 1215-c.
1290 .... **CMLC 90**

Guild, Nicholas M. 1944- .... **CLC 33**
See also CA 93-96

Guillemin, Jacques
See Sartre, Jean-Paul

Guillen, Jorge 1893-1984 . **CLC 11; HLCS 1; PC 35**
See also CA 89-92; CAAS 112; DAM
MULT, POET; DLB 108; EWL 3; HW 1;
RGWL 2, 3

Guillen, Nicolas (Cristobal)
1902-1989 .... **BLC 2; CLC 48, 79; HLC 1; PC 23**
See also BW 2; CA 125; CAAE 116; CAAS
129; CANR 84; DAM MST, MULT,
POET; DLB 283; EWL 3; HW 1; LAW;
RGWL 2, 3; WP

Guillen y Alvarez, Jorge
See Guillen, Jorge

Guillevic, (Eugene) 1907-1997 .... **CLC 33**
See also CA 93-96; CWW 2

Guillois
See Desnos, Robert

Guillois, Valentin
See Desnos, Robert

Guimaraes Rosa, Joao 1908-1967 .... **HLCS 2**
See Rosa, Joao Guimaraes
See also CA 175; LAW; RGSF 2; RGWL 2,
3

Guiney, Louise Imogen
1861-1920 .... **TCLC 41**
See also CA 160; DLB 54; RGAL 4

Guinizelli, Guido c. 1230-1276 ...... **CMLC 49**
See Guinizzelli, Guido

Guinizzelli, Guido
See Guinizelli, Guido
See also WLIT 7

Guiraldes, Ricardo (Guillermo)
1886-1927 .... **TCLC 39**
See also CA 131; EWL 3; HW 1; LAW;
MTCW 1

Gumilev, Nikolai (Stepanovich)
1886-1921 .... **TCLC 60**
See Gumilyov, Nikolay Stepanovich
See also CA 165; DLB 295

Gumilyov, Nikolay Stepanovich
See Gumilev, Nikolai (Stepanovich)
See also EWL 3

Gump, P. Q.
See Card, Orson Scott

Gunesekera, Romesh 1954- .... **CLC 91**
See also BRWS 10; CA 159; CANR 140;
CN 6, 7; DLB 267, 323

Gunn, Bill .... **CLC 5**
See Gunn, William Harrison
See also DLB 38

Gunn, Thom(son William)
1929-2004 . **CLC 3, 6, 18, 32, 81; PC 26**
See also BRWS 4; CA 17-20R; CAAS 227;
CANR 9, 33, 116; CDBLB 1960 to
Present; CP 1, 2, 3, 4, 5, 6, 7; DAM
POET; DLB 27; INT CANR-33; MTCW
1; PFS 9; RGEL 2

Gunn, William Harrison 1934(?)-1989
See Gunn, Bill
See also AITN 1; BW 1, 3; CA 13-16R;
CAAS 128; CANR 12, 25, 76

Gunn Allen, Paula
See Allen, Paula Gunn

Gunnars, Kristjana 1948- .... **CLC 69**
See also CA 113; CCA 1; CP 6, 7; CWP;
DLB 60

Gunter, Erich
See Eich, Gunter

Gurdjieff, G(eorgei) I(vanovich)
1877(?)-1949 .... **TCLC 71**
See also CA 157

Gurganus, Allan 1947- .... **CLC 70**
See also BEST 90:1; CA 135; CANR 114;
CN 6, 7; CPW; CSW; DAM POP; GLL 1

Gurney, A. R.
See Gurney, A(lbert) R(amsdell), Jr.
See also DLB 266

Gurney, A(lbert) R(amsdell), Jr.
1930- .... **CLC 32, 50, 54**
See Gurney, A. R.
See also AMWS 5; CA 77-80; CAD; CANR
32, 64, 121; CD 5, 6; DAM DRAM; EWL
3

Gurney, Ivor (Bertie) 1890-1937 ... **TCLC 33**
See also BRW 6; CA 167; DLBY 2002;
PAB; RGEL 2

Gurney, Peter
See Gurney, A(lbert) R(amsdell), Jr.

Guro, Elena (Genrikhovna)
1877-1913 .... **TCLC 56**
See also DLB 295

Gustafson, James M(oody) 1925- ... **CLC 100**
See also CA 25-28R; CANR 37

Gustafson, Ralph (Barker)
1909-1995 .... **CLC 36**
See also CA 21-24R; CANR 8, 45, 84; CP
1, 2, 3, 4, 5, 6; DLB 88; RGEL 2

Gut, Gom
See Simenon, Georges (Jacques Christian)

Guterson, David 1956- .... **CLC 91**
See also CA 132; CANR 73, 126; CN 7;
DLB 292; MTCW 2; MTFW 2005; NFS
13

Guthrie, A(lfred) B(ertram), Jr.
1901-1991 .... **CLC 23**
See also CA 57-60; CAAS 134; CANR 24;
CN 1, 2, 3; DLB 6, 212; MAL 5; SATA
62; SATA-Obit 67; TCWW 1, 2

Guthrie, Isobel
See Grieve, C(hristopher) M(urray)

Guthrie, Woodrow Wilson 1912-1967
See Guthrie, Woody
See also CA 113; CAAS 93-96

Guthrie, Woody .... **CLC 35**
See Guthrie, Woodrow Wilson
See also DLB 303; LAIT 3

Gutierrez Najera, Manuel
1859-1895 .... **HLCS 2; NCLC 133**
See also DLB 290; LAW

Guy, Rosa (Cuthbert) 1925- .... **CLC 26**
See also AAYA 4, 37; BW 2; CA 17-20R;
CANR 14, 34, 83; CLR 13; DLB 33;
DNFS 1; JRDA; MAICYA 1, 2; SATA 14,
62, 122; YAW

Gwendolyn
See Bennett, (Enoch) Arnold

H. D. .... **CLC 3, 8, 14, 31, 34, 73; PC 5**
See Doolittle, Hilda
See also FL 1:5

H. de V.
See Buchan, John

Haavikko, Paavo Juhani 1931- .. **CLC 18, 34**
See also CA 106; CWW 2; EWL 3

Habbema, Koos
See Heijermans, Herman

Habermas, Juergen 1929- .... **CLC 104**
See also CA 109; CANR 85, 162; DLB 242

Habermas, Jurgen
See Habermas, Juergen

Hacker, Marilyn 1942- ...... **CLC 5, 9, 23, 72, 91; PC 47**
See also CA 77-80; CANR 68, 129; CP 3,
4, 5, 6, 7; CWP; DAM POET; DLB 120,
282; FW; GLL 2; MAL 5; PFS 19

Hadewijch of Antwerp fl. 1250- ... **CMLC 61**
See also RGWL 3

Hadrian 76-138 .... **CMLC 52**

Haeckel, Ernst Heinrich (Philipp August)
1834-1919 .... **TCLC 83**
See also CA 157

Hafiz c. 1326-1389(?) .... **CMLC 34**
See also RGWL 2, 3; WLIT 6

Hagedorn, Jessica T(arahata)
1949- .... **CLC 185**
See also CA 139; CANR 69; CWP; DLB
312; RGAL 4

Haggard, H(enry) Rider
1856-1925 .... **TCLC 11**
See also BRWS 3; BYA 4, 5; CA 148;
CAAE 108; CANR 112; DLB 70, 156,
174, 178; FANT; LMFS 1; MTCW 2;
RGEL 2; RHW; SATA 16; SCFW 1, 2;
SFW 4; SUFW 1; WLIT 4

Hagiosy, L.
See Larbaud, Valery (Nicolas)

Hagiwara, Sakutaro 1886-1942 .... **PC 18; TCLC 60**
See Hagiwara Sakutaro
See also CA 154; RGWL 3

Hagiwara Sakutaro
See Hagiwara, Sakutaro
See also EWL 3

Haig, Fenil
See Ford, Ford Madox

Haig-Brown, Roderick (Langmere)
1908-1976 .... **CLC 21**
See also CA 5-8R; CAAS 69-72; CANR 4, 38, 83; CLR 31; CWRI 5; DLB 88; MAICYA 1, 2; SATA 12; TCWW 2
Haight, Rip
See Carpenter, John (Howard)
Haij, Vera
See Jansson, Tove (Marika)
Hailey, Arthur 1920-2004 .... **CLC 5**
See also AITN 2; BEST 90:3; BPFB 2; CA 1-4R; CAAS 233; CANR 2, 36, 75; CCA 1; CN 1, 2, 3, 4, 5, 6, 7; CPW; DAM NOV, POP; DLB 88; DLBY 1982; MTCW 1, 2; MTFW 2005
Hailey, Elizabeth Forsythe 1938- ..... **CLC 40**
See also CA 188; 93-96, 188; 1; CANR 15, 48; INT CANR-15
Haines, John (Meade) 1924- .... **CLC 58**
See also AMWS 12; CA 17-20R; CANR 13, 34; CP 1, 2, 3, 4, 5; CSW; DLB 5, 212; TCLE 1:1
Ha Jin 1956- .... **CLC 109**
See Jin, Xuefei
See also CA 152; CANR 91, 130; DLB 244, 292; MTFW 2005; NFS 25; SSFS 17
Hakluyt, Richard 1552-1616 .... **LC 31**
See also DLB 136; RGEL 2
Haldeman, Joe 1943- .... **CLC 61**
See Graham, Robert
See also AAYA 38; CA 179; 53-56, 179; 25; CANR 6, 70, 72, 130; DLB 8; INT CANR-6; SCFW 2; SFW 4
Haldeman, Joe William
See Haldeman, Joe
Hale, Janet Campbell 1947- .... **NNAL**
See also CA 49-52; CANR 45, 75; DAM MULT; DLB 175; MTCW 2; MTFW 2005
Hale, Sarah Josepha (Buell)
1788-1879 .... **NCLC 75**
See also DLB 1, 42, 73, 243
Halevy, Elie 1870-1937 .... **TCLC 104**
Haley, Alex(ander Murray Palmer)
1921-1992 .... **BLC 2; CLC 8, 12, 76; TCLC 147**
See also AAYA 26; BPFB 2; BW 2, 3; CA 77-80; CAAS 136; CANR 61; CDALBS; CPW; CSW; DA; DA3; DAB; DAC; DAM MST, MULT, POP; DLB 38; LAIT 5; MTCW 1, 2; NFS 9
Haliburton, Thomas Chandler
1796-1865 .... **NCLC 15, 149**
See also DLB 11, 99; RGEL 2; RGSF 2
Hall, Donald 1928- ... **CLC 1, 13, 37, 59, 151, 240; PC 70**
See also AAYA 63; CA 5-8R; 7; CANR 2, 44, 64, 106, 133; CP 1, 2, 3, 4, 5, 6, 7; DAM POET; DLB 5; MAL 5; MTCW 2; MTFW 2005; RGAL 4; SATA 23, 97
Hall, Donald Andrew, Jr.
See Hall, Donald
Hall, Frederic Sauser
See Sauser-Hall, Frederic
Hall, James
See Kuttner, Henry
Hall, James Norman 1887-1951 ..... **TCLC 23**
See also CA 173; CAAE 123; LAIT 1; RHW 1; SATA 21
Hall, Joseph 1574-1656 .... **LC 91**
See also DLB 121, 151; RGEL 2
Hall, Marguerite Radclyffe
See Hall, Radclyffe
Hall, Radclyffe 1880-1943 .... **TCLC 12**
See also BRWS 6; CA 150; CAAE 110; CANR 83; DLB 191; MTCW 2; MTFW 2005; RGEL 2; RHW
Hall, Rodney 1935- .... **CLC 51**
See also CA 109; CANR 69; CN 6, 7; CP 1, 2, 3, 4, 5, 6, 7; DLB 289

Hallam, Arthur Henry
1811-1833 .... **NCLC 110**
See also DLB 32
Halldor Laxness .... **CLC 25**
See Gudjonsson, Halldor Kiljan
See also DLB 293; EW 12; EWL 3; RGWL 2, 3
Halleck, Fitz-Greene 1790-1867 .... **NCLC 47**
See also DLB 3, 250; RGAL 4
Halliday, Michael
See Creasey, John
Halpern, Daniel 1945- .... **CLC 14**
See also CA 33-36R; CANR 93; CP 3, 4, 5, 6, 7
Hamburger, Michael 1924-2007 .... **CLC 5, 14**
See also CA 196; 5-8R, 196; 4; CANR 2, 47; CP 1, 2, 3, 4, 5, 6, 7; DLB 27
Hamburger, Michael Peter Leopold
See Hamburger, Michael
Hamill, Pete 1935- .... **CLC 10**
See also CA 25-28R; CANR 18, 71, 127
Hamilton, Alexander
1755(?)-1804 .... **NCLC 49**
See also DLB 37
Hamilton, Clive
See Lewis, C.S.
Hamilton, Edmond 1904-1977 .... **CLC 1**
See also CA 1-4R; CANR 3, 84; DLB 8; SATA 118; SFW 4
Hamilton, Elizabeth 1758-1816 ... **NCLC 153**
See also DLB 116, 158
Hamilton, Eugene (Jacob) Lee
See Lee-Hamilton, Eugene (Jacob)
Hamilton, Franklin
See Silverberg, Robert
Hamilton, Gail
See Corcoran, Barbara (Asenath)
Hamilton, (Robert) Ian 1938-2001 . **CLC 191**
See also CA 106; CAAS 203; CANR 41, 67; CP 1, 2, 3, 4, 5, 6, 7; DLB 40, 155
Hamilton, Jane 1957- .... **CLC 179**
See also CA 147; CANR 85, 128; CN 7; MTFW 2005
Hamilton, Mollie
See Kaye, M.M.
Hamilton, (Anthony Walter) Patrick
1904-1962 .... **CLC 51**
See also CA 176; CAAS 113; DLB 10, 191
Hamilton, Virginia 1936-2002 .... **CLC 26**
See also AAYA 2, 21; BW 2, 3; BYA 1, 2, 8; CA 25-28R; CAAS 206; CANR 20, 37, 73, 126; CLR 1, 11, 40; DAM MULT; DLB 33, 52; DLBY 2001; INT CANR-20; JRDA; LAIT 5; MAICYA 1, 2; MAICYAS 1; MTCW 1, 2; MTFW 2005; SATA 4, 56, 79, 123; SATA-Obit 132; WYA; YAW
Hammett, (Samuel) Dashiell
1894-1961 .... **CLC 3, 5, 10, 19, 47; SSC 17; TCLC 187**
See also AAYA 59; AITN 1; AMWS 4; BPFB 2; CA 81-84; CANR 42; CDALB 1929-1941; CMW 4; DA3; DLB 226, 280; DLBD 6; DLBY 1996; EWL 3; LAIT 3; MAL 5; MSW; MTCW 1, 2; MTFW 2005; NFS 21; RGAL 4; RGSF 2; TUS
Hammon, Jupiter 1720(?)-1800(?) .... **BLC 2; NCLC 5; PC 16**
See also DAM MULT, POET; DLB 31, 50
Hammond, Keith
See Kuttner, Henry
Hamner, Earl (Henry), Jr. 1923- .... **CLC 12**
See also AITN 1; CA 73-76; DLB 6
Hampton, Christopher 1946- .... **CLC 4**
See also CA 25-28R; CD 5, 6; DLB 13; MTCW 1
Hampton, Christopher James
See Hampton, Christopher

Hamsun, Knut .... **TCLC 2, 14, 49, 151**
See Pedersen, Knut
See also DLB 297, 330; EW 8; EWL 3; RGWL 2, 3
Handke, Peter 1942- .... **CLC 5, 8, 10, 15, 38, 134; DC 17**
See also CA 77-80; CANR 33, 75, 104, 133; CWW 2; DAM DRAM, NOV; DLB 85, 124; EWL 3; MTCW 1, 2; MTFW 2005; TWA
Handy, W(illiam) C(hristopher)
1873-1958 .... **TCLC 97**
See also BW 3; CA 167; CAAE 121
Hanley, James 1901-1985 ..... **CLC 3, 5, 8, 13**
See also CA 73-76; CAAS 117; CANR 36; CBD; CN 1, 2, 3; DLB 191; EWL 3; MTCW 1; RGEL 2
Hannah, Barry 1942- .. **CLC 23, 38, 90; SSC 94**
See also BPFB 2; CA 110; CAAE 108; CANR 43, 68, 113; CN 4, 5, 6, 7; CSW; DLB 6, 234; INT CA-110; MTCW 1; RGSF 2
Hannon, Ezra
See Hunter, Evan
Hansberry, Lorraine (Vivian)
1930-1965 .. **BLC 2; CLC 17, 62; DC 2; TCLC 192**
See also AAYA 25; AFAW 1, 2; AMWS 4; BW 1, 3; CA 109; CAAS 25-28R; CABS 3; CAD; CANR 58; CDALB 1941-1968; CWD; DA; DA3; DAB; DAC; DAM DRAM, MST, MULT; DFS 2; DLB 7, 38; EWL 3; FL 1:6; FW; LAIT 4; MAL 5; MTCW 1, 2; MTFW 2005; RGAL 4; TUS
Hansen, Joseph 1923-2004 .... **CLC 38**
See Brock, Rose; Colton, James
See also BPFB 2; CA 29-32R; 17; CAAS 233; CANR 16, 44, 66, 125; CMW 4; DLB 226; GLL 1; INT CANR-16
Hansen, Karen V. 1955- .... **CLC 65**
See also CA 149; CANR 102
Hansen, Martin A(lfred)
1909-1955 .... **TCLC 32**
See also CA 167; DLB 214; EWL 3
Hanson, Kenneth O(stlin) 1922- .... **CLC 13**
See also CA 53-56; CANR 7; CP 1, 2, 3, 4, 5
Hardwick, Elizabeth 1916- .... **CLC 13**
See also AMWS 3; CA 5-8R; CANR 3, 32, 70, 100, 139; CN 4, 5, 6; CSW; DA3; DAM NOV; DLB 6; MBL; MTCW 1, 2; MTFW 2005; TCLE 1:1
Hardy, Thomas 1840-1928 .... **PC 8; SSC 2, 60; TCLC 4, 10, 18, 32, 48, 53, 72, 143, 153; WLC 3**
See also AAYA 69; BRW 6; BRWC 1, 2; BRWR 1; CA 123; CAAE 104; CDBLB 1890-1914; DA; DA3; DAB; DAC; DAM MST, NOV, POET; DLB 18, 19, 135, 284; EWL 3; EXPN; EXPP; LAIT 2; MTCW 1, 2; MTFW 2005; NFS 3, 11, 15, 19; PFS 3, 4, 18; RGEL 2; RGSF 2; TEA; WLIT 4
Hare, David 1947- . **CLC 29, 58, 136; DC 26**
See also BRWS 4; CA 97-100; CANR 39, 91; CBD; CD 5, 6; DFS 4, 7, 16; DLB 13, 310; MTCW 1; TEA
Harewood, John
See Van Druten, John (William)
Harford, Henry
See Hudson, W(illiam) H(enry)
Hargrave, Leonie
See Disch, Thomas M.
Hariri, Al- al-Qasim ibn 'Ali Abu Muhammad al-Basri
See al-Hariri, al-Qasim ibn 'Ali Abu Muhammad al-Basri

Hooker, Richard 1554-1600 .... **LC 95**
    See also BRW 1; DLB 132; RGEL 2
Hooker, Thomas 1586-1647 .... **LC 137**
    See also DLB 24
hooks, bell 1952(?)- .... **CLC 94**
    See also BW 2; CA 143; CANR 87, 126;
    DLB 246; MTCW 2; MTFW 2005; SATA
    115, 170
Hooper, Johnson Jones
    1815-1862 .... **NCLC 177**
    See also DLB 3, 11, 248; RGAL 4
Hope, A(lec) D(erwent) 1907-2000 .... **CLC 3,
51; PC 56**
    See also BRWS 7; CA 21-24R; CAAS 188;
    CANR 33, 74; CP 1, 2, 3, 4, 5; DLB 289;
    EWL 3; MTCW 1, 2; MTFW 2005; PFS
    8; RGEL 2
Hope, Anthony 1863-1933 .... **TCLC 83**
    See also CA 157; DLB 153, 156; RGEL 2;
    RHW
Hope, Brian
    See Creasey, John
Hope, Christopher (David Tully)
    1944- .... **CLC 52**
    See also AFW; CA 106; CANR 47, 101;
    CN 4, 5, 6, 7; DLB 225; SATA 62
Hopkins, Gerard Manley
    1844-1889 .... **NCLC 17; PC 15; WLC 3**
    See also BRW 5; BRWR 2; CDBLB 1890-
    1914; DA; DA3; DAB; DAC; DAM MST,
    POET; DLB 35, 57; EXPP; PAB; PFS 26;
    RGEL 2; TEA; WP
Hopkins, John (Richard) 1931-1998 .. **CLC 4**
    See also CA 85-88; CAAS 169; CBD; CD
    5, 6
Hopkins, Pauline Elizabeth
    1859-1930 .... **BLC 2; TCLC 28**
    See also AFAW 2; BW 2, 3; CA 141; CANR
    82; DAM MULT; DLB 50
Hopkinson, Francis 1737-1791 .... **LC 25**
    See also DLB 31; RGAL 4
Hopley-Woolrich, Cornell George 1903-1968
    See Woolrich, Cornell
    See also CA 13-14; CANR 58, 156; CAP 1;
    CMW 4; DLB 226; MTCW 2
Horace 65B.C.-8B.C. .... **CMLC 39; PC 46**
    See also AW 2; CDWLB 1; DLB 211;
    RGWL 2, 3; WLIT 8
Horatio
    See Proust, (Valentin-Louis-George-Eugene)
    Marcel
**Horgan, Paul (George Vincent
O'Shaughnessy)** 1903-1995 .. **CLC 9, 53**
    See also BPFB 2; CA 13-16R; CAAS 147;
    CANR 9, 35; CN 1, 2, 3, 4, 5; DAM
    NOV; DLB 102, 212; DLBY 1985; INT
    CANR-9; MTCW 1, 2; MTFW 2005;
    SATA 13; SATA-Obit 84; TCWW 1, 2
Horkheimer, Max 1895-1973 .... **TCLC 132**
    See also CA 216; CAAS 41-44R; DLB 296
Horn, Peter
    See Kuttner, Henry
Hornby, Nick 19 .... **CLC 243**
    See also AAYA 74; CA 151; CANR 104,
    151; CN 7; DLB 207; MBL
Horne, Frank (Smith) 1899-1974 ...... **HR 1:2**
    See also BW 1; CA 125; CAAS 53-56; DLB
    51; WP
Horne, Richard Henry Hengist
    1802(?)-1884 .... **NCLC 127**
    See also DLB 32; SATA 29
Hornem, Horace Esq.
    See Byron, George Gordon (Noel)
**Horney, Karen (Clementine Theodore
Danielsen)** 1885-1952 .... **TCLC 71**
    See also CA 165; CAAE 114; DLB 246;
    FW

Hornung, E(rnest) W(illiam)
    1866-1921 .... **TCLC 59**
    See also CA 160; CAAE 108; CMW 4;
    DLB 70
Horovitz, Israel (Arthur) 1939- .... **CLC 56**
    See also CA 33-36R; CAD; CANR 46, 59;
    CD 5, 6; DAM DRAM; DLB 7; MAL 5
Horton, George Moses
    1797(?)-1883(?) .... **NCLC 87**
    See also DLB 50
Horvath, odon von 1901-1938
    See von Horvath, Odon
    See also EWL 3
Horvath, Oedoen von -1938
    See von Horvath, Odon
Horwitz, Julius 1920-1986 .... **CLC 14**
    See also CA 9-12R; CAAS 119; CANR 12
Horwitz, Ronald
    See Harwood, Ronald
Hospital, Janette Turner 1942- .... **CLC 42,
145**
    See also CA 108; CANR 48, 166; CN 5, 6,
    7; DLB 325; DLBY 2002; RGSF 2
Hostos, E. M. de
    See Hostos (y Bonilla), Eugenio Maria de
Hostos, Eugenio M. de
    See Hostos (y Bonilla), Eugenio Maria de
Hostos, Eugenio Maria
    See Hostos (y Bonilla), Eugenio Maria de
Hostos (y Bonilla), Eugenio Maria de
    1839-1903 .... **TCLC 24**
    See also CA 131; CAAE 123; HW 1
Houdini
    See Lovecraft, H. P.
Houellebecq, Michel 1958- .... **CLC 179**
    See also CA 185; CANR 140; MTFW 2005
Hougan, Carolyn 1943-2007 .... **CLC 34**
    See also CA 139; CAAS 257
Household, Geoffrey (Edward West)
    1900-1988 .... **CLC 11**
    See also CA 77-80; CAAS 126; CANR 58;
    CMW 4; CN 1, 2, 3, 4; DLB 87; SATA
    14; SATA-Obit 59
Housman, A(lfred) E(dward)
    1859-1936 .... **PC 2, 43; TCLC 1, 10;
WLCS**
    See also AAYA 66; BRW 6; CA 125; CAAE
    104; DA; DA3; DAB; DAC; DAM MST,
    POET; DLB 19, 284; EWL 3; EXPP;
    MTCW 1, 2; MTFW 2005; PAB; PFS 4,
    7; RGEL 2; TEA; WP
Housman, Laurence 1865-1959 .... **TCLC 7**
    See also CA 155; CAAE 106; DLB 10;
    FANT; RGEL 2; SATA 25
Houston, Jeanne Wakatsuki 1934- .... **AAL**
    See also AAYA 49; CA 232; 103, 232; 16;
    CANR 29, 123; LAIT 4; SATA 78, 168;
    SATA-Essay 168
Howard, Elizabeth Jane 1923- ..... **CLC 7, 29**
    See also BRWS 11; CA 5-8R; CANR 8, 62,
    146; CN 1, 2, 3, 4, 5, 6, 7
Howard, Maureen 1930- .... **CLC 5, 14, 46,
151**
    See also CA 53-56; CANR 31, 75, 140; CN
    4, 5, 6, 7; DLBY 1983; INT CANR-31;
    MTCW 1, 2; MTFW 2005
Howard, Richard 1929- .... **CLC 7, 10, 47**
    See also AITN 1; CA 85-88; CANR 25, 80,
    154; CP 1, 2, 3, 4, 5, 6, 7; DLB 5; INT
    CANR-25; MAL 5
Howard, Robert E 1906-1936 .... **TCLC 8**
    See also BPFB 2; BYA 5; CA 157; CAAE
    105; CANR 155; FANT; SUFW 1;
    TCWW 1, 2
Howard, Robert Ervin
    See Howard, Robert E
Howard, Warren F.
    See Pohl, Frederik

Howe, Fanny (Quincy) 1940- .... **CLC 47**
    See also CA 187; 117, 187; 27; CANR 70,
    116; CP 6, 7; CWP; SATA-Brief 52
Howe, Irving 1920-1993 .... **CLC 85**
    See also AMWS 6; CA 9-12R; CAAS 141;
    CANR 21, 50; DLB 67; EWL 3; MAL 5;
    MTCW 1, 2; MTFW 2005
Howe, Julia Ward 1819-1910 .... **TCLC 21**
    See also CA 191; CAAE 117; DLB 1, 189,
    235; FW
Howe, Susan 1937- .... **CLC 72, 152; PC 54**
    See also AMWS 4; CA 160; CP 5, 6, 7;
    CWP; DLB 120; FW; RGAL 4
Howe, Tina 1937- .... **CLC 48**
    See also CA 109; CAD; CANR 125; CD 5,
    6; CWD
Howell, James 1594(?)-1666 .... **LC 13**
    See also DLB 151
Howells, W. D.
    See Howells, William Dean
Howells, William D.
    See Howells, William Dean
Howells, William Dean 1837-1920 ... **SSC 36;
TCLC 7, 17, 41**
    See also AMW; CA 134; CAAE 104;
    CDALB 1865-1917; DLB 12, 64, 74, 79,
    189; LMFS 1; MAL 5; MTCW 2; RGAL
    4; TUS
Howes, Barbara 1914-1996 .... **CLC 15**
    See also CA 9-12R; 3; CAAS 151; CANR
    53; CP 1, 2, 3, 4, 5, 6; SATA 5; TCLE 1:1
Hrabal, Bohumil 1914-1997 ...... **CLC 13, 67;
TCLC 155**
    See also CA 106; 12; CAAS 156; CANR
    57; CWW 2; DLB 232; EWL 3; RGSF 2
Hrabanus Maurus 776(?)-856 .... **CMLC 78**
    See also DLB 148
Hrotsvit of Gandersheim c. 935-c.
    1000 .... **CMLC 29**
    See also DLB 148
Hsi, Chu 1130-1200 .... **CMLC 42**
Hsun, Lu
    See Lu Hsun
Hubbard, L. Ron 1911-1986 .... **CLC 43**
    See also AAYA 64; CA 77-80; CAAS 118;
    CANR 52; CPW; DA3; DAM POP;
    FANT; MTCW 2; MTFW 2005; SFW 4
Hubbard, Lafayette Ronald
    See Hubbard, L. Ron
Huch, Ricarda (Octavia)
    1864-1947 .... **TCLC 13**
    See also CA 189; CAAE 111; DLB 66;
    EWL 3
Huddle, David 1942- .... **CLC 49**
    See also CA 57-60; 20; CANR 89; DLB
    130
Hudson, Jeffrey
    See Crichton, Michael
Hudson, W(illiam) H(enry)
    1841-1922 .... **TCLC 29**
    See also CA 190; CAAE 115; DLB 98, 153,
    174; RGEL 2; SATA 35
Hueffer, Ford Madox
    See Ford, Ford Madox
Hughart, Barry 1934- .... **CLC 39**
    See also CA 137; FANT; SFW 4; SUFW 2
Hughes, Colin
    See Creasey, John
Hughes, David (John) 1930-2005 ..... **CLC 48**
    See also CA 129; CAAE 116; CAAS 238;
    CN 4, 5, 6, 7; DLB 14
Hughes, Edward James
    See Hughes, Ted
    See also DA3; DAM MST, POET

Lardner, Ring W., Jr.
See Lardner, Ring(gold) W(ilmer)
Lardner, Ring(gold) W(ilmer)
1885-1933 .... **SSC 32; TCLC 2, 14**
See Lardner, Ring
See also AMW; CA 131; CAAE 104;
MTCW 1, 2; MTFW 2005; TUS
Laredo, Betty
See Codrescu, Andrei
Larkin, Maia
See Wojciechowska, Maia (Teresa)
Larkin, Philip (Arthur) 1922-1985 ... **CLC 3,
5, 8, 9, 13, 18, 33, 39, 64; PC 21**
See also BRWS 1; CA 5-8R; CAAS 117;
CANR 24, 62; CDBLB 1960 to Present;
CP 1, 2, 3, 4; DA3; DAB; DAM MST,
POET; DLB 27; EWL 3; MTCW 1, 2;
MTFW 2005; PFS 3, 4, 12; RGEL 2
La Roche, Sophie von
1730-1807 .... **NCLC 121**
See also DLB 94
La Rochefoucauld, Francois
1613-1680 .... **LC 108**
**Larra (y Sanchez de Castro), Mariano Jose
de** 1809-1837 .... **NCLC 17, 130**
Larsen, Eric 1941- .... **CLC 55**
See also CA 132
Larsen, Nella 1893(?)-1963 .... **BLC 2; CLC
37; HR 1:3**
See also AFAW 1, 2; BW 1; CA 125; CANR
83; DAM MULT; DLB 51; FW; LATS
1:1; LMFS 2
Larson, Charles R(aymond) 1938- ... **CLC 31**
See also CA 53-56; CANR 4, 121
Larson, Jonathan 1960-1996 .... **CLC 99**
See also AAYA 28; CA 156; DFS 23;
MTFW 2005
La Sale, Antoine de c. 1386-1460(?) . **LC 104**
See also DLB 208
Las Casas, Bartolome de
1474-1566 .... **HLCS; LC 31**
See Casas, Bartolome de las
See also DLB 318; LAW
Lasch, Christopher 1932-1994 .... **CLC 102**
See also CA 73-76; CAAS 144; CANR 25,
118; DLB 246; MTCW 1, 2; MTFW 2005
Lasker-Schueler, Else 1869-1945 ... **TCLC 57**
See Lasker-Schuler, Else
See also CA 183; DLB 66, 124
Lasker-Schuler, Else
See Lasker-Schueler, Else
See also EWL 3
Laski, Harold J(oseph) 1893-1950 . **TCLC 79**
See also CA 188
Latham, Jean Lee 1902-1995 .... **CLC 12**
See also AITN 1; BYA 1; CA 5-8R; CANR
7, 84; CLR 50; MAICYA 1, 2; SATA 2,
68; YAW
Latham, Mavis
See Clark, Mavis Thorpe
Lathen, Emma .... **CLC 2**
See Hennissart, Martha; Latsis, Mary J(ane)
See also BPFB 2; CMW 4; DLB 306
Lathrop, Francis
See Leiber, Fritz (Reuter, Jr.)
Latsis, Mary J(ane) 1927-1997
See Lathen, Emma
See also CA 85-88; CAAS 162; CMW 4
Lattany, Kristin
See Lattany, Kristin (Elaine Eggleston)
Hunter
Lattany, Kristin (Elaine Eggleston) Hunter
1931- .... **CLC 35**
See Hunter, Kristin
See also AITN 1; BW 1; BYA 3; CA 13-
16R; CANR 13, 108; CLR 3; CN 7; DLB
33; INT CANR-13; MAICYA 1, 2; SAAS
10; SATA 12, 132; YAW

Lattimore, Richmond (Alexander)
1906-1984 .... **CLC 3**
See also CA 1-4R; CAAS 112; CANR 1;
CP 1, 2, 3; MAL 5
Laughlin, James 1914-1997 .... **CLC 49**
See also CA 21-24R; 22; CAAS 162; CANR
9, 47; CP 1, 2, 3, 4, 5, 6; DLB 48; DLBY
1996, 1997
Laurence, Margaret 1926-1987 ..... **CLC 3, 6,
13, 50, 62; SSC 7**
See also BYA 13; CA 5-8R; CAAS 121;
CANR 33; CN 1, 2, 3, 4; DAC; DAM
MST; DLB 53; EWL 3; FW; MTCW 1, 2;
MTFW 2005; NFS 11; RGEL 2; RGSF 2;
SATA-Obit 50; TCWW 2
Laurent, Antoine 1952- .... **CLC 50**
Lauscher, Hermann
See Hesse, Hermann
Lautreamont 1846-1870 .. **NCLC 12; SSC 14**
See Lautreamont, Isidore Lucien Ducasse
See also GFL 1789 to the Present; RGWL
2, 3
Lautreamont, Isidore Lucien Ducasse
See Lautreamont
See also DLB 217
Lavater, Johann Kaspar
1741-1801 .... **NCLC 142**
See also DLB 97
Laverty, Donald
See Blish, James (Benjamin)
Lavin, Mary 1912-1996 . **CLC 4, 18, 99; SSC
4, 67**
See also CA 9-12R; CAAS 151; CANR 33;
CN 1, 2, 3, 4, 5, 6; DLB 15, 319; FW;
MTCW 1; RGEL 2; RGSF 2; SSFS 23
Lavond, Paul Dennis
See Kornbluth, C(yril) M.; Pohl, Frederik
Lawes, Henry 1596-1662 .... **LC 113**
See also DLB 126
Lawler, Ray
See Lawler, Raymond Evenor
See also DLB 289
Lawler, Raymond Evenor 1922- .... **CLC 58**
See Lawler, Ray
See also CA 103; CD 5, 6; RGEL 2
Lawrence, D(avid) H(erbert Richards)
1885-1930 .... **PC 54; SSC 4, 19, 73;
TCLC 2, 9, 16, 33, 48, 61, 93; WLC 3**
See Chambers, Jessie
See also BPFB 2; BRW 7; BRWR 2; CA
121; CAAE 104; CANR 131; CDBLB
1914-1945; DA; DA3; DAB; DAC; DAM
MST, NOV, POET; DLB 10, 19, 36, 98,
162, 195; EWL 3; EXPP; EXPS; LAIT 2,
3; MTCW 1, 2; MTFW 2005; NFS 18;
PFS 6; RGEL 2; RGSF 2; SSFS 2, 6;
TEA; WLIT 4; WP
Lawrence, T(homas) E(dward)
1888-1935 .... **TCLC 18**
See Dale, Colin
See also BRWS 2; CA 167; CAAE 115;
DLB 195
Lawrence of Arabia
See Lawrence, T(homas) E(dward)
Lawson, Henry (Archibald Hertzberg)
1867-1922 .... **SSC 18; TCLC 27**
See also CA 181; CAAE 120; DLB 230;
RGEL 2; RGSF 2
Lawton, Dennis
See Faust, Frederick (Schiller)
Layamon fl. c. 1200- .... **CMLC 10**
See also DLB 146; RGEL 2
Laye, Camara 1928-1980 ..... **BLC 2; CLC 4,
38**
See Camara Laye
See also AFW; BW 1; CA 85-88; CAAS
97-100; CANR 25; DAM MULT; MTCW
1, 2; WLIT 2

Layton, Irving 1912-2006 ..... **CLC 2, 15, 164**
See also CA 1-4R; CAAS 247; CANR 2,
33, 43, 66, 129; CP 1, 2, 3, 4, 5, 6, 7;
DAC; DAM MST, POET; DLB 88; EWL
3; MTCW 1, 2; PFS 12; RGEL 2
Layton, Irving Peter
See Layton, Irving
Lazarus, Emma 1849-1887 .... **NCLC 8, 109**
Lazarus, Felix
See Cable, George Washington
Lazarus, Henry
See Slavitt, David R.
Lea, Joan
See Neufeld, John (Arthur)
Leacock, Stephen (Butler)
1869-1944 .... **SSC 39; TCLC 2**
See also CA 141; CAAE 104; CANR 80;
DAC; DAM MST; DLB 92; EWL 3;
MTCW 2; MTFW 2005; RGEL 2; RGSF
2
Lead, Jane Ward 1623-1704 .... **LC 72**
See also DLB 131
Leapor, Mary 1722-1746 .... **LC 80**
See also DLB 109
Lear, Edward 1812-1888 ..... **NCLC 3; PC 65**
See also AAYA 48; BRW 5; CLR 1, 75;
DLB 32, 163, 166; MAICYA 1, 2; RGEL
2; SATA 18, 100; WCH; WP
Lear, Norman (Milton) 1922- .... **CLC 12**
See also CA 73-76
Leautaud, Paul 1872-1956 .... **TCLC 83**
See also CA 203; DLB 65; GFL 1789 to the
Present
Leavis, F(rank) R(aymond)
1895-1978 .... **CLC 24**
See also BRW 7; CA 21-24R; CAAS 77-
80; CANR 44; DLB 242; EWL 3; MTCW
1, 2; RGEL 2
Leavitt, David 1961- .... **CLC 34**
See also CA 122; CAAE 116; CANR 50,
62, 101, 134; CPW; DA3; DAM POP;
DLB 130; GLL 1; INT CA-122; MAL 5;
MTCW 2; MTFW 2005
Leblanc, Maurice (Marie Emile)
1864-1941 .... **TCLC 49**
See also CAAE 110; CMW 4
Lebowitz, Fran(ces Ann) 1951(?)- ... **CLC 11,
36**
See also CA 81-84; CANR 14, 60, 70; INT
CANR-14; MTCW 1
Lebrecht, Peter
See Tieck, (Johann) Ludwig
le Carre, John 1931- .... **CLC 9, 15**
See also AAYA 42; BEST 89:4; BPFB 2;
BRWS 2; CA 5-8R; CANR 13, 33, 59,
107, 132; CDBLB 1960 to Present; CMW
4; CN 1, 2, 3, 4, 5, 6, 7; CPW; DA3;
DAM POP; DLB 87; EWL 3; MSW;
MTCW 1, 2; MTFW 2005; RGEL 2; TEA
Le Clezio, J. M.G. 1940- .... **CLC 31, 155**
See also CA 128; CAAE 116; CANR 147;
CWW 2; DLB 83; EWL 3; GFL 1789 to
the Present; RGSF 2
Le Clezio, Jean Marie Gustave
See Le Clezio, J. M.G.
Leconte de Lisle, Charles-Marie-Rene
1818-1894 .... **NCLC 29**
See also DLB 217; EW 6; GFL 1789 to the
Present
Le Coq, Monsieur
See Simenon, Georges (Jacques Christian)
Leduc, Violette 1907-1972 .... **CLC 22**
See also CA 13-14; CAAS 33-36R; CANR
69; CAP 1; EWL 3; GFL 1789 to the
Present; GLL 1
Ledwidge, Francis 1887(?)-1917 .... **TCLC 23**
See also CA 203; CAAE 123; DLB 20

Leskov, Nikolai Semenovich
See Leskov, Nikolai (Semyonovich)
See also DLB 238
Lesser, Milton
See Marlowe, Stephen
Lessing, Doris 1919- .. **CLC 1, 2, 3, 6, 10, 15, 22, 40, 94, 170; SSC 6, 61; WLCS**
See also AAYA 57; AFW; BRWS 1; CA 9-12R; 14; CANR 33, 54, 76, 122; CBD; CD 5, 6; CDBLB 1960 to Present; CN 1, 2, 3, 4, 5, 6, 7; CWD; DA; DA3; DAB; DAC; DAM MST, NOV; DFS 20; DLB 15, 139; DLBY 1985; EWL 3; EXPS; FL 1:6; FW; LAIT 4; MTCW 1, 2; MTFW 2005; RGEL 2; RGSF 2; SFW 4; SSFS 1, 12, 20; TEA; WLIT 2, 4
Lessing, Doris May
See Lessing, Doris
Lessing, Gotthold Ephraim
1729-1781 .... **DC 26; LC 8, 124**
See also CDWLB 2; DLB 97; EW 4; RGWL 2, 3
Lester, Richard 1932- .... **CLC 20**
Levenson, Jay .... **CLC 70**
Lever, Charles (James)
1806-1872 .... **NCLC 23**
See also DLB 21; RGEL 2
Leverson, Ada Esther
1862(?)-1933(?) .... **TCLC 18**
See Elaine
See also CA 202; CAAE 117; DLB 153; RGEL 2
Levertov, Denise 1923-1997 .. **CLC 1, 2, 3, 5, 8, 15, 28, 66; PC 11**
See also AMWS 3; CA 178; 1-4R, 178; 19; CAAS 163; CANR 3, 29, 50, 108; CDALBS; CP 1, 2, 3, 4, 5, 6; CWP; DAM POET; DLB 5, 165; EWL 3; EXPP; FW; INT CANR-29; MAL 5; MTCW 1, 2; PAB; PFS 7, 17; RGAL 4; RGHL; TUS; WP
Levi, Carlo 1902-1975 .... **TCLC 125**
See also CA 65-68; CAAS 53-56; CANR 10; EWL 3; RGWL 2, 3
Levi, Jonathan .... **CLC 76**
See also CA 197
Levi, Peter (Chad Tigar)
1931-2000 .... **CLC 41**
See also CA 5-8R; CAAS 187; CANR 34, 80; CP 1, 2, 3, 4, 5, 6, 7; DLB 40
Levi, Primo 1919-1987 ...... **CLC 37, 50; SSC 12; TCLC 109**
See also CA 13-16R; CAAS 122; CANR 12, 33, 61, 70, 132; DLB 177, 299; EWL 3; MTCW 1, 2; MTFW 2005; RGHL; RGWL 2, 3; WLIT 7
Levin, Ira 1929- .... **CLC 3, 6**
See also CA 21-24R; CANR 17, 44, 74, 139; CMW 4; CN 1, 2, 3, 4, 5, 6, 7; CPW; DA3; DAM POP; HGG; MTCW 1, 2; MTFW 2005; SATA 66; SFW 4
Levin, Meyer 1905-1981 .... **CLC 7**
See also AITN 1; CA 9-12R; CAAS 104; CANR 15; CN 1, 2, 3; DAM POP; DLB 9, 28; DLBY 1981; MAL 5; RGHL; SATA 21; SATA-Obit 27
Levine, Albert Norman
See Levine, Norman
See also CN 7
Levine, Norman 1923-2005 .... **CLC 54**
See Levine, Albert Norman
See also CA 73-76; 23; CAAS 240; CANR 14, 70; CN 1, 2, 3, 4, 5, 6; CP 1; DLB 88
Levine, Norman Albert
See Levine, Norman
Levine, Philip 1928- .. **CLC 2, 4, 5, 9, 14, 33, 118; PC 22**
See also AMWS 5; CA 9-12R; CANR 9, 37, 52, 116, 156; CP 1, 2, 3, 4, 5, 6, 7; DAM POET; DLB 5; EWL 3; MAL 5; PFS 8

Levinson, Deirdre 1931- .... **CLC 49**
See also CA 73-76; CANR 70
Levi-Strauss, Claude 1908- .... **CLC 38**
See also CA 1-4R; CANR 6, 32, 57; DLB 242; EWL 3; GFL 1789 to the Present; MTCW 1, 2; TWA
Levitin, Sonia (Wolff) 1934- .... **CLC 17**
See also AAYA 13, 48; CA 29-32R; CANR 14, 32, 79; CLR 53; JRDA; MAICYA 1, 2; SAAS 2; SATA 4, 68, 119, 131; SATA-Essay 131; YAW
Levon, O. U.
See Kesey, Ken
Levy, Amy 1861-1889 .... **NCLC 59**
See also DLB 156, 240
Lewes, George Henry 1817-1878 ... **NCLC 25**
See also DLB 55, 144
Lewis, Alun 1915-1944 .... **SSC 40; TCLC 3**
See also BRW 7; CA 188; CAAE 104; DLB 20, 162; PAB; RGEL 2
Lewis, C. Day
See Day Lewis, C(ecil)
See also CN 1
Lewis, Cecil Day
See Day Lewis, C(ecil)
Lewis, Clive Staples
See Lewis, C.S.
Lewis, C.S. 1898-1963 ... **CLC 1, 3, 6, 14, 27, 124; WLC 4**
See also AAYA 3, 39; BPFB 2; BRWS 3; BYA 15, 16; CA 81-84; CANR 33, 71, 132; CDBLB 1945-1960; CLR 3, 27, 109; CWRI 5; DA; DA3; DAB; DAC; DAM MST, NOV, POP; DLB 15, 100, 160, 255; EWL 3; FANT; JRDA; LMFS 2; MAICYA 1, 2; MTCW 1, 2; MTFW 2005; NFS 24; RGEL 2; SATA 13, 100; SCFW 1, 2; SFW 4; SUFW 1; TEA; WCH; WYA; YAW
Lewis, Janet 1899-1998 .... **CLC 41**
See Winters, Janet Lewis
See also CA 9-12R; CAAS 172; CANR 29, 63; CAP 1; CN 1, 2, 3, 4, 5, 6; DLBY 1987; RHW; TCWW 2
Lewis, Matthew Gregory
1775-1818 .... **NCLC 11, 62**
See also DLB 39, 158, 178; GL 3; HGG; LMFS 1; RGEL 2; SUFW
Lewis, (Harry) Sinclair 1885-1951 . **TCLC 4, 13, 23, 39; WLC 4**
See also AMW; AMWC 1; BPFB 2; CA 133; CAAE 104; CANR 132; CDALB 1917-1929; DA; DA3; DAB; DAC; DAM MST, NOV; DLB 9, 102, 284, 331; DLBD 1; EWL 3; LAIT 3; MAL 5; MTCW 1, 2; MTFW 2005; NFS 15, 19, 22; RGAL 4; TUS
Lewis, (Percy) Wyndham
1884(?)-1957 .. **SSC 34; TCLC 2, 9, 104**
See also BRW 7; CA 157; CAAE 104; DLB 15; EWL 3; FANT; MTCW 2; MTFW 2005; RGEL 2
Lewisohn, Ludwig 1883-1955 .... **TCLC 19**
See also CA 203; CAAE 107; DLB 4, 9, 28, 102; MAL 5
Lewton, Val 1904-1951 .... **TCLC 76**
See also CA 199; IDFW 3, 4
Leyner, Mark 1956- .... **CLC 92**
See also CA 110; CANR 28, 53; DA3; DLB 292; MTCW 2; MTFW 2005
Lezama Lima, Jose 1910-1976 .... **CLC 4, 10, 101; HLCS 2**
See also CA 77-80; CANR 71; DAM MULT; DLB 113, 283; EWL 3; HW 1, 2; LAW; RGWL 2, 3
L'Heureux, John (Clarke) 1934- ...... **CLC 52**
See also CA 13-16R; CANR 23, 45, 88; CP 1, 2, 3, 4; DLB 244

Li Ch'ing-chao 1081(?)-1141(?) .... **CMLC 71**
Liddell, C. H.
See Kuttner, Henry
Lie, Jonas (Lauritz Idemil)
1833-1908(?) .... **TCLC 5**
See also CAAE 115
Lieber, Joel 1937-1971 .... **CLC 6**
See also CA 73-76; CAAS 29-32R
Lieber, Stanley Martin
See Lee, Stan
Lieberman, Laurence (James)
1935- .... **CLC 4, 36**
See also CA 17-20R; CANR 8, 36, 89; CP 1, 2, 3, 4, 5, 6, 7
Lieh Tzu fl. 7th cent. B.C.-5th cent.
B.C. .... **CMLC 27**
Lieksman, Anders
See Haavikko, Paavo Juhani
Lifton, Robert Jay 1926- .... **CLC 67**
See also CA 17-20R; CANR 27, 78, 161; INT CANR-27; SATA 66
Lightfoot, Gordon 1938- .... **CLC 26**
See also CA 242; CAAE 109
Lightfoot, Gordon Meredith
See Lightfoot, Gordon
Lightman, Alan P(aige) 1948- .... **CLC 81**
See also CA 141; CANR 63, 105, 138; MTFW 2005
Ligotti, Thomas (Robert) 1953- ...... **CLC 44; SSC 16**
See also CA 123; CANR 49, 135; HGG; SUFW 2
Li Ho 791-817 .... **PC 13**
Li Ju-chen c. 1763-c. 1830 .... **NCLC 137**
Lilar, Francoise
See Mallet-Joris, Francoise
Liliencron, Detlev
See Liliencron, Detlev von
Liliencron, Detlev von 1844-1909 .. **TCLC 18**
See also CAAE 117
Liliencron, Friedrich Adolf Axel Detlev von
See Liliencron, Detlev von
Liliencron, Friedrich Detlev von
See Liliencron, Detlev von
Lille, Alain de
See Alain de Lille
Lillo, George 1691-1739 .... **LC 131**
See also DLB 84; RGEL 2
Lilly, William 1602-1681 .... **LC 27**
Lima, Jose Lezama
See Lezama Lima, Jose
Lima Barreto, Afonso Henrique de
1881-1922 .... **TCLC 23**
See Lima Barreto, Afonso Henriques de
See also CA 181; CAAE 117; LAW
Lima Barreto, Afonso Henriques de
See Lima Barreto, Afonso Henrique de
See also DLB 307
Limonov, Eduard
See Limonov, Edward
See also DLB 317
Limonov, Edward 1944- .... **CLC 67**
See Limonov, Eduard
See also CA 137
Lin, Frank
See Atherton, Gertrude (Franklin Horn)
Lin, Yutang 1895-1976 .... **TCLC 149**
See also CA 45-48; CAAS 65-68; CANR 2; RGAL 4
Lincoln, Abraham 1809-1865 .... **NCLC 18**
See also LAIT 2
Lind, Jakov 1927-2007 ... **CLC 1, 2, 4, 27, 82**
See Landwirth, Heinz
See also CA 4; CAAS 257; DLB 299; EWL 3; RGHL

MacDonald, Anson
See Heinlein, Robert A.

Macdonald, Cynthia 1928- .... **CLC 13, 19**
See also CA 49-52; CANR 4, 44, 146; DLB
105

Macdonald, George 1824-1905 .... **TCLC 9,
113**
See also AAYA 57; BYA 5; CA 137; CAAE
106; CANR 80; CLR 67; DLB 18, 163,
178; FANT; MAICYA 1, 2; RGEL 2;
SATA 33, 100; SFW 4; SUFW; WCH

Macdonald, John
See Millar, Kenneth

MacDonald, John D. 1916-1986 .. **CLC 3, 27,
44**
See also BPFB 2; CA 1-4R; CAAS 121;
CANR 1, 19, 60; CMW 4; CPW; DAM
NOV, POP; DLB 8, 306; DLBY 1986;
MSW; MTCW 1, 2; MTFW 2005; SFW 4

Macdonald, John Ross
See Millar, Kenneth

Macdonald, Ross ..... **CLC 1, 2, 3, 14, 34, 41**
See Millar, Kenneth
See also AMWS 4; BPFB 2; CN 1, 2, 3;
DLBD 6; MAL 5; MSW; RGAL 4

MacDougal, John
See Blish, James (Benjamin)

MacDougal, John
See Blish, James (Benjamin)

MacDowell, John
See Parks, Tim(othy Harold)

MacEwen, Gwendolyn (Margaret)
1941-1987 .... **CLC 13, 55**
See also CA 9-12R; CAAS 124; CANR 7,
22; CP 1, 2, 3, 4; DLB 53, 251; SATA 50;
SATA-Obit 55

Macha, Karel Hynek 1810-1846 .... **NCLC 46**

Machado (y Ruiz), Antonio
1875-1939 .... **TCLC 3**
See also CA 174; CAAE 104; DLB 108;
EW 9; EWL 3; HW 2; PFS 23; RGWL 2,
3

Machado de Assis, Joaquim Maria
1839-1908 .... **BLC 2; HLCS 2; SSC 24;
TCLC 10**
See also CA 153; CAAE 107; CANR 91;
DLB 307; LAW; RGSF 2; RGWL 2, 3;
TWA; WLIT 1

Machaut, Guillaume de c.
1300-1377 .... **CMLC 64**
See also DLB 208

Machen, Arthur .... **SSC 20; TCLC 4**
See Jones, Arthur Llewellyn
See also CA 179; DLB 156, 178; RGEL 2;
SUFW 1

Machiavelli, Niccolo 1469-1527 ... **DC 16; LC
8, 36, 140; WLCS**
See also AAYA 58; DA; DAB; DAC; DAM
MST; EW 2; LAIT 1; LMFS 1; NFS 9;
RGWL 2, 3; TWA; WLIT 7

MacInnes, Colin 1914-1976 .... **CLC 4, 23**
See also CA 69-72; CAAS 65-68; CANR
21; CN 1, 2; DLB 14; MTCW 1, 2; RGEL
2; RHW

MacInnes, Helen (Clark)
1907-1985 .... **CLC 27, 39**
See also BPFB 2; CA 1-4R; CAAS 117;
CANR 1, 28, 58; CMW 4; CN 1, 2; CPW;
DAM POP; DLB 87; MSW; MTCW 1, 2;
MTFW 2005; SATA 22; SATA-Obit 44

Mackay, Mary 1855-1924
See Corelli, Marie
See also CA 177; CAAE 118; FANT; RHW

Mackay, Shena 1944- .... **CLC 195**
See also CA 104; CANR 88, 139; DLB 231,
319; MTFW 2005

Mackenzie, Compton (Edward Montague)
1883-1972 .... **CLC 18; TCLC 116**
See also CA 21-22; CAAS 37-40R; CAP 2;
CN 1; DLB 34, 100; RGEL 2

Mackenzie, Henry 1745-1831 .... **NCLC 41**
See also DLB 39; RGEL 2

Mackey, Nathaniel 1947- .... **PC 49**
See also CA 153; CANR 114; CP 6, 7; DLB
169

Mackey, Nathaniel Ernest
See Mackey, Nathaniel

MacKinnon, Catharine A. 1946- .... **CLC 181**
See also CA 132; CAAE 128; CANR 73,
140; FW; MTCW 2; MTFW 2005

Mackintosh, Elizabeth 1896(?)-1952
See Tey, Josephine
See also CAAE 110; CMW 4

Macklin, Charles 1699-1797 .... **LC 132**
See also DLB 89; RGEL 2

MacLaren, James
See Grieve, C(hristopher) M(urray)

MacLaverty, Bernard 1942- ..... **CLC 31, 243**
See also CA 118; CAAE 116; CANR 43,
88; CN 5, 6, 7; DLB 267; INT CA-118;
RGSF 2

MacLean, Alistair (Stuart)
1922(?)-1987 .... **CLC 3, 13, 50, 63**
See also CA 57-60; CAAS 121; CANR 28,
61; CMW 4; CP 2, 3, 4, 5, 6, 7; CPW;
DAM POP; DLB 276; MTCW 1; SATA
23; SATA-Obit 50; TCWW 2

Maclean, Norman (Fitzroy)
1902-1990 .... **CLC 78; SSC 13**
See also AMWS 14; CA 102; CAAS 132;
CANR 49; CPW; DAM POP; DLB 206;
TCWW 2

MacLeish, Archibald 1892-1982 ... **CLC 3, 8,
14, 68; PC 47**
See also AMW; CA 9-12R; CAAS 106;
CAD; CANR 33, 63; CDALBS; CP 1, 2;
DAM POET; DFS 15; DLB 4, 7, 45;
DLBY 1982; EWL 3; EXPP; MAL 5;
MTCW 1, 2; MTFW 2005; PAB; PFS 5;
RGAL 4; TUS

MacLennan, (John) Hugh
1907-1990 .... **CLC 2, 14, 92**
See also CA 5-8R; CAAS 142; CANR 33;
CN 1, 2, 3, 4; DAC; DAM MST; DLB
68; EWL 3; MTCW 1, 2; MTFW 2005;
RGEL 2; TWA

MacLeod, Alistair 1936- .. **CLC 56, 165; SSC
90**
See also CA 123; CCA 1; DAC; DAM
MST; DLB 60; MTCW 2; MTFW 2005;
RGSF 2; TCLE 1:2

Macleod, Fiona
See Sharp, William
See also RGEL 2; SUFW

MacNeice, (Frederick) Louis
1907-1963 .... **CLC 1, 4, 10, 53; PC 61**
See also BRW 7; CA 85-88; CANR 61;
DAB; DAM POET; DLB 10, 20; EWL 3;
MTCW 1, 2; MTFW 2005; RGEL 2

MacNeill, Dand
See Fraser, George MacDonald

Macpherson, James 1736-1796 .... **LC 29**
See Ossian
See also BRWS 8; DLB 109, 336; RGEL 2

Macpherson, (Jean) Jay 1931- .... **CLC 14**
See also CA 5-8R; CANR 90; CP 1, 2, 3, 4,
6, 7; CWP; DLB 53

Macrobius fl. 430- .... **CMLC 48**

MacShane, Frank 1927-1999 .... **CLC 39**
See also CA 9-12R; CAAS 186; CANR 3,
33; DLB 111

Macumber, Mari
See Sandoz, Mari(e Susette)

Madach, Imre 1823-1864 .... **NCLC 19**

Madden, (Jerry) David 1933- .... **CLC 5, 15**
See also CA 1-4R; 3; CANR 4, 45; CN 3,
4, 5, 6, 7; CSW; DLB 6; MTCW 1

Maddern, Al(an)
See Ellison, Harlan

Madhubuti, Haki R. 1942- ... **BLC 2; CLC 6,
73; PC 5**
See Lee, Don L.
See also BW 2, 3; CA 73-76; CANR 24,
51, 73, 139; CP 6, 7; CSW; DAM MULT,
POET; DLB 5, 41; DLBD 8; EWL 3;
MAL 5; MTCW 2; MTFW 2005; RGAL
4

Madison, James 1751-1836 .... **NCLC 126**
See also DLB 37

Maepenn, Hugh
See Kuttner, Henry

Maepenn, K. H.
See Kuttner, Henry

Maeterlinck, Maurice 1862-1949 ..... **TCLC 3**
See also CA 136; CAAE 104; CANR 80;
DAM DRAM; DLB 192, 331; EW 8;
EWL 3; GFL 1789 to the Present; LMFS
2; RGWL 2, 3; SATA 66; TWA

Maginn, William 1794-1842 .... **NCLC 8**
See also DLB 110, 159

Mahapatra, Jayanta 1928- .... **CLC 33**
See also CA 73-76; 9; CANR 15, 33, 66,
87; CP 4, 5, 6, 7; DAM MULT; DLB 323

Mahfouz, Nagib
See Mahfouz, Naguib

Mahfouz, Naguib 1911(?)-2006 ..... **CLC 153;
SSC 66**
See Mahfuz, Najib
See also AAYA 49; BEST 89:2; CA 128;
CAAS 253; CANR 55, 101; DA3; DAM
NOV; MTCW 1, 2; MTFW 2005; RGWL
2, 3; SSFS 9

Mahfouz, Naguib Abdel Aziz Al-Sabilgi
See Mahfouz, Naguib

Mahfouz, Najib
See Mahfouz, Naguib

Mahfuz, Najib .... **CLC 52, 55**
See Mahfouz, Naguib
See also AFW; CWW 2; DLB 331; DLBY
1988; EWL 3; RGSF 2; WLIT 6

Mahon, Derek 1941- .... **CLC 27; PC 60**
See also BRWS 6; CA 128; CAAE 113;
CANR 88; CP 1, 2, 3, 4, 5, 6, 7; DLB 40;
EWL 3

Maiakovskii, Vladimir
See Mayakovski, Vladimir (Vladimirovich)
See also IDTP; RGWL 2, 3

Mailer, Norman 1923- ... **CLC 1, 2, 3, 4, 5, 8,
11, 14, 28, 39, 74, 111, 234**
See also AAYA 31; AITN 2; AMW; AMWC
2; AMWR 2; BPFB 2; CA 9-12R; CABS
1; CANR 28, 74, 77, 130; CDALB 1968-
1988; CN 1, 2, 3, 4, 5, 6, 7; CPW; DA;
DA3; DAB; DAC; DAM MST, NOV
POP; DLB 2, 16, 28, 185, 278; DLBD 3;
DLBY 1980, 1983; EWL 3; MAL 5;
MTCW 1, 2; MTFW 2005; NFS 10;
RGAL 4; TUS

Mailer, Norman Kingsley
See Mailer, Norman

Maillet, Antonine 1929- .... **CLC 54, 118**
See also CA 120; CAAE 115; CANR 46,
74, 77, 134; CCA 1; CWW 2; DAC; DLB
60; INT CA-120; MTCW 2; MTFW 2005

Maimonides, Moses 1135-1204 ..... **CMLC 76**
See also DLB 115

Mais, Roger 1905-1955 .... **TCLC 8**
See also BW 1, 3; CA 124; CAAE 105
CANR 82; CDWLB 3; DLB 125; EWL 3
MTCW 1; RGEL 2

Maistre, Joseph 1753-1821 .... **NCLC 37**
See also GFL 1789 to the Present

Margulies, Donald 1954- .... **CLC 76**
    See also AAYA 57; CA 200; CD 6; DFS 13;
    DLB 228
Marias, Javier 1951- .... **CLC 239**
    See also CA 167; CANR 109, 139; DLB
    322; HW 2; MTFW 2005
Marie de France c. 12th cent. - ..... **CMLC 8;**
PC 22
    See also DLB 208; FW; RGWL 2, 3
Marie de l'Incarnation 1599-1672 ...... **LC 10**
Marier, Captain Victor
    See Griffith, D(avid Lewelyn) W(ark)
Mariner, Scott
    See Pohl, Frederik
Marinetti, Filippo Tommaso
    1876-1944 .... **TCLC 10**
    See also CAAE 107; DLB 114, 264; EW 9;
    EWL 3; WLIT 7
Marivaux, Pierre Carlet de Chamblain de
    1688-1763 .... **DC 7; LC 4, 123**
    See also DLB 314; GFL Beginnings to
    1789; RGWL 2, 3; TWA
Markandaya, Kamala .... **CLC 8, 38**
    See Taylor, Kamala
    See also BYA 13; CN 1, 2, 3, 4, 5, 6, 7;
    DLB 323; EWL 3
Markfield, Wallace (Arthur)
    1926-2002 .... **CLC 8**
    See also CA 69-72; 3; CAAS 208; CN 1, 2,
    3, 4, 5, 6, 7; DLB 2, 28; DLBY 2002
Markham, Edwin 1852-1940 .... **TCLC 47**
    See also CA 160; DLB 54, 186; MAL 5;
    RGAL 4
Markham, Robert
    See Amis, Kingsley
Marks, J.
    See Highwater, Jamake (Mamake)
Marks-Highwater, J.
    See Highwater, Jamake (Mamake)
Markson, David M. 1927- .... **CLC 67**
    See also AMWS 17; CA 49-52; CANR 1,
    91, 158; CN 5, 6
Markson, David Merrill
    See Markson, David M.
Marlatt, Daphne (Buckle) 1942- .... **CLC 168**
    See also CA 25-28R; CANR 17, 39; CN 6,
    7; CP 4, 5, 6, 7; CWP; DLB 60; FW
Marley, Bob .... **CLC 17**
    See Marley, Robert Nesta
Marley, Robert Nesta 1945-1981
    See Marley, Bob
    See also CA 107; CAAS 103
Marlowe, Christopher 1564-1593 . **DC 1; LC**
    22, 47, 117; PC 57; WLC 4
    See also BRW 1; BRWR 1; CDBLB Before
    1660; DA; DA3; DAB; DAC; DAM
    DRAM, MST; DFS 1, 5, 13, 21; DLB 62;
    EXPP; LMFS 1; PFS 22; RGEL 2; TEA;
    WLIT 3
Marlowe, Stephen 1928- .... **CLC 70**
    See Queen, Ellery
    See also CA 13-16R; CANR 6, 55; CMW
    4; SFW 4
Marmion, Shakerley 1603-1639 .... **LC 89**
    See also DLB 58; RGEL 2
Marmontel, Jean-Francois 1723-1799 .. **LC 2**
    See also DLB 314
Maron, Monika 1941- .... **CLC 165**
    See also CA 201
Marot, Clement c. 1496-1544 .... **LC 133**
    See also DLB 327; GFL Beginnings to 1789
Marquand, John P(hillips)
    1893-1960 .... **CLC 2, 10**
    See also AMW; BPFB 2; CA 85-88; CANR
    73; CMW 4; DLB 9, 102; EWL 3; MAL
    5; MTCW 2; RGAL 4

Marques, Rene 1919-1979 .. **CLC 96; HLC 2**
    See also CA 97-100; CAAS 85-88; CANR
    78; DAM MULT; DLB 305; EWL 3; HW
    1, 2; LAW; RGSF 2
Marquez, Gabriel Garcia
    See Garcia Marquez, Gabriel
Marquis, Don(ald Robert Perry)
    1878-1937 .... **TCLC 7**
    See also CA 166; CAAE 104; DLB 11, 25;
    MAL 5; RGAL 4
Marquis de Sade
    See Sade, Donatien Alphonse Francois
Marric, J. J.
    See Creasey, John
    See also MSW
Marryat, Frederick 1792-1848 .... **NCLC 3**
    See also DLB 21, 163; RGEL 2; WCH
Marsden, James
    See Creasey, John
Marsh, Edward 1872-1953 .... **TCLC 99**
Marsh, (Edith) Ngaio 1895-1982 .. **CLC 7, 53**
    See also CA 9-12R; CANR 6, 58; CMW 4;
    CN 1, 2, 3; CPW; DAM POP; DLB 77;
    MSW; MTCW 1, 2; RGEL 2; TEA
Marshall, Allen
    See Westlake, Donald E.
Marshall, Garry 1934- .... **CLC 17**
    See also AAYA 3; CA 111; SATA 60
Marshall, Paule 1929- .. **BLC 3; CLC 27, 72;**
    SSC 3
    See also AFAW 1, 2; AMWS 11; BPFB 2;
    BW 2, 3; CA 77-80; CANR 25, 73, 129;
    CN 1, 2, 3, 4, 5, 6, 7; DA3; DAM MULT;
    DLB 33, 157, 227; EWL 3; LATS 1:2;
    MAL 5; MTCW 1, 2; MTFW 2005;
    RGAL 4; SSFS 15
Marshallik
    See Zangwill, Israel
Marsten, Richard
    See Hunter, Evan
Marston, John 1576-1634 .... **LC 33**
    See also BRW 2; DAM DRAM; DLB 58,
    172; RGEL 2
Martel, Yann 1963- .... **CLC 192**
    See also AAYA 67; CA 146; CANR 114;
    DLB 326, 334; MTFW 2005
Martens, Adolphe-Adhemar
    See Ghelderode, Michel de
Martha, Henry
    See Harris, Mark
Marti, Jose .... **PC 76**
    See Marti (y Perez), Jose (Julian)
    See also DLB 290
Marti (y Perez), Jose (Julian)
    1853-1895 .... **HLC 2; NCLC 63**
    See Marti, Jose
    See also DAM MULT; HW 2; LAW; RGWL
    2, 3; WLIT 1
Martial c. 40-c. 104 .... **CMLC 35; PC 10**
    See also AW 2; CDWLB 1; DLB 211;
    RGWL 2, 3
Martin, Ken
    See Hubbard, L. Ron
Martin, Richard
    See Creasey, John
Martin, Steve 1945- .... **CLC 30, 217**
    See also AAYA 53; CA 97-100; CANR 30,
    100, 140; DFS 19; MTCW 1; MTFW
    2005
Martin, Valerie 1948- .... **CLC 89**
    See also BEST 90:2; CA 85-88; CANR 49,
    89, 165
Martin, Violet Florence 1862-1915 .. **SSC 56;**
    TCLC 51
Martin, Webber
    See Silverberg, Robert
Martindale, Patrick Victor
    See White, Patrick (Victor Martindale)

Martin du Gard, Roger
    1881-1958 .... **TCLC 24**
    See also CAAE 118; CANR 94; DLB 65,
    331; EWL 3; GFL 1789 to the Present;
    RGWL 2, 3
Martineau, Harriet 1802-1876 ...... **NCLC 26,**
    137
    See also DLB 21, 55, 159, 163, 166, 190;
    FW; RGEL 2; YABC 2
Martines, Julia
    See O'Faolain, Julia
Martinez, Enrique Gonzalez
    See Gonzalez Martinez, Enrique
Martinez, Jacinto Benavente y
    See Benavente (y Martinez), Jacinto
Martinez de la Rosa, Francisco de Paula
    1787-1862 .... **NCLC 102**
    See also TWA
Martinez Ruiz, Jose 1873-1967
    See Azorin; Ruiz, Jose Martinez
    See also CA 93-96; HW 1
Martinez Sierra, Gregorio
    See Martinez Sierra, Maria
Martinez Sierra, Gregorio
    1881-1947 .... **TCLC 6**
    See also CAAE 115; EWL 3
Martinez Sierra, Maria 1874-1974 .. **TCLC 6**
    See also CA 250; CAAS 115; EWL 3
Martinsen, Martin
    See Follett, Ken
Martinson, Harry (Edmund)
    1904-1978 .... **CLC 14**
    See also CA 77-80; CANR 34, 130; DLB
    259, 331; EWL 3
Martyn, Edward 1859-1923 .... **TCLC 131**
    See also CA 179; DLB 10; RGEL 2
Marut, Ret
    See Traven, B.
Marut, Robert
    See Traven, B.
Marvell, Andrew 1621-1678 .... **LC 4, 43; PC**
    10; WLC 4
    See also BRW 2; BRWR 2; CDBLB 1660-
    1789; DA; DAB; DAC; DAM MST,
    POET; DLB 131; EXPP; PFS 5; RGEL 2;
    TEA; WP
Marx, Karl (Heinrich)
    1818-1883 .... **NCLC 17, 114**
    See also DLB 129; LATS 1:1; TWA
Masaoka, Shiki -1902 .... **TCLC 18**
    See Masaoka, Tsunenori
    See also RGWL 3
Masaoka, Tsunenori 1867-1902
    See Masaoka, Shiki
    See also CA 191; CAAE 117; TWA
Masefield, John (Edward)
    1878-1967 .... **CLC 11, 47; PC 78**
    See also CA 19-20; CAAS 25-28R; CANR
    33; CAP 2; CDBLB 1890-1914; DAM
    POET; DLB 10, 19, 153, 160; EWL 3;
    EXPP; FANT; MTCW 1, 2; PFS 5; RGEL
    2; SATA 19
Maso, Carole 1955(?)- .... **CLC 44**
    See also CA 170; CANR 148; CN 7; GLL
    2; RGAL 4
Mason, Bobbie Ann 1940- ... **CLC 28, 43, 82,**
    154; SSC 4, 101
    See also AAYA 5, 42; AMWS 8; BPFB 2;
    CA 53-56; CANR 11, 31, 58, 83, 125;
    CDALBS; CN 5, 6, 7; CSW; DA3; DLB
    173; DLBY 1987; EWL 3; EXPS; INT
    CANR-31; MAL 5; MTCW 1, 2; MTFW
    2005; NFS 4; RGAL 4; RGSF 2; SSFS 3,
    8, 20; TCLE 1:2; YAW
Mason, Ernst
    See Pohl, Frederik
Mason, Hunni B.
    See Sternheim, (William Adolf) Carl

Mason, Lee W.
 See Malzberg, Barry N(athaniel)
Mason, Nick 1945- .... **CLC 35**
Mason, Tally
 See Derleth, August (William)
Mass, Anna .... **CLC 59**
Mass, William
 See Gibson, William
Massinger, Philip 1583-1640 .... **LC 70**
 See also BRWS 11; DLB 58; RGEL 2
Master Lao
 See Lao Tzu
Masters, Edgar Lee 1868-1950 ...... **PC 1, 36;**
 TCLC 2, 25; WLCS
 See also AMWS 1; CA 133; CAAE 104;
 CDALB 1865-1917; DA; DAC; DAM
 MST, POET; DLB 54; EWL 3; EXPP;
 MAL 5; MTCW 1, 2; MTFW 2005;
 RGAL 4; TUS; WP
Masters, Hilary 1928- .... **CLC 48**
 See also CA 217; 25-28R, 217; CANR 13,
 47, 97; CN 6, 7; DLB 244
Mastrosimone, William 1947- .... **CLC 36**
 See also CA 186; CAD; CD 5, 6
Mathe, Albert
 See Camus, Albert
Mather, Cotton 1663-1728 .... **LC 38**
 See also AMWS 2; CDALB 1640-1865;
 DLB 24, 30, 140; RGAL 4; TUS
Mather, Increase 1639-1723 .... **LC 38**
 See also DLB 24
Mathers, Marshall
 See Eminem
Mathers, Marshall Bruce
 See Eminem
Matheson, Richard (Burton) 1926- .. **CLC 37**
 See also AAYA 31; CA 97-100; CANR 88,
 99; DLB 8, 44; HGG; INT CA-97-100;
 SCFW 1, 2; SFW 4; SUFW 2
Mathews, Harry 1930- .... **CLC 6, 52**
 See also CA 21-24R; 6; CANR 18, 40, 98,
 160; CN 5, 6, 7
Mathews, John Joseph 1894-1979 .. **CLC 84;**
 NNAL
 See also CA 19-20; CAAS 142; CANR 45;
 CAP 2; DAM MULT; DLB 175; TCWW
 1, 2
Mathias, Roland 1915-2007 .... **CLC 45**
 See also CA 97-100; CANR 19, 41; CP 1,
 2, 3, 4, 5, 6, 7; DLB 27
Mathias, Roland Glyn
 See Mathias, Roland
Matsuo Basho 1644(?)-1694 ...... **LC 62; PC 3**
 See Basho, Matsuo
 See also DAM POET; PFS 2, 7, 18
Mattheson, Rodney
 See Creasey, John
Matthews, (James) Brander
 1852-1929 .... **TCLC 95**
 See also CA 181; DLB 71, 78; DLBD 13
Matthews, Greg 1949- .... **CLC 45**
 See also CA 135
Matthews, William (Procter III)
 1942-1997 .... **CLC 40**
 See also AMWS 9; CA 29-32R; 18; CAAS
 162; CANR 12, 57; CP 2, 3, 4, 5, 6; DLB
 5
Matthias, John (Edward) 1941- .... **CLC 9**
 See also CA 33-36R; CANR 56; CP 4, 5, 6,
 7
Matthiessen, F(rancis) O(tto)
 1902-1950 .... **TCLC 100**
 See also CA 185; DLB 63; MAL 5

Matthiessen, Peter 1927- ... **CLC 5, 7, 11, 32,**
 64
 See also AAYA 6, 40; AMWS 5; ANW;
 BEST 90:4; BPFB 2; CA 9-12R; CANR
 21, 50, 73, 100, 138; CN 1, 2, 3, 4, 5, 6,
 7; DA3; DAM NOV; DLB 6, 173, 275;
 MAL 5; MTCW 1, 2; MTFW 2005; SATA
 27
Maturin, Charles Robert
 1780(?)-1824 .... **NCLC 6, 169**
 See also BRWS 8; DLB 178; GL 3; HGG;
 LMFS 1; RGEL 2; SUFW
Matute (Ausejo), Ana Maria 1925- .. **CLC 11**
 See also CA 89-92; CANR 129; CWW 2;
 DLB 322; EWL 3; MTCW 1; RGSF 2
Maugham, W. S.
 See Maugham, W(illiam) Somerset
Maugham, W(illiam) Somerset
 1874-1965 .. **CLC 1, 11, 15, 67, 93; SSC**
 8, 94; WLC 4
 See also AAYA 55; BPFB 2; BRW 6; CA
 5-8R; CAAS 25-28R; CANR 40, 127;
 CDBLB 1914-1945; CMW 4; DA; DA3;
 DAB; DAC; DAM DRAM, MST, NOV;
 DFS 22; DLB 10, 36, 77, 100, 162, 195;
 EWL 3; LAIT 3; MTCW 1, 2; MTFW
 2005; NFS 23; RGEL 2; RGSF 2; SATA
 54; SSFS 17
Maugham, William Somerset
 See Maugham, W(illiam) Somerset
Maupassant, (Henri Rene Albert) Guy de
 1850-1893 . **NCLC 1, 42, 83; SSC 1, 64;**
 WLC 4
 See also BYA 14; DA; DA3; DAB; DAC;
 DAM MST; DLB 123; EW 7; EXPS; GFL
 1789 to the Present; LAIT 2; LMFS 1;
 RGSF 2; RGWL 2, 3; SSFS 4, 21; SUFW;
 TWA
Maupin, Armistead 1944- .... **CLC 95**
 See also CA 130; CAAE 125; CANR 58,
 101; CPW; DA3; DAM POP; DLB 278;
 GLL 1; INT CA-130; MTCW 2; MTFW
 2005
Maupin, Armistead Jones, Jr.
 See Maupin, Armistead
Maurhut, Richard
 See Traven, B.
Mauriac, Claude 1914-1996 .... **CLC 9**
 See also CA 89-92; CAAS 152; CWW 2;
 DLB 83; EWL 3; GFL 1789 to the Present
Mauriac, Francois (Charles)
 1885-1970 .... **CLC 4, 9, 56; SSC 24**
 See also CA 25-28; CAP 2; DLB 65, 331;
 EW 10; EWL 3; GFL 1789 to the Present;
 MTCW 1, 2; MTFW 2005; RGWL 2, 3;
 TWA
Mavor, Osborne Henry 1888-1951
 See Bridie, James
 See also CAAE 104
Maxwell, Glyn 1962- .... **CLC 238**
 See also CA 154; CANR 88; CP 6, 7; PFS
 23
Maxwell, William (Keepers, Jr.)
 1908-2000 .... **CLC 19**
 See also AMWS 8; CA 93-96; CAAS 189;
 CANR 54, 95; CN 1, 2, 3, 4, 5, 6, 7; DLB
 218, 278; DLBY 1980; INT CA-93-96;
 MAL 5; SATA-Obit 128
May, Elaine 1932- .... **CLC 16**
 See also CA 142; CAAE 124; CAD; CWD;
 DLB 44
Mayakovski, Vladimir (Vladimirovich)
 1893-1930 .... **TCLC 4, 18**
 See Maiakovskii, Vladimir; Mayakovsky,
 Vladimir
 See also CA 158; CAAE 104; EWL 3;
 MTCW 2; MTFW 2005; SFW 4; TWA
Mayakovsky, Vladimir
 See Mayakovski, Vladimir (Vladimirovich)
 See also EW 11; WP

Mayhew, Henry 1812-1887 .... **NCLC 31**
 See also DLB 18, 55, 190
Mayle, Peter 1939(?)- .... **CLC 89**
 See also CA 139; CANR 64, 109
Maynard, Joyce 1953- .... **CLC 23**
 See also CA 129; CAAE 111; CANR 64
Mayne, William (James Carter)
 1928- .... **CLC 12**
 See also AAYA 20; CA 9-12R; CANR 37,
 80, 100; CLR 25, 123; FANT; JRDA;
 MAICYA 1, 2; MAICYAS 1; SAAS 11;
 SATA 6, 68, 122; SUFW 2; YAW
Mayo, Jim
 See L'Amour, Louis
Maysles, Albert 1926- .... **CLC 16**
 See also CA 29-32R
Maysles, David 1932-1987 .... **CLC 16**
 See also CA 191
Mazer, Norma Fox 1931- .... **CLC 26**
 See also AAYA 5, 36; BYA 1, 8; CA 69-72;
 CANR 12, 32, 66, 129; CLR 23; JRDA;
 MAICYA 1, 2; SAAS 1; SATA 24, 67,
 105, 168; WYA; YAW
Mazzini, Guiseppe 1805-1872 .... **NCLC 34**
McAlmon, Robert (Menzies)
 1895-1956 .... **TCLC 97**
 See also CA 168; CAAE 107; DLB 4, 45;
 DLBD 15; GLL 1
McAuley, James Phillip 1917-1976 .. **CLC 45**
 See also CA 97-100; CP 1, 2; DLB 260;
 RGEL 2
McBain, Ed
 See Hunter, Evan
 See also MSW
McBrien, William (Augustine)
 1930- .... **CLC 44**
 See also CA 107; CANR 90
McCabe, Patrick 1955- .... **CLC 133**
 See also BRWS 9; CA 130; CANR 50, 90;
 CN 6, 7; DLB 194
McCaffrey, Anne 1926- .... **CLC 17**
 See also AAYA 6, 34; AITN 2; BEST 89:2;
 BPFB 2; BYA 5; CA 227; 25-28R, 227;
 CANR 15, 35, 55, 96; CLR 49; CPW;
 DA3; DAM NOV, POP; DLB 8; JRDA;
 MAICYA 1, 2; MTCW 1, 2; MTFW 2005;
 SAAS 11; SATA 8, 70, 116, 152; SATA-
 Essay 152; SFW 4; SUFW 2; WYA; YAW
McCaffrey, Anne Inez
 See McCaffrey, Anne
McCall, Nathan 1955(?)- .... **CLC 86**
 See also AAYA 59; BW 3; CA 146; CANR
 88
McCann, Arthur
 See Campbell, John W(ood, Jr.)
McCann, Edson
 See Pohl, Frederik
McCarthy, Charles, Jr.
 See McCarthy, Cormac
McCarthy, Cormac 1933- .... **CLC 4, 57, 101,**
 204
 See also AAYA 41; AMWS 8; BPFB 2; CA
 13-16R; CANR 10, 42, 69, 101, 161; CN
 6, 7; CPW; CSW; DA3; DAM POP; DLB
 6, 143, 256; EWL 3; LATS 1:2; MAL 5;
 MTCW 2; MTFW 2005; TCLE 1:2;
 TCWW 2
McCarthy, Mary (Therese)
 1912-1989 .. **CLC 1, 3, 5, 14, 24, 39, 59;**
 SSC 24
 See also AMW; BPFB 2; CA 5-8R; CAAS
 129; CANR 16, 50, 64; CN 1, 2, 3, 4;
 DA3; DLB 2; DLBY 1981; EWL 3; FW;
 INT CANR-16; MAL 5; MBL; MTCW 1,
 2; MTFW 2005; RGAL 4; TUS
McCartney, James Paul
 See McCartney, Paul
McCartney, Paul 1942- .... **CLC 12, 35**
 See also CA 146; CANR 111

Medoff, Mark (Howard) 1940- .... **CLC 6, 23**
  See also AITN 1; CA 53-56; CAD; CANR
  5; CD 5, 6; DAM DRAM; DFS 4; DLB
  7; INT CANR-5
Medvedev, P. N.
  See Bakhtin, Mikhail Mikhailovich
Meged, Aharon
  See Megged, Aharon
Meged, Aron
  See Megged, Aharon
Megged, Aharon 1920- .... **CLC 9**
  See also CA 49-52; 13; CANR 1, 140; EWL
  3; RGHL
Mehta, Deepa 1950- .... **CLC 208**
Mehta, Gita 1943- .... **CLC 179**
  See also CA 225; CN 7; DNFS 2
Mehta, Ved 1934- .... **CLC 37**
  See also CA 212; 1-4R, 212; CANR 2, 23,
  69; DLB 323; MTCW 1; MTFW 2005
Melanchthon, Philipp 1497-1560 .... **LC 90**
  See also DLB 179
Melanter
  See Blackmore, R(ichard) D(oddridge)
Meleager c. 140B.C.-c. 70B.C. ...... **CMLC 53**
Melies, Georges 1861-1938 .... **TCLC 81**
Melikow, Loris
  See Hofmannsthal, Hugo von
Melmoth, Sebastian
  See Wilde, Oscar (Fingal O'Flahertie Wills)
Melo Neto, Joao Cabral de
  See Cabral de Melo Neto, Joao
  See also CWW 2; EWL 3
Meltzer, Milton 1915- .... **CLC 26**
  See also AAYA 8, 45; BYA 2, 6; CA 13-
  16R; CANR 38, 92, 107; CLR 13; DLB
  61; JRDA; MAICYA 1, 2; SAAS 1; SATA
  1, 50, 80, 128; SATA-Essay 124; WYA;
  YAW
Melville, Herman 1819-1891 ..... **NCLC 3, 12,
  29, 45, 49, 91, 93, 123, 157, 181; SSC 1,
  17, 46, 95; WLC 4**
  See also AAYA 25; AMW; AMWR 1;
  CDALB 1640-1865; DA; DA3; DAB;
  DAC; DAM MST, NOV; DLB 3, 74, 250,
  254; EXPN; EXPS; GL 3; LAIT 1, 2; NFS
  7, 9; RGAL 4; RGSF 2; SATA 59; SSFS
  3; TUS
Members, Mark
  See Powell, Anthony
Membreno, Alejandro .... **CLC 59**
Menand, Louis 1952- .... **CLC 208**
  See also CA 200
Menander c. 342B.C.-c. 293B.C. .... **CMLC 9,
  51; DC 3**
  See also AW 1; CDWLB 1; DAM DRAM;
  DLB 176; LMFS 1; RGWL 2, 3
Menchu, Rigoberta 1959- .. **CLC 160; HLCS
  2**
  See also CA 175; CANR 135; DNFS 1;
  WLIT 1
Mencken, H(enry) L(ouis)
  1880-1956 .... **TCLC 13**
  See also AMW; CA 125; CAAE 105;
  CDALB 1917-1929; DLB 11, 29, 63, 137,
  222; EWL 3; MAL 5; MTCW 1, 2;
  MTFW 2005; NCFS 4; RGAL 4; TUS
Mendelsohn, Jane 1965- .... **CLC 99**
  See also CA 154; CANR 94
Mendoza, Inigo Lopez de
  See Santillana, Inigo Lopez de Mendoza,
  Marques de
Menton, Francisco de
  See Chin, Frank (Chew, Jr.)
Mercer, David 1928-1980 .... **CLC 5**
  See also CA 9-12R; CAAS 102; CANR 23;
  CBD; DAM DRAM; DLB 13, 310;
  MTCW 1; RGEL 2
Merchant, Paul
  See Ellison, Harlan

Meredith, George 1828-1909 .. **PC 60; TCLC
  17, 43**
  See also CA 153; CAAE 117; CANR 80;
  CDBLB 1832-1890; DAM POET; DLB
  18, 35, 57, 159; RGEL 2; TEA
Meredith, William 1919-2007 ...... **CLC 4, 13,
  22, 55; PC 28**
  See also CA 9-12R; 14; CAAS 260; CANR
  6, 40, 129; CP 1, 2, 3, 4, 5, 6, 7; DAM
  POET; DLB 5; MAL 5
Meredith, William Morris
  See Meredith, William
Merezhkovsky, Dmitrii Sergeevich
  See Merezhkovsky, Dmitry Sergeyevich
  See also DLB 295
Merezhkovsky, Dmitry Sergeyevich
  See Merezhkovsky, Dmitry Sergeyevich
  See also EWL 3
Merezhkovsky, Dmitry Sergeyevich
  1865-1941 .... **TCLC 29**
  See Merezhkovsky, Dmitrii Sergeevich;
  Merezhkovsky, Dmitry Sergeevich
  See also CA 169
Merimee, Prosper 1803-1870 ... **NCLC 6, 65;
  SSC 7, 77**
  See also DLB 119, 192; EW 6; EXPS; GFL
  1789 to the Present; RGSF 2; RGWL 2,
  3; SSFS 8; SUFW
Merkin, Daphne 1954- .... **CLC 44**
  See also CA 123
Merleau-Ponty, Maurice
  1908-1961 .... **TCLC 156**
  See also CA 114; CAAS 89-92; DLB 296;
  GFL 1789 to the Present
Merlin, Arthur
  See Blish, James (Benjamin)
Mernissi, Fatima 1940- .... **CLC 171**
  See also CA 152; FW
Merrill, James 1926-1995 ...... **CLC 2, 3, 6, 8,
  13, 18, 34, 91; PC 28; TCLC 173**
  See also AMWS 3; CA 13-16R; CAAS 147;
  CANR 10, 49, 63, 108; CP 1, 2, 3, 4;
  DA3; DAM POET; DLB 5, 165; DLBY
  1985; EWL 3; INT CANR-10; MAL 5;
  MTCW 1, 2; MTFW 2005; PAB; PFS 23;
  RGAL 4
Merrill, James Ingram
  See Merrill, James
Merriman, Alex
  See Silverberg, Robert
Merriman, Brian 1747-1805 .... **NCLC 70**
Merritt, E. B.
  See Waddington, Miriam
Merton, Thomas (James)
  1915-1968 . **CLC 1, 3, 11, 34, 83; PC 10**
  See also AAYA 61; AMWS 8; CA 5-8R;
  CAAS 25-28R; CANR 22, 53, 111, 131;
  DA3; DLB 48; DLBY 1981; MAL 5;
  MTCW 1, 2; MTFW 2005
Merwin, W.S. 1927- ..... **CLC 1, 2, 3, 5, 8, 13,
  18, 45, 88; PC 45**
  See also AMWS 3; CA 13-16R; CANR 15,
  51, 112, 140; CP 1, 2, 3, 4, 5, 6, 7; DA3;
  DAM POET; DLB 5, 169; EWL 3; INT
  CANR-15; MAL 5; MTCW 1, 2; MTFW
  2005; PAB; PFS 5, 15; RGAL 4
Metastasio, Pietro 1698-1782 .... **LC 115**
  See also RGWL 2, 3
Metcalf, John 1938- .... **CLC 37; SSC 43**
  See also CA 113; CN 4, 5, 6, 7; DLB 60;
  RGSF 2; TWA
Metcalf, Suzanne
  See Baum, L(yman) Frank
Mew, Charlotte (Mary) 1870-1928 .. **TCLC 8**
  See also CA 189; CAAE 105; DLB 19, 135;
  RGEL 2
Mewshaw, Michael 1943- .... **CLC 9**
  See also CA 53-56; CANR 7, 47, 147;
  DLBY 1980

Meyer, Conrad Ferdinand
  1825-1898 .... **NCLC 81; SSC 30**
  See also DLB 129; EW; RGWL 2, 3
Meyer, Gustav 1868-1932
  See Meyrink, Gustav
  See also CA 190; CAAE 117
Meyer, June
  See Jordan, June
Meyer, Lynn
  See Slavitt, David R.
Meyers, Jeffrey 1939- .... **CLC 39**
  See also CA 186; 73-76, 186; CANR 54,
  102, 159; DLB 111
**Meynell, Alice (Christina Gertrude
  Thompson)** 1847-1922 .... **TCLC 6**
  See also CA 177; CAAE 104; DLB 19, 98;
  RGEL 2
Meyrink, Gustav .... **TCLC 21**
  See Meyer, Gustav
  See also DLB 81; EWL 3
Michaels, Leonard 1933-2003 ..... **CLC 6, 25;
  SSC 16**
  See also AMWS 16; CA 61-64; CAAS 216;
  CANR 21, 62, 119; CN 3, 45, 6, 7; DLB
  130; MTCW 1; TCLE 1:2
Michaux, Henri 1899-1984 .... **CLC 8, 19**
  See also CA 85-88; CAAS 114; DLB 258;
  EWL 3; GFL 1789 to the Present; RGWL
  2, 3
Micheaux, Oscar (Devereaux)
  1884-1951 .... **TCLC 76**
  See also BW 3; CA 174; DLB 50; TCWW
  2
Michelangelo 1475-1564 .... **LC 12**
  See also AAYA 43
Michelet, Jules 1798-1874 .... **NCLC 31**
  See also EW 5; GFL 1789 to the Present
Michels, Robert 1876-1936 .... **TCLC 88**
  See also CA 212
Michener, James A. 1907(?)-1997 . **CLC 1, 5,
  11, 29, 60, 109**
  See also AAYA 27; AITN 1; BEST 90:1;
  BPFB 2; CA 5-8R; CAAS 161; CANR
  21, 45, 68; CN 1, 2, 3, 4, 5, 6; CPW; DA3;
  DAM NOV, POP; DLB 6; MAL 5;
  MTCW 1, 2; MTFW 2005; RHW; TCWW
  1, 2
Mickiewicz, Adam 1798-1855 . **NCLC 3, 101;
  PC 38**
  See also EW 5; RGWL 2, 3
Middleton, (John) Christopher
  1926- .... **CLC 13**
  See also CA 13-16R; CANR 29, 54, 117;
  CP 1, 2, 3, 4, 5, 6, 7; DLB 40
Middleton, Richard (Barham)
  1882-1911 .... **TCLC 56**
  See also CA 187; DLB 156; HGG
Middleton, Stanley 1919- .... **CLC 7, 38**
  See also CA 25-28R; 23; CANR 21, 46, 81,
  157; CN 1, 2, 3, 4, 5, 6, 7; DLB 14, 326
Middleton, Thomas 1580-1627 ...... **DC 5; LC
  33, 123**
  See also BRW 2; DAM DRAM, MST; DFS
  18, 22; DLB 58; RGEL 2
Mieville, China 1972(?)- .... **CLC 235**
  See also AAYA 52; CA 196; CANR 138;
  MTFW 2005
Migueis, Jose Rodrigues 1901-1980 . **CLC 10**
  See also DLB 287
Mikszath, Kalman 1847-1910 .... **TCLC 31**
  See also CA 170
Miles, Jack .... **CLC 100**
  See also CA 200
Miles, John Russiano
  See Miles, Jack

NOV; DLB 53; EWL 3; MTCW 1, 2; MTFW 2005; RGEL 2; RGSF 2; SATA 29; SSFS 5, 13, 19; TCLE 1:2; WWE 1

Munro, H(ector) H(ugh) 1870-1916
See Saki
See also AAYA 56; CA 130; CAAE 104; CANR 104; CDBLB 1890-1914; DA; DA3; DAB; DAC; DAM MST, NOV; DLB 34, 162; EXPS; MTCW 1, 2; MTFW 2005; RGEL 2; SSFS 15

Murakami, Haruki 1949- .... **CLC 150**
See Murakami Haruki
See also CA 165; CANR 102, 146; MJW; RGWL 3; SFW 4; SSFS 23

Murakami Haruki
See Murakami, Haruki
See also CWW 2; DLB 182; EWL 3

Murasaki, Lady
See Murasaki Shikibu

Murasaki Shikibu 978(?)-1026(?) .. **CMLC 1, 79**
See also EFS 2; LATS 1:1; RGWL 2, 3

Murdoch, Iris 1919-1999 .. **CLC 1, 2, 3, 4, 6, 8, 11, 15, 22, 31, 51; TCLC 171**
See also BRWS 1; CA 13-16R; CAAS 179; CANR 8, 43, 68, 103, 142; CBD; CDBLB 1960 to Present; CN 1, 2, 3, 4, 5, 6; CWD; DA3; DAB; DAC; DAM MST, NOV; DLB 14, 194, 233, 326; EWL 3; INT CANR-8; MTCW 1, 2; MTFW 2005; NFS 18; RGEL 2; TCLE 1:2; TEA; WLIT 4

Murfree, Mary Noailles 1850-1922 .. **SSC 22; TCLC 135**
See also CA 176; CAAE 122; DLB 12, 74; RGAL 4

Murglie
See Murnau, F.W.

Murnau, Friedrich Wilhelm
See Murnau, F.W.

Murnau, F.W. 1888-1931 .... **TCLC 53**
See also CAAE 112

Murphy, Richard 1927- .... **CLC 41**
See also BRWS 5; CA 29-32R; CP 1, 2, 3, 4, 5, 6, 7; DLB 40; EWL 3

Murphy, Sylvia 1937- .... **CLC 34**
See also CA 121

Murphy, Thomas (Bernard) 1935- ... **CLC 51**
See Murphy, Tom
See also CA 101

Murphy, Tom
See Murphy, Thomas (Bernard)
See also DLB 310

Murray, Albert 1916- .... **CLC 73**
See also BW 2; CA 49-52; CANR 26, 52, 78, 160; CN 7; CSW; DLB 38; MTFW 2005

Murray, Albert L.
See Murray, Albert

Murray, James Augustus Henry 1837-1915 .... **TCLC 117**

Murray, Judith Sargent 1751-1820 .... **NCLC 63**
See also DLB 37, 200

Murray, Les(lie Allan) 1938- .... **CLC 40**
See also BRWS 7; CA 21-24R; CANR 11, 27, 56, 103; CP 1, 2, 3, 4, 5, 6, 7; DAM POET; DLB 289; DLBY 2001; EWL 3; RGEL 2

Murry, J. Middleton
See Murry, John Middleton

Murry, John Middleton 1889-1957 .... **TCLC 16**
See also CA 217; CAAE 118; DLB 149

Musgrave, Susan 1951- .... **CLC 13, 54**
See also CA 69-72; CANR 45, 84; CCA 1; CP 2, 3, 4, 5, 6, 7; CWP

Musil, Robert (Edler von) 1880-1942 .... **SSC 18; TCLC 12, 68**
See also CAAE 109; CANR 55, 84; CD-WLB 2; DLB 81, 124; EW 9; EWL 3; MTCW 2; RGSF 2; RGWL 2, 3

Muske, Carol .... **CLC 90**
See Muske-Dukes, Carol (Anne)

Muske-Dukes, Carol (Anne) 1945-
See Muske, Carol
See also CA 203; 65-68, 203; CANR 32, 70; CWP; PFS 24

Musset, Alfred de 1810-1857 . **DC 27; NCLC 7, 150**
See also DLB 192, 217; EW 6; GFL 1789 to the Present; RGWL 2, 3; TWA

Musset, Louis Charles Alfred de
See Musset, Alfred de

Mussolini, Benito (Amilcare Andrea) 1883-1945 .... **TCLC 96**
See also CAAE 116

Mutanabbi, Al-
See al-Mutanabbi, Ahmad ibn al-Husayn Abu al-Tayyib al-Jufi al-Kindi
See also WLIT 6

My Brother's Brother
See Chekhov, Anton (Pavlovich)

Myers, L(eopold) H(amilton) 1881-1944 .... **TCLC 59**
See also CA 157; DLB 15; EWL 3; RGEL 2

Myers, Walter Dean 1937- .. **BLC 3; CLC 35**
See Myers, Walter M.
See also AAYA 4, 23; BW 2; BYA 6, 8, 11; CA 33-36R; CANR 20, 42, 67, 108; CLR 4, 16, 35, 110; DAM MULT, NOV; DLB 33; INT CANR-20; JRDA; LAIT 5; MAICYA 1, 2; MAICYAS 1; MTCW 2; MTFW 2005; SAAS 2; SATA 41, 71, 109, 157; SATA-Brief 27; WYA; YAW

Myers, Walter M.
See Myers, Walter Dean

Myles, Symon
See Follett, Ken

Nabokov, Vladimir (Vladimirovich) 1899-1977 .... **CLC 1, 2, 3, 6, 8, 11, 15, 23, 44, 46, 64; SSC 11, 86; TCLC 108, 189; WLC 4**
See also AAYA 45; AMW; AMWC 1; AMWR 1; BPFB 2; CA 5-8R; CAAS 69-72; CANR 20, 102; CDALB 1941-1968; CN 1, 2; CP 2; DA; DA3; DAB; DAC; DAM MST, NOV; DLB 2, 244, 278, 317; DLBD 3; DLBY 1980, 1991; EWL 3; EXPS; LATS 1:2; MAL 5; MTCW 1, 2; MTFW 2005; NCFS 4; NFS 9; RGAL 4; RGSF 2; SSFS 6, 15; TUS

Naevius c. 265B.C.-201B.C. .... **CMLC 37**
See also DLB 211

Nagai, Kafu .... **TCLC 51**
See Nagai, Sokichi
See also DLB 180

Nagai, Sokichi 1879-1959
See Nagai, Kafu
See also CAAE 117

Nagy, Laszlo 1925-1978 .... **CLC 7**
See also CA 129; CAAS 112

Naidu, Sarojini 1879-1949 .... **TCLC 80**
See also EWL 3; RGEL 2

Naipaul, Shiva 1945-1985 .... **CLC 32, 39; TCLC 153**
See also CA 112; CAAE 110; CAAS 116; CANR 33; CN 2, 3; DA3; DAM NOV; DLB 157; DLBY 1985; EWL 3; MTCW 1, 2; MTFW 2005

Naipaul, V.S. 1932- .. **CLC 4, 7, 9, 13, 18, 37, 105, 199; SSC 38**
See also BPFB 2; BRWS 1; CA 1-4R; CANR 1, 33, 51, 91, 126; CDBLB 1960 to Present; CDWLB 3; CN 1, 2, 3, 4, 5, 6, 7; DA3; DAB; DAC; DAM MST,

NOV; DLB 125, 204, 207, 326, 331; DLBY 1985, 2001; EWL 3; LATS 1:2; MTCW 1, 2; MTFW 2005; RGEL 2; RGSF 2; TWA; WLIT 4; WWE 1

Nakos, Lilika 1903(?)-1989 .... **CLC 29**

Napoleon
See Yamamoto, Hisaye

Narayan, R.K. 1906-2001 ...... **CLC 7, 28, 47, 121, 211; SSC 25**
See also BPFB 2; CA 81-84; CAAS 196; CANR 33, 61, 112; CN 1, 2, 3, 4, 5, 6, 7; DA3; DAM NOV; DLB 323; DNFS 1; EWL 3; MTCW 1, 2; MTFW 2005; RGEL 2; RGSF 2; SATA 62; SSFS 5; WWE 1

Nash, (Fredric) Ogden 1902-1971 . **CLC 23; PC 21; TCLC 109**
See also CA 13-14; CAAS 29-32R; CANR 34, 61; CAP 1; CP 1; DAM POET; DLB 11; MAICYA 1, 2; MAL 5; MTCW 1, 2; RGAL 4; SATA 2, 46; WP

Nashe, Thomas 1567-1601(?) .... **LC 41, 89**
See also DLB 167; RGEL 2

Nathan, Daniel
See Dannay, Frederic

Nathan, George Jean 1882-1958 .... **TCLC 18**
See Hatteras, Owen
See also CA 169; CAAE 114; DLB 137; MAL 5

Natsume, Kinnosuke
See Natsume, Soseki

Natsume, Soseki 1867-1916 .... **TCLC 2, 10**
See Natsume Soseki; Soseki
See also CA 195; CAAE 104; RGWL 2, 3; TWA

Natsume Soseki
See Natsume, Soseki
See also DLB 180; EWL 3

Natti, (Mary) Lee 1919-
See Kingman, Lee
See also CA 5-8R; CANR 2

Navarre, Marguerite de
See de Navarre, Marguerite

Naylor, Gloria 1950- ..... **BLC 3; CLC 28, 52, 156; WLCS**
See also AAYA 6, 39; AFAW 1, 2; AMWS 8; BW 2, 3; CA 107; CANR 27, 51, 74, 130; CN 4, 5, 6, 7; CPW; DA; DA3; DAC; DAM MST, MULT, NOV, POP; DLB 173; EWL 3; FW; MAL 5; MTCW 1, 2; MTFW 2005; NFS 4, 7; RGAL 4; TCLE 1:2; TUS

Neal, John 1793-1876 .... **NCLC 161**
See also DLB 1, 59, 243; FW; RGAL 4

Neff, Debra .... **CLC 59**

Neihardt, John Gneisenau 1881-1973 .... **CLC 32**
See also CA 13-14; CANR 65; CAP 1; DLB 9, 54, 256; LAIT 2; TCWW 1, 2

Nekrasov, Nikolai Alekseevich 1821-1878 .... **NCLC 11**
See also DLB 277

Nelligan, Emile 1879-1941 .... **TCLC 14**
See also CA 204; CAAE 114; DLB 92; EWL 3

Nelson, Willie 1933- .... **CLC 17**
See also CA 107; CANR 114

Nemerov, Howard 1920-1991 .... **CLC 2, 6, 9, 36; PC 24; TCLC 124**
See also AMW; CA 1-4R; CAAS 134; CABS 2; CANR 1, 27, 53; CN 1, 2, 3; CP 1, 2, 3, 4, 5; DAM POET; DLB 5, 6; DLBY 1983; EWL 3; INT CANR-27; MAL 5; MTCW 1, 2; MTFW 2005; PFS 10, 14; RGAL 4

Nepos, Cornelius c. 99B.C.-c. 24B.C. .... **CMLC 89**
See also DLB 211

MTFW 2005; NFS 14; RGAL 4; RGSF 2;
SATA 39; SATA-Obit 23; SSFS 1, 8, 11,
16, 23; TCWW 2; TUS

Porter, Peter (Neville Frederick)
1929- .... **CLC 5, 13, 33**
See also CA 85-88; CP 1, 2, 3, 4, 5, 6, 7;
DLB 40, 289; WWE 1

Porter, William Sydney 1862-1910
See Henry, O.
See also CA 131; CAAE 104; CDALB
1865-1917; DA; DA3; DAB; DAC; DAM
MST; DLB 12, 78, 79; MTCW 1, 2;
MTFW 2005; TUS; YABC 2

Portillo (y Pacheco), Jose Lopez
See Lopez Portillo (y Pacheco), Jose

Portillo Trambley, Estela 1927-1998 .. **HLC 2**
See Trambley, Estela Portillo
See also CANR 32; DAM MULT; DLB
209; HW 1

Posey, Alexander (Lawrence)
1873-1908 .... **NNAL**
See also CA 144; CANR 80; DAM MULT;
DLB 175

Posse, Abel .... **CLC 70**
See also CA 252

Post, Melville Davisson
1869-1930 .... **TCLC 39**
See also CA 202; CAAE 110; CMW 4

Potok, Chaim 1929-2002 ... **CLC 2, 7, 14, 26,
112**
See also AAYA 15, 50; AITN 1, 2; BPFB 3;
BYA 1; CA 17-20R; CAAS 208; CANR
19, 35, 64, 98; CLR 92; CN 4, 5, 6; DA3;
DAM NOV; DLB 28, 152; EXPN; INT
CANR-19; LAIT 4; MTCW 1, 2; MTFW
2005; NFS 4; RGHL; SATA 33, 106;
SATA-Obit 134; TUS; YAW

Potok, Herbert Harold -2002
See Potok, Chaim

Potok, Herman Harold
See Potok, Chaim

Potter, Dennis (Christopher George)
1935-1994 .... **CLC 58, 86, 123**
See also BRWS 10; CA 107; CAAS 145;
CANR 33, 61; CBD; DLB 233; MTCW 1

Pound, Ezra (Weston Loomis)
1885-1972 .. **CLC 1, 2, 3, 4, 5, 7, 10, 13,
18, 34, 48, 50, 112; PC 4; WLC 5**
See also AAYA 47; AMW; AMWR 1; CA
5-8R; CAAS 37-40R; CANR 40; CDALB
1917-1929; CP 1; DA; DA3; DAB; DAC;
DAM MST, POET; DLB 4, 45, 63; DLBD
15; EFS 2; EWL 3; EXPP; LMFS 2; MAL
5; MTCW 1, 2; MTFW 2005; PAB; PFS
2, 8, 16; RGAL 4; TUS; WP

Povod, Reinaldo 1959-1994 .... **CLC 44**
See also CA 136; CAAS 146; CANR 83

Powell, Adam Clayton, Jr.
1908-1972 .... **BLC 3; CLC 89**
See also BW 1, 3; CA 102; CAAS 33-36R;
CANR 86; DAM MULT

Powell, Anthony 1905-2000 ... **CLC 1, 3, 7, 9,
10, 31**
See also BRW 7; CA 1-4R; CAAS 189;
CANR 1, 32, 62, 107; CDBLB 1945-
1960; CN 1, 2, 3, 4, 5, 6; DLB 15; EWL
3; MTCW 1, 2; MTFW 2005; RGEL 2;
TEA

Powell, Dawn 1896(?)-1965 .... **CLC 66**
See also CA 5-8R; CANR 121; DLBY 1997

Powell, Padgett 1952- .... **CLC 34**
See also CA 126; CANR 63, 101; CSW;
DLB 234; DLBY 01; SSFS 25

Powell, (Oval) Talmage 1920-2000
See Queen, Ellery
See also CA 5-8R; CANR 2, 80

Power, Susan 1961- .... **CLC 91**
See also BYA 14; CA 160; CANR 135; NFS
11

Powers, J(ames) F(arl) 1917-1999 ..... **CLC 1,
4, 8, 57; SSC 4**
See also CA 1-4R; CAAS 181; CANR 2,
61; CN 1, 2, 3, 4, 5, 6; DLB 130; MTCW
1; RGAL 4; RGSF 2

Powers, John J(ames) 1945-
See Powers, John R.
See also CA 69-72

Powers, John R. .... **CLC 66**
See Powers, John J(ames)

Powers, Richard 1957- .... **CLC 93**
See also AMWS 9; BPFB 3; CA 148;
CANR 80; CN 6, 7; MTFW 2005; TCLE
1:2

Powers, Richard S.
See Powers, Richard

Pownall, David 1938- .... **CLC 10**
See also CA 89-92, 180; 18; CANR 49, 101;
CBD; CD 5, 6; CN 4, 5, 6, 7; DLB 14

Powys, John Cowper 1872-1963 ... **CLC 7, 9,
15, 46, 125**
See also CA 85-88; CANR 106; DLB 15,
255; EWL 3; FANT; MTCW 1, 2; MTFW
2005; RGEL 2; SUFW

Powys, T(heodore) F(rancis)
1875-1953 .... **TCLC 9**
See also BRWS 8; CA 189; CAAE 106;
DLB 36, 162; EWL 3; FANT; RGEL 2;
SUFW

Pozzo, Modesta
See Fonte, Moderata

Prado (Calvo), Pedro 1886-1952 ... **TCLC 75**
See also CA 131; DLB 283; HW 1; LAW

Prager, Emily 1952- .... **CLC 56**
See also CA 204

Pratchett, Terry 1948- .... **CLC 197**
See also AAYA 19, 54; BPFB 3; CA 143;
CANR 87, 126; CLR 64; CN 6, 7; CPW;
CWRI 5; FANT; MTFW 2005; SATA 82,
139; SFW 4; SUFW 2

Pratolini, Vasco 1913-1991 .... **TCLC 124**
See also CA 211; DLB 177; EWL 3; RGWL
2, 3

Pratt, E(dwin) J(ohn) 1883(?)-1964 . **CLC 19**
See also CA 141; CAAS 93-96; CANR 77;
DAC; DAM POET; DLB 92; EWL 3;
RGEL 2; TWA

Premchand .... **TCLC 21**
See Srivastava, Dhanpat Rai
See also EWL 3

Prescott, William Hickling
1796-1859 .... **NCLC 163**
See also DLB 1, 30, 59, 235

Preseren, France 1800-1849 .... **NCLC 127**
See also CDWLB 4; DLB 147

Preussler, Otfried 1923- .... **CLC 17**
See also CA 77-80; SATA 24

Prevert, Jacques (Henri Marie)
1900-1977 .... **CLC 15**
See also CA 77-80; CAAS 69-72; CANR
29, 61; DLB 258; EWL 3; GFL 1789 to
the Present; IDFW 3, 4; MTCW 1; RGWL
2, 3; SATA-Obit 30

Prevost, (Antoine Francois)
1697-1763 .... **LC 1**
See also DLB 314; EW 4; GFL Beginnings
to 1789; RGWL 2, 3

Price, Reynolds 1933- .. **CLC 3, 6, 13, 43, 50,
63, 212; SSC 22**
See also AMWS 6; CA 1-4R; CANR 1, 37,
57, 87, 128; CN 1, 2, 3, 4, 5, 6, 7; CSW;
DAM NOV; DLB 2, 218, 278; EWL 3;
INT CANR-37; MAL 5; MTFW 2005;
NFS 18

Price, Richard 1949- .... **CLC 6, 12**
See also CA 49-52; CANR 3, 147; CN 7;
DLBY 1981

Prichard, Katharine Susannah
1883-1969 .... **CLC 46**
See also CA 11-12; CANR 33; CAP 1; DLB
260; MTCW 1; RGEL 2; RGSF 2; SATA
66

Priestley, J(ohn) B(oynton)
1894-1984 .... **CLC 2, 5, 9, 34**
See also BRW 7; CA 9-12R; CAAS 113;
CANR 33; CDBLB 1914-1945; CN 1, 2,
3; DA3; DAM DRAM, NOV; DLB 10,
34, 77, 100, 139; DLBY 1984; EWL 3;
MTCW 1, 2; MTFW 2005; RGEL 2; SFW
4

Prince 1958- .... **CLC 35**
See also CA 213

Prince, F(rank) T(empleton)
1912-2003 .... **CLC 22**
See also CA 101; CAAS 219; CANR 43,
79; CP 1, 2, 3, 4, 5, 6, 7; DLB 20

Prince Kropotkin
See Kropotkin, Peter (Aleksieevich)

Prior, Matthew 1664-1721 .... **LC 4**
See also DLB 95; RGEL 2

Prishvin, Mikhail 1873-1954 .... **TCLC 75**
See Prishvin, Mikhail Mikhailovich

Prishvin, Mikhail Mikhailovich
See Prishvin, Mikhail
See also DLB 272; EWL 3

Pritchard, William H(arrison)
1932- .... **CLC 34**
See also CA 65-68; CANR 23, 95; DLB
111

Pritchett, V(ictor) S(awdon)
1900-1997 ... **CLC 5, 13, 15, 41; SSC 14**
See also BPFB 3; BRWS 3; CA 61-64;
CAAS 157; CANR 31, 63; CN 1, 2, 3, 4,
5, 6; DA3; DAM NOV; DLB 15, 139;
EWL 3; MTCW 1, 2; MTFW 2005; RGEL
2; RGSF 2; TEA

Private 19022
See Manning, Frederic

Probst, Mark 1925- .... **CLC 59**
See also CA 130

Procaccino, Michael
See Cristofer, Michael

Proclus c. 412-c. 485 .... **CMLC 81**

Prokosch, Frederic 1908-1989 ...... **CLC 4, 48**
See also CA 73-76; CAAS 128; CANR 82;
CN 1, 2, 3, 4; CP 1, 2, 3, 4; DLB 48;
MTCW 2

Propertius, Sextus c. 50B.C.-c.
16B.C. .... **CMLC 32**
See also AW 2; CDWLB 1; DLB 211;
RGWL 2, 3; WLIT 8

Prophet, The
See Dreiser, Theodore

Prose, Francine 1947- .... **CLC 45, 231**
See also AMWS 16; CA 112; CAAE 109;
CANR 46, 95, 132; DLB 234; MTFW
2005; SATA 101, 149

Protagoras c. 490B.C.-420B.C. ...... **CMLC 85**
See also DLB 176

Proudhon
See Cunha, Euclides (Rodrigues Pimenta)
da

Proulx, Annie
See Proulx, E. Annie

Proulx, E. Annie 1935- .... **CLC 81, 158**
See also AMWS 7; BPFB 3; CA 145;
CANR 65, 110; CN 6, 7; CPW 1; DA3;
DAM POP; DLB 335; MAL 5; MTCW 2;
MTFW 2005; SSFS 18, 23

Proulx, Edna Annie
See Proulx, E. Annie

**Proust, (Valentin-Louis-George-Eugene)
Marcel** 1871-1922 ..... **SSC 75; TCLC 7,
13, 33; WLC 5**
See also AAYA 58; BPFB 3; CA 120;
CAAE 104; CANR 110; DA; DA3; DAB;

Rae, Ben
See Griffiths, Trevor

Raeburn, John (Hay) 1941- .... **CLC 34**
See also CA 57-60

Ragni, Gerome 1942-1991 .... **CLC 17**
See also CA 105; CAAS 134

Rahv, Philip .... **CLC 24**
See Greenberg, Ivan
See also DLB 137; MAL 5

Raimund, Ferdinand Jakob
1790-1836 .... **NCLC 69**
See also DLB 90

Raine, Craig (Anthony) 1944- .. **CLC 32, 103**
See also BRWS 13; CA 108; CANR 29, 51,
103; CP 3, 4, 5, 6, 7; DLB 40; PFS 7

Raine, Kathleen (Jessie) 1908-2003 .. **CLC 7,
45**
See also CA 85-88; CAAS 218; CANR 46,
109; CP 1, 2, 3, 4, 5, 6, 7; DLB 20; EWL
3; MTCW 1; RGEL 2

Rainis, Janis 1865-1929 .... **TCLC 29**
See also CA 170; CDWLB 4; DLB 220;
EWL 3

Rakosi, Carl .... **CLC 47**
See Rawley, Callman
See also CA 5; CAAS 228; CP 1, 2, 3, 4, 5,
6, 7; DLB 193

Ralegh, Sir Walter
See Raleigh, Sir Walter
See also BRW 1; RGEL 2; WP

Raleigh, Richard
See Lovecraft, H. P.

Raleigh, Sir Walter 1554(?)-1618 .... **LC 31,
39; PC 31**
See Ralegh, Sir Walter
See also CDBLB Before 1660; DLB 172;
EXPP; PFS 14; TEA

Rallentando, H. P.
See Sayers, Dorothy L(eigh)

Ramal, Walter
See de la Mare, Walter (John)

Ramana Maharshi 1879-1950 .... **TCLC 84**

Ramoacn y Cajal, Santiago
1852-1934 .... **TCLC 93**

Ramon, Juan
See Jimenez (Mantecon), Juan Ramon

Ramos, Graciliano 1892-1953 .... **TCLC 32**
See also CA 167; DLB 307; EWL 3; HW 2;
LAW; WLIT 1

Rampersad, Arnold 1941- .... **CLC 44**
See also BW 2, 3; CA 133; CAAE 127;
CANR 81; DLB 111; INT CA-133

Rampling, Anne
See Rice, Anne
See also GLL 2

Ramsay, Allan 1686(?)-1758 .... **LC 29**
See also DLB 95; RGEL 2

Ramsay, Jay
See Campbell, (John) Ramsey

Ramuz, Charles-Ferdinand
1878-1947 .... **TCLC 33**
See also CA 165; EWL 3

Rand, Ayn 1905-1982 ...... **CLC 3, 30, 44, 79;
WLC 5**
See also AAYA 10; AMWS 4; BPFB 3;
BYA 12; CA 13-16R; CAAS 105; CANR
27, 73; CDALBS; CN 1, 2, 3; CPW; DA;
DA3; DAC; DAM MST, NOV, POP; DLB
227, 279; MTCW 1, 2; MTFW 2005; NFS
10, 16; RGAL 4; SFW 4; TUS; YAW

Randall, Dudley (Felker) 1914-2000 . **BLC 3;
CLC 1, 135**
See also BW 1, 3; CA 25-28R; CAAS 189;
CANR 23, 82; CP 1, 2, 3, 4, 5; DAM
MULT; DLB 41; PFS 5

Randall, Robert
See Silverberg, Robert

Ranger, Ken
See Creasey, John

Rank, Otto 1884-1939 .... **TCLC 115**

Ransom, John Crowe 1888-1974 .. **CLC 2, 4,
5, 11, 24; PC 61**
See also AMW; CA 5-8R; CAAS 49-52;
CANR 6, 34; CDALBS; CP 1, 2; DA3;
DAM POET; DLB 45, 63; EWL 3; EXPP;
MAL 5; MTCW 1, 2; MTFW 2005;
RGAL 4; TUS

Rao, Raja 1908-2006 .... **CLC 25, 56; SSC 99**
See also CA 73-76; CAAS 252; CANR 51;
CN 1, 2, 3, 4, 5, 6; DAM NOV; DLB 323;
EWL 3; MTCW 1, 2; MTFW 2005; RGEL
2; RGSF 2

Raphael, Frederic (Michael) 1931- ... **CLC 2,
14**
See also CA 1-4R; CANR 1, 86; CN 1, 2,
3, 4, 5, 6, 7; DLB 14, 319; TCLE 1:2

Raphael, Lev 1954- .... **CLC 232**
See also CA 134; CANR 72, 145; GLL 1

Ratcliffe, James P.
See Mencken, H(enry) L(ouis)

Rathbone, Julian 1935- .... **CLC 41**
See also CA 101; CANR 34, 73, 152

Rattigan, Terence (Mervyn)
1911-1977 .... **CLC 7; DC 18**
See also BRWS 7; CA 85-88; CAAS 73-76;
CBD; CDBLB 1945-1960; DAM DRAM;
DFS 8; DLB 13; IDFW 3, 4; MTCW 1,
2; MTFW 2005; RGEL 2

Ratushinskaya, Irina 1954- .... **CLC 54**
See also CA 129; CANR 68; CWW 2

Raven, Simon (Arthur Noel)
1927-2001 .... **CLC 14**
See also CA 81-84; CAAS 197; CANR 86;
CN 1, 2, 3, 4, 5, 6; DLB 271

Ravenna, Michael
See Welty, Eudora

Rawley, Callman 1903-2004
See Rakosi, Carl
See also CA 21-24R; CAAS 228; CANR
12, 32, 91

Rawlings, Marjorie Kinnan
1896-1953 .... **TCLC 4**
See also AAYA 20; AMWS 10; ANW;
BPFB 3; BYA 3; CA 137; CAAE 104;
CANR 74; CLR 63; DLB 9, 22, 102;
DLBD 17; JRDA; MAICYA 1, 2; MAL 5;
MTCW 2; MTFW 2005; RGAL 4; SATA
100; WCH; YABC 1; YAW

Ray, Satyajit 1921-1992 .... **CLC 16, 76**
See also CA 114; CAAS 137; DAM MULT

Read, Herbert Edward 1893-1968 ..... **CLC 4**
See also BRW 6; CA 85-88; CANR 25-28R;
DLB 20, 149; EWL 3; PAB; RGEL 2

Read, Piers Paul 1941- .... **CLC 4, 10, 25**
See also CA 21-24R; CANR 38, 86, 150;
CN 2, 3, 4, 5, 6, 7; DLB 14; SATA 21

Reade, Charles 1814-1884 .... **NCLC 2, 74**
See also DLB 21; RGEL 2

Reade, Hamish
See Gray, Simon (James Holliday)

Reading, Peter 1946- .... **CLC 47**
See also BRWS 8; CA 103; CANR 46, 96;
CP 5, 6, 7; DLB 40

Reaney, James 1926- .... **CLC 13**
See also CA 41-44R; 15; CANR 42; CD 5,
6; CP 1, 2, 3, 4, 5, 6, 7; DAC; DAM MST;
DLB 68; RGEL 2; SATA 43

Rebreanu, Liviu 1885-1944 .... **TCLC 28**
See also CA 165; DLB 220; EWL 3

Rechy, John 1934- ..... **CLC 1, 7, 14, 18, 107;
HLC 2**
See also CA 195; 5-8R, 195; 4; CANR 6,
32, 64, 152; CN 1, 2, 3, 4, 5, 6, 7; DAM
MULT; DLB 122, 278; DLBY 1982; HW
1, 2; INT CANR-6; LLW; MAL 5; RGAL
4

Rechy, John Francisco
See Rechy, John

Redcam, Tom 1870-1933 .... **TCLC 25**

Reddin, Keith 1956- .... **CLC 67**
See also CAD; CD 6

Redgrove, Peter (William)
1932-2003 .... **CLC 6, 41**
See also BRWS 6; CA 1-4R; CAAS 217;
CANR 3, 39, 77; CP 1, 2, 3, 4, 5, 6, 7;
DLB 40; TCLE 1:2

Redmon, Anne .... **CLC 22**
See Nightingale, Anne Redmon
See also DLBY 1986

Reed, Eliot
See Ambler, Eric

Reed, Ishmael 1938- ..... **BLC 3; CLC 2, 3, 5,
6, 13, 32, 60, 174; PC 68**
See also AFAW 1, 2; AMWS 10; BPFB 3;
BW 2, 3; CA 21-24R; CANR 25, 48, 74,
128; CN 1, 2, 3, 4, 5, 6, 7; CP 1, 2, 3, 4,
5, 6, 7; CSW; DA3; DAM MULT; DLB
2, 5, 33, 169, 227; DLBD 8; EWL 3;
LMFS 2; MAL 5; MSW; MTCW 1, 2;
MTFW 2005; PFS 6; RGAL 4; TCWW 2

Reed, John (Silas) 1887-1920 .... **TCLC 9**
See also CA 195; CAAE 106; MAL 5; TUS

Reed, Lou .... **CLC 21**
See Firbank, Louis

Reese, Lizette Woodworth
1856-1935 .... **PC 29; TCLC 181**
See also CA 180; DLB 54

Reeve, Clara 1729-1807 .... **NCLC 19**
See also DLB 39; RGEL 2

Reich, Wilhelm 1897-1957 .... **TCLC 57**
See also CA 199

Reid, Christopher (John) 1949- .... **CLC 33**
See also CA 140; CANR 89; CP 4, 5, 6, 7;
DLB 40; EWL 3

Reid, Desmond
See Moorcock, Michael

Reid Banks, Lynne 1929-
See Banks, Lynne Reid
See also AAYA 49; CA 1-4R; CANR 6, 22,
38, 87; CLR 24; CN 1, 2, 3, 7; JRDA;
MAICYA 1, 2; SATA 22, 75, 111, 165;
YAW

Reilly, William K.
See Creasey, John

Reiner, Max
See Caldwell, (Janet Miriam) Taylor
(Holland)

Reis, Ricardo
See Pessoa, Fernando (Antonio Nogueira)

Reizenstein, Elmer Leopold
See Rice, Elmer (Leopold)
See also EWL 3

Remarque, Erich Maria 1898-1970 . **CLC 21**
See also AAYA 27; BPFB 3; CA 77-80;
CAAS 29-32R; CDWLB 2; DA; DA3;
DAB; DAC; DAM MST, NOV; DLB 56;
EWL 3; EXPN; LAIT 3; MTCW 1, 2;
MTFW 2005; NFS 4; RGHL; RGWL 2, 3

Remington, Frederic S(ackrider)
1861-1909 .... **TCLC 89**
See also CA 169; CAAE 108; DLB 12, 186,
188; SATA 41; TCWW 2

Remizov, A.
See Remizov, Aleksei (Mikhailovich)

Remizov, A. M.
See Remizov, Aleksei (Mikhailovich)

Remizov, Aleksei (Mikhailovich)
1877-1957 .... **TCLC 27**
See Remizov, Alexey Mikhaylovich
See also CA 133; CAAE 125; DLB 295

Remizov, Alexey Mikhaylovich
See Remizov, Aleksei (Mikhailovich)
See also EWL 3

Renan, Joseph Ernest 1823-1892 . **NCLC 26,
145**
See also GFL 1789 to the Present

Rio, Michel 1945(?)- .... **CLC 43**
See also CA 201

Rios, Alberto 1952- .... **PC 57**
See also AAYA 66; AMWS 4; CA 113;
CANR 34, 79, 137; CP 6, 7; DLB 122;
HW 2; MTFW 2005; PFS 11

Ritsos, Giannes
See Ritsos, Yannis

Ritsos, Yannis 1909-1990 .... **CLC 6, 13, 31**
See also CA 77-80; CAAS 133; CANR 39,
61; EW 12; EWL 3; MTCW 1; RGWL 2,
3

Ritter, Erika 1948(?)- .... **CLC 52**
See also CD 5, 6; CWD

Rivera, Jose Eustasio 1889-1928 ... **TCLC 35**
See also CA 162; EWL 3; HW 1, 2; LAW

Rivera, Tomas 1935-1984 .... **HLCS 2**
See also CA 49-52; CANR 32; DLB 82;
HW 1; LLW; RGAL 4; SSFS 15; TCWW
2; WLIT 1

Rivers, Conrad Kent 1933-1968 .... **CLC 1**
See also BW 1; CA 85-88; DLB 41

Rivers, Elfrida
See Bradley, Marion Zimmer
See also GLL 1

Riverside, John
See Heinlein, Robert A.

Rizal, Jose 1861-1896 .... **NCLC 27**

Roa Bastos, Augusto 1917-2005 ...... **CLC 45;**
HLC 2
See also CA 131; CAAS 238; CWW 2;
DAM MULT; DLB 113; EWL 3; HW 1;
LAW; RGSF 2; WLIT 1

Roa Bastos, Augusto Jose Antonio
See Roa Bastos, Augusto

Robbe-Grillet, Alain 1922- .... **CLC 1, 2, 4, 6,**
8, 10, 14, 43, 128
See also BPFB 3; CA 9-12R; CANR 33,
65, 115; CWW 2; DLB 83; EW 13; EWL
3; GFL 1789 to the Present; IDFW 3, 4;
MTCW 1, 2; MTFW 2005; RGWL 2, 3;
SSFS 15

Robbins, Harold 1916-1997 .... **CLC 5**
See also BPFB 3; CA 73-76; CAAS 162;
CANR 26, 54, 112, 156; DA3; DAM
NOV; MTCW 1, 2

Robbins, Thomas Eugene 1936-
See Robbins, Tom
See also CA 81-84; CANR 29, 59, 95, 139;
CN 7; CPW; CSW; DA3; DAM NOV,
POP; MTCW 1, 2; MTFW 2005

Robbins, Tom .... **CLC 9, 32, 64**
See Robbins, Thomas Eugene
See also AAYA 32; AMWS 10; BEST 90:3;
BPFB 3; CN 3, 4, 5, 6, 7; DLBY 1980

Robbins, Trina 1938- .... **CLC 21**
See also AAYA 61; CA 128; CANR 152

Robert de Boron fl. 12th cent. - .... **CMLC 94**

Roberts, Charles G(eorge) D(ouglas)
1860-1943 .... **SSC 91; TCLC 8**
See also CA 188; CAAE 105; CLR 33;
CWRI 5; DLB 92; RGEL 2; RGSF 2;
SATA 88; SATA-Brief 29

Roberts, Elizabeth Madox
1886-1941 .... **TCLC 68**
See also CA 166; CAAE 111; CLR 100;
CWRI 5; DLB 9, 54, 102; RGAL 4;
RHW; SATA 33; SATA-Brief 27; TCWW
2; WCH

Roberts, Kate 1891-1985 .... **CLC 15**
See also CA 107; CAAS 116; DLB 319

Roberts, Keith (John Kingston)
1935-2000 .... **CLC 14**
See also BRWS 10; CA 25-28R; CANR 46;
DLB 261; SFW 4

Roberts, Kenneth (Lewis)
1885-1957 .... **TCLC 23**
See also CA 199; CAAE 109; DLB 9; MAL
5; RGAL 4; RHW

Roberts, Michele 1949- .... **CLC 48, 178**
See also CA 115; CANR 58, 120, 164; CN
6, 7; DLB 231; FW

Roberts, Michele Brigitte
See Roberts, Michele

Robertson, Ellis
See Ellison, Harlan; Silverberg, Robert

Robertson, Thomas William
1829-1871 .... **NCLC 35**
See Robertson, Tom
See also DAM DRAM

Robertson, Tom
See Robertson, Thomas William
See also RGEL 2

Robeson, Kenneth
See Dent, Lester

Robinson, Edwin Arlington
1869-1935 .... **PC 1, 35; TCLC 5, 101**
See also AAYA 72; AMW; CA 133; CAAE
104; CDALB 1865-1917; DA; DAC;
DAM MST, POET; DLB 54; EWL 3;
EXPP; MAL 5; MTCW 1, 2; MTFW
2005; PAB; PFS 4; RGAL 4; WP

Robinson, Henry Crabb
1775-1867 .... **NCLC 15**
See also DLB 107

Robinson, Jill 1936- .... **CLC 10**
See also CA 102; CANR 120; INT CA-102

Robinson, Kim Stanley 1952- .... **CLC 34**
See also AAYA 26; CA 126; CANR 113,
139; CN 6, 7; MTFW 2005; SATA 109;
SCFW 2; SFW 4

Robinson, Lloyd
See Silverberg, Robert

Robinson, Marilynne 1944- ...... **CLC 25, 180**
See also AAYA 69; CA 116; CANR 80, 140;
CN 4, 5, 6, 7; DLB 206; MTFW 2005;
NFS 24

Robinson, Mary 1758-1800 .... **NCLC 142**
See also BRWS 13; DLB 158; FW

Robinson, Smokey .... **CLC 21**
See Robinson, William, Jr.

Robinson, William, Jr. 1940-
See Robinson, Smokey
See also CAAE 116

Robison, Mary 1949- .... **CLC 42, 98**
See also CA 116; CAAE 113; CANR 87;
CN 4, 5, 6, 7; DLB 130; INT CA-116;
RGSF 2

Roches, Catherine des 1542-1587 ...... **LC 117**
See also DLB 327

Rochester
See Wilmot, John
See also RGEL 2

Rod, Edouard 1857-1910 .... **TCLC 52**

Roddenberry, Eugene Wesley 1921-1991
See Roddenberry, Gene
See also CA 110; CAAS 135; CANR 37;
SATA 45; SATA-Obit 69

Roddenberry, Gene .... **CLC 17**
See Roddenberry, Eugene Wesley
See also AAYA 5; SATA-Obit 69

Rodgers, Mary 1931- .... **CLC 12**
See also BYA 5; CA 49-52; CANR 8, 55,
90; CLR 20; CWRI 5; INT CANR-8;
JRDA; MAICYA 1, 2; SATA 8, 130

Rodgers, W(illiam) R(obert)
1909-1969 .... **CLC 7**
See also CA 85-88; DLB 20; RGEL 2

Rodman, Eric
See Silverberg, Robert

Rodman, Howard 1920(?)-1985 .... **CLC 65**
See also CAAS 118

Rodman, Maia
See Wojciechowska, Maia (Teresa)

Rodo, Jose Enrique 1871(?)-1917 .... **HLCS 2**
See also CA 178; EWL 3; HW 2; LAW

Rodolph, Utto
See Ouologuem, Yambo

Rodriguez, Claudio 1934-1999 .... **CLC 10**
See also CA 188; DLB 134

Rodriguez, Richard 1944- .... **CLC 155; HLC**
2
See also AMWS 14; CA 110; CANR 66,
116; DAM MULT; DLB 82, 256; HW 1,
2; LAIT 5; LLW; MTFW 2005; NCFS 3;
WLIT 1

Roelvaag, O(le) E(dvart) 1876-1931
See Rolvaag, O(le) E(dvart)
See also AAYA 75; CA 171; CAAE 117

Roethke, Theodore (Huebner)
1908-1963 .... **CLC 1, 3, 8, 11, 19, 46,**
101; PC 15
See also AMW; CA 81-84; CABS 2;
CDALB 1941-1968; DA3; DAM POET;
DLB 5, 206; EWL 3; EXPP; MAL 5;
MTCW 1, 2; PAB; PFS 3; RGAL 4; WP

Rogers, Carl R(ansom)
1902-1987 .... **TCLC 125**
See also CA 1-4R; CAAS 121; CANR 1,
18; MTCW 1

Rogers, Samuel 1763-1855 .... **NCLC 69**
See also DLB 93; RGEL 2

Rogers, Thomas 1927-2007 .... **CLC 57**
See also CA 89-92; CAAS 259; CANR 163;
INT CA-89-92

Rogers, Thomas Hunton
See Rogers, Thomas

Rogers, Will(iam Penn Adair)
1879-1935 .... **NNAL; TCLC 8, 71**
See also CA 144; CAAE 105; DA3; DAM
MULT; DLB 11; MTCW 2

Rogin, Gilbert 1929- .... **CLC 18**
See also CA 65-68; CANR 15

Rohan, Koda
See Koda Shigeyuki

Rohlfs, Anna Katharine Green
See Green, Anna Katharine

Rohmer, Eric .... **CLC 16**
See Scherer, Jean-Marie Maurice

Rohmer, Sax .... **TCLC 28**
See Ward, Arthur Henry Sarsfield
See also DLB 70; MSW; SUFW

Roiphe, Anne 1935- .... **CLC 3, 9**
See also CA 89-92; CANR 45, 73, 138;
DLBY 1980; INT CA-89-92

Roiphe, Anne Richardson
See Roiphe, Anne

Rojas, Fernando de 1475-1541 ... **HLCS 1, 2;**
LC 23
See also DLB 286; RGWL 2, 3

Rojas, Gonzalo 1917- .... **HLCS 2**
See also CA 178; HW 2; LAWS 1

Roland (de la Platiere), Marie-Jeanne
1754-1793 .... **LC 98**
See also DLB 314

Rolfe, Frederick (William Serafino Austin
Lewis Mary) 1860-1913 .... **TCLC 12**
See Al Siddik
See also CA 210; CAAE 107; DLB 34, 156;
RGEL 2

Rolland, Romain 1866-1944 .... **TCLC 23**
See also CA 197; CAAE 118; DLB 65, 284,
332; EWL 3; GFL 1789 to the Present;
RGWL 2, 3

Rolle, Richard c. 1300-c. 1349 ...... **CMLC 21**
See also DLB 146; LMFS 1; RGEL 2

Rolvaag, O(le) E(dvart) .... **TCLC 17**
See Roelvaag, O(le) E(dvart)
See also DLB 9, 212; MAL 5; NFS 5;
RGAL 4

Romain Arnaud, Saint
See Aragon, Louis

Romains, Jules 1885-1972 .... **CLC 7**
See also CA 85-88; CANR 34; DLB 65,
321; EWL 3; GFL 1789 to the Present;
MTCW 1

Romero, Jose Ruben 1890-1952 .... **TCLC 14**
See also CA 131; CAAE 114; EWL 3; HW
1; LAW

Ronsard, Pierre de 1524-1585 . **LC 6, 54; PC
11**
See also DLB 327; EW 2; GFL Beginnings
to 1789; RGWL 2, 3; TWA

Rooke, Leon 1934- .... **CLC 25, 34**
See also CA 25-28R; CANR 23, 53; CCA
1; CPW; DAM POP

Roosevelt, Franklin Delano
1882-1945 .... **TCLC 93**
See also CA 173; CAAE 116; LAIT 3

Roosevelt, Theodore 1858-1919 ..... **TCLC 69**
See also CA 170; CAAE 115; DLB 47, 186,
275

Roper, William 1498-1578 .... **LC 10**

Roquelaure, A. N.
See Rice, Anne

Rosa, Joao Guimaraes 1908-1967 ... **CLC 23;
HLCS 1**
See Guimaraes Rosa, Joao
See also CAAS 89-92; DLB 113, 307; EWL
3; WLIT 1

Rose, Wendy 1948- . **CLC 85; NNAL; PC 13**
See also CA 53-56; CANR 5, 51; CWP;
DAM MULT; DLB 175; PFS 13; RGAL
4; SATA 12

Rosen, R. D.
See Rosen, Richard (Dean)

Rosen, Richard (Dean) 1949- .... **CLC 39**
See also CA 77-80; CANR 62, 120; CMW
4; INT CANR-30

Rosenberg, Isaac 1890-1918 .... **TCLC 12**
See also BRW 6; CA 188; CAAE 107; DLB
20, 216; EWL 3; PAB; RGEL 2

Rosenblatt, Joe .... **CLC 15**
See Rosenblatt, Joseph
See also CP 3, 4, 5, 6, 7

Rosenblatt, Joseph 1933-
See Rosenblatt, Joe
See also CA 89-92; CP 1, 2; INT CA-89-92

Rosenfeld, Samuel
See Tzara, Tristan

Rosenstock, Sami
See Tzara, Tristan

Rosenstock, Samuel
See Tzara, Tristan

Rosenthal, M(acha) L(ouis)
1917-1996 .... **CLC 28**
See also CA 1-4R; 6; CAAS 152; CANR 4,
51; CP 1, 2, 3, 4, 5, 6; DLB 5; SATA 59

Ross, Barnaby
See Dannay, Frederic; Lee, Manfred B.

Ross, Bernard L.
See Follett, Ken

Ross, J. H.
See Lawrence, T(homas) E(dward)

Ross, John Hume
See Lawrence, T(homas) E(dward)

Ross, Martin 1862-1915
See Martin, Violet Florence
See also DLB 135; GLL 2; RGEL 2; RGSF
2

Ross, (James) Sinclair 1908-1996 ... **CLC 13;
SSC 24**
See also CA 73-76; CANR 81; CN 1, 2, 3,
4, 5, 6; DAC; DAM MST; DLB 88;
RGEL 2; RGSF 2; TCWW 1, 2

Rossetti, Christina 1830-1894 ... **NCLC 2, 50,
66, 186; PC 7; WLC 5**
See also AAYA 51; BRW 5; BYA 4; CLR
115; DA; DA3; DAB; DAC; DAM MST,
POET; DLB 35, 163, 240; EXPP; FL 1:3;
LATS 1:1; MAICYA 1, 2; PFS 10, 14;
RGEL 2; SATA 20; TEA; WCH

Rossetti, Christina Georgina
See Rossetti, Christina

Rossetti, Dante Gabriel 1828-1882 . **NCLC 4,
77; PC 44; WLC 5**
See also AAYA 51; BRW 5; CDBLB 1832-
1890; DA; DAB; DAC; DAM MST,
POET; DLB 35; EXPP; RGEL 2; TEA

Rossi, Cristina Peri
See Peri Rossi, Cristina

Rossi, Jean-Baptiste 1931-2003
See Japrisot, Sebastien
See also CA 201; CAAS 215

Rossner, Judith 1935-2005 .... **CLC 6, 9, 29**
See also AITN 2; BEST 90:3; BPFB 3; CA
17-20R; CAAS 242; CANR 18, 51, 73;
CN 4, 5, 6, 7; DLB 6; INT CANR-18;
MAL 5; MTCW 1, 2; MTFW 2005

Rossner, Judith Perelman
See Rossner, Judith

Rostand, Edmond (Eugene Alexis)
1868-1918 .... **DC 10; TCLC 6, 37**
See also CA 126; CAAE 104; DA; DA3;
DAB; DAC; DAM DRAM, MST; DFS 1;
DLB 192; LAIT 1; MTCW 1; RGWL 2,
3; TWA

Roth, Henry 1906-1995 ..... **CLC 2, 6, 11, 104**
See also AMWS 9; CA 11-12; CAAS 149;
CANR 38, 63; CAP 1; CN 1, 2, 3, 4, 5, 6;
DA3; DLB 28; EWL 3; MAL 5; MTCW
1, 2; MTFW 2005; RGAL 4

Roth, (Moses) Joseph 1894-1939 ... **TCLC 33**
See also CA 160; DLB 85; EWL 3; RGWL
2, 3

Roth, Philip 1933- ... **CLC 1, 2, 3, 4, 6, 9, 15,
22, 31, 47, 66, 86, 119, 201; SSC 26,
102; WLC 5**
See also AAYA 67; AMWR 2; AMWS 3;
BEST 90:3; BPFB 3; CA 1-4R; CANR 1,
22, 36, 55, 89, 132; CDALB 1968-1988;
CN 3, 4, 5, 6, 7; CPW 1; DA; DA3; DAB;
DAC; DAM MST, NOV, POP; DLB 2,
28, 173; DLBY 1982; EWL 3; MAL 5;
MTCW 1, 2; MTFW 2005; NFS 25;
RGAL 4; RGHL; RGSF 2; SSFS 12, 18;
TUS

Roth, Philip Milton
See Roth, Philip

Rothenberg, Jerome 1931- .... **CLC 6, 57**
See also CA 45-48; CANR 1, 106; CP 1, 2,
3, 4, 5, 6, 7; DLB 5, 193

Rotter, Pat .... **CLC 65**

Roumain, Jacques (Jean Baptiste)
1907-1944 .... **BLC 3; TCLC 19**
See also BW 1; CA 125; CAAE 117; DAM
MULT; EWL 3

Rourke, Constance Mayfield
1885-1941 .... **TCLC 12**
See also CA 200; CAAE 107; MAL 5;
YABC 1

Rousseau, Jean-Baptiste 1671-1741 ...... **LC 9**

Rousseau, Jean-Jacques 1712-1778 .... **LC 14,
36, 122; WLC 5**
See also DA; DA3; DAB; DAC; DAM
MST; DLB 314; EW 4; GFL Beginnings
to 1789; LMFS 1; RGWL 2, 3; TWA

Roussel, Raymond 1877-1933 .... **TCLC 20**
See also CA 201; CAAE 117; EWL 3; GFL
1789 to the Present

Rovit, Earl (Herbert) 1927- .... **CLC 7**
See also CA 5-8R; CANR 12

Rowe, Elizabeth Singer 1674-1737 ..... **LC 44**
See also DLB 39, 95

Rowe, Nicholas 1674-1718 .... **LC 8**
See also DLB 84; RGEL 2

Rowlandson, Mary 1637(?)-1678 .... **LC 66**
See also DLB 24, 200; RGAL 4

Rowley, Ames Dorrance
See Lovecraft, H. P.

Rowley, William 1585(?)-1626 ... **LC 100, 123**
See also DFS 22; DLB 58; RGEL 2

Rowling, J.K. 1965- .... **CLC 137, 217**
See also AAYA 34; BYA 11, 13, 14; CA
173; CANR 128, 157; CLR 66, 80, 112;
MAICYA 2; MTFW 2005; SATA 109,
174; SUFW 2

Rowling, Joanne Kathleen
See Rowling, J.K.

Rowson, Susanna Haswell
1762(?)-1824 .... **NCLC 5, 69, 182**
See also AMWS 15; DLB 37, 200; RGAL 4

Roy, Arundhati 1960(?)- .... **CLC 109, 210**
See also CA 163; CANR 90, 126; CN 7;
DLB 323, 326; DLBY 1997; EWL 3;
LATS 1:2; MTFW 2005; NFS 22; WWE
1

Roy, Gabrielle 1909-1983 .... **CLC 10, 14**
See also CA 53-56; CAAS 110; CANR 5,
61; CCA 1; DAB; DAC; DAM MST;
DLB 68; EWL 3; MTCW 1; RGWL 2, 3;
SATA 104; TCLE 1:2

Royko, Mike 1932-1997 .... **CLC 109**
See also CA 89-92; CAAS 157; CANR 26,
111; CPW

Rozanov, Vasilii Vasil'evich
See Rozanov, Vassili
See also DLB 295

Rozanov, Vasily Vasilyevich
See Rozanov, Vassili
See also EWL 3

Rozanov, Vassili 1856-1919 .... **TCLC 104**
See Rozanov, Vasilii Vasil'evich; Rozanov,
Vasily Vasilyevich

Rozewicz, Tadeusz 1921- ...... **CLC 9, 23, 139**
See also CA 108; CANR 36, 66; CWW 2;
DA3; DAM POET; DLB 232; EWL 3;
MTCW 1, 2; MTFW 2005; RGHL;
RGWL 3

Ruark, Gibbons 1941- .... **CLC 3**
See also CA 33-36R; 23; CANR 14, 31, 57;
DLB 120

Rubens, Bernice (Ruth) 1923-2004 . **CLC 19,
31**
See also CA 25-28R; CAAS 232; CANR
33, 65, 128; CN 1, 2, 3, 4, 5, 6, 7; DLB
14, 207, 326; MTCW 1

Rubin, Harold
See Robbins, Harold

Rudkin, (James) David 1936- .... **CLC 14**
See also CA 89-92; CBD; CD 5, 6; DLB 13

Rudnik, Raphael 1933- .... **CLC 7**
See also CA 29-32R

Ruffian, M.
See Hasek, Jaroslav (Matej Frantisek)

Ruiz, Jose Martinez .... **CLC 11**
See Martinez Ruiz, Jose

Ruiz, Juan c. 1283-c. 1350 .... **CMLC 66**

Rukeyser, Muriel 1913-1980 . **CLC 6, 10, 15,
27; PC 12**
See also AMWS 6; CA 5-8R; CAAS 93-96;
CANR 26, 60; CP 1, 2, 3; DA3; DAM
POET; DLB 48; EWL 3; FW; GLL 2;
MAL 5; MTCW 1, 2; PFS 10; RGAL 4;
SATA-Obit 22

Rule, Jane (Vance) 1931- .... **CLC 27**
See also CA 25-28R; 18; CANR 12, 87;
CN 4, 5, 6, 7; DLB 60; FW

Rulfo, Juan 1918-1986 .. **CLC 8, 80; HLC 1;
SSC 25**
See also CA 85-88; CAAS 118; CANR 26;
CDWLB 3; DAM MULT; DLB 113; EWL
3; HW 1, 2; LAW; MTCW 1, 2; RGSF 2;
RGWL 2, 3; WLIT 1

Rumi, Jalal al-Din 1207-1273 ...... **CMLC 20;
PC 45**
See also AAYA 64; RGWL 2, 3; WLIT 6;
WP

Salinger, J. D. 1919- ...... **CLC 1, 3, 8, 12, 55, 56, 138, 243; SSC 2, 28, 65; WLC 5**
See also AAYA 2, 36; AMW; AMWC 1; BPFB 3; CA 5-8R; CANR 39, 129; CDALB 1941-1968; CLR 18; CN 1, 2, 3, 4, 5, 6, 7; CPW 1; DA; DA3; DAB; DAC; DAM MST, NOV, POP; DLB 2, 102, 173; EWL 3; EXPN; LAIT 4; MAICYA 1, 2; MAL 5; MTCW 1, 2; MTFW 2005; NFS 1; RGAL 4; RGSF 2; SATA 67; SSFS 17; TUS; WYA; YAW
Salisbury, John
See Caute, (John) David
Sallust c. 86B.C.-35B.C. .... **CMLC 68**
See also AW 2; CDWLB 1; DLB 211; RGWL 2, 3
Salter, James 1925- .. **CLC 7, 52, 59; SSC 58**
See also AMWS 9; CA 73-76; CANR 107, 160; DLB 130; SSFS 25
Saltus, Edgar (Everton) 1855-1921 . **TCLC 8**
See also CAAE 105; DLB 202; RGAL 4
Saltykov, Mikhail Evgrafovich
1826-1889 .... **NCLC 16**
See also DLB 238;
Saltykov-Shchedrin, N.
See Saltykov, Mikhail Evgrafovich
Samarakis, Andonis
See Samarakis, Antonis
See also EWL 3
Samarakis, Antonis 1919-2003 .... **CLC 5**
See Samarakis, Andonis
See also CA 25-28R; 16; CAAS 224; CANR 36
Sanchez, Florencio 1875-1910 .... **TCLC 37**
See also CA 153; DLB 305; EWL 3; HW 1; LAW
Sanchez, Luis Rafael 1936- .... **CLC 23**
See also CA 128; DLB 305; EWL 3; HW 1; WLIT 1
Sanchez, Sonia 1934- .... **BLC 3; CLC 5, 116, 215; PC 9**
See also BW 2, 3; CA 33-36R; CANR 24, 49, 74, 115; CLR 18; CP 2, 3, 4, 5, 6, 7; CSW; CWP; DA3; DAM MULT; DLB 41; DLBD 8; EWL 3; MAICYA 1, 2; MAL 5; MTCW 1, 2; MTFW 2005; PFS 26; SATA 22, 136; WP
Sancho, Ignatius 1729-1780 .... **LC 84**
Sand, George 1804-1876 ..... **NCLC 2, 42, 57, 174; WLC 5**
See also DA; DA3; DAB; DAC; DAM MST, NOV; DLB 119, 192; EW 6; FL 1:3; FW; GFL 1789 to the Present; RGWL 2, 3; TWA
Sandburg, Carl (August) 1878-1967 . **CLC 1, 4, 10, 15, 35; PC 2, 41; WLC 5**
See also AAYA 24; AMW; BYA 1, 3; CA 5-8R; CAAS 25-28R; CANR 35; CDALB 1865-1917; CLR 67; DA; DA3; DAB; DAC; DAM MST, POET; DLB 17, 54, 284; EWL 3; EXPP; LAIT 2; MAICYA 1, 2; MAL 5; MTCW 1, 2; MTFW 2005; PAB; PFS 3, 6, 12; RGAL 4; SATA 8; TUS; WCH; WP; WYA
Sandburg, Charles
See Sandburg, Carl (August)
Sandburg, Charles A.
See Sandburg, Carl (August)
Sanders, (James) Ed(ward) 1939- .... **CLC 53**
See Sanders, Edward
See also BG 1:3; CA 13-16R; 21; CANR 13, 44, 78; CP 1, 2, 3, 4, 5, 6, 7; DAM POET; DLB 16, 244
Sanders, Edward
See Sanders, (James) Ed(ward)
See also DLB 244
Sanders, Lawrence 1920-1998 .... **CLC 41**
See also BEST 89:4; BPFB 3; CA 81-84; CAAS 165; CANR 33, 62; CMW 4; CPW; DA3; DAM POP; MTCW 1

Sanders, Noah
See Blount, Roy (Alton), Jr.
Sanders, Winston P.
See Anderson, Poul
Sandoz, Mari(e Susette) 1900-1966 .. **CLC 28**
See also CA 1-4R; CAAS 25-28R; CANR 17, 64; DLB 9, 212; LAIT 2; MTCW 1, 2; SATA 5; TCWW 1, 2
Sandys, George 1578-1644 .... **LC 80**
See also DLB 24, 121
Saner, Reg(inald Anthony) 1931- .... **CLC 9**
See also CA 65-68; CP 3, 4, 5, 6, 7
Sankara 788-820 .... **CMLC 32**
Sannazaro, Jacopo 1456(?)-1530 .... **LC 8**
See also RGWL 2, 3; WLIT 7
Sansom, William 1912-1976 . **CLC 2, 6; SSC 21**
See also CA 5-8R; CAAS 65-68; CANR 42; CN 1, 2; DAM NOV; DLB 139; EWL 3; MTCW 1; RGEL 2; RGSF 2
Santayana, George 1863-1952 .... **TCLC 40**
See also AMW; CA 194; CAAE 115; DLB 54, 71, 246, 270; DLBD 13; EWL 3; MAL 5; RGAL 4; TUS
Santiago, Danny .... **CLC 33**
See James, Daniel (Lewis)
See also DLB 122
Santillana, Inigo Lopez de Mendoza, Marques de 1398-1458 .... **LC 111**
See also DLB 286
Santmyer, Helen Hooven
1895-1986 .... **CLC 33; TCLC 133**
See also CA 1-4R; CAAS 118; CANR 15, 33; DLBY 1984; MTCW 1; RHW
Santoka, Taneda 1882-1940 .... **TCLC 72**
Santos, Bienvenido N(uqui)
1911-1996 ... **AAL; CLC 22; TCLC 156**
See also CA 101; CAAS 151; CANR 19, 46; CP 1; DAM MULT; DLB 312; EWL; RGAL 4; SSFS 19
Sapir, Edward 1884-1939 .... **TCLC 108**
See also CA 211; DLB 92
Sapper .... **TCLC 44**
See McNeile, Herman Cyril
Sapphire
See Sapphire, Brenda
Sapphire, Brenda 1950- .... **CLC 99**
Sappho fl. 6th cent. B.C.- ... **CMLC 3, 67; PC 5**
See also CDWLB 1; DA3; DAM POET; DLB 176; FL 1:1; PFS 20; RGWL 2, 3; WLIT 8; WP
Saramago, Jose 1922- ..... **CLC 119; HLCS 1**
See also CA 153; CANR 96, 164; CWW 2; DLB 287, 332; EWL 3; LATS 1:2; SSFS 23
Sarduy, Severo 1937-1993 .... **CLC 6, 97; HLCS 2; TCLC 167**
See also CA 89-92; CAAS 142; CANR 58, 81; CWW 2; DLB 113; EWL 3; HW 1, 2; LAW
Sargeson, Frank 1903-1982 ..... **CLC 31; SSC 99**
See also CA 25-28R; CAAS 106; CANR 38, 79; CN 1, 2, 3; EWL 3; GLL 2; RGEL 2; RGSF 2; SSFS 20
Sarmiento, Domingo Faustino
1811-1888 .... **HLCS 2; NCLC 123**
See also LAW; WLIT 1
Sarmiento, Felix Ruben Garcia
See Dario, Ruben
Saro-Wiwa, Ken(ule Beeson)
1941-1995 .... **CLC 114**
See also BW 2; CA 142; CAAS 150; CANR 60; DLB 157

Saroyan, William 1908-1981 ... **CLC 1, 8, 10, 29, 34, 56; SSC 21; TCLC 137; WLC 5**
See also AAYA 66; CA 5-8R; CAAS 103; CAD; CANR 30; CDALBS; CN 1, 2; DA; DA3; DAB; DAC; DAM DRAM, MST, NOV; DFS 17; DLB 7, 9, 86; DLBY 1981; EWL 3; LAIT 4; MAL 5; MTCW 1, 2; MTFW 2005; RGAL 4; RGSF 2; SATA 23; SATA-Obit 24; SSFS 14; TUS
Sarraute, Nathalie 1900-1999 .... **CLC 1, 2, 4, 8, 10, 31, 80; TCLC 145**
See also BPFB 3; CA 9-12R; CAAS 187; CANR 23, 66, 134; CWW 2; DLB 83, 321; EW 12; EWL 3; GFL 1789 to the Present; MTCW 1, 2; MTFW 2005; RGWL 2, 3
Sarton, May 1912-1995 ... **CLC 4, 14, 49, 91; PC 39; TCLC 120**
See also AMWS 8; CA 1-4R; CAAS 149; CANR 1, 34, 55, 116; CN 1, 2, 3, 4, 5, 6; CP 1, 2, 3, 4, 5, 6; DAM POET; DLB 48; DLBY 1981; EWL 3; FW; INT CANR-34; MAL 5; MTCW 1, 2; MTFW 2005; RGAL 4; SATA 36; SATA-Obit 86; TUS
Sartre, Jean-Paul 1905-1980 . **CLC 1, 4, 7, 9, 13, 18, 24, 44, 50, 52; DC 3; SSC 32; WLC 5**
See also AAYA 62; CA 9-12R; CAAS 97-100; CANR 21; DA; DA3; DAB; DAC; DAM DRAM, MST, NOV; DFS 5; DLB 72, 296, 321, 332; EW 12; EWL 3; GFL 1789 to the Present; LMFS 2; MTCW 1, 2; MTFW 2005; NFS 21; RGHL; RGSF 2; RGWL 2, 3; SSFS 9; TWA
Sassoon, Siegfried (Lorraine)
1886-1967 .... **CLC 36, 130; PC 12**
See also BRW 6; CA 104; CAAS 25-28R; CANR 36; DAB; DAM MST, NOV, POET; DLB 20, 191; DLBD 18; EWL 3; MTCW 1, 2; MTFW 2005; PAB; RGEL 2; TEA
Satterfield, Charles
See Pohl, Frederik
Satyremont
See Peret, Benjamin
Saul, John (W. III) 1942- .... **CLC 46**
See also AAYA 10, 62; BEST 90:4; CA 81-84; CANR 16, 40, 81; CPW; DAM NOV, POP; HGG; SATA 98
Saunders, Caleb
See Heinlein, Robert A.
Saura (Atares), Carlos 1932-1998 .... **CLC 20**
See also CA 131; CAAE 114; CANR 79; HW 1
Sauser, Frederic Louis
See Sauser-Hall, Frederic
Sauser-Hall, Frederic 1887-1961 ...... **CLC 18**
See Cendrars, Blaise
See also CA 102; CAAS 93-96; CANR 36, 62; MTCW 1
Saussure, Ferdinand de
1857-1913 .... **TCLC 49**
See also DLB 242
Savage, Catharine
See Brosman, Catharine Savage
Savage, Richard 1697(?)-1743 .... **LC 96**
See also DLB 95; RGEL 2
Savage, Thomas 1915-2003 .... **CLC 40**
See also CA 132; 15; CAAE 126; CAAS 218; CN 6, 7; INT CA-132; SATA-Obit 147; TCWW 2
Savan, Glenn 1953-2003 .... **CLC 50**
See also CA 225
Sax, Robert
See Johnson, Robert
Saxo Grammaticus c. 1150-c.
1222 .... **CMLC 58**
Saxton, Robert
See Johnson, Robert

Shanley, John Patrick 1950- .... **CLC 75**
See also AAYA 74; AMWS 14; CA 133; CAAE 128; CAD; CANR 83, 154; CD 5, 6; DFS 23

Shapcott, Thomas W(illiam) 1935- .. **CLC 38**
See also CA 69-72; CANR 49, 83, 103; CP 1, 2, 3, 4, 5, 6, 7; DLB 289

Shapiro, Jane 1942- .... **CLC 76**
See also CA 196

Shapiro, Karl 1913-2000 ... **CLC 4, 8, 15, 53; PC 25**
See also AMWS 2; CA 1-4R; 6; CAAS 188; CANR 1, 36, 66; CP 1, 2, 3, 4, 5, 6; DLB 48; EWL 3; EXPP; MAL 5; MTCW 1, 2; MTFW 2005; PFS 3; RGAL 4

Sharp, William 1855-1905 .... **TCLC 39**
See Macleod, Fiona
See also CA 160; DLB 156; RGEL 2

Sharpe, Thomas Ridley 1928-
See Sharpe, Tom
See also CA 122; CAAE 114; CANR 85; INT CA-122

Sharpe, Tom .... **CLC 36**
See Sharpe, Thomas Ridley
See also CN 4, 5, 6, 7; DLB 14, 231

Shatrov, Mikhail .... **CLC 59**

Shaw, Bernard
See Shaw, George Bernard
See also DLB 10, 57, 190

Shaw, G. Bernard
See Shaw, George Bernard

Shaw, George Bernard 1856-1950 ..... **DC 23; TCLC 3, 9, 21, 45; WLC 5**
See Shaw, Bernard
See also AAYA 61; BRW 6; BRWC 1; BRWR 2; CA 128; CAAE 104; CDBLB 1914-1945; DA; DA3; DAB; DAC; DAM DRAM, MST; DFS 1, 3, 6, 11, 19, 22; DLB 332; EWL 3; LAIT 3; LATS 1:1; MTCW 1, 2; MTFW 2005; RGEL 2; TEA; WLIT 4

Shaw, Henry Wheeler 1818-1885 .. **NCLC 15**
See also DLB 11; RGAL 4

Shaw, Irwin 1913-1984 .... **CLC 7, 23, 34**
See also AITN 1; BPFB 3; CA 13-16R; CAAS 112; CANR 21; CDALB 1941-1968; CN 1, 2, 3; CPW; DAM DRAM; POP; DLB 6, 102; DLBY 1984; MAL 5; MTCW 1, 21; MTFW 2005

Shaw, Robert (Archibald)
1927-1978 .... **CLC 5**
See also AITN 1; CA 1-4R; CAAS 81-84; CANR 4; CN 1, 2; DLB 13, 14

Shaw, T. E.
See Lawrence, T(homas) E(dward)

Shawn, Wallace 1943- .... **CLC 41**
See also CA 112; CAD; CD 5, 6; DLB 266

Shaykh, al- Hanan
See al-Shaykh, Hanan
See also CWW 2; EWL 3

Shchedrin, N.
See Saltykov, Mikhail Evgrafovich

Shea, Lisa 1953- .... **CLC 86**
See also CA 147

Sheed, Wilfrid (John Joseph) 1930- . **CLC 2, 4, 10, 53**
See also CA 65-68; CANR 30, 66; CN 1, 2, 3, 4, 5, 6, 7; DLB 6; MAL 5; MTCW 1, 2; MTFW 2005

Sheehy, Gail 1937- .... **CLC 171**
See also CA 49-52; CANR 1, 33, 55, 92; CPW; MTCW 1

Sheldon, Alice Hastings Bradley
1915(?)-1987
See Tiptree, James, Jr.
See also CA 108; CAAS 122; CANR 34; INT CA-108; MTCW 1

Sheldon, John
See Bloch, Robert (Albert)

Sheldon, Walter J(ames) 1917-1996
See Queen, Ellery
See also AITN 1; CA 25-28R; CANR 10

Shelley, Mary Wollstonecraft (Godwin)
1797-1851 .... **NCLC 14, 59, 103, 170; SSC 92; WLC 5**
See also AAYA 20; BPFB 3; BRW 3; BRWC 2; BRWS 3; BYA 5; CDBLB 1789-1832; DA; DA3; DAB; DAC; DAM MST, NOV; DLB 110, 116, 159, 178; EXPN; FL 1:3; GL 3; HGG; LAIT 1; LMFS 1, 2; NFS 1; RGEL 2; SATA 29; SCFW 1, 2; SFW 4; TEA; WLIT 3

Shelley, Percy Bysshe 1792-1822 .. **NCLC 18, 93, 143, 175; PC 14, 67; WLC 5**
See also AAYA 61; BRW 4; BRWR 1; CDBLB 1789-1832; DA; DA3; DAB; DAC; DAM MST, POET; DLB 96, 110, 158; EXPP; LMFS 1; PAB; PFS 2; RGEL 2; TEA; WLIT 3; WP

Shepard, James R.
See Shepard, Jim

Shepard, Jim 1956- .... **CLC 36**
See also AAYA 73; CA 137; CANR 59, 104, 160; SATA 90, 164

Shepard, Lucius 1947- .... **CLC 34**
See also CA 141; CAAE 128; CANR 81, 124; HGG; SCFW 2; SFW 4; SUFW 2

Shepard, Sam 1943- .... **CLC 4, 6, 17, 34, 41, 44, 169; DC 5**
See also AAYA 1, 58; AMWS 3; CA 69-72; CABS 3; CAD; CANR 22, 120, 140; CD 5, 6; DA3; DAM DRAM; DFS 3, 6, 7, 14; DLB 7, 212; EWL 3; IDFW 3, 4; MAL 5; MTCW 1, 2; MTFW 2005; RGAL 4

Shepherd, Jean (Parker)
1921-1999 .... **TCLC 177**
See also AAYA 69; AITN 2; CA 77-80; CAAS 187

Shepherd, Michael
See Ludlum, Robert

Sherburne, Zoa (Lillian Morin)
1912-1995 .... **CLC 30**
See also AAYA 13; CA 1-4R; CAAS 176; CANR 3, 37; MAICYA 1, 2; SAAS 18; SATA 3; YAW

Sheridan, Frances 1724-1766 .... **LC 7**
See also DLB 39, 84

Sheridan, Richard Brinsley
1751-1816 . **DC 1; NCLC 5, 91; WLC 5**
See also BRW 3; CDBLB 1660-1789; DA; DAB; DAC; DAM DRAM, MST; DFS 15; DLB 89; WLIT 3

Sherman, Jonathan Marc 1968- .... **CLC 55**
See also CA 230

Sherman, Martin 1941(?)- .... **CLC 19**
See also CA 123; CAAE 116; CAD; CANR 86; CD 5, 6; DFS 20; DLB 228; GLL 1; IDTP; RGHL

Sherwin, Judith Johnson
See Johnson, Judith (Emlyn)
See also CANR 85; CP 2, 3, 4, 5; CWP

Sherwood, Frances 1940- .... **CLC 81**
See also CA 220; 146, 220; CANR 158

Sherwood, Robert E(mmet)
1896-1955 .... **TCLC 3**
See also CA 153; CAAE 104; CANR 86; DAM DRAM; DFS 11, 15, 17; DLB 7, 26, 249; IDFW 3, 4; MAL 5; RGAL 4

Shestov, Lev 1866-1938 .... **TCLC 56**

Shevchenko, Taras 1814-1861 .... **NCLC 54**

Shiel, M(atthew) P(hipps)
1865-1947 .... **TCLC 8**
See Holmes, Gordon
See also CA 160; CAAE 106; DLB 153; HGG; MTCW 2; MTFW 2005; SCFW 1, 2; SFW 4; SUFW

Shields, Carol 1935-2003 .. **CLC 91, 113, 193**
See also AMWS 7; CA 81-84; CAAS 218; CANR 51, 74, 98, 133; CCA 1; CN 6, 7; CPW; DA3; DAC; DLB 334; MTCW 2; MTFW 2005; NFS 23

Shields, David 1956- .... **CLC 97**
See also CA 124; CANR 48, 99, 112, 157

Shields, David Jonathan
See Shields, David

Shiga, Naoya 1883-1971 .... **CLC 33; SSC 23; TCLC 172**
See Shiga Naoya
See also CA 101; CAAS 33-36R; MJW; RGWL 3

Shiga Naoya
See Shiga, Naoya
See also DLB 180; EWL 3; RGWL 3

Shilts, Randy 1951-1994 .... **CLC 85**
See also AAYA 19; CA 127; CAAE 115; CAAS 144; CANR 45; DA3; GLL 1; INT CA-127; MTCW 2; MTFW 2005

Shimazaki, Haruki 1872-1943
See Shimazaki Toson
See also CA 134; CAAE 105; CANR 84; RGWL 3

Shimazaki Toson .... **TCLC 5**
See Shimazaki, Haruki
See also DLB 180; EWL 3

Shirley, James 1596-1666 .... **DC 25; LC 96**
See also DLB 58; RGEL 2

Shirley Hastings, Selina
See Hastings, Selina

Sholokhov, Mikhail (Aleksandrovich)
1905-1984 .... **CLC 7, 15**
See also CA 101; CAAS 112; DLB 272, 332; EWL 3; MTCW 1, 2; MTFW 2005; RGWL 2, 3; SATA-Obit 36

Sholom Aleichem 1859-1916 .... **SSC 33; TCLC 1, 35**
See Rabinovitch, Sholem
See also DLB 333; TWA

Shone, Patric
See Hanley, James

Showalter, Elaine 1941- .... **CLC 169**
See also CA 57-60; CANR 58, 106; DLB 67; FW; GLL 2

Shreve, Susan
See Shreve, Susan Richards

Shreve, Susan Richards 1939- .... **CLC 23**
See also CA 49-52; 5; CANR 5, 38, 69, 100, 159; MAICYA 1, 2; SATA 46, 95, 152; SATA-Brief 41

Shue, Larry 1946-1985 .... **CLC 52**
See also CA 145; CAAS 117; DAM DRAM; DFS 7

Shu-Jen, Chou 1881-1936
See Lu Hsun
See also CAAE 104

Shulman, Alix Kates 1932- .... **CLC 2, 10**
See also CA 29-32R; CANR 43; FW; SATA 7

Shuster, Joe 1914-1992 .... **CLC 21**
See also AAYA 50

Shute, Nevil .... **CLC 30**
See Norway, Nevil Shute
See also BPFB 3; DLB 255; NFS 9; RHW; SFW 4

Shuttle, Penelope (Diane) 1947- .... **CLC 7**
See also CA 93-96; CANR 39, 84, 92, 108; CP 3, 4, 5, 6, 7; CWP; DLB 14, 40

Shvarts, Elena 1948- .... **PC 50**
See also CA 147

Sidhwa, Bapsi 1939-
See Sidhwa, Bapsy (N.)
See also CN 6, 7; DLB 323

Sidhwa, Bapsy (N.) 1938- .... **CLC 168**
See Sidhwa, Bapsi
See also CA 108; CANR 25, 57; FW

Sidney, Mary 1561-1621 .... **LC 19, 39**
See Sidney Herbert, Mary

Sidney, Sir Philip 1554-1586 .... **LC 19, 39, 131; PC 32**
See also BRW 1; BRWR 2; CDBLB Before 1660; DA; DA3; DAB; DAC; DAM MST, POET; DLB 167; EXPP; PAB; RGEL 2; TEA; WP

Sidney Herbert, Mary
See Sidney, Mary
See also DLB 167

Siegel, Jerome 1914-1996 .... **CLC 21**
See Siegel, Jerry
See also CA 169; CAAE 116; CAAS 151

Siegel, Jerry
See Siegel, Jerome
See also AAYA 50

Sienkiewicz, Henryk (Adam Alexander Pius) 1846-1916 .... **TCLC 3**
See also CA 134; CAAE 104; CANR 84; DLB 332; EWL 3; RGSF 2; RGWL 2, 3

Sierra, Gregorio Martinez
See Martinez Sierra, Gregorio

Sierra, Maria de la O'LeJarraga Martinez
See Martinez Sierra, Maria

Sigal, Clancy 1926- .... **CLC 7**
See also CA 1-4R; CANR 85; CN 1, 2, 3, 4, 5, 6, 7

Siger of Brabant 1240(?)-1284(?) . **CMLC 69**
See also DLB 115

Sigourney, Lydia H.
See Sigourney, Lydia Howard (Huntley)
See also DLB 73, 183

Sigourney, Lydia Howard (Huntley) 1791-1865 .... **NCLC 21, 87**
See Sigourney, Lydia H.; Sigourney, Lydia Huntley
See also DLB 1

Sigourney, Lydia Huntley
See Sigourney, Lydia Howard (Huntley)
See also DLB 42, 239, 243

Siguenza y Gongora, Carlos de 1645-1700 .... **HLCS 2; LC 8**
See also LAW

Sigurjonsson, Johann
See Sigurjonsson, Johann

Sigurjonsson, Johann 1880-1919 ... **TCLC 27**
See also CA 170; DLB 293; EWL 3

Sikelianos, Angelos 1884-1951 .... **PC 29; TCLC 39**
See also EWL 3; RGWL 2, 3

Silkin, Jon 1930-1997 .... **CLC 2, 6, 43**
See also CA 5-8R; 5; CANR 89; CP 1, 2, 3, 4, 5, 6; DLB 27

Silko, Leslie 1948- ...... **CLC 23, 74, 114, 211; NNAL; SSC 37, 66; WLCS**
See also AAYA 14; AMWS 4; ANW; BYA 12; CA 122; CAAE 115; CANR 45, 65, 118; CN 4, 5, 6, 7; CP 4, 5, 6, 7; CPW 1; CWP; DA; DA3; DAC; DAM MST, MULT, POP; DLB 143, 175, 256, 275; EWL 3; EXPP; EXPS; LAIT 4; MAL 5; MTCW 2; MTFW 2005; NFS 4; PFS 9, 16; RGAL 4; RGSF 2; SSFS 4, 8, 10, 11; TCWW 1, 2

Sillanpaa, Frans Eemil 1888-1964 ... **CLC 19**
See also CA 129; CAAS 93-96; DLB 332; EWL 3; MTCW 1

Sillitoe, Alan 1928- .. **CLC 1, 3, 6, 10, 19, 57, 148**
See also AITN 1; BRWS 5; CA 191; 9-12R, 191; 2; CANR 8, 26, 55, 139; CDBLB 1960 to Present; CN 1, 2, 3, 4, 5, 6; CP 1, 2, 3, 4, 5; DLB 14, 139; EWL 3; MTCW 1, 2; MTFW 2005; RGEL 2; RGSF 2; SATA 61

Silone, Ignazio 1900-1978 .... **CLC 4**
See also CA 25-28; CAAS 81-84; CANR 34; CAP 2; DLB 264; EW 12; EWL 3; MTCW 1; RGSF 2; RGWL 2, 3

Silone, Ignazione
See Silone, Ignazio

Silver, Joan Micklin 1935- .... **CLC 20**
See also CA 121; CAAE 114; INT CA-121

Silver, Nicholas
See Faust, Frederick (Schiller)

Silverberg, Robert 1935- .... **CLC 7, 140**
See also AAYA 24; BPFB 3; BYA 7; CA 186; 1-4R, 186; 3; CANR 1, 20, 36, 85, 140; CLR 59; CN 6, 7; CPW; DAM POP; DLB 8; INT CANR-20; MAICYA 1, 2; MTCW 1, 2; MTFW 2005; SATA 13, 91; SATA-Essay 104; SCFW 1, 2; SFW 4; SUFW 2

Silverstein, Alvin 1933- .... **CLC 17**
See also CA 49-52; CANR 2; CLR 25; JRDA; MAICYA 1, 2; SATA 8, 69, 124

Silverstein, Shel 1932-1999 .... **PC 49**
See also AAYA 40; BW 3; CA 107; CAAS 179; CANR 47, 74, 81; CLR 5, 96; CWRI 5; JRDA; MAICYA 1, 2; MTCW 2; MTFW 2005; SATA 33, 92; SATA-Brief 27; SATA-Obit 116

Silverstein, Virginia B(arbara Opshelor) 1937- .... **CLC 17**
See also CA 49-52; CANR 2; CLR 25; JRDA; MAICYA 1, 2; SATA 8, 69, 124

Sim, Georges
See Simenon, Georges (Jacques Christian)

Simak, Clifford D(onald) 1904-1988 . **CLC 1, 55**
See also CA 1-4R; CAAS 125; CANR 1, 35; DLB 8; MTCW 1; SATA-Obit 56; SCFW 1, 2; SFW 4

Simenon, Georges (Jacques Christian) 1903-1989 .... **CLC 1, 2, 3, 8, 18, 47**
See also BPFB 3; CA 85-88; CAAS 129; CANR 35; CMW 4; DA3; DAM POP; DLB 72; DLBY 1989; EW 12; EWL 3; GFL 1789 to the Present; MSW; MTCW 1, 2; MTFW 2005; RGWL 2, 3

Simic, Charles 1938- .... **CLC 6, 9, 22, 49, 68, 130; PC 69**
See also AMWS 8; CA 29-32R; 4; CANR 12, 33, 52, 61, 96, 140; CP 2, 3, 4, 5, 6, 7; DA3; DAM POET; DLB 105; MAL 5; MTCW 2; MTFW 2005; PFS 7; RGAL 4; WP

Simmel, Georg 1858-1918 .... **TCLC 64**
See also CA 157; DLB 296

Simmons, Charles (Paul) 1924- .... **CLC 57**
See also CA 89-92; INT CA-89-92

Simmons, Dan 1948- .... **CLC 44**
See also AAYA 16, 54; CA 138; CANR 53, 81, 126; CPW; DAM POP; HGG; SUFW 2

Simmons, James (Stewart Alexander) 1933- .... **CLC 43**
See also CA 105; 21; CP 1, 2, 3, 4, 5, 6, 7; DLB 40

Simms, William Gilmore 1806-1870 .... **NCLC 3**
See also DLB 3, 30, 59, 73, 248, 254; RGAL 4

Simon, Carly 1945- .... **CLC 26**
See also CA 105

Simon, Claude 1913-2005 ... **CLC 4, 9, 15, 39**
See also CA 89-92; CAAS 241; CANR 33, 117; CWW 2; DAM NOV; DLB 83, 332; EW 13; EWL 3; GFL 1789 to the Present; MTCW 1

Simon, Claude Eugene Henri
See Simon, Claude

Simon, Claude Henri Eugene
See Simon, Claude

Simon, Marvin Neil
See Simon, Neil

Simon, Myles
See Follett, Ken

Simon, Neil 1927- .... **CLC 6, 11, 31, 39, 70, 233; DC 14**
See also AAYA 32; AITN 1; AMWS 4; CA 21-24R; CAD; CANR 26, 54, 87, 126; CD 5, 6; DA3; DAM DRAM; DFS 2, 6, 12, 18,, 24; DLB 7, 266; LAIT 4; MAL 5; MTCW 1, 2; MTFW 2005; RGAL 4; TUS

Simon, Paul 1941-)- .... **CLC 17**
See also CA 153; CAAE 116; CANR 152

Simon, Paul Frederick
See Simon, Paul

Simonon, Paul 1956(?)- .... **CLC 30**

Simonson, Rick .... **CLC 70**

Simpson, Harriette
See Arnow, Harriette (Louisa) Simpson

Simpson, Louis 1923- ... **CLC 4, 7, 9, 32, 149**
See also AMWS 9; CA 1-4R; 4; CANR 1, 61, 140; CP 1, 2, 3, 4, 5, 6, 7; DAM POET; DLB 5; MAL 5; MTCW 1, 2; MTFW 2005; PFS 7, 11, 14; RGAL 4

Simpson, Mona 1957- .... **CLC 44, 146**
See also CA 135; CAAE 122; CANR 68, 103; CN 6, 7; EWL 3

Simpson, Mona Elizabeth
See Simpson, Mona

Simpson, N(orman) F(rederick) 1919- .... **CLC 29**
See also CA 13-16R; CBD; DLB 13; RGEL 2

Sinclair, Andrew (Annandale) 1935- . **CLC 2, 14**
See also CA 9-12R; 5; CANR 14, 38, 91; CN 1, 2, 3, 4, 5, 6, 7; DLB 14; FANT; MTCW 1

Sinclair, Emil
See Hesse, Hermann

Sinclair, Iain 1943- .... **CLC 76**
See also CA 132; CANR 81, 157; CP 5, 6, 7; HGG

Sinclair, Iain MacGregor
See Sinclair, Iain

Sinclair, Irene
See Griffith, D(avid Lewelyn) W(ark)

Sinclair, Julian
See Sinclair, May

Sinclair, Mary Amelia St. Clair (?)-
See Sinclair, May

Sinclair, May 1865-1946 .... **TCLC 3, 11**
See also CA 166; CAAE 104; DLB 36, 135; EWL 3; HGG; RGEL 2; RHW; SUFW

Sinclair, Roy
See Griffith, D(avid Lewelyn) W(ark)

Sinclair, Upton 1878-1968 ...... **CLC 1, 11, 15, 63; TCLC 160; WLC 5**
See also AAYA 63; AMWS 5; BPFB 3; BYA 2; CA 5-8R; CAAS 25-28R; CANR 7; CDALB 1929-1941; DA; DA3; DAB; DAC; DAM MST, NOV; DLB 9; EWL 3; INT CANR-7; LAIT 3; MAL 5; MTCW 1, 2; MTFW 2005; NFS 6; RGAL 4; SATA 9; TUS; YAW

Sinclair, Upton Beall
See Sinclair, Upton

Singe, (Edmund) J(ohn) M(illington) 1871-1909 .... **WLC**

Singer, Isaac
See Singer, Isaac Bashevis

Singer, Isaac Bashevis 1904-1991 .. **CLC 1, 3, 6, 9, 11, 15, 23, 38, 69, 111; SSC 3, 53, 80; WLC 5**
See also AAYA 32; AITN 1, 2; AMW; AMWR 2; BPFB 3; BYA 1, 4; CA 1-4R; CAAS 134; CANR 1, 39, 106; CDALB 1941-1968; CLR 1; CN 1, 2, 3, 4; CWRI 5; DA; DA3; DAB; DAC; DAM MST,

NOV; DLB 6, 28, 52, 278, 332, 333;
DLBY 1991; EWL 3; EXPS; HGG;
JRDA; LAIT 3; MAICYA 1, 2; MAL 5;
MTCW 1, 2; MTFW 2005; RGAL
4; RGHL; RGSF 2; SATA 3, 27; SATA-Obit
68; SSFS 2, 12, 16; TUS; TWA

Singer, Israel Joshua 1893-1944 .... **TCLC 33**
See Zinger, Yisroel-Yehoyshue
See also CA 169; DLB 333; EWL 3

Singh, Khushwant 1915- .... **CLC 11**
See also CA 9-12R; 9; CANR 6, 84; CN 1,
2, 3, 4, 5, 6, 7; DLB 323; EWL 3; RGEL
2

Singleton, Ann
See Benedict, Ruth

Singleton, John 1968(?)- .... **CLC 156**
See also AAYA 50; BW 2, 3; CA 138;
CANR 67, 82; DAM MULT

Siniavskii, Andrei
See Sinyavsky, Andrei (Donatevich)
See also CWW 2

Sinjohn, John
See Galsworthy, John

Sinyavsky, Andrei (Donatevich)
1925-1997 .... **CLC 8**
See Siniavskii, Andrei; Sinyavsky, Andrey
Donatovich; Tertz, Abram
See also CA 85-88; CAAS 159

Sinyavsky, Andrey Donatovich
See Sinyavsky, Andrei (Donatevich)
See also EWL 3

Sirin, V.
See Nabokov, Vladimir (Vladimirovich)

Sissman, L(ouis) E(dward)
1928-1976 .... **CLC 9, 18**
See also CA 21-24R; CAAS 65-68; CANR
13; CP 2; DLB 5

Sisson, C(harles) H(ubert)
1914-2003 .... **CLC 8**
See also BRWS 11; CA 1-4R; 3; CAAS
220; CANR 3, 48, 84; CP 1, 2, 3, 4, 5, 6,
7; DLB 27

Sitting Bull 1831(?)-1890 .... **NNAL**
See also DA3; DAM MULT

Sitwell, Dame Edith 1887-1964 ..... **CLC 2, 9,
67; PC 3**
See also BRW 7; CA 9-12R; CANR 35;
CDBLB 1945-1960; DAM POET; DLB
20; EWL 3; MTCW 1, 2; MTFW 2005;
RGEL 2; TEA

Siwaarmill, H. P.
See Sharp, William

Sjoewall, Maj 1935- .... **CLC 7**
See Sjowall, Maj
See also CA 65-68; CANR 73

Sjowall, Maj
See Sjoewall, Maj
See also BPFB 3; CMW 4; MSW

Skelton, John 1460(?)-1529 ..... **LC 71; PC 25**
See also BRW 1; DLB 136; RGEL 2

Skelton, Robin 1925-1997 .... **CLC 13**
See Zuk, Georges
See also AITN 2; CA 5-8R; 5; CAAS 160;
CANR 28, 89; CCA 1; CP 1, 2, 3, 4, 5, 6;
DLB 27, 53

Skolimowski, Jerzy 1938- .... **CLC 20**
See also CA 128

Skram, Amalie (Bertha)
1847-1905 .... **TCLC 25**
See also CA 165

Skvorecky, Josef 1924- . **CLC 15, 39, 69, 152**
See also CA 61-64; 1; CANR 10, 34, 63,
108; CDWLB 4; CWW 2; DA3; DAC;
DAM NOV; DLB 232; EWL 3; MTCW
1, 2; MTFW 2005

Slade, Bernard 1930- .... **CLC 11, 46**
See Newbound, Bernard Slade
See also CA 9; CCA 1; CD 6; DLB 53

Slaughter, Carolyn 1946- .... **CLC 56**
See also CA 85-88; CANR 85; CN 5, 6, 7

Slaughter, Frank G(ill) 1908-2001 ... **CLC 29**
See also AITN 2; CA 5-8R; CAAS 197;
CANR 5, 85; INT CANR-5; RHW

Slavitt, David R. 1935- .... **CLC 5, 14**
See also CA 21-24R; 3; CANR 41, 83, 166;
CN 1, 2; CP 1, 2, 3, 4, 5, 6, 7; DLB 5, 6

Slavitt, David Rytman
See Slavitt, David R.

Slesinger, Tess 1905-1945 .... **TCLC 10**
See also CA 199; CAAE 107; DLB 102

Slessor, Kenneth 1901-1971 .... **CLC 14**
See also CA 102; CAAS 89-92; DLB 260;
RGEL 2

Slowacki, Juliusz 1809-1849 .... **NCLC 15**
See also RGWL 3

Smart, Christopher 1722-1771 .... **LC 3, 134;
PC 13**
See also DAM POET; DLB 109; RGEL 2

Smart, Elizabeth 1913-1986 .... **CLC 54**
See also CA 81-84; CAAS 118; CN 4; DLB
88

Smiley, Jane 1949- ...... **CLC 53, 76, 144, 236**
See also AAYA 66; AMWS 6; BPFB 3; CA
104; CANR 30, 50, 74, 96, 158; CN 6, 7;
CPW 1; DA3; DAM POP; DLB 227, 234;
EWL 3; INT CANR-30; MAL 5; MTFW
2005; SSFS 19

Smiley, Jane Graves
See Smiley, Jane

Smith, A(rthur) J(ames) M(arshall)
1902-1980 .... **CLC 15**
See also CA 1-4R; CAAS 102; CANR 4;
CP 1, 2, 3; DAC; DLB 88; RGEL 2

Smith, Adam 1723(?)-1790 .... **LC 36**
See also DLB 104, 252, 336; RGEL 2

Smith, Alexander 1829-1867 .... **NCLC 59**
See also DLB 32, 55

Smith, Anna Deavere 1950- ...... **CLC 86, 241**
See also CA 133; CANR 103; CD 5, 6; DFS
2, 22

Smith, Betty (Wehner) 1904-1972 .... **CLC 19**
See also AAYA 72; BPFB 3; BYA 3; CA
5-8R; CAAS 33-36R; DLBY 1982; LAIT
3; RGAL 4; SATA 6

Smith, Charlotte (Turner)
1749-1806 .... **NCLC 23, 115**
See also DLB 39, 109; RGEL 2; TEA

Smith, Clark Ashton 1893-1961 .... **CLC 43**
See also AAYA 76; CA 143; CANR 81;
FANT; HGG; MTCW 2; SCFW 1, 2; SFW
4; SUFW

Smith, Dave .... **CLC 22, 42**
See Smith, David (Jeddie)
See also CA 7; CP 3, 4, 5, 6, 7; DLB 5

Smith, David (Jeddie) 1942-
See Smith, Dave
See also CA 49-52; CANR 1, 59, 120;
CSW; DAM POET

Smith, Iain Crichton 1928-1998 .... **CLC 64**
See also BRWS 9; CA 21-24R; CAAS 171;
CN 1, 2, 3, 4, 5, 6; CP 1, 2, 3, 4, 5, 6;
DLB 40, 139, 319; RGSF 2

Smith, John 1580(?)-1631 .... **LC 9**
See also DLB 24, 30; TUS

Smith, Johnston
See Crane, Stephen (Townley)

Smith, Joseph, Jr. 1805-1844 .... **NCLC 53**

Smith, Kevin 1970- .... **CLC 223**
See also AAYA 37; CA 166; CANR 131

Smith, Lee 1944- .... **CLC 25, 73**
See also CA 119; CAAE 114; CANR 46,
118; CN 7; CSW; DLB 143; DLBY 1983;
EWL 3; INT CA-119; RGAL 4

Smith, Martin
See Smith, Martin Cruz

Smith, Martin Cruz 1942- .. **CLC 25; NNAL**
See also BEST 89:4; BPFB 3; CA 85-88;
CANR 6, 23, 43, 65, 119; CMW 4; CPW;
DAM MULT, POP; HGG; INT CANR-
23; MTCW 2; MTFW 2005; RGAL 4

Smith, Patti 1946- .... **CLC 12**
See also CA 93-96; CANR 63

Smith, Pauline (Urmson)
1882-1959 .... **TCLC 25**
See also DLB 225; EWL 3

Smith, Rosamond
See Oates, Joyce Carol

Smith, Seba 1792-1868 .... **NCLC 187**
See also DLB 1, 11, 243

Smith, Sheila Kaye
See Kaye-Smith, Sheila

Smith, Stevie 1902-1971 .... **CLC 3, 8, 25, 44;
PC 12**
See also BRWS 2; CA 17-18; CAAS 29-
32R; CANR 35; CAP 2; CP 1; DAM
POET; DLB 20; EWL 3; MTCW 1, 2;
PAB; PFS 3; RGEL 2; TEA

Smith, Wilbur 1933- .... **CLC 33**
See also CA 13-16R; CANR 7, 46, 66, 134;
CPW; MTCW 1, 2; MTFW 2005

Smith, William Jay 1918- .... **CLC 6**
See also AMWS 13; CA 5-8R; CANR 44,
106; CP 1, 2, 3, 4, 5, 6, 7; CSW; CWRI
5; DLB 5; MAICYA 1, 2; SAAS 22;
SATA 2, 68, 154; SATA-Essay 154; TCLE
1:2

Smith, Woodrow Wilson
See Kuttner, Henry

Smith, Zadie 1975- .... **CLC 158**
See also AAYA 50; CA 193; MTFW 2005

Smolenskin, Peretz 1842-1885 .... **NCLC 30**

Smollett, Tobias (George) 1721-1771 ... **LC 2,
46**
See also BRW 3; CDBLB 1660-1789; DLB
39, 104; RGEL 2; TEA

Snodgrass, W.D. 1926- .... **CLC 2, 6, 10, 18,
68; PC 10**
See also AMWS 6; CA 1-4R; CANR 6, 36,
65, 85; CP 1, 2, 3, 4, 5, 6, 7; DAM POET;
DLB 5; MAL 5; MTCW 1, 2; MTFW
2005; RGAL 4; TCLE 1:2

Snorri Sturluson 1179-1241 .... **CMLC 56**
See also RGWL 2, 3

Snow, C(harles) P(ercy) 1905-1980 ... **CLC 1,
4, 6, 9, 13, 19**
See also BRW 7; CA 5-8R; CAAS 101;
CANR 28; CDBLB 1945-1960; CN 1, 2;
DAM NOV; DLB 15, 77; DLBD 17;
EWL 3; MTCW 1, 2; MTFW 2005; RGEL
2; TEA

Snow, Frances Compton
See Adams, Henry (Brooks)

Snyder, Gary 1930- . **CLC 1, 2, 5, 9, 32, 120;
PC 21**
See also AAYA 72; AMWS 8; ANW; BG
1:3; CA 17-20R; CANR 30, 60, 125; CP
1, 2, 3, 4, 5, 6, 7; DA3; DAM POET; DLB
5, 16, 165, 212, 237, 275; EWL 3; MAL
5; MTCW 2; MTFW 2005; PFS 9, 19;
RGAL 4; WP

Snyder, Zilpha Keatley 1927- .... **CLC 17**
See also AAYA 15; BYA 1; CA 252; 9-12R,
252; CANR 38; CLR 31, 121; JRDA;
MAICYA 1, 2; SAAS 2; SATA 1, 28, 75,
110, 163; SATA-Essay 112, 163; YAW

Soares, Bernardo
See Pessoa, Fernando (Antonio Nogueira)

Sobh, A.
See Shamlu, Ahmad

Sobh, Alef
See Shamlu, Ahmad

Sobol, Joshua 1939- .... **CLC 60**
See Sobol, Yehoshua
See also CA 200; RGHL

Sobol, Yehoshua 1939-
See Sobol, Joshua
See also CWW 2

Socrates 470B.C.-399B.C. .... **CMLC 27**

Soderberg, Hjalmar 1869-1941 ...... **TCLC 39**
See also DLB 259; EWL 3; RGSF 2

Soderbergh, Steven 1963- .... **CLC 154**
See also AAYA 43; CA 243

Soderbergh, Steven Andrew
See Soderbergh, Steven

Sodergran, Edith (Irene) 1892-1923
See Soedergran, Edith (Irene)
See also CA 202; DLB 259; EW 11; EWL 3; RGWL 2, 3

Soedergran, Edith (Irene)
1892-1923 .... **TCLC 31**
See Sodergran, Edith (Irene)

Softly, Edgar
See Lovecraft, H. P.

Softly, Edward
See Lovecraft, H. P.

Sokolov, Alexander V(sevolodovich) 1943-
See Sokolov, Sasha
See also CA 73-76

Sokolov, Raymond 1941- .... **CLC 7**
See also CA 85-88

Sokolov, Sasha .... **CLC 59**
See Sokolov, Alexander V(sevolodovich)
See also CWW 2; DLB 285; EWL 3; RGWL 2, 3

Solo, Jay
See Ellison, Harlan

Sologub, Fyodor .... **TCLC 9**
See Teternikov, Fyodor Kuzmich
See also EWL 3

Solomons, Ikey Esquir
See Thackeray, William Makepeace

Solomos, Dionysios 1798-1857 .... **NCLC 15**

Solwoska, Mara
See French, Marilyn

Solzhenitsyn, Aleksandr I. 1918- .. **CLC 1, 2, 4, 7, 9, 10, 18, 26, 34, 78, 134, 235; SSC 32; WLC 5**
See Solzhenitsyn, Aleksandr Isayevich
See also AAYA 49; AITN 1; BPFB 3; CA 69-72; CANR 40, 65, 116; DA; DA3; DAB; DAC; DAM MST, NOV; DLB 302, 332; EW 13; EXPS; LAIT 4; MTCW 1, 2; MTFW 2005; NFS 6; RGSF 2; RGWL 2, 3; SSFS 9; TWA

Solzhenitsyn, Aleksandr Isayevich
See Solzhenitsyn, Aleksandr I.
See also CWW 2; EWL 3

Somers, Jane
See Lessing, Doris

Somerville, Edith Oenone
1858-1949 .... **SSC 56; TCLC 51**
See also CA 196; DLB 135; RGEL 2; RGSF 2

Somerville & Ross
See Martin, Violet Florence; Somerville, Edith Oenone

Sommer, Scott 1951- .... **CLC 25**
See also CA 106

Sommers, Christina Hoff 1950- ...... **CLC 197**
See also CA 153; CANR 95

Sondheim, Stephen (Joshua) 1930- . **CLC 30, 39, 147; DC 22**
See also AAYA 11, 66; CA 103; CANR 47, 67, 125; DAM DRAM; LAIT 4

Sone, Monica 1919- .... **AAL**
See also DLB 312

Song, Cathy 1955- .... **AAL; PC 21**
See also CA 154; CANR 118; CWP; DLB 169, 312; EXPP; FW; PFS 5

Sontag, Susan 1933-2004 ... **CLC 1, 2, 10, 13, 31, 105, 195**
See also AMWS 3; CA 17-20R; CAAS 234; CANR 25, 51, 74, 97; CN 1, 2, 3, 4, 5, 6, 7; CPW; DA3; DAM POP; DLB 2, 67; EWL 3; MAL 5; MBL; MTCW 1, 2; MTFW 2005; RGAL 4; RHW; SSFS 10

Sophocles 496(?)B.C.-406(?)B.C. .... **CMLC 2, 47, 51, 86; DC 1; WLCS**
See also AW 1; CDWLB 1; DA; DA3; DAB; DAC; DAM DRAM, MST; DFS 1, 4, 8, 24; DLB 176; LAIT 1; LATS 1:1; LMFS 1; RGWL 2, 3; TWA; WLIT 8

Sordello 1189-1269 .... **CMLC 15**

Sorel, Georges 1847-1922 .... **TCLC 91**
See also CA 188; CAAE 118

Sorel, Julia
See Drexler, Rosalyn

Sorokin, Vladimir .... **CLC 59**
See Sorokin, Vladimir Georgievich
See also CA 258

Sorokin, Vladimir Georgievich
See Sorokin, Vladimir
See also DLB 285

Sorrentino, Gilbert 1929-2006 .... **CLC 3, 7, 14, 22, 40**
See also CA 77-80; CAAS 250; CANR 14, 33, 115, 157; CN 3, 4, 5, 6, 7; CP 1, 2, 3, 4, 5, 6, 7; DLB 5, 173; DLBY 1980; INT CANR-14

Soseki
See Natsume, Soseki
See also MJW

Soto, Gary 1952- ... **CLC 32, 80; HLC 2; PC 28**
See also AAYA 10, 37; BYA 11; CA 125; CAAE 119; CANR 50, 74, 107, 157; CLR 38; CP 4, 5, 6, 7; DAM MULT; DLB 82; EWL 3; EXPP; HW 1, 2; INT CA-125; JRDA; LLW; MAICYA 2; MAICYAS 1; MAL 5; MTCW 2; MTFW 2005; PFS 7; RGAL 4; SATA 80, 120, 174; WYA; YAW

Soupault, Philippe 1897-1990 .... **CLC 68**
See also CA 147; CAAE 116; CAAS 131; EWL 3; GFL 1789 to the Present; LMFS 2

Souster, (Holmes) Raymond 1921- .... **CLC 5, 14**
See also CA 13-16R; 14; CANR 13, 29, 53; CP 1, 2, 3, 4, 5, 6, 7; DA3; DAC; DAM POET; DLB 88; RGEL 2; SATA 63

Southern, Terry 1924(?)-1995 .... **CLC 7**
See also AMWS 11; BPFB 3; CA 1-4R; CAAS 150; CANR 1, 55, 107; CN 1, 2, 3, 4, 5, 6; DLB 2; IDFW 3, 4

Southerne, Thomas 1660-1746 .... **LC 99**
See also DLB 80; RGEL 2

Southey, Robert 1774-1843 .... **NCLC 8, 97**
See also BRW 4; DLB 93, 107, 142; RGEL 2; SATA 54

Southwell, Robert 1561(?)-1595 .... **LC 108**
See also DLB 167; RGEL 2; TEA

Southworth, Emma Dorothy Eliza Nevitte
1819-1899 .... **NCLC 26**
See also DLB 239

Souza, Ernest
See Scott, Evelyn

Soyinka, Wole 1934- .. **BLC 3; CLC 3, 5, 14, 36, 44, 179; DC 2; WLC 5**
See also AFW; BW 2, 3; CA 13-16R; CANR 27, 39, 82, 136; CD 5, 6; CDWLB 3; CN 6, 7; CP 1, 2, 3, 4, 5, 6 ,7; DA; DA3; DAB; DAC; DAM DRAM, MST, MULT; DFS 10; DLB 125, 332; EWL 3; MTCW 1, 2; MTFW 2005; RGEL 2; TWA; WLIT 2; WWE 1

Spackman, W(illiam) M(ode)
1905-1990 .... **CLC 46**
See also CA 81-84; CAAS 132

Spacks, Barry (Bernard) 1931- .... **CLC 14**
See also CA 154; CANR 33, 109; CP 3, 4, 5, 6, 7; DLB 105

Spanidou, Irini 1946- .... **CLC 44**
See also CA 185

Spark, Muriel 1918-2006 .... **CLC 2, 3, 5, 8, 13, 18, 40, 94, 242; PC 72; SSC 10**
See also BRWS 1; CA 5-8R; CAAS 251; CANR 12, 36, 76, 89, 131; CDBLB 1945-1960; CN 1, 2, 3, 4, 5, 6, 7; CP 1, 2, 3, 4, 5, 6, 7; DA3; DAB; DAC; DAM MST, NOV; DLB 15, 139; EWL 3; FW; INT CANR-12; LAIT 4; MTCW 1, 2; MTFW 2005; NFS 22; RGEL 2; TEA; WLIT 4; YAW

Spark, Muriel Sarah
See Spark, Muriel

Spaulding, Douglas
See Bradbury, Ray

Spaulding, Leonard
See Bradbury, Ray

Speght, Rachel 1597-c. 1630 .... **LC 97**
See also DLB 126

Spence, J. A. D.
See Eliot, T(homas) S(tearns)

Spencer, Anne 1882-1975 ...... **HR 1:3; PC 77**
See also BW 2; CA 161; DLB 51, 54

Spencer, Elizabeth 1921- .... **CLC 22; SSC 57**
See also CA 13-16R; CANR 32, 65, 87; CN 1, 2, 3, 4, 5, 6, 7; CSW; DLB 6, 218; EWL 3; MTCW 1; RGAL 4; SATA 14

Spencer, Leonard G.
See Silverberg, Robert

Spencer, Scott 1945- .... **CLC 30**
See also CA 113; CANR 51, 148; DLBY 1986

Spender, Stephen 1909-1995 ..... **CLC 1, 2, 5, 10, 41, 91; PC 71**
See also BRWS 2; CA 9-12R; CAAS 149; CANR 31, 54; CDBLB 1945-1960; CP 1, 2, 3, 4, 5, 6; DA3; DAM POET; DLB 20; EWL 3; MTCW 1, 2; MTFW 2005; PAB; PFS 23; RGEL 2; TEA

Spengler, Oswald (Arnold Gottfried)
1880-1936 .... **TCLC 25**
See also CA 189; CAAE 118

Spenser, Edmund 1552(?)-1599 ...... **LC 5, 39, 117; PC 8, 42; WLC 5**
See also AAYA 60; BRW 1; CDBLB Before 1660; DA; DA3; DAB; DAC; DAM MST, POET; DLB 167; EFS 2; EXPP; PAB; RGEL 2; TEA; WLIT 3; WP

Spicer, Jack 1925-1965 .... **CLC 8, 18, 72**
See also BG 1:3; CA 85-88; DAM POET; DLB 5, 16, 193; GLL 1; WP

Spiegelman, Art 1948- .... **CLC 76, 178**
See also AAYA 10, 46; CA 125; CANR 41, 55, 74, 124; DLB 299; MTCW 2; MTFW 2005; RGHL; SATA 109, 158; YAW

Spielberg, Peter 1929- .... **CLC 6**
See also CA 5-8R; CANR 4, 48; DLBY 1981

Spielberg, Steven 1947- .... **CLC 20, 188**
See also AAYA 8, 24; CA 77-80; CANR 32; SATA 32

Spillane, Frank Morrison
See Spillane, Mickey
See also BPFB 3; CMW 4; DLB 226; MSW

Spillane, Mickey 1918-2006 .. **CLC 3, 13, 241**
See Spillane, Frank Morrison
See also CA 25-28R; CAAS 252; CANR 28, 63, 125; DA3; MTCW 1, 2; MTFW 2005; SATA 66; SATA-Obit 176

Spinoza, Benedictus de 1632-1677 .. **LC 9, 58**

Spinrad, Norman (Richard) 1940- ... **CLC 46**
See also BPFB 3; CA 233; 37-40R, 233; 19; CANR 20, 91; DLB 8; INT CANR-20; SFW 4

Vergil 70B.C.-19B.C. ... **CMLC 9, 40; PC 12; WLCS**
See Virgil
See also AW 2; DA; DA3; DAB; DAC; DAM MST, POET; EFS 1; LMFS 1

Vergil, Polydore c. 1470-1555 .... **LC 108**
See also DLB 132

Verhaeren, Emile (Adolphe Gustave) 1855-1916 .... **TCLC 12**
See also CAAE 109; EWL 3; GFL 1789 to the Present

Verlaine, Paul (Marie) 1844-1896 .. **NCLC 2, 51; PC 2, 32**
See also DAM POET; DLB 217; EW 7; GFL 1789 to the Present; LMFS 2; RGWL 2, 3; TWA

Verne, Jules (Gabriel) 1828-1905 ... **TCLC 6, 52**
See also AAYA 16; BYA 4; CA 131; CAAE 110; CLR 88; DA3; DLB 123; GFL 1789 to the Present; JRDA; LAIT 2; LMFS 2; MAICYA 1, 2; MTFW 2005; RGWL 2, 3; SATA 21; SCFW 1, 2; SFW 4; TWA; WCH

Verus, Marcus Annius
See Aurelius, Marcus

Very, Jones 1813-1880 .... **NCLC 9**
See also DLB 1, 243; RGAL 4

Vesaas, Tarjei 1897-1970 .... **CLC 48**
See also CA 190; CAAS 29-32R; DLB 297; EW 11; EWL 3; RGWL 3

Vialis, Gaston
See Simenon, Georges (Jacques Christian)

Vian, Boris 1920-1959(?) .... **TCLC 9**
See also CA 164; CAAE 106; CANR 111; DLB 72, 321; EWL 3; GFL 1789 to the Present; MTCW 2; RGWL 2, 3

Viaud, (Louis Marie) Julien 1850-1923
See Loti, Pierre
See also CAAE 107

Vicar, Henry
See Felsen, Henry Gregor

Vicente, Gil 1465-c. 1536 .... **LC 99**
See also DLB 318; IDTP; RGWL 2, 3

Vicker, Angus
See Felsen, Henry Gregor

Vico, Giambattista .... **LC 138**
See Vico, Giovanni Battista
See also WLIT 7

Vico, Giovanni Battista 1668-1744
See Vico, Giambattista
See also EW 3

Vidal, Eugene Luther Gore
See Vidal, Gore

Vidal, Gore 1925- ...... **CLC 2, 4, 6, 8, 10, 22, 33, 72, 142**
See Box, Edgar
See also AAYA 64; AITN 1; AMWS 4; BEST 90:2; BPFB 3; CA 5-8R; CAD; CANR 13, 45, 65, 100, 132; CD 5, 6; CDALBS; CN 1, 2, 3, 4, 5, 6, 7; CPW; DA3; DAM NOV, POP; DFS 2; DLB 6, 152; EWL 3; INT CANR-13; MAL 5; MTCW 1, 2; MTFW 2005; RGAL 4; RHW; TUS

Viereck, Peter 1916-2006 .... **CLC 4; PC 27**
See also CA 1-4R; CAAS 250; CANR 1, 47; CP 1, 2, 3, 4, 5, 6, 7; DLB 5; MAL 5; PFS 9, 14

Viereck, Peter Robert Edwin
See Viereck, Peter

Vigny, Alfred (Victor) de 1797-1863 .... **NCLC 7, 102; PC 26**
See also DAM POET; DLB 119, 192, 217; EW 5; GFL 1789 to the Present; RGWL 2, 3

Vilakazi, Benedict Wallet 1906-1947 .... **TCLC 37**
See also CA 168

Vile, Curt
See Moore, Alan

Villa, Jose Garcia 1914-1997 ... **AAL; PC 22; TCLC 176**
See also CA 25-28R; CANR 12, 118; CP 1, 2, 3, 4; DLB 312; EWL 3; EXPP

Villard, Oswald Garrison 1872-1949 .... **TCLC 160**
See also CA 162; CAAE 113; DLB 25, 91

Villarreal, Jose Antonio 1924- .... **HLC 2**
See also CA 133; CANR 93; DAM MULT; DLB 82; HW 1; LAIT 4; RGAL 4

Villaurrutia, Xavier 1903-1950 .... **TCLC 80**
See also CA 192; EWL 3; HW 1; LAW

Villaverde, Cirilo 1812-1894 .... **NCLC 121**
See also LAW

Villehardouin, Geoffroi de 1150(?)-1218(?) .... **CMLC 38**

Villiers, George 1628-1687 .... **LC 107**
See also DLB 80; RGEL 2

Villiers de l'Isle Adam, Jean Marie Mathias Philippe Auguste 1838-1889 ... **NCLC 3; SSC 14**
See also DLB 123, 192; GFL 1789 to the Present; RGSF 2

Villon, Francois 1431-1463(?) . **LC 62; PC 13**
See also DLB 208; EW 2; RGWL 2, 3; TWA

Vine, Barbara .... **CLC 50**
See Rendell, Ruth
See also BEST 90:4

Vinge, Joan (Carol) D(ennison) 1948- .... **CLC 30; SSC 24**
See also AAYA 32; BPFB 3; CA 93-96; CANR 72; SATA 36, 113; SFW 4; YAW

Viola, Herman J(oseph) 1938- .... **CLC 70**
See also CA 61-64; CANR 8, 23, 48, 91; SATA 126

Violis, G.
See Simenon, Georges (Jacques Christian)

Viramontes, Helena Maria 1954- .... **HLCS 2**
See also CA 159; DLB 122; HW 2; LLW

Virgil
See Vergil
See also CDWLB 1; DLB 211; LAIT 1; RGWL 2, 3; WLIT 8; WP

Visconti, Luchino 1906-1976 .... **CLC 16**
See also CA 81-84; CAAS 65-68; CANR 39

Vitry, Jacques de
See Jacques de Vitry

Vittorini, Elio 1908-1966 .... **CLC 6, 9, 14**
See also CA 133; CAAS 25-28R; DLB 264; EW 12; EWL 3; RGWL 2, 3

Vivekananda, Swami 1863-1902 .... **TCLC 88**

Vizenor, Gerald Robert 1934- .... **CLC 103; NNAL**
See also CA 205; 13-16R, 205; 22; CANR 5, 21, 44, 67; DAM MULT; DLB 175, 227; MTCW 2; MTFW 2005; TCWW 2

Vizinczey, Stephen 1933- .... **CLC 40**
See also CA 128; CCA 1; INT CA-128

Vliet, R(ussell) G(ordon) 1929-1984 .... **CLC 22**
See also CA 37-40R; CAAS 112; CANR 18; CP 2, 3

Vogau, Boris Andreyevich 1894-1938
See Pilnyak, Boris
See also CA 218; CAAE 123

Vogel, Paula A. 1951- .... **CLC 76; DC 19**
See also CA 108; CAD; CANR 119, 140; CD 5, 6; CWD; DFS 14; MTFW 2005; RGAL 4

Voigt, Cynthia 1942- .... **CLC 30**
See also AAYA 3, 30; BYA 1, 3, 6, 7, 8; CA 106; CANR 18, 37, 40, 94, 145; CLR 13, 48; INT CANR-18; JRDA; LAIT 5; MAICYA 1, 2; MAICYAS 1; MTFW 2005; SATA 48, 79, 116, 160; SATA-Brief 33; WYA; YAW

Voigt, Ellen Bryant 1943- .... **CLC 54**
See also CA 69-72; CANR 11, 29, 55, 115; CP 5, 6, 7; CSW; CWP; DLB 120; PFS 23

Voinovich, Vladimir 1932- .. **CLC 10, 49, 147**
See also CA 81-84; 12; CANR 33, 67, 150; CWW 2; DLB 302; MTCW 1

Voinovich, Vladimir Nikolaevich
See Voinovich, Vladimir

Vollmann, William T. 1959- ...... **CLC 89, 227**
See also AMWS 17; CA 134; CANR 67, 116; CN 7; CPW; DA3; DAM NOV, POP; MTCW 2; MTFW 2005

Voloshinov, V. N.
See Bakhtin, Mikhail Mikhailovich

Voltaire 1694-1778 . **LC 14, 79, 110; SSC 12; WLC 6**
See also BYA 13; DA; DA3; DAB; DAC; DAM DRAM, MST; DLB 314; EW 4; GFL Beginnings to 1789; LATS 1:1; LMFS 1; NFS 7; RGWL 2, 3; TWA

von Aschendrof, Baron Ignatz
See Ford, Ford Madox

von Chamisso, Adelbert
See Chamisso, Adelbert von

von Daeniken, Erich 1935- .... **CLC 30**
See also AITN 1; CA 37-40R; CANR 17, 44

von Daniken, Erich
See von Daeniken, Erich

von Eschenbach, Wolfram c. 1170-c. 1220 .... **CMLC 5**
See Eschenbach, Wolfram von
See also CDWLB 2; DLB 138; EW 1; RGWL 2

von Hartmann, Eduard 1842-1906 .... **TCLC 96**

von Hayek, Friedrich August
See Hayek, F(riedrich) A(ugust von)

von Heidenstam, (Carl Gustaf) Verner
See Heidenstam, (Carl Gustaf) Verner von

von Heyse, Paul (Johann Ludwig)
See Heyse, Paul (Johann Ludwig von)

von Hofmannsthal, Hugo
See Hofmannsthal, Hugo von

von Horvath, Odon
See von Horvath, Odon

von Horvath, Odon
See von Horvath, Odon

von Horvath, Odon 1901-1938 .... **TCLC 45**
See von Horvath, Oedoen
See also CA 194; CAAE 118; DLB 85, 124; RGWL 2, 3

von Horvath, Oedoen
See von Horvath, Odon
See also CA 184

von Kleist, Heinrich
See Kleist, Heinrich von

Vonnegut, Kurt, Jr.
See Vonnegut, Kurt

Vonnegut, Kurt 1922-2007 .... **CLC 1, 2, 3, 4, 5, 8, 12, 22, 40, 60, 111, 212; SSC 8; WLC 6**
See also AAYA 6, 44; AITN 1; AMWS 2; BEST 90:4; BPFB 3; BYA 3, 14; CA 1-4R; CAAS 259; CANR 1, 25, 49, 75, 92; CDALB 1968-1988; CN 1, 2, 3, 4, 5, 6, 7; CPW 1; DA; DA3; DAB; DAC; DAM MST, NOV, POP; DLB 2, 8, 152; DLBD 3; DLBY 1980; EWL 3; EXPN; EXPS; LAIT 4; LMFS 2; MAL 5; MTCW 1, 2; MTFW 2005; NFS 3; RGAL 4; SCFW; SFW 4; SSFS 5; TUS; YAW

Von Rachen, Kurt
See Hubbard, L. Ron

von Sternberg, Josef
See Sternberg, Josef von

Vorster, Gordon 1924- .... **CLC 34**
See also CA 133

Warren, Robert Penn 1905-1989 .. **CLC 1, 4, 6, 8, 10, 13, 18, 39, 53, 59; PC 37; SSC 4, 58; WLC 6**
  See also AITN 1; AMW; AMWC 2; BPFB 3; BYA 1; CA 13-16R; CAAS 129; CANR 10, 47; CDALB 1968-1988; CN 1, 2, 3, 4; CP 1, 2, 3, 4; DA; DA3; DAB; DAC; DAM MST, NOV, POET; DLB 2, 48, 152, 320; DLBY 1980, 1989; EWL 3; INT CANR-10; MAL 5; MTCW 1, 2; MTFW 2005; NFS 13; RGAL 4; RGSF 2; RHW; SATA 46; SATA-Obit 63; SSFS 8; TUS

Warrigal, Jack
  See Furphy, Joseph

Warshofsky, Isaac
  See Singer, Isaac Bashevis

Warton, Joseph 1722-1800 ... **LC 128; NCLC 118**
  See also DLB 104, 109; RGEL 2

Warton, Thomas 1728-1790 .... **LC 15, 82**
  See also DAM POET; DLB 104, 109, 336; RGEL 2

Waruk, Kona
  See Harris, (Theodore) Wilson

Warung, Price .... **TCLC 45**
  See Astley, William
  See also DLB 230; RGEL 2

Warwick, Jarvis
  See Garner, Hugh
  See also CCA 1

Washington, Alex
  See Harris, Mark

Washington, Booker T(aliaferro) 1856-1915 .... **BLC 3; TCLC 10**
  See also BW 1; CA 125; CAAE 114; DA3; DAM MULT; LAIT 2; RGAL 4; SATA 28

Washington, George 1732-1799 .... **LC 25**
  See also DLB 31

Wassermann, (Karl) Jakob 1873-1934 .... **TCLC 6**
  See also CA 163; CAAE 104; DLB 66; EWL 3

Wasserstein, Wendy 1950-2006 . **CLC 32, 59, 90, 183; DC 4**
  See also AAYA 73; AMWS 15; CA 129; CAAE 121; CAAS 247; CABS 3; CAD; CANR 53, 75, 128; CD 5, 6; CWD; DA3; DAM DRAM; DFS 5, 17; DLB 228; EWL 3; FW; INT CA-129; MAL 5; MTCW 2; MTFW 2005; SATA 94; SATA-Obit 174

Waterhouse, Keith (Spencer) 1929- . **CLC 47**
  See also BRWS 13; CA 5-8R; CANR 38, 67, 109; CBD; CD 6; CN 1, 2, 3, 4, 5, 6, 7; DLB 13, 15; MTCW 1, 2; MTFW 2005

Waters, Frank (Joseph) 1902-1995 .. **CLC 88**
  See also CA 5-8R; 13; CAAS 149; CANR 3, 18, 63, 121; DLB 212; DLBY 1986; RGAL 4; TCWW 1, 2

Waters, Mary C. .... **CLC 70**

Waters, Roger 1944- .... **CLC 35**

Watkins, Frances Ellen
  See Harper, Frances Ellen Watkins

Watkins, Gerrold
  See Malzberg, Barry N(athaniel)

Watkins, Gloria Jean
  See hooks, bell

Watkins, Paul 1964- .... **CLC 55**
  See also CA 132; CANR 62, 98

Watkins, Vernon Phillips 1906-1967 .... **CLC 43**
  See also CA 9-10; CAAS 25-28R; CAP 1; DLB 20; EWL 3; RGEL 2

Watson, Irving S.
  See Mencken, H(enry) L(ouis)

Watson, John H.
  See Farmer, Philip Jose

Watson, Richard F.
  See Silverberg, Robert

Watts, Ephraim
  See Horne, Richard Henry Hengist

Watts, Isaac 1674-1748 .... **LC 98**
  See also DLB 95; RGEL 2; SATA 52

Waugh, Auberon (Alexander) 1939-2001 .... **CLC 7**
  See also CA 45-48; CAAS 192; CANR 6, 22, 92; CN 1, 2, 3; DLB 14, 194

Waugh, Evelyn (Arthur St. John) 1903-1966 .. **CLC 1, 3, 8, 13, 19, 27, 44, 107; SSC 41; WLC 6**
  See also BPFB 3; BRW 7; CA 85-88; CAAS 25-28R; CANR 22; CDBLB 1914-1945; DA; DA3; DAB; DAC; DAM MST, NOV, POP; DLB 15, 162, 195; EWL 3; MTCW 1, 2; MTFW 2005; NFS 13, 17; RGEL 2; RGSF 2; TEA; WLIT 4

Waugh, Harriet 1944- .... **CLC 6**
  See also CA 85-88; CANR 22

Ways, C. R.
  See Blount, Roy (Alton), Jr.

Waystaff, Simon
  See Swift, Jonathan

Webb, Beatrice (Martha Potter) 1858-1943 .... **TCLC 22**
  See also CA 162; CAAE 117; DLB 190; FW

Webb, Charles (Richard) 1939- .... **CLC 7**
  See also CA 25-28R; CANR 114

Webb, Frank J. .... **NCLC 143**
  See also DLB 50

Webb, James, Jr.
  See Webb, James

Webb, James 1946- .... **CLC 22**
  See also CA 81-84; CANR 156

Webb, James H.
  See Webb, James

Webb, James Henry
  See Webb, James

Webb, Mary Gladys (Meredith) 1881-1927 .... **TCLC 24**
  See also CA 182; CAAS 123; DLB 34; FW; RGEL 2

Webb, Mrs. Sidney
  See Webb, Beatrice (Martha Potter)

Webb, Phyllis 1927- .... **CLC 18**
  See also CA 104; CANR 23; CCA 1; CP 1, 2, 3, 4, 5, 6, 7; CWP; DLB 53

Webb, Sidney (James) 1859-1947 .. **TCLC 22**
  See also CA 163; CAAE 117; DLB 190

Webber, Andrew Lloyd .... **CLC 21**
  See Lloyd Webber, Andrew
  See also DFS 7

Weber, Lenora Mattingly 1895-1971 .... **CLC 12**
  See also CA 19-20; CAAS 29-32R; CAP 1; SATA 2; SATA-Obit 26

Weber, Max 1864-1920 .... **TCLC 69**
  See also CA 189; CAAE 109; DLB 296

Webster, John 1580(?)-1634(?) ...... **DC 2; LC 33, 84, 124; WLC 6**
  See also BRW 2; CDBLB Before 1660; DA; DAB; DAC; DAM DRAM, MST; DFS 17, 19; DLB 58; IDTP; RGEL 2; WLIT 3

Webster, Noah 1758-1843 .... **NCLC 30**
  See also DLB 1, 37, 42, 43, 73, 243

Wedekind, Benjamin Franklin
  See Wedekind, Frank

Wedekind, Frank 1864-1918 .... **TCLC 7**
  See also CA 153; CAAE 104; CANR 121, 122; CDWLB 2; DAM DRAM; DLB 118; EW 8; EWL 3; LMFS 2; RGWL 2, 3

Wehr, Demaris .... **CLC 65**

Weidman, Jerome 1913-1998 .... **CLC 7**
  See also AITN 2; CA 1-4R; CAAS 171; CAD; CANR 1; CD 1, 2, 3, 4, 5; DLB 28

Weil, Simone (Adolphine) 1909-1943 .... **TCLC 23**
  See also CA 159; CAAE 117; EW 12; EWL 3; FW; GFL 1789 to the Present; MTCW 2

Weininger, Otto 1880-1903 .... **TCLC 84**

Weinstein, Nathan
  See West, Nathanael

Weinstein, Nathan von Wallenstein
  See West, Nathanael

Weir, Peter (Lindsay) 1944- .... **CLC 20**
  See also CA 123; CAAE 113

Weiss, Peter (Ulrich) 1916-1982 .. **CLC 3, 15, 51; TCLC 152**
  See also CA 45-48; CAAS 106; CANR 3; DAM DRAM; DFS 3; DLB 69, 124; EWL 3; RGHL; RGWL 2, 3

Weiss, Theodore (Russell) 1916-2003 .... **CLC 3, 8, 14**
  See also CA 189; 9-12R, 189; 2; CAAS 216; CANR 46, 94; CP 1, 2, 3, 4, 5, 6, 7; DLB 5; TCLE 1:2

Welch, (Maurice) Denton 1915-1948 .... **TCLC 22**
  See also BRWS 8, 9; CA 148; CAAE 121; RGEL 2

Welch, James (Phillip) 1940-2003 ..... **CLC 6, 14, 52; NNAL; PC 62**
  See also CA 85-88; CAAS 219; CANR 42, 66, 107; CN 5, 6, 7; CP 2, 3, 4, 5, 6, 7; CPW; DAM MULT, POP; DLB 175, 256; LATS 1:1; NFS 23; RGAL 4; TCWW 1, 2

Weldon, Fay 1931- . **CLC 6, 9, 11, 19, 36, 59, 122**
  See also BRWS 4; CA 21-24R; CANR 16, 46, 63, 97, 137; CDBLB 1960 to Present; CN 3, 4, 5, 6, 7; CPW; DAM POP; DLB 14, 194, 319; EWL 3; FW; HGG; INT CANR-16; MTCW 1, 2; MTFW 2005; RGEL 2; RGSF 2

Wellek, Rene 1903-1995 .... **CLC 28**
  See also CA 5-8R; 7; CAAS 150; CANR 8; DLB 63; EWL 3; INT CANR-8

Weller, Michael 1942- .... **CLC 10, 53**
  See also CA 85-88; CAD; CD 5, 6

Weller, Paul 1958- .... **CLC 26**

Wellershoff, Dieter 1925- .... **CLC 46**
  See also CA 89-92; CANR 16, 37

Welles, (George) Orson 1915-1985 .. **CLC 20, 80**
  See also AAYA 40; CA 93-96; CAAS 117

Wellman, John McDowell 1945-
  See Wellman, Mac
  See also CA 166; CD 5

Wellman, Mac .... **CLC 65**
  See Wellman, John McDowell; Wellman, John McDowell
  See also CAD; CD 6; RGAL 4

Wellman, Manly Wade 1903-1986 ... **CLC 49**
  See also CA 1-4R; CAAS 118; CANR 6, 16, 44; FANT; SATA 6; SATA-Obit 47; SFW 4; SUFW

Wells, Carolyn 1869(?)-1942 .... **TCLC 35**
  See also CA 185; CAAE 113; CMW 4; DLB 11

Wells, H(erbert) G(eorge) 1866-1946 . **SSC 6, 70; TCLC 6, 12, 19, 133; WLC 6**
  See also AAYA 18; BPFB 3; BRW 6; CA 121; CAAE 110; CDBLB 1914-1945; CLR 64; DA; DA3; DAB; DAC; DAM MST, NOV; DLB 34, 70, 156, 178; EWL 3; EXPS; HGG; LAIT 3; LMFS 2; MTCW 1, 2; MTFW 2005; NFS 17, 20; RGEL 2; RGSF 2; SATA 20; SCFW 1, 2; SFW 4; SSFS 3; SUFW; TEA; WCH; WLIT 4; YAW

Wells, Rosemary 1943- .... **CLC 12**
 See also AAYA 13; BYA 7, 8; CA 85-88;
 CANR 48, 120; CLR 16, 69; CWRI 5;
 MAICYA 1, 2; SAAS 1; SATA 18, 69,
 114, 156; YAW

Wells-Barnett, Ida B(ell)
 1862-1931 .... **TCLC 125**
 See also CA 182; DLB 23, 221

Welsh, Irvine 1958- .... **CLC 144**
 See also CA 173; CANR 146; CN 7; DLB
 271

Welty, Eudora 1909-2001 .... **CLC 1, 2, 5, 14,
 22, 33, 105, 220; SSC 1, 27, 51; WLC 6**
 See also AAYA 48; AMW; AMWR 1; BPFB
 3; CA 9-12R; CAAS 199; CABS 1; CANR
 32, 65, 128; CDALB 1941-1968; CN 1,
 2, 3, 4, 5, 6, 7; CSW; DA; DA3; DAB;
 DAC; DAM MST, NOV; DLB 2, 102,
 143; DLBD 12; DLBY 1987, 2001; EWL
 3; EXPS; HGG; LAIT 3; MAL 5; MBL;
 MTCW 1, 2; MTFW 2005; NFS 13, 15;
 RGAL 4; RGSF 2; RHW; SSFS 2, 10;
 TUS

Welty, Eudora Alice
 See Welty, Eudora

Wen I-to 1899-1946 .... **TCLC 28**
 See also EWL 3

Wentworth, Robert
 See Hamilton, Edmond

Werfel, Franz (Viktor) 1890-1945 ... **TCLC 8**
 See also CA 161; CAAE 104; DLB 81, 124;
 EWL 3; RGWL 2, 3

Wergeland, Henrik Arnold
 1808-1845 .... **NCLC 5**

Wersba, Barbara 1932- .... **CLC 30**
 See also AAYA 2, 30; BYA 6, 12, 13; CA
 182; 29-32R, 182; CANR 16, 38; CLR 3,
 78; DLB 52; JRDA; MAICYA 1, 2; SAAS
 2; SATA 1, 58; SATA-Essay 103; WYA;
 YAW

Wertmueller, Lina 1928- .... **CLC 16**
 See also CA 97-100; CANR 39, 78

Wescott, Glenway 1901-1987 .. **CLC 13; SSC
 35**
 See also CA 13-16R; CAAS 121; CANR
 23, 70; CN 1, 2, 3, 4; DLB 4, 9, 102;
 MAL 5; RGAL 4

Wesker, Arnold 1932- .... **CLC 3, 5, 42**
 See also CA 1-4R; 7; CANR 1, 33; CBD;
 CD 5, 6; CDBLB 1960 to Present; DAB;
 DAM DRAM; DLB 13, 310, 319; EWL
 3; MTCW 1; RGEL 2; TEA

Wesley, Charles 1707-1788 .... **LC 128**
 See also DLB 95; RGEL 2

Wesley, John 1703-1791 .... **LC 88**
 See also DLB 104

Wesley, Richard (Errol) 1945- .... **CLC 7**
 See also BW 1; CA 57-60; CAD; CANR
 27; CD 5, 6; DLB 38

Wessel, Johan Herman 1742-1785 .... **LC 7**
 See also DLB 300

West, Anthony (Panther)
 1914-1987 .... **CLC 50**
 See also CA 45-48; CAAS 124; CANR 3,
 19; CN 1, 2, 3, 4; DLB 15

West, C. P.
 See Wodehouse, P(elham) G(renville)

West, Cornel 1953- .... **BLCS; CLC 134**
 See also CA 144; CANR 91, 159; DLB 246

West, Cornel Ronald
 See West, Cornel

West, Delno C(loyde), Jr. 1936- .... **CLC 70**
 See also CA 57-60

West, Dorothy 1907-1998 ...... **HR 1:3; TCLC
 108**
 See also BW 2; CA 143; CAAS 169; DLB
 76

West, (Mary) Jessamyn 1902-1984 ... **CLC 7,
 17**
 See also CA 9-12R; CAAS 112; CANR 27;
 CN 1, 2, 3; DLB 6; DLBY 1984; MTCW
 1, 2; RGAL 4; RHW; SATA-Obit 37;
 TCWW 2; TUS; YAW

West, Morris L(anglo) 1916-1999 ..... **CLC 6,
 33**
 See also BPFB 3; CA 5-8R; CAAS 187;
 CANR 24, 49, 64; CN 1, 2, 3, 4, 5, 6;
 CPW; DLB 289; MTCW 1, 2; MTFW
 2005

West, Nathanael 1903-1940 .. **SSC 16; TCLC
 1, 14, 44**
 See also AMW; AMWR 2; BPFB 3; CA
 125; CAAE 104; CDALB 1929-1941;
 DA3; DLB 4, 9, 28; EWL 3; MAL 5;
 MTCW 1, 2; MTFW 2005; NFS 16;
 RGAL 4; TUS

West, Owen
 See Koontz, Dean R.

West, Paul 1930- .... **CLC 7, 14, 96, 226**
 See also CA 13-16R; 7; CANR 22, 53, 76,
 89, 136; CN 1, 2, 3, 4, 5, 6, 7; DLB 14;
 INT CANR-22; MTCW 2; MTFW 2005

West, Rebecca 1892-1983 ... **CLC 7, 9, 31, 50**
 See also BPFB 3; BRWS 3; CA 5-8R;
 CAAS 109; CANR 19; CN 1, 2, 3; DLB
 36; DLBY 1983; EWL 3; FW; MTCW 1,
 2; MTFW 2005; NCFS 4; RGEL 2; TEA

Westall, Robert (Atkinson)
 1929-1993 .... **CLC 17**
 See also AAYA 12; BYA 2, 6, 7, 8, 9, 15;
 CA 69-72; CAAS 141; CANR 18, 68;
 CLR 13; FANT; JRDA; MAICYA 1, 2;
 MAICYAS 1; SAAS 2; SATA 23, 69;
 SATA-Obit 75; WYA; YAW

Westermarck, Edward 1862-1939 . **TCLC 87**

Westlake, Donald E. 1933- .... **CLC 7, 33**
 See also BPFB 3; CA 17-20R; 13; CANR
 16, 44, 65, 94, 137; CMW 4; CPW; DAM
 POP; INT CANR-16; MSW; MTCW 2;
 MTFW 2005

Westlake, Donald Edwin
 See Westlake, Donald E.

Westmacott, Mary
 See Christie, Agatha (Mary Clarissa)

Weston, Allen
 See Norton, Andre

Wetcheek, J. L.
 See Feuchtwanger, Lion

Wetering, Janwillem van de
 See van de Wetering, Janwillem

Wetherald, Agnes Ethelwyn
 1857-1940 .... **TCLC 81**
 See also CA 202; DLB 99

Wetherell, Elizabeth
 See Warner, Susan (Bogert)

Whale, James 1889-1957 .... **TCLC 63**
 See also AAYA 75

Whalen, Philip (Glenn) 1923-2002 .... **CLC 6,
 29**
 See also BG 1:3; CA 9-12R; CAAS 209;
 CANR 5, 39; CP 1, 2, 3, 4, 5, 6, 7; DLB
 16; WP

Wharton, Edith (Newbold Jones)
 1862-1937 ... **SSC 6, 84; TCLC 3, 9, 27,
 53, 129, 149; WLC 6**
 See also AAYA 25; AMW; AMWC 2;
 AMWR 1; BPFB 3; CA 132; CAAE 104;
 CDALB 1865-1917; DA; DA3; DAB;
 DAC; DAM MST, NOV; DLB 4, 9, 12,
 78, 189; DLBD 13; EWL 3; EXPS; FL
 1:6; GL 3; HGG; LAIT 2, 3; LATS 1:1;
 MAL 5; MBL; MTCW 1, 2; MTFW 2005;
 NFS 5, 11, 15, 20; RGAL 4; RGSF 2;
 RHW; SSFS 6, 7; SUFW; TUS

Wharton, James
 See Mencken, H(enry) L(ouis)

Wharton, William (a pseudonym)
 1925- .... **CLC 18, 37**
 See also CA 93-96; CN 4, 5, 6, 7; DLBY
 1980; INT CA-93-96

Wheatley (Peters), Phillis
 1753(?)-1784 ... **BLC 3; LC 3, 50; PC 3;
 WLC 6**
 See also AFAW 1, 2; CDALB 1640-1865;
 DA; DA3; DAC; DAM MST, MULT,
 POET; DLB 31, 50; EXPP; FL 1:1; PFS
 13; RGAL 4

Wheelock, John Hall 1886-1978 .... **CLC 14**
 See also CA 13-16R; CAAS 77-80; CANR
 14; CP 1, 2; DLB 45; MAL 5

Whim-Wham
 See Curnow, (Thomas) Allen (Monro)

Whisp, Kennilworthy
 See Rowling, J.K.

Whitaker, Rod 1931-2005
 See Trevanian
 See also CA 29-32R; CAAS 246; CANR
 45, 153; CMW 4

White, Babington
 See Braddon, Mary Elizabeth

White, E. B. 1899-1985 .... **CLC 10, 34, 39**
 See also AAYA 62; AITN 2; AMWS 1; CA
 13-16R; CAAS 116; CANR 16, 37;
 CDALBS; CLR 1, 21, 107; CPW; DA3;
 DAM POP; DLB 11, 22; EWL 3; FANT;
 MAICYA 1, 2; MAL 5; MTCW 1, 2;
 MTFW 2005; NCFS 5; RGAL 4; SATA 2,
 29, 100; SATA-Obit 44; TUS

White, Edmund 1940- .... **CLC 27, 110**
 See also AAYA 7; CA 45-48; CANR 3, 19,
 36, 62, 107, 133; CN 5, 6, 7; DA3; DAM
 POP; DLB 227; MTCW 1, 2; MTFW
 2005

White, Elwyn Brooks
 See White, E. B.

White, Hayden V. 1928- .... **CLC 148**
 See also CA 128; CANR 135; DLB 246

White, Patrick (Victor Martindale)
 1912-1990 ...... **CLC 3, 4, 5, 7, 9, 18, 65,
 69; SSC 39; TCLC 176**
 See also BRWS 1; CA 81-84; CAAS 132;
 CANR 43; CN 1, 2, 3, 4; DLB 260, 332;
 EWL 3; MTCW 1; RGEL 2; RGSF 2;
 RHW; TWA; WWE 1

White, Phyllis Dorothy James 1920-
 See James, P. D.
 See also CA 21-24R; CANR 17, 43, 65,
 112; CMW 4; CN 7; CPW; DA3; DAM
 POP; MTCW 1, 2; MTFW 2005; TEA

White, T(erence) H(anbury)
 1906-1964 .... **CLC 30**
 See also AAYA 22; BPFB 3; BYA 4, 5; CA
 73-76; CANR 37; DLB 160; FANT;
 JRDA; LAIT 1; MAICYA 1, 2; RGEL 2;
 SATA 12; SUFW 1; YAW

White, Terence de Vere 1912-1994 ... **CLC 49**
 See also CA 49-52; CAAS 145; CANR 3

White, Walter
 See White, Walter F(rancis)

White, Walter F(rancis) 1893-1955 ... **BLC 3;
 HR 1:3; TCLC 15**
 See also BW 1; CA 124; CAAE 115; DAM
 MULT; DLB 51

White, William Hale 1831-1913
 See Rutherford, Mark
 See also CA 189; CAAE 121

Whitehead, Alfred North
 1861-1947 .... **TCLC 97**
 See also CA 165; CAAE 117; DLB 100,
 262

Whitehead, Colson 1970- .... **CLC 232**
 See also CA 202; CANR 162

Wolfe, Tom .... **CLC 1, 2, 9, 15, 35, 51**
See Wolfe, Thomas Kennerly, Jr.
See also AAYA 8, 67; AITN 2; AMWS 3;
BEST 89:1; BPFB 3; CN 5, 6, 7; CPW;
CSW; DLB 152; LAIT 5; RGAL 4

Wolff, Geoffrey 1937- .... **CLC 41**
See also CA 29-32R; CANR 29, 43, 78, 154

Wolff, Geoffrey Ansell
See Wolff, Geoffrey

Wolff, Sonia
See Levitin, Sonia (Wolff)

Wolff, Tobias 1945- .... **CLC 39, 64, 172; SSC 63**
See also AAYA 16; AMWS 7; BEST 90:2;
BYA 12; CA 117; 22; CAAE 114; CANR
54, 76, 96; CN 5, 6, 7; CSW; DA3; DLB
130; EWL 3; INT CA-117; MTCW 2;
MTFW 2005; RGAL 4; RGSF 2; SSFS 4, 11

Wolitzer, Hilma 1930- .... **CLC 17**
See also CA 65-68; CANR 18, 40; INT
CANR-18; SATA 31; YAW

Wollstonecraft, Mary 1759-1797 .... **LC 5, 50, 90**
See also BRWS 3; CDBLB 1789-1832;
DLB 39, 104, 158, 252; FL 1:1; FW;
LAIT 1; RGEL 2; TEA; WLIT 3

Wonder, Stevie 1950- .... **CLC 12**
See also CAAE 111

Wong, Jade Snow 1922-2006 .... **CLC 17**
See also CA 109; CAAS 249; CANR 91;
SATA 112; SATA-Obit 175

Wood, Ellen Price
See Wood, Mrs. Henry

Wood, Mrs. Henry 1814-1887 ...... **NCLC 178**
See also CMW 4; DLB 18; SUFW

Wood, James 1965- .... **CLC 238**
See also CA 235

Woodberry, George Edward
1855-1930 .... **TCLC 73**
See also CA 165; DLB 71, 103

Woodcott, Keith
See Brunner, John (Kilian Houston)

Woodruff, Robert W.
See Mencken, H(enry) L(ouis)

Woodward, Bob
See Woodward, Robert Upshur

Woodward, Robert Upshur 1943- .. **CLC 240**
See also CA 69-72; CANR 31, 67, 107;
MTCW 1

Woolf, (Adeline) Virginia 1882-1941 .. **SSC 7, 79; TCLC 1, 5, 20, 43, 56, 101, 123, 128; WLC 6**
See also AAYA 44; BPFB 3; BRW 7;
BRWC 2; BRWR 1; CA 130; CAAE 104;
CANR 64, 132; CDBLB 1914-1945; DA;
DA3; DAB; DAC; DAM MST, NOV;
DLB 36, 100, 162; DLBD 10; EWL 3;
EXPS; FL 1:6; FW; LAIT 3; LATS 1:1;
LMFS 2; MTCW 1, 2; MTFW 2005;
NCFS 2; NFS 8, 12; RGEL 2; RGSF 2;
SSFS 4, 12; TEA; WLIT 4

Woollcott, Alexander (Humphreys)
1887-1943 .... **TCLC 5**
See also CA 161; CAAE 105; DLB 29

Woolrich, Cornell .... **CLC 77**
See Hopley-Woolrich, Cornell George
See also MSW

Woolson, Constance Fenimore
1840-1894 .... **NCLC 82; SSC 90**
See also DLB 12, 74, 189, 221; RGAL 4

Wordsworth, Dorothy 1771-1855 . **NCLC 25, 138**
See also DLB 107

Wordsworth, William 1770-1850 .. **NCLC 12, 38, 111, 166; PC 4, 67; WLC 6**
See also AAYA 70; BRW 4; BRWC 1; CD-
BLB 1789-1832; DA; DA3; DAB; DAC;
DAM MST, POET; DLB 93, 107; EXPP;
LATS 1:1; LMFS 1; PAB; PFS 2; RGEL
2; TEA; WLIT 3; WP

Wotton, Sir Henry 1568-1639 .... **LC 68**
See also DLB 121; RGEL 2

Wouk, Herman 1915- .... **CLC 1, 9, 38**
See also BPFB 2, 3; CA 5-8R; CANR 6,
33, 67, 146; CDALBS; CN 1, 2, 3, 4, 5,
6; CPW; DA3; DAM NOV, POP; DLBY
1982; INT CANR-6; LAIT 4; MAL 5;
MTCW 1, 2; MTFW 2005; NFS 7; TUS

Wright, Charles 1935- ... **CLC 6, 13, 28, 119, 146**
See also AMWS 5; CA 29-32R; 7; CANR
23, 36, 62, 88, 135; CP 3, 4, 5, 6, 7; DLB
165; DLBY 1982; EWL 3; MTCW 1, 2;
MTFW 2005; PFS 10

Wright, Charles Stevenson 1932- ..... **BLC 3; CLC 49**
See also BW 1; CA 9-12R; CANR 26; CN
1, 2, 3, 4, 5, 6, 7; DAM MULT, POET;
DLB 33

Wright, Frances 1795-1852 .... **NCLC 74**
See also DLB 73

Wright, Frank Lloyd 1867-1959 .... **TCLC 95**
See also AAYA 33; CA 174

Wright, Harold Bell 1872-1944 .... **TCLC 183**
See also BPFB 3; CAAE 110; DLB 9;
TCWW 2

Wright, Jack R.
See Harris, Mark

Wright, James (Arlington)
1927-1980 .... **CLC 3, 5, 10, 28; PC 36**
See also AITN 2; AMWS 3; CA 49-52;
CAAS 97-100; CANR 4, 34, 64;
CDALBS; CP 1, 2; DAM POET; DLB 5,
169; EWL 3; EXPP; MAL 5; MTCW 1,
2; MTFW 2005; PFS 7, 8; RGAL 4; TUS;
WP

Wright, Judith 1915-2000 ... **CLC 11, 53; PC 14**
See also CA 13-16R; CAAS 188; CANR
31, 76, 93; CP 1, 2, 3, 4, 5, 6, 7; CWP;
DLB 260; EWL 3; MTCW 1, 2; MTFW
2005; PFS 8; RGEL 2; SATA 14; SATA-
Obit 121

Wright, L(aurali) R. 1939- .... **CLC 44**
See also CA 138; CMW 4

Wright, Richard (Nathaniel)
1908-1960 ... **BLC 3; CLC 1, 3, 4, 9, 14, 21, 48, 74; SSC 2; TCLC 136, 180; WLC 6**
See also AAYA 5, 42; AFAW 1, 2; AMW;
BPFB 3; BW 1; BYA 2; CA 108; CANR
64; CDALB 1929-1941; DA; DA3; DAB;
DAC; DAM MST, MULT, NOV; DLB 76,
102; DLBD 2; EWL 3; EXPN; LAIT 3,
4; MAL 5; MTCW 1, 2; MTFW 2005;
NCFS 1; NFS 1, 7; RGAL 4; RGSF 2;
SSFS 3, 9, 15, 20; TUS; YAW

Wright, Richard B(ruce) 1937- .... **CLC 6**
See also CA 85-88; CANR 120; DLB 53

Wright, Rick 1945- .... **CLC 35**

Wright, Rowland
See Wells, Carolyn

Wright, Stephen 1946- .... **CLC 33**
See also CA 237

Wright, Willard Huntington 1888-1939
See Van Dine, S. S.
See also CA 189; CAAE 115; CMW 4;
DLBD 16

Wright, William 1930- .... **CLC 44**
See also CA 53-56; CANR 7, 23, 154

Wroth, Lady Mary 1587-1653(?) .... **LC 30, 139; PC 38**
See also DLB 121

Wu Ch'eng-en 1500(?)-1582(?) .... **LC 7**

Wu Ching-tzu 1701-1754 .... **LC 2**

Wulfstan c. 10th cent. -1023 .... **CMLC 59**

Wurlitzer, Rudolph 1938(?)- .... **CLC 2, 4, 15**
See also CA 85-88; CN 4, 5, 6, 7; DLB 173

Wyatt, Sir Thomas c. 1503-1542 . **LC 70; PC 27**
See also BRW 1; DLB 132; EXPP; PFS 25;
RGEL 2; TEA

Wycherley, William 1640-1716 .... **LC 8, 21, 102, 136**
See also BRW 2; CDBLB 1660-1789; DAM
DRAM; DLB 80; RGEL 2

Wyclif, John c. 1330-1384 .... **CMLC 70**
See also DLB 146

Wylie, Elinor (Morton Hoyt)
1885-1928 .... **PC 23; TCLC 8**
See also AMWS 1; CA 162; CAAE 105;
DLB 9, 45; EXPP; MAL 5; RGAL 4

Wylie, Philip (Gordon) 1902-1971 ... **CLC 43**
See also CA 21-22; CAAS 33-36R; CAP 2;
CN 1; DLB 9; SFW 4

Wyndham, John .... **CLC 19**
See Harris, John (Wyndham Parkes Lucas)
Beynon
See also BRWS 13; DLB 255; SCFW 1, 2

Wyss, Johann David Von
1743-1818 .... **NCLC 10**
See also CLR 92; JRDA; MAICYA 1, 2;
SATA 29; SATA-Brief 27

Xenophon c. 430B.C.-c. 354B.C. ... **CMLC 17**
See also AW 1; DLB 176; RGWL 2, 3;
WLIT 8

Xingjian, Gao 1940-
See Gao Xingjian
See also CA 193; DFS 21; DLB 330;
RGWL 3

Yakamochi 718-785 .... **CMLC 45; PC 48**

Yakumo Koizumi
See Hearn, (Patricio) Lafcadio (Tessima
Carlos)

Yamada, Mitsuye (May) 1923- .... **PC 44**
See also CA 77-80

Yamamoto, Hisaye 1921- .... **AAL; SSC 34**
See also CA 214; DAM MULT; DLB 312;
LAIT 4; SSFS 14

Yamauchi, Wakako 1924- .... **AAL**
See also CA 214; DLB 312

Yanez, Jose Donoso
See Donoso (Yanez), Jose

Yanovsky, Basile S.
See Yanovsky, V(assily) S(emenovich)

Yanovsky, V(assily) S(emenovich)
1906-1989 .... **CLC 2, 18**
See also CA 97-100; CAAS 129

Yates, Richard 1926-1992 .... **CLC 7, 8, 23**
See also AMWS 11; CA 5-8R; CAAS 139;
CANR 10, 43; CN 1, 2, 3, 4, 5; DLB 2,
234; DLBY 1981, 1992; INT CANR-10;
SSFS 24

Yau, John 1950- .... **PC 61**
See also CA 154; CANR 89; CP 4, 5, 6, 7;
DLB 234, 312; PFS 26

Yearsley, Ann 1753-1806 .... **NCLC 174**
See also DLB 109

Yeats, W. B.
See Yeats, William Butler

Yeats, William Butler 1865-1939 . **PC 20, 51; TCLC 1, 11, 18, 31, 93, 116; WLC 6**
See also AAYA 48; BRW 6; BRWR 1; CA
127; CAAE 104; CANR 45; CDBLB
1890-1914; DA; DA3; DAB; DAC; DAM
DRAM, MST, POET; DLB 10, 19, 98,
156, 332; EWL 3; EXPP; MTCW 1, 2;
MTFW 2005; NCFS 3; PAB; PFS 1, 2, 5,
7, 13, 15; RGEL 2; TEA; WLIT 4; WP

Yehoshua, A. B. 1936- .... **CLC 13, 31, 243**
See also CA 33-36R; CANR 43, 90, 145;
CWW 2; EWL 3; RGHL; RGSF 2; RGWL
3; WLIT 6

Yehoshua, Abraham B.
See Yehoshua, A.B.

Yellow Bird
See Ridge, John Rollin

Yep, Laurence 1948- .... **CLC 35**
See also AAYA 5, 31; BYA 7; CA 49-52;
CANR 1, 46, 92, 161; CLR 3, 17, 54;
DLB 52, 312; FANT; JRDA; MAICYA 1,
2; MAICYAS 1; SATA 7, 69, 123, 176;
WYA; YAW

Yep, Laurence Michael
See Yep, Laurence

Yerby, Frank G(arvin) 1916-1991 ..... **BLC 3;
CLC 1, 7, 22**
See also BPFB 3; BW 1, 3; CA 9-12R;
CAAS 136; CANR 16, 52; CN 1, 2, 3, 4,
5; DAM MULT; DLB 76; INT CANR-16;
MTCW 1; RGAL 4; RHW

Yesenin, Sergei Aleksandrovich
See Esenin, Sergei

Yevtushenko, Yevgeny (Alexandrovich)
1933- ...... **CLC 1, 3, 13, 26, 51, 126; PC
40**
See Evtushenko, Evgenii Aleksandrovich
See also CA 81-84; CANR 33, 54; DAM
POET; EWL 3; MTCW 1; RGHL

Yezierska, Anzia 1885(?)-1970 .... **CLC 46**
See also CA 126; CAAS 89-92; DLB 28,
221; FW; MTCW 1; RGAL 4; SSFS 15

Yglesias, Helen 1915- .... **CLC 7, 22**
See also CA 37-40R; 20; CANR 15, 65, 95;
CN 4, 5, 6, 7; INT CANR-15; MTCW 1

Yokomitsu, Riichi 1898-1947 .... **TCLC 47**
See also CA 170; EWL 3

Yonge, Charlotte (Mary)
1823-1901 .... **TCLC 48**
See also CA 163; CAAE 109; DLB 18, 163;
RGEL 2; SATA 17; WCH

York, Jeremy
See Creasey, John

York, Simon
See Heinlein, Robert A.

Yorke, Henry Vincent 1905-1974 ..... **CLC 13**
See Green, Henry
See also CA 85-88; CAAS 49-52

Yosano, Akiko 1878-1942 ... **PC 11; TCLC 59**
See also CA 161; EWL 3; RGWL 3

Yoshimoto, Banana .... **CLC 84**
See Yoshimoto, Mahoko
See also AAYA 50; NFS 7

Yoshimoto, Mahoko 1964-
See Yoshimoto, Banana
See also CA 144; CANR 98, 160; SSFS 16

Young, Al(bert James) 1939- ... **BLC 3; CLC
19**
See also BW 2, 3; CA 29-32R; CANR 26,
65, 109; CN 2, 3, 4, 5, 6, 7; CP 1, 2, 3, 4,
5, 6, 7; DAM MULT; DLB 33

Young, Andrew (John) 1885-1971 ...... **CLC 5**
See also CA 5-8R; CANR 7, 29; CP 1;
RGEL 2

Young, Collier
See Bloch, Robert (Albert)

Young, Edward 1683-1765 .... **LC 3, 40**
See also DLB 95; RGEL 2

Young, Marguerite (Vivian)
1909-1995 .... **CLC 82**
See also CA 13-16; CAAS 150; CAP 1; CN
1, 2, 3, 4, 5, 6

Young, Neil 1945- .... **CLC 17**
See also CA 110; CCA 1

Young Bear, Ray A. 1950- ... **CLC 94; NNAL**
See also CA 146; DAM MULT; DLB 175;
MAL 5

Yourcenar, Marguerite 1903-1987 ... **CLC 19,
38, 50, 87; TCLC 193**
See also BPFB 3; CA 69-72; CANR 23, 60,
93; DAM NOV; DLB 72; DLBY 1988;
EW 12; EWL 3; GFL 1789 to the Present;
GLL 1; MTCW 1, 2; MTFW 2005;
RGWL 2, 3

Yuan, Chu 340(?)B.C.-278(?)B.C. . **CMLC 36**
Yurick, Sol 1925- .... **CLC 6**
See also CA 13-16R; CANR 25; CN 1, 2,
3, 4, 5, 6, 7; MAL 5

Zabolotsky, Nikolai Alekseevich
1903-1958 .... **TCLC 52**
See Zabolotsky, Nikolay Alekseevich
See also CA 164; CAAE 116

Zabolotsky, Nikolay Alekseevich
See Zabolotsky, Nikolai Alekseevich
See also EWL 3

Zagajewski, Adam 1945- .... **PC 27**
See also CA 186; DLB 232; EWL 3; PFS
25

Zalygin, Sergei -2000 .... **CLC 59**
Zalygin, Sergei (Pavlovich)
1913-2000 .... **CLC 59**
See also DLB 302

Zamiatin, Evgenii
See Zamyatin, Evgeny Ivanovich
See also RGSF 2; RGWL 2, 3

Zamiatin, Evgenii Ivanovich
See Zamyatin, Evgeny Ivanovich
See also DLB 272

Zamiatin, Yevgenii
See Zamyatin, Evgeny Ivanovich

Zamora, Bernice (B. Ortiz) 1938- .. **CLC 89;
HLC 2**
See also CA 151; CANR 80; DAM MULT;
DLB 82; HW 1, 2

Zamyatin, Evgeny Ivanovich
1884-1937 .... **SSC 89; TCLC 8, 37**
See Zamiatin, Evgenii; Zamiatin, Evgenii
Ivanovich; Zamyatin, Yevgeny Ivanovich
See also CA 166; CAAE 105; SFW 4

Zamyatin, Yevgeny Ivanovich
See Zamyatin, Evgeny Ivanovich
See also EW 10; EWL 3

Zangwill, Israel 1864-1926 ... **SSC 44; TCLC
16**
See also CA 167; CAAE 109; CMW 4;
DLB 10, 135, 197; RGEL 2

Zanzotto, Andrea 1921- .... **PC 65**
See also CA 208; CWW 2; DLB 128; EWL
3

Zappa, Francis Vincent, Jr. 1940-1993
See Zappa, Frank
See also CA 108; CAAS 143; CANR 57

Zappa, Frank .... **CLC 17**
See Zappa, Francis Vincent, Jr.

Zaturenska, Marya 1902-1982 ..... **CLC 6, 11**
See also CA 13-16R; CAAS 105; CANR
22; CP 1, 2, 3

Zayas y Sotomayor, Maria de 1590-c.
1661 .... **LC 102; SSC 94**
See also RGSF 2

Zeami 1363-1443 .... **DC 7; LC 86**
See also DLB 203; RGWL 2, 3

Zelazny, Roger 1937-1995 .... **CLC 21**
See also AAYA 7, 68; BPFB 3; CA 21-24R;
CAAS 148; CANR 26, 60; CN 6; DLB 8;
FANT; MTCW 1, 2; MTFW 2005; SATA
57; SATA-Brief 39; SCFW 1, 2; SFW 4;
SUFW 1, 2

Zhang Ailing
See Chang, Eileen
See also CWW 2; DLB 328; RGSF 2

Zhdanov, Andrei Alexandrovich
1896-1948 .... **TCLC 18**
See also CA 167; CAAE 117

Zhukovsky, Vasilii Andreevich
See Zhukovsky, Vasily (Andreevich)
See also DLB 205

Zhukovsky, Vasily (Andreevich)
1783-1852 .... **NCLC 35**
See Zhukovsky, Vasilii Andreevich

Ziegenhagen, Eric .... **CLC 55**
Zimmer, Jill Schary
See Robinson, Jill

Zimmerman, Robert
See Dylan, Bob

Zindel, Paul 1936-2003 ...... **CLC 6, 26; DC 5**
See also AAYA 2, 37; BYA 2, 3, 8, 11, 14;
CA 73-76; CAAS 213; CAD; CANR 31,
65, 108; CD 5, 6; CDALBS; CLR 3, 45,
85; DA; DA3; DAB; DAC; DAM DRAM,
MST, NOV; DFS 12; DLB 7, 52; JRDA;
LAIT 5; MAICYA 1, 2; MTCW 1, 2;
MTFW 2005; NFS 14; SATA 16, 58, 102;
SATA-Obit 142; WYA; YAW

Zinger, Yisroel-Yehoyshue
See Singer, Israel Joshua

Zinger, Yitskhok
See Singer, Isaac Bashevis

Zinn, Howard 1922- .... **CLC 199**
See also CA 1-4R; CANR 2, 33, 90, 159

Zinov'Ev, A.A.
See Zinoviev, Alexander

Zinov'ev, Aleksandr
See Zinoviev, Alexander
See also DLB 302

Zinoviev, Alexander 1922-2006 .... **CLC 19**
See Zinov'ev, Aleksandr
See also CA 133; 10; CAAE 116; CAAS
250

Zinoviev, Alexander Aleksandrovich
See Zinoviev, Alexander

Zizek, Slavoj 1949- .... **CLC 188**
See also CA 201; MTFW 2005

Zoilus
See Lovecraft, H. P.

Zola, Emile (Edouard Charles Antoine)
1840-1902 .. **TCLC 1, 6, 21, 41; WLC 6**
See also CA 138; CAAE 104; DA; DA3;
DAB; DAC; DAM MST, NOV; DLB 123;
EW 7; GFL 1789 to the Present; IDTP;
LMFS 1, 2; RGWL 2; TWA

Zoline, Pamela 1941- .... **CLC 62**
See also CA 161; SFW 4

Zoroaster 628(?)B.C.-551(?)B.C. ... **CMLC 40**
Zorrilla y Moral, Jose 1817-1893 .... **NCLC 6**
Zoshchenko, Mikhail 1895-1958 ...... **SSC 15;
TCLC 15**
See also CA 160; CAAE 115; EWL 3;
RGSF 2; RGWL 3

Zoshchenko, Mikhail Mikhailovich
See Zoshchenko, Mikhail

Zuckmayer, Carl 1896-1977 .... **CLC 18;
TCLC 191**
See also CA 69-72; DLB 56, 124; EWL 3;
RGWL 2, 3

Zuk, Georges
See Skelton, Robin
See also CCA 1

Zukofsky, Louis 1904-1978 ... **CLC 1, 2, 4, 7,
11, 18; PC 11**
See also AMWS 3; CA 9-12R; CAAS 77-
80; CANR 39; CP 1, 2; DAM POET; DLB
5, 165; EWL 3; MAL 5; MTCW 1; RGAL
4

Zweig, Paul 1935-1984 .... **CLC 34, 42**
See also CA 85-88; CAAS 113

Zweig, Stefan 1881-1942 .... **TCLC 17**
See also CA 170; CAAE 112; DLB 81, 118;
EWL 3; RGHL

Zwingli, Huldreich 1484-1531 .... **LC 37**
See also DLB 179

Literary Criticism Series
Cumulative Topic Index

This index lists all topic entries in Thomson Gale's *Children's Literature Review* (CLR), *Classical and Medieval Literature Criticism* (CMLC), *Contemporary Literary Criticism* (CLC), *Drama Criticism* (DC), *Literature Criticism from 1400 to 1800* (LC), *Nineteenth-Century Literature Criticism* (NCLC), *Short Story Criticism* (SSC), and *Twentieth-Century Literary Criticism* (TCLC). The index also lists topic entries in the Gale Critical Companion Collection, which includes the following publications: *The Beat Generation* (BG), *Feminism in Literature* (FL), *Gothic Literature* (GL), and *Harlem Renaissance* (HR).

Topic Index

TCLC Cumulative Nationality Index

Bernanos, (Paul Louis) Georges **3**
Bernhardt, Sarah (Henriette Rosine) **75**
Bloy, Léon **22**
Bourget, Paul (Charles Joseph) **12**
Claudel, Paul (Louis Charles Marie) **2, 10**
Cocteau, Jean (Maurice Eugene Clement) **119**
Colette, (Sidonie-Gabrielle) **1, 5, 16**
Coppee, Francois **25**
Crevel, Rene **112**
Daumal, Rene **14**
Deleuze, Gilles **116**
Desnos, Robert **22**
Drieu la Rochelle, Pierre(-Eugène) **21**
Dujardin, Edouard (Emile Louis) **13**
Durkheim, Emile **55**
Epstein, Jean **92**
Fargue, Leon-Paul **11**
Feydeau, Georges (Léon Jules Marie) **22**
Fondane, Benjamin **159**
Genet, Jean **128**
Gide, André (Paul Guillaume) **5, 12, 36, 177**
Giono, Jean **124**
Giraudoux, Jean(-Hippolyte) **2, 7**
Gourmont, Remy(-Marie-Charles) de **17**
Halévy, Elie **104**
Huysmans, Joris-Karl **7, 69**
Jacob, (Cyprien-)Max **6**
Jammes, Francis **75**
Jarry, Alfred **2, 14, 147**
Larbaud, Valery (Nicolas) **9**
Léautaud, Paul **83**
Leblanc, Maurice (Marie Emile) **49**
Leroux, Gaston **25**
Lyotard, Jean-François **103**
Martin du Gard, Roger **24**
Melies, Georges **81**
Merlau-Ponty, Maurice **156**
Mirbeau, Octave **55**
Mistral, Frédéric **51**
Nizan, Paul **40**
Péguy, Charles (Pierre) **10**
Péret, Benjamin **20**
Proust, (Valentin-Louis-George-Eugène-)Marcel **7, 13, 33, 161**
Radiguet, Raymond **29**
Renard, Jules **17**
Rolland, Romain **23**
Rostand, Edmond (Eugene Alexis) **6, 37**
Roussel, Raymond **20**
Saint-Exupéry, Antoine (Jean Baptiste Marie Roger) de **2, 56, 169**
Schwob, Marcel (Mayer André) **20**
Sorel, Georges **91**
Sully Prudhomme, René-François-Armand **31**
Teilhard de Chardin, (Marie Joseph) Pierre **9**
Tzara, Tristan **168**
Valéry, (Ambroise) Paul (Toussaint Jules) **4, 15**
Vallette, Marguerite Eymery **67**
Verne, Jules (Gabriel) **6, 52**
Vian, Boris **9**
Weil, Simone (Adolphine) **23**
Yourcenar, Marguerite **193**
Zola, Émile (Édouard Charles Antoine) **1, 6, 21, 41**

GERMAN

Adorno, Theodor W(iesengrund) **111**
Andreas-Salome, Lou **56**
Arendt, Hannah **193**
Arp, Jean **115**
Auerbach, Erich **43**
Ball, Hugo **104**
Barlach, Ernst (Heinrich) **84**
Benjamin, Walter **39**
Benn, Gottfried **3**
Böll, Heinrich **185**
Borchert, Wolfgang **5**
Brecht, (Eugen) Bertolt (Friedrich) **1, 6, 13, 35, 169**

Carossa, Hans **48**
Cassirer, Ernst **61**
Doeblin, Alfred **13**
Einstein, Albert **65**
Ewers, Hanns Heinz **12**
Feuchtwanger, Lion **3**
Frank, Bruno **81**
George, Stefan (Anton) **2, 14**
Goebbels, (Paul) Joseph **68**
Haeckel, Ernst Heinrich (Philipp August) **83**
Hauptmann, Gerhart (Johann Robert) **4**
Heym, Georg (Theodor Franz Arthur) **9**
Heyse, Paul (Johann Ludwig von) **8**
Hitler, Adolf **53**
Horkheimer, Max **132**
Horney, Karen (Clementine Theodore Danielsen) **71**
Huch, Ricarda (Octavia) **13**
Husserl, Edmund (Gustav Albrecht) **100**
Kaiser, Georg **9**
Klabund **44**
Kolmar, Gertrud **40**
Lasker-Schueler, Else **57**
Liliencron, (Friedrich Adolf Axel) Detlev von **18**
Luxemburg, Rosa **63**
Mann, (Luiz) Heinrich **9**
Mann, (Paul) Thomas **2, 8, 14, 21, 35, 44, 60, 168**
Mannheim, Karl **65**
Michels, Robert **88**
Morgenstern, Christian (Otto Josef Wolfgang) **8**
Neumann, Alfred **100**
Nietzsche, Friedrich (Wilhelm) **10, 18, 55**
Ophuls, Max **79**
Otto, Rudolf **85**
Plumpe, Friedrich Wilhelm **53**
Raabe, Wilhelm (Karl) **45**
Rilke, Rainer Maria **1, 6, 19**
Schreber, Daniel Paul **123**
Schwitters, Kurt (Hermann Edward Karl Julius) **95**
Simmel, Georg **64**
Spengler, Oswald (Arnold Gottfried) **25**
Sternheim, (William Adolf) Carl **8**
Strauss, Leo **141**
Sudermann, Hermann **15**
Toller, Ernst **10**
Vaihinger, Hans **71**
von Hartmann, Eduard **96**
Wassermann, (Karl) Jakob **6**
Weber, Max **69**
Wedekind, (Benjamin) Frank(lin) **7**
Wiene, Robert **56**
Zuckmayer, Carl **191**

GHANIAN

Casely-Hayford, J(oseph) E(phraim) **24**

GREEK

Cavafy, C(onstantine) P(eter) **2, 7**
Kazantzakis, Nikos **2, 5, 33, 181**
Palamas, Kostes **5**
Papadiamantis, Alexandros **29**
Sikelianos, Angelos **39**

GUATEMALAN

Asturias, Miguel Ángel **184**

HAITIAN

Roumain, Jacques (Jean Baptiste) **19**

HUNGARIAN

Ady, Endre **11**
Babits, Mihaly **14**
Csath, Geza **13**
Herzl, Theodor **36**
Horváth, Ödön von **45**
Jozsef, Attila **22**

Karinthy, Frigyes **47**
Mikszath, Kalman **31**
Molnár, Ferenc **20**
Moricz, Zsigmond **33**
Radnóti, Miklós **16**

ICELANDIC

Sigurjonsson, Johann **27**

INDIAN

Chatterji, Saratchandra **13**
Dasgupta, Surendranath **81**
Gandhi, Mohandas Karamchand **59**
Ghose, Aurabinda **63**
Iqbal, Muhammad **28**
Naidu, Sarojini **80**
Premchand **21**
Ramana Maharshi **84**
Tagore, Rabindranath **3, 53**
Vivekananda, Swami **88**

INDONESIAN

Anwar, Chairil **22**

IRANIAN

Hedabayat, Sãdeq **21**

IRISH

A.E. **3, 10**
Baker, Jean H. **3, 10**
Cary, (Arthur) Joyce (Lunel) **1, 29**
Gogarty, Oliver St. John **15**
Gregory, Isabella Augusta (Persse) **1, 176**
Harris, Frank **24**
Joyce, James (Augustine Aloysius) **3, 8, 16, 35, 52, 159**
Ledwidge, Francis **23**
Martin, Violet Florence **51**
Martyn, Edward **131**
Moore, George Augustus **7**
Murdoch, Iris **171**
O'Faolain, Sean **143**
O'Grady, Standish (James) **5**
Shaw, George Bernard **3, 9, 21, 45**
Somerville, Edith Oenone **51**
Stephens, James **4**
Stoker, Bram **8, 144**
Synge, (Edmund) J(ohn) M(illington) **6, 37**
Tynan, Katharine **3**
Wilde, Oscar (Fingal O'Flahertie Wills) **1, 8, 23, 41, 175**
Yeats, William Butler **1, 11, 18, 31, 93, 116**

ISRAELI

Agnon, S(hmuel) Y(osef Halevi) **151**

ITALIAN

Alvaro, Corrado **60**
Betti, Ugo **5**
Brancati, Vitaliano **12**
Calvino, Italo **183**
Campana, Dino **20**
Carducci, Giosuè (Alessandro Giuseppe) **32**
Croce, Benedetto **37**
D'Annunzio, Gabriele **6, 40**
de Filippo, Eduardo **127**
Deledda, Grazia (Cosima) **23**
Gadda, Carlo Emilio **144**
Gentile, Giovanni **96**
Giacosa, Giuseppe **7**
Ginzburg, Natalia **156**
Jovine, Francesco **79**
Levi, Carlo **125**
Levi, Primo **109**
Malaparte, Curzio **52**
Marinetti, Filippo Tommaso **10**
Montessori, Maria **103**
Mosca, Gaetano **75**
Mussolini, Benito (Amilcare Andrea) **96**

Papini, Giovanni **22**
Pareto, Vilfredo **69**
Pascoli, Giovanni **45**
Pavese, Cesare **3**
Pirandello, Luigi **4, 29, 172**
Protolini, Vasco **124**
Saba, Umberto **33**
Tozzi, Federigo **31**
Verga, Giovanni (Carmelo) **3**

JAMAICAN

De Lisser, H(erbert) G(eorge) **12**
Garvey, Marcus (Moziah Jr.) **41**
Mais, Roger **8**
Redcam, Tom **25**

JAPANESE

Abé, Kōbō **131**
Akutagawa Ryunosuke **16**
Dazai Osamu **11**
Endō, Shūsaku **152**
Futabatei, Shimei **44**
Hagiwara, Sakutaro **60**
Hayashi, Fumiko **27**
Ishikawa, Takuboku **15**
Kunikida, Doppo **99**
Masaoka, Shiki **18**
Mishima, Yukio **161**
Miyamoto, (Chujo) Yuriko **37**
Miyazawa, Kenji **76**
Mizoguchi, Kenji **72**
Mori Ogai **14**
Nagai, Kafu **51**
Nishida, Kitaro **83**
Noguchi, Yone **80**
Santoka, Taneda **72**
Shiga, Naoya **172**
Shimazaki Toson **5**
Suzuki, Daisetz Teitaro **109**
Yokomitsu, Riichi **47**
Yosano Akiko **59**

LATVIAN

Berlin, Isaiah **105**
Rainis, Jānis **29**

LEBANESE

Gibran, Kahlil **1, 9**

LESOTHAN

Mofolo, Thomas (Mokopu) **22**

LITHUANIAN

Kreve (Mickevicius), Vincas **27**

MARTINIQUE

Fanon, Frantz **188**

MEXICAN

Azuela, Mariano **3**
Gamboa, Federico **36**
Garro, Elena **153**
Gonzalez Martinez, Enrique **72**
Ibargüengoitia, Jorge **148**
Nervo, (Jose) Amado (Ruiz de) **11**
Reyes, Alfonso **33**
Romero, José Rubén **14**
Villaurrutia, Xavier **80**

NEPALI

Devkota, Laxmiprasad **23**

NEW ZEALANDER

Mander, (Mary) Jane **31**
Mansfield, Katherine **2, 8, 39, 164**

NICARAGUAN

Darío, Rubén **4**

NIGERIAN

Okigbo, Christopher **171**
Tutuola, Amos **188**

NORWEGIAN

Bjoernson, Bjoernstjerne (Martinius) **7, 37**
Bojer, Johan **64**
Grieg, (Johan) Nordahl (Brun) **10**
Hamsun, Knut **151**
Ibsen, Henrik (Johan) **2, 8, 16, 37, 52**
Kielland, Alexander Lange **5**
Lie, Jonas (Lauritz Idemil) **5**
Obstfelder, Sigbjoern **23**
Skram, Amalie (Bertha) **25**
Undset, Sigrid **3**

PAKISTANI

Iqbal, Muhammad **28**

PERUVIAN

Arguedas, José María **147**
Palma, Ricardo **29**
Vallejo, César (Abraham) **3, 56**

POLISH

Asch, Sholem **3**
Borowski, Tadeusz **9**
Conrad, Joseph **1, 6, 13, 25, 43, 57**
Herbert, Zbigniew **168**
Peretz, Isaac Loeb **16**
Prus, Boleslaw **48**
Przybyszewski, Stanislaw **36**
Reymont, Wladyslaw (Stanislaw) **5**
Schulz, Bruno **5, 51**
Sienkiewicz, Henryk (Adam Alexander Pius) **3**
Singer, Israel Joshua **33**
Witkiewicz, Stanislaw Ignacy **8**

PORTUGUESE

Pessoa, Fernando (António Nogueira) **27**
Sa-Carniero, Mario de **83**

PUERTO RICAN

Hostos (y Bonilla), Eugenio Maria de **24**

ROMANIAN

Bacovia, George **24**
Caragiale, Ion Luca **76**
Rebreanu, Liviu **28**

RUSSIAN

Adamov, Arthur **189**
Aldanov, Mark (Alexandrovich) **23**
Andreyev, Leonid (Nikolaevich) **3**
Annensky, Innokenty (Fyodorovich) **14**
Artsybashev, Mikhail (Petrovich) **31**
Babel, Isaak (Emmanuilovich) **2, 13, 171**
Bagritsky, Eduard **60**
Bakhtin, Mikhail **160**
Balmont, Konstantin (Dmitriyevich) **11**
Bely, Andrey **7**
Berdyaev, Nikolai (Aleksandrovich) **67**
Bergelson, David **81**
Blok, Alexander (Alexandrovich) **5**
Bryusov, Valery Yakovlevich **10**
Bulgakov, Mikhail (Afanas'evich) **2, 16, 159**
Bulgya, Alexander Alexandrovich **53**
Bunin, Ivan Alexeyevich **6**
Chekhov, Anton (Pavlovich) **3, 10, 31, 55, 96, 163**
Der Nister **56**
Eisenstein, Sergei (Mikhailovich) **57**
Esenin, Sergei (Alexandrovich) **4**
Fadeyev, Alexander **53**
Gladkov, Fyodor (Vasilyevich) **27**
Gumilev, Nikolai (Stepanovich) **60**
Gurdjieff, G(eorgei) I(vanovich) **71**
Guro, Elena **56**

Hippius, Zinaida **9**
Ilf, Ilya **21**
Ivanov, Vyacheslav Ivanovich **33**
Kandinsky, Wassily **92**
Khlebnikov, Velimir **20**
Khodasevich, Vladislav (Felitsianovich) **15**
Klimentov, Andrei Platonovich **14**
Korolenko, Vladimir Galaktionovich **22**
Kropotkin, Peter (Aleksieevich) **36**
Kuprin, Aleksander Ivanovich **5**
Kuzmin, Mikhail **40**
Lenin, V. I. **67**
Mandelstam, Osip (Emilievich) **2, 6**
Mayakovski, Vladimir (Vladimirovich) **4, 18**
Merezhkovsky, Dmitry Sergeyevich **29**
Nabokov, Vladimir (Vladimirovich) **108, 189**
Olesha, Yuri **136**
Pasternak, Boris **188**
Pavlov, Ivan Petrovich **91**
Petrov, Evgeny **21**
Pilnyak, Boris **23**
Prishvin, Mikhail **75**
Remizov, Aleksei (Mikhailovich) **27**
Rozanov, Vassili **104**
Shestov, Lev **56**
Sologub, Fyodor **9**
Stalin, Joseph **92**
Stanislavsky, Konstantin **167**
Tolstoy, Alexey Nikolaevich **18**
Tolstoy, Leo (Nikolaevich) **4, 11, 17, 28, 44, 79, 173**
Trotsky, Leon **22**
Tsvetaeva (Efron), Marina (Ivanovna) **7, 35**
Zabolotsky, Nikolai Alekseevich **52**
Zamyatin, Evgeny Ivanovich **8, 37**
Zhdanov, Andrei Alexandrovich **18**
Zoshchenko, Mikhail (Mikhailovich) **15**

SCOTTISH

Barrie, J(ames) M(atthew) **2, 164**
Brown, George Douglas **28**
Buchan, John **41**
Cunninghame Graham, Robert (Gallnigad) Bontine **19**
Davidson, John **24**
Doyle, Arthur Conan **7**
Frazer, J(ames) G(eorge) **32**
Lang, Andrew **16**
MacDonald, George **9, 113**
Muir, Edwin **2, 87**
Murray, James Augustus Henry **117**
Sharp, William **39**
Tey, Josephine **14**

SLOVENIAN

Cankar, Ivan **105**

SOUTH AFRICAN

Bosman, Herman Charles **49**
Campbell, (Ignatius) Roy (Dunnachie) **5**
La Guma, Alex **140**
Mqhayi, S(amuel) E(dward) K(rune Loliwe) **25**
Paton, Alan **165**
Plaatje, Sol(omon) T(shekisho) **73**
Schreiner, Olive (Emilie Albertina) **9**
Smith, Pauline (Urmson) **25**
Vilakazi, Benedict Wallet **37**

SPANISH

Alas (y Urena), Leopoldo (Enrique Garcia) **29**
Aleixandre, Vicente **113**
Barea, Arturo **14**
Baroja (y Nessi), Pio **8**
Benavente (y Martinez), Jacinto **3**
Blasco Ibáñez, Vicente **12**
Echegaray (y Eizaguirre), Jose (Maria Waldo) **4**
García Lorca, Federico **1, 7, 49, 181**
Jiménez (Mantecón), Juan Ramón **4, 183**

ISBN-13:978-0-7876-9969-7
ISBN-10:0-7876-9969-1